# Global Marketing

## FOURTH EDITION

Warren J. Keegan

*Lubin Graduate School of Business*
*Pace University—New York City and Westchester, New York*

Mark C. Green

*Department of Accounting, Economics, Management, and Marketing*
*Simpson College—Indianola, Iowa*

PEARSON

Prentice
Hall

**Pearson Education International**

**Editorial Director:** Jeff Shelstad
**Project Manager:** Ashley Santora
**Editorial Assistant:** Rebecca Lembo
**Media Project Manager:** Peter Snell
**Executive Marketing Manager:** Michelle O'Brien
**Marketing Assistant:** Joanna Sabella
**Senior Managing Editor (Production):** Judy Leale
**Production Editor:** Kelly Warsak
**Permissions Coordinator:** Charles Morris
**Manufacturing Buyer:** Michelle Klein
**Design Director:** Maria Lange
**Designer:** Michael Fruhbeis
**Interior Design:** Michael Fruhbeis
**Cover Design:** Michael Fruhbeis
**Cover Photo:** Corbis/Laffont
**Director, Image Resource Center:** Melinda Reo
**Manager, Rights and Permissions:** Zina Arabia
**Manager, Visual Research:** Beth Brenzel
**Manager, Cover Visual Research & Permissions:** Karen Sanatar
**Image Permission Coordinator:** Debbie Latronica
**Photo Researcher:** Melinda Alexander
**Manager, Print Production:** Christy Mahon
**Composition:** Integra Software Services
**Full-Service Project Management:** Jennifer Welsch/BookMasters, Inc.
**Printer/Binder:** Courier/Westford
**Cover Printer:** Phoenix Color Corp.
**Typeface:** 10/12 Palatino

Credits and acknowledgments borrowed from other sources and reproduced, with permission, in this textbook appear on pages 604–605.

If you purchased this book within the United States or Canada you should be aware that it has been wrongfully imported without the approval of the Publisher or the Author.

Pearson Education LTD.
Pearson Education Singapore, Pte. Ltd
Pearson Education, Canada, Ltd
Pearson Education—Japan
Pearson Education Australia PTY, Limited

Pearson Education North Asia Ltd
Pearson Educación de Mexico, S.A. de C.V.
Pearson Education Malaysia, Pte. Ltd
Pearson Education, Upper Saddle River, New Jersey

10 9 8 7 6 5 4 3 2 1
ISBN 0-13-196854-8

To Cynthia
WJK

*Ad memoriam:* George W. Smalley, Professor Emeritus, Lawrence University
MCG

# BRIEF CONTENTS

**PART I        INTRODUCTION        1**

Chapter 1        Introduction to Global Marketing        1

Case 1-1        McDonald's Expands Globally While Adjusting Its Local Recipe        31

Case 1-2        Acer, Inc. (A)        35

**PART II        THE GLOBAL MARKETING ENVIRONMENT        45**

Chapter 2        The Global Economic Environment        45

Case 2-1        Vietnam's Market Potential        77

Case 2-2        Acer, Inc. (B)        79

Chapter 3        The Global Trade Environment: Regional Market Characteristics and Preferential Trade Agreements        81

Case 3-1        Ecuador Adopts the Dollar        112

Case 3-2        The Euro Yo-yo        114

Chapter 4        Social and Cultural Environments        117

Case 4-1        Fair Trade Coffee: Ethics, Religion, and Sustainable Production        147

Case 4-2        Barbie: The American Girl Goes Global        148

Chapter 5        The Political, Legal, and Regulatory Environments of Global Marketing        151

Case 5-1        Bud Versus Bud        184

Case 5-2        America's Cuban Conundrum        185

**PART III        APPROACHING GLOBAL MARKETS        189**

Chapter 6        Global Information Systems and Market Research        189

Case 6-1        Research Helps Whirlpool Act Local in the Global Market        223

Chapter 7        Segmentation, Targeting, and Positioning        225

Case 7-1        Nokia Segments the Global Cell Phone Market        259

Case 7-2        Carmakers Target Gen Y        260

Chapter 8        Importing, Exporting, and Sourcing        262

Case 8-1        Concerns About Factory Safety and Worker Exploitation in Developing Countries        288

Case 8-2        U.S. Sugar Subsidies: Too Sweet a Deal?        291

Chapter 9        Global Market Entry Strategies: Licensing, Investment, and Strategic Alliances        293

Case 9-1        DHL Shakes Up the Global Package Express Business        324

Case 9-2        Harry Potter        325

PART IV     THE GLOBAL MARKETING MIX    328

Chapter 10     Product and Brand Decisions    328

Case 10-1   Boeing Versus Airbus: A Battle for the Skies    360

Case 10-2   The Smart Car    361

Chapter 11     Pricing Decisions    364

Case 11-1   Pricing AIDS Drugs in Emerging Markets    395

Case 11-2   LVMH and Luxury Goods Marketing    396

Chapter 12     Global Marketing Channels and Physical Distribution    401

Case 12-1   Wal-Mart's Global Expansion    431

Case 12-2   The Future of Radio Frequency Identification    433

Chapter 13     Global Marketing Communications Decisions I: Advertising and Public Relations    435

Case 13-1   Benetton Group S.p.A.: Raising Consciousness and Controversy with Global Advertising    466

Case 13-2   Adidas-Salomon AG    468

Chapter 14     Global Marketing Communications Decisions II: Sales Promotion, Personal Selling, Special Forms of Marketing Communication    471

Case 14-1   Marketing an Industrial Product in Latin America    500

PART V     STRATEGY AND LEADERSHIP IN THE TWENTY-FIRST CENTURY    502

Chapter 15     Strategic Elements of Competitive Advantage    502

Case 15-1   Kodak in the Twenty-First Century: The Search for New Sources of Competitive Advantage    528

Case 15-2   Lego    529

Chapter 16     Leading, Organizing, and Controlling the Global Marketing Effort    530

Case 16-1   A Marketer Takes the Wheel at Volkswagen AG    556

Case 16-2   Kazuo Inamori: Spiritual Leadership at Kyocera Corp.    558

Chapter 17     The Digital Revolution and Global Electronic Marketplace    561

Case 17-1   Napster and the Global Music Industry    583

# CONTENTS

Preface    xv

## PART I    INTRODUCTION    1

Chapter 1    Introduction to Global Marketing    1

Overview of Marketing    3
*Competitive Advantage, Globalization, and Global Industries    4*

Global Marketing: What It Is and What It Isn't    8

The Importance of Global Marketing    13

Management Orientations    15
*Ethnocentric Orientation    16*
*Polycentric Orientation    18*
*Regiocentric and Geocentric Orientations    19*

Forces Affecting Global Integration and Global Marketing    21
*Driving Forces    21*
*Restraining Forces    27*

Outline of This Book    28

## PART II    THE GLOBAL MARKETING ENVIRONMENT    45

Chapter 2    Global Economic Environment    45

The World Economy—An Overview    46

Economic Systems    49
*Market Capitalism    49*
*Centrally Planned Socialism    49*
*Centrally Planned Capitalism and Market Socialism    50*

Stages of Market Development    53
*Low-Income Countries    55*
*Lower-Middle-Income Countries    57*
*Upper-Middle-Income Countries    57*
*Marketing Opportunities in LDCs and Developing Countries    59*
*High-Income Countries    61*
*The Triad    63*
*Marketing Implications of the Stages of Development    65*

Balance of Payments    66

World Trade in Merchandise and Services    68

Overview of International Finance    69
*Managed Dirty Float    70*
*Foreign Exchange Market Dynamics    71*
*Purchasing Power Parity    71*
*Economic Exposure    72*
*Managing Exchange Rate Exposure    73*

Chapter 3    The Global Trade Environment: Regional Market
Characteristics and Preferential Trade Agreements    81

The World Trade Organization and GATT    82

Preferential Trade Agreements    83
*Free Trade Area    83*

*Customs Union    84*
*Common Market    85*
*Economic Union    85*

North America    87

Latin America: SICA, Andean Community, Mercosur, CARICOM    89
*Central American Integration System    89*
*Andean Community    90*
*Common Market of the South (Mercosur)    92*
*Caribbean Community and Common Market (CARICOM)    94*
*Current Trade-Related Issues    95*
*ASIA-PACIFIC: The Association of Southeast Asian Nations (ASEAN)    96*
*Marketing Issues in the Asia-Pacific Region    97*

Western, Central, and Easter Europe    98
*The European Union (EU)    98*
*The European Free Trade Area (EFTA) and European Economic Area (EEA)    100*
*Marketing Issues in the European Union    101*
*The Lomé Convention and the Cotonou Agreement    103*
*Central European Free Trade Association (CEFTA)    103*

The Middle East    104
*Cooperation Council for the Arab States of the Gulf    104*
*Marketing Issues in the Middle East    106*

Africa    106
*Economic Community of West African States (ECOWAS)    106*
*East African Cooperation    107*
*Southern African Development Community (SADC)    108*

Chapter 4    Social and Cultural Environments    117

Society, Culture, and Global Consumer Culture    119
*Attitudes, Beliefs, and Values    120*
*Religion    120*
*Aesthetics    121*
*Dietary Preferences    124*
*Language and Communication    126*
*Marketing's Impact on Culture    129*

High- and Low-Context Cultures    132

Hofstede's Cultural Typology    133

The Self-Reference Criterion and Perception    138

Diffusion Theory    139
*The Adoption Process    140*
*Characteristics of Innovations    140*
*Adopter Categories    141*
*Diffusion of Innovations in Pacific Rim Countries    142*

Marketing Implications of Social and Cultural Environments    143

Chapter 5    The Political, Legal, and Regulatory Environments of Global Marketing    151

The Political Environment    152
*Nation States and Sovereignty    153*
*Political Risk    154*
*Taxes    157*
*Seizure of Assets    160*

The Legal Environment    161
*Common Law Versus Civil Law    162*
*Sidestepping Legal Problems: Important Business Issues    164*
*Conflict Resolution, Dispute Settlement, and Litigation    176*

The Regulatory Environment    180
    *Regional Economic Organizations: The European Union Example*    *180*

# PART III    APPROACHING GLOBAL MARKETS    189

Chapter 6    Global Information Systems and Market
             Research    189

Information Technology for Global Marketing    190

Information Subject Agenda and Environmental Scanning
Modes    195

Sources of Market Information    197

Formal Market Research    199
    *Step 1: Identify the Information Requirement*    *200*
    *Step 2: Problem Definition—Overcoming the SRC*    *201*
    *Step 3: Choose Unit of Analysis*    *203*
    *Step 4: Examine Data Availability*    *203*
    *Step 5: Assess Value of Research*    *205*
    *Step 6: Research Design*    *205*
    *Step 7: Analyzing Data*    *214*
    *Step 8: Presenting the Findings*    *218*
    *Headquarters Control of Marketing Research*    *219*
    *An Integrated Approach to Information Collection*    *220*

Chapter 7    Segmentation, Targeting, and Positioning    225

Global Market Segmentation    226
    *Demographic Segmentation*    *228*
    *Psychographic Segmentation*    *235*
    *Behavior Segmentation*    *237*
    *Benefit Segmentation*    *240*
    *Ethnic Segmentation*    *241*

Assessing Market Potential and Choosing Target Markets
or Segments    242
    *Current Segment Size and Growth Potential*    *242*
    *Potential Competition*    *243*
    *Feasibility and Compatibility*    *244*
    *A Framework for Selecting Target Markets*    *245*

Product-Market Decisions    247

Target Market Strategy Options    248
    *Standardized Global Marketing*    *248*
    *Concentrated Global Marketing*    *249*
    *Differentiated Global Marketing*    *250*

Positioning    250
    *Attribute or Benefit*    *251*
    *Quality and Price*    *251*
    *Use or User*    *252*
    *Competitor*    *253*
    *Global, Foreign, and Local Consumer Culture Positioning*    *254*

Chapter 8    Importing, Exporting, and Sourcing    262

Organizational Export Activities    264

National Policies Governing Exports and Imports    265
    *Government Programs that Support Exports*    *266*
    *Governmental Actions to Discourage Imports and
    Block Market Access*    *267*

Tariff Systems    271
    *Customs Duties*    *274*
    *Other Duties and Import Charges*    *275*

Key Export Participants      275

Organizing for Exporting in the Manufacturer's Country      277

Organizing for Exporting in the Market Country      278

Export Financing and Methods of Payment      279
*Documentary Credit*      279
*Documentary Collections (Sight or Time Drafts)*      280
*Cash in Advance*      281
*Sales on Open Account*      282
*Sales on a Consignment Basis*      282

Sourcing      282
*Management Vision*      283
*Factor Costs and Conditions*      284
*Customer Needs*      285
*Logistics*      285
*Country Infrastructure*      285
*Political Factors*      286
*Foreign Exchange Rates*      286

**Chapter 9**      **Global Market Entry Strategies: Licensing, Investment, and Strategic Alliances**      **293**

Licensing      295
*Special Licensing Arrangements*      297

Investment      298
*Joint Ventures*      299
*Investment via Ownership or Equity Stake*      303

Global Strategic Partnerships      306

The Nature of Global Strategic Partnerships      309
*Success Factors*      311
*Alliances with Asian Competitors*      312
*CFM International, GE, and Snecma: A Success Story*      313
*AT&T and Olivetti: A Failure*      313
*Boeing and Japan: A Controversy*      314
*International Partnerships in Developing Countries*      315

Cooperative Strategies in Japan: *Keiretsu*      316
*How* Keiretsu *Affect American Business: Two Examples*      319

Cooperative Strategies in South Korea: *Chaebol*      319

Twenty-First Century Cooperative Strategies: Targeting the Digital Future      320
*Beyond Strategic Alliances*      320

Market Expansion Strategies      321

**PART IV**      **THE GLOBAL MARKETING MIX**      **328**

**Chapter 10**      **Product and Brand Decisions**      **328**

Basic Product and Brand Concepts      329
*Product Types*      330
*Brands*      330
*Local Products and Brands*      332
*International Products and Brands*      333
*Global Products and Brands*      333
*Global Brand Development*      335
*Local Versus Global Products and Brands: A Needs-Based Approach*      339

"Country of Origin" as Brand Element      341

Packaging      344
*Labeling*      344
*Aesthetics*      345

Product Warranties    346

Extend, Adapt, Create: Strategic Alternatives in Global
Marketing    346
  *Strategy 1: Product-Communication Extension    348*
  *Strategy 2: Product Extension–Communication Adaptation    349*
  *Strategy 3: Product Adaptation–Communication Adaptation    350*
  *Strategy 4: Product–Communication Adaptation    351*
  *Strategy 5: Product Invention    351*
  *How to Choose a Strategy    353*

New Products in Global Marketing    354
  *Identifying New-Product Ideas    355*
  *New-Product Development    356*
  *The International New-Product Department    357*
  *Testing New Products    358*


**Chapter 11    Pricing Decisions    364**

Basic Pricing Concepts    365

Global Pricing Objectives and Strategies    366
  *Market Skimming and Financial Objectives    366*
  *Penetration Pricing and Nonfinancial Objectives    367*
  *Companion Products: "Razors and Blades" Pricing    368*
  *Target Costing    369*
  *Calculating Prices: Cost-Based Pricing and Price Escalation    369*
  *Terms of the Sale    371*

Environmental Influences on Pricing Decisions    373
  *Currency Fluctuations    373*
  *Inflationary Environment    376*
  *Government Controls, Subsidies, and Regulations    378*
  *Competitive Behavior    379*
  *Using Sourcing as a Strategic Pricing Tool    380*

Global Pricing: Three Policy Alternatives    380
  *Extension or Ethnocentric    380*
  *Adaptation or Polycentric    381*
  *Geocentric    381*

Gray Market Goods    383

Dumping    385

Price Fixing    387

Transfer Pricing    388
  *Tax Regulations and Transfer Prices    389*
  *Sales of Tangible and Intangible Property    389*
  *Competitive Pricing    389*
  *Importance of Section 482 Regulations    389*

Countertrade    390
  *Barter    391*
  *Counterpurchase    392*
  *Offset    392*
  *Compensation Trading    393*
  *Switch Trading    393*


**Chapter 12    Global Marketing Channels and Physical
               Distribution    401**

Channel Objectives    402

Distribution Channels: Terminology and Structure    403
  *Consumer Products and Services    403*
  *Industrial Products    407*

Establishing Channels and Working with Channel
Intermediaries    410

Global Retailing    413

Innovation in Global Retailing    421

Physical Distribution, Supply Chains, and Logistics
Management    423
  *Order Processing    424*
  *Warehousing    424*
  *Inventory Management    424*
  *Transportation    425*
  *Logistics Management: A Brief Case Study    429*

**Chapter 13    Global Marketing Communications Decisions I:
Advertising and Public Relations    435**

Global Advertising    437
  *Global Advertising Content: The "Standardization" Versus
  "Adaptation" Debate    439*

Advertising Agencies: Organizations and Brands    443
  *Selecting an Advertising Agency    446*

Creating Global Advertising    447
  *Art Directors and Art Direction    450*
  *Copy    450*
  *Cultural Considerations    452*

Global Media Decisions    456
  *Media Vehicles and Expenditures    457*
  *Media Decisions    459*

Public Relations and Publicity    459
  *The Growing Role of Public Relations in Global Marketing
  Communications    462*
  *How Public Relations Practices Differ Around the World    463*

**Chapter 14    Global Marketing Communications Decisions II:
Sales Promotion, Personal Selling, Special Forms
of Marketing Communication    471**

Sales Promotion    472
  *Sampling    474*
  *Couponing    476*
  *Sales Promotions: Issues and Problems    477*

Personal Selling    479
  *The Strategic/Consultative Selling Model    481*
  *Sales Force Nationality    485*

Special Forms of Marketing Communications: Direct Marketing,
Event Sponsorship, and Product Placement    488
  *Direct Mail    490*
  *Catalogs    492*
  *Infomercials and Teleshopping    493*
  *Sponsorship    495*
  *Product Placement in Motion Pictures, Television Shows, and Other
  Performances    496*

**PART V    STRATEGY AND LEADERSHIP IN THE TWENTY-FIRST
CENTURY    502**

**Chapter 15    Strategic Elements of Competitive Advantage    502**

Industry Analysis: Forces Influencing Competition    503
  *Threat of New Entrants    503*
  *Threat of Substitute Products    505*

*Bargaining Power of Buyers*    505
*Bargaining Power of Suppliers*    506
*Rivalry Among Competitors*    507

Competitive Advantage    507
*Generic Strategies for Creating Competitive Advantage*    508
*The Flagship Firm: The Business Network with Five Partners*    512
*Creating Competitive Advantage via Strategic Intent*    513

Global Competition and National Competitive Advantage    516
*Demand Conditions*    519
*Related and Supporting Industries*    520
*Firm Strategy, Structure, and Rivalry*    521
*Chance*    522
*Government*    522

Current Issues in Competitive Advantage    522

Chapter 16    Leading, Organizing, and Controlling the Global Marketing Effort    530

Leadership    531
*Top Management Nationality*    533
*Leadership and Core Competence*    534

Organization    535
*Patterns of International Organization Development*    539

Lean Production: Organizing the Japanese Way    545

Global Marketing Management Control    548
*Formal Control Methods*    550
*Informal Control Methods*    552

The Global Marketing Audit    552
*Setting Objectives and Scope of the Audit*    553

Chapter 17    The Digital Revolution and the Global Electronic Marketplace    561

The Digital Revolution: A Brief History    562

Convergence    564

Value Networks and Disruptive Technologies    565

Global E-Commerce    567

Web Site Design    571

New Products and Services    576
*Broadband*    576

Mobile Commerce and Wireless Connectivity    579
*Smart Cell Phones*    580
*Internet Phone Service*    581

Conclusion    582

Glossary    588

Credits    604

Author /Name Index    606

Subject/Organization Index    612

# PREFACE

*Global Marketing*, Fourth Edition, builds on the worldwide success of *Principles of Global Marketing* and *Global Marketing,* Second Edition and Third Edition. Those books took an environmental and strategic approach by outlining the major dimensions of the global business environment. The authors also provided a set of conceptual and analytical tools that would prepare students to successfully apply the 4Ps to global marketing. The authors have approached all four editions with the same goal: to write a book that is authoritative in content, yet relaxed and assured in style and tone. The following student comments suggest that we accomplished our goal: "the textbook is very clear and easy to understand"; "an excellent textbook with many real-life examples"; "the authors use simple language and clearly state the important points"; "this is the best textbook that I am using this term"; "the authors have done an excellent job of writing a text than can be read easily." *Principles of Global Marketing* was the first textbook on the subject to be published in a full four-color format. In addition, when it appeared in fall 1996, the first edition invited students to "look ahead" to such developments as the ending of America's trade embargo with Vietnam, Europe's new currency, Daimler-Benz's Smart car project, and the controversy concerning Benetton's advertising. Those topics represented "big stories" in the global marketing arena and continue to receive press coverage on a regular basis.

As was the case with the first three editions, we approached *Global Marketing*, Fourth Edition, with today's students and instructors in mind. Guided by our experience using the text in undergraduate and graduate classrooms and in corporate training seminars, we have revised, updated, and expanded *Global Marketing*, Third Edition. We have benefited tremendously from adopter feedback and input; we also continue to draw on our direct experience in the Americas, Asia, Europe, Africa, and the Middle East. The result is a text that addresses the needs of students and instructors in every part of the world. The English-language edition of *Global Marketing* has been used in many countries, including Australia, Canada, China, Ireland, Japan, Malaysia, and Sri Lanka; the text is also available in Spanish, Portuguese, and Chinese editions.

## WHAT'S NEW

The fourth edition includes new material on newsworthy and relevant topics such as the expanded European Union, China's growing importance as an export powerhouse and a giant consumer market, the impact of religion on global marketing activities, and the global music industry's ongoing efforts to combat music piracy. Current research findings have been incorporated into each of the chapters. For example, Shaoming Zou and S. Tamer Cavusgil's work on global marketing strategy (from *Journal of Marketing*, October 2002) is an important addition to Chapter 1 "Introduction to Global Marketing." Similarly, our thinking about global market segmentation and targeting has been influenced by David Arnold's recent book, *The Mirage of Global Markets*. We have added scores of current examples of global marketing practices as well as quotations from global marketing practitioners and industry experts. New to the fourth edition is Chapter 17, "The Digital Revolution and Global Electronic Marketplace."

Adopters of earlier editions will note that the chapter on strategy and competitive advantage has been moved to Part V; it now is Chapter 15. This change means that the global marketing mix chapters now appear earlier in the book. Throughout the text, organizational Web sites are referenced for further student study and exploration. A Companion Web site (**www.prenhall.com/keegan**) is integrated with the text as well.

Each chapter contains several illustrations that bring global marketing to life. Chapter opening vignettes introduce a company, country, product, or global marketing issue that directly relates to chapter themes and content. Half the opening vignettes in the fourth edition are new, including: "Furniture Exports from China" (Chapter 8); "LCD TV" (Chapter 10); and "Xbox" (Chapter 14). In addition, every chapter contains one or more sidebars on various themes including global marketing in action, risks and gambles, a look behind the scenes of global marketing, issues that are "open to discussion," and the cultural differences that challenge the global marketer. A new sidebar, "Global Marketing Q&A," features interview excerpts with top executives of well-known global companies.

## CASES

The case set in *Global Marketing*, Fourth Edition, strikes a 50/50 balance between revisions of earlier cases (e.g., Case 1-1 McDonald's Expands Globally While Adjusting Its Local Recipe and Case 17-1 Napster and the Global Music Industry) and entirely new cases (e.g., Case 3-1 Ecuador Adopts the Dollar, Case 4-1 Fair Trade Coffee: Ethics, Religion, and Sustainable Production, and Case 7-1 Nokia Segments the Global Cell Phone Market). The cases vary in length from a few hundred words to more than 2,600 words, yet they are all short enough to be covered in an efficient manner. The cases were written with the same objectives in mind: to raise issues that will encourage student interest and learning, to stimulate class discussion, and to enhance the classroom experience for students and instructors alike. Every chapter and case has been classroom tested.

## SUPPLEMENTS

All teaching supplements have been revised! We're pleased to offer an instructor's resource manual, video segments, PowerPoint slides, online study guide, and a test bank prepared by the authors. Special consideration was given to the test bank, with considerable effort devoted to minimizing the number of simplistic, superficial multiple-choice questions with "all of the above"-type answers.

All teaching supplements, except the video segments, are delivered on a CD-ROM and can be downloaded from Prentice Hall's password-protected Instructor Resource Center.

- **Instructor's Resource Center (IRC) on CD-ROM**: ISBN 0-13-146922-3
- **Instructor's Resource Center (IRC) Online**: **www.prenhall.com/keegan**
- **Video Segments on VHS**: ISBN 0-13-146920-7

One of the constant challenges to authors of books about global marketing is the rate of change in the global business environment. Yesterday's impossibility becomes today's reality. Books are quickly outdated by events. Even so, we believe that adopters will find *Global Marketing*, Fourth Edition, to be as up-to-date, relevant, and useful to today's students of global marketing as any comparable text on the market, perhaps even more so.

# ACKNOWLEDGMENTS

We are grateful to the reviewers of this book for their many insights and helpful suggestions.

Inigo Arroniz, *University of Central Florida*
David Campbell, *University of Mississippi*
Chanaz Gargouri, *St. Peters College*
Betsy Holloway, *Samford University*
Kenneth Lord, *Mercer University*
Min Lu, *Monmouth University*
Lois Olson, *San Diego State University*
Mark Peterson, *University of Texas at Arlington*
Fred Pragasam, *University of North Florida*

This book reflects the contributions, labor, and insights of many persons.

I would like to thank my students, colleagues, associates, and clients, for their many insights and contributions. It is impossible to single out all of the people who have contributed to this edition, but I would especially like to thank:

Peter Allen, Stephen Blank, Jean Boddewyn, Lawrence G. Bridwell, Steve Burgess, Arthur Centonze, Marcos Cobra, Fernando de Campos, Bertrand de Frondeville, John Dory, Bob Fulmer, Pradeep Gopalakrisna, Doug Jebb, Steve Kobrin, Jean-Marc de Leersnyder, Susan Douglas, Donald Gibson, Jim Gould, Tayfur Gullulu, Salah Hassan, David Heenan, Peter Hoefer, Robert Isaak, Hermawan Kartajaya, Suren Kaushik, Mark Keegan, Hermann Kopp, Jem Li, Raymond Lopez, Malcolm McDonald, Dorothy Minkus-McKenna, Jan Morgan, Stan Paliwoda, Howard Perlmutter, Robert Radway, Alan Rugman, John Ryans, Bodo B. Schlegelmilch, Donald Sexton, Barbara Stöttinger, Francoise Simon, Oleg Smirnoff, Ralph Z. Sorenson, Earl Spencer, Moshe Speter, William Stolze, John Stopford, Jim Stoner, Martin Topol, Robert Vambery, Terry Vavra, Len Vickers, Dianna Powell Ward, Colin Watson, Kathy Winsted, Dominique Xardel, George Yip, Philip Young, and Alan Zimmerman.

I would especially like to acknowledge the many contributions of the students in my doctoral seminar on global strategic marketing. My research assistants, Tayfur Gullulu and Thomas Sillery, provided invaluable research assistance in many areas, including the very difficult task of creating the Global Income and Population data that appears in this edition. My office managers, Gail Pietrangolare Weldon and Lisa DeFonce and my secretaries Mary O'Connor, Vicki Underwood, and Marie Loprieno have provided outstanding and creative support above and beyond the call of duty, and always with a cheerful attitude.

Special thanks are due the superb librarians at Pace University: Michelle Lang, Head, Graduate Center Library; Anne B. Campbell, Reference Librarian; and Christa Burns, Head of Research & Information Services have a remarkable ability to find anything. Like the Canadian Mounties who always get their man, Michelle, Anne, and Christa always get the document. My admiration for their talent and appreciation for their effort is unbounded.

Whitney Blake, our editor at Prentice Hall, was quick to endorse and support this text as was Ashley Santora, our new project manager. We are grateful for the continuity of the support at Prentice Hall.

**Warren J. Keegan**

I am indebted to the many colleagues and friends who carefully read and critiqued individual manuscript sections and chapters. Their comments improved the clarity and readability of the text. In particular, I would like to thank Hunter Clark, Frank

Colella, Dave Collins, Thomas Schmidt, Mark Freyberg, Alexandre Gilfanov, Carl Halgren, Kathy Hill, Mark Juffernbruch, Peter Kvetko, Liz Miller, Keith Miller, Gayle Moberg, Marilyn Mueller, James Palmieri, Alexandre Plokhov, Thomas Schmidt, and Wendy Vasquez.

I would also like to thank the many present and former Simpson College students who offered feedback on the fourth edition of *Global Marketing* and suggested improvements to the manuscript as it evolved between 2003 and 2004. Beth Dorrell graciously contributed her story for this edition's "A Day in the Life" sidebar. The authors are indebted to Alexandra Kennedy-Scott, David Henderson, and Michel Phan of the ESSEC Business School for permission to include "Barbie: An American Girl Goes Global" and "Harry Potter" in this edition's case set. Thanks also to Alanah Davis for her work on Acer, Inc. (B) and to Katie McCool for her research on Ecuador's dollarization program. Caleb Sellers kindly supplied me with important data about the white goods market in Germany. Yuri Toda translated copy from L. L. Bean's Japanese Web site. In addition, several industry professionals were kind enough to contribute their knowledge and expertise to the fourth edition. Special thanks to Kimberley Gardiner, Lexus Marketing; Meredith Rule, Klipsch Audio Technologies; and Rhonda Milliken, Whirlpool.

It was a great pleasure working with the Prentice Hall team that supervised production of this edition. My heartfelt thanks to Ashley Santora and Kelly Warsak. Kudos also to our photo researcher, Melinda Alexander, for demonstrating once again that "every picture tells a story," and to Kathy Weisbrod for additional permissions research. Thanks also to Michelle O'Brien for her great work on marketing support materials, and to the entire PH sales team for helping promote the book in the field. I also want to acknowledge the contributions of Susan Leshnower at Midlands College for her fine work on the Instructor's Manual, and Kristopher Blanchard at North Central University for preparing a new set of PowerPoint slides. As was the case with the first three editions, several friends and colleagues at Simpson College were very supportive of my research and writing endeavors. In particular, I would like to thank Robyn Copeland for graciously extending special consideration regarding "due dates" of books and periodicals that I checked out.

A writing project of this magnitude sometimes requires an author to sacrifice precious family time. I want to thank Lauren, Tommy, and Jonny for their patience, understanding, and unconditional love during the past year.

**Mark C. Green**

# ABOUT THE AUTHORS

## Dr. Warren J. Keegan

Dr. Keegan is Distinguished Professor of Marketing and International Business and Director of the Institute for Global Business Strategy at the Lubin School of Business, Pace University, New York City and Westchester. He is Visiting University Professor, Cranfield School of Management (UK), CEIBS (China European International Business School) Shanghai, the Wharton School, University of Pennsylvania Executive Programs, and ESSEC, Cergy – Pontoise (France). He is the founder of Warren Keegan Associates, Inc., a consulting consortium of experts in global strategic management and marketing and Keegan & Company LLP, a firm specializing in litigation support. The firm is affiliated with MarkPlus, the leading marketing consulting firm of Indonesia.

Dr. Keegan is the author of many books. His text, *Global Marketing Management*, Seventh Edition (2002, Prentice Hall, Inc.) is recognized as the leading Global Marketing text for M.B.A. courses around the world. His other books include *Offensive Marketing* (2004), *Global Marketing*, Third Edition (2003, Prentice Hall), *Marketing Plans That Work*, Second Edition (2002, Butterworth-Heinemann), *Marketing*, Second Edition (1995, Prentice Hall), *Marketing Sans Frontieres* (1994, InterEditions), *Advertising Worldwide* (1991, Prentice Hall), and *Judgments, Choices and Decisions* (1984, Wiley). He has published in leading business journals including the *Harvard Business Review, Journal of Marketing, Journal of International Business Studies, Administrative Science Quarterly*, and the *Columbia Journal of World Business*.

He is a former MIT Fellow in Africa where he served as Assistant Secretary, Ministry of Development Planning and Secretary of the Economic Development Commission for the Government of Tanzania. He was a consultant with Boston Consulting Group and Arthur D. Little, and Chairman of Douglas A. Edwards, a New York corporate real estate firm.

Dr. Keegan holds an M.B.A. and doctorate from the Harvard Business School. He has been a visiting professor at New York University, INSEAD (France), IMD (Switzerland), The Stockholm School of Economics, Emmanuel College of Cambridge University, and at the University of Hawaii. He is a former faculty member of Columbia Business School, Baruch College, and The School of Government and Business Administration of The George Washington University.

He is a Lifetime Fellow of the Academy of International Business, Individual Eminent Person (IEP) Appointed by Asian Global Business Leaders Society (other awardees include: Noel Tichy, Rosabeth Moss Kanter, and Gary Wendt). His biography is listed in *Marquis Who's Who in America*. He is a member of the International Advisory Board of École des Hautes Études Commerciales (HEC), Montreal; the Editorial Advisory Board, Cranfield School of Management; and Financial Times Management Monograph Series and is a current or former director of The S.M. Stoller Company, Inc., The Cooper Companies, Inc. (NYSE), Inter-Ad, Inc., American Thermal Corporation, Inc., Halfway Houses of Westchester, Inc., Wainwright House, and The Rye Arts Center.

## Dr. Mark C. Green

Dr. Green is Professor of Management and Marketing at Simpson College in Indianola, Iowa, where he teaches courses in management, marketing, advertising, international marketing, innovation, and Russian language. He earned his B.A. degree in Russian literature from Lawrence University, M.A. and Ph.D. degrees in Russian linguistics from Cornell University and an M.B.A. degree in marketing management from Syracuse University.

In addition to co-authoring *Global Marketing*, Fourth Edition with Warren Keegan, Dr. Green has also contributed case studies and chapter materials to several other textbooks published by Prentice Hall. These include: *Advertising Principles and Practices*, Fourth Edition, by William Wells, John Burnett, and Sandra Moriarty (1997); *Behavior in Organizations*, Sixth Edition, by Jerald Greenberg and Robert Baron (1996); *Business*, Fourth Edition, by Ricky Griffin and Ronald Ebert (1995); and *Principles of Marketing* by Warren Keegan, Sandra Moriarty, and Thomas Duncan (1992). Dr. Green has also written essays on technology and global business that have appeared in the *Des Moines Register* and other newspapers.

Dr. Green has traveled to the former Soviet Union on numerous occasions. In 1995 and 1996, he participated in a grant project funded by the U.S. Agency for International Development (USAID) and presented marketing seminars to audiences in Nizhny Novgorod. In addition, Dr. Green has served as a consultant to several Iowa organizations that have business and cultural ties with Russia and other former Soviet republics. Dr. Green has lectured in Russia and Ukraine on topics relating to emerging market economies. His 1992 monograph, *Developing the Russian Market in the 1990s*, received an award from the Iowa-based International Network on Trade.

In 1997, Dr. Green was the recipient of Simpson College's Distinguished Research and Writing Award. Dr. Green also received the 1995 Distinguished Teaching Award for senior faculty. In 1990, he was the recipient of Simpson's Excellence in Teaching Award for junior faculty. He also received the 1988 Outstanding Faculty of the Year awarded by the Alpha Sigma Lambda adult student honorary at Simpson College.

## Part I

INTRODUCTION

# 1

# Introduction to Global Marketing

Consider the following proposition: *We live in a global marketplace.* McDonald's restaurants, Sony TVs, Nokia cell phones, Lego toys, Swatch watches, and Caterpillar earthmoving equipment are found practically everywhere on the planet. Now consider a second proposition: *We live in a world in which markets are local.* In the Philippines, for example, Western fast-food companies compete with local restaurant chains such as Jollibee. In China, appliances from Whirlpool and Electrolux compete with products manufactured and marketed by Haier Group. France's domestic film industry generates about 40 percent of motion picture box office receipts; U.S.-made movies account for about 50 percent. In Turkey, local artists such as Sertab Erena account for more than 80 percent of recorded music sales. *Kiki*, a Japanese magazine for teenage girls, competes for newsstand sales with *Vogue Girl*, *Cosmo Girl*, and other titles from Western publishers. In Brazil, many consumers are partial to Antarctica and other local soft drink brands made from guaraná, a berry that grows in the Amazon region.

At first glance, the two propositions set forth above may strike readers as contradictory. In fact, both are valid; the resulting paradox lies at the heart of this textbook. In later chapters, we will investigate the nature of the global marketplace/local markets paradox in more detail. For now, however, we will focus on the first part of the paradox. Think for a moment about brands and products that are found throughout the world. Ask the average consumer where this global "horn of plenty" comes from, and you'll likely hear a variety of answers that reflect widely differing perceptions. It's certainly true that some brands—McDonald's, Corona Extra, Swatch, Waterford, Benetton, and Dr. Martens, for instance—are strongly identified with a particular country. In much of the world, McDonald's is the quintessential American fast-food restaurant, just as Dr. Martens are synonymous with British youth culture. However, for many

Dr. Martens have long been popular with rock stars and club kids. Recently, people from all walks of life—including the pope—have taken to the rugged shoes with the distinctive yellow "Z Welt" stitching. The brand's owner, R. Griggs Group, is headquartered in Northamptonshire, but 85 percent of the company's footwear sales are generated outside of the United Kingdom.

other products, brands, and companies, the sense of identity with a particular country is becoming blurred. Which brands are Japanese—or American—or Korean—or German? In what country is Nokia headquartered? Does a Big Mac taste the same everywhere in the world?

The global marketplace finds expression in many ways; some quite subtle, others less so. While shopping, you may have noticed more multi-language labeling on your favorite products and brands. If you had an Amoco or Standard Oil credit card, it has been replaced by a card from BP. Wal-Mart buys about $10 billion worth of goods from China each year. When you shop at your local gourmet coffee store, you may have noticed that some beans are labeled "Free Trade Certified." Your toll-free telephone call to a software technical support service or an airline customer service center may be answered in Bombay. Quentin Tarantino's movie *Kill Bill* was filmed on soundstages in China. Possibly you heard or read recent news accounts of antiglobalization protesters disrupting meetings of the World Trade Organization in Cancún, Mexico.

The preceding paragraphs provide some clues to the sweeping transformation that has profoundly affected the people and industries of many nations during the past 150 years. International trade has existed for centuries; beginning in 200 B.C., for example, the legendary Silk Road connected the East with the West. Even so, prior to 1840, students sitting at their desks would not have had any item in their possession that was manufactured more than a few miles from where they lived—with the possible exception of the books they were reading. From the mid-1800s to the early 1920s, with Great Britain the dominant economic power in the world, international trade flourished. A series of global upheavals, including World War I, the Bolshevik Revolution, and the Great Depression, brought that era to an end. Then, following World War II, a new era began. This new global era is characterized by unparalleled expansion into global markets by companies that previously served only customers located in their home country.

Two decades ago, the phrase *global marketing* did not even exist. Today, savvy business people utilize global marketing for the realization of their companies' full commercial potential. That is why, no matter whether you live in Asia, Europe, or North or South America, you may be familiar with the brands mentioned in the opening paragraphs. However, there is another, even more critical reason why companies need to take global marketing seriously: survival. A company that fails to understand the importance of global marketing risks losing its domestic business to competitors with lower costs, more experience, and better products. But what is global marketing? How does it differ from "regular" marketing? *Marketing* is the process of planning and executing the conception, pricing, promotion, and distribution of ideas, goods, and services to create exchanges that satisfy individual and organization goals.[1] Marketing activities center on an organization's efforts to satisfy customer wants and needs with products and services that offer competitive value. The marketing mix (product, price, place, and promotion) comprises a contemporary marketer's primary tools. Marketing is a universal discipline, as applicable in Argentina as it is in Zimbabwe.

This book is about *global marketing*. An organization that engages in **global marketing** focuses its resources on global market opportunities and threats. One difference between "regular" marketing and "global" marketing is the scope of activities. A company that engages in global marketing conducts important business activities outside the home-country market. Another difference is that global marketing involves an understanding of specific concepts, considerations, and strategies that must be skillfully applied in conjunction with universal marketing fundamentals to ensure success in global markets. This book concentrates on the major dimensions of global marketing. A brief overview of marketing is presented next, although the authors assume that the reader has completed an introductory marketing course or has equivalent experience.

## OVERVIEW OF MARKETING

Marketing can be described as one of the functional areas of a business, distinct from finance and operations. Marketing can also be thought of as one of the activities that, along with product design, manufacturing, and transportation logistics, comprise a firm's **value chain**. Decisions at every stage, from idea conception to support after the sale, should be assessed in terms of their ability to create value for customers. Historically, marketing was considered just another link in the chain. Today, however, many organizations are emphasizing the effective coordination of marketing with other functional areas. Competitive pressures have prompted many firms to involve marketers in design, manufacturing, and other value-related decisions from the start. This approach is known in some circles as *boundaryless marketing*. Rather than linking marketing sequentially with other activities, the goal is to eliminate the communication barriers between marketing and other functional areas. Properly implemented, boundaryless marketing ensures that a marketing orientation permeates *all* value-creating activities in a company. This change in emphasis is reflected in Figure 1-1. GE and other companies that subscribe to the "boundaryless" concept give employees at all levels and in all departments the opportunity to be involved in marketing.

For any organization operating anywhere in the world, the essence of marketing is to surpass the competition at the task of creating perceived value for customers. The **value equation** is a guide to this task:

$$\text{Value} = \text{Benefits}/\text{Price (money, time, effort, etc.)}$$

---

[1] Peter D. Bennett, ed., *Dictionary of Marketing Terms,* 2d ed. (Chicago: NTC Business Books, 1995), p. 166.

**Figure 1-1**

*The Value Chain and Boundaryless Marketing*

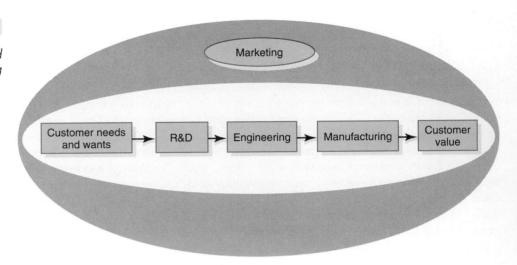

The marketing mix is integral to the equation because benefits are a combination of the product, promotion, and distribution. As a general rule, value, as perceived by the customer, can be increased in two basic ways. Markets can offer customers an improved bundle of benefits or lower prices (or both!). Marketers may strive to improve the product itself, to design new channels of distribution, to create better communications strategies, or a combination of all three. Marketers may also seek to increase value by finding ways to cut costs and prices. Nonmonetary costs are also a factor, and marketers may be able to decrease the time and effort that customers must expend to learn about or seek out the product.[2] Companies that use price as a competitive weapon may enjoy an ample supply of low-wage labor or access to cheap raw materials. Companies can also reduce prices if costs are low because of process efficiencies in manufacturing.

If a company is able to offer a combination of superior product, distribution, or promotion benefits *and* lower prices than the competition, it enjoys an extremely advantageous position. This is precisely how Toyota, Nissan, and other Japanese automakers made significant gains in the American market in the 1980s. They offered cars with higher quality and lower prices than those made by Chrysler, Ford, and General Motors. Needless to say, to become a market success, a product must measure up to a threshold of acceptable quality. Some of Japan's initial auto exports were market failures. In the late 1960s, for example, Subaru of America began importing the Subaru 360 automobile and offering it for sale with a sticker price of $1,297. After *Consumer Reports* judged the 360 "not acceptable," however, sales ground to a halt. Similarly, the Yugo automobile achieved a modest level of U.S. sales in the 1980s (despite a "don't buy" rating from a consumer magazine) because its sticker price of $3,999 made it the cheapest new car available. Low quality was the primary reason for the market failure of both the Subaru 360 and the Yugo.[3]

## Competitive Advantage, Globalization, and Global Industries

When a company succeeds in creating more value for customers than its competitors do, that company is said to enjoy **competitive advantage** in an industry. Competitive advantage is measured relative to rivals in a given industry. For example, your local

---

2   With certain categories of differentiated goods, including designer clothing and other luxury products, higher price is often associated with increased value.

3   The history of the Subaru 360 is documented in Randall Rothman, *Where the Suckers Moon: The Life and Death of an Advertising Campaign* (New York: Vintage Books, 1994), chapter 4.

laundromat is in a local industry; its competitors are local. In a national industry, competitors are national. In a global industry—automobiles, consumer electronics, athletic shoes, watches, pharmaceuticals, steel, furniture, and dozens of other sectors—the competition is, likewise, global. Global marketing is essential if a company competes in a global industry or one that is globalizing. The transformation of formerly local or national industries into global ones is part of a broader process of *globalization*, which Thomas L. Friedman defines as follows:

> Globalization is the inexorable integration of markets, nation-states and technologies to a degree never witnessed before—in a way that is enabling individuals, corporations and nation-states to reach around the world farther, faster, deeper and cheaper than ever before, and in a way that is enabling the world to reach into individuals, corporations and nation-states farther, faster, deeper, and cheaper than ever before.[4]

From a marketing point of view, globalization presents companies with tantalizing opportunities—and challenges—as executives decide whether or not to offer their products and services everywhere. At the same time, globalization presents companies with unprecedented opportunities to reconfigure themselves; as John Micklethwait and Adrian Wooldridge put it, "the same global bazaar that allows consumers to buy the best that the world can offer also allows producers to find the best partners."[5]

What, then, is a global industry? As management guru Michael Porter has noted, a **global industry** is one in which competitive advantage can be achieved by integrating and leveraging operations on a worldwide scale. Put another way, an industry is global to the extent that a company's industry position in one country is interdependent with its industry position in other countries. Indicators of globalization include the ratio of cross-border trade to total worldwide production, the ratio of cross-border investment to total capital investment, and the proportion of industry revenue generated by companies that compete in all key world regions.[6]

Achieving competitive advantage in a global industry requires executives and managers to maintain a well-defined strategic focus. **Focus** is simply the concentration of attention on a core business or competence. The importance of focus for a global company is evident in the following comment by Helmut Maucher, former chairman of Nestlé SA:

> Nestlé is focused: We are food and beverages. We are not running bicycle shops. Even in food we are not in all fields. There are certain areas we do not touch. For the time being we have no biscuits [cookies] in Europe and the United States for competitive reasons, and no margarine. We have no soft drinks because I have said we either buy Coca-Cola or we leave it alone. This is focus.[7]

However, company management may choose to initiate a change in focus as part of an overall strategy shift. Even Coca-Cola has been forced to sharpen its focus on its core beverage brands. Following sluggish sales in 2000–2001, chief executive Douglas Daft announced a new alliance with Nestlé that will jointly develop and market coffees and teas. Daft also set about the task of transforming Coca-Cola's Minute Maid unit into a global division that will market juice brands worldwide. As Daft explained:

> We're a network of brands and businesses. You don't just want to be a total beverage company. Each brand has a different return on investment, is sold differently, drunk

---

4   Thomas L. Friedman, *The Lexus and the Olive Tree* (New York: Anchor Books, 2000), p. 9.
5   John Micklethwait and Adrian Wooldridge, *A Future Perfect: The Challenge and Hidden Promise of Globalization* (New York: Crown Publishers, 2000), p. xxvii.
6   Vijay Govindarajan and Anil Gupta, "Setting a Course for the New Global Landscape," *Financial Times—Mastering Global Business*, part I (1998), p. 3.
7   Elizabeth Ashcroft, "Nestlé and the Twenty-First Century," Harvard Business School Case 9-595-074, 1995. See also Ernest Beck, "Nestlé Feels Little Pressure to Make Big Acquisitions," *The Wall Street Journal* (June 22, 2000), p. B4.

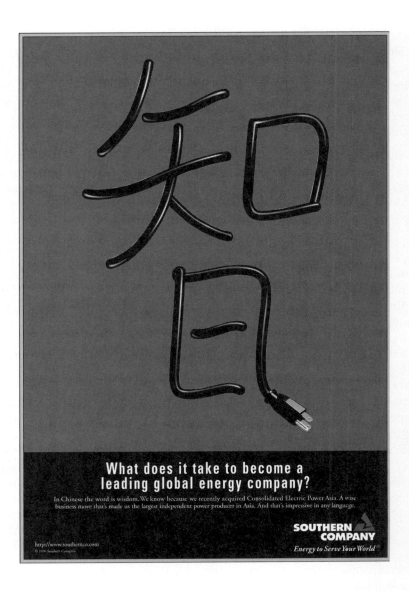

**What does it take to become a leading global energy company?**

In Chinese the word is wisdom. We know because we recently acquired Consolidated Electric Power Asia. A wise business move that's made us the largest independent power producer in Asia. And that's impressive in any language.

http://www.southernco.com
© 1996 Southern Company

**SOUTHERN COMPANY**
*Energy to Serve Your World*

for different reasons, and has different managing structures. If you mix them all together, you lose the focus.[8]

Examples abound of corporate executives addressing the issue of focus, often in response to changes in the global business environment. In recent years Fiat, Volvo, Electrolux, Toshiba, Colgate, and many other companies have stepped up efforts to sharpen their strategic focus on core businesses. Specific actions can take a number of different forms besides alliances, including mergers, acquisitions, divestitures, and folding some businesses into other company divisions.[9]

IBM originally succeeded in the data-processing industry by focusing on customer needs and wants better than Univac. After decades of success, however, IBM remained focused on mainframe computers, despite customers who were increasingly turning to PCs. IBM was a key player in the early days of the PC revolution, but its corporate culture was still oriented toward mainframes. "Big Blue" faltered in the early 1990s—it lost more than $8 billion in 1993—in part because competitors

---

8   Betsy McKay, "Coke's 'Think Local' Strategy has Yet to Prove Itself," *The Wall Street Journal* (March 1, 2001), p. B6.
9   Robert A. Guth, "How Japan's Toshiba Got Its Focus Back," *The Wall Street Journal* (December 12, 2000), p. A6.
10  Scott Miller, "BMW Bucks Diversification to Focus on Luxury Models," *The Wall Street Journal* (March 20, 2002), p. B4.

### Managing Global Growth

The first years of the twenty-first century have proved challenging for deal-making top executives at several global companies. In 1998, Edgar Bronfman, Jr., the CEO of Montreal-based Seagram Company, paid $1 billion for music giant PolyGram NV and sold Seagram's Tropicana orange juice unit to PepsiCo. Bronfman then sold Chivas Regal, several other major spirits brands, and Seagram's wine business to Diageo PLC and Pernod-Ricard SA. Collectively, these transactions shifted Seagram's focus from beverages to entertainment; the combination of PolyGram with Seagram's MCA record unit created a global music powerhouse. In 2000, Bronfman agreed to a $32 billion takeover by France's Vivendi. The resulting company, Vivendi Universal, was tightly focused in two industry sectors: environmental services and communications. The strategic plan for the communications businesses called for distributing Universal's entertainment content via an Internet portal that could be accessed by PCs, wireless phones, and other electronic devices. However, Vivendi Universal had taken on too much debt, and chairman Jean-Marie Messier was forced to resign in 2002.

ABB Inc., the Swiss/Swedish electrical and engineering firm that was once comprised of 1,300 companies in 140 countries, is another global giant that has fallen on hard times. During the 1990s, ABB was frequently cited as a textbook example of a successful transnational company. Former chief executive Percy Barnevik was legendary in business circles for his charismatic

and visionary leadership. However, one of his acquisitions, Combustion Engineering, an American producer of powerplant boilers, proved disastrous because of asbestos-related liability claims. Although his decentralized management structure helped the company grow, it also resulted in conflict and breakdowns in communication between far-flung management units. Between 1997 and 2003, two chief executives—Göran Lindahl and Jörgen Centerman—came and went in quick succession. The company lost nearly $700 million in 2001; also in 2001, Barnevik, who had remained with the company as a non-executive chairman, was forced to resign after a scandal involving pension benefits. The following year, losses totaled nearly $800 million. ABB's current chief executive, Jürgen Dormann, is selling non-core assets such as its finance unit in an effort to reduce debt; the slimmed-down company's two core businesses will be focused around automation and power technologies. Commenting on Barnevik's legacy, Dormann noted "We had a lack of focus as Percy went on an acquisition spree...The company wasn't disciplined enough."

*Sources: Bruce Orwall, "Universal Script: Vivendi-Seagram Deal Has the Former MCA Playing Familiar Role," The Wall Street Journal (June 20, 2000), pp. A1, A8; John Carreyrou and Martin Peers, "Damage Control: How Messier Kept Cash Crisis at Vivendi Hidden for Months," The Wall Street Journal (October 31, 2002), pp. A1, A15; Dan Bilefsky and Anita Raghavan, "Blown Fuse: How 'Europe's GE' and Its Star CEO Tumbled to Earth," The Wall Street Journal (January 23, 2003), pp. A1, A8.*

specializing in PCs had become even *more* clearly focused on what PC customers needed and wanted; namely, low prices and increased speed. Within a few years, however, then-CEO Lou Gerstner succeeded in refocusing the company's PC business and broadening its scope to higher-margin products such as servers for electronic commerce and the Thinkpad laptop. Gerstner and e-business marketing chief Abby Kohnstamm also leveraged IBM's reputation for providing expertise-based solutions for its customers; in 2003, global services accounted for 48 percent of revenues and 41 percent of profits.

Value, competitive advantage, and the focus required to achieve them are universal in their relevance and they should guide marketing efforts in any part of the world. Global marketing requires attention to these issues on a worldwide basis and utilization of an information system capable of monitoring the globe for opportunities and threats. A fundamental premise of this book can be stated as follows: Companies that understand and engage in global marketing can offer more overall value to customers than companies that do not have that understanding. There are many who share this conviction. For example, C. Samuel Craig and Susan P. Douglas recently noted:

> Globalization is no longer an abstraction but a stark reality. . . . Choosing not to participate in global markets is no longer an option. All firms, regardless of their size, have to craft strategies in the broader context of world markets to anticipate, respond, and adapt to the changing configuration of these markets.[11]

---

[11] C. Samuel Craig and Susan P. Douglas, "Responding to the Challenges of Global Markets: Change, Complexity, Competition, and Conscience," *Columbia Journal of World Business* 31, no. 4 (Winter 1996), pp. 6–18.

# GLOBAL marketing in action ▄

## Whirlpool Thinks Globally

Assessment of an industry's actual or potential degree of globalization may vary among companies. Recalling Whirlpool's assessment of the changing business environment, CEO David Whitwam noted, "The closer we looked, the more we said to ourselves, 'This is becoming a global industry. One of these days someone is going to figure that out and build lots of competitive advantage. That someone should be us.'" Today, Whirlpool produces white goods (as major appliances are known in the industry) in 11 countries and is the only appliance manufacturer with strategic positions in North America, Latin America, Europe, and Asia. To date, however, the European strategy has not paid off as expected, because large competitors such as Bosch-Siemens and Electrolux invested heavily in product and efficiency improvements. Meanwhile, Whirlpool made

marketing and management mistakes. Executives were forced to scale back the objective of capturing 20 percent of the European appliance market by 2000. Despite its disappointments, Whirlpool is proceeding with plans to globalize the development of new products by creating "platforms" (core design elements) that can be used throughout the world. It is noteworthy that appliance makers in Japan have not targeted the United States, in part because they do not share the view that the appliance industry is global.

Sources: William C. Taylor and Alan M. Webber, Going Global: Four Entrepreneurs Map the New World Marketplace (New York: Penguin Books USA, 1996), p. 7; Greg Steinmetz and Carl Quintanilla, "Tough Target: Whirlpool Expected Easy Going in Europe, and It Got a Big Shock," The Wall Street Journal (April 10, 1998), pp. A1, A6. See also Peter Marsh and Nikki Tait, "Whirlpool's Platform for Growth," Financial Times (March 26, 1998), p. 8.

## GLOBAL MARKETING: WHAT IT IS AND WHAT IT ISN'T

The discipline of marketing is universal. It is natural, however, that marketing practices will vary from country to country, for the simple reason that the countries and peoples of the world are different. These differences mean that a marketing approach that has proven successful in one country will not *necessarily* succeed in another country. Customer preferences, competitors, channels of distribution, and communication media may differ. An important task in global marketing is learning to recognize the extent to which marketing plans and programs can be extended worldwide, as well as the extent to which they must be adapted.

The way a company addresses this task is a reflection of its **global marketing strategy** (GMS). Recall that in single country marketing, strategy development addresses two fundamental issues: choosing a target market and developing a marketing mix. The same two issues are at the heart of a firm's GMS, although they are viewed from a somewhat different perspective (see Table 1-1). **Global market participation** is the extent to which a company has operations in major world markets. *Standardization versus adaptation* is the extent to which each marketing mix element can be standardized (i.e., executed the same way) or adapted (i.e., executed in different ways) in various country markets. GMS has three additional dimensions that pertain to marketing management. First, *concentration of marketing activities* is the extent to which activities related to the marketing mix

***Table 1-1***

*Comparison of Single-Country Marketing Strategy and Global Marketing Strategy*

| Single-Country Marketing Strategy | Global Marketing Strategy |
|---|---|
| Target Market Strategy | Global Market Participation |
| Marketing Mix Development | Marketing Mix Development |
|     Product |     Product adaptation or standardization |
|     Price |     Price adaptation or standardization |
|     Promotion |     Promotion adaptation or standardization |
|     Place |     Place adaptation or standardization |
| | Concentration of Marketing Activities |
| | Coordination of Marketing Activities |
| | Integration of Competitive Moves |

(e.g., promotional campaigns or pricing decisions) are performed in one or a few country locations. *Coordination of marketing activities* refers to the extent to which marketing activities related to the marketing mix are planned and executed interdependently around the globe. Finally, *integration of competitive moves* is the extent to which a firm's competitive marketing tactics in different parts of the world are interdependent. The GMS should be designed to enhance the firm's performance on a worldwide basis.[12]

Companies that engage in global marketing do not necessarily conduct business in every one of the world's 200-plus country markets. Global marketing *does* mean widening business horizons to encompass the world in scanning for opportunity and threat. The decision to enter one or more particular markets outside the home country depends on a company's resources, its managerial mind-set, and the nature of opportunity and threat. Some brands are, indeed, found in virtually every country; Coke is a case in point. Coke is the best-known, strongest brand in the world; its enviable global position has resulted in part from the Coca-Cola Company's willingness and ability to back its flagship brand with a network of local bottlers and a strong local marketing effort.

The issue of standardization versus adaptation has been at the center of a long-standing controversy among both academicians and business practitioners. Much of the controversy dates back to Professor Theodore Levitt's 1983 article in the *Harvard Business Review*, "The Globalization of Markets." Levitt argued that marketers were confronted with a "homogeneous global village." He advised organizations to develop standardized, high-quality world products and market them around the globe by using standardized advertising, pricing, and distribution. Some well-publicized failures by Parker Pen and other companies that tried to follow Levitt's advice brought his proposals into question. The business press frequently quoted industry observers who disputed Levitt's views. As Carl Spielvogel, chairman and CEO of the Backer Spielvogel Bates Worldwide advertising agency, told *The Wall Street Journal* in the late 1980s, "Theodore Levitt's comment about the world becoming homogenized is bunk. There are about two products that lend themselves to global marketing—and one of them is Coca-Cola."[13]

Indeed, global marketing made Coke a worldwide success. However, that success was *not* based on a total standardization of marketing mix elements. For example, Coca-Cola achieved success in Japan by spending a great deal of time and money to become an insider; that is, the company built a complete local infrastructure with its sales force and vending machine operations. Coke's success in Japan is a function of its ability to achieve "global localization," being as much of an insider as a local company but still reaping the benefits that result from worldscale operations.[14] Similarly, in India, the company's local Thums Up cola brand competes with—and even outsells—the flagship cola.[15]

What does the phrase *global localization* really mean? In a nutshell, it means that a successful global marketer must have the ability to "think globally and act locally." As we will see many times in this book, "global" marketing may include a combination of standard (e.g., the actual product itself) and nonstandard (e.g., distribution or packaging) approaches. A global product may be the same product everywhere and yet different. Global marketing requires marketers to behave in a way that is

---

12 Shaoming Zou and S. Tamer Cavusgil, "The GMS: A Broad Conceptualization of Global Marketing Strategy and Its Effect on Performance," *Journal of Marketing* 66, no. 4 (October 2002), pp. 40–56.

13 Joanne Lipman, "Ad Fad: Marketers Turn Sour on Global Sales Pitch Harvard Guru Makes," *The Wall Street Journal* (May 12, 1988), p. 1.

14 Kenichi Ohmae, *The Borderless World: Power and Strategy* (New York: Harper Perennial, 1991), pp. 26–27.

15 Nikhil Deogun and Jonathan Karp, "For Coke in India, Thums Up Is the Real Thing," *The Wall Street Journal* (April 29, 1998), pp. B1, B2.

global *and* local at the same time by responding to similarities and differences in world markets. Kenichi Ohmae recently summed up this paradox as follows:

> The essence of being a global company is to maintain a kind of tension within the organization without being undone by it. Some companies say the new world requires homogeneous products—"one size fits all"—everywhere. Others say the world requires endless customization —special products for every region. The best global companies understand it's neither and it's both. They keep the two perspectives in mind simultaneously.[16]

As the Coca-Cola Company has convincingly demonstrated, the ability to think globally and act locally can be a source of competitive advantage. Because the company is adept at adapting sales promotion, distribution, and customer service efforts to local needs, Coke has become a billion-dollar-plus brand in six markets outside the United States: Brazil, Germany, Great Britain, Japan, Mexico, and Spain. Of course, this type of success does not happen overnight. For example, Coca-Cola managers initially did not understand the Japanese distribution system. However, with considerable investment of time and money, they succeeded in establishing a sales force that was as effective in Japan as it was in the United States. The Japanese unit has also created numerous new beverage products expressly for the Japanese market; these include Georgia-brand canned coffee and Qoo, a noncarbonated juice drink. Today, Japan accounts for nearly 20 percent of the Coca-Cola Company's total worldwide operating revenues.

The Coca-Cola Company supports its Coke, Fanta, and Powerade brands with marketing mix elements that are both global and local. Dozens of other companies also have successfully pursued global marketing by creating strong global brands. This has been accomplished in various ways. The Altria Group (formerly Philip Morris), for example, made Marlboro the world's number one cigarette by identifying the brand with a cowboy. By creating distinctive, user-friendly handset designs, Nokia has become the world's leading cell phone brand. In automobiles, DaimlerChrysler's Mercedes nameplate enjoys global recognition thanks to Germany's reputation for excellence in automotive engineering. Virtually all Nokia phones are manufactured in Finland; by contrast, some Mercedes models are manufactured outside Germany. Gillette uses the same packaging for its flagship Mach3 razor everywhere in the world. Italy's Benetton utilizes a sophisticated distribution system to quickly deliver the latest fashions to its worldwide network of stores. The backbone of Caterpillar's global success is a network of dealers who support a promise of "24-hour parts and service" anywhere in the world. As these examples indicate, there are many different paths to success in global markets. In this book, we do *not* propose that global marketing is a knee-jerk attempt to impose a totally standardized approach to marketing around the world. A central issue in global marketing is how to tailor the global marketing concept to fit particular products, businesses, and markets.[17]

As shown in Table 1-2, McDonald's global marketing strategy is based on a combination of global and local marketing mix elements. For example, a core element in McDonald's business model is a restaurant system that can be set up virtually anywhere in the world. McDonald's offers core menu items—hamburgers, French fries, and soft drinks—in most countries, and the company also customizes menu offerings in accordance with local eating customs. The average price of a Big Mac in the United States is $2.80. By contrast, in China, Big Macs sell for the equivalent of $1.23. In absolute terms, Chinese Big Macs are cheaper than American ones.

---

[16] William C. Taylor and Alan M. Webber, *Going Global: Four Entrepreneurs Map the New World Marketplace* (New York: Penguin Books USA, 1996), pp. 48–49.

[17] John A. Quelch and Edward J. Hoff, "Customizing Global Marketing," *Harvard Business Review* 64, no. 3 (May–June 1986), p. 59.

Some of Coke's many faces around the world. Although the basic design of the label is the same (white letters against a red background), the Coca-Cola name is frequently transliterated into local languages. In the left-hand column, the Arabic label (second from top) is read from right to left; the Chinese label (fourth from the top) translates "delicious/happiness."

But is it a fair comparison? Real estate costs vary from country to country, as do per capita incomes. McDonald's prices can be understood in terms of the length of time a person must work to earn enough money to buy a Big Mac. Each year UBS, a Swiss bank, publishes a study of purchasing power based on a weighted average of hourly wages across 13 occupations. For example, in Los Angeles and Tokyo, earnings from 10 minutes of work can buy a Big Mac; by contrast, in Bombay, the corresponding figure is 112 minutes.[18]

**Table 1-2**

*Examples of Effective Global Marketing—McDonald's*

| Marketing Mix Element | Standardized | Localized |
|---|---|---|
| Product | Big Mac | McAloo Tikka potato burger (India) |
| Promotion | Brand name | Slang nicknames, e.g., "Macca's" (Australia), MakDo (Philippines), "McDoof" (Germany) |
| | Advertising slogan "I'm Loving It" | McJoy magazine "Hawaii Surfing Hula" promotion (Japan) |
| Place | Free-standing restaurants in high-traffic public areas | McDonald's Switzerland operates themed dining cars on Swiss national rail system; McDonald's served on Stena Line ferry from Helsinki to Oslo; home delivery (India) |
| Price | Average price of Big Mac is $2.80 (USA); same in Korea | $5.11 (Switzerland); $1.23 (China) |

---

[18] Frances Williams, "Price of a Big Mac: 10 Minutes in Miami, Three Hours in Nairobi," *Financial Times* (August 21, 2003), p. 4.

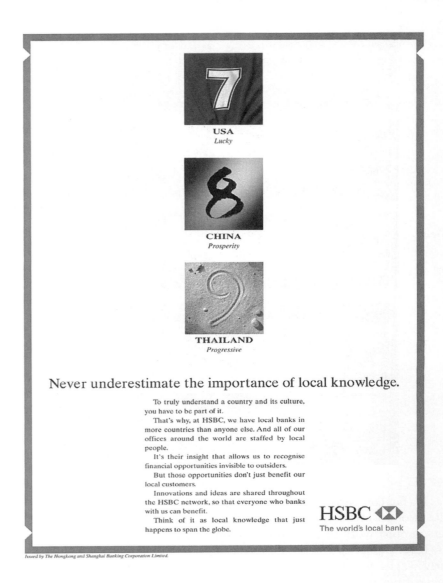

The particular approach to global marketing that a company adopts will depend on industry conditions and its source or sources of competitive advantage. For example:

- Harley-Davidson's motorcycles are perceived around the world as *the* all-American bike. Should Harley-Davidson start manufacturing motorcycles in a low-wage country such as Mexico?

- The success of Honda and Toyota in world markets was initially based on exporting cars from factories in Japan. Now, both companies have invested in manufacturing and assembly facilities in the Americas, Asia, and Europe. From these sites, the automakers supply customers in the local market and also export to the rest of the world. For example, each year Honda exports tens of thousands of Accords and Civics from U.S. plants to Japan and dozens of other countries. Will European consumers continue to buy Honda vehicles exported from America? Will American consumers continue to snap up American-built Toyotas?

- About 85 percent of Gap's 3,000 stores are located in the United States, and its design group is based in New York. However, the company relies on apparel factories in Honduras, the Philippines, India, and other low-wage countries to supply most of its clothing. Should Gap open more stores in Japan?

The answer to these questions is: "It all depends." Because Harley's competitive advantage is based in part on its "Made in the USA" positioning, shifting production outside the United States is not advisable. The company has opened a new production facility in Kansas and taken a majority stake in Buell Motorcycle, a manufacturer of "American street bikes." Toyota's success in the United States is partly attributable to its ability to transfer world-class manufacturing skills to America while using advertising to stress that its Camry is built by Americans with many components purchased from American suppliers. Gap has more than 500 stores outside the United States, including Canada, the United Kingdom, Japan, and France. Japan may present an opportunity for Gap to increase revenues and profits in a major non-U.S. market. A recent annual report noted that, in terms of sales revenues, the apparel market outside the United States is twice as large as that within the United States. Also, "American style" is in high demand in Japan and other parts of the world. Gap's management team has responded to this situation by selectively targeting key country markets—especially areas with high population densities—while continuing to concentrate on trends in the U.S. fashion marketplace. However, recent operating difficulties in the core U.S. market led to the departure of several executives, suggesting management's top priority at this time should be the domestic market.[19]

## THE IMPORTANCE OF GLOBAL MARKETING

The largest single market in the world in terms of national income, the United States represents roughly 25 percent of the total world market for all products and services. Thus, U.S. companies that wish to achieve maximum growth potential must "go global" because 75 percent of world market potential is outside their home country. Management at Coca-Cola clearly understands this; about 75 percent of the company's operating income and two-thirds of operating revenue are generated outside North America. Non-U.S. companies have an even greater motivation to seek market opportunities beyond their own borders; their opportunities include the 290 million people in the United States. For example, even though the dollar value of the home market for Japanese companies is the second largest in the world (after the United States), the market *outside* Japan is 85 percent of the world potential for Japanese companies. For European countries, the picture is even more dramatic. Even though Germany is the largest single country market in Europe, 94 percent of the world market potential for German companies is outside Germany.

Many companies have recognized the importance of conducting business activities outside the home country. Industries that were essentially national in scope only a few years ago are dominated today by a handful of global companies. The rise of the global corporation closely parallels the rise of the national corporation, which emerged from the local and regional corporation in the 1880s and 1890s in the United States. The auto industry provides a dramatic example: In the early twentieth century, there were thousands of auto companies scattered around the globe. The United States alone was home to more than 500 automakers. Today, fewer than 20 major companies remain worldwide. A dramatic illustration of the ongoing consolidation in the auto industry is Daimler-Benz's $36 billion takeover of Chrysler in 1998. In most industries, the companies that will survive and prosper in the twenty-first century will be

---

[19] Gap's transformation into a global brand is chronicled in Nina Munk, "Gap Gets It," *Fortune* (August 3, 1998), pp. 68–74+; see also Calmetta Coleman, "Gap is Making Management Changes to Fight Sales Slump," *The Wall Street Journal* (November 7, 2000), p. B4.

**Table 1-3**

The Largest Corporations by
Market Capitalization

| Company | Market Value (US$ millions) |
|---|---|
| 1. General Electric (USA) | 294,206 |
| 2. Microsoft (USA) | 283,576 |
| 3. Wal-Mart Stores (USA) | 259,501 |
| 4. Exxon Mobil (USA) | 251,813 |
| 5. Pfizer (USA) | 226,203 |
| 6. Citigroup (USA) | 222,849 |
| 7. Intel (USA) | 187,003 |
| 8. American International Group (USA) | 155,382 |
| 9. Royal Dutch/Shell Group (UK/Netherlands) | 154,194 |
| 10. BP (UK) | 151,431 |
| 11. Johnson & Johnson (USA) | 147,194 |
| 12. International Business Machines (USA) | 141,713 |
| 13. HSBC Holdings (UK) | 137,526 |
| 14. Cisco Systems (SA) | 134,409 |
| 15. NTT DoCoMo (Japan) | 128,766 |
| 16. Vodafone Group (UK) | 124,425 |
| 17. Bank of America (USA) | 118,613 |
| 18. GlaxoSmithKline (UK) | 114,811 |
| 19. Procter & Gamble (USA) | 112,858 |
| 20. Merck (USA) | 112,834 |
| 21. Coca-Cola (USA) | 107,201 |
| 22. Total (France) | 105,437 |
| 23. Novartis (Switzerland) | 99,873 |
| 24. Toyota Motor (Japan) | 99,429 |
| 25. Berkshire Hathaway (USA) | 98,255 |

*Source:* "The World's 100 Largest Public Companies," *The Wall Street Journal* (September 22, 2003), p. R9. Data reflect market value on August 29, 2003. *Wall Street Journal.* Online (Staff Produced Copy Only) by Unknown. Copyright 2003 by Dow Jones & Co. Inc. Reproduced with permission of Dow Jones & Co. Inc. in the format Textbook via Copyright Clearance Center.

global enterprises. Some companies that fail to formulate adequate responses to the challenges and opportunities of globalization will be absorbed by more dynamic, visionary enterprises. Others—ABB, for example—will undergo wrenching transformations and, if the effort succeeds, will emerge from the process greatly transformed. There is a third, grimmer, scenario as well: Some companies will simply disappear. Table 1-3 shows 25 of *The Wall Street Journal*'s top 100 companies in terms of market capitalization; that is, the market value of all shares of stock outstanding. Table 1-4 provides a different perspective: the top 25 of *Fortune* magazine's 2003 ranking of the 500 largest service and manufacturing companies by revenues.

Comparing the two tables, one is struck by GE's strong showing: It is first in market capitalization and ninth in revenues. Much credit for this outstanding performance goes to former CEO Jack Welch, who set out in the mid-1980s to globalize his company. Note too that, measured by market capitalization, Toyota is the world's most valuable car company; today, Toyota sells more cars worldwide than Ford. Ford and GM were not in the top 100 market value rankings in 2003. Not every company in the tables is truly global, however; Nippon Telegraph and Telephone (NTT), for example, ranks fifteenth in revenues. In 2000, NTT ranked twentieth in market value; by 2003, the company had dropped to forty-third. A downturn in the telecommunications sector and Japan's ongoing economic woes help explain the poor profit and market value performance. Until recently, Japanese regulations severely limited NTT's reach outside of Japan. After regulations were relaxed in 1999, NTT embarked on a global shopping spree. Acquisitions include Verio Inc., a U.S.-based Internet company; NTT also bought a stake in the mobile phone unit of a Dutch

**Table 1-4**

The Fortune Global 500: Largest Corporations by Revenues

company, KPN NV. The company's strategic goal is to become a global company with a strong base in Asia.[20] Similarly, Wal-Mart, the world's number one retailer, currently generates only about 5 percent of revenues outside the United States. However, global expansion is the key to the company's growth strategy over the next few years.

Examining the size of individual product markets, measured in terms of annual sales, provides another perspective on global marketing's importance. Not surprisingly, many of the companies identified in Tables 1-3 and 1-4 are key players in the global marketplace. Annual sales in select global industry sectors markets are shown in Table 1-5. Table 1-6 shows annual sales in individual countries for select product categories.

## MANAGEMENT ORIENTATIONS

The form and substance of a company's response to global market opportunities depend greatly on management's assumptions or beliefs—both conscious and unconscious—about the nature of the world. The world view of a company's personnel can be described as ethnocentric, polycentric, regiocentric, or geocentric.[21] Management at a company with a prevailing ethnocentric orientation may consciously make a decision to move in the direction of geocentrism.

---

[20] Robert Guth, "Japan's NTT Steps Up Its Push into U.S. and Europe," *The Wall Street Journal* (May 26, 2000), pp. A16, A19.

[21] Adapted from Howard Perlmutter, "The Tortuous Evolution of the Multinational Corporation," *Columbia Journal of World Business* (January–February 1969)

**Table 1-5**

*How Big Is the Market?*
*I—Product Category*

| Product or Service | Size of Market | Key Players/Brands |
|---|---|---|
| Cigarettes | $295 billion | Altria Group (USA); B.A.T Industries (UK); Japan Tobacco (Japan); Gallaher Group (UK) |
| Personal computers | $175 billion | Hewlett Packard (USA); Dell (USA) |
| Computer software | $95 billion | IBM (USA); Microsoft (USA); Oracle (USA); SAP (Germany) |
| White goods (major appliances) | $85 billion | Whirlpool (USA); Electrolux (Sweden); Bosch-Siemens (Germany) |
| Construction equipment | $70 billion | Caterpillar (USA); Komatsu (Japan); Volvo (Sweden) |
| Cell phones | $60 billion | Nokia (Finland); Motorola (USA); Samsung (South Korea) |
| Luxury goods | $55 billion | LVMH Group (France); Giorgio Armani (Italy) |
| Recorded music | $32 billion | Sony Music (Japan); Warner Music (USA); BMG (Germany); EMI (UK); Universal Music Group (France) |
| Pet food | $30 billion | Iams (Procter & Gamble USA); Ralston Purina (Nestlé Switzerland); Pedigree (Mars USA) |
| Flat panel displays | $29 billion | LG Philips (South Korea/Netherlands); Samsung (South Korea); Sharp (Japan) |
| Customer relationship management (CRM) services | $6 billion | Siebel (USA); Oracle (USA); SAP (Germany) |
| Regional jet aircraft | $5.9 billion | Bombardier (Canada); Embraer (Brazil) |

The orientations—collectively known as the EPRG framework—are summarized in Figure 1-2.

## Ethnocentric Orientation

A person who assumes that his or her home country is superior to the rest of the world is said to have an **ethnocentric orientation**. Ethnocentrism is sometimes associated with attitudes of national arrogance or assumptions of national superiority. Company personnel with an ethnocentric orientation see only similarities in markets, and *assume* that products and practices that succeed in the home country will be successful anywhere. At some companies, the ethnocentric orientation means that opportunities outside the home country are largely ignored. Such companies are sometimes called **domestic companies.** Ethnocentric companies that conduct business outside the home country can be described as **international companies;** they adhere to the notion that the products that succeed in the home country are superior. This point of view leads to a **standardized** or **extension approach** to marketing based on the premise that products can be sold everywhere without adaptation.

| Country | Product Category | Annual Sales |
|---|---|---|
| United States | Wood furniture | $23.0 billion |
| | Video game consoles and games | $10.0 billion |
| | Toothpaste | $1.5 billion |
| Japan | Pharmaceuticals | $50.0 billion |
| | Luxury goods | $10.5 billion |
| India | Soft drinks | $2.3 billion |
| | Chocolate | $157 million |
| Europe | Cigarettes | $18.0 billion |
| | Home appliances (wholesale) | €20.0 billion |

# OPEN *to* discussion

## Are We Ready for "One World"?

William Greider believes that the globalization of industries and markets will have some unintended, possibly dire, consequences in the coming years. In his book *One World, Ready or Not*, Greider describes how the logic of commerce and capital in the closing years of the twentieth century has created an economic revolution and launched great social transformations. As Greider sees it, the message of globalization contains good news and bad news. The good news is that modern technology and global marketing are enabling people and nations throughout the world to leap into the modern era. The bad news, Greider warns, is that modern technology tends to be more individualistic and anti-egalitarian than the mass assembly technology that revolutionized production in the first part of the twentieth century. As a result, disregard for basic human rights and the exploitation of the weak in developing nations may result in great social upheavals and, eventually, a breakdown in the global system.

One issue that concerns Greider is the fact that productivity and revenues at many global corporations have risen dramatically, while overall worldwide employment has not. Meanwhile, a dispersal of productive wealth is underway as global corporations establish operations in key developing countries like Brazil and China. Many economists agree that this dispersal will narrow the gap between poor and rich nations. Back in the industrialized nations, however, there is an increasing sense of social distress as workers see their plants close and jobs shipped out of the country. One byproduct of globalization, Greider observes, is that it pits the interests of the older, more prosperous workers against the interests of newly recruited, lower-paid workers. Greider warns that deeper political instability lies ahead for the United States, Germany, France, and Britain as workers take up the fight to save their jobs.

In addition, the globalization of industries such as steel, automobiles, and consumer electronics has created surplus production capacity on a massive scale. Greider notes that the U.S. economy serves as a sort of safety valve for the global system. Because the U.S. market places relatively few restrictions on imports, this "benevolent openness" means that the United States serves as a "buyer of last resort" by absorbing much of the world's excess production. As a result of the chronic imbalance in the trading system, the United States continues to post massive trade deficits that defy conventional economic analysis.

What can, or should, be done? Greider argues that U.S.-based global companies that create jobs overseas at the expense of domestic jobs should not be permitted to finance export deals by borrowing from tax-supported agencies such as the Export-Import Bank. At the same time, Greider says that American public interest would be better served if government policy shifted away from supporting and underwriting the interests of global companies and focused instead on jobs and wages. Finally, Greider advocates the use of emergency tariffs to reduce the trade deficit if American policymakers are unable to gain more access in foreign markets to U.S. export.

*Sources: William Greider, One World, Ready or Not: The Manic Logic of Global Capitalism (Upper Saddle River, NJ: Simon & Schuster, 1997); Greider, "Who Governs Globalism?" The American Prospect, no. 30 (January–February 1997), pp. 73–80.*

In the ethnocentric international company, foreign operations or markets are typically viewed as being secondary or subordinate to domestic ones. (We are using the term *domestic* to mean the country in which a company is headquartered.) An ethnocentric company operates under the assumption that "tried and true" headquarters knowledge and organizational capabilities can be applied in other parts of the world. Although this can sometimes work to a company's advantage, valuable managerial knowledge and experience in local markets may go unnoticed. For a manufacturing firm, ethnocentrism may mean foreign markets are viewed as a dumping ground for surplus domestic production. Plans for overseas markets are developed utilizing policies and procedures modeled on those employed at home. Little or no systematic marketing research is conducted outside the home country, and no major modifications are made to products. Even if customer needs or wants differ from those in the home country, those differences are ignored at headquarters.

Nissan's ethnocentric orientation was quite apparent during its first few years of exporting cars and trucks to America. Designed for mild Japanese winters, the vehicles were difficult to start in many parts of the United States during the cold winter months. In northern Japan, many car owners would put blankets over the hoods of their cars. Nissan's assumption—which turned out to be false—was that Americans would do the same thing. As a Nissan spokesman said recently, "We tried for a long time to design cars in Japan and shove them down the American consumer's throat. That didn't work very well."[22] Until the 1980s, Eli Lilly and

---

[22] Norihiko Shirouzu, "Tailoring World's Cars to U.S. Tastes," *The Wall Street Journal* (January 1, 2001), pp. B1, B6.

**Figure 1-2**

Management Orientations

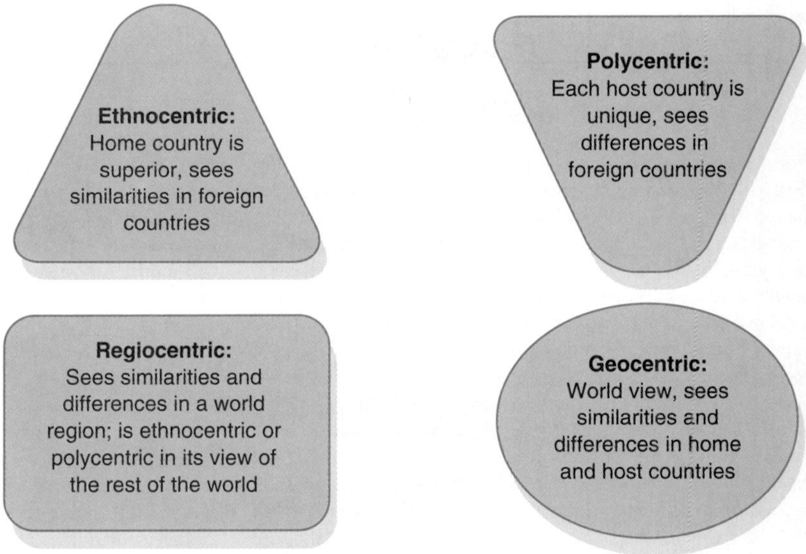

**Ethnocentric:**
Home country is superior, sees similarities in foreign countries

**Polycentric:**
Each host country is unique, sees differences in foreign countries

**Regiocentric:**
Sees similarities and differences in a world region; is ethnocentric or polycentric in its view of the rest of the world

**Geocentric:**
World view, sees similarities and differences in home and host countries

Company operated as an ethnocentric company: Activity outside the United States was tightly controlled by headquarters and the focus was on selling products originally developed for the U.S. market.[23] Similarly, executives at California's Robert Mondavi Corporation operated the company for many years as an ethnocentric international entity. As CEO Michael Mondavi explains:

> Robert Mondavi was a local winery that thought locally, grew locally, produced locally, and sold globally .... To be a truly global company, I believe it's imperative to grow and produce great wines in the world in the best wine-growing regions of the world, regardless of the country or the borders.[24]

Fifty years ago, most business enterprises—and especially those located in a large country like the United States—could operate quite successfully with an ethnocentric orientation. Today, however, as CEO Mondavi's words make clear, ethnocentrism is one of the major internal weaknesses that must be overcome if a company is to transform itself into an effective global competitor.

## Polycentric Orientation

The **polycentric orientation** is the opposite of ethnocentrism. The term *polycentric* describes management's belief or assumption that each country in which a company does business is unique. This assumption lays the groundwork for each subsidiary to develop its own unique business and marketing strategies in order to succeed; the term **multinational company** is often used to describe such a structure. This point of view leads to a **localized** or **adaptation approach** that assumes products must be adapted in response to different market conditions. Until the mid-1990s, Citicorp's financial services around the world operated on a polycentric basis. James Bailey, a Citicorp executive, offered this description of the company: "We were like a medieval state. There was the king and his court and they were in charge, right? No. It was the land barons who were in charge. The king and his court might declare this or that, but the land barons went and did their thing."[25] Realizing that the financial services

---

[23] T.W. Malnight, "Globalization of an Ethnocentric Firm: An Evolutionary Perspective," *Strategic Management Journal* 16, no. 2 (February 1995), p. 125.

[24] Robert Mondavi, *Harvests of Joy: My Passion for Excellence* (New York: Harcourt Brace & Company, 1998), p. 333.

[25] Saul Hansell, "Uniting the Feudal Lords at Citicorp," *The New York Times* (January 16, 1994), Sec. 3, p. 1.

**The Global Marketplace**

Now that we've got you thinking about global marketing, it's time to test your knowledge of global current events. Some well-known companies and brands are listed in the left-hand column. The question is, in what country is the parent corporation located? Possible answers are shown in the right-hand column. Write the letter corresponding to the country of your choice in the space provided; each country can be used more than once. Answers are provided at the bottom of the box.

|  |  |
|---|---|
| ____ 1. Firestone Tire & Rubber | a. Germany |
| ____ 2. Ray Ban | b. France |
| ____ 3. Rolls-Royce | c. Japan |
| ____ 4. RCA Electronics | d. Great Britain |
| ____ 5. Dr Pepper | e. United States |
| ____ 6. Ben & Jerry's Homemade | f. Switzerland |
| ____ 7. Gerber | g. Italy |
| ____ 8. Miller Beer | h. Sweden |
| ____ 9. Rollerblade | |
| ____ 10. Dunkin' Donuts | |
| ____ 11. Weed Eater | |
| ____ 12. Holiday Inn | |
| ____ 13. Wild Turkey bourbon | |
| ____ 14. Eddie Bauer | |

*Answers: 1. Japan (Bridgestone) 2. Italy (Luxottica SpA) 3. Germany (Volkswagen) 4. France (Thomson SA) 5. Great Britain (Cadbury-Schweppes) 6. Britain/Netherlands (Unilever) 7. Switzerland (Novartis) 8. Great Britain (SABMiller) 9. Italy (Benetton) 10. Great Britain (Allied Domecq) 11. Sweden (AB Electrolux) 12. Great Britain (InterContinental Hotels Group PLC) 13. France (Groupe Pernod Ricard) 14. Germany (Otto Versand)*

industry was globalizing, then-CEO John Reed attempted to achieve a higher degree of integration between Citicorp's operating units. Reed sought to instill a geocentric orientation throughout his company.

Prior to 1994, Ford Motor Company was also organized as a multinational corporation. Each of the company's four geographical regions operated autonomously. That meant four separate development centers, each designing vehicles to be marketed in their respective regions. In January 1994, CEO Alex Trotman launched Ford 2000, an ambitious reorganization designed to transform Ford into a global company as opposed to a multinational one. A key element in the plan was the centralization of worldwide product development. In November 1999, Trotman's successor announced plans to reintroduce some of the regional focus. Jacques Nasser's reversal was viewed as an effort to ensure that Ford products and the Ford brand are responsive to local preferences, especially in Europe.

## Regiocentric and Geocentric Orientations

In a company with a **regiocentric orientation**, a region becomes the relevant geographic unit; management's goal is to develop an integrated regional strategy. For example, a U.S. company that focuses on the countries included in the North American Free Trade Agreement (NAFTA), the United States, Canada, and Mexico, has a regiocentric orientation. Similarly, a European company that focuses its attention on Europe is regiocentric. A company with a **geocentric orientation** views the entire world as a potential market and strives to develop integrated world market strategies. A company whose management has a regiocentric or geocentric orientation is sometimes known as a **global** or **transnational company.**[26] A global company can be further described as one that pursues either a strategy of serving world markets from a single country, or that sources globally for the purposes of focusing on select country markets. In addition, global companies tend to retain their association with a particular headquarters country. Harley-Davidson and Waterford serve world markets from the United States and Ireland, respectively; Gap sources its apparel from low-wage countries in all parts of the world and focuses primarily on the key U.S. market. All three may be thought of as global companies. Transnational companies both serve global markets and source globally; in addition, there is often a blurring of national identity. A true transnational would be characterized as "stateless." Toyota is a good example of a company that is coming close to fulfilling the criteria of transnationality. At global and transnational companies, management uses a combination of standardized (extension) and localized (adaptation) elements in the marketing program. A key factor that distinguishes global and transnational companies from international or multinational companies is *mind-set*: at global and transnational companies, decisions regarding extension and adaptation are not based on assumptions. Rather, such decisions are made on the basis of ongoing research into market needs and wants. In addition, global operations are integrated and coordinated.

"As the saying goes, if you are not manufacturing in China or selling in India, you are as good as finished."
Dipankar Halder, associate director
KSA Technopak, India[27]

One way to assess the extent to which a company is transnational is to compute an average of three figures: sales outside the home country to total sales; assets outside the home country to total assets; and employees outside the home country to total employees. Viewed in terms of this type of analysis, Nestlé, Unilever, Northern Telecom, Royal Philips Electronics, GlaxoWellcome, and the News Corporation are all transnational companies. Each is headquartered in a relatively small home country market, a fact of life that has compelled management to adopt regiocentric or geocentric orientations to achieve revenue and profit growth.

The geocentric orientation represents a synthesis of ethnocentrism and polycentrism; it is a "world view" that sees similarities and differences in markets and countries and seeks to create a global strategy that is fully responsive to local needs and wants. A regiocentric manager might be said to have a world view on a regional scale; the world outside the region of interest will be viewed with an ethnocentric or a polycentric orientation, or a combination of the two. However, recent research suggests that many companies are seeking to strengthen their regional competitiveness rather than moving directly to develop global responses to changes in the competitive environment.[28]

The ethnocentric company is centralized in its marketing management, the polycentric company is decentralized, and the regiocentric and geocentric companies are integrated on a regional and global scale, respectively. A crucial difference between the orientations is the underlying assumption for each. The ethnocentric orientation is based on a belief in home-country superiority. The underlying assumption of the polycentric approach is that there are so many differences in cultural, economic, and marketing conditions in the world that it is futile to

---

26 Although the definitions provided here are important, to avoid confusion we will use the term *global marketing* when describing the general activities of global companies. Another note of caution is in order: Usage of the terms *international, multinational,* and *global* varies widely. Alert readers of the business press are likely to recognize inconsistencies; usage does not always reflect the definitions provided here. In particular, companies that are (in the view of the authors as well as numerous other academics) global, are often described as *multinational enterprises* (abbreviated MNE) or *multinational corporations* (abbreviated MNC). The United Nations prefers the term *transnational company* rather than *global company*. When we refer to an "international company" or a "multinational," we will do so in a way that maintains the distinctions described in the text.
27 Saritha Rai, "Tastes of India in U.S. Wrappers," *The New York Times* (April 29, 2003), p. W7.
28 Allan J. Morrison, David A. Ricks, and Kendall Roth, "Globalization Versus Regionalization: Which Way for the Multinational?" *Organizational Dynamics* (Winter 1991), p. 18.

attempt to transfer experience across national boundaries. A key challenge facing organizational leaders today is managing a company's evolution beyond an ethnocentric or polycentric orientation toward a regiocentric or geocentric one. As noted in one book on global business, "The multinational solution encounters problems by ignoring a number of organizational impediments to the implementation of a global strategy and underestimating the impact of global competition."[29] At many companies, management realizes the need to change. For example, Louis R. Hughes, a General Motors executive, said, "We are on our way to becoming a transnational corporation." His view was echoed by Basil Drossos, president of GM de Argentina, who noted, "We are talking about becoming a global corporation as opposed to a multinational company; that implies that the centers of expertise may reside anywhere they best reside."[30]

# FORCES AFFECTING GLOBAL INTEGRATION AND GLOBAL MARKETING

The remarkable growth of the global economy over the past 50 years has been shaped by the dynamic interplay of various driving and restraining forces. During most of those decades, companies from different parts of the world in different industries achieved great success by pursuing international, multinational, or global strategies. During the 1990s, changes in the business environment presented a number of challenges to established ways of doing business. Today, the growing importance of global marketing stems from the fact that driving forces have more momentum than the restraining forces. The forces affecting global integration are shown in Figure 1-3.

Regional economic agreements, converging market needs and wants, technology advances, pressure to cut costs, pressure to improve quality, improvements in communication and transportation technology, global economic growth, and opportunities for leverage all represent important driving forces; any industry subject to these forces is a candidate for globalization.

## Driving Forces

### Regional Economic Agreements

A number of multilateral trade agreements have accelerated the pace of global integration. NAFTA is already expanding trade among the United States, Canada, and Mexico. The General Agreement on Tariffs and Trade (GATT), which was ratified by more than 120 nations in 1994, has created the World Trade Organization to promote and protect free trade. In Europe, the expanding membership of the European Union is lowering boundaries to trade within the region.

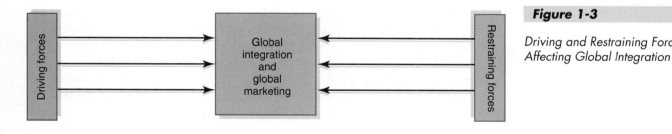

**Figure 1-3**

*Driving and Restraining Forces Affecting Global Integration*

---

29 Michael A. Yoshino and U. Srinivasa Rangan, *Strategic Alliances: An Entrepreneurial Approach to Globalization* (Boston: Harvard Business School Press, 1995), p. 64.
30 Rebecca Blumenstein, "Global Strategy: GM Is Building Plants in Developing Nations to Woo New Markets," *The Wall Street Journal* (August 4, 1997), p. A4.

### Philips Electronics: How Global Companies Win

Royal Philips Electronics is a giant $41 billion consumer electronics company headquartered in the Netherlands. Philips manufactures a vast array of products. For example, Philips Lighting is the largest manufacturer of light bulbs in the world; in Western Europe alone, the Philips brand commands more than one-third share of the light bulb market. Other divisions include domestic appliances, consumer electronics, industrial electronics, semiconductors, and medical systems.

Philips is a company that has changed with the times. For example, to meet the challenge of Japanese consumer electronics manufacturers such as Sony and Matsushita, Philips management abandoned its polycentric, multinational approach and adopted a more geocentric orientation. A first step in this direction was to create industry groups in the Netherlands responsible for developing global strategies for research and development (R&D), marketing, and manufacturing. The change has paid off in Europe, where today Philips is the number one selling color television brand.

Despite such successes, the company lost $3.4 billion in 2002. Part of the problem is the fact that the company's U.S. consumer electronics division has been losing money for years. Even though Philips was a pioneer in developing new product categories such as CD players, the company was mostly known for Philips-Magnavox, a low-end brand of television. Not surprisingly, Philips is stepping up its marketing efforts in the key North American market, which accounts for about 26 percent of overall consumer electronics sales. In 2001, Larry Blanford, formerly president of Maytag Corp's appliance division, was assigned the task of revitalizing Philips's U.S. business. The stakes are high: Soon after Blanford took the job, the word was passed along from headquarters that if the U.S. unit didn't show a profit for 2004, it would be shut down.

Blanford mapped out a strategy designed to position Philips as a premium, high-tech brand and to boost sales of high-margin, must-have digital products such as wide-screen flat-panel HDTV monitors, DVD recorders, and portable MP3 music players. The U.S. sales team was quadrupled in size to 50 people; Blanford also instituted a policy requiring salespeople to visit at least two retail stores each week. Even as Philips works to improve relations with specialty electronics retailers, it has spent $100 million on a consumer brand awareness advertising campaign keyed to the theme "Getting Better." Some industry observers warn that Blanford has his work cut out for him. As a Dutch consumer electronics analyst noted recently, "In the U.S., Philips has been seen as a clunky brand, not at all sexy. They have a long road ahead to change people's minds."

*Sources: Dan Bilefsky, "Lost in Translation: A European Electronics Giant Races to Undo Mistakes in U.S.," The Wall Street Journal (January 7, 2004), pp. A1, A10; Gregory Crouch, "Philips Electronics Reports Best Profit in Three Years," The New York Times (October 15, 2003), p. W1; Crouch, "Philips Electronics Lost $3.4 Billion Last Year," The New York Times (February 12, 2003), p. W1; Bilefsky, "Famed Philips Tries to Raise U.S. Profile," The Wall Street Journal (October 3, 2002), p. B4; Dave Pringle and Dan Bilefsky, "Philips Plans to Unveil Digital Videodisc Recorder," The Wall Street Journal (August 24, 2001), p. B7.*

The creation of a single currency zone and the introduction of the euro are also expected to dramatically expand European trade in the twenty-first century.

### Converging Market Needs and Wants and the Information Revolution

A person studying markets around the world will discover cultural universals as well as differences. The common elements in human nature provide an underlying basis for the opportunity to create and serve global markets. The word *create* is deliberate. Most global markets do not exist in nature; they must be created by marketing effort. For example, no one *needs* soft drinks, and yet today in some countries per capita soft drink consumption *exceeds* the consumption of water. Marketing has driven this change in behavior, and today, the soft drink industry is a truly global one. Evidence is mounting that consumer needs and wants around the world are converging today as never before. This creates an opportunity for global marketing. Multinational companies pursuing strategies of product adaptation run the risk of falling victim to global competitors that have recognized opportunities to serve global customers.

The information revolution—what Thomas L. Friedman refers to as the democratization of information—is one reason for the trend toward convergence. Thanks to satellite dishes and globe-spanning TV networks such as CNN and MTV, people in even the remotest corners of the globe can compare their own lifestyles and standards of living with those in other countries. In regional markets such as Europe and Asia, the increasing overlap of advertising across national boundaries and the mobility of consumers have created opportunities for marketers to pursue pan-European product positionings. The Internet is an even stronger driving force:

When a company establishes a site on the Internet, it automatically becomes global. In addition, the Internet allows people everywhere in the world to reach out, buying and selling a virtually unlimited assortment products and services.

## Transportation and Communication Improvements

The time and cost barriers associated with distance have fallen tremendously over the past 100 years. The jet airplane revolutionized communication by making it possible for people to travel around the world in less than 48 hours. Tourism enables people from many countries to see and experience the newest products being sold abroad. In 1970, 75 million passengers traveled internationally; according to figures compiled by the International Air Transport Association, that figure increased to nearly 540 million passengers in 2003. One essential characteristic of the effective global business is face-to-face communication among employees and between the company and its customers. Modern jet travel made such communication feasible. Today's information technology allows airline alliance partners such as United Airlines and Lufthansa to sell seats on each other's flights, thereby helping travelers get from point to point more easily. Meanwhile, the cost of international telephone calls has fallen dramatically over the past several decades. That fact, plus the advent of new communication technologies such as e-mail, fax, video teleconferencing, wi-fi, and broadband Internet means that managers, executives, and customers can link up electronically from virtually any part of the world without traveling at all.

A similar revolution has occurred in transportation technology. The costs associated with physical distribution, both in terms of money and time, have been greatly reduced as well. The per-unit cost of shipping automobiles from Japan and Korea to the United States by specially designed auto-transport ships is less than the cost of overland shipping from Detroit to either U.S. coast. Another key innovation has been increased utilization of 20- and 40-foot metal containers that can be transferred from trucks to railroad cars to ships.

## Product Development Costs

The pressure for globalization is intense when new products require major investments and long periods of development time. The pharmaceuticals industry provides a striking illustration of this driving force. According to the Pharmaceutical Research and Manufacturers Association, the cost of developing a new drug in 1976 was $54 million; by 1982, the cost had increased to $87 million. By 1993, the figure had reached $359 million. Today, it may take 14 years for a new drug to be approved; the average total cost of bringing a new drug to market is estimated to exceed $400 million.[31] Such costs must be recovered in the global marketplace, because no single national market is likely to be large enough to support investments of this size. Thus Pfizer, Merck, GlaxoSmithKline, Novartis, Bristol-Myers Squibb, Aventis, and other leading pharmaceutical companies have little choice but to engage in global marketing. As noted earlier, however, global marketing does not necessarily mean operating everywhere; in the $200 billion pharmaceutical industry, for example, seven countries account for 75 percent of sales. Similarly, in the $30 billion market for recorded music, 12 countries—including the United States, Japan, the United Kingdom, and France—account for 70 percent of sales.

## Quality

Global marketing strategies can generate greater revenue and greater operating margins which, in turn, support design and manufacturing quality. A global and a domestic company may each spend 5 percent of sales on R&D, but the global company may have many times the total revenue of the domestic because it serves the

---

[31] Joseph A. DiMasi, Ronald W. Hansen, and Henry G. Grabowski, "The Price of Innovation: New Estimates of Drug Development Costs," *Journal of Health Economics* 22, no. 2 (March 2003), p. 151.

world market. It is easy to understand how Nissan, Matsushita, Caterpillar, and other global companies can achieve world-class quality. Global companies "raise the bar" for all competitors in an industry. When a global company establishes a benchmark in quality, competitors must quickly make their own improvements and come up to par. For example, the U.S. auto manufacturers have seen their market share erode over the past three decades as Japanese manufacturers built reputations for quality and durability. Now Detroit faces a new threat: even as Ford rolled out its new F-150 pickup truck in January 2003, Nissan and other Japanese automakers were introducing their own full-sized truck models for the first time. For truly global products, uniformity can drive down research, engineering, design, and production costs across business functions. Quality, uniformity, and cost reduction were all driving forces behind Ford's $6 billion investment in a "World Car," which is sold in the United States as the Ford Contour and Mercury Mystique and in Europe as the Mondeo. The same imperatives drove the 1998 launch of the Ford Focus in Europe; company plans call for offering the Focus in a total of 60 countries.

## World Economic Trends

Economic growth has been a driving force in the expansion of the international economy and the growth of global marketing for three reasons: First, economic growth in key developing countries has created market opportunities that provide

*With annual sales of $48 billion, Pfizer is the world's largest research-based pharmaceutical company. Pfizer depends on global sales of blockbuster drugs such as Lipitor to generate the revenues necessary to support drug research and development.*

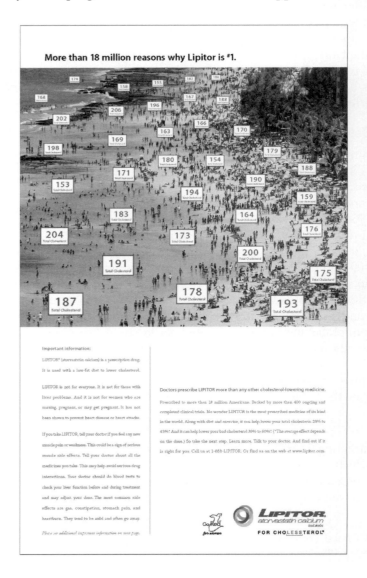

a major incentive for companies to expand globally. At the same time, slow growth in industrialized countries has compelled management to look abroad for opportunities in nations or regions with high rates of growth.

Second, economic growth has reduced resistance that might otherwise have developed in response to the entry of foreign firms into domestic economies. When a country such as China is experiencing rapid economic growth, policymakers are likely to look more favorably on outsiders. A growing country means growing markets; there is often plenty of opportunity for everyone. It is possible for a "foreign" company to enter a domestic economy and establish itself without threatening the existence of local firms. Indeed, the latter can ultimately be strengthened by the new competitive environment. Without economic growth, however, global enterprises may take business away from domestic ones. Domestic businesses are more likely to seek governmental intervention to protect their local position if markets are not growing. Predictably, the worldwide recession of the early 1990s created pressure in most countries to limit foreign access to domestic markets.

The worldwide movement toward free markets, deregulation, and privatization is a third driving force. The trend toward privatization is opening up formerly closed markets; tremendous opportunities are being created as a result. Authors Daniel Yergin and Joseph Stanislaw described these trends as follows:

> It is the greatest sale in the history of the world. Governments are getting out of businesses by disposing of what amounts to trillions of dollars of assets. Everything is going—from steel plants and phone companies and electric utilities to airlines and railroads to hotels, restaurants, and nightclubs. It is happening not only in the former Soviet Union, Eastern Europe, and China but also in Western Europe, Asia, Latin America, and Africa—and in the United States.[32]

For example, when a nation's telephone company is a state monopoly, it is much easier to require it to buy only from national companies. An independent, private company will be more inclined to look for the best offer, regardless of the nationality of the supplier. Privatization of telephone systems around the world is creating huge opportunities for companies such as Lucent Technologies and Northern Telcom.

## Leverage

A global company possesses the unique opportunity to develop leverage. In the context of global marketing, **leverage** means some type of advantage that a company enjoys by virtue of the fact that it has experience in more than one country. Leverage allows a company to conserve resources when pursuing opportunities in new geographical markets. In other words, leverage enables a company to expend less time, less effort, or less money. Four important types of leverage are experience transfers, scale economies, resource utilization, and global strategy.

**Experience Transfers** A global company can leverage its experience in any market in the world. It can draw upon management practices, strategies, products, advertising appeals, or sales or promotional ideas that have been market tested in one country or region and apply them in other comparable markets. For example, Whirlpool has considerable experience in the United States dealing with powerful retail buyers such as Sears and Circuit City. The majority of European appliance retailers have plans to establish their own cross-border "power" retailing systems; as Whirlpool CEO David Whitwam explains, "When power retailers

---

[32] Daniel Yergin and Joseph Stanislaw, *The Commanding Heights* (New York: Simon & Schuster, 1998), p. 13.

take hold in Europe, we will be ready for it. The skills we've developed here are directly transferable."[33]

Chevron is another example of a global company that gains leverage through experience transfers. As H. F. Iskander, general manager of Chevron's Kuwait office, explains:

> Chevron is pumping oil in different locations all over the world. There is no problem we have not confronted and solved somewhere. There isn't a rock we haven't drilled through. We centralize all that knowledge at our headquarters, analyze it, sort it out, and that enables us to solve any oil-drilling problem anywhere. As a developing country you may have a national oil company that has been pumping your own oil for twenty years. But we tell them, "Look, you have twenty years of experience, but there's no diversity. It is just one year of knowledge twenty times over." When you are operating in a multitude of countries, like Chevron, you see a multitude of different problems and you have to come up with a multitude of solutions. You have to, or you won't be in business. All those solutions are then stored in Chevron's corporate memory. The key to our business now is to tap that memory, and bring out the solution that we used to solve a problem in Nigeria in order to solve the same problem in China or Kuwait.[34]

**Scale Economies** The global company can take advantage of its greater manufacturing volume to obtain traditional scale advantages within a single factory. Also, finished products can be manufactured by combining components manufactured in scale-efficient plants in different countries. Japan's giant Matsushita Electric Company is a classic example of global marketing in action; it achieved scale economies by exporting VCRs, televisions, and other consumer electronics products throughout the world from world-scale factories in Japan. The importance of manufacturing scale has diminished somewhat as companies implement flexible manufacturing techniques and invest in factories outside the home country. However, scale economies were a cornerstone of Japanese success in the 1970s and 1980s.

Leverage from scale economies is not limited to manufacturing. Just as a domestic company can achieve economies in staffing by eliminating duplicate positions after an acquisition, a global company can achieve the same economies on a global scale by centralizing functional activities. The larger scale of the global company also creates opportunities to improve corporate staff competence and quality.

**Resource Utilization** A major strength of the global company is its ability to scan the entire world to identify people, money, and raw materials that will enable it to compete most effectively in world markets. For a global company, it is not problematic if the value of the "home" currency rises or falls dramatically, because for this company there really is no such thing as a home currency. The world is full of currencies, and a global company seeks financial resources on the best available terms. In turn, it uses them where there is the greatest opportunity to serve a need at a profit.

**Global Strategy** The global company's greatest single advantage can be its global strategy. A global strategy is built on an information system that scans the world business environment to identify opportunities, trends, threats, and resources. When opportunities are identified, the global company adheres to the three principles identified earlier: It leverages its skills and focuses its resources to create superior perceived value for customers and achieve competitive advantage.

---

[33] William C. Taylor and Alan M. Webber, *Going Global: Four Entrepreneurs Map the New World Marketplace* (New York: Penguin USA, 1996), p. 18.

[34] Friedman, pp. 221–222.

*The global strategy is a design to create a winning offering on a global scale.* This takes great discipline, much creativity, and constant effort. The reward is not just success, it's survival. For example, French automaker Renault operated for many years as a regional company. During that time, its primary struggle was a two-way race with Peugeot Citroën for dominance in the French auto industry. However, in an industry dominated by Toyota and other global competitors, chairman Louis Schweitzer had no choice but to formulate a global strategy. Recent initiatives include acquiring a majority stake in Nissan Motor and Romania's Dacia. Schweitzer has also invested $1 billion in a plant in Brazil and is spending hundreds of millions of dollars in South Korea.[35]

A note of caution is in order: A global strategy is no guarantee of ongoing organizational success. The severe downturn in the business environment in the early years of the twenty-first century has wreaked havoc with strategic plans. As noted earlier in the chapter, ABB and Vivendi Universal have struggled as their chief executives' ambitious global visions have come to grief and expensive strategic bets have not paid off. Although both companies will no doubt survive, they will be much smaller, focused entities than they were in the mid-1990s. Companies that cannot formulate or successfully implement a coherent global strategy may lose their independence, as evidenced by the fortunes of Gerber, Helene Curtis, and others. Some strategic bets do not yield the expected results, as seen in the deals that created DaimlerChrysler and AOL Time Warner.

## Restraining Forces

Despite the impact of the driving forces identified previously, several restraining forces may slow a company's efforts to engage in global marketing. In addition to the market differences discussed earlier, important restraining forces include management myopia, organizational culture, national controls, and opposition to globalization. As we have noted, however, in today's world the driving forces predominate over the restraining forces. That is why the importance of global marketing is steadily growing.

### Management Myopia and Organizational Culture

In many cases, management simply ignores opportunities to pursue global marketing. A company that is "nearsighted" and ethnocentric will not expand geographically. Myopia is also a recipe for market disaster if headquarters attempts to dictate when it should listen. Global marketing does not work without a strong local team that can provide information about local market conditions. Executives at Parker Pen once attempted to implement a top-down marketing strategy that ignored experience gained by local market representatives. Costly market failures resulted in Parker's buyout by managers of the former UK subsidiary. Eventually, the Gillette Company acquired Parker.

In companies where subsidiary management "knows it all," there is no room for vision from the top. In companies where headquarters management is all-knowing, there is no room for local initiative or an in-depth knowledge of local needs and conditions. Executives and managers at successful global companies have learned how to integrate global vision and perspective with local market initiative and input. A striking theme emerged during interviews conducted by one of the authors with executives of successful global companies. That theme was the respect for local initiative and input by headquarters executives, and the corresponding respect for headquarters' vision by local executives.

---

[35] John Tagliabue, "Renault Pins Its Survival on a Global Gamble," *The New York Times* (July 2, 2000), sec. 3, pp. 1, 6; Don Kirk and Peter S. Green, "Renault Rolls the Dice on Two Auto Projects Abroad," *The New York Times* (August 29, 2002), pp. W1, W7.

## National Controls

Every country protects the commercial interests of local enterprises by maintaining control over market access and entry in both low- and high-tech industries. Such control ranges from a monopoly controlling access to tobacco markets to national government control of broadcast, equipment, and data transmission markets. Today, tariff barriers have been largely removed in the high-income countries, thanks to the World Trade Organization (WTO), GATT, NAFTA, and other economic agreements. However, **non-tariff barriers** (NTBs) such as "buy local" campaigns, food safety rules, and other bureaucratic obstacles still make it difficult for companies to gain access to some individual country and regional markets.

## Opposition to Globalization

To many people around the world, globalization and global marketing represent a threat. The term *globaphobia* is sometimes used to describe an attitude of hostility toward trade agreements, global brands, or company policies that appear to result in hardship for some individuals or countries while benefiting others. Globaphobia manifests itself in various ways, including protests or violence directed at policymakers or well-known global companies. Opponents of globalization include labor unions, college and university students, special interest groups, and others. In the United States, for example, some people believe that globalization has depressed the wages of American workers and resulted in the loss of both blue-collar and white-collar jobs even as companies post record profits. In many developing countries, there is a growing suspicion that the world's advanced countries—starting with the United States—are reaping most of the rewards of free trade. As an unemployed miner in Bolivia put it, "Globalization is just another name for submission and domination. We've had to live with that here for 500 years and now we want to be our own masters."[36]

# OUTLINE OF THIS BOOK

This book has been written for students and businesspersons interested in global marketing. Throughout the book, we present and discuss important concepts and tools specifically applicable to global marketing.

The book is divided into five parts. Part I consists of Chapter 1, an overview of global marketing and the basic theory of global marketing. Chapters 2 through 5 comprise Part II, in which we cover the environments of global marketing. Chapters 2 and 3 cover economic and regional market characteristics, including the location of income and population, patterns of trade and investment, and stages of market development. In Chapter 4, social and cultural elements are examined; the legal, political, and regulatory dimensions are presented in Chapter 5.

Part III is devoted to topics that must be considered when approaching global markets. We cover marketing information systems and research in Chapter 6. Chapter 7 discusses market segmentation, targeting, and positioning. Chapter 8 covers the basics of importing, exporting, and sourcing. Chapter 9 is devoted to various aspects of global strategy, including strategy alternatives for market entry and expansion.

Part IV is devoted to global considerations pertaining to the marketing mix. The application of product, price, channel, and marketing communications decisions in response to global market opportunity and threat is covered in detail in Chapters 10 through 15.

---

[36] Larry Rohter, "Bolivia's Poor Proclaim Abiding Distrust of Globalization," *The New York Times* (October 17, 2003), p. A3.

The three chapters in Part V address issues of corporate strategy, leadership, and the impact of the digital revolution on global marketing. Chapter 15 includes an overview of strategy and competitive advantage. Chapter 16 addresses some of the leadership challenges facing the chief executives of global companies. In addition, the chapter covers the organization and control of global marketing programs and examines the integrating and managerial dimensions of global marketing. The book closes with Chapter 17, a new chapter that explores the ways that the Internet, e-commerce, and other aspects of the digital revolution are creating new opportunities and challenges for global marketers.

## summary

A company that engages in **global marketing** focuses its resources on global market opportunities and threats. Successful global marketers such as Nestlé, Coca-Cola, and Honda use familiar **marketing mix** elements—the four Ps—to create global marketing programs. Marketing, R&D, manufacturing, and other activities comprise a firm's **value chain;** firms configure these activities to create superior customer **value** on a global basis. Global companies also maintain strategic **focus** while relentlessly pursuing **competitive advantage.** The marketing mix, value chain, competitive advantage, and focus are universal in their applicability, irrespective of whether a company does business only in the home country or has a presence in many markets around the world. However, in a **global industry,** companies that fail to pursue global opportunities risk being pushed aside by stronger global competitors.

A firm's **global marketing strategy (GMS)** can enhance its worldwide performance. The GMS addresses several issues. First is the nature of the marketing program in terms of the balance between a **standardization (extension) approach** to the marketing mix elements and a **localization (adaptation) approach** that is responsive to country or regional differences. Second is the **concentration of marketing activities** in a few countries or the dispersal of such activities across many countries. Third, the pursuit of global marketing opportunities requires cross border **coordination of marketing activities.** Finally, a firm's GMS will address the issue of **global market participation.**

The importance of global marketing today can be seen in the company rankings compiled by *The Wall Street Journal, Fortune, Financial Times,* and other publications. Whether ranked by revenues, market capitalization, or some other measure, most of the world's major corporations are active regionally or globally. The size of global markets for individual industries or product categories helps explain why companies "go global." Global markets for some product categories represent hundreds of billions of dollars in annual sales; other markets are much smaller. Whatever the size of the opportunity, successful industry competitors find that increasing revenues and profits means seeking markets outside the home country.

Company management can be classified in terms of its orientation toward the world: **ethnocentric, polycentric, regiocentric,** or **geocentric.** An ethnocentric orientation characterizes **domestic** and **international companies;** international companies pursue marketing opportunities outside the home market by extending various elements of the marketing mix. A polycentric world view predominates at a **multinational company,** where the marketing mix is adapted by country managers operating autonomously. Managers at **global** and **transnational companies** are regiocentric or geocentric in their orientation and pursue both extension and adaptation strategies in global markets.

Global marketing's importance today is shaped by the dynamic interplay of several driving and restraining forces. The former include market needs and wants, technology, transportation and communication improvements, product costs, quality, world economic trends, and a recognition of opportunities to develop **leverage** by operating globally. Restraining forces include market differences, management myopia, organizational culture, and national controls such as **nontariff barriers.**

1. What are the basic goals of marketing? Are these goals relevant to global marketing?

2. What is meant by "global localization"? Is Coca-Cola a global product? Explain.

3. Describe some of the global marketing strategies available to companies. Give examples of companies that use the different strategies.

4. How do the global marketing strategies of Harley-Davidson and Toyota differ?

5. Describe the difference between ethnocentric, polycentric, regiocentric, and geocentric management orientations.

6. Identify and briefly describe some of the forces that have resulted in increased global integration and the growing importance of global marketing.

7. Define *leverage* and explain the different types of leverage utilized by companies with global operations.

Virtually every company mentioned in this chapter is using the Internet as a communications tool. You can learn a great deal about a company's geographic scope and marketing activities by visiting its Web site. Many companies also post their annual reports online; you can read and print them if your computer is equipped with Adobe's Acrobat software. A company's universal resource locator (URL) is often based on its name (e.g., **www.caterpillar.com**) or initials (e.g., **www.ibm.com**). If, after a couple of tries, you are unable to locate a company's homepage, consult Hoover's (**www.hoovers.com**). You may already be familiar with the company's printed reference book, *Hoover's Handbook*. Hoover's Web site offers free company capsules that contain basic information including names of top executives, headquarters address, annual sales, and links to other corporate Web sites.

1. Each August, *Fortune* magazine publishes its survey of the Global 500. The top-ranked companies for 2003 are shown in Table 1-3. Browse through the list and choose any company that interests you. Compare its 2003 ranking with the most recent ranking (that you can find either by referring to the print version of *Fortune* or by visiting **www.fortune.com**). How has the company's ranking changed? Consult additional sources (e.g., magazine articles, annual reports, the company's Web site) to enhance your understanding of the factors and forces that contributed to the company's move up or down in the rankings.

2. The following is a list of countries from various regions of the world. What category of goods do you think is the number one export from each? Possible answers are shown in the right-hand column. Write the letter corresponding to the product or product category of your choice in the space provided; each product answer can be used more than once. The answers follow.

| | | |
|---|---|---|
| _____ 1. Brazil | a. | cocoa |
| _____ 2. Finland | b. | gold |
| _____ 3. Ghana | c. | telecommunication/technology products |
| _____ 4. Saudi Arabia | d. | aircraft equipment and parts |
| _____ 5. Nigeria | e. | petroleum |
| _____ 6. Australia | f. | metal ores and extractive commodities |
| _____ 7. Russia | g. | electronics |
| _____ 8. Singapore | h. | motor vehicles |
| _____ 9. Germany | i. | coffee beans |
| _____ 10. Peru | | |

Answers: 1.d 2.c 3.a 4.e 5.e 6.f 7.e 8.g 9.h 10.b

# Case 1-1

## McDonald's Expands Globally While Adjusting Its Local Recipe

At the end of 2002, McDonald's Corporation reported its first quarterly loss in nearly 40 years. The disappointing financial news was a wake-up call for the fast-food legend whose famous golden arches can be found in more than 120 different countries. The company built its reputation by promising and delivering three things to customers: inexpensive food with consistent taste regardless of location; quick service; and a clean, familiar environment. The company was also a pioneer in the development of convenience-oriented features such as drive-through windows and indoor playgrounds for children. Today, thanks to memorable advertising and intensive promotion efforts, McDonald's is one of the world's most valuable brands. In fact, the golden arches are said to be the second most recognized symbol in the world, behind the Olympic rings. In the United States alone, McDonald's spent nearly $575 million on advertising in 2002, about twice as much as Burger King and Wendy's. Indeed, in a recent issue devoted to twentieth century advertising milestones, *Advertising Age* magazine ranked McDonald's "You Deserve A Break Today" ad campaign from the 1970s and 1980s as the fifth most popular campaign in the last 100 years. The company's Ronald McDonald personality ranked number 2 on *Advertising Age's* list of Top Ten Icons.

In short, the company is the undisputed leader in the QSR ("quick service restaurant") segment of the industry, with more than twice the systemwide revenues of Burger King. However, after a decade of torrid growth, overall U.S. sales at McDonald's outlets open at least 1 year ("same-store sales" in industry parlance) increased by only 3 percent from 1999 to 2000; sales were flat or negative in the 2-year period 2000 to 2001. The decline reflected, among other things, a drop in the percentage of U.S fast-food dollars spent at McDonald's. The company faces competitive attacks from several directions. During the 1990s, a wide range of upscale food and beverage purveyors arrived on the scene. For example, consumers are flocking to Starbucks coffee bars where they spend freely on lattes and other coffee-based specialty drinks.

The "fast-casual" segment of the industry that includes companies such as Panera Bread, Cosi, and Baja Fresh is attracting customers seeking higher-quality menu items in more comfortable surroundings. Meanwhile, Subway overtook McDonald's as the restaurant chain with the most outlets in the United States. Some industry observers suggested that, in terms of both food offerings and marketing, McDonald's was losing touch with modern American lifestyles.

Ironically, until recently the picture appeared brighter outside the United States. Thanks to changing lifestyles around the globe, more and more people are embracing the notion of fast food. Also, the competitive picture is different in other countries. The United States boasts 25 hamburger restaurants for every 100,000 people, but the figure is much lower elsewhere. In Japan, for example, there are only 5 hamburger restaurants per 100,000 people; in many European countries, the ratio is approximately 2 for every 100,000 people. McDonald's responded to these opportunities by stepping up its rate of new unit openings during the 1990s. In 1991, the company had 3,355 units in 53 countries; by the end of 2002, there were more than 16,530 non-U.S. restaurants. These comprise about 55 percent of the total number of restaurants (in all, there were 30,025 McDonald's restaurants worldwide in 2002) and account for nearly 50 percent of sales. In dollar terms, $20 billion of McDonald's $41.5 billion in 2002 systemwide sales came from outside the United States. Over the 10-year period from 1987 to 1997, operating profits from outside the United States grew at a compounded annual rate of 23.3 percent, compared with 3.5 percent in the United States. Results for the past several years are shown in Table 1. In the Asia/Pacific region, sales growth has been as high as 10 percent, and Latin American sales have experienced 7 percent annual growth.

McDonald's International is organized into four geographic regions: (1) Europe, which currently accounts for about 52 percent of international sales; (2) Asia/Pacific, Middle East, and Africa (APMEA), with 37 percent; (3) Latin America; and (4) Canada, with about 7 percent each. McDonald's frequently adapts its food to suit local tastes. In Asia, for example, fried chicken is often on the menu. Other offerings include banana fruit pies in Latin America, kiwi burgers (served with beet root sauce) in New Zealand, beer in Germany, McSpaghetti noodles and a sweeter Burger McDo in the Philippines, and chili sauce to go with fries in Singapore. In some countries, McDonald's changes its food processing methods to comply with religious customs; in Singapore and Malaysia, for example, the beef that goes into Halal burgers must be slaughtered according to Muslim law. In the words of one market analyst, "McDonald's is similar to Coca-Cola ten years ago. It's on the verge of becoming an international giant, with the United States as a major market, but overseas as the driving force."

### Asia/Pacific

McDonald's opened its first Japanese location in 1972; by 1998, the company's 2,500 locations accounted for about 50 percent of the fast-food hamburger market in Japan.

**Table 1**  McDonald's Operating Income 1996–2002 (US$ millions)

|  | 2002 | 2001 | 2000 | 1999 | 1998 | 1997 | 1996 |
|---|---|---|---|---|---|---|---|
| U.S. operating income | 1,673 | 1,622 | 1,795 | 1,653 | 1,202 | 1,211 | 1,144[a] |
| Operating income outside the U.S.* | 1,211 | 1,523 | 1,860 | 1,832 | 1,716 | 1,659 | 1,541[b] |

*1999 and earlier figures exclude Canada, Africa, and the Middle East
[a]Includes $72 million special charge.
[b]Includes $16 million asset impairment charge

Source: Adapted from McDonald's Corporation *Annual Report* 2002 and 2000.

Approximately 80 percent of the restaurants are company owned, with about 20 percent operated by franchisees (the ratios are reversed in the United States). Skyrocketing real estate and construction costs during the so-called bubble years of the late 1980s translated into a slow rate of new store openings. As Japan's economy cooled off in the late 1990s, McDonald's took advantage of lower costs and stepped up the pace of store openings. The company is also experimenting with new locations such as placing restaurants within gas stations.

Among the menu items tailored to local palates are the soy-flavored Teriyaki McBurger and Chicken Tatsuta. McDonald's marketing strategy for Japan also contains some global elements. For example, TV ads feature idealized images of family men sharing quality time with the kids while enjoying McDonald's french fries. Such scenes of family interaction are part of a global campaign that features consistent images. Even so, they have struck a responsive chord in Japan where the balance between work life and family life has become a hotly debated topic.

The Indian market appears to hold huge potential for McDonald's. In fall 1996, the company opened its first restaurants in New Delhi and Bombay. In New Delhi, the golden arches compete with Nirula's, a quick-service restaurant chain with about two dozen outlets; in addition, there are hundreds of smaller regional chains throughout India. The U.S.-based Subway chain opened its first Indian location in 2001; Pizza Hut, KFC, and Domino's Pizza are also setting up shop. The Pizza Hut on Juhu Road in Bombay is housed in a three-story-tall building with large plate glass windows and central air conditioning; on most nights, a long line of customers forms outside. Indian demand for meals from the major fast-food chains is growing at an estimated rate of 40 percent annually; analysts forecast that the market will grow to $1.3 billion by 2005. By the end of 2003, McDonald's had 53 stores in India. Management identifies strategic locations in areas with a great deal of pedestrian traffic such as the shopping street in Bandra in the Bombay suburbs. Other restaurant locations include a site near a college in Vile Parle and another opposite the Andheri train station. Prices are lower than in other countries; most sandwiches cost about 40 rupees (less than one dollar). Drinks cost 15 rupees, and a packet of French fries is 25 rupees. A complete meal costs the equivalent of about $2.

Because the Hindu religion prohibits eating beef, McDonald's developed the lamb-based Maharaja Mac specifically for India. Despite protests from several Hindu nationalist groups, the first McDonald's attracted huge crowds to its site near the Victoria railway terminal; customers included many tourists from across India and from abroad as well as locals commuting to and from work. In short order, however, Hindu activists renewed their protests, this time accusing the company of using beef tallow in its cooking. Management responded by posting signs reading "No beef or beef products sold here," but the doubts raised by the controversy kept many potential customers away. In an effort to bring back the crowds, McDonald's has worked steadily to prove that it is sensitive to Indian tastes and traditions. As is the case throughout the world, McDonald's emphasizes that most of the food ingredients it uses—as much as 95 percent—are produced locally. In addition, to accommodate vegetarians, each restaurant has two separate food preparation areas. The "green" kitchen is devoted to vegetarian fare such as the spicy McAloo Tikka potato burger, Pizza McPuff, and Paneer Salsa McWrap. The meat items are prepared on the red side. Even the mayonnaise is made without eggs. Some of the new menu items developed for India are being introduced in Europe and the United States.

*"The tastes of the urban, upwardly mobile Indian are evolving, and more Indians are looking to eat out and experiment. The potential Indian customer base for a McDonald's or a Subway is larger than the size of entire developed countries."*

Sapna Nayak, food analyst at Raobank India

China is currently home to the world's largest McDonald's. The first Chinese location opened in mid-1992 in central Beijing, a few blocks from the infamous Tiananmen Square. By mid-1995, McDonald's had 12 restaurants in the Chinese capital and 40 throughout the rest of the country. The restaurants source 95 percent of their supplies, including lettuce, from within China. Despite McDonald's 20-year lease for its central Beijing location, the company found itself in the middle of a dispute between the central government and Beijing's city government. City officials decided to build a new $1.2 billion commercial complex in the city center and demanded that McDonald's vacate the site. However, central government officials had not approved the city's plans.

McDonald's was adversely affected by the currency crisis in Asia that started in July 1997. In Indonesia, for example, where the rupiah's value fell 80 percent, the company was forced to close 14 of its 101 restaurants as a result of slow sales. An additional 6 restaurants were destroyed in May 1998 in rioting that led to the ouster of President Suharto. Then again, it now costs about 80 percent less to build a new restaurant, thanks to lower labor and real estate costs. McDonald's protects itself from currency fluctuations by purchasing as much as possible from local suppliers. For example, the company's Singapore locations now buy chicken patties from Thailand rather than from the United States. However, french fries must still be imported from Australia or the United States. To help offset higher costs, McDonald's offers customers the choice of rice as a side dish at a lower price.

## Western Europe

The golden arches are a familiar sight in Europe, particularly in England, France, and Germany; there is even a four-star Golden Arch hotel in Zurich. Overall, Europe contributes 25 percent of sales and 45 percent of operating income, making it a key world region. However, from 1999 to 2000, Europe posted a 3 percent decline in sales, due in large part to consumer concerns about mad cow disease. The chain's British business was hit especially hard; the public health scare about mad cow disease that began in 1996 resulted in bans on British beef exports to continental Europe. Responding to public concerns, McDonald's immediately substituted imported beef at its British restaurants. By mid-1997, convinced that British beef was safe, McDonald's put it back on the menu. Ironically, no sooner had the beef furor subsided than Burger King brought its aptly named Big King sandwich ("20 percent more beef than a Big Mac") to England. In 2000 and 2001, concerns over the safety of the meat supply surfaced again amid an outbreak of hoof-and-mouth disease and ongoing media reports about mad cow disease. The public's reduced appetite for beef was reflected in decreases in systemwide sales, revenues, and operating income for McDonald's European division in 2000.

Meanwhile, another controversy kept McDonald's in the public eye in Britain during the 1990s. The company became embroiled in a highly publicized lawsuit that eventually earned the dubious distinction as the longest-running trial in British legal history. McDonald's sued several environmental activists for defamation after they distributed pamphlets that criticized the company's food and environmental policies. The lawsuit quickly took on David and Goliath overtones. The defendants, unable to obtain legal aid, represented themselves. McDonald's, by contrast, established a legal fund of more than $16 million. McDonald's ultimately won the battle; the judge ruled that the defendants were guilty of defamation and ordered them to pay about $100,000 in damages.

Across the channel, France's tradition of culinary excellence makes it a special case in Europe; dining options range from legendary three-star Michelin restaurants to humble neighborhood bistros. From the time McDonald's opened its first French outlet in 1972, policy makers and media commentators have voiced concerns about the impact of fast food on French culture. Even so, with nearly 1,000 outlets, France today represents McDonald's third-largest market in Europe. However, controversy has kept the company in the public eye. For example, some French citizens objected when McDonald's became the official food of the World Cup finals that were held in France in 1998. In August 1999, a sheep farmer named Jose Bové led a protest against construction of the eight hundred and fifty-first French McDonald's near the village of Millau. The group used construction tools to dismantle the partially finished structure. Bové told the press that the group had singled out McDonald's because, in his words, it is a symbol of America, "the place where they not only promote globalization and industrially produced food but also unfairly penalize our peasants." In 2002, executives at McDonald's France even ran an ad in *Femme Actuelle* magazine suggesting that children should eat only one meal at McDonald's per week.

McDonald's French franchisees experience some of the same competitive pressures facing the U.S. units; there are also key differences. On the plus side, for example, Burger King closed its last restaurant in France in 1998. However, local bistros operators have enjoyed great success selling fresh-baked baguettes filled with ham and brie, effectively neutralizing McDonald's advantage of fast service and low prices. In response, executives hired an architecture firm to develop new restaurant designs specifically for the French market. A total of eight different themes were developed; many of the redesigned stores have hardwood floors and exposed brick walls. Signs are in muted colors rather than the chain's signature red and yellow and the golden arches are displayed more subtly. In short, the restaurants don't look like McDonald's elsewhere. The first redesigned store is located on the Champs Elysees on a site previously occupied by a Burger King; called "Music," the restaurant provides diners with the opportunity to listen to music CDs and watch music videos on TV monitors. To date, about half of McDonald's locations in France have been redesigned; some franchisees report sales increases of 10 percent to 20 percent. Impressed by these results, some American franchisees are undertaking similar renovations.

## Central and Eastern Europe

On January 31, 1990, after 14 years of negotiation and preparation, the first Bolshoi Mac went on sale in what was then the Soviet Union; by the end of the decade, there were more than two dozen McDonald's restaurants in Russia. The first Moscow McDonald's was built on Pushkin Square, near a major metro station just a few blocks from the Kremlin. It has 700 indoor seats and another 200 outside. It boasts 800 employees and features a 70-foot counter with 27 cash registers, equivalent to 20 ordinary McDonald's rolled into one. At present, there are more than 70 McDonald's locations in Russia, but the original Pushkin Square store enjoys the distinction of being the busiest McDonald's in the world. To ensure a steady supply of high-quality raw materials, the company built McComplex, a huge $45 million processing facility on the outskirts of Moscow. McDonald's also worked closely with local farmers to boost yields and quality; today, the company sources 75 percent of its ingredients from a network of 100 in-country suppliers.

From the outset, George Cohon, the Canadian who is senior chairman of McDonald's Russia, decreed that the restaurants would accept rubles, which was the only currency ordinary Russian citizens were allowed to possess. It was a gutsy decision, because the ruble was not convertible; in other words, rubles were worthless outside Russia. Among the handful of other Western eateries in Moscow at the time, some (e.g., the Baskin Robbins ice cream shop at the Rossiya Hotel) required that customers pay in dollars or other "hard" (i.e., convertible) currencies; by contrast, Pizza Hut's Moscow restaurant offered separate service lines for ruble patrons and those paying in hard currency. Although McDonald's Russia could not initially send any profits out of the country, there was another alternative: reinvesting rubles in choice Moscow real estate and opening additional restaurants.

The turmoil stemming from the dissolution of the Soviet Union and Russia's sometimes tortuous journey toward a market economy during the 1990s has presented the management of McDonald's Russia with a number of challenges. Although massive public demonstrations followed a failed coup attempt in August 1991, the protesters did not target McDonald's. Perhaps management's biggest challenge to date was the currency crisis that began in the summer of 1998 when the Russian government devalued the ruble and defaulted on its foreign debt. Many companies immediately raised prices to compensate for the precipitous drop in the ruble's value, and customers stopped buying.

Ukraine and Belarus are among the other members of the Commonwealth of Independent States with newly opened restaurants. The first Ukrainian McDonald's opened in Kiev in 1997; the company envisions 100 locations by 2007 for a total investment of $120 million. McDonald's has also set its sights on Central Europe, where plans call for hundreds of new restaurants to be opened in Croatia, Slovakia, Romania, and other countries.

## Refocusing on the U.S. Market

Back in the United States, there were some bright spots in the 1990s such as the company's wildly successful promotions featuring Beanie Babies and toys based on characters from Disney movies such as *101 Dalmatians*. However, McDonald's 10-year licensing agreement with Disney rules out any promotions tied to competing media companies. Unfortunately for both parties, several of Disney's recent features have performed relatively poorly at the box office. By contrast, Burger King promotions tied to popular characters such as Nickelodeon's SpongeBob SquarePants have enjoyed great success. By the late 1990s, McDonald's strategy of growing its U.S. business by opening new restaurants was not yielding the desired results.

In 1998, McDonald's struggles led to a management shakeup: Chairman and CEO Michael R. Quinlan relinquished the top position to Jack M. Greenberg, who had headed McDonald's USA. Greenberg immediately launched a new food preparation initiative called Made For You. The goal was to improve customer perceptions of the taste and freshness of menu items. The quest for new ideas to fuel growth also prompted executives to make their first forays outside the core business. In February 1998, McDonald's acquired a majority stake in the Chipotle Mexican Grill chain. The move signaled McDonald's recognition both of the increasing popularity of ethnic foods and of heightened interest among consumers in healthy eating. In 1998, McDonald's also acquired Aroma, a coffeehouse chain in London. The acquisition trend continued over the next 2 years as McDonald's snapped up Donatos Pizza and Boston Market, a floundering chain featuring home-style cooking. As Greenberg conceded, "There are pieces of the business we can't do under the arches. When you're out with friends on a Saturday night for pizza and wine, you don't go to McDonald's." Greenberg envisioned these partner brands adding at least 2 percent to McDonald's growth rate within a few years. In addition, McCafé, a gourmet coffee shop modeled on a successful Australian concept, was tested in downtown Chicago, and a McTreat ice cream parlor had a trial run in Houston.

*"McDonald's comes off as uncool.*
*If you want to be chic, you eat sushi. Indian food is even more cutting edge.*
*McDonald's is like white bread."*

Daniel, a 26-year-old architectural draftsman in San Francisco

Despite these changes, sales of key menu items continued to disappoint. For example, demand for the all-important Happy Meal, which represents about one out of five transactions, was declining, and McDonald's continued to struggle in its efforts to increase its appeal to grown-ups. In spring 2001, McDonald's was faced with a consumer lawsuit charging the company with "fraudulently concealing the existence of beef in their french fries." For years, the company had promoted its fries as being cooking in 100 percent vegetable oil. In response to the lawsuit, McDonald's conceded that a small amount of beef extract was added to the potatoes as they were being processed. The company settled the suit in 2002 for $12.5 million. Meanwhile, CEO Greenberg's highly touted redesigned cooking system resulted in slower service at many restaurants; also, the Chicago McCafe was closed after failing to generate much interest. At the end of 2002, Greenberg abruptly announced that he would retire.

His successor, Jim Cantalupo, is a retired vice chairman whose 28-year career at McDonald's included considerable international experience. He pledged to review all of his predecessor's initiatives, including the new cooking system and the non-core acquisitions. He also vowed to get the company back on track by focusing on the basics, namely customer service, clean restaurants, and reliable food. Unhappy with the company's recent advertising "Smile" advertising theme, Cantalupo took the extraordinary step of calling a summit meeting of senior creative personnel from 14 advertising agencies representing McDonald's 10 largest international markets. Foremost among them was New York-based DDB Worldwide, the lead agency on the McDonald's account that handles advertising in 34 countries including Australia, the United States, and Germany. In addition, Leo Burnett is responsible for ads targeting children. McDonald's marketing and advertising managers from key countries were also summoned to the meeting at company headquarters in Oakbrook, Illinois.

As Larry Light, global chief marketing officer for McDonald's, noted:

Creative talent is a rare talent, and creative people don't belong to geographies, to Brazil or France or

Australia. We're going to challenge our agencies to be more open-minded about sharing between geographies.

Charlie Bell, a former executive at McDonald's Europe who was promoted to chief operating officer, believes the company needs more relevance in its advertising. "For one of the world's best brands, we have missed the mark," he said before the summit meeting. In June 2003, the company announced that it had picked the phrase "I'm loving it" as its new global marketing theme; the idea was proposed by Heye & Partner, a DDB Worldwide unit located in Germany.

Not surprisingly, even as McDonald's executives attempt to come to grips with the problems facing their company, various business experts are offering advice of their own. Adrian J. Slywotzky, author of *Value Migration*, noted, "McDonald's needs to move the question from 'How can we sell more hamburgers?' to 'What does our brand allow us to consider selling to our customers?'" Mark DiMassimo, chief executive of a New York-based company that specializes in brand advertising, calls McDonald's "a large lost organization that is searching for a strategy." In his view, "The company must focus, focus, focus, and stand for one thing."

## Discussion Questions

1. Identify the key elements in McDonald's global marketing strategy. In particular, how does McDonald's approach the issue of standardization?

2. Do you think government officials in developing countries such as Russia, China, and India welcome McDonald's? Do consumers in these countries welcome McDonald's? Why or why not?

3. At the end of 2003, McDonald's announced it was selling the Donatos Pizza unit. In light of this decision, assess McDonald's prospects for success beyond the burger-and-fries model.

4. Is it realistic to expect that McDonald's—or any well-known company—can expand globally without occasionally making mistakes or generating controversy? Why do antiglobalization protesters around the world frequently target McDonald's?

*Visit the Web site*
**www.mcdonalds.com**

*Sources:* Saritha Rai, "Tastes of India in U.S. Wrappers," *The New York Times* (April 29, 2003), pp. W1, W7; Bruce Horovitz, "It's Back to Basics for McDonald's," *USA Today* (May 21, 2003), pp. 1B, 2B; Sherri Day, "After Years at Top, McDonald's Strives to Regain Ground," *The New York Times* (March 3, 2003), pp. A1, A19; Day and Stuart Elliot, "At McDonald's, an Effort to Restore Lost Luster," *The New York Times* (April 8, 2003), pp. B1, B4; Leung and Suzanne Vranica, "Happy Meals Are No Longer Bringing Smiles at McDonald's," *The Wall Street Journal* (January 31, 2003), p. B1; Shirley Leung and Ron Lieber, "The New Menu Option at McDonald's: Plastic," *The Wall Street Journal* (November 26, 2002), pp. D1, D2; Leung, "McHaute Cuisine: Armchairs, TVs and Espresso—Is It McDonald's?" *The Wall Street Journal* (August 30, 2002), pp. A1, A6; Bruce Horovitz, "McDonald's Tries a New Recipe to Revive Sales," *USA Today* (July 10, 2001), pp. 1A, 2A; Geoff Winestock and Yaroslav Trofimov, "McDonald's Reassures Italians About Beef," *The Wall Street Journal* (January 16, 2001), pp. A3, A6; Kevin Helliker and Richard Gibson, "The New Chief Is Ordering Up Changes at McDonald's," *The Wall Street Journal* (August 24, 1998), pp. B1, B4; Bethan Hutton, "Fast-Food Group Blows a McBubble in Slow Economy," *Financial Times* (May 8, 1998), p. 24; Bruce Horovitz, "'My Job Is Always on the Line,'" *USA Today* (March 16, 1998), p. 8B; David Leonhardt, "McDonald's: Can It Regain Its Golden Touch?" *Business Week* (March 9, 1998), pp. 70–74+; Richard Tomkins, "When the Chips Are Down," *Financial Times* (August 16, 1997), p. 13; Yumiko Ono, "Japan Warms to McDonald's Doting Dad Ads," *The Wall Street Journal* (May 8, 1997), pp. B1, B12.

# Case 1-2

## Acer, Inc. (A)

Despite McDonald's recent problems (see Case 1-1), the company's business model has served as a source of inspiration for Taiwan businessman Stan Shih. However, Shih is not in the fast-food business; his company, Acer Inc., manufactures and markets personal computers for the consumer and home office markets as well as chips, monitors, keyboards, CD-ROM drives, and other hardware. Just as hungry consumers will shun a restaurant that serves warmed-over food, most computer buyers want the absolute latest technology. For more than 15 years, Acer manufactured computers in Taiwan and shipped them to dealers throughout the world. By building and marketing computers under its own brand name as well as supplying Hitachi, Siemens, and other companies on an "original equipment manufacturer" (OEM) basis, Acer became Taiwan's number one exporter. Acer's success also helped change the public's perception that "Made in Taiwan" was synonymous with cheap, low-tech products.

However, because of the fast pace of technological change in the computer industry, Acer's PCs sometimes became obsolete by the time they were shipped to their destinations. Shih realized that one of the keys to McDonald's success was the company's system of delivering beef patties, buns, and other ingredients to local restaurants, where they are assembled into sandwiches as needed. He decided to decentralize computer assembly in nearly three dozen locations around the globe and use a combination of locally purchased components plus components shipped in from Taiwan. As Shih explains, "We are providing the customer with the freshest technology at the most reasonable price."

McDonald's hasn't been Shih's only source of inspiration. When Shih first founded his company in the 1970s, it was called Multitech International Corporation. After a decade, Shih decided a name change was in order. For one thing, the original name was too long. Another problem: It didn't convey the image of technical innovation the way names like Sony, BMW, and Honda do. Shih spent 2 years searching for a new name; a consulting firm helped generate some 20,000 possible alternatives. From the short list of finalists, Acer was the top choice for several reasons: it means "sharp" in Latin and implies "energetic" and "capable." It also sounds like *ace*, which has a positive connotation for many people.

Once the name change had been implemented, Shih made a number of deeper changes. He developed a policy of "global brand, local touch," a break from the traditional Asian preference for hierarchical, top-down corporate structures and corporate cultures that stress deference to authority. Shih realized that hierarchies couldn't act quickly enough in the fast-moving computer industry. Now Acer is organized into strategic business units for manufacturing and regional business units for marketing. Acer's local management teams in individual country or regional markets are empowered to make decisions on a wide range of marketing mix elements. Acer America, for example, is a wholly owned subsidiary, but Marketing Vice President Marlene Williamson was afforded free rein to target the home-user market segment by distributing Acer's sleek and stylish Aspire line through the Best Buy chain.

"Local touch" also has financial ramifications: Because joint venture partners have their own investments at stake, Shih believes he can trust them to make prudent decisions. This trust has paid off handsomely. In South Africa, for example, Acer became the number two brand by expanding during the shift from apartheid to majority rule; some competitors marked time out of fear of market volatility. In Mexico, the government's devaluation of the peso in December 1994 prompted several computer companies to cut back on marketing. Managers at Acer Computec Latinoamerica adjusted to the new financial circumstances and, within a year, Acer commanded a 30 percent share of the market.

Back in Taiwan, Shih also made fundamental changes in how his company is run. Acer's executive teams encouraged employees to speak up and share ideas without bowing their heads in deference to higher-ranking personnel. Simon Lin, the chief executive of the information products unit, explained, "Sometimes I have to keep my opinions to myself so that others will speak. You need to have different voices speak up—that's how innovation comes about. I tell our people, 'You can bring up anything that you want to discuss.'" To encourage a free exchange of ideas, Shih, Lin, and their colleagues practice "management by wandering around"; that is, they drop in on employees to exchange ideas and glean bits of information that may not be available through more formal channels. Lin

says, "We come in to communicate with each other, to create a spirit of teamwork. This is part of our new way of thinking."

Shih has used a number of different approaches to build his company. A joint venture with Texas Instruments produces dynamic random-access memory chips (DRAMs) in Hsinchu, Taiwan. Acer acquired Counterpoint Computers in the United States and bought a stake in Germany's Cetec Data Technology. Acer also has built assembly plants in Australia, Britain, Germany, Japan, the Netherlands, New Zealand, the Philippines, South Korea, and the United States.

Of the regional and global issues that will have an impact on the company, perhaps the most significant is the economic crisis in Asia that began in 1997. Acer's sales in the region are likely to suffer as consumer spending falls. Then there are broader geopolitical issues involving Taiwan's relationship with China, which has long claimed sovereignty over its smaller neighbor. Taiwan lobbied to join 18 other nations in the Asia-Pacific Economic Cooperation forum. However, thanks to maneuvering by Beijing, Taiwan was allowed to join only as "Chinese Taipei." Similarly, Taiwan's hopes to join the World Trade Organization have been stymied by Beijing's insistence that mainland China become a member first. For now, Taiwan is shut out of the world's most important organization for resolving trade disputes.

Meanwhile, in the United States, Acer's market share fell from nearly 15 percent in 1995 to only 5 percent by the end of 1997. The Aspire line of home PCs failed to achieve profitability in the face of aggressive price cutting by Compaq and other competitors. Despite a $20 million advertising budget in 1996, the Acer brand name was still not nearly as well known as Compaq, Dell, Gateway, IBM, or Sony. In 1997, Acer America shifted its communication emphasis from brand-image advertising to product-oriented advertising. Also, more money was allocated to retail promotions, trade shows, and public relations communications efforts. In terms of products, Shih and marketing VP Williamson hope to achieve more success by targeting small and medium-size businesses with a new modular desktop PC called AcerPower. Shih also acquired Texas Instrument's global computer notebook business; the deal brought an 80-person sales force on board.

Despite these setbacks and challenges, Shih continues to set ambitious goals for his company. One goal was to be the fifth-largest computer company by the turn of the century; by mid-1998, Acer already ranked number eight. To position Acer for the next century, Shih envisions a corporate structure that he calls "21 in 21." Shih intends to break up Acer into a borderless network of 21 independent companies that maintain close ties with Taipei. *Fortune* magazine described Shih's vision as "a global federation of highly autonomous Acer companies." "Eventually," Shih said in 1995, "Acer will have a majority of local ownership in each country, and no one will be able to say that we are a Taiwanese company."

The problems in the U.S. market, however, may make it more difficult to reach $15 billion in sales by 2010. Shih still aspires to challenge Japan's dominance in the consumer electronics industry. To achieve these goals, Shih hopes to move beyond PCs and attain leadership in next-generation low-priced "information appliances." One new product is the AcerBasic, a computer that provides Internet access when hooked up to a television set. By competing in this segment, Acer will come face-to-face with a new set of competitors, such as marketing heavyweight Sony. Some industry observers believe that Shih should concentrate on supplying PCs to other companies. Shih maintains, "Brand is critical to our long-term success." Some industry observers disagree; as one analyst noted, "Brand name doesn't bring investors any benefit." He advises Stan Shih to give up his dream of becoming a global brand. To be blunt, the analyst said, "I'd pull the plug."

## Discussion Questions

1. How would you classify Acer in terms of the stages of development described in Chapter 1?
2. Assess the market potential for Acer's new lines, including children's computers, "information appliances," and video game players.
3. Can you think of any risks associated with Shih's vision of "21 in 21"?
4. Advise Shih on global marketing strategy. Should Acer continue its quest to establish Acer as a global consumer brand, or pull the plug and focus on being a top-tier supplier to global brand marketers?

*Visit the Web Site*
**www.acer.com**

*Sources:* Jonathan Moore and Peter Burrows, "A New Attack Plan for Acer America," *Business Week* (December 8, 1997), pp. 82–83; Bradley Johnson, "Struggling Acer Exits Branding," *Advertising Age* (April 7, 1997), p. 19; Richard Halloran, "Parallel Lives," *World Business* (November–December 1996), pp. 24–29; Emily Thornton, "The Reckoning," *Far Eastern Economic Review* (July 25, 1996), pp. 74–76; Pete Engardio and Peter Burrows, "Acer: A Global Powerhouse," *Business Week* (July 1, 1996), pp. 94–96; Dan Shapiro, "Ronald McDonald, Meet Stan Shih," *Sales & Marketing Management* (November 1995), pp. 85–86+; Louis Kraar, "Acer's Edge: PCs to Go," *Fortune* (October 30, 1995), pp. 187–188+.

# Appendix 1.1

# The 18 Guiding Principles of the Marketing Company

## Introduction

### The Marketing Company

Welcome to the global marketplace! Regardless of the size, profit, and market strength, every company on the earth has entered a new era of competition.

The change drivers such as technology, economy, and market conditions have increasingly redefined almost every sector of industries, and the way we do business. The advance of information technology has transformed the marketplace; it has provided industry players with a vast array of alternatives to compete more strategically and forcefully.

The dynamic change of economic and social conditions have revolutionized consumer behavior and attitudes. With a dizzying array of product choices in the marketplace, consumers, to the highest degree, have more demanding expectations than ever before. They do not just expect a high-quality product; product quality has become a norm and requirement. This new breed of consumers want high product quality with an affordable price within their convenient reach.

The traditional strategy that brought companies success will lose the applicability in this new marketplace. The conventional disciplines that guaranteed market leadership during the past years will lose their adaptability. In order to survive in this new marketplace, companies need a new set of strategies and tools. They need a set of guiding principles that will create a sustainable competitive advantage. They need to become a new breed of company: the Marketing Company!

What is the Marketing Company? As you will soon explore the characters of the company in the following pages, you will discover that it is not just a market-oriented company. Company is not just a market-driven company. The Marketing Company is an organization that adopts the 18 Guiding Principles of the Marketing Company as its credo—as its guiding values, its principles to compete in the new marketplace. It endures external and internal change drivers, more demanding customers, and even fiercer competitors. After all, a new competition needs a different kind of rules and principles to survive and win the race. *Be ready to rewrite your credo, or your company will die!*

### Principle #1—The Principle of the Company: Marketing is a Strategic Business Concept

This principle is the first foundation of the Marketing Company. In the chaotic marketplace in the global economy era, the traditional concept of lowercase marketing has lost its adaptability in market competition. As companies are squeezed by external change drivers such as technology, economy, and market—and as they face internal organizational changes within themselves (shareholders, people, and organization culture)—marketing is no longer about selling, advertising or even 4Ps introduced by Jerome McCarthy.

Marketing should become the strategic business concept within corporations. It is no longer functional tasks and respon-

sibilities carried by a department. Marketing is strategic because it should be *formulated by top-level management, long-term oriented, navigate a company's direction, and hold the responsibilities of creating loyal business customers (internal, external, and investor customers).*

A1 Ries, in his book, *Focus*, says that, "A good Chief Executive Officer should also be a Chief Marketing Officer." David Packard, a cofounder of Hewlett-Packard, once said that "Marketing is too important for a marketing department." Peter Drucker long ago envisioned that, "Business has only two basic functions: marketing and innovation. Marketing and innovation produce results, the rest are cost!"

Admittedly, their statements are definitely true. In other words, they agree with this first principle: *Marketing is a strategic business concept.*

### Principle #2—The Principle of the Community: Marketing is Everyone's Business

This principle is the second foundation of the Marketing Company. Within the Marketing Company, marketing should be adopted as a strategic business concept. Ideally, the organizational structure in the company should be flat and layerless. There is no marketing department and function in the Marketing Company because marketing is not a department, and marketing as a department is becoming weaker. *Therefore, all departments are marketing departments, and all functions are marketing functions.*

All people within the Marketing Company form a community, called a *marketing community.* So, in the community everyone is a *marketer,* meaning that the responsibilities and tasks of acquiring, satisfying, and retaining customers lie on the shoulders of everyone. Regardless of what level and department a person works in, he or she should be involved in the process of retaining customers.

New roles such as Accounting–Marketer, Operations–Marketer, R&D–Marketer, Janitor–Marketer, Maintenance–Marketer, and the like will be emerging as this principle is instilled in the Marketing Company. While their jobs will not be exactly similar, the responsibility to create customer loyalty becomes the central theme of their works.

Thus, everyone led by the Chief Executive Officer (acting as Chief Marketing Officer) of the company, should march in the same direction. They should carry a similar mission: It is the responsibility of everyone to attract, satisfy, and retain customers. *Everyone is a marketer, whatever his or her job description is.*

### Principle #3—The Principle of Competition: Marketing War is About Value War

This principle is the third foundation of the Marketing Company. The Marketing Company does not pursue short-term profits; it creates customer value for long-term relationships. Unfortunately, the company's principle does not parallel with stockholders' short-term orientation in stock exchange institutions. While they rely upon companies' quarterly financial reports to buy and sell stocks, the Marketing Company looks beyond this short-term time frame for result.

The company regards profit as short term and value creation as long term. By continuously and consistently creating customer value, the Marketing Company will generate profits. Hence, profit follows value. This is because marketing war is not merely marketing war. Marketing war is value war.

While value is defined as total get (customer benefits) divided by total give (customer expenses), there are five value-creating formula alternatives to win competition. First, increase benefits and lower expenses. Second, increase benefits and hold expenses constant. Third, hold benefits constant and lower expenses. Fourth, increase benefits significantly and increase expenses. Fifth, lower benefits and significantly lower expenses.

As the value impact among the formula alternatives above varies significantly, the core idea behind the principle remains unchanged: Value is the key to winning and keeping customers. *Therefore, improve customer value to win the marketing war.*

### Principle #4—The Principle of Retention: Concentrate on Loyalty, Not Just on Satisfaction

In addition to the three previous founding principles, the Marketing Company concentrates on loyalty, not just on satisfaction.

As marketing war becomes value war and as industry competition becomes value competition, it is inadequate for the Marketing Company to concentrate merely on customer satisfaction. The ultimate objective of the Marketing Company should be customer loyalty.

As we enter the *era of choices*, there is no guarantee that satisfied customers will become loyal customers. Satisfaction has increasingly become a commodity. It is only the process, not the end result. The final goal of the Marketing Company is customer loyalty. *Customer loyalty has become the moving target* every Marketing Company must pursue to remain competitive. What matters most to the Marketing Company is now *the quality of profit, not just the quantity of profit.* It is already evident that customer attraction activities cost a company much more than a customer retention program; the cost to acquire a new customer will cost more than retaining one good customer. Profits, therefore, should come more from old, existing customers than from new, first-time buyers.

A company's profit record, accordingly, provides an insight on the level of customer loyalty. As customer attraction, customer satisfaction, and customer retention will become an endless process of company survival, the ultimate effort of the Marketing Company should remain clear: *Concentrate on loyalty, not just on satisfaction.*

### Principle #5—The Principle of Integration: Concentrate on Differences, Not Just on Averages

The Marketing Company concentrates on differences, not just averages.

In order for the Marketing Company to create the loyal customer base mentioned in the first topping principle, it has to concentrate on customers individually. The principle commands the company to build intimate relationships with customers—intimate enough to learn about customers' needs and wants; close enough to understand customers' expectations. In the chaotic competitive setting, every customer will become unique.

Underlying this principle is a profound fact that *all customers are not created equal.* Many companies are tempted to think that their customers have roughly similar needs and wants. This dangerous assumption, however, will lead them to create mediocre and average offers for their diversified customers.

The principle emphasizes that by no means are customers equal. *They are uniquely different and their needs are distinctively diversified.* In other words, *there are no average customers.* The Marketing Company, as a result, has to integrate itself with customers to create a bond that produces a vivid picture about customers' needs, wants, and expectations.

There are no average customers. *In order to build customer loyalty, a company has to concentrate on differences, not just on averages.*

### Principle #6—The Principle of Anticipation: Concentrate on Proactivity, Not Just on Reactivity

The Marketing Company concentrates on proactivity, not just reactivity.

To fully integrate with customers, as described in the second topping principle, the Marketing Company should be ready for change. It must adapt to the current state of industry and be able to anticipate and cope with change in order to be proactive.

Stephen Covey, in his landmark book, *The Seven Habits of Highly Effective People,* defines *proactivity as responsibility.* In this context, responsibility means the ability of an organization to choose responses within a given circumstance and environment. Between a stimulus and a response, there is a gap. It is the gap of freedom to react, freedom to choose a response.

Thus, to be competitive, a company has to be ready for change in its environment. It has to be able to anticipate change of technology, economy, and markets. It has to have proactivity to operate in an uncertain and unpredictable environment. To be fluid and dynamic operationally, the Marketing Company concentrates on proactivity, not just reactivity. Be a *change agent, change driver,* or even *change surpriser* to your competitors.

### Principle #7—The Principle of Brand: Avoid the Commodity-Like Trap

This is the first value-creating principle of the Marketing Company. To the company, brand is not just a name, nor is it a logo and symbols. Brand is the *value indicator* of the Marketing Company. It is the umbrella that represents the product or service, companies, persons, or even countries. It is determined by the company's new product development, customer satisfaction and retention, and value-chain management.

It is the equity of the firm that adds value to products and services it offers. It is an asset that creates value to consumers by enhancing satisfaction and recognition of quality. Through its brand, the company is able to liberate itself from the supply–demand curve.

When the firm successfully liberates itself from the supply–demand curve, the price of the firm's offers will not be dependent on the price equilibrium point. The firm, as a result, is able to be the *price maker, not price taker.*

Unfortunately, macroeconomists, to a certain extent, do not realize the power of brand. They view economy from a global perspective and derive numbers from a macro point of view. This ignores the most crucial element of a price driver: brand.

It is brand that determines a price. It is brand that liberates the company to create values for internal customers, external customers, and investor customers. It is brand that indicates a value of the firm's products and services. Therefore, use, build, and protect your brand. *It is the brand that will enable the company to avoid the commodity-like trap.*

### Principle #8—The Principle of Service: Avoid the Business-Category Trap

This is the second value-creating principle of the Marketing Company. To the company, service is not just after-sales service, before-sales service, or even during-sales service. Service is not customer toll-free numbers, maintenance service, or customer service. Service is a *value enhancer* of the Marketing Company. It is the paradigm of the company to create a lasting value to customers through products (small "p") and services (small "s"). Service in this principle refers to service with a big "S," not a small "s." It is the answer to Peter Drucker's question: "What business are you in?" The only answer to the question is, "We are in the service business!" There is only one business category: service. Why? It is because *service means solution.* Companies must give the true solution to customers.

Whether the company's business is a restaurant, hotel, or shoe manufacturing, the only category for all businesses must become a service business. To become a real service company, a firm has to continuously enhance the small "p" and the small "s." To create a long-lasting value and build relationships with customers, the firm's offers should provide constant value to customers. Therefore, a CEO acting as CMO has the key role between *corporate governance* and *corporate management* to maintain, and even develop this sense of service throughout the whole organization.

In this sense, service is a paradigm. It is the spirit of the company. It is the attitude to sustain and win tomorrow's competition. *It is the strategy to avoid the business-category trap.*

### Principle #9—The Principle of Process: Avoid the Function-Orientation Trap

This is the third value-creating principle of the Marketing Company. It refers to the process of creating value to customers. It reflects the product quality, cost, and delivery of a company to customers. It is the *value enabler* of a company.

The principle commands the company to be the captain of supply-chain process. It should manage the supply-chain process, from raw materials to finished products, in a way that would enhance value-creating activities and reduce and eliminate value-eroding activities within the company.

In addition, it requires a firm to be *the hub of network organizations* where it could establish relationships with organizations that have the potential to add value. The renowned term

for this is *strategic alliance.* These partnering organizations may be the company's suppliers, customers, or even competitors. Benchmarking, reengineering, outsourcing, merger, and acquisition are examples of strategic actions to improve process.

The value-creating drivers such as brand, service, and process (as the value enabler) should not only create value to external customers and investor customers, but also become the credo of internal customers, who are people. People within the organization should be marketers. They should avoid functional arrogance within the company because everyone holds a similar belief: Customer value is the end result, not titles and job positions in the company. *Brand, service, and process as three value-creating principles are drivers to win the heart share of customers.*

### Principle #10—The Principle of Segmentation: View Your Market Creatively

Another crucial part of a company is marketing strategy. The strategy comprises three elements, namely segmentation, targeting, and positioning. Together they are *driven to win shares of customers.*

The first element of marketing strategy is segmentation. Segmentation is the process of partitioning the market into several divisions. However, segmentation to us is about *viewing a market creatively*. It is about mapping a market into several categories by gathering similar behavior of consumers into a segment. It is the *mapping strategy* of a company.

Segmentation is an art to identify and pinpoint opportunity emerging in the markets. At the same time, it is a science to view the market based on *geographic, demographic, psychographic,* and *behavior* variables or even a *segment of one.* Whatever segmentation variables are used, please make sure that each person in a segment has similar behavior, especially in purchasing, using, or servicing the products.

The Marketing Company should be creative enough to view a market from a unique angle. It also has to clearly identify the market from an advanced perspective, using segmentation variables. Segmentation is the first marketing strategy element. It is the initial step that determines the life of the company. *Market opportunities are in the eyes of the beholder. In order to exploit the opportunity arising in the market, that beholder must first view the market creatively.*

### Principle #11—The Principle of Targeting: Allocate Your Resources Effectively

The second element of marketing strategy is *targeting.* By the traditional definition, targeting is the process of selecting the right target market for a company's products and services. We however, define targeting as the strategy to *allocate the company's resources effectively.* Why? Because resources are always limited. It is about how to fit the company within a selected target market segment. Hence, we call it the *fitting strategy of a company.*

There are several criteria used to select an appropriate market segment for the company's resources. The first criterion is market size. The company has to select the market segment that has "good" size to generate expected financial returns. The bigger the market size, the more lucrative the segment is to the company.

The second criterion used to choose market segment is growth. The potential growth of a market segment is a crucial attribute for the company. The better and higher the growth is the more promising the market segment to the company.

The third criterion is competitive advantage. Competitive advantage is a way to measure whether the company has such strength and expertise to dominate the chosen market segment.

The fourth criterion is competitive situation. The company has to consider the competition intensity within the industry including the number of players, suppliers, and entry barriers. Using these main criteria, the company has to find its "fit" with the right market segment.

## Principle #12—The Principle of Positioning: Lead Your Customers Credibly

The third criterion of marketing strategy is *positioning*. By the traditional definition, positioning is the strategy to occupy the consumers' minds with our company's offerings. In this principle, however, we define positioning as the strategy to *lead the company's customers credibly*. It is about how to establish trustworthiness, confidence, and competence for customers. If the company has those elements, customers will then have the "being" of the company or product within their minds. Therefore, positioning is about the *being strategy* of the company or product in the customers' minds. It is about earning customers' trust to make them willingly follow the company.

Yoram Wind, a marketing strategy professor, defines positioning as the *reason for being*. He advocates that positioning is about defining the company's identity and personality in the customers' minds. As we move toward the era of choices, the company can no longer force customers to buy their products: they no longer can manage the customers. In this era, the company should have credibility in the minds of customers. Because customers cannot be managed, they have to be led. In order to successfully lead customers, companies have to have credibility. So positioning is not just about persuading and creating image in the consumers' minds, it is about earning consumers' trust. It is about *the quest of trustworthiness. It is about creating a being in the consumers' minds and leading them credibly.*

## Principle #13—The Principle of Differentiation: Integrate Your Content, Context, and Infrastructure

The first element of marketing tactics is *differentiation*. Traditionally, differentiation is the act of designing a set of meaningful differences in the company's offers. To us, this definition by Philip Kotler is still valid. We define differentiation as "integrating the content, context, and infrastructure of our offers to customers." Different products are the core tactic of the company to support its positioning. Differentiation, therefore, is the *core tactic* of the Marketing Company.

As the first marketing tactic element, differentiation should create a truly different and unique product for customers. The product not only has to be perceived differently by customers (positioning), it has to be really different in content, context, and infrastructure (differentiation).

A company can ideally create a unique offer by concentrating on three aspects of differentiation: *content, context, and infrastructure*. Content (what to offer), is the core benefit of the product itself. Context (how to offer), in addition, refers to the way the company offers the product. Infrastructure (enabler), is the technology, facilities, and people used to create the content and context.

When positioning strategy is not supported by differentiation, the company may overpromise and underdeliver to customers, which could ruin the company's brand and reputation. On the other hand, if the positioning is supported by differentiation, the company will establish *strong brand integrity*. It means the brand image in the consumers' minds is similar to brand identity communicated by companies.

## Principle #14—The Principle of Marketing Mix: Integrate Your Offer, Logistics, and Communications

The second element of marketing tactics is *marketing mix*. To many practitioners, this is considered as the whole marketing concept. The 4Ps (product, price, place, promotion), initially introduced by Jerome McCarthy, is often thought of as the complete marketing principle. To us, marketing mix is only an element of marketing tactic. It is also the tip of an iceberg—the most visible part of the company in the market.

The marketing mix, to us, is about *integrating the company's offers, logistics, and communications*. The company's offers, consisting of products and prices, should be well-integrated with logistics (including channel distribution) and communications to create a powerful marketing force in the marketplace. Therefore, we call it the *creation tactic* of the company. Why? Because marketing mix has to be the creation of content–context–infrastructure differentiation. There are three types of marketing mix in the market. First, is *destructive marketing mix*. It is a marketing mix that does not add customer value and does not build the company's brand. Second, is *me-too marketing mix*. It is a marketing mix that often imitates existing marketing mix from other players in an industry. Third, is *creative marketing mix*. It is the marketing mix that supports the marketing strategy (segmentation–targeting–positioning) and other marketing tactic principles (differentiation–selling) of the company and builds marketing value (brand–service–process).

## Principle #15—The Principle of Selling: Integrate Your Company, Customers, and Relationships

The last element of marketing tactics is *selling*. The principle of selling does not refer to personal selling at all, nor is it related to the activities of selling products to customers. What we mean by selling is, "the tactic to create long-term relationship with customers through company's products." It is the tactic to *integrate company, customers, and relationships*.

After developing marketing strategy and creating marketing mix, the company should be able to generate financial returns through selling. Thus, it is the *capture tactic* of the company. There are three main levels of selling: feature selling, benefit selling, and solution selling. As the choice of products in the marketplace overwhelm customers, companies have to sell solutions to customers, not just features and benefits. There is a relevant framework called *customer bonding* that emphasizes the importance of this principle. In the concept, customers have to go through five steps, from consumers to loyalists, as follows: awareness–identity–relationship–community–advocacy.

Hence, consumers should be made aware of our products and drive them to become advocacies. The principle of differentiation, marketing mix, and selling are *drivers to win the market share*.

## Principle #16—The Principle of Totality: Balance Your Strategy, Tactics, and Value

After focusing on the nine core elements of marketing (segmentation, targeting, positioning, differentiation, marketing mix, selling, brand, service, and process) individually, in the implementation, the Marketing Company should be able to balance those elements operationally as well as strategically. The Marketing Company should be able to balance the strategy, tactic, and value in the implementation. Marketing strategy is about how to win *the mind share*. Marketing tactic is about how to win the *market share*. Marketing value is about how to win *the heart share*. Together, they will win the mind, market, and heart shares.

As the business environment changes dynamically, the strategy, tactic, and value of the company may not be as precise as when it was developed. The maneuvers of competitors, the revolution of technology, and the changes in consumer behavior will require the company to adjust and readjust the strategy, tactic, and value. It demands the company to align strategy, tactic, and value to adapt to the most current business environment. The dynamic business environment will necessitate the company to constantly monitor or review the balance of strategy, tactic, and value; to build the totality of the business. The Marketing Company should also *balance the time allocation* in strategy, tactic, and value activities.

## Principle #17—The Principle of Agility: Integrate Your What, Why, and How

To operate in a competitive, dynamic environment, where technology, consumer behavior, and competitor movement change in a chaotic pattern, a company has to be agile to survive. The question, then, is, "What does it take to be agile?"

In this principle, an agile company continually engages in three main activities: First, it constantly monitors the competitors' movement and consumer behavior (what). It has marketing intelligence and information systems to take a picture of the business environment. Second, it continuously uses and analyzes the information gathered from the first activity to get a useful insight about the environment (why). Third, the gathered and analyzed information is incorporated in its strategy and tactic development process (how).

To put it simply, an agile company monitors, scans, and reviews the business environment continually. It analyzes the information and uses it to respond and preempt the competitor movement.

This principle will allow the company to be informed about the changes in the marketplace. This principle will allow the company to be not just a change agent and a change driver, but also a *change surpriser*. A change sur-

priser is a company who is agile. It is the organization that can balance what, why, and how. Balance your time allocation on what–why–how activities in the implementation.

## Principle #18—The Principle of Utility: Integrate Your Present, Future, and Gap

The Marketing Company does not just create profit for today and lose tomorrow. It does not just think about tomorrow and forget about today. The Marketing Company knows exactly the utility to integrate the present, future, and gap.

Together with the principles of totality and agility, utility *is the driver to win the activity share*, which is important, as mentioned by Michael Porter in one of his writings in *Harvard Business Review*. In the implementation, finally, the Marketing Company can successfully balance present activities, future activities, and gap activities.

Present activities are about today's products, which create profit by servicing today's customers. Future activities, meanwhile, are about developing tomorrow's products, which create sustainable growth by servicing tomorrow's different customers.

Gap activities are about enhancing capabilities of the technology and people, internally and externally, or by creating a strategic alliance or merger and acquisition in order to create future's activities.

Living by this principle, the company can maintain its competitiveness today and tomorrow and pursue whatever it lacks (the gap) to stay competitive in the present and future.

## Final Thought

### The Company Making

Throughout this writing, we have learned about the new principles of marketing. It is not just a set of static principles. It is a set of dynamic, guiding principles of the Marketing Company.

The 18 principles are organized around six dimensions—Foundation, Topping, Strategy, Tactic, Value, and Implementation—in which each dimension contains three principles.

Using these principles, a company's transformation from production oriented, selling oriented, marketing oriented, and market driven to a customer-driven company should be clearly guided along the way to become the Marketing Company.

The making of the Marketing Company involves strategic processes and steps as follows: The company should conduct an internal and external marketing audit. The results of the audit will produce what we call CAP (company alignment profile) and CSP (competitive setting profile). The gap between CAP and CSP portrays what the company should do.

In addition, the Marketing Company should adopt the 18 Guiding Principles as the corporate guiding credo and value that determines how it should act and react in the marketplace. The set of principles should become the guidance, culture, and foundation to live by.

Furthermore, the Marketing Company should be navigated by top management or a CEO who acts as a CMO. How the company behaves in the marketplace—and which direction it should take—must be decided by the top management based on the gap.

One final word: *The Marketing Company is not a destination*. It is not a goal or objective. Becoming the Marketing Company is a *process*. It is the never-ending pursuit of excellence. It is a *moving target* every company should pursue if it wants to survive and remain competitive.

### The Anatomy of Marketing

Many people who come to the subject of marketing with little or no business experiences think of it as a study of selling. Those who already have extensive professional experience or have undergone intensive academic training regard marketing as marketing mix. We at MarkPlus define marketing with three strategic dimensions: marketing strategy, marketing tactic, and marketing value (STV). The integrated concept of marketing is illustrated in Figure 1A-1.

In the global marketplace of the new millennium, marketing should be redefined to reflect the increasingly intensified competition in almost every sector of industries.

### Marketing Strategy: How to Win the Mind Share

According to Figure 1A-1, the first element of marketing strategy is the first dimension in the marketing concept. Its role is to *win the share* of consumers. Because of its strategic importance, it is in the Strategic Business Unit (SBU) level of a company.

The first element of marketing strategy is segmentation. Segmentation is defined as a way to view a market creatively. We call it the *mapping strategy* of a company.

After the market is mapped and segmented into groups of potential customers with similar characteristics and behavior, the company needs to select which segments to enter. This act is called *trageting*, which is the second element of the marketing strategy. Targeting is defined as a way to allocate

company's resources effectively—by selecting the right target market. We also define it as a company's *fitting strategy*.

**The 18 Guiding Principles of the Marketing Company**
Rewrite your credo, or your company will die.

1. **The Principle of the Company** Marketing Is a Strategic Business Concept
2. **The Principle of the Community** Marketing Is Everyone's Business
3. **The Principle of Competition** Marketing War Is about Value War
4. **The Principle of Retention** Concentrate on Loyalty, Not Just on Satisfaction
5. **The Principle of Integration** Concentrate on Differences, Not Just on Averages
6. **The Principle of Anticipation** Concentrate on Proactivity, Not Just on Reactivity
7. **The Principle of Brand** Avoid the Commodity-like Trap
8. **The Principle of Service** Avoid the Business-Category Trap
9. **The Principle of Process** Avoid the Function-Orientation Trap
10. **The Principle of Segmentation** View Your Market Creatively
11. **The Principle of Targeting** Allocate Your Resources Effectively
12. **The Principle of Positioning** Lead Your Customers Credibly
13. **The Principle of Differentiation** Integrate Your Content, Context, and Infrastructure
14. **The Principle of the Marketing Mix** Integrate Your Offer, Logistics, and Communications
15. **The Principle of Selling** Integrate Your Company, Customers, and Relationships
16. **The Principle of Totality** Balance Your Strategy, Tactic, and Value
17. **The Principle of Agility** Balance Your What, Why, and How
18. **The Principle of Utility** Balance Your Present, Future, and Gap

The last element of strategy is *positioning*. Positioning is defined as a way to lead customers credibly. We call it the *being strategy* of a company. After mapping the market and fitting the company's resources into its selected market segment, a company has to define its being in the mind of the target market—in order to have a credible position in their minds.

### Marketing Tactic: How to Win the Market Share

The second dimension of *The STV Model* is marketing tactic. Marketing tactic, because of its role, is regarded as elements to *win the market share*. Whereas marketing strategy is in the SBU level, marketing tactics is in operational level.

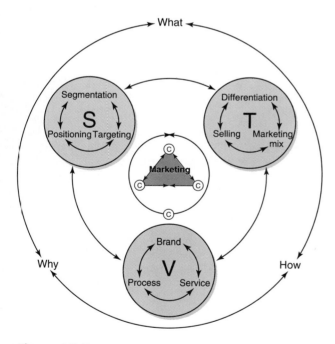

**Figure 1A-1**

*Strategy, Tactic, and Value Model*

The first element of marketing tactic is differentiation. Differentiation is the *core tactic* to differentiate the content, context, and infrastructure of a company's offers to the target markets. Meanwhile, we call marketing mix a *creation tactic*, which integrates a company's offer, logistics, and communications. Selling, furthermore, is the third element of the marketing tactic, which we define as the capture *tactic* to generate cash inflows for the company and to integrate the customer and company in a long-term, satisfying relationship.

Marketing Value: How to Win the Heart Share

Marketing value is the last dimension of *The STV Model.* It is the corporate-level responsibility and is intended to *win the heart share* of target markets.

The first element of marketing value is brand. Brand is the *value indicator* of a company, which enables the company to avoid the commodity trap. Service is the second element of marketing. It is the paradigm of a company to always meet or exceed the customers' needs, wants, and expectations. We define it as the *value enhancer* of a company.

The last element of marketing value is process. It is the *value enabler* of a company that enables it to deliver value to customers through the process within and without the firm.

**Discussion Questions**

1. What do you think of The 18 Guiding Principles of the Marketing Company? How do these principles compare to the marketing concepts and principles that you learned in your basic marketing course or that you have acquired through your experience as a marketer?

2. Hermawan Kartajaya is an Asian marketer. Do his 18 Guiding Principles apply in your country? Is marketing a universal discipline? Do the marketing concepts, tools, and methods that are used in a home country need to be modified or changed when used in other countries? Explain your answer.

3. What, in your view, are the key principles of marketing? List your principles (no more than six), and explain their importance to marketing success.

# 2 The Global Economic Environment

I n August 1998, the Russian economy imploded. The ruble plunged in value and the government defaulted on its foreign debt obligations. Many Russians faced wage cuts and layoffs; savings were wiped out as banks collapsed. The meltdown sent shock waves through global financial markets. Russia was down, but it was not out; in the years since the crisis, Russia's economy has experienced substantial growth. By 2003, a country that had teetered on the brink of bankruptcy could boast $60 billion in foreign currency reserves. The recovery was due in part to high world prices for oil and gas; the energy sector is Russian's most important source of export revenue. A second explanation for the rebounding economy was politics. In 2000, Vladimir Putin succeeded Boris Yeltsin as president. Putin initiated a reform program that included a new tax code, streamlined customs regulations, and made other improvements in the business climate. A third factor was the manner in which price increases for imports, caused by the ruble's devaluation, stimulated local production of a wide range of goods. At the same time, wealthy Russians continued to spend lavishly on luxury imports such as German cars, French wine, and Italian designer fashions. Moreover, during the 1990s, Russia's wealthy business people were sending a great deal of money out of the country; annual outflows of private capital were estimated to be as high as $30 billion. By 2003, the situation had improved dramatically and Russia was able to post a small surplus in capital flows. Putin confidently predicted that national income in Russia would double by 2010.

The collapse of Russia's economy in 1998, and its subsequent rebound in the first years of the new millennium, vividly illustrate the dynamic nature of today's economic environment. Recall the basic definition of a **market**: people or organizations with needs and wants and both the willingness and ability to buy or sell. As noted in Chapter 1, many companies engage in global marketing in an effort to reach new customers outside the home country and thereby

*Fine dining options in Russia were limited during the Soviet era. Today, upscale restaurants catering to wealthy "New Russians" are found in most large cities. In Moscow, affluent Russians can shop at boutiques that offer Versace, Burberry, Bulgari, and other exclusive brands. Although per capita GNP in Russia is only $1,800, Russian shoppers spend an estimated $4 billion each year on luxury goods.*

increase sales, profits, and market share. Today, Russia represents a major growth opportunity for global companies. This chapter will identify the most salient characteristics of the world economic environment, starting with an overview of the world economy, a survey of economic system types, a discussion of stages of market development, and balance of payments. Foreign exchange is discussed in the final section of this chapter.

## THE WORLD ECONOMY—AN OVERVIEW

The world economy has changed profoundly since World War II.[1] Perhaps the most fundamental change is the emergence of global markets; responding to new opportunities, global competitors have steadily displaced or absorbed local ones. Concurrently, the integration of the world economy has increased significantly. Economic integration stood at 10 percent at the beginning of the twentieth century; today, it is approximately 50 percent. Integration is particularly striking in the European Union (EU) and the North American Free Trade Area.

Just 35 years ago, the world was far less integrated than it is today. As evidence of the changes that have taken place, consider the automobile. Cars with European nameplates such as Renault, Citroen, Peugeot, Morris, Volvo, and others were radically different from the American Chevrolet, Ford, or Plymouth, or Japanese models from Toyota or Nissan. These were local cars built by local companies, mostly destined for local or regional markets. Even today, global and regional auto companies make cars for their home markets that would not be marketable in North America and vice versa, but it is also true that the world car is a reality for Toyota, Nissan, Honda, and Ford. Product changes reflect organizational changes as well. The world's largest automakers have, for the most part, evolved into global companies. At Ford Motor Company, for example, change is reflected in the Ford 2000 restructuring plan announced in the mid-1990s. Ford 2000 represented a dramatic rethinking in the way the company designs and manufactures cars; the fact that former CEO Jacques Nasser altered some key elements of the program during his tenure illustrates that globalization is a process to which companies must continually adapt.

---

1    Numerous books and articles survey this subject, for example Lowell Bryan et al., *Race for the World: Strategies to Build a Great Global Firm* (Boston: Harvard Business School Press, 1999).

During the past two decades, the world economic environment has become increasingly dynamic; change has been dramatic and far reaching. To achieve success, executives and marketers must take into account the following new realities.[2]

- Capital movements have replaced trade as the driving force of the world economy.
- Production has become "uncoupled" from employment.
- The world economy dominates the scene; individual country economies play a subordinate role.
- The 75-year struggle between capitalism and socialism is largely over.
- The growth of e-commerce diminishes the importance of national barriers and forces companies to re-evaluate their business models.

The first change is the increased volume of capital movements. The dollar value of world trade in merchandise is running at roughly $9.2 trillion per year. However, the London foreign exchange market turns over $450 billion each working day; overall, foreign exchange transactions are running at approximately $1.5 trillion per day worldwide—far surpassing the dollar volume of world trade in goods and services.[3] There is an inescapable conclusion in these data: Global capital movements far exceed the dollar volume of global trade. This explains the paradoxical combination of U.S. trade deficits and a strong dollar during the first half of the 1980s and again in the early twenty-first century. According to orthodox economic theory, when a country runs a deficit on its trade accounts, its currency should depreciate in value. Today, it is capital movements and trade that determine currency value.

The second change concerns the relationship between productivity and employment. Although employment in manufacturing remains steady or has declined, productivity continues to grow. The pattern is especially clear in American agriculture, where fewer farm employees produce more output. In the United States, manufacturing's share of gross domestic product (GDP) has declined from 19.2 percent in 1989 to 16.1 percent in 1999.[4] In 2001, about 13 percent of U.S. workers were employed by factories; in 1971, the figure was 26 percent. During that 30-year period, productivity has increased dramatically. Similar trends can be found in many other major industrial economies as well. One recent study of 20 large economies found that, between 1995 and 2002, more than 22 million factory jobs have been eliminated. Manufacturing is not in decline; it is *employment* in manufacturing that is in decline.[5]

The third major change is the emergence of the world economy as the dominant economic unit. Company executives and national leaders who recognize this have the greatest chance of success. For example, the real secret of the economic success of Germany and Japan is the fact that business leaders and policy makers

---

2  William Greider offers a thought-provoking analysis of these new realities in *One World, Ready or Not: The Manic Logic of Global Capitalism* (New York: Simon & Schuster, 1997).

3  Alan C. Shapiro, *Multinational Financial Management*, 7th ed. (Hoboken, NJ: John Wiley & Sons, 2003), p. 137. A Eurodollar is a U.S. dollar held outside the United States. U.S. dollars are subject to U.S. banking regulations; Eurodollars are not.

4  Gross national product (GNP) is a numerical representation of the economic activity in a country for a given time period. It is calculated as the sum of the value of *finished* goods and services produced in a country by its citizens and domestic business enterprises, plus the value of output produced by citizens working outside their home country. Gross domestic product (GDP) also measures economic activity; however, GDP includes *all* income produced within a country's borders by its citizens and domestic enterprises as well as foreign-owned enterprises. Income earned by citizens working abroad is *not* included. For example, Ireland has attracted a great deal of foreign investment by companies that generate a significant amount of economic output within the country's borders. As a result, Ireland's GDP figures have been running 10 to 12 percent ahead of those for GNP. However, as a practical matter, GNP and GDP figures for many countries will be roughly the same.

5  Jon E. Hilsenrath and Rebecca Buckman, "Factory Employment is Falling World-Wide," *The Wall Street Journal* (October 20, 2003), p. A2. Some companies have cut employment by outsourcing or subcontracting nonmanufacturing activities such as data processing, accounting, and customer service.

focus on world markets and their respective countries' competitive positions in the world economy. This change has brought two questions to the fore: How does the global economy work, and who is in charge? Unfortunately, the answers to these questions are not clearcut.

The fourth change is the end of the Cold War. The demise of communism as an economic and political system can be explained in a straightforward manner: Communism is not an effective economic system. The overwhelmingly superior performance of the world's market economies has given leaders in socialist countries little choice but to renounce their ideology. A key policy change in such countries has been the abandonment of futile attempts to manage national economies with a single central plan. This policy change frequently goes hand in hand with governmental efforts to foster increased public participation in matters of state by introducing democratic reforms.[6]

Finally, the personal computer revolution and the advent of the Internet era have in some ways diminished the importance of national boundaries. Two-thirds of American households have PCs; worldwide, nearly 600 million personal computers are installed in homes and businesses. In the so-called Information Age, barriers of time and place have been subverted by a transnational cyberworld that functions "24/7." Apple Computer, Google, and eBay are just a few of the companies that are pushing the envelope in this brave new world.

## the rest of the story

### Russia's Economic Rebound

Will President Putin be able to realize his vision for economic growth in Russia? Can the current recovery be sustained? Despite the many positive indicators, much work remains to be done. For one thing, the country is so dependent on revenues from the energy sector that a major decline in world oil prices would likely have a destabilizing effect. A related problem is the fact that Russia's energy industry is dominated by a handful of huge conglomerates. The men who run these companies are known as oligarchs; Yukos Oil chief Mikhail Khodorkovsky, Sibneft's Roman Abramovich, and their peers are Russia's ultra-rich elite. However, there is widespread resentment among the Russian citizenry about the manner in which the oligarchs gained control of their respective companies. A controversial privatization program in the 1990s enabled the oligarchs to pay rock-bottom prices for the assets of enterprises formerly owned by the government. For example, Khodorkovsky paid $300 million for Yukos; today the company has a market capitalization of $20 billion, and Khodorkovsky's personal fortune is estimated to be $11 billion. In July 2003, the Putin government sent a message to the oligarchs by arresting billionaire businessman Platon Lebedev on charges of paying too little for a fertilizer plant that he acquired in 1994.

There are other problems as well. Putin's tax reform program was relatively easy to implement; however, further reforms may face more opposition. Russia's entrenched bureaucracy is a barrier to increased economic freedom. The banking system remains fragile and in need of reform. Yevgeny Yasin, a former economy minister and an advocate of liberal reforms, noted recently, "The Russian economy is constrained by bureaucratic shackles. If the economy is to grow, these chains must be dropped. If we can overcome this feudal system of using power, we will create a stimulus for strong and sustainable economic growth and improve the standards of living."

Many observers believe that, if Putin's goal is to be achieved, investment in Russia will have to increase. Capital investment in 2003 was about 5 percent; foreign investment remains at a low level as well. One positive sign is the announcement that BP will invest $7 billion in a joint venture with Tyumen Oil, a Russian energy company. In fall 2003, Moody's Investors Service upgraded Russia's foreign currency debt, a move that should lead to increased investment. Another positive sign: Ikea, the furniture retailer, plans to open dozens of new stores across Russia. Putin must ensure that the needs of ordinary Russians are satisfied and, at the same time, reign in the oligarchs. If he succeeds, he may well be credited with creating an economic miracle in Russia.

*Sources:* Peter Weinberg, "Russia Merits a Welcome Into the Trade Fold," *Financial Times* (October 27, 2003), p. 13; Mark Medish, "Russia's Economic Strength Begins at Home," *Financial Times* (September 22, 2003), p. 15; Andrew Jack and Stefan Wagstyl, "In 1998, Russia Was Nearly Bankrupt. Today It Has Reserves of $60 Bn. But Its Economic Future Remains Insecure," *Financial Times* (August 18, 2003), p. 9; Gregory L. White and Jeanne Whalen, "Why Russian Oil is a Sticky Business," *The Wall Street Journal* (August 1, 2003), p. A7; Marshall Goldman, "Russia Will Pay Twice for the Fortunes of Its Oligarchs," *Financial Times* (July 26/27, 2003), p. 10.

---

[6] Marcus W. Brauchli, "Poll Vaults: More Nations Embrace Democracy—and Find It Can Often Be Messy," *The Wall Street Journal* (June 25, 1996), pp. A1, A6.

# ECONOMIC SYSTEMS

There are four main types of economic systems: market capitalism, centrally planned socialism, centrally planned capitalism, and market socialism (see Figure 2-1). This classification is based on the dominant method of resource allocation (market versus command) and the dominant form of resource ownership (private versus state).

## Market Capitalism

**Market capitalism** is an economic system in which individuals and firms allocate resources and production resources are privately owned. Simply put, consumers decide what goods they desire and firms determine what and how much to produce; the role of the state in market capitalism is to promote competition among firms and ensure consumer protection. Today, market capitalism is widely practiced around the world, most notably in North America and Western Europe.

It would be a gross oversimplification, however, to assume that all market-oriented economies function in an identical manner. Economist Paul Krugman has remarked that the United States is distinguished by its competitive, "wild free-for-all" and decentralized initiative. By contrast, outsiders sometimes refer to Japan as "Japan Inc." The label can be interpreted in different ways, but it basically refers to a tightly run, highly regulated economic system that is also market oriented.

## Centrally Planned Socialism

At the opposite end of the spectrum from market capitalism is **centrally planned socialism.** In this type of economic system, the state has broad powers to serve the public interest as it sees fit. State planners make "top-down" decisions about what goods and services are produced and in what quantities; consumers can spend their money on what is available. Government ownership of entire industries, as well as individual enterprises, is characteristic of centrally planned socialism. Because demand typically exceeds supply, the elements of the marketing mix are not used as strategic variables.[7] Little reliance is placed on product differentiation, advertising, or promotion; to eliminate "exploitation" by intermediaries, the government also controls distribution.

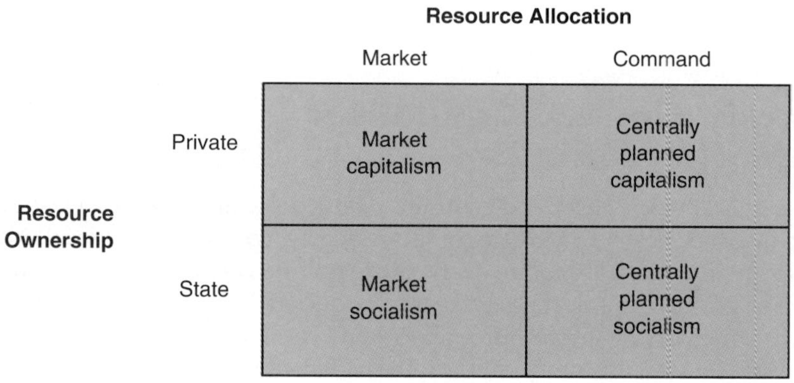

**Resource Allocation**

|  | | Market | Command |
|---|---|---|---|
| **Resource Ownership** | Private | Market capitalism | Centrally planned capitalism |
|  | State | Market socialism | Centrally planned socialism |

**Figure 2-1**

*Economic Systems*

---

[7] Peggy A. Golden, Patricia M. Doney, Denise M. Johnson, and Jerald R. Smith, "The Dynamics of a Marketing Orientation in Transition Economies: A Study of Russian Firms," *Journal of International Marketing* 3, no. 2 (1995), pp. 29–49.

The clear superiority of market capitalism in delivering the goods and services that people need and want has led to its adoption in many formerly socialist countries. An ideology developed in the nineteenth century by Karl Marx, and perpetuated in the twentieth century by Lenin and others, has been resoundingly refuted. As William Greider writes:

> Marxism is utterly vanquished, if not yet entirely extinct, as an alternative economic system. Capitalism is triumphant. The ideological conflict first joined in the mid-nineteenth century in response to the rise of industrial capitalism, the deep argument that has preoccupied political imagination for 150 years, is ended.[8]

For decades, the economies of China, the former Soviet Union, and India functioned according to the tenets of centrally planned socialism. All three countries are now engaged in economic reforms characterized, in varying proportions, by increased reliance on market allocation and private ownership. Even as China's leaders attempt to maintain control over society, they acknowledge the importance of economic reform. At a recent plenum, the Communist Party said that reform "is an inevitable road for invigorating the country's economy and promoting social progress, and a great pioneering undertaking without parallel in history."

## Centrally Planned Capitalism and Market Socialism

In reality, market capitalism and centrally planned socialism do not exist in "pure" form. In most countries, to a greater or lesser degree, command and market resource allocation are practiced simultaneously, as are private and state resource ownership. The role of government in modern market economies varies widely. An economic system in which command resource allocation is utilized extensively in an environment of private resource ownership can be called **centrally planned capitalism.** In Sweden, for example, where two-thirds of all expenditures are controlled by the

---

8  William Greider, *One World, Ready or Not: The Manic Logic of Global Capitalism* (New York: Simon & Schuster, 1997), p. 37.

government, resource allocation is more "command" oriented than "market" oriented. To a certain extent, the same is true in Japan. This type of system is represented by the upper-right quadrant in Figure 2-1.

A fourth variant, **market socialism,** is also possible. In such a system, market allocation policies are permitted within an overall environment of state ownership. For example, China has given considerable freedom to businesses and individuals in the Guangdong Province to operate within a market system. Today, China's private sector accounts for more than 75 percent of national output. Even so, state enterprises still receive more than two-thirds of the credit available from the country's banks. In the late 1980s and early 1990s, Mikhail Gorbachev tried to preserve socialist principles in the USSR while pursuing a policy of gradual economic reform known as *perestroika*. Ultimately, however, Gorbachev was unable to reconcile the conflicting demands of Communist hard-liners with those of an increasingly discontented, democracy-minded population. His failure to establish a system of "capitalism with a human face" contributed to the dissolution of the Soviet Union.

Market reforms and nascent capitalism in many parts of the world are creating opportunities for large-scale investments by global companies. Indeed, Coca-Cola returned to India in 1994, two decades after being forced out by the government. A new law allowing 100 percent foreign ownership of enterprises helped pave the way. By contrast, Cuba stands as one of the last bastions of the command allocation approach. Daniel Yergin and Joseph Stanislaw sum up the situation in the following way:

> Socialists are embracing capitalism, governments are selling off companies they had nationalized, and countries are seeking to entice multinational corporations expelled just two decades earlier. Today, politicians on the left admit that their governments can no longer afford the expansive welfare state. . . . The decamping of the

*"Countries with planned economies have never been part of economic globalization. China's economy must become a market economy."*

Long Yongtu, chief WTO negotiator for China[9]

# **OPEN** *to* discussion

## Which Operating System Do You Use?

Author Thomas L. Friedman compares and contrasts various types of economic systems by drawing an analogy with the main elements of a computer system. First is the "hardware," the basic shell around a country's economy. In the Cold War era, there were three basic types of hardware: free-market capitalism, communism, and hybrid. Second is the "operating system," which Friedman compares to a country's broad economic policies. Utilizing a pun on the title of Marx's classic work *Das Kapital*, Friedman categorizes these operating systems in a continuum ranging from DOScapital 0.0 through DOScapital 6.0. The basic "economic operating system" in communist countries, as noted previously, was central planning, which is version 0.0. The liberalized economies of the United States, Hong Kong, Taiwan, and the United Kingdom appear at the other end of the continuum. The hybrid states are characterized by various combinations of socialism, free markets, and crony capitalism.

For example, Friedman classifies Hungary as DOScapital 1.0 and China is running version 1.0 in rural provinces but

4.0 in Shanghai. Thailand and Indonesia are both DOScapital 3.0, and Korea is 4.0. To get the most out of its hardware and operating system, of course, a computer needs software. In Friedman's analysis, a country's "software" is comprised of the basic institutions of a free society. These include a functioning judicial system, a free press, free speech, economic reform, civic institutions, and multiple political parties. In short, a country's software is a reflection of how well developed its legal and regulatory systems are and the degree to which laws are understood, embraced, and made workable.

As Friedman asserts, with the end of the Cold War, virtually every country in the world is using the same basic hardware: free-market capitalism. Even so, some countries have yet to find the optimum balance between software and hardware; for example, Friedman views Russia and Venezuela as "illiberal democracies" because their governments currently emphasize hardware more than software.

*Source: Thomas L. Friedman, "Needed: Iraqi Software," The New York Times (May 7, 2003), p. A29; Friedman, The Lexus and the Olive Tree (New York: Anchor Books, 2000), pp. 151–152.*

---

9   Nicholas R. Lardy, *Integrating China into the Global Economy* (Washington, D.C.: The Brookings Institution, 2003), p. 21.

*Vladimir Ilyich Lenin was the Bolshevik revolutionary who brought communism to Russia and laid the groundwork for the modern Soviet state. A crowd in the Latvian capital of Riga pulls down a statue of Lenin in August 1991 after Latvia's break with the Soviet Union. Similar actions were repeated many times in Eastern Europe in the early 1990s. In Vilnius, Lithuania, a statue of Frank Zappa was erected on a plinth where Lenin's statue had once stood; nonconformity and free expression were hallmarks of the late musician's career.*

state from the "commanding heights" marks a great divide between the 20th and 21st centuries. It is opening the doors of many formerly closed countries to trade and investment, and vastly increasing the global market.[10]

The Washington, D.C.-based Heritage Foundation, a conservative think tank, takes a more conventional approach classifying economies: It compiles a survey of more than 150 countries ranked by degree of **economic freedom index** (Table 2-1). A number of key economic variables are considered: trade policy, taxation policy, government consumption of economic output, monetary policy, capital flows and foreign investment, banking policy, wage and price controls, property rights, regulations, and the black market. The rankings form a continuum from "free" to "repressed," with "mostly free" and "mostly unfree" in between. Hong Kong and Singapore are ranked first and second in terms of economic freedom; Cuba, Laos, and North Korea are ranked lowest.

There is a high correlation between the degree of economic freedom and the extent to which a nation's mixed economy is heavily market-oriented. However, the validity of the ranking has been subject to some debate. For example, author William Greider has observed that the authoritarian state capitalism practiced in Singapore deprives the nation's citizens of free speech, a free press, and free assembly. For example, in 1992, Singapore banned the import, manufacture, and sale of chewing gum, because discarded wads of gum were making a mess on sidewalks, and in buildings, buses, and subway trains. Greider notes, "Singaporeans are comfortably provided for by a harshly autocratic government that administers paranoid control over press and politics and an effective welfare state that keeps everyone well housed and fed, but not free."[11] As Greider's observation makes clear, some aspects of "free economies" bear more than a passing resemblance to command-style economic systems.

---

10  Daniel Yergin and Joseph Stanislaw, "Sale of the Century," *Financial Times Weekend* (January 24–25, 1998), p. I.

11  William Greider, *One World, Ready or Not: The Manic Logic of Global Capitalism* (New York: Simon & Schuster, 1997), pp. 36–37. See also Steve Glain, "Political Grudges? For South Korean Firms, Speaking Too Freely May Carry Steep Price," *The Wall Street Journal* (August 18, 1995), pp. A1, A10.

**Table 2-1**

*Index of Economic Freedom*

| FREE | | | |
|---|---|---|---|
| 1. Hong Kong | 41. Bolivia | 83. Colombia | 124. Chad |
| 2. Singapore | 42. Hungary | Guyana | Gambia |
| 3. New Zealand | UAE | Lebanon | 126. Ecuador |
| 4. Luxembourg | 44. Armenia | 86. Madagascar | 127. Cameroon |
| 5. Ireland | France | 87. Guatemala | 128. China |
| 6. Estonia | 46. Belize | Malaysia | 129. Romania |
| 7. United Kingdom | South Korea | 89. Ivory Coast | 130. Equatorial Guinea |
| 8. Denmark | 48. Kuwait | Swaziland | 131. Bangladesh |
| 9. Switzerland | Uganda | 91. Georgia | Kazakhstan |
| 10. United States | 50. Costa Rica | 92. Djibouti | Yemen |
| 11. Australia | 51. Jordan | 93. Guinea | 134. Sierra Leone |
| 12. Sweden | 52. Slovenia | 94. Kenya | Togo |
| 13. Chile | 53. South Africa | 95. Burkina Faso | 136. Indonesia |
| 14. Cyprus | 54. Greece | Egypt | 137. Haiti |
| Finland | Oman | Mozambique | 138. Syria |
| 16. Canada | 56. Jamaica | 98. Tanzania | 139. Congo, Rep. |
| **MOSTLY FREE** | Poland | 99. Bosnia | Guinea Bissau |
| 17. Iceland | 58. Panama | 100. Algeria | 141. Vietnam |
| 18. Germany | Peru | 101. Ethiopia | 142. Nigeria |
| 19. Netherlands | 60. Cape Verde | 102. Mali | 143. Suriname |
| 20. Austria | Qatar | 103. Kyrgyzstan | **REPRESSED** |
| Bahrain | Thailand | Rwanda | 144. Cuba |
| 22. Belgium | 63. Cambodia | 105. Central | 145. Belarus |
| Lithuania | Mexico | African Rep. | 146. Tajikistan |
| 24. El Salvador | Mongolia | 106. Azerbaijan | 147. Venezuela |
| 25. Bahamas | 66. Morocco | Paraguay | 148. Iran |
| 26. Italy | 67. Mauritania | Turkey | 149. Uzbekistan |
| 27. Spain | Nicaragua | 109. Ghana | 150. Turkmenistan |
| 28. Norway | Tunisia | Pakistan | 151. Burma |
| 29. Israel | 70. Namibia | 111. Gabon | Laos |
| Latvia | 71. Mauritius | Niger | 153. Zimbabwe |
| 31. Portugal | **MOSTLY UNFREE** | 113. Benin | 154. Libya |
| 32. Czech Republic | 72. Senegal | 114. Malawi | 155. North Korea |
| 33. Barbados | 73. Macedonia | Russia | **UNRATED** |
| 34. Taiwan | 74. Philippines | 116. Argentina | Angola |
| 35. Slovak Republic | Saudi Arabia | 117. Ukraine | Burundi |
| 36. Trinidad and | 76. Fiji | 118. Lesotho | Congo (Dem. Rep.) |
| Tobago | Sri Lanka | Zambia | Iraq |
| 37. Malta | 78. Bulgaria | 120. Dominican | Sudan |
| 38. Japan | 79. Moldova | Republic | Serbia and |
| 39. Botswana | 80. Albania | 121. Honduras | Montenegro |
| Uruguay | Brazil | India | |
| | 82. Croatia | Nepal | |

Source: Mary Anastasia O'Grady, "Free Markets, Free People," *The Wall Street Journal* (January 9, 2004), p. A10. *The Wall Street Journal.* Online. [Staff Produced Copy Only] by Mary Anastasia O'Grady. Copyright 2004 by *Dow Jones & Co. Inc.* Reproduced with permission of *Dow Jones & Co. Inc.* in the format Textbook via Copyright Clearance Center.

# STAGES OF MARKET DEVELOPMENT

At any point in time, individual country markets are at different stages of economic development. The World Bank has developed a four-category system of classification that uses per capita gross national product (GNP) as a base. Although the income definition for each of the stages is arbitrary, countries within a given category generally have a number of characteristics in common. Thus, the stages provide a useful basis for global market segmentation and target marketing. The categories are shown in Table 2-2 on page 55.

A handful of countries in Central Europe, Latin America, and Asia have experienced rapid economic growth throughout most of the past decade. Because this fast

### The Asian Flu

On July 2, 1997, Thailand's minister of finance cut his country's currency from its peg to the U.S. dollar. Because the dollar had strengthened over the course of previous months, exports from Thailand and other Asian countries were gradually becoming uncompetitive in world markets. However, a bigger problem for Thailand was the fact that financial institutions such as Finance One were overextended with questionable loans. The Thai government itself had seen its financial reserves dwindle to dangerously low levels. By allowing the baht to fluctuate in value or "float," government officials ensured that Thailand would not default on its debts to international lenders. The action also signaled the onset of a crisis that has been called the "Asian flu." Words like "contagion" and "domino effect" were used to describe what happened next. On July 14, Malaysia's central bank stopped supporting its national currency, the ringgit; on July 17, Singapore's central bank allowed the Singapore dollar to depreciate. In August, finance officials in Indonesia followed suit and allowed the rupiah to float. Even South Korea fell into line with the others; despite the country's tightly closed economy, officials took action on November 17 when they floated the won. Taken together, these actions signaled to the world that the phenomenal "bubble" of growth enjoyed by the tiger economies had occurred despite fundamental structural problems in the countries' economic and financial systems. In the future, policies such as "crony capitalism" whereby bank loans were freely given to the well-connected, would be replaced by more rigorous, Western-style approaches.

By October, Hong Kong's currency was put to the test as currency speculators sold Hong Kong dollars and bought U.S. dollars. Fortunately, the Hong Kong Monetary Authority had US$90 billion in foreign exchange reserves that were sufficient to maintain the peg. Even so, investor concern around the world was reflected in falling stock prices on the world's major exchanges. On Wall Street, the Dow Jones Industrial Average plummeted more than 500 points, the biggest one-day loss ever. To help rebuild the shell-shocked Asian economies, the International Monetary Fund (IMF) extended loans to bail out the worst-hit victims: $17 billion to Thailand, $40 billion to Indonesia, and a record $58 billion to South Korea.

During the first year after the crisis began, capital took flight as some $200 billion was transferred out of the region. Meanwhile, Western investors were quick to snap up companies,

factories, and other assets in Asia at fire-sale prices. Some observers warned that foreign businesses could face a backlash if investors were perceived as exploiting the situation. However, the impact of the Asian crisis in the West spread beyond the financial and investment communities. Global marketers were affected in several ways.

First, with Asia's tiger economies in recession, exports to the region fell sharply. Rising unemployment and a decline in real income prevented many consumers from making purchases, and credit-strapped Asian importers were unable to obtain the letters of credit needed to pay for imports. Earnings at French luxury goods marketer LVMH were negatively impacted because Asia accounts for 40 percent of annual sales. Nike reported a loss for the quarter ended on May 31, 1998. Hewlett-Packard saw earnings drop 13 percent in the second quarter. Tourist and airline revenues in important travel destinations such as Australia also dropped. Industrial companies, including those in construction and power generation, were hurt as important infrastructure projects such as dams, bridges, and highways were canceled.

Second, because of the devalued currencies, exports from Asia soared as Asian companies slashed prices. American bike-maker Huffy, hit hard by price cuts on the part of Asian manufacturers, was forced to cut 25 percent of its workforce. A third issue concerns pricing of products produced locally by global corporations. Toyota produces Soluna sedans in Thailand; production costs since the crisis began rose 30 to 40 percent in baht terms. Rather than raise prices to compensate the weaker baht, Toyota managers hoped to retain market share. Toyota raised prices by a modest 6 percent, with another 15 percent increase scheduled later. Mazda slashed the U.S. price of its 1999 Millenia model by $5,000.

Some companies hoped to use the short-term situation as an opportunity for brand building and increasing market share. Early in 1998, for example, Coca-Cola's regional manager for Southeast and West Asia said, "Our attitude to the economic blip in Thailand is to go ahead and aggressively build our brand. There will be a substantial increase in our investment in advertising and marketing this year."

*Sources: John Ridding, Ted Bardacke, and Sander Thoenes, "Tough Message for Regional Advertisers," Financial Times (February 19, 1998), p. 20; Paul M. Sherer, "Thai Baht Devaluations Fails to Trigger Classic Inflation," The Wall Street Journal (February 3, 1998), p. A17.*

growth presents significant marketing opportunities, the countries are known as **big emerging markets** (BEMs). Ten countries generally recognized as BEMs are China, India, Indonesia, South Korea, Brazil, Mexico, Argentina, South Africa, Poland, and Turkey.[12] These BEMs cut across the four stages of economic development; per capita income ranges from $10,879 in South Korea to $489 in India. China is the largest, with a population of 1.3 billion people; Argentina is the smallest, with a population of 38 million people. Despite these contrasts, experts predict that the BEMs will be key players in global trade even as their track records on human rights, environmental protection, and other issues come under closer scrutiny by their trading partners. The

[12] For an excellent discussion of BEMs, see Jeffrey E. Garten, *The Big Ten: The Big Emerging Markets and How They Will Change Our Lives* (New York: Basic Books, 1997).

Table 2-2

Stages of Market Development

| Income Group by Per Capita GNP | 2003 GNP ($ millions) | 2003 GNP Per Capita ($) | % of World GNP | 2003 Population (millions) |
|---|---|---|---|---|
| **High-income countries** | | | | |
| GNP per capita >$9,266 | 27,370,922 | 28,396 | 80.8 | 964 |
| **Upper-middle-income countries** | | | | |
| GNP per capita >$2,995 but ≤$9,266 | 2,750,743 | 4,723 | 8.1 | 582 |
| **Lower-middle-income countries** | | | | |
| GNP per capita ≥$755 but ≤$2,995 | 2,642,056 | 1,254 | 7.8 | 2,106 |
| **Low-income countries** | | | | |
| GNP per capita <$755 | 1,107,982 | 434 | 3.2 | 2,554 |

BEM government leaders will also come under pressure at home as their developing market economies create greater income disparity. For each of the stages of economic development discussed here, special attention is given to the BEMs.

## Low-Income Countries

Low-income countries have a GNP per capita of less than $755. The general characteristics shared by countries at this income level are:

1. Limited industrialization and a high percentage of the population engaged in agriculture and subsistence farming
2. High birth rates
3. Low literacy rates
4. Heavy reliance on foreign aid
5. Political instability and unrest
6. Concentration in Africa south of the Sahara

Although about 40 percent of the world's population is included in this economic category, many low-income countries represent limited markets for products. Still, there are exceptions; for example, in Bangladesh, where per capita GNP is approximately $380, the garment industry has enjoyed burgeoning exports. Finished clothing exports to the United States alone amounted to $2.4 billion in 2002; an estimated 1.8 million Bangladeshis—mostly women—work in the industry for an

The rural family in this photo lives in a world that is deeply rooted in tradition but that has also been touched by Western civilization. As is often the case in low-income countries, self-sufficiency is a way of life in Ethiopia. The farm animals are sources of both food and labor. The mortar in the left foreground is an important traditional cooking utensil in Africa. This family produces food for its own needs and sells the excess in the market, thereby earning money to purchase a few goods and to pay for the children's schooling. The family members are wearing both traditional and Western-style clothes, including plastic shoes that will survive wet weather.

average month wage of about $35. Bangladesh received preferential treatment under the Multifiber Arrangement (MFA), an international pact dating to the mid-1970s that established import quotas to regulate the global trade in garments. Unfortunately, the MFA is set to expire at the end of 2004; some observers expect a shakeout in the garment industry that will lead to widespread unemployment and social and political unrest.[13]

Many low-income countries have such serious economic, social, and political problems that they represent extremely limited opportunities for investment and operations. Some are low-income, no-growth countries such as Burundi and Rwanda that are beset by one disaster after another. Others were once growing, relatively stable countries that have become divided by political struggles. The result is a tinderbox or flash point environment characterized by civil strife, declining income, and often, considerable danger to residents. Haiti is a case in point. Countries embroiled in civil wars are dangerous areas; most companies find it prudent to avoid them.

The newly independent countries of the former Soviet Union present an interesting situation: Income is declining, and there is considerable economic hardship. The potential for disruption is certainly high. Are they problem cases, or are they attractive opportunities with good potential for moving out of the low-income category? These countries present an interesting risk-reward trade-off; some companies have taken the plunge, but many others are still assessing whether to take the risk. Table 2-1 rates three low-income former Soviet republics—Tajikistan, Uzbekistan, and Turkmenistan—"repressed" in terms of economic freedom. This is one indication of a risky business environment. Russia itself, a lower-middle income country, is below the middle of the ranking (number 114); as evidenced by the events of 1998 and recent terror attacks, economic and political instability are present here as well.

Of all the countries in the low-income category, only India and Indonesia are considered BEMs. In 1997, India commemorated the fiftieth anniversary of its independence from Great Britain. During that half century, economic growth was weak. As the decade of the 1990s began, India was in the throes of economic crisis: Inflation was high, and foreign exchange reserves were low. Country leaders opened India's economy to trade and investment and dramatically improved market opportunities. Following the assassination of Rajiv Gandhi and the election of P. V. Narasimha Rao to the office of prime minister in 1991, Monmohan Singh was placed in charge of India's economy. Singh, former governor of the Indian central bank and finance minister, noted, "For years, India has been taking the wrong road." Accordingly, he set about dismantling the planned economy by eliminating import licensing requirements for many products, reducing tariffs, easing restrictions on foreign investment, and liberalizing the rupee. The results were impressive: Foreign exchange reserves jumped to $13 billion in 1993 from $1 billion in 1991. Yashwant Sinha, the country's former finance minister, declared that the twenty-first century will be "the century of India." Although India's economy has faltered in recent years and the pace of economic reform has slowed, during his tenure, Sinha outlined steps for achieving annual economic growth of 9 percent over the next decade.

Prior to the onset of the Asian flu, Indonesia's fast-growing economy attracted billions of dollars in foreign investment. The world's fourth most populous nation, Indonesia is the largest noncommunist country in Southeast Asia; per capita GNP rose from $250 in 1985 to $751 in 2003. Indonesia plays a key economic role in Southeast Asia. Several factories there produce athletic shoes under contract for Nike. Following student protests in 1998, President Suharto was forced to resign.

---

[13]  Peter Fritsch, "Looming Trouble: As End of a Quota System nears, Bangladesh Fears for Its Jobs," *The Wall Street Journal* (November 20, 2003), pp. A1, A12.

# Lower-Middle-Income Countries

The United Nations designates fifty countries in the bottom ranks of the low-income category as **least-developed countries (LDCs)**; the term is sometimes used to indicate a contrast with **developing** (i.e., upper ranks of low-income plus lower-middle and upper-middle-income) **countries** and **developed** (high-income) **countries**. Lower-middle-income countries are those with a GNP per capita between $755 and $2,995. Consumer markets in these countries are expanding rapidly. Countries such as China and Thailand represent an increasing competitive threat as they mobilize their relatively cheap—and often highly motivated—labor forces to serve target markets in the rest of the world. The developing countries in the lower-middle-income category have a major competitive advantage in mature, standardized, labor-intensive industries such as making toys and textiles.

There are two BEMs in this category: China and South Africa. China represents the largest single destination for foreign investment in the developing world. Attracted by the country's vast size and market potential, companies in Japan, Europe, and the United States are making China a key country in their global strategies. Despite ongoing market reforms, Chinese society does not have democratic foundations. Although China has joined the World Trade Organization (WTO), trading partners are still concerned about human rights, protection of intellectual property rights, and other issues. The country's leaders must deal with China's sprawling bureaucracy while reforming the banking system and the state enterprise sector. General Motors, Ford, Honda, Volkswagen, Motorola, Procter & Gamble, Avon, Siemens AG, and McDonald's are actively pursuing opportunities in China.

South Africa boasts the largest economy in Africa south of the Sahara, with a GDP that represents 45 percent of the continent's output of goods and services. South Africa has a modern infrastructure and several well-developed industry sectors including finance, communications, and energy. The best-known South African company is the De Beers diamond cooperative.

# Upper-Middle-Income Countries

Upper-middle-income countries, are those with GNP per capita ranging from $2,996 to $9,266. In these countries, the percentage of population engaged in agriculture drops sharply as people move to the industrial sector and the degree of urbanization increases. Malaysia, Brazil, Chile, Hungary, and many other countries in this stage are rapidly industrializing. They have rising wages and high rates of literacy and advanced education but significantly lower wage costs than the advanced countries. Innovative local companies can become formidable competitors and help contribute to their nations' rapid, export-driven economic growth.

Upper-middle-income countries that achieve the highest rates of economic growth are sometimes referred to collectively as **newly industrializing economies (NIEs)**. In Hungary and other upper-middle-income countries, scores of manufacturing companies have received ISO-9000 certification for documenting compliance with recognized quality standards. The influx of technology, particularly the computer revolution, creates startling juxtapositions of the old and the new in these countries. In Brazil, for example, grocery distribution companies use logistics software to route their trucks; meanwhile, horse-drawn carts are still a common sight on many roads. Likewise, to help them keep pace with the volatile financial environment, many local retailers have invested in sophisticated computer and communications systems. They utilize sophisticated inventory management software to help them maintain financial control.

Three BEMs in the upper-middle-income category are located in Latin America. In Argentina, the runaway inflation of the 1980s has been brought under control. A massive privatization effort has transferred ownership of many enterprises from

A portable cassette player, looms and tools, dolls for the kids, and religious objects figure prominently in the lives of this family in Guatemala. Guatemala is a lower-middle-income country where per capita income is $1,759. Elsewhere in Central America, El Salvador and Honduras are also lower-middle-income countries, Costa Rica is an upper-middle-income country, and Nicaragua is in the low-income category.

the government into the hands of private investors. Key export markets include the United States, Brazil, and Germany. Patent protection is a key issue, especially in the pharmaceuticals industry. Brazil is the largest country in South America in terms of the size of its economy, population, and geographic territory. Brazil also boasts the richest reserves of natural resources in the hemisphere. Like Argentina, Brazil has tamed hyperinflation. Liberalized trade is replacing tariff protection and an import quota system as Brazil joins Argentina in the Mercosur customs union. Global companies doing business in Brazil include Whirlpool, Electrolux, Raytheon, Fiat, and Ford. French President Jacques Chirac underscored Brazil's importance on the world trade scene when he noted, "Geographically, Brazil is part of America. But it's European because of its culture and global because of its interests."[14]

Mexico is the second-largest country in Latin America after Brazil. It is a key trading partner of the United States, thanks to a thousand-mile shared border and the North American Free Trade Agreement. Companies that want to take advantage of Mexico's low wage levels can set up a wholly owned subsidiary, a joint venture, or a maquiladora program. The term **maquiladora** refers to a Mexican corporation that is permitted to import materials, components, equipment, and other production inputs duty-free if they are used to produce goods for export. When the completed product is exported to the United States, the manufacturer pays duty only on the value added in Mexico. The advantages of maquiladora manufacturing attracted many Asian companies to Mexico; however, effective January 1, 2001, import duties were no longer waived for production inputs that originate outside of NAFTA. In addition, products produced in maquiladora plants can now be sold in Mexico instead of being exported.

In the post-Soviet era, Poland established a democratic government and has moved quickly to privatize banking, the state telephone monopoly, and other enterprises. Two-thirds of both export and import trade is conducted with the European Union, which Poland joined in 2004; Germany is Poland's single most important trading partner. Poland, along with Hungary and the Czech Republic, joined NATO in 1999.

---

[14] Matt Moffett and Helene Cooper, "Silent Invasion: In Backyard of the U.S., Europe Gains Ground in Trade, Diplomacy," *The Wall Street Journal* (September 18, 1997), pp. A1, A8.

The relative affluence of this Brazilian family can be judged by the fact that the stucco covering on their brick dwelling has been painted. Brazil's per capita income of $3,494 qualifies it as an upper-middle-income country. The open-air design and lack of window screens is typical of Brazilian residences; armoires are necessary because few homes have closets. Like most Brazilians, this family owns a TV and a large stereo, but has no washer or dryer.

Strategically located at the intersection of Asia and Europe, Turkey is a member of NATO. An industrialized country with a strong economy, Turkey has suffered from high inflation; in 2000, a three-year plan was launched to bring inflation down to single digits. Germany is Turkey's top trading partner, receiving about 24 percent of exports and providing about 19 percent of imports. Children in the labor force and human rights issues concern trading partners. An Islamic opposition party is active, but radicalism is not spreading. A major issue is whether the EU will extend an offer of membership to Turkey. Global companies in Turkey include American Express, Citibank, Coca-Cola, Kodak, Procter & Gamble, and Siemens.

## Marketing Opportunities in LDCs and Developing Countries

Despite many problems in LDCs and developing countries, it is possible to nurture long-term market opportunities. Today, Nike produces and sells only a small portion of its output in China, but when the firm refers to China as a "two-billion-foot market," it clearly has the future in mind. C. K. Prahalad and Allen Hammond have identified several assumptions and misconceptions about the "bottom of the pyramid" (BOP) that need to be corrected:

- Mistaken assumption #1: *The poor have no money.* In fact, the aggregate buying power of poor communities can be substantial. In rural Bangladesh, for example, villagers spend considerable sums to use village phones operated by local entrepreneurs.
- Mistaken assumption #2: *The poor are too concerned with fulfilling basic needs to "waste" money on non-essential goods.* In fact, consumers who are too poor to purchase a house do buy "luxury" items such as television sets and gas stoves to improve their lives.
- Mistaken assumption #3: *The goods sold in developing markets are so inexpensive that there is no room for a new market entrant to make a profit.* In fact, because the poor often pay higher prices for many goods, there is an opportunity for efficient competitors to realize attractive margins by offering quality and low prices.

- Mistaken assumption #4: *People in BOP markets cannot use advanced technology.* In fact, residents of rural areas can and do quickly learn to use cell phones, PCs, and similar devices.
- Mistaken assumption #5: *Global companies that target BOP markets will be criticized for exploiting the poor.* In fact, the informal economies in many poor countries are highly exploitative. A global company offering basic goods and services that improve a country's standard of living can earn a reasonable return while benefiting society.

Despite the difficult economic conditions in parts of Southeast Asia, Latin America, Africa, and Eastern Europe, many nations in these regions will evolve into attractive markets. One of marketing's roles in developing countries is to focus resources on the task of creating and delivering products that are best suited to local needs and incomes. Appropriate marketing communications techniques can also be applied to accelerate acceptance of these products. Marketing can be the link that relates resources to opportunity and facilitates need satisfaction on the consumer's terms.

An interesting debate in marketing is whether it has any relevance to the process of economic development. Some people believe that marketing is relevant only in affluent, industrialized countries, where the major problem is directing society's resources into ever-changing output or production to satisfy a dynamic marketplace. In the less-developed country, the argument goes, the major problem is the allocation of scarce resources toward obvious production needs. Efforts should focus on production and how to increase output, not on customer needs and wants.

Conversely, it can be argued that the marketing process of focusing an organization's resources on environmental opportunities is a process of universal relevance. The role of marketing—to identify people's needs and wants and to focus individual and organizational efforts to respond to these needs and wants—is the same in all countries, irrespective of level of economic development. For example, pursuing alternative sources of energy such as wind and solar power is important for two reasons: the lack of coal reserves in many countries and concerns that heavy reliance on fossil fuels contributes to global warming. There is also an opportunity to help developing countries join the Information Age. Hewlett-Packard CEO Carly Fiorina unveiled an ambitious program to market communication products in LDCs. Dubbed World e-Inclusion, HP will sell, lease, or donate products and services valued at $1 billion to governments and nonprofit groups in Bangladesh and other low-income countries. Fiorina has directed the company's engineers to develop solar-powered communication devices that can link remote areas to the Internet.[15] The Coca-Cola Company recently began to address dietary and health needs in low-income countries by developing a beverage product, Vitango, that can help fight anemia, blindness, and other ailments related to malnutrition.

Global companies can also contribute to economic development by finding creative ways to preserve old-growth forests and other resources while creating economic opportunities for local inhabitants. In Brazil, for example, DaimlerChrysler works with a cooperative of farmers who transform coconut husks into natural rubber to be used in auto seats, headrests, and sun visors. French luxury-goods marketer Hermes has created a line of handbags called "Amazonia" made of latex extracted by traditional rubber tappers. Both DaimlerChrysler and Hermes are responding to the opportunity to promote themselves as environmentally conscious while appealing to "green"-oriented consumers. As Isabela Fortes, director of a company in Rio de Janeiro that retrains forest workers, notes, "You can only

---

[15] David Kirkpatrick, "Looking for Profits in Poverty," *Fortune* (February 5, 2001), pp. 174–176.

*The Fur Council of Canada recently took out full-page newspaper ads promoting the fur industry. The ads were designed to inform consumers of the fur trade's role in Canada's heritage and its importance to indigenous people living in remote regions.*

prevent forest people from destroying the jungle by giving them viable economic alternatives."[16]

## High-Income Countries

High-income countries, also known as advanced, developed, industrialized, or postindustrial countries, are those with GNP per capita above $9,266. With the exception of a few oil-rich nations, the countries in this category reached their present income level through a process of sustained economic growth.

The phrase *postindustrial countries* was first used by Daniel Bell of Harvard to describe the United States, Sweden, Japan, and other advanced, high-income societies. Bell suggests that there is a difference between the industrial and the postindustrial societies that goes beyond mere measures of income. Bell's thesis is that the sources of innovation in postindustrial societies are derived increasingly from the codification of theoretical knowledge rather than from "random" inventions.

---

[16] Miriam Jordan, "From the Amazon to Your Armrest," *The Wall Street Journal* (May 1, 2001), pp. B1, B4.

Other characteristics are the importance of the service sector (more than 50 percent of GNP); the crucial importance of information processing and exchange; and the ascendancy of knowledge over capital as the key strategic resource, of intellectual technology over machine technology, of scientists and professionals over engineers and semi-skilled workers. Other aspects of the postindustrial society are an orientation toward the future and the importance of interpersonal relationships in the functioning of society.

Product and market opportunities in a postindustrial society are more heavily dependent upon new products and innovations than in industrial societies. Ownership levels for basic products are extremely high in most households. Organizations seeking to grow often face a difficult task if they attempt to expand their share of existing markets. Alternatively, they can endeavor to create new markets. Today, for example, global companies in a range of communication-related industries are seeking to create new e-commerce markets for interactive forms of electronic communication. A case in point is Barry Diller's InterActiveCorp (IAC), which includes Expedia.com, Hotels.com, and other Internet businesses.

South Korea occupies a unique position among the BEMs in that it is the only one of the ten to have achieved the status of a high-income country. The most industrialized BEM nation, South Korea is home to Samsung Electronics, LG Group, Kia Motors Corporation, Daewoo Corporation, Hyundai Corporation, and other well-known global enterprises. Per capita income doubled in the decade from 1985 to 1995. In place of substantial barriers to free trade, South Korea has initiated major reforms in its political and economic system in response to the Asian flu.

Among the high-income countries, the United States, Japan, Germany, France, Britain, Canada, and Italy are known as the **Group of Seven (G-7).** Finance ministers, central bankers, and heads of state from the seven nations have worked together for a quarter of a century in an effort to steer the global economy in the direction of prosperity and to ensure monetary stability. Whenever a global crisis looms—be it the Latin American debt crisis of the 1980s or Russia's struggle to transform its economy in the 1990s—representatives from the G-7 nations gather and try to coordinate policy. An advantage of the G-7 is "strength in numbers"; however, talk is one thing and action is another. As a former official at the U.S. Federal Reserve Bank observed, "Governments rarely want to do what outsiders want them to do."[17] In 1998, as Japan's recession deepened and the value of the yen plummeted, the G-7 leaders devoted a great deal of attention to the economic crisis in Asia. Other items on the agenda at the group's 1998 annual meeting included India's nuclear tests and the debt crisis in Africa's poorest nations. With regard to Africa, British Prime Minister Tony Blair said in an interview, "There's an increasing recognition in our countries that—providing we're not just throwing money at the problem, but geared to real economic reform and progress—it's in our interest, too, that countries in Africa can exploit the huge potential they have there without being submerged in this burden of debt from which they can't escape."[18]

Another institution comprised of high-income countries is the **Organization for Economic Cooperation and Development (OECD; www.oecd.org).** The 30 nations that belong to the OECD believe in market-allocation economic systems and pluralistic democracy. The organization has been variously described as an "economic think tank" and a "rich-man's club"; in any event, the OECD's fundamental task is to "enable its members to achieve the highest sustainable

---

[17] David Wessel, "Dollar Days: Can Wealthy Nations Save Japan from Itself? They're Going to Try," *The Wall Street Journal* (June 18, 1998), pp. A1, A9.
[18] "Talks of the Rich Focus on Debt of the Poor," *The New York Times* (May 17, 1998), p. 11.

This middle-class family has a typical Japanese lifestyle. The head of the household is a "salaryman" who works 50-hour weeks and is expected to go drinking after work to talk business with his boss and coworkers. The children in the family have many toys and personal possessions; most Japanese insist that children attend after-school classes for extra tutoring in mathematics, English, or Japanese. Because houses lack central heat, the dining table in the foreground has a heater under it; in the wintertime, family members might sit at the table to stay warm while they watch TV. Because space is at a premium in Japan, the dining room also serves as the living room. The combination washer-dryer unit takes less space than separate units; however, most families do not use the dryer, preferring instead to hang clothes to conserve energy.

economic growth and improve the economic and social well-being of their populations." Today's organization is based in Paris and evolved from a group of European nations that worked together after World War II to rebuild the region's economy. Canada and the United States have been members since 1961; Japan joined in 1964. Evidence of the increasing importance of the BEMs is the fact that China, India, Indonesia, Brazil, and Russia have all formally announced their intention to join the OECD. Applicants must demonstrate progress toward economic reform.[19]

Representatives from OECD member nations work together in committees to review economic and social policies that affect world trade. The secretary-general presides over a council that meets regularly and has decision-making power. Committees comprised of specialists from member countries provide a forum for discussion of trade and other issues. Consultation, peer pressure, and diplomacy are the keys to helping member nations candidly assess their own economic policies and actions. The OECD publishes country surveys and an annual economic outlook. Recently, the OECD has become more focused on global issues, social policy, and labor market deregulation. For example, the OECD tackled the vexing problem of bribery; the goal is to establish a treaty aimed at outlawing bribery of foreign officials.[20]

## The Triad

The ascendancy of the global economy has been noted by many observers in recent years. One of the most astute is Kenichi Ohmae, former chairman of McKinsey & Company Japan. His 1985 book *Triad Power* represented one of the first attempts to develop a coherent conceptualization of the new emerging order. Ohmae argued that successful global companies had to be equally strong in Japan, Western Europe, and the United States. These three regions, which Ohmae collectively called the **Triad,** represented the dominant economic centers of the world.

---

[19] Wolfgang Münchau, "Think-Tank Has Clearer Goals," *Financial Times—World Economy and Finance* (September 19, 1997), p. XV.
[20] Michael Hershman, "A Blow Against Bribery," *Financial Times* (February 28, 1998), p. 14.

Today, nearly 75 percent of world income as measured by GNP is located in the Triad. Ohmae has recently revised his view of the world; in the **expanded Triad,** the Japanese leg encompasses the entire Pacific region; the American leg includes Canada and Mexico; and the boundary in Europe is moving eastward. Coca-Cola is a perfect illustration of a company with a balanced revenue stream. Approximately one-quarter of the company's revenues are generated in Asia. Another 25 percent come from Europe, Eurasia, and the Middle East. North America accounts for about 40 percent.

# OPEN <sup>to</sup>discussion

### Is Ireland Truly a "Celtic Tiger"?

The term "tiger" has frequently been used to describe fast-growing economies in Asia. For years, Hong Kong, Singapore, Taiwan, and South Korea were considered tigers because they posted double-digit rates of economic growth. As the decade of the 1990s came to an end, however, the Asian "economic miracle" had given way to hard times. Concurrently, some observers began calling Ireland the "Celtic Tiger." Riding the wave of the technology boom of the late 1990s, Ireland's economy grew at an annual rate of 9.6 percent. Lured by low corporate tax rates and a skilled work force, companies from the United States, the United Kingdom, Germany, and Japan established subsidiaries in Ireland. The country best known for exports such as Waterford crystal, Guinness stout, Riverdance, and U2 had been transformed into a preferred location for high-tech manufacturing. More than 500 U.S. companies created tens of thousands of jobs as Intel, Motorola, and Gateway built factories to keep pace with burgeoning global demand for personal computers and other high-tech products. Before long, however, there were signs that Ireland's economic bubble might burst. The country's infrastructure was showing signs of stress, labor was in short supply, and inflation soared. By mid-2000, the pot of gold at the end of the rainbow gave way to gray and gloom. As the U.S. economy slowed down and the technology sector slumped, the impact on Ireland was immediate. Exports fell as foreign companies severely curtailed operations in Ireland or even closed down altogether.

A potential bright spot for Ireland is the Media Lab Europe, which opened in July 2000 in Dublin in a building that once was the site of a Guinness brewery. Media Lab Europe is an offshoot of the original Media Lab that was established at the Massachusetts Institute of Technology (MIT) more than 20 years ago. The Media Lab is a research facility; in exchange for sponsorship contributions of $5 million or more, global companies such as BT, Intel, the Lego Group, and Swatch AG get a first look at the lab's innovations in such areas as robotic design, speech synthesis, and holographic imaging. Total corporate funding for the original lab has passed the $500 million mark, and 50 new companies have been spun off after being incubated at the lab.

The Irish government allocated nearly $50 million in funding to establish the Media Lab Europe, including a $10 million payment to MIT for the right to use the Media Lab name. Government officials believe the investment will pay off by strengthening the country's position in advanced information-technology research. By the end of 2001, several organizational sponsors had signed on and pledged an additional $7.5 million in support. However, there were problems. For one thing, some researchers at MIT have been reluctant to move their work to Ireland. By mid-2001, only six researchers and about two dozen research associates, assistants, and graduate students were working in a facility designed to accommodate 250 people.

Some Irish academics are offended by the notion that Ireland needs outside help; critics also question whether the lab will contribute to economic growth to the extent envisioned by the government. To placate such critics, the government has increased funding for local research efforts. Science Foundation Ireland (SFI) is an initiative funded by the Irish government to create an economic base in information technology, telecommunications, and biotechnology. Currently, 130 scientists from around the globe are conducting research at Irish universities; a typical SFI research grant provides €1 million in annual support for five years. The Irish government hopes that, attracted by the skills and talent of students graduating from local universities, global companies currently operating in Ireland will increase their level of investment. Ultimately, the government hopes to create its own world-class companies.

**Visit the Web site**
**www.medialabeurope.org**

*Sources:* John Murray Brown, "Ireland Extends Its Hospitality to Top Scientists," Financial Times (November 8, 2003), p. 12; Alana Cowell, "Ireland, Once a Celtic Tiger, Slackens Its Stride," The New York Times (February 19, 2003), pp. C1, C4; Saritha Rai, "Rift in India Leads M.I.T. to Abandon a Media Lab," The New York Times (May 8, 2003), p. C4; David Armstrong, "Many Irish Eyes Aren't Smiling on MIT Import," The Wall Street Journal (July 5, 2001), p. B1, B4; Jeffrey R. Young, "MIT's Media Lab, a Media Darling, Seeks Global Role and New Missions," The Chronicle of Higher Education (October 12, 2001), pp. A41–A43; Christopher Rhoads, "U.S. Slowdown Muffles the Volume of Ireland's Boom," The Wall Street Journal (March 6, 2001), p. A18; Mike Burns, "High-tech Shudders for the Celtic Tiger," Europe, no. 406 (May 2001), pp. 14–15; Stewart Brand, The Media Lab: Inventing the Future at M.I.T. (New York: Viking Penguin, 1988).

## Marketing Implications of the Stages of Development

The stages of economic development described previously can serve as a guide to marketers in evaluating **product saturation levels**, or the percentage of potential buyers or households who own a particular product. In countries with low per capita income, product saturation levels for many products are low. In India, for example, ownership of private telephones is limited to about 1 percent of the population (see Figure 2-2). In China, saturation levels of private cars and personal computers are similarly low; there is only one car for every 20,000 Chinese, and

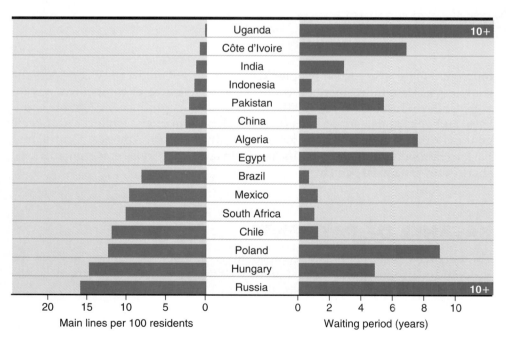

**Figure 2-2**

*Telephone Coverage in Developing Countries*

### Currency Crisis in Mexico

On December 20, 1994, the Bank of Mexico embarked on a course of action that sent shock waves around the world. A combination of circumstances, including a $28 billion current-account deficit, dwindling reserves, the murder of presidential candidate Donaldo Colosio, and eroding investor confidence, forced the Bank of Mexico to devalue the peso. The Clinton administration quickly arranged $20 billion in loans and loan guarantees, secured in part by some of Mexico's $7 billion in annual oil export revenues. Opponents of NAFTA—notably Ross Perot—seized the opportunity to denounce both the loans and the trade agreement itself. The devalued peso, critics predicted, would make U.S. exports to Mexico more expensive and reduce the $2 billion trade surplus that the U.S. enjoys with Mexico. NAFTA opponents also noted that increased imports of Mexican goods into the United States would constitute a new threat to U.S. jobs.

The Bank of Mexico's decision to devalue the peso meant that the Mexican currency declined nearly 40 percent relative to key currencies such as the dollar, the mark, and the yen. One immediate effect of the devaluation was a sharp decline in Mexican purchases of U.S. imports. For example, Westinghouse and Lennox had been aggressively selling air conditioners after NAFTA reduced tariffs; sales quickly slowed down after the devaluation. McDonald's, Kentucky Fried Chicken, Dunkin' Donuts, and other U.S. restaurant chains were also hard hit as they were forced to raise prices. Many franchisors had contracted to pay rent for their facilities in dollars; after the devaluation, franchisors who couldn't pay the rent were forced to shut down. Simply put, the purchasing power of Mexican consumers was cut nearly in half. To reduce the risk of inflation, the Mexican government pledged to cut spending and allow interest rates to rise. Meanwhile, investors who had poured money into Mexico since the late 1980s, lured by the promise of low inflation and a stable currency, faced huge declines in the value of their holdings.

For many manufacturing companies, the weaker peso wreaked havoc with 1995 sales forecasts. GM, for example, had hoped to export 15,000 vehicles to Mexico in 1995, a goal rendered unattainable by the financial crisis. Ford raised vehicle prices in Mexico; the increases applied to vehicles built in Mexico as well as those imported from Canada and the United States. Shares of Avon Products, whose Mexican sales comprise 11 percent of the company's $4 billion in annual revenue, declined sharply on Wall Street. Hoping to calm investors' fears, company executives predicted that a decline in Mexican sales would be offset in 1995 by gains in other countries.

Supporters and opponents of NAFTA debated the long-term effects of the devaluation. Harley Shaiken, a labor professor at the University of California and NAFTA critic, noted, "It will have a dual impact: It will diminish the market for U.S. goods in Mexico, but the more sizable impact will be the transfer of production to Mexico. It's going to make Mexico less desirable as a place to sell things and far more desirable as a place to make things." Persons holding opposing views acknowledged that the devaluation cut Mexican wages in dollar terms. However, NAFTA supporters have pointed out that labor's percentage of total cost in autos and auto parts, which constitute Mexico's largest export sector, is relatively low. Thus, despite the devaluation, NAFTA supporters denied that there would be a "giant sucking sound" caused by an exodus of U.S. jobs south of the border. In 2004, the tenth anniversary of NAFTA, policymakers and the general public were still divided. Perhaps the best assessment came from a recent report by the Carnegie Endowment of International Peace which noted, "NAFTA has been neither the disaster its opponents predicted nor the savior hailed by its supporters."

Sources: James Cox, "10 Years Ago, NAFTA Was Born," USA Today (December 31, 2003), p. 3B; Craig Torres, "Headed South: Mexico's Devaluation Stuns Latin America—and U.S. Investors," The Wall Street Journal (December 22, 1994), pp. A1, A12; "Ford Lifts Prices, Avon Tries to Calm Holders, Dina Estimates Loss as Peso Fallout Continues," The Wall Street Journal (January 13, 1995); Michael Clements and Bill Montague, "Will Peso's Fall Prove Perot Right?" USA Today (January 17, 1995), pp. B1, B2.

only one PC for every 6,000 people. Management at Unilever NV considers the company's strength in emerging countries to be a source of competitive advantage. Unilever has operations in 90 countries, sells its products in 70 more countries, and gets 30 percent of sales from developing markets. Unilever's strategic goal over the next decade is to focus on southern South America, Central and Eastern Europe, and the Asia-Pacific region in an effort to raise emerging markets' share of revenue to 50 percent.[21]

## BALANCE OF PAYMENTS

The **balance of payments** is a record of all economic transactions between the residents of a country and the rest of the world. U.S. balance of payments statistics for the period 1999 to 2003 are shown in Table 2-3. International trade data

---

[21] Tara Parker-Pope, "Unilever Plans a Long-Overdue Pruning," *The Wall Street Journal* (September 3, 1996), p. A11.

| | 1999 | 2000 | 2001 | 2002 | 2003 | |
|---|---|---|---|---|---|---|
| **A. Current Account** | **−290.84** | **−411.45** | **−393.74** | **−480.86** | **−541.83** | |
| 1. Goods Exports (BoP basis) | 683.96 | 771.99 | 718.71 | 681.97 | 713.76 | |
| 2. Goods Imports (BoP basis) | −1,029.98 | −1,224.41 | −1,145.92 | −1,164.74 | −1,263.17 | |
| 3. Balance on Goods | −346.0 | −452.42 | −427.21 | −482.87 | −549.40 | |
| 4. Services: Credit | 281.5 | 298.00 | 288.86 | 292.23 | 304.93 | |
| 5. Services: Debit | −196.68 | −221.00 | −219.47 | −227.39 | −245.68 | |
| 6. Balance on Services | 84.82 | 77.03 | 69.39 | 64.83 | 59.24 | |
| 7. Balance on Goods and Services | −261.2 | −375.38 | −357.8 | −418.0 | −490.16 | |
| **B. Capital Account** | **−4,843** | **−799** | **−1,062** | **−1,285** | **−3,050** | |

**Table 2-3**

*U.S. Balance of Payments, 1999–2003 (US$ billions)*

Source: Adapted from **www.bea.gov**.

for the United States is available from the U.S. Bureau of Economic Analysis (**www.bea.gov**); the bureau's interactive Web site enables users to generate customized reports. Trade statistics and summaries of economic activity for all countries in the world can be found in International Monetary Fund's *Balance of Payments Statistics Yearbook*.[22]

The balance of payments is divided into the current and capital accounts. The **current account** is a broad measure that includes trade in merchandise and services plus certain categories of financial transfers such as humanitarian aid. A country with a negative current account balance has a **trade deficit**; that is, the outflow of money to pay for imports exceeds the inflow of money for sales of exports. Conversely, a country with a positive current account balance has a **trade surplus.** The **capital account** is a record of all long-term direct investment, portfolio investment, and other short- and long-term capital flows. The minus signs signify outflows of cash; for example, in Table 2-3, line 2 shows an outflow of $1.26 trillion in 2003 that represents payment for U.S. merchandise imports. Other entries not shown in Table 2-3 represent changes in net errors and omissions, foreign liabilities, and reserves. These are the entries that make the balance of payments balance. In general, a country accumulates reserves when the net of its current and capital account transactions shows a surplus; it gives up reserves when the net shows a deficit. The important fact to recognize about the overall balance of payments is that it is always in balance. Imbalances occur in subsets of the overall balance. For example, a commonly reported balance is the trade balance on goods (line 3 in Table 2-3).

A close examination of Table 2-3 reveals that, for several years, the United States has posted deficits in both the current account and the trade balance in goods. The United States' growing trade deficit reflects a number of factors, including increased imports from China, historically low interest rates that drive demand for imported goods, and the enormous cost of military operations in the Middle East. Table 2-4 shows a record of goods and services trade between the United States and Japan for 1999 through 2003. A comparison of lines 4 and 5 in the two tables shows a bright spot from the U.S. perspective: The United States has maintained an overall surplus in services trade with the world, including Japan. From the mid-1990s until 2000, the U.S. merchandise trade deficit with Japan grew by about $10 billion per year; in 2000, the deficit peaked at $83 billion. The merchandise trade deficit with Japan has declined in the years since 2000. This decline is explained, in part, by increasing

[22] Balance of payments data are available from a number of different sources, each of which may show slightly different figures for a given line item.

Table 2-4

U.S. Goods and Services Trade
with Japan, 1999–2003
(US$ billions)

| | 1999 | 2000 | 2001 | 2002 | 2003 |
|---|---|---|---|---|---|
| 1. U.S. Goods Exports | 56.07 | 63.47 | 55.87 | 49.66 | 50.30 |
| 2. Goods Imports from Japan | −130.87 | 146.49 | −126.48 | −121.42 | −118.84 |
| 3. Balance on Goods | −74.80 | −83.02 | −70.60 | −71.76 | −67.73 |
| 4. U.S. Services Exports | 31.88 | 33.72 | 30.553 | 30.39 | 30.12 |
| 5. Services Imports from Japan | −17.39 | −18.79 | −18.01 | −18.93 | −19.95 |
| 6. U.S. Balance on Services | 14.48 | 14.92 | 12.52 | 11.45 | 10.17 |
| 7. U.S. Balance on Goods and Services | −60.31 | −68.09 | −58.08 | −60.30 | −57.56 |

Source: Adapted from **www.bea.gov**.

U.S. trade with China; in 2003, for example, the United States posted a $125 billion trade deficit with China. Overall, the United States posts balance of payments deficits while Japan has surpluses. Japan offsets its trade surplus with an outflow of capital, while the United States offsets its trade deficit with an inflow of capital. As trading partners, U.S. consumers and businesses own an increasing quantity of Japanese products, while the Japanese own more U.S. land, real estate, and government securities.

# WORLD TRADE IN MERCHANDISE AND SERVICES

Thanks in part to the achievements of General Agreement on Tariffs and Trade (GATT) and the WTO, world merchandise trade has grown at a faster rate than world production since the end of World War II. Put differently, import and export growth has outpaced the rate of increase in GNP. Moreover, since 1983, foreign direct investment has grown five times faster than world trade and 10 times faster than GNP. According to figures compiled by the International Monetary Fund, the dollar value of world trade in 2003 totaled $9.2 trillion. Exports worth $4 trillion—about 43 percent of the total—were generated by the world's major advanced economies. The 12 nations in the Euro zone accounted for about one-third of the total, with $3 trillion in exports. The top exporting and importing countries are shown in Table 2-5. China's fourth place in the export rankings underscores its role as an export powerhouse. Even in the face of Asia's economic downturn in the late 1990s and the SARS outbreak, China demonstrated continued economic strength by achieving double-digit export growth. Chinese exports to the United States are surging now that China has joined the World Trade Organization; in fact, policymakers in Washington are pressuring Beijing to boost the value of the yuan in an effort to stem the tide of imports. In the Western Hemisphere, Mexico's

Table 2-5

Top Exporters and Importers in
World Merchandise Trade, 2001
(US$ billions)

| Leading Exporters | 2001 | Leading Importers | 2001 |
|---|---|---|---|
| 1. European Union | 874.1 | 1. European Union | 1,180.2 |
| 2. United States | 730.8 | 2. United States | 912.8 |
| 3. Japan | 403.5 | 3. Japan | 349.1 |
| 4. China | 266.2 | 4. China | 243.6 |
| 5. Canada | 259.2 | 5. Canada | 227.2 |
| 6. Hong Kong | 191.1 | 6. Hong Kong | 202.0 |
| 7. Taiwan | 182.3 | 7. Mexico | 176.2 |
| 8. Mexico | 158.5 | 8. South Korea | 141.1 |
| 9. South Korea | 150.4 | 9. Singapore | 116.0 |
| 10. Singapore | 146.5 | 10. Taiwan | 107.3 |

Source: Adapted from International Monetary Fund, *Direction of Trade Statistics Yearbook* (Washington, D.C.: IMF, June 2003), pp. 2–4.

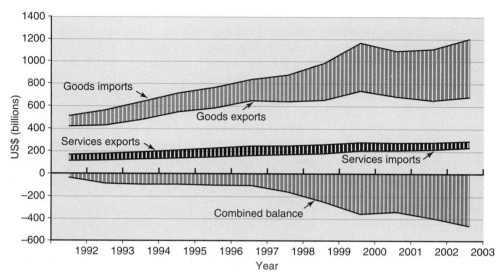

**Figure 2-3**

U.S. Trade Balance on Services
and on Merchandise Trade
(US$ billions)

Source: U.S. Census Bureau.

robust export growth since the mid-1990s shows the continuing impact of NAFTA. For the past several years, Mexico has been running a trade surplus with the United States. Much of the surplus can be attributed to American firms that assemble products at factories in Mexico for the American market. By comparison, Mexico's exports grew only 9 percent from 1992 to 1993.

Probably the fastest-growing sector of world trade is trade in services. Services include travel and entertainment; education; business services such as engineering, accounting, and legal services; and payments of royalties and license fees. One of the major issues in trade relations between the high- and lower-income countries is trade in services. As a group, low-, lower-middle, and even upper-middle-income countries are lax in enforcing international copyrights and protecting intellectual property and patent laws. As a result, countries that export service products such as computer software, music, and video entertainment suffer a loss of income. According to the Software Publishers Association, annual worldwide losses due to software piracy amount to $8 billion. In China and the countries of the former Soviet Union, it is estimated that more than 95 percent of the personal computer software currently in use is pirated.

The United States is a major service trader. As shown in Figure 2-3, U.S. services exports in 2003 totaled $305 billion. This represents nearly one-third of total U.S. exports. The U.S. services surplus (service exports minus imports) stood at $60 billion. This surplus partially offset the U.S. merchandise trade deficit, which reached a record $549 billion in 2003. American Express, Walt Disney, IBM, and Microsoft are a few of the U.S. companies currently enjoying rapid growth in demand for their services around the world.

## OVERVIEW OF INTERNATIONAL FINANCE

The Asian crisis described earlier in the chapter highlights the importance of one specific aspect of the economic environment: foreign exchange rates. Foreign exchange makes it possible for a company in one country to conduct business in other countries with different currencies. However, foreign exchange is an aspect of global marketing that involves certain financial risks, decisions, and activities that are completely different than those facing a domestic marketer. Moreover, those risks can be even higher in developing markets such as Thailand, Malaysia, and South Korea. When a company conducts business within a single country with domestic customers and suppliers paying in the domestic currency, there is no exchange risk. All prices, payments, receipts, assets, and liabilities are in the national currency. However, when a company conducts business across boundaries, it is thrust into the turbulent world of exchange risk.

The foreign exchange market consists literally of a buyer's and a seller's market where currencies are traded for both spot and future delivery on a continuous basis. The *spot market* is for immediate delivery; the market for future delivery is called the *forward market*. This is a true market where prices are based on the combined forces of supply and demand that come into play at the moment of any transaction. A currency in this market is worth what people are willing to pay for it; put another way, it is worth what people are prepared to sell it for. It is a commodity. The principal players in the foreign exchange market are major banks such as Citicorp, Bankers Trust, and J.P. Morgan whose trading activities comprise nearly 80 percent of foreign exchange transactions. Other players include the International Monetary Market (IMM) of the Chicago Mercantile Exchange, which trades currency futures; the London International Financial Futures Exchange (LIFFE); and the Philadelphia Stock Exchange (PSE), which specializes in currency options.

The volume of trading in the foreign exchange market is enormous. The Bank for International Settlements estimates that daily turnover in the spot market exceeds $1.5 trillion, making foreign exchange the world's largest financial market. This figure is so huge it is hard to get a handle on; $1.5 trillion dollars represents one-fifth of U.S. GNP, one-third of Japan's GNP, and two-thirds of Germany's GNP. In any 2 weeks, foreign exchange traders do as much business as importers and exporters of goods and services do in a year. Put differently, it takes the New York Stock Exchange 2 months to ring up a dollar volume equivalent to the value of foreign exchange transactions recorded in a single day. The dollar is the most heavily traded currency, accounting for 80 percent of transactions. London is the world's leading foreign exchange market. London's daily turnover totals $450 billion, which represents about 40 percent of the average daily foreign exchange turnover. Each market has its own focus: London is dollars per pound sterling (£), New York is dollars per euro (€), and Tokyo is dollars per yen (¥).

## Managed Dirty Float

Today's global financial system can be described as a "managed dirty float with SDRs." What does this mean? *Float* refers to the system of fluctuating exchange rates. As currency trader Andrew Krieger has described this system, currencies are "up for auction," with rates "floating" or adjusting in the foreign exchange market subject to all the forces of supply and demand. In other words, the buying and selling activities of currency traders partially determine a specific currency's value on a given day. *Managed* refers to the specific use of fiscal and monetary policy by governments to influence exchange rates.

**Devaluation** can result from government action that decrees a reduction in the value of the local currency that was previously fixed against other currencies. In 1994, for example, the Chinese devalued the yuan (also known as *renminbhi* or "people's money"). The immediate result was to ensure the low-cost position of Chinese exporters. However, the action also set the stage for the 1997 devaluations of the Thai baht, Malaysian ringgit, and Indonesian rupiah; the expression "beggar thy neighbor" is sometimes used to describe devaluations designed to increase export competitiveness.

Market forces can also trigger devaluation; once the governments of Thailand, Malaysia, and Indonesia allowed their respective currencies to float, market forces led to the subsequent depreciation in value. *Dirty* refers to the fact that, besides currency traders, central banks buy and sell currencies in the foreign exchange market in an effort to influence exchange rates. Such interventions may be intended to dampen fluctuations in foreign exchange rates. A good illustration occurred in October 1997, when currency speculators mounted an attack on the Hong Kong dollar, which was still pegged to the U.S. dollar. The head of the Hong Kong Monetary Authority defended the peg by using his country's ample reserves to buy and therefore support the value of the Hong Kong dollar. Central bank intervention can also represent government attempts to change the relative values of currencies over the short and medium term.

## Foreign Exchange Market Dynamics

Some of the trading in the foreign exchange market represents the forces of supply and demand driven by the need to settle accounts for the global trade in goods and services. To the extent that a country sells more goods and services abroad than it buys, there will be a greater demand for its currency and a tendency for it to *appreciate* in value. The strength of the Japanese yen in the mid-1990s was a case in point. High demand for Japanese goods resulted in high demand for yen; the strong demand for yen caused its value to increase. If the foreign exchange market were influenced only by purchases and sales to settle accounts for merchandise and services trade, it would be a fairly simple matter to forecast foreign exchange rates. However, short- and long-term capital flows and speculative purchases and sales are a major source of supply and demand for foreign exchange. Short-term capital is sensitive to interest rates and long-term capital to return expectations, and both are sensitive to perceptions of risk. Today, currency speculators appear to have more power to move currency markets than government central bankers do.[23]

Table 2-6 shows how fluctuating currency values can affect financial risk, depending on the terms of payment specified in the contract. Suppose, at the time a deal is made, the exchange rate is €1.10 = $1. How is a U.S. exporter affected if the dollar strengthens against the euro (e.g., trades at €1.25 = $1) and the contract specifies payment in dollars? What happens if the dollar weakens (e.g., €0.85 = $1)? Conversely, what if the European buyer contracts to pay in euros rather than dollars?

## Purchasing Power Parity

Given that currencies fluctuate in value, a reasonable question to ask is whether due either to market forces or government intervention, a given currency is over- or undervalued compared with another. One way to answer the question is to compare world prices for a single well-known product: McDonald's Big Mac hamburger. The so-called Big Mac Index is a "quick and dirty" way of determining which of the world's currencies are too weak or strong (**www.economist.com/markets/ bigmac**). The underlying assumption is that the price of a Big Mac in any world currency should, after being converted to dollars, equal the price of a Big Mac in the

| Foreign Exchange Rates | $1,000,000 Contract | | €1,100,000 Contract | | Table 2-6 |
| | U.S. Seller Receives | European Buyer Pays | U.S. Seller Receives | European Buyer Pays | |
| --- | --- | --- | --- | --- | --- |
| €1.25 = $1 | $1,000,000 | €1,250,000 | $ 880,000 | €1,100,000 | *Exchange Risks and Gains in Foreign Transactions* |
| €1.10 = $1 | $1,000,000 | €1,100,000 | $1,000,000 | €1,100,000 | |
| €1.00 = $1 | $1,000,000 | €1,000,000 | $1,100,000 | €1,100,000 | |
| €0.85 = $1 | $1,000,000 | € 850,000 | $1,294,118 | €1,100,000 | |

---

[23] Thomas L. Friedman's discussion of this topic is an excellent source for additional information. See *The Lexus and the Olive Tree* (New York: Anchor Books, 2000), Chapter 7, "The Electronic Herd."

**Table 2-7**

The Big Mac Index

| Country | Big Mac Price Converted to $ | Official Exchange Rate | Over- or Undervaluation of Local Currency (%) |
|---|---|---|---|
| Switzerland | 5.11 | 1.22170/$1 | +78 |
| Euro zone | 3.48 | .78345/$1 | +24 |
| U.S. | 2.80 | – | – |
| Japan | 2.47 | 106.26/$1 | −12 |
| Russia | 1.42 | 28.88/$1 | −50 |
| China | 1.23 | 8.26/$1 | −56 |

Source: Adapted from "The Big Mac Index;" **www.economist.com/markets/bigmac**, accessed May 25, 2004.

United States. A country's currency would be overvalued if the Big Mac price (converted to dollars) is higher than the U.S. price. Conversely, a country's currency would be undervalued if the converted Big Mac price is lower than the U.S. price. Economists use the concept of **purchasing power parity (PPP)** when adjusting national income data to improve comparability. Table 2-7 shows the Big Mac Index for selected countries in 2003. The first column of figures shows the price of a Big Mac converted from the local currency to dollars at the prevailing exchange rate on January 14, 2004. Thus, we can see that the Chinese yuan is undervalued against the dollar by about 56 percent. In other words, based on the U.S price for a Big Mac, the yuan/dollar exchange rate ought to be closer to 4 to 1 rather than 8.3 to 1.

In its survey of earnings around the world, Zurich-based UBS also uses the Big Mac as a reference point. The survey assesses purchasing power around the world in terms of how long the average wage earner must work to earn enough money to pay for a Big Mac. According to its 2003 survey, employees in Zurich, Geneva, Tokyo, Luxembourg, and New York have the highest take-home pay. Workers in Nairobi, Bombay, Shanghai, Budapest, Moscow, and Manila rank at the bottom in terms of take-home pay. Table 2-8 shows the longest and shortest average times required to earn enough for a Big Mac.

## Economic Exposure

The degree to which exchange rates affect a company's market value as measured by its stock price is known as economic exposure. **Economic exposure** refers to the impact of currency fluctuations on the present value of a company's expected future cash flows. For example, Mexican sales account for 11 percent of Avon Products'

**Table 2-8**

Time Worked to Pay for a Big Mac

| Longest Time | | Shortest Time | |
|---|---|---|---|
| City | Minutes | City | Minutes |
| Nairobi | 185 | Los Angeles, Miami, Chicago, Tokyo | 10 |
| Karachi | 132 | New York | 12 |
| Bombay | 112 | Hong Kong | 13 |
| Bogotá | 93 | Zurich, Toronto, Montreal | 14 |
| Kiev | 84 | Basle, Luxembourg, Dublin, Frankfurt, Vienna | 15 |
| Bucharest, Lima | 79 | Geneva, Copenhagen, Amsterdam, Berlin, London | 16 |
| Caracas | 76 | Lugano | 17 |
| Mexico City | 75 | Oslo, Brussels, Taipei | 18 |
| Jakarta | 67 | Auckland, Helsinki, Stockholm, Sydney, Paris | 19 |
| Vilnius | 62 | Madrid, Milan, Athens, Singapore | 21 |

Source: UBS, **www.ubs.com/economic research,** accessed August 21, 2003.

annual sales; thus, Avon had a great deal of economic exposure to the peso's devaluation in 1994. The extent of the exposure prompted many investors to sell Avon stock.

Economic exposure can be further divided into two categories: transaction exposure and real operating exposure. **Transaction exposure** arises when the company's activities result in sales or purchases denominated in foreign currencies. Guinness, for example faces transaction exposure to the extent that it agrees to accept payment for exports of scotch at one exchange rate but actually settles its accounts at a different rate of exchange.[24] The importance of transaction exposure is directly proportional to the amount of business a company conducts outside the home market. Obviously, currency exposure is a critical issue for Nestlé, with 98 percent of annual sales taking place outside Switzerland. By contrast, GE generated about 70 percent of its 2001 revenues in the United States, so the relative extent of GE's exposure is less than that of Nestlé.

Transaction exposure may vary among a company's business units. Consider, for example, DaimlerChrysler's aircraft group, DaimlerChrysler Aerospace Airbus (Dasa). World prices for aircraft are denominated in dollars, and 75 percent of Dasa's revenues are in dollars. In the early 1990s, this had serious implications in view of the mark's strength. Compounding the problem was the fact that most of Dasa's employees were paid in marks. Dasa's net losses for 1992 to 1994 totaled nearly 1.5 billion marks. Company executives simply misforecast how far the dollar would fall against the mark. Budgets for 1995 were based on an exchange rate of 1.6 marks to the dollar, but by mid-1995 the actual rate was 1.38 to 1.[25]

*Real operating exposure* arises when currency fluctuations, together with price changes, alter a company's future revenues and costs. According to this definition, the firms that face operating exposure include not only those that have overseas operations but also those whose manufacturing plan calls for sourcing goods abroad. Economic exposure arises whenever companies commit to setting up new product development centers and distribution systems, getting foreign supply, or investing in foreign production facilities.

In dealing with the economic exposure introduced by currency fluctuations, a key issue is whether the company can use price as a strategic tool for maintaining its profit margins. Can the company adjust prices in response to a rise or fall of foreign exchange rates in various markets? That depends on the price elasticity of demand. The less price sensitive the demand, the greater the flexibility a company has in responding to exchange rate changes. Price elasticity, in turn, depends on the degree of competition and the location of the competitors. Ford managers believed a 10 percent price increase following the peso devaluation in Mexico was feasible. In the case of DaimlerChrysler's Dasa unit, the presence of numerous regional competitors constrained the company's ability to push through price increases. In 1995, Dasa executives launched a Competition Initiative to examine various measures such as cutting jobs and rethinking supplier agreements. Dasa purchased only 25 percent of its parts outside Germany, so one option was to switch to suppliers in the United States or other countries with relatively weak currencies. Another option is to persuade German suppliers to "share the pain" by accepting payment in dollars. Finally, Dasa may be forced to exit some segments of the industry.

## Managing Exchange Rate Exposure

As the Dasa example illustrates, it is difficult to accurately forecast the movement of exchange rates. Over the years, the search for other ways of managing cash flows to eliminate or reduce exchange rate risks has resulted in the development of

---

[24] John Willman, "Currency Squeeze on Guinness," *Financial Times—Weekend Money* (September 27–28, 1997), p. 5.
[25] Brian Coleman, "Daimler Aerospace Comes Down to Earth," *The Wall Street Journal* (July 27, 1995), p. A7.

numerous techniques and financial strategies. For example, it may be desirable to sell products in the company's home country currency. When this is not possible, techniques are available to reduce both transaction and operating exposure.

**Hedging** exchange rate exposure involves establishing an offsetting currency position such that the loss or gain of one currency position is offset by a corresponding gain or loss in some other currency. The practice is common among global companies that sell products and maintain operations in different countries. For example, DaimlerChrysler spends tens of millions of dollars each year on foreign currency and hedging transactions. A basic rule of thumb is this: If company forecasts indicate that the value of the foreign currency will weaken against the home currency, a hedge to protect against potential transaction losses is a prudent course of action. Conversely, for predictions that the foreign currency will appreciate (strengthen) against the home currency, then a gain, rather than a loss, can be expected on foreign transactions when revenues are converted into the home currency. Given this expectation, the best decision may be not to hedge at all. (The operative word is "may"; many companies hedge anyway unless management is convinced the foreign currency will strengthen.) External hedging methods for managing both transaction and translation exposure require companies to participate in the foreign currency market. Specific hedging tools include forward contracts and currency options. Internal hedging methods include price adjustment clauses and intra-corporate borrowing or lending in foreign currencies.

The **forward market** is a mechanism for buying and selling currencies at a preset price for future delivery. If it is known that a certain amount of foreign currency is going to be paid out or received at some future date, a company can insure itself against exchange loss by buying or selling forward. With a forward contract, the company can lock in a specific fixed exchange rate for a future date and thus immunize itself from the loss (or gain) caused by the exchange rate fluctuation. By consulting sources such as *Financial Times, The Wall Street Journal*, or **www.ozforex.com,** it is possible to determine exchange rates on any given day. In addition to spot prices, 30-, 60-, and 180-day forward prices are quoted for dozens of world currencies.

Companies use the forward market when the currency exposure is known in advance (e.g., when a firm contract of sale exists). In some situations, however, companies are not certain about the future foreign currency cash inflow or outflow. Consider the risk exposure of a U.S. company that bids for a foreign project but won't know if the project will be granted until sometime later. The company needs to protect the dollar value of the contract by hedging the *potential* foreign currency cash inflow that will be generated if the company turns out to be the winning bidder. In such an instance, forward contracts are not the appropriate hedging tool.

A foreign currency **option** is best for such situations. A **put option** gives the buyer the right, not the obligation, to sell a specified number of foreign currency units at a fixed price, up to the option's expiration date. (Conversely, a **call option** is the right, but not the obligation, to buy the foreign currency.) In the example of bidding the foreign project, the company can take out a put option to sell the foreign currency for dollars at a set price in the future. In other words, the U.S. company locks in the value of the contract in dollars. Thus, if the project is granted, the future foreign currency cash inflow has been hedged by means of the put option. If the project is *not* granted, the company can trade the put option in the options market without exercising it; remember, options are rights, not obligations. The only money the company stands to lose is the difference between what it paid for the option and what it receives upon selling it.

Avon Products' attitude that "turmoil presents opportunities" served it well in the wake of the Asian currency crisis. In 1996, Asian sales accounted for $751 million of Avon's $4.8 billion in worldwide revenues. Avon purchases most raw materials locally and has factories in China, Indonesia, the Philippines, and Japan. Rather than borrow in dollars, country managers who need capital for operations arrange for loans denominated in local currencies. When the crisis unfolded in Thailand in the summer of 1997, Joe Ferreira Jr., head of Avon's Asia-Pacific region, and treasurer Dennis Ling stipulated that the 10 country units in Asia remit earnings on a weekly, rather than monthly basis. This allowed for quicker conversion of local currencies into dollars. As of August 1997, however, the company had not hedged in Asia; Ferreira and Ling agreed to spend about $3 million to protect $50 million in Asian currency exposure. The two Avon executives also took other steps that reflected the changes in the financial environment: Avon's Latin American managers were invited to Asia to share their experiences of the peso devaluation with the Asian managers; a European lace vendor was replaced by a Thai company; and a contract was renegotiated with a South Korean supplier of jewelry for the United States. As Ling said, "Part of my job is to help our managers understand and take advantage of the impact of currencies on their business."[26]

Financial officers of global firms can avoid transaction exposure altogether by demanding a particular currency as the payment for its foreign sales. As noted, a U.S-based company might demand U.S. dollars as the payment currency for its foreign sales. This, however, does not eliminate currency risk; it simply shifts that risk to the customers. In common practice, companies typically attempt to invoice exports (receivables) in strong currencies and imports (payables) in weak currencies. However, in today's highly competitive world market, such practice may reduce a company's competitive edge.

**summary**

The economic environment is a major determinant of global market potential and opportunity. In today's global economy, capital movements are the key driving force, production has become uncoupled from employment, and capitalism has vanquished communism. Based on patterns of resource allocation and ownership, the world's national economies can be categorized as **market capitalism, centrally planned capitalism, centrally planned socialism**, and **market socialism.** The final years of the twentieth century were marked by a transition toward market capitalism in many countries that had been centrally controlled. However, there still exists a great disparity among the nations of the world in terms of **economic freedom.**

Countries can be categorized in terms of their stage of economic development: **low income, lower-middle income, upper-middle income**, and **high income.** Countries in the first two categories are sometimes known as **less-developed countries (LDCs).** Upper-middle-income countries with high growth rates are often called **newly industrializing economies (NIEs).** Several of the world's economies are notable for their fast growth; the **big emerging markets (BEMs)** include China and India (low income), Poland, Turkey, and Indonesia (lower-middle income), Argentina, Brazil, Mexico, and

South Africa (upper-middle income), and South Korea (high income). The **Group of Seven (G7)** and **Organization for Economic Cooperation and Development (OECD)** represent two initiatives by high-income nations to promote democratic ideals and free-market policies throughout the rest of the world. Most of the world's income is located in the **Triad**, which is comprised of Japan, the United States, and Western Europe. Companies with global aspirations generally have operations in all three areas. Market potential for a product can be evaluated by determining **product saturation levels** in light of income levels.

A country's **balance of payments** is a record of its economic transactions with the rest of the world; this record shows whether a country has a **trade surplus** (value of exports exceeds value of imports) or a **trade deficit** (value of imports exceeds value of exports). Trade figures can be further divided into **merchandise trade** and **services trade** accounts; a country can run a surplus in both accounts, a deficit in both accounts, or a combination of the two. The U.S. merchandise trade deficit was $549 billion in 2003. However, the U.S. enjoys an annual service trade surplus. Overall, the United States is a debtor; Japan enjoys an overall trade surplus and serves as a creditor nation.

---

[26] Fred R. Bleakley, "How U.S. Firm Copes with Asia Crisis," *The Wall Street Journal* (December 26, 1997), pp. A2, A4.

Foreign exchange provides a means for settling accounts in different currencies. The dynamics of international finance can have a significant impact on a nation's economy as well as the fortunes of individual companies. Currencies can be subject to **devaluation** as a result of actions taken by a country's central banker. Currency trading by international speculators can also lead to devaluation.

When a country's economy is strong or when demand for its goods is high, its currency tends to appreciate in value. When currency values fluctuate, firms face various types of economic exposure. These include **transaction exposure** and **operating exposure**. Firms can manage exchange rate exposure by **hedging,** for example, by buying and selling currencies in the **forward market.**

## discussion questions

1. Explain the difference between market capitalism, centrally planned capitalism, centrally planned socialism, and market socialism. Give an example of a country that illustrates each type of system.

2. What is a Big Emerging Market (BEM)? Identify the BEMs according to their respective stages of economic development.

3. Turn to the Index of Economic Freedom (Table 2-1) and identify where the BEMs are ranked. What does the result tell you in terms of the relevance of the index to global marketers?

4. A manufacturer of satellite dishes is assessing the world market potential for his products. He asks you if he should consider developing countries as potential markets. How would you advise him?

5. A friend is distressed to learn that America's merchandise trade deficit hit a record $549 billion in 2003. You want to cheer your friend up by demonstrating that the trade picture is not as bleak as it sounds. What do you say?

## research exercise

1. The big emerging markets (BEMs) discussed in this chapter are frequently in the news. Choose one of the countries to follow during the semester; keep a journal with notes or pasted-up articles from the press. What issues identified in the chapter continue to affect trade prospects in your country? What new issues, if any, have developed?

## web resources

*Economist* magazine's Web site offers briefings on more than 60 countries representing all stages of development at: **www.economist.com/countries.**

The U.S. Census Bureau compiles data on U.S. trade and makes it available on the Web. You can find this data under the headings "FT900" and "Supplement" at: **www.census.gov/foreign-trade/www.**

The United States Bureau of Economic Analysis posts a great deal of information about the U.S. economy. You can access the database at: **www.bea.doc.gov.**

# Case 2-1

## Vietnam's Market Potential

In October 2001, U.S. President George Bush signed an agreement that created a U.S.–Vietnam free trade area. The signing marked yet another milestone along Vietnam's path toward a more open market, the timeline for which includes the following:

- In February 1994, U.S. President Bill Clinton ended America's 19-year economic embargo of Vietnam and opened the door for U.S. companies to target the world's twelfth most populous country.

- In July 1995, President Clinton reestablished diplomatic relations with Vietnam. In the absence of diplomatic relations, many Vietnamese manufactured exports to the United States faced prohibitive tariffs.

- In 1995, Vietnam joined the Association of Southeast Asian Nations (ASEAN).

- In 1998, the White House announced that it would exempt Vietnam from the Jackson-Vanik amendment. The exemption meant that, pending congressional approval, American companies investing in Vietnam could apply for financial assistance from the Overseas Private Investment Corporation (OPIC) and the Export-Import Bank.

- In July 2000, U.S. President Bill Clinton signed a trade pact with Vietnam.

- Vietnam hopes to join the World Trade Organization by 2005.

After being ratified by Congress, President Clinton's actions in the mid-1990s established normal trading relations (NTR) between the two countries. In particular, Vietnam benefited from an immediate lowering of duties on a number of goods produced by its light industry sector (see Figure 1). Vietnamese tariffs and quotas on imports from the United States would be lowered more gradually. A number of U.S. companies immediately seized the opportunity. As Brian Watson, a Hong Kong-based deputy regional director for the McCann-Erickson advertising agency, said in the mid-1990s, "Vietnam is the next great frontier. There is an enormous amount of interest among clients. Every meeting starts with a question about going into Vietnam."

While the U.S. business community hailed the U.S. government's initiatives, many American firms found themselves playing catch up; by the early 1990s, many non-U.S. global companies had preceded the Americans into Vietnam. For example, South Korean industrial giant Daewoo was a key investor; other companies with major commitments included Sony, Toshiba, Honda, Peugeot, and British Petroleum. Carrier was among the first U.S. companies to legally market in Vietnam in 1994; the company's window air conditioners appeared in stores in Hanoi and Ho Chi Minh City. Gillette began shipping razor blades and disposable razors, and AT&T began selling home and office telephone products

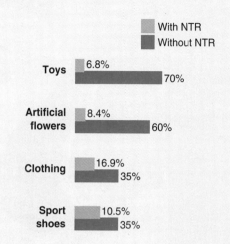

**Figure 1**

*Duty Rates on Vietnamese Exports to the United States with and Without NTR*

Source: Vietnam Economic Times.

through a distributor in Taiwan. Mobil began exploring for oil, Caterpillar set up equipment-leasing operations, and the Otis Elevator division of United Technologies joined in the construction boom. J. Walter Thompson, Ogilvy & Mather, and Backer Spielvogel Bates Worldwide became the first Western ad agencies to open liaison offices in Vietnam.

In view of the fact that 60 percent of Vietnam's population is under the age of 25, it is no surprise that PepsiCo and the Coca-Cola Company were also quick to make moves in Vietnam. In fact, at the time of the official announcement about ending the embargo, McCann-Erickson had already produced a TV commercial for Coca-Cola that included the global slogan "Always"; likewise, Ogilvy & Mather had a Pepsi ad ready for TV. Coca-Cola is building a $20 million bottling plant outside of Hanoi, but was denied permission to build in Ho Chi Minh City (formerly Saigon). Pepsi's joint venture with a Vietnamese firm in Ho Chi Minh City is bottling Pepsi; local production began within hours of President Clinton's 1994 announcement. To supply the market in the south, Coca-Cola imported canned soda from Singapore. As a result, a can of Coke cost twice as much as a bottle of Pepsi.

Experts agree that the Vietnamese market holds tremendous potential over the long term. It may be two decades before Vietnam reaches the level of economic development found in Thailand today. Meanwhile, the country's location in the heart of Asia and the presence of an ample low-wage workforce are powerful magnets for foreign companies. By the end of 1999, France ranked first in foreign investment while Japan was the top trading partner. Overall foreign direct investment peaked at about $3.1 billion in 1997 after rising steadily since the early

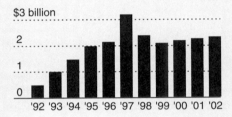

**Figure 2**

*Foreign Direct Investment in Vietnam, 1992–2002*

"whether it's possible to carry on free-market reforms and maintain absolute political power."

Yvonne Gupwell, a business consultant who was born in Vietnam, believes that "The biggest mistake companies make is they think because the Vietnamese are so polite, they're a little bit dim. The Vietnamese are poor, but they are not mentally poor at all." Statistics support this view; for example, adult literacy is nearly 90 percent. In fact, an emerging entrepreneurial class has developed a taste for expensive products such as Nikon cameras and Ray Ban sunglasses, both of which are available in stores. Notes Do Duc Dinh of the Institute on the World Economy, "There is a huge unofficial economy. For most people, we can live only 5 days or 10 days a month on our salary. But people build houses. Where does the money come from? Even in government ministries, there are two sets of books—one for the official money and one for unofficial."

*"In 1996, you were told where to invest, and you also had to build the road, the school, the hospital. You said, 'Thank you very much; my new address is Malaysia.'"*

A foreign businessman in Vietnam

Euphoria over Vietnam's potential showed signs of waning at the end of the 1990s. Part of the problem was the "currency contagion" that struck Asia in mid-1997; Asian countries that had been major investors were forced to scale back their activities in Vietnam. More generally, many companies were finding it difficult to make a profit. Cross-border smuggling from Thailand depressed legitimate sales of products produced locally by Procter & Gamble, Unilever, American Standard, and other companies. Foreign companies were also frustrated by the shallow pool of qualified local managers. It was also clear that China was attracting a great deal of foreign investment away from other countries in the region.

Today, many companies are discovering that Vietnam is an excellent source of low-cost labor. Burgeoning apparel and textile exports to the United States led to an agreement on export quotas in 2003. The fledgling tech sector also appears to hold great promise. Vietnam's universities turn out graduates who are highly trained in information technology. One company, Glass Egg Digital Media, provides software-writing services to leading global videogame developers such as Frances Infogames and U.S.-based Electronic Arts. Glass Egg founder Phil Tran pays programmers annual salaries of about $4,000, tens of thousands less than programmers in the United States are paid.

Although still strongly influenced by Communist hardliners, the bureaucrats in Hanoi have demonstrated an increased willingness to adopt much-needed reforms to foreign investment laws. In January 2000, for example, the regulatory environment improved with the enactment of an enterprise law that streamlined the process of market entry and setting up a business; a stock market was also opened. Increasingly, decisions about foreign investment are being made at the provincial level, and local officials are offering incentives and issuing import licenses more quickly. Investors

1990s (see Figure 2). After falling to about $2.1 billion in 1999, investment rebounded to $2.3 billion in 2002. As encouraging as those figures are, however, investment levels in China are much higher.

There are still many challenges for companies seeking to invest in Vietnam. The population is very poor, with 2000 annual per capita income of only about $350. However, urbanites with savings estimated at $1 to $2 billion comprise one-quarter of the population. The infrastructure is undeveloped: Only 10 percent of roads are paved, electricity sources are unreliable, there is less than one telephone per 100 people, and the banking system is undeveloped. The Communist Party of Vietnam (CPV) is struggling to adapt to the principles of a market economy, and the layers of bureaucracy built up over decades of Communist rule slow the pace of change. A key agency is the State Committee for Cooperation and Investment (SCCI); as Vu Tien Phuc, a deputy director of the agency, explained, "Every authority would like to have the last say. We have to improve the investment climate." William Ratliff, an analyst with the Hoover Institute, points out that the question for Vietnam is in many industry sectors are now able to set up wholly foreign-owned firms; previously, the government rarely approved such arrangements. Instead, foreign companies were encouraged to form joint ventures with state-owned enterprises. The improved investment climate helps explain why a number of foreign carmakers, including Ford, GM, Toyota, and DaimlerChrysler, have established operations in Vietnam. Noted one local businessman approvingly, "In the past, it was absolutely horrendous to set up a private company. Now 99 percent of the difficulties are gone."

Vietnam's free trade area agreement with the United States entered into force in December 2001. The effect was immediate: The value of U.S. imports from Vietnam more than doubled in 2002, to nearly $2.4 billion. At the end of 2003, the two nations signed an air services agreement that will make it easy for travelers to book flights to Vietnam. The agreement comes as Vietnam's government is marketing the country as an attractive vacation destination. Despite such positive news, however, many problems remain. For example, Vietnam's legal system is still bewildering, and regulations can change on a moment's notice. Relations between the new trading partners have shown some signs of strain, as evidenced by U.S. charges that Vietnam has been dumping catfish in the U.S. market at artificially low prices.

## Discussion Questions

1. Assess the market opportunities in Vietnam for both American consumer-products companies and American industrial-products companies. What is the nature of the opportunity?

2. Nike and several other well-known American companies are sourcing some of their production in Vietnam, thereby taking advantage of a labor force that is paid the equivalent of $2 per day or less. Are goods labeled "Made in Vietnam" likely to find widespread acceptance among American consumers?

3. Some critics have argued that Cuba is more deserving of diplomatic and trade relations with the United States than Vietnam is. What are some of the factors behind this argument?

*Sources:* Dan Reed, "Ex-Enemies Make a Deal," *USA Today* (December 9, 2003), p. 5B; Reginald Chua and Margot Cohen, "Vietnamese Tiger Growls Again; Investors Want a Change of Stripes," *The Wall Street Journal* (March 13, 2003), p. A10; Margot Cohen, "Foreign Investors Take New Look at Vietnam and Like What They See," *The Wall Street Journal* (January 28, 2003), p. A14; Bruce Knecht, "Vietnam Taps Videogame Talent," *The New York Times* (October 21, 2001), p. B5; Frederik Balfour, "Back on the Radar Screen," *Business Week* (November 20, 2000), pp. 56–57; Wayne Arnold, "Clearing the Decks for a Trade Pact's Riches," *The New York Times* (August 27, 2000), sec. 3, pp. 1, 12; Samantha Marshall, "Vietnam Pullout: This Time, Investors Pack Up Gear, Stymied by Bureaucracy, Lack of Reforms," *The Wall Street Journal* (June 30, 1998), p. A15; Marshall, "P&G Squabbles with Vietnamese Partner," *The Wall Street Journal* (February 27, 1998), p. A10; Chua, "Vietnam Frustrates Foreign Investors as Leaders Waffle on Market Economy," *The Wall Street Journal* (November 25, 1996), p. A10; "Vietnam," *The Economist* (July 8, 1995), pp. 1–18 (survey); William J. Ardrey, Anthony Pecotich, and Clifford J. Schultz, "American Involvement in Vietnam, Part II: Prospects for U.S. Business in a New Era," *Business Horizons* 38 (March/April 1995), pp. 21–27; Edward A. Gargan, "For U.S. Business, a Hard Road to Vietnam," *The New York Times* (July 14, 1995), p. C1; Marilyn Greene, "'Very Soon, Vietnam Will Be Very Good,'" *USA Today* (April 1, 1994), p. 8A; Robert Keatley, "Vietnam, Despite Promise, Faces Climb," *The Wall Street Journal* (August 18, 1994), p. A8; Philip Shenon, "Vietnam: Behind a Red-Tape Curtain," *The New York Times* (November 13, 1994), Sec. 3, p. 6; James Cox, "Vietnamese Look Forward to Trade, Jobs," *USA Today* (July 12, 1995), pp. 1A, 2A; Kevin Goldman, "Agencies Get Ready for Vietnam Business," *The Wall Street Journal* (February 7, 1994), p. B10.

# Case 2-2

## Acer, Inc. (B)

Acer Inc. is a leading manufacturer of notebook and desktop PCs. The company, which posted sales of $4.6 billion in 2003, also produces a wide range of hardware components including motherboards, monitors, keyboards, and CD-ROM drives. As Taiwan gained a reputation as the "tech workshop of the world," Acer was able to become Taiwan's number one exporter by manufacturing and marketing computers sold under its own brand name. Acer also produced equipment on an OEM ("original equipment manufacturer") basis for well-known global companies such as IBM, Dell, and Hitachi.

Company founder, chairman, and CEO Stan Shih built Acer Inc. into one of Taiwan's most successful companies.

Despite Acer's success, the company had trouble breaking into the American market. Between 1995 and 1997, Acer's U.S. market share dropped from 15 percent to 5 percent. In the late 1990s, Shih noted, "In the United States and Europe, we are relatively weak. The local players there are very strong. The problem is that we don't have good experience in marketing in those regions. It's a people issue, not a product issue." Shih has discovered that building brands in the business-to-business market is easier than building brands in the business-to-consumer market. "Business-to-consumer brands have more value but also face more challenges. People involved in business-to-business are usually rational, but consumers in business-to-consumer are usually emotional in choosing their brands," asserted Shih.

In 1999, Shih decided to pull out of the United States altogether and focus Acer's manufacturing and marketing on a vast, fast-growing market much closer to home: China. In 2001, China joined the WTO. Acer and other key players in Taiwan's high-tech industry stand to benefit from closer economic ties with China. From China's standpoint this new membership is also a benefit: WTO rules require that both China and Taiwan eliminate limitations on foreign investment. Taiwan manufacturers are expected to quickly increase the rate of investment in various Chinese businesses.

Shih wants to convert Acer Inc. from a top-10 global PC manufacturer into a "marketing and services powerhouse." He envisions Acer marketing its PCs and IT expertise to greater China (mainland China, Taiwan, and Hong Kong) and expanding from there to the rest of the world. "The market in China is very critical for Taiwanese companies to become global companies," Shih says. "Innovation is not necessarily related to whether you are smart or not. The reality is that if you don't have a big market it's not easy to innovate because the return on investment is too low. The potential of China is not just big markets and low cost labor. Actually, it's also for highly educated engineers or professionals." Shih believes that, if greater China becomes the company's "home" market (as opposed to just Taiwan), Acer will capture critical economies of scale that will allow it to develop innovative new products that will succeed in China as well as the rest of the world. Global PC sales were near 9 million units in 2001, and are expected to grow to more than 22 million units in 2005. Shih's goal is for Acer to capture approximately 20 percent of the worldwide total.

Shih understands that it is crucial for Acer to develop a strong brand image in China. "The challenge for this region is really the poor image that is often associated with products here," says Shih. Shih believes that it is necessary for all companies to be stable and secure in the local market before pursuing regional, then global markets. He continues, "Another important feature is also the government and the general public. They have to understand the role of supporting activities for local brands. If they do not support or use the locally made products, there will be no improvement in this area."

Ronald Chwang, Acer's chief technology officer, anticipates that Acer's knowledge of China's market will help the company achieve its growth and market share objectives; as he puts it, "Now we have a market where we understand the culture and the people's needs. That should enable Acer to move a lot of hardware." J.T. Wang, Acer's new president, points out, "China and Taiwan share not just the same language and culture, but a lot of our Taiwanese suppliers are already there. We can take our brand global by building a strong home market." Currently, Acer has only 3 percent of the mainland's computer market and ranks eighth in share of the PC market. Legend, a local mainland brand, dominates with 35 percent of the market. However, Acer's notebook computers rank fourth and the company has an impressive nation-wide network of nearly 1,000 distributors. Wang believes Acer is well positioned to overtake local mainland firms such as Legend and Founder to become a leader in PC sales in China.

A cornerstone of Acer's strategy for the mainland is its first PC made in China from start to finish. This new model, the Acer Aspire, is comparable to currently available Legend products in quality and price. Wang is confident that Acer can challenge Legend as China's number one PC maker. Shih believes Acer will have an advantage over Legend and other local PC makers because Acer is more "global." At the same time, Shih is convinced his company will be able to compete with better-known global companies that are entering China because Acer is more "local" than them. Acer's international identity gives the company access to advanced business practices, technology, and economies of scale that companies like Legend do not have. For example, Legend does not manufacture its own notebook computers, which are much more technically complex than desktops. Instead, Legend buys notebooks from Taiwanese companies. "We have more technology than Legend. We have more global exposure than Legend. We have more international know-how. . . . We can gradually gain more market share," Shih says.

Shih admits that sales of Acer's desktop PCs in China have developed more slowly than he expected. He attributes this to Acer's poor brand recognition in the mainland. Shih claims the company's position among the top three vendors in China's small but growing notebook PC market has "helped Acer establish a quality name and high-end image." However, Shih promised his wife he would retire at the end of 2004 when he turns 60 years old. Would he realize his vision for Acer before then?

## Discussion Questions

1. How does the "global markets/local markets" paradox figure into Stan Shih's strategy for China?

2. Shih cites McDonald's as a source for many of his business ideas. If, in turn, managers at Legend were to learn from Acer's successes and mistakes, what would those lessons be?

3. If Shih decides to relaunch the Acer brand in the United States, what strategy do you recommend? Should he focus on the consumer market? Or should he target corporate users?

This case was prepared by Research Assistant Alanah Davis under the supervision of Professor Mark Green.

*Sources:* Bruce Einhorn, Amy Reinhardt, and Maureen Kline, "Acer: How Far Can It Ride This Hot Streak?" *Business Week* (May 17, 2004), p. 52; Hiawatha Bray, "Acer Embodies Taiwanese Climb Up Manufacturing Food Chain," *The Boston Globe* (June 24, 2002); Simon Burns and Kathy Wilhelm, "Acer Who?" *Far Eastern Economic Review* (May 24, 2001), pp. 47; Wai-Chan Chan, Martin Hirt, and Stephen M. Shaw, "The Greater China High-Tech Highway," *The McKinsey Quarterly* no. 4 (October 11, 2002); Charles S. Lee, "Acer's Last Stand?" *Fortune* (June 10, 2002); Yu Wui Wui, "Marketing Asian Brands," *New Straits Times — Management Times* (October 4, 2000).

# 3 The Global Trade Environment

## REGIONAL MARKET CHARACTERISTICS AND PREFERENTIAL TRADE AGREEMENTS

n the fall of 2003, leaders from 34 North, Central, and South American nations convened the fifth Summit of the Americas in Miami, Florida, to discuss plans for a proposed Free Trade Area of the Americas (FTAA). If negotiations are successfully completed by January 2005, the FTAA will stretch from Alaska to Tierra del Fuego, Argentina; the area will account for $11 trillion in annual economic output (approximately one-third of the world total) and encompass 800 million people. However, as evidenced by the hundreds of protesters who demonstrated against the talks in Miami and elsewhere, President George W. Bush and U.S. trade representative Robert Zoellick are under pressure from a variety of constituents. For example, American farmers want assurances that subsidy programs will not be cut back. America's steel producers are concerned about the influx of low-priced steel imports. Meanwhile, in Latin America, opinion polls indicate growing opposition to closer trade ties with the United States. The prospect of improved access to one of the world's most attractive consumer market holds considerable allure for some Latin American nations, particularly Costa Rica and Colombia. However, in other parts of the region, there is a widespread perception that a trade deal would be most beneficial to the United States.

Since World War II, there has been a tremendous interest among nations toward economic cooperation. As we will discuss in this chapter, trade negotiations can be quite broad in scope, resulting in global agreements such as the World Trade Organization (WTO). Conversely, negotiations can be limited to two nations and result in bilateral arrangements such as the new free agreement between the United States and Chile. The regional nature of the FTAA represents a third type of agreement that is narrower in scope than a global arrangement but broader than a bilateral one.

Our survey of the world trade environment begins at the global level with the WTO and its predecessor, the GATT. Next, the four main types of regional and bilateral preferential trade

agreements are identified and described. An introduction to individual countries in the world's major market regions follows; each section also includes detailed discussion of the specific preferential trade agreements in which those countries participate. Important marketing issues in each region are also discussed. Several important emerging country markets were described in Chapter 2; in this chapter, special attention will be given to individual country markets that were not previously discussed.

## THE WORLD TRADE ORGANIZATION AND GATT

The year 1997 marked the fiftieth anniversary of the General Agreement on Tariffs and Trade (GATT), a treaty among nations whose governments agree, at least in principle, to promote trade among members. GATT was intended to be a multilateral, global initiative, and GATT negotiators did indeed succeed in liberalizing world merchandise trade. GATT was also an organization that handled 300 trade disputes—many involving food—during its half century of existence. GATT itself had no enforcement power (the losing party in a dispute was entitled to ignore the ruling), and the process of dealing with disputes sometimes stretched on for years. Little wonder, then, that some critics referred to GATT as the "General Agreement to Talk and Talk."

The successor to GATT, the World Trade Organization (WTO), came into existence on January 1, 1995. From its base in Geneva, the WTO provides a forum for trade-related negotiations among its 147 members. The WTO's staff of neutral trade experts also serve as mediators in global trade disputes. The WTO has a Dispute Settlement Body (DSB) that mediates complaints concerning unfair trade barriers and other issues between the WTO's member countries. During a 60-day consultation period, parties to a complaint are expected to engage in good-faith negotiations and reach an amicable resolution. Failing that, the complainant can ask the DSB to appoint a three-member panel of trade experts to hear the case behind closed doors. After convening, the panel has 9 months within which to issue its ruling. The DSB is empowered to act on the panel's recommendations. The losing party has the option of turning to a seven-member appellate body. If, after due process, a country's trade policies are found to violate WTO rules, it is expected to change those policies. If changes are not forthcoming, the WTO can authorize trade sanctions against the loser. Table 3-1 lists some recent cases that have been brought to the WTO.

| Countries Involved in Dispute | Nature of Dispute | **Table 3-1** |
| --- | --- | --- |
| United States; European Union | In 2002, U.S. President Bush imposed 30 percent tariffs on a range of steel imports for a period of 3 years. The EU lodged a protest, and in 2003, the WTO ruled that the tariffs were illegal. President Bush responded by lifting the tariffs. | *Recent WTO Cases* |
| European Union; Philippines and Thailand | In 2002, the EU imposed 24 percent tariffs on canned tuna imports from the Philippines and Thailand but granted imports from former Africa, Caribbean, and Pacific (ACP) colonies duty-free status. Dispute was resolved in 2003 when Philippines and Thailand agreed to minimum access volumes of tuna exports to EU. | |
| United States; European Union | In 1999, the United States imposed tariffs on select imports from the EU in retaliation for the EU's policy of giving preference to bananas imported from ACP countries. WTO ruled in favor of the United States; in 2001, the EU agreed to revise its import scheme, and the United States lifted the tariffs. | |

Trade ministers representing the WTO member nations meet annually to work on improving world trade. It remains to be seen whether the WTO will live up to expectations when it comes to additional major policy initiatives on such vexing issues as foreign investment and agricultural subsidies. One problem is that politicians in many countries are resisting the WTO's plans to move swiftly in removing trade barriers. A Norwegian trade group told reporters that the WTO's motto should be, "If you can decide it tomorrow, why decide it today?" Still, as Renato Ruggiero, former director general of the WTO, said recently, "Free trade is a process that cannot be stopped."[1] At present, WTO negotiations known as the Doha Development Round are underway; the goal is further reduction of trade barriers.

## PREFERENTIAL TRADE AGREEMENTS

The GATT treaty promotes free trade on a global basis; in addition, countries in each of the world's regions are seeking to liberalize trade within their regions. A **preferential trade agreement** is a mechanism that confers special treatment on select trading partners. By favoring certain countries, such agreements frequently discriminate against others. For that reason, it is customary for countries to notify the WTO when they enter into preference agreements. Over the past 10 years, more than 150 preferential trade agreements have been notified to the WTO. Strictly speaking, few fully conform with WTO requirements; none, however, has been disallowed.

### Free Trade Area

A **free trade area** (FTA) is formed when two or more countries agree to eliminate tariffs and other barriers that restrict trade. A free trade area comes into being when trading partners successfully negotiate a **free trade agreement** (also abbreviated FTA), the ultimate goal of which is zero duties on goods that cross borders

---

[1]  Helene Cooper and Bhushan Bahree, "No 'Gattzilla': World's Best Hope for Global Trade Topples Few Barriers," *The Wall Street Journal* (December 3, 1996), p. A8.

| Table 3-2 | United States | Chile |
|---|---|---|
| *Free Trade Agreements* | Canada and Mexico (North American Free Trade Agreement or NAFTA) | Canada |
| | Jordan | Mexico |
| | Israel | European Union |
| | Singapore | South Korea |
| | Chile | United States |
| | El Salvador, Guatemala, Honduras, Nicaragua (Central American Free Trade Agreement or CAFTA) | Bolivia |
| | Morocco | |
| | South Africa, Botswana, Lesotho, Namibia, and Swaziland (Southern Africa Free Trade and Development Agreement or SAFTDA) | |
| | Australia | |
| | Vietnam | |

between the partners. In some instances, duties are eliminated on the day the agreement takes effect; in other cases, duties are phased out over a set period of time. Countries that belong to an FTA can maintain independent trade policies with respect to third countries. **Rules of origin** are used to discourage the importation of goods into the member country with the lowest external tariff for transshipment to one or more FTA members with higher external tariffs; customs inspectors police the borders between members. For example, because Chile and Canada established an FTA in 1997, a Canadian-built Caterpillar grader tractor imported into Chile would not be subject to duty. If the same piece of equipment were imported from a factory in the United States, the importer would pay about $13,000 in duties. Could Caterpillar send the U.S.-built tractor to Chile by way of Canada, thereby allowing the importer to avoid paying the duty? No, because the tractor would bear a "Made in the U.S.A." certificate of origin indicating it was subject to the duty. Little wonder, then, that the United States government negotiated its own bilateral free trade agreement with Chile that entered into force in 2003.

To date, dozens of free trade agreements, many of them bilateral, have been successfully negotiated; for example, Mexico has free trade agreements with 31 countries. Table 3-2 lists free trade agreements that the United States and Chile have, respectively, established with other countries. Additional examples of FTAs include the European Economic Area, a free trade area that includes the 25-nation European Union plus Norway, Liechtenstein, and Iceland; the Group of Three (G3), an FTA encompassing Colombia, Mexico, and Venezuela; and the Closer Economic Partnership Agreement (CEPA), a free trade agreement between China and Hong Kong.

## Customs Union

A **customs union** represents the logical evolution of a free trade area. In addition to eliminating internal barriers to trade, members of a customs union agree to the establishment of **common external tariffs (CETs)**. On January 1, 1996, the European Union (EU) and Turkey initiated a customs union in an effort to boost two-way trade above the average annual level of $20 billion. The arrangement called for elimination of tariffs averaging 14 percent that added $1.5 billion each year to the cost of European goods imported by Turkey. Other customs unions discussed in this chapter are the Andean Community, the Central American Integration System (SICA), Mercosur, and CARICOM.

# the rest of the story

## FTAA

Former U.S. President Bill Clinton first formally proposed the idea for a hemispheric free trade area in 1994 during a summit of heads of state in Miami. Meeting in Brazil in May 1997, trade ministers from the 34 participating countries agreed to create "preparatory committees" in anticipation of formal talks that would begin in 1998. The Clinton administration was keen to open the region's fast-growing, big emerging markets to U.S. companies. In particular, the president wanted talks to focus immediately on tariffs and "early harvest" agreements on individual industry sectors such as information technology. The FTAA was formally launched in April 1998 during the second Summit of the Americas in Santiago, Chile.

After President George W. Bush took office, he viewed FTAA as one aspect of a multilevel approach to trade issues. Bush also hoped to pursue bilateral agreements between the United States and individual nations as well as global negotiations within the framework of the World Trade Organization. Prospects for the latter had been dimmed somewhat by the disastrous global trade talks in Seattle in the fall of 1999; protesters succeeded in disrupting the event.

The Canadian government went to unprecedented lengths to ensure security during the 2001 Summit of the Americas meeting in Quebec City, spending about $100 million on the effort. The meeting venue was enclosed by a 2.3 mile concrete and chain-link fence that demonstrators called the "Wall of Shame." As thousands of labor and environmental activists gathered behind barricades, Mexican President Vicente Fox, Brazilian President Henrique Cardoso, and their colleagues hoped for a clear signal from President George W. Bush that the United States was serious about free trade. One positive sign: The U.S. Congress granted the president trade promotion authority (TPA). TPA enables the president to negotiate trade agreements, which Congress then has to vote on without making any changes or amendments.

Opposition to the FTAA has been strongest in Brazil, despite the fact that its textile industry stands to benefit greatly if U.S. import quotas are lifted. By contrast, Brazil's paper and chemical industries could be severely hurt by strong American competitors. Executives in these and other industries have pleaded with the Brazilian government for more time to improve productivity and marketing. In some circles, a preference has been expressed for a trade pact with the European Union.

The 2003 summit ended with the United States and Brazil agreeing to a draft declaration. Celso Amorim, Brazil's foreign minister, noted, "Things are moving in the right direction." Representatives of American companies disagreed. The declaration reduced the scope of the trade deal so that minimum common rights and obligations would be agreed on while giving individual nations leeway about whether or not to make additional commitments. A representative for the National Association of Manufacturers said that a "low quality" agreement was not worth having.

*Sources: David Luhnow, "Latin America Looks Hard at U.S.," The Wall Street Journal (November 28, 2003), p. A15; Guy de Jonquières, "US Business Lobby Groups Unhappy at 'Low-Quality' FTAA Compromise," Financial Times (November 20, 2003), p. 6; "All in the Familia," The Economist (April 21, 2001), pp. 19–21; "Breaking Barriers in the Americas," The Economist (April 21, 2001), p. 14; Jonathan Karp, "Brazil to Be Vocal in Americas Trade Talks," The Wall Street Journal (April 19, 2001), p. A13; Kenneth Maxwell, "Brazil's Free Traders Are in Dire Need of a U.S. Boost," The Wall Street Journal (April 6, 2001), p. A15.*

## Common Market

A **common market** is the next level of economic integration. In addition to the removal of internal barriers to trade and the establishment of common external tariffs, the common market allows for free movement of factors of production, including labor, capital, and information. The Andean Community and the Central American Integration System (SICA), which currently function as customs unions, may ultimately evolve into true common markets.

## Economic Union

An **economic union** builds upon the elimination of the internal tariff barriers, the establishment of common external barriers, and the free flow of factors. It seeks to coordinate and harmonize economic and social policy within the union to facilitate the free flow of capital, labor, and goods and services from country to country. An economic union is a common marketplace not only for goods but also for services and capital. For example, if professionals are going to be able to work anywhere in the EU, the members must harmonize their practice licensing so that a doctor or lawyer qualified in one country may practice in any other. The full evolution of an economic union would involve the creation of a unified central bank, the use of a single currency, and common policies on agriculture, social services and welfare, regional development, transport, taxation, competition, and mergers.

**Table 3-3**

*Forms of Regional Economic Integration*

| Stage of Integration | Elimination of Tariffs and Quotas Among Members | Common External Tariff (CET) and Quota System | Elimination of Restrictions on Factor Movements | Harmonization and Unification of Economic and Social Policies and Institutions |
|---|---|---|---|---|
| Free Trade Area | Yes | No | No | No |
| Customs Union | Yes | Yes | No | No |
| Common Market | Yes | Yes | Yes | No |
| Economic Union | Yes | Yes | Yes | Yes |

A true economic union requires extensive political unity, which makes it similar to a nation. The further integration of nations that were members of fully developed economic unions would be the formation of a central government that would bring together independent political states into a single political framework. The European Union is approaching its target of completing most of the steps required to become a full economic union. The various forms of regional economic integration are compared in Table 3-3.

# behind the scenes

## A Half Century of Trade Negotiation

Between 1947 and 1994, the member countries of GATT completed eight rounds of multilateral trade negotiations. Tariffs have been reduced from an average of 40 percent in 1945 to 5 percent today. The result has been a tremendous growth in trade: In the three decades from 1945 to 1975, the volume of world trade expanded by roughly 500 percent. The seventh round of negotiations was launched in Tokyo and ran from 1973 to 1979. These talks succeeded in cutting duties on industrial products valued at $150 billion by another 30 percent so that the remaining tariffs averaged about 6 percent. In terms of agricultural trade, there was a major clash between the United States and protectionist European and Japanese markets. The clash pitted the American farmer—the world's most efficient producer—against the high-cost, but politically powerful, farmers of Europe and Japan. These deep-rooted differences resulted in little change in the agricultural area during the Tokyo round. The most notable feature of the Tokyo round was not the duty cuts, but rather a series of nine new agreements on nontariff trade barriers.

GATT officials also devoted considerable attention to the services industry, addressing market-entry barriers in banking, insurance, telecommunications, and other sectors. The services issue was so volatile that the opening of the Uruguay round was delayed from 1982 until 1986. In addition to trade in services, these negotiations focused on the aforementioned nontariff measures that restrict or distort trade, including agricultural trade policy, intellectual property protection, and restrictions on foreign investment.

Agricultural subsidies and quotas that developed outside the multilateral framework have also been a divisive issue. Affluent countries protect and subsidize farm production. While home-market consumers pay higher prices, surplus output is sold abroad at artificially low prices. Sugar subsidies in the European Union cost European shoppers an estimated $7.5 billion extra because high sugar prices result in higher prices for ice cream, soft drinks, and candy bars. In France, government expenditures for agricultural subsidies in 1992

amounted to $44 billion; French consumers paid an additional $85 billion for higher-priced food products. According to the Organization for Economic Cooperation and Development (OECD) the total cost of these subsidies to rich-country taxpayers and consumers is more than $200 billion a year. Poor countries (including those in Eastern Europe) are denied their natural path out of poverty, namely food exports. The Uruguay negotiations were suspended in December 1990 after 30,000 French farmers took to the streets of Brussels to protest a proposed 30 percent cut in agricultural export subsidies. Negotiations resumed a few months later against the background of the united Western war effort in the Persian Gulf war. Negotiators finally succeeded in reaching agreement by the December 15, 1993, deadline. A stalemate over agricultural subsidies was broken, with France and the EU nations agreeing to reductions. The U.S. Congress voted in favor of GATT at the end of 1994.

Competitive companies will benefit as tariffs are cut or eliminated entirely. The Triad nations agreed to end tariffs in pharmaceuticals, construction and agricultural equipment, scotch whiskey, furniture, paper, steel, and medical equipment. Also, U.S. restrictions on textile and apparel imports from Third World countries will be phased out over a 10-year period. Another breakthrough was the Chemical Tariff Harmonization Agreement (CTHA), whose signatories agreed to reduce tariffs on chemicals to a maximum of 6.5 percent. Major issues remain unresolved in the entertainment industry; France has insisted on preferences and subsidies for French producers of television programming and motion pictures in order to limit what they feel is "cultural imperialism." Efforts to reduce European broadcast restrictions on U.S.-produced movies and television programming were unsuccessful.

*Sources: Shailagh Murray, "Subsidies Shackle EU Competitiveness," The Wall Street Journal (October 28, 1996), p. A13; "GATT's Last Gasp," The Economist (December 1, 1990), p. 16; Joseph A. McKinney, "How Multilateral Trade Talks Affect the U.S.," Baylor Business Review (Fall 1991), pp. 24–25; Bob Davis, "Squeaky Wheels: GATT Talks Resume, with France and India Calling Many of the Shots," The Wall Street Journal (January 31, 1992), pp. A1, A13; "Free Trade's Fading Champion," The Economist (April 11, 1992), p. 65; Davis and Lawrence Ingrassia, "Trade Acceptance: After Years of Talks, GATT Is at Last Ready to Sign Off On a Pact," The Wall Street Journal (December 15, 1993), pp. A1, A7.*

# NORTH AMERICA

North America, which includes Canada, the United States, and Mexico, comprises a distinctive regional market. The United States combines great wealth, a large population, vast space, and plentiful natural resources in a single national economic and political environment and thus presents unique marketing characteristics. High product ownership levels are associated with high income and relatively high receptivity to innovations and new ideas both in consumer and industrial products. The United States is home to more global industry leaders than any other nation in the world. For example, U.S. companies are the dominant producers in the computer, software, aerospace, entertainment, medical equipment, and jet engine industry sectors.

In 1988, the United States and Canada signed a free trade agreement (U.S.-Canada Free Trade Agreement, or CFTA); the Canada-U.S. Free Trade Area formally came into existence in 1989. This helps explain the fact that almost $400 billion per year in goods and services flows between Canada and the United States, the biggest trading relationship between any two single nations. Canada takes 20 percent of U.S. exports and the United States buys approximately 85 percent of Canada's exports. Figure 3-1 illustrates the economic integration of North America: Canada is the number one trading partner of the United States, Mexico is second, and Japan ranks third as a market for U.S. exports in spite of the fact that Mexico's GNP is only 12 percent of Japan's. American companies have more invested in Canada than in any other country. Many U.S. manufacturers, including GE and IBM, use their Canadian operations as major global suppliers for some product lines. By participating in the Canadian auto market, U.S. automakers gain greater economies of scale. The CFTA, which was fully implemented when all duties were eliminated effective January 1998, is creating a true continental market for most other products.

On August 12, 1992, representatives from the United States, Canada, and Mexico concluded negotiations for the **North American Free Trade Agreement (NAFTA).**

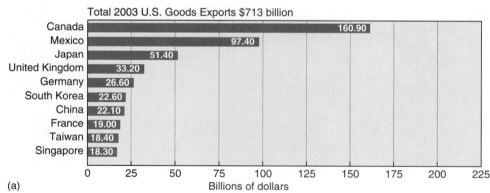

(a)

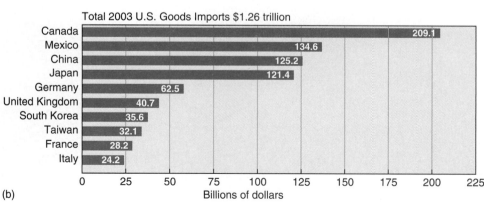

(b)

**Figure 3-1**

*U.S. Trade Partners*

Source: U.S. Bureau of the Census, 2003.

**Table 3-4**

*NAFTA Income and Population*

| | 2003 GNP (in millions) | 2003 Population (in thousands) | 2003 GNP Per Capita |
|---|---|---|---|
| United States | $10,580,779 | 288,361 | $36,693 |
| Canada | 733,604 | 31,870 | 23,018 |
| Mexico | 629,659 | 103,962 | 6,057 |
| **Total/Mean GNP per capita*** | $11,944,042 | 424,193 | $28,157* |

Source: Reprinted by permission of Warren Keegan Associates, Inc., 2003.

The agreement was approved by both houses of the U.S. Congress and became effective on January 1, 1994. The result is a free trade area with a combined population of roughly 425 million and a total GNP of $11.9 trillion (see Table 3-4 and Figure 3-2).

Why does NAFTA create a free trade area as opposed to a customs union or a common market? The governments of all three nations pledge to promote economic growth through tariff elimination and expanded trade and investment. At present, however, there are no common external tariffs nor have restrictions on labor and other factor movements been eliminated. The issue of illegal immigration from Mexico into the United States remains a contentious one. The benefits of continental free trade will enable all three countries to meet the economic challenges of the decades to come. The gradual elimination of barriers to the flow of goods, services, and investment, coupled with strong protection of intellectual property rights (patents, trademarks, and copyrights), will further benefit businesses, workers, farmers, and consumers.

The agreement does leave the door open for discretionary protectionism, however. For example, California avocado growers won government protection for a market worth $250 million; Mexican avocado growers can only ship their

**Figure 3-2**

*NAFTA Countries*

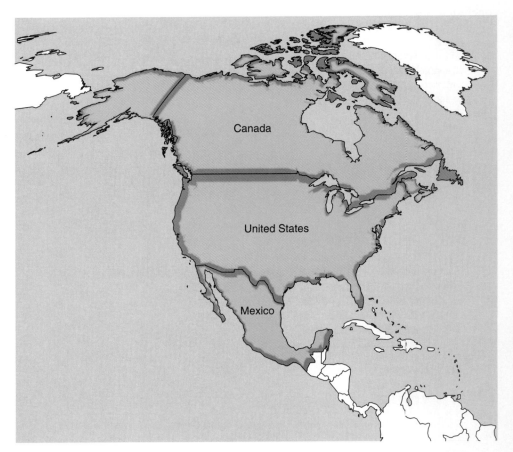

fruit to the United States during the winter months, and only to states in the northeast. Moreover, Mexican avocados are subject to quotas, so only $30 million worth of avocados reach the United States each year. Mexican farmer Ricardo Salgado complained, "The California growers want to control all of the supply—that way they get the best prices. We'd love to have a bigger selling season, but right now we have to wait for the U.S. Congress to give us permission."[2] Mexico engages in some protectionism of its own; for example, in 2003, a 98.8 percent tariff was imposed on chicken leg quarters beyond the first 50,000 metric tons imported. In addition, Mexico imposed a 46.6 percent tariff on red and golden delicious apples.

# LATIN AMERICA: SICA, ANDEAN COMMUNITY, MERCOSUR, CARICOM

Latin America includes the Caribbean and Central and South America (because of NAFTA, Mexico is grouped with North America). The allure of the Latin American market has been its considerable size and huge resource base. After a decade of no growth, crippling inflation, increasing foreign debt, protectionism, and bloated government payrolls, the countries of Latin America have begun the process of economic transformation. Balanced budgets are a priority and privatization is underway. Free markets, open economies, and deregulation have begun to replace the policies of the past. With the exception of Cuba, democratically elected governments are found throughout Latin America. Policy makers have recognized the benefits of free-market forces and the advantages of participating fully in the global economy. In many countries, tariffs that sometimes reached as much as 100 percent or more have been lowered to 10 to 20 percent. Global corporations are watching developments closely. They are encouraged by import liberalization, the prospects for lower tariffs within subregional trading groups, and the potential for establishing more efficient regional production. Many observers envision a free trade area throughout the hemisphere. The four most important preferential trading arrangements in Latin America are the Central American Integration System (SICA), the Andean Community, the Common Market of the South (Mercosur), and the Caribbean Community and Common Market (CARICOM).

## Central American Integration System

Central America is trying to revive its common market, which was set up in the early 1960s. The five original members—El Salvador, Honduras, Guatemala, Nicaragua, and Costa Rica—decided in July 1991 to reestablish the Central American Common Market (CACM) by 1994. Efforts to improve regional integration gained momentum with the granting of observer status to Panama. Between 1994 and 1996, the volume of intra-regional trade grew from $1.1 billion to $1.6 billion. In 1997, with Panama as a member, the group's name was changed to the Central American Integration System (Sistema de la Integración Centroamericana or SICA).

The Secretariat for Central American Economic Integration, headquartered in Guatemala City, is charged with helping to coordinate the movement toward a Central American common market. Common rules of origin were also adopted, allowing for freer movement of goods among current SICA countries. SICA countries agreed to conform to a common external tariff (CET) of 5 to 20 percent for most goods by the mid-1990s; many tariffs had previously exceeded 100 percent. For example, the Costa Rican government had previously benefited from the revenues generated by triple-digit tariffs on automobiles imported from Japan and elsewhere. As a practical

---

[2]  Joel Millman, "Bitter Fruit: Spats Persist Despite NAFTA," *The Wall Street Journal* (June 19, 2000), p. A23.

**Figure 3-3**

SICA Countries

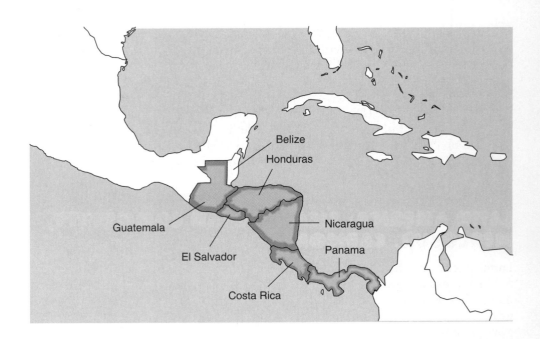

matter, there was considerable variation in tariff rates until the end of the 1990s. Starting in 2000, import duties charged by the five SICA members converged to a range of 0 to 15 percent. Still, the region's attempts to achieve integration have been described as uncoordinated, inefficient, and costly. There are still tariffs on imports of products—sugar, coffee, and alcoholic beverages, for example—that are also produced in the importing country. As one Guatemalan analyst remarked, "Only when I see Salvadoran beer on sale in Guatemala and Guatemalan beer on sale in El Salvador will I believe that trade liberalization and integration is a reality."[3] The SICA group is shown in Figure 3-3; income and population data are in Table 3-5.

## Andean Community

The Andean Community (formerly the Andean Pact; see Figure 3-4 and Table 3-6) was formed in 1969 to accelerate development of member states Bolivia, Colombia, Ecuador, Peru, and Venezuela through economic and social integration. Members agreed to lower tariffs on intra-group trade and work together to decide what products each country should produce. At the same time, foreign goods and companies were kept out as much as possible. One Bolivian described the unfortunate result of

**Table 3-5**

SICA Income and Population

|  | 2003 GNP (in millions) | 2003 Population (in thousands) | 2003 GNP Per Capita |
|---|---|---|---|
| Costa Rica | $16,688 | 4,068 | $4,102 |
| El Salvador | 15,009 | 6,602 | 2,273 |
| Guatemala | 21,697 | 12,332 | 1,759 |
| Honduras | 6,405 | 6,992 | 916 |
| Nicaragua | 2,367 | 5,541 | 427 |
| Panama | 10,386 | 3,004 | 3,457 |
| **Total/Mean GNP per capita*** | **$72,552** | **38,539** | **$1,882*** |

*Source:* Reprinted by permission of Warren Keegan Associates, Inc., 2003.

---

3    Johanna Tuckman, "Central Americans Start to Act Together," *Financial Times* (July 9, 1997), p. 4.

**Figure 3-4**

*The Andean Community and Mercosur*

this lack of competition in the following way: "We had agreed, 'You buy our over-priced goods and we'll buy yours.'"[4]

In 1988, the group members decided to get a fresh start. Beginning in 1992, the Andean Pact signatories agreed to form Latin America's first operating subregional free trade area. More than 100 million consumers would be affected by the pact, which abolished all foreign exchange, financial and fiscal incentives, and export subsidies at the end of 1992. Common external tariffs were established, marking the transition to a true customs union. The new approach yielded some successes; for example, Peru now boasts one of the fastest-growing economies in the region. Ecuador, meanwhile, has experienced years of economic and political instability. In

| | 2003 GNP (in millions) | 2003 Population (in thousands) | 2003 GNP Per Capita |
|---|---|---|---|
| Bolivia | $9,010 | 8,865 | $1,016 |
| Colombia | 88,446 | 44,625 | 1,982 |
| Ecuador | 13,449 | 13,499 | 996 |
| Peru | 59,255 | 27,152 | 2,182 |
| Venezuela | 136,165 | 25,952 | 5,247 |
| **Total/Mean GNP per capita*** | **$306,325** | **120,093** | **$2,551*** |

*Source:* Reprinted by permission of Warren Keegan Associates, Inc., 2003.

**Table 3-6**

*Andean Community Income and Population*

---

[4] "NAFTA Is Not Alone," *The Economist* (June 18, 1994), pp. 47–48.

2000, in an attempt to bring rampant inflation under control, the government adopted the U.S. dollar as Ecuador's official currency (see Case 3-1). Overall, rural residents and the urban poor in the region have become frustrated and impatient with the lack of progress. As one Andean scholar put it, "After 10 or 15 years of operating with free-market policies, paradise hasn't come. People start wondering if the gospel was as good as advertised."[5]

## Common Market of the South (Mercosur)

March 2001 marked the tenth anniversary of the signing of the Asunción Treaty. With this action, the governments of Argentina, Brazil, Paraguay, and Uruguay agreed to form the Common Market of the South (Mercado Comun del Sur or Mercosur; see Figure 3-4 and Table 3-7). The presidents of the four countries had agreed to begin phasing in tariff reform on January 1, 1995. Internal tariffs were eliminated, and CETs of up to 20 percent were established. In theory, goods, services, and factors of production will ultimately move freely throughout the member countries; until this goal is achieved, however, Mercosur will actually operate as a customs union rather than a true common market. Today, about 90 percent of goods are traded freely; however, individual members of Mercosur can change both internal and external tariffs when it suits the respective government. For example, Argentina and Brazil maintained separate internal tariff barriers on cars and trucks for several years. Also, Argentina was allowed to break from the CET and raise duties on consumer goods in response to its recent financial crisis.

Much depends on the successful outcome of this experiment in regional cooperation. The early signs were positive, as trade between the four full member nations grew from $4.2 billion in 1990 to peak at $20 billion in 1998. Brazil and Argentina must work well together if increased integration is to take place in the region. By mid-1996, more than 150 joint ventures had been formed between companies in Argentina and Brazil. A major impediment to further integration is the lack of economic and political discipline and responsibility, a situation reflected in the volatility of currencies in the Mercosur countries. For example, in early 1995, much to the dismay of the other three Mercosur members Brazil devalued its currency; the real was devalued again in 1999. In the 1990s, Argentina's currency was pegged to the U.S. dollar. However, by the end of the decade Argentina's economy had become mired in recession and concern mounted that the country might default on $130 billion in foreign debt. In January 2002, economy minister Jorge Remes Lenicov announced emergency measures that included a 29 percent currency devaluation for exports and capital transactions.

In 1996, Chile became an associate member of Mercosur. Policy makers opted against full membership because Chile already had lower external tariffs than the

| | 2003 GNP (in millions) | 2003 Population (in thousands) | 2003 GNP Per Capita |
|---|---|---|---|
| Argentina | $312,086 | 38,381 | $8,131 |
| Bolivia[a] | 9,010 | 8,865 | 1,016 |
| Brazil | 622,603 | 178,190 | 3,494 |
| Chile[a] | 78,882 | 15,906 | 4,959 |
| Paraguay | 8,497 | 5,919 | 1,436 |
| Uruguay | 21,366 | 3,408 | 6,270 |
| **Total/Mean GNP per capita*** | **$1,052,444** | **250,669** | **$4,198*** |

**Table 3-7**

*Mercosur Income and Population*

[a]Associate members that participate in free trade area only.
*Source:* Reprinted by permission of Warren Keegan Associates, Inc., 2003.

<hr/>

[5]   Marc Lifsher, "The Andean Arc of Instability," *The Wall Street Journal* (February 24, 2003), p. A13.

Chile's winemakers are gaining international acclaim; quality has increased dramatically as wines that were once produced for local consumption only are crafted to appeal to discerning palates around the globe. ProChile, an agency of the Ministry of Foreign Affairs, spends about $3 million annually on print advertising in export markets. Because Chile's climate is ideally suited for grape growing, the country has attracted a great deal of foreign investment. For example, Robert Mondavi recently established a 50/50 partnership with Vina Errazuriz.

rest of Mercosur; ironically, full membership would have required raising them. (In other words, Chile participates in the free-trade-area aspect of Mercosur, not the customs union.) Chile had been negotiating for inclusion in NAFTA; however, after Mexico's trade deficit with the United States turned into a trade surplus following the peso crisis, Washington's interest in expanding NAFTA cooled. Chile's export-driven success makes it a role model for the rest of Latin America as well as Central and Eastern Europe. Like Chile, Bolivia is an associate member of Mercosur. Mercosur member countries recently agreed to merge with the Andean Community. The EU is Mercosur's number one trading partner; Mercosur has signed an agreement with the European Union to establish a free trade area by 2005. Germany and France are opposed to such an agreement on the grounds that low-cost agricultural exports will harm farmers in Europe.

# OPEN *to* discussion

## Are Free Trade Areas Really Discriminatory Trade Agreements?

Despite the increasing willingness of many nations to enter into trade agreements, some observers are disturbed by the trend. For example, Columbia University professor Jagdish Bhagwati calls NAFTA, Mercosur, and similar agreements a "spaghetti bowl" that represent "a pox on the world trading system." Professor Bhagwati's concern is that regional trade preferences are discriminatory. They can result in diversion of imports away from cheaper country sources toward more expensive country sources that are signatories to a given agreement. For example, one researcher has concluded that the added cost to Mexico of buying goods and services from its NAFTA partners amounts to more than $3 billion annually.

Professor Bhagwati is not the only critic of trade agreements. An executive at the World Bank noted, "Our view is it's easy to get overly enthusiastic about preferential trade agreements. They might confer significant benefits, but there are also very significant dangers." In a 1996 report, World Bank economist Alexander Yeats acknowledged that Mercosur has generated

a great deal of trade and investment; the problem is that much intra-Mercosur trade is in cars, agricultural machinery, and other industry sectors for which the four full-trading partners are inefficient producers. Efficient foreign producers that would like to export to Mercosur are deterred because of tariffs and quotas. Meanwhile, Mercosur partners buy goods from each other at prices that do not reflect global competition. In particular, because Mercosur's auto producers are uncompetitive, exports to countries outside of the customs union have suffered. Yeats' conclusion: Mercosur distorts international trade.

According to an opposing viewpoint, Mercosur has not become a fortress. Edward Hudgins of the Cato Institute attributes Mercosur's reduced exports to Western Europe to the fall of communism. Western European countries have stepped up trade with their neighbors to the east, partly at the expense of Mercosur.

*Sources: Jagdish Bhagwati, "Short on Trade Vision," Financial Times (June 3, 1997), p. 12; Edward L. Hudgins, "Mercosur Gets a 'Not Guilty' on Trade Diversion," The Wall Street Journal (March 21, 1997), p. A19; Martin Wolf, "Fast Track to Nowhere," Financial Times (November 11, 1997), p. 19; Wolf, "An Unhealthy Trade-off," Financial Times (October 29, 1996), p. 14; Michael M. Phillips, "South American Trade Pact Is Under Fire," The Wall Street Journal (October 23, 1996), pp. A2, A4.*

# Caribbean Community and Common Market (CARICOM)

**CARICOM** was formed in 1973 as a movement toward unity in the Caribbean. It replaced the Caribbean Free Trade Association (CARIFTA) founded in 1965. The members are Antigua and Barbuda, Bahamas, Barbados, Belize, Dominica, Grenada, Guyana, Haiti, Jamaica, Montserrat, St. Kitts and Nevis, St. Lucia, St. Vincent and the Grenadines, and Trinidad and Tobago. The population of the entire 15-member CARICOM is about 15 million; disparate levels of economic development can be seen by comparing GNP per capita in Antigua and Barbuda with that of Haiti (see Table 3-8).

To date, CARICOM's main objective has been to achieve a deepening of economic integration by means of a Caribbean common market. During the 1980s, the economic difficulties of member states hindered the development of inter-regional trade. Another problem concerned applying rules of origin to verify that imported goods genuinely come from within the community. As a result, CARICOM was largely stagnant during its first two decades of existence. At its annual meeting in July 1991, member countries agreed to speed integration; a customs union was established with common external tariffs. At the 1998 summit meeting, leaders from the 15 countries agreed to move quickly to establish an economic union with a common currency. A recent study of the issue has suggested, however, that the limited extent of intra-regional trade would limit the potential gains from lower transaction costs.[6]

If achieved, such actions would qualify CARICOM for membership in the proposed Free Trade Area of the Americas (FTAA) in 2005. CARICOM nations could join if the original 1973 treaty were revised. As Owen Arthur, prime minister of Barbados explained, "The old treaty limited the movement of capital, skills, and business in the region. The treaty has to be changed so that regional trade policy can be widened to deal with the FTAA and the EU, and such matters as bilateral investments treaties, intellectual property rights, and trade in services."[7]

| Table 3-8 | | 2003 GNP (in millions) | 2003 Population (in thousands) | 2003 GNP Per Capita |
|---|---|---|---|---|
| CARICOM Income and Population | Antigua and Barbuda | $703 | 69 | $10,218 |
| | Bahamas | 4,856 | 317 | 15,327 |
| | Barbados | 2,674 | 278 | 9,897 |
| | Belize | 888 | 258 | 3,445 |
| | Dominica | 262 | 73 | 3,582 |
| | Grenada | 413 | 99 | 4,178 |
| | Guyana | 688 | 891 | 891 |
| | Haiti | 4,300 | 8,421 | 511 |
| | Jamaica | 7,844 | 2,705 | 2,900 |
| | Montserrat | na | 12 | na |
| | St. Kitts and Nevis | 313 | 44 | 7,192 |
| | St. Lucia | 753 | 166 | 4,546 |
| | St. Vincent & Grenadines | 351 | 122 | 2,876 |
| | Suriname | 871 | 444 | 1,962 |
| | Trinidad and Tobago | 7,111 | 1,332 | 5,337 |
| | **Total/Mean GNP per capita*** | **$32,027[a]** | **15,231** | **$2,113[a]*** |

[a]Excluding Montserrat.
*Source:* Reprinted by permission of Warren Keegan Associates, Inc., 2003.

---

6  Myrvin L. Anthony and Andrew Hughes Hallett, "Is the Case for Economic and Monetary Union in the Caribbean Realistic?" *World Economy* 23, no. 1 (January 2000), pp. 119–144.
7  Canute James, "Caribbean Community Grapples with Challenge of Creating a Single Market," *Financial Times* (July 10, 1998), p. 7.

**Figure 3-5**

CARICOM

The English-speaking CARICOM members in the eastern Caribbean are also concerned with defending their privileged trading position with the United States. That status dates to the Caribbean Basin Initiative (CBI) of 1984, which promoted export production of certain products by providing duty-free U.S. market access to 20 countries, including members of CARICOM. Guatemala quickly attracted manufacturers based in Taiwan and South Korea and subsequently became the region's leading exporter of apparel to the United States.[8] Unfortunately for CARICOM, the Enterprise for the Americas Initiative—with the Mexican free trade agreement as its centerpiece—has overtaken the CBI as the flagship U.S. trade policy in the area. In response to the situation, the CBI members requested that the CBI be expanded and its members granted the same trade privileges that are available to Mexico. The Caribbean Basin Trade Partnership Act, which went into effect on October 1, 2000, exempts textile and apparel exports from the Caribbean to the United States from duties and tariffs. (Students studying in the United States take note: Check the labels on your school's sports apparel. Chances are they read "Made in Guatemala," "Assembled in El Salvador," etc.) CARICOM is shown in Figure 3-5.

## Current Trade-Related Issues

One of the biggest issues pertaining to trade in the Western Hemisphere is the Free Trade Area of the Americas (FTAA). As noted earlier, leaders in many Latin American countries—Brazil in particular—are frustrated by what they perceive as America's failure to follow through on its promises in the region. As a result, Brazil and its Mercosur partners are advocating a slower, three-stage approach to negotiations. The first stage would include discussions on business facilitation issues such as standardized customs forms and industry deregulation; the second would focus on dispute settlement and rules of origin; and the third would focus on tariffs. Meanwhile, Mercosur, CARICOM, SICA, and the Andean Community intend to pursue further integration among themselves as well as with Europe.

---

[8] Lucy Martinez-Mont, "Sweatshops Are Better Than No Shops," *The Wall Street Journal* (June 25, 1996), p. A14.

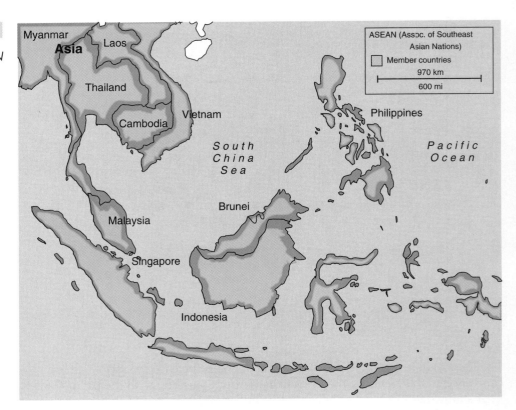

**Figure 3-6**

ASEAN

## ASIA-PACIFIC: The Association of Southeast Asian Nations (ASEAN)

The Association of Southeast Asian Nations (ASEAN) is the flagship preferential trade agreement in the Asia-Pacific area, although Japan is not a member. ASEAN was established in 1967 as an organization for economic, political, social, and cultural cooperation among its member countries. The United States, which at the time was embroiled in the Vietnam War, played a role in establishing ASEAN with the signing of the Bangkok Declaration. Brunei, Indonesia, Malaysia, the Philippines, Singapore, and Thailand were the original six members. Vietnam became the first Communist nation in the group when it was admitted to ASEAN in July 1995. Cambodia and Laos were admitted to ASEAN at the organization's thirtieth anniversary meeting in July 1997 (see Figure 3-6 and Table 3-9). Burma (known as

**Table 3-9**

ASEAN Income and Population

| | 2003 GNP (in millions) | 2003 Population (in thousands) | 2003 GNP Per Capita |
|---|---|---|---|
| Brunei | na | 363 | na |
| Cambodia | $3,673 | 12,983 | $283 |
| Indonesia | 165,143 | 220,033 | 751 |
| Laos | 1,933 | 5,752 | 336 |
| Malaysia | 95,379 | 24,840 | 3,840 |
| Myanmar | na | 50,226 | na |
| Philippines | 91,819 | 80,442 | 1,141 |
| Singapore | 112,261 | 4,226 | 26,562 |
| Thailand | 139,545 | 62,941 | 2,217 |
| Vietnam | 36,285 | 85,305 | 425 |
| **Total/Mean GNP per capita*** | $646,038[a] | 547,111 | $1,180*,[a] |

[a]Excluding Brunei and Myanmar.
Source: Reprinted by permission of Warren Keegan Associates, Inc., 2003.

Myanmar by the ruling military junta) joined in 1998, following delays related to the country's internal politics and human rights record.

Individually and collectively, ASEAN countries are active in regional and global trade. ASEAN's top trading partners include the United States ($52.8 billion in 2002 exports), the European Union ($48 billion in 2002 exports), and China ($23 billion in 2002). A few years ago, ASEAN officials realized that broad common goals and perceptions were not enough to keep the association alive. A constant problem was the strict need for consensus among all members before proceeding with any form of cooperative effort. Although the ASEAN member countries are geographically close, they have historically been divided in many respects. One of the reasons the association remained in existence is that for many years it accomplished almost nothing. The situation is changing today, however; in 1994, economic ministers from the member nations agreed to implement an ASEAN Free Trade Area (AFTA) by 2003, 5 years earlier than previously discussed. Under the agreement, tariffs of 20 percent have been reduced to 0 to 5 percent; in the oldest ASEAN members, tariffs will fall to 0 by 2010. In 2002, intra-ASEAN trade surpassed $80 billion. That same year, China and ASEAN signed agreements that will create a free trade area by 2010. Although the action was opposed by some, China's dynamic growth and increasing power in the region required a response. As ASEAN secretary general Rodolfo Severino noted, "You can either close yourself off from China and crouch in fear or engage more closely. Although some industries will get hurt, the overall impact on both China and ASEAN would be beneficial."[9]

Singapore represents a special case among the ASEAN nations. In fewer than three decades, Singapore has transformed itself from a British colony to a vibrant, 240-square-mile industrial power. Singapore has an extremely efficient infrastructure—the Port of Singapore is the world's second-largest container port (Hong Kong's ranks first)—and a standard of living second in the region only to Japan's. Singapore's 4.2 million citizens have played a critical role in the country's economic achievements by readily accepting the notion that "the country with the most knowledge will win" in global competition. Excellent training programs and a 97 percent literacy rate help explain why Singapore has more engineers per capita than the United States. Singapore's Economic Development Board has also actively recruited business interest in the nation. The manufacturing companies that have been attracted to Singapore read like a "who's who" of global marketing and include Hewlett-Packard, IBM, Philips, and Apple Computer; in all, more than 3,000 companies have operations or investments in Singapore.

Singapore alone accounts for more than one-third of U.S. trading activities with ASEAN countries; U.S. exports to Singapore in 2003 totaled $16.5 billion, while imports totaled $15.1 billion. Singapore's efforts to fashion a civil society have gained the country some notoriety; crime is nearly nonexistent, thanks to the government's severe treatment of criminals. Some people in the United States objected after an American youth living in Singapore was sentenced to a caning after being arrested and convicted of vandalism. Singaporeans believe the United States has given individuals too many liberties; in Singapore, the interests of society take precedence over those of the individual.

## Marketing Issues in the Asia-Pacific Region

Mastering the Japanese market takes flexibility, ambition, and a long-term commitment. Japan has changed from being a closed market to one that's just tough. There are barriers in Japan in terms of attitudes as well as laws. Any organization wishing to compete in Japan must be committed to providing top-quality products and

---

[9] Amy Kazmin, "ASEAN and China Sign Deal for Free Trade Area," *Financial Times* (November 5, 2002), p. 6.

services. In many cases, products and marketing must be tailored to local tastes. Countless visits and socializing with distributors are necessary to build trust. Marketers must also master the *keiretsu* system of tightly knit corporate alliances. All of these factors served as a backdrop to the trade dispute between Japan and the United States that escalated in mid-1995. In an effort to pry open Japan's market for auto parts, the U.S. government threatened to impose stiff tariffs on Japanese luxury car imports.

India's huge population base also presents attractive opportunities. Several automakers—including Suzuki, Hyundai, General Motors, and Ford—are present in the market. Other companies currently investing in India are DuPont, Fujitsu, IBM, Unilever, and Coca-Cola. However, the political climate remains volatile. The nationalistic Bharatiya Janata Party (BJP) has been a vocal and powerful opponent of reform; in 2004, the BJP was ousted in national elections and the left-leaning Congress party came to power. Manmohan Singh, India's former finance minister and the architect of the country's economic reforms, is the new prime minister. Financial markets reacted negatively to uncertainty over India's future direction; as one analyst put it, "This feels like the Asia crisis and the Mexico crisis times again."[10]

## WESTERN, CENTRAL, AND EASTERN EUROPE

The countries of Western Europe are among the most prosperous in the world. Despite the fact that there are significant differences in income between the north and the south and obvious differences in language and culture, the once-varied societies of Western Europe have grown remarkably alike. Still, enough differences remain that many observers view Western Europe in terms of three tiers. Many Britons view themselves as somewhat apart from the rest of the continent; Euro-skepticism is widespread, and the country still has problems seeing eye-to-eye with historic rivals Germany and France. Meanwhile, across the English Channel, Portugal, Italy, Greece, and Spain have struggled mightily to overcome the stigma of being called "Club Med" nations and other derogatory nicknames by their northern neighbors.[11] Still, as they enter the first decade of the twenty-first century, the governments of Western Europe are achieving unprecedented levels of economic integration.

## The European Union (EU)

The origins of the European Union (EU) can be traced back to the 1958 Treaty of Rome. The six original members of the European Community (EC), as the group was called then, were Belgium, France, Holland, Italy, Luxembourg, and West Germany. In 1973, Great Britain, Denmark, and Ireland were admitted, followed by Greece in 1981, and Spain and Portugal in 1986. Beginning in 1987, the 12 countries that were EC members set about the difficult task of creating a genuine single market in goods, services, and capital; in other words, an economic union. Adopting the Single European Act by the end of 1992 was a major EC achievement; the Council of Ministers adopted 282 pieces of legislation and regulations to make the single market a reality.

---

[10] Daniel Pearl, "In India, Other Firms Feel Enron's Pain," *The Wall Street Journal* (July 5, 2001), p. A8; see also Jonathan Karp and Kathryn Kranhold, "Power Politics: Enron's Plant in India Was Dead; This Month, It Will Go On Stream," *The Wall Street Journal* (February 5, 1999), pp. A1, A6.

[11] Thomas Kamm, "Snobbery: The Latest Hitch in Unifying Europe," *The Wall Street Journal* (November 6, 1996), p. A17; Kyle Pope, "More Than Water Divides U.K., Europe," *The Wall Street Journal* (June 30, 1995), p. A12.

| | 2003 GNP (in millions) | 2003 Population (in thousands) | 2003 GNP Per Capita | |
|---|---|---|---|---|
| Austria | $198,532 | 8,232 | $24,116 | Table 3-10a |
| Belgium | 244,510 | 10,345 | 23,637 | |
| Denmark | 172,416 | 5,368 | 32,119 | *EU Income and Population Prior to May 1, 2004* |
| Finland | 132,379 | 5,255 | 25,191 | |
| France | 1,400,852 | 59,780 | 23,434 | |
| Germany | 1,996,350 | 83,140 | 24,012 | |
| Greece | 122,513 | 10,719 | 11,429 | |
| Ireland | 91,534 | 3,817 | 23,982 | |
| Italy | 1,128,687 | 58,037 | 19,448 | |
| Luxembourg | 18,478 | 451 | 40,947 | |
| Netherlands | 400,453 | 16,159 | 24,782 | |
| Portugal | 114,467 | 10,068 | 11,369 | |
| Spain | 601,866 | 41,881 | 14,371 | |
| Sweden | 240,323 | 9,030 | 26,615 | |
| United Kingdom | 1,530,501 | 60,278 | 25,391 | |
| **Total/Mean GNP per capita*** | **$8,393,861** | **382,560** | **$21,941*** | |

Source: Reprinted by permission of Warren Keegan Associates, Inc., 2003.

The objective of the EU member countries is to harmonize national laws and regulations so that goods, services, people, and eventually money can flow freely across national boundaries. December 31, 1992, marked the dawn of the new economic era in Europe. Finland, Sweden, and Austria officially joined on January 1, 1995. (In November 1994, voters in Norway rejected a membership proposal.) Evidence that this is more than a free trade area, customs union, or common market is the fact that citizens of the member countries are now able to freely cross borders within the union. The EU is encouraging the development of a community-wide labor pool; it is also attempting to shake up Europe's cartel mentality by handing down rules of competition patterned after U.S. antitrust law. Improvements to highway and rail networks are now being coordinated as well.

Further EU enlargement is the big story in this region today. In December 1991, Czechoslovakia, Hungary, and Poland became associate members through the so-called "European Agreements." Cyprus, the Czech Republic, Estonia, Hungary, Poland, Latvia, Lithuania, Malta, the Slovak Republic, and Slovenia became full EU members on May 1, 2004. Today, the 25 nations of the EU represent 458 million people and a combined GNP of $8.8 trillion (see Table 3-10 a and b). The map in Figure 3-7 shows the EU membership.

| | 2003 GNP (in millions) | 2003 Population (in thousands) | 2003 GNP Per Capita | |
|---|---|---|---|---|
| Cyprus | $9,906 | 782 | $12,664 | Table 3-10b |
| Czech Republic | 54,651 | 10,304 | 5,304 | |
| Estonia | 5,186 | 1,373 | 3,777 | *Ten Newest EU Members* |
| Hungary | 48,147 | 10,022 | 4,804 | |
| Latvia | 7,615 | 2,393 | 3,182 | |
| Lithuania | 12,329 | 3,762 | 3,277 | |
| Malta | 4,007 | 398 | 10,060 | |
| Poland | 181,019 | 39,233 | 4,614 | |
| Slovak Republic | 21,110 | 5,467 | 3,861 | |
| Slovenia | 20,325 | 2,000 | 10,163 | |
| **Total/Mean GNP per capita*** | **$364,295** | **75,734** | **$6,170*** | |

Source: Reprinted by permission of Warren Keegan Associates, Inc., 2003.

**Figure 3-7**

*The EU*

Ten newest members

During the two decades between 1979 and 1999, the European Monetary System (EMS) was an important foundation of Western European commerce. The EMS was based on the European Currency Unit (ECU), a unit of account comprised of a hypothetical basket of "weighted" currencies. The ECU did not take the form of an actual currency; it existed physically in the form of checks and electronically in computers. Some companies priced their raw materials and products in ECU, thereby saving the time and cost of exchange transactions. The 1991 **Maastricht Treaty** set the stage for the transition from the EMS to an economic and monetary union (EMU) that includes a European central bank and a single European currency known as the **euro**. In May 1998, Austria, Belgium, Finland, Ireland, the Netherlands, France, Germany, Italy, Luxembourg, Portugal, and Spain were chosen as the 11 charter members of the **euro zone**. Greece became the twelfth member in January 2001. The single currency era, which officially began on January 1, 1999, is expected to bring many benefits to companies in the euro zone such as eliminating costs associated with currency conversion and exchange rate uncertainty. The euro existed as a unit of account until 2002, when actual coins and paper money were issued and national currencies such as the French franc were withdrawn from circulation.

## The European Free Trade Area (EFTA) and European Economic Area (EEA)

Since 1990, the EU has concluded more than 20 trade pacts with other nations. For example, in October 1991, the then-EC and the seven-nation European Free Trade Association (EFTA) reached agreement on the creation of the European

Economic Area (EEA) beginning January 1993. The ultimate goal is to achieve the free movement of goods, services, capital, and labor between the two groups, but the EEA is a free trade area, not a customs union with common external tariffs. With Austria, Finland, and Sweden now members of the EU, Norway, Iceland, and Liechtenstein are the only remaining EFTA countries that are not EU members (Switzerland voted not to be part of the EEA). The three non-EU members of the new EEA are expected to adopt all the EU's single-market legislation. Meanwhile, the four members of EFTA (Norway, Iceland, Liechtenstein, and Switzerland) maintain free trade agreements with Israel and Turkey as well as nations in Central and Eastern Europe. EFTA also has cooperation agreements with Morocco, Tunisia, and Egypt.

## Marketing Issues in the European Union

The European Commission establishes directives and sets deadlines for their implementation by legislation in individual nations. The business environment in Europe has undergone considerable transformation since 1992, with significant implications for all elements of the marketing mix. Table 3-11 summarizes some of the marketing mix issues that must be addressed in Europe's single market. For example, content and other product standards that varied among nations have been harmonized. As a result, companies may have an opportunity to reap economies by cutting back on the number of product adaptations. Case Europe, for example, manufactures and markets farm machinery. When it introduced the Magnum tractor in Europe in 1988, it offered 17 different versions because of country regulations regarding placement of lights and brakes. Thanks to harmonization, Case offers the current model, the Magnum MX, in one version. However, because different types of implements and trailers are used in different countries, the MX is available with different kinds of hitches.[12] The advent of the euro on January 1, 1999, brought about more changes. Direct comparability of prices in the euro zone will force companies to review pricing policies. The marketing challenge is to develop strategies to take advantage of opportunities in one of the largest, wealthiest, most stable markets in the world. Corporations must assess the extent to which they can treat the region as one entity and how to change organizational policies and structures to adapt to and take advantage of a unified Europe.

The music industry is a case in point; long before online music distribution and MP3 file swapping had become issues, the major record companies faced a number of challenges. The single market meant that, for the first time, music retailers in Europe were allowed to buy CDs and tapes from distributors throughout the EU. This practice, known as *transshipment*, had not been permitted prior to the single market. Now, for example, a music retailer in Germany is no longer tied to a local supplier in Germany if better prices are available elsewhere. The change means that Sony, Warner, Bertelsmann, EMI, and the other major record companies have been forced to adopt more uniform pricing policies across Europe. This, in turn, has required them to find ways to cut costs without compromising the need to respond quickly to consumer demand. One solution has been to realign distribution via joint ventures or other arrangements; previously, each company had maintained its own distribution system. In 1998, however, Warner and Sony merged their distribution facilities in the United Kingdom.[13]

---

[12] George Russel, "Marketing in the 'Old Country': The Diversity of Europe Presents Unique Challenges," *Agri Marketing* 37, no. 1 (January 1999), p. 38.

[13] Jeff Clark-Meads, "The Year in Europe: Union Members Confront Parallel Imports and Universes," *Billboard* 107 (December 23, 1995), p. YE14; Alice Rawsthorn, "Music's 'Big Five' Dip Toes in Common Distribution Pool," *Financial Times* (August 14, 1998), p. 60.

**Table 3-11**

*Marketing Strategies in the European Union*

| | Changes Affecting Strategies | Threats to Marketers' Planning | Management's Strategic Options |
|---|---|---|---|
| **Product Strategies** | Harmonization in product standards, testing, and certification process<br>Common patenting and branding<br>Harmonization in packaging, labeling, and processing requirements | Incorporating changes mandated by EC directives<br>Complying with rules of origin<br>Local content rules<br>Differences in marketing research | Consolidate production<br>Seek marketing economies<br>Shift from brand to benefit segmentation<br>Standardize packaging and labeling where possible |
| **Pricing Strategies** | More competitive environment<br>Lifting of restrictions on foreign products<br>Antimonopoly measures<br>Opening up of the public procurement market | Parallel importing<br>Different taxation of goods<br>Less freedom in setting transfer prices | Exploit different excise and value-added taxes<br>Understand price elasticity of consumer demand<br>Emphasize high-margin products<br>Introduce low-cost brand |
| **Promotion Strategies** | Common guidelines on TV broadcasting<br>Deregulation of national broadcasting monopolies<br>Uniform standards for TV commercials | Restrictions on alcohol and tobacco advertising<br>Limits on foreign TV production<br>Differences in permissible promotional techniques | Coordinate components of promotional mix via Integrated Marketing Communications (IMC)<br>Exploit advantage of pan-European media<br>Position products according to local market preferences |
| **Distribution Strategies** | Simplification of transit documents and procedures<br>Elimination of customs formalities | Increase in distributors' margins<br>Lack of direct marketing infrastructure<br>Restrictions in the use of computer databases | Consolidate manufacturing facilities<br>Centralize distribution<br>Develop nontraditional channels (direct marketing, telemarketing) |

*Source:* Reprinted from G. Guido, "Implementing a Pan-European Marketing Strategy," *Long Range Planning* 5 (1991), p. 32. With permission from Elsevier.

The enlargement of the EU will further impact marketing strategies. For example, food safety laws in the EU are different from those in some Central European countries. As a result, Coca-Cola had to delay launching its Powerade sports drink and other beverage products. Specifically, Polish and EU food law require the use of different ingredients. In addition to the harmonization of laws, the very size of the expanded EU offers opportunities. For example, Procter & Gamble executives foresee that, in the event of shortages in a particular country, they will be able to shift products from one market to another. A 25-nation EU also allows for more flexibility in the placement of factories. There will also be challenges. For example, South American banana growers now face 75 percent tariffs on exports to the new EU countries; previously, tariffs on bananas were virtually nonexistent. Also, because sugar production in the EU is protected by tariffs and quotas, both consumers and food producers such as Kraft will face rising costs.[14]

---

[14] Scott Miller, "Trading Partners Meet New EU," *The Wall Street Journal* (May 4, 2004), p. A17.

# The Lomé Convention and the Cotonou Agreement

The EU maintains an accord with 71 countries in Africa, the Caribbean, and the Pacific (ACP). The Lomé Convention (named for the capital city of the West African nation of Togo) took effect in 1975. It was designed to promote trade and provide poor countries with financial assistance from a European Development Fund. The ACP signatories generally considered the treaty to be a success, as it allowed for preferential access to the EU for such commodities as sugar, bananas, rum, and rice. However, the WTO has ruled that some of the banana preferences are unfair. Recently, budget pressures at home have prompted some EU nations to push for cuts in Lomé aid. The convention expired in 2000; in June 2000, the EU and ACP nations signed a new 20-year pact known as the Cotonou Agreement. The new convention will be headquartered in the capital of Fiji. Government officials in Cuba have expressed a desire to become part of a post-Lomé arrangement in order to get better prices for sugar exports; Cuba is also interested in joining CARICOM.

# Central European Free Trade Association (CEFTA)

In the early 1990s, the extraordinary political and economic reforms that swept through Central and Eastern Europe focused attention on a new 430-million-person market. The transition in the region from command to market economies—a process that is ongoing today—has toppled a number of entrenched institutions, including the Council for Mutual Economic Assistance. COMECON (or CMEA, as it was also known) was a group of Communist bloc countries allied with the Soviet Union. In the years since COMECON's demise in 1992, a number of proposals for a multilateral cooperation have been advanced. In December 1992, Hungary, Poland, the Czech Republic, and Slovakia signed an agreement creating the Central European Free Trade Association (CEFTA). Slovenia, which declared its autonomy from the Yugoslav federation in 1992, is also a member. The signatories pledged cooperation in a number of areas, including infrastructure and telecommunications; an overriding common goal was to join the EU as a group. As noted earlier, this goal has now been accomplished. Meanwhile, within the Commonwealth of Independent States, formal economic integration between the former Soviet republics is proceeding slowly. In May 1995, the governments of Russia and Belarus agreed to form a customs union and remove border posts between their two countries. Hoping to capitalize on the opportunity to export to Russia without incurring prohibitive tariffs, Ford opened a $10 million vehicle assembly plant outside Minsk.

Because they are in transition, the markets of Central and Eastern Europe present interesting opportunities and challenges. Global companies view the region as an important new source of growth, and the first company to penetrate a country market often emerges as the industry leader. Exporting has been favored as a market entry mode, but direct investment in the region is on the rise; with wage rates much lower than those in Spain, Portugal, and Greece, the region offers attractive locations for low-cost manufacturing. For consumer products, distribution is a critical marketing mix element because availability is the key to sales.

A recent study examined the approaches utilized by 3M International, McDonald's, Philips Electronics, Henkel, Südzucker AG, and several other companies operating in Central Europe. Consumers and businesses in the region are eagerly embracing well-known global brands that were once available only to government elites and others in privileged positions. The study found a high degree of standardization of marketing program elements; in particular, the core product and brand elements were largely unchanged from those used in Western Europe. Consumer companies generally target high-end segments of the market and focus on brand image and product quality; industrial marketers concentrate on opportunities to do business with the largest firms in a given country.[15]

## THE MIDDLE EAST

The Middle East includes 16 countries: Afghanistan, Bahrain, Cyprus, Egypt, Iran, Iraq, Israel, Jordan, Kuwait, Lebanon, Oman, Qatar, Saudi Arabia, Syria, the United Arab Emirates, and the reunited Yemen. The majority of the population is Arab, a large percentage is Persian, and a small percentage is Jewish. Persians and most Arabs share the same religion, beliefs, and Islamic traditions, making the population 95 percent Muslim and 5 percent Christian and Jewish.

Despite this apparent homogeneity, many differences exist. Middle Eastern countries fall into all categories of the index of economic freedom discussed in Chapter 2, including "mostly free" (e.g., Bahrain, United Arab Emirates, Kuwait and Qatar), "mostly unfree" (e.g., Saudi Arabia), and "repressed" (Iran and, until the 2003 regime change, Iraq). Moreover, the Middle East does not have a single societal type with a typical belief, behavior, and tradition. Each capital and major city in the Middle East has a variety of social groups that can be differentiated on the basis of religion, social class, education, and degree of wealth.

Business in the Middle East is driven by the price of oil. Seven of the countries have high oil revenues: Bahrain, Iraq, Iran, Kuwait, Oman, Qatar, and Saudi Arabia hold significant world oil reserves. Oil revenues have widened the gap between poor and rich nations in the Middle East, and the disparities contribute to political and social instability in the area. Saudi Arabia, a monarchy with 22 million people and 25 percent of the world's known oil reserves, remains the most important market in this region.

In the past, the region was characterized by pan-Arabism, a form of nationalism and loyalty that transcended borders and amounted to anti-Western dogma. During the Persian Gulf in the early 1990s, this pan-Arabism weakened somewhat. To defeat Iraq, the Gulf Arabs and their allies broke many of their unwritten rules including accepting help from the United States, a traditional ally of Israel. However, anti-Americanism was ignited in 2003 following President George W. Bush's decision to invade Iraq and remove Saddam Hussein from power. The repercussions of America's military action continue to be felt throughout the region. The world community is watching to see whether political and social reform can take root in Iraq.

## Cooperation Council for the Arab States of the Gulf

The key regional organization is the Gulf Cooperation Council (GCC), which was established in 1981 by Bahrain, Kuwait, Oman, Qatar, Saudi Arabia, and the United Arab Emirates (Table 3-12 and Figure 3-8). These six countries hold about 45 percent of the world's known oil reserves, but production is only about 18 percent of world oil output. Ironically, Saudi Arabia and several other Middle Eastern countries post current-account deficits, largely because they must import most of the goods and services that their citizens consume. The countries are heavily dependent on oil revenues to pay for their imports; efforts toward economic diversification are underway. For example, Saudi Arabia has developed new businesses in the petrochemical, cement, and iron industries; Bahrain is expanding its banking and insurance sectors;

---

[15] Arnold Shuh, "Global Standardization as a Success Formula for Marketing in Central Eastern Europe," *Journal of World Business* 35, no. 2 (Summer 2000), pp. 133–148.

Table 3-12

GCC Income and Population

| | 2003 GNP (in millions) | 2003 Population (in thousands) | 2003 GNP Per Capita |
|---|---|---|---|
| Bahrain | $8,426 | 755 | $11,160 |
| Kuwait | 48,420 | 2,044 | 23,688 |
| Oman | na | 2,663 | na |
| Qatar | na | 664 | na |
| Saudi Arabia | 189,760 | 22,121 | 8,578 |
| United Arab Emirates | na | 3,174 | na |
| **Total/Mean GNP per capita*** | **246,606** | **31,421** | |

Excludes Oman, Qatar, and United Arab Emirates.
*Source:* Reprinted by permission of Warren Keegan Associates, Inc., 2003.

and the United Arab Emirates is focusing on information technology, media, and telecommunications.[16]

The organization provides a means of realizing coordination, integration, and cooperation in all economic, social, and cultural affairs. Gulf finance ministers drew up an economic cooperation agreement covering investment, petroleum, the abolition of customs duties, harmonization of banking regulations, and financial and monetary coordination. GCC committees coordinate trade development in the region, industrial strategy, agricultural policy, and uniform petroleum policies and prices. Current goals include establishing an Arab common market and increasing trade ties with Asia.

The GCC is one of three newer regional organizations. In 1989, two other organizations were established. Morocco, Algeria, Mauritania, Tunisia, and Libya banded together in the Arab Maghreb Union (AMU); Egypt, Iraq, Jordan, and North Yemen created the Arab Cooperation Council (ACC). Many Arabs see their new regional

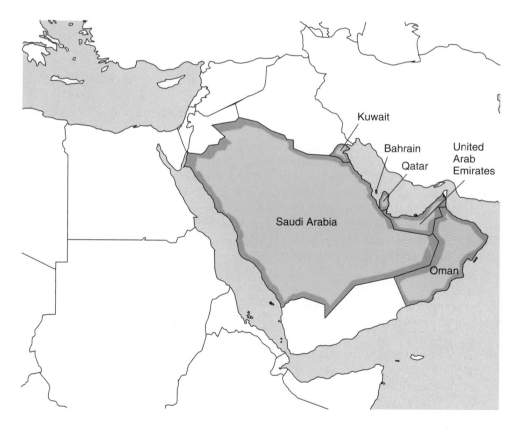

**Figure 3-8**

The GCC Countries

---

[16] Moin A. Siddiqi, "GCC: A Force to Be Reckoned With," *Middle East* (December 2003).

groups—the GCC, ACC, and AMU—as embryonic economic communities that will foster the development of inter-Arab trade and investment. The newer organizations are more promising than the Arab League, which consists of 21 member states and has a constitution that requires unanimous decisions.

## Marketing Issues in the Middle East

*Connection* is a key word in conducting business in the Middle East. Those who take the time to develop relationships with key business and government figures are more likely to cut through red tape than those who do not. A predilection for bargaining is culturally ingrained, and the visiting businessperson must be prepared for some old-fashioned haggling. Establishing personal rapport, mutual trust, and respect are essentially the most important factors leading to a successful business relationship. Decisions are usually not made by correspondence or telephone. The Arab businessperson does business with the individual, not with the company. Most social customs are based on the Arab male-dominated society. Women are usually not part of the business or entertainment scene for traditional Muslim Arabs.

## AFRICA

The African continent is an enormous landmass with a territory of 11.7 million square miles; the United States would fit into Africa about three and a half times. It is not really possible to treat Africa as a single economic unit. The 54 nations on the continent can be divided into three distinct areas: the Republic of South Africa, North Africa, and sub-Saharan or Black Africa, located between the Sahara in the north and the Zambezi River in the south. With 1.3 percent of the world's wealth and 11.5 percent of its population, Africa is a developing region with an average per capita income of less than $600. Many African nations are former colonies of Europe, and the EU remains the continent's most important trading partner.

The Arabs living in North Africa are differentiated politically and economically. The six northern nations are richer and more developed, and several—notably Libya, Algeria, and Egypt—benefit from large oil resources. The Arab states have been independent for a longer period than have the black African nations. The Middle East and North Africa are sometimes viewed as a regional entity known as "Mena." Since oil prices slumped in the 1980s, the region has been marked by slow economic growth. Most governments are working to reduce their reliance on oil revenues and their public aid levels. The economies of non-oil "emerging Mena" countries, which include Jordan, Lebanon, Morocco, and Tunisia, have performed best in recent years.[17]

## Economic Community of West African States (ECOWAS)

The Treaty of Lagos establishing the Economic Community of West African States (ECOWAS) was signed in May 1975 by 16 states with the object of promoting trade, cooperation, and self-reliance in West Africa. The members are Benin,

---

[17] Roula Khalaf, "World's Slowest Growing Developing Region," *Financial Times, Survey—World Economy and Finance* (September 19, 1997), p. 28.

| | 2003 GNP (in millions) | 2003 Population (in thousands) | 2003 GNP Per Capita |
|---|---|---|---|
| Benin | $2,418 | 6,794 | $356 |
| Burkina Faso | 2,457 | 12,212 | 201 |
| Cape Verde | 626 | 467 | 1,342 |
| Côte d'Ivoire | 9,973 | 17,498 | 570 |
| The Gambia | 434 | 1,457 | 298 |
| Ghana | 5,666 | 20,912 | 271 |
| Guinea | 228 | 8,032 | 28 |
| Guinea-Bissau | 3,297 | 1,265 | 2,606 |
| Liberia | na | 3,331 | na |
| Mali | 2,542 | 11,742 | 217 |
| Mauritania | 1,023 | 2,853 | 358 |
| Niger | 2,027 | 11,871 | 171 |
| Nigeria | 41,193 | 137,872 | 299 |
| Senegal | 4,821 | 10,323 | 467 |
| Sierra Leone | 673 | 5,261 | 128 |
| Togo | 1,344 | 4,932 | 273 |
| **Total/Mean GNP per capita*** | **$78,722[a]** | **256,822** | **$306[a]*** |

**Table 3-13**

ECOWAS Income and Population

[a]Excludes Liberia.

Source: Reprinted by permission of Warren Keegan Associates, Inc., 2003.

Burkina Faso, Cape Verde, Côte d'Ivoire, The Gambia, Ghana, Guinea, Guinea-Bissau, Liberia, Mali, Mauritania, Niger, Nigeria, Senegal, Sierra Leone, and Togo (see Table 3-13 and Figure 3-9). In 1980, the member countries agreed to establish a free trade area for unprocessed agricultural products and handicrafts. Tariffs on industrial goods were also to be abolished; however, there were implementation delays. By January 1990, tariffs on 25 items manufactured in ECOWAS member states had been eliminated. The organization installed a computer system to process customs and trade statistics and to calculate the loss of revenue resulting from the liberalization of inter-community trade. In June 1990, ECOWAS adopted measures that would create a single monetary zone in the region by 1994. Despite such achievements, economic development has occurred unevenly in the region. In recent years, the economies of Benin, Côte d'Ivoire and Ghana have performed impressively, while Liberia and Sierra Leone are still experiencing political conflict and economic decline.

## East African Cooperation

In 1996, the presidents of Kenya, Uganda, and Tanzania established a formal mechanism to promote free trade and economic integration. Tariff issues will be resolved and prospects for a customs union are being explored. Efforts are also underway to develop regional ties in tourism and coordinate energy projects. Although Kenya is the most developed of the three nations, Francis Muthaura, the executive secretary of the secretariat of the Commission of East African Cooperation, expressed optimism that all three will benefit. "A free market is going to generate competition and already we are seeing a lot of cross-border investment. If you have free movement of capital and goods and labor, imbalances will be sorted out in the long term."[18]

---

[18] Michael Holman, "Learning from the Past," *Financial Times Survey* (November 5, 1996), p. 1.

**Figure 3-9**

ECOWAS and SADC Countries

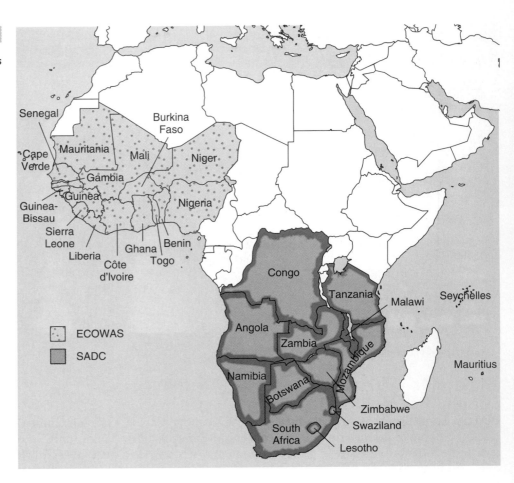

## Southern African Development Community (SADC)

In 1992, the SADC superseded the South African Development Coordination Council as a mechanism by which the region's black-ruled states could promote trade, cooperation, and economic integration. The members are Angola, Botswana, Democratic Republic of Congo (formerly Zaire), Lesotho, Malawi, Mauritius, Mozambique, Namibia, South Africa, Seychelles, Swaziland, Tanzania, Zambia, and Zimbabwe (see Figure 3-9 and Table 3-14). South Africa joined the community in 1994; it represents about 75 percent of the income in the region and 86 percent of intra-regional exports. The SADC's ultimate goal is a fully developed customs union; in 2000, an 11-nation free trade area was finally established (Angola, the DRC, and Seychelles are not participants). South Africa has been in discussions with the European Union about the formation of a free trade area; other SADC members are concerned that such an arrangement would provide European global companies with a base from which to dominate the continent. South Africa, Botswana, Lesotho, Namibia, and Swaziland also belong to the Southern African Customs Union (SACU). Another concern is war in the Congo, which threatens to have a severe impact on economic growth in the region.[19]

---

[19] Tony Hawkins and Michael Holman, "Trade Tensions Send Southern Africa Regional Link-Up Reeling," *Financial Times* (September 2, 1998), p. 4.

# OPEN *to* discussion

## An American Trade Bill with Africa

In March 1998, U.S. President Bill Clinton toured six African nations in an effort to promote the region's political and economic accomplishments to the American people. The tour came just days after the U.S. House of Representatives passed the African Growth and Opportunities Act. Keyed to a theme of "Trade, not Aid," the bill's sponsors intended to support nations that had made significant progress toward economic liberalization. The bill would make it easier for African nations to gain access to financing from the U.S. Export-Import Bank; it also represented a formal step toward a U.S.-Africa free trade area. One of the bill's key provisions granted textile and apparel manufacturers in Kenya and Mauritius free access to the American market on up to $3.5 billion in exports each year. As Benjamin Kipkorir, Kenya's ambassador to the United States, observed, "Every country that has industrialized, starting from England in the eighteenth century, began with textiles. We'd like to do the same thing."

Under the Agreement on Textiles and Clothing negotiated during the Uruguay Round of GATT negotiations, global textile quotas will be eliminated in 2005. Nevertheless, the textile provision in the bill is proving to be controversial. The United States imports about $50 billion in textiles and apparel each year, much of it from Asia, Latin America, and Africa. Wary legislators from textile-producing U.S. states fear job losses among their constituents if the bill becomes law. The bill's opponents point out that, by the mid-1990s, dozens of Asian companies had established operations in Kenya to take advantage of quota-free exports to the United States. Kenya's flourishing textile export industry eventually caught the attention of U.S. officials, who imposed import restrictions. As a result, dozens of companies shut down and 10,000 Kenyans lost their jobs.

More generally, there is concern that the act will not, in fact, "create a transition path from development assistance to economic self-reliance." One especially harsh critic is Representative Jesse Jackson Jr., who voted against the act. In a letter to *The Wall Street Journal*, he wrote:

> In my view, this bill will not benefit the common people of Africa or America, black or white. It will benefit multinational corporations operating in the global economy, but not African-American or American workers. Protection of African workers' rights, assurance of safe working conditions, prohibition of child labor or sweatshop conditions, and protection of the African environment are markedly absent. . . . The bill will force 48 subSaharan African nations into a straitjacket of economic austerity and deepening poverty in order to benefit transnational financial institutions, wealthy investors, and large corporations.

Beyond the ethical concerns expressed by Representative Jackson, other questions have been raised about general prospects for improved trade with Africa. Communications are unreliable, the overall infrastructure remains underdeveloped, and basic legal protections for businesses are lacking. Exporters and importers quickly learn that the cost of moving freight, including port charges and air transport rates, are much higher than in Asia. Import barriers remain high in many nations. Although some observers believe that Africa is poised for an era of growth similar to that in Asia, others feel that such comparisons are not justified.

*Sources: Robert Block and Michael K. Frisby, "Clinton Tour Aims to Sell New Image of Africa," The Wall Street Journal (March 20, 1998), p. A13; Tony Hawkins and Michael Holman, "Clinton Talks Up Africa's Prospects for Investment," Financial Times (March 31, 1998), p. A10; Michael M. Phillips, "Some Blacks Are Torn by Africa Trade Bill," The Wall Street Journal (March 11, 1998), pp. A2, A8; Nicholas D. Kristof, "Why Africa Can Thrive Like Asia," The New York Times (May 25, 1997), sec. 4, pp. 1, 4; Phillips, "U.S. is Seeking to Build Its Trade with Africa," The Wall Street Journal (June 2, 1996), p. A1; Phillips, "U.S. Rethinks Trade Policy with Africa," The Wall Street Journal (July 15, 1996), p. A2.*

| | 2003 GNP (in millions) | 2003 Population (in thousands) | 2003 GNP Per Capita |
|---|---|---|---|
| Angola | $5,343 | 14,144 | $378 |
| Botswana | 6,058 | 1,740 | 3,481 |
| DR of Congo | 5,218 | 55,672 | 94 |
| Lesotho | 1,327 | 2,179 | 609 |
| Malawi | 1,922 | 11,234 | 171 |
| Mauritius | 4,892 | 1,215 | 4,027 |
| Mozambique | 4,082 | 18,609 | 219 |
| Namibia | 4,015 | 1,898 | 2,116 |
| Seychelles | 651 | 84 | 7,781 |
| South Africa | 135,976 | 45,421 | 2,994 |
| Swaziland | 1,704 | 1,139 | 1,497 |
| Tanzania | 10,106 | 36,713 | 275 |
| Zambia | 3,014 | 10,865 | 277 |
| Zimbabwe | 7,782 | 13,638 | 571 |
| **Total/Mean GNP per capita*** | **$192,090** | **214,551** | **$895*** |

*Source: Reprinted by permission of Warren Keegan Associates, Inc., 2003.*

**Table 3-14**

*SADC Income and Population*

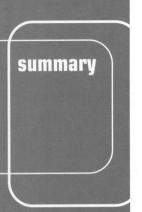
This chapter examines the environment for world trade, focusing on the institutions and regional cooperation agreements that affect trade patterns. The multilateral **World Trade Organization**, created in 1995 as the successor to the General Agreement on Tariffs and Trade, provides a forum for settling disputes among member nations and tries to set policy for world trade. The world trading environment is also characterized by **preferential trade agreements** among smaller numbers of countries on a regional and subregional basis. These agreements can be conceptualized on a continuum of increasing economic integration. **Free trade areas** such as the one created by the North American Free Trade Agreement (NAFTA) represent the lowest level of economic integration. The purpose of a free trade area is to eliminate tariffs and quotas. **Rules of origin** are used to verify the country from which goods are shipped. A **customs union** (e.g., Mercosur) represents a further degree of integration in the form of common external tariffs. In a **common market** such as the Central American Integration System (SICA), restrictions on the movement of labor and capital are eased in an effort to further increase integration. In an **economic union**, such as the European Union (EU), the highest level of economic integration is achieved by unification of economic policies and institutions. Other important cooperation arrangements include the Association of Southeast Asian Nations (ASEAN) and the Cooperation Council for the Arab States of the Gulf (GCC). In Africa, the two main cooperation agreements are the Economic Community of West African States (ECOWAS) and the South African Development Community (SADC).

1. Explain the role of the World Trade Organization.

2. Describe the similarities and differences between a free trade area, a customs union, a common market, and an economic union. Give an example of each.

3. Identify a regional economic organization or agreement in each of the following areas: Latin America, Asia-Pacific, Western Europe, Central Europe, the Middle East, and Africa.

The Inter-American Development Bank (IADB) is the oldest regional development institution for the Western Hemisphere. To learn more about the functions of the IADB and the services it provides, visit the Web site at: **www.iadb.org.**

Several key dates mentioned in the chapter are listed here. Can you identify the event associated with each? (The answers follow.)

December 31, 1992
January 1, 1994
January 1, 1995

January 1, 1999
January 1, 2002
May 1, 2004

**Answers:** *December 31, 1992—Single Market Act goes into effect; January 1, 1994—NAFTA becomes effective; January 1, 1995—GATT is renamed the WTO; January 1, 1999—Introduction of the euro as unit of account; January 1, 2002—Euro currency goes into circulation; May 1, 2004—EU enlargement.*

The American Enterprise Institute, the Institute of International Economics, the Council on Hemispheric Affairs, the Cato Institute, and a number of other think tanks offer analysis and position papers on the FTAA and other trade-related topics. Visit them at:

**www.iie.org**

**www.aei.org**

**www.coha.org**

**www.cato.org**

The secretariat of CARICOM maintains a Web site offering information, publications, and membership information. It can be accessed at:

**www.caricom.org**

There has been considerable grassroots opposition to the FTAA. For a sampling, visit:

**www.globalexchange.com**

**wtoaction.org/ftaa**

**www.stopftaa.org**

**www.corpwatch.org/globalization/treaties**

# Case 3-1

## Ecuador Adopts the Dollar

In January 2000, Ecuador's economy was in shambles. President Jamil Muhuad faced a host of challenges, including interventionist actions by the nation's military, increasing activism by disgruntled indigenous groups, and a government system weakened by years of corrupt practices. Ecuador's economic problems, while a long time in the making, had become acute in the final years of the twentieth century: Between January 1 and December 31, 1999, Ecuador's economy shrank 7.3 percent, the sucre lost 65 percent of its value against the dollar, and inflation reached 60 percent. In 1998, the exchange rate was 7,000 sucre to the dollar, but by 1999, with the sucre in freefall, the exchange rate plunged to 29,000 to the dollar. Ecuador was on the brink of hyperinflation. By March 1999, Ecuador had accumulated an external debt of $13.7 billion—an amount almost equal to its GDP. The state operated 70 percent of the country's banks, and under government orders, most bank deposits were frozen. Nearly two-thirds of the country's banks collapsed due to mismanagement and loan losses. Compounding these problems, flooding caused by El Niño wreaked havoc with an already struggling agricultural sector; meanwhile, world prices for oil, the country's main export, collapsed.

As conditions worsened, pressure increased on Muhuad to take steps to ward off hyperinflation. Muhuad, a Harvard graduate and political centrist, had become Ecuador's president in August of 1998. Dollarization was at the center of his plan to strengthen the economy. Simply stated, dollarization meant that the American dollar would replace the sucre as Ecuador's official currency. On January 9, 2000, when Muhuad announced that the sucre would be replaced with the American dollar, Ecuador became the first South American country to use the greenback. Panama and nine other countries had preceded Ecuador in making the dollar the official currency, but, in the view of many experts, Ecuador's dollarization plan was a test case for other ailing South American economies.

The plan was simple: A 6-month phase-out period began on April 1, 2000, to replace the sucre with the greenback. The change required an estimated $420 million, which the government held in foreign reserves. Each night the Central Bank determined how many sucres were in circulation in banks. The sucre notes were then destroyed and replaced with greenbacks, which were shipped from the Federal Reserve in the United States via heavily armored and guarded jets. The change was to be finalized by March 9, 2001, but by that date, 2 percent of sucres were still in circulation so the date was extended.

The currency conversion was intended to stabilize the economy and curb inflation. Inflation would be slowed because the government could no longer alter interest rates; thus, monetary policy could no longer fuel inflation. Control of inflation would be out of the hands of the nation's policy makers; instead, any changes would reflect decisions by the U.S. Federal Reserve. According to one poll conducted by The

Economist, 59 percent of Ecuadorians supported the change. At a time when the average monthly wage was only $48, the promise of increased wages and stable employment from dollarization seemed attractive. Indeed, many Ecuadorians, especially businesspeople and government officials, already held their assets in dollars rather than sucres and foreign investors had switched to greenbacks at the first sign of trouble. With transactions occurring in American dollars, money could be borrowed at lower U.S. interest rates, which in turn would help attract foreign investors.

However, support for the change was not universal. Ecuador's population includes 3.5 million indigenous people representing more than 20 tribes. Many indigenous Ecuadorians perceive the government as advancing the interests of the wealthy while ignoring the needs of minorities. In short, the indigenous people saw dollarization as one more example of betrayal, as a threat to their national identity, and as another ploy to cover up years of corruption. Many also worried that the change would open the door to increased money laundering and drug trafficking.

Turmoil and tension increased as the political climate in Ecuador heated up. Indigenous groups threatened protests and riots, of which a handful materialized. Many denounced the use of the American dollar and called for the president's resignation. On one occasion in January 2000, police used tear gas to disband a group of protesters. Oil workers joined the protests and went on strike in opposition to Muhuad's reforms. The turning point came soon after when a bloodless coup forced President Muhuad to resign only 12 days after announcing his plan to dollarize. Thousands of poor Indian farmers from the Andean highlands and a group of junior officers and troops led by Colonel Lucio Gutierrez stormed the congress building on January 21, 2000. U.S. officials declared that a military government would not be tolerated; Colonel Gutierrez was arrested and Vice President Gustavo Noboa became the fifth president of Ecuador in as many years. Gutierrez was released after spending 6 months in prison.

Noboa, a 63-year-old former law professor, was quickly recognized as a more adept leader than Muhuad. His presidency had the potential to establish more political stability than his predecessor's because he enjoyed support from several key groups: the businesspeople in Quayaquil, Ecuador's center of commerce; both dominant political groups in the coastal lowlands, the right-wing Social Christian party and the populist Roldosists; and his own Democratic party.

With a new president in office, the question facing Ecuadorians was whether or not Noboa would continue down the path to dollarization. He did. Noboa's reforms centered on privatization of the power, telephone, and oil industries, as well as more flexible labor laws. It was hoped that privatization would lead to more direct foreign investment, increase Ecuador's competitiveness, and revive the economy. Sweeping reforms also included cutting government subsidies as a condition for receiving aid from the International Monetary Fund. The IMF agreed to a $304 million funding program to get Ecuador's economy back on its feet. The IMF's conditions to phase out subsidies doubled public transportation fares and home cooking costs as the prices of fuel, gasoline, and other consumer items rose sharply.

Noboa's accession was also accompanied by hopes for decreasing political risk, uncertainty, and national tensions; however, such hopes were short-lived as indigenous groups continued to protest the new reforms. In April 2000, hundreds of students, union members, and grassroots organizations took to the streets of Quito to protest rising consumer products. Riot police used tear gas after nearly 200 participants threw rocks at them. Elsewhere in the city, more than 300 rioters hijacked 13 public buses. The protesters forced passengers off the buses and then demanded the drivers take the buses to the Central University campus. When all was over, at least 30 students were arrested but no serious injuries were reported. Much of the social unrest could be traced to the 49 percent inflation rate coupled with the $48 per month minimum wage. The average family needed $245 a month for the basic "family basket" but only earned $113.70. By the end of 2000, support for dollarization was waning. One poll showed that 76 percent of Ecuadorians were unhappy with the new currency.

In an interview with the Associated Press, President Noboa declared his intention to "transform Ecuador from a corruption-ridden banana republic to a competitive force in the world market . . . [but the] process is being complicated by competing internal interests and the possibility of spillover from a U.S.-backed drug war in Colombia." In Noboa's view, privatization would be the driving force behind increased exports of oil, coffee, bananas, shrimp, and flowers. Noboa also announced plans to spend money on improving the country's infrastructure with new schools and roads, especially in the Indian areas.

Ecuadorians finally exchanged all of their sucres for dollars on June 9, 2001. Today, Ecuador's 13 million citizens still face high unemployment and poverty rates. Ecuador's economic situation, although still dire, is improving, while many of Ecuador's South American neighbors still struggle. Private foreign investment in Latin America was forecast to drop from $80 billion to $50 billion while the overall GDP for Latin America was expected to fall 1.5 percent. Dollarization has had other benefits for Ecuador's economy as well. Historically, the volume of trade triples between countries that share a currency, so Ecuador stands to gain from increased trade with the United States. Exports to the United States already accounted for 42 percent of Ecuador's foreign trade. By the end of 2001, Ecuador's economy was finally showing a much-needed improvement. Inflation was only 2.5 percent per month compared to 14.3 percent one year earlier. Interest rates were coming down, and banks that had previously been seeking bankruptcy were now solvent again. In fact, Ecuador led Latin America with the highest projected economic growth rate of 2001 and was able to boast that international development had doubled, wages were rising, and unemployment was declining.

In short, Ecuador's economy was finally showing the positive effects of its dollarization program. Broad political support for the dollar now replaced the strong opposition of the prior year. Members of the indigenous groups even acknowledged the benefits of the stability that the dollar brought to their country. Carlos Emanuel, the new minister of the economy, said that the dollarization helped "provide greater security, stability, and better knowledge of costs and it facilitates long-term credits." Despite the positive indicators, however, Ecuador's recovery is far from complete. Much of the improvement in the economy was only making up for the losses suffered in the 1999 collapse. Ecuador's growth is heavily dependent on the rebound in oil prices and remittances into the country.

External trade issues continue to be problematic. In 2001, a dispute between the EU and the United States over banana exports resulted in Ecuador's banana exports declining 15.22 percent from the previous year. As the world's largest exporter of bananas, Ecuador was caught in the middle of an international dispute involving wealthy nations. Although that situation was ultimately resolved, Ecuador faces a new challenge: tariffs and quotas on bananas exported to the 10 new members of the European Union. Poland, the Czech Republic, and the other new members represent a 500,000-ton annual market for bananas; now, a whopping 750 percent tariff will apply to banana exports to the EU beyond 300,000 tons. When the enlargement of the EU went into effect in May 2004, Ecuador supplied 70 percent of Eastern Europe's bananas.

Meanwhile, other South American countries, especially Argentina, Uruguay, and Brazil, are experiencing sliding currencies. Ecuador faces increasing competition from some of its neighbors. For example, Ecuador's flower exports to the United States are now being challenged by Colombian flower exports, and low-priced ceramics from Peru are saturating Ecuador's markets. Declines in the manufacturing sector have resulted in a 14 percent unemployment rate. Economists say the solution lies in investment and increased oil production. Ecuador's inability to compete globally does not stem, however, from the dollarization. Rather, it is an age-old problem.

Ecuador's government is working hard to address the problem. For example, a new $1.1 billion pipeline will link oil reserves in the Amazon to ports on the Pacific Ocean. Formally known as Oledoducto de Crudo Pesado (Heavy Crude Pipeline or OCP), the new project will parallel the existing Trans-Ecuadorian Oil Pipeline (Sistema Oledoducta TransEcuatoriana or SOTE). Each day Ecuador produces 380,000 barrels of oil and exports only 220,000 due to a lack of pipeline capacity. According to some estimates, the pipeline will attract more than $2 billion in foreign investment in oil production and increase exports significantly. However, further development of Ecuador's oil resources is a highly political issue because indigenous people are opposed to the oil companies interfering with the natural habitat. Specifically, opponents of the OCP assert that industry development is destroying the fragile ecosystems in the jungle and interfering with native hunting patterns.

Another problem is the fact that, with cocoa prices and plantings decreasing in many parts of South America, increasing numbers of drug farmers are crossing the border from Colombia and setting up operations in the Ecuadorian jungle. For this reason, a new cocoa-bean tree is being developed specifically for the Andean jungle. The Chocolate Manufacturers Association, the U.S. State Department, and the U.S. Department of Agriculture are collaborating on a program to create strong cocoa trees. Areas where coca plants are currently cultivated to supply the drug trade would be prime locations for growing cocoa. This would be advantageous for both the war on drugs and for the increased exports for Ecuador.

Foreign money is also streaming into Ecuador from a new source: tourism. The influx of visitors has spurred hundreds of tourism-related building projects such as hotels. Ecuador's geographical features include coastal lowlands, the Andes mountain range, the fabled jungles of the Amazon, and the legendary Galapagos Islands. Government officials hope that tourism can be a driving force behind an invigorated economy that is less dependent on oil exports. Environmentalists hope that tourists, anxious to see the pristine jungles and exotic Galapagos Islands, will influence natives to stop destroying the rain forests. One plan calls for lining up investors who will finance the conversion of some vulnerable parts of the rain forest into protected preserves. There are concerns, however, that ecotourism will actually accelerate the area's environmental degradation. Meanwhile, the livelihoods of the twenty thousand Ecuadorians who live on the Galapagos are increasingly dependent on exotic sea species. China's growing demand for shark fins and sea cucumbers is resulting in overfishing. Environmentalists are concerned that Ecuador's environment ministry and parks service are giving in to the demands of the local fishing cooperative.

Ecuador also stands to benefit from the creation of the Free Trade Area of the Americas (FTAA). Many obstacles must be overcome before a hemisphere-wide free trade zone becomes a reality. Some observers doubt that the developed world will extend new trade benefits to Andean nations such as Ecuador until they change current labor conditions and seek to end corruption and drug trafficking. These are problems that Ecuador's policymakers are working to overcome.

The last boost for Ecuador's economy has come in the form of IMF loans directly related to the dollarization program. In 2000, when President Muhuad announced his decision to switch to greenbacks, the IMF offered an emergency loan program including $425 million from the World Bank, $300 million from the IMF, and $620 million from the Inter-American Development Bank. The Corporacion Andina de Fomento pledged another $700 million. Only $900 million was available, however, over the 12-month period that began in March 2000. The funds were designated for social programs to support health, education, and welfare during the dollarization process. IMF loan funds were to be dispersed over a 3-year period.

Ecuador's long-term outlook is still unclear. Inflation that was near 100 percent at the beginning of the new millennium has declined to less than 10 percent. Foreign investment is showing signs of improvement as interest rates fall, making investment cheaper. However, concerns are growing over public expenditures and the pace of economic reforms. Ecuador's current account deficit stood at $1.2 billion in 2002. In November 2002, Lucio Gutierrez was elected president with backing from left-wing and indigenous groups. He spent his first year in office trying to implement a reform agenda in accordance with IMF guidelines. However, Gutierrez' coalition collapsed in August 2003. As Professor Julio Carrión, an Andean expert at the University of Delaware, noted, "After 10 or 15 years of operating with free-market policies, paradise hasn't come. People start wondering if the gospel was as good as advertised."

## Discussion Questions

1. Do you agree with President Muhuad's decision to dollarize Ecuador's economy?

2. What market opportunities does Ecuador offer?

3. What steps should policymakers in Ecuador and other countries take to further decrease the production of crops that supply the drug trade?

4. President Gutierrez must find a way to balance the imperatives of economic development while maintaining a social safety net and preserving Ecuador's unique natural resources. What course of action should he take?

This case was prepared by Research Assistant Katie McCool under the supervision of Professor Mark Green.

Sources: Richard Lapper, "China's Dynamism Puts Galapagos at Risk," Financial Times (May 4, 2004), p. 2; Marc Lifsher, "The Andean Arc of Instability," The Wall Street Journal (February 24, 2003), p. A13; Jill Carroll, "Can Chocolate Help to Fight War on Drugs?" The Wall Street Journal (August 28, 2002), p. B1; Richard Chacon, "With Its Economy Hurting, Ecuador Warily Switches to the Dollar," The Boston Globe (June 1, 2000); Jane Bussey, "Ecuador's Plan to Convert to Dollars Is Simple but Risky, Experts Say," The Miami Herald (January 21, 2000); Dora de Ampueoro, "Ecuador Bounced Back With the Dollar, Argentina Could Too," The Wall Street Journal (November 2, 2001), p. A15; "Ecuador on the Brink," The Economist (January 1, 2000), pp. 33-34; Andres Oppenheimer, "Ecuador's President Discusses Virtues of Dollarization," The Miami Herald (October 13, 2002).

# Case 3-2

## The Euro Yo-yo

Since the inception of the European Monetary Union (EMU) on January 1, 1999, the ups and downs of the euro have created challenges and opportunities for global companies. The euro's volatility has also compounded the economic problems of the 12 countries in the euro zone. The euro began its life as an electronic medium with an exchange rate set at €1 equal to $1.161. Then, the unexpected happened: The euro's value plunged relative to the currencies of Europe's major trading partners. The lowest point came in October 2000, when one euro was worth only about 83 cents. By December, the euro had strengthened to about 97 cents; it then plunged again in mid-2001. Euro coins and bills began to circulate on January 1, 2002, after which the euro began to steadily gain strength. By mid-2003, as the war in Iraq and the ballooning deficit raised concerns about the U.S. economy, the euro's value had strengthened to a monthly average of $1.17.

The euro's volatility forces businesses that export to Europe to think carefully about business strategies and policies. One such company is Markel Corp, a Philadelphia-based manufacturer of cable-control tubing and insulated wire used in the automotive and appliance industries. About 40 percent of Markel's $26 million in sales is generated in Europe; important euro zone customers are located in Spain, the Netherlands, and Germany. In an effort to build up market share, company president Kim Reynolds aims to hold prices steady for Markel's euro zone customers; contracts with euro zone customers call for payment in euros. The strategy is paying off; today, Markel commands about 70 percent of the global market for high-performance tubing. This success came at a cost, however; as the euro plunged in value, Markel's losses mounted. In 2000, the company suffered a currency loss of $650,000; losses in 2001 and 2002 amounted to $400,000 and $225,000, respectively. However, Reynolds hedges his exchange risk by buying forward contracts that guarantee him a set number of dollars for each euro his customers pay. Even so, Reynolds was forced to institute pay cuts for salaried employees and cancel year-end bonuses and dividends to shareholders. The situation has changed dramatically as the euro has gained strength again; in 2003, Reynolds expects a currency gain of up to $500,000.

Policy makers in the 12 euro zone nations are also facing challenges. Here too, an analysis of the Euroland economy must begin by addressing issues related to the currency's volatility. Twelve nations make up Euroland: Germany, France, Spain, Portugal, Luxembourg, the Netherlands, Ireland, Italy, Austria, Finland, Belgium, and Greece. Sweden voted in late summer of 2003 to retain the krona. No doubt the volatility of the euro was a consideration, as was the desire to preserve Sweden's generous social welfare system. There is more support for the euro in the remaining two holdouts. According to Eurobarometer, an EU public opinion poll, 53 percent of the citizens of Denmark now favor the common currency. By contrast, in the United Kingdom, only 24 percent support a change to the euro. It is possible that both countries will wait until 2006 to put the euro to a vote again.

Ten additional states acceded to the European Union in May 2004: Poland, the Czech Republic, Hungary, Slovakia, Estonia, Latvia, Lithuania, Slovenia, Cyprus, and Malta. Support for joining the euro zone has risen to 72 percent in the acceding states, thus ensuring growth of the economic union. Measured in euros in 2002, Euroland GDP was €7.064 trillion; in the 15-nation European Union as a whole, GDP was €8.824 trillion, and for the United States it was €9.287 trillion. Population figures were 307.8 million, 382.2 million, and 287.5 million for Euroland, the European Union, and the United States, respectively. With the accession of the 10 new states to the European Union, the United States is, by a much wider margin, the world's second-largest market in terms of population. By size of GDP, it may also soon be playing second fiddle. Thus, Euroland will be a formidable competitor on the world stage.

However, there are two big problems ahead for both the acceding countries and the current Euroland 12. The first problem relates to the convergence criteria and related protocols of the Maastricht Treaty. Nations in the euro zone must have the following:

- inflation rates within 1.5 percent of average inflation in the three best performers
- long-term government bond rates no more than 2 percent higher than the average of the three best performers on inflation
- budget deficits less than 3 percent of GDP and government debt less than 60 percent of GDP

It will be impossible for some of the acceding countries to meet these targets for many years. Moreover, two of the existing members of the euro zone, France and Germany, no longer comply on budget deficits—and they have not been fined the required 0.5 percent of GDP, which would translate into $7.8 billion for France and $11 billion for Germany. The French deficit reached 4.2 percent of GDP in 2003. The European Commission allowed France and Germany (both out of compliance for 3 years running) an additional year to reduce deficits, despite calls from Austria and the Netherlands to be tough. The commission indicated that Paris must reduce spending on its generous health programs.

The second problem is more of an EU issue and does not relate to only the euro zone. In the fourth quarter of 2003, Germany, Italy, the Netherlands, indeed, nearly half of Europe, was in or near recession. As noted in *The Wall Street Journal*, Europe faces a choice. It must not only reject the old notion of nation state, it must even reject the thought of developing as a trade bloc. Instead it must make the most of globalization of markets. His agenda includes tax competition with the United States and Asia rather than tax harmonization; deregulation and de-subsidization of industry; free trade and free market competition; and a more flexible labor market. The European Union should no longer be content with low inflation and high unemployment. Eliminating decades-long double-digit unemployment will also help to reduce the deficits in France and Germany, but changes in the labor market will be necessary. European employers must be able to hire and lay off workers as the market changes. Employers must also take a look at popular policies such as generous 1- and 2-year severance packages.

Given the challenges faced by companies such as Markel and the governments in the euro zone, it is fair to ask whether the euro experiment has been a success or a failure. Is there a bright future ahead for the new currency zone or will the old problems of an inflexible labor market and slow growth continue to plague Europe? European economic success will depend on flexibility, openness, and competitiveness. It also depends on a strong American economy. Trade with the United States will create economic growth in Europe. Increasingly stressed relations resulting from American export tax relief and European Union preferential tariffs work to limit free trade and growth.

Enlargement of the European Union is sustaining the drive toward open free trade and competitiveness that began with the coal and steel communities, but Europe needs to wake up to the fact that globalization has passed enlargement by. Global capital flows, global sourcing of products, and global movement of people are facts of modern economic life. While Europe goes about the business of building its federal nation state, it must also go about the business of building institutions and attitudes that are necessary to accommodate the global market. On November 1, 2003, Jean-Claude Trichet took up his post as president of the European Central Bank (ECB). He began his 8-year term with a very strong euro and the shrinking trade surplus and growth rate that go with it.

## Discussion Questions

1. Will Trichet be more pragmatic about Euroland's problems or continue with ECB tunnel vision for low inflation?

2. Will the current trade dispute between Europe and the U.S. over export taxes grow into a real trade war of ever-increasing sanctions or will trade liberalization return to the agenda?

3. Will Europe adopt the tax competition and labor market reforms suggested as appropriate in the age of global markets?

This case was prepared by Professor Francis J. Colella.

*Sources: Monthly Bulletin*, European Central Bank, March 1999 and August 2003; Eurobarometer 59, Spring 2003; *Statistics Pocket Book*, European Central Bank, August 2003; Michael Sesit, "U.S. Investors Reap Gains in Euro-Zone Stocks," *The Wall Street Journal* (October 15, 2003); Daniel Schwammenthal, "France Gets More Time to Comply on Budget," *The Wall Street Journal* Online (October 21, 2003); Gordon Brown, "Old Europe's Choice," *The Wall Street Journal* (October 16, 2003), p. A22; George Parker, "Paris Gets Off the Hook with an Extra Year to Comply," *Financial Times* (October 8, 2003), p. 6; Christopher Rhoads and G. Thomas Sims, "Money Trouble: Rising Deficits in Europe Give Euro Its Toughest Challenge Yet," *The Wall Street Journal* (September 15, 2003), pp. A1, A14; Michael M. Phillips, "Ship Those Boxes; Check the Euro!" *The Wall Street Journal* (February 7, 2003), pp. C1, C7.

# 4 Social and Cultural Environments

France and the United States have a relationship that dates back hundreds of years. For example, in the late 1700s, French troops helped the Americans defeat the British at the Battle of Yorktown. In the twentieth century, the United States returned the favor by helping to liberate France from Hitler's army. Today, the two countries ring up about $50 billion in two-way trade each year, with the United States running a trade deficit of about $11 billion. In the months after President George W. Bush ordered military action in Iraq, however, America's relationship with France entered a phase that might be described as "chilly" at best. On the diplomatic front, the Bush administration was irate that French President Jacques Chirac did not support the decision to invade Iraq. That lack of support was also evident among many French citizens, who do not feel threatened by global terror networks. There were other points of disagreement as well, including opposition to the death penalty, disapproval of the apparently insatiable profit motive of American companies, and concern about the threat of American-style eating habits and fast food to France's culinary tradition.

The big chill in U.S.-French relations is an example of the way that differences in the social and cultural environments—in particular, a cultural gap—impact marketing opportunities around the globe. This chapter focuses on the social and cultural forces that shape and affect individual and corporate behavior in the marketplace. Because the world's cultures are characterized by both differences and similarities, the task of the global marketer is twofold. First, marketers must study and understand the country cultures in which they will be doing business. Second, this understanding must be incorporated into the marketing planning process. In some instances, strategies and marketing programs will have to be adapted; however, marketers should also take advantage of shared cultural characteristics and avoid unneeded and costly

*The United States is the world's top wine importing country. In recent years, France has slipped from first to third place in the ranks of wine exporters to America, behind Italy and Australia. France's opposition to the U.S. military action in Iraq angered many Americans. A grassroots boycott of French products had an immediate negative impact on wine sales in 2003; one importer reported that sales of French wines declined 10 percent.*

*Across the Atlantic, public opinion was equally strong. Anti-American graffiti was visible in many places, and the French called for their own boycott against "arrogant Americans."*

adaptations of the marketing mix. Deep cultural understanding can actually be a source of competitive advantage for global companies. The aggressive expansion of Spain's Telefónica in Latin America provides a case in point. As Juan Villalonga, former chairman of Telefónica, noted recently, "It is not just speaking a common language. It is sharing a culture and understanding friendships in the same way."[1]

Any systematic study of a new geographic market requires a combination of tough mindedness and generosity. While marketers should be secure in their own convictions and traditions, generosity is required to appreciate the integrity and value of other ways of life and points of view. People must, in other words, overcome the prejudices that are a natural result of the human tendency toward ethnocentricity. Although "culture shock" is a normal human

---

[1]    Tom Burns, "Spanish Telecoms Visionary Beholds a Brave New World," *Financial Times* (May 2, 1998), p. 24.

reaction to the new and unknown, successful global marketers strive to comprehend human experience from the local point of view. One reason cultural factors challenge global marketers is that many of them are hidden from view. Because culture is a learned behavior passed on from generation to generation, it can be difficult for the inexperienced or untrained outsider to fathom. As they endeavor to understand cultural factors, outsiders gradually become insiders and develop cultural empathy. There are many different paths to the same goals in life. The global marketer understands this and rejoices in life's rich diversity.

This chapter begins with a general discussion of the basic aspects of culture and society and the emergence of a twenty-first century global consumer culture. To help marketers better understand social and cultural dynamics in the global marketplace, this chapter discusses several useful conceptual frameworks for understanding culture: Hall's notion of high- and low-context cultures, Maslow's Hierarchy of Needs, Hofstede's cultural typology, the self-reference criterion, and diffusion theory. Next is a discussion of specific examples of the impact of culture and society on the marketing of both consumer and industrial products. The chapter ends with suggested solutions to cross-cultural challenges and a review of global companies' cross-cultural training procedures.

# SOCIETY, CULTURE, AND GLOBAL CONSUMER CULTURE

Anthropologists and sociologists have offered scores of different definitions of culture. As a starting point, **culture** can be defined as "ways of living, built up by a group of human beings, that are transmitted from one generation to another." A culture acts out its ways of living in the context of *social institutions*, including family, educational, religious, governmental, and business institutions. Those institutions, in turn, function to reinforce cultural norms. Culture includes both conscious and unconscious values, ideas, attitudes, and symbols that shape human behavior *and that are transmitted from one generation to the next*. Organizational anthropologist Geert Hofstede defines *culture* as "the collective programming of the mind that distinguishes the members of one category of people from those of another."[2] A particular "category of people" may constitute a nation, an ethnic group, a gender group, an organization, a family, or some other unit.

Some anthropologists and sociologists divide cultural elements into two broad categories: material culture and nonmaterial culture. The former is sometimes referred to as the *physical component* or *physical culture* and includes physical objects and artifacts created by humans such as clothing and tools. Nonmaterial culture (also known as *subjective* or *abstract culture*) includes intangibles such as religion, perceptions, attitudes, beliefs, and values. There is general agreement that the material and nonmaterial elements of culture are interrelated and interactive. Cultural anthropologist George P. Murdock studied material and nonmaterial culture and identified dozens of "cultural universals," including athletic sports, body adornment, cooking, courtship, dancing, decorative art, education, ethics, etiquette, family feasting, food taboos, language, marriage, mealtime, medicine, mourning, music, property rights, religious rituals, residence rules, status differentiation, and trade.[3]

It is against this background of traditional definitions that global marketers should understand a worldwide sociocultural phenomenon of the late twentieth and early twenty-first centuries.[4] It has been argued that consumption has become

---

2   Geert Hofstede and Michael Harris Bond, "The Confucius Connection: From Cultural Roots to Economic Growth," *Organizational Dynamics* (Spring 1988), p. 5.
3   George P. Murdock, "The Common Denominator of Culture," in *The Science of Man in the World Crisis*, Ralph Linton, ed. (New York: Columbia University Press, 1945), p. 145.
4   The following discussion is adapted from Dana L. Alden, Jan-Benedict Steenkamp, and Rajeev Batra, "Brand Positioning Through Advertising in Asia, North America, and Europe: The Role of Global Consumer Culture," *Journal of Marketing* 63, no. 1 (January 1999), pp. 75–87.

the hallmark of postmodern society. As cultural information and imagery flow freely across borders via satellite TV, the Internet, and similar communication channels, new global consumer cultures are emerging. Persons who identify with these cultures share meaningful sets of consumption-related symbols. Some of these cultures are associated with specific product categories; marketers speak of "fast-food culture," "credit card culture," "pub culture," "coffee culture," and so on. This cosmopolitan culture, which is comprised of various segments, owes its existence in large part to a wired world in which there is increasing interconnectedness of various local cultures. It can be exploited by global consumer culture positioning (GCCP), a marketing tool that will be explained in more detail in Chapter 7. In particular, marketers can use advertising to communicate the notion that people everywhere consume a particular brand or to appeal to human universals.

## Attitudes, Beliefs, and Values

If we accept Hofstede's notion of culture as "the collective programming of the mind," then it makes sense to learn about culture by studying the attitudes, beliefs, and values shared by a specific group of people. An **attitude** is a learned tendency to respond in a consistent way to a given object or entity. Attitudes are clusters of interrelated beliefs. A **belief** is an organized pattern of knowledge that an individual holds to be true about the world. Attitudes and beliefs, in turn, are closely related to values. A **value** can be defined as an enduring belief or feeling that a specific mode of conduct is personally or socially preferable to another mode of conduct.[5] In the view of Hofstede and others, values represent the deepest level of a culture and are present in the majority of the members of a particular culture.

Some specific examples will allow us to illustrate these definitions by comparing and contrasting attitudes, beliefs, and values. The Japanese, for example, strive to achieve cooperation, consensus, self-denial, and harmony. Because these all represent feelings about modes of conduct, they are *values*. Japan's monocultural society reflects the *belief* among the Japanese that they are unique in the world. Many Japanese, especially young people, also believe that the West is the source of important fashion trends. As a result, many Japanese share a favorable *attitude* toward American brands. Within any large, dominant cultural group, there are likely to be **subcultures**; that is, smaller groups of people with their own shared subset of attitudes, beliefs, and values. Values, attitudes, and beliefs can also be surveyed at the level of any "category of people" that is embedded within a broad culture. For example, if you are a vegetarian, then eating meat represents a mode of conduct that you and others who share your views avoid. Subcultures often represent attractive niche marketing opportunities.

## Religion

Religion is one important source of a society's beliefs, attitudes, and values. The world's major religions include Buddhism, Hinduism, Islam, Judaism, and Christianity; the latter is comprised of Roman Catholicism and numerous Protestant denominations. Examples abound of religious tenets, practices, holidays, and history directly impacting the way people of different faiths react to global marketing activities. For example, Hindus do not eat beef, which means that McDonald's does not serve hamburgers in India (see Case 1-1). Issues related to Jewish history and the Holocaust have been raised in the wake of the 1998 merger of Germany's Daimler-Benz and the American Chrysler Corporation. For example, several Jewish organizations in the United States objected to DaimlerChrysler's 2002 corporate advertising campaign that used references to scientists Wernher

---

[5] Milton Rokeach, *Beliefs, Attitudes, and Values* (San Francisco: Jossey-Bass, 1968), p. 160.

Von Braun and Albert Einstein to promote the quality of Chrysler's cars. For one thing, critics noted, Von Braun was the leader of the Nazi rocket program. A second issue is the fact that Einstein was actually a Swiss citizen who fled Germany in 1933 and settled in the United States.[6]

In the aftermath of the September 2001 terror attacks in New York and Washington, D.C. and the subsequent American military actions in the Middle East, some Muslims have tapped into anti-American sentiment by urging a boycott of American brands. One entrepreneur, Tunisian-born Tawfik Mathlouthi, launched a soft drink brand, Mecca-Cola, as an alternative to Coca-Cola for Muslims living in the United Kingdom and France. The brand's name is both an intentional reference to the holy city of Islam as well as an ironic swipe at Coca-Cola, which Mathlouthi calls "the Mecca of capitalism." London's *Sunday Times* called Mecca-Cola "the drink now seen as politically preferable to Pepsi or Coke."[7] In 2003, Qibla Cola (the name comes from an Arabic word for "direction") was launched in the United Kingdom. Founder Zahida Parveen hopes to reach a broader market than Mecca-Cola by positioning the brand "for any consumer with a conscience, irrespective of ethnicity or religion."[8] Some global companies have successfully capitalized on the love-hate relationship between Muslims and the United States. In the Islamic world, Ramadan is a month of fasting that begins at the end of October. In Indonesia, home to the world's largest Muslim population, KFC uses Ramadan-themed outdoor advertising to encourage Indonesians to come to the restaurants at *buka puasa*, the end of each day's fast. Business at KFC Indonesia's 200 units is up as much as 20 percent during Ramadan.[9]

Religious issues have also been at the heart of a dispute about whether references to God and Christianity should be included in a new European constitution that will be adopted now that the European Union has expanded its membership from 15 to 25 countries. On one side of the dispute are Europe's Catholic countries, including Ireland, Spain, Italy, and Poland. As Italy's deputy prime minister said, "The Italian government believes that [Europe's] common religious heritage should be explicitly referred to with the values of Judeo-Christian tradition." By contrast, the official position in France and Belgium is one of church-state separation. According to this view, religion has no place in the founding documents of the enlarged European Union. In addition, Muslims constitute a politically active minority in France and other countries; Turkey is predominately Muslim. Representatives of Europe's Muslim population are resisting any reference to Christianity in the new constitution.[10]

## Aesthetics

Within every culture, there is an overall sense of what is beautiful and what is not beautiful, what represents good taste as opposed to tastelessness or even obscenity, and so on. Such considerations are matters of **aesthetics**. Global marketers must

---

[6] Joseph B. White, "Jewish Groups Say DaimlerChrysler Ads 'Whitewash' History," *The Wall Street Journal* (July 11, 2002), p. B1. See also Arch G. Woodside and Jean-Charles Chebat, "Updating Heider's Balance Theory in Consumer Behavior: A Jewish Couple Buys a German Car and Additional Buying-Consuming Transformation Stories," *Psychology & Marketing* 18, no. 5 (May 2001), pp. 475–495.

[7] Bill Britt, "Upstart Cola Taps Anti-War Vibe," *Advertising Age* (February 24, 2003), p. 1. See also Digby Lidstone, "Pop Idols," *Middle East Economic Digest* (August 22, 2003), p. 4.

[8] Meg Carter, "New Colas Wage Battle for Hearts and Minds," *Financial Times* (January 8, 2004), p. 9.

[9] Shawn Donnan, "Ramadan Sees Finger-Licking Sales at Outlets for Fast Foods," *Financial Times* (November 13, 2003), p. 6.

[10] Richard Bernstein, "Continent Wrings Its Hands Over Proclaiming Its Faith," *The New York Times* (November 12, 2003), p. A4. See also Brandon Mitchener, "Birth of a Nation? As Europe Unites, Religion, Defense Still Stand in Way," *The Wall Street Journal* (July 11, 2003), pp. A1, A6.

*Opinion polls in some Muslim countries indicate increasingly negative attitudes toward the United States. Even so, in Indonesia, Malaysia, Singapore, and elsewhere, American fast-food companies are still attracting customers. This billboard in Jakarta features men in conservative Islamic clothing posing with a giant drum that is used to call worshippers to prayer. The headline reads, "Let's drum up the Ramadan spirit."*

understand the importance of *visual aesthetics* embodied in the color or shape of a product, label, or package. Likewise, *aesthetic styles*—various degrees of complexity, for example—are perceived differently in different parts of the world. Aesthetic elements that are deemed attractive, appealing, and in good taste in one country may be perceived differently in another. In some cases, a standardized color can be used in all countries; examples include the distinctive yellow color on Caterpillar's earth-moving equipment and its licensed outdoor gear and the red chevron on a pack of Marlboro cigarettes. A number of companies seem to be experiencing a case of the "blues," as evidenced by names such as Bluetooth, Blue Moon, and JetBlue Airways; likewise, Skyy vodka is packaged in a distinctive blue bottle.[11] However, because color perceptions can vary among cultures, adaptation to local preferences

*Qibla Cola was launched in 2003. Company executives hope to position Qibla as an alternative to mainstream American brands. As one executive noted, "We want to show that you can develop a brand that is global, ethical, quality, and commercially viable. We are not trying to do so by being anti-American but by being anti-injustice." As of mid-2004, Qibla Cola was available in the United Kingdom, the Netherlands, Norway, Canada, and Pakistan.*

---

[11] Susan Carey, "More U.S. Companies Are Blue, and It's Not Just the Stock Market," *The Wall Street Journal* (August 30, 2001), pp. A1, A2.

may be required. Such perceptions should be taken into account when making decisions about product packaging and other brand-related communications. In highly competitive markets, inappropriate or unattractive product packaging may put a company or brand at a disadvantage. New color schemes may also be mandated by a changing competitive environment. For example, in the wake of Wal-Mart's expansion into Germany in the 1990s, retailer Metro AG added blue, white, and yellow to the logo of its Real hypermarket stores.

There is nothing inherently "good" or "bad" about any color of the spectrum; all associations and perceptions regarding color arise from culture. Red is a popular color in most parts of the world; besides being the color of blood, in many countries red also is tied to centuries-old traditions of viticulture and winemaking. Blue, because of its associations with sky and water, has an elemental connotation with undertones of dependability, constancy, and eternity. One recent study of perceptions in eight countries found that red is associated with "active," "hot," and "vibrant"; in most countries studied, it also conveys meanings such as "emotional" and "sharp."[12] As such, red has positive connotations in many societies. However, red is poorly received in some African countries. White connotes purity and cleanliness in the West, but it is associated with death in parts of Asia. In the Middle East, purple is associated with death. Another research team concluded that gray connotes inexpensive in China and Japan, while it is associated with high quality and expensive in the United States. The researchers also found that the Chinese associated brown with soft drink labels and associated the color with good tasting; South Korean and Japanese consumers associated yellow with soft drinks and good tasting. For Americans, the color red has those associations.[13]

Sensitivity and a willingness to accommodate such perceptions can help generate rapport and build goodwill. For example, when GM was vying for the right to build a sedan in China, company executives gave Chinese officials gifts from upscale Tiffany & Company in the jeweler's signature blue box. (It has been said that Tiffany & Company is in the "blue box business" rather than the jewelry business.) However, the Americans replaced Tiffany's white ribbons with red ones, because red is considered a lucky color in China and white has negative connotations. GM ultimately won government approval of its proposal.[14]

Music is an aesthetic component of all cultures, accepted as a form of artistic expression and source of entertainment. In one sense, music represents a "transculture" that is not identified with any particular nation. For example, rhythm, or movement through time, is a universal aspect of music. However, music is also characterized by considerable stylistic variation with regional- or country-specific associations. For example, bossa nova rhythms are associated with Argentina, samba with Brazil, salsa with Cuba, reggae with Jamaica, merengue with the Dominican Republic, and blues, driving rock rhythms, hip hop, and rap with the United States. Sociologists have noted that national identity derives in part from a country's indigenous or popular music; a unique music style can "represent the uniqueness of the cultural entity and of the community."[15] In fact, music provides an interesting example of the "think global, act local" theme of this book. Musicians in different countries draw from, absorb, adapt, and synthesize transcultural music influences as well as country-specific ones, as they create hybrid

---

[12] Thomas J. Madden, Kelly Hewett, and Martin S. Roth, "Managing Images in Different Cultures: A Cross-National Study of Color Meanings and Preferences," *Journal of International Marketing* 8, no. 4 (2000), p. 98.

[13] Laurence E. Jacobs, Charles Keown, Reginald Worthley, and Kyung-I Ghymn, "Cross-Cultural Colour Comparisons: Global Marketers Beware!" *International Marketing Review* 8, no. 3 (1991), pp. 21–30.

[14] Craig S. Smith and Rebecca Blumenstein, "Uncertain Terrain: In China, GM Bets Billions on a Market Strewn with Casualties," *The Wall Street Journal* (February 11, 1998), p. A11.

[15] Martin Stokes, *Ethnicity, Identity, and Music: The Musical Construction of Place* (Oxford: Berg, 1994).

styles such as Polish reggae or Italian hip hop. Motti Regev describes this paradox as follows:

> Producers of and listeners to these types of music feel, at one and the same time, participants in a specific contemporary, global-universal form of expression *and* innovators of local, national, ethnic, and other identities. A cultural form associated with American culture and with the powerful commercial interests of the international music industry is being used in order to construct a sense of local difference and authenticity.[16]

Because music plays an important role in advertising, marketers must understand what style is appropriate in a given national market. Although background music can be used effectively in broadcast commercials, the type of music appropriate for a commercial in one part of the world may not be acceptable or effective in another part. For example, when Nissan Motor Company challenged its U.S. advertising agency to create unconventional TV spots, the agency's creative team chose a popular Van Halen recording to communicate hipness and vitality. Nissan's Japanese agency, however, created quieter, more philosophical TV ads. Needless to say, Van Halen's music was not used. The different ads reflect Nissan's corporate philosophy that consumer tastes and values vary from country to country. Advertising at Nissan is decentralized, and local country managers have considerable autonomy.[17] Similarly, to promote movies in Hong Kong, Taiwan, and other Asian countries, Hollywood studios often enlist the services of local artists. For example, Warner Brothers commissioned a theme song and music video by Beyond, a hugely popular Hong Kong heavy metal band, to promote *Lethal Weapon 4* in Asia.[18]

Across Asia, the under-16 segment totals 500 million people; this group is particularly receptive to the idea of joining the "credit card culture." To ensure that the message gets across, the credit card companies are carefully tailoring communications for individual country markets. In Indonesia and Thailand, for example, MasterCard presents itself as hip and cutting edge with ads featuring the classic tune "Money (That's What I Want)." In Singapore and Hong Kong, the pitch is smoother. Ads have featured tag lines such as "Don't let possessions possess you" and music from British pop singer Des'ree. Visa International also believes in a local touch; as Suresh Nanoo, Visa's director of marketing for Asia-Pacific, noted, "With the diversity of Asia, we have to address local needs before getting wrapped up in the global campaign."[19]

## Dietary Preferences

Cultural influences are also quite apparent in food preparation and consumption patterns and habits. Russians eat caviar from sturgeon harvested in the Caspian Sea. In Finland, reindeer meat is on the menu; the French consider rabbit to be a delicacy. Rice and grilled fish are regularly eaten for breakfast in Japan. When eating, Hindus in India serve themselves with the right hand rather than use utensils; they prepare food with spices that create a level of hotness that many Westerners would find unpalatable. Hindus enculturate their children to hot food at a very early age by starting with small quantities and gradually increasing the amount.

A solid understanding of food-related cultural preferences is important for any company that markets food or beverage products globally. Titoo Ahluwalia,

[16] Motti Regev, "Rock Aesthetics and Musics of the World," *Theory, Culture & Society* 14, no. 3 (August 1997), pp. 125–142.

[17] Yumiko Ono, "McCann Finds Global a Tough Sell in Japan," *The Wall Street Journal* (June 19, 1997), p. B12.

[18] Louise Lee, "To Sell Movies in Asia, Sing a Local Tune," *The Wall Street Journal* (September 22, 1998), pp. B1, B4.

[19] Steven Lipin, "Pick a Card: Visa, American Express and MasterCard Vie in Overseas Strategies," *The Wall Street Journal* (February 5, 1994), p. A1; Fara Warner, "Booming Asia Lures Credit-Card Firms," *The Wall Street Journal* (November 24, 1995), p. B10.

# the rest of the story

## French-American Culture Clash

American consumers took out their frustration at France by launching boycotts and other forms of protest. French fries were renamed "freedom fries," and restaurateurs poured expensive French wines down the drain. Some Americans put out the word on the Internet; one site, **www.howtobuyamerican.com**, claimed to have the most comprehensive list of French companies to boycott. Rush Limbaugh, Jay Leno, Willie (the groundskeeper on *The Simpsons*), and other media personalities and commentators expressed displeasure and frustration at the French position.

Some companies used public relations to minimize or neutralize potential losses. For example, Reckitt Benckiser, the company that markets French's mustard, issued a press release stating, "The only thing French about French's Mustard is the name! Robert T. French's All-American Dream Lives On." As a spokeswoman noted, "We issued the press release in response to some confusion that was going on. We are not anti-French. We're not anti-anybody." (One commentator pointed out that, in fact, Reckitt Benckiser is a *British* company.) Likewise, Michelin responded to telephone, e-mail, and postal inquiries by reminding the public that it employs 20,000 Americans and supplies tires to the U.S. Army.

Meanwhile, on the other side of the Atlantic, the French Government Tourist Office estimated that losses associated with reduced American tourism in 2003 would total $500 million. Some French citizens responded to the American boycott with symbolic acts of their own. For example, the staff of a bar in Bayonne poured Coca-Cola into the gutter. The anti-American sentiment was shared by French citizens working elsewhere in the European Union—Germany in particular. For example, some French restaurant owners in Germany took American cigarettes and liquor off their menus. As one restaurateur said, "If the Americans won't calm down, I'll start refusing to accept American Express and other U.S. credit cards."

European ads for Heineken beer, Dr. Pepper, and I Can't Believe It's Not Butter satirized American manners and behavior. As Marie Ridgley, a strategic marketing consultant in Great Britain, explained, "People have gone through the love affair with Americana. It's not necessarily totally anti-Americanism that's going on, but it's a reappraisal of that relationship." Some entrepreneurial individuals are finding ways to capitalize on the cultural gap. America's gun culture is a good example. *Bowling for Columbine*, the Academy Award-winning documentary, was a huge hit in France, perhaps not coincidentally because director Michael Moore is an outspoken critic of President Bush's policies. Boom Chicago, an American comedy troupe that performs in Europe, had a runaway hit with its show "Yankee Go Home! Americans and Why You Love to Hate Us."

### American Imports from France, 2001 (in billions)

| Imports | Value |
| --- | --- |
| Aircraft and equipment | $5.73 |
| Engines, motors | $3.15 |
| Art, antiques, collectors' items | $2.20 |
| Alcoholic beverages | $1.48 |
| Medicines | $1.25 |

*Sources: Erin White, "Europeans Take a Satiric Jab at the U.S., The Wall Street Journal (April 28, 2003), pp. B1, B4; Elaine Sciolino, "Iraq Aside, French View the U.S. with a Mixture of Attraction and Repulsion," The New York Times (November 13, 2003), p. A12; Katy McLaughlin, "Hey, Buddy, Wanna Score Some Cheese?" The Wall Street Journal (June 10, 2003), pp. D1, D2; Melissa Eddy, "Europeans Boycott U.S. Goods in Show of Anti-War Sentiment," Associated Press (April 1, 2003); Floyd Norris, "French's Has an Unmentioned British Flavor," The New York Times (March 28, 2003), p. C1; Kathy Kiely, "Angry Americans Aim Ire at France," USA Today (February 20, 2003), p. 8A; Craig S. Smith, "Joking Aside, A Serious Antipathy to Things American Rises in Europe," The New York Times (February 14, 2003), p. A11.*

chairman of a market research firm in Bombay, points out that local companies can also leverage superior cultural understanding to compete effectively with large foreign firms. He says, "Indian companies have an advantage when they are drawing from tradition. When it comes to food, drink, and medicine, you have to be culturally sensitive."[20] Companies that lack such sensitivity are bound to make marketing mistakes. For example, U.S. companies once introduced mixes for fluffy frosted cakes to the United Kingdom, where cake is eaten at tea time with the fingers rather than as a dessert with a fork. Green Giant Foods attempted to market corn in Europe where the prevailing attitude is that corn is a grain fed to hogs, not to people. In both instances, cultural differences resulted in market failures.

These blunders notwithstanding, there is plenty of evidence that global dietary preferences are converging. For example, "fast food" is gaining increased acceptance around the world. There are several explanations. Heads of families in many countries are pressed for time and are disinclined to prepare home-cooked meals. Also, young people are experimenting with different foods, and the global tourism boom has exposed travelers to pizza, pasta, and other ethnic foods. Shorter lunch hours and tighter budgets are forcing workers to find a place

---

[20] Fara Warner, "Savvy Indian Marketers Hold Their Ground," *The Wall Street Journal Asia* (December 1, 1997), p. 8.

to grab a quick, cheap bite before returning to work.[21] As cultural differences become less relevant, such convenience products will be purchased in any country when consumer disposable income is high enough.

As we have seen, such processes can provoke a nationalist backlash. To counteract the exposure of its young citizens to *le Big Mac* and other American-style fast foods, the French National Council of Culinary Arts designed a course on French cuisine and "good taste" for elementary school students. The director of the council, Alexandre Lazareff, recently published *The French Culinary Exception*. Lazareff warns that France's vaunted *haute cuisine* is under attack by the globalization of taste. More generally, Lazareff is speaking out against perceived challenges to France's culinary identity and way of life. His concerns are real enough; while McDonald's continues to open new restaurants in France (there were 600 by the end of 1997), the number of traditional bistros has declined from 55,000 to 25,000 over the past decade.[22] Meanwhile, the French have coined a new buzzword, *le fooding*, to express the notion that the nation's passion for food goes beyond mere gastronomy:

> To eat with feeling in France is to eat with your head and your spirit, with your nose, your eyes, and your ears, not simply your palate. *Le fooding* seeks to give witness to the modernity and new reality of drinking and eating in the 21st century. . . Everything is *fooding* so long as audacity, sense, and the senses mix.[23]

## Language and Communication

The diversity of cultures around the world is also reflected in language. A person can learn a great deal about another culture without leaving home by studying its language and literature; such study is the next best thing to actually living in another country. Linguists have divided the study of *spoken* or *verbal* language into four main areas: syntax (rules of sentence formation), semantics (system of meaning), phonology (system of sound patterns), and morphology (word formation). *Unspoken* or

---

21  John Willman, "'Fast Food' Spreads as Lifestyles Change," *Financial Times* (March 27, 1998), p. 7.
22  Marlow Hood, "The Holy Terroir," *Financial Times Weekend* (July 4–5, 1998), p. I.
23  Jacqueline Friedrich, "All the Rage in Paris? Le Fooding," *The Wall Street Journal* (February 9, 2001), p. W11.

# CULTURE *watch*

## Jollibee Takes on Ronald McDonald

Quick! What's the most popular fast-food restaurant in the Philippines? If you answered "McDonald's," then you're probably not familiar with Jollibee. With 440 restaurants, Jollibee has twice as many outlets in the Philippines as McDonald's. In the late 1970s, company president Tony Tan decided against acquiring the local McDonald's franchise. Instead, he studied the American fast-food icon, then built a regional empire from the ground up by tailoring menus, advertising, and store atmospherics to the preferences of the 70 million people who live in the Philippines. Even Jollibee's marketing vice president concedes that McDonald's provided the basic blueprint. "They have playlands, we have playgrounds. They have a mascot, we have a mascot. In terms of service and execution, we are all the same." However, at Jollibee, sweet and spicy flavors predominate in the burgers and chicken dishes, and Jollibee's menu offerings are much more varied than competitors'. Advertising stresses interaction among closely knit family members and national pride; a 1998 ad campaign theme was the centennial anniversary of the nation's independence from Spain. Restaurant interiors are kid-friendly, with play areas and decorations reflecting a cheerful, carnival theme.

In 1989, Jollibee got an unexpected boost when the threat of a military coup prompted McDonald's to temporarily suspend operations. Jollibee has even managed to ride out the Asian currency crisis. Manolo Tingzon, the general manager for the international division explained, "People will cut back on everything except food. And even when they do cut back on food spending, they usually will skip fancy and expensive restaurants in times of crisis. We therefore expect fast-food sales to go up." Tan's formula has been so well received that Jollibee commands 56 percent of the fast-food market, compared with McDonald's 19 percent.

Since the mid-1990s, the company has been pursuing growth both abroad and at home. There are now dozens of Jollibee

restaurants in Hong Kong, China, Guam, Indonesia, and other Asian countries, plus units in the Middle East and the United States. Recently, Tan began applying his fast-food techniques to Chinese food. Noting the impact of Chinese culture in the Philippines and the rest of Asia, in 2000 Tan acquired the 200-unit Chowking chain. During the next 2 years, Chowking's sales increased fivefold to $80 million. As Tan said recently, "We Filipinos like Chinese food. It was just a case of finding the right way to present it." With 2002 revenues of $377 million, Jollibee is on the move.

Sources: James Hookway, "Fast-Food Maven in the Philippines Raises the Ante," The Wall Street Journal (October 4, 2002), p. A11; Gertrude Chavez, "The Buzz: Jollibee Hungers to Export Filipino Tastes, Dominate Asian Fast Food," Advertising Age (March 9, 1998), p. 14; William McGurn, "Home Advantage: Local Chain Upstages McDonald's in the Philippines," Far Eastern Economic Review (November 20, 1997), p. 70; Andrew Tanzer, "Bee Bites Clown," Forbes (October 20, 1997), pp. 182–183; Hugh Filman, "Happy Meals for a McDonald's Rival," Business Week (July 29, 1996), p. 77.

---

*nonverbal* communication includes gestures, touching, and other forms of body language that supplement spoken communication. (Nonverbal communication is sometimes called the silent language.) Both the spoken and unspoken aspects of language are included in the broader linguistic field of *semiotics*, which is the study of signs and their meanings. Several examples of linguistic differences are shown in Table 4-1.

In global marketing, of course, language is a crucial tool for communicating with customers, channel intermediaries, and others. The marketing literature is full of anecdotal references to costly blunders caused by incorrect or inept translations of product names and advertising copy. In some countries, marketers must be

| Linguistic Category | Language Example |
|---|---|
| Syntax | English has relatively fixed word order; Russian has relatively free word order. |
| Semantics | Japanese words convey nuances of feeling for which other languages lack exact correlations; "yes" and "no" can be interpreted differently than in other languages. |
| Phonology | Japanese does not distinguish between the sounds "l" and "r"; English and Russian both have "l" and "r" sounds. |
| Morphology | Russian is a highly inflected language, with six different case endings for nouns and adjectives; English has fewer inflections. |

**Table 4-1**

*English, Russian, and Japanese: A Brief Linguistic Comparison*

aware of subcultures created by intranational language or dialect differences. In Switzerland, for example, in addition to Swiss German dialects, there are communities of French, Italian, and Romansch speakers. In addition, of course, Swiss German and standard German differ in significant ways. American English and British English provide another illustration of how the same language in different countries can be characterized by linguistic differences.

Semantic issues frequently arise in global marketing. For example, when British retail-development firm BAA McArthurGlen set up a U.S.-style factory outlet mall in Austria, local officials wanted to know, "Where's the factory?" To win approval for the project, McArthurGlen was forced to call its development a "designer outlet center."[24] Before Hearst Corporation launched *Good Housekeeping* magazine in Japan, managers experimented with Japanese translations. The closest word in Japanese, *kaji*, means "domestic duties." However, that word can be interpreted as tasks performed by servants. In the end, the American title was retained, with the word "Good" in much larger type on the front cover than the word "Housekeeping." Inside the magazine, some of the editorial content has also been adapted to appeal to Japanese women; the famous Seal of Approval was eliminated because the concept confused readers. Editor-in-chief Ellen Levine said, "We have no interest in trying to export our product exactly as it is. That would be cultural suicide."[25]

Phonology can also come into play; Colgate discovered that, in Spanish, *colgate* is a command that means "go hang yourself." Whirlpool spent considerable sums of money on brand advertising in Europe only to discover that consumers in Italy, France, and Germany had trouble pronouncing the company's name.[26] Conversely, Renzo Rosso deliberately chose "Diesel" for a new jeans brand because, as he notes, "It's one of the few words pronounced the same in every language." Rosso has built Diesel into a successful global youth brand distributed in more than 80 countries with annual sales of more than $300 million.[27] Technology is providing interesting new opportunities for exploiting linguistics in the name of marketing. For example, young people throughout the world are using mobile phones to send text messages; it turns out that certain number combinations have meaning in particular languages. For example, in Korean, the phonetic pronunciation of the numerical sequence 8282 means "hurry up" and 7170 sounds like "close friend"; also, on most keypads, 4 5683 968 can be interpreted as "I love you."[28] Korean marketers are using these and other numerical sequences in their advertising.

One impact of globalization on culture is the diffusion of the English language around the globe. Today there are more people who speak English as a foreign language than there are people whose native language is English. Nearly 85 percent of the teenagers in the European Union are studying English. Despite the fact that Sony Corp. is headquartered in Japan, the company makes it clear to job applicants in any part of the world that it does not consider English to be a "foreign language." The same is true for Finland's Nokia. Matsushita Corp. recently introduced a policy that requires all managers to pass an English language-competency test before being considered for promotion. Top management at Matsushita concluded that the company's competitiveness in the global market was being eroded by a staid corporate culture that was exclusively Japanese. The English-language requirement is a potent symbol that a Japanese company is globalizing.[29]

---

24  Ernest Beck, "American-Style Outlet Malls in Europe Make Headway Despite Local Resistance," *The Wall Street Journal* (September 17, 1998), p. A17.
25  Yumiko Ono, "Will Good Housekeeping Translate into Japanese?" *The Wall Street Journal* (December 30, 1997), p. B1.
26  Greg Steinmetz and Carl Quintanilla, "Tough Target: Whirlpool Expected Easy Going in Europe, and It Got a Big Shock," *The Wall Street Journal* (April 10, 1998), pp. A1, A6.
27  Alice Rawsthorn, "A Hipster on Jean Therapy," *Financial Times* (August 20, 1998), p. 8.
28  Meeyoung Song, "How to Sell in Korea? Marketers Count the Ways," *The Wall Street Journal* (August 24, 2001), p. A6.
29  Kevin Voigt, "At Matsushita, It's a New Word Order," *Asian Wall Street Journal Weekly* (June 18–24, 2001), p. 1.

It goes without saying that people interested in international business and global marketing will benefit many times over from the time they invest in learning one or more new languages. The difficult part is convincing people to invest the time and effort in the first place! Foreign language study imparts many benefits. For Americans in particular, language study can help individuals develop rapport with persons who speak English as a second language. Rather than belittling or mocking persons who mispronounce English words, those who have studied another language have insights into the underlying linguistic sources of those mistakes. While acquiring language performance skills, students also gain important cross-cultural insights. Such knowledge can be crucial during negotiations. Negotiations put global marketers face-to-face with counterparts from diverse cultural backgrounds, challenging both sides to surmount verbal and nonverbal communications barriers. Training and a heightened sense of the host country cultural context are necessary to counteract the tendency to bring one's cultural ethnocentrism to the negotiating table.

The challenges presented by nonverbal communication are perhaps even more formidable. For example, Westerners doing business in the Middle East must be careful not to reveal the soles of their shoes to hosts or pass documents with the left hand. In Japan, bowing is an important form of nonverbal communication that has many nuances. People who grow up in the West tend to be verbal; those from Asia exhibit behavior that places more weight on nonverbal aspects of interpersonal communication. Not surprisingly, there is a greater expectation in the East that people will pick up nonverbal cues and understand intuitively without being told.[30] Westerners must pay close attention not only to what they hear but also to what they see when conducting business in such cultures.

Several important communication issues may emerge. One is *sequencing*, which concerns whether the discussion goes directly from point A to point B or seems to go off on tangents. Another is *phasing*, which pertains to whether certain important agenda items are discussed immediately or after the parties have taken some time to establish rapport. According to two experts on international negotiations, there are 10 distinctly American tactics that frequently emerge during negotiations. These tactics are often effective with other Americans, but may require modification for people from other cultural backgrounds. In any communication situation, speakers offer a variety of verbal cues that can help astute observers understand the speaker's mind-set and mental programming. Table 4-2 summarizes some typical American English cues, the underlying culture-influenced attitudes and behaviors they signify, and suggested adaptations.

> *"Global business makes sense, but it's much more difficult to do it than to talk about it. The American manager prides himself or herself on directness, frankness, being in-your-face, being accountable. But that's almost unique in the world."*
>
> A. Paul Flask, managing partner, Korn/Ferry International[31]

## Marketing's Impact on Culture

Universal aspects of the cultural environment represent opportunities for global marketers to standardize some or all elements of a marketing program. The astute global marketer often discovers that much of the apparent cultural diversity in the world turns out to be different ways of accomplishing the same thing. Widespread shared preference for convenience foods, disposable products, popular music, and movies in the United States, Europe, and Asia suggests that many consumer products have broad, even universal, appeal. Increasing travel and improving communications have contributed to a convergence of

---

[30] See Anthony C. Di Benedetto, Miriko Tamate, and Rajan Chandran, "Developing Strategy for the Japanese Marketplace," *Journal of Advertising Research* (January–February 1992), pp. 39–48.

[31] Robert Frank and Thomas M. Burton, "Side Effects: Cross-Border Merger Results in Headaches for a Drug Company," *The Wall Street Journal* (February 4, 1997), p. A1.

**Table 4-2**

American Communication Styles:
Verbal Cues, Underlying
Realities, and Suggested
Adaptations

| Verbal Cues | Underlying Reality | Adaptation Required |
|---|---|---|
| 1. "I can go it alone." | Americans are typically outnumbered in negotiations. Reflects culture of individualism. | Greater reliance cn teamwork and division of negotiating labor, especially in collectivist culture. |
| 2. "Just call me 'John.'" | Americans place a high value on informality and equality of participants in negotiations. This may conflict with the customs and class structures of foreign cultures. | Respect the customs, hierarchies, and class structure of other cultures. Learn more via self study; ask country nationals to explain local attitudes and values. |
| 3. "Do you speak English?" | Americans are culturally monolingual. (Old joke: Q: What do you call someone who speaks two languages? A: Bilingual. Q: What do you call someone who speaks one language? A: American!) | Ignore the conventional wisdom about how difficult it is to learn a foreign language; if you have ongoing business in a country, make the effort to study the language. At a minimum, develop a good working relationship with a skilled interpreter. |
| 4. "Get to the point." | Americans' short term orientation manifests itself as a tendency to be blunt and impatient. | Understand that people from other cultures need to develop a sense of connection and personal trust in order to feel comfortable about doing business. This takes time. |
| 5. "Lay your cards on the table." | Americans like to state the case up front, and are not accustomed to "feeling out" prospective partners. | Slow down, and recognize the need to rephrase the question, several times if necessary. Prepare to spend double the time you think is needed to get the information you seek. |
| 6. "Why doesn't somebody say something?" | Americans are uncomfortable with silence during negotiations and often deal with their discomfort by continuing to speak. | Recognize that silence is golden in many cultures. It can be detrimental to keep up a constant stream of chatter. If there is silence, let it be. Reflect. Take in nonverbal information. *Value* the silence. Take advantage of it. |
| 7. "Don't take 'no' for an answer." | Tenacity and the hard sell are highly valued in the United States. | If the answer is "no," stop selling and find out why. Respond to the reasons for the answer "no." |
| 8. "One thing at a time." | Many Americans favor a linear, organized "left brain" negotiation style. "Point One, Point Two"–style sequencing is not a universal approach. | Recognize your own right brain capability. Embrace a more holistic approach toward negotiations. Be patient if the discussion seems to proceed in loops and spirals. |
| 9. "A deal is a deal." | Expectations and perceptions may not be shared by all parties. Have you agreed on all the points in the contract, or have you agreed to work together? | Accept a more gradual, supplemental view of negotiations and joint effort. |
| 10. "I am what I am." | Americans have a tendency to see things in black-and-white terms. | Adopt a more flexible standpoint. Be willing to change your mind and manner and to adapt to your opposite. |

*Source:* Adapted from John L. Graham and Roy A. Heberger Jr., "Negotiators Abroad—Don't Shoot from the Hip," *Harvard Business Review* 61, no. 4 (July–August 1983), pp. 160–168.

# CULTURE *watch*

## Using English as a Marketing Tool in Japan

In Japan, many consumer packaged goods—including some that are not imported—have English, French, or German on the labels to suggest a stylish image and Western look. A Westerner may wonder, however, what point the copywriters are actually trying to get across. For example, English on the label of City Original Coffee proclaims "Ease Your Bosoms. This coffee has carefully selected high quality beans and roasted by our all the experience." The intended message: Drinking the coffee provides a relaxing break and "takes a load off your chest." Other products, such as casual wear and sports apparel, are also emblazoned with fractured messages. These words appeared on the back of a jacket: "Vigorous throw up. Go on a journey." A sports bag bore the message, "A drop of sweat is the precious gift for your guts."

Finally, consider the message printed on the cover of a notebook: "Be a man I recommend it with confidence as like a most intelligent stationary of basic design." One expert on "Japanese English" believes messages like these highlight basic differences between Japanese and other languages. Many Western languages lack exact equivalents for the rich variety of Japanese words that convey feelings. This presents difficulties for copywriters trying to render feelings in a language other than Japanese. The message on the black notebook was supposed to convey manliness. As the English-speaking Japanese copywriter explained, "I wanted to say I'm proud to present the product to the consumer because it's got a simple, masculine image." Although a Westerner might wonder whether the copywriter succeeded, the fact is that some people actually *do* read the labels and like the

sayings. Sometimes the intended message *does* get interpreted correctly in the Japanese consumer's mind. Japanese retailers do not seem at all concerned that the messages are syntactically suspect. As one retailer explained, the point is that a message in English, French, or German can convey hipness and help sell a product. "I don't expect people to *read* it," she said.

Sources: Howrd W. French, "To Grandparents, English Word Trend Isn't 'Naisu,'" The New York Times (October 23, 2002), p. A4; Nicholas D. Kristof, "Japan's Favorite Import from America: English," The New York Times (February 21, 1995), p. A3; Yumiko Ono, "A Little Bad English Goes a Long Way in Japan's Boutiques," The Wall Street Journal (May 20, 1992), pp. A1, A6; Charles Goldsmith, "Look See! Anyone Do Read This And It Will Make You Laughable," The Wall Street Journal (November 19, 1992), p. B1.

---

tastes and preferences in a number of product categories. The cultural change and the globalization of culture have been capitalized upon, and even significantly accelerated, by companies that have seized opportunities to find customers around the world. However, as noted at the beginning of this chapter, the impact of marketing and, more generally, of global capitalism on culture can be controversial. For example, sociologist George Ritzer and others lament the so-called "McDonaldization of culture" that, they say, occurs when global companies break down cultural barriers while expanding into new markets with their products. As Ritzer noted in a recent book:

> Eating is at the heart of most cultures and for many it is something on which much time, attention and money are lavished. In attempting to alter the way people eat, McDonaldization poses a profound threat to the entire cultural complex of many societies.[32]

Fabien Ouaki is living proof that persons outside of academe and government have also joined the battle against McDonaldization. Ouaki is the managing director of Tati, a discount retailer based in France. Ouaki is opening new stores in select countries, including the United States. Ouaki claims that "personal revenge" is one motivation for entering the U.S. market. "As a Frenchman, it makes me sick to see kids crying to go see 'Titanic,' eat at McDonald's, or

---

[32] George Ritzer, *The McDonaldization Thesis* (London: Sage Publications, 1998), p. 8.

drink Coke. I want to see New Yorkers crying to have a Tati wedding dress," he said recently.[33] Similarly, the international Slow Food movement boasts 70,000 members in 35 countries. Slow Food grew out of a 1986 protest over the opening of a McDonald's on a popular plaza in Rome; every 2 years, Slow Food stages a Salone del Gusto in Italy that is designed to showcase traditional food preparation. As a spokesperson said, "Slow Food is about the idea that things should not taste the same everywhere."[34]

## HIGH- AND LOW-CONTEXT CULTURES

Edward T. Hall has suggested the concept of high and low context as a way of understanding different cultural orientations.[35] In a **low-context culture**, messages are explicit and specific; words carry most of the communication power. In a **high-context culture**, less information is contained in the verbal part of a message. Much more information resides in the context of communication, including the background, associations, and basic values of the communicators. In general, high-context cultures function with much less legal paperwork than is deemed essential in low-context cultures. Japan, Saudi Arabia, and other high-context cultures place a great deal of emphasis on a person's values and position or place in society. In such cultures, a business loan is more likely to be based on "who you are" than on formal analysis of pro forma financial documents. In a low-context culture such as the United States, Switzerland, or Germany, deals are made with much less information about the character, background, and values of the participants. Much more reliance is placed upon the words and numbers in the loan application. Similarly, Japanese companies such as Sony traditionally paid a great deal of attention to the university background of a new hire; preference would be given to graduates of Tokyo University. Specific elements on a resume were less important.

In a high-context culture, a person's word is his or her bond. There is less need to anticipate contingencies and provide for external legal sanctions because the culture emphasizes obligations and trust as important values. In these cultures, shared feelings of obligation and honor take the place of impersonal legal sanctions. This helps explain the importance of long and protracted negotiations that never seem to get to the point. Part of the purpose of negotiating, for a person from a high-context culture, is to get to know the potential partner.

For example, insisting on competitive bidding can cause complications in low-context cultures. In a high-context culture, the job is given to the person who will do the best work and whom you can trust and control. In a low-context culture, one tries to make the specifications so precise that a builder is forced by the threat of legal sanction to do a good job. As Hall has noted, a builder in Japan is likely to say, "What has that piece of paper got to do with the situation? If we can't trust each other enough to go ahead without it, why bother?"

Although countries can be classified as high- or low-context in their overall tendency, there are exceptions to the general tendency. These exceptions are found in subcultures. The United States is a low-context culture with subcultures that operate in the high-context mode. The world of the central banker, for example, is a "gentleman's" world; that is, a high-context culture. Even during the most hectic

---

33  Amy Barrett, "French Discounter Takes Cheap Chic World-Wide," *The Wall Street Journal* (May 27, 1998), p. B8.

34  Jerry Shriver, "At Slow Food Fest, Taste Trumps Time," *USA Today* (November 9, 1998), p. 1D. See also Alexander Stille, "Slow Food's Pleasure Principles," *The Utne Reader* (May/June 2002), pp. 56–58.

35  Edward T. Hall, "How Cultures Collide," *Psychology Today* (July 1976), pp. 66–97.

| Factors/Dimensions | High Context | Low Context | |
|---|---|---|---|
| Lawyers | Less important | Very important | **Table 4-3** |
| A person's word | Is his or her bond | Is not to be relied upon; "get it in writing" | *High- and Low-Context Cultures* |
| Responsibility for organizational error | Taken by highest level | Pushed to lowest level | |
| Space | People breathe on each other | People maintain a bubble of private space and resent intrusions | |
| Time | Polychronic—everything in life must be dealt with in terms of its own time | Monochronic—time is money. Linear—one thing at a time | |
| Negotiations | Are lengthy—a major purpose is to allow the parties to get to know each other | Proceed quickly | |
| Competitive bidding | Infrequent | Common | |
| Country/regional examples | Japan, Middle East | United States, Northern Europe | |

day of trading in the foreign exchange markets, a central banker's word is sufficient for him or her to borrow millions of dollars. In a high-context culture there is trust, a sense of fair play, and a widespread acceptance of the rules of the game as it is played. Table 4-3 summarizes some of the ways in which high- and low-context cultures differ.

## HOFSTEDE'S CULTURAL TYPOLOGY

Organizational anthropologist Geert Hofstede was introduced earlier in this chapter in a discussion of his widely quoted definition of culture. Hofstede is also well-known for research studies of social values suggesting that the cultures of different nations can be compared in terms of five dimensions.[36] Hofstede notes that three of the dimensions refer to expected social behavior, the fourth dimension is concerned with "man's search for Truth," and a fifth reflects the importance of time. A summary of Triad country rankings, plus Hong Kong and Taiwan, is shown in Table 4-4.

The first dimension, **power distance**, is the extent to which the less powerful members of a society accept—even expect—power to be distributed unequally. To paraphrase George Orwell, all societies are unequal, but some are more unequal than others. Hong Kong and France are both high-power distance cultures; low-power distance characterizes Germany, Austria, the Netherlands, and Scandinavia.

The second dimension is a reflection of the degree to which individuals in a society are integrated into groups. In **individualist cultures**, each member of society is primarily concerned with his or her own interest and those of the immediate family. In **collectivist cultures**, all of society's members are integrated into cohesive in-groups. High individualism is a general aspect of culture in the United States and Europe; low individualism is characteristic of Japanese and other Asian culture patterns.

**Masculinity**, the third dimension, describes a society in which men are expected to be assertive, competitive, and concerned with material success, and

---

[36] Geert Hofstede and Michael Harris Bond, "The Confucius Connection: From Cultural Roots to Economic Growth," *Organizational Dynamics* (Spring 1988), p. 5.

# CULTURE *watch*

## Music in India

When Madonna appeared onstage during the 1998 MTV Video Music Awards, she struck a pose intended to evoke a deep Indian spirituality. Wearing a bindhi on her forehead and draped in white linen cloth, she chanted, "Om shanti om," an ancient Hindu mantra. Abruptly, as Madonna tossed aside her faux-Indian costume to reveal tight leather pants, she began singing "And I feel like I just got home!" to the driving beat of her "Ray of Light" dance track. While Madonna has based her career on appropriating various cultural symbols her current imagery reflects an intense interest in Kabbalah her MTV performance was interpreted by many in India as yet another neo-colonial act of cultural insensitivity.

Even as Channel V and MTV have attracted new viewers in India in the 1990s, middle- and upper-class youths in large cities such as New Delhi and Mumbai can purchase many of the same recordings that are popular in the West. Local music stores stock Madonna's compact disks as well as dance mix compilations featuring music from all over the world. Even cassettes by relatively new bands are available in the stores within months of their commercial breakthrough at home. This globalization of music is due primarily to the vast distribution networks established by global giants Sony, Bertelsmann, EMI, Warner, and Polygram. Despite the growing popularity of Western music, however, regional artists and Hindi film music continue to dominate India's music industry. American pop music accounts for less than 5 percent of total sales.

Lucky Ali, Silk Route, and other regional artists that incorporate Western instrumentation and music styles enjoy great popularity in India. By singing lyrics in Hindi or Urdu, these artists are perceived as having vocal styles that are "more Indian." In addition, their performances are felt to come from a South Asian perspective. Such artists avoid the risk of cultural *faux pas* such as Madonna's.

Looking at the Top 40 charts in India reveals one aspect of American pop music's global reach. However, a more compelling approach would be to look not at the *content* but rather at the *form* of popular music. This approach was first employed by Marshall McLuhan (the person who coined the term *global village*). In his 1967 book, *The Medium Is the Message*, McLuhan argued that the form of a new technology and its impact on social organization is vastly more significant than the specific content the new technology delivers. For example, the observation that "Mad About You" is a popular TV show in Nigeria may disguise the fact that television as a media form has had a profound effect on the daily lives of many Nigerian households. In India, then, the wide availability of Madonna's recordings may be less notable than the growing significance of a Western-style music industry based on music television and massive advertising campaigns. The latter aspects point to a dramatic change for the place of music in Indian society.

Globalization has come to India's rural communities in other forms as well. Even in the smallest villages, one can see the occasional vendor's cart painted with the familiar blue Pepsi logo. Nevertheless, the uneven flow of global commerce is starkly evident, as many Western products and sensibilities have yet to penetrate the provincial areas to the extent that they have in the big cities. For reasons of language, aesthetics, and world view, consumption of Western pop music is mostly confined to the relatively wealthy inhabitants of India's largest cities. Responding to the influx of Western visitors, however, rural shopkeepers make an effort to cater primarily to the tastes of the tourists. At the local music shop, the recordings of Hindu devotional singers have been displaced by global pop stars such as Madonna, Celine Dion, Van Halen, and Jamiroquai.

*Source: Personal communication, Peter Kvetko, 2001.*

---

women fulfill the role of nurturer and are concerned with issues such as the welfare of children. **Femininity**, by contrast, describes a society in which the social roles of men and women overlap, with neither gender exhibiting overly ambitious or competitive behavior. Japan and Austria ranked highest in masculinity; Spain, Taiwan, the Netherlands, and the Scandinavian countries were among the lowest.

**Uncertainty avoidance** is the extent to which the members of a society are uncomfortable with unclear, ambiguous, or unstructured situations. Members of some cultures express strong uncertainty avoidance by resorting to aggressive, emotional, intolerant behavior; they are characterized by a belief in absolute truth.

Greece and Portugal outrank the others in Table 4-4 in uncertainty avoidance; other Mediterranean countries and much of Latin America ranks high in uncertainty avoidance as well. Acceptance of uncertainty generally manifests itself in behavior that is more contemplative, relativistic, and tolerant; these values are evident in Southeast Asia and India.

Hofstede's research convinced him that, although these four dimensions yielded interesting and useful interpretations, they did not provide sufficient insight into possible cultural bases for economic growth. Hofstede was also disturbed by the fact that the surveys used in the research had been developed by Western social scientists. Because many economists had failed to predict the explosive economic development of Japan and the tigers (i.e., South Korea, Taiwan, Hong Kong, and Singapore),

**Table 4-4**

*Hofstede's Cultural Dimension Rankings: Triad*

| Country | Power Distance (PDI) | | Individualism | | Masculinity | | Uncertainty Avoidance | | Long-Term Orientation (LTO) | |
|---|---|---|---|---|---|---|---|---|---|---|
| | **Index** | **Rank** | **Index** | **Rank** | **Index** | **Rank** | **Index** | **Rank** | **Index** | **Rank** |
| Austria | 11 | 53 | 55 | 18 | 79 | **2** | 70 | 24–25 | 31 | 22–24 |
| Belgium | 65 | 20 | 75 | 8 | 54 | 22 | 94 | 5–6 | 38 | 18 |
| Denmark | 18 | 51 | 74 | 9 | 16 | 50 | 23 | 51 | 46 | 10 |
| Finland | 33 | 46 | 63 | 17 | 26 | 47 | 59 | 31–32 | 41 | 14 |
| France | 68 | **15–16** | 71 | 10–11 | 43 | 35–36 | 86 | 10–15 | 39 | 17 |
| Germany | 35 | 42–44 | 67 | 15 | 66 | 9–10 | 65 | 29 | 31 | 22–24 |
| Greece | 60 | 27–28 | 35 | 30 | 57 | 18–19 | 112 | **1** | – | – |
| Ireland | 28 | 49 | 70 | 12 | 68 | 7–8 | 35 | 47–48 | 43 | 13 |
| Italy | 50 | 34 | 76 | 7 | 70 | 4–5 | 75 | 23 | 34 | 19 |
| Netherlands | 38 | 40 | 80 | 4–5 | 14 | 51 | 53 | 35 | 44 | 11–12 |
| Portugal | 63 | 24–25 | 69 | 13 | 31 | 45 | 104 | 2 | 30 | 25–26 |
| Spain | 57 | 31 | 51 | 20 | 42 | 37–38 | 86 | 10–15 | 19 | 31–32 |
| Sweden | 31 | 47–48 | 71 | 10–11 | 5 | 52 | 29 | 49–50 | 33 | 20 |
| UK | 65 | 42–44 | 89 | 3 | 66 | 9–10 | 35 | 47–48 | 25 | 28–29 |
| USA | 40 | 38 | 91 | **1** | 62 | 15 | 41 | 43 | 29 | 27 |
| Japan | 54 | 33 | 46 | 22–23 | 95 | **1** | 92 | 7 | 80 | 4 |
| Hong Kong | 68 | **15–16** | 25 | 37 | 57 | 18–19 | 29 | 49–50 | 96 | **2** |
| Taiwan | 58 | 29–30 | 17 | 44 | 45 | 32–33 | 69 | 26 | 87 | 3 |

*Source:* Geert Hofstede, *Culture's Consequences* (Thousand Oaks, CA: Sage, 2001), pp. 500–502.

Hofstede surmised that some cultural dimensions in Asia were eluding the researchers. This methodological problem was remedied by a Chinese Value Survey (CVS) developed by Chinese social scientists in Hong Kong and Taiwan. The CVS data supported the first three "social behavior" dimensions of culture: power distance, individualism/collectivism, and masculinity/femininity. Uncertainty avoidance, however, did not show up in the CVS. Instead, the CVS revealed a dimension, **long-term orientation** (LTO) versus **short-term orientation**, that had eluded Western researchers.[37] Hofstede interpreted this dimension as concerning "a society's search for virtue," rather than a search for truth. It assesses the sense of immediacy within a culture, whether gratification should be immediate or deferred.

Long-term values include *persistence* (perseverance), defined as a general tenacity in the pursuit of a goal. *Ordering relationships* by status reflects the presence of societal hierarchies, and *observing this order* indicates the acceptance of complementary relations. *Thrift* manifests itself in high savings rates. Finally, *a sense of shame* leads to sensitivity in social contacts. Hofstede notes that these values are widely held within high-performing Asian countries such as Hong Kong, Taiwan, and Japan, but that the presence of these values by themselves is not sufficient to lead to economic growth. Two other conditions are necessary: the existence of a market and a supportive political context. Thus, although Hofstede determined that India ranked quite high on the LTO dimension, market restrictions and political forces have, until recently, held back that nation's economic growth.

By studying Hofstede's work, marketers gain insights that can guide them in a range of activities, including product development, interacting with joint venture partners, and conducting sales meetings. For example, understanding the time orientation of one's native culture compared to others' is crucial. In Japan, Brazil, and India, building a relationship with a potential business

---

[37] In some articles, Hofstede refers to this dimension as "Confucian Dynamism" because it is highest in Japan, Hong Kong, and Taiwan.

partner takes precedence over transacting the deal. People from cultures that emphasize the short term must adapt to the slower pace of business in some countries. As noted earlier, language can offer some insights into cultural differences. For example, the phrase "in a New York minute" captures the urgent pace of American urban life.

Conversely, the Japanese notion of *gaman* (persistence) provides insight into the willingness of Japanese corporations to pursue research and development projects for which the odds of short-term success appear low. When Sony licensed the newly invented transistor from Bell Laboratories in the mid-1950s, for example, the limited high-frequency yield (sound output) of the device suggested to American engineers that the most appropriate application would be for a hearing aid. However, *gaman* meant that Sony engineers were not deterred by the slow progress of their efforts to increase the yield. As Sony cofounder Masaru Ibuka recalled, "To challenge the yield is a very interesting point for us. At that time no one recognized the importance of it." Sony's persistence was rewarded when company engineers eventually made the yield breakthrough that resulted in a wildly successful global product—the pocket-sized transistor radio.[38]

By understanding the dimension of uncertainty avoidance, global marketers are better equipped to assess the amount of risk with which buyers are comfortable. In Japan and other Asian cultures characterized by a low tolerance for ambiguity, buyers will be conscious of brand names and are likely to exhibit high brand loyalty. Advertising copy in countries with high levels of uncertainty avoidance should provide reassurance by stressing warranties, money-back guarantees, and other risk-reducing features. Interestingly, Hong Kong is characterized by an even higher tolerance for ambiguity than the United States; Japan, however, ranks quite high in uncertainty avoidance, as do France and Spain.

The power distance dimension reflects the degree of trust among members of society. The higher the power distance (PDI), the lower the level of trust. Organizationally, high PDI finds expression in tall, hierarchical designs, a preference for centralization, and relatively more supervisory personnel. The PDI dimension also provides insights into the dynamics between superiors and subordinates. In cultures where respect for hierarchy is high, subordinates may have to navigate through several layers of assistants to get to the boss. If so, the latter is likely to be isolated in an office with the door closed. In such cultures, lower-level employees may be easily intimidated by superiors. Recent research has suggested that, when evaluating alternatives for entering global markets, companies in high PDI cultures prefer sole ownership of subsidiaries because it provides them with more control. Conversely, companies in low PDI cultures are more apt to use joint ventures.[39] Of the Triad countries in Table 4-4, France has the highest PDI. Other countries with high PDI scores are Mexico, India, and Hong Kong.

The masculinity-femininity dimension is likely to manifest itself in the relative importance of achievement and possessions (masculine values) compared with a spirit of helpfulness and social support (feminine values). Overall, an aggressive, achievement-oriented salesperson is better matched to the culture of Austria, Japan, or Mexico than that of Denmark. (Of course, such a salesperson would also have to bear in mind that both Japan and Mexico rank high in LTO, a dimension that can be at odds with transaction-oriented assertiveness.) Similarly, a Western woman who is sent to make a presentation to a Japanese company will undoubtedly find that her audience consists of men. The Japanese managers may react negatively to a woman, especially if she is younger than they are.

---

[38] James Lardner, *Fast Forward: Hollywood, the Japanese, and the VCR Wars* (New York: NAL Penguin, 1987), p. 45.

[39] Scott A. Shane, "The Effect of Cultural Differences in Perceptions of Transactions Costs on National Differences in the Preference for International Joint Ventures," *Asia Pacific Journal of Management* 10, no. 1 (1993), pp. 57–69.

The collective-individual orientation deserves special comment because there is wide agreement that it is an important component of culture. Knowing which cultures value the collective and which value the individual can help marketers in various ways. In Japan, for example, the team orientation and desire for *wa* (harmony) means that singling out one person for distinction and praise in front of peers can be awkward for those involved. Again, language provides important cues about these cultural dimensions; as the saying goes in Japan, "The nail that sticks up gets hammered down." Throughout much of Asia, the collectivist orientation is dominant. In the highly individualist U.S. culture, however, a person whose individual accomplishments are publicly acknowledged is likely to be pleased by the recognition.[40]

Several teams of researchers have attempted to determine whether cross-national collective/individual differences are reflected in print and television advertisements. In theory, a global company's communication efforts should be adapted in accordance with a particular country's orientation. For example, in cultures where individualism is highly valued, ads would typically feature one person; in countries where individualism is less highly valued, ads would feature groups. Although one team[41] claimed to have found a strong correlation, the findings were not confirmed by a later study.[42] However, Cutler argues that print advertising is, by its very nature, designed to communicate to an individual reader. This suggests that the individualism-collectivism distinction may be a moot issue in print advertising.

In highly collectivist cultures, however, products or services that enjoy an early word-of-mouth buzz among influential consumer groups can quickly achieve phenomenon status that then spreads to other countries. The Tamagotchi craze of the late 1990s is a perfect example. The virtual pets were test marketed in central Tokyo in a shopping area frequented by teenage girls. *Kuchikomi* (word of mouth) was so strong among schoolgirls that toymaker Bandai was hard-pressed to keep up with demand. By the time Tamagotchis reached New York toy retailer FAO Schwartz, the prerelease buzz ensured that the initial 10,000-unit shipment sold out immediately. Although Japanese teens also pay attention to print and television advertising, it is clear that marketers can reach this segment by providing selected youngsters with product samples.[43]

Other recent research suggests that Hofstede's framework can provide useful insights for global marketers hoping to create culturally appropriate consumer brand images. For example, researcher Martin Ross described three types of brand images: functional, social, and sensory. A product with a *functional brand image* is oriented toward problem solving and problem prevention; products with a *social brand image* fulfill consumers' needs for group membership and affiliation; a product with *sensory appeal* provides novelty, variety, and sensory gratification. In the United States, for example, the Crest, Ultra Brite, and Aim toothpaste brands respectively embody these images. Ross surveyed marketing managers at U.S. companies that market blue jeans and athletic shoes. His research suggests that in countries where power distance is high, social brand images enhance brand performance. Conversely, by limiting the use of social and sensory images and emphasizing functional benefits, marketers can enhance brand performance in countries or

---

[40] Adapted from Anne Macquin and Dominique Rouziès, "Selling across the Culture Gap," *Financial Times—Mastering Global Business*, Part 7, 1998, pp. 10–11.

[41] Katherine Toland Frith and Subir Sengupta, "Individualism: A Cross-Cultural Analysis of Print Advertisements from the U.S. and India," paper presented at 1991 Annual Conference of Advertising Division of Association for Education in Journalism and Mass Communication, Boston, MA.

[42] Bob D. Cutler, S. Altan Erdem, and Rajshekhar G. Javalgi, "Advertisers' Relative Reliance on Collectivism-Individualism Appeals," *Journal of International Consumer Marketing* 9, no. 3 (1997), pp. 43–55.

[43] Bethan Hutton, "Winning Word-of-Mouth Approval," *Financial Times* (September 8, 1997), p. 10.

regions with low power distance. Ross also found strong evidence that sensory brand images would perform well in countries where high individualism is a dominant cultural pattern and that social brand image strategies would be effective in countries characterized by low individualism.[44]

## THE SELF-REFERENCE CRITERION AND PERCEPTION

As we have shown, a person's perception of market needs is framed by his or her own cultural experience. A framework for systematically reducing perceptual blockage and distortion was developed by James Lee and published in the *Harvard Business Review* in 1966. Lee termed the unconscious reference to one's own cultural values the **self-reference criterion**, or **SRC.** To address this problem and eliminate or reduce cultural myopia, he proposed a systematic four-step framework:

1. Define the problem or goal in terms of home-country cultural traits, habits, and norms.
2. Define the problem or goal in terms of host-country cultural traits, habits, and norms. Make no value judgments.
3. Isolate the SRC influence and examine it carefully to see how it complicates the problem.
4. Redefine the problem without the SRC influence and solve for the host-country market situation.[45]

The Walt Disney Company's decision to build a theme park in France provides an excellent vehicle for understanding SRC. As they planned their entry into the French market, how might Disney executives have done things differently had they used the steps of SRC?

Step 1. Disney executives believe there is virtually unlimited demand for American cultural exports around the world. Evidence includes the success of McDonald's, Coca-Cola, Hollywood movies, and American rock music. Disney has a stellar track record in exporting its American management system and business style. Tokyo Disneyland, a virtual carbon copy of the park in Anaheim, California, has been a runaway success. Disney policies prohibit the sale or consumption of alcohol inside its theme parks.

Step 2. Europeans in general, and the French in particular, are sensitive about American cultural imperialism. Consuming wine with the midday meal is a long-established custom. Europeans have their own real castles, and many popular Disney characters come from European folk tales.

Step 3. The significant differences revealed by comparing the findings in steps 1 and 2 suggest strongly that the needs upon which the American and Japanese Disney theme parks were based did not exist in France. A modification of this design was needed for European success.

Step 4. This would require the design of a theme park that is more in keeping with French and European cultural norms. Allow the French to put their own identity on the park.

The lesson that the SRC teaches is that a vital, critical skill of the global marketer is unbiased perception, the ability to see what is so in a culture. Although

---

44 Martin S. Ross, "The Effects of Culture and Socioeconomics on the Performance of Global Brand Image Strategies," *Journal of Marketing Research* 32 (May 1995), pp. 163–175.
45 James A. Lee, "Cultural Analysis in Overseas Operations," *Harvard Business Review* (March–April 1966), pp. 106–114.

# CULTURE *watch*

## What's for Breakfast? Lunch? Snack Time?

The globalization of food tastes is one sign of broader cultural shifts that are taking place in many countries. Changes in eating habits are being driven by changing lifestyles as well as global retailing and food processing trends. Many Europeans, for example, are eating bigger breakfasts because lunch breaks have been shortened. Options for breakfast foods, in turn, have multiplied because supermarkets are popping up in neighborhoods in competition with small mom-and-pop stores. Supermarkets can stock a broader selection of food items and are more likely to offer new products to their customers. Global companies such as Kellogg and Cereal Partners Worldwide are engaged in fierce competition with each other and with smaller, local firms for a share of palates and pocketbooks.

Europeans are also developing a taste for salty snacks like tortilla chips. As with breakfast cereal, consumption of tortilla chips in Europe has historically been much lower than in the United States. However, the Tex-Mex concept is gaining momentum. Although Frito-Lay introduced its Doritos brand in Europe in 1994, Europeans viewed the chips as a snack for special occasions and sales were below expectations. In 1998, Frito-Lay relaunched Doritos in the United Kingdom, France, Spain, Portugal, Belgium, the Netherlands, and Luxembourg. A $20 million advertising campaign, identical across the seven countries except for the individual languages, was intended to raise European consumption of the snack chips. Following the recommendations of a brand consultant, Frito-Lay made two significant changes to the packaging. First, it dropped the America-style "see-through window" in favor of the type of sealed foil package that is used for potato chips in Europe. Second, the dominant color of the package was changed from white to black.

In another global food trend that some have likened to "taking coals to Newcastle," food items are being introduced in some countries from unlikely sources. American versions of cheddar cheese are being exported to southwest England, where cheddar was first produced. German imports of American wine increased sevenfold between 1991 and 1996. A Hong Kong noodle maker has achieved great success exporting to China. Grass-fed beef from Argentina is becoming popular in the United States.

Despite these trends, some local food preferences are likely to remain entrenched—at least for a while. For example, many Japanese prefer a traditional breakfast of *okayu* (rice porridge) with *umeboshi* (pickled plums). In Vietnam, street venders offer *pho* ('fuh') for breakfast, lunch, dinner, or as a snack. It consists of a broth made of oxtail, beef, and shrimp paste, seasoned with spices and served over rice noodles. One sign of the times: *Pho* is now being sold from street carts in New York, Chicago, and Los Angeles.

*Sources: Ernest Beck and Rekha Balu, "Europe Is Deaf to Snap! Crackle! Pop!" The Wall Street Journal (June 28, 1998), pp. B1, B8; Helene Cooper and Scott Kilman, "Exotic Tastes: Trade Wars Aside, U.S. and Europe Buy More of Each Other's Foods," The Wall Street Journal (June 28, 1998), pp. A1, A8; Anna Wilde Mathews, "Modern Menus Star Flown-in Fish, Game," The Wall Street Journal (July 7, 1998), pp. B1, B2; John Willman, "Salty Snack Attack on Europe," Financial Times (February 2, 1998), p. 11.*

this skill is as valuable at home as it is abroad, it is critical to the global marketer because of the widespread tendency toward ethnocentrism and use of the self-reference criterion. The SRC can be a powerful negative force in global business, and forgetting to check for it can lead to misunderstanding and failure. While planning Euro Disney, chairman Michael Eisner and other company executives were blinded by a potent combination of their own prior success and ethnocentrism. Avoiding the SRC requires a person to suspend assumptions based on prior experience and success and be prepared to acquire new knowledge about human behavior and motivation.

## DIFFUSION THEORY[46]

Hundreds of studies have described the process by which an individual adopts a new idea. Sociologist Everett Rogers reviewed these studies and discovered a pattern of remarkably similar findings. In *Diffusion of Innovations*, Rogers distilled the research into three concepts that are extremely useful to global marketers: the adoption process, characteristics of innovations, and adopter categories.

An innovation is something new. When applied to a product, "new" can mean different things. In an absolute sense, once a product has been introduced anywhere in the world, it is no longer an innovation because it is no longer new to the world. Relatively speaking, however, a product already introduced in one market may be an innovation elsewhere because it is new and different for the targeted

---

[46] This section draws from Everett M. Rogers, *Diffusion of Innovations* (New York: Free Press, 1962).

market. Global marketing often entails just such product introductions. Managers find themselves marketing products that may be, simultaneously, innovations in some markets and mature or declining products in other markets.

## The Adoption Process

One of the basic elements of Rogers's diffusion theory is the concept of an **adoption process**—the mental stages through which an individual passes from the time of his or her first knowledge of an innovation to the time of product adoption or purchase. Rogers suggests that an individual passes through five different stages in proceeding from first knowledge of a product to the final adoption or purchase of that product: awareness, interest, evaluation, trial, and adoption.

1. *Awareness.* In the first stage the customer becomes aware for the first time of the product or innovation. Studies have shown that at this stage impersonal sources of information such as mass media advertising are most important. An important early communication objective in global marketing is to create awareness of a new product through general exposure to advertising messages.
2. *Interest.* During this stage, the customer is interested enough to learn more. The customer has focused his or her attention on communications relating to the product and will engage in research activities and seek out additional information.
3. *Evaluation.* In this stage the individual mentally assesses the product's benefits in relation to present and anticipated future needs and, based on this judgment, decides whether or not to try it.
4. *Trial.* Most customers will not purchase expensive products without the "hands-on" experience marketers call "trial." A good example of a product trial that does not involve purchase is the automobile test drive. For health care products and other inexpensive consumer packaged goods, trial often involves actual purchase. Marketers frequently induce trial by distributing free samples. For inexpensive products, an initial single purchase is defined as trial.
5. *Adoption.* At this point, the individual either makes an initial purchase (in the case of the more expensive product) or continues to purchase—adopts and exhibits brand loyalty to—the less expensive product. Studies show that, as a person moves from the evaluation through trial to adoption, personal sources of information are more important than impersonal sources. It is during these stages that sales representatives and word of mouth become major persuasive forces affecting the decision to buy.

## Characteristics of Innovations

In addition to describing the product adoption process, Rogers also identifies five major factors affecting the rate at which innovations are adopted: relative advantage, compatibility, complexity, divisibility, and communicability.

1. *Relative advantage*: How a new product compares with existing products or methods in the eyes of customers. The perceived relative advantage of a new product versus existing products is a major influence on the rate of adoption. If a product has a substantial relative advantage vis-à-vis the competition, it is likely to gain quick acceptance. When compact disc players were first introduced in the early 1980s, industry observers predicted that only audiophiles would care enough about digital sound—and have the money—to purchase them. However, the sonic advantages of CDs compared to LPs were obvious to the mass market; as prices for CD players plummeted, the 12-inch black vinyl LP was rendered virtually extinct in less than a decade.

2. *Compatibility*: The extent to which a product is consistent with existing values and past experiences of adopters. The history of innovations in international marketing is replete with failures caused by the lack of compatibility of new products in the target market. For example, the first consumer VCR, the Sony Betamax, ultimately failed because it could only record for 1 hour. Most buyers wanted to record movies and sports events; they shunned the Betamax in favor of VHS-format VCRs that could record 4 hours of programming.

3. *Complexity*: The degree to which an innovation or new product is difficult to understand and use. Product complexity is a factor that can slow down the rate of adoption, particularly in developing country markets with low rates of literacy. In the 1990s, dozens of global companies are developing new interactive multimedia consumer electronics products. Complexity is a key design issue; it is a standing joke that in most households, VCR clocks flash 12:00 because users don't know how to set them. To achieve mass success, new products will have to be as simple to use as slipping a prerecorded videocassette into a VCR.

4. *Divisibility*: The ability of a product to be tried and used on a limited basis without great expense. Wide discrepancies in income levels around the globe result in major differences in preferred purchase quantities, serving sizes, and product portions. CPC International's Hellmann's mayonnaise was simply not selling in U.S.-size jars in Latin America. Sales took off after the company placed the mayonnaise in small plastic packets. The plastic packets were within the food budgets of local consumers, and they required no refrigeration—another plus.

5. *Communicability*. The degree to which benefits of an innovation or the value of a product may be communicated to a potential market. A new digital cassette recorder from Philips was a market failure, in part because advertisements did not clearly communicate the fact that the product could make CD-quality recordings using new cassette technology while still playing older analog tapes.

## Adopter Categories

**Adopter categories** are classifications of individuals within a market on the basis of their innovativeness. Hundreds of studies of the diffusion of innovation demonstrate that, at least in the West, adoption is a social phenomenon that is characterized by a normal distribution curve, as shown in Figure 4-1.

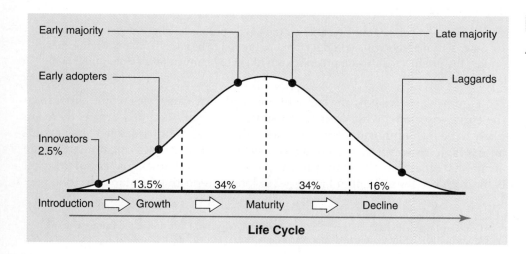

**Figure 4-1**

*Adopter Categories*

Five categories have been assigned to the segments of this normal distribution. The first 2.5 percent of people to purchase a product are defined as innovators. The next 13.5 percent are early adopters, the next 34 percent are the early majority, the next 34 percent are the late majority, and the final 16 percent are laggards. Studies show that innovators tend to be venturesome, more cosmopolitan in their social relationships, and wealthier than those who adopt later. Early adopters are the most influential people in their communities, even more than the innovators. Thus, the early adopters are a critical group in the adoption process, and they have great influence on the early and late majority, who comprise the bulk of the adopters of any product. Several characteristics of early adopters stand out. First, they tend to be younger, with higher social status, and in a more favorable financial position than later adopters. They must be responsive to mass media information sources and must learn about innovations from these sources because they cannot simply copy the behavior of early adopters.

One of the major reasons for the normal distribution of adopter categories is the *interaction effect*; that is, the process through which individuals who have adopted an innovation influence others. Adoption of a new idea or product is the result of human interaction in a social system. If the first adopter of an innovation or new product discusses it with two other people, and each of these two adopters passes the new idea along to two other people, and so on, the resulting distribution yields a normal bell shape when plotted.

From the point of view of the marketing manager, steps taken to persuade innovators and early adopters to purchase a product are critical. These groups must make the first move and are the basis for the eventual penetration of a product into a new market because, over time, the majority copy their behavior.

## Diffusion of Innovations in Pacific Rim Countries

In a recent cross-national comparison of the United States, Japan, South Korea, and Taiwan, Takada and Jain present evidence that different country characteristics—in particular, culture and communication patterns—affect diffusion processes for room air conditioners, washing machines, and calculators. Proceeding from the observation that Japan, South Korea, and Taiwan are high-context cultures with relatively homogeneous populations and the United States is a low-context, heterogeneous culture, Takada and Jain surmised that Asia would show faster rates of diffusion than the United States. A second hypothesis supported by the research was that adoption would proceed more quickly in markets where innovations were introduced relatively late. Presumably, the lag time would give potential consumers more opportunity to assess the relative advantages, compatibility, and other product attributes. Takada and Jain's research has important marketing implications. They note:

> If a marketing manager plans to enter the newly industrializing countries (NICs) or other Asia markets with a product that has proved to be successful in the home market, the product's diffusion processes are likely to be much faster than in the home market.[47]

Figure 4-2 shows how the curve of Asian adopter categories would differ from the curve associated with Western consumer behavior. As noted before, there are likely to be fewer innovators in Japan and other Asian countries, where risk avoidance is high. However, as the Tamagotchi story illustrated, once consumers become aware that others have tried the product, they follow suit quickly so as not to be left behind. Hence the left tail in Figure 4-2 is longer, reflecting hesitancy to try a new

---

[47] Hirokazu Takada and Dipak Jain, "Cross-National Analysis of Diffusion of Consumer Durable Goods in Pacific Rim Countries," *Journal of Marketing* 55 (April 1991), pp. 48–53.

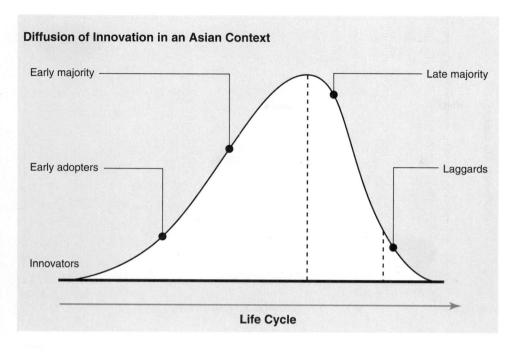

**Diffusion of Innovation in an Asian Context**

Early majority

Late majority

Early adopters

Laggards

Innovators

**Life Cycle**

**Figure 4-2**

*Adopter Categories in Asia*

Source: Hellmut Schütte, "Asian Culture and the Global Consumer," Financial Times—Mastering Marketing, Part Two (September 21, 1998), p. 2.

product; moreover, the curve is steeper and less symmetrical, reflecting the speed with which early adopters and early majority try the product.[48]

# MARKETING IMPLICATIONS OF SOCIAL AND CULTURAL ENVIRONMENTS

The various cultural factors described earlier can exert important influences on consumer and industrial products marketing around the globe. These factors must be recognized in formulating a global marketing plan. **Environmental sensitivity** reflects the extent to which products must be adapted to the culture-specific needs of different national markets. A useful approach is to view products on a continuum of environmental sensitivity. At one end of the continuum are environmentally insensitive products that do not require significant adaptation to the environments of various world markets. At the other end of the continuum are products that are highly sensitive to different environmental factors. A company with environmentally insensitive products will spend relatively less time determining the specific and unique conditions of local markets because the product is basically universal. The greater a product's environmental sensitivity, the greater the need for managers to address country-specific economic, regulatory, technological, social, and cultural environmental conditions.

The sensitivity of products can be represented on a two-dimensional scale as shown in Figure 4-3. The horizontal axis shows environmental sensitivity, the vertical axis the degree for product adaptation needed. Any product exhibiting low levels of environmental sensitivity—integrated circuits, for example—belongs in the lower left of the figure. Intel has sold more than 100 million microprocessors because a chip is a chip anywhere around the world. Moving to the right on the horizontal axis, the level of sensitivity increases, as does the amount of adaptation. Computers are characterized by moderate levels of environmental sensitivity; variations in country voltage requirements require some adaptation. In addition,

---

[48]  Helmitt Schütte, "Asian Culture and the Global Consumer," *Financial Times—Mastering Marketing, Part Two* (September 21, 1998), p. 2

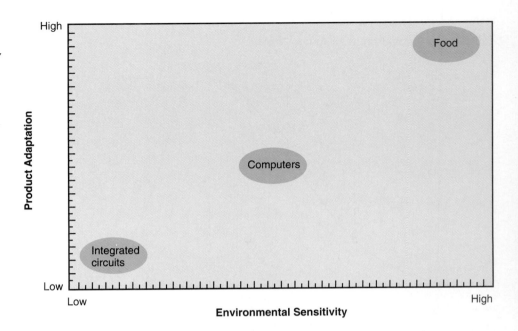

**Figure 4-3**

*Environmental Sensitivity*

the computer's software documentation should be in the local language. At the upper right of Figure 4-3 are products with high environmental sensitivity. Food sometimes falls into this category because it is sensitive to climate and culture. As we saw in the McDonald's case at the end of Chapter 1, the fast-food giant has achieved great success outside the United States by adapting its menu items to local tastes. GE's turbine generating equipment may also appear on the high-sensitivity end of the continuum; in many countries, local equipment manufacturers receive preferential treatment when bidding on national projects.

Research studies show that, independent of social class and income, culture is a significant influence on consumption behavior and durable goods ownership.[49] Consumer products are probably more sensitive to cultural difference than are industrial products. Hunger is a basic physiological need in Maslow's hierarchy; everyone needs to eat, but what we want to eat can be strongly influenced by culture. Evidence from the front lines of the marketing wars suggests that food is probably the most sensitive category of consumer products. CPC International failed to win popularity for Knorr dehydrated soups among Americans. The U.S. soup market was dominated by Campbell Soup Company; 90 percent of the soup consumed by households was canned. Knorr was a Swiss company acquired by CPC that had a major share of the European prepared food market, where bouillon and dehydrated soups account for 80 percent of consumer soup sales. Despite CPC's failure to change the soup-eating habits of Americans, the company (now called Bestfoods and a unit of Unilever) is a successful global marketer with operations in more than 60 countries and sales in 110 countries.

At Campbell, by contrast, the figures are reversed: 75 percent of 2001 revenues were generated in the United States and 25 percent from global markets. Despite the fact that Campbell is one of the world's best-known brand names, the company has discovered that the attitude of homemakers toward food preparation is a major cultural factor in marketing prepared foods. Recall that cooking was one of the cultural universals identified by Murdock. However, cooking habits and customs vary from country to country. Campbell's research revealed that Italian housewives devote approximately 4.5 hours per day to food preparation, versus 60 minutes a day spent by their U.S. counterparts. The difference reflects cultural norms regarding the

49  Charles M. Schaninger, Jacques C. Bourgeois, and Christian W. Buss, "French-English Canadian Subcultural Consumption Differences," *Journal of Marketing* 49 (Spring 1985), pp. 82–92.

kitchen as well as the fact that a higher percentage of American women work outside the home.

Campbell discovered a strong negative opinion toward convenience food in Italy. A panel of randomly selected Italian housewives was asked, "Would you want your son to marry a canned soup user?" The response to this question was sobering: All but a small fraction of a percent of the respondents answered, "No." Increased incomes as well as product innovations may have an impact on Italian attitudes toward time and convenience, with a corresponding positive effect on the market for convenience foods. Already, taste improvements in frozen pizza have boosted sales in Italy.

When David Johnson was Campbell's CEO in the mid-1990s, he acquired a majority stake in Arnotts, Australia's leading biscuit company. Johnson was setting his sights on the $1 billion Asian cracker market, which he expected to triple or quadruple in size in the coming years. Will consumers in Beijing and Bangkok clamor for Australian baked goods? Only time will tell, but Johnson—a native of Australia—was relying on sophisticated market research to guide the company's product adaptation effort.[50] Other Campbell executives share Johnson's global vision. As C. David Clark, former CEO of Campbell Canada, noted, "The strategy for North America is very simple. You market locally, manufacture regionally, and resource globally—with common technology, knowledge, and supplies."[51]

Thirst also shows how needs differ from wants. Liquid intake is a universal physiological need. As is the case with food and cooking, however, the particular beverages people *want* to drink can be strongly influenced by culture. Coffee is a beverage category that illustrates the point. On the European continent, coffee has been consumed for centuries. Britain has historically been a nation of tea drinkers, and the notion of afternoon tea is firmly entrenched in British culture. In the 1970s, tea outsold coffee by a ration of 4-to-1. Brits who did drink coffee tended to buy it in instant form, because the preparation of instant is similar to that of tea. By the 1990s, however, Britain was experiencing an economic boom and an explosion of new nightclubs and restaurants. Trendy Londoners looking for a non-pub "third place" found it in the form of Seattle Coffee Company cafés. An instant success after the first store was opened by coffee-starved Americans in 1995, by 1998 Seattle Coffee had 55 locations around London. Starbucks bought the business from its founders for $84 million.[52]

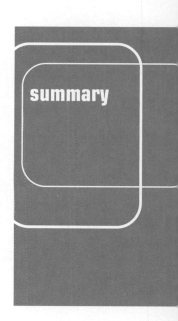

**summary**

**Culture**, a society's "programming of the mind," has both a pervasive and changing influence on each national market environment. Global marketers must recognize the influence of culture and be prepared to either respond to it or change it. Human behavior is a function of a person's own unique personality and that person's interaction with the collective forces of the particular society and culture in which he or she has lived. In particular, **attitudes**, **values**, and **beliefs** can vary significantly from country to country. Also, differences pertaining to **religion**, **aesthetics**, dietary customs, and language and communication can affect local reaction to a company's brands or products as well as the ability of company personnel to function effectively in different cultures. A number of concepts and theoretical frameworks provide insights into these and other cultural issues.

Cultures can be classified as **high-** or **low-context**; communication and negotiation styles can differ from country to country. Hofstede's **social values typology** helps marketers understand culture in terms of **power distance**, **individualism** versus **collectivism**, **masculinity** versus **feminity**, **uncertainty avoidance**, and **long** versus **short-term orientation**. By

50 Stephen W. Quickel, "Can Campbell Survive the Global Food Wars? M'm! M'm! Maybe!" *CFO* (February 1994), p. 26.
51 Bill Saporito, "Campbell Soup Gets Piping Hot," *Fortune* (September 9, 1991), p. 143.
52 Marco R. della Cava, "Brewing a British Coup," *USA Today* (September 16, 1998), pp. D1, D2.

understanding the **self-reference criterion**, global marketers can overcome the unconscious tendency for perceptual blockage and distortion. Rogers' classic study on the **diffusion of innovations** helps explain how products are adopted over time by different **adopter categories**. Rogers' findings concerning the **characteristics of innovations** can also help marketers successfully launch new products in global markets. Recent research has suggested that Asian adopter categories differ from the Western model. An awareness of **environmental sensitivity** can help marketers determine whether consumer and industry products must be adapted to the needs of different markets.

**discussion questions**

1. What are some of the elements that make up culture? How do these find expression in your native culture?

2. What is the difference between a low-context culture and a high-context culture? Give an example of a country that is an example of each type and provide evidence for your answer.

3. How can Hofstede's cultural typologies help Western marketers better understand Asian culture?

4. Explain the self-reference criterion. Go to the library and find examples of product failures that might have been avoided through the application of the SRC.

5. Briefly explain the social research of Everett Rogers regarding diffusion of innovations, characteristics of innovations, and adopter categories. How does the adoption process in Asia differ from the traditional Western model?

6. Compare and contrast the United States and Japan in terms of traditions and organizational behavior and norms.

# Case 4-1

## Fair Trade Coffee: Ethics, Religion, and Sustainable Production

It's a basic law of economics: When supply goes up, price goes down. That is the situation facing the coffee industry today, as a glut of coffee beans led to sharply lower prices on world commodities markets. Historically, coffee has been one of the most lucrative exports in many developing nations. Green, unroasted coffee beans are traded on the London and New York futures markets; Volcafe and Neumann Gruppe are large coffee traders that buy about 25 percent of the world's coffee supply. Other major players include Procter & Gamble (P&G), Kraft, and Nestlé; all three are key suppliers to the grocery industry, where the greatest percentage of coffee is purchased. For example, P&G sells about $1 billion worth of Folgers brand coffee each year. Specialty coffees such as those marketed by Starbucks are regarded as niche products that account for only about 2 percent of the world supply of coffee beans.

In 1999, the wholesale price for coffee was about $1.40 per pound; in 2001, the price dropped to 42 cents. By the end of 2003, prices had recovered to about 50 cents per pound; however, the cost of producing and processing green coffee beans is between 80 cents and 90 cents per pound. Oversupply is another problem. Between 1990 and 2000, Vietnam's production soared from 84,000 tons to 950,000 tons; Vietnam produces mostly robusta beans, which are cheaper and have a harsher taste than arabica beans. According to the International Coffee Organization,

Rainforest Alliance works with big corporations to monitor environmental and working conditions in developing countries. It was a pioneer in certifying lumber sourced from forests in the tropics. It certifies about $12.5 billion worth of coffee beans each year. The Fairtrade Labeling Organization International (FLO; **www.fairtrade.net**) is a certification authority based in Bonn, Germany, that licenses its trademark to organizations such as the United Kingdom's Fairtrade Foundation (**www.fairtrade.org.uk**). The Fairtrade label on a bag or can of coffee indicates that growers were paid a fair price for their crops. TransFair USA is a fair-trade certification organization in the United States (**www.transfairusa.org**).

Coffee bearing the Fairtrade label is often marketed with the help of charitable organizations; for example, Oxfam, a private charity in Britain, created a new coffee brand called cafédirect (**www.cafedirect.co.uk**). In addition to providing price supports, such organizations also sponsor training and development programs to help growers become more knowledgeable about market prices and learn ways to reach export markets. Catholic Relief Services (CRS) recently launched an effort to encourage America's 65 million Catholics to buy fair trade coffee (**www.catholicrelief.org/coffee/trade**). The CRS Coffee Project is part of a larger organization, the Interfaith Coffee Program of Equal Exchange; the latter includes participants from Lutheran, Presbyterian, and Methodist groups. The bottom line: Wholesale coffee buyers that participate in the fair trade program agree to pay farmers $1.26 per pound for regular coffee beans and $1.41 for higher quality, organic beans.

the 2001–2002 harvest yielded 115 million sacks of coffee. However, worldwide consumption only absorbed 105 million bags. Low prices and excess supply all adds up to bad news for 25 million coffee farmers in Latin American and Africa.

Since the mid-1990s, Starbucks has pursued a policy of improving working conditions at its suppliers; however, Starbucks' annual coffee purchases amount to only about $180 million. A number of different nongovernmental organizations have begun to address the situation faced by farmers who supply the broader coffee market. For example, the

The Fairtrade coffee movement is gaining momentum among socially conscious consumers. For example, in 2002, the interfaith partnership in the United States sold nearly $1.7 million of fair trade coffee at 7,500 houses of worship; sales in 2003 reached $2.7 million. Although impressive, that figure is a mere drop in the bucket; annually, Americans spend about $19 billion on coffee. However, as Paul Rice, President and CEO of Transfair, noted, "If we could get every Catholic in the country to drink fair-trade coffee, that would be a huge market right there." He added, "But it's the ripple effect—getting all those people kind of up to speed on what fair trade is all about and getting them to ask for it at their local stores—that's going to have a much broader effect on the market."

*"We've been in this business for 100 years and want to be in it for another 100. . . . This is not philanthropy. This is about incorporating sustainable coffee into our mainstream brands as a way to have a more efficient and competitive way of doing business"*

Annemieke Wijm, senior director for commodity sustainability programs, Kraft Foods

Kraft recently signed an accord with the Rainforest Alliance; Kraft, which buys about 10 percent of the world's coffee crop, agreed to buy beans that are certified as produced with sustainable agricultural practices and blend them into their mass market brands. The purchases will amount to about $3.1 billion annually and will benefit farmers in Brazil, Colombia, Mexico, and Central America. Tensie Whelen, executive director for the Rainforest Alliance, hailed the accord, noting, "This step by Kraft marks the beginning of transforming the coffee industry. You have a company capable of shaping markets commit to buying a significant amount of coffee and to mainstreaming across their brands and not 'ghettoising' it in one brand."

Meanwhile, industry experts disagree about ways to reduce the supply of low-quality beans. A recent Oxfam report recommended government financing to destroy five million bags of robusta beans currently being stored in warehouses in developing countries. Others would prefer not to ask for government intervention. Peter A. Reiling, president and chief executive of Technoserve, a nonprofit organization that promotes socially responsible entrepreneurship in developing countries, noted, "It's an emotional issue and everyone seems to have a different solution. I'd say there's no one silver bullet, but there are market solutions."

## Discussion Questions

1. Is it important for coffee marketers such as Starbucks, Kraft, and Nestlé to create "ethical supply chains"? Why?

2. A recent study by the United Kingdom's Institute of Grocery Distribution determined that the majority of consumers do not buy fair trade products. The report noted, "Self-interest is at the center of food choice for most consumers. Few consumers consider the impact of their purchase decisions on anyone or anything but themselves and their family." Do you agree with this finding?

3. What recommendations would you make to help cure the ills of the coffee market?

*Sources:* Mary Beth Marklein, "Goodness—To the Last Drop," *USA Today* (February 16, 2004), pp. 1D, 2D; Tony Smith, "Difficult Times for the Coffee Industry," *The New York Times* (November 25, 2003), p. W1; Sara Silver, "Kraft Blends Ethics with Coffee Beans," *Financial Times* (October 7, 2003), p. 10; Tim Harford, "Fairtrade Tries a Commercial Blend for Coffee," *Financial Times* (September 12, 2003), p. 10; In-Sung Yoo, "Faith Organizations Throw Weight Behind 'Fair Trade' Coffee Movement," *USA Today* (December 2, 2003), p. 7D; Peter Fritsche, "Bitter Brew: An Oversupply of Coffee Beans Deepens Latin America's Woes," *The Wall Street Journal* (July 8, 2002), pp. A1, A10.

# Case 4-2

## Barbie: The American Girl Goes Global

In 1976, a time capsule was buried to commemorate the U.S. bicentennial. The capsule contained items that captured the essence of America and included a Barbie doll, described as the "quintessential American." More than 25 years later, Barbie has become much more cosmopolitan: She has been adopted as one of the favorite toys for girls around the world and is sold in more than 150 countries. Indeed, despite her 1950s American heritage, Barbie is still a best seller for Mattel, Inc.

What is the secret to Barbie's timeless success? Ruth Handler, Barbie's creator, believed that all children need to play with mature dolls to effectively project their fantasies of growing up. Ironically, Barbie was modeled on a doll for men, Lill, who was a cartoon character in a men's sporting newspaper. Though Mattel's executives initially believed that a doll with breasts was improper and would never sell, Barbie became an instant success with American children.

Over time, Barbie's look has changed to reflect changing fashion and cultural trends. In 1968, for example, the first black Barbie was introduced to cater to the growing African-American market. Hispanic and Asian-American Barbies have also been created in response to the growth of America's other ethnic markets. Despite these successes, Barbie is reaching maturity in the United States. In 1999, U.S. Barbie sales were down 14 percent. Consequently, Mattel executives are searching for new avenues for profit.

Not surprisingly, the company is targeting untapped groups of children in other parts of the world. A strategy dubbed "Mattel 2000" focused on the company's direction during the decade of the 1990s. As John Amerman, former CEO of Mattel, noted, "There are twice as many children in Europe as in the U.S . . . three times as many in South America and fifteen times as many in Asia . . . the potential market for products like Barbie . . . is mind boggling." However, although Barbie has been successfully adapted to cultural differences in the United States, the international challenge will be more formidable—and yet, according to current CEO Robert Eckert, Mattel is "dedicated to becoming a truly global company."

Mattel adopted a pan-European, regiocentric approach to the Western European market. Barbie is a huge success in Europe; children in Italy, France, and Germany average five Barbie dolls in their toy collections. In the early 1990s, Mattel developed a new "Friendship Barbie" to sell in Central and Eastern Europe. The new doll was less elaborate than its Western European counterpart, which sports designer clothes and accessories. By contrast, Friendship Barbie reflects the more basic lifestyle children had experienced under communism. However, although Mattel has experimented with multicultural dolls, the company discovered that little girls in Europe prefer the well-known American Barbie to the local versions.

In other areas of the world Barbie has encountered barriers of a different kind. Since being introduced in the Middle East, Barbie has faced opposition on political, religious, and social grounds. Parents and religious leaders alike are at odds with the cultural values that Barbie and Ken portray. Writing in the *Cairo Journal*, Douglas Jehl noted, "To put it plainly, the plastic icon of Western girlhood is seen in the Middle East, where modesty matters, as something of a tramp."

In Egypt and Iran, Barbie faces competition from two new products aimed at providing an Islamic alternative to Barbie. However, the dolls have not originated from commercial competitors but from government agencies set on reducing the impact of Barbie in their nations. As one Arab toy seller noted, "I think that Barbie is more harmful than an American missile." Barbie's challengers include demure looking dolls such as Laila, who was designed according to recommendations of participants at the Arab League children's celebrations in 1998. Laila wears simple contemporary clothes such as a short-sleeve blouse and skirt and traditional Arab costumes. Abala Ibrahim, director of the Arab League's Department of Childhood, believes "there is a cultural gap when an Arab girl plays with a doll like Barbie. . . the average Arab girl's reality is different from Barbie's with her swimming pool, Cadillac, blond hair, and boyfriend Ken."

Despite the cultural differences and a price equal to seven times the average monthly salary, Barbie has been highly successful in Iran. It remains to be seen whether Barbie, who is "forbidden by Islam," will struggle against new local competitors Sara and Dara which have been created expressly to compete against Barbie. The dolls feature traditional clothing and headscarves and are available with family members, thus reinforcing the importance of family for Iranian children. The dolls were launched in 2002 at prices about one-third of Barbie's.

In Brazil, Barbie faces stiff competition from a cheaper local rival. Latin America was one of the first non-U.S. markets Barbie entered. Brazil is an important market for Mattel because dolls account for 37 percent of the country's annual $430 million in toy sales. However, Barbie has been losing market share to the Susi doll manufactured by Estrela, the company once licensed to distribute Barbie in Brazil. According to Synesio Batista da Costa, president of the Brazilian Association of Toy Manufacturers, five Susi dolls were sold for every two Barbies during the 1999 Christmas season. In fact, due to Susi's overwhelming popularity, Estrela introduced Susi in Chile, Argentina, Paraguay, and Uruguay in 2000. Susi's success can be attributed to both a lower price and the inclusion of realistic Brazilian touches allowing Brazilian children to identify with Susi. Susi is a blonde with a small chest and waist but wide thighs and dark skin, similar to Brazilian girls. Susi represents the philosophy that "young girls want dolls that show them as they are, not as they want to be." Mattel faces strong competition from this new doll and needs to assert its prominence to ensure success in the Latin region.

However, Mattel has learned that to be successful within a foreign culture, Barbie does not need a total overhaul, but instead can be very profitable with small cosmetic changes. For example, Barbie was successfully launched in India in 1995 and while the core product remains unchanged, Indian dolls are painted with a head spot and dressed in a sari. In short, Mattel tailors its product to Indian tastes while still offering the universally recognized Barbie.

Mattel has had great difficulty conquering the world's second-largest toy market, Japan. The Japanese toy market is worth $8 billion in annual sales and is vital if Mattel is to achieve its goal of becoming more global. The Japanese market is notoriously difficult to penetrate as Mattel has found during 20 years of doing business in the country. Companies entering Japan must contend with complex distribution systems and intense competition from Japanese brands. Furthermore, dolls have a strong tradition in the Japanese culture with a heritage of over 800 years and ceremonial importance. Mattel's initial attempts to market Barbie in Japan met with limited success. Mattel had entered the market without thoroughly understanding it. Management simply presumed that Barbie's success in other markets would be replicated in Japan. As John Amerman, CEO of Mattel in the mid-1990s, noted, "They didn't know what that product was, and it didn't work." To address the problem of low sales, Mattel enlisted the services of Takara, a Japanese toy specialist. Through focus groups, Mattel learned that Barbie's legs were too long, and her chest too large—in short, Japanese girls didn't relate to Barbie's physical attributes. Also, Barbie's eyes were changed from blue to brown, and the doll ultimately took on a look that was appealing to the Japanese children's sense of aesthetics. The Takara Barbie was born.

Although sales improved, a licensing disagreement prompted Mattel to terminate the relationship with Takara and search for a new partner in Japan. Takara continued selling the doll as Jenny, which, ironically, became a competitor to the new Japanese Barbie. In 1986, Mattel joined forces with Bandai, Japan's largest toy company. Bandai produced Maba Barbies ("Ma" for Mattel and "ba" for Bandai) with wide brown eyes. Due to its similarities to the Jenny doll, however, Maba Barbie was withdrawn from the market before it achieved success. Maba was replaced by Bandai Barbies which were again similar to Jenny, possessing the wide-eye look but wearing mainly ball gowns and unimaginative clothing.

Once again, market success eluded Mattel. Indeed, Mattel was committed to neither Japanese nor an American style and thus competed poorly against dolls whose identity was well defined. However, Mattel realized that its competitive advantage lay with its American culture. Though Mattel had attempted to adapt to the Japanese culture, Mattel discovered once again that girls prefer the well-known Barbie to the local versions. In 1991, Mattel ended its relationship with Bandai and opened its own marketing and sales office in Tokyo. Mattel introduced its American Barbie to Japan and experienced success with "Long Hair Star Barbie" which became one of the top-selling dolls in Japan. Although financial losses mounted until 1993, in 1994 Barbie made a profit in Japan with sales almost doubling since its reintroduction.

In 1999, Mattel refocused its Japanese efforts. Then-CEO Jill Barad promised to double Mattel's international sales within 5 years. To this end, a Japanese native named Sam Sugiyama was placed in charge of Mattel's Japanese operations; previously, the position had been held by American expatriates. Mr. Sugiyama stated that Mattel was "very anxious to do something quickly," understandable considering its past problems in the market. After almost 20 years of perseverance in Japan, it was imperative that Mattel improve its position. Therefore, the company joined forces once again with Bandai to form a marketing, sales, and product development alliance in an effort to tackle the complex Japanese distribution system.

At the end of 2001, CEO Robert Eckert reported that Mattel's strategic partnership with Bandai had "eliminated chronic operating losses" in Japan. Indeed, international revenues had grown by 10 percent, an important indicator because international markets account for 31 percent of Mattel's total revenue. Barbie is a huge success story. However, in terms of financial performance, Barbie experiences peaks and troughs. For example, in 1999 Mattel experienced a 7 percent decrease in international sales with poor performance by Barbie. This was due in part to the strength of the American dollar; another factor was the company's new just-in-time inventory management practices in Europe. Therefore, Mattel launched the "Market by Market" initiative in 2000. Writing in Mattel's 1999 *Annual Report*, acting CEO Ronald Loeb promised that the company "will proactively adapt its products to local tastes, economic conditions, and pricing, rather than viewing the rest of the world as an extension of our U.S. strategy." The Market by Market approach has been successful with Mattel's "wheels products," resulting in 20 percent growth in international sales in the first year of implementation. Results for Barbie have been less dramatic. Barbie experienced a 5 percent growth in international sales in 2000, mainly due to the joint venture with Bandai in Japan. Mattel ramped up international branding support for Barbie with the creation and marketing of **www.Barbie.com** Web sites tailored to girls around the world.

Richard Dickson, senior vice president of Mattel's girl's consumer products worldwide, believes Barbie's global strategy must originate from a perspective of worldwide cohesion. He noted, "If I go on a plane from France to Japan to the United States and there's a Barbie billboard, you're going to sense that it's the same Barbie [in all three countries]." To facilitate its global approach, Mattel has given the U.S. president of Barbie the full responsibility for the brand around the world. Mattel's constant reassessment of its operations is vital for Barbie's continued success. Indeed, Barbie carries a huge weight on her tiny shoulders, representing 40 percent of Mattel's annual profit. As long as international sales continue to increase, the future looks bright for this tiny icon.

## Discussion Questions

1. Describe Mattel's global marketing strategy for Barbie and assess its success.
2. Mattel has experienced problems in entering the Japanese market. How could Mattel have achieved greater success in Japan?
3. What strategies should Mattel employ to combat the threat from the Susi doll in Latin America?
4. How important is culture in children's toy preference? Will cultural differences result in failure for Mattel as the company faces new competitors in the Middle East?

This case was prepared by Alexandra Kennedy-Scott, David Henderson, Michel Phan, ESSEC Business School. Used by permission.

*Sources*: Queena Sook Kim and Ichiko Fuyuno, "Barbie's New Clothes," *The Wall Street Journal* (January 30, 2004), pp. B1, B3; Richard Dickson, "Marketers of the Next Generation: Richard Dickson," *Brandweek* (April 8, 2002), p. 30; David Finnigan, "Mattel Dolls Up Barbie 'Nutcracker' with a Little Help from McD, CBS," *Brandweek* (July 16, 2001), p. 6; Jan Golab, "King Barbie: How I Gussied up America's Favorite Toy and Turned My Struggling Company into a Megatoyopoly," *Los Angeles Magazine* (August 1, 1994), p. 66; Lawrence B. Chonko, "Case Study: Alliance Formation with Direct Selling Companies: Avon and Mattel," *Journal of Personal Selling & Sales Management* 19, no. 1 (Winter 1999), p. 6; "Big Game Hunting," *The Economist* (April 17, 1999), p. 68; Mattel Inc. *Annual Report* (various years).

# 5 The Political, Legal, and Regulatory Environments of Global Marketing

Since the late 1990s, a growing debate about genetically modified organisms (GMOs) has put the biotechnology industry at odds with a broad coalition of environmentalists and small-scale farmers. For a number of years, giant global companies such as Monsanto, DuPont, Novartis, and Zeneca PLC have reaped significant revenue and profits from sales of genetically modified seeds for soybeans, corn, cotton, tomatoes, and other crops. Farmers, in turn, generate higher yields by planting crops with an enhanced ability to withstand stressors such as insects, drought, and disease. In the United States alone, more than one-third of the yearly corn harvest is produced from genetically modified seed. Depending on the variety, transgenic crops can be processed into food for humans or feed for animals; some are designed specifically for industrial or pharmaceutical use. As one industry executive enthusiastically noted, "The next Silicon Valley is plant biotechnology." GMOs are present in a wide range of food products from well-known companies such as Coca-Cola, H.J. Heinz, Quaker Oats, and Nestlé. Future breakthroughs are expected to include healthier cooking oil and soybean protein that doesn't taste "beany."

There is a problem, however: A growing number of consumers around the world are deeply concerned about food products that have not been produced naturally. Now regulators are taking up the cause. In 1998, for example, the European Union (EU) imposed a moratorium on biotech crop approvals. The ban costs Pioneer Hi-Bred International and other U.S. companies about $300 million annually in lost sales of seed corn alone. In addition, the European Union has begun to require mandatory labeling for some foods containing GMOs, and regulators in Australia, New Zealand, Japan, and several other countries also have begun devising labeling strategies.

A protester dressed as a "killer tomato" marches through downtown San Diego in 2001 en route to the Convention Center where the Biotechnology Industry Organization was holding its annual conference. The goal of this demonstration, and others like it in other cities, is to warn about long-term effects of introducing food from genetically-modified crops into the food supply. The biotech industry contends that such products will be accepted by consumers as long as they are fully informed about the benefits and potential risks.

The GMO issue illustrates the impact that the political, legal, and regulatory environments can have on international trade and global marketing activities. Each of the world's national governments regulates trade and commerce with other countries and attempts to control the access of outside enterprises to national resources. Every country has its own unique legal and regulatory system that affects the operations and activities of the global enterprise, including the global marketer's ability to address market opportunities and threats. Laws and regulations constrain the cross-border movement of products, services, people, money, and know-how. The global marketer must attempt to comply with each set of national—and, in some instances, regional—constraints. These efforts are hampered by the fact that laws and regulations are frequently ambiguous and continually changing.

In this chapter, we consider the basic elements of the political, legal, and regulatory environments of global marketing, including the most pressing current issues and some suggested approaches for dealing with those issues. Some specific topics, such as rules for exporting and importing industrial and consumer products, standards for health and safety, and regulations regarding packaging, labeling, advertising, and promotion, are covered in later chapters devoted to individual marketing mix elements.

## THE POLITICAL ENVIRONMENT

Global marketing activities take place within the political environment of governmental institutions, political parties, and organizations through which a country's people and rulers exercise power. As we saw in Chapter 4, each nation has a unique culture that reflects its society. Each nation also has a *political culture*, which reflects the relative importance of the government and legal system, and provides a context within which individuals and corporations understand their relationship to the political system. Any company doing business outside its home country should carefully study the political culture in the target country and analyze salient issues arising from the political environment. These include the governing party's attitude toward sovereignty, political risk, taxes, the threat of equity dilution, and expropriation.

# Nation-States and Sovereignty

**Sovereignty** can be defined as supreme and independent political authority. A century ago, U.S. Supreme Court Chief Justice Fuller said, "Every sovereign state is bound to respect the independence of every other sovereign state, and the courts in one country will not sit in judgment on the acts of government of another done within its territory." More recently, Richard Stanley, president of the Stanley Foundation, offered the following concise description:

> A sovereign state was considered free and independent. It regulated trade, managed the flow of people into and out of its boundaries, and exercised undivided jurisdiction over all persons and property within its territory. It had the right, authority, and ability to conduct its domestic affairs without outside interference and to use its international power and influence with full discretion.[1]

Government actions taken in the name of sovereignty occur in the context of two important criteria: a country's stage of development and the political and economic system in place in the country.

As outlined in Chapter 2, the economies of individual nations may be classified as industrialized, newly industrializing, or developing. Many governments in developing countries exercise control over their nations' economic development by passing protectionist laws and regulations. Their objective is to encourage economic development by protecting emerging or strategic industries. Government leaders can also engage in cronyism and provide favors for family members or "good friends." For example, former Indonesian president Suharto established a national car program that granted tax breaks and tariff privileges to a company established in South Korea by his youngest son. The United States, EU, and Japan responded by taking the matter to the World Trade Organization. Conversely, when many nations reach advanced stages of economic development, their governments declare that (in theory, at least) any practice or policy that restrains free trade is illegal. Antitrust laws and regulations are established to promote fair competition. Advanced country laws often define and preserve a nation's social order; laws may extend to political, cultural, and even intellectual activities and social conduct. In France, for example, laws forbid the use of foreign words such as *le weekend* or *le marketing* in official documents. Also, a French law passed in 1996 requires that at least 40 percent of the songs played by popular radio stations must be French.

We also noted in Chapter 2 that most of the world's economies combine elements of market and nonmarket systems. The sovereign political power of a government in a predominantly nonmarket economy reaches quite far into the economic life of a country. By contrast, in a capitalist, market-oriented democracy, that power tends to be much more constrained. A current global phenomenon in both nonmarket and market structures is the trend toward privatization, which reduces direct governmental involvement as a supplier of goods and services in a given economy. In essence, each act of privatization moves a nation's economy farther in the free-market direction. The trend is clearly evident in Mexico, where, at one time, the government controlled over 1,000 "parastatals." By the early 1990s, most had been sold, as President Carlos Salinas de Gortari presided over the sale of full or partial stakes in enterprises worth $23 billion, including the two Mexican airlines, mines, and banks. Privatization in Mexico and elsewhere is evidence that national governments are changing *how* they exercise sovereign power.

---

[1]  See *Changing Concepts of Sovereignty: Can the United Nations Keep Pace?* (Muscatine, IA: The Stanley Foundation, 1992), p. 7.

Some observers believe global market integration is eroding national economic sovereignty. Economic consultant Neal Soss notes, "The ultimate resource of a government is power, and we've seen repeatedly that the willpower of governments can be overcome by persistent attacks from the marketplace."[2] Is this a disturbing trend? If the issue is framed in terms of marketing, the concept of the exchange comes to the fore: Nations may be willing to give up sovereignty in return for something of value. If countries can increase their share of world trade and increase national income, perhaps they will be willing to cede some sovereignty. In Europe, the individual EU countries are giving up the right to have their own currencies, ceding the right to set their own product standards, and are making other sacrifices in exchange for improved market access.

## Political Risk

**Political risk** is the risk of a change in political environment or government policy that would adversely affect a company's ability to operate effectively and profitably. It can deter a company from investing abroad. When the perceived level of

---

[2] Cited in Karen Pennar, "Is the Nation-State Obsolete in a Global Economy?" *Business Week* (July 17, 1995), p. 80.

*Table 5-1*

*Categories of Political Risk*

| Economist Intelligence Unit (EIU) | Business Environment Risk Intelligence (BERI) | PRS Group |
|---|---|---|
| War | Fractionalization of the political spectrum | Political turmoil probability |
| Social unrest | Fractionalization by language, ethnic, and/or religious groups | Equity restrictions |
| Orderly political transfer | Restrictive/coercive measures required to retain power | Local operations restrictions |
| Politically motivated violence | Mentality (xenophobia, nationalism, corruption, nepotism) | Taxation discrimination |
| International disputes | Social conditions (including population density and wealth distribution) | Repatriation restrictions |
| Change in government/ pro-business orientation | Organization and strength of forces for a radical government | Exchange controls |
| Institutional effectiveness | Dependence on and/or importance to a major hostile power | Tariff barriers |
| Bureaucracy | Negative influences of regional political forces | Other barriers |
| Transparency/fairness | Societal conflict involving demonstrations, strikes, and street violence | Payment delays |
| Corruption | Instability as perceived by assassinations and guerilla war | Fiscal/monetary expansion |
| Crime |  | Labor costs |
|  |  | Foreign debt |

*Source:* Adapted from Llewellyn D. Howell, *The Handbook of Country and Political Risk Analysis*, 2d ed. (Syracuse, NY: PRS Group, 1998).

political risk is high, a country will have greater difficulty in attracting foreign investment. Unfortunately, it is often the case that managers fail to include political risk assessment in the global strategic planning process because they think it is esoteric, too expensive, or unreliable. Political forces can drastically change the business environment with little advance notice. For example, businesspeople need to stay apprised of the formation and evolution of political parties. Valuable sources of information include *The Economist, Financial Times*, and other business periodicals. A number of organizations such as the Economist Intelligence Unit (EIU; **www.eiu.com**), the Geneva-based Business Environment Risk Intelligence (BERI SA; **www.beri.com**), and the PRS Group (**www.prsgroup.com**) specialize in providing up-to-date political risk reports on individual country markets. These commercial sources, however, vary somewhat in the criteria that constitute political risk. For example, BERI is concerned with societal and system attributes, whereas PRS Group focuses more directly on government actions and economic functions. The EIU analyzes political risk in terms of five subcategories of political stability, and five subcategories of political effectiveness. Political risk, in turn, is one of four components in an overall country risk rating. The BERI system examines six internal causes of political risk, two external causes, and two symptoms. (See Table 5-1.)

## Causes of Political Risk

The fundamental cause of political risk is tension between the residents' aspirations and goals and the real conditions at a given time. Whenever the public perceives a wide gap between its aspirations and reality, there is political risk.

The gap between aspirations and reality in high-income countries is seldom great enough to generate a significant level of political risk. When political risk is present in a high-income country, it can be traced to identifiable, long-standing issues in the country such as the conflict between the Protestants and Catholics in Northern Ireland.

In lower- and lower-middle-income countries, an economic crisis can trigger political risk. Indonesia is a prime example: After the rupiah plunged from 2,300 to 18,000 to the U.S. dollar and then settled at a rate of 10,000 rupiah to the dollar, Indonesia went into a free fall of economic decline. What had been the most stable country in Southeast Asia overnight became a country where all bets were off. The incompetence of the government and private sector in Indonesia provoked the expulsion of President Suharto and ushered in a period of significant risk to marketers and investors.

The political maneuverings of former president Boris Yeltsin's government in Russia similarly created a high level of political risk. Vladimir Putin, Yeltsin's successor, is implementing reforms in an effort to pave the way for Russia's membership in the WTO and to attract foreign investment. Thanks to high world oil prices, Russia's economy grew at an average rate of about 6.5 percent between 1998 and 2003. The government has a number of bills pending that, if adopted, will strengthen intellectual property and contract law. Medium-term prospects for the transformation of the Russian market appear good. The current political climate in the rest of Central and Eastern Europe is still characterized by varying degrees of uncertainty. Hungary, Latvia, and Albania represent three different levels of risk. Hungary and Latvia have already achieved upper-middle-income status, although Latvia is projected to grow more slowly. In Albania, the transition to a market economy has been hampered by an ongoing feud between the country's socialist prime minister and the leader of the opposition Democratic party.[3]

## Expressions and Symptoms of Political Risk

The level of political risk is inversely related to a country's stage of economic development: All other things being equal, the less developed a country, the greater the political risk (Figure 5-1). A number of symptoms can indicate possible increases in political risk. Currency depreciation is frequently accompanied by economic decline, which, in turn, churns up the political waters. In a country such as China with a nonconvertible currency, there is risk that the government will block repatriation of profit by foreign companies. The threat of civil disorder or ethnic conflict is also a symptom of political risk. Risk in the Triad and high-income countries, for example, is quite limited as compared with a country in low-middle-income and low-income categories.

Southeast Asia, and Indonesia in particular, illustrate how economic and political risk are intertwined. For the past 30 years, Southeast Asia was a paragon of political calm. Even the poorest countries in the region, like Indonesia, were stable because the Indonesians had accepted a single-party government and restrictions on freedom of expression and democracy in exchange for a government that promised economic growth. In Indonesia, everyone referred to President Suharto and his family as the Royal Family. Indonesians looked the other way at the clear evidence of cronyism and favoritism of the Suharto children. They remained silent about their lack of political freedom and choice. The reason is simple: They thought they were getting rich.

---

[3] Leyla Boulton, "Political Discord Slows EU March," *Financial Times—Albania: Special Report* (May 18, 2004), p. 22.

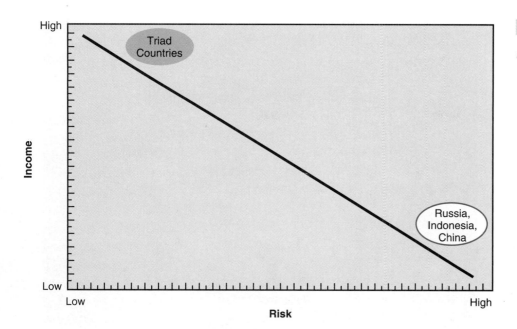

**Figure 5-1**

*Income Versus Political Risk*

The economic collapse of Indonesia has changed all of that. Today, Indonesia is a country with a high degree of political risk. When Indonesians realized that they were not as rich as they thought, and that they were getting poorer under Suharto, they decided that they wanted more political expression. The old order (Suharto) was forced out of office, and a new era of political turmoil was launched. In the long term, the change is surely for the good; in the short term, where previously there had been calm and predictability, today there is great uncertainty.

Because political risk cannot be accurately predicted, the corporate culture also must be considered when making a strategic decision. For the aggressive, entrepreneurial company wishing to make a minimum investment, a country with some political risk may have great market potential. For a conservative company or one considering a multimillion-dollar investment, the same country may have potential for a great market loss.

Companies can purchase insurance to offset potential risks arising from the political environment. In Japan, Germany, France, Britain, the United States, and other industrialized nations, various agencies offer investment insurance to corporations doing business abroad. The Overseas Private Investment Corporation (OPIC; **www.opic.gov**) provides various types of political risk insurance to U.S. companies; in Canada, the Export Development Corporation performs a similar function. OPIC's activities came under scrutiny in 1997 when the Clinton administration proposed reauthorizing it, along with the Ex-Im Bank. Some legislators wanted to dismantle both agencies as part of an effort to reduce government involvement in business. These legislators criticized the agencies for providing unnecessary subsidies to large corporations.[4]

## Taxes

Governments rely on tax revenues to generate funds necessary for social services, the military, and other expenditures. Unfortunately, government taxation policies on the sale of goods and services frequently motivate companies and individuals to profit by *not* paying taxes. In China, for example, most imports are subject to high duties, plus a 17 percent value-added tax (VAT). As a result, significant quantities

---

[4]  Nancy Dunne, "Eximbank and Opic Face Survival Test in U.S." *Financial Times* (May 8, 1997), p. 8.

of oil, cigarettes, photographic film, personal computers, and other products are smuggled into China. In some instances, customs documents are falsified to under-count goods in a shipment; the Chinese military has allegedly escorted goods into the country as well. Ironically, global companies can still profit from the practice; it has been estimated, for example, that 90 percent of the foreign cigarettes sold in China are smuggled in. For Philip Morris, this means annual sales of $100 million to distributors in Hong Kong, who then smuggle the smokes across the border.[5] High excise and VAT taxes can also encourage legal cross-border shopping as consumers go abroad in search of good values. In Great Britain, for example, the Wine and Spirit Association estimates that, on average, cars returning from France are loaded with 80 bottles of wine.

Corporate taxation is another issue. The high level of political risk currently evident in Russia can be attributed in part to excessively high taxes on business operations. High taxes encourage many enterprises to engage in cash or barter transactions that are off the books and sheltered from the eyes of tax authorities. This, in turn, has created a liquidity squeeze that prevents companies from paying wages to employees. Needless to say, unpaid, disgruntled workers can contribute

---

[5] Craig S. Smith and Wayne Arnold, "China's Antismuggling Drive to Hurt U.S. Exporters that Support Crackdown," *The Wall Street Journal* (August 5, 1998), p. A12.

# the rest of the story

## Genetically Altered Crops

In Europe, a number of activist groups, including Greenpeace and Friends of the Earth (FoE), have taken up the fight against GMOs. They claim that GMOs pose threats to both people and the environment; terms such as "Frankenfoods" have been used to put the point across. The general public, already cynical thanks to perceived governmental mishandling of the "mad cow" scare, has been receptive.

The GMO controversy is not limited to the industrialized world, however. In 2002, Zambia's president rejected a 26,000-ton shipment of genetically modified corn from the United States that was intended for famine relief. Robert Zoellick, the United States trade represented, pointed the finger at Europe. "The European antiscientific policies are spreading to other corners of the world," he said. "I find it immoral that people are not being supplied food to live in Africa because people have invented dangers about biotechnology." Concerned that anti-GMO sentiment could spread to Asia, Latin America, and the Middle East, Zoellick indicated that the United States might take its complaint to the World Trade Organization. Meanwhile, the EU's executive arm was lobbying several member states to drop opposition to lifting the ban.

Monsanto and other biotech companies have begun to work more closely with government regulators. The companies had already been supplying regulatory agencies with their research; now, the companies are advocating certain changes in the U.S. Food and Drug Administration's policies concerning GMOs. The FDA currently regards most modified crops as identical to conventional ones as long as there is no change in nutrient content or composition. The agribusiness companies are hoping that the FDA can help reassure consumers so that mandatory labeling along the lines of the European model won't be required. American companies are also frustrated by lengthy regulatory delays in Europe, where all 15 EU governments are involved in the process of approving new food products for sale to the public. A product is approved if a qualified majority is reached as a result of a weighted vote. At the European Commission itself, five separate directorates are involved in biotechnology issues, and two—DG Sanco and DG Environment—have responsibility for assessing the safety of the food supply.

Some biotech companies are presenting their case directly to consumers. Zeneca, a British chemical company, began distributing leaflets in supermarkets explaining the benefits of genetically altered crops. Meanwhile, in the summer of 1998, Monsanto launched an unusual advertising campaign in British and French newspapers. Featuring headlines such as, "Qu'est-ce que la biotechnologie vegetale?", the ads encouraged consumers to directly contact advocacy groups such as Greenpeace. As Philip S. Angell, former director of corporate relations at Monsanto, said, "We believe the facts about biotechnology stand up under scrutiny. And we're ready to debate." Despite this effort, Sainsbury, Marks and Spencer, and other British retailers responded to the labeling requirements and pressure from consumer activists by touting the fact that their "own-brand" (private label) food products are GMO free.

Sources: John Mason and David Firn, "Monsanto Sees Seeds of Food Revolution in Europe," Financial Times (March 19, 2004), p. 6; Alison Maitland, "An Ethical Answer to Consumers' Fears," Financial Times (December 4, 2003), p. 11; Tony Smith, "Brazil to Lift Ban on Crops with Genetic Modification," The New York Times (September 25, 2003), p. W1; Norman E. Borlaug, "Science vs. Hysteria," The Wall Street Journal (January 22, 2003), p. A14; Elizabeth Becker, "U.S. Threatens to Act Against Europeans Over Modified Foods," The New York Times (January 10, 2003), p. A4; Neil King Jr., "U.S. Ponders Next Course in EU Food Fight," The Wall Street Journal (December 2, 2002), p. A4; Scott Kilman, "Food Fright: Biotech Scare Sweeps Europe, and Companies Wonder if U.S. is Next," The Wall Street Journal (October 9, 1999), pp. A1, A15; Kilman, "Green Genes: If Fat-Free Pork Is Your Idea of Savory, It's a Bright Future," The Wall Street Journal (January 29, 1998), pp. A1, A10; Clive Cookson, "Field of Genes," Financial Times (August 11, 1998), p. 10; Guy de Jonquieres, "One Man's Meat," Financial Times (April 15, 1998), p. 13.

to political instability. Meanwhile, the Putin government is pursuing a tough new tax policy in an effort to shrink Russia's budget deficit and qualify for IMF loans. However, such policies should not have the effect of deterring foreign investment. As Bruce Bean, head of the American Chamber of Commerce in Moscow, summed up the situation:

> Change the name of the country, change the flag, change the border. Yes, this was done overnight. But build a market economy, introduce a meaningful tax system, create new accounting rules, accept the concept that companies which cannot compete should go bankrupt and the workers there lose their jobs? These things take time.[6]

Meanwhile, global companies are being caught up in the chaos. In July 1998, tax collectors seized dozens of automobiles belonging to Johnson & Johnson's Russian division and froze the group's assets. The authorities claimed J&J owed $19 million in back taxes.

The diverse geographical activity of the global corporation also requires special attention to tax laws. Many companies make efforts to minimize their tax liability by

---

[6] Andrew Higgins, "Go Figure: At Russian Companies, Hard Numbers Often Hard to Come By," *The Wall Street Journal* (August 20, 1998), p. A9.

shifting the location of income. For example, it has been estimated that tax minimization by foreign companies doing business in the United States costs the U.S. government $3 billion each year in lost revenue. In one approach, called "earnings stripping," foreign companies reduce earnings by making loans to U.S. affiliates rather than using direct investment to finance U.S. activities. The U.S. subsidiary can deduct the interest it pays on such loans and thereby reduce its tax burden.

## Seizure of Assets

The ultimate threat a government can pose toward a company is seizing assets. **Expropriation** refers to governmental action to dispossess a foreign company or investor. Compensation is generally provided, although not often in the "prompt, effective, and adequate" manner provided for by international standards. If no compensation is provided, the action is referred to as *confiscation*.[7] International law is generally interpreted as prohibiting any act by a government to take foreign property without compensation. **Nationalization** is generally broader in scope than expropriation; it occurs when the government takes control of some or all of the enterprises in a particular industry. International law recognizes nationalization as a legitimate exercise of government power, as long as the act satisfies a "public purpose" and is accompanied by "adequate payment" (i.e., one that reflects fair market value of the property). In 1959, for example, the newly empowered Castro government nationalized property belonging to American sugar producers in retaliation for new American import quotas on sugar. Cuban-owned production sources were not nationalized. Castro offered compensation in the form of Cuban government bonds, which was adequate under Cuban law. The U.S. State Department viewed this particular act of nationalization as discriminatory and the compensation offered as inadequate.[8] More recently, South Korea nationalized Kia, the nation's number three automaker, in the wake of the Asian currency crisis. Some industry observers believe that a much-needed reform of Japan's banking system will require nationalization.

Short of outright expropriation or nationalization, the phrase *creeping expropriation* has been applied to limitations on economic activities of foreign firms in particular countries. These have included limitations on repatriation of profits, dividends, royalties, and technical assistance fees from local investments or technology arrangements. Other issues are increased local content requirements, quotas for hiring local nationals, price controls, and other restrictions affecting return on investment (ROI). Global companies have also suffered discriminatory tariffs and nontariff barriers that limit market entry of certain industrial and consumer goods, as well as discriminatory laws on patents and trademarks. Intellectual property restrictions have had the practical effect of eliminating or drastically reducing protection of pharmaceutical products.

In April 1997, for example, the Canadian government banned a gasoline additive known as MMT. The U.S.-based Ethyl Corporation is the world's sole manufacturer of MMT. Ethyl sued the Canadian government for $231 million, citing the "expropriation and compensation" rule in the NAFTA agreement. In essence, Ethyl claimed that the Canadian government's ban had the effect of restricting Ethyl's ability to make a profit and thus constituted an expropriation of assets.

In the mid-1970s, Johnson & Johnson and other foreign investors in India had to submit to a host of government regulations to retain majority equity positions in companies already established. Many of these rules were later copied in whole or in part by Malaysia, Indonesia, the Philippines, Nigeria, and Brazil. By the late 1980s, after a "lost decade" in Latin America characterized by debt crises and low GNP growth, lawmakers reversed many of these restrictive and discriminatory laws. The goal was to again attract foreign direct investment and badly needed

---

[7]   Franklin R. Root, *Entry Strategies for International Markets* (New York: Lexington Books, 1994), p. 154.
[8]   William R. Slomanson, *Fundamental Perspectives on International Law* (St. Paul, MN: West Publishing, 1990), p. 356.

Located in The Hague, the International Court of Justice (ICJ) is the judicial arm of the United Nations. The court's 15 judges are elected to 9-year terms. The primary function of the ICJ is to settle disputes among different countries according to international law. The ICJ also offers advice on legal issues submitted by various international agencies.

Western technology. The end of the Cold War and restructuring of political allegiances contributed significantly to these changes.

When governments expropriate foreign property, there are impediments to action to reclaim that property. For example, according to the U.S. Act of State Doctrine, if the government of a foreign state is involved in a specific act, the U.S. court will not get involved. Representatives of expropriated companies may seek recourse through arbitration at the World Bank Investment Dispute Settlement Center. It is also possible to buy expropriation insurance from either a private company or a government agency such as OPIC. The expropriation of U.S. copper companies operating in Chile in 1970 to 1971 shows the impact that companies can have on their own fate. Companies that strenuously resisted government efforts to introduce home-country nationals into the company management were expropriated outright; other companies that made genuine efforts to follow Chilean guidelines were allowed to remain under joint Chilean-U.S. management.

## THE LEGAL ENVIRONMENT

**International law** may be defined as the rules and principles that nation-states consider binding upon themselves. International law pertains to property, trade, immigration, and other areas that have traditionally been under the jurisdiction of individual nations. International law applies only to the extent that countries are willing to assume all rights and obligations in these areas. The roots of modern international law can be traced back to the seventeenth century Peace of Westphalia. Early international law was concerned with waging war, establishing peace, and other political issues such as diplomatic recognition of new national entities and governments. Although elaborate international rules gradually emerged—covering, for example, the status of neutral nations—the creation of laws governing commerce proceeded on a state-by-state basis in the nineteenth century. International law still has the function of upholding order, although in a broader sense than dealing with problems arising from war. At first, international law was essentially an amalgam of treaties, covenants, codes, and agreements. As trade grew among nations, order in commercial affairs assumed increasing importance. The law had originally dealt only with nations as entities, but a growing body of law rejected the idea that only nations can be subject to international law.

Paralleling the expanding body of international case law in the twentieth century, new international judiciary organizations have contributed to the creation of an established rule of international law: The Permanent Court of International Justice (1920–1945); the International Court of Justice (ICJ; **www.icj-cij.org**), the judicial arm of the United Nations, founded in 1946; and the International Law Commission, established by the United States in 1947. Disputes arising between nations are issues of **public international law**, and they may be taken before the ICJ or the World Court, located in The Hague. In supplemental documents to the United Nations Charter, article 38 of the ICJ Statute concerns international law:

> The Court, whose function is to decide in accordance with international law such disputes as are submitted to it, shall apply:
>
> a. international conventions, whether general or particular, establishing rules expressly recognized by the contesting states;
>
> b. international custom, as evidence of a general practice accepted as law;
>
> c. the general principles of law recognized by civilized nations;
>
> d. subject to the provisions of Article 59, judicial decisions and the teachings of the most highly qualified publicists of the various nations, as subsidiary means for the determination of rules of law.

Other sources of modern international law include treaties, international custom, judicial case decisions in the courts of law of various nations, and scholarly writings. What happens if a nation has allowed a case against it to be brought before the International Court of Justice and then refuses to accept a judgment against it? The plaintiff nation can seek recourse through the United Nations Security Council, which can use its full range of powers to enforce the judgment.

## Common Law Versus Civil Law

**Private international law** is the body of law that applies to disputes arising from commercial transactions between companies of different nations. As noted, laws governing commerce emerged gradually, leading to a major split in legal systems between various countries.[9] The story of law in the Western world can be traced to two sources: Rome, from which the continental European civil law tradition originated, and English common law, from which the U.S. legal system originated.

A **civil-law country** is one in which the legal system reflects the structural concepts and principles of the Roman Empire in the sixth century.

> For complex historical reasons, Roman law was received differently and at vastly different times in various regions of Europe, and in the nineteenth century each European country made a new start and adopted its own set of national private-law codes, for which the *Code Napoleon* of 1804 was the prototype. But the new national codes drew largely on Roman law in conceptual structure and substantive content. In civil-law countries, the codes in which private law is cast are formulated in broad general terms and are thought of as completely comprehensive, that, is, as the all-inclusive source of authority by reference to which every disputed case must be referred for decision.[10]

In **common-law countries**, many disputes are decided by reliance on the authority of past judicial decisions (cases). Although much of contemporary American and English law is legislative in origin, the law inferred from past judicial decisions is equal in importance to the law set down in codes. Common-law countries often rely on codification in certain areas—the U.S. Uniform Commercial Code is one example—but these codes are not the all-inclusive, systematic statements found in civil-law countries.

---

9   Much of the material in this section is adapted from Randall Kelso and Charles D. Kelso, *Studying Law: An Introduction* (St. Paul, MN: West Publishing, 1984).

10   Harry Jones, "Our Uncommon Common Law," *Tennessee Law Review* 30 (1975), p. 447.

The Uniform Commercial Code (UCC), fully adopted by 49 U.S. states, codifies a body of specifically designed rules covering commercial conduct. (Louisiana has adopted parts of the UCC, but its laws are still heavily influenced by the French civil code.) The host country's legal system—that is common or civil law—directly affects the form a legal business entity will take. In common-law countries, companies are legally incorporated by state authority. In civil-law countries, companies are formed by contract between two or more parties, who are fully liable for the actions of the company.

The United States, 9 of Canada's 10 provinces, and other former colonies with an Anglo-Saxon history, founded their systems on common law. Historically, much of continental Europe was influenced by Roman law and, later, the Napoleonic Code. Asian countries are split: India, Pakistan, Malaysia, Singapore, and Hong Kong are common-law jurisdictions. Japan, Korea, Thailand, Indochina, Taiwan, Indonesia, and China are civil-law jurisdictions. The legal systems in Scandinavia are mixed, displaying some civil-law attributes and some common-law attributes. Today, the majority of countries have legal systems based on civil-law traditions.

As various countries in Eastern and Central Europe wrestle with establishing legal systems in the post-Communist era, a struggle of sorts has broken out; consultants representing both common-law and civil-law countries are trying to influence the process. In much of Central Europe, including Poland, Hungary, and the Czech Republic, the German civil-law tradition prevails. As a result, banks not only take deposits and make loans but also engage in the buying and selling of securities. In Eastern Europe, particularly Russia, the United States has had greater influence. Germany has accused the United States of promoting a system so complex that it requires legions of lawyers. The U.S. response is that the German system is outdated.[11] In any event, the constant stream of laws and decrees issued by the Russian government creates an unpredictable, evolving legal environment. Specialized publications such as *The Russian and Commonwealth Business Law Report* are important resources for anyone doing business in Russia or the CIS.

*Napoleon's code of 1804 was the prototype for the code law system that predominates in Europe today.*

---

[11] Mark M. Nelson, "Two Styles of Business Vie in East Europe," *The Wall Street Journal* (April 3, 1995), p. A14.

## Islamic Law

The legal system in many Middle Eastern countries is identified with the laws of Islam, which are associated with "the one and only one God, the Almighty."[12] In **Islamic law**, the *sharia* is a comprehensive code governing Muslim conduct in all areas of life, including business. The code is derived from two sources. First is the Koran, the Holy Book written in Arabic that is a record of the revelations made to the Prophet Mohammed by Allah. The second source is the Hadith, which is based on the life, sayings, and practices of Muhammad. In particular, the Hadith spells out the products and practices that are *haram* (forbidden). The orders and instructions found in the Koran are analogous to code laws; the guidelines of the Hadith correspond to common law. Any Westerner doing business in the Middle East should have, at minimum, a rudimentary understanding of Islamic law and its implications for commercial activities. Brewers, for example, must refrain from advertising beer on billboards or in local-language newspapers.

## Sidestepping Legal Problems: Important Business Issues

Clearly, the global legal environment is dynamic and complex. Therefore, the best course to follow is to get expert legal help. However, the astute, proactive marketer can do a great deal to prevent conflicts from arising in the first place, especially concerning issues such as establishment, jurisdiction, patents and trademarks, antitrust, licensing and trade secrets, bribery, and advertising and other promotion tools. Regulation of specific promotion activities is discussed in Chapters 13 and 14.

### Jurisdiction

Company personnel working abroad should understand the extent to which they are subject to the jurisdiction of host-country courts. In the context of global marketing, **jurisdiction** refers to a court's authority to rule on particular types of controversies arising outside of a nation's borders or to exercise power over individuals or entities from different countries. Employees of foreign companies working in the United States must understand that courts have jurisdiction to the extent that the company can be demonstrated to be doing business in the state in which the court sits. The court may examine whether the foreign company maintains an office, solicits business, maintains bank accounts or other property, or has agents or other employees in the state in question. For example, in the mid-1990s, Revlon sued United Overseas Limited (UOL) in U.S. District Court for the Southern District of New York. Revlon charged the British company with breach of contract, contending that UOL had failed to purchase some specialty shampoos as agreed. Claiming lack of jurisdiction, UOL asked the court to dismiss the complaint. Revlon countered with the argument that UOL was, in fact, subject to the court's jurisdiction; Revlon cited the presence of a UOL sign above the entrance to the offices of a New York company in which UOL had a 50 percent ownership interest. The court denied UOL's motion to dismiss.[13]

Jurisdiction played an important role in two recent trade-related disputes. One pitted Volkswagen AG against General Motors. After GM's worldwide head of purchasing, José Ignacio López de Arriortúa, was hired by Volkswagen in 1992, his former employer accused him of taking trade secrets. Volkswagen accepted U.S. court jurisdiction in the dispute, although the company's lawyers requested

---

12  This section is adapted from Mushtaq Luqmani, Ugur Yavas, and Zahir Quraeshi, "Advertising in Saudi Arabia: Content and Regulation," *International Marketing Review* 6, no. 1 (1989), pp. 61–63.

13  Joseph Ortego and Josh Kardisch, "Foreign Companies Can Limit the Risk of Being Subject to U.S. Courts," *National Law Journal* 17, no. 3 (September 19, 1994), p. C2.

that the U.S. District Court in Detroit transfer the case to Germany. Jurisdiction was also an issue in a trade dispute that pitted Eastman Kodak against Fuji Photo Film. Kodak alleged that the Japanese government helped Fuji in Japan by blocking the distribution of Kodak film. The U.S. government turned the case over to the World Trade Organization, despite the opinion expressed by many experts that the WTO lacks jurisdiction in complaints over trade and competition policy.

## Intellectual Property: Patents, Trademarks, and Copyrights

Patents and trademarks that are protected in one country are not necessarily protected in another, so global marketers must ensure that patents and trademarks are registered in each country where business is conducted. A **patent** is a formal legal document that gives an inventor the exclusive right to make, use, and sell an invention for a specified period of time. Typically, the invention represents an "inventive leap" that is novel or nonobvious. A **trademark** is defined as a distinctive mark, motto, device, or emblem that a manufacturer affixes to a particular product or package to distinguish it from goods produced by other manufacturers. A **copyright** establishes ownership of a written, recorded, performed, or filmed creative work.

Infringement of intellectual property can take a variety of forms. **Counterfeiting** is the unauthorized copying and production of a product. An *associative counterfeit*, or *imitation*, uses a product name that differs slightly from a well-known brand but is close enough that consumers will associate it with the genuine product. A third type of counterfeiting is *piracy*, the unauthorized publication or reproduction of copyrighted work. Counterfeiting and piracy are particularly important in industries such as motion pictures, recorded music, computer software, and textbook publishing. Companies in these industries produce products that can be easily duplicated and distributed on a mass basis. The United States in particular has a vested interest in intellectual property protection around the globe because it is home to many companies in the industries just mentioned. However, the United States faces significant challenges in countries such as China. As one expert has noted:

> Current attempts to establish intellectual property law, particularly on the Chinese mainland, have been deeply flawed in their failure to address the difficulties of reconciling legal values, institutions, and forms generated in the West with the legacy of China's past and the constraints imposed by its present circumstances.[14]

Case 5-1 at the end of this chapter describes some of the problems companies encounter as they try to enforce trademarks around the world.

In the United States, where patents, trademarks, and copyrights are registered with the Federal Patent Office, the patent holder retains all rights for the life of the patent even if the product is not produced or sold. Trademarks in the United States are covered by the Trademark Act of 1946, also known as the Lanham Act. President Reagan signed the Trademark Law Revision Act into law in November 1988. The law makes it easier for companies to register new trademarks. Patent and trademark protection in the United States is very good, and U.S. law relies on the precedent of previously decided court cases for guidance. To register a patent in Europe, a company has the option of filing on a country-by-country basis or applying to the European Patent Office in Munich for patent registration in a specific number of countries. A third option will soon be available: The Community Patent Convention will make it possible for an inventor to file for a patent that is effective in the 25 signatory nations. Currently, patent procedures in Europe are quite expensive, in part because of the cost of translating

---

[14] William P. Alford, *To Steal a Book Is an Elegant Offense: Intellectual Property Law in Chinese Civilization* (Stanford, CA: Stanford University Press, 1995), p. 2.

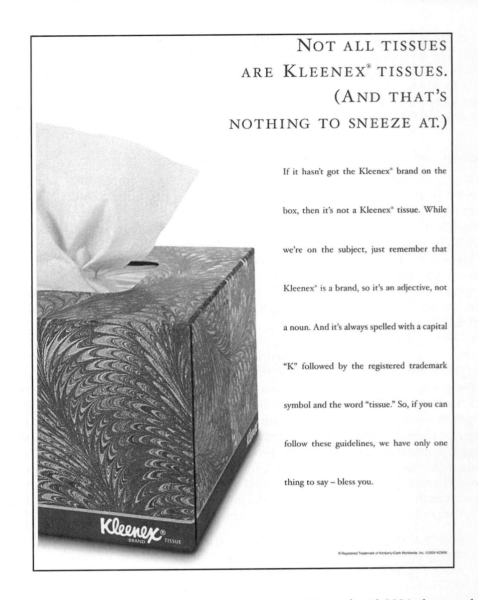

**NOT ALL TISSUES ARE KLEENEX® TISSUES. (AND THAT'S NOTHING TO SNEEZE AT.)**

If it hasn't got the Kleenex® brand on the box, then it's not a Kleenex® tissue. While we're on the subject, just remember that Kleenex® is a brand, so it's an adjective, not a noun. And it's always spelled with a capital "K" followed by the registered trademark symbol and the word "tissue." So, if you can follow these guidelines, we have only one thing to say – bless you.

© Registered Trademark of Kimberly-Clark Worldwide, Inc. ©2004 KCWW.

technical documents into all the languages of the EU as of mid-2004, the translation issue remained unresolved.[15] In July 1997, in response to complaints, the European Patent Office instituted a 19 percent reduction in the average cost of an eight-country patent registration. The United States recently joined the World Intellectual Property Organization (WIPO); governed by the Madrid agreement of 1891 and the more flexible 1996 Madrid protocol, the system allows trademark owners to seek protection in as many as 74 countries with a single application.

Companies sometimes find ways to exploit loopholes or other unique opportunities offered by patent and trademark laws in individual nations. In France, designer Yves St. Laurent was barred from marketing a new luxury perfume called Champagne because French laws allow the name to be applied only to sparkling wines produced in the Champagne region. St. Laurent proceeded to launch Champagne in the United States, Great Britain, Germany, and Belgium where Champagne and other geographic names are not protected trademarks. In France, the perfume is sold without a name.[16] In 1992, Germany's Bayer AG received permission from Russia's patent office to register *aspirin* as a trademark

[15]  Frances Williams, "Call for Stronger EU Patent Laws," *Financial Times* (May 22, 1997).

[16]  Karla Vermeulen, "Champagne Perfume Launched in United States but Barred in France," *Wine Spectator* (October 31, 1994), p. 9.

Headquartered in Geneva, Switzerland, the World Intellectual Property Organization (Wipo) is one of 16 specialized subunits of the United Nations. Wipo's mission is to promote and protect intellectual property throughout the world. Wipo views intellectual property as a critical element in economic development; it has created illustrated booklets that explain trademarks, copyright, and other intellectual property issues in a straightforward, easy-to-understand manner. Local agencies can access and print the booklets directly from Wipo's Internet site.

in that country. Rival pharmaceutical companies, such as France's Laboratoire UPSA, were infuriated because the ruling meant that they would effectively be shut out of the Russian market of 150 million people. According to a spokesperson for the French company, "The word never should have been registered in the first place. It's a universally accepted generic name." In June 1994, the Russian patent office rescinded permission; Bayer immediately announced its intention to appeal.[17]

International concern about intellectual property issues in the nineteenth century resulted in two important agreements. The first is the International Convention for the Protection of Industrial Property. Also known as the Paris Union or Paris Convention, the convention dates to 1883 and is now honored by nearly 100 countries. This treaty facilitates multicountry patent registrations by ensuring that, once a company files in a signatory country, it will be afforded a "right of priority" in other countries for 1 year from the date of the original filing. A U.S. company wishing to obtain foreign patent rights must apply to the Paris Union within 1 year of filing in the United States or risk a permanent loss of patent rights abroad.[18] In 1886, the International Union for the Protection of Literary and Artistic Property was formed. Also known as the Berne Convention, this was a landmark agreement on copyright protection.

Two other treaties deserve mention. The Patent Cooperation Treaty (PCT) has more than 100 contracting states, including Australia, Brazil, France, Germany, Japan, North Korea, South Korea, the Netherlands, Switzerland, the Russian

---

[17]  Marya Fogel, "Bayer Trademarks the Word 'Aspirin' in Russia, Leaving Rivals Apoplectic," *The Wall Street Journal* (October 29, 1993), p. A13.
[18]  Franklin R. Root, *Entry Strategies for International Markets* (New York: Lexington Books, 1994), p. 113.

Federation and other former Soviet republics, and the United States. The members constitute a union that provides certain technical services and cooperates in the filing, searching, and examination of patent applications in all member countries. The European Patent Office administers applications for the European Patent Convention, which is effective in the EU and Switzerland. An applicant can file a single patent application covering all of the convention states; the advantage is that the application will be subject to only one procedure of grant. Although national patent laws remain effective under this system, approved patents are effective in all member countries for a period of 20 years from the filing date.

In recent years, the U.S. government has devoted considerable diplomatic effort to improving the worldwide environment for intellectual property protection. For example, China agreed to accede to the Berne Convention in 1992; on January 1, 1994, China became an official signatory of the PCT. After years of discussion, the United States and Japan have agreed to make changes in their respective patent systems; Japan has promised to speed up patent examinations, eliminate challenges to patent submissions, and allow patent applications to be filed in English. Effective June 7, 1995, in accordance with GATT, new U.S. patents are granted for a period of 20 years from the filing date. Previously, patents had been valid for a 17-year term effective after being granted. Thus, U.S. patent laws now harmonize with those in the EU as well as Japan. Even with the changes, however, patents in Japan are narrower than those in the United States. As a result, companies such as Caterpillar have been unable to protect critical innovations in Japan because products very similar to those made by U.S. companies can be patented without fear of infringement.[19]

Another key issue is global patent protection for software. Although copyright laws protect the computer code, it does not apply to the idea embodied in the software. The U.S. Patent and Trademark Office has extended patent protection to software since 1981; Microsoft has more than 500 software patents. In Europe, software patents were not allowed under the Munich Convention; in June 1997, however, the EU indicated it was ready to revise patent laws so they cover software.[20] Table 5-2 ranks the 10 companies that received the most U.S. patents in 2002. Six of the 10 are Japanese companies; IBM has topped the rankings every year since 1993. IBM generates more than $1 billion in revenues by licensing patents and other forms of intellectual property; Hewlitt-Packard has more than 16,000 patents worldwide.

**Table 5-2**

Companies Receiving the Most
U.S. Patents, 2002

| Company | No. of Patents |
|---|---|
| 1. IBM | 3,288 |
| 2. Canon Kabushiki Kaisha | 1,893 |
| 3. Micron Technology | 1,833 |
| 4. NEC | 1,821 |
| 5. Hitachi | 1,601 |
| 6. Matsushita Electric Industrial | 1,544 |
| 7. Sony | 1,434 |
| 8. General Electric | 1,416 |
| 9. Mitsubishi | 1,373 |
| 10. Samsung | 1,328 |

Source: U.S. Patent and Trademark Office.

19 John Carey, "Inching Toward a Borderless Patent," *Business Week* (September 5, 1994), p. 35.
20 Richard Pynder, "Intellectual Property in Need of Protection," *Financial Times* (July 7, 1998), p. 22.

## Antitrust

Antitrust laws in the United States and other countries are designed to combat restrictive business practices and to encourage competition. The laws are enforced by agencies such as the U.S. Federal Trade Commission, Japan's Fair Trade Commission, and the European Commission. Some legal experts believe that the pressures of global competition have resulted in an increased incidence of price-fixing and collusion among companies. As then, FTC chairman Robert Pitofsky said, "For years, tariffs and trade barriers blocked global trade. Now those are falling, and we are forced to confront the private anticompetitive behavior that often remains."[21]

A recent rash of antitrust actions brought in the United States against foreign companies has raised concerns that the United States is violating international law as well as the sovereignty of other nations. The U.S. antitrust laws are a legacy of the nineteenth-century trust-busting era and are intended to maintain free competition by limiting the concentration of economic power. The Sherman Act of 1890 prohibits certain restrictive business practices, including fixing prices, limiting production, allocating markets, or any other scheme designed to limit or avoid competition. The law applies to the activities of U.S. companies outside U.S. boundaries, as well as to foreign companies conducting business in the United States. In a precedent-setting case, Nippon Paper Industries was found guilty in a U.S. court of conspiring with other Japanese companies to raise fax paper prices in the United States. The Japanese government denounced the U.S. indictment of Nippon Paper in December 1995 as a violation of international law and Japan's sovereignty. The meetings at which pricing strategies were allegedly discussed took place outside the United States; a U.S. federal judge struck down the indictment, ruling that the Sherman Act does not apply to foreign conduct. However, a federal appeals court in Boston reversed the decision. In his opinion, U.S. Circuit Judge Bruce Selya wrote, "We live in an age of international commerce, where decisions reached in one corner of the world can reverberate around the globe."[22]

Although similar antitrust laws are on the books in many countries, they are often weak or loosely enforced. In the fall of 1996, the Organization for Economic Cooperation and Development (OECD) began working on an agreement to coordinate antitrust laws. Meanwhile, antitrust is taking on increasing importance in emerging country markets. For example, Colgate-Palmolive's 1995 acquisition of Brazil's Kolynos oral care company for $1 billion was subject to review by that country's Administrative Council of Economic Defense (CADE). Rival Procter & Gamble instigated the review by complaining that the acquisition would give Colgate a 79 percent share of the market. CADE ruled that Colgate must either license the trademark to another company for 20 years or halt sales of Kolynos brand toothpaste in Brazil for 4 years; Colgate agreed to the latter. The Miller Brewing unit of Philip Morris also ran into antitrust problems in Brazil following its 1995 investment of $50 million in a 50/50 joint venture with Cia Cervejaria Brahma SA. CADE ruled that the venture, which produced and distributed Miller Genuine Draft beer, deprived consumers of head-to-head competition between the two brewing companies. CADE also criticized Miller for choosing a market entry strategy that required a relatively low level of investment. Nelio Weiss, a consultant at Coopers & Lybrand's Sao Paulo office, noted, "The message is that foreign companies shouldn't assume that antitrust authorities will be passive."[23]

---

[21] John R. Wilke, "Hunting Cartels: U.S. Trust-Busters Increasingly Target International Business," *The Wall Street Journal* (February 5, 1997), p. A10.

[22] John R. Wilke, "U.S. Court Rules Antitrust Laws Apply to Foreigners," *The Wall Street Journal* (March 19, 1997), p. B5.

[23] Yumiko Ono, "Colgate Purchase Gets Brazil's Blessing but with Restrictions on Brand Name," *The Wall Street Journal* (September 20, 1996), p. A11; Matt Moffett, "Miller Brewing Is Ordered to Sell Its Stake in Brazilian Joint Venture," *The Wall Street Journal* (June 13, 1997), p. A15.

For the past four decades, the competition authority of the European Commission has had the power to prohibit agreements and practices that prevent, restrict, and/or distort competition. The commission has jurisdiction over European-based companies as well as non-European ones such as Microsoft that generate significant revenues in Europe. For example, the commission can block a proposed merger or joint venture, approve it with only minor modifications, or demand substantial concessions before granting approval. The commission begins with a preliminary study of a proposed deal; serious concerns can lead to an in-depth investigation lasting several months. Since the mid-1990s, the commission has taken an increasingly activist approach. The current competition minister is Mario Monti, an Italian with an economics background. Nicknamed "Super Mario" by the European press, Monti blocked the proposed $115 merger of WorldCom and Sprint in 2000. He also demanded major concessions before allowing America Online to acquire Time Warner.[24] There have been calls for the EU to revamp its approach to antitrust issues and reduce its caseload. Any proposed changes will pit modernists against traditionalists. As one European attorney complained, "The commission is putting resources into regulating cases that don't actually restrict competition, which means that the cases that do need to be looked at are not being resolved efficiently."[25] Table 5-3 summarizes some recent joint ventures, mergers, and other global business deals that have been subject to review by antitrust authorities on both sides of the Atlantic.

The interstate trade clause of the Treaty of Rome applies to trade with third countries, so that a company must be aware of the conduct of its affiliates. The

| **Table 5-3** | **Companies Involved** | **Antitrust Review in EU** | **Antitrust Review in USA** |
|---|---|---|---|
| *Antitrust Investigations* | Merger of Sony Music (Japan) and BMG (Germany), 2004 | Approved | Approved |
| | Acquisition of Honeywell (USA) by GE (USA), 2001, $40 billion | Deal was vetoed on grounds that merged firm would be stronger than competitors in aviation equipment | Deal was on track for approval, subject to conditions |
| | Joint venture between music businesses of EMI Group PLC (Great Britain) and Time Warner (USA), 2000, $20 billion | Regulators expressed concern that the new EMI-Time Warner would dominate growing market for digital music distribution | Deal was scrapped in October 2000 before regulatory review began |
| | Merger of WorldCom (USA) and MCI (USA), 1998, $37 billion | MCI ordered to divest all Internet-related assets | U.S. concerns were incorporated into review by EU, which occurred first; EU's terms were acceptable to Federal Communications Commission and Department of Justice |
| | Strategic alliance between British Airways (UK) and American Airlines (USA), 1998 | Commission required the two carriers to give up 267 weekly slots at London's Heathrow Airport | Washington has demanded an "open skies" agreement with the UK, allowing U.S. carriers other than United and American to fly into Heathrow |

*Source:* Compiled by the authors.

---

[24] Anita Raghavan and Brandon Mitchener, "'Super Mario': EU's Antitrust Czar Isn't Afraid to Say No; Just Ask Time Warner," *The Wall Street Journal* (October 2, 2000), pp. A1, A10.
[25] Emma Tucker, "Europe's Paper Mountain," *Financial Times* (February 11, 1998), p. 21.

commission also exempts certain cartels from Articles 85 and 86 of the treaty in an effort to encourage the growth of important businesses. The intent is to allow European companies to compete on an equal footing with Japan and the United States. In some instances, individual country laws in Europe apply to specific marketing mix elements. For example, some countries permit selective or exclusive product distribution. However, European Community law can take precedence.

In one case, Consten, a French company, had exclusive French rights to import and distribute consumer electronics products from the German Grundig company. Consten sued another French firm, charging the latter with bringing "parallel imports" into France illegally; that is, Consten charged that the competitor bought Grundig products from various foreign suppliers without Consten's knowledge and was selling them in France. Although Consten's complaint was upheld by two French courts, the Paris Court of Appeals suspended the judgment, pending a ruling by the European Commission on whether the Grundig-Consten arrangement violated Articles 85 and 86 of the Treaty of Rome. The commission ruled against Consten on the grounds that "territorial protection proved to be particularly damaging to the realization of the Common Market."[26]

A recent high-profile antitrust case pitted the European Union against U.S. based Microsoft. The case dates back to 1998 when Sun Microsystems alleged that Microsoft was restricting the ability of servers built by Sun and other companies to interface with PCs running Windows. As the case gained momentum, the European Commission investigated whether Microsoft was creating a monopoly in new market segments by bundling Windows with its Media Player program. The Commission finally issued a ruling in Spring 2004 that found Microsoft had violated antitrust laws. Three penalties were issued. First, Microsoft must allow computer makers to market PCs equipped with Windows and alternative brands of media software for playing music and videos. Second, Microsoft must provide competitors with more information about Windows codes and protocols; the action is designed to spur innovation in new software products. Finally, Microsoft was ordered to pay a record fine of $602 million.[27]

In some instances, companies or entire industries have been able to secure exemption from antitrust rules. In the airline industry, for example, KLM and Northwestern won an exemption from the U.S. government and now share computer codes and set prices jointly. Similarly, the European Commission permitted United International Pictures (UIP), a joint venture between Paramount, Universal, and MGM/UA, to cut costs by collaborating on motion picture distribution in Europe. In 1998, the commission reversed itself and notified the three studios that they must distribute their films independently in Europe.[28] A **cartel** is a group of separate companies that collectively sets prices, controls output, or takes other actions to maximize profits. For example, the group of oil producing countries known as OPEC is a cartel. In the United States, most cartels are illegal. One notable exception, however, has a direct impact on global marketing. A number of the world's major shipping lines, including the U.S.-based Sea-Land Service and Denmark's A. P. Moller/Maersk line, have enjoyed exemption from antitrust laws since the passage of the Shipping Act of 1916.

---

[26] Detlev Vagts, *Transnational Business Problems* (Mineola, NY: The Foundation Press, 1986), pp. 285–291.

[27] Brandon Mitchener, James Kanter, and Don Clark, "Regulatory Jolt: EU Warns Microsoft Is Abusing Its Control of Certain Software," *The Wall Street Journal* (August 7, 2003), pp. A1, A2. See also Mitchener, "EU Backs Plans to Punish Microsoft," *The Wall Street Journal* (March 6, 2004), p. B3.

[28] Alice Rawsthorn and Emma Tucker, "Movie Studios May Have to Scrap Joint Distributor," *Financial Times* (February 6, 1998), p. 1.

The law was originally enacted to ensure reliability; today, it has been estimated that the cartel results in shipping prices that are 18 percent higher than they would be if shippers set prices independently. Attempts in recent years to change the law have not been successful.[29]

## Licensing and Trade Secrets

**Licensing** is a contractual agreement in which a licensor allows a licensee to use patents, trademarks, trade secrets, technology, or other intangible assets in return for royalty payments or other forms of compensation. U.S. laws do not regulate the licensing process per se as do technology transfer laws in the European Union, Australia, Japan, and many developing countries. The duration of the licensing agreement and the amount of royalties a company can receive are considered a matter of commercial negotiation between licensor and licensee, and there are no government restrictions on remittances of royalties abroad. Important considerations in licensing include analysis of what assets a firm may offer for license, how to price the assets, and whether to grant only the right to "make" the product or to grant the rights to "use" and to "sell" the product as well. The right to sublicense is another important issue. As with distribution agreements, decisions must also be made regarding exclusive or nonexclusive arrangements and the size of the licensee's territory.

To prevent the licensee from using the licensed technology to compete directly with the licensor, the latter may try to limit the licensee to selling only in its home country. The licensor may also seek to contractually bind the licensee to discontinue use of the technology after the contract has expired. In practice, host-government laws and even U.S. antitrust laws may make such agreements impossible to obtain. Licensing is a potentially dangerous action: It may be instrumental in creating a competitor. Therefore, licensors should be careful to ensure that their own competitive position remains advantageous. This requires constant innovation.

As noted, licensing agreements can come under antitrust scrutiny. In one recent case, Bayer AG granted an exclusive patent license for a new household insecticide to S. C. Johnson & Sons. The German firm's decision to license was based in part on the time required for EPA approval, which had stretched to 3 years. Bayer decided it made better business sense to let the U.S. firm deal with regulatory authorities in return for a 5 percent royalty on sales. However, a class-action suit filed against the companies alleged that the licensing deal would allow Johnson to monopolize the $450 million home insecticide market. Then the U.S. Justice Department stepped in, calling the licensing agreement anticompetitive. In a statement, Anne Bingaman, then head of the justice department's antitrust unit, said, "The cozy arrangement that Bayer and Johnson maintained is unacceptable in a highly concentrated market." Bayer agreed to offer licenses to any interested company on better terms than the original contract with Johnson. Johnson agreed to notify the U.S. government of any future pending exclusive licensing agreements for household insecticides. If Bayer is party to any such agreements, the Justice Department has the right to veto them. Not surprisingly, the reaction from the legal community has been negative. One Washington lawyer who specializes in intellectual property law noted that the case "really attacks traditional licensing practices." As Melvin Jager, president of the Licensing Executives Society, explained, "An exclusive license is a very valuable tool to promote intellectual property and get it out into the marketplace."[30]

---

[29] Anna Wilde Mathews, "Making Waves: As U.S. Trade Grows, Shipping Cartels Get a Bit More Scrutiny," *The Wall Street Journal* (October 7, 1997), pp. A1, A8.
[30] Brigid McMenamin, "Eroding Patent Rights," *Forbes* (October 24, 1994), p. 92.

What happens if a licensee gains knowledge of the licensor's trade secrets? **Trade secrets** are confidential information or knowledge that has commercial value and is not in the public domain, and for which steps have been taken to keep it secret. Trade secrets include manufacturing processes, formulas, designs, and customer lists. To prevent disclosure, the licensing of unpatented trade secrets should be linked to confidentiality contracts with each employee who has access to the protected information. In the United States, trade secrets are protected by state law rather than federal statute; most states have adopted the Uniform Trade Secrets Act (UTSA). The U.S. law provides trade secret liability against third parties that obtain confidential information through an intermediary. Remedies include damages and other forms of relief.

The 1990s have seen widespread improvements in laws pertaining to trade secrets. Several countries have recently adopted trade secret statutes for the first time. Mexico's first statute protecting trade secrets became effective on June 28, 1991; China's first trade secret law took effect December 1, 1993. In both countries, the new laws were part of broader revisions of intellectual property laws. Japan and South Korea have also recently amended their intellectual property laws to include trade secrets. Many countries in Central and Eastern Europe have also enacted laws to protect trade secrets. When NAFTA became effective on January 1, 1994, it marked the first international trade agreement with provisions for protecting trade secrets. This milestone was quickly followed by the Agreement on Trade-Related Aspects of Intellectual Property Rights (TRIPs) that resulted from the Uruguay Round of GATT negotiations. The TRIPs agreement requires signatory countries to protect against acquisition, disclosure, or use of trade secrets "in a manner contrary to honest commercial practices."[31] Despite these formal legal developments, in practice, enforcement is the key issue. Companies transferring trade secrets across borders should apprise themselves not only of the existence of legal protection but also of the risks associated with lax enforcement.

## Bribery and Corruption: Legal and Ethical Issues

History does not record a burst of international outrage when Charles M. Schwab, head of Bethlehem Steel at the beginning of the twentieth century, presented a $200,000 diamond and pearl necklace to the mistress of Czar Alexander III's nephew.[32] In return for that consideration, Bethlehem Steel won the contract to supply the rails for the Trans-Siberian railroad. Today, in the post-Soviet era, Western companies are again being lured by emerging opportunities in Eastern Europe. Here, as in the Middle East and other parts of the world, they are finding that bribery is a way of life, and that corruption is widespread. U.S. companies in particular are constrained in their responses to such a situation by U.S. government policies of the post-Watergate age. **Bribery** is the corrupt business practice of demanding or offering some type of consideration—typically cash payment—when negotiating a cross-border deal. Transparency International (**www.transparency.org**) compiles an annual report ranking countries by Corruption Perceptions Index (CPI). The "cleanest" score is 10. The 2003 ranking of the top 10 and bottom 10 countries is shown in Table 5-4.

In the United States, the **Foreign Corrupt Practices Act (FCPA)** is a legacy of the Watergate scandal during Richard Nixon's presidency. In the course of his investigation, the Watergate special prosecutor discovered that more than

---

[31] Salem M. Katsh and Michael P. Dierks, "Globally, Trade Secrets Laws Are All Over the Map," *The National Law Journal* 17, no. 36 (May 8, 1995), p. C12.

[32] Much of the material in this section is adapted from Daniel Pines, "Amending the Foreign Corrupt Practices Act to Include a Private Right of Action," *California Law Review* (January 1994), pp. 185–229.

**Table 5-4**

*2003 Corruption Rankings*

| Rank/Country | 2003 CPI Score | Rank/Country | 2003 CPI Score |
|---|---|---|---|
| 1. Finland | 9.7 | 124. Angola | 1.8 |
| 2. Iceland | 9.6 | 124. Azerbaijan | 1.8 |
| 3. Denmark | 9.5 | 124. Cameroon | 1.8 |
| 3. New Zealand | 9.5 | 124. Georgia | 1.8 |
| 5. Singapore | 9.4 | 124. Tajikistan | 1.8 |
| 6. Sweden | 9.3 | 129. Myanmar | 1.6 |
| 7. Netherlands | 8.9 | 129. Paraguay | 1.6 |
| 8. Australia | 8.8 | 131. Haiti | 1.5 |
| 8. Norway | 8.8 | 132. Nigeria | 1.4 |
| 8. Switzerland | 8.8 | 133. Bangladesh | 1.3 |

*Source:* Transparency International, 2004.

300 American companies had made undisclosed payments to foreign officials totaling hundreds of millions of dollars. The act was unanimously passed by Congress and signed into law by President Jimmy Carter on December 17, 1977. Administered by the U.S. Department of Justice and the Securities and Exchange Commission, the act was concerned with disclosure and prohibition. The disclosure part of the act required publicly held companies to institute internal accounting controls that would record all transactions. The prohibition part made it a crime for U.S. corporations to bribe an official of a foreign government or political party to obtain or retain business. Payments to third parties were also prohibited when the company had reason to believe that part or all of the money would be channeled to foreign officials.

The U.S. business community immediately began lobbying for changes to the act, complaining that the statute was too vague and so broad in scope that it threatened to severely curtail U.S. business activities abroad. Amendments to the statutes were signed into law by President Ronald Reagan in 1988 as part of the Omnibus Trade and Competitiveness Act. Among the changes were exclusions for "grease" payments to low-level officials to cut red tape and expedite "routine governmental actions" such as clearing shipments through customs, securing permits, or getting airport passport clearance to leave a country.

Although several well-known U.S. companies have pleaded guilty to violations of the antibribery provisions, enforcement of the act has generally been lax. A total of 23 cases were filed between 1977 and 1988. In one such case, a business executive was convicted of giving money and honeymoon airplane tickets to a Nigerian government official in the hopes of securing a contract.[33] There are stiff penalties for violating the law: Convictions carry severe jail sentences (in excess of 1 to 5 years) and heavy fines (in excess of $1 million). Fines cannot be paid or reimbursed by the company, under the theory that individuals commit such crimes. It has also been made clear that the law will not let a person do indirectly (e.g., through an agent, joint venture partner, or other third party) what it prohibits directly.

Some critics of the FCPA decry it as a regrettable display of moral imperialism. At issue is the extraterritorial sovereignty of U.S. law. It is wrong, according to these critics, to impose U.S. laws, standards, values, and mores on American companies and citizens worldwide. As one legal expert points out, however, this criticism has one fundamental flaw: There is no nation in which the letter of the law condones bribery of government officials. Thus, the standard set by the FCPA is shared, in principle at least, by other nations.[34]

---

[33] Katherine Albright and Grace Won, "Foreign Corrupt Practices Act," *American Criminal Law Review* (Spring 1993), p. 787.

[34] Daniel Pines, "Amending the Foreign Corrupt Practices Act to Include a Private Right of Action," *California Law Review* (January 1994), p. 205.

A second criticism of the FCPA is that it puts U.S. companies in a difficult position vis-à-vis foreign competitors, especially those in Japan and Europe. Several opinion polls and surveys of the business community have revealed the widespread perception that the act adversely affects U.S. businesses overseas. Some academic researchers have concluded that the FCPA has not negatively affected the export performance of U.S. industry. However, a U.S. Commerce Department report prepared with the help of U.S. intelligence services indicated that in 1994 alone, bribes offered by non-U.S. companies were a factor in 100 business deals valued at $45 billion. Foreign companies prevailed in 80 percent of those deals.[35] Although accurate statistics are hard to come by, the rankings shown in Table 5-4 highlight some areas of the world where bribery is still rampant.

The existence of bribery as a fact of life in world markets will not change because it is condemned by the U.S. Congress. In fact, bribery payments are considered a deductible business expense in many European countries. According to one estimate, the annual price tag for illegal payments by German firms alone is more than $5 billion. Still, increasing numbers of global companies are adopting codes of conduct designed to reduce illegal activities. Moreover, in May 1997, the 29-member OECD adopted a formal standard against bribery by drafting a binding international convention that makes it a crime for a company bidding on a contract to bribe foreign officials. Representatives of OECD member nations put the legislation before their respective parliaments in 1998; the convention went into effect in February 1999. The OECD is also working on a smaller scale to create so-called islands of integrity. The goal is to achieve transparency at the level of an individual deal, with all the players pledging not to bribe. In one recent example, Cable & Wireless PLC from the United Kingdom was selected over GTE to acquire 49 percent of Panama's telephone company. The Panamanian government pledged to make all documents public after the bidding process was completed.[36]

Despite the progress made to date on the new agreement, industry observers have expressed several concerns about the proposed treaty. First, it is unclear whether the new law will be enforced with equal rigor everywhere, and, if not, what sanctions will be imposed. Second, the treaty contains legal loopholes, such as the provision that business contracts can be linked to public aid projects such as building hospitals. Third, there is disagreement on what constitutes a "normal" versus an "abnormal" payment. Finally, it will be necessary to arrive at a workable definition of what constitutes a "public official."[37]

When companies operate abroad in the absence of home-country legal constraints, they face a continuum of choices concerning company ethics. At one extreme, they can maintain home-country ethics worldwide with absolutely no adjustment or adaptation to local practice. At the other extreme, they can abandon any attempt to maintain company ethics and adapt entirely to local conditions and circumstances as they are perceived by company managers in each local environment. Between these extremes, one approach that companies may select is to utilize varying degrees of extension of home-country ethics. Alternatively, they may adapt in varying degrees to local customs and practices.

What should a U.S. company do if competitors are willing to offer a bribe? Two alternative courses of action are possible. One is to ignore bribery and act as if it does not exist. The other is to recognize the existence of bribery and evaluate its effect on the customer's purchase decision as if it were just another element of

---

[35] Amy Borrus, "Inside the World of Greased Palms," *Business Week* (November 6, 1995), pp. 36–38.
[36] Neil King Jr., "Coming Clean: EU Firms Await Pact on Banning Bribery with Mixed Feelings," *The Wall Street Journal Europe* (September 23, 1997), pp. 1, 7.
[37] John Mason and Guy de Jonquières, "Goodbye Mr. 10%," *Financial Times* (July 22, 1997), p. 13.

**Table 5-5**

*Lawyers: An International Comparison*

| Country | Lawyers per 100,000 People |
|---|---|
| USA | 290 |
| Australia | 242 |
| United Kingdom | 141 |
| France | 80 |
| Germany | 79 |
| Hungary | 79 |
| Japan | 11 |
| Korea | 3 |

Source: Adapted from Frank B. Cross, "Lawyers, the Economy, and Society," *American Business Law Journal* (Summer 1998), pp. 477+.

the marketing mix. The overall value of a company's offer must be as good as, or better than, the competitor's overall offering, bribe included. It may be possible to offer a lower price, a better product, better distribution, or better advertising to offset the value added by the bribe. The best line of defense is to have a product that is clearly superior to that of the competition. In such a case, a bribe should not sway the purchase decision. Alternatively, clear superiority in service and in local representation may tip the scales.

## Conflict Resolution, Dispute Settlement, and Litigation

The degree of legal cooperation and harmony in the EU is unique and stems in part from the existence of code law as a common bond. Other regional organizations have made far less progress toward harmonization. Countries vary in their approach toward conflict resolution. Table 5-5 shows the number of practicing lawyers per 200,000 people in selected countries. The United States has more lawyers than any other country in the world and is arguably the most

*global* MARKETING Q&A

**Wall Street Journal:** "How do you deal with developing countries that have oi , but where there are governments and people with their hands out to you?"

**Lord John Browne, chairman, BP PLC:** "I think that the first thing you have recognize is that in the vast majority of the world, corruption, whether it's dormant or active, lies very close below the surface. So, unless it is carefully policed it becomes a monster that eats everybody. The first thing you must do is to look to the boundaries of the company and make sure that the payments we make are for services rendered, of a legal nature, and equal to the services obtained. We cannot be a nation's keeper. But we can influence. If corruption is around, it sort of says to people, well, maybe we can get away with something. So it will be very clear that we must always be reinforcing what we do and take swift and speedy action if someone does something bad."

**Wall Street Journal:** "Have you ever had to deal with someone with his hand out?"

**Lord Browne:** "Oh yes. Not recently. It's very easy to say 'goodbye.'"

Source: Bhushan Bahree, "Beyond BP's Catchphrase," The Wall Street Journal (November 25, 2003), p. B11.

litigious nation on earth. In part, this is a reflection of the low-context nature of American culture and the spirit of confrontational competitiveness. Other factors can contribute to differing attitudes toward litigation. For example, in many European nations, class action lawsuits are not allowed. Also, European lawyers cannot undertake cases on a contingency fee basis. However, change is in the air, as Europe experiences a broad political shift away from the welfare state.[38]

Conflicts inevitably arise in business anywhere, especially when different cultures come together to buy, sell, establish joint ventures, compete, and cooperate in global markets. For American companies, the dispute with a foreign party is frequently in the home-country jurisdiction. The issue can be litigated in the United States, where the company and its attorneys might be said to enjoy "home court" advantage. Litigation in foreign courts, however, becomes vastly more complex, partly because of differences in language, legal systems, currencies, and traditional business customs and patterns. In addition, problems arise from differences in procedures relating to discovery. In essence, *discovery* is the process of obtaining evidence to prove claims and determining which evidence may be admissible in which countries under which conditions. A further complication is the fact that judgments handed down in courts in another country may not be enforceable in the home country. For all these reasons, many companies prefer to pursue arbitration before proceeding to litigate.

## Alternatives to Litigation for Dispute Settlement[39]

In 1995, the Cuban government abruptly cancelled contracts with Endesa, a Spanish utility company. Rather than seek restitution in a Cuban court, Endesa turned to the International Arbitration Tribunal in Paris, seeking damages of $12 million. Endesa's actions illustrate how alternative dispute resolution (ADR) methods allow parties to resolve international commercial disputes without resorting to the court system. Formal arbitration is one means of settling international business disputes outside the courtroom. **Arbitration** is a negotiation process that the two parties have, by prior agreement, committed themselves to using. It is a fair process in the sense that the parties using it have created it themselves. Generally, arbitration involves a hearing of the parties before a three-member panel; each party selects one panel member, and those two panel members in turn select the third member. The panel renders a judgment that the parties agree in advance to abide by.

The most important treaty regarding international arbitration is the 1958 United Nations Convention on the Recognition and Enforcement of Foreign Arbitral Awards. Also known as the New York Convention, the treaty has 107 signatory countries, including China. Brazil is notable among the big emerging markets for not being a signatory. The framework created by the New York Convention is important for several reasons. First, when parties enter into agreements that provide for international arbitration, the signatory countries can hold the parties to their pledge to use arbitration. Second, after arbitration has taken place and the arbitrators have made an award, the signatories recognize and can enforce the judgment. Third, the signatories agree that there are limited grounds for challenging arbitration decisions. The grounds that are recognized are different than the typical appeals that are permitted in a court of law.

---

[38] Charles Fleming, "Europe Learns Litigious Ways," *The Wall Street Journal* (February 24, 2004), p. A17.
[39] The authors are indebted to Louis B. Kimmelman of O'Melveny & Meyers LLP, New York City, New York, for his contributions to this section.

Some firms and lawyers inexperienced in the practice of international commercial arbitration approach the arbitration clauses in a contract as "just another clause." In fact, the terms of every contract are different and therefore no two arbitration clauses should be the same. Consider, for example, the case of a contract between an American firm and a Japanese one. If the parties resort to arbitration, where will it take place? The American side will be reluctant to go to Japan; conversely, the Japanese side will not want to arbitrate in the United States. An alternative, "neutral" location—Singapore or London, for example—must be considered and specified in the arbitration clause. In what language will the proceedings be conducted? If no language is specified in the arbitration clause, the arbitrators themselves will choose.

In addition to location and language, other issues must be addressed as well. For example, if the parties to a patent-licensing arrangement agree in the arbitration clause that the validity of the patent cannot be contested, such a provision may not be enforceable in some countries. Which country's laws will be used as the standard for invalidity? Pursuing such an issue on a country-by-country basis would be inordinately time-consuming. In addition, there is the issue of acceptance: By law, U.S. courts must accept an arbitrator's decision in patent disputes; in other countries, however, there is no general rule of acceptance. To reduce delays relating to such issues, one expert suggests drafting arbitration clauses with as much specificity as possible. To the extent possible, for example, patent policies in various countries should be addressed; arbitration clauses may also include a provision that all foreign patent issues will be judged according to the standard of home-country law. Another provision could forbid the parties from commencing separate legal actions in other countries. The goal is to help the arbitration tribunal zero in on the express intentions of the parties.[40]

For decades, business arbitration has also been promoted through the International Court of Arbitration at the Paris-based International Chamber of Commerce (ICC; **www.iccwbo.org**). The ICC recently modernized some of its older rules. However, because it is such a well-known organization, it has an extensive backlog of cases. Overall, the ICC has gained a reputation for being slower, more expensive, and more cumbersome than some alternatives. As U.S. involvement in global commerce grew dramatically during the post–World War II period, the American Arbitration Association (AAA) also became recognized as an effective institution within which to resolve disputes. In 1992, the AAA signed a cooperation agreement with China's Beijing Conciliation Center. Each year, the AAA uses mediation to help resolve thousands of disputes. The AAA has entered into cooperation agreements with the ICC and other global organizations to promote the use of alternative dispute resolution methods; it serves as the agent to administer arbitrations in the United States under ICC auspices. In one recent case, Toys "R" Us was the losing party in a dispute brought to the AAA. The dispute's origins date back to a 1982 licensing agreement between the toy retailer and Alghanin & Sons regarding toy stores in the Middle East. The AAA ruled that Toys "R" Us was to pay a $55 million arbitration award.

Another agency for settling disputes is the Swedish Arbitration Institute of the Stockholm Chamber of Commerce. This agency frequently administers disputes between Western and Eastern European countries and has gained credibility for its evenhanded administration. However, a favorable ruling from the arbitration tribunal is one thing; enforcement is another. For example, Canada's IMP Group took its case against a Russian hotel development partner to Stockholm and was awarded $9.4 million. When payment was not forthcoming, IMP's representatives took matters into their own hands: They commandeered an Aeroflot jet in Canada and released it only after the Russians paid up![41] Other alternatives have proliferated in recent years. In addition to those mentioned, active centers for arbitration exist in Vancouver, Hong Kong, Cairo, Kuala Lumpur, Singapore, Buenos Aires, Bogotá, and Mexico City. A World Arbitration Institute was established in New York; in the United Kingdom, Advisory, Conciliation and Arbitration Service (ACAS) has achieved great success at handling industrial disputes. An International Council for Commercial Arbitration (ICCA) was established to coordinate the far-flung activities of arbitration organizations. The ICCA meets in different locations around the world every 4 years.

The United Nations Conference on International Trade Law (UNCITRAL; **www.un.or.at/uncitral**) has also been a significant force in the area of arbitration. Its rules have become more or less standard, as many of the organizations just named have adopted them with some modifications. Many developing countries, for example, long held prejudices against the ICC, AAA, and other developed-country organizations. Representatives of developing nations assumed that such organizations would be biased in favor of multinational corporations. Developing nations insisted on settlement in national courts, which was unacceptable to the multinational firms. This was especially true in Latin America, where the Calvo Doctrine required disputes arising with foreign investors be resolved in national courts under national laws. The

[40] Bruce Londa, "An Agreement to Arbitrate Disputes Isn't the Same in Every Language," *Brandweek* (September 26, 1994), p. 18. See also John M. Allen, Jr. and Bruce G. Merritt, "Drafters of Arbitration Clauses Face a Variety of Unforeseen Perils," *National Law Journal* 17, no. 33 (April 17, 1995), pp. C6–C7.

[41] Dorothee J. Feils and Florin M. Sabac, "The Impact of Political Risk on the Foreign Direct Investment Decision: A Capital Budgeting Analysis," *Engineering* 45, no. 2 (2000), p. 129.

growing influence of the ICCA and UNCITRAL rules, coupled with the proliferation of regional arbitration centers, have contributed to changing attitudes in developing countries and resulted in the increased use of arbitration around the world.

# THE REGULATORY ENVIRONMENT

The regulatory environment of global marketing consists of a variety of governmental and nongovernmental agencies that enforce laws or set guidelines for conducting business. These regulatory agencies address a wide range of marketing issues, including price control, valuation of imports and exports, trade practices, labeling, food and drug regulations, employment conditions, collective bargaining, advertising content, and competitive practices. As noted in *The Wall Street Journal:*

> Each nation's regulations reflect and reinforce its brand of capitalism—predatory in the U.S., paternal in Germany, and protected in Japan—and its social values. It's easier to open a business in the U.S. than in Germany because Germans value social consensus above risk-taking, but it's harder to hire people because Americans worry more about discrimination lawsuits. It's easier to import children's clothes in the U.S. than Japan because Japanese bureaucrats defend a jumble of import restrictions, but it's harder to open bank branches across the U.S. because Americans strongly defend state prerogatives.[42]

In most countries, the influence of regulatory agencies is pervasive, and an understanding of how they operate is essential to protect business interests and advance new programs. Executives at many global companies are realizing the need to hire lobbyists to represent their interests and to influence the direction of the regulatory process. For example, in the early 1990s, McDonald's, Nike, and Toyota didn't have a single representative in Brussels. Today, each of the companies has several people representing its interests to the European Commission. U.S. law firms and consulting firms also have sharply increased their presence in Brussels; in an effort to gain insight into EU politics and access to its policy makers, some have hired EU officials. In all, there are currently approximately 10,000 lobbyists in Brussels representing about 1,400 companies and nonprofit organizations from around the world.[43]

## Regional Economic Organizations: The European Union Example

The overall importance of regional organizations such as the World Trade Organization and the European Union (EU) was discussed in Chapter 3. The legal dimensions are important, however, and will be briefly mentioned here. The Treaty of Rome established the European Community (EC), the precursor to the European Union. The treaty created an institutional framework in which a council (the Council of Ministers) serves as the main decision-making body, with each country member having direct representation. The European Commission, the European Parliament, and the European Court of Justice are the other three main institutions of the community. The 1987 Single European Act amended the Treaty of Rome and provided strong impetus for the creation of a single market beginning January 1, 1993. Although technically the target was not completely met, approximately 85 percent of the new recommendations were implemented into national law by most member states by the target date, resulting in substantial harmonization. A relatively new body known as the European Council (a distinct entity from the Council

[42] Bob Davis, "Red-Tape Traumas: To All U.S. Managers Upset by Regulations: Try Germany or Japan," *The Wall Street Journal* (December 14, 1995), p. A1.

[43] Brandon Mitchener, "Standard Bearers: Increasingly, Rules of Global Economy Are Set in Brussels," *The Wall Street Journal* (April 23, 2002), p. A1.

of Ministers) was formally incorporated into the EC institutional structure by Article 2 of the 1987 act. Comprised of heads of member states plus the president of the commission, the European Council's role is to define general political guidelines for the union and provide direction on integration-related issues such as monetary union.[44] Governments in Central and Eastern European countries that hope to join are currently getting their laws in line with those of the EU.

The Treaty of Rome contains hundreds of articles, several of which are directly applicable to global companies and global marketers. Articles 30 through 36 establish the general policy referred to as "Free Flow of Goods, People, Capital and Technology" among the member states. Articles 85 through 86 contain competition rules, as amended by various directives of the 20-member EU Commission. The commission is the administrative arm of the EU; from its base in Brussels, the commission proposes laws and policies, monitors the observance of EU laws, administers and implements EU legislation, and represents the EU to international organizations.[45] Commission members represent the union rather than their respective nations. The laws, regulations, directives, and policies that originate in the commission must be submitted to the parliament for an opinion and then passed along to the council for a final decision. Once the council approves a prospective law, it becomes union law, which is somewhat analogous to U.S. federal law. Regulations automatically become law throughout the union; directives include a time frame for implementation by legislation in each member state. For example, in 1994 the commission issued a directive regarding use of trademarks in comparative advertising. Individual member nations of the EU have been working to implement the directive; for example, in the United Kingdom, the 1994 Trade Marks Act gave companies the right to apply for trademark protection of smells, sounds, and images and also provides improved protection against trademark counterfeiting.

The Single Market era is one in which many industries face new regulatory environments. The European Court of Justice, based in Luxembourg, is the European Union's highest legal authority. It is responsible for ensuring that EU laws and treaties are upheld throughout the union. Based in Luxembourg, it consists of two separate tribunals. The senior body is known as the Court of Justice; a separate entity, the Court of First Instance, hears cases involving commerce and competition (see Table 5-6).

**Table 5-6**

*Recent and Pending Actions by the European Court of Justice*

| Country/Plaintiffs Involved | Issue |
| --- | --- |
| USA/Microsoft | The Court of First Instance will make a preliminary ruling on antitrust sanctions imposed by the European Commission on Microsoft, e.g., the separation of Windows Media from the Windows OS. The Court of Justice will render a final judgment in 2006. |
| UK/Airtours | In 1999, the European Commission blocked a takeover by UK-based Airtours of rival travel company First Choice. In 2002, the Court ruled that Airtours could appeal. The court's action marked the first time it overturned an antitrust ruling by the European Commission. |
| Italy/Monsanto, Syngenta, Pioneer Hi-Bred International | In 2000, fearing risk to human health, Italy banned foods containing four strains of genetically modified corn. The Italian court hearing the plaintiffs' appeal asked for ECJ intervention; in 2003, the ECJ ruled that the ban was not justified. The case was returned to Italy for final a ruling. |

---

[44] Klaus-Dieter Borchardt, *European Integration: The Origins and Growth of the European Union* (Luxembourg: Office for Official Publications of the European Communities, 1995), p. 30.
[45] Klaus-Dieter Borchardt, *The ABC of Community Law* (Luxembourg: Office for Official Publications of the European Communities, 1994), p. 25.

Although the European Court of Justice plays a role similar to that of the U.S. Supreme Court, there are important differences. The European court cannot decide which cases it will hear, and it does not issue dissenting opinions. The court exercises jurisdiction over a range of civil matters involving trade, individual rights, and environmental law. For example, the court can assess damages against countries that fail to introduce directives by the date set. The court also hears disputes that arise among the 25 EU member nations on trade issues such as mergers, monopolies, trade barriers and regulations, and exports. The court is also empowered to resolve conflicts between national law and EU law. In most cases, the latter supersedes national laws of individual European countries.

A case from Germany helps illustrate the point. A German court ruled that Pronuptia, a French wedding dress manufacturer and retailer, couldn't require its German franchisees to buy all their goods from the parent company. Pronuptia took its case to the European Court of Appeals, the EU's main forum for arbitration that makes recommendations to the Court of Justice. Had the German court's ruling been upheld on antitrust grounds, *all* franchisors doing business in Europe—including such well-known companies as McDonald's, Midas Muffler, and PepsiCo's Kentucky Fried Chicken and Pizza Hut units—would have been stripped of their ability to operate U.S.-style franchises in Europe. Key policies, including the right to dictate corporate logos, store designs, and outside suppliers, would have been nullified. After intense lobbying by the International Franchising Association, the court issued a ruling that was generally favorable to franchisors. Still, the new regulations prohibit franchisors from requiring franchisees to sell specific *branded* products from outside suppliers. Thus, while McDonald's retains the right to designate suppliers for commodities such as meat and potatoes, it can't force franchisees to conform to the U.S. policy that calls for selling only Coca-Cola beverages at its restaurants.[46]

## summary

The **political environment** of global marketing is the set of governmental institutions, political parties, and organizations that are the expression of the people in the nations of the world. In particular, anyone engaged in global marketing should have an overall understanding of the importance of **sovereignty** to national governments. The political environment varies from country to country, and **political risk** assessment is crucial. It is also important to understand a particular government's actions with respect to taxes and seizure of assets. Historically, the latter have taken the form of **expropriation, confiscation,** and **nationalization.**

The **legal environment** consists of laws, courts, attorneys, legal customs, and practices. The countries of the world can be broadly categorized in terms of common-law system or civil-law legal systems. The United States and Canada and many former British colonies are **common law** countries; most other countries use **code law.** A third system, **Islamic law,** predominates in the Middle East.

Some of the most important legal issues pertain to **jurisdiction, intellectual property protection, antitrust, licensing,** and **bribery.** In particular, **counterfeiting** is a major problem in global marketing; it often involves infringement of a company's **copyright** or **trademark** ownership. When legal conflicts arise, companies can pursue the matter in court or use **arbitration.**

The **regulatory environment** consists of agencies, both governmental and non-governmental, that enforce laws or set guidelines for conducting business. Global marketing activities can be affected by a number of international or regional economic organizations; in Europe, for example, the European Union makes laws governing member states. The World Trade Organization will have a broad impact on global marketing activities in the years to come. Although all three environments are complex, astute marketers plan ahead to avoid situations that might result in conflict, misunderstanding, or outright violation of national laws.

[46] Philip Revzin, "European Bureaucrats Are Writing the Rules Americans Will Live By," *The Wall Street Journal* (May 17, 1989), pp. A1, A12.

1. What is sovereignty? Why is it an important consideration in the political environment of global marketing?

2. Describe some of the sources of political risk. Specifically, what forms can political risk take?

3. Briefly describe some of the differences between the legal environment of a country that embraces common law and one that observes civil law.

4. Global marketers can avoid legal conflicts by understanding the reasons conflicts arise in the first place. Identify and describe several legal issues that relate to global commerce.

5. You are an American traveling on business in the Middle East. As you are leaving country X, the passport control officer at the airport tells you there will be a passport "processing" delay of 12 hours. You explain that your plane leaves in 30 minutes, and the official suggests that a contribution of $50 would probably speed things up. If you comply with the suggestion, have you violated U.S. law? Explain.

6. "See you in court" is one way to respond when legal issues arise. What other approaches are possible?

# Case 5-1

## Bud Versus Bud

What's in a name? If the name is Budweiser, the answer is, "Quite a bit." Budweiser, of course, is a registered trademark of St. Louis-based Anheuser-Busch, the world's largest brewing company. At the present time, however, Anheuser-Busch can't use the Budweiser brand name on a global basis. The reason is firmly rooted in history: The European brewing industry dates to the fourteenth century. During the days of the Austro-Hungarian Empire, Bohemia was famous for its beers; beers from the Bohemian town of Budweis were held in especially high esteem. A person from Budweis would be known as a Budweiser; the same would be true of the town's beer. While traveling in Europe in the mid-1800s, Adolphus Busch, the founder of Anheuser-Busch, became familiar with beers from Budweis—Budweisers, in other words. After emigrating to the United States, Busch married into the Anheuser brewing family; in the 1870s, he registered Budweiser as a trademark. Two decades later, in 1895, the Budejovicky Budvar brewery was established in Budweis, and its beer was officially named Budweiser, "the beer of kings." Adolphus Busch dubbed his company's Budweiser "the king of beers."

In 1911, representatives of Anheuser-Busch and Budvar signed an agreement that entitled the European company to market Budweiser beer in continental Europe. The American company would have rights to the name in the United States and Latin America. Later, the name of the town was changed from Budweis to Ceske Budejovice. In several European countries, including France, Italy, and Spain, Anheuser-Busch markets beer using the "Bud" brand name. The American company also won a court decision in Britain allowing it to sell Budweiser in Britain alongside the Czech brew with the same name.

Today, Anheuser-Busch's various brands command a 45 percent share of the U.S. beer market. Although it is the world's largest brewer, nearly 94 percent of its output is consumed in the United States. Faced with slackening demand at home, competition from microbreweries and imported brands, and increased scrutiny by regulators, executives at Anheuser-Busch are looking to international markets for growth in the twenty-first century. In Japan, Anheuser-Busch has established a joint venture with Kirin Brewery, the local market leader. Similarly, the company has acquired a 5 percent share in China's Tsingtao Brewery. After communist rule ended in Czechoslovakia in 1989, many breweries and other government-owned enterprises were privatized. For example, in 1992 the Czech government sold all but an 18 percent stake in Plzensky Prazdoj, maker of the Pilsner Urquell brand that competes directly with Budvar. Anheuser-Busch officials hoped to capitalize on the opportunity in 1993 by investing in Budejovicky Budvar and, at the same time, resolving the trademark issue. August Busch III, the chairman and president of Anheuser-Busch and the great-great-grandson of Adolphus Busch, wrote to Czech officials promising to invest capital in the brewery and share management and marketing expertise.

The Czech response to Anheuser-Busch's overtures was less than enthusiastic. For one thing, Czechs consider Budweiser to be more than a mere brand name; it is a geographic name that indicates a product's origin and is a source of Czech national pride. According to a 1958 agreement signed by the Czech government but not the United States, brand names that denote geographic origin are protected. Strictly speaking, therefore, only wine made from grapes grown in the Burgundy region of France can be called Burgundy, Champagne refers only to sparkling wine made from grapes grown in the Champagne region of France, and the Czechs firmly believe that their beer is the only one entitled to the name "Budweiser." However, the World Trade Organization does not currently recognize so-called "geographic indicators" for beer.

A second concern is related to the general issue of privatization. Germany's Volkswagen AG bought a stake in Skoda, the Czech automaker, and Air France invested in Czechoslovak Airlines. Many Czechs are uneasy about selling off these industrial crown jewels (or "family silver," as they are known in the Czech language) to Western companies, and there is concern about allowing Budvar to have a similar fate. In the case of Skoda, autoworkers were disappointed that wage levels after the deal were still far below those of workers in the company's plants in Germany. Also, Volkswagen officials scaled back the amount of money that they had originally promised to invest for expansion of Skoda's facilities.

Third, there is the matter of taste. Simply put, the Czechs consider American beer to be markedly inferior to European brews in general and Budvar's in particular. The Czechs know what they are talking about; per capita beer consumption in the Czech Republic is 160 liters per year. By comparison, the Irish consume 153 liters per capita each year; in American, the figure is 83 liters. Independent experts agree side with the Czechs. For example, beer authority and master taster Michael Jackson says, "Budweiser Budvar is one of the world's truly great beers. It just has a wonderful creamy malt character and a very, very delicate, almost perfumy flowery hop aroma." As one middle-aged Czech put it, "I like Americans, their culture, their films. But I know American beer doesn't reach the quality of Czech beer. It's much poorer, much weaker."

To help win over the Czechs, Anheuser-Busch embarked upon an extensive public relations effort. It spent $1 million on a cultural center in Ceske Budejovice, started a baseball team and equipped it with red and white Cardinals uniforms, opened a cafe´, and began offering English-language lessons—all, apparently, to no avail. The two sides continued to differ as to who would reap the most benefit from a new business arrangement. The sheer size of the American company made its intentions seem more imperialistic than honorable. Petr Jansky, finance director at Budvar, said, "Foreign partners need us as a strategic partner to help them. We don't need Anheuser-Busch, they need us." If Budvar began producing American-style Budweiser, Jansky added, "It could end up being the same as asking Rolls-Royce to produce mass cars." Not surprisingly, Anheuser-Busch representatives took a different view. John Koykka, chief financial officer for Anheuser-Busch International, believes that both companies could benefit. "The consumer base is quite different and the products quite different. We have a younger consumer base. We don't see a direct consumer competition."

*"Beer doesn't qualify for appellation of origin. It can be made anywhere. There is nothing unique about location."*

Steve Burrows, Anheuser-Busch International

*"Modern European consumers expect diversity, choice, and local produce. Yet large brewers often forget this in their battle to dominate the world with 'global brands'. Such companies would do well to respond to consumers and celebrate the heritage and regionality of beer."*

Mike Benner, Campaign for Real Ale (UK)

Ultimately, the Czech government decided not to proceed with the privatization of the Budvar brewery planned for 1993. At a meeting in St. Louis in September 1996, the parties disagreed on how much Budvar was worth, and Anheuser-Busch broke off negotiations. In a prepared statement, Jack H. Purcell, chairman and chief executive of Anheuser-Busch International, said, "Due to our success in selling our Budweiser beer in disputed markets in Europe under the Bud brand name, coupled with recent litigation successes with both the Budweiser and Bud brand names, it is no longer necessary for us to have a trademark settlement to develop our Budweiser business in Europe." Purcell was referring to the company's new strategy of suing on a country-by-country basis to win the right to the Budweiser name. By the end of 1996, it had won cases in Ireland, Portugal, Sweden, and six other European countries. Anheuser-Busch even pulled out of a $145 million proposed joint venture in Vietnam because Budvar had registered the Budweiser name there in 1960. Anheuser-Busch officials believe they will prevail in Vietnamese courts and that country officials will award them the right to register the Budweiser name. Currently, there are about 30 cases pending in 25 countries.

## Discussion Questions

1. Assess Anheuser-Busch's effort to reach an agreement with the Czechs to invest in Budvar. What, if anything, should the American company have done differently?

2. Do you agree with Anheuser-Busch's decision to break off negotiations and go to court on a country-by-country basis to assert its rights to the Budweiser name?

3. Assess the differing positions of A-B's Steve Burrows and Mike Benner of the Campaign for Real Ale. Is beer a "local" product?

*Sources:* Robert Anderson, "Battle of the Budweiser Brand May Come to a Head," *Financial Times* (December 2, 2003), p. 16; Vincent Boland and Roderick Oram, "U.S. Brewer Leaves Budvar Fighting for Identity," *Financial Times* (November 1, 1996), p. 20; Boland, "Budvar Takes Lid off U.S. Rival's Offer," *Financial Times* (December 20, 1996), p. 22; Jane Perlez, "This Bud's Not for You," *The New York Times* (June 30, 1995), pp. D1, D4; Shaillagh Murray, "Prazdoj's Beer: Rich History, Poor Sales," *The Wall Street Journal Europe* (June 16–17, 1995), p. 4; Yumiko Ono, "'King of Beers' Wants to Rule More of Japan," *The Wall Street Journal* (October 28, 1993), pp. B1, B8.

# Case 5-2

## America's Cuban Conundrum

On March 12, 1996, President Clinton signed the Cuban Liberty and Democratic Solidarity Act, also known as the Helms-Burton Act. The president's actions came after Cuban MiGs shot down two U.S. civilian airplanes, killing the four Cuban-Americans who were on board. The act has two key provisions. First, it denies entry into the United States to corporate officers of companies from other countries doing business on U.S. property in Cuba that was confiscated by the Cuban government. Second, it allows U.S. companies and citizens to sue foreign firms and investors doing business on U.S. property confiscated in Cuba. However, in July 1996, the president ordered a 6-month moratorium on lawsuits. Washington pledged to keep the embargo in place until Cuban President Fidel Castro held free elections and released political prisoners.

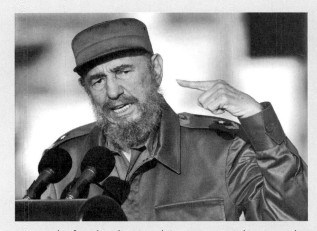

*Despite the fact that the United States is currently engaged in limited trading with Castro's Cuba, the Comandante himself remains unrepentant and appears determined to cling to his economic policies. In denouncing "neo-liberal globalization," Castro said, "The more contact we have with capitalism, the more repugnance I feel."*

## Cuba-U.S. Relations Prior to 1996

Cuba is a communist outpost in the Caribbean where "socialism or death" is the national motto. After Fidel Castro came to power in 1959, his government took control of most private companies without providing compensation to the owners. American assets owned by both consumer and industrial companies worth approximately $1.8 billion were among those expropriated; today, those assets are worth about $6 billion (See Table 1). President Kennedy responded by imposing a trade embargo on the island nation. Four decades later, Fidel Castro was still in power, despite the fact that his politics had fallen from fashion in many parts of the world. In 1990, Cuba opened its economy to foreign investment; by the mid-1990s, foreign commitments to invest in Cuba totaled more than half a billion dollars.

In 1993, Castro decreed that the U.S. dollar was legal tender although the peso would still be Cuba's official currency. As a result, hundreds of millions of dollars are injected into Cuba's economy each year; much of the money is sent by Cuban exiles living in the United States. Cubans can spend their dollars in special stores that stock imported foods and other hard-to-find products. In a country where doctors are among the highest paid workers with salaries equal to about $20 per month, the cash infusions can significantly improve a family's standard of living. In 1994, *mercados agropecuarios* (farmers markets) were created as a mechanism to enable farmers to earn more money.

Cuba desperately needs investment and U.S. dollars, in part to compensate for the end of subsidies following the demise of the Soviet Union. Oil companies from Europe and Canada were among the first to seek potential opportunities in Cuba. Many American executives are concerned that lucrative opportunities will be lost as Spain, Mexico, Italy, Canada, and other countries move aggressively into Cuba. Anticipating a softening in the U.S. government's stance, representatives from scores of U.S. companies visit Cuba regularly to meet with officials from state enterprises.

Those U.S. companies that are found guilty of violating trade embargoes, including the one on Cuba, are subject to fines of up to $1 million. Cuba remained officially off-limits to all but a handful of U.S. companies. Some telecommunications and financial services were allowed; AT&T, Sprint, and other companies have offered direct-dial service between the United States and Cuba since 1994. Also, a limited number of charter flights were available each day between Miami and Havana. Sale of medicines was also permitted under the embargo. At a state department briefing for business executives, Assistant Secretary of State for Inter-American Affairs Alexander Watson told his audience, "The Europeans and the Asians are knocking on the door in Latin America. The game is on and we can compete effectively, but it will be a big mistake if we leave the game to others." Secretary Watson was asked whether his comments on free trade applied to Cuba. "No, no. That simply can't be, not for now," Watson replied. "Cuba is a special case. This administration will maintain the embargo until major democratic changes take place in Cuba."

Within the United States, the government's stance toward Cuba has both supporters and opponents. Senator Jesse Helms pushed for a tougher embargo and sponsored a bill in Congress that would penalize foreign countries and companies for doing business with Cuba. The Cuban-American National Foundation actively engaged in anti-Cuba and anti-Castro lobbying. Companies that have openly spoken out against the embargo include Carlson Companies, owner of the Radisson Hotel chain; grain-processing giant Archer Daniels Midland; and the Otis Elevator division of United Technologies. A spokesperson for Carlson noted, "We see Cuba as an exciting new opportunity—the forbidden fruit of the Caribbean." A number of executives, including Ron Perelman, whose corporate holdings include Revlon and Consolidated Cigar Corporation, are optimistic that the embargo will be lifted within a few years.

Meanwhile, opinion was divided on the question of whether the embargo was costing U.S. companies once-in-a-lifetime opportunities. Some observers argued that many European and Latin American investments in Cuba were short-term, high-risk propositions that would not create barriers to U.S. companies. The opponents of the embargo, however, pointed to evidence that some investments were substantial. Three thousand new hotel rooms have been added by Spain's Grupo Sol Melia and Germany's LTI International Hotels. Both companies were taking advantage of the Cuban government's goal to increase tourism. Moreover, Italian and Mexican companies were snapping up contracts to overhaul the country's telecommunications infrastructure. Wayne Andreas, chairman of Archer Daniels Midland, summed up the views of many American executives when he said, "Our embargo has been a total failure for 30 years. We ought to have all the Americans in Cuba doing all the business they can. It's time for a change."

## The Helms-Burton Era

The Helms-Burton Act brought change, but not the type advocated by ADM's Andreas. The toughened U.S. stance signaled by Helms-Burton greatly concerned key trading partners, even though Washington insisted that the act was consistent with international law. In particular, supporters noted, the "effects doctrine" of international law permits a nation to take "reasonable" measures to protect its interests when an act outside its boundaries produces a direct effect inside its boundaries. Unmoved by such rationalizations, the European Commission responded in mid-1996 by proposing

**Table 1**  *American Companies Seeking Restitution from Cuba*

| Company | Amount of Claim (millions) |
| --- | --- |
| American Brands | $10.6 |
| Coca-Cola | $27.5 |
| General Dynamics | $10.4 |
| ITT | $47.6 |
| Lone Star Cement | $24.9 |
| Standard Oil | $71.6 |
| Texaco | $50.1 |

Source: U.S. Justice Department.

legislation barring European companies from complying with Helms-Burton. Although such a "blocking statute" was permitted under Article 235 of the EU treaty, Denmark threatened to veto the action on the grounds that doing so exceeded the European Commission's authority; its concerns were accommodated, and the legislation was adopted. Similarly, the Canadian government enacted legislation that would allow Canadian companies to retaliate against U.S. court orders regarding sanctions. Also, Canadian companies that complied with the U.S. sanctions could be fined $1 million dollars for doing so.

Meanwhile, executives at Canada's Sherritt International Corp. and Mexico's Grupo Domos received letters from the U.S. government informing them that they would be barred from entering the United States because of their business ties with Cuba. Sherritt operated a Cuban nickel mine, and Grupo Domos owned a 37 percent stake in Cuba's national telephone company. Both assets had been confiscated from U.S. companies. Canada and Mexico initiated arbitration proceedings as provided for under NAFTA. Meanwhile, in the fall of 1996, Canada registered its defiance of Helms-Burton by hosting Cuba's vice president for a 4-day visit.

In August 1996, President Clinton signed another piece of legislation designed to put economic pressure on foreign governments. The Iran and Libya Sanctions Act stipulated that foreign governments and companies that invest $40 million or more in the oil or gas industry sectors in Iran or Libya would be subject to U.S. sanctions. Expert opinion was divided as to whether such sanctions would be effective.

In the fall of 1996, the World Trade Organization agreed to a request by the EU to convene a three-person trade panel that would determine whether Helms-Burton violated international trade rules. The official U.S. position was that Helms-Burton was a foreign policy measure designed to promote the transition to democracy in Cuba. The United States also hinted that, if necessary, it could legitimize Helms-Burton by invoking the WTO's national security exemption. That exemption, in turn, hinged on whether the United States faced "an emergency in international relations."

Meanwhile, efforts were underway to resolve the issue on a diplomatic basis. Sir Leon Brittan, trade commissioner for the EU, visited the United States in early November with an invitation for the United States and EU to put aside misunderstandings and join forces in promoting democracy and human rights in Cuba. He noted:

> By opposing Helms-Burton, Europe is challenging one country's presumed right to impose its foreign policy on others by using the threat of trade sanctions. This has nothing whatever to do with human rights. We are merely attacking a precedent which the U.S. would oppose in many other circumstances, with the full support of the EU.

In December, senior EU officials approved a resolution sponsored by Spain that formally clarified the EU's intention to step up pressure on Castro. The U.S. State Department hailed the move as "a breakthrough in U.S.-EU relations." The EU insisted that the policy statement did not represent a change in its position or a concession to the United States. Even so, Spain's move surprised Havana, because Spain is Cuba's biggest foreign investor. However, Spain's newly elected conservative government was taking a harder line. Spain's prime minister and Castro even engaged in a bit of public name-calling.

In January 1997, President Clinton extended the moratorium on lawsuits against foreign investors in Cuba. In the months since the Helms-Burton Act had been in effect, a dozen companies had ceased operating on confiscated U.S. property in Cuba. Stet, the Italian telecommunications company, agreed to pay ITT for confiscated assets thereby exempting itself from possible sanctions. However, in some parts of the world, reaction to the president's action was lukewarm. The EU issued a statement noting that the action "falls short of the European Commission's hopes for a more comprehensive resolution of this difficult issue in trans-Atlantic relations." The EU also reiterated its intention of pursuing the case at the WTO. Art Eggleton, Canada's international trade minister responded with a less guarded tone: "It continues to be unacceptable behavior by the United States in foisting its foreign policy onto Canada, and other countries, and threatening Canadian business and anybody who wants to do business legally with Cuba."

Meanwhile, there was evidence that the U.S. sanctions, combined with other factors, were hurting Cuba. Sherritt and other foreign investors found the going slower than they expected. A number of legal reforms had still not been implemented. Also, the 1997 sugar crop, critical to Cuba's export earnings, was lower than anticipated. Another interesting twist occurred in Canada, where Wal-Mart temporarily removed Cuban-made pajamas from its 136 retail outlets. The issue was whether Wal-Mart was in violation of the Cuban Democracy Act, which makes U.S. global firms responsible for any boycott violations committed by foreign subsidiaries. After spending 2 weeks studying the matter and consulting with legal experts, Wal-Mart executives ordered the Cuban goods to be returned to the shelves.

In February, the WTO appointed the panel that would consider the dispute. However, Washington declared that it would boycott the panel proceedings on the grounds that the panel's members weren't competent to review U.S. foreign policy interests. Stuart Eizenstat, undersecretary for international trade at the U.S. Commerce Department, said, "The WTO was not created to decide foreign-policy and national-security issues." One expert on international trade law cautioned that the United States was jeopardizing the future of the WTO. Professor John Jackson of the University of Michigan School of Law said, "If the U.S. takes these kinds of unilateral stonewalling tactics, then it may find itself against other countries doing the same thing in the future."

The parties averted a confrontation at the WTO when the EU suspended its complaint in April, following President Clinton's pledge to seek congressional amendments to Helms-Burton. In particular, the president agreed to seek a waiver of the provision denying U.S. visas to employees of companies using expropriated property. A few days later, the EU and the United States announced plans to develop an agreement on property claims in

Cuba with "common disciplines" designed to deter and inhibit investment in confiscated property. Washington hoped such a bilateral agreement could be introduced into the negotiations at the OECD pertaining to the Multilateral Agreement on Investment. However, the agreement spelled out the EU's right to resume the trade panel or launch new proceedings if the United States took action against any European companies. The EU had 1 year to reactivate its complaint; it chose not to, however, and the panel was allowed to lapse in April 1998.

The U.S. stance was seen in a new perspective following the pope's visit to Cuba in January 1998. Many observers were heartened by Cuban authorities' decision to release nearly 300 political prisoners in February. Opinion within the Cuban-American community in Miami, which had historically supported the embargo, now appeared to be divided. In the fall of 1998, several former U.S. secretaries of state called upon President Clinton to create a National Bipartisan Commission on Cuba to review U.S. policy. In the fall of 2000, President Clinton signed a law that permits Cuba to buy unlimited amounts of food and medicine from the United States. The slight liberalization of trade represented a victory for the U.S. farm lobby, although all purchases must be made in cash. In 2002, several pieces of legislation were introduced in the U.S. Congress that would effectively undercut the embargo. One bill prohibited funding that would be used to enforce sanctions on private sales of medicine and agricultural products. Another proposal would have the effect of withholding budget money earmarked for enforcing both the ban on U.S. travel to Cuba and limits on monthly dollar remittances. Also in 2002, Castro began to clamp down on the growing democracy movement; about 70 writers and activists were jailed. President George W. Bush responded by phasing out cultural travel exchanges between the United States and Cuba.

## Discussion Questions

1. What was the key issue that prompted the EU to take the Helms-Burton dispute to the WTO?

2. Who benefits the most from an embargo of this type? Who suffers?

3. Assess attempts by some U.S. policymakers to limit or end *enforcement* of the embargo rather than the embargo itself. Do you agree with this approach?

*Sources:* Jerry Perkins, "Making American Dollar Legal Tenderizes Tough Cuban Economy," *The Des Moines Register* (April 6, 2003), pp. 1D, 5D; Mary Anastasia O'Grady, "Threshing Out a Deal Between the Farmers and Fidel," *The Wall Street Journal* (September 20, 2002), p. A11; Pascal Fletcher, "Cuba Sees Itself as Shining Example Amid Global Troubles," *Financial Times* (September 19–20, 1998), p. 3; Carl Gershman, "Thanks to the Pope, Civil Society Stirs in Cuba," *The Wall Street Journal* (September 18, 1998), p. A11; Stuart E. Eizenstat, "A Multilateral Approach to Property Rights," *The Wall Street Journal* (April 11, 1997), p. A18; Therese Raphael, "U.S. and Europe Clash over Cuba," *The Wall Street Journal* (March 31, 1997), p. A14; Robert Greenberger, "Washington Will Boycott WTO Panel," *The Wall Street Journal* (February 21, 1997), p. A2; Greenberger, "U.S. Holds Up Cuba Suits, Pleasing Few," *The Wall Street Journal* (January 6, 1997), p. A7; Brian Coleman, "EU to Push for Human Rights in Cuba," *The Wall Street Journal* (December 2, 1996), p. A12; Guy de Jonquières, "Brittan Calls for End to Cuba Row," *Financial Times* (November 7, 1996), p. 10; Julie Wolf and Brian Coleman, "EU Challenges U.S. Plan to Penalize Foreign Firms that Trade with Cuba," *The Wall Street Journal* (July 31, 1996), p. A1; Gail DeGeorge, "U.S. Business Isn't Afraid to Shout *Cuba Si!*" *Business Week* (November 6, 1995), p. 39; Jose De Cordoba, "Cuba's Business Law Puts Off Foreigners," *The Wall Street Journal* (October 10, 1995), p. A14; Sam Dillon, "Companies Press Clinton to Lift Embargo on Cuba," *The New York Times* (August 27, 1995), pp. 1, 4; Thomas T. Vogel, Jr., "Havana Headaches: Investors Find Cuba Tantalizing yet Murky in Financial Matters," *The Wall Street Journal* (August 7, 1995), pp. A1, A4.

# 6 Global Information Systems and Market Research

K. M. S. "Titoo" Ahuwalia is the president of ORG-MARG, the largest marketing research company in India. His client list reads like a who's who of global companies: Avon Products, Gillette, Coca-Cola, and Unilever. And, as Ahuwalia is fond of telling them, they are finding that "India is different." India is the second most populous nation on earth, with a middle class of more than 200 million people. Despite increasing affluence, however, centuries-old cultural traditions and customs still prevail. As a result, consumer behavior sometimes confounds Western expectations. Despite summer temperatures that frequently reach triple digits, only 2 percent of urban dwellers use deodorant. Instead, Indians bathe twice daily. Only 1 percent of households own air conditioners, and a recent Gallup survey revealed that only 1 percent intended to buy an air conditioner in the near future. The virtues of frugality once preached by Gandhi remain uppermost in the minds of many; smokers refill disposable lighters, and women recycle old sheets instead of spending money on feminine protection products. Likewise, in a country where food is believed to shape personality and mood and hot breakfasts are thought to be a source of energy, Kellogg had little luck at winning converts to cold cereal. The company positioned Frosties and other cereal brands as "convenient to prepare," and advertising was designed to raise awareness of the benefits of eating a healthy breakfast. Despite these efforts, sales results were disappointing.

For marketers who hope to achieve success in India and other emerging markets, information about buyer behavior and the overall business environment is vital to effective managerial decision making. When researching any market, marketers must know where to go to obtain information, what subject areas to investigate and information to look for, the different ways information can be acquired, and the various analysis approaches that will yield important insights and understanding. Obviously, India's 16 languages, 200 dialects, and low level of urbanization create

As these billboards demonstrate, the Coke/Pepsi rivalry is as intense in India as it is in the rest of the world. For much of the 1990s, Coke was promoted in India as a global brand. By contrast, Pepsi achieved market dominance in the cola segment by pursuing a more local approach. Here, Pepsi appeals to national sentiments by appending the phrase "yeh hi hai" (literally "This only is") to the global "right choice Baby" tag line. Recently, Coke brought its strategy more in line with Pepsi's; now both companies use local film stars in their advertising and sponsor sports, music, and religious events.

special research challenges. However, similar challenges are likely to present themselves wherever the marketer goes. It is the marketer's good fortune that a veritable cornucopia of market information is available on the Internet. A few keystrokes can yield literally hundreds of articles, research findings, and Web sites that offer a wealth of information about particular country markets. Even so, marketers need to study several important topics to make the most of modern information technology. First, they need to understand the importance of information technology and marketing information systems as strategic assets. Second, they need a framework for information scanning and opportunity identification. Third, they should have a general understanding of the formal market research process. Finally, they should know how to manage the marketing information collection system and the marketing research effort. These topics are the focus of this chapter.

## INFORMATION TECHNOLOGY FOR GLOBAL MARKETING

The phrase **information technology (IT)** refers to an organization's processes for creating, storing, exchanging, using, and managing information. For example, a **management information system (MIS)** provides managers and other decision makers with a continuous flow of information about company operations. MIS is a general term that can be used in reference to a system of hardware and software that a company uses to manage information. (The term can also be used to describe an IT department; in this case, it refers to people, hardware, and software.) An MIS should provide a means for gathering, analyzing, classifying, storing, retrieving, and reporting relevant data. The MIS should also cover important aspects of a company's external environment, including customers and competitors. Global competition intensifies the need for an effective MIS that is accessible throughout the company. As Jean-Pierre Corniou, chief information officer (CIO) at Renault, noted recently:

> My vision is to design, build, sell, and maintain cars. Everything I do is directly linked to this, to the urgent need to increase turnover, margins, and brand image. Every single investment and expense in the IT field has to be driven by this vision of the automotive business.[1]

---

[1] Jean-Pierre Corniu, "Bringing Business Technology Out Into the Open," *Financial Times—Information Technology Review* (September 17, 2003), p. 2.

Caterpillar, GE, Boeing, Federal Express, Diageo, Ford, Texas Instruments, and many other the companies with global operations have made significant investments in IT in recent years.

Such investment is typically directed at upgrading a company's computer hardware and software. One beneficiary is Microsoft, thanks to high global acceptance of its Windows operating system. Unlike the public Internet, an **intranet** is a private network that allows authorized company personnel or outsiders to share information electronically in a secure fashion without generating mountains of paper. Intranets allow a company's information system to serve as a 24-hour nerve center, enabling Amazon.com, Dell, and other companies to operate as real-time enterprises (RTEs). The RTE model is expected to grow in popularity as wireless Internet access becomes more widely available. Boeing used intranet technology to create an online database known as Boeing Online Data (BOLD). The system provides suppliers and airline customers with electronic access to engineering drawings, maintenance manuals, service bulletins, and other data. A typical airline requires a library of 40,000 information cards for each type of Boeing aircraft in its fleet plus 30,000 updates each year; BOLD cuts down on the amount of paper needed, with annual savings that can total $200,000 per aircraft.[2]

An **electronic data interchange (EDI)** system allows a company's business units to submit orders, issue invoices, and conduct business electronically with other company units as well as outside companies. One of the key features of EDI is that its transaction formats are universal. This allows computer systems at different companies to speak the same language. Wal-Mart is legendary for its sophisticated EDI system; for years, vendors have received orders from the retailer on personal computers using dial-up modems connected to third-party transmission networks. In 2002, Wal-Mart informed vendors it was switching to an Internet-based EDI system. The switch has saved both time and money; the modem-based system was susceptible to transmission interruptions, and the cost was between 10 and 20 cents per thousand characters transmitted. Any vendor that wishes to do business with Wal-Mart in the future must purchase and install the necessary computer software.[3]

Poor operating results can often be traced to insufficient data and information about events both inside and outside the company. For example, when a new management team was installed at the U.S. unit of Adidas AG, the German athletic shoe marketer, data were not even available on normal inventory turnover rates. A new reporting system revealed that arch-rivals Reebok and Nike turned inventories five times a year, compared with twice a year at Adidas. This information was used to tighten the marketing focus on the best-selling Adidas products. Benetton SpA's use of MIS as a strategic competitive tool is described later. In Japan, 7-Eleven's computerized distribution system also provides it with a competitive advantage in the convenience store industry. Every 7-Eleven store is linked with each other and with distribution centers. As one retail analyst noted:

> With the system they have established, whatever time you go, the shelves are never empty. If people come in at 4 A.M. and the stores don't have what they want, that will have a big impact on what people think of the store.[4]

Globalization puts increased pressure on companies to achieve as many economies as possible. IT provides a number of helpful tools. As noted, EDI links with vendors enable retailers to improve inventory management and restock hot-selling products in a timely, cost-effective manner. In addition to EDI, retailers are

---

2  Geoffrey Nairn, "Business Benefits Come First," *Financial Times—Information Technology Review* (March 4, 1998), p. 9.
3  Ann Zimmerman, "To Sell Goods to Wal-Mart, Get on the Net," *The Wall Street Journal* (November 21, 2003), pp. B1, B6.
4  Bethan Hutton, "Japan's 7-Eleven Sets Store by Computer Links," *Financial Times* (March 17, 1998), p. 26.

increasingly using a technique known as **efficient consumer response (ECR)** in an effort to work more closely with vendors on stock replenishment. ECR can be defined as a joint initiative by members of a supply chain to work toward improving and optimizing aspects of the supply chain to benefit customers. ECR systems utilize **electronic point of sale (EPOS)** data gathered by checkout scanners to help retailers identify product sales patterns and how consumer preferences vary with geography. Although currently most popular in the United States, the ECR movement is also gaining traction in Europe. Companies such as Carrefour, Metro, Coca-Cola, and Henkel have all embraced ECR. Supply chain innovations such as radio frequency identification tags (RFID) are likely to provide increased momentum for ECR (see Case 12-2).

EPOS, ECR, and other IT tools are also helping businesses improve their ability to target consumers and increase loyalty. The trend among retailers is to develop customer-focused strategies that will personalize and differentiate the business. In addition to point-of-sale scanner data, loyalty programs that use electronic smart cards will provide retailers with important information about shopping habits. A new business model that helps companies collect, store, and analyze customer data is called **customer relationship management (CRM).** A recent special report in *Advertising Age* magazine was devoted to CRM. Although industry experts interviewed for the report offered varying descriptions and definitions of CRM, the prevailing view is that CRM is a philosophy that values two-way communication between company and customer. Every point of contact ("touchpoint" in CRM-speak) a company has with a consumer or business customer—through a Web site, a warranty card or sweepstakes entry, payment on credit card account, or inquiry to a call center—is an opportunity to collect data. CRM tools allow companies such as Credit Suisse, AT&T, and Hewlett-Packard to determine which customers are most valuable and to react in a timely manner with customized product and service offerings that closely match customer needs. If implemented correctly, CRM can make employees more productive and enhance corporate profitability; it also benefits customers by providing value-added products and services.

A company's use of CRM can manifest itself in various ways. Some are visible to consumers, others are not; some make extensive use of leading-edge information technology, others do not. In the hotel industry, for example, CRM can take the form of front desk staff who monitor, respond to, and anticipate the needs of repeat customers. A visitor to Amazon.com who buys "The Red Hot Chili Peppers Greatest Hits" CD encounters CRM when he or she is prompted by the message "Customers who bought this title also bought 'In Time: The Very Best of REM 1988–2003.'" A television viewer who owns a TiVo digital video recorder gets messages from TiVo alerting him or her to upcoming shows that, based on previous viewing patterns, may be of interest. CRM can also be based on the click path that a Web site visitor follows. In this case, however, Internet users may be unaware that a company is tracking their behavior and interests.

One challenge is to integrate data into a complete picture of the customer and his or her relationship to the company and its products or services. This is sometimes referred to as a "360-degree view of the customer." The challenge is compounded for global marketers. Subsidiaries in different parts of the world may use different customer data formats, and commercial CRM products may not support all the target languages. In view of such issues, industry experts recommend implementing global CRM programs in phases. The first could focus on a specific task such as **sales force automation (SFA);** the term refers to a software system that automates routine aspects of sales and marketing functions such as lead assignment, contact follow-up, and opportunity reporting. An SFA system can also analyze the cost of sales and the effectiveness of marketing campaigns. Some SFA software can assist with quote preparation and management of other aspects of a sales campaign such as mass mailings and conference or convention attendee follow-up.

*"The major thing is, 'One size fits all' is not true. CRM is designed to support the sales process, and if I develop a system that works in the U.S., it might not work in Europe."*

Jim Dickie, Insight Technology Group

Siebel Systems is the world's leading supplier of CRM software. Client companies use Siebel's products to distribute customer information to call centers, sales teams, and marketing and customer service departments. Siebel is committed to 100% customer satisfaction, a difficult thing to achieve with complex software systems. As company founder Thomas Siebel explained in an interview with Harvard Business Review in 2001, "Siebel Systems is a global company, not a multinational company. I believe the notion of the multinational company—where a division is free to follow its own set of business rules—is obsolete, though there are still plenty around. Our customers—global companies like IBM, Zurich Financial Services, and Citicorp—expect the same high level of service and quality, and the same licensing policies, no matter where we do business with them around the world. Our human resources and legal departments help us create policies that respect local cultures and requirements worldwide, while at the same time maintaining the highest standards. We have one brand, one image, one set of corporate colors, one set of messages, across every place on the planet."

For example, an important first step in implementing a CRM system could be to utilize SFA software from a company such as Siebel Systems or Onyx Software. The objective at this stage of the CRM effort would be to provide sales representatives in all country locations with access via an Internet portal to sales activities throughout the organization. To simplify the implementation, the company could require that all sales activities be recorded in English. Subsequently, marketing, customer service, and other functions could be added to the system.[5]

Privacy issues also vary widely from country to country. In the European Union, for example, a Directive on Data Collection has been in effect since 1998. Companies that use CRM to collect data about individual consumers must satisfy the regulations in each of the EU's 25 member countries. There are also restrictions about sharing such information across national borders. In 2000, the U.S. Department of Commerce and the European Union concluded a Safe Harbor agreement that establishes principles for privacy protection for companies that wish to transfer data to the United States from Europe. The principles, which are posted in detail at **www.export.gov/safeharbor**, include:

- The purposes for which information is collected and used and the means by which individuals can direct inquiries to the company

---

[5] Gina Fraone, "Facing Up to Global CRM," *eWeek* (July 30, 2001), pp. 37–41.

- An "opt out" option to prevent the disclosure of personal information to third parties
- An agreement that information can only be transferred to third parties that are in compliance with Safe Harbor Principles
- Individuals must have access to information collected about them and must be able to correct or delete inaccurate information

Databases called **data warehouses** are frequently an integral part of a company's CRM system. Data warehouses can serve other purposes as well. For example, they can help retailers with multiple store locations fine-tune product assortments. Company personnel, including persons who are not computer specialists, can access data warehouses via standard Web browsers. Behind the familiar interfaces, however, is specialized software capable of performing multidimensional analysis by using sophisticated techniques such as linear programming and regression. This enhances the ability of managers to respond to changing business conditions by adjusting marketing mix elements. MicroStrategy, an information services company in the United Kingdom, is one of several companies creating data warehouses for clients. As manager Stewart Holness explains, "Many corporations have a vast amount of information which they have spent money accumulating, but they have not been able to distribute it. The Web is the perfect vehicle for it."[6]

As Holness' comment makes clear, the Internet is revolutionizing corporate information processing (see Chapter 17). Companies that are slow to recognize the revolution risk falling behind competitors. For example, Germany is home to the *Mittelstand*, a group of three million small and mid-size manufacturers that have traditionally been focused and successful global marketers. The *Mittelstand* are often cited as an illustration of how small companies can help propel economic growth and sustain prosperity. As Dietmar Hopp, chief executive of Germany's largest software firm, noted in the mid-1990s:

> With globalization there is no difference now between the *Mittelstand* and big companies—the business processes are comparable. It is only a matter of time before foreign competitors use the Internet to strengthen their foothold in Germany. German companies should follow their example and build up their U.S. and Asian activities through electronic marketing and commerce.[7]

Evidence exists that *Mittelstand* companies have gotten the message. According to a recent study conducted by IBM Germany and *Impulse*, a German magazine for entrepreneurs, most *Mittelstand* companies now have Web homepages. Approximately one-third use the Web for e-business activities such as ordering and cross-linking with suppliers.[8]

These examples show just some of the ways that information technology is affecting global marketing. However, EDI, ECR, EPOS, SFA, CRM, and other aspects of IT do not simply represent marketing issues; they are organizational imperatives. The tasks of designing, organizing, and implementing information systems must be coordinated in a coherent manner that contributes to the overall strategic direction of the organization. Modern information technology tools provide the means for a company's marketing information system and research functions to provide relevant information in a timely, cost-efficient, and actionable manner.

A more detailed discussion of the information technology issues is beyond the scope of this book. The discussion that follows in this section focuses on the subject agenda, scanning modes, and information sources characteristic of a global information system that is oriented toward the external environment.

---

6   Vanessa Houlder, "Warehouse Parties," *Financial Times* (October 23, 1996), p. 8. See also John W. Verity, "Coaxing Meaning Out of Raw Data," *Business Week* (February 3, 1997), pp. 134+.
7   Graham Bowley, "In the Information Technology Slow Lane," *Financial Times* (November 11, 1997), p. 14.
8   "E-Business in the *Mittelstand*," **www.impulse.de** (January 23, 2002).

| Category | Coverage | |
|---|---|---|
| 1. Market potential | Demand estimates, consumer behavior, review of products, channels, communication media. | **Table 6-1** |
| 2. Competitor information | Corporate, business, and functional strategies. Resources and intentions. Capabilities. | *Subject Agenda Categories for a Global Marketing Information System* |
| 3. Foreign exchange | Balance of payments, interest rates, attractiveness of country currency, expectations of analysts. | |
| 4. Prescriptive information | Laws, regulations, rulings concerning taxes, earnings, dividends in both host and home countries. | |
| 5. Resource information | Availability of human, financial, physical, and information resources. | |
| 6. General conditions | Overall review of sociocultural, political, technological environments. | |

# INFORMATION SUBJECT AGENDA AND ENVIRONMENTAL SCANNING MODES

A starting point for a global marketing information system is a list of subjects about which information is desired. The resulting "subject agenda" should be tailored to the specific needs and objectives of the company. The general framework suggested in Table 6-1 consists of six broad information areas. The framework satisfies two essential criteria. First, it is all the information subject areas relevant to a company with global operations. Second, the categories in the framework are mutually exclusive; any kind of information encompassed by the framework can be correctly placed in one and only one category. The basic elements of the external environment outlined in the last four chapters—economic, social and cultural, legal and regulatory, and financial factors—will undoubtedly be on the information agenda of most companies, as shown in the table.

Once the subject agenda has been determined, the next step is the actual collection of information. This can be accomplished by using either surveillance or search. In the **surveillance** mode, the marketer engages in informal information gathering. Globally oriented marketers are constantly on the lookout for information about potential opportunities and threats in various parts of the world. They want to know everything about the industry, the business, the marketplace, and consumers. This passion shows up in the way they keep their ears and eyes tuned for clues, rumors, nuggets of information, and insights. Browsing through newspapers and magazines is one way to ensure exposure to information on a regular basis. Global marketers may also develop a habit of watching news programs from around the world via satellite. This type of general exposure to information is known as **viewing.** If a particular news story has special relevance for a company—for example, renewal of China's most-favored-nation status or the currency crisis in Asia—the marketer will pay special attention, tracking the story as it develops. This is known as **monitoring.**

The **search** mode is characterized by more formal activity. Search involves the deliberate seeking out of specific information. Search often includes **investigation,** a relatively limited and informal type of search. Investigation often means seeking out books or articles in trade publications on a particular topic or issue. Search may also consist of **research,** a formally organized effort to acquire specific information for a specific purpose. This type of formal, organized research is described later in the chapter.

## the rest of the story

### Market Research in Developing Countries

Kellogg has achieved greater success in India with new products that are better suited to local eating habits. Its Chocos brand breakfast biscuits cost the equivalent of about 10 cents for a 50-gram pack and are widely available at roadside tea stalls. Nestlé's experience also demonstrates that understanding the needs in an emerging market can lead to success. It successfully positioned its Maggi brand noodles in India as a between-meal snack food rather than a pasta meal item. Nestlé also caters to the Indian preference for local brands; although Nescafé is the company's flagship global coffee brand in many countries, Nestlé created chicory-flavored Sunrise especially for the Indian market. Nestlé managers have also learned that the 20 million wealthy households in its core target market exhibit a value orientation traditionally associated with mass markets. As Arvind Sharma, chairman and chief executive of Leo Burnett India, said recently, "The Indian purse is tough to open. Its owner is discriminating. She must be convinced the product you are marketing will make a difference." Nestlé has responded by keeping prices down; more than half of the products it sells in India cost less than 25 rupees—about 70 cents.

The tobacco industry is also learning about India. Sixty percent of adult Indian males smoke, although many prefer the native *bidi*, which is hand-rolled with a leaf outer wrapper rather than

paper. As Darryl Jayson, economist at the Tobacco Merchants Association (TMA), noted recently, "Many companies, local and international, are hoping that these bidi-smokers move up to cigarettes as India becomes more affluent." Although Western brands enjoy high levels of awareness, the government taxes make up 70 percent of the retail price of a single pack. As a result, premium European brands such as Dunhill cost $4 per pack, whereas Indian brands from Indian Tobacco Company and other local manufacturers sell for $.50 to $1.50. Taste is an issue facing American tobacco companies; Indian smokers prefer Virginia blend tobaccos, while the typical American smoke uses oriental and burley blends. The TMA's Jayson says, "Indian smokers perceive U.S. cigarettes as roasted and harsh. I think it is very difficult to change the smoking habits of the Indians. It may take up to 20 years to bring about the change."

*Sources: Rasul Bailay, "In India, Shopping Takes on a Whole New Meaning," The Wall Street Journal (December 16, 2003), p. A13; Khozem Merchant, "India's Luminaries Take a Bow," Financial Times (November 6, 2003), p. 9; Merchant, "Sweet Rivals Find Love in a Warm Climate," Financial Times (July 24, 2003), p. 9; Daniel Pearle, "The Rigors of Cracking India's Markets," The Wall Street Journal (November 27, 2000), pp. A25, A28; Miriam Jordan, "Marketing Gurus Say: In India, Think Cheap, Lose the Cold Cereal," The Wall Street Journal (October 11, 1996), p. A7; O. P. Malik, "The World's Tobacco Marketers Think 20 Million Indians Can't Be Wrong," Brandweek (October 9, 1995), pp. 46, 48; Malik, "The Great Indian Brand Bazaar," Brandweek (June 5, 1995), pp. 31–32.*

One study found that nearly 75 percent of the information acquired by headquarters executives at U.S. global companies comes from surveillance as opposed to search. However, the viewing mode generated only 13 percent of important external information and monitoring generated 60 percent. Two factors contribute to the paucity of information generated by viewing. One is the limited extent to which executives are exposed to information that is not included in a clearly defined subject agenda. The other is the limited receptivity of the typical executive to information outside this agenda. Every executive limits his or her exposure to information that will not have a high probability of being relevant to the job or company. This is rational; a person can absorb only a minute fraction of the data available. Exposure to and retention of information stimuli must be selective.

Nevertheless, the organization as a whole must be receptive to information not explicitly recognized as important. To be effective, a scanning system must ensure that the organization is viewing areas where developments that could be important to the company might occur. Innovations in information technology have increased the speed with which information is transmitted and simultaneously shortened the life of its usefulness to the company. Advances in technology have also placed new demands on the global firm in terms of shrinking reaction times to information acquired. In some instances, the creation of a full-time scanning unit with explicit responsibility for acquiring and disseminating strategic information may be required.

Of all the changes in recent years that have affected the availability of information, perhaps none is more apparent than the explosion of documentary and electronic information. An overabundance of information has created a major problem for anyone attempting to stay abreast of key developments in multiple national markets. Today, **information overload** occurs when executives and other company personnel cannot effectively assimilate all the information available to them. Unfortunately, too few companies employ a formal system for coordinating scanning activities. This situation results in considerable duplication of effort.

For example, it is not uncommon for members of an entire management group to read a single publication covering a particular subject area despite the fact that several other excellent publications covering the same area may be available.

The best way to identify unnecessary duplication is to carry out an audit of reading activity by asking each person involved to list the publications he or she reads regularly. A consolidation of the lists will reveal the surveillance coverage. Often, the scope of the group will be limited to a handful of publications to the exclusion of other worthwhile ones. A good remedy for this situation is consultation with outside experts regarding the availability and quality of publications in relevant fields or subject areas.

Information technology can also provide solutions to the problem of information overload. For example, Swiss Bank Corporation (SBC) determined that, in theory, staff members would have to spend several hours reading each day if they were to keep up with internal documents, let alone material from outside sources. SBC also estimated that 80 percent of the publications produced for in-house use were read either sporadically or not at all. SBC developed a "know-how pool project" utilizing an artificial intelligence technique known as case-based reasoning (CBR). The majority of SBC's documents are available in the company's database; a user can query the system with a request such as "I would like to have information about private banking." The computer then retrieves the necessary information. Users can also define their information needs so that "intelligent agent" software searches for new information that matches the user's profile.[9] Boeing, Andersen Consulting, and other companies are making similar progress in using information technology for knowledge management.

Overall, then, the global organization is faced with the following needs:

- An efficient, effective system that will scan and digest published sources and technical journals in the headquarter's country as well as all countries in which the company has operations or customers.
- Daily scanning, translating, digesting, abstracting, and electronic input of information into a market intelligence system. Today, thanks to advances in IT, full-text versions of many sources are available on line. Print documentary material can be easily scanned, digitized, and added to a company's information system.
- Expanding information coverage to other regions of the world.

## SOURCES OF MARKET INFORMATION

Although scanning is a vital source of information, research has shown that headquarters executives of global companies obtain as much as two-thirds of the information they need from *personal sources*. A great deal of external information comes from executives based abroad in company subsidiaries, affiliates, and branches. These executives are likely to have established communication with distributors, consumers, customers, suppliers, and government officials. Indeed, a striking feature of the global corporation—and a major source of competitive strength—is the role that executives abroad play in acquiring and disseminating information about the world environment. Headquarters executives generally acknowledge that company executives overseas are the people who know best what is going on in their areas. The following is a typical comment of headquarters executives:

> Our principal sources are internal. We have a very well-informed and able overseas establishment. The local people have a double advantage. They know the local scene and they know our business. Therefore, they are an excellent source. They know

---

[9] Vanessa Houlder, "Intelligent Reading," *Financial Times* (June 11, 1997), p. 8.

what we are interested in learning, and because of their local knowledge they are able to effectively cover available information from all sources.

The information issue exposes one of the key weaknesses of a domestic company: Although more attractive opportunities may be present outside existing areas of operation, they are likely to go unnoticed by inside sources in a domestic company because the scanning horizon tends to end at the home-country border. Similarly, a company with only limited geographical operations may be at risk because internal sources abroad tend to scan only information about their own countries or regions.

Other important information sources are friends, acquaintances, professional colleagues, consultants, and prospective new employees. The last are particularly important if they have worked for competitors. Sometimes information-related ethical and legal issues arise when a person changes jobs. As noted in Chapter 5, J. Ignacio López de Arriortúa was head of purchasing at General Motors when he accepted a job as production chief with Volkswagen. GM charged that he had taken important documents and computer files when he moved to VW. The resulting publicity was the source of considerable embarrassment to Volkswagen.

As noted in Chapter 4, it is hard to overstate the importance of travel and contact for building rapport and personal relationships. Moreover, one study found that three-quarters of the information acquired from human sources is gained in face-to-face conversation. Why? Some information is too sensitive to transmit in any other way. For example, highly placed government employees could find their careers compromised if they are identified as information sources. In such cases, the most secure way of transmitting information is face to face rather than in writing. Information that includes estimates of future developments or even appraisals of the significance of current happenings is often considered too uncertain to commit to writing. Commenting upon this point, one executive said:

> People are reluctant to commit themselves in writing to highly "iffy" things. They are not cowards or overly cautious; they simply know that you are bound to be wrong in trying to predict the future, and they prefer to not have their names associated with documents that will someday look foolish.

The great importance of face-to-face communication lies also in the dynamics of personal interaction. Personal contact provides an occasion for executives to get together long enough to permit communication in some depth. Face-to-face discussion also exposes highly significant forms of nonverbal communication, as discussed in Chapter 4. One executive described the value of face-to-face contact in these terms:

> If you really want to find out about an area, you must see people personally. There is no comparison between written reports and actually sitting down with a man and talking. A personal meeting is worth 4,000 written reports.

*Direct sensory perception* provides a vital background for the information that comes from human and documentary sources. Direct perception gets all the senses involved. It means seeing, feeling, hearing, smelling, or tasting for oneself to find out what is going on in a particular country, rather than getting secondhand information by hearing or reading about a particular issue. Some information is easily available from other sources but requires sensory experience to sink in. Often, the background information or context one gets from observing a situation can help fill in the big picture. For example, Wal-Mart's first stores in China stocked a number of products—extension ladders and giant bottles of soy sauce, for example—that were inappropriate for local customers. Joe Hatfield, Wal-Mart's top executive for Asia, began roaming the streets of Shenzhen in search of ideas. His observations paid off; when Wal-Mart's giant

# behind the scenes

store in Dalian opened in April 2000, a million shoppers passed through its doors in the first week. They snapped up products ranging from lunch boxes to pizza topped with corn and pineapple.[10]

Direct perception can also be important when a company's domestic market is dominated by a global player. Such was the case with Microsoft and its Xbox video game system, which was launched in a market dominated by Sony. Cindy Spodek-Dickey, group manager for national consumer promotions and sponsorships, took Xbox "on the road" with various promotional partners such as the Association of Volleyball Professionals (AVP). At AVP tournaments in different cities, spectators (and potential customers) had the opportunity to visit the Xbox hospitality tent to try out the new machine. At one tournament event, Spodek-Dickey explained the importance of informal market research:

> What are the other sponsors doing? What's the crowd into? What brands are they wearing? How are they interacting with our property? I'll stop them as they come out of the tent and say: 'What do you think? What do you like about Xbox? What do you think of your PlayStation?' It's mother-in-law research. I wouldn't want to stake a $10 million ad campaign on it, but I think it keeps you credible and real. When you start to hear the same feedback, three, four, five times, you'd better be paying attention. . . . I believe it is part of any good marketer's job to be in touch with their audience and their product. There's no substitute for face-to-face, eye-to-eye, hand-to-hand.[11]

# FORMAL MARKET RESEARCH

Information is a critical ingredient in formulating and implementing a successful marketing strategy. As described earlier, a marketing information system should produce a continuous flow of information. **Market research,** by contrast,

---

[10] Peter Wonacott, "Wal-Mart Finds Market Footing in China," *The Wall Street Journal* (July 17, 2000), p. A31.

[11] Kenneth Hein, "We Know What Guys Want," *Brandweek* (November 14, 2002), p. M48.

is the project-specific, systematic gathering of data in the search scanning mode. The American Marketing Association defines *marketing research* as "the activity that links the consumer, customer, and public to the marketer through information."[12] In **global market research,** this activity is carried out on a global scale. The challenge of global marketing research is to recognize and respond to the important national differences that influence the way information can be obtained. These include cultural, linguistic, economic, political, religious, historical, and market differences.

Michael Czinkota and Illka Ronkainen note that the objectives of international market research are the same as the objectives of domestic research. However, they have identified four specific environmental factors that may require international research efforts to be conducted differently than domestic research. First, researchers must be prepared for new parameters of doing business. Not only will there be different requirements, but the ways in which rules are applied may differ as well. Second, "cultural megashock" may occur as company personnel come to grips with a new set of culture-based assumptions about conducting business. Third, a company entering more than one new geographic market faces a burgeoning network of interacting factors; research may help prevent psychological overload. Fourth, company researchers may have to broaden the definition of competitors in international markets to include competitive pressures that would not be present in the domestic market.[13]

According to a recent report by Datamonitor, expenditures on global market research totaled $16.6 billion in 2002.[14] There are two basic ways to conduct marketing research. One is to design and implement a study with in-house staff. The other is to use an outside firm specializing in marketing research. In global marketing, a combination of in-house and outside research efforts is often advisable. Many outside firms have considerable international expertise; some specialize in particular industry segments. VNU is the world's largest market research organization; its Nielsen Media Research unit is the source of the well-known Nielsen TV ratings. Some research firms limit their scope to specific industry sectors. For example, IMS Health focuses on the pharmaceuticals and health care industries; London-based Ovum Limited specializes in IT, telecommunications, and new media; and Canadean Limited's expertise is the global beverage industry. In some country markets, smaller local agencies such as ORG-MARG offer advantages such as valuable contacts and cultural insight. The top global marketing research companies are shown in Table 6-2.

The process of collecting data and converting it into useful information can be quite detailed as shown in Figure 6-1 on page 202. In the discussion that follows, we will focus on eight basic steps: information requirement, problem definition, choosing unit of analysis, examining data availability, assessing the value of research, research design, data analysis, and presenting the research findings.

## Step 1: Identify the Information Requirement

The following story illustrates the first step in the formal marketing research process:

> The vice presidents of finance and marketing of a shoe company were traveling around the world to estimate the market potential for their products. They arrived in a very poor country and both immediately noticed that none of the local citizens wore shoes. The vice president of finance said, "We might as well

---

12  Peter D. Bennett, ed., *Dictionary of Marketing Terms*, 2d ed. (Chicago: American Marketing Association, 1995), p. 169.
13  Michael R. Czinkota and Ilkka A. Ronkainen, "Market Research for Your Export Operations: Part I—Using Secondary Sources of Research," *International Trade Forum* 30, no. 3 (1994), pp. 22–33.
14  Datamonitor, "Global Market Research—Industry Profile," (November 2003), p. 6.

| Company (Home Country) | 2003 Revenues ($ millions) | Competitive Focus |
|---|---|---|
| 1. VNU NV (Netherlands) | 4.872 | Units include ACNielsen, Nielsen Media Research, Claritas, and Spectra. Focus on media monitoring and business information. |
| 2. IMS Health (USA) | 1.381 | Pharmaceuticals/health care. |
| 3. TNS (UK) | 233 | Consumer panels. |
| 4. Dentsu (Japan) | 2.358 | |
| 5. Kantar Group (USA; unit of WPP Group) | 1.033 | Units include Millward Brown, Research International. Focus on brand awareness and media analysis. |
| 6. GfK (Germany) | 747 | Specialist in Europe, consumer panels, media, healthcare. |

**Table 6-2**

*Leading Global Market Research Companies*

get back on the plane. There is no market for shoes in this country." The vice president of marketing replied, "What an opportunity! Everyone in this country is a potential customer!"

The potential market for shoes was enormous in the eyes of the marketing executive. To formally confirm his instinct, some research would be required. As this story shows, research is often undertaken after a problem or opportunity has presented itself. Perhaps a competitor is making inroads in one or more important markets around the world. Maybe research on local taste preferences is required to determine if a food product must be adapted. Or, as in this story, a company may wish to determine whether a particular country or regional market offers good growth potential. What is the likelihood that potential customers can be converted into *actual* customers? It is a truism of market research that a problem well defined is a problem half solved. Thus, regardless of what situation sets the research effort in motion, the first two questions a marketer should ask are "What information do I need?" and "Why do I need this information?"

## Step 2: Problem Definition—Overcoming the SRC

As noted in Chapter 4, when a person's values and beliefs intrude on the assessment of a foreign culture or country, the self-reference criterion (SRC) is at work. For example, when Mattel first introduced Barbie in Japan, managers assumed that Japanese girls would find the doll's design just as appealing as American girls did. They didn't. Likewise, when the Walt Disney Company opened Disneyland Paris, park employees were expected to comply with a detailed written code regarding clothing, jewelry, and other aspects of personal appearance. The goal was to ensure that guests receive the kind of experience associated with the Disney name. However, the French considered the code to be an insult to French culture, individualism, and privacy. Also, in designing hotel restaurants, Disney officials assumed that Europeans don't eat breakfast. The restaurants were scaled down as a result. In reality, most guests wanted to eat more than just a continental breakfast consisting of coffee and pastry; the result was long waits and disgruntled guests. A similar problem occurred inside the park at lunchtime. The United States is a nation of snackers, and the Disney team assumed that European guests would be content to "graze" and then eat in shifts. It turned out that at 1 P.M. each day, the park's restaurants were inundated with hungry patrons.

As these examples show, assumptions that companies make based on home-country experience can turn out to be wrong. When approaching global markets, it is best to have "eyes wide open." In other words, marketers must be aware of the impact that SRC can have. Such awareness can have several positive effects.

## Figure 6-1

The International Marketing Research Process

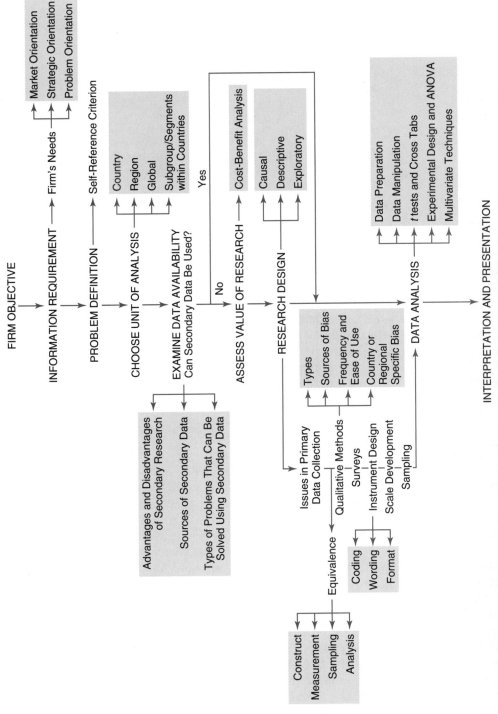

Source: *International Marketing Research* by Kumar, V., © Reprinted by permission of Pearson Education, Inc. Upper Saddle River, NJ.

First, it can enhance management's willingness to conduct market research in the first place. Second, an awareness of SRC can help ensure that the research effort is designed with minimal home-country bias. Third, it can enhance management's receptiveness to accepting research findings—even if they contradict "tried and true" marketing experience in the home country.

## Step 3: Choose Unit of Analysis

The next step involves the need to identify in what part(s) of the world the company should be doing business and finding out as much as possible about the business environment in the area(s) identified. These issues are reflected in the subject agenda categories in Table 6-1. The unit of analysis may be a single country; it may also be a region such as Europe or South America. In some instances, the marketer is interested in a segment that is global. Country-wide data are not required for all market entry decisions. Rather, a specific city, state, or province may be the relevant unit of analysis. For example, a company that is considering entering China may focus initially on Shanghai. Located in the Jiangsu province, Shanghai is China's largest city and main seaport. Because Shanghai is a manufacturing center, has a well-developed infrastructure, and is home to a population with relatively high per capita income, it is the logical focus of a market research effort.

## Step 4: Examine Data Availability

The first task at this stage is to answer several questions regarding the availability of data. What type of data should be gathered? Are data available in company files, a library, industry or trade journals, or online? Can secondary data be used? When does management need the information in order to make a decision regarding market entry? Marketers must address these issues before proceeding to the next step of the research process. Using data that are readily available saves both money and time. A formal market study can cost hundreds of thousands of dollars and take many months to complete.

A low-cost approach to market research and data collection begins with desk research. In other words, "the key to creating a cost-effective way of surveying foreign markets is to climb on the shoulders of those who have gone before."[15] Suppose a marketer wants to assess the basic market potential for a particular product. To find the answer, secondary sources are a good place to start. Personal files, company or public libraries, online databases, government census records, and trade associations are just a few of the data sources that can be tapped with minimal effort and cost. Data from these sources already exist. Such data are known as secondary data because they were not gathered for the specific project at hand. Statistical Abstract of the United States is just one of the annual publications issued by the U.S. government that contains myriad facts about international markets. The U.S. government's most comprehensive source of world trade data is the National Trade Data Base (NTDB), an online resource from the Department of Commerce. Another commerce department Web site, STAT-USA/Internet (**www.stat-usa.gov**), is an excellent online source for merchandise trade, gross domestic product, and other current and historical data. Most countries compile national accounts estimates of gross national product (GNP), gross domestic product (GDP), consumption, investment, government expenditures, and price levels. Demographic data indicating the population size, distribution of population by age category, and rates of population growth are also available. Market

---

[15] Michael R. Czinkota and Ilkka A. Ronkainen, "Market Research for Your Export Operations: Part I—Using Secondary Sources of Research," *International Trade Forum* 30, no. 3 (1994), p. 22.

information is also available from export census documents compiled by the department of commerce on the basis of shipper's export declarations (known as "ex-decs" or SEDs, these must be filled out for any export valued at $1,500 or more). Another important source of market data is the Foreign Commercial Service. Many countries have set up Web sites to help small firms find opportunities in world markets. For example, the Virtual Trade Commissioner (**www.infoexport.gc.ca**) is a service of Canada's Department of Foreign Affairs and International Trade (DFAIT). The site is a computerized database containing the names of Canadian companies that export.

These do not exhaust the types of data available, however. A single source, *The Statistical Yearbook of the United Nations*, contains global data on agriculture, mining, manufacturing, construction, energy production and consumption, internal and external trade, railroad and air transport, wages and prices, health, housing, education, communication infrastructure, and availability of mass communication media. The U.S. Central Intelligence Agency (CIA) publishes *World Factbook*, which is revised yearly. Other important sources are the World Bank, the International Monetary Fund (IMF), and Japan's Ministry of International Trade and Industry (MITI). *The Economist* and *Financial Times* regularly compile comprehensive surveys of regional and country markets and include them in their publications. Data from these sources are generally available in both print and electronic form.

How can such data be useful? Take industrial growth patterns as one example. Because they generally reveal consumption patterns, production patterns are helpful in assessing market opportunities. Additionally, trends in manufacturing production indicate potential markets for companies that supply manufacturing inputs. At the early stages of growth in a country, when per capita incomes are low, manufacturing centers on such necessities as food and beverages, textiles, and other forms of light industry. As incomes rise, the relative importance of these industries declines as heavy industry begins to develop.

A word of caution is in order at this point: Remember that data are compiled from various sources, some of which may not be reliable. Even when the sources are reliable, there is likely to be some variability from source to source. Anyone using data should be clear on exactly what the data are measuring. For example, studying income data requires understanding whether one is working with GNP or GDP figures. Also, anyone using the Internet as an information source should evaluate the credibility of the person(s) responsible for the Web site. Moreover, as Czinkota and Ronkainen note,[16] secondary data may support the decision to pursue a market opportunity outside the home country, but it is unlikely to shed light on specific questions: What is the market potential for our furniture in Indonesia? How much does the typical Nigerian consumer spend on soft drinks? If a packaging change is made to ensure compliance with Germany's Green Dot Ordinance, what effect, if any, will the change have on consumer purchasing behavior?

Syndicated studies published by private research companies are another source of secondary data and information (the word "syndicated" comes from the newspaper industry and refers the practice of selling articles, cartoons, or guest columns to a number of different organizations). For example, MarketResearch.com (**www.marketresearch.com**) sells reports on a wide range of global business sectors; the company partners with 350 research firms to offer a comprehensive set of reports. A sampling of reports available from MarketResearch.com is shown in Table 6-3; while the cost of a single report can run into thousands of dollars, a company may be able to get the market information it needs without incurring the cost associated with primary research.

---

16  Michael R. Czinkota and Ilkka A. Ronkainen, "Market Research for Your Export Operations: Part II—Conducting Primary Marketing Research," *International Trade Forum* 31, no. 1 (1995), p. 16.

| Title of Study | Length in Pages | Price |
|---|---|---|
| World Pharmaceutical Chemicals | 438 | $4,500 |
| Internet Commerce in Canada 2000–2006 | 22 | $4,500 |
| World Alcohol—Strategic Review | 900 | $3,950 |
| Global Airport Retailing | 185 | $1,115 |
| The Market for Travel and Tourism in Russia | 73 | $1,000 |
| Pet Food and Pet Products in India | 36 | $1,000 |
| Online Music in Japan | 12 | $995 |
| The 2000–2005 World Ice Cream Outlook | 110 | $795 |
| Automobiles and Automotive Parts in Brazil | 170 | $136 |

Source: The Information Catalog, 2nd Quarter 2002, MarketResearch.com.

**Table 6-3**

*Global Market Research Reports from MarketResearch.com*

## Step 5: Assess Value of Research

When data are not available through published statistics or studies, management may wish to conduct further study of the country market, region, or global segment. However, collecting information costs money. Thus, the plan should also spell out what this information is worth to the company in dollars (or euro, or yen, etc.) compared with what it would cost to collect it. What will the company gain by collecting this data? What would be the cost of not getting the data that could be converted into useful information? Research requires investment of both money and managerial time, and it is necessary to perform a cost-benefit analysis before proceeding further. In some instances, a company may pursue the same course of action no matter what the research reveals. Even when more information is needed to ensure a high-quality decision, a realistic estimate of a formal study may reveal that the cost to perform research is simply too high.

The small markets around the world pose a special problem for the researcher. The relatively low profit potential in smaller markets justifies only modest expenditures for marketing research. Therefore, the global researcher must devise techniques and methods that keep expenditures in line with the market's profit potential. In smaller markets, there is pressure on the researcher to discover economic and demographic relationships that permit estimates of demand based on a minimum of information. It may also be necessary to use inexpensive survey research that sacrifices some elegance or statistical rigor to achieve results within the constraints of the smaller market research budget.

## Step 6: Research Design

As indicated in Figure 6-1, if secondary data can be used, the researcher can go directly to the data analysis step. Suppose, however, data are not available through published statistics or studies; in addition, suppose that the cost-benefit analysis indicated in Step 4 has been performed and that the decision has been made to carry on with the research effort. **Primary data** are gathered through original research pertaining to the particular problem identified in Step 1. At this point, it is time to establish a research design.

Global marketing guru David Arnold offers the following guidelines regarding data gathering:[17]

- Use multiple indicators rather than a single measure. This approach will decrease the level of uncertainty for decision makers. As the saying goes, "There are three sides to every story: your side, my side, and the truth." A land surveyor can pinpoint the location of a third object given the known

---

[17] David Arnold, *The Mirage of Global Markets* (Upper Saddle River, NJ: Financial Times Prentice Hall, 2004), pp. 41–43.

location of two objects. This technique, known as *triangulation*, is equally useful in global market research.

- Individual companies should develop customized indicators specific to the industry, product market, or business model. Such indicators should leverage a company's previous experience in global markets. For example, in some developing markets, Mary Kay Cosmetics uses the average wage of a female secretary as a basis for estimate income potential for its beauty consultants.
- Always conduct comparative assessments in multiple markets. Do not assess a particular market in isolation. Comparative assessment enables management to develop a "portfolio" approach in which alternative priorities and scenarios can be developed. For example, to better understand Czech consumers in general, a company might also conduct research in nearby Poland and Hungary. By contrast, if a brewing company wished to learn more about beer consumption patterns in the Czech Republic, it might also conduct research in Ireland and Germany where per capita beer consumption is high.
- Observation of purchasing patterns and other behavior should be weighted more heavily than reports or opinion regarding purchase intention or price sensitivity. Particularly in developing markets, it is difficult to accurately survey consumer perceptions.

With these guidelines in mind, the marketer must address a new set of questions and issues in primary data collection. Should the research effort be geared toward quantitative, numerical data that can be subjected to statistical analysis or should qualitative techniques be used? In global marketing research, it is advisable for the plan to call for a mix of techniques. For consumer products, qualitative research is especially well-suited to accomplish the following tasks:[18]

- To provide consumer understanding; to "get close" to the consumer
- To describe the social and cultural context of consumer behavior, including cultural, religious, and political factors that impact decision making
- Identify core brand equity and "get under the skin" of brands
- To "mine" the consumer and identify what people really feel

**Issues in Data Collection** The research problem may be more narrowly focused on marketing issues, such as the need to adapt products and other mix elements to local tastes and assessing demand and profit potential. Demand and profit potential, in turn, depend in part on whether the market being studied can be classified as existing or potential. *Existing markets* are those in which customer needs are already being served by one or more companies. In many countries, data about the size of existing markets—in terms of dollar volume and unit sales—are readily available. In some countries, however, formal market research is a relatively new phenomenon and data are scarce. McKinsey & Company, Gartner Group Asia, and Grey China Advertising have been very active in China. For example, using focus groups and other techniques, Grey China gathers a wealth of information about attitudes and buying patterns that it publishes in its Grey ChinaBase Annual Consumer Study. Recent findings point to growing concerns about the future, Westernization of grocery purchases, growing market saturation, increasingly discerning customers, and a rise in consumer willingness to try new products. Even so, data gathered by different sources may be inconsistent. What is the level of soft drink consumption in China? Euromonitor International estimates consumption at 23 billion liters, while Coca-Cola's in-house marketing research team places the figure at 39 billion liters. Likewise, CSM, a Chinese

---

[18] John Pawle, "Mining the International Consumer," *Journal of the Market Research Society* 41, no. 1 (1999), p. 20.

television-rating agency, estimates the TV-advertising market at $2.8 billion per year. According to Nielsen Media Research, the figure is closer to $7.5 billion.[19]

In such situations, and in countries where such data are not available, researchers must first estimate the market size, the level of demand, or the rate of product purchase or consumption. A second research objective in existing markets may be assessment of the company's overall competitiveness in terms of product appeal, price, distribution, and promotional coverage and effectiveness. Researchers may be able to pinpoint a weakness in the competitor's product or identify an unserved market segment. The minivan and sport utility vehicle segments of the auto industry illustrate the opportunity that can be presented by an existing market. Chrysler dominates the U.S. minivan market, for which annual sales total about 1.2 million vehicles. Most global marketers compete in this segment. For example, Toyota introduced its Japanese-built Previa in the United States in 1991; critics mocked the teardrop styling and dismissed it as being underpowered. For the 1998 model year, the Previa was replaced with the American-built Sienna. To ensure that Sienna suited American tastes, Toyota designers and engineers studied Chrysler minivans and duplicated key features such as numerous cupholders and a sliding driver-side rear door.

In some instances, there is no existing market to research. Such *potential markets* can be further subdivided into latent and incipient markets. A **latent market** is, in essence, an undiscovered segment. It is a market in which demand would materialize *if* an appropriate product were made available. In a latent market, demand is zero before the product is offered. In the case of existing markets such as the one for minivans described previously, the main research challenge is to understand the extent to which competition fully meets customer needs. As J. Davis Illingworth, an executive at Toyota Motor Sales USA, explained, "I think the American public will look at Sienna as an American product that meets their needs."[20] With latent markets, initial success is not based on a company's competitiveness. Rather, it depends on the prime mover advantage—a company's ability to uncover the opportunity and launch a marketing program that taps the latent demand. This is precisely what Chrysler achieved by single-handedly creating the minivan market.

Sometimes, traditional marketing research is not an effective means for identifying latent markets. In a *Wall Street Journal* article, Peter Drucker pointed out that the failure of American companies to successfully commercialize fax machines—an American innovation—can be traced to research that indicated no potential demand for such a product. The problem, in Drucker's view, stems from the typical survey question for a product targeted at a latent market. Suppose a researcher asks, "Would you buy a telephone accessory that costs upwards of $1,500 and enables you to send, for $1 a page, the same letter the post office delivers for 25 cents?" On the basis of economics alone, the respondent most likely will answer, "No."

Drucker explained that Japanese companies are the leading sellers of fax machines today because their understanding of the market was not based on survey research. Instead, they reviewed the early days of mainframe computers, photocopy machines, cellular telephones, and other information and communications products. The Japanese realized that, judging only by the initial economics of buying and using these new products, the prospects of market acceptance were low. However, each of these products had become a huge success after people began to use them. This realization prompted the Japanese to focus on the market for the *benefits* provided by fax machines, rather than the market for the machines themselves. By looking at the success of courier

---

[19] Gabriel Kahn, "Chinese Puzzle: Spotty Consumer Data," *The Wall Street Journal* (October 15, 2003), p. B1.

[20] Kathleen Kerwin, "Can This Minivan Dent Detroit?" *Business Week* (February 3, 1997), p. 37.

# challenges of the global marketplace

## Motorola Loses a Big Bet with Iridium

Motorola spent more than a decade and billions of dollars developing Iridium, an ambitious new business that would offer satellite-global personal communications services to supplement ground-based wire and cellular telephone services. If it succeeded, Iridium would be an historic first: A business that was truly global from day one of operations. Iridium's first customers were expected to include globetrotting business executives who need to send and receive voice messages and data and who want a single telephone number that will work anywhere on the planet. In addition, the business concept was based on the fact that 90 percent of the world's population lacks access to telephones. Iridium could bring wireless telephone service to rural areas in South America, India, and Africa.

Motorola executives projected that Iridium would attract 5 million users by the year 2002. Each subscriber was expected to contribute $1,000 per year in net revenues to Iridium. In essence, Iridium was a huge bet that the varying technology standards of conventional cellular telephone systems would provide the key to Iridium's success. At the time, cellular phone standards were different in Europe and the United States, so a European businessperson's cell phone unit was rendered inoperable across the Atlantic in the United States. Iridium's early customers would have to pay approximately $3,000 for new telephones. Usage fees for satellite telephone calls were set in a range from $1.75 to $7.00 per minute

Industry observers were skeptical. Some wondered whether Motorola could really recoup its investment. One consultant got to the heart of the matter when he asked, "The biggest single issue is, can they sell it? There is no good head count of international businessmen who need this." For their part, Iridium executives reasoned that some 40 million people travel from the United States each year. Even if a small percentage of them became Iridium users, the service would be a success.

Early in 1997, Iridium management announced a number of strategic changes. The company was now aiming to sign up 3 million businesspeople such as contractors, people employed in the oil and gas industries, maritime workers, and employees of heavy construction firms such as Schlumberger and Bechtel. Such professional travelers, it was hoped, would account for about two-thirds of Iridium's revenues. As Iridium vice chairman and chief executive Dr. Edward Staiano said, "The guy who's going to pay for this system is the guy who doesn't look at his phone bill." This change de-emphasized the opportunity in emerging markets with undeveloped telephone systems.

A $140 million global print advertising campaign created by Ammirati Puris Lintas was launched in June 1998. Voice services began on November 1, with paging services available November 15. However, the required number of actual customers never materialized, and by 2000, Iridium was dead. The lesson: There was no latent market for global satellite telephone service.

*Sources: Quentin Hardy, "'Iridium Gets U.S. as First Big Customer of Wireless Communications System," The Wall Street Journal (January 26, 1998), p. B6; Sally Beatty, "Iridium Hopes to Ring Up Global Sales," The Wall Street Journal (June 22, 1998), p. B8; Hardy, "Iridium Creates New Plan for Global Cellular Service," The Wall Street Journal (August 18, 1997), p. B4.*

---

services such as Federal Express, the Japanese realized that, in essence, the fax machine market already existed.[21]

An **incipient market** is a market that will emerge if a particular economic, demographic, political, or sociocultural trend continues. A company is not likely to achieve satisfactory results if it offers a product in an incipient market before the trends have taken root. After the trends have had a chance to unfold, the incipient market will become latent and, later, existing. For example, one-third of Indonesia's 200 million people are under the age of 15. This represents a huge incipient market for cigarette marketers: About 4.4 million teenagers will become old enough to smoke each year.[22] The concept of incipient markets can also be illustrated by the impact of rising income on demand for automobiles and other expensive consumer durables. As per capita income rises in a country, the demand for automobiles will also rise. Therefore, if a company can predict a country's future rate of income growth, it can also predict the growth rate of its automobile market. For example, to capitalize on China's rapid economic growth, Volkswagen, Peugeot, Chrysler, and other global automakers have established in-country manufacturing operations. There is even incipient demand in China for imported exotic cars; in early 1994, Ferrari opened its first showroom in Beijing. Because of a 150 percent import tax, China's first Ferrari buyers were entrepreneurs who had profited from China's increasing openness to Western-style marketing and capitalism. By the end of the 1990s, demand for

---

[21] Peter F. Drucker, "Marketing 101 for a Fast-Changing Decade," *The Wall Street Journal* (November 20, 1990), p. A17.

[22] Michael Shari, "Will Cloves Lite Set the World on Fire?" *Business Week* (April 28, 1997), p. 55.

luxury cars had grown at a faster rate than anticipated. Today, there are 3 million private sedans for China's 1.3 billion people. Clearly, China is a very attractive market opportunity for carmakers.

By contrast, some companies have concluded that China has limited potential at present. For example, UK-based retailer Marks & Spencer recently closed its office in Shanghai and tabled plans to open a store in China. Commenting to the press, a company representative directly addressed the issue of whether or not China represents an incipient market:

> After three years of research, we have come to the conclusion that the timing is not right. The majority of our customers are from middle income groups. But, our interest is in Shanghai, and the size of the middle income group, although it is growing, is not yet at a level that would justify us opening a store there.[23]

**Research Methodologies** Survey research, interviews, consumer panels, observation, and focus groups are some of the tools used to collect primary market data. These are the same tools used by marketers whose activities are not global; however, some adaptations and special considerations for global marketing may be required.

**Survey research** utilizes questionnaires designed to elicit either quantitative data ("How much would you buy?"), qualitative data ("Why would you buy?"), or both. Survey research often obtains data from customers or some other designated group by means of a questionnaire distributed through the mail, by telephone, or in person. Many good marketing research textbooks provide details on questionnaire design and administration.

In global marketing research, a number of survey design and administration issues may arise. For example, telephone directories or lists may not be available; also, important differences may exist between urban dwellers and people in rural areas. Open-ended questions may help the researcher identify a respondent's frame of reference. In some cultures, respondents may be unwilling to answer certain questions, or they may intentionally give inaccurate answers.

Recall that Step 2 of the global market research process calls for identifying possible sources of SRC bias. This issue is especially important in survey research: SRC bias can originate from the cultural backgrounds of those designing the questionnaire. For example, a survey designed and administered in the United States may be inappropriate in non-Western cultures, even if it is carefully translated. This is especially true if the person designing the questionnaire is not familiar with the self-reference criterion. A technique known as **back translation** can help increase comprehension and validity; the technique requires that, after a questionnaire or survey instrument is translated into a particular target language, it is translated once again into the original by a different translator. For even greater accuracy, **parallel translations**—that is, two versions by different translators—can be used as input to the back translation. The same techniques can be used to ensure that advertising copy is accurately translated into different languages.

Sometimes bias is introduced when a survey is sponsored by a company with a financial stake in the outcome plans to publicize the results. For example, American Express joined with the French tourist bureau in producing a study that, among other things, covered the personality of the French people. The report ostensibly showed that, contrary to a long-standing stereotype, the French are not "unfriendly" to foreigners. However, the survey respondents were people who

---

[23] James Harding, "Foreign Investors Face New Curbs on Ownership of Stores," *Financial Times* (November 10, 1998), p. 7.

already had traveled to France on pleasure trips in the previous 2 years—a fact that likely biased the result.[24]

**Personal interviews** allow researchers to ask why and then explore answers. Interviews may be conducted in person or by telephone. However, what is customary in one country may be impossible in others because of infrastructure differences, cultural barriers, or other reasons. For example, telephone interviewing is a popular mass market research tool in the United States and other countries where most households have at least one telephone. However, the technique is quite inappropriate as a research tool in emerging markets where only 1 or 2 percent of households have telephones. At a deeper level, culture shapes attitudes and values in a way that will directly affect people's willingness to respond to interviewer questions.

A **consumer panel** is a sample of respondents whose behavior is tracked over time. For example, a number of companies, including the Nielsen Media Research unit of Netherlands-based VNU, AGB, GfK, and TNS, conduct television audience measurement (TAM) by studying the viewing habits of household panels. Broadcasters use audience share data to set advertising rates; advertisers such as Procter & Gamble, Unilever, and Coca-Cola use the data to choose programs during which to advertise. In the United States, Nielsen has enjoyed a virtual monopoly on viewership research for half a century. For years, however, the four major U.S. television networks have complained that they lose advertising revenues because Nielsen's data collection methods undercount viewership. Nielsen has responded to these concerns by upgrading its survey methodology; the company now uses an electronic device known as a **peoplemeter** to collect national audience data. Peoplemeter systems are currently in use in dozens of countries around the world, including China; Nielsen is also rolling out peoplemeters to collect local audience viewership data in key metropolitan markets such as New York City.

The peoplemeter is actually a system consisting of a monitor unit (one for each TV in a given panel household) that detects when a TV set is turned on and the channel to which it is tuned. The monitor prompts individual household members to identify themselves using a remote control. Another component identifies whether a VCR is being used. The final component is a data storage unit that is accessed once daily by the service provider. Even as Nielsen and its competitors attempt to provide a more accurate picture of TV viewing habits, however, media consumption patterns are changing. In a key finding, Nielsen reported a significant drop-off in viewership among American men aged 18-34. This group is spending more time surfing the Internet and playing video games, often during prime TV viewing hours. Because this age group represents an important demographic for advertisers, Nielsen Entertainment, a separate unit of VNU, is developing new tools to monitor their media habits. For example, Nielsen is teaming with Activision, a video game company whose titles include *Tony Hawk's Pro Skater 4*; one of Nielsen's goals is to measure whether branded product placement in video games results in increased awareness and purchase intention among gamers. Nielsen is also working with TiVo, the leading personal video recorder service in the United States.[25]

When **observation** is used as a data collection method, one or more trained observers (or a mechanical device such as a video camera) watch and record the behavior of actual or prospective buyers. Observation can take the form of home visits. For example, Toyota used observation when redesigning its flagship luxury car, the Lexus LS 400, for the 1995 model year. The chief engineer of Lexus and a

---

[24] Cynthia Crossen, "Margin of Error: Studies Galore Support Products and Positions, But Are They Reliable?" *The Wall Street Journal* (November 4, 1991), pp. A1, A7.

[25] John Schwartz, "Leisure Pursuits of Today's Young Man," *The New York Times* (March 29, 2004), p. C1. See also Christopher Parkes, "Nielsen to Interact with Gaming Group," *Financial Times* (April 8, 2004), p. 22.

five-person team came to the United States in 1991. They stayed in luxury hotels to gain an understanding of the level of service Lexus customers demanded. Design team members visited customers' homes and took notes on preferences for such things as furniture, paintings—even briefcases. As Ron Brown, a U.S.-based product planning manager for Lexus, recalled, "It's like if you just bought a new washer-dryer, and the Kenmore people called and said they wanted to bring a bunch of people out to watch you wash your clothes." One thing the team discovered was that the coat hooks in the first-generation LS 400 were too small. The Japanese thought a coat hook was, literally, for hanging a coat. In reality, Lexus owners regularly hang their dry-cleaning in the car. The hook was redesigned for 1995. "You can get five coat hangers on it. But now it's big enough that you wouldn't want it out all the time, so it retracts," says Brown.[26] The research effort paid off; by 2001, Lexus ranked in the top three of luxury car nameplates sold in the United States; Cadillac, meanwhile, had fallen from first place to sixth. How did Cadillac respond? The company sent *its* designers and engineers to Los Angeles and New York for "luxury immersions." Teams stayed in luxury hotels, drove BMWs and Mercedes, and shopped in upscale stores. As one designer noted, "You've got to live the lifestyle for a couple of days."[27]

A marketer of breakfast cereals might send researchers to preselected households at 6 A.M. to watch families go about their morning routines. The client could also assign a researcher to accompany family members to the grocery store to observe their behavior under actual shopping conditions. The client might wish to know about the shoppers' reactions to in-store promotions linked to an advertising campaign. The researcher could record comments using a cassette recorder or discretely take photographs with a small camera. Companies using observation as a research methodology must be sensitive to public concerns about privacy issues. A second problem with observation is **reactivity,** which is the tendency of research subjects to behave differently for the simple reason that they know they are under study.

Procter & Gamble has recently undertaken an ambitious observation program that will send video crews into 80 households in the United Kingdom, Italy, Germany, and China. The filmmakers will arrive each day when the subject family rises and film until bedtime. Faced with sluggish annual sales growth, marketers at the packaged-goods giant are hoping to gain insights into consumer behavior that other forms of research might miss. Those insights could be translated directly into product and package design improvements that could provide a competitive advantage for P&G. P&G's ultimate goal is to amass an in-house video library that can be directly accessed by key word searches. Stan Joosten, an information-technology manager, noted, "You could search for 'eating snacks' and find all clips from all over the world on that topic. Immediately, it gives you a global perspective on certain topics."[28]

In **focus group** research, a trained moderator facilitates discussion of a product concept, a brand's image and personality, advertisement, social trend, or other topic with a group comprised of 6 to 10 people. Global marketers can use focus groups to arrive at important insights. For example:

- Reebok International discovered that young consumers' initial impressions of the company's shoes were positive when the brand wasn't identified; the same consumers responded negatively when it was revealed to be Reebok. As chief executive Paul Fireman noted, "We have a brand that hasn't been held in the highest regard." To give its marketing a new twist, Reebok

---

[26] James R. Healy, "Toyota Strives for New Look, Same Edge," *USA Today* (October 13, 1994), pp. 1B–2B.

[27] Gregory White, "GM Shifts Into Overdrive in Luxury Sport-Sedan Race," *The Wall Street Journal* (August 17, 2001), p. B4.

[28] Emily Nelson, "P&G Checks Out Real Life," *The Wall Street Journal* (May 17, 2001), pp. B1, B4.

launched a advertising campaign featuring tennis star Venus Williams with the theme of "Defy Convention."[29]

- In the mid-1990s, Whirlpool launched a European advertising campaign that featured fantasy characters such as a drying diva and a washing-machine goddess. The campaign's success prompted management to adapt it for use in the United States and Latin America. First, however, the company conducted nearly two dozen focus groups to gauge reaction to the ads. Nick Mote is Whirlpool's worldwide account director at France's Publicis advertising agency. "We've had some incredible research results. It was just like somebody switched the lights on," he said.[30]

- In Singapore, focus groups comprised of young teens were used to help guide development of Coca-Cola's advertising program. As Karen Wong, Coke's country marketing director for Singapore, explained, "We tested everything from extreme to borderline boring: body-piercing all over, grungy kids in a car listening to rock music and head-banging all the way. Youth doing things that youth in America do." Some participants found much of Coke's imagery—for example, a shirtless young man crowd surfing at a rock concert and careening down a store aisle on a grocery cart—too rebellious. As one young Singaporean remarked, "They look like they're on drugs. And if they're on drugs, then how can they be performing at school?" Armed with the focus group results, Coca-Cola's managers devised an ad campaign for Singapore that was well within the bounds of societal approval.[31]

- When Blockbuster Video was planning its entry into Japan, the world's number two video rental market, the company convened focus groups to learn more about Japanese preferences and perceptions of existing video rental outlets. In the mid-1990s, most video stores in Japan were tiny operations with limited display space. Video titles were piled up from the floor to the ceilings, making it difficult to find and retrieve individual titles. Acting on the information provided by the focus groups, Blockbuster designed its Japanese stores with 3,000 square feet of floor space and display shelves that were more accessible.[32]

A typical focus group meets at a facility equipped with recording equipment and a one-way mirror behind which representatives of the client company observe the proceedings. The moderator can utilize a number of approaches to elicit reactions and responses, including projective techniques, visualization, and role plays. When using a **projective technique,** the researcher presents open-ended or ambiguous stimuli to a subject. Presumably, when verbalizing a response, the subject will "project"—that is, reveal—his or her unconscious attitudes and biases. By analyzing the responses, researchers are better able understand how consumers perceive a particular product, brand, or company. For example, in a focus group convened to assess car-buying preferences among a Striver-type segment, the researcher might ask participants to describe a party where various automotive brands are present. What is Nissan wearing, eating, and drinking? What kind of sneakers does Honda have on? What are their personalities like? Who's shy? Who's loud? Who gets the girl (or guy)? Interaction among group members can result in synergies that yield important qualitative insights that are likely to differ from those based on data gathered through more direct questioning. Focus group research is a technique has grown in popularity.

[29] Joseph Pereira, "Reebok Serves Up Tennis Star in New Ads," *The Wall Street Journal* (January 18, 2001), p. B2.

[30] Katheryn Kranhold, "Whirlpool Conjures Up Appliance Divas," *The Wall Street Journal* (April 27, 2000), p. B1.

[31] Cris Prystay, "Selling to Singapore's Teens is Tricky," *The Wall Street Journal* (October 4, 2002), p. B4.

[32] Khanh T. L. Tran, "Blockbuster Finds Success in Japan that Eluded the Chain in Germany," *The Wall Street Journal* (August 28, 1998), p. A14.

However, some industry observers caution that the technique has been used so much that participants, especially those who are used on a regular basis, have become overly familiar with its workings.

Focus group research yields qualitative data that does not lend itself to statistical projection. Such data suggests rather than confirms hypotheses; also, qualitative data tends to be directional rather than conclusive. Such data is extremely valuable in the exploratory phase of a project and is typically used in conjunction with data gathered via observation and other methods. For example, the Coca-Cola Company convened focus groups in Japan, England, and the United States to explore potential consumer reaction to a prototype 12-ounce contoured aluminum soft drink can. Coca-Cola was searching for ways to counteract competition from private-label colas in key markets; in England, for example, Sainsbury's store brand cola has an 18 percent market share.[33] Similarly, focus groups have helped PepsiCo's Frito-Lay snack unit build its business in Asia. In Thailand, focus group research indicated that *tom yan* (prawn) was the favorite flavor; in China, focus groups prefer dog. However, that did not automatically mean that Thai consumers would prefer prawn-flavored potato chips. The researchers discovered that a "good" snack is one with a Western flavor such as barbeque.[34]

**Scale Development** Market research requires assigning some type of measure, ranking, or interval to a response. To take a simple example of measurement, a *nominal scale* is used to establish the identity of a survey element. For example, male respondents could be labeled "1" and female respondents could be labeled "2." Scaling can also entail placing each response in some kind of continuum; a common example is the Likert scale that asks respondents to indicate whether they "strongly agree" with a statement, "strongly disagree," or whether their attitude falls somewhere in the middle. In a multicountry research project it is important to have **scalar equivalence**, which means that two respondents in different countries with the same value for a given variable receive equivalent scores on the same survey item.

Even with standard data-gathering techniques, the application of a particular technique may differ from country to country. Matthew Draper, vice president at New Jersey-based Total Research Corporation, cites "scalar bias" as a major problem: "There are substantial differences in the way people use scales, and research data based on scales such as rating product usefulness on a scale of 1 to 10 is therefore frequently cluttered with biases disguising the truth." For example, while the typical American scale would equate a high number such as 10 with "most" or "best" and 1 with "least," Germans prefer scales in which 1 is "most/best." Also, while American survey items pertaining to spending provide a range of figures, Germans prefer the opportunity to provide an exact answer.[35]

When collecting data, researchers generally cannot administer a survey to every possible person in the designated group. A sample is a selected subset of a population that is representative of the entire population. The two best-known types of samples are *probability samples* and *nonprobability samples*. A probability sample is generated by following statistical rules that ensure that each member of the population under study has an equal chance—or probability—of being included in the sample. The results of a probability sample can be projected to the

[33] Karen Benezra, "Coke Queries on Contour Can," *Brandweek* (November 7, 1994), p. 4.
[34] G. Pascal Zachary, "Strategic Shift: Major U.S. Companies Expand Efforts to Sell to Consumers Abroad," *The Wall Street Journal* (June 13, 1996), pp. A1, A6.
[35] Jack Edmonston, "U.S., Overseas Differences Abound," *Business Marketing* (January 1998), p. 32.

entire population with statistical reliability reflecting sampling error, degree of confidence, and standard deviation.

The results of a nonprobability sample cannot be projected with statistical reliability. One form of nonprobability sample is a *convenience sample*. As the name implies, researchers select people who are easy to reach. For example, in one study that compared consumer shopping attitudes in the United States, Jordan, Singapore, and Turkey, data for the latter three countries were gathered from convenience samples recruited by an acquaintance of the researcher. Although data gathered in this way are not subject to statistical inference, they may be adequate to address the problem defined in Step 1. In this study, for example, the researchers were able to identify a clear trend toward cultural convergence in shopping attitudes and customs that cut across modern industrial countries, emerging industrial countries, and developing countries.[36]

To obtain a *quota sample*, the researcher divides the population under study into categories; a sample is taken from each category. The term *quota* refers to the need to make sure that enough people are chosen in each category to reflect the overall makeup of the population. For example, assume a country's population may be divided into six categories according to monthly income as follows:

| Percent of population | 10 | 15 | 25 | 25 | 15 | 10 |
|---|---|---|---|---|---|---|
| Earnings per month | 0–9 | 10–19 | 20–39 | 40–59 | 60–69 | 70–100 |

If it is assumed that income is the characteristic that adequately differentiates the population for study purposes, then a quota sample would include respondents of different income levels in the same proportion as they occurred in the population, that is, 15 percent with monthly earnings from 10 to 19, and so on.

## Step 7: Analyzing Data[37]

The data collected up to this point must be subjected to some form of analysis if it to be useful to decision makers. Although a detailed discussion is beyond the scope of this text, a brief overview is in order. First, the data must be prepared—the term "cleaned" is sometimes used—before further analysis is possible. It must be logged and stored in a central location or database; obviously, when research has been conducted in various parts of the world, rounding up data can pose some difficulties. Are data comparable across samples so that multicountry analysis can be performed? Some amount of editing may be required; for example, some responses may be missing or difficult to interpret. Next, questionnaires must be coded. Simply put, coding involves identifying the respondents and the variables. Finally, some data adjustment may be required.

Data analysis continues with *tabulation*, that is, the arrangement of data in tabular form. Researchers may wish to determine various things: the mean, median, and mode; range and standard deviation; and the shape of the distribution (e.g., normal curve). For nominally-scaled variables such as "male" and "female," a simple cross tabulation may be performed. Suppose, for example, Nielsen Media Research surveyed video gamers to determine how they felt about products (e.g., soft drinks) and advertisements (e.g., a billboard for a cell phone) embedded in video games. Nielsen could use cross-tabulation to separately examine the responses of male and female subjects to see if their responses differed significantly. If females were equally or more positive in their responses than males, video game companies could use this information to persuade consumer products companies to pay to have select products targeted at

---

[36] Eugene H. Fram and Riad Ajami, "Globalization of Markets and Shopping Stress: Cross-Country Comparisons," *Business Horizons* 37, no. 1 (January–February 1994), pp. 17–23.

[37] Parts of this section are adapted from Glen L. Urban, John R. Hauser, and Nikhilesh Dholakia, *Essentials of New Product Management* (Upper Saddle River, NJ: Prentice Hall, 1987), Chapters 6 and 7.

| Product Characteristic/Benefit | Rating | | | | | Table 6-4 |
|---|---|---|---|---|---|---|
| | Low 1 | 2 | 3 | 4 | High 5 | |

| Product Characteristic/Benefit | Low 1 | 2 | 3 | 4 | High 5 |
|---|---|---|---|---|---|
| 1. Long battery life | ___ | ___ | ___ | ___ | ___ |
| 2. Many games available | ___ | ___ | ___ | ___ | ___ |
| 3. Wireless Internet access | ___ | ___ | ___ | ___ | ___ |
| 4. Easy to use | ___ | ___ | ___ | ___ | ___ |
| 5. Attractive styling | ___ | ___ | ___ | ___ | ___ |
| 6. Plays MP3 music files | ___ | ___ | ___ | ___ | ___ |
| 7. Bright display screen | ___ | ___ | ___ | ___ | ___ |
| 8. Fits hand comfortably | ___ | ___ | ___ | ___ | ___ |
| 9. Works anywhere in the world | ___ | ___ | ___ | ___ | ___ |
| 10. Custom face plates available | ___ | ___ | ___ | ___ | ___ |

**Table 6-4**

*Hypothetical Scales for Obtaining Consumer Perceptions of Nokia N-Gage*

*Instructions: Please rate the Nokia N-Gage on the following product characteristics or benefits.*

women featured as integral parts of the game. Researchers can also use various relatively simple statistical techniques such as hypothesis testing and chi-square testing; advanced data analysis such as analysis of variance (ANOVA), correlation analysis, and regression analysis can also be used.

If the researcher is interested in the interaction between variables, *interdependence techniques* such as factor analysis, cluster analysis, and multi-dimensional scaling (MDS) can be used. **Factor analysis** can be used to transform large amounts of data into manageable units; specialized computer programs perform data reduction by "distilling out" a few meaningful factors that underlie attitudes and perceptions from a multitude of survey responses. Factor analysis is useful in psychographic segmentation studies; it can also be used to create perceptual maps. In this form of analysis, variables are not classified as dependent or independent. Subjects are asked to rate specific product benefits on five-point scales; Table 6-4 shows a hypothetical scale that Nokia might use to assess consumer perceptions of the new N-Gage cell phone. Although the scale shown in Table 6-4 lists 10 characteristics/benefits, factor analysis will generate *factor loadings* that enable the researcher to determine two or three factors that underlie the benefits. For the N-Gage, the researcher might label the factors "easy to use" and "stylish." The computer will also output *factor scores* for each respondent; respondent #1 might have a factor score of .35 "easy to use"; respondent #2 might have .42, and so on. When all respondents' factor scores for N-Gage are averaged, N-Gage's position on a perceptual map can be determined. Similar determinations can be made for other cell phone brands.

**Cluster analysis** allows the researcher to group variables into clusters that maximize within-group similarities and between-group differences. Cluster analysis shares some characteristics of factor analysis: It does not classify variables as dependent or independent, and it can be used in psychographic segmentation. Cluster analysis is well-suited to global marketing research because similarities and differences can be established between local, national, and regional markets of the world. For example, Claritas/NPDC uses geodemographic data to cluster neighborhoods into types. Claritas has begun matching some U.S. cities to "twins" in Canada.[38] Cluster analysis can also be used to perform benefit segmentation and identify new product opportunities.

**MDS** is another technique for creating perceptual maps. When the researcher is using MDS, the respondent is given the task of comparing products, one pair at a time, and judging them in terms of similarity. The researcher then infers

---

[38] Claudi Montague, "Is Calgary Denver's Long-Lost Twin?" *American Demographics* (June 1993), pp. 12–13.

| | Very Similar | | | | Very Different |
|---|---|---|---|---|---|
| | 1 | 2 | 3 | 4 | 5 |
| Acura MDX/Volvo XC90 | ____ | ____ | ____ | ____ | ____ |
| Acura MDX/Infiniti FX45 | ____ | ____ | ____ | ____ | ____ |
| Acura MDX/Lexus RX330 | ____ | ____ | ____ | ____ | ____ |
| Acura MDX/Honda Pilot | ____ | ____ | ____ | ____ | ____ |
| Acura MDX/Nissan Murano | ____ | ____ | ____ | ____ | ____ |
| Acura MDX/Buick Rendezvous | ____ | ____ | ____ | ____ | ____ |
| Acura MDX/Toyota Highlander | ____ | ____ | ____ | ____ | ____ |
| Volvo XC90/Infiniti FX45 | ____ | ____ | ____ | ____ | ____ |
| Volvo XC90/Lexus RX330 | ____ | ____ | ____ | ____ | ____ |
| Volvo XC90/Honda Pilot | ____ | ____ | ____ | ____ | ____ |
| Volvo XC90/Nissan Murano | ____ | ____ | ____ | ____ | ____ |
| Volvo XC90/Buick Rendezvous | ____ | ____ | ____ | ____ | ____ |
| Volvo XC90/Toyota Highlander | ____ | ____ | ____ | ____ | ____ |

the dimensions that underlie the judgments. MDS is particularly useful when there are many products from which to choose and when consumers may have difficulty verbalizing their perceptions. To create a well-defined spatial map, a minimum of eight products or brands should be used. Suppose, for example, that a consumer uses an underlying perceptual dimension of "distinct image" in assessing the similarity of pairs of crossover SUVs. Table 6-5 shows a five-point similarity judgment scale for eight current crossover SUV models. Figure 6-2 shows the position of the eight SUVs on the "distinct image" dimension for a hypothetical respondent. The figure shows that the Infiniti/Volvo pair are the most similar while Infiniti and Buick are the farthest apart. The responses help marketers understand which brands in a particular category—crossover SUVs in this example—are in direct competition with each other and which are not. The responses are input into a computer running an MDS program; the output is a perceptual map such as that shown in Figure 6-3. Once the computer has generated the map, the marketer examines the positions of different SUV models and infers the dimensions, which in this case are "comfort" and "distinct image." This map would be helpful to, say, Kia, if management was considering rolling out the company's first crossover SUV.

*Dependence techniques* assess the interdependence of two or more dependent variables with one or more independent variables. To continue with the SUV example, suppose Kia's new product team has selected an ideal position on Figure 6-3; now the task is to select specific product features that will deliver that positioning. The researchers want to determine the relative importance of a product's *salient attributes* in consumer decision making; that is, the relevance or importance that consumers attach to a product's qualities or properties. If the target position is a "smooth, car-like ride while protecting your family," the team must determine relevant physical product characteristics, for example, 6-cylinder engine, rollover sensors, side-curtain airbags, and onboard global positioning system. The team must also determine other

**Figure 6-2**

Hypothetical One-Dimensional
Illustration of Similarity Judgments

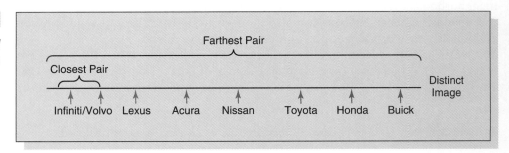

216    Part 3    Approaching Global Markets

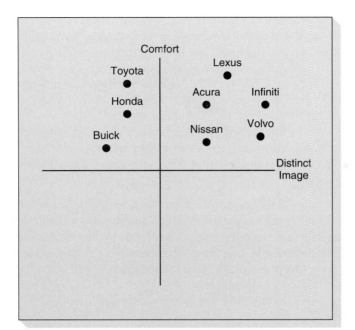

**Figure 6-3**

Hypothetical MDS-based
Perceptual Map for Crossover
SUVs

characteristics (e.g., price, mileage, warranty, etc.) that consumers most prefer. Each attribute should be available in different levels, e.g., 5-year or 10-year warranty. **Conjoint analysis** is a tool that researchers can use to gain insights into the combination of features that will be most attractive to consumers; it is assumed that features affect both perception and preferences. Table 6-6 shows a listing of possible features; a total of 36 combinations are possible. In a full-profile approach, each of these combinations (e.g., 6 cylinder, side-curtain airbags for all three rows, 5-year warranty, $27,500) is printed on an index card, and consumers are asked to rank them in order by preference. Conjoint analysis then determines the values or *utilities* of the various levels of product features and plots them graphically. Because the number of combinations can overwhelm subjects and lead to fatigue, it is sometimes preferable to use a pair-wise approach that allows them to consider two attributes at a time.

**Comparative Analysis and Market Estimation by Analogy** One of the unique opportunities in global marketing analysis is to conduct comparisons of market potential and marketing performance in different country or regional markets at the same point in time. A common form of comparative analysis is the intracompany cross-national comparison. For example, general market conditions in two or more countries (as measured by income, stage of industrialization, or some other indicator) may be similar. If there is a significant discrepancy between per capita sales of a given product in the countries, the marketer might reasonably wonder about it and determine what actions need to be taken.

- Soon after George Fisher became CEO of Kodak, he asked for a review of market share in color film on a country-by-country basis. Fisher was shocked to learn that Kodak's market share in Japan was only 7 percent, compared with

| | Engine size | Side-curtain Airbags | Warranty | Price |
|---|---|---|---|---|
| Level 1 | – | Side-curtain airbags for front seat passengers only | – | $22,500 |
| Level 2 | 6 cylinder | Side-curtain airbags for front seat and middle passengers | 5 years | $27,500 |
| Level 3 | 8 cylinder | Side-curtain airbags for front, middle, and third row passengers | 10 years | $32,500 |

**Table 6-6**

Product Feature Combinations for
Crossover SUV

40 percent in most other countries. The situation prompted Fisher to lodge a petition with the U.S. trade representative seeking removal of alleged anti-competitive barriers in Japan. The WTO ultimately ruled against Kodak.

- Campbell's commands nearly 80 percent of the U.S. canned soup market. However, former CEO Dale Morrison set aggressive growth goals for Campbell based on figures showing that Campbell's has just 10 percent market share throughout the rest of the world.[39]
- Catalog sales in the United States represent about 3 percent of overall retail sales. By comparison, catalog sales in Germany account for 5.8 percent of overall sales. This suggests that there is a catalog marketing opportunity in Germany.[40]

In these examples, data are, for the most part, available. However, global marketers may find that certain types of desired data are unavailable for a particular country market. This is especially true in developing country markets. If this is the case, it is sometimes possible to estimate market size or potential demand by analogy. Drawing an **analogy** is simply stating a partial resemblance. For example, the advertising and computer industries in the United States both have geographic nicknames. The advertising industry is often referred to as "Madison Avenue," while the phrase "Silicon Valley" is synonymous with California's high-tech industry center. Thus, Silicon Valley is to the computer industry as Madison Avenue is to the advertising industry. Statements such as this are analogies.

David Arnold notes that there are four possible approaches to forecasting by analogy.[41]

- Data is available on a comparable product in the same country.
- Data is available on the same product in a comparable country.
- Data is available on the same product from an independent distributor in a neighboring country.
- Data is available about a comparable company in the same country.

*Time-series displacement* is an analogy technique based on the assumption that an analogy between markets exists in different time periods. Displacing time is a useful form of market analysis when data are available for two markets at different levels of development. The time displacement method requires a marketer to estimate when two markets are at similar stages of development. For example, the market for Polaroid instant cameras in Russia at the present time is comparable to the instant camera market in the United States in the mid-1960s. By obtaining data on the factors associated with demand for instant cameras in the United States in 1964 and in Russia today, as well as actual U.S. demand in 1964, one could current estimate potential in Russia.

## Step 8: Presenting the Findings

The report based on the market research must be useful to managers as input to the decision-making process. Whether the report is presented in written form, orally, or electronically via videotape, it must relate clearly to the problem or opportunity identified in Step 1. Generally, it is advisable for major findings to be summarized concisely in a memo that indicates the answer or answers to the problem first proposed in Step 1. Many managers are uncomfortable with research jargon and complex quantitative analysis. Results should be clearly stated and provide a basis for managerial action. Otherwise, the report may end up on the shelf, where it will

[39] Amy Barrett, "Souping Up Campbell's," *Business Week* (November 3, 1997), p. 70.
[40] Cacilie Rohwedder, "U.S. Mail-Order Firms Shake Up Europe," *The Wall Street Journal* (January 6, 1998), p. A15.
[41] David Arnold, *The Mirage of Global Markets* (Upper Saddle River, NJ: Financial Times Prentice Hall, 2004), pp. 41–43.

gather dust and serve as a reminder of wasted time and money. As the data provided by a corporate information system and market research become increasingly available on a worldwide basis, it becomes possible to analyze marketing expenditure effectiveness across national boundaries. Managers can then decide where they are achieving the greatest marginal effectiveness for their marketing expenditures and can adjust expenditures accordingly.

## Headquarter's Control of Marketing Research

An important issue for the global company is where to locate control of the organization's research capability. The difference between a multinational, polycentric company and a global, geocentric company on this issue is significant. In the multinational company, responsibility for research is delegated to the operating subsidiary. The global company delegates responsibility for research to operating subsidiaries but retains overall responsibility and control of research as a headquarters' function. A key difference between single country market research and global market research is the importance of comparability. In practice, this means that the global company must ensure that research is designed and executed so as to yield comparable data.

Simply put, **comparability** means that the results can be used to make valid comparisons between the countries covered by the research.[42] To achieve this, the company must inject a level of control and review of marketing research at the global level. The director of worldwide marketing research must respond to local conditions as he or she develops a research program that can be implemented on a global basis. The research director must pay particular attention to whether data gathered is based on emic analysis or etic analysis. These terms, which come from anthropology, refer to the perspective taken in the study of another culture. **Emic analysis** is similar to ethnography in that it attempts to study a culture from within, using its own system of meanings and values. **Etic analysis** is "from the outside"; in other words, it is a more detached perspective that is often used in comparative or multicountry studies. In a particular research study, an etic scale would entail using the same set of items across all countries. This approach enhances comparability but some precision is lost. By contrast, an emic study would be tailored to fit a particular country; inferences about cross-cultural similarities based on emic research have to be made subjectively. A good compromise is to use a survey instrument that incorporates elements of both types of analysis. It is likely that the marketing director will end up with a number of marketing programs tailored to clusters of countries that exhibit within-group similarities. The agenda of a coordinated worldwide research program might look like the one in Table 6-7.

The director of worldwide research should not simply direct the efforts of country research managers. His or her job is to ensure that the corporation achieves maximum results worldwide from the total allocation of its research resources. Achieving this requires that personnel in each country are aware of research being carried out in the rest of the world and are involved in influencing the design of their own in-country research as well as the overall research program. Ultimately, the director of worldwide research must be responsible for the

| Research Objective | Country Cluster A | Country Cluster B | Country Cluster C |
|---|---|---|---|
| Identify market potential | | | X |
| Appraise competitive intentions | | X | X |
| Evaluate product appeal | X | X | X |
| Study market response to price | X | | |
| Appraise distribution channels | X | X | X |

**Table 6-7**

Worldwide Marketing Research Plan

42 V. Kumar, *International Marketing Research* (Upper Saddle River, NJ: Prentice Hall, 1999), p. 15.

overall research design and program. It is his or her job to take inputs from the entire world and produce a coordinated research strategy that generates the information needed to achieve global sales and profit objectives.

## The Marketing Information System as a Strategic Asset

The advent of the transnational enterprise means that boundaries between the firm and the outside world are dissolving. Marketing has historically been responsible for managing many of the relationships across that boundary. The boundary between marketing and other functions is also dissolving, and the traditional notion of marketing as a distinct functional area within the firm may be giving way to a new model. The process of marketing decision making is also changing, largely because of the changing role of information from a support tool to a wealth-generating, strategic asset.

Some firms are experimenting with flattened organizations, with less hierarchical, less centralized decision-making structures. Such organizations facilitate the exchange and flow of information between otherwise noncommunicative departments. The more information intensive the firm, the greater the degree to which marketing is involved in activities traditionally associated with other functional areas. In such firms there is parallel processing of information.

Information intensity in the firm has an impact on perceptions of market attractiveness, competitive position, and organizational structure. The greater a company's information intensity, the more the traditional product and market boundaries shift. In essence, companies increasingly face new sources of competition from other firms in historically noncompetitive industries, particularly if those firms are also information intensive. The most obvious and dramatic example is the emergence of the "superindustry," combining telecommunications, computers, financial services, and retailing into what is essentially an information industry. Such diverse firms as AT&T, IBM, Merrill Lynch, Citicorp, and Sears now find themselves in direct competition with each other. They offer essentially the same products, although not as a result of diversification. Rather, the new competition reflects a natural extension and redefinition of traditional product lines and marketing activities. Today, when a company speaks of "value added," it is less likely to be referring to unique product features. Rather, the emphasis is on the information exchanged as part of customer transactions, much of which cuts across traditional product lines.

## An Integrated Approach to Information Collection[43]

Coordinated organization activity is required to maintain surveillance of those aspects of the environment about which the organization wishes to stay informed. The goal of this activity, which may be termed *organized intelligence*, is to systematize the collecting and analysis of competitive intelligence to serve the needs of the organization as a whole. Organizing for intelligence requires more than gathering and disseminating good intelligence. Many companies that simply assign an analyst to the task of gathering, analyzing, and disseminating intelligence encounter problems in getting managers to use the output, in gaining credibility for the output and its function, and in establishing the relevance of the output for users.

The role of organized competitive intelligence in shaping strategy will depend on its ability to supplement, rather than replace, the informal activities of employees, especially top management. One obstacle to a fully integrated marketing information

---

[43] This section is adapted from Benjamin Gilad, "The Role of Organized Competitive Intelligence in Corporate Strategy," *Columbia Journal of World Business* 24 (Winter 1989), pp. 29–35.

system that encompasses both formal and informal information-gathering techniques is that monitoring activities are not usually fully integrated with the decision-making process. If the information isn't used, the monitoring effort invariably fails to increase a company's competitiveness. Michael Porter's influential work on competitive strategy, together with increasing global competitive pressures and loss of market dominance by many U.S. companies, has helped bring environmental scanning into a new focus. The emphasis has been on competitive intelligence rather than on broader environmental scanning.

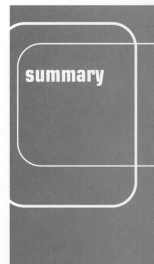

**summary**

Information is one of the most basic ingredients of a successful marketing strategy. A company's **management information system** provides decision makers with a continuous flow of information. **Information technology** is profoundly affecting global marketing activities by allowing managers to access and manipulate data to assist in decision making. **Electronic data interchange, electronic point of sale data, efficient consumer response, customer relationship management,** and **data warehouses** are some of the new tools and techniques available. The global marketer must scan the world for information about opportunities and threats and make information available via a management information system. Environmental **scanning** can be accomplished by keeping in touch with an area of information via **surveillance** or by actively seeking out information via **search.** Information can be obtained from human and documentary sources or from **direct perception.**

Formal research is often required before specific marketing decisions can be made. The research process begins when marketers define the problem and set research objectives; this step may entail assessing whether a particular market should be classified as **latent** or **incipient.** A research plan specifies the relative amounts of **qualitative** and **quantitative** information desired. Information is collected using either **primary** or **secondary data** sources. In today's wired world, the Internet has taken its place alongside more traditional channels as an important secondary information source. In some instances, the cost of collecting primary data may outweigh the potential benefits. Secondary sources are especially useful for researching a market that is too small to justify a large commitment of time and money.

If collection of primary data can be justified on a cost-benefit basis, research can be conducted via **surveys, personal interviews, consumer panels, observation,** and **focus groups.** Before collecting data, researchers must determine whether a probability sample is required. In global marketing, careful attention must be paid to issues such as eliminating cultural bias in research, accurately translating surveys, and ensuring data comparability in different markets. A number of techniques are available for analyzing survey data, including **factor analysis, cluster analysis, multidimensional scaling,** and **conjoint analysis.** Research findings and recommendations must be presented clearly. A final issue is how much control headquarters will have over research and the overall management of the organization's information system. To ensure comparability of data, the researcher should utilize both **emic** and **etic** approaches.

**discussion questions**

1. Explain how information technology puts powerful tools in the hands of global marketers.

2. What are the different modes of information acquisition? Which is the most important for gathering strategic information?

3. Assume that you have been asked by the president of your organization to devise a systematic approach to scanning. The president does not want to be surprised by major market or competitive developments. What would you recommend?

4. Outline the basic steps of the market research process.

5. What is the difference between existing, latent, and incipient demand? How might these differences affect the design of a marketing research project?

6. Describe some of the analytical techniques used by global marketers. When is it appropriate to use each technique?

1. See for yourself how the Internet can help with marketing research needs. Suppose your boss asks you to find a market research firm that can help your company in India. Using Google or another search engine, type "India market research" and see what happens.

www.imf.org

www.jetro.org

www.unsystem.org

www.worldbank.org

www.odci.gov/cia/publications/factbook

www.miti.go.jp

www.euromonitor.com

www.ft.com

www.marketresearch.com

www.euromonitor.com

www.qrca.org

www.aqrp.co.uk

Focus group moderators are also known as *qualitative researchers*. Many belong to the Qualitative Research Consultants Association. The QRCA Web site includes the association's code of ethics and links to other research-oriented sites. The Web site for the UK-based Association of Qualitative Research Practitioners (AQRP) includes a concise history of qualitative research.

# Case 6-1

## Research Helps Whirlpool Act Local in the Global Market

Whirlpool Corporation, headquartered in Benton Harbor, Michigan, is the number one appliance company in the United States and number two worldwide. The company sells more than $11 billion worth of "white goods" each year; this category includes refrigerators, stoves, washing machines, and microwave ovens. Whirlpool's success has been achieved in part by offering products in three different price ranges: top-of-the-line Kitchen Aid appliances, the medium-priced Whirlpool and Sears Kenmore lines, and Roper and Estate at the low end. In part, the impetus for overseas expansion comes from a mature domestic market that is only growing 2 or 3 percent annually. However, Whirlpool is not new to foreign markets; the company has been in Latin America since 1957. Today, it is the market share leader in that region.

At the beginning of 1993, David Whitwam, chairman and CEO of Whirlpool Corporation, told an interviewer, "Five years ago we were essentially a domestic company. Today about 40 percent of our revenues are overseas, and by the latter part of this decade, a majority will be." The CEO's comments came 3 years after he placed his first bet that the appliance industry is globalizing. By acquiring Philips Electronics' European appliance business for $1 billion, Whirlpool vaulted into the number three position in Europe. Whitwam pledged another $2 billion investment in Europe alone. As the decade of the 1990s drew to a close, however, Whitwam's ambitious plans for expanding beyond Europe into Japan and the developing nations in Asia and Latin America hadn't yet achieved the desired results. Noting that Whirlpool stock underperformed the bull market of the 1990s, analysts began questioning whether Whitwam's global vision was on target. As one analyst put it, "The strategy has been a failure. Whirlpool went big into global markets and investors have paid for it." Others fault the company on execution. Another analyst said, "I respect Whirlpool's strategy. They just missed on the blocking and tackling."

The challenge facing Whirlpool is rooted partially in the structure of the appliance industry. In Europe, for example, the presence of more than 200 brands and 170 factories makes the appliance industry highly fragmented and highly competitive. Electrolux, a Swedish company, ranks number one. European appliance sales have been flat for years, with sales volumes growing at a mere 1 or 2 percent; industry overcapacity is a major issue. Although analysts expect to see a surge in demand from Central and Eastern Europe within a few years, there will also be an influx of products from low-cost producers in those regions. To cut costs and bring margins up, the company has streamlined its European organization. Four regional sales offices replaced sales organizations in 17 separate countries. Hank Bowman, president of Whirlpool Europe BV, trimmed the number of warehouses from 30 to 16 and hopes eventually to have as few as 5 or 6. A global parts-sourcing strategy has helped reduce the number of suppliers by 40 percent. Over the course of several years, Whirlpool invested hundreds of millions of dollars in new-product development. It has already begun marketing a new clothes dryer designed to operate more efficiently and provide higher quality despite containing fewer parts.

Bowman believes that a global market segmentation approach is the key to success in Europe. Whirlpool relies heavily on market research to maintain its leadership in the United States; listening to consumers is important in Europe and Latin America as well. "Research tells us that the trends, preferences and biases of consumers, country by country, are reducing as opposed to increasing," Bowman said recently. He believes that European homemakers fall into distinct "Euro-segments"—traditionalists and aspirers, for example—allowing Whirlpool to duplicate the three-tiered approach to brands that has worked so well in the United States. The Bauknecht brand is positioned at the high end of the market, with Whirlpool in the middle, and Ignis at the lower end. For example, appliance shoppers in Germany visiting a department store such as Saturn can choose a Bauknecht Neptun 1400 priced at ¢699 or a Whirlpool for ¢369.

Research has also indicated that consumers in different countries prefer different types of features. Thus, Whirlpool has begun emphasizing product platforms as a means to produce localized versions of ovens, refrigerators, and other appliance lines more economically. A platform is essentially a technological core underneath the metal casing of an appliance. The platform—for example, the compressor and sealant system in a refrigerator—can be the same throughout the world. Country or region-specific capabilities can be added late in the production cycle. The goal was to cut 10 percent from Whirlpool's $200 million annual production development budget and achieve a 30 percent productivity increase among the company's 2,000 member product-development staff. Ultimately, the platform project team hopes to reduce the total number of platforms in the company from 135 to 65. Specific goals include reducing the number of dishwasher platforms from 6 to 3, and refrigerator platforms from 48 to 25.

Market research also drives the search for new products that address the specific needs of developing markets. In Brazil, for example, Whirlpool's market entry strategy included acquiring two local established appliance brands, Brastemp and Consul. However, with a basic washer priced at $300, even the low end of Whirlpool's product lines proved to be too expensive for many Brazilians. Economic data indicated that Brazil's 30 million low-income households, many with monthly incomes of about $220, account for about one-third of national consumption. Moreover, studies showed that these households ranked an automatic washer second only to a cell phone as an aspirational purchase. Whirlpool's researchers convened focus groups and made visits to representative low-income households. Marcele Rodrigues is director of laundry technology at Multibrás SA Eletrodomésticos, Whirlpool's Brazilian division. "It wasn't a matter of stripping down an existing model," he noted recently. "We had to innovate for the masses."

Whirlpool's response was to develop what it proudly calls the world's least expensive automatic washer. The company has a strong team of engineers and industrial designers in

Focus group research also indicated that consumers would find a smaller capacity washer acceptable because low-income families do laundry more often. Because Brazilian housewives like to wash floors underneath furniture, the Ideale sits high on four legs as opposed to resting on the floor as most conventional units do. Perhaps the most significant thing that the Ideale design team learned from its research was that form matters too. As Emerson do Valle, vice president of Multibrás, explained, "We realized the washer should be aesthetically pleasing; it's a status symbol for these people." The team selected a rounded design with a yellow start button and blue lettering on the control panel. Because white is widely associated with cleanliness in Brazil, the Ideale is only available in white.

Despite the fact that the Brazilian Ideale incorporates many design features that appeal to consumers in Brazil, the Ideale is also being manufactured and marketed in China and India with additional adaptations. In China, for example, an appliance with a white exterior would be undesirable because of the prevailing belief that white shows dirt easily. For that reason, the Ideale is available in light blue and gray in China. In India, the color options are green, blue, and white. In addition, the heavy duty wash cycle in China is labeled "grease removal" for the simple reason that many Chinese use bicycles for daily transportation. Similarly, in India, the setting for delicate fabrics is labeled "sari." Also, the Indian units are mounted on casters so they can be moved easily. Whirlpool executives hope that low-income consumers in Brazil, China, India, and other emerging markets who are pleased with their Ideale washers will also one day purchase some of the company's other appliances. If they do, emerging markets could fulfill CEO Whitwam's vision for achieving global growth.

## Discussion Questions

1. Describe Whirlpool's global marketing strategy.
2. Summarize the role of market research in Whirlpool's globalization strategy. What different types of research methodologies does the company use? What are the advantages of each methodology described in the case?
3. Do you believe developing products for low-income consumers in emerging markets is the right strategy?

Brazil, as well as some of its most technologically advanced factories. Despite the fact that Brazil's economy was in turmoil, Whirlpool invested $30 million to develop the new washer, the Ideale, to meet the needs of a large class of consumers who still wash clothes by hand. One cost-saving design breakthrough was a patentable technology that allows the machine to switch from the wash cycle to the spin cycle without shifting gears. The design involves some performance compromises: Compared with more expensive models, the spin cycle takes longer and clothes come out damper. However, research indicated that these were not critical issues for most consumers.

# 7 Segmentation, Targeting, and Positioning

**J**anet Jackson's "wardrobe malfunction" during the halftime show of the 2004 Super Bowl caused a worldwide sensation. For better or for worse, MTV, which produced the show, demonstrated that it still had the ability to shake things up. Worldwide, musical tastes and trends have changed significantly since MTV first went on the air in 1981. Indeed, few current viewers are likely to remember the Buggles, the British duo whose song "Video Killed the Radio Star" was featured in the first clip aired. In some ways, MTV looks the same in the twenty-first century as it did in the 1980s. Today, however, MTV's reach extends far beyond the United States; together with sister channels VH1 and Nickelodeon, it comprises the world's largest network with nearly 340 million viewing households around the globe. However, MTV has not prospered by offering the same sights and sounds in every market. Rather, its owes much of its success to the realization that viewer sensibilities and tastes vary on a regional and country-by-country basis. MTV carefully researches those sensibilities and tastes, and then caters to them. MTV is especially popular with persons aged 15 to 34, with 15-to-24 year olds—a pure youth audience, as executives proudly note—as the core consumer. MTV executives are quick to point out that the channel's programming is extremely audience driven; shows like *Total Request Live (TRL)* allow the channel to stay close to its viewing audience.

MTV's worldwide success is a convincing example of the power of superior global market segmentation and targeting. *Market segmentation* represents an effort to identify and categorize groups of customers and countries according to common characteristics. *Targeting* is the process of evaluating the segments and focusing marketing efforts on a country, region, or group of people that has significant potential to respond. Such targeting reflects the reality that a company should identify those consumers it can reach most effectively, efficiently, and profitably. Finally, proper *positioning* is required to influence perceptions of target customers.

Def Jam recording artist Jay-Z performs at the MTV Europe Music Awards in Frankfurt, Germany, on November 8, 2001. Musicians and other celebrities offer an alternative for global companies exploring unconventional ways to connect with young people. For example, a Motorola pager is an integral part of a recent Jay-Z music video. The rapper has also appeared on posters for Zino Platinum Series cigars from Davidoff of Geneva. In 2002, Reebok created a line of image-oriented shoes especially for Jay-Z.

Consider the following examples of market segmentation and targeting by global companies:

- The personal computer market can divided into home users, corporate (also known as "enterprise") users, and educational users. Dell originally targeted corporate customers; even today, sales of products for home use only account for 20 percent of revenues. After focusing on the PC market only, Dell then branched out into other computer categories such as servers and storage hardware. In 2003, Dell cropped the word "Computer" from its corporate name as it ramped up sales of new categories of consumer electronics products including PDAs, flat-panel TVs, and digital cameras.
- In 2003, after convening worldwide employee conferences to study women's shaving preferences, Schick-Wilkinson Sword introduced a shaving system for women that features a replaceable blade cartridge. Intuition, as the system is known, incorporates a "skin-conditioning solid" that allows a woman to lather and shave her legs simultaneously. Intuition is a premium product targeted directly at users of Venus, Gillette's three-blade razor system for women.[1]
- Nokia recently introduced N-Gage, a combination cell phone and portable game machine targeted at adult gamers as old as 35 (see Case 7-1).

As these examples show, global markets can be segmented according to buyer category (e.g., consumer or enterprise), gender, age, and a number of other criteria. These examples also illustrate the fact that market segmentation and targeting are two separate but closely related activities. These activities serve as the link between market needs and wants and specific decisions on the part of company management to develop products that meet the specific needs of one or more segments. Segmentation, targeting, and positioning are all examined in this chapter.

## GLOBAL MARKET SEGMENTATION

"We are very humbled by the fact that there are virtually no other companies that are both consumer and enterprise brands."

Mike George, Chief Marketing Officer, Dell Inc.[2]

**Global market segmentation** has been defined as the process of identifying specific segments—whether they be country groups or individual consumer groups—of potential customers with homogeneous attributes who are likely to exhibit similar

---

1  Charles Forelle, "Schick Puts a Nick in Gillette's Razor Cycle," *The Wall Street Journal* (October 3, 2003), p. B7.
2  Richard Waters, "Dell Aims to Stretch Its Way of Business," *Financial Times* (November 13, 2003), p. 8.

responses to a company's marketing mix.[3] Interest in global market segmentation dates back several decades. In the late 1960s, one observer suggested that the European market could be divided into three broad categories—international sophisticate, semi-sophisticate, and provincial—solely on the basis of consumers' presumed receptivity to a common advertising approach.[4] Another writer suggested that some themes—for example, the desire to be beautiful, the desire to be healthy and free of pain, the love of mother and child—were universal and could be used in advertising around the globe.[5]

As noted in earlier chapters, two decades ago Professor Theodore Levitt advanced the thesis that consumers in different countries increasingly seek variety, and that the same new segments are likely to show up in multiple national markets. Thus, ethnic or regional foods such as sushi, falafel, or pizza might be in demand anywhere in the world. Levitt suggested that this trend, known variously as the *pluralization of consumption* and *segment simultaneity*, provides an opportunity for marketers to pursue one or more segments on a global scale. Frank Brown, president of MTV Networks Asia, acknowledged this trend in explaining MTV's success in Asia despite the recent economic turmoil in the region. "When marketing budgets are tight, advertisers look for a more effective buy, and we can deliver a niche audience with truly panregional reach," he said.[6] Authors John Micklethwait and Adrian Wooldridge sum up the situation this way:

> The audience for a new recording of a Michael Tippett symphony or for a nature documentary about the mating habits of flamingos may be minuscule in any one country, but round up all the Tippett and flamingo fanatics around the world, and you have attractive commercial propositions. The cheap distribution offered by the Internet will probably make these niches even more attractive financially.[7]

Global market segmentation is based on the premise that companies should attempt to identify consumers in different countries who share similar needs and desires. However, the fact that significant numbers of pizza-loving consumers are found in many countries does not mean they are eating the exact same thing. In France, for example, Domino's serves pizza with goat cheese and strips of pork fat known as *lardoons*. In Taiwan, toppings include squid, crab, shrimp, and pineapple; Brazilians can order their pies with mashed bananas and cinnamon. As Patrick Doyle, executive vice president of Domino's international division, explains, "Pizza is beautifully adaptable to consumer needs around the world, simply by changing the toppings."[8]

A. Coskun Samli has developed a useful approach to global market segmentation that compares and contrasts "conventional" versus "unconventional" wisdom (see Table 7-1). For example, conventional wisdom might assume that consumers in Europe and Latin America are interested in World Cup soccer while those in America are not. Unconventional wisdom would note that the "global jock" segment exists in many countries, including the United States.[9] Similarly, conventional wisdom might assume that, because per capita income in India is about $490, all Indians have low incomes. Unconventional wisdom would note

3   Salah S. Hassan and Lea Prevel Katsanis, "Identification of Global Consumer Segments: A Behavioral Framework," *Journal of International Consumer Marketing* 3, no. 2 (1991), p. 17.

4   John K. Ryans, Jr., "Is It Too Soon to Put a Tiger in Every Tank?" *Columbia Journal of World Business* (March–April 1969), p. 73.

5   Arther C. Fatt, "The Danger of 'Local' International Advertising," *Journal of Marketing* 31, no. 1 (January 1967), pp. 60–62.

6   Magz Osborne, "Second Chance in Japan," *Ad Age Global* 1, no. 9 (May 2001), p. 28.

7   John Micklethwait and Adrian Wooldridge. *A Future Perfect: The Challenge and Hidden Promise of Globalization* (New York: Crown Publishers, 2000), p. 198.

8   Neil Buckley, "Domino's Returns to Fast Food's Fast Lane," *Financial Times* (November 26, 2003), p. 10.

9   Robert Frank, "When World Cup Soccer Starts, World-Wide Productivity Stalls," *The Wall Street Journal* (June 12, 1998), pp. B1, B2; Daniela Deane, "Their Cup Runneth Over: Ethnic Americans Going Soccer Crazy," *USA Today* (July 2, 1998), p. 13A.

| **Table 7-1** | **Conventional Wisdom** | **Unconventional Wisdom** |
| --- | --- | --- |
| *Contrasting Views of Global Segmentation* | 1. Assumes heterogeneity between countries | 1. Assumes the emergence of segments that transcend national boundaries |
| | 2. Assumes homogeneity within any given country | 2. Acknowledges the existence of within-country differences |
| | 3. Focuses heavily on cultural differences at a macro level | 3. Emphasizes differences and commonalities in micro-level values, consumption patterns, etc. |
| | 4. Segmentation relies heavily on clustering of national markets | 4. Segmentation relies on grouping micro markets within a country or between countries |
| | 5. Within-country micro segments are assigned secondary priority | 5. Micro segments based on consumer behavior are assigned high priority |

*Source:* Adapted from A. Coskun Samli, *International Consumer Behavior* (Westport, CT: Quorum, 1995), p. 130.

the presence of a higher-income, middle-class segment. As Sapna Nayak, a food analyst at Raobank India, noted recently, "The potential Indian customer base for a McDonald's or a Subway is larger than the size of entire developed countries."[10] The same is true of China; the average annual income of people living in eastern China is approximately $1,200. This is the equivalent to a lower-middle-income country market with 470 million people, larger than every other single country market except India.[11]

Today, global companies (and the research and advertising agencies that serve them) use market segmentation to identify, define, understand, and respond to customer wants and needs on a worldwide, rather than strictly local, basis. As we have noted many times in this book, global marketers must determine whether a standarized or adapted marketing mix is required to best serve those wants and needs. By performing market segmentation, marketers can generate the insights needed to devise the most effective approach.

The process of global market segmentation begins with the choice of one or more variables to use as a basis for grouping customers. Common variables include demographics (including national income and size of population), psychographics (values, attitudes, and lifestyles), behavioral characteristics, and benefits sought. It is also possible to cluster different national markets in terms of their environments—for example, the presence or absence of government regulation in a particular industry—to establish groupings.

## Demographic Segmentation

**Demographic segmentation** is based on measurable characteristics of populations such as income, population, age distribution, gender, education, and occupation. A number of global demographic trends—fewer married couples, smaller family size, changing roles of women, higher incomes and living standards, for example—have contributed to the emergence of global market segments. Here are several key demographic facts and trends from around the world:

- A widening age gap exists between the older populations in the West and the large working-age populations in developing countries.
- In the European Union, the number of consumers aged 16 and under is rapidly approaching the number of consumers aged 60-plus.
- Asia is home to 500 million consumers aged 16 and under.
- Half of Japan's population will be age 50 or older by 2025.

---

[10] Saritha Rai, "Tastes of India in U.S. Wrappers," *The New York Times* (April 29, 2003), p. W7.
[11] Joseph Kahn, "Made in China, Bought in China," *The New York Times* (January 5, 2003), sec. 3, p. 10.

# the rest of the story

## The Youth of the World Proclaim, "We Want Our MTV!"

Within 6 years of its launch, MTV had penetrated some 50 million U.S. households, virtually the entire domestic cable audience at the time. Having conquered America, and with support from youth-oriented advertisers such as Coca-Cola, Levi's, and Nike, MTV Europe was launched in Rotterdam in 1987. Today, MTV has 16 local feeds in Europe with coverage stretching from Ireland to Russia. The local feeds are important, because as much as 70 percent of revenues come from advertisers in local markets. One driver of local ad revenues is MTV's commitment to introducing its viewers to local music groups. Despite its sensitivity to local preferences, however, executives and producers still seek economies. As Bill Roedy, president of MTV Networks International, told *Billboard* magazine in 2000, "MTV looks for format opportunities to make content from one area travel to another with a local look and feel."

The blend of global and local elements in proportions that reflect local preferences is especially clear in Asia. When MTV first entered Japan in 1992, it met with limited success because a licensing agreement with several electronics manufacturers restricted the control that channel executives had over content; the result was an overemphasis on international pop music that was out of sync with viewers. MTV Japan was relaunched with an emphasis on extensive audience research and a new focus on local music and artists.

Today, MTV Asia reaches 125 million households and is comprised of seven channels: Japan, Taiwan, Hong Kong, China, Korea, MTV India, and MTV Southeast Asia (with English-language local feeds for Singapore, Indonesia, Malaysia, Thailand, and the Philippines). In India, the channel presents itself as zany, colorful, and light-hearted. For example, comedian

Cyrus Barocha hosts a show called MTV Bakra that plays hidden camera pranks on unsuspecting victims. Programming in Taiwan, by contrast, is similar to that in the United States: edgy and in your face. Overall, MTV Mandarin's playlist contains about 80 percent local music, while MTV Philippines features predominantly international artists.

In 2003, Roedy unveiled a new "gain market scale" strategy. As he noted, "We've built up a big infrastructure. It's now time to leverage our resources and develop programming that can cross borders, regions, and even go global." New programming can cost between $200,000 and $350,000 per 30-minute episode; Roedy hopes to develop shows that will have appeal no matter where the viewers live.

*Top Two Most Domestic Music Markets (in percent)*

| Country | Domestic Artists | International Artists |
| --- | --- | --- |
| Turkey | 95.7 | 4.1 |
| China | 92.6 | 0.5 |

Sources: Tim Burt, "Veteran Leads MTV's Attack," Financial Times (August 12, 2003), p. 6; Charles Goldsmith, "MTV Seeks Global Appeal," The Wall Street Journal (January 21, 2003), pp. B1, B3; Anne-Marie Crawford, "MTV: Out of its Teens," Ad Age Global 1, no. 9 (May 2001), pp. 25–26; Magz Osborne, "Second Chance in Japan," Ad Age Global 1, no. 9 (May 2001), pp. 26, 28; Claudia Penteado, "MTV Brazil Wins Success with Local Programming," Ad Age Global 1, no. 9 (May 2001), p. 29; Mimi Turner, "A Q&A with Bill Roedy," Billboard 112, no. 36 (September 2, 2000), pp. 48, 54; Owen Hughes, "MTV Asia's Five Branches," Billboard 112, no. 36 (September 2, 2000), pp. 48, 54; Sally Beatty and Carol Hymowitz, "How MTV Stays Tuned In to Teens," The Wall Street Journal (March 21, 2000), pp. B1, B4.

- America's three main ethnic groups—African/Black Americans, Hispanic Americans, and Asian Americans—represent a combined annual buying power of $1 trillion.
- The United States is home to 28.4 million foreign-born residents with a combined income of $233 billion.
- By 2030, 20 percent of the U.S. population—70 million Americans—will be 65 or older versus 13 percent (36 million) today.
- India has the youngest demographic profile among the world's large nations: More than half its population is under the age of 25.

Statistics such as these can provide valuable insights to marketers who are scanning the globe for opportunities. Managers at global companies must be alert to the possibility that marketing strategies will have to be adjusted in response to the aging of the population and other demographic trends. For example, consumer products companies will need to convene focus groups consisting of people over the age of 50 who are nearing retirement. These same companies will also have to target developing country markets such as Vietnam, Brazil, and Mexico to achieve growth objectives in the years to come.

Demographic changes can create opportunities for marketing innovation. In France, for example, two entrepreneurs began rewriting the rules of retailing years before Sam Walton founded the Wal-Mart chain. Marcel Fournier and Louis Defforey opened the first Carrefour ("crossroads") hypermarket in 1963. At the time, France had a fragmented shop system that consisted of small, specialized stores with only about 5,000 square feet of floor space such as the *boulangerie* and *charcuterie*. The shop system was part of France's national heritage, and shoppers developed personal relationships with a shop's proprietor. However, time pressed, dual-parent working families had less time to stop at several stores for daily shopping. The same trend was occurring in other countries. By 1993, Carrefour SA was a global chain with $21 billion in sales and a market capitalization of $10 billion. By 2002, sales had reached $72 billion; today, Carrefour operates 9,500 stores in 30 countries. As Adrian Slywotzky has noted, it was a demographic shift that provided the opportunity for Fournier and Defforey to create a novel, customer-matched, cost-effective business design.[12]

## Segmenting Global Markets by Income and Population

When a company charts a plan for global market expansion, it often finds that income is a valuable segmentation variable. After all, a market consists of those who are willing and *able* to buy. For cigarettes, soft drinks, photographic film, candy, and other consumer products that have a low per-unit cost, population is often a more valuable segmentation variable than income. Nevertheless, for a vast range of industrial and consumer products offered in global markets today, income is a valuable and important macro indicator of market potential. About 75 percent of world GNP is generated in the Triad; however, only about 13 percent of the world's population is located in Triad countries. The concentration of wealth in a handful of industrialized countries has significant implications for global marketers. After segmenting in terms of a single demographic variable—income—a company can reach the most affluent markets by targeting fewer than 20 nations: the European Union, North America, and Japan. By doing so, however, the marketers are *not* reaching almost 90 percent of the world's population! A word of caution is in order here. Data about income (and population) have the advantage of being widely available and inexpensive to access. However, management may unconsciously "read too much" into such data. In other words, while providing some measure of market potential, such macro-level demographic data should not necessarily be used as the sole indicator of presence (or absence) of a market opportunity. This is especially true when an emerging country market or region is being investigated.

Ideally, GNP and other measures of national income converted to U.S. dollars should be calculated on the basis of purchasing power parities (i.e., what the currency will buy in the country of issue) or through direct comparisons of actual prices for a given product. This would provide an actual comparison of the standards of living in the countries of the world. Table 7-2 ranks the top 10 countries in terms of 2003 per capita income followed by a ranking adjusted for purchasing power parity. Although the United States ranks fourth in per capita income, its standard of living—as measured by what money can buy—is second only to Luxembourg's.[13] By most measures, the U.S. market is enormous: more than $10.5 trillion in 2003 national income, a population of 288 million people, and per capita income of nearly $37,000. Little wonder, then, that so many non-U.S. companies target and cater to American consumers and organizational buyers! A case in point is Mitsubishi Motors, which had begun redesigning its Montero Sport SUV with the goal of creating a "global vehicle" that could be sold worldwide with little adaptation. Now the design program has changed course; the new goal is to make the vehicle more "American" by providing more interior space and more horsepower. Hiroshi Yajima, a Mitsubishi executive in North America,

---

[12] Adrian Slywotzky, *Value Migration* (Cambridge, MA: Harvard Business School Press, 1996), p. 37.
[13] For a more detailed discussion, see Malcolm Gillis et. al., *Economics of Development* (New York: Norton, 1996), pp. 37–40.

| Table 7-2 |
| --- |
| *Per Capita Income, 2003* |

| 2003 Per Capita Income | | 2003 Income Adjusted for Purchasing Power | |
| --- | --- | --- | --- |
| 1. Japan | $40,986 | 1. Luxembourg | $47,569 |
| 2. Luxembourg | $40,947 | 2. United States | $35,855 |
| 3. Norway | $38,748 | 3. Norway | $32,184 |
| 4. Switzerland | $36,947 | 4. Switzerland | $31,831 |
| 5. United States | $36,693 | 5. Iceland | $30,367 |
| 6. Denmark | $32,119 | 6. Denmark | $29,166 |
| 7. Iceland | $31,142 | 7. Belgium | $29,058 |
| 8. Sweden | $26,615 | 8. Ireland | $28,950 |
| 9. Singapore | $26,562 | 9. Japan | $28,735 |
| 10. Hong Kong, China | $26,421 | 10. Canada | $28,647 |

*Source:* Reprinted by permission of Warren Keegan Associates, Inc., 2003.

attributes the change to the vibrancy and sheer size of the American auto market. "We wouldn't care if the vehicle didn't sell outside the U.S.," he said.[14]

Despite having comparable per capita incomes, other industrialized countries are nevertheless quite small in terms of *total* annual income. In Sweden, for example, per capita GNP is $26,615; however, Sweden's smaller population—9 million—means that annual national income is only about $240 billion. This helps explain why Ericsson, IKEA, Saab, and other companies based in Sweden have looked beyond their borders for significant growth opportunities.

While Table 7-2 highlights differences between straightforward income statistics and standard of living in the world's most affluent nations, such differences can be even more pronounced in less-developed countries. A visit to a mud house in Tanzania will reveal many of the things that money can buy: an iron bed frame, a corrugated metal roof, beer and soft drinks, bicycles, shoes, photographs, radios, and even televisions. What Tanzania's per capita income of $275 does not reflect is the fact that instead of utility bills, Tanzanians have the local well and the sun. Instead of nursing homes, tradition and custom ensure that families will take care of the elderly at home. Instead of expensive doctors and hospitals, villagers may utilize the services of witch doctors and healers.

In industrialized countries, a significant portion of national income is the value of goods and services that would be free in a poor country. Thus, the standard of living in many low-income countries is often higher than income data might suggest. In low-income countries, the *actual* purchasing power of the local currency may be much higher than that implied by exchange values. For example, the per capita income average for China of $970 equals 7,719 Chinese Renminbi (8.3 Renminbi = US$1.00), but 7,719 Renminbi will buy much more in China than $970 will buy in the United States. Adjusted for purchasing power parity, per capita income in China is estimated to be $4,507; this amount is nearly five times higher than the unadjusted figure suggests. Similarly, calculated in terms of purchasing power, per capita income in Tanzania is approximately $537. Indeed, a visit to the capital city of Dar Es Salaam reveals that stores are stocked with televisions and CD players, and businesspeople can be seen negotiating deals using their cellular phones.[15]

No one knows with certainty what the future will bring, but using 2003 GNP data as a baseline (Table 7-3) and extrapolating current economic growth trends to the year 2010 produces interesting results (Table 7-4). The United States, Japan,

---

[14] Norihiko Shirouzu, "Tailoring World's Cars to U.S. Tastes," *The Wall Street Journal* (January 1, 2001), p. B1.

[15] Robert S. Greenberger, "Africa Ascendant: New Leaders Replace Yesteryear's 'Big Men,' and Tanzania Benefits," *The Wall Street Journal* (December 10, 1996), pp. A1, A6.

| *Table 7-3* | Country | GNP (in millions) |
|---|---|---|
| *Top 10 Nations Ranked by GNP, 2003* | United States | 10,580,779 |
| | Japan | 5,262,577 |
| | Germany | 1,996,350 |
| | United Kingdom | 1,530,501 |
| | France | 1,400,852 |
| | China | 1,268,769 |
| | Italy | 1,128,687 |
| | Canada | 733,604 |
| | Mexico | 629,659 |
| | Brazil | 622,603 |

*Source:* Reprinted by permission of Warren Keegan Associates, Inc., 2003.

and Germany retain their rankings in the first three positions; China moves up to fourth place. These extrapolation results suggest that China, with its combination of high real income growth and relatively low population growth, is a strong candidate to become a leading world economic power. Even if this forecast turns out to be overly optimistic in the face of the current economic slowdown, China is expected to fare better than other Asian countries.

In 2003, the 10 most populous countries in the world accounted for 52 percent of world income; the 5 most populous accounted for 35 percent (see Table 7-5). Although population is not as concentrated as income, there is, in terms of size of nations, a pattern of considerable concentration. The 10 most populous countries in the world account for roughly 60 percent of the world's population today. The concentration of income in the high-income and large-population countries means that a company can be "global" by targeting buyers in 10 or fewer countries. World population is now approximately 6.4 billion; at the present rate of growth it will reach 12 billion by the middle of the century. Simply put, global population will probably double during the lifetime of many students using this textbook.

As noted previously, for products whose price is low enough, population is a more important variable than income in determining market potential. As former Kodak CEO George Fisher commented a decade ago, "Half the people in the world have yet to take their first picture. The opportunity is huge, and it's nothing fancy. We just have to sell yellow boxes of film."[16] Thus, China and India, with respective populations of 1.3 billion and 1 billion, represent attractive target markets. In a country like China, one segmentation approach would call for serving the existing mass market for inexpensive consumer products. Procter & Gamble, Unilever, Kao, Johnson & Johnson, and other packaged goods companies are targeting and developing the

| *Table 7-4* | Country | GNP (in millions) |
|---|---|---|
| *Top 10 Nations Ranked by GNP, 2010 Projections* | 1. United States | 12,577,221 |
| | 2. Japan | 6,212,955 |
| | 3. Germany | 2,356,874 |
| | 4. China | 1,907,760 |
| | 5. United Kingdom | 1,831,746 |
| | 6. France | 1,653,834 |
| | 7. Italy | 1,287,635 |
| | 8. Canada | 902,241 |
| | 9. Mexico | 828,589 |
| | 10. Brazil | 765,723 |

*Source:* Reprinted by permission of Warren Keegan Associates, Inc., 2003.

---

[16] Mark Maremont, "Kodak's New Focus," *Business Week* (January 30, 1995), p. 63.

**Table 7-5**

The 10 Most Populous Countries, 2003 and 2010 Projections

| Global Income and Population | 2003 Population (thousands) | Percent of World Population | Projected Population 2010 | 2003 GNP (millions) | Per Capita GNP | Percent of World GNP |
|---|---|---|---|---|---|---|
| World Total | 6,401,708 | 100.00 | 7,203,265 | 33,871,703 | – | 100.0 |
| 1. China | 1,308,456 | 20.44 | 1,428,781 | 1,268,769 | 723 | 3.75 |
| 2. India | 1,071,776 | 16.74 | 1,225,550 | 524,611 | 489 | 1.55 |
| 3. USA | 288,361 | 4.50 | 30?,592 | 10,580,779 | 29,953 | 27.3 |
| 4. Indonesia | 220,033 | 3.44 | 247,045 | 165,143 | 751 | .49 |
| 5. Brazil | 178,190 | 2.78 | 200,019 | 622,603 | 3,494 | 1.84 |
| 6. Pakistan | 150,007 | 2.34 | 15?,331 | 67,064 | 447 | .20 |
| 7. Russia | 147,309 | 2.30 | 15?,483 | 265,269 | 1,801 | .78 |
| 8. Bangladesh | 138,663 | 2.17 | 158,058 | 52,739 | 380 | .16 |
| 9. Nigeria | 137,872 | 2.15 | 167,273 | 41,193 | 299 | .12 |
| 10. Japan | 128,399 | 2.01 | 132,411 | 5,262,577 | 40,986 | 15.54 |

Source: Reprinted by permission of Warren Keegan Associates, Inc., 2003.

China market, lured in part by the possibility that as many as 100 million Chinese customers are affluent enough to spend, say, 14 cents for a single-use pouch of shampoo. GM's original strategy for entering China was based on its success in reaching the segment comprised of government and company officials who are entitled to a large sedan-style automobile. Today, GM's lineup for China includes the Buick Century, targeted at the country's middle class, and the $10,000 Buick Sail.

McDonald's global expansion illustrates the significance of both income and population on marketing activities. On the one hand, as noted in Case 1-1, McDonald's operates in more than 120 countries. What this figure conceals, however is that 80 percent of McDonald's restaurants are located in nine country markets: Australia, Brazil, Canada, China, France, Germany, Japan, the United Kingdom, and the United States. These nine countries generate about 75 percent of the company's total revenues. Eight of these countries appear in the top 10 GNP ranking shown in Table 7-4; however, only four appear in the Table 7-5 population rankings. At present, the restaurants in the company's approximately 100 non-major country markets contribute less than 20 percent to operating income. McDonald's is counting on an expanded presence in China and other high population country markets to drive corporate growth in the twenty-first century.

As noted earlier, marketers must be careful not to be overly optimistic when using macro-level data such as income or population to segment markets. It is also possible to underestimate a market's potential. Marketers should keep in mind, for example, that national income figures such as those cited for China and India are averages. Large, fast-growing, higher-income segments are present in both of these countries. An estimated 100 million Indians can be classified as "upper-middle-class," with average incomes of more than $1,400. Pinning down a demographic segment may require additional information; according to some estimates, India's middle class totals 300 million people. However, if middle class is defined more narrowly as "households that own cars, computers, and washing machines," the figure would be much lower. According to one Indian expert, India's population can be further segmented to include a "bike" segment of 25 million households in which telephones and motorbikes are present. However, the vast majority of India's population comprises a "bullock cart" segment whose households lack most comforts but typically own a television.[17] The lesson is to

---

[17] Sundeep Waslekar, "India Can Get Ahead if It Gets on a Bike," *Financial Times* (November 12, 2002), p. 15.

guard from being blinded by averages; as Samli has suggested, do not *assume* homogeneity.

## Age Segmentation

Age is another useful demographic variable in global marketing. One global segment based on demographics is **global teens,** young people between the ages of 12 and 19. Teens, by virtue of their shared interest in fashion, music, and a youthful lifestyle, exhibit consumption behavior that is remarkably consistent across borders. As Renzo Rosso, creator of the Diesel designer jeans brand, explains, "A group of teenagers randomly chosen from different parts of the world will share many of the same tastes."[19] Young consumers may not yet have conformed to cultural norms; indeed, they may be rebelling against them. This fact, combined with shared universal wants, needs, desires, and fantasies (for name brands, novelty, entertainment, trendy, and image-oriented products), make it possible to reach the global teen segment with a unified marketing program. This segment is attractive both in terms of its size (about 1.3 billion) and its multi-billion dollar purchasing power. Coca-Cola, Benetton, Swatch, and Sony are some of the companies pursuing the global teenage segment. The global telecommunications revolution is a critical driving force behind the emergence of this segment. Global media such as MTV and the Internet are perfect vehicles for reaching this segment. Satellites such as AsiaSatI are beaming Western programming and commercials to millions of viewers in China, India, and other countries.

Another global segment is the so-called **global elite:** affluent consumers who are well traveled and have the money to spend on prestigious products with an image of exclusivity. Although this segment is often associated with older individuals who have accumulated wealth over the course of long careers, it also includes movie stars, musicians, elite athletes, entrepreneurs, and others who have achieved great financial success at a relatively young age. This segment's needs and wants are spread over various product categories: durable goods (luxury automobiles such as Mercedes Benz), nondurables (upscale beverages such as Perrier mineral water or Grey Goose Vodka), and financial services (American Express Gold and Platinum cards).

## Gender Segmentation

For obvious reasons, segmenting markets by gender is an approach that makes sense for many companies. Less obvious, however, is the need to ensure that opportunities for sharpening the focus on the needs and wants of one gender or the other do not go unnoticed. Although some companies—fashion designers and cosmetics companies, for example—market primarily or exclusively to women, other companies offer different lines of products to both genders. For example, in 2000, Nike generated $1.4 billion in global sales of women's shoes and apparel, a figure representing 16 percent of total Nike sales. Nike executives believe its global women's business is poised for big growth. To make it happen, Nike is opening concept shops inside department stores and creating free-standing retail stores devoted exclusively to women.[20] In Europe, Levi Strauss is taking a similar approach. In 2003, the company opened its first boutique for young women, Levi's for Girls, in Paris. As Suzanne Gallacher, associate brand manager for Levi's in Europe, the Middle East, and Africa, noted, "In Europe, denim is for girls."[21]

18  Chris Prystay, "Companies Market to India's Have-Littles," *The Wall Street Journal* (June 5, 2003), p. B1.

19  Alice Rawsthorn, "A Hipster on Jean Therapy," *Financial Times* (August 20, 1998), p. 8.

20  Paula Stepanowsky, "Nike Tones Up Its Marketing to Women with Concept Shops, New Apparel Lines," *The Wall Street Journal* (September 5, 2001), p. B19.

21  John Tagliabue, "2 Sexes Separated by a Common Levi's," *The New York Times* (September 30, 2003), p. W1.

The move is part of a broader strategy to boost Levi Strauss' performance in the face of strong competition from Calvin Klein and The Gap in the United States and Diesel in Europe. Gallacher predicts that, if Levi's for Girls is a success in France, similar stores will be opened in other European countries.

## Psychographic Segmentation

**Psychographic segmentation** involves grouping people in terms of their attitudes, values, and lifestyles. Data are obtained from questionnaires that require respondents to indicate the extent to which they agree or disagree with a series of statements. Psychographics is primarily associated with SRI International, a market research organization whose original VALS and updated VALS 2 analyses of consumers are widely known. Finland's Nokia relies heavily on psychographic segmentation of mobile phone users; its most important segments are "poseurs," "trendsetters," "social contact seekers," and "highfliers." By carefully studying these segments and tailoring products to each, Nokia has captured 40 percent of the world's market for mobile communication devices.[22]

Porsche AG, the German sports car maker, turned to psychographics after experiencing a worldwide sales decline from 50,000 units in 1986 to about 14,000 in 1993. Its U.S. subsidiary, Porsche Cars North America, already had a clear demographic profile of its typical customer: a 40-plus-year-old male college graduate whose annual income exceeded $200,000. A psychographic study showed that, demographics aside, Porsche buyers could be divided into five distinct categories (see Table 7-6). Top Guns, for example, buy Porsches and expect to be noticed; for Proud Patrons and Fantasists, on the other hand, such conspicuous consumption is irrelevant. Porsche will use the profiles to develop advertising tailored to each type. As Richard Ford, Porsche vice president of sales and marketing, noted: "We were selling to people whose profiles were diametrically opposed. You wouldn't want to tell an elitist how good he looks in the car or how fast he could go." The results were impressive; Porsche's U.S. sales improved nearly 50 percent after a new advertising campaign was launched.[23]

Honda's recent experience in Europe demonstrates the potential value of using psychographic segmentation to supplement the use of more traditional variables such as demographics. When Honda executives were developing a communication strategy to support the European launch of the company's new HR-V sport utility

| Category | Percent of all Owners | Description |
|---|---|---|
| Top Guns | 27 | Driven and ambitious. Care about power and control. Expect to be noticed. |
| Elitists | 24 | Old money. A car—even an expensive one—is just a car, not an extension of one's personality. |
| Proud Patrons | 23 | Ownership is what counts. A car is a trophy, a reward for working hard. Being noticed doesn't matter. |
| Bon Vivants | 17 | Cosmopolitan jet setters and thrill seekers; car heightens excitement. |
| Fantasists | 9 | Car represents a form of escape. Don't care about impressing others; may even feel guilty about owning a car. |

*Source:* Alex Taylor III, "Porsche Slices Up Its Buyers," *Fortune* (January 16, 1995), p. 24.

**Table 7-6**

*Psychographic Profiles of Porsche's American Customers*

---

22 John Micklethwait and Adrian Wooldridge, *Future Perfect: The Challenge and Hidden Promise of Globalization* (New York: Crown Business, 2000), p. 131.
23 Alex Taylor III, "Porsche Slices Up Its Buyers," *Fortune* (January 16, 1995), p. 24.

vehicle in the late 1990s, they brought together a panel of experts from the United Kingdom, Germany, France, and Italy. The goal was to develop a pan-European advertising campaign targeted squarely at a relatively young demographic. The researchers agreed that, irrespective of nationality, European youth exhibit more similarities than differences: They listen to the same music, enjoy the same films, and pursue the same recreational activities. The resulting ad campaign, dubbed "Joy Machine," was targeted at 25- to 35-year-olds. However, the HR-V proved to be popular with Europeans of *all* ages; in fact, one out of six buyers was a grandparent! Reflecting on this turn of events, Chris Brown, an advertising executive at Honda Motor Europe, noted, "The decision within advertising should be about attitudes, not ages. I was recently reminded that [former British prime minister] John Major and Mick Jagger of the Rolling Stones are the same age."[24] Brown's statement underscores the insight that people of the same age don't necessarily have the same attitudes, just as people in one age bracket sometimes share attitudes with those in other age brackets. Sometimes it is preferable to market to a mind-set rather than a particular age group; in such an instance, psychographic studies can help marketers arrive at a deeper understanding of consumer behavior than is possible with traditional segmentation variables such as demographics.

However, such understanding does come at a price. Psychographic market profiles are available from a number of different sources; companies may pay thousands of dollars to use these studies. SRI International has recently created psychographic profiles of the Japanese market; broader-scope studies have been undertaken by several global advertising agencies. For example, a research team at D'arcy Massius Benton & Bowles (DMBB) focused on Europe and produced a 15-country study entitled "The Euroconsumer: Marketing Myth or Cultural Certainty?"[25] The researchers identified four lifestyle groups: Successful Idealists, Affluent Materialists, Comfortable Belongers, and Disaffected Survivors. The first two groups represent the elite, the latter two, mainstream European consumers:

> *Successful Idealists*  Comprising from 5 to 20 percent of the population, this segment consists of persons who have achieved professional and material success while maintaining commitment to abstract or socially responsible ideals.
>
> *Affluent Materialists*  These status-conscious "up-and-comers"—many of whom are business professionals—use conspicuous consumption to communicate their success to others.
>
> *Comfortable Belongers*  Comprising one-fourth to one-half of a country's population, this group, like Global Scan's Adapters and Traditionals, is conservative and most comfortable with the familiar. Belongers are content with the comfort of home, family, friends, and community.
>
> *Disaffected Survivors*  Lacking power and affluence, this segment harbors little hope for upward mobility and tends to be either resentful or resigned. This segment is concentrated in high-crime urban inner city–type neighborhoods. Despite Disaffecteds' lack of societal status, their attitudes nevertheless tend to affect the rest of society.

DMBB has also recently completed a psychographic profile of the Russian market. The study divides Russians into five categories, based on their outlook, behavior, and openness to Western products. The categories include *kuptsy*, Cossacks, students, business executives, and Russian Souls. Members of the largest group, the *kuptsy* (the label comes from the Russian word for "merchant"), theoretically prefer Russian products but look down on mass-produced goods of

24  Ian Morton, "Target Advertising Is Not an Exact Science," *Automotive News Europe* (June 19, 2000), p. 28.
25  The following discussion is adapted from Rebecca Piirto, *Beyond Mind Games: The Marketing Power of Psychographics* (Ithaca, NY: American Demographics Books, 1991).

inferior quality. *Kuptsy* are most likely to admire automobiles and stereo equipment from countries with good reputations for engineering, such as Germany and Scandinavia. Nigel Clarke, the author of the study, notes that segmentation and targeting are appropriate in Russia, despite the fact that its broad consumer market is still in its infancy. "If you're dealing with a market as different as Russia is, even if you want to go 'broad,' it's best to think: 'Which group would go most for my brand? Where is my natural center of gravity?'"[26]

The study's marketing implications became more clear in the late 1990s. Market share growth for many Western brands began to slow; the trend accelerated after the economic crisis of 1998. As Sergei Platinin, director of a Russian company that markets fruit juices, noted, "People used to want only to buy things that looked foreign. Now they want Russian." In the world of fashion, expensive blue jeans from designer Valentin Yudashkin are supplanting Armani as *the* hip jeans. At the other end of the price spectrum, McDonald's has begun offering *pirozhki*, meat and cheese pies. The local Nestlé subsidiary has revived several brands of Russian chocolate candies. According to a survey conducted by Comcon 2, nearly two-thirds of upper-income Russians prefer to buy domestic chocolates, even though they can afford to buy imported brands.[27]

The segmentation and targeting approach used by a company can vary from country to country. As just noted, in Europe Levi Strauss is relying heavily on gender segmentation. By contrast, CEO Phil Marineau believes that a psychographic segmentation strategy is the key to revitalizing the venerable jeans brand in its home market. Marineau's team has identified several different segments, including "fashionistas," trendy teens, middle-aged men, and budget shoppers. The goal is to create different styles of jeans at different price points for each segment and to make them available at stores ranging from Wal-Mart to Neiman Marcus.[28] Likewise, Sony Electronics, a unit of Sony Corp. of America, recently undertook a reorganization of its marketing function. Traditionally, Sony had approached marketing from a product category point of view. In the future, a new unit, the Consumer Segment Marketing Division, will be responsible for getting closer to consumers in the United States (see Table 7-7).[29] What variables did Sony use to develop these categories?

## Behavior Segmentation

**Behavior segmentation** focuses on whether or not people buy and use a product, as well as how often, and how much they use or consume. Consumers can be categorized in terms of **usage rates:** for example, heavy, medium, light, and

| Segment | Description |
|---|---|
| Affluent | High-income consumers |
| CE Alphas | Early adopters of high-tech consumer electronics products, irrespective of age |
| Zoomers | Age 55+ |
| SoHo | Small office/home office |
| Families | Ages 35 to 54 |
| Young professionals/D.I.N.K.S. | Dual income no kids, ages 25 to 34 |
| Gen Y | Under 25 (includes tweens, teens, college students) |

**Table 7-7**

*Sony's U.S. Consumer Segments*

26  Stuart Elliot, "Figuring Out the Russian Consumer," *The New York Times* (April 1, 1992), pp. C1, C19.
27  Betsy McKay, "In Russia, West No Longer Means Best; Consumers Shift to Home-Grown Goods," *The Wall Street Journal* (December 9, 1996), p. A9.
28  Sally Beatty, "At Levi Strauss, Trouble Comes from All Angles," *The Wall Street Journal* (October 13, 2003), pp. B1, B3.
29  Tobi Elkin, "Sony Marketing Aims at Lifestyle Segments," *Advertising Age* (March 18, 2002), pp. 1, 72.

## OPEN *to* discussion

### Segmenting Europe's Single Market

It may be a single market, but the demographics of twenty-first century Europe still offer ample opportunities for market segmentation. One approach known as "3G" addresses issues pertaining to three distinct segments: youth aged 16 and under (Generation Y), adults aged 60 and over (the Golden Grays), and transnational corporations ("Globerations"). The following trends and traits associated with each have major implications for marketing strategy in the year 2005 and beyond.

#### Generation Y

- share few family activities
- display less reverence toward established authorities
- approach leisure time as "pay-per-play"
- maintain a heavy diet that is heavily weighted toward "convenience food"
- are tech savvy
- are deluged with passive information

#### Golden Grays

- consider it important to mix fun and work
- are relatively affluent, meaning more out-of-home activities
- enjoy high-tech gaming
- expect home health-care devices and biotechnology to extend life expectancy
- are deluged with passive information

#### Globerations

- employees will be less inclined to leave their companies as nations gradually reduce the benefits associated with the "social safety net"
- knowledge workers will be challenged finding work-life balance
- customers will want build-to-order solutions
- online auctions will be a significant sales channel
- a few, powerful consumer-to-business buying groups will emerge

Given these trends, which industries will be the winners and which will be the losers? Likely losers in the leisure sector will include general interest consumer magazines and national newspapers; winners will include interactive services, audio books, and social sports such as golf and tennis. Business services losers will likely be newspaper publishers, grocery coupon distributors, and mass market retailers. Winning services offerings will likely be corporate concierges, personalized telecom networks, and domestic services. Marketers are particularly advised to take the Golden Grays seriously and market brands that provide happiness, convenience, and time savings.

*Source: Allyson L. Stewart-Allen, "EU's Future Consumers: Three Groups to Watch," Marketing News 35, no. 12 (June 4, 2001), pp. 9–10.*

non-user. Consumers can also be segmented according to **user status:** potential users, non-users, ex-users, regulars, first-timers, and users of competitors' products. Marketers sometimes refer to the **80/20 rule** when assessing usage rates. This rule, (also known as the *law of disproportionality* or Pareto's Law), suggests that 80 percent of a company's revenues or profits are accounted for by 20 percent of a firm's products or customers. As noted earlier, nine country markets generate about 80 percent of McDonald's revenues. This situation presents McDonald's executives with strategy alternatives: Should the company pursue growth in the handful of countries where it is already well known and popular? Or, should it focus on expansion and growth opportunities in the scores of countries that, as yet, contribute little to revenues and profits?

Behavioral segmentation in global marketing can be illustrated with two examples. The first example is a product that is not widely used around the globe. Worldwide, only about 100 million women use tampons; the total market potential is estimated to be 1.7 billion women. In the mid-1990s, Tambrands Inc., marketers of Tampax brand tampons, approached market segmentation in terms of how resistant women are to using tampons. Cluster 1 (the United States, the United Kingdom, and Australia) is comprised of women who use tampons and believe themselves to be well informed about them. Tampon use in Cluster 2 (France, Israel, and South Africa) is limited to about 50 percent of women; some women in this cluster are concerned that tampon use may result in a loss of virginity. Advertising to women in Cluster 2 will focus on endorsements by gynecologists. Cluster 3, which includes big emerging markets such as Brazil, China, and Russia, presents the biggest marketing challenge. Tambrands must deal with two issues: virginity concerns and the fact that most women in the cluster have little or no experience using tampons. Despite the fact that advertising messages will vary by cluster, each ad will end with the slogan "Tampax. Women Know." Tambrands allocated $65 million for an advertising campaign targeted at the three clusters in 27 countries. One risk: The campaign's frank language would offend women. Commenting on Tambrands' plans, Jeffrey Hill of Meridian Consulting Group commented, "The greatest challenge in the global expansion of tampons is to address the religious and cultural mores that suggest that vaginal insertion is fundamentally prohibited by culture."[30]

The second example of behavior segmentation is vodka consumption. Diageo PLC, V&S Vin & Spirit AB, Seagram, and other marketers of distilled spirits know that Russians are heavy drinkers who consume a great deal of vodka. (In fact, the word *vodka* is derived from the Russian word for "water," and Russians believe vodka originated in their country in the fourteenth century.) Estimated 2002 vodka consumption in Russia was four billion liters—about 14.4 liters per capita, the highest in the world. However, as noted previously, Russian consumers have recently shown an increased preference for domestic brands. Production of home-made vodka, known as *samogon*, and illegal bootleg vodka surpasses official production by a ratio of 2 to 1 (see Figure 7-1) and the Russian government loses an estimated $1.9 billion in annual tax revenues. As a result of high duties, as well as the marketing goal of retaining a premium image, imports such as Smirnoff and Absolut are priced significantly higher than local brands. To date, imported vodka brands have only captured about 1 percent of the Russian market.

At a time when economic uncertainty is high and workers can go months without being paid, price is a significant factor for the average Russian. An entrepreneur named Vladimir Dovgan has prospered by launching several different brands of vodka priced between $5 and $10 per bottle. Dovgan's picture is featured on the label, and he also appears in print and television ads. Meanwhile, in the late 1990s, Diageo PLC began producing Smirnoff in St. Petersburg. Ironically, Smirnoff's heritage is truly Russian, although for decades the brand was produced only in the West. As a company executive

Home-brew vodka made from grain or beets is a long-standing tradition in Russia. Consider the following excerpt from Vladimir Voinovich's satirical novel The Life and Extraordinary Adventures of Private Ivan Chonkin:

> They clinked glasses. Ivan downed the contents of his glass and nearly fell off his chair. He instantly lost his breath, just as if he'd been punched in the stomach . . .
> Gladishev, who had downed his own glass without any difficulty, looked over at Ivan with a sly grin. "Well, Ivan, how's the home brew?"
> "First-rate stuff," praised Chonkin, wiping the tears from his eyes with the palm of his hand. "Takes your breath away."

<hr />

[30] Emily Nelson and Miriam Jordan, "Sensitive Export: Seeking New Markets for Tampons, P&G Faces Cultural Barriers," *The Wall Street Journal* (December 8, 2000), pp. A1, A8; Yumiko Ono, "Tambrands Ads Aim to Overcome Cultural and Religious Obstacles," *The Wall Street Journal* (March 17, 1997), p. B8. See also Dyan Machan, "Will the Chinese Use Tampons?" *Forbes* (January 16, 1995), pp. 86–87.

**Figure 7-1**

*Russia's Vodka Industry*

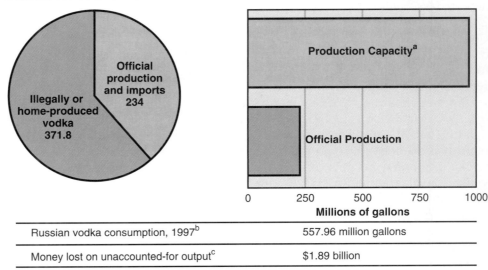

Official vs. Total Production . . . . . . And vs. Total Capacity

| Russian vodka consumption, 1997[b] | 557.96 million gallons |
|---|---|
| Money lost on unaccounted-for output[c] | $1.89 billion |

[a]For 800 enterprises licensed to produce hard, or 128-proof, liquor
[b]Consumption level is believed to be much higher
[c]Converted to U.S. dollars from rubles at current rate

noted, "This should make Smirnoff seem more Russian. We want Russians to realize that Smirnoff came to Russia to produce for Russians."[31] Even as marketers of distilled spirits adjust their strategies, market preferences are changing; young Russians are turning to beer, with demand up 25 percent in the 5-year period between 1995 and 2000. In 2002, expenditures on beer surpassed vodka for the first time. Local brands are favored, as the weak ruble priced imports out of the reach of the average consumer. Some observers attribute the change to the influence of healthier, Western lifestyles. Also, vodka is associated with heavy drinking during Russia's often tumultuous transition to a market economy in the 1990s.[32]

## Benefit Segmentation

Global **benefit segmentation** focuses on the numerator of the value equation: the B in $V = B/P$. This approach is based on marketers' superior understanding of the problem a product solves, the benefit it offers, or the issue it addresses, regardless of geography. Food marketers are finding success creating products that can help parents create nutritious family meals with a minimal investment of time. Campbell Soup is making significant inroads into Japan's $500 million soup market as time-pressed homemakers place a premium on convenience. Marketers of health and beauty aids also use benefit segmentation. Many toothpaste brands are straightforward cavity fighters, and as such they reach a very broad market. However, as consumers become more concerned about whitening, sensitive teeth, gum disease, and other oral care issues, marketers are developing new toothpaste brands suited to the different sets of perceived needs.

---

31  Ernest Beck, "Absolut Frustration: Why Foreign Distillers Find It So Hard to Sell Vodka to the Russians," *The Wall Street Journal* (January 15, 1998), pp. A1, A9; Betsy McKay, "Vladimir Dovgan Is a Constant Presence in Capitalist Russia," *The Wall Street Journal* (March 20, 1998), pp. A1, A8.
32  John Varoli, "Bored by Vodka, Russians Find More Style in Beer," *The New York Times* (December 19, 1999), sec. 3, p. 7. See also Nick Paton Walsh, "Russia Lite: Nyet to Vodka, Da to Beer," *The Observer* (October 20), 2002.

The European pet food market represents $30 billion in annual sales. Nestlé discovered that cat owners' attitudes toward feeding their pets are the same everywhere. In response, a pan-European campaign was created for Friskies Dry Cat Food. The appeal was that dry cat food better suits a cat's universally recognized independent nature. Likewise, many Europeans are concerned with improving the health and longevity of their pets. Accordingly, Procter & Gamble is marketing its Iams brand premium pet food as a way to improve pets' health.[33]

## Ethnic Segmentation

In many countries, the population includes ethnic groups of significant size. In the United States, for example, there are three major ethnic segments: African/black Americans, Asian Americans, and Hispanic Americans. Each segment shows great diversity and can be further subdivided. For example, Asian-Americans include Thai Americans, Vietnamese Americans, and Chinese Americans, each of whom speak a different language. By contrast, America's Hispanic population includes Mexican Americans, Puerto-Rican Americans, Cuban Americans, and others who share a common language. According to the U.S Census Bureau, Hispanic Americans numbered 35 million in 2000 and comprised the fifth-largest Hispanic population in the world with $560 billion in annual buying power. As a group, Hispanic Americans are hard working and exhibit a strong family and religious orientation. In addition, consider the following statistics:

- Mexican households in California have after-tax income of $100 billion, half the total of all Mexican Americans.
- The number of Hispanic teens is projected to swell from 12 percent of the U.S. teen population to 18 percent in the next decade.

From a marketing point of view, these groups offer great opportunity. Companies in a variety of industry sectors, including food and beverages, consumer durables, and leisure and financial services are recognizing the need to include these segments when preparing marketing programs for the United States. For example, companies based in Mexico are zeroing in on opportunities to the north. Three Mexican retailers—Famso, Grupo Gigant SA, and Grupo Comercial Chedraui SA—have opened stores in the United States. As Famsa president Humberto Garza Valdez explained at the grand opening of a store in San Fernando, California, "We're not coming to the U.S. to face big companies like Circuit City or Best Buy. Our focus is the Hispanic market."[34]

In the 2-year period 1999–2000, new-vehicle registrations by Hispanics in the United States grew 20 percent, twice the overall national growth rate. Honda, Toyota, and other Japanese automakers have been courting U.S. Hispanics for years and have built up a great deal of brand loyalty. Ford and GM are playing catch up, with mixed results; despite large increases in advertising targeting Hispanics, GM's market share is slipping.[35] Sales of Corona Extra beer in the United States have grown dramatically recently, thanks in part to savvy marketing to the Hispanic segment. In lower-income neighborhoods, imported premium beer brands represent "affordable luxuries." Although a six-pack of Corona typically costs at least a dollar more than Budweiser at a local bodega, it is usually priced

---

[33] Sarah Ellison and Emily Nelson, "Pet-Food Companies Compete to Be the Pick of the Litter," *The Wall Street Journal* (July 31, 2001), p. B11.

[34] Joel Millman, "Mexican Retailers Enter U.S. to Capture Latino Dollars," *The Wall Street Journal* (February 8, 2001), p. A18.

[35] Eduardo Porter, "Ford, Other Auto Makers Target Hispanic Community," *The Wall Street Journal* (November 9, 2000), p. B4.

lower than Heineken. Marketers must understand, though, that many Hispanic Americans live in two worlds; while they identify strongly with the United States, there is also a sense of pride associated with brands that connect to their heritage.[36]

## ASSESSING MARKET POTENTIAL AND CHOOSING TARGET MARKETS OR SEGMENTS[37]

After segmenting the market by one or more of the criteria just discussed, the next step is to assess the attractiveness of the identified segments. This part of the process is especially important when sizing up emerging country markets as potential targets. It is at this stage that global marketers should be mindful of several potential pitfalls associated with the market segmentation process. First, there is a tendency to overstate the size and short-term attractiveness of individual country markets, especially when estimates are based primarily on demographic data such as income and population. For example, while China, India, Brazil, and other emerging markets undoubtedly offer potential in the long run, management must realize that short-term profit and revenue growth objectives may be hard to achieve. During the 1990s, Procter & Gamble and other consumer packaged-goods companies learned this lesson in Latin America. By contrast, the success of McDonald's Russia during the same period is a case study in the rewards of persistence and long-term outlook. A second trap that global marketers can set for themselves is to target a country because shareholders or competitors exert pressure on management not to "miss out" on a strategic opportunity. Recall from Chapter 2, for example, the statement by India's finance minister that the twenty-first century will be "the century of India." Such pronouncements can create the impression that management must "act now" to take advantage of a limited window of opportunity. Third, there is a danger that management's network of contacts will emerge as a primary criterion for targeting. The result can be market entry based on convenience rather than rigorous market analysis. For example, a company may enter into a distribution agreement with a non-national employee who wants to represent the company after returning to his or her home country. The issue of choosing the right foreign distributor will be discussed in detail in Chapter 12.

With these pitfalls in mind, marketers can utilize three basic criteria for assessing opportunity in global target markets: current size of the segment and anticipated growth potential, competition, and compatibility with the company's overall objectives and the feasibility of successfully reaching a designated target.

## Current Segment Size and Growth Potential

Is the market segment currently large enough to present a company with the opportunity to make a profit? If the answer is "no" today, does it have significant growth potential to make it attractive in terms of a company's long-term strategy? As noted earlier, one of the advantages of targeting a market segment globally is that, while the segment in a single-country market might be small, even a narrow segment can be served profitably if the segment exists in several countries. The billion-plus members of the global MTV Generation is a case in point. Moreover, by virtue of its size and purchasing power, the global teen segment is extremely

---

[36] Suein L. Hwang, "Corona Ads Target Hispanics in Effort to Hop to Head of U.S. Beer Market," *The Wall Street Journal Europe* (November 21–22, 1997), p. 9; Michael Barone, "How Hispanics Are Americanizing," *The Wall Street Journal* (February 6, 1998), p. A22.

[37] Parts of the following discussion are adapted from David Arnold, *The Mirage of Global Markets* (Upper Saddle River, NJ: Pearson Education, 2004), Chapter 2.

attractive to consumer goods companies. In the case of a huge country market such as India or China, segment size and growth potential may be assessed in a different manner. From the perspective of a consumer packaged-goods company, for example, low incomes and the absence of a distribution infrastructure offset the fact that 75 percent of India's population lives in rural areas. The appropriate decision may be to target urban areas only, even though they are home to only 25 percent of the population. Visa's strategy in China perfectly illustrates this criterion as it relates to demographics: Visa is targeting persons with a monthly salary equivalent to $300 or more. The company estimates that currently 60 million people fit that description; by 2010, the number could include as many as 200 million people.

Thanks to a combination of favorable demographics and lifestyle-related needs, the United States has been a very attractive market for foreign automakers. For example, demand for sports utility vehicles exploded during the 1990s. From 1990 to 2000, SUV sales tripled, growing from nearly 1 million units in 1990, reaching the two-million unit mark in 1996, and passing three million sold in 2000. Why are these vehicles so popular? Primarily it is the security of four-wheel drive and the higher clearance for extra traction in adverse driving conditions. They also typically have more space for hauling cargo. Reacting to high demand for the Jeep Cherokee, Ford Explorer, and Chevy Blazer, manufacturers from outside the United States introduced models of their own at a variety of price points (see Table 7-8). AutoPacific consultancy predicts that by 2006, at least 79 SUV models will be available as Toyota, Nissan, Rover, BMW, Mercedes, Volkswagen, and other global automakers target American buyers. Even as growth slows in the United States, SUVs are growing in popularity in many other countries. In China, for example, SUVs represent the fastest-growing sector in the auto industry; SUVs account for about 40 percent of auto imports. Officials at GM's Cadillac division are considering exporting the company's popular $50,000-plus Escalade model to China.[38]

## Potential Competition

A market segment or country market characterized by strong competition may be a segment to avoid. However, if the competition is vulnerable in terms of price or quality disadvantages, it is possible for a market newcomer to make significant inroads. Over the past several decades, for example, Japanese companies in a variety of industries targeted the U.S. market despite the presence of entrenched domestic market leaders. Some of the newcomers

**Table 7-8**

Global Automakers Targeting the U.S. Market with SUVs

| Automaker | Current SUV model | Current Price* (or range) | Country of Assembly or Manufacture | Year Introduced |
|---|---|---|---|---|
| Porsche | Cayenne | $42,000–$100,000 | Germany | 2003 |
| Volkswagen | Touareg | $35,000–$54,000 | Slovakia | 2004 |
| Honda | CR-V | $21,000 | Japan | 1995 |
| Toyota | RAV-4 | $19,000–$25,000 | Japan | 1994 |
| Kia | Sorento | $20,500–$29,000 | South Korea | 2003 |
| BMW | X5 | $40,000–$70,000 | USA | 2000 |
| Mercedes-Benz | ML 350 | $42,000–$50,000 | USA | 2003 |

\* Price variations due to engine, drive train, trim, and other options.

---

[38] Peter Wonacott and Lee Hawkins Jr., "Saying 'Beamer' in Chinese," *The Wall Street Journal* (November 6, 2003), p. B1. See also Joseph B. White, "Rollback: America's Love Affair with Sport Utilities Is Now Cooling Off," *The Wall Street Journal* (May 30, 2001), pp. A1, A8.

proved to be extremely adept at segmenting and targeting; as a result, they made significant inroads. In the motorcycle industry, for example, Honda first created the market for small-displacement dirt bikes. The company then moved upmarket with bigger bikes targeted at casual riders whose psychographic profile was quite different than that of the hard-core Harley-Davidson rider. In document imaging, Canon outflanked Xerox by offering compact desktop copiers and targeting department managers and secretaries. Similar case studies can be found in earth-moving equipment (Komatsu versus Caterpillar), photography (Fuji versus Kodak), and numerous other industries. By contrast, there are many examples of companies whose efforts to develop a position in the United States ended in failure. For example, in the computer industry, Acer failed to make headway in a U.S. market dominated by such strong brand names such as Dell (see Case 1-2).

## Feasibility and Compatibility

If a market segment is judged to be large enough, and if strong competitors are either absent or deemed to be vulnerable, then the final consideration is whether a company can and should target that market. The feasibility of targeting a particular segment can be negatively impacted by various factors. For example, significant regulatory hurdles may be present that limit market access. This issue is especially important in China today. The company may also encounter cultural barriers, as was the case with Tambrands' efforts to build its feminine-hygiene market. Other marketing-specific issues can arise; in India, for example, 3 to 5 years are required to build an effective distribution system for many consumer products. This fact may serve as a deterrent to foreign companies that might otherwise be attracted by the apparent potential of India's large population.[39]

Managers must decide how well a company's product fits the country market in question—or, as noted, if the company does not currently offer a suitable product, can it develop one? To make this decision, a marketer must consider several criteria:

- Will adaptation be required? If so, is this economically justifiable in terms of the expected sales volume?
- Will import restrictions, high tariffs, or a strong home country currency drive up the price of the product in the target market currency and effectively dampen demand?
- Is it advisable to source locally? In many cases, reaching global market segments requires considerable expenditures for distribution and travel by company personnel. Would it make sense to source products in the country for export elsewhere in the region?

Finally, it is important to address the question of whether targeting a particular segment is compatible with the company's overall goals, its brand image, or established sources of competitive advantage. For example, BMW is one of the world's premium auto brands. Should BMW add a minivan to its product lineup? As BMW CEO Helmut Panke explained recently, "There is a segment in the market which BMW is not catering to and that is the minivan or MPV segment. We don't have a van because a van as it is in the market today does not fulfill any of the BMW group brand values. We all as a team said 'no'."[40]

---

[39] Khozem Merchant, "Sweet Rivals Find Love in a Warm Climate," *Financial Times* (July 24, 2003), p. 9.
[40] Neal E. Boudette, "BMW's CEO Just Says 'No' to Protect Brand," *The Wall Street Journal* (November 26, 2003), p. B1.

| Market | Market Size | Competitive Advantage | | Market Potential | Terms of Access | Market Potential |
|---|---|---|---|---|---|---|
| China (1.3 billion) | 100 | .07 | = | 7 | .20 | 1.4 |
| Russia (150 million) | 50 | .10 | = | 5 | .60 | 3.0 |
| Mexico (100 million) | 20 | .20 | = | 4 | .90 | 3.6 |

**Table 7-9**

*Market Selection Framework*

# A Framework for Selecting Target Markets

As one can infer from this discussion, it would be extremely useful to have formal tools or frameworks available when assessing emerging country markets. Table 7-9 presents a market selection framework that incorporates some of the elements just discussed. Suppose an American company has identified China, Russia, and Mexico as potential country target markets. The table shows the countries arranged in declining rank by market size. At first glance, China might appear to hold the greatest potential simply on the basis of size. However, the competitive advantage of our hypothetical firm is 0.07 in China, 0.10 in Russia, and 0.20 in Mexico. Multiplying the market size and competitive advantage index yields a market potential of 7 in China, 5 in Russia, and 4 in Mexico.

The next stage in the analysis requires an assessment of the various market access considerations. In Table 7-9 all these conditions or terms are reduced to an index number of terms of access, which is 0.20 for China, 0.60 for Russia and 0.90 Mexico. In other words, the "market access considerations" are more favorable in Mexico than in Russia, perhaps in this instance due to NAFTA. Multiplying the market potential by the terms of access index suggests that Mexico, despite its small size, holds greater export potential than China or Russia.

Although the framework in Table 7-9 should prove useful as a preliminary screening tool for intercountry comparisons, it does not go far enough in terms of assessing actual market potential. Global marketing expert David Arnold has developed a framework that goes beyond demographic data and considers other, marketing-oriented assessments of market size and growth potential. Instead of a "top-down" segmentation analysis beginning with, say, income or population data from a particular country, Arnold's framework is based on a "bottom-up" analysis that begins at the product-market level. The term **product-market** refers to a market defined by a product category; in the automotive industry, for example, phrases such as "luxury car market," "SUV market," and "minivan market" refer to specific product-markets. By contrast, phrases such as "the Russian market" or "the Indian market" refer to country markets.

As shown in Figure 7-2, Arnold's framework incorporates two core concepts: marketing model drivers and enabling conditions. **Marketing model drivers** are key elements or factors required for a business to take root and grow in a particular country market environment. The drivers may differ depending on whether a company serves consumer or industrial markets. Does success hinge on establishing or leveraging a brand name? Or, is distribution or a tech-savvy sales staff the key element? Marketing executives seeking an opportunity must arrive at insights into the true driving force(s) that will affect success for their particular product-market. **Enabling conditions** are structural market characteristics whose presence or absence can determine whether the marketing model can succeed. For example, in India, refrigeration is not widely available in shops and market food stalls. This creates challenges for Nestlé and Cadbury Schweppes as they attempt to capitalize on Indians' increasing appetite for chocolate confections. Although Nestlé's KitKat and Cadbury's Dairy Milk bars have been reformulated to better withstand heat, the absence or rudimentary nature of refrigeration hampers the companies' efforts to ensure their products are in saleable condition.

After marketing-model drivers and enabling conditions have been identified, the third step is for management to weigh the estimated costs associated with

**Figure 7-2**

Screening Criteria for Market
Segments

Source: David Arnold. The Mirage of Global
Markets: How Globalizing Companies Can
Succeed As Markets Localize, © 2004. Reprinted
by Permission of Pearson Education, Inc., Upper
Saddle River, NJ.

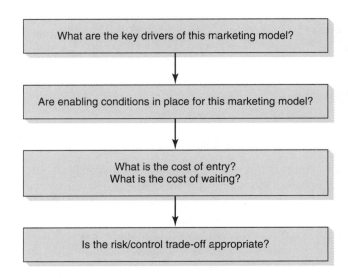

entering and serving the market with potential short- and long-term revenue streams. Does this segment or country market merit entry now? Or, would it be better to wait until, say, specific enabling conditions are established? The issue of timing is often framed in terms of the quest for **first-mover advantage.** The conventional wisdom is that the first company to enter a market has the best chance of becoming the market leader. Examples from the history of global marketing that appear to support this notion include the Coca-Cola Company, which established itself globally during World War II. However, there are also first-mover *disadvantages.* The first company to enter a market often makes substantial investments in marketing only to find that a late-arriving competitor reaps some of the benefits. Indeed, there is ample evidence that late entrants into global markets can also achieve success. One way they do this is by benchmarking established companies and then outmaneuvering them, first locally and then globally. Jollibee, the Philippines-based fast-food chain that was discussed in Chapter 4, is a case in point. Late movers can also succeed by developing innovative business models. This approach was used by Stephen Millar, chief executive of Australian wine producer BRL Hardy. Millar's insight was that no leading global brand had emerged in the wine business; in other words, there was no equivalent to Coca-Cola. During the 1990s, Hardy established itself as a leading global brand. It accomplished this by moving on several fronts. First, it took control of the sales function. Second, the company made sure its wines were crafted to appeal to a broader demographic than "wine snobs" who tend to favor bottles from France and Italy. Third, it supplemented its line of Australian brands with select brands from other countries. In 2002 Hardy sold 20 million cases of wine worldwide. Today, Hardy is one of the world's top 10 wine companies.[41]

One way to determine the marketing model drivers and enabling conditions is to create a product-market profile. The profile should address some or all of the following basic questions:

1. Who buys our product or brand?
2. Who does not buy our product or brand?
3. What need or function does our product serve? Does our product or brand address that need?
4. Is there a market need that is not being met by current product/brand offerings?
5. What problem does our product solve?
6. What are customers currently buying to satisfy the need and/or solve the problem for which our product is targeted?

---

[41] Christopher A. Bartlett and Sumantra Ghoshal, "Going Global: Lessons from the Late Movers," *Harvard Business Review* 78, no. 2 (March–April 2000), pp. 138–140. See also Christopher Lawton, "Aussie Wines Star at Spirits Marketer Constellation Brands," *The Wall Street Journal* (January 16, 2004), pp. B1, B4.

7. What price are they paying for the product they are currently buying?
8. When is our product purchased?
9. Where is our product purchased?

## PRODUCT-MARKET DECISIONS

The next step is in assessing market segments is a company review of current and potential product offerings in terms of their suitability for the country market or segment. This assessment can be performed by creating a product-market grid that maps markets as horizontal rows on a spreadsheet and products as vertical columns. Each cell represents the possible intersection of a product and a market segment. In the case of the candy companies just discussed, both Nestlé and Cadbury determined that a liquid chocolate confection would be one way to address the issue of India's hot weather. The companies are also working to improve the enabling conditions for selling traditional chocolate treats by supplying coolers to merchants.

Table 7-10 shows a product-market grid for Lexus. Toyota launched the Lexus brand in 1989 with two sedan models. In market segmentation terms, the

*Table 7-10*

Product-Market Grid for Lexus, Select Country Markets

| Country Segment | Vehicle Model | | | | | | | |
|---|---|---|---|---|---|---|---|---|
| | LS430 | GS300/430 | IS200/300 | IS300SC | ES330 | LX 470 | RX330/330 | SC430 |
| **Asia** | | | | | | | | |
| Japan | | | | | | | | |
| China | X | X | X | | X | | | |
| S. Korea | X | X | X | | X | | X | X |
| **North America** | | | | | | | | |
| Canada | X | X | X | X | X | X | X | X |
| USA | X | X | X | X | X | X | X | X |
| **Europe** | | | | | | | | |
| Austria | X | X | X | X | | | X | X |
| Belgium | X | X | X | X | | X | X | X |
| Denmark | X | X | X | X | | | X | X |
| Finland | X | X | X | X | | | X | X |
| France | X | X | X | X | | | X | X |
| Germany | X | X | X | X | | | X | X |
| Gr. Britain | X | X | X | X | | | X | X |
| Greece | X | X | X | X | | X | X | X |
| Ireland | X | X | X | X | | | X | X |
| Luxembourg | X | X | X | X | | | X | X |
| Netherlands | X | X | X | X | | | X | X |
| Portugal | X | X | X | X | | | X | X |
| Sweden | X | X | X | X | | | X | X |
| Switzerland | X | X | X | X | | | X | X |
| **Middle East** | | | | | | | | |
| Israel | X | | | | | | | |
| Bahrain | X | X | | | X | X | X | X |
| Kuwait | X | X | | | X | X | X | X |
| Saudi Arabia | X | X | | | X | X | X | X |

*Source:* Lexus Marketing.

luxury car buyer Lexus hoped to attract is associated with an upper-income demographic. In 1996, Lexus launched its first sport utility vehicle. The decision to enter the SUV product market represented management's desire to reach upper-income consumers whose lifestyles required something other than a luxury sedan. In 2004, Lexus offered a total of eight different models in the United States; in addition to the LX470 luxury utility vehicle ($64,800), there is the LS430 luxury sedan ($55,750) and the SC430, a four-seat convertible priced at about $65,000. Lexus vehicles are marketed in more than 60 countries; the United States is the number one market. Ironically, in Japan the vehicles were sold for years under the Toyota nameplate; the line is to be relaunched under the Lexus brand in 2005. The company sells about 20,000 vehicles in Europe each year, with the United Kingdom accounting for half of those sales.

Management intends to build Lexus into a global luxury brand; the goal is to sell 60,000 cars in Europe by the end of the decade. That, in turn, means that the company has to target Germany, the largest market in Europe where 1 in 10 vehicles bought are luxury models. In 2003, Lexus sold about 2,500 cars in Germany; by comparison, Mercedes and BMW sold a combined total of more than 500,000 vehicles. Can Lexus succeed on the home turf of two of the world's leading luxury carmakers? To appeal to Germany's famously finicky car buyers, Lexus vehicles are undergoing significant adaptation. For example, because Germans want the option of buying vehicles with diesel engines, Lexus developed new diesel models for 2004 as well as a gas-electric hybrid engine for the RX330 SUV. Note that, in Europe, Lexus offers the top-of-the-line LX470 in only two countries. Can you explain this decision?

## TARGET MARKET STRATEGY OPTIONS

After evaluating the identified segments in terms of the three criteria presented, a decision is made whether to pursue a particular opportunity or not. If the decision is made to proceed, an appropriate targeting strategy must be developed. There are three basic categories of target marketing strategies: standardized marketing, concentrated marketing, and differentiated marketing.

## Standardized Global Marketing

**Standardized global marketing** is analogous to mass marketing in a single country. Strictly speaking, it involves creating the same marketing mix for a broad mass market of potential buyers. Standardized global marketing, also known as *undifferentiated target marketing*, is based on the premise that a mass market exists around the world. In addition, that mass market is served with a marketing mix of standardized elements. Product adaptation is minimized, and a strategy of intensive distribution ensures that the product is available in the maximum number of retail outlets. The appeal of standardized global marketing is clear: lower production costs. The same is true of standardized global communications.

Executives at Revlon International recently adopted a standardized strategy when they announced their intention of making Revlon a global name. President Paul Block declared, "All Revlon North American advertising for all products, whether they are cosmetics, skincare, haircare, or Almay, will now be used worldwide."[42] The global theme is keyed to a "Shake Your Body" campaign. Revlon's strategy calls for developing the huge consumer markets emerging in Central and Eastern Europe, including Hungary and the former Soviet republics.

---

[42] Pat Sloan, "Revlon Eyes Global Image; Picks Y & R," *Advertising Age* (January 1, 1993), p. 1.

# GLOBAL *marketing in action*

## Targeting Adventure Seekers with an American Classic

In 2003, Harley-Davidson (H-D) celebrated its hundredth anniversary. The company grew impressively during its first 100 years of operation; as the twenty-first century began, H-D had sales of $2.1 billion, 8,000 employees worldwide, and a network of 1,300 dealerships in 48 countries. Savvy export marketing enabled H-D to dramatically increase worldwide sales of its heavyweight motorcycles. From Australia to Germany to Mexico City, Harley enthusiasts are paying the equivalent of up to $25,000 to own an American-built classic. In many countries, dealers must put would-be buyers on a 6-month waiting list because of high demand.

H-D's international success came after years of neglecting overseas markets. The company was also slow to react to a growing threat from Japanese manufacturers. Early on, the company used an export-selling approach, symbolized by its underdeveloped dealer network. Moreover, print advertising simply used word-for-word translations of the U.S. ads. By the late 1980s, after recruiting dealers in the important Japanese and European markets, company executives discovered a basic principle of global marketing. "As the saying goes, we needed to think global but act local," said Jerry G. Wilke, vice president for worldwide marketing during that time. Managers began to adapt the company's international marketing to make it more responsive to local conditions.

In Japan, for example, Harley's rugged image and high quality helped make it the best-selling imported motorcycle. Still, Toshifumi Okui, president of Harley's Japanese division, was not satisfied. He worried that the tag line from the U.S. ads, "One steady constant in an increasingly screwed-up world," didn't connect with Japanese riders. Okui finally convinced Milwaukee to allow him to launch a Japan-only advertising campaign juxtaposing images from both Japan and the United States, such as American cyclists passing a rickshaw carrying a geisha. After learning that riders in Tokyo consider fashion and customized bikes to be essential, Harley opened two stores specializing in clothes and bike accessories.

In Europe, Harley discovered that an "evening out" means something different than it does in America. The company sponsored a rally in France, where beer and live rock music were available until midnight. Recalls Wilke, "People asked us why we were ending the rally just as the evening was starting. So I had to go persuade the band to keep playing and reopen the bar until 3 or 4 A.M." Still, rallies are less common in Europe than in the United State, so Harley encourages its dealers to hold open houses at their dealerships. While biking through Europe, Wilke also learned that German bikers often travel at speeds exceeding 100 miles per hour. The company made design changes to create a smoother ride at Autobahn speeds. Harley's German marketing effort began focusing on accessories to increase rider protection. Today, the company has a clear picture of its core European customers; as Klaus Stobel, European affairs director for Harley-Davidson Europe, explained, "The people who buy Harleys in Europe are like the people who buy BMWs in the U.S. They are dentists and lawyers." Even so, in 2002, Europe accounted for just 8 percent of 2002 global revenues.

*"Everyone thinks we produce big, showy, custom motorcycles. We actually have a broad range of bikes that well suit European riding habits. We have a perception problem around Harley which is an issue we need to tackle."*

John Russell, managing director, Harley-Davidson Europe

Despite high demand from brand-loyal enthusiasts, the company intentionally limits production increases to keep quality high and to keep the product supply limited in relation to demand. The company's total motorcycle production recently passed the 250,000 mark. Even so, there are not enough bikes to go around, a situation that seems to suit company executives just fine. Notes Harley's James H. Patterson, "Enough motorcycles is too many motorcycles."

*Sources: Jeremy Grand and Harald Ehren, "Harley-Davidson Eyes Europe," Financial Times (July 28, 2003), p. 17; Kevin Kelly and Karen Lowry Miller, "The Rumble Heard Round the World: Harleys," Business Week (May 24, 1993), pp. 58, 60; Robert L. Rose, "Vrooming Back: After Nearly Stalling, Harley-Davidson Finds New Crowd of Riders," The Wall Street Journal (August 31, 1990), pp. A1, A6; John Holusha, "How Harley Outfoxed Japan with Exports," New York Times (August 12, 1990), p. F5; Robert C. Reid, "How Harley Beat Back the Japanese," Fortune (September 25, 1989), pp. 155+.*

## Concentrated Global Marketing

The second global targeting strategy, **concentrated global marketing,** involves devising a marketing mix to reach a **niche.** A niche is simply a single segment of the global market. In cosmetics, the House of Lauder, Chanel, and other cosmetics marketers have used this approach successfully to target the upscale, prestige segment of the market. Similarly, Body Shop International PLC caters to consumers in many countries who wish to purchase "natural" beauty aids and cosmetics that have not been tested on animals. Concentrated targeting is also the strategy employed by the hidden champions of global marketing: companies unknown to most people that have succeeded by serving a niche market that exists in many countries. These companies define their markets narrowly and strive for global depth rather than national breadth. For example, Germany's Winterhalter is a hidden champion in the dishwasher market, but the company has never sold a dishwasher to a consumer, hospital, or school. Instead, it focuses exclusively on dishwashers and water conditioners for hotels and restaurants.

As Jürgen Winterhalter noted recently, "The narrowing of our market definition was the most important strategic decision we ever made. It is the very foundation of our success in the past decade."[43]

## Differentiated Global Marketing

The third target marketing strategy, **differentiated global marketing,** represents a more ambitious approach than concentrated target marketing. Also known as **multisegment targeting,** this approach entails targeting two or more distinct market segments with multiple marketing mix offerings. This strategy enables a company to achieve wider market coverage. For example, in the sport utility vehicle segment described previously, Rover has a $68,000 Range Rover at the high end of the market. A scaled-down version, the Land Rover Discovery, competes directly with the Jeep Grand Cherokee and is available in two models priced from $33,350 to $37,450. Rover's newest vehicle, the Freelander, has been on sale in Europe for several years. Freelander was introduced in the U.S. market in December 2001 with prices starting at $25,000. Likewise, Stolichnaya produces three brands of Russian vodka, each targeted at a different market segment: superpremium Stolichnaya Gold, the premium "base" brand Stolichnaya, and low-priced Privet (the name means "greetings" in Russian).

In the cosmetics industry, Unilever NV and Cosmair Inc. pursue differentiated global marketing strategies by targeting both ends of the perfume market. Unilever targets the luxury market with Calvin Klein and Elizabeth Taylor's Passion; Wind Song and Brut are its mass-market brands. Cosmair sells Tresnor and Giorgio Armani Gio to the upper end of the market and Gloria Vanderbilt to the lower end. Mass marketer Procter & Gamble, known for its Old Spice and Incognito brands, also embarked upon this strategy with its 1991 acquisition of Revlon's EuroCos, marketer of Hugo Boss for men and Laura Biagiotti's Roma perfume. In the mid-1990s, P&G launched a new prestige fragrance, Venezia, in the United States and several European countries. Conversely, in 1997 Estee Lauder acquired Sassaby Inc., owner of the mass-market Jane brand. The move marked the first move by Lauder outside the prestige segment.[44]

## POSITIONING

The term *positioning* is attributed to marketing gurus Al Ries and Jack Trout, who first introduced it in a 1969 article published in *Industrial Marketing* magazine. **Positioning** refers to the act of differentiating a brand in customers' minds over and against competitors in terms of attributes and benefits that the brand does and does not offer. Put differently, positioning is the process of developing strategies for "staking out turf" or "filling a slot" in the mind of target customers.[45] Positioning is frequently used in conjunction with the segmentation variables and targeting strategies discussed previously. For example, Unilever and other consumer goods companies often engage in differentiated target marketing, offering a full range of brands within a given product category. Unilever's 10 detergent brands include All, Wisk, Surf, and Persil; each is positioned slightly differently. In some instances, extensions of a popular brand can be positioned in different ways. For example, Procter & Gamble's Crest toothpaste is positioned

[43] Hermann Simon, *Hidden Champions: Lessons from 500 of the World's Best Unknown Companies* (Boston: Harvard Business School Press, 1996), p. 54.
[44] Tara Parker-Pope, "Estee Lauder Buys Jane Brand's Owner for Its First Venture into Mass Market," *The Wall Street Journal* (September 27, 1997), p. B8.
[45] Al Ries and Jack Trout, *Positioning: The Battle for Your Mind* (New York: Warner Books, 1982), p. 44.

| Brand Name | Table 7-11 |
| --- | --- |
| Crest Rejuvenating Effects<br>Crest Whitening Plus Scope<br>Crest Tartar Control Whitening Plus Scope Liquid Gel<br>Crest Plus Scope Liquid Gel<br>Crest Dual Action Whitening<br>Crest Advanced Cleaning<br>Crest MultiCare<br>Crest Extra Whitening<br>Crest Cavity Protection<br>Crest Tartar Protection<br>Crest Baking Soda and Peroxide Whitening<br>Crest Sensitivity Protection<br>Crest Kid's Cavity Protection | *Crest's Many Formulations* |

as an all-around cavity fighter. As shown in Table 7-11, Crest is also available in more than one dozen other formulations; one of the newest products, Crest Whitening Expressions, comes in cinnamon and other flavors that were created under the supervision of New Orleans celebrity chef Emeril Lagasse. Whitening Expressions is designed to appeal to women.[46] Effective positioning differentiates each variety from the others.

In the decades since Ries and Trout first focused attention on the importance of the concept, marketers have utilized a number of general positioning strategies. These include positioning by attribute or benefit, quality and price, use or user, and competitor.[47] Recent research has identified three additional positioning strategies that are particularly useful in global marketing: global consumer culture positioning, local consumer culture positioning, and foreign consumer culture positioning.

## Attribute or Benefit

A frequently used positioning strategy exploits a particular product attribute, benefit, or feature. Economy, reliability, and durability are frequently used attribute/benefit positions. Volvo automobiles are known for solid construction that offers safety in the event of a crash. By contrast, BMW is positioned as "the ultimate driving machine," a reference that signifies performance. In the ongoing credit card wars, Visa's advertising theme "It's Everywhere You Want to Be" draws attention to the benefit of worldwide merchant acceptance. In global marketing, it may be deemed important to communicate the fact that a brand is imported. This approach is known as *foreign consumer culture positioning* (FCCP).

## Quality and Price

This strategy can be thought of in terms of a continuum from high fashion/quality and high price to good value (rather than "low quality") at a reasonable price. A legendary print ad campaign for Belgium's Stella Artois beer juxtaposes a cap pried off a bottle of Stella with images of prized possessions such as a Steinway piano. The tagline "Reassuring expensive" is the only copy; upon close inspection of the ad with the Steinway, the reader can see that one of the keys is broken

---

46  Sarah Ellison, "P&G's Latest Growth Strategy: His and Hers Toothpaste," *The Wall Street Journal* (September 5, 2002), p. B1.
47  David A. Aaker and J. Gary Shansby, "Positioning Your Product," *Business Horizons* 25, no. 2 (May–June 1982), pp. 56–62.

because it was used to open the bottle! At the high end of the distilled spirits industry, marketers of imported vodkas such as Belvedere and Stolichnaya Gold have successfully positioned their brands as superpremium entities selling for twice the price of premium ("ordinary") vodka. Ads for several export vodka brands emphasize their national origins, demonstrating how quality and price positioning can be reinforced by FCCP. Marketers sometimes use the phrase "transformation advertising" to describe advertising that seeks to change the experience of buying and using a product—in other words, the product benefit—to justify a higher price/quality position. Presumably, buying and drinking Grey Goose (from France), Belvedere (Poland), Ketel One (the Netherlands), or Stolichnaya Gold (Russia) is a more gratifying consumption experience than that of buying and drinking a "bar brand" such as Popov (who knows where it is made?).

## Use or User

Another positioning strategy represents how a product is used or associates the brand with a user or class of users. For example, to capitalize on the global success and high visibility of the *Lord of the Rings* trilogy, Gillette Company's Duracell battery unit ran print and TV ads proclaiming that, on location in

Ten years, ago, South Korea's Lucky GoldStar was known for inexpensive consumer electronics and home appliances. Today, the company's name is LG Group, and GoldStar is a top brand in the global mass market for appliances. However, the company's LG Electronics unit has also successfully charted a path as a high-end niche marketer of sleek, fashionable refrigerators, washing machines, and flat-panel TVs bearing the LG brand. This print ad combines elements of two positioning strategies: quality/price and user. The headline refers to Cristal, a famous brand of expensive French Champagne. LG is targeting people who know about and appreciate the finer things in life. This audience will also appreciate the subtle humor implied by the "sacrifice" required to purchase a flat-panel TV.

remote areas of New Zealand, *Rings* director Peter Jackson and his crew used Duracell exclusively. Likewise, Max Factor makeup is positioned as "the makeup that makeup artists use."

## Competitor

Implicit or explicit reference to competitors can provide the basis for an effective positioning strategy. For example, Body Shop International founder Anita Roddick achieved early success by emphasizing the difference between the principles pursued by "mainstream" cosmetics manufacturers and retailers and those of her company. The Body Shop brand stands for natural ingredients, no animal testing, and recyclable containers. Moreover, Roddick broke with the conventional industry approach of promising miracles. At Body Shop, women were given realistic expectations of what health and beauty aids can accomplish. Unfortunately, competitors such as Bath & Body Works quickly took notice and began mimicking both the Body Shop's positioning and its merchandising approach. After years of aggressive expansion, especially in the United States and Britain, the Body Shop brand remains well known but is not as distinctive as it was. Roddick resigned as the company's chief executive in 1998; the company no longer manufactures its own products. Instead, it focuses exclusively on retailing and marketing.

500 years ago, while others tried to turn lead into gold, Poland discovered a way to turn rye into vodka.

Following Old World traditions, Belvedere is handcrafted from 100% Polish rye and distilled 4 times for a creamy smoothness.

IMPORTED BY MILLENNIUM® IMPORT CO., MINNEAPOLIS, MINNESOTA U.S.A.
100% neutral spirits distilled from rye grain 40% ALC./VOL. (80 Proof) ©2000 Millennium® Import Co.

To justify high prices, marketers of ultra-premium vodka must differentiate their brands through packaging, distinctive flavors, or, as this ad for top-selling Belvedere illustrates, by positioning with respect to a country's distilling heritage. Competition in the category has increased dramatically in recent years; in 2001 alone, 42 new vodka brands were launched. Meanwhile, following years of explosive growth, the category is cooling as recession-pinched consumers trade down to lower-priced brands.

# Global, Foreign, and Local Consumer Culture Positioning[48]

As noted in Chapter 4 and discussed briefly in this chapter, global consumer culture positioning is a strategy that can be used to target various segments associated with the emerging global consumer culture. **Global consumer culture positioning** (GCCP) is defined as a strategy that identifies the brand as a symbol of a particular global culture or segment. It has proven to be an effective strategy for communicating with global teens, cosmopolitan elites, globetrotting laptop warriors who consider themselves members of a "transnational commerce culture," and other groups. For example, Sony's brightly colored "My First Sony" line is positioned as *the* electronics brand for youngsters around the globe with discerning parents. Philips's global corporate image campaign features people from all parts of the world with the theme "Let's make things better." Benetton uses the slogan "United Colors of Benetton" to position itself as a brand concerned with the unity of humankind. Heineken's strong brand equity around the globe can be attributed in good measure to a GCCP strategy that reinforces consumers' cosmopolitan self-image.

Certain categories of products lend themselves especially well to GCCP. High-tech and high-touch products are both associated with high levels of customer involvement and by a shared "language" among users.[49] *High-tech products* are sophisticated, technologically complex, and/or difficult to explain or understand. When shopping for them, consumers often have specialized needs or interests and rational buying motives. High-tech brands and products are frequently evaluated in terms of their performance against established objective standards. Portable MP3 players, cellular phones, personal computers, home theater audio/video components, luxury automobiles, and financial services are some of the high-tech product categories for which companies have established strong global positions. Buyers typically already possess—or wish to acquire—considerable technical information. Generally speaking, for example, computer buyers in all parts of the world are equally knowledgeable about Pentium microprocessors, 40 gigabyte hard drives, software RAM requirements, and flat-panel displays. High-tech global consumer positioning also works well for special interest products associated with leisure or recreation. Fuji bicycles, Adidas sports equipment, and Canon cameras are examples of successful global special-interest products. Because most people who buy and use high-tech products "speak the same language" and share the same mind-set, marketing communications should be informative and emphasize performance-related attributes and features to establish the desired GCCP.

By contrast, when shopping for *high-touch products*, consumers are generally energized by emotional motives rather than rational ones. Consumers may feel an emotional or spiritual connection with high-touch products, the performance of which is evaluated in subjective, aesthetic terms rather than objective, technical terms. Consumption of high-touch products may represent an act of personal indulgence, reflect the user's actual or ideal self-image, or reinforce interpersonal relationships between the user and family members or friends. High-touch products appeal to the senses more than the intellect; if a product comes with a detailed user's manual, it's probably high tech; by contrast, the consumption experience associated with a high-touch product probably does not entail referring to an instruction manual. Luxury perfume, designer fashions, and fine champagne are

---

[48] The following discussion is adapted from Dana L. Alden, Jan-Benedict Steenkamp, and Rajeev Batra, "Brand Positioning Through Advertising in Asia, North America, and Europe: The Role of Global Consumer Culture," *Journal of Marketing* 63, no. 1 (January 1999), pp. 75–87.

[49] Teresa J. Domzal and Lynette Unger, "Emerging Positioning Strategies in Global Marketing," *Journal of Consumer Marketing* 4, no. 4 (Fall 1987), pp. 26–27.

THE WYNNEWOOD CHAMPAGNE FLUTE, LIKE ALL WATERFORD PATTERNS, WILL NEVER BE DISCONTINUED. FOR A BROCHURE, CALL 1-800-523-0009.

**WATERFORD**
WORTHY OF THE MOMENT
FOR OVER TWO CENTURIES.

This long-running print advertising campaign from the Waterford Crystal division of Ireland's Waterford Wedgwood PLC is consistent with the company's status as the world's premier purveyor of luxury crystal. By choosing black-and-white photography and minimizing the amount of copy, the ad's creators evoke understated elegance, simplicity, and intimacy—a quintessential example of high-touch positioning.

all examples of high-touch products that lend themselves to GCCP. Some high-touch products are linked with the joy or pleasure found in "life's little moments." Ads that show friends chatting over a cup of coffee in a cafe or someone's kitchen put the product at the center of everyday life. As Nestlé has convincingly demonstrated with its Nescafé brand, this type of high-touch, emotional appeal is understood worldwide.

A brand's GCCP can be reinforced by the careful selection of the thematic, verbal, or visual components that are incorporated into advertising and other communications. For marketers seeking to establish a high-touch GCCP, leisure, romance, and materialism are three themes that cross borders well. By contrast, professionalism and experience are advertising themes that work well for high-tech products such as global financial services. Several years ago, for example, Chase Manhattan bank launched a $75 million global advertising campaign geared to the theme "Profit from experience." According to Aubrey Hawes, a vice president and corporate director of marketing for the bank, Chase's business and private banking clients "span the globe and travel the globe. They can only know one Chase in their minds, so why should we try to confuse them?"[50] Presumably, Chase's target audience is sophisticated enough to appreciate the subtlety of the copywriter's craft—"profit" can be interpreted as either a noun ("monetary gain") or a verb ("reap an advantage").

In some instances, products may be positioned globally in a "bipolar" fashion (i.e., as both high tech and high touch). This approach can be used when products satisfy buyers' rational criteria while evoking an emotional response.

---

[50] Gary Levin, "Ads Going Global," *Advertising Age* (July 22, 1991) p. 42.

For example, audio-video components from Denmark's Bang & Olufsen, by virtue of their performance and elegant styling, are perceived as both high tech ("advanced engineering and sonically superior") and high touch ("modern design blends in nicely with the rest of the décor"). Nokia has become the world's leading cellular phone brand because the company combines state-of-the-art technical performance with a fashion orientation that allows users to view their phones as extensions of themselves. Likewise, Apple Computer positions its products on the basis of both performance ("two G5 processors operating in parallel") and design (the unorthodox iMac's flat-screen display mounted on a swiveling stainless-steel neck).

To the extent that English is the primary language of international business, mass media, and the Internet, one can make the case that English signifies modernism and a cosmopolitan outlook. Therefore, the use of English in advertising and labeling throughout the world is another way to achieve GCCP. Benetton's tag line "United Colors of Benetton" appears in English in all of the company's advertising. The implication is that fashion-minded consumers everywhere in the world shop at Benetton. Recall the Chapter 4 discussion of the use of English as a marketing tool in Japan. Even though a native English speaker would doubtless find the syntax to be muddled, it is the symbolism associated with the use of English that counts rather than specific meanings that the words might (or might not) convey. A third way to reinforce a GCCP is to use brand symbols that cannot be interpreted as associated with a specific country culture. Examples include Nestlé's "little nest" logo with an adult bird feeding its babies, the Nike swoosh, and the Mercedes-Benz star.

A second option is **foreign consumer culture positioning** (FCCP), which associates the brand's users, use occasions, or production origins with a foreign country or culture. Foster's Brewing Group's U.S. advertising proudly trumpets the brand's national origin; print ads feature the tag line "Foster's. Australian for beer" while TV and radio spots are keyed to the theme "How to speak Australian." Needless to say, these ads are not used in Australia itself. Advertising for Grupo Modelo's Corona Extra brand is identified generally with Latin America. The "American-ness" of Levi jeans, Marlboro cigarettes, and

Harley-Davidson motorcycles—sometimes conveyed with subtlety, sometimes not—enhances their appeal to cosmopolitans around the world and offers opportunities for FCCP. FCCP is sometimes used in automobile advertising; in the early 1990s, for example, Volkswagen ran an advertising campaign featuring a German word, "Fahrvergnügen," that was meant to signify both the cars' German origins and a European joy of driving. Sometimes, brand names suggest an FCCP even though a product is of local origin. For example, the name "Häagen-Dazs" was made up to imply Scandinavian origin even though the ice cream was launched by an American company. Conversely, a popular chewing gum in Italy marketed by Perfett bears the brand name Brooklyn.

Marketers can also utilize **local consumer culture positioning** (LCCP), a strategy that associates the brand with local cultural meanings, reflects the local culture's norms, portrays the brand as consumed by local people in the national culture, or depicts the product as locally produced for local consumers. An LCCP approach can be seen in Budweiser's U.S. advertising; ads featuring the Clydesdale horses, for example, associate the brand with small-town American culture. Researchers studying television advertising in seven countries found that LCCP predominated, particularly in ads for food, personal nondurables, and household nondurables.

Wine and beer brands from Australia's Foster's Group are available in more than 150 countries, but about three fourths of the company's sales are in the Asia/Pacific region. In the United States, ads for Foster's lager play up the brand's Australian heritage and emphasize the sense of adventure associated with the country's exotic outback.

**summary**

The global environment must be analyzed before a company pursues expansion into new geographic markets. Through **global market segmentation,** a company can identify and group customers or countries according to common needs and wants. **Demographic segmentation** can be based on country income and population, age, ethnic heritage, or other variables. **Psychographic segmentation** groups people according to attitudes, interests, opinions, and lifestyles. **Behavioral segmentation** utilizes **user status** and **usage rate** as segmentation variables. Segmentation can also be based on the **benefits** buyers seek. **Global teens** and **global elites** are two examples of global market segments.

After marketers have identified segments, the next step is **targeting**: The identified groups are evaluated and compared, and one or more segments with the greatest potential is selected from them. The groups are evaluated on the basis of several factors, including segment size and growth potential, competition, and compatibility and feasibility. Target market assessment also entails a thorough understanding of the **product-market** in question and determining marketing **model drivers** and **enabling conditions** in the countries under study. The timing of market entry should take into account whether a **first-mover** advantage is likely to be gained. After evaluating the identified segments, marketers must decide on an appropriate targeting strategy. The three basic categories of global target marketing strategies are **standardized marketing, concentrated (niche) marketing,** and **differentiated (multisegment) marketing.**

Positioning a product or brand in the minds of target customers can be accomplished in various ways: **positioning by attribute** or **benefit, positioning by quality/price, positioning by use** or **user,** and **positioning by competition.** In global marketing, **global consumer culture positioning (GCCP), foreign consumer culture positioning (FCCP),** and **local consumer culture positioning (LCCP)** are additional strategic options.

**discussion questions**

1. Identify the five basic segmentation strategies. Give an example of a company that has used each one.

2. Explain the difference between segmenting and targeting.

3. Compare and contrast standardized, concentrated, and differentiated global marketing. Illustrate each strategy with an example from a global company.

4. American Isuzu Motors recently introduced the AXIOM SUV in the United States with a base sticker price of $25,985. The base price for a Honda CR-V is $18,750; prices for Toyota's RAV-4 start at $19,000. Assess Isuzu's decision to target the U.S. market for sport utility vehicles.

5. What is positioning? Identify the different positioning strategies presented in the chapter and give examples of companies or products that illustrate each.

6. What is global consumer culture positioning (GCCP)? What other strategic positioning choices do global marketers have?

7. What is a high-touch product? Explain the difference between high-tech product positioning and high-touch product positioning. Can some products be positioned using both strategies? Explain.

# Case 7-1

## Nokia Segments the Global Cell Phone Market

Nokia Corporation, headquartered in Finland, enjoys an enviable position in the cell phone industry: With 2003 sales totaling $37 billion, Nokia is the world's leading manufacturer of mobile telephone products. The company commands a 40 percent share of the global market, more than twice the share of archrival Motorola. More than 400 million people use Nokia's products on a daily basis. Has Nokia achieved this success by pursuing a "one size fits all" approach to the market? Hardly. The company's mobile phones division is a skilled practitioner of the art and science of segmenting consumer markets. Nokia also serves the business segment; its networks division markets wireless switching and transmission equipment. In addition, the company makes set-top boxes for television sets and home satellite systems. In 2003, the company announced the formation of a new enterprise solutions division. The aim of the new division is to tap into the fast-growing business handset market.

However, Nokia is best known as the marketer of mobile phones to individual consumers. In the mid-1990s, Nokia's Communicator digital cell phone created a new market for devices that also function as a wireless pager and personal digital assistant (PDA). Today, Nokia offers a wide range of mobile telephone products that address different user needs and lifestyles. These include "smart phones" based on the Symbian operating system that allows users to access a full range of voice and high-speed data services. There is, however, a guiding principle that is incorporated into every Nokia phone: usability. Chairman and chief executive Jorma Ollila believes that the company has succeeded in part because it was one of the first manufacturers to realize that "ease of use" had to be a primary design goal. As a result, many Nokia users are so satisfied with their phones' "user interface" (UI) that they are reluctant to switch to other brands.

Consumers are exhibiting an appetite for phones that can be used for more than voice calling. For example, in 2003, sales of mobile phones with built-in cameras surpassed the sales of regular digital cameras for the first time. Depending on the model, phones can also function as portable digital music players, game devices, and walkie-talkies. Nokia is setting out to redefine how consumers use cell phones. The company is targeting a new and growing segment: the market for mobile Internet devices that can be used for gaming and other activities. Nokia's competitive weapon is the N-Gage, an all-in-one unit that allows users to play video games in full color. N-Gage also functions as an MP3 player and has a built-in FM radio. In fact, it is the first Nokia product whose telephone function is not its primary selling point.

An online community, N-Gage Arena, allows users to post scores and receive rankings. Currently, gaming one-on-one with an opponent in real-time is possible via Bluetooth, the short-range wireless radio standard in Europe. Eventually, two players will be able compete against each other, no matter whether they are in the same room or on different continents. This will be possible thanks to a radio technology for telecommunication devices that use GSM networks known as General Packet Radio Service (GPRS). At the time N-Gage was launched, real-time, "head-to-head" gaming was not possible over long distances because of "latency," or significant time lag. As Paul Jackson, an analyst at Forrester Research, noted, "If you take a shooting game, you are going to need to get lag times down sharply. Otherwise by the time you have fired your bullet, your rival is three rooms away." Nokia's plans called for launching a game that would allow real-time competition over GPRS networks sometime in 2004.

> "This is the first gaming device you will take everywhere. We are talking about global, mobile gaming."
>
> John Kuner, global manager
> Nokia N-Gage Arena operations

Nokia is targeting a different consumer than the 13-to-15 year old who typically plays games on Sony's popular Game Boy. As one industry analyst explained, "Nokia is going after the console gaming market, consumers in their late 20s." In the mid-1990s, Sony's PlayStation increased the age of the console game player from adolescents to people 16 to 24. Nokia wants to do a similar thing with the hand-held market." Nokia kept development costs low by basing N-Gage on an existing phone unit, the model 3650. However, the strategy resulted in a design peculiarity: To change game cards, users have to remove the back cover and take out the battery. A Nokia spokesman offered assurances that the issue could be addressed in the next-generation unit. Industry analysts were quick to point out that N-Gage would have a 12-to-18 month product cycle, compared to 3 or more years for typical game consoles. As Keith Westhead, a telecom equipment analyst for Deutsche Bank, explained, "The first-generation N-Gage establishes the brand. A new model will likely be announced in the spring, and then be formally launched at the 2004 E3 gaming show in Los Angeles in May 2004."

N-Gage carried a retail price of $299 (€299 in Europe) when it was launched in October 2003; by comparison, Nintendo's Gameboy Advance SP cost about $100. Game cards for popular titles such as Tony Hawk's Pro Skater were priced at about $40. Nokia's distribution strategy for N-Gage was focused on two retail channels. Phone shops that carried Nokia's regular lines were an obvious choice; such retailers typically discount the price of the unit if it is purchased in conjunction with a phone service contract. The second channel was game shops that do not normally sell phones. Nokia expected these retailers to offer a bundle including N-Gage with a selection of games at a reduced price. However, as a Nokia spokesperson noted, "We have some way to go in educating the game retailers."

## Discussion Questions

1. How does Nokia segment the market for cell phones?

2. What factors were paramount in Nokia's decision to enter the game-playing market?

3. Evaluate the appropriateness of Nokia's marketing program for the N-Gage in terms of the desired target market.

*Sources:* Robert Budden and Chris Brown-Humes, "Nokia Tries to Learn a New Game," *Financial Times* (February 5, 2004), p. 8; Brown-Humes, "Mobility Awaits Its Moment," *Financial Times — IT Review Mobile and Online Games* (December 10, 2003), p. 5; Budden, "Nokia Moves to Head Off an Asian Invasion," *Financial Times* (October 29, 2003), p. 11; Eric A. Taub, "A Game Player that Happens to Be a Phone," *The New York Times* (October 20, 2003), pp. C1, C5; Neil McCartney, "Squaring Up to Usability at Nokia," *Financial Times — IT Review Telecom World* (October 13, 2003), p. 4; Budden and Brown-Humes, "Nokia Dials into Business Market," *Financial Times* (September 9, 2003), p. 20; Pui-Wing Tam, "Gameboys for Grown-Ups," *The Wall Street Journal* (October 1, 2003), pp. D1, D5.

# Case 7-2

## Carmakers Target Gen Y

The world's automakers have Generation Y in their sights. Gen Y is the cohort of 71 million Americans born between 1977 and 1994. As their customer base ages, the automakers want to build brand loyalty among the nation's youth. For example, the average Toyota buyer is 47 years old; for Honda, the figure is 44 years old (see Table 1). Moreover, at home in Japan, the population is not only rapidly aging, it is expected to stop growing entirely by 2007. In a reversal of the orthodox notion in some parts of the world that "globalization = Americanization," young American car buyers are equating Japanese-designed cars with coolness. The trend began in California; the letters JDM ("Japanese Domestic Market") are shorthand for car accessories that, due to different regulations, are only available in Japan. Using the Internet, car buffs—many of whom favor the Honda Civic—ordered turbo chargers and other parts and customized their vehicles. The West coast "tuner" trend gained nationwide traction with the release of the movie *The Fast and the Furious* in 2002.

Honda is targeting Gen Y consumers with the Element, a compact SUV that features dramatic exterior styling, a dash-mounted shifter, and waterproof seat fabric. Launched in 2003, the Element is available in both 2-wheel and 4-wheel drive models. First-year sales exceeded the target of 50,000 units; half the people who bought Elements had never owned a Honda before.

Betting that Gen Y car buyers are ready to try something new, Toyota, Honda, and other companies are using a variety of product strategies. In spring 2003, Honda launched Element, a boxy sport utility vehicle that is manufactured in the United States. With a base price of $18,300, the vehicle is targeted at 24-year-old males. Toyota responded by launching the Scion xB miniwagon in the United States; the vehicle was already available in Japan, where it is known as a youthmobile.

*"Somehow the idea got propagated that young people like really weird automobiles and that'll attract young people because they wear their baseball caps backwards and trousers that look like they're about to slip off their butts. Well, they don't. If you go to university campuses in the U.S., I dare say that if you look at the parking lot you'll see a very heavy proportion of BMW 3-series. Now, they're not new 3-series . . . but the aspirational vehicle for them is the*

**Table 1**  *Average Buyer Age for Select Auto Brands*

| | Average Age of Buyer |
|---|---|
| Toyota | 47 |
| Chevrolet | 45 |
| Ford | 45 |
| Honda | 44 |
| Pontiac | 44 |
| Mitsubishi | 41 |
| Volkswagen | 41 |
| Toyota Scion | 39 |

BMW 3-series. *To sort of give them some goofy-looking contraption and say 'look, we designed this just for you,' that's the kiss of death. My answer is: sell them a three- or four-year-old used car. That's the way it's always been."*

Bob Lutz, vice chairman, General Motors

Other automakers are sizing up the potential and attractiveness of the Gen Y segment. Hyundai fields Hyundai Investigative Teams (HIT) in an effort to better understand the needs, wants, and preferences of young car buyers. For example, early in 2004, an HIT unit comprised of eight teens aged 16 to 18 visited the Chicago Motor Show. They spent a day looking at vehicles and provided feedback. Hyundai does not currently specifically target the youth market. However, the company is using HIT to assess the strength of competitors. After viewing the Scion xB, one female HIT member described it as, "A clown bus. I laughed when I saw it. *That's* what everyone thinks we'd like?" However, Japanese auto makers can be encouraged be HIT members' other responses. First, they prefer Japanese cars to American brands. Also, they are attracted by sporty styling and low prices—two traditional Japanese strengths.

## Discussion Questions

1. Why are Japanese automakers targeting Gen Y?
2. Do you think Honda and Toyota are using the right strategy to appeal to Gen Y?

*Sources:* Jeremy Grant, "Carmakers Try to Fathom the Teenage Taste," *Financial Times* (February 10, 2004), p. 10; Sholnn Freeman and Norihiko Shirouzu, "Toyota's Gen Y Gamble," *The Wall Street Journal* (July 30, 2003), p. B1; Norihiko Shirouzu and Todd Zaun, "Big Wheels: Japan Auto Makers Train Their Sights on the U.S. Again," *The Wall Street Journal* (January 3, 2003), pp. A1, A6. Jeremy Grant, "In the Driving Seat of a Car Giant: Bob Lutz," *Financial Times* (January 3-4, 2004), p. W3.

# 8 Importing, Exporting, and Sourcing

Furniture imports are flooding into the United States from China. Until recently, a Chinese-made wooden table might have suffered from obvious flaws such as a warped top or loose legs. Today, however, the situation is quite different: Chinese manufacturers are improving quality and offering designs that appeal to traditional American tastes in décor. The improvements have coincided with historically low mortgage rates in the United States; as a result, a record number of Americans are buying new homes or moving into bigger existing ones. To be sure, there are drawbacks to buying something made halfway around the world. For one thing, oceangoing container ships can encounter delays, and replacement parts can be hard to obtain if a piece breaks. In the case of leather furniture, low prices may be due in part to lower quality leather or a narrower range of color choices. However, China's low labor rates—a typical worker in a furniture factory earns monthly wages equivalent to about $100—translate into reasonable prices that are attractive to budget-conscious American furniture shoppers. For example, some leather sofas from China are priced below $1,000, hundreds less than pieces made in America or Europe. Likewise, an eight-piece dining room set sells for $2,500 to $3,500; a comparable American set would cost twice as much.

The success of China's furniture industry serves as a reminder of the impact exporting can have on a country's economy. It also demonstrates the difference between **export selling** and **export marketing**. Export selling does not involve tailoring the product, the price, or the promotional material to suit the requirements of global markets. The only marketing mix element that differs is the "place"; that is, the country where the product is sold. This selling approach may work for some products or services; for unique products with

Lecong, a city in Guangdong Province, can boast that it is the "furniture capital of the world": approximately 6,000 production facilities are located nearby in the Pearl River delta. The Chinese are adept at carving and other special woodworking skills, and monthly wages are as low as $100. In 2003, China's furniture exports to the United States totaled nearly $14 billion. In mid-2004, the U.S. government imposed antidumping duties on wooden bedroom furniture imports to provide some relief for American producers. Meanwhile, Ethan Allen Interiors, Furniture Brands International, Howard Miller Company, and other U.S manufacturers have little choice but to source at least some of their production in China.

little or no international competition, such an approach is possible. Similarly, companies new to exporting may initially experience success with selling. Even today, the managerial mind-set in many companies still favors export selling. However, as companies mature in the global marketplace or as new competitors enter the picture, export *marketing* becomes necessary.

Export marketing targets the customer in the context of the total market environment. The export marketer does not simply take the domestic product "as is" and sell it to international customers. To the export marketer, the product offered in the home market represents a starting point. It is modified as needed to meet the preferences of international target markets; this is the approach the Chinese have adopted in the U.S. furniture market. Similarly, the export marketer sets prices to fit the marketing strategy and does not merely extend home-country pricing to the target market. Charges incurred in export preparation, transportation, and financing must be taken into account in determining prices. Finally, the export marketer also adjusts strategies and plans for communications and distribution to fit the market. In other words, effective communication about product features or uses to buyers in export markets may require creating brochures with different copy, photographs, or artwork. As the vice president of sales and marketing of one manufacturer noted, "We have to approach the international market with *marketing* literature as opposed to *sales* literature."

Export marketing is the integrated marketing of goods and services that are destined for customers in international markets. Export marketing requires:

1. An understanding of the target market environment
2. The use of marketing research and identification of market potential
3. Decisions concerning product design, pricing, distribution and channels, advertising, and communications—the marketing mix

After the research effort has zeroed in on potential markets, there is no substitute for a personal visit to size up the market firsthand and begin the development of an actual export marketing program. A market visit should do several things. First, it should confirm (or contradict) assumptions regarding market potential. A second major purpose is to gather the additional data necessary to reach the final go/no-go decision regarding an export marketing program. Certain kinds of information simply cannot be obtained from secondary sources. For example, an export manager or international marketing manager may have a list of potential distributors provided by the U.S. Department of Commerce.

He or she may have corresponded with distributors on the list and formed some tentative idea of whether they meet the company's international criteria. It is difficult, however, to negotiate a suitable arrangement with international distributors without actually meeting face to face to allow each side of the contract to appraise the capabilities and character of the other party. A third reason for a visit to the export market is to develop a marketing plan in cooperation with the local agent or distributor. Agreement should be reached on necessary product modifications, pricing, advertising and promotion expenditures, and a distribution plan. If the plan calls for investment, agreement on the allocation of costs must also be reached.

One way to visit a potential market is through a **trade show** or a state- or federally-sponsored **trade mission.** Each year hundreds of trade fairs, usually organized around a product category or industry, are held in major markets. For example, Bauma 2001, a construction industry trade show held in Munich, Germany, attracted nearly 400,000 visitors from 43 countries. By attending trade shows and missions, company representatives can conduct market assessment, develop or expand markets, find distributors or agents, or locate potential end users. Perhaps most important, attending a trade show enables company representatives to learn a great deal about competitors' technology, pricing, and depth of market penetration. For example, exhibits often offer product literature with strategically useful technological information. Overall, company managers or sales personnel should be able to get a good general impression of competitors in the marketplace as they try to sell their own company's product.

## ORGANIZATIONAL EXPORT ACTIVITIES

Exporting is becoming increasingly important as companies in all parts of the world step up their efforts to supply and service markets outside their national boundaries.[1] Research has shown that exporting is essentially a developmental process that can be divided into the following distinct stages:

1. The firm is unwilling to export; it will not even fill an unsolicited export order. This may be due to perceived lack of time ("too busy to fill the order") or to apathy or ignorance.
2. The firm fills unsolicited export orders but does not pursue unsolicited orders. Such a firm is an export seller.
3. The firm explores the feasibility of exporting (this stage may bypass Stage 2).
4. The firm exports to one or more markets on a trial basis.
5. The firm is an experienced exporter to one or more markets.
6. After this success, the firm pursues country- or region-focused marketing based on certain criteria (e.g., all countries where English is spoken or all countries where it is not necessary to transport by water).
7. The firm evaluates global market potential before screening for the "best" target markets to include in its marketing strategy and plan. *All* markets—domestic and international—are regarded as equally worthy of consideration.

The probability that a firm will advance from one stage to the next depends on different factors. Moving from Stage 2 to Stage 3 depends on management's attitude toward the attractiveness of exporting and their confidence in the firm's ability to compete internationally. However, *commitment* is the most important aspect of a company's international orientation. Before a firm can

---

[1]    This section relies heavily on Warren J. Bilkey, "Attempted Integration of the Literature on the Export Behavior of Firms," *Journal of International Business Studies* 8, no. 1 (1978) pp. 33–46. The stages are based on Rogers' adoption process. See Everett M. Rogers, *Diffusion of Innovations* (New York: Free Press, 1995).

| LOGISTICS | SERVICING EXPORTS | **Table 8-1** |
|---|---|---|
| Arranging transportation | Providing parts availability | *Potential Export Problems* |
| Transport rate determination | Providing repair service | |
| Handling documentation | Providing technical advice | |
| Obtaining financial information | Providing warehousing | |
| Distribution coordination | **SALES PROMOTION** | |
| Packaging | Advertising | |
| Obtaining insurance | Sales effort | |
| **LEGAL PROCEDURE** | Marketing information | |
| Government red tape | **FOREIGN MARKET INTELLIGENCE** | |
| Product liability | Locating markets | |
| Licensing | Trade restrictions | |
| Customs/duty | Competition overseas | |
| Contract | | |
| Agent/distributor agreements | | |

reach Stage 4, it must receive and respond to unsolicited export orders. The quality and dynamism of management are important factors that can lead to such orders. Success in Stage 4 can lead a firm to Stages 5 and 6. A company that reaches Stage 7 is a mature, geocentric enterprise that is relating global resources to global opportunity. To reach this stage requires management with vision and commitment.

One recent study noted that export procedural expertise and sufficient corporate resources are required for successful exporting. An interesting finding was that even the most experienced exporters express lack of confidence in their knowledge about shipping arrangements, payment procedures, and regulations. The study also showed that, although profitability is an important expected benefit of exporting, other advantages include increased flexibility and resiliency and improved ability to deal with sales fluctuations in the home market. Although research generally supports the proposition that the probability of being an exporter increases with firm size, it is less clear that export intensity—the ratio of export sales to total sales—is positively correlated with firm size. Table 8-1 lists some of the export-related problems that a company typically faces.[2]

## NATIONAL POLICIES GOVERNING EXPORTS AND IMPORTS

It is hard to overstate the impact of exporting and importing on the world's national economies. In 1997, for example, total imports of goods and services by the United States passed the $1 trillion mark for the first time; in 2003, the combined figure was $1.5 trillion. China's pace-setting economic growth in the Asia-Pacific region is reflected by trends in both exports and imports. Since 1979, exports from China have grown significantly; they will grow at a faster rate now that China has joined the WTO. As shown in Table 8-2, more than $6.5 billion worth of Chinese textiles and apparel were exported to the United States in 2000. Historically, China protected its own producers by imposing double-digit import tariffs. These will gradually be reduced as China complies with WTO regulations. Needless to say, representatives of the furniture, textile, and apparel industries in the United States are deeply concerned about the

[2]  Masaaki Kotabe and Michael R. Czinkota, "State Government Promotion of Manufacturing Exports: A Gap Analysis," *Journal of International Business Studies* 23, no. 4 (Fourth Quarter 1992), pp. 637–658.

**Table 8-2**

Top 15 Apparel and Textile
Exporting Countries to the United
States, 2000 ($ billions)

| | |
|---|---|
| Mexico | $9.70 |
| China | 6.52 |
| Hong Kong | 4.71 |
| Canada | 3.30 |
| South Korea | 3.01 |
| Taiwan | 2.75 |
| India | 2.74 |
| Dominican Republic | 2.45 |
| Thailand | 2.44 |
| Indonesia | 2.38 |
| Honduras | 2.32 |
| Bangladesh | 2.20 |
| Philippines | 2.20 |
| Italy | 2.10 |
| Pakistan | 1.83 |

Source: U.S. Department of Commerce.

impact increased trade with China will have on the sector. As this example suggests, national policies toward exports and imports can be summarized in one word: contradictory. For centuries, nations have combined two opposing policy attitudes toward the movement of goods across national boundaries. On the one hand, nations directly encourage exports; the flow of imports, on the other hand, is generally restricted.

## Government Programs that Support Exports

To see the tremendous results that can come from a government-encouraged export strategy, consider Japan, Singapore, South Korea and the so-called greater-China or "China triangle" market, which includes Taiwan, Hong Kong, and the People's Republic of China. Japan totally recovered from the destruction of World War II and became an economic superpower as a direct result of export strategies devised by the Ministry for International Trade and Industry (MITI). The four tigers—Singapore, South Korea, Taiwan, and Hong Kong—learned from the Japanese experience and built strong export-based economies of their own. Although Asia's "economic bubble" burst in 1997 as a result of uncontrolled growth, Japan and the tigers are moving forward in the twenty-first century at a more moderate rate. China, an economy unto itself, has attracted increased foreign investment from DaimlerChrysler, Hewlett-Packard, GM, and other companies that are setting up production facilities to support local sales, as well as exports to world markets.

Any government concerned with trade deficits or economic development should focus on educating firms about the potential gains from exporting. This is true at the national, regional, and local government levels. Governments commonly use three activities to support export activities of national firms. First, *tax incentives* treat earnings from export activities preferentially either by applying a lower rate to earnings from these activities or by refunding taxes already paid on income associated with exporting. The tax benefits offered by export-conscious governments include varying degrees of tax exemption or tax deferral on export income, accelerated depreciation of export-related assets, and generous tax treatment of overseas market development activities. Naturally, in many cases, the actual treatment of export-related income is even more favorable than tax statutes would imply. East Asian, Latin American, and European trading nations have been particularly generous in providing these kinds of special aids to exporting companies.

From 1985 until 2000, the major tax incentive under U.S. law was the **foreign sales corporation** (FSC), through which American exporters could obtain a

15 percent exclusion on earnings from international sales. Big exporters benefited the most from the arrangement; Boeing, for example, saved about $100 million per year, and Eastman Kodak saved about $40 million annually. However, in 2000, the World Trade Organization ruled that any tax break that was contingent on exports amounted to an illegal subsidy. Accordingly, the U.S. Congress has set about the task of overhauling the FSC system; failure to do so would entitle the EU to impose up to $4 billion in retaliatory tariffs. So far, congressional efforts have been hampered by the fact that potential winners and losers from a change in the FSC law are lobbying furiously. One proposed version of a new law would benefit General Motors, Procter & Gamble, Wal-Mart, and other U.S. companies with extensive factories or retail operations overseas. By contrast, Boeing would no longer benefit. As Rudy de Leon, a Boeing executive in charge of government affairs, noted, "As we look at the bill, the export of U.S. commercial aircraft would become considerably more expensive."[3]

Governments also support export performance by providing outright **subsidies,** which are direct or indirect financial contributions that benefit producers. Subsidies can severely distort trade patterns when less competitive but subsidized producers displace competitive producers in world markets (see Case 8-2). OECD members spend nearly $400 billion annually on farm subsidies; currently, total annual farm support in the European Union is estimated at $100 billion. With about $40 billion in annual support, the United States has the highest subsidies of any single nation. Agricultural subsidies are particularly controversial because, although they protect the interests of farmers in developed countries, they work to the detriment of farmers in developing areas such as Africa. The EU has undertaken an overhaul of its **Common Agricultural Policy (CAP),** a system of guaranteed prices that dates back to the end of World War II. In some instances, CAP pays farmers not to grow crops. Critics have called "as egregious a system of protection as any" and "the single most harmful piece of protectionism in the world."[4] In May 2002, much to Europe's dismay, President George W. Bush signed a $118 billion farm bill that actually *increased* subsidies to American farmers over a 6-year period. The Bush administration takes the position that, despite the increases, overall U.S. subsidies are still lower than those in Europe and Japan.

The third support area is *governmental assistance* to exporters. Companies can avail themselves of a great deal of government information concerning the location of markets and credit risks. Assistance may also be oriented toward export promotion. Government agencies at various levels often take the lead in setting up trade fairs and trade missions designed to promote sales to foreign customers.

## Governmental Actions to Discourage Imports and Block Market Access

Measures such as tariffs, import controls, and a host of nontariff barriers are designed to limit the inward flow of goods. **Tariffs** can be thought of as the "three R's" of global business: rules, rate schedules (duties), and regulations of individual countries. **Duties** on individual products or services are listed in the schedule of rates (see Table 8-3 on p. 271). As defined by one expert on global trade, **duties** are "taxes that punish individuals for making choices of which their governments disapprove."[5]

---

[3] Edmund L. Andrews, "A Civil War Within a Trade Dispute," *The New York Times* (September 20, 2002), pp. C1, C2.

[4] John Micklethwait and Adrian Wooldridge, *A Future Perfect: The Challenge and Hidden Promise of Globalization* (New York: Crown Publishers, 2000), p. 261.

[5] Edward L. Hudgins, "Mercosur Gets a 'Not Guilty' on Trade Diversion," *The Wall Street Journal* (March 21, 1997), p. A19.

# the rest of the story

## Furniture Exports from China

The furniture industry has become one of the fastest-growing sectors of China's economy. China currently accounts for about 10 percent of global furniture exports, and some industry experts believe exports could increase 30 percent annually through the end of the decade. However, such forecasts are subject to unexpected changes in the business environment. Once such change was the Asian SARS crisis. New furniture orders fell precipitously as foreign buyers stayed away from Chinese factories and fewer Chinese traveled abroad. At the retail level, many American furniture stores began stocking pieces from non-Asian sources. Some American furniture shoppers were reluctant to buy Chinese-made goods for fear that the disease could somehow be transmitted to humans via inanimate objects. As Lynn Chipperfield, senior vice president at Furniture Brands International, the biggest furniture importer in the United States, noted, "Importing is a constant challenge even under normal circumstances. This doesn't help."

Although the SARS crisis quickly passed, China's export success has caught the attention of American manufacturers and policymakers. American furniture companies, many of which are located in North Carolina and Virginia, have been laying off employees and closing plants. A recent study by an economist at the University of California–Santa Cruz found 500,000 U.S. furniture workers lost their jobs between 1979 and 1999; 38 percent were unable to find new jobs. In response, a coalition group called the American Furniture Manufacturers Committee for Legal Trade, has petitioned U.S. trade officials. The group is asking investigators to examine whether Chinese furniture prices violate U.S. antidumping statutes.

Sources: Dan Morse and Katy McLaughlin, "China's Latest Export: Your Living Room," The Wall Street Journal (January 17, 2003), p. D1; Karby Leggett and Peter Wonacott, "The World's Economy: Surge in Exports from China Jolts Global Industry," The Wall Street Journal (October 10, 2002), pp. A1, A8; Jon E. Hilsenrath and Peter Wonacott, "Imports Hammer Furniture Makers," The Wall Street Journal (September 20, 2002), p. A2.

Developed under the auspices of the Customs Cooperation Council (now the World Customs Organization), the **Harmonized Tariff System** (HTS) went into effect in January 1989 and has since been adopted by the majority of trading nations. Under this system, importers and exporters have to determine the correct classification number for a given product or service that will cross borders. With the Harmonized Tariff Schedule B, the export classification number for any exported item is the same as the import classification number. Also, exporters must include the Harmonized Tariff Schedule B number on their export documents to facilitate customs clearance. Accuracy, especially in the eyes of customs officials, is essential. The U.S. Census Bureau compiles trade statistics from the HTS system. In its quest for a more precise picture of U.S. trade flows, the U.S. Census Bureau is cracking down on exporters whose documentation is incorrect. Even so, any HTS with a value of less than $2,500 is not counted as a U.S. export. However, *all* imports, regardless of value, are counted.

As noted in earlier chapters, a major U.S. objective in the Uruguay round of GATT negotiations was to improve market access for U.S. companies with major U.S. trading partners. When the round ended in December 1993, the United States had secured reductions or total elimination of tariffs on 11 categories of U.S. goods exported to the EU, Japan, five of the EFTA nations (Austria, Switzerland, Sweden, Finland, and Norway), New Zealand, South Korea, Hong Kong, and Singapore. The categories affected included equipment for the construction, agricultural, medical, and scientific industry sectors, as well as steel, beer, brown distilled spirits, pharmaceuticals, paper, pulp and printed matter, furniture, and toys. Most of the remaining tariffs were phased out over a 5-year period. A key goal of the Doha round of trade talks is the reduction in agricultural tariffs, which currently average 12 percent in the United States, 31 percent in the European Union, and 51 percent in Japan.

In spite of the progress made in simplifying tariff procedures, administering a tariff is an enormous problem. People who work with imports and exports must familiarize themselves with the different classifications and use them accurately. Even a tariff schedule of several thousand items cannot clearly describe every product traded globally. The introduction of new products and new materials used in manufacturing processes creates new problems. Often, determining the duty rate on a particular article requires assessing how the item is used or determining its main component material. Two or more alternative classifications may have to be considered. A product's classification can make a substantial difference in the duty applied. For example, is a Chinese-made X-Men action figure a doll or a toy? For many years, dolls were subject to a 12 percent duty when imported into the United States; the rate was 6.8 percent for toys. Moreover, action figures that represent non-human creatures such as monsters or robots were categorized as toys and thus qualified for lower duties than human figures that the Customs Service classifies as dolls. Duties on both categories have been eliminated; however, the Toy Biz subsidiary of Marvel Enterprises spent nearly 6 years on an action in the U.S. Court of International Trade to prove that its X-Men action figures do not represent humans. Although the move appalled many fans of the mutant super heroes, Toy Biz hoped to be reimbursed for overpayment of past duties made when the U.S. Customs Service had classified imports of Wolverine and his fellow figures as dolls.[6]

A **nontariff trade barrier (NTB)** is any measure other than a tariff that is a deterrent or obstacle to the sale of products in a foreign market. Also known as *hidden trade barriers*, NTBs include quotas, discriminatory procurement policies, restrictive customs procedures, arbitrary monetary policies, and restrictive regulations. A **quota** is a government-imposed limit or restriction on the number of units or the total value of a particular product or product category that can be imported. The trade distortion caused by a quota is even more severe than that due to tariffs because once the quota has been reached, market price mechanisms are not allowed to operate. The phrase *state trade controls* refers to the practice of monopolizing trade in certain commodities. The Swedish government, for example, controls the import of all alcoholic beverages and tobacco products, and the French government controls all imports of coal.

The United States has more than 8,000 different tariff classifications, half of which are restricted by quotas and other control mechanisms. For example, there are machine tool agreements with Japan and Taiwan, 20 steel trade agreements, textile quotas for most Southeast Asian and developing countries, the U.S.-Japan Semiconductor Agreement, and Japanese "voluntary" restraints on the export of cars and TVs to the United States. The United States and the EU have a combined total of 250 quotas on imports of Chinese textiles.[7] The extent of these and other similar agreements on a worldwide basis has led some critics to argue that the United States engages in "managed" trade rather than free trade.

A recent case involving Ukraine and the United States shows how politics and export-import issues are often intertwined. The United States is encouraging Ukraine's transition to a market economy and provides foreign aid totaling hundreds of millions of dollars each year. Yet, after Ukrainian imports of women's coats grew dramatically in the early 1990s, the Clinton administration imposed an import quota in November 1994. The stylish, well-made coats retailed in the United States at prices ranging from $89 to $139. (By 1994, only the Dominican Republic and Guatemala surpassed Ukraine in unit imports of wool coats to the United States; the Latin American countries are exempt from quotas under the Caribbean Basin Initiative.) The popularity of the Ukrainian goods provoked accusations of unfair trade from the American woolen industry and, in particular, from the coat-making industry that is

[6] Neil King Jr., "Is Wolverine Human? A Judge Answers No; Fans Howl in Protest," *The Wall Street Journal* (January 20, 2003), p. A1.

[7] Joseph Kahn, "Dragon Flies: China Swiftly Becomes an Exporting Colossus, Straining Western Ties," *The Wall Street Journal* (November 13, 1995), p. A6.

# OPEN *to* discussion

## Why Doesn't the United States Export More?

Many nations export up to 20 percent of their total production; the United States exports only about 10 percent. Businesses in smaller industrialized countries easily exhaust the potential of their home market and are forced to search internationally for expansion opportunities. Meanwhile, their U.S. counterparts appear to have fallen victim to one or more barriers to successful exporting. First, the limited ambition of many American business managers may result in complacency and a lack of export consciousness. A second barrier is lack of knowledge of market opportunities abroad or misperceptions about those markets. The perceived lack of necessary resources—managerial skill, time, financing, and productive capacity—are often cited as reasons for not pursuing export opportunities. Unrealistic fears are a fourth type of barrier to exporting. When weighing export expansion opportunities, managers may express concerns about operating difficulties, environmental differences, credit or other types of risks, and possible strains upon the company. A fifth type of barrier is management inertia, the simple inability of company personnel to overcome export myopia.

U.S. exports have historically been dominated by the large companies of the *Fortune* 500. By contrast, in Germany, small businesses are the export powerhouses. Studies have shown that, in the United States, it is smaller-sized businesses rather than the *Fortune* 500 that are the major source of new jobs. Until recently, relatively few of these smaller companies were involved with exports. Dun & Bradstreet tracks U.S. exports in 70 industries; its figures now show that the majority of companies exporting employ less than 100 people. The U.S. Department of Commerce found that after participating in trade missions in 1987, 3,000 companies (most of which were small) generated $200 million in new export business—yet, the U.S. Small Business Administration estimates that there are tens of thousands of small companies that could export but do not. For many of these firms, exporting represents a major untapped market opportunity. To address this issue, in October 2001 the U.S. Commercial Service launched BuyUSA.com, a Web site that helps companies set up e-commerce operations to serve customers outside the United States.

A quick survey of the suggested readings on the Web at www.prenhall.com/keegan highlights the fact that export activities at small and medium-sized enterprises (SMEs) is a popular research topic. For example, one recent study of 114 companies in California questioned the potential of standardized promotional messages in mass-produced government pamphlets to motivate managers at SME to investigate exporting. The researcher found that company personnel were more likely to be persuaded by arguments that stated exporting's benefits in microeconomic terms. Another recent study examined companies with previous export experience; the researchers examined the relationship between management's intention to continue exporting and the extent to which management valued the learning gained from export activities. The researchers determined that, in addition to meeting financial criteria, management at companies with export experience welcomed the opportunity to acquire new knowledge and new skills and to broaden organizational capabilities.

*Sources: Tahi J. Gnepa, "Persuading Small Manufacturing Companies to Become Active Exporters: The Effect of Message Framing and Focus on Behavioral Intentions," Journal of Global Marketing 14, no. 4 (2001), pp. 49–66, William J. Burpitt and Dennis A. Rondinelli, "Small Firms' Motivations for Exporting: To Earn and Learn?" Journal of Small Business Management 38, no. 4 (October 2000), pp. 1–14.*

---

centered in Maine. Wool coat imports were already subject to a 21.5 percent tariff. The quota, which was supported by Senator George Mitchell of Maine and the U.S. Commerce Department, limited Ukrainian imports in 1995 to one million coats, approximately the level of 1994 imports. Ukrainian producers had expected 1995 orders to double compared with 1994.[8]

**Discriminatory procurement policies** can take the form of government rules and administrative regulations specifying that local vendors or suppliers receive priority consideration. For example, the Buy American Act of 1933 stipulates that U.S. federal agencies must buy articles produced in the United States unless domestically produced goods are not available, the cost is unreasonable, or purchasing U.S. materials would be inconsistent with the public interest. Similarly, the Fly American Act stipulates that employees of the U.S. government must fly on domestic airlines whenever possible. Formal or informal company policies can also discriminate against foreign suppliers. In the automotive industry, the relatively low level of Japanese imports of U.S.-made auto parts is a contentious issue that centers on procurement policies.

**Customs procedures** are considered restrictive if they are administered in a way that makes compliance difficult and expensive. For example, the U.S. Department of Commerce might classify a product under a certain harmonized

---

[8] Jane Perlez, "In Ukraine, a Free-Market Lesson Learned Too Well," *The New York Times* (January 1, 1995), sec. 3, p. 5. See also James Dean, "Ukraine: Europe's Forgotten Economy," *Challenge* 43, no. 6 (November/December 2000), pp. 93–108.

number; Canadian customs may disagree. The U.S. exporter may have to attend a hearing with Canadian customs officials to reach an agreement. Such delays cost time and money for both the importer and exporter.

**Discriminatory exchange rate policies** distort trade in much the same way as selective import duties and export subsidies. A country may require importers to place on deposit—at no interest—an amount equal to the value of imported goods. Such an action constitutes an **arbitrary monetary policy** that, in effect, raises the price of foreign goods by the cost of money for the term of the required deposit.

Finally, **restrictive administrative and technical regulations** can create barriers to trade. These may take the form of antidumping regulations, size regulations, and safety and health regulations. Some of these regulations are intended to keep out foreign goods; others are directed toward legitimate domestic objectives. For example, the safety and pollution regulations being developed in the United States for automobiles are motivated almost entirely by legitimate concerns about highway safety and pollution. However, an effect of these regulations has been to make it so expensive to comply with U.S. safety requirements that some automakers have withdrawn certain models from the market. Volkswagen, for example, was forced to stop selling diesel automobiles in the United States for several years.

Despite a GATT agreement concerning technical barriers to trade, Japan used technical standards unrelated to performance to bar U.S. forest products from its market. In May 1989, these restrictive technical regulations became part of the basis for listing Japan as guilty of unfair trade practices under Section 301 of the 1988 Trade Act.

As discussed in earlier chapters, there is a growing trend to remove all such restrictive trade barriers on a regional basis. The largest single effort was undertaken by the European Union in an effort to create a single market starting January 1, 1993. The intent is to have one standard for all of Europe for such things as automobile safety, drug testing and certification, and food and product quality controls, as well as the development of a single currency, the euro, to facilitate trade and commerce. Some observers believe that elimination of these intra-European barriers will result in the creation of a so-called Fortress Europe with new external barriers designed to keep out the foreign (e.g., Japanese) competition.

# TARIFF SYSTEMS

Tariff systems provide either a single rate of duty for each item applicable to all countries or two or more rates, applicable to different countries or groups of countries. Tariffs are usually grouped into two classifications.

The **single-column tariff** is the simplest type of tariff; a schedule of duties in which the rate applies to imports from all countries on the same basis. Under the **two-column tariff** (see Table 8-3), column 1 includes "general" duties plus "special"

| Column 1 | | Column 2 |
|---|---|---|
| **General** | **Special** | **Non-NTR** |
| 1.5% | Free (A, E, IL, J, MX)<br>0.4% (CA) | 30% |

A, Generalized System of Preferences
E, Caribbean Basin Initiative (CBI) Preference
IL, Israel Free Trade Agreement (FTA) Preference
J, Andean Agreement Preference
CA, NAFTA Canada Preference
MX, NAFTA Mexico Preference

**Table 8-3**

*Sample Rates of Duty for U.S. Imports*

# GLOBAL *marketing in action*

## A Day in the Life of an Export Coordinator

Beth Dorrell is an export coordinator with a multimillion dollar company that manufactures writing and marking inks. From its headquarters in Southern California, the company exports ink to more than 30 countries. Beth is responsible for all exports from the main manufacturing plant in Tennessee. Beth's background includes a BA degree in international management and French from a small liberal arts college in the Midwest.

During the summer after her sophomore year, Beth traveled in Europe and studied a number of corporations including Swarski Crystal, Club Med, and Moet Chandon. During the fall of her junior year, Beth attended a 10-week Import & Export Seminar led by a representative of the state economic development commission. Beth is convinced that the seminar gave her the upper hand during her job search. "In interviews, I was able to confidently answer questions about documentary credits and Incoterms. I have utilized and expanded upon that knowledge on a daily basis in my job," says Beth. "We have hundreds of different customers, each with different shipping terms and different payment terms. It is essential that I know the difference, and know the document requirements of each."

Beth's workday begins early. Because the company has offices on the West coast, manufacturing facilities on the East coast, and customers throughout the world, time zones are always an issue. Beth arrives at work early to take late night phone calls from Europe and Asia; she also must deal with any problems on the East coast that need to be solved that day. She also checks correspondence received overnight via fax and e-mail. This may consist of new order inquiries, requests for cost quotes or product availability, changes to existing orders, or payment advice from Poland, China, Taiwan, or Pakistan.

"Because the majority of our international customers are in Asia, I usually have the full work day to compose responses and/or proforma invoices for those customers. The exceptions are our customers in Mexico, Venezuela, and Argentina and other Latin American countries. I try to structure my day so that I can reply to those inquiries early in the day thereby providing same day service to those customers," Beth explains.

On any given day, a freight forwarder may call and inform Beth that freight did not arrive at the port in time to meet an expected ocean booking. Beth must then track down the shipment through the trucking company, establish a new booking, ensure that the freight is delivered, advise the customer of the delay, and if necessary, arrange to air freight a portion of the freight. "One of the worst things that can happen," notes Beth, "is that a customer's plant has to stop production because we were late in delivering product. With so much of the world operating on just-in-time systems, one little slip can backlog multiple companies. If one of our suppliers is delayed in providing a raw material, then we are delayed in providing ink, our customer is delayed in providing pens, and *their* retail customer is delayed in putting product on the shelf. No one wants to put a Christmas product on the shelf in January, or a Back To School product on the shelf in October."

Another important part of Beth's job involves documents and banks. Company policy requires that orders over a certain established dollar amount move under a letter of credit (L/C). Before the shipment can leave the factory, Beth must ensure that the letter of credit has been received, that the details of the L/C are accurate, and that the company is capable of satisfying the date and document requirements of the L/C. She must then check that every single detail of the L/C is abided by. Beth provides all the documents demanded of the company (invoice, packing lists, certificates of quality, etc.) under the L/C and double checks all of the documents that must be provided by other sources (bills of lading, certificates of insurance) and sends them all to the advising bank in the United States. Beth says, "I love the way L/Cs work—how they enable companies around the world to contract large business deals with little to no risk for either party. But I'll take a DP (documents against payment) over an L/C any day! The work involved in processing an L/C properly is extensive. It requires incredible attention to detail, and sometimes even that isn't enough. Every once in a while you simply cannot determine how the document examiner will interpret some phrasing."

Beth concludes, "Global marketing is amazing. A commodity raw material from Africa can be refined in Asia, then shipped to South America to be incorporated into a component of a final product that is produced in the Middle East and then sold around the world. The things we all use every day are truly products of the world."

duties indicating reduced rates determined by tariff negotiations with other countries. Rates agreed upon by "convention" are extended to all countries that qualify for **normal trade relations** (NTR; formerly most-favored nation or MFN) status within the framework of the WTO. Under the WTO, nations agree to apply their most favorable tariff or lowest tariff rate to all nations—subject to some exceptions—that are signatories to the WTO. Column 2 shows rates for countries that do not enjoy NTR status.

Table 8-4 shows a detailed entry from Chapter 89 of the harmonized system pertaining to "Ships, Boats, and Floating Structures" (for explanatory purposes, each column has been identified with an alphabet letter). Column A contains the heading level numbers that uniquely identify each product. For example, the product entry for heading level 8903 is "yachts and other vessels for pleasure or sports; row boats and canoes." Subheading level 8903.10 identifies "inflatable";

**Table 8-4**

Chapter 89 of the Harmonized System

| A | B | C | D | E | F | G |
|---|---|---|---|---|---|---|
| 8903 | | Yachts and other vessels for pleasure or sports; row boats and canoes | | | | |
| 8903.10 | | Inflatable | | 2.4% | Free (A,E,IL,J,MX) 0.4% (CA) | |
| | | Valued over $500 | | | | |
| | 15 | With attached rigid hull ...................... | No | | | |
| | 45 | Other ................................................ | No | | | |
| | 60 | Other ................................................ | No | | | |
| | | Other: | | 1.5% | Free (A,E,IL,J,MX) 0.3% (CA) | |
| 8903.91 | | Sailboats, with or without auxiliary motor | | | | |

A, Generalized System of Preferences
E, Caribbean Basin Initiative (CBI) Preference
IL, Israel Free Trade Agreement (FTA) Preference
J, Andean Agreement Preference
CA, NAFTA Canada Preference
MX, NAFTA Mexico Preference

8903.91 designates "sailboats with or without auxiliary motor." These six-digit numbers are used by more than 100 countries that have signed on to the harmonized system. Entries can extend to as many as 10 digits, with the last four used on a country-specific basis for each nation's individual tariff and data collection purposes. Taken together, E and F correspond to Column 1 as shown in Table 8-3, while G corresponds to Column 2.

The United States has given NTR status to some 180 countries around the world, so the name is really a misnomer. Only North Korea, Iran, Cuba, and Libya are excluded, showing that NTR is really a political tool more than an economic one. In the past, China had been threatened with the loss of NTR status because of alleged human rights violations. The landed prices of its products would have risen significantly, which would have priced many Chinese products out of the U.S. market. The U.S. Congress recently granted China permanent NTR as a precursor to its joining the WTO. Table 8-5 illustrates what a loss of NTR status would have meant to China.

A **preferential tariff** is a reduced tariff rate applied to imports from certain countries. GATT prohibits the use of preferential tariffs, with three major exceptions. First are historical preference arrangements such as the British Commonwealth preferences and similar arrangements that existed before GATT. Second, preference schemes that are part of a formal economic integration treaty, such as free trade areas or common markets, are excluded. Third, industrial countries are permitted to grant preferential market access to companies based in less-developed countries.

The United States is now a signatory to the GATT customs valuation code. U.S. customs value law was amended in 1980 to conform to the GATT

| | NTR (%) | Non-NTR (%) |
|---|---|---|
| Gold jewelry, such as plated neckchains | 6.5 | 80 |
| Screws, lock washers, misc. iron/steel parts | 5.8 | 35 |
| Steel products | 0–5 | 66 |
| Rubber footwear | 0 | 66 |
| Women's overcoats | 19 | 35 |

Source: U.S. Customs Service.

**Table 8-5**

Tariff Rates for China, NTR Versus Non-NTR

valuation standards. Under the code, the primary basis of customs valuation is "transaction value." As the name implies, **transaction value** is defined as the actual individual transaction price paid by the buyer to the seller of the goods being valued. In instances where the buyer and seller are related parties (e.g., when Honda's U.S. manufacturing subsidiaries purchase parts from Japan), customs authorities have the right to scrutinize the transfer price to make sure it is a fair reflection of market value. If there is no established transaction value for the good, alternative methods that are used to compute the customs value sometimes result in increased values and, consequently, increased duties. In the late 1980s, the U.S. Treasury Department began a major investigation into the transfer prices charged by the Japanese automakers to their U.S. subsidiaries. It charged that the Japanese paid virtually no U.S. income taxes because of their "losses" on the millions of cars they import into the United States each year.

During the Uruguay round of GATT negotiations, the United States successfully sought a number of amendments to the Agreement on Customs Valuations. Most important, the United States wanted clarification of the rights and obligations of importing and exporting countries in cases where fraud was suspected. Two overall categories of products were frequently targeted for investigation. The first included exports of textiles, cosmetics, and consumer durables; the second included entertainment software such as videotapes, audiotapes, and compact disks. Such amendments improve the ability of U.S. exporters to defend their interests if charged with fraudulent practices. The amendments were also designed to encourage nonsignatories, especially developing countries, to become parties to the agreement.

## Customs Duties

Customs duties are divided into two categories. They may be calculated either as a percentage of the value of the goods (ad valorem duty), as a specific amount per unit (specific duty), or as a combination of both of these methods. Before World War II, specific duties were widely used and the tariffs of many countries, particularly those in Europe and Latin America, were extremely complex. Since the war, the trend has been toward the conversion to ad valorem duties; that is, duties expressed as a certain percentage of the value of the goods.

An **ad valorem duty** is expressed as a percentage of the value of goods. The definition of customs value varies from country to country. An exporter is well advised to secure information about the valuation practices applied to his or her product in the country of destination. The reason is simple: to be price competitive with local competitiors. In countries adhering to GATT conventions on customs valuation, the customs value is landed cost, insurance, and freight (CIF) amount at the port of importation. This cost should reflect the arm's-length price of the goods at the time the duty becomes payable.

A **specific duty** is expressed as a specific amount of currency per unit of weight, volume, length, or other units of measurement; for example, "50 cents U.S. per pound," "$1.00 U.S. per pair," or "25 cents U.S. per square yard." Specific duties are usually expressed in the currency of the importing country, but there are exceptions, particularly in countries that have experienced sustained inflation.

Both ad valorem and specific duties are occasionally set out in the custom tariff for a given product. Normally, the applicable rate is the one that yields the higher amount of duty, although there are cases where the lower is specified. These duties provide for specific, plus ad valorem, rates to be levied on the same articles. Compound or mixed duties provide for specific, plus ad valorem, rates to be levied on the same articles.

# Other Duties and Import Charges

**Dumping,** which is the sale of merchandise in export markets at unfair prices, is discussed in detail in Chapter 11. To offset the impact of dumping and to penalize guilty companies, most countries have introduced legislation providing for the imposition of **antidumping duties** if injury is caused to domestic producers. Such duties take the form of special additional import charges equal to the dumping margin. Antidumping duties are almost invariably applied to products that are also manufactured or grown in the importing country. In the United States, antidumping duties are assessed after the commerce department finds a foreign company guilty of dumping and the International Trade Commission rules that the dumped products injured American companies.

**Countervailing duties (CVDs)** are additional duties levied to offset subsidies granted in the exporting country. In the United States, countervailing duty legislation and procedures are very similar to those pertaining to dumping. The U.S. Commerce Department and the International Trade Commission jointly administer both the countervailing duty and antidumping laws under provisions of the Trade and Tariff Act of 1984. Subsidies and countervailing measures received a great deal of attention during the Uruguay GATT negotiations. In 2001, the ITC and commerce department imposed both countervailing and antidumping duties on Canadian lumber producers. The CVDs were intended to offset subsidies to Canadian sawmills in the form of low fees for cutting trees in forests owned by the Canadian government. The antidumping duties on imports of softwood lumber, flooring, and siding were in response to complaints by American producers that the Canadians were exporting lumber at prices below their production cost.

Several countries, including Sweden and some other members of the EU, apply a system of **variable import levies** to certain categories of imported agricultural products. If prices of imported products would undercut those of domestic products, the effect of these levies would be to raise the price of imported products to the domestic price level. **Temporary surcharges** have been introduced from time to time by certain countries, such as the United Kingdom and the United States, to provide additional protection for local industry and, in particular, in response to balance-of-payments deficits.

# KEY EXPORT PARTICIPANTS

Anyone with responsibilities for exporting should be familiar with some of the people and organizations who can assist with various tasks. Some of these, including purchasing agents, export brokers, and export merchants, have no assignment of responsibility from the client. Others, including export management companies, manufacturers' export representatives, export distributors, and freight forwarders, are assigned responsibilities by the exporter.

**Foreign purchasing agents** are variously referred to as *buyer for export, export commission house,* or *export confirming house.* They operate on behalf of, and are remunerated by, an overseas customer. They generally seek out the U.S. manufacturer whose price and quality match the demands of their overseas principal.

Foreign purchasing agents often represent governments, utilities, railroads, and other large users of materials abroad. Foreign purchasing agents do not offer the manufacturer stable volume except when long-term supply contracts are agreed upon. Purchases may be completed as domestic transactions with the purchasing agent handling all export packing and shipping details, or the agent may rely on the manufacturer to handle the shipping arrangements.

The **export broker** receives a fee for bringing together the seller and the overseas buyer. The fee is usually paid by the seller, but sometimes the buyer pays it. The broker takes no title to the goods and assumes no financial responsibility. A broker usually specializes in a specific commodity, such as grain or cotton, and is less frequently involved in the export of manufactured goods.

**Export merchants** are sometimes referred to as *jobbers*. They seek out needs in foreign markets and make purchases in world markets to fill these needs. Export merchants often handle staple, openly traded products, for which brand names or manufacturers' identifications are not important. **Export management company (EMC)** is the term used to designate an independent export firm that acts as the export department for more than one manufacturer. The EMC usually operates in the name of a manufacturer-client for export markets, but it may operate in its own name. It may act as an independent distributor, purchasing and reselling goods at an established price or profit margin, or as a commission representative, taking no title and bearing no financial risks in the sale. Combination export management firms often refer to themselves as **manufacturer's export representatives** whether they act as export distributors or as export commission representatives. An **export distributor** assumes financial risk. The firm usually has the exclusive right to sell a manufacturer's products in all or some markets outside the country of origin. The distributor pays for the goods and assumes all financial risks associated with the foreign sale. The firm ordinarily sells at manufacturer's list price abroad, receiving an agreed percentage of list price as remuneration. The distributor may operate in its own name or in the manufacturer's. It handles all shipping details. The export distributor usually represents several manufacturers and hence is a combination export manager.

The **export commission representative** assumes no financial risk and is sometimes termed an *agent*, although this term is generally avoided because of the legal connotations. The commission representative is assigned all or some foreign markets by the manufacturer. The manufacturer carries all accounts, although the representative often provides credit checks and arranges financing. The representative may operate in his or her own name or in the manufacturer's. Generally, the export commission representative handles several accounts and hence is a combination export management company. The **cooperative exporter**, sometimes called a *mother hen, piggyback exporter*, or *export vendor*, is an export organization of a manufacturing company retained by other independent manufacturers to sell their products in some or all foreign markets. Cooperative exporters usually operate as export distributors for other manufacturers, but in special cases they operate as export commission representatives. They are regarded as a form of export management company.

**Freight forwarders** are licensed specialists in traffic operations, customs clearance, and shipping tariffs and schedules; simply put, they can be thought of as travel agents for freight. They seek out the best routing and the best prices for transporting freight and assist exporters in determining and paying fees and insurance charges. Forwarders may also do export packing, when necessary. They usually handle freight from port of export to overseas port of import. They may also move inland freight from factory to port of export and, through affiliates abroad, handle freight from port of import to customer. Freight forwarders also perform consolidation services for land, air, and ocean freight. Because they contract for large blocks of space on a ship or airplane, they can resell that space to various shippers at a rate lower than is generally available to individual shippers dealing directly with the export carrier.

A licensed forwarder receives brokerage or rebates from shipping companies for booked space. Some companies and manufacturers engage in freight forwarding or some phase of it on their own, but they may not, under law, receive brokerage from shipping lines.

*U.S. customs agents on the job in Texas. Beginning exporters can utilize the services of freight forwarders, export management companies, and other firms that specialize in moving goods across borders.*

# ORGANIZING FOR EXPORTING IN THE MANUFACTURER'S COUNTRY

Home-country issues involve deciding whether to assign export responsibility inside the company or to work with an external organization specializing in a product or geographic area. Most companies handle export operations within their own in-house export organization. Depending on the company's size, responsibilities may be incorporated into an employee's domestic job description. Alternatively, these responsibilities may be handled as part of a separate division or organizational structure.

The possible arrangements for handling exports include the following:

1. As a part-time activity performed by domestic employees
2. Through an export partner affiliated with the domestic marketing structure that takes possession of the goods before they leave the country
3. Through an export department that is independent of the domestic marketing structure
4. Through an export department within an international division
5. For multidivisional companies, each of the foregoing possibilities exists within each division

A company that assigns a sufficiently high priority to its export business will establish an in-house organization. It then faces the question of how to organize effectively. This depends on two things: the company's appraisal of the opportunities in export marketing and its strategy for allocating resources to markets on a global basis. It may be possible for a company to make export responsibility part of a domestic employee's job description. The advantage of this arrangement is obvious: It is a low-cost arrangement requiring no additional personnel. However, this approach can work under only two conditions: First, the domestic employee assigned to the task must be thoroughly competent in terms of product and customer knowledge; second, that competence must be applicable to the target international market(s). The key issue underlying the second condition is the extent to which the target export market is different from the domestic market. If customer circumstances and characteristics are similar, the requirements for specialized regional knowledge are reduced.

The company that chooses not to perform its own marketing and promotion in-house has numerous external export service providers from which to choose. As described previously, these include export trading companies (ETCs), export management companies (EMCs), export merchants, export brokers, combination export managers, manufacturers' export representatives or commission agents, and export distributors. However, because these terms and labels may be used inconsistently, the reader is urged to check and confirm the services performed by a particular independent export organization.

A typical export management company acts as the export department for several unrelated companies that lack export experience. EMCs perform a variety of services, including marketing research, channel selection, arrangement of financing and shipping, and documentation. According to one recent survey of U.S.-based EMCs, the most important activities for export success are marketing information gathering, communication with markets, setting prices, and ensuring parts availability. The same survey ranked export activities in terms of degree of difficulty; analyzing political risk, sales force management, setting pricing, and obtaining financial information were deemed most difficult to accomplish. One of the study's conclusions was that the U.S. government should do a better job of helping EMCs and their clients analyze the political risk associated with foreign markets.[9]

## ORGANIZING FOR EXPORTING IN THE MARKET COUNTRY

In addition to deciding whether to rely on in-house or external export specialists in the home country, a company must also make arrangements to distribute the product in the target market country. Every exporting organization faces one basic decision: To what extent do we rely on direct market representation as opposed to representation by independent intermediaries?

There are two major advantages to *direct representation* in a market: control and communications. Direct market representation allows decisions concerning program development, resource allocation, or price changes to be implemented unilaterally. Moreover, when a product is not yet established in a market, special efforts are necessary to achieve sales. The advantage of direct representation is that these special efforts are ensured by the marketer's investment. With indirect or independent representation, such efforts and investment are often not forthcoming; in many cases, there is simply not enough incentive for independents to invest significant time and money in representing a product. The other great advantage to direct representation is that the possibilities for feedback and information from the market are much greater. This information can vastly improve export marketing decisions concerning product, price, communications, and distribution.

Direct representation does not mean that the exporter is selling directly to the consumer or customer. In most cases, direct representation involves selling to wholesalers or retailers. For example, the major automobile exporters in Germany and Japan rely upon direct representation in the U.S. market in the form of their distributing agencies, which are owned and controlled by the manufacturing organization. The distributing agencies sell products to franchised dealers.

In smaller markets, it is usually not feasible to establish direct representation because the low sales volume does not justify the cost. Even in larger markets,

---

9  Donald G. Howard, "The Role of Export Management Companies in Global Marketing," *Journal of Global Marketing* 8, no. 1 (1994), pp. 95–110.

a small manufacturer usually lacks adequate sales volume to justify the cost of direct representation. Whenever sales volume is small, use of an independent distributor is an effective method of sales distribution. Finding "good" distributors can be the key to export success.

# EXPORT FINANCING AND METHODS OF PAYMENT

The appropriate method of payment for a given international sale is a basic credit decision. A number of factors must be considered, including currency availability in the buyer's country, creditworthiness of the buyer, and the seller's relationship to the buyer. Finance managers at companies that have never exported often express concern regarding payment. Many CFOs with international experience know that there are generally fewer collections problems on international sales than on domestic sales, provided the proper financial instruments are used. The reason is simple: A letter of credit can be used to guarantee payment for a product.

The export sale begins when the exporter/seller and the importer/buyer agree to do business. The agreement is formalized when the terms of the deal are set down in a pro forma invoice contract, fax, or some other document. Among other things, the **pro forma invoice** spells out how much, and by what means, the exporter-seller wants to be paid.

## Documentary Credit

Documentary credits (also known as letters of credit or L/Cs) are widely used as a payment method in international trade. A **letter of credit** is essentially a document stating that a bank has substituted its creditworthiness for that of the importer/buyer. Next to cash in advance, an L/C offers the exporter the best assurance of being paid. That assurance arises from the fact that the payment obligation under an L/C lies with the buyer's bank and not with the buyer. The international standard by which L/Cs are interpreted is ICC Publication No. 500 of the Uniform Customs and Practice for Documentary Credits, also known as UCP 500.

The importer-buyer's bank is the "issuing" bank; the importer-buyer is, in essence, asking the issuing bank to extend credit. The importer-buyer is thus considered the applicant. The issuing bank may require that the importer/buyer deposit funds in the bank or use some other method to secure a line of credit. After agreeing to extend the credit, the issuing bank requests that the exporter-seller's bank advise and/or confirm the L/C. (A bank "confirms" an L/C by adding its name to the document.) The seller's bank becomes the "advising" and/or "confirming" bank. Whether it is advised or confirmed, the L/C represents a guarantee that assures payment contingent on the exporter-seller's (the beneficiary in the transaction) complying with the terms set forth in the L/C.

The actual payment process is set in motion when the exporter/seller physically ships the goods and submits the necessary documents as requested in the L/C. These could include a transportation bill of lading (which may represent title to the product), a commercial invoice, a packing list, a certificate of origin, or insurance certificates. For most of the world, a commercial invoice and bill of lading represent the minimum documentation required for customs clearance. If the pro forma invoice specifies a confirmed L/C as the method of payment, the exporter-seller receives payment at the time the correct shipping documents are presented to the confirming bank. The confirming bank, in turn, requests payment from the issuing bank. In the case of an irrevocable L/C, the exporter-seller receives payment only after the advising bank negotiates the documents and requests payment from the issuing bank in accordance with terms set forth in the L/C. Once the shipper sends the documents to the advising bank, the advising bank negotiates those documents and is referred to as the negotiating bank. Specifically, it takes each shipping document and closely compares it to the L/C. If there are no discrepancies, the negotiating or confirming bank transfers the money to the exporter/seller's account.

The fee for an irrevocable L/C—for example, "1/8 of 1 percent of the value of the credit, with an $80 minimum"—is lower than that for a confirmed L/C. The higher bank fees associated with confirmation can drive up the final cost of the sale; fees are also higher when the transaction involves a country with a high level of risk. Good communication between the exporter/seller and the advising or confirming bank regarding fees is important; the selling price indicated on the pro forma invoice should reflect these and other costs associated with exporting. The process described here is illustrated in Figures 8-1 and 8-2.

## Documentary Collections (Sight or Time Drafts)

After an exporter and an importer have established a good working relationship and the finance manager's level of confidence increases, it may be possible to move to a documentary collection or open-account method of payment. A **documentary collection** is a method of payment that uses a bill of exchange, also known as a *draft*. A **bill of exchange** is a negotiable instrument that is easily transferable from one party to another. In its simplest form, it is a written order from one party (the *drawer*) directing a second party (the *drawee*) to pay to the order of a third party (the *payee*). Drafts are distinctly different from L/Cs; a **draft** is a payment instrument that transfers all the risk of nonpayment onto the exporter/seller. Banks are involved as intermediaries but they do not bear financial risk. Because a draft is negotiable, however, a bank may be willing to buy the draft from the seller at a discount and thus assume the risk. Also, because bank fees for drafts are lower than those for L/Cs, drafts are frequently used when the monetary value of an export transaction is relatively low.

With a documentary draft, the exporter delivers documents such as the bill of lading, the commercial invoice, a certificate of origin, and an insurance certificate

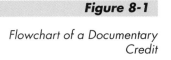

**Figure 8-1**

*Flowchart of a Documentary Credit*

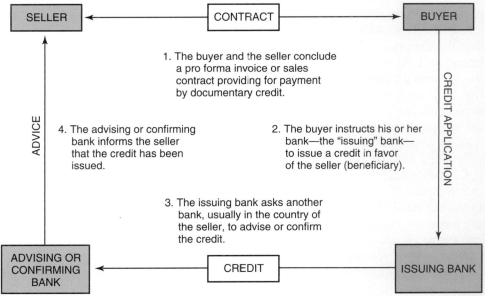

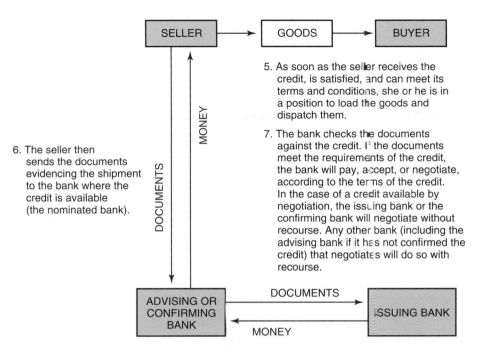

**Figure 8-2**

Flowchart of Documentary Credit Documents

5. As soon as the seller receives the credit, is satisfied, and can meet its terms and conditions, she or he is in a position to load the goods and dispatch them.

6. The seller then sends the documents evidencing the shipment to the bank where the credit is available (the nominated bank).

7. The bank checks the documents against the credit. If the documents meet the requirements of the credit, the bank will pay, accept, or negotiate, according to the terms of the credit. In the case of a credit available by negotiation, the issuing bank or the confirming bank will negotiate without recourse. Any other bank (including the advising bank if it has not confirmed the credit) that negotiates will do so with recourse.

8. The bank, if other than the issuing bank, sends the documents to the issuing bank.

9. The issuing bank checks the documents and, if they meet the credit requirements, either (a) effects payment in accordance with the terms of the credit, either to the seller if the documents were sent directly to the issuing bank, to the bank that has made funds available to the issuing bank, or to the bank that has made funds available to the seller in anticipation, or (b) reimburses in the preagreed manner the confirming bank or any bank that has paid, accepted, or negotiated under the credit.

to a bank in the exporter's country. The shipper or bank prepares a collection letter (draft) and sends it via courier to a correspondent bank in the importer/buyer's country. The draft is presented to the importer; payment takes place in accordance with the terms specified in the draft. In the case of a *sight draft* (also known as a D/P or *documents against payment*), the importer-buyer is required in principle to make payment when presented with both the draft and the shipping documents, even though the buyer may not have taken possession of the goods yet. *Time drafts* can take two forms. As the name implies, an *arrival draft* specifies that payment is due when the importer/buyer receives the goods; a *date draft* requires payment on a particular date, irrespective of whether the importer has the goods in hand.

## Cash in Advance

A number of conditions may prompt the exporter to request cash payment—in whole or in part—in advance of shipment. Examples include times when credit risks abroad are high, when exchange restrictions within the country of destination may delay return of funds for an unreasonable period, or when, for any other reason, the exporter may be unwilling to sell on credit terms. Because of competition and restrictions against cash payment in many countries, the volume of business handled on a cash-in-advance basis is small. Cash in advance can also be used by a company that manufactures a unique product for which there are no substitutes available. For example, Compressor Control Corporation is a midwestern firm that manufactures special equipment for the oil industry. It can stipulate cash in advance because no other company offers a competing product.

## Sales on Open Account

Goods that are sold on open account are paid for after delivery. Intracorporate sales to branches or subsidiaries of an exporter are frequently on open-account terms. Open-account terms also generally prevail in areas where exchange controls are minimal and exporters have had long-standing relations with good buyers in nearby or long-established markets. For example, Jimmy Fand is the owner of the Tile Connection in Tampa, Florida. He imports high-quality ceramic tile from Italy, Spain, Portugal, Colombia, Brazil, and other countries. Fand takes pride in the excellent credit rating that he has built up with his vendors. The manufacturers from whom he buys no longer require an L/C; Fand's philosophy is "pay in time," and he makes sure that his payables are sent electronically on the day they are due.

The main objection to open-account sales is the absence of a tangible obligation. Normally, if a time draft is drawn and then dishonored after acceptance, it can be used as a basis of legal action. By contrast, if an open-account transaction is dishonored, the legal procedure may be more complicated. Starting in 1995, the Export-Import Bank expanded insurance coverage on open-account transactions to limit the risk for exporters.

## Sales on a Consignment Basis

A **free trade zone (FTZ)** is a geographic entity that may include a manufacturing facility and a warehouse. Goods sold on consignment are delivered by the exporter-consignor to the importer-consignee who then sells them. As in the case of sales on open account, no tangible obligation is created by consignment sales. In countries with free ports or free trade zones, consigned merchandise can be placed under bonded warehouse control in the name of a foreign bank. Sales can then be arranged by the selling agent and arrangements made to release partial lots out of the consigned stock against regular payment terms. The merchandise is not cleared through customs until after the sale has been completed. The import duty is not paid until the goods come out of the FTZ and are cleared through customs.

## SOURCING

In global marketing, the issue of customer value is inextricably tied to the **sourcing decision:** whether a company makes or buys the products it markets as well as where it makes or buys them. **Outsourcing** means shifting production jobs or work assignments to another company to cut costs. When the outsourced work moves to another country, the terms **global outsourcing** or **offshoring** are sometimes used. In today's competitive marketplace, companies are under intense pressure to lower costs; one way to do this is to locate manufacturing and other activities in China, India, and other low-wage countries. And why not? Many consumers do not know where the products they buy—sneakers, for example—are manufactured. It is also true that, as the quiz in Chapter 1 indicated, people often can't match corporate and brand names with particular countries. In theory, this situation bestows great flexibility on companies. However, in the United States, the sourcing issue became highly politicized during the 2004 presidential campaign. Several Democratic candidates tapped into Americans' fears and concerns over a "jobless" economic recovery. The first wave of nonmanufacturing outsourcing primarily affected **call centers.** These are sophisticated telephone operations that provide customer support and other services to in-bound callers from around the world. Call centers also perform outbound services such as telemarketing. Now, however, outsourcing is expanding and includes white collar, high-tech service sector jobs. Workers in low wage countries are performing a variety of tasks, including completing tax returns, performing

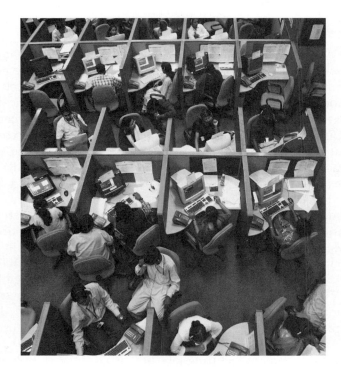

In Bangalore, India and other locations, call centers such as this one specialize in "long-distance" or "arm's length" services. India's well-educated workforce and the growing availability of broadband Internet connections mean that more Western service jobs and industries are subject to global outsourcing. Among the tasks being outsourced to India are medical record transcription, tax return preparation, and technical writing. In fact, the book you are reading was typeset in Jawahar Nagar, Pondicherry, India.

research for financial services companies, reading medical CAT scans and X-rays, and drawing up architectural blueprints. American companies that transfer work abroad are finding themselves in the spotlight.

As this discussion suggests, the decision of where to locate key business activities depends on other factors besides cost. There are no simple rules to guide sourcing decisions. Indeed, the sourcing decision is one of the most complex and important decisions faced by a global company. Several factors may figure in the sourcing decision: management vision, factor costs and conditions, customer needs, public opinion, logistics, country infrastructure, political factors, and exchange rates.

## Management Vision

Some chief executives are determined to retain some or all manufacturing in their home country. Nicolas Hayek, head of the Swatch Group, is one such executive. Hayek presided over the spectacular revitalization of the Swiss watch industry. The Swatch Group's portfolio of brands includes Blancpain, Omega, Breguet, Rado, and, of course the inexpensive Swatch brand itself. Hayek demonstrated that the fantasy and imagination of childhood and youth can be translated into breakthroughs that allow mass-market products to be manufactured in high-wage countries side-by-side with handcrafted luxury products. The Swatch story is a triumph of engineering, as well as a triumph of the imagination. Similarly, top management at Canon has chosen to maintain a strategic focus on high value-added products rather than manufacturing location. The company aims to keep 60 percent of its manufacturing at home in Japan. The company offers a full line of office equipment, including popular products such printers and copiers; it is also one of the top producers of digital cameras. Instead of increasing the level of automation in its Japanese factories, it has converted from assembly lines to so-called cell production.[10]

---

[10] Sebastian Moffett, "Canon Manufacturing Strategy Pays Off with Strong Earnings," *The Wall Street Journal* (January 4, 2004), p. B3.

# Factor Costs and Conditions

Factor costs are land, labor, and capital costs (remember Economics 101!). Labor includes the cost of workers at every level: manufacturing and production, professional and technical, and management. Basic manufacturing direct labor costs today range from less than $1 per hour in the typical emerging country to $6 to $12 per hour in the typical developed country. In certain industries in the United States, direct labor costs in manufacturing exceed $20 per hour without benefits. German hourly compensation costs for production workers in manufacturing are 160 percent of those in the United States while those in Mexico are only 15 percent of those in the United States. For Volkswagen, the wage differential between Mexico and Germany, combined with the strength of the mark and, most recently, the euro, dictate a Mexican manufacturing facility that builds Golf and Jetta models destined for the United States. The company's new Touareg SUV is assembled in Bratislava, Slovakia. Do lower wage rates demand that a company relocate 100 percent of its manufacturing to low-wage countries? Not necessarily. During his tenure as chairman at VW, Ferdinand Piech improved his company's competitiveness by convincing unions to accept flexible work schedules. For example, during peak demand, employees work 6-day weeks; when demand slows, factories produce cars only 3 days per week.

Labor costs in nonmanufacturing jobs are also dramatically lower in some parts of the world. For example, a software engineer in India may receive an annual salary of $12,000; by contrast, an American with the same educational credentials might earn $80,000. The other factors of production are land, materials, and capital. The cost of these factors depends upon their availability and relative abundance. Often, the differences in factor costs will offset each other so that, on balance, companies have a level field in the competitive arena. For example, some countries have abundant land and Japan has abundant capital. These advantages partially offset each other. When this is the case, the critical factor is management, professional, and worker team effectiveness.

The application of advanced computer controls and other new manufacturing technologies has reduced the proportion of labor relative to capital for many businesses. In formulating a sourcing strategy, company managers and executives should also recognize the declining importance of direct manufacturing labor as a percentage of total product cost. It is certainly true that, for many companies in high-wage countries, the availability of cheap labor is a prime consideration when choosing manufacturing locations; this is why China has become "the world's workplace." However, it is also true that direct labor cost may be a relatively small percentage of the total production cost. As a result, it may not be worthwhile to incur the costs and risks of establishing a manufacturing activity in a distant location. For example, Greg Petsch, senior vice president of manufacturing at Compaq, had to decide whether to close plants in Houston and Scotland and contract out assembly work to East Asia. After determining that the human labor content in a PC is only about 15 minutes, he opted to run Compaq's existing Houston factory 24 hours a day. Another decision was whether to source motherboards from a vendor in Asia. Petsch calculated that Compaq could produce the boards—which account for 40 percent of the cost of a PC—for $25 less than suppliers in East Asia. Manufacturing in Houston also saved 2 weeks in shipping time, which translated into inventory savings.[11]

---

[11] Doron P. Levin, "Compaq Storms the PC Heights from Its Factory Floor," *The New York Times* (November 4, 1994), sec. 3, p. 5.

## Customer Needs

Although outsourcing can help reduce costs, sometimes customers are seeking something besides the lowest possible price. Dell Computer recently rerouted some of its call center jobs back to the United States after complaints from key business customers that Indian tech support workers were offering scripted responses and having difficulty solving complex problems. In such instances, the need to keep customers satisfied justifies the higher cost of home-country support operations.

## Logistics

In general, the greater the distance between the product source and the target market, the greater the time delay for delivery and the higher the transportation cost. However, innovation and new transportation technologies are cutting both time and dollar costs. To facilitate global delivery, transportation companies such as CSX Corporation are forming alliances and becoming an important part of industry value systems. Manufacturers can take advantage of intermodal services that allow containers to be transferred between rail, boat, air, and truck carriers. In Europe, Latin America, and elsewhere, the trend toward regional economic integration means fewer border controls, which greatly speeds up delivery times and lowers costs.

Despite these overall trends, a number of specific issues pertaining to logistics can affect the sourcing decision. For example, in the wake of the 2001 terror attacks, importers are required to send electronic lists to the U.S. government prior to shipping. The goal is to help the U.S. Customs Service identify high-risk cargo that could be linked to the global terror network. In fall 2002, a 10-day strike on the West Coast shut down 29 docks and cost the United States economy an estimated $20 billion. Such incidents can delay shipments by weeks or even months.

*"Supply Chain 101 says the most important thing is continuity of supply. When you establish a supply line that is 12,000 miles long, you have to weigh the costs of additional inventory and logistics costs versus what you can save in terms of lower costs per unit or labor costs."*

Norbert Ore, Institute for Supply Management[12]

## Country Infrastructure

In order to present an attractive setting for a manufacturing operation, it is important that the country's infrastructure be sufficiently developed to support a manufacturing operation. The required infrastructure will vary from company to company, but minimally, it will include power, transportation and roads, communications, service and component suppliers, a labor pool, civil order, and effective governance. In addition, a country must offer reliable access to foreign exchange for the purchase of necessary material and components from abroad as well as a physically secure setting where work can be done and product can be shipped to customers.

A country may have cheap labor, but does it have the necessary supporting services or infrastructure to support a manufacturing activity? Many countries offer these conditions, including Hong Kong, Taiwan, and Singapore. There are many other countries that do not, such as Lebanon, Uganda, and El Salvador. One of the challenges of doing business in the new Russian market is an infrastructure that is woefully inadequate to handle the increased volume of shipments. The Mexican government, anticipating much heavier trade volume because of NAFTA, has committed billions of dollars for infrastructure improvements.

---

[12] Barbara Hagenbaugh, "Moving Work Abroad Tough for Some Firms," *USA Today* (December 3, 2003), p. 2B.

## Political Factors

As discussed in Chapter 5, political risk is a deterrent to investment in local sourcing. Conversely, the lower the level of political risk, the less likely it is that an investor will avoid a country or market. The difficulty of assessing political risk is inversely proportional to a country's stage of economic development: All other things being equal, the less developed a country, the more difficult it is to predict political risk. The political risk of the Triad countries, for example, is quite limited as compared to that of a less developed country in Africa, Latin America, or Asia. The recent rapid changes in Central and Eastern Europe and the dissolution of the Soviet Union have clearly demonstrated the risks *and* opportunities resulting from political upheavals.

Other political factors may influence the sourcing decision. For example, with protectionist sentiment on the rise, for example, the U.S. Senate recently passed an amendment that would prohibit the U.S. Treasury and Department of Transportation from accepting bids from private companies that use offshore workers. In a highly publicized move, the state of New Jersey changed a call center contract that had shifted jobs offshore. About one dozen jobs were brought back instate—at a cost of about $900,000.

Market access is another type of political factor. If a country or a region limits market access because of local content laws, balance-of-payments problems, or any other reason, it may be necessary to establish a production facility within the country itself. The Japanese automobile companies invested in U.S. plant capacity because of concerns about market access. By producing cars in the United States, they have a source of supply that is not exposed to the threat of tariff or import quotas. Market access figured heavily in Boeing's decision to produce airplane components in China. China ordered 100 airplanes valued at $4.5 billion; in return, Boeing is making investments and transferring engineering and manufacturing expertise.[13]

## Foreign Exchange Rates

In deciding where to source a product or locate a manufacturing activity, a manager must take into account foreign exchange rate trends in various parts of the world. Exchange rates are so volatile today that many companies pursue global sourcing strategies as a way of limiting exchange-related risk. At any point in time, what has been an attractive location for production may become much less attractive due to exchange rate fluctuation. For example, *endaka* is the Japanese term for a strong yen. In 2003, the exchange rate went from ¥122/$1 to ¥107/$1. For every one yen increase relative to the American dollar, Canon's operating income declines six billion yen! As noted earlier, Canon's management is counting on R&D investment to ensure that its products deliver superior margins that offset **endaka.**

The dramatic shifts in price levels of commodities and currencies are a major characteristic of the world economy today. Such volatility argues for a sourcing strategy that provides alternative country options for supplying markets. Thus, if the dollar, the yen, or the mark becomes seriously overvalued, a company with production capacity in other locations can achieve competitive advantage by shifting production among different sites.

---

[13] Jeff Cole, Marcus W. Brauchli, and Craig S. Smith, "Orient Express: Boeing Flies into Flap over Technology Shift in Dealings with China," *The Wall Street Journal* (October 13, 1995), pp. A1, A11. See also Joseph Kahn, "Clipped Wings: McDonnell Douglas's High Hopes for China Never Really Soared," *The Wall Street Journal* (May 22, 1996), pp. A1, A10.

summary

A company's first business dealings outside the home country often take the form of **exporting** or **importing.** Such companies should recognize the difference between **export marketing** and **export selling.** By attending **trade shows** and participating in **trade missions,** company personnel can learn a great deal about new markets. Governments use a variety of programs to support exports, including tax incentives, subsidies, and export assistance. Governments also discourage imports with a combination of **tariffs** and **nontariff barriers.** The latter include **quotas** and **discriminatory procurement policies.**

The **Harmonized Tariff System** has been adopted by most countries that are actively involved in export-import trade. **Two-column tariffs** include special rates such as those available to countries with **most favored nation status.** Customs duties can take the form of **ad valorem** or **specific duties.** Governments can also impose special types of duties. These include **antidumping duties** imposed on products whose prices government officials deem too low and **countervailing duties** to offset government subsidies.

Key participants in the export-import process include **foreign purchasing agents, export brokers, export merchants, export management companies, manufacturers' export representatives,** and **export distributors.**

A number of export-import payment methods are available. A transaction begins with the issue of a **pro forma invoice** or some other formal document. A basic payment instrument is the **letter of credit** that assures payment from the buyer's bank. Sales may also be made using a **bill of exchange, cash in advance, sales on open account,** or a **consignment** agreement.

Exporting and importing is directly related to a company's **sourcing strategy.** A number of factors determine whether a company makes or buys its products as well as *where* it makes or buys. A paramount consideration is **factor costs;** other issues include customer needs **logistics, country infrastructure, political risk,** ease of **market access,** and **foreign exchange rates.** However, concern is mounting in the United States and Europe about job losses linked to **outsourcing.**

discussion questions

1. What is the difference between export marketing and export selling?

2. Why is exporting from the United States dominated by large companies? What, if anything, could be done to increase exports from smaller companies?

3. Describe the stages a company typically goes through as it learns about exporting.

4. Governments often pursue policies that promote exports while limiting imports. What are some of those policies?

5. What are the various types of duties that export marketers should be aware of?

6. What is the difference between a letter of credit and other forms of export-import financing? Why do sellers often require letters of credit in international transactions?

7. What criteria should company management consider when making sourcing decisions?

web resources

The U.S. Department of Commerce provides export support through its Market Access and Compliance Web site. Visit MAC Online at:
**www.mac.doc.gov**

The U.S. federal government provides information on the HTS at:
**www.usitc.gov/taffairs.htm**

The database maintained by the U.S. International Trade Commission can be accessed at:
**dataweb.usitc.gov**

# Case 8-1

## Concerns About Factory Safety and Worker Exploitation in Developing Countries

In April 1997, President Bill Clinton announced the creation of a code of conduct aimed at combating sweatshops on a worldwide basis. Representatives from Phillips-Van Heusen (PVH), Nike, Reebok, Liz Claiborne, and six other manufacturers had served on a task force that spent 8 months studying the sweatshop issue. The code established a minimum age of 14 for apparel workers and a maximum work week of 60 hours. Companies were required to pay the prevailing minimum wage in the country where the factory was located. Michael Posner, executive director of the Lawyers Committee for Human Rights, hailed the code as a breakthrough agreement. "It establishes a framework that provides consumers with confidence that companies are making good-faith efforts to address sweatshop practices," he said. Despite such optimism, the manufacturers and human rights advocates that were task force members disagreed on several issues. One concern was countries in which the official minimum wage was not a true "living wage" sufficient to support a family. Another issue was monitoring labor practices; the manufacturers wanted the right to select accounting firms, while activists and labor groups wanted nonprofit groups to perform the task of monitoring.

### Background to the Code of Conduct

In August 1995, federal agents raided a garment-manufacturing facility near Los Angeles. The agents discovered 60 people, all from Thailand, who worked as many as 22 hours per day for $1.60 an hour to repay expenses for travel to the United States. The U.S. Labor Department charged the six Thai nationals believed to be running the sweatshop operation with harboring illegal immigrants and smuggling immigrants. The labor department also alleged that May Department Stores, Sears, and other retailers were selling goods that originated in the Los Angeles factory. Under the Fair Labor Standards Act, the labor department was authorized to hold the various apparel manufacturers that bought goods from the sweatshop legally liable for $5 million in worker back pay.

A year later, the sweatshop issue stayed in the news thanks to Kathie Lee Gifford, who was best known to television viewers as the host of a popular talk show and as a celebrity endorser who appeared in ads for Carnival Cruise Lines and Ultra Slim-Fast. Many Wal-Mart shoppers also associated Kathie Lee's name with a line of moderately priced apparel. Some items in the Kathie Lee clothing line were produced under contract in factories in Honduras and other developing countries. Labor rights activist Charles Kernaghan charged that working conditions in many of those factories fit the definition of "sweatshop": long hours, low wages, and abusive supervisors. Moreover, many employees in the factories were alleged to be minors. Kernaghan accused Kathie Lee and other endorsers of profiting from worker exploitation.

### Sweatshops in the Spotlight

The sweatshop bust in Los Angeles and the revelations surrounding Kathy Lee Gifford finally focused the public's

attention on an issue that had been gathering momentum for years. Catastrophic industrial fires in several countries have resulted in extensive loss of life. In Dongguan, China, 80 workers died in a fire at a raincoat factory in 1991. In 1993, 84 people were killed in a handicrafts factory fire in the Chinese city of Shenzhen. The most deadly industrial fire in history broke out on May 10, 1993, in a four-story toy factory near Bangkok, Thailand. Nearly 200 workers—most of whom were women and teenage girls—died in the blaze. The factory was owned by Kader Industrial Toy Company, which supplies toys to well-known U.S. companies such as Fisher-Price, Toys 'R' Us, and Hasbro. One reason so many perished is that several emergency exit doors were locked.

Government support is just one reason that companies can rely on far-flung manufacturing; 900 million, about 15 percent, of the world's six billion people are unemployed. Thus, governments in many countries encourage foreign investment that will create jobs. Moreover, manufacturing companies account for nearly three-fourths of the dollar value of world trade. Improved communications technology allows company headquarters to closely monitor operations throughout the world. As John Cavanagh, a fellow at Washington's Institute for Policy Studies, explains, "Companies can coordinate production in plants scattered all over the world on a real-time, minute-to-minute basis."

Not surprisingly, many U.S. companies are scouring the globe for low-cost sources of labor. As wages have increased in South Korea, Taiwan, and Singapore, offshore assembly and manufacturing has moved to developing countries such as Indonesia, Thailand, India, Mexico, and China. For example, almost half of all the toys sold in the United States are produced in Asia; in 1992, Chinese factories turned out $3.3 billion worth of toys for the United States. The minimum wage in China is about 80 cents per day.

Disturbed by the trend, many U.S. observers had long characterized factories in developing countries as sweatshops where "semi-slave labor" was forced to work in inhumane, unsafe working conditions for extremely low wages. These critics suggest that profit-hungry American executives often turn a blind eye to working conditions outside the United States. For their part, executives and industry spokespersons point out that, in many cases, U.S. companies do not own the factories where goods are made. Labor movement representatives in the United States, concerned that U.S. companies are unwilling to support improved working conditions abroad, have even attempted to align with labor movements in developing countries.

Despite the terrible tragedies in Thailand and China, not everyone in the United States agrees with the view that workers in developing countries are being exploited. Although wages in some countries may seem low by U.S. standards, they are relatively high by Asian standards. Compared to an agriculture-based subsistence standard of living, these wages represent both an improvement and an important step forward in terms of economic development. As advocates of global production point out, wages in Japan, Taiwan, and South Korea were low in the years after World War II, but increased as those countries' economies developed. The first

step toward a developed economy involved sweatshops. As economist Paul Krugman noted recently, "The overwhelming mainstream view among economists is that the growth of this kind of employment is tremendous good news for the world's poor." Krugman has adopted a pragmatic viewpoint on the child labor issue. Noting that some impoverished parents sell their children to syndicates who force them to work as beggars, Krugman says, "If that is the alternative, it is not so easy to say that children should not be working in factories."

Still, some experts predict that business executives are starting to realize that it is simply good business to be concerned with factory conditions. Notes Professor Elliot Schrage of Columbia University, "Many companies are being forced to examine their labor practices around the world by consumer pressure or fear of consumer backlash." Indeed, the U.S. government hoped that publicizing the names of retailers who bought from the Los Angeles manufacturers would encourage retailers to improve their social responsibility policies.

## Nike and the Sneaker Controversy

The truth in Schrage's observation has been amply illustrated in the athletic shoe industry. Nike, Reebok, and other sneaker marketers source virtually 100 percent of their shoes in Asia, where contractors are responsible for the production of the shoes. For example, 80 million pairs of Nikes are manufactured each year in dozens of factories outside the United States. During the 1980s, most of Nike's manufacturing was located in South Korea and Taiwan. As workers there gained the right to organize and strike, wage rates increased. Nike responded by shifting production to China, Malaysia, Indonesia, and Thailand and leaving 20 closed factories in its wake. In Indonesia, where 50 factories make shoes for Nike, the nonunion workforce is made up mostly of young women paid wages starting at about $1.35 a day. In all, an estimated 300,000 young Asian women are employed by Nike subcontractors.

Nike's practice of following cheap labor around the globe made it the target of criticism from the ranks of workers and scholars alike. For example, Solidarity magazine, published by the United Auto Workers, once urged union members to send their "dirty, smelly, worn-out" running shoes to Nike as a way of protesting overseas production. John Cavanagh and others have written numerous articles criticizing Nike for profiting at the expense of low-wage workers. Cavanagh has pointed out that, although 2.5 million people enter the Indonesian job market each year, employment options are so limited that most people can only find work making athletic shoes. Low wages permit only subsistence living in shanties without electricity or plumbing and also result in malnutrition. Nike pays superstar Michael Jordan $20 million annually in endorsement fees, an amount that has been estimated to exceed the total annual wages for Indonesian workers who make the sneakers.

For several years, Nike executives responded to inquiries about working conditions in contract factories by noting that the company focuses on marketing and design rather than manufacturing. Still, the company was coming under increased pressure from both human rights groups and the

# Doonesbury

general public to address the sweatshop issue. In 1997, Nike commissioned former U.N. ambassador Andrew Young to visit some of the Asian factories and report his findings. After spending 15 days personally inspecting working conditions, Young reported that he did not find abuse or mistreatment of workers. Critics took Nike to task for asking Young to focus only on working conditions and failing to investigate wage rates as well. However, in September 1997, Nike canceled contracts with four factories in Indonesia where pay was below minimum government levels. By 1998, the controversy began to affect Nike's bottom line. Nike's profits dropped as sneaker sales slumped. The sweatshop backlash was not the only cause, however; increasing numbers of consumers were turning to "brown shoes," snapping up casual wear from Hush Puppies, Timberland, and other makers.

Nike was not the only company caught up in the controversy. Allegations surfaced that a subcontractor for Adidas-Salomon AG employed Chinese political prisoners in labor camps near Shanghai to sew soccer balls that commemorated the 1998 World Cup. Adidas, like Nike, has adopted a code of conduct and closely monitors production to prevent such things from occurring. The allegations came as President Clinton was visiting China with an agenda that downplayed human rights issues. An estimated 230,000 Chinese are held in camps dedicated to "reeducation through labor." Soccer balls are hand sewn from 32 precut panels, a process that is so labor-intensive that the work is often done in rural "stitching centers" with the country's lowest labor costs. Adidas confirmed that the allegations were based in fact but that the prison labor had been utilized without the company's knowledge. Adidas announced that it would not source soccer balls in China until production was centralized in one location that excluded the possibility of using prison labor.

**Visit the Web Site**

*Read Nike's Revised Code of Conduct and learn more about the company's labor practices at:*

### www.nikebiz.com

*Global Exchange, a human rights group, offers information on efforts to combat sweatshops:*

### www.globalexchange.org

## Discussion Questions

1. Do you think toy company executives—in Japan, the United States, and elsewhere—should take steps to ensure the safety and welfare of factory workers in developing countries? Why or why not?

2. How have the low wages paid in developing country manufacturing operations affected the number of manufacturing jobs in the high-wage Triad countries?

3. If higher wages in toy factories led to higher prices in the United States for toys, how would the toy industry be affected?

4. Should the subject of working conditions be included in international trade agreements?

5. Do you think companies are doing enough to act responsibly and ensure that human rights standards are upheld for workers both inside and outside their home countries?

*Sources:* Craig S. Smith and A. Craig Copetas, "For Adidas, China Could Prove Trouble," *The Wall Street Journal* (June 26, 1998), p. A13; Holman W. Jenkins, Jr. "The Rise and Stumble of Nike," *The Wall Street Journal* (June 3, 1998), p. A19; Steven Greenhouse, "Accord to Battle Sweatshop Labor Faces Obstacles," *The New York Times* (April 13, 1997), pp. 1, 13; Allen R. Myerson, "In Principle, a Case for More 'Sweatshops,'" *The New York Times* (June 22, 1997), p. 5; Asra Q. Nomani, "Labor Department Asks $5 million for Alleged Worker Enslavement," *The Wall Street Journal* (August 16, 1995), p. B4; Lori Ioannou, "Capitalizing on Global Surplus Labor," *International Business* (April, 1995), pp. 32–34+; G. Pascal Zachary, "Multinationals Can Aid Some Foreign Workers," *The Wall Street Journal* (April 24, 1995), p. A1; Bob Herbert, "Terror in Toyland," *The New York Times* (December 21, 1994), p. A27; "102 Dead in Thai Factory Fire; Higher Toll Seen," *The New York Times* (May 11, 1993), p. A3; "Thai Factory Fire's 200 Victims Were Locked Inside, Guards Say," *The New York Times* (May 12, 1993), p. A5; Jeffrey Ballinger, "The New Free-Trade Heel," *Harper's Magazine* (August, 1992) pp. 46–47; Geraldine E. Willigan, "High-Performance Marketing: An Interview with Nike's Phil Knight," *Harvard Business Review* (July–August 1992) pp. 91–101; Richard J. Barnet and John Cavanagh, "Just Undo It: Nike's Exploited Workers," *The New York Times* (February 13, 1994), sec. 3, p. 11.

# Case 8-2

## U.S. Sugar Subsidies: Too Sweet a Deal?

A turf war has broken out over one of the humblest commodities traded on world markets: sugar. On one side are small-scale farmers in some of the poorest regions the world; desperate to increase their incomes and improve their living standards, these farmers seek increased exports of sugar cane. On the other side are farmers in some of the richest nations in the world who are equally intent on preserving a system of quotas and subsidies to support production of sugar cane and sugar beets. Caught in the middle are processed food and beverage companies that use sugar in baked goods, ice cream, jams and jellies, soft drinks, and a range of other products. Of course, there is also an impact on consumers: Sugar subsidies result in higher prices for popular food and beverage products.

The debate over agricultural policy is at the heart of the struggle. Worldwide, agricultural subsidies amount to approximately $300 billion each year. The subsidies issue has been central to the current round of global trade negotiations; it has also been debated at the World Summit on Sustainable Development. Brazil, Australia, and Thailand rank first, third, and fourth, respectively, among top sugar exporters; the European Union ranks second. Collectively, Brazil, Australia, and Thailand have challenged the European Union's sugar export policy at the World Trade Organization.

In Europe, protection of the agricultural sector was a response to the shortages and rationing that occurred during World War II. Thanks to an initiative known as the Common Agricultural Policy (CAP), European farmers supply virtually all of Europe's food consumption needs. Ag producers also made gains in the 1960s in negotiations relating to the creation of the Common Market—the precursor to today's European Union. Today, the European Union spends more than $90 billion each year to support domestic agriculture; ironically, the EU also spends $25 billion in development aid for low-income nations. French president Jacques Chirac is a particularly vocal advocate of EU farm policy, and farmers in France are well organized. The current EU farm bill expires in 2006.

Europe's agricultural policies have led to sugar beet production in Sweden and Finland—countries not renowned for favorable growing conditions—as well as France. The impact of the sugar regime is clear: European farmers operate with quotas that specify how much they can produce. The farmers are also guaranteed prices for their crops that are roughly three times higher than the world price. Furthermore, the EU produces much more sugar than it can use; as a result, about 6 tons of European sugar are dumped on the world market each year. Moreover, EU sugar supports benefit former colonies such as Mauritius and Fiji which sell raw sugar to the EU at the higher, protected prices. However, these imports are offset by an equivalent amount of exports from the EU; the annual cost of this practice to EU taxpayers is estimated at $800 million.

In the United States, the current sugar regime can be traced back to the Sugar Act of 1934. The act was designed to stabilize prices; today, as in Europe, the U.S. price for raw sugar is about three times the world market price. The General Accounting Office estimates that the program costs Americans $2 billion annually in inflated sugar prices; it will cost an additional $2 billion to store surplus sugar over the course of 10 years. In contrast to Europe, however, the United States exports only a fraction of the 8 tons of sugar it produces each year; quotas limit sugar imports to about 15 percent of U.S. consumption. The U.S. government pays approximately $50 billion in farm aid each year; in May 2002, president George W. Bush signed a new farm bill that actually increased support to some farmers. Not surprisingly, the Europeans point to the bill as evidence that the United States is hypocritical on trade issues. U.S. sugarcane and sugar beet producers rank first in contributions to political campaigns, ahead of both tobacco farmers and dairy farmers. Florida, the key sugar producing state, is a crucial swing state in national elections. However, sugar beets are also grown in North Dakota and other states in the northern plains.

The Sugar Association heads the industry's lobbying effort in the United States. However, the industry flexes its political muscle in other ways. For example, the World Health Organization and the Food and Agriculture Organization have identified sugar as a key contributor to obesity. A recent report titled "Diet, Nutrition and the Prevention of Chronic Diseases" recommended that no more than 10 percent of an individual's caloric intake should come from "added sugars." The Sugar Association assailed the "'dubious nature" of the report, and implied that congressional funding to the WHO of more than $400 million per year could be jeopardized. Andrew Briscoe, president of the association, said, "We are not opposed to a global strategy in the fight against obesity. No one, including the sugar industry, wants anybody to be obese and we want to be part of the solution. But we want that solution to be based on the preponderance of science."

President Bush's administration has actively pursued bilateral and regional trade agreements, a fact that also has the sugar industry up in arms. For example, as part of the newly-negotiated Central American Free Trade Agreement, the United States agreed to import 100,000 tons of sugar—about 1 percent of the U.S. market—from Guatemala and its neighbors. Industry reaction was swift. Robert Coker, senior vice president of Florida-based U.S. Sugar Corporation said, "If the U.S. agrees in regional trade negotiations to open up the U.S. sugar market, American sugar producers, including our company, will be wiped out." The president of the American Sugarbeet Growers Association summed up the situation more succinctly. "If you go to free trade, Brazil wins and everybody else gets killed," he said. As noted earlier, Australia is the world's number 3 sugar exporter; however, when the United States and Australia completed negotiations on a free trade agreement in 2004, sugar was not included.

## Discussion Questions

1. Why do Europe and the United States spend so much on agricultural subsidies?
2. Do individual consumers care where their sugar comes from? If not, should they?

3. Which poses the biggest threat to sugar producers in wealthy countries, the growing concern over obesity or increased imports from developing countries?

*Sources:* Tobia Buck, "EU to Consider Sugar Subsidy Reform," *Financial Times* (June 24, 2004), p. 7; Robert B. Zoellick, "Don't Get Bitter about Sugar," *The Wall Street Journal* (February 25, 2004), p. A14; Edward Alden and Neil Buckley, "Sweet Deals: 'Big Sugar' Fights Threats from Free Trade and a Global Drive to Limit Consumption," *Financial Times* (February 27, 2004), p. 11; Roger Thurow and Geoff Winestock, "Bittersweet: How an Addiction to Sugar Subsidies Hurts Development," *The Wall Street Journal* (September 16, 2002), pp. A1, A10.

# 9 Global Market Entry Strategies

## LICENSING, INVESTMENT, AND STRATEGIC ALLIANCES

South African Breweries PLC had a problem. The company owned more than 100 breweries in 24 countries. South Africa alone, where the company has a commanding 98 percent share of the beer market, accounted for about 14 percent of annual revenues. However, South Africa's currency, the rand, was quite volatile. Moreover, most of the company's brands, which include Castle Lager, Pilsner Urquell, and Carling Black Label, were sold on a local or regional basis; none had the global status of Heineken, Amstel, or Guinness. Nor were the company's brands well known in the key U.S. market, where a growing number of the "echo boom"—the children of the nation's 75 million baby boomers—were reaching drinking age. In 2002, a solution presented itself: South African Breweries had an opportunity to buy the Miller Brewing unit from Philip Morris. The $3.6 billion deal created a new company, SABMiller, that ranks as the world's number-2 brewer in terms of production volume. Miller operates nine breweries in the United States, where its flagship brand, Miller Lite, has been losing marketing share for years. The challenge facing Graham McKay, SABMiller's CEO, is to revitalize the Miller Lite brand in the United States and then launch Miller in Europe as a premium brand.

South African Breweries' acquisition of Miller illustrates the fact that every firm, at various points in its history, faces a broad range of strategy alternatives. As trade barriers fall around the world, companies face growing pressure to expand outside their home country markets. Some companies are making the decision to go global for the first time; others, including SABMiller, are seeking to expand their existing shares of world markets. The various entry mode options form a continuum; as shown in Figure 9-1, the level of involvement, risk, and financial reward increases as a company moves from market entry strategies such as licensing to joint ventures and ultimately,

*A few years ago, South African Breweries was a local company that dominated its domestic market. Building on that base, the company expanded into the rest of Africa as well as key emerging markets such as China, India, and Central Europe. The company's expansion strategy included joint ventures and acquisitions. Today, following the acquisition of Miller, SABMiller is the world's second largest brewer with a strong presence in the U.S. market.*

various forms of investment. When a global company seeks to enter a developing country market, there is an additional strategy issue to address: whether to replicate the strategy that served the company well in developed markets without significant adaptation. To the extent that the objective of entering the market is to achieve penetration, executives at global companies are well advised to consider embracing a mass-market mind-set. This may well mandate an adaptation strategy.[1] Formulating a market entry strategy means that management must decide which of several options to use in pursuing opportunities outside the home country: licensing, some form of foreign direct investment, or global strategic partnership. The particular market entry strategy company executives choose will depend on their vision, attitude toward risk, how much investment capital is available, and how much control is sought.

**Figure 9-1**

*Involvement and Cost Levels for Five Methods of Entering the Global Marketplace*

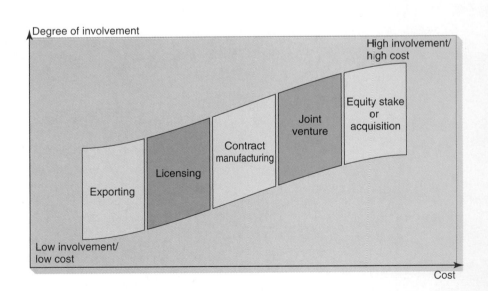

---

1    David Arnold, *The Mirage of Global Markets: How Globalizing Companies Can Succeed as Markets Localize* (Upper Saddle River, NJ: Prentice Hall, 2004), pp. 78–79.

# LICENSING

**Licensing** is a contractual arrangement whereby one company (the licensor) makes a legally protected asset available to another company (the licensee) in exchange for royalties, license fees, or some other form of compensation.[2] The licensed asset may be a brand name, company name, patent, trade secret, or product formulation. Licensing is widely used in the fashion industry. For example, the namesake companies associated with Bill Blass, Hugo Boss, and other global design icons typically generate more revenue from licensing deals for jeans, fragrances, and watches than from their high-priced couture lines. Organizations as diverse as Disney, Caterpillar Inc., the National Basketball Association, and Coca-Cola also make extensive use of licensing. None is an apparel manufacturer; however, licensing agreements allow them to leverage their brand names and generate substantial revenue streams. As these examples suggest, licensing is a global market entry and expansion strategy with considerable appeal. It can offer an attractive return on investment for the life of the agreement, provided that the necessary performance clauses are included in the contract. The only cost is signing the agreement and policing its implementation.

Two key advantages are associated with licensing as a market entry mode. First, because the licensee is typically a local business that will produce and market the goods on a local or regional basis, licensing enables companies to circumvent tariffs, quotas, or similar export barriers discussed in Chapter 8. Disney's success with licensing illustrates a second key advantage of this entry mode. When appropriate, licensees are granted considerable autonomy and are free to adapt the licensed goods to local tastes. Disney licenses trademarked cartoon characters, names, and logos to producers of clothing, toys, and watches for sale throughout the world. Licensing allows Disney to create synergies based on its core theme park, motion picture, and television businesses. Its licensees are allowed considerable leeway to adapt colors, materials, or other design elements to local tastes. This helps explain why, in the Asia-Pacific region alone, sales of licensed Disney products doubled between 1988 and 1990 and doubled again by 1994. In China, licensed goods were practically unknown until a few years ago; by 2001, annual sales of all licensed goods totaled $600 million. Industry observers expect that figure to more than double by 2010. Similarly, yearly worldwide sales of licensed Caterpillar merchandise are running at $900 million as consumers make a fashion statement with boots, jeans, and handbags bearing the distinctive black-and-yellow Cat label. Stephen Palmer is the head of London-based Overland Ltd., which holds the world-wide license for Cat apparel. He notes, "Even if people here don't know the brand, they have a feeling that they know it. They have seen Caterpillar tractors from an early age. It's subliminal, and that's why it's working."[3]

Sanofi-Aventis, a French pharmaceutical company, has pursued a licensing strategy with great success. Drug research is extremely expensive; even so, Sanofi has dozens of drugs under development, with each program costing as much as $400 million. Sanofi's chief executive turns to rivals such as Bristol-Myers Squibb to help fund the research; licensees are then permitted to market the new drugs in return for royalties of up to 15 percent of total sales.[4] Licensing was also the cornerstone of Pilkington's market expansion strategy. In the 1950s, after 7 years of research and an investment of $21 million, the British company developed a process innovation that dramatically lowered the cost of producing high-quality plate glass for the automotive and building industries. In addition to exporting its new "float

---

2   Franklin R. Root, *Entry Strategies for International Markets* (New York: Lexington Books, 1994), p. 107.
3   Cecilie Rohwedder and Joseph T. Hallinan, "In Europe, Hot New Fashion for Urban Hipsters Comes from Peoria," *The Wall Street Journal* (August 8, 2001), p. B1.
4   Stephen D. Moore, "French Drug Maker Reaps Profits with Offbeat Strategy," *The Wall Street Journal* (November 14, 1996), p. B4.

*Licensed merchandise generates nearly $15 billion in annual revenues for the Walt Disney Company. Thanks to the popularity of the company's theme parks, movies, and television shows, Mickey Mouse, Winnie the Pooh, and other popular characters are familiar faces throughout the world. The president of Disney Consumer Products recently predicted that the company's license-related revenues will eventually reach $75 billion.*

glass" to dozens of countries, Pilkington licensed its technology to competitors and created a worldwide industry standard. As Richard D'Aveni has noted, this strategy "generated substantial income for Pilkington, helping to assure its continued technological leadership in the industry for decades."[5]

Licensing is associated with several disadvantages and opportunity costs. First, licensing agreements offer limited market control. Because the licensor typically does not become involved in the licensee's marketing program, potential returns from marketing may be lost. The second disadvantage is that the agreement may have a short life if the licensee develops its own know-how and begins to innovate in the licensed product or technology area. In a worst-case scenario (from the licensor's point of view), licensees, especially those working with process technologies, can develop into strong competitors in the local market and, eventually, into industry leaders. This is because licensing, by its very nature, enables a company to "borrow"—that is, leverage and exploit—another company's resources. A case in point is Pilkington, which has seen its leadership position in the glass industry erode as Glaverbel, Saint-Gobain, PPG, and other competitors have achieved higher levels of production efficiency and lower costs.[6] The ice cream industry in Japan provides another example. Meiji Milk produced and marketed Lady Borden premium ice cream under a licensing agreement with Borden Inc. Meiji learned important skills in dairy product processing; as the expiration dates of the licensing contracts drew near, Meiji rolled out its own premium ice cream brands. When Borden tried to market ice cream without Meiji's help, it had problems developing new sales channels.[7]

Perhaps the most famous example of the opportunity costs associated with licensing dates back to the mid-1950s, when Sony cofounder Masaru Ibuka obtained a licensing agreement for the transistor from AT&T's Bell Laboratories. Ibuka dreamed of using transistors to make small, battery-powered radios. However, the Bell engineers with whom he spoke insisted that it was impossible to manufacture transistors that could handle the high frequencies required for a radio; they advised him to try making hearing aids. Undeterred, Ibuka presented the challenge to his Japanese engineers who spent many months

5   Richard D'Aveni, *Hypercompetition: Managing the Dynamics of Strategic Maneuvering* (New York: The Free Press, 1994), pp. 59–60.
6   Charis Gresser, "A Real Test of Endurance," *Financial Times—Weekend* (November 1–2, 1997), p. 5.
7   Yumiko Ono, "Borden's Breakup with Meiji Milk Shows How a Japanese Partnership Can Curdle," *The Wall Street Journal* (February 21, 1991), p. B1.

improving high-frequency output. Sony was not the first company to unveil a transistor radio; a U.S.-built product, the Regency, featured transistors from Texas Instruments and a colorful plastic case. However, it was Sony's high quality, distinctive approach to styling, and marketing savvy that ultimately translated into worldwide success.

Conversely, the *failure* to seize an opportunity to license can also lead to dire consequences. In the mid-1980s, Apple Computer chairman John Sculley decided against a broad licensing program for Apple's famed operating system (OS). Such a move would have allowed other computer manufacturers to produce Mac-compatible units. Meanwhile, Microsoft's growing world dominance in both OS and applications got a boost in 1985 from Windows, which featured a Mac-like graphic interface. Apple sued Microsoft for infringing on its intellectual property; however, attorneys for the software giant successfully argued in court that Apple had in fact shared crucial aspects of its OS without limiting Microsoft's right to adapt and improve it. Belatedly, in the mid-1990s, Apple began licensing its operating system to other manufacturers. However, the global market share for machines running the Mac OS continues to hover in the low single digits. The return of Steve Jobs and Apple's introduction of the new iMac in 1998 marked the start of a new era for Apple. More recently, the popularity of the company's iPod music players and iTunes Music Store have boosted its fortunes. However, Apple's failure to license its technology in the pre-Windows era arguably cost the company tens of billions of dollars. What's the basis for this assertion? According to *The Wall Street Journal*, Microsoft, the winner in the operating systems war, had a market capitalization of nearly $300 billion in 2003.

As the Borden and transistor stories make clear, companies may find that the up-front easy money obtained from licensing turns out to be an expensive source of revenue. To prevent a licensor-competitor from gaining unilateral benefit, licensing agreements should provide for a cross-technology exchange between all parties. At the absolute minimum, any company that plans to remain in business must ensure that its license agreements include a provision for full cross-licensing (i.e., that the licensee shares its developments with the licensor). Overall, the licensing strategy must ensure ongoing competitive advantage. For example, license arrangements can create export market opportunities and open the door to low-risk manufacturing relationships. They can also speed diffusion of new products or technologies.

## Special Licensing Arrangements

**Contract manufacturing** such as that discussed in Case 8-1 requires a global company—Nike, for example—to provide technical specifications to a subcontractor or local manufacturer. The subcontractor then oversees production. Such arrangements offer several advantages. The licensing firm can specialize in product design and marketing, while transferring responsibility for ownership of manufacturing facilities to contractors and subcontractors. Other advantages include limited commitment of financial and managerial resources and quick entry into target countries, especially when the target market is too small to justify significant investment.[8] One disadvantage, as already noted, is that companies may open themselves to public scrutiny and criticism if workers in contract factories are poorly paid or labor in inhumane circumstances.

**Franchising** is another variation of licensing strategy. A franchise is a contract between a parent company-franchisor and a franchisee that allows the franchisee to operate a business developed by the franchisor in return for a fee and adherence to franchise-wide policies and practices. Franchising has great appeal to local entrepreneurs anxious to learn and apply Western-style marketing techniques.

---

[8] Franklin R. Root, *Entry Strategies for International Markets* (New York: Lexington Books, 1994), p. 138.

William Le Sante, a franchising consultant in Miami, suggests that would-be franchisors ask the following questions before expanding overseas:

- Will local consumers buy your product?
- How tough is the local competition?
- Does the government respect trademark and franchisor rights?
- Can your profits be easily repatriated?
- Can you buy all the supplies you need locally?
- Is commercial space available and are rents affordable?
- Are your local partners financially sound and do they understand the basics of franchising?[9]

The specialty retailing industry favors franchising as a market entry mode. For example, there are nearly 2,000 Body Shop stores around the world; 70 percent of the stores are operated by franchisees. Franchising is also a cornerstone of global growth in the fast-food industry; McDonald's reliance on franchising to expand globally is a case in point. The fast-food giant has a well-known global brand name and a business system that can be easily replicated in multiple country markets. Crucially, McDonald's headquarters has learned the wisdom of leveraging local market knowledge by granting franchisees considerable leeway to tailor restaurant interior designs and menu offerings to suit country-specific preferences and tastes (see Case 1-1). Generally speaking, however, franchising is a market entry strategy that is typically executed with less localization than licensing.

When companies do decide to license, they should sign agreements that anticipate more extensive market participation in the future. Insofar as is possible, a company should keep options and paths open for other forms of market participation. Many of these forms require investment and give the investing company more control than is possible with licensing.

## INVESTMENT

After companies gain experience outside the home country via exporting or licensing, the time often comes when executives desire a more extensive form of participation. In particular, the desire to have partial or full ownership of operations outside the home country can drive the decision to invest. **Foreign direct investment (FDI)** figures reflect investment flows out of the home country as companies invest in or acquire plants, equipment, or other assets. Foreign direct investment allows companies to produce, sell, and compete locally in key markets. Examples of FDI abound: United Parcel Service (UPS) plans to invest more than $1 billion in Europe over 5 years, Ford Motor Company is building a $500 million factory in Thailand, South Korea's LG Electronics purchased a 58 percent stake in Zenith Electronics, and Coca-Cola has spent $600 million on bottling plants in Russia. Each of these represents foreign direct investment.

The final years of the twentieth century were a boom time for cross-border mergers and acquisitions. At the end of 2000, cumulative foreign investment by U.S. companies totaled $1.2 trillion. The top three target countries for U.S. investment were the United Kingdom, Canada, and the Netherlands. Investment in the United States by foreign companies also totaled $1.2 trillion; the United Kingdom, Japan, and the Netherlands were the top three sources of investment.[11]

---

9    Eve Tahmincioglu, "It's Not Only the Giants with Franchises Abroad," *The New York Times* (February 12, 2004), p. C4.
10   Sarah Murray, "Big Names Don Camouflage," *Financial Times* (February 5, 2004), p. 9.
11   Maria Borga and Raymond J. Mataloni, Jr., "Direct Investment Positions for 2000: Country and Industry Detail," *Survey of Current Business* 81, no. 7 (July 2001), pp. 16–29.

| Country | Amount ($ billions) |
|---------|--------------------:|
| USA | 7.1 |
| UK | 1.5 |
| Mauritius | 1.3 |
| Japan | 1.2 |

*Source:* Jonathan Karp, "Japanese Companies Dash into India in Challenge to U.S. Firms' Dominance," *The Wall Street Journal.* (March 13, 1997), p. A19. *Wall Street Journal* Online [Staff Produced Copy Only] by Jonathan Karp. Copyright 2004 by Dow Jones & Co. Inc. Reproduced with permission of Dow Jones & Co. Inc. in the format Textbook via Copyright Clearance Center.

**Table 9-1**

*Approved Foreign Direct Investment in India (Cumulative 1991–1996)*

Investment in developing nations also grew rapidly in the 1990s. For example, as noted in Case 2-1, investment interest in Vietnam is increasing, especially in the automobile industry and other sectors critical to the country's economic development. Table 9-1 shows approved FDI for India. Central and Eastern Europe have also attracted a great deal of investment; Table 9-2 summarizes investment in the former Soviet Union. Daewoo Group's investment in the former Soviet bloc is shown in Table 9-3.

Foreign investments may take the form of minority or majority shares in joint ventures, minority or majority equity stakes in another company, or, as in the case of Sandoz and Gerber, outright acquisition. A company may choose to use a combination of these entry strategies by acquiring one company, buying an equity stake in another, and operating a joint venture with a third. In recent years, for example, UPS has made more than 16 acquisitions in Europe and has also expanded its transportation hubs.

## Joint Ventures

A joint venture with a local partner represents a more extensive form of participation in foreign markets than either exporting or licensing. Strictly speaking, a **joint venture** is an entry strategy for a single target country in which the partners share ownership of a newly created business entity.[12] This strategy is attractive for several reasons. First and foremost is the sharing of risk. By pursuing a joint venture entry strategy, a company can limit its financial risk as well

| Country | 2000 ($ millions) | 2001 ($ millions) |
|---------|------------------:|------------------:|
| Russia | 2,000 | 2,500 |
| Kazakhstan | 1,150 | 1,810 |
| Azerbaijan | 500 | 1,000 |
| Ukraine | 594 | 800 |
| Armenia | 150 | 200 |
| Turkmenistan | 100 | 150 |
| Georgia | 101 | 124 |
| Belarus | 90 | 100 |
| Uzbekistan | 73 | 71 |
| Kyrgyzstan | 41 | 65 |
| Moldova | 100 | 60 |
| Tajikistan | 22 | 19 |

**Table 9-2**

*Foreign Direct Investment in Former Soviet Union 2000 and 2001*

*Source:* Guy Chazan, "For Western Business, Uzbekistan Beckons," *The Wall Street Journal* (November 6, 2001), p. A20. *Wall Street Journal.* Online [Staff Produced Copy Only] by Guy Chazan. Copyright 2004 by Dow Jones & Co. Inc. Reproduced with permission of Dow Jones & Co. Inc. in the format Textbook via Copyright Clearance Center.

---

12 Franklin R. Root, *Entry Strategies for International Markets* (New York: Lexington Books, 1994), p. 309.

| Table 9-3 | Country | Amount ($ millions) |
|---|---|---|
| *Daewoo Group Investment in Central/Eastern Europe* | Poland | 1,540 |
| | Hungary | 198 |
| | Romania | 654 |
| | Czech Republic | 200 |
| | Uzbekistan | 1,860 |
| | Russia | 195 |

Source: Matthew Brzezinski, "Daewoo Boldly Invades Old Soviet Bloc," *The Wall Street Journal* (May 7, 1997), p. A14. *Wall Street Journal.* Online (Staff Produced Copy Only) by Matthew Brzezinski. Copyright 2004 by Dow Jones & Co. Inc. Reproduced with permission of Dow Jones & Co. Inc. in the format Textbook via Copyright Clearance Center.

as its exposure to political uncertainty. Second, a company can use the joint venture experience to learn about a new market environment. If it succeeds in becoming an insider, it may later increase the level of commitment and exposure. Third, joint ventures allow partners to achieve synergy by combining different value chain strengths. One company might have in-depth knowledge of a local market, an extensive distribution system, or access to low-cost labor or raw materials. Such a company might link up with a foreign partner possessing well-known brands or cutting-edge technology, manufacturing know-how, or advanced process applications. A company that lacks sufficient capital resources might seek partners to jointly finance a project. Finally, a joint venture may be the only way to enter a country or region if government bid award practices routinely favor local companies, if import tariffs are high, or if laws prohibit foreign control but permit joint ventures.

# the rest of the story

## SABMiller

In 1998 South Africa Breweries shifted its stock listing from Johannesburg to the London Stock Exchange; the move meant the company was in a better position to raise equity capital. Recognizing the need for global scale, Graham McKay immediately went on an acquisition drive in Europe, starting in Hungary. He noted, "All the growth to be had is outside the developed world." In the former communist countries of Central and Eastern Europe, the strategy took the form of buying privatized breweries, modernizing them, and using Western marketing techniques to build the brands locally. McKay also acquired several breweries in China, the world's second-largest beer market behind the United States.

As for the new Miller unit, Norman Adami was named CEO 6 months after the acquisition. Miller had just under 20 percent of the $67 billion U.S. market for domestic beer with brands such as Miller Lite, Miller Genuine Draft, and Miller High Life; archrival Anheuser-Busch had about 50 percent. New packaging was the first step in revitalizing the brand; the color of Miller's label was changed from silver to royal blue, and the typography was made bolder. In January 2003, Miller launched a controversial TV advertising campaign featuring two attractive women whose argument about whether Miller "tastes great" or is "less filling" escalates into a catfight. Some industry observers interpreted the ads as indicating that SABMiller was prepared to take greater creative risks than Miller's former corporate parent. Bob Garfield, the influential advertising critic for *Advertising Age* magazine, denounced the spots for their "*Maxim*-style neo-pinupism." Despite all the publicity surrounding the campaign, Miller contin-

ues to struggle. CEO Adami expects the U.S. sales picture to worsen before it improves. The brewery launched a corporate branding ad campaign designed to highlight the brand's history as an innovator.

Meanwhile, some of SABMiller's local brands are being introduced in the United States. The company hopes to build Pilsner Urquell, the number one beer in the Czech Republic, into a national brand in the United States. If that effort succeeds, it can be the foundation for building Urquell into a global premium brand that rivals Heineken. SABMiller is also launching Tyskie, a popular Polish brand, in cities such as Chicago that are home to large Polish immigrant communities. The company hopes to successfully position Miller Genuine Draft as a premium global brand in Eastern Europe. Some industry observers predict it will be a hard sell. As one analyst noted, "American beer has a bad reputation in Eastern Europe, because beer drinkers think it tastes like water." Will all these efforts succeed? SABMiller's chief harbors no doubts; if the Miller acquisition does *not* pay off, he says, "I'll fall on my sword."

Sources: Maggie Urry and Adam Jones, "SABMiller Chief Preaches the Lite Fantastic," Financial Times (November 21, 2003), p. 22; Dan Bilefsky and Christopher Lawton, "SABMiller Has U.S. Hangover," The Wall Street Journal (November 20, 2003), p. B5; Christopher Lawton and Dan Bilefsky, "Miller Lite Now: Haste Great, Less Selling," The Wall Street Journal (October 4, 2002), pp. B1, B6; Nicol Deglil Innocenti, "Fearless Embracer of Challenge," Financial Times Special Report—Investing in South Africa (October 2, 2003), p. 6; David Pringle, "Miller Deal Brings Stability to SAB," The Wall Street Journal (May 31, 2002), p. B6; John Willman, "Time for Another Round," Financial Times (June 21, 1999), p. 15.

Many companies have experienced difficulties when attempting to enter the Japanese market. Anheuser-Busch's experience in Japan illustrates both the interactions of the entry modes discussed so far and the advantages and disadvantages of the joint venture approach. Access to distribution is critical to success in the Japanese market; Anheuser-Busch first entered by means of a licensing agreement with Suntory, the smallest of Japan's four top brewers. Although Budweiser had become Japan's top-selling imported beer within a decade, Bud's market share in the early 1990s was still less than 2 percent. Anheuser-Busch then created a joint venture with Kirin Brewery, the market leader. Anheuser-Busch's 90 percent stake in the venture entitled it to market and distribute beer produced in a Los Angeles brewery through Kirin's channels. Anheuser-Busch also had the option to use some of Kirin's brewing capacity to brew Bud locally. For its part, Kirin was well positioned to learn more about the global market for beer from the world's largest brewer. By the end of the decade, however, Bud's market share hadn't increased and the venture was losing money. On January 1, 2000, Anheuser-Busch dissolved the joint venture and eliminated most of the associated job positions in Japan; it reverted instead to a licensing agreement with Kirin. The lesson for consumer products marketers considering market entry in Japan is clear. It may make more sense to give control to a local partner via a licensing agreement rather than making a major investment.[13]

Joint venture investment in the big emerging markets (BEMs) is growing rapidly. China is a case in point; for many companies, the price of market entry is the willingness to pursue a joint venture with a local partner. Procter & Gamble has several joint ventures in China. China Great Wall Computer Group is a joint-venture factory in which IBM is the majority partner with a 51 percent stake. In automotive joint ventures, the Chinese government limits foreign companies to minority stakes. Despite this, Japan's Isuzu Motors has been a joint-venture partner with Jiangling Motors for more than a decade. The venture produces 20,000 pickup trucks and one-ton trucks annually. As indicated in Table 9-4, in 1995 General Motors pledged $1.1 billion for a joint venture with Shanghai Automotive Industry to build Buicks for government and business use. GM was selected after giving high-level Chinese officials a tour of GM's operations in Brazil and agreeing to the government's conditions regarding technology transfer and investment capital.[14] In 1997, GM was chosen by the Chinese government as the sole Western partner in a joint venture in

| Companies Involved | Purpose of Joint Venture |
|---|---|
| GM (USA), Toyota (Japan) | NUMMI—a jointly operated plant in Freemont, California |
| GM (USA), Shanghai Automotive Industry (China) | 50/50 joint venture to build an assembly plant to produce 100,000 midsized sedans for the Chinese market beginning in 1997 (total investment of $1 billion) |
| GM (USA), Hindustan Motors (India) | Joint venture to build up to 20,000 Opel Astras annually (GM's investment, $100 million) |
| GM (USA), governments of Russia and Tatarstan | 25/75 joint venture to assemble Blazers from imported parts; venture currently manufactures Niva SUV |
| Ford (USA), Mazda (Japan) | Joint operation of a plant in Flat Rock, Michigan |
| Ford (USA), Mahindra Ltd. (Japan) | 50/50 joint venture to build Ford Fiestas in the Indian state of Tamil Nadu ($800 million) |
| Chrysler (USA), BMW (Germany) | 50/50 joint venture to build a plant in South America to produce small-displacement 4-cylinder engines ($500 million) |

**Table 9-4**

*Market Entry and Expansion by Joint Venture*

[13] Yumiko Ono, "Beer Venture of Anheuser, Kirin Goes Down Drain on Tepid Sales," *The Wall Street Journal* (November 3, 1999), p. A23.

[14] Keith Naughton, "How GM Got the Inside Track in China," *Business Week* (November 6, 1995), pp. 56–57.

Guangzhou that has begun producing smaller, less expensive cars for the general public. Other global carmakers competing with GM for the project were BMW, Mercedes-Benz, Honda Motor, and Hyundai Motor.

Although Russia is not currently considered a BEM, it represents a huge, barely tapped market for a number of industries. The number of joint ventures is increasing. In 2003, sales of autos with global nameplates totaled 200,000 units; Toyota is the most popular brand. In 1997, GM became the first Western automaker to begin assembling vehicles in Russia. To avoid hefty tariffs that pushed the street price of an imported Blazer above $65,000, GM invested in a 25/75 joint venture with the government of the autonomous Tatarstan republic. Elaz-GM assembled Blazer sport utility vehicles from imported components until the end of 2000. Young Russian professionals were expected to snap up the vehicles as long as the price was less than $30,000. However, after about 15,000 vehicles had been sold, market demand evaporated. At the end of 2001, GM terminated the joint venture.

GM executives are counting on better results with AvtoVAZ, the largest carmaker in the former Soviet Union. AvtoVAZ is home to Russia's top technical design center and also has access to low-cost Russian titanium and other materials. GM originally intended to assemble a stripped-down, reengineered car based on its Opel model. However, market research revealed that a "Made in Russia" car would only be acceptable if it sported a low sticker price; GM had anticipated a price of approximately $15,000. The same research pointed GM toward an opportunity to put the Chevrolet nameplate on a redesigned domestic model, the Niva. With financial support from GM, the Chevrolet Niva was launched in fall 2002 with a sticker price equal to $8,500.[15] In addition to GM, several other automakers are joining with Russian partners. BMW Group AG has already begun the local manufacture of its 5-series sedans; Renault SA is producing Megane and Clio Symbol models at a plant near Moscow. Fiat SpA and Ford have also started production at joint venture plants. Some other recent joint venture alliances are outlined in Table 9-4.

The disadvantages of joint venturing can be significant. Joint venture partners must share rewards as well as risks. The main disadvantage associated with joint ventures is that a company incurs significant costs associated with control and coordination issues that arise when working with a partner. (However, in some instances, country-specific restrictions limit the share of capital help by foreign companies.)

A second disadvantage is the potential for conflict between partners. These often arise out of cultural differences, as was the case in a failed $130 million joint venture between Corning Glass and Vitro, Mexico's largest industrial manufacturer. The venture's Mexican managers sometimes viewed the Americans as too direct and aggressive; the Americans believed their partners took too much time to make important decisions.[16] Such conflicts can multiply when there are several partners in the venture. For example, James River's European joint venture, Jamont, was actually a consortium of 13 companies from 10 countries. Major problems included incompatible computer systems and varying measures of production efficiency; Jamont used committees to solve these and other problems as they arose. For example, agreement had to be reached on a standardized table napkin size; for some country markets, the norm was 30 by 30 centimeters; for others, 35 by 35 centimeters was preferred.[17] Conflict can also arise when a joint venture is a source of supply for third-country markets. Disagreements about third-country markets where partners face each other as actual or potential competitors can lead to "divorce." To avoid

15  Gregory L. White, "Off Road: How the Chevy Name Landed on SUV Using Russian Technology," *The Wall Street Journal* (February 20, 2001), pp. A1, A8.
16  Anthony DePalma, "It Takes More than a Visa to Do Business in Mexico," *The New York Times* (June 26, 1994), sec. 3, p. 5.
17  James Guyon, "A Joint-Venture Papermaker Casts Net Across Europe," *The Wall Street Journal* (December 7, 1992), p. B6.

this, it is essential to work out a plan for approaching third-country markets as part of the venture agreement.

A third issue, also noted in the discussion of licensing, is that a dynamic joint venture partner can evolve into a stronger competitor. Many developing countries are forthright in this regard. Yuan Sutai, a member of China's Ministry of Electronics Industry, told *The Wall Street Journal*, "The purpose of any joint venture, or even a wholly-owned investment, is to allow Chinese companies to learn from foreign companies. We want them to bring their technology to the soil of the People's Republic of China."[18] GM and South Korea's Daewoo Group formed a joint venture in 1978 to produce cars for the Korean market. By the mid-1990s, GM had helped Daewoo improve its competitiveness as an auto producer, but Daewoo chairman Kim Woo-Choong terminated the venture because its provisions prevented the export of cars bearing the Daewoo name.[19]

As one global marketing expert warns, "In an alliance you have to learn skills of the partner, rather than just see it as a way to get a product to sell while avoiding a big investment." However, compared with U.S. and European firms, Japanese and Korean firms seem to excel in their ability to leverage new knowledge that comes out of a joint venture. For example, Toyota learned many new things from its partnership with GM, about U.S. supply and transportation and managing American workers, that have been subsequently applied at its Camry plant in Kentucky. However, some American managers involved in the venture complained that the manufacturing expertise they gained was not applied broadly throughout GM. To the extent that this complaint has validity, GM missed opportunities to leverage new learning. Still, many companies have achieved great successes in joint ventures. Gillette, for example, used this strategy to introduce its shaving products in the Middle East and Africa.

## Investment via Ownership or Equity Stake

The most extensive form of participation in global markets is investment that results in majority or 100 percent ownership. This may be achieved by start-up of new operations, known as **greenfield operations** or **greenfield investment,** or by merger or acquisition of an existing enterprise. According to Thomson Financial Securities Data, worldwide merger and acquisition (M&A) deals worth nearly $3 trillion were struck in 2000. Significantly, about one-third of these were cross-border transactions. M&A activity in Europe and Latin America grew at a faster rate than in the United States. Ownership requires the greatest commitment of capital and managerial effort and offers the fullest means of participating in a market. Companies may move from licensing or joint venture strategies to ownership in order to achieve faster expansion in a market, greater control, or higher profits. In 1991, for example, Ralston Purina ended a 20-year joint venture with a Japanese company to start its own pet food subsidiary. Monsanto and Bayer AG, the German pharmaceutical company, are two other companies that have also recently disbanded partnerships in favor of wholly owned subsidiaries in Japan.

If government restrictions prevent majority or 100 percent ownership by foreign companies, the investing company will have to settle for a minority equity stake. In Russia, for example, the government restricts foreign ownership in joint ventures to a 49 percent stake. A minority equity stake may also suit a company's business interests. For example, Samsung was content to purchase a 40 percent stake in computer maker AST. As Samsung manager Michael

---

18 David P. Hamilton, "China, with Foreign Partners' Help, Becomes a Budding Technology Giant," *The Wall Street Journal* (December 7, 1995), p. A10.
19 "Mr. Kim's Big Picture," *The Economist* (September 16, 1995), pp. 74–75.

Yang noted, "We thought 100 percent would be very risky, because any time you have a switch of ownership, that creates a lot of uncertainty among the employees."[20] In other instances, the investing company may start with a minority stake and then increase its share. In 1991, Volkswagen AG made its first investment in the Czech auto industry by purchasing a 31 percent share in Skoda. By 1995, Volkswagen had increased its equity stake to 70 percent (the government of the Czech Republic owns the rest). Similarly, Ford purchased a 25 percent stake in Mazda in 1979; in 1996, Ford spent another $408 million to raise its stake to 33.4 percent.

Large-scale direct expansion by means of establishing new facilities can be expensive and require a major commitment of managerial time and energy. However, political or other environmental factors sometimes dictate this approach. For example, Japan's Fuji Photo Film Company invested hundreds of millions of dollars in the United States after the U.S. government ruled that Fuji was guilty of dumping (i.e., selling photographic paper at substantially lower prices than in Japan). As an alternative to greenfield investment in new facilities, acquisition is an instantaneous—and sometimes, less expensive—approach to market entry or expansion. Although full ownership can yield the additional advantage of avoiding communication and conflict of interest problems that may arise with a joint venture or coproduction partner, acquisitions still present the demanding and challenging task of integrating the acquired company into the worldwide organization and coordinating activities.

Tables 9-5, 9-6, and 9-7 provide a sense of how companies in the automotive industry utilize a variety of market entry options discussed previously, including equity stakes, investments to establish new operations, and acquisition. Table 9-5 shows that GM favors minority stakes in non-U.S. automakers; in the 3-year period 1998–2000, the company spent $4.7 billion on such deals. Ford spent twice as much on acquisitions. Despite the fact that GM losses from the deals resulted in substantial write-offs, the strategy reflects management's skepticism about

**Table 9-5**

*Investment in Equity Stake*

| Investing Company (Home country) | Investment (Share, Amount, Date) |
|---|---|
| General Motors (USA) | Suzuki Motor Co. (Japan, 3.5% stake, 1981; increased to 10%, 1998; increased to 20%, $490 million, 2000) |
| | Fiat SpA auto unit (Italy, 20% stake, share swap, 2000) |
| | Fuji Heavy Industries (Japan, 20% stake, $1.4 billion, 1999) |
| | Saab Automobiles AB (Sweden, 50% stake, $500 million, 1990; remaining 50%, 2000) |
| Volkswagen AG (Germany) | Skoda (Czech Republic, 31% stake, $6 billion, 1991; increased to 50.5%, 1994; currently owns 70% stake) |
| Ford (USA) | Mazda Motor Corp. (Japan, 25% stake, 1979; increased to 33.4%, $408 million, 1996) |
| DaimlerChrysler (Germany/USA) | Mitsubishi Motors Corp. (Japan, 34% stake, 2000) |
| Renault SA (France) | Nissan Motors (Japan, 35% stake, $5 billion, 2000) |
| Proton (Malaysia) | Lotus Cars (Great Britain, 80% stake, $100 million, 1996) |

20 Ross Kerber, "Chairman Predicts Samsung Deal Will Make AST a Giant," *The Los Angeles Times* (March 2, 1995), p. D1.

| Investing Company (Home Country) | Investment (Location) |
|---|---|
| Mercedes-Benz AG (Germany) | $300 million auto assembly plant (South Carolina, USA) |
| Bayerische Motoren Werke AG (Germany) | $400 million auto assembly plant (South Carolina, USA, 1995) |
| Toyota (Japan) | $3.4 billion manufacturing plant producing Camry, Avalon, and minivan models (Kentucky, USA); $400 million engine plant (West Virginia, USA) |

**Table 9-6**

*Investment to Establish New Operations*

making big mergers work. As GM chairman and CEO Rick Wagoner said, "We could have bought 100 percent of somebody, but that probably wouldn't have been a good use of capital." Meanwhile, the investments in minority stakes are finally paying off: The company enjoys scale-related savings in purchasing, it has gained access to diesel technology, and Saab produced a new model in record time with the help of Subaru.[21]

What is the driving force behind many of these acquisitions? It is globalization. At Gerber, management realized that the path to globalization could not be undertaken independently; the company was acquired by Sandoz (see p. 308). Management at Helene Curtis Industries came to a similar realization and agreed to be acquired by Unilever. Ronald J. Gidwitz, president and CEO, said, "It was very clear to us that Helene Curtis did not have the capacity to project itself in emerging markets around the world. As markets get larger, that forces the smaller players to take action."[22] Still, management's decision to invest abroad sometimes clashes with investors' short-term profitability goals. Although this is an especially important issue for publicly held U.S. companies, there is an increasing trend toward foreign investment by U.S. companies. For example, U.S. direct investment in Canada totaled $228 billion between 1994 and 2003.

Several of the advantages of joint ventures also apply to ownership, including access to markets and avoidance of tariff or quota barriers. Like joint ventures, ownership also permits important technology experience transfers and provides a company with access to new manufacturing techniques. For example, the Stanley Works, a tool maker with headquarters in New Britain, Connecticut, has acquired more than a dozen companies since 1986, among them is Taiwan's National Hand Tool/Chiro company, a socket wrench manufacturer and developer of a "cold-forming" process that speeds up production and reduces waste. Stanley is now using that technology in the manufacture of other tools. Former chairman Richard H. Ayers presided over the acquisitions and envisioned such global cross-fertilization and "blended technology" as

| Acquiring Company | Target (Country, Date, Amount) |
|---|---|
| Daimler Benz (Germany) | Merger with Chrysler Corporation (USA, 1998, $40 billion) |
| Volkswagen AG (Germany) | Sociedad Española de Automoviles de Turisme (SEAT, Spain, $600 million, purchase completed in 1990) |
| BMW (Germany) | Rover (UK, $1.2 billion, 1994) |
| Ford Motor Company (USA) | Jaguar (UK, $2.6 billion, 1989) |
| | Volvo car unit (Sweden, $6.5 billion, 1999) |
| Paccar (USA) | DAF Trucks (Netherlands, $543 million, 1996) |

**Table 9-7**

*Market Entry and Expansion by Acquisition*

[21] James Mackintosh, "GM Stands by Its Strategy for Expansion," *Financial Times* (February 2, 2004), p. 5.

[22] Richard Gibson and Sara Calian, "Unilever to Buy Helene Curtis for $770 Million," *The Wall Street Journal* (February 19, 1996), p. A3.

a key benefit of globalization.[23] In 1998, former GE executive John Trani succeeded Ayers as CEO; Trani brought considerable experience with international acquisitions, and his selection was widely viewed as evidence that Stanley intended to boost global sales even more.

The alternatives discussed here—licensing, joint ventures, minority or majority equity stake, and ownership—are, in fact, points along a continuum of alternative strategies for global market entry and expansion. The overall design of a company's global strategy may call for combinations of exporting-importing, licensing, joint ventures, and ownership among different operating units. Avon Products uses both acquisition and joint ventures to enter developing markets. Similarly, Jamont, the European paper-products company discussed earlier, utilizes both joint ventures and acquisitions. A company's strategy preference may change over time. For example, Borden Inc. ended licensing and joint venture arrangements for branded food products in Japan and set up its own production, distribution, and marketing capabilities for dairy products. Meanwhile, in non-food products, Borden has maintained joint venture relationships with Japanese partners in flexible packaging and foundry materials.

It can also be the case that competitors within a given industry pursue different strategies. For example, Cummins Engine and Caterpillar both face extremely high costs, in the $300 to $400 million range, for developing new diesel engines suited to new applications. However, the two companies vary in their strategic approaches to the world market for engines. Cummins management looks favorably on collaboration; also, the company's relatively modest $6 billion in annual revenues presents financial limitations. Thus, Cummins prefers joint ventures. Indeed, the biggest joint venture between an American company and the Soviet Union linked Cummins with the KamAZ truck company in Tatarstan. The joint venture allowed the Russians to implement new manufacturing technologies while providing Cummins with access to the Russian market. Cummins also has joint ventures in Japan, Finland, and Italy. Management at Caterpillar, by contrast, prefers the higher degree of control that comes with full ownership. The company has spent more than $2 billion on purchases of Germany's MaK, British engine-maker Perkins, and others. Management believes that it is often less expensive to buy existing firms than to develop new applications independently. Also, Caterpillar is concerned about safeguarding proprietary knowledge that is basic to manufacturing in its core construction equipment business.[24]

## GLOBAL STRATEGIC PARTNERSHIPS

In Chapter 8 and the first half of Chapter 9, we surveyed the range of options—exporting, licensing, joint ventures, and ownership—traditionally used by companies wishing either to enter global markets for the first time or to expand their activities beyond present levels. However, recent changes in the political, economic, sociocultural, and technological environments of the global firm have combined to change the relative importance of those strategies. Trade barriers have fallen, markets have globalized, consumer needs and wants have converged, product life cycles have shortened, and new communications technologies and trends have emerged. Although these developments provide unprecedented market opportunities, there are strong strategic implications for the global organization and new challenges for the global marketer. Such strategies will undoubtedly incorporate—or may even be structured around—a variety of collaborations.

---

23  Louis Uchitelle, "The Stanley Works Goes Global," *The New York Times* (July 23, 1989), sec. 3, pp. 1, 10.
24  Peter Marsh, "Engine Makers Take Different Routes," *Financial Times* (July 14, 1998), p. 11.

# GLOBAL *marketing in action*

## Ford Bets Billions on Jaguar

In 1989, the Ford Motor Company acquired Jaguar PLC of Coventry, England, for $2.6 billion. L. Lindsay Halstead, then chairman of Ford of Europe, said the acquisition fulfilled "a longtime strategic objective of entering the luxury car market in a significant way." Ford lacked a high-end luxury model for both the U.S. and European markets, and the company was betting it could leverage an exclusive nameplate by launching a new, less expensive line of Jaguars and selling it to more people. The challenge was to execute this strategy without diminishing Jaguar's reputation; as Daniel Jones, a professor at the University of Cardiff and an auto industry expert, noted, the Ford name is synonymous with "bread and butter" cars. Meanwhile, Ford's Japanese competitors, including Honda, Nissan, and Toyota, pursued a different strategy: They launched new nameplates and upgraded their dealer organizations. In the past decade, status- and quality-conscious car buyers have embraced Lexus, Infiniti, and other new luxury sedans that offer high performance and out-standing dealer organizations.

In 1988, its best sales year before the acquisition, Jaguar sold just under 50,000 cars worldwide. Ford set a production target of 150,000 cars by the end of the 1990s, two-thirds of which would be the lower-priced sporty sedan. Ford executives also expected Jaguar to show a positive cash flow by the end of 1992. Unfortunately, the Jaguar acquisition coincided with the global recession that hurt sales in Japan, Germany, and the United States. To make matters worse, a 10 percent luxury tax imposed in the United States scared off potential buyers. By 1991, Jaguar sales slipped to 25,676 cars. In the face of losses totaling $431 million in 1990 and 1991, Ford scaled back its original end-of-decade volume target to 100,000 cars.

Ford also confronted other challenges. Despite Jaguar's classy image and distinguished racing heritage, the cars were also legendary for their unreliability. Gears sometimes wouldn't shift, headlights wouldn't light, and the brakes sometimes caught fire. Part of the problem could be traced to

manufacturing: In 1990, there were 2,500 defects per 100 cars produced. By 1992, that number had been reduced to 500 defects per 100 cars. Even so, in the closely watched J. D. Power rankings, Jaguar's quality in 1992 was rated just a notch above that of the lowly Yugo. Ironically, die-hard Jaguar loyalists seemed to thrive on the misery associated with owning an unreliable car. In fact, Jaguar clubs in the United States bestowed Cat Bite awards on members with the best tales of woe.

Because Jaguar was arguably one of the world's worst auto-manufacturing operations, Ford invested heavily to update and upgrade Jaguar's plant facilities and improve productivity. As a benchmark, Ford's manufacturing experts knew that German luxury carmakers could build a vehicle in 80 hours; in Japan, the figure was 20 hours. If Jaguar were ever to achieve world-class status, Jaguar's assembly time of 110 hours per car had to be drastically reduced. Jaguar chief executive Sir Nicholas Scheele attacked the quality problem on a number of different fronts. For example, line employees made telephone calls to Jaguar owners who were experiencing problems with their vehicles.

In 1998, amid industry estimates that Ford's total investment had reached $6 billion, Jaguar unveiled its S-type sedan to widespread acclaim. One observer called it a "handsome car, instantly recognizable as a Jaguar, yet totally contemporary." In 2000, Jaguar sold 90,000 cars worldwide. In 2001, the long-awaited "baby Jaguar," the X-type, was launched. Company executives hope to capture a significant share of the entry-level luxury market dominated by the BMW 3-series and another newcomer, the Mercedes C-Class.

*Sources:* Danny Hakim, "Restoring the Heart of Ford," The New York Times (November 14, 2001), pp. C1, C6; Haig Simonian, "Jag's Faces for the Future," Financial Times (November 7–8, 1998), p. 12; Joann S. Lublin and Craig Forman, "Going Upscale: Ford Snares Jaguar, but $2.5 Billion Is High Price for Prestige," The Wall Street Journal (November 3, 1989), pp. A1, A4; Steven Prokesch, "Jaguar Battle at a Turning Point," The New York Times (October 29, 1990), p. C1; Steven Prokesch, "Ford's Jaguar Bet: Payoff Isn't Close," The New York Times (April 21, 1992), p. C1; Robert Johnson, "Jaguar Owners Love Company and Sharing Their Horror Stories," The Wall Street Journal (September 28, 1993), p. A1.

*Jaguar's S-type represented the venerable automaker's bid to become a mainstream luxury nameplate and double its North American sales to 80,000 cars each year. In terms of styling, the $45,000 S-type recalls the classic Jaguar designs of the 1950s and 1960s. Worldwide, Jaguar executives hope to quadruple sales from 50,000 units to 200,000 within 5 years.*

### Gerber

Gerber Products is the undisputed leader in the U.S. baby food market. Despite a 70 percent market share, Gerber faces a mature market and stagnant growth at home. Because 9 out of 10 of the world's births take place outside the United States, Gerber executives hoped to make international sales a greater part of the company's $1.17 billion in annual revenues. Overall, Gerber's international sales increased 150 percent between 1989 and 1993, from $86.5 million to $216.1 million.

Still, for two decades Gerber's globalization effort had been slowed by a combination of changing market conditions, management inconsistency, and decisions that didn't pay off. Gerber entered the Latin American market in the 1970s, but then closed down operations in Venezuela in the wake of government-imposed price controls. Management's focus on the U.S. market resulted in a series of diversifications into nonfood categories that were not successful. Meanwhile, management was not willing to sacrifice short-term quarterly earnings growth to finance an international effort. As Michael A. Cipollaro, Gerber's former president of international operations, remarked, "If you are going to sow in the international arena today to reap tomorrow, you couldn't have that [earnings] growth on a regular basis." In the 1980s, Gerber pursued a strategy of licensing the manufacture and distribution of its baby food products to other companies. In France, for example, Gerber selected CPC International as a licensee.

Unfortunately, Gerber couldn't force its licensees to make baby food a priority business. In France, for example, baby food represented a meager 2 percent of CPC's European revenues. When CPC closed down its French plant, Gerber had to find another manufacturing source. It bought a stake in a Polish factory, but production was held up for months while quality improvements were made. The delay ended up costing Gerber its market position in France.

Belatedly, Gerber discovered that strong competitors already dominated many markets around the globe. Heinz has about one-third of the $1.5 billion baby food market outside the United States; Gerber's share of the global market is 17 percent. Competitors with less global share than Gerber—including France's BSN Group (15 percent market share), and Switzerland's Nestlé SA (8 percent)—have been aggressively building brand loyalty. In France, for example, parents traveling with infants can get free baby food and diapers through Nestlé's system of roadside changing stations. Another barrier is that many European mothers think homemade baby food is healthier than food from a jar.

Meanwhile, Gerber's global efforts were interrupted by the resignations of several key executives. Cipollaro, the chief of international operations, left, as did the vice president for Europe and the international director of business development. Gerber's management team was forced to rethink its strategy: In May 1994, it agreed to be acquired by Sandoz AG, a $10.3 billion Swiss pharmaceutical and chemical company. As market analyst David Adelman noted, "It was very expensive for Gerber to build business internationally. This was one of the driving reasons why Gerber wanted to team up with a larger company."

Some industry analysts expressed doubts about the logic behind the acquisition. London broker Peter Smith said, "I'm sorry: Baby food and anticancer drugs don't really come together." Nevertheless, the deal gave Gerber immediate access to a global marketing and distribution network that is particularly strong in developing countries such as China and India. Sandoz, which faces expiring patents for some of its most profitable drugs, instantly assumed a strong position in the U.S. nutrition market.

Sources: Jennifer Reingold, "The Pope of Basel," Financial World (July 18, 1995), pp. 36–38; Margaret Studer, "Sandoz AG Is Foraging for Additional Food Holdings," The Wall Street Journal (February 21, 1995), p. B4; Richard Gibson, "Growth Formula: Gerber Missed the Boat in Quest to Go Global, so It Turned to Sandoz," The Wall Street Journal (May 24, 1994), pp. A1, A7; Leah Rickard and Laurel Wentz, "Sandoz Opens World for Gerber," Advertising Age (May 30, 1994), p. 4; Margaret Studer and Ron Winslow, "Sandoz, Under Pressure, Looks to Gerber for Protection," The Wall Street Journal (May 25, 1994), p. B3.

Once thought of only as joint ventures with the more dominant party reaping most of the benefits (or losses) of the partnership, cross-border alliances are taking on surprising new configurations and even more surprising players.

Why would any firm—global or otherwise—seek to collaborate with another firm, be it local or foreign? For example, despite its commanding 37 percent share of the global cellular handset market, Nokia recently announced that it would make the source code for its proprietary Series 60 software available to competing handset manufacturers such as Siemens AG. Why did Nokia's top executives decide to collaborate, thereby putting the company's competitive advantage with software development (and healthy profit margins) at risk? As noted, a "perfect storm" of converging environmental forces is rendering traditional competitive strategies obsolete. Today's competitive environment is characterized by unprecedented degrees of turbulence, dynamism, and unpredictability; global firms must respond and adapt quickly. To succeed in global markets, firms can no longer rely exclusively on the technological superiority or core competence that brought them past success. In the twenty-first century, firms must look toward new strategies that will enhance environmental responsiveness. In particular, they must pursue "entrepreneurial globalization" by developing flexible organizational capabilities, innovating continuously, and revising global strategies accordingly."[25] In the second half of this chapter, we will focus on global strategic partnerships. In addition, we will examine the Japanese *keiretsu* and various other types of cooperation strategies that global firms are using today.

## THE NATURE OF GLOBAL STRATEGIC PARTNERSHIPS

The terminology used to describe the new forms of cooperation strategies varies widely. The phrases **collaborative agreements**, **strategic alliances**, **strategic international alliances**, and **global strategic partnerships (GSPs)** are frequently used to refer to linkages between companies from different countries to jointly pursue a common goal. A broad spectrum of interfirm agreements, including joint ventures, can be covered by this terminology. However, the strategic alliances discussed here exhibit three characteristics (see Figure 9-2).[26]

1. The participants remain independent subsequent to the formation of the alliance
2. The participants share the benefits of the alliance as well as control over the performance of assigned tasks
3. The participants make ongoing contributions in technology, products, and other key strategic areas

According to estimates, the number of strategic alliances has been growing at a rate of 20 to 30 percent since the mid-1980s. The upward trend for GSPs comes in part at the expense of traditional cross-border mergers and acquisitions. Since the mid-1990s, a key force driving partnership formation is the realization that

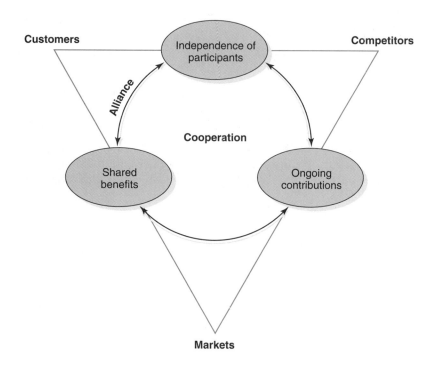

**Figure 9-2**

*Three Characteristics of Strategic Alliances*

---

[25] Michael Y. Yoshino and U. Srinivasa Rangan, *Strategic Alliances: An Entrepreneurial Approach to Globalization* (Boston: Harvard Business School Press, 1995), p. 51.

[26] Yoshino and Rangan, p. 5. For an alternative description see Riad Ajami and Dara Khambata, "Global Strategic Alliances: The New Transnationals," *Journal of Global Marketing* 5, no. 1/2, (1991), pp. 55–59.

**Table 9-8**

*Examples of Global Strategic Partnerships*

| Name of Alliance | Major Participants | Purpose of Alliance |
|---|---|---|
| Beverage Partners Worldwide | Coca-Cola and Nestlé | Offer new coffee, tea, and herbal beverage products in "rejuvenation" category. |
| Star Alliance | Air Canada, Air New Zealand, ANA, Asiana, Austrian, Airlines Group, bmi, LOT Polish Airlines, Lufthansa, SAS, Singapore Airlines, SpanAir, Thai, United Airlines, US Airways, and Varig | Create a global travel network by linking airlines and providing better service for international travelers. |
| Cereal Partners Worldwide | General Mills and Nestlé | Market cereals in more than 80 countries not including the United States and Canada. |

globalization and the Internet will require new intercorporate configurations. According to data compiled by Thomson Financial, 5,200 new strategic alliances were formed in 1996; that number had almost doubled by 2000.[27] Table 9-8 lists some of the GSPs that have been formed recently.

Roland Smith, chairman of British Aerospace, offers a straightforward reason why a firm would enter into a GSP: "A partnership is one of the quickest and cheapest ways to develop a global strategy."[28] Like traditional joint ventures, GSPs have some disadvantages. Partners share control over assigned tasks, a situation that creates management challenges. Also, there are potential risks associated with strengthening a competitor from another country.

Despite these drawbacks, GSPs are attractive for several reasons. First, high product development costs in the face of resource constraints may force a company to seek partners; this was part of the rationale for Boeing's partnership with a Japanese consortium to develop a new jet aircraft, the 777. Second, the technology requirements of many contemporary products mean that an individual company may lack the skills, capital, or know-how to go it alone.[29] Third, partnerships may be the best means of securing access to national and regional markets. Fourth, partnerships provide important learning opportunities; in fact, one expert regards GSPs as a "race to learn." Professor Gary Hamel of the London Business School has observed that the partner that proves to be the fastest learner can ultimately dominate the relationship.[30]

As noted earlier, GSPs differ significantly from the market entry modes discussed in the first half of the chapter. Because licensing agreements do not call for continuous transfer of technology or skills among partners, such agreements are not strategic alliances.[31] Traditional joint ventures are basically alliances focusing on a single national market or a specific problem. The Chinese joint venture described previously between GM and Shanghai Automotive fits this description; the basic goal is to make cars for the Chinese

---

[27] Matthew Schifrin, "Partner or Perish," *Forbes* (May 21, 2001), pp. 26–28.

[28] Jeremy Main, "Making Global Alliances Work," *Fortune* (December 17, 1990), p. 121.

[29] Kenichi Ohmae, "The Global Logic of Strategic Alliances," *Harvard Business Review* 67, no. 2 (March–April 1989), p. 145.

[30] Jeremy Main, "Making Global Alliances Work," *Fortune* (December 17, 1990), p. 122.

[31] Michael A. Yoshino and U. Srinivasa Rangan, *Strategic Alliances: An Entrepreneurial Approach to Globalization* (Boston: Harvard Business School Press, 1995), p. 6.

market. A true global strategic partnership is different; it is distinguished by the following five attributes:[32]

1. Two or more companies develop a joint long-term strategy aimed at achieving world leadership by pursuing cost-leadership, differentiation, or a combination of the two.
2. The relationship is reciprocal. Each partner possesses specific strengths that it shares with the other; learning must take place on both sides.
3. The partners' vision and efforts are truly global, extending beyond home countries and the home regions to the rest of the world.
4. The relationship is organized along horizontal, not vertical, lines. Continual transfer of resources laterally between partners is required, with technology sharing and resource pooling representing norms.
5. When competing in markets excluded from the partnership, the participants retain their national and ideological identities.

## Success Factors

Assuming that a proposed alliance meets these five prerequisites, it is necessary to consider six basic factors deemed to have significant impact on the success of GSPs: mission, strategy, governance, culture, organization, and management.[33]

1. *Mission*. Successful GSPs create win-win situations, where participants pursue objectives on the basis of mutual need or advantage.
2. *Strategy*. A company may establish separate GSPs with different partners; strategy must be thought out up front to avoid conflicts.
3. *Governance*. Discussion and consensus must be the norms. Partners must be viewed as equals.
4. *Culture*. Personal chemistry is important, as is the successful development of a shared set of values. The failure of a partnership between Great Britain's General Electric Company and Siemens AG was blamed in part on the fact that the former was run by finance-oriented executives, the latter by engineers.
5. *Organization*. Innovative structures and designs may be needed to offset the complexity of multicountry management.
6. *Management*. GSPs invariably involve a different type of decision making. Potentially divisive issues must be identified in advance and clear, unitary lines of authority established that will result in commitment by all partners.

Companies forming GSPs must keep these factors in mind. Moreover, successful collaborators will be guided by the following four principles. First, despite the fact that partners are pursuing mutual goals in some areas, partners must remember that they are competitors in others. Second, harmony is not the most important measure of success; some conflict is to be expected. Third, all employees, engineers, and managers must understand where cooperation ends and competitive compromise begins. Finally, as noted earlier, learning from partners is critically important.[34]

---

[32] Howard V. Perlmutter and David A. Heenan, "Cooperate to Compete Globally," *Harvard Business Review* 64, no. 2 (March–April 1986), p. 137.
[33] Howard V. Perlmutter and David A. Heenan, "Cooperate to Compete Globally," *Harvard Business Review* 64, no. 2 (March–April 1986), p. 137.
[34] Gary Hamel, Yves L. Doz, and C. K. Prahalad, "Collaborate with Your Competitors—and Win," *Harvard Business Review* 67, no. 1 (January–February 1989), pp. 133–139.

The issue of learning deserves special attention. As one team of researchers notes,

> The challenge is to share enough skills to create advantage vis-à-vis companies outside the alliance while preventing a wholesale transfer of core skills to the partner. This is a very thin line to walk. Companies must carefully select what skills and technologies they pass to their partners. They must develop safeguards against unintended, informal transfers of information. The goal is to limit the transparency of their operations.[35]

## Alliances with Asian Competitors

Western companies may find themselves at a disadvantage in GSPs with an Asian competitor, especially if the latter's manufacturing skills are the attractive quality. Unfortunately for Western companies, manufacturing excellence represents a multifaceted competence that is not easily transferred. Non-Asian managers and engineers must also learn to be more receptive and attentive; they must overcome the "not-invented-here" syndrome and begin to think of themselves as students, not teachers. At the same time, they must learn to be less eager to show off proprietary lab and engineering successes. To limit transparency, some companies involved in GSPs establish a "collaboration section." Much like a corporate communications department, this department is designed to serve as a gatekeeper through which requests for access to people and information must be channeled. Such gatekeeping serves an important control function that guards against unintended transfers.

A 1991 report by McKinsey and Company shed additional light on the specific problems of alliances between Western and Japanese firms.[36] Often, problems between partners had less to do with objective levels of performance than with a feeling of mutual disillusionment and missed opportunity. The study identified four common problem areas in alliances gone wrong. The first problem was that each partner had a "different dream"; the Japanese partner saw itself emerging from the alliance as a leader in its business or entering new sectors and building a new basis for the future; the Western partner sought relatively quick and risk-free financial returns. Said one Japanese manager, "Our partner came in looking for a return. They got it. Now they complain that they didn't build a business. But that isn't what they set out to create."

A second area of concern is the balance between partners. Each must contribute to the alliance and each must depend on the other to a degree that justifies participation in the alliance. The most attractive partner in the short run is likely to be a company that is already established and competent in the business with the need to master, say, some new technological skills. The best long-term partner, however, is likely to be a less competent player or even one from outside the industry.

Another common cause of problems is "frictional loss," caused by differences in management philosophy, expectations, and approaches. All functions within the alliance may be affected, and performance is likely to suffer as a consequence. Speaking of his Japanese counterpart, a Western businessperson said, "Our partner just wanted to go ahead and invest without considering whether there would be a return or not." The Japanese partner stated that "the foreign partner took so long to decide on obvious points that we were always too slow." Such differences often lead to frustration and time-consuming debates that stifle decision making.

---

[35] Gary Hamel, Yves L. Doz, C. K. Prahalad, "Collaborate with your Competitors—and Win," *Harvard Business Review* 67, no. 1 (January–February 1989), p. 136.

[36] Kevin K. Jones and Walter E. Schill, "Allying for Advantage," *The McKinsey Quarterly*, no. 3 (1991), pp. 73–101.

Last, the McKinsy study found that short-term goals can result in the foreign partner limiting the number of people allocated to the joint venture. Those involved in the venture may perform only 2- or 3-year assignments. The result is "corporate amnesia"; that is, little or no corporate memory is built up on how to compete in Japan. The original goals of the venture will be lost as each new group of managers takes their turn. When taken collectively, these four problems will almost ensure that the Japanese partner will be the only one in it for the long haul.

## CFM International, GE, and Snecma: A Success Story

Commercial Fan Moteur (CFM) International, a partnership between GE's jet engine division and Snecma, a government-owned French aerospace company, is a frequently cited example of a successful GSP. GE was motivated, in part, by the desire to gain access to the European market so it could sell engines to Airbus Industrie; also, the $800 million in development costs was more than GE could risk on its own. While GE focused on system design and high-tech work, the French side handled fans, boosters, and other components. Today CFM International has more than 300 commercial and military customers worldwide including Boeing, Airbus, and the U.S. Air Force. In 2000, the partnership generated sales of $6.7 billion.

The alliance got off to a strong start because of the personal chemistry between two top executives, GE's Gerhard Neumann and the late General René Ravaud of Snecma. The partnership thrives despite each side's differing views regarding governance, management, and organization. Brian Rowe, senior vice president of GE's engine group, has noted that the French like to bring in senior executives from outside the industry, whereas GE prefers to bring in experienced people from within the organization. Also, the French prefer to approach problem solving with copious amounts of data, and Americans may take a more intuitive approach. Still, senior executives from both sides of the partnership have been delegated substantial responsibility.

## AT&T and Olivetti: A Failure

In theory, the partnership in the mid-1980s between AT&T and Italy's Olivetti appeared to be a winner: The collective mission was to capture a major share of the global market for information processing and communications.[37] Olivetti had what appeared to be a strong presence in the European office equipment market; AT&T executives, having just presided over the divestiture of their company's regional telephone units, had set their sights on overseas growth with Europe as the starting point. AT&T promised its partner $260 million and access to microprocessor and telecommunications technology. The partnership called for AT&T to sell Olivetti's personal computers in the United States; Olivetti, in turn, would sell AT&T computers and switching equipment in Europe. Underpinning the alliance was the expectation that synergies would result from the pairing of companies from different industries: communications and computers.

Unfortunately, that vision was nothing more than a hope: There was no real strength in Olivetti in the computer market, and Olivetti had no experience or capability in communications equipment. Tensions ran high when sales did not reach expected levels. AT&T group executive Robert Kavner cited communication and cultural differences as important factors leading to the breakdown of the alliance. "I don't think we or Olivetti spent enough time understanding behavior patterns," Kavner said. "We knew the culture was different but we never really penetrated.

---

[37] Howard V. Perlmutter and David A. Heenan, "Cooperate to Compete Globally," *Harvard Business Review* 64, no. 2 (March–April 1986), p. 145.

We would get angry, and they would get upset."[38] In 1989, AT&T cashed in its Olivetti stake for a share in the parent company Compagnie Industriali Riunite SpA (CIR). In 1993, citing a decline in CIR's value, AT&T sold its remaining stake.

## Boeing and Japan: A Controversy

In some circles, GSPs have been the target of criticism. Critics warn that employees of a company that becomes reliant on outside suppliers for critical components will lose expertise and experience erosion of their engineering skills. Such criticism is often directed at GSPs involving U.S. and Japanese firms. For example, a proposed alliance between Boeing and a Japanese consortium to build a new fuel-efficient airliner, the 7J7, generated a great deal of controversy. The project's $4 billion price tag was too high for Boeing to shoulder alone. The Japanese were to contribute between $1 billion and $2 billion; in return, they would get a chance to learn manufacturing and marketing techniques from Boeing. Although the 7J7 project was shelved in 1988, a new widebody aircraft, the 777, was developed with about 20 percent of the work subcontracted out to Mitsubishi, Fuji, and Kawasaki.[39]

Critics envision a scenario in which the Japanese use what they learn to build their own aircraft and compete directly with Boeing in the future—a disturbing thought since Boeing is a major exporter to world markets. One team of researchers has developed a framework outlining the stages that a company can go through as it becomes increasingly dependent on partnerships:[40]

Stage One: Outsourcing of assembly for inexpensive labor

Stage Two: Outsourcing of low-value components to reduce product price

Stage Three: Growing levels of value-added components move abroad

Stage Four: Manufacturing skills, designs, and functionally related technologies move abroad

Stage Five: Disciplines related to quality, precision manufacturing, testing, and future avenues of product derivatives move abroad

Stage Six: Core skills surrounding components, miniaturization, and complex systems integration move abroad

Stage Seven: Competitor learns the entire spectrum of skills related to the underlying core competence

Yoshino and Rangan have described the interaction and evolution of the various market entry strategies in terms of cross-market dependencies (Figure 9-2).[41] Many firms start with an export-based approach as described in Chapter 8. For example, the striking success of Japanese firms in the automobile and consumer electronics industries can be traced back to an export drive. Nissan, Toyota, and Honda initially concentrated production in Japan, thereby achieving economies of scale. Eventually, an export-driven strategy gives way to an affiliate-based one. The various types of investment strategies described previously—equity stake, investment to establish new operations, acquisitions, and joint ventures—create operational interdependence within the firm. By operating in different markets, firms have the opportunity to transfer production from place to place, depending on exchange rates, resource costs, or other considerations. Although at some companies, foreign affiliates operate as autonomous fiefdoms (the prototypical multinational business with a polycentric

[38] Bernard Wysocki, "Global Reach: Cross Border Alliances Become Favorite Way to Crack New Markets," *The Wall Street Journal* (March 26, 1990), p. A12.

[39] John Holusha, "Pushing the Envelope at Boeing," *The New York Times* (November 10, 1991), sec. 3, pp. 1, 6.

[40] David Lei and John W. Slocum Jr., "Global Strategy, Competence-Building and Strategic Alliances," *California Management Review* 35, no. 1 (Fall 1992), pp. 81–97.

[41] Michael A. Yoshino and U. Srinivasa Rangan, *Strategic Alliances: An Entrepreneurial Approach to Globalization* (Boston: Harvard Business School Press, 1995), pp. 56–59.

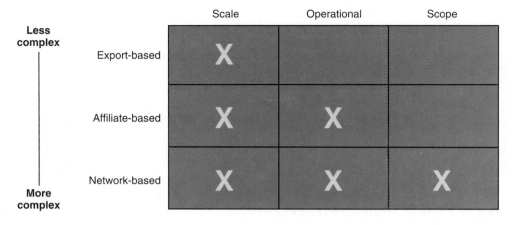

**Figure 9-3**

*Evolution and Interaction
of Entry Strategies*

Source: Adapted from Michael Y. Yoshino and
U. Srinivasa Rangan, Strategic Alliances: An
Entrepreneurial Approach to Globalization
(Boston: Harvard Business School Press, 1995),
p. 51.

orientation), other companies realize the benefits that operational flexibility can bring. The third and most complex stage in the evolution of a global strategy comes with management's realization that full integration and a network of shared knowledge from different country markets can greatly enhance the firm's overall competitive position. As implied by Figure 9-3, as company personnel opt to pursue increasingly complex strategies, they must simultaneously manage each new interdependency as well as preceding ones. The stages described here are reflected in the evolution of Taiwan's Acer Group as described in Case 1-2.

## International Partnerships in Developing Countries

Central and Eastern Europe, Asia, India, and Mexico offer exciting opportunities for firms that seek to enter gigantic and largely untapped markets. An obvious strategic alternative for entering these markets is the strategic alliance. Like the early joint ventures between U.S. and Japanese firms, potential partners will trade market access for know-how. Other entry strategies are also possible, of course; in 1996, for example, Chrysler and BMW agreed to invest $500 million in a joint venture plant in Latin America capable of producing 400,000 small engines annually. Although then-Chrysler chairman Robert Eaton was skeptical of strategic partnerships, he believed that limited forms of cooperation such as joint ventures make sense in some situations. Eaton said, "The majority of world vehicle sales are in vehicles with engines of less than 2.0 liters, outside of the United States. We have simply not been able to be competitive in those areas because of not having a smaller engine. In the international market, there's no question that in many cases such as this, the economies of scale suggest you really ought to have a partner."[42]

Assuming that risks can be minimized and problems overcome, joint ventures in the transition economies of Central and Eastern Europe could evolve at a more accelerated pace than past joint ventures with Asian partners. A number of factors combine to make Russia an excellent location for an alliance: There is a well-educated workforce, and quality is very important to Russian consumers. However, several problems are frequently cited in connection with joint ventures in Russia; these include organized crime, supply shortages, and outdated regulatory and legal systems in a constant state of flux. Despite the risks, the number of joint ventures in Russia is growing, particularly in the services and manufacturing sectors. In the early–post Soviet era, most of the manufacturing ventures were limited to assembly work, but higher value-added activities such as component manufacture are now being performed.

---

[42] Angelo B. Henderson, "Chrysler and BMW Team Up to Build Small-Engine Plant in South America," *The Wall Street Journal* (October 2, 1996), p. A4.

A Central European market with interesting potential is Hungary. Hungary already has the most liberal financial and commercial system in the region. It has also provided investment incentives to Westerners, especially in high-tech industries. Like Russia, this former communist economy has its share of problems. Digital's recent joint venture agreement with the Hungarian Research Institute for Physics and the state-supervised computer systems design firm Szamalk is a case in point. Although the venture was formed so Digital would be able to sell and service its equipment in Hungary, the underlying importance of the venture was to stop the cloning of Digital's computers by Central European firms.

## COOPERATIVE STRATEGIES IN JAPAN: *KEIRETSU*

Japan's *keiretsu* represent a special category of cooperative strategy. A **keiretsu** is an interbusiness alliance or enterprise group that, in the words of one observer, "resembles a fighting clan in which business families join together to vie for market share."[43] *Keiretsu* exist in a broad spectrum of markets, including the capital market, primary goods markets, and component parts markets.[44] *Keiretsu* relationships are often cemented by bank ownership of large blocks of stock and by cross-ownership of stock between a company and its buyers and nonfinancial suppliers. Further, *keiretsu* executives can legally sit on each other's boards, share information, and coordinate prices in closed-door meetings of "presidents' councils." Thus, *keiretsu* are essentially cartels that have the government's blessing. Although not a market entry strategy per se, *keiretsu* played an integral role in the international success of Japanese companies as they sought new markets.

Some observers have disputed charges that *keiretsu* have an impact on market relationships in Japan and claim instead that the groups primarily serve a social function. Others acknowledge the past significance of preferential trading patterns associated with *keiretsu* but assert that the latter's influence is now weakening. Although it is beyond the scope of this chapter to address these issues in detail, there can be no doubt that, for companies competing with the Japanese or wishing to enter the Japanese market, a general understanding of *keiretsu* is crucial. Imagine, for example, what it would mean in the United States if an automaker (e.g., GM), an electrical products company (e.g., GE), a steelmaker (e.g., USX), and a computer firm (e.g., IBM) were interconnected, rather than separate, firms. Global competition in the era of *keiretsu* means that competition exists not only among products, but between different systems of corporate governance and industrial organization.[45]

As the hypothetical example from the United States suggests, some of Japan's biggest and best-known companies are at the center of *keiretsu*. For example, several large companies with common ties to a bank are at the center of the Mitsui Group and Mitsubishi Group. These two, together with the Sumimoto, Fuyo, Sanwa, and DKB groups make up the "big six" *keiretsu* (in Japanese, *roku dai kigyo shudan* or six big industrial groups). The big six strive for a strong position in each major sector of the Japanese economy; because intra-group relationships often involve shared stockholdings and trading relations, the big six are

---

[43] Robert L. Cutts, "Capitalism in Japan: Cartels and Keiretsu," *Harvard Business Review* 70, no. 4 (July–August 1992), p. 49.
[44] Michael L. Gerlach, "Twilight of the *Kereitsu*? A Critical Assessment," *Journal of Japanese Studies* 18, no. 1 (Winter 1992), p. 79.
[45] Ronald J. Gilson and Mark J. Roe, "Understanding the Japanese Keiretsu Overlaps Between Corporate Governance and Industrial Organization," *The Yale Law Journal* 102, no. 4 (January 1993), p. 883.

sometimes known as *horizontal keiretsu*.[46] Annual revenues in each group are in the hundreds of billions of dollars. In absolute terms, *keiretsu* constitute a small percentage of all Japanese companies. However, these alliances can effectively block foreign suppliers from entering the market and result in higher prices to Japanese consumers, while at the same time resulting in corporate stability, risk sharing, and long-term employment. The Mitsubishi Group's *keiretsu* structure is shown in detail in Figure 9-4.

In addition to the big six, several other *keiretsu* have formed, bringing new configurations to the basic forms described previously. *Vertical* (i.e., supply and distribution) *keiretsu* are hierarchical alliances between manufacturers and retailers. For example, Matsushita controls a chain of 25,000 National stores in Japan through which it sells its Panasonic, Technics, and Quasar brands. About half of Matsushita's domestic sales are generated through the National chain, 50 to 80 percent of whose inventory consists of Matsushita's brands. Japan's other major consumer electronics manufacturers, including Toshiba and Hitachi, have similar alliances. (Sony's chain of stores is much smaller and weaker by comparison.) All are fierce competitors in the Japanese market.[47]

Another type of manufacturing *keiretsu* consists of vertical hierarchical alliances between automakers and suppliers and component manufacturers. Intergroup operations and systems are closely integrated, with suppliers receiving long-term contracts. Toyota, for example, has a network of about 175 primary and 4,000 secondary suppliers. One supplier is Koito; Toyota owns about one-fifth of Koito's shares and buys about half of its production. The net result of this arrangement is that Toyota produces about 25 percent of the sales value of its cars, compared with 50 percent for GM. Manufacturing *keiretsu* show the gains that can result from an optimal balance of supplier and buyer power. Because Toyota buys a given component from several suppliers (some are in the *keiretsu*, some are independent), discipline is imposed down the network. Also, because Toyota's suppliers do not work exclusively for Toyota, they have an incentive to be flexible and adaptable.[48]

The *keiretsu* system ensured that high-quality parts were delivered on a just-in-time basis, a key factor in the high quality for which Japan's auto industry is well known. However, as U.S. and European automakers have closed the quality gap, larger Western parts makers are building economies of scale that enable them to operate at lower costs than small Japanese parts makers. Moreover, the stock holdings that Toyota, Nissan, and others have in their supplier network ties up capital that could be used for product development and other purposes. At Nissan, for example, a new management team from France recently began divesting some of the company's 1,300 *keiretsu* investments.[49]

Some observers have questioned whether *keiretsu* violate antitrust laws. As many observers have noted, the Japanese government frequently puts the interests of producers ahead of the interests of consumers. In fact, the *keiretsu* were formed in the early 1950s as regroupings of four large conglomerates—*zaibatsu*—that dominated the Japanese economy until 1945. *Zaibatsu* were dissolved after the occupational forces introduced antitrust as part of the reconstruction. Today, Japan's Fair Trade Commission appears to favor harmony rather than pursuing anticompetitive behavior. As a result, the U.S. Federal Trade Commission has launched several investigations of price fixing, price discrimination, and exclusive

[46] Kenichi Miyashita and David Russell, *Keiretsu: Inside the Hidden Japanese Conglomerates* (New York: McGraw-Hill, 1996), p. 9.

[47] The importance of the chain stores is eroding due to increasing sales at mass merchandisers not under the manufacturers' control.

[48] "Japanology, Inc.—Survey," *The Economist* (March 6, 1993), p. 15.

[49] Norihiko Shirouzu, "U-Turn: A Revival at Nissan Shows There's Hope for Ailing Japan Inc.," *The Wall Street Journal* (November 16, 2000), pp. A1, A10.

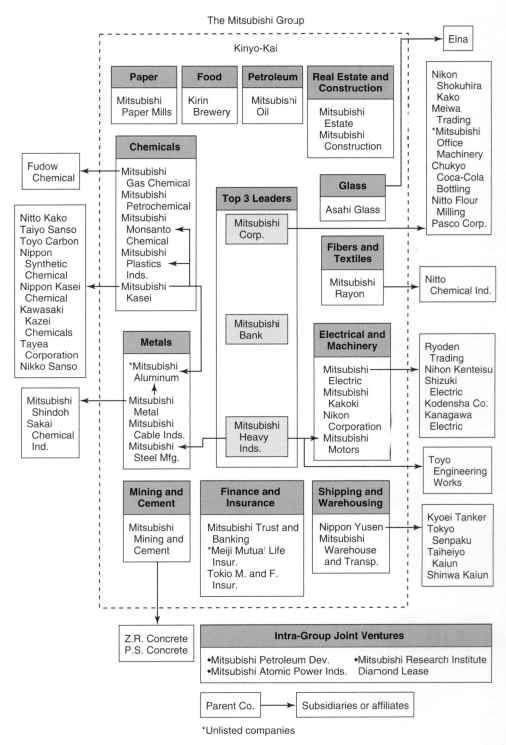

**Figure 9-4**

*Mitsubishi Group's* Keiretsu *Structure*

*Source: Courtesy of the Mitsubishi Group, from Collins and Doorley,* Teaming Up for the '90s. *(Deloitte & Touche, 1991).*

supply arrangements. Hitachi, Canon, and other Japanese companies have also been accused of restricting the availability of high-tech products in the U.S. market. The U.S. Justice Department has considered prosecuting the U.S. subsidiaries of Japanese companies if the parent company is found guilty of unfair trade practices in the Japanese market.[50]

---

[50]  Carla Rapoport, "Why Japan Keeps on Winning," *Fortune* (July 15, 1991), p. 84.

# How *Keiretsu* Affect American Business: Two Examples

Clyde Prestowitz provides the following example to show how *keiretsu* relationships have a potential impact on U.S. businesses. In the early 1980s, Nissan was in the market for a supercomputer to use in its car design. Two vendors under consideration were Cray, the worldwide leader in supercomputers at the time, and Hitachi, which had no functional product to offer. When it appeared that the purchase of a Cray computer was pending, Hitachi executives called for solidarity; both Nissan and Hitachi were members of the same big six *keiretsu*, the Fuyo group. Hitachi essentially mandated that Nissan show preference to Hitachi, a situation that rankled U.S. trade officials. Meanwhile, a coalition within Nissan was pushing for a Cray computer; ultimately, thanks to U.S. pressure on both Nissan and the Japanese government, the business went to Cray.

Prestowitz describes the Japanese attitude toward this type of business practice:[51]

> . . . It respects mutual obligation by providing a cushion against shocks. Today Nissan may buy a Hitachi computer. Tomorrow it may ask Hitachi to take some of its redundant workers. The slightly lesser performance it may get from the Hitachi computer is balanced against the broader considerations. Moreover, because the decision to buy Hitachi would be a favor, it would bind Hitachi closer and guarantee slavish service and future Hitachi loyalty to Nissan products. . . . This attitude of sticking together is what the Japanese mean by the long-term view; it is what enables them to withstand shocks and to survive over the long term.[52]

Because *keiretsu* relationships are crossing the Pacific and directly affecting the American market, U.S. companies have reason to be concerned with *keiretsu* outside the Japanese market as well. According to 1991 data compiled by Dodwell Marketing Consultants, in California alone *keiretsu* own more than half of the Japanese-affiliated manufacturing facilities. However, the impact of *keiretsu* extends beyond the West Coast. Illinois-based Tenneco Automotive, a maker of shock absorbers and exhaust systems, does a great deal of worldwide business with the Toyota *keiretsu*. In 1990, however, Mazda dropped Tenneco as a supplier to its U.S. plant in Kentucky. Part of the business was shifted to Tokico Manufacturing, a Japanese transplant and a member of the Mazda *keiretsu*; a non-*keiretsu* Japanese company, KYB Industries, was also made a vendor. A Japanese auto executive explained the rationale behind the change: "First choice is a *keiretsu* company, second choice is a Japanese supplier, third is a local company."[53]

# COOPERATIVE STRATEGIES IN SOUTH KOREA: *CHAEBOL*

South Korea has its own type of corporate alliance groups, known as *chaebol*. Like the Japanese *keiretsu*, *chaebol* are composed of dozens of companies, centered around a central bank or holding company, and dominated by a founding family. However, *chaebol* are a more recent phenomenon; in the early 1960s, Korea's military dictator granted government subsidies and export credits to a select

---

[51] For years, Prestowitz has argued that Japan's industry structure—*keiretsu* included—gives its companies unfair advantages. A more moderate view might be that any business decision must have an economic justification. Thus, a moderate would caution against overstating the effect of *keiretsu*.

[52] Clyde V. Prestowitz, Jr., *Trading Places: How We Are Giving Our Future to Japan and How to Reclaim It* (New York: Basic Books, 1989), pp. 299–300.

[53] Carla Rappoport, "Why Japan Keeps on Winning," *Fortune* (July 15, 1991), p. 84.

group of companies. By the 1980s, Daewoo, Hyundai, LG, and Samsung had become leading producers of low-cost consumer electronics products. The *chaebol* were a driving force behind South Korea's economic miracle; GNP increased from $1.9 billion in 1960 to $238 billion in 1990. Since the economic crisis of 1997, however, former South Korean President Kim Dae Jung pressured *chaebol* leaders to initiate reform. Prior to the crisis, the *chaebol* had become bloated and heavily leveraged; recently, some progress has been made in improving corporate governance, changing corporate cultures, and reducing debt levels.[54]

## TWENTY-FIRST CENTURY COOPERATIVE STRATEGIES: TARGETING THE DIGITAL FUTURE

Increasing numbers of companies in all parts of the world are entering into alliances that resemble *keiretsu*. In fact, the phrase *digital keiretsu* is frequently used to describe alliances between companies in several industries—computers, communications, consumer electronics, and entertainment—that are undergoing transformation and convergence. These processes are the result of tremendous advances in the ability to transmit and manipulate vast quantities of audio, video, and data and the rapidly approaching era of a global electronic "superhighway" composed of fiber optic cable and digital switching equipment.

One U.S. technology alliance, Sematech, is unique in that it is the direct result of government industrial policy. The U.S. government, concerned that key companies in the domestic semiconductor industry were having difficulty competing with Japan, agreed to subsidize a consortium of 14 technology companies beginning in 1987. Sematech was originally comprised of 700 employees, some permanent and some on loan from IBM, AT&T, Advanced Micro Devices (AMD), Intel, and other companies. The task facing the consortium was to save the U.S. chipmaking equipment industry, whose manufacturers were rapidly losing market share in the face of intense competition from Japan. Although initially plagued by attitudinal and cultural differences between different factions, Sematech eventually helped chipmakers try new approaches with their equipment vendors. By 1991, the Sematech initiative, along with other factors such as the economic downturn in Japan, reversed the market share slide of the semiconductor equipment industry. Sematech's creation heralded a new era in cooperation among technology companies. The company has expanded internationally; its membership roster now includes AMD, Freescale Semiconductor, Hewlett-Packard, Infineon Technologies, IBM, Intel, Philips, TSMC, and Texas Instruments. Companies in a variety of industries are pursuing similar types of alliances.

### Beyond Strategic Alliances

The "relationship enterprise" is said to be the next stage of evolution of the strategic alliance. Groupings of firms in different industries and countries, they will be held together by common goals that encourage them to act almost as a single firm. Cyrus Freidheim, vice chairman of the Booz, Allen, & Hamilton consulting firm, recently outlined an alliance that, in his opinion, might be representative of an early relationship enterprise. He suggests that, within the next few decades, Boeing, British Airways, Siemens, TNT, and Snecma might jointly build 10 new airports in China. As part of the package, British Airways and TNT would be granted preferential routes and landing slots, the Chinese government would contract to buy all its aircraft from Boeing/Snecma, and Siemens would provide air traffic control systems for all 10 airports.[55]

[54] "The *Chaebol* Spurn Change," *The Economist* (July 27, 2000), pp. 59–60.
[55] "The Global Firm: R.I.P." *The Economist* (February 6, 1993), p. 69.

More than the simple strategic alliances we know today, relationship enterprises will be super-alliances among global giants, with revenues approaching $1 trillion. They would be able to draw on extensive cash resources, circumvent antitrust barriers, and, with home bases in all major markets, enjoy the political advantage of being a "local" firm almost anywhere. This type of alliance is not driven simply by technological change, but by the political necessity of having multiple home bases.

Another perspective on the future of cooperative strategies envisions the emergence of the "virtual corporation." As described in a *Business Week* cover story, the virtual corporation "will seem to be a single entity with vast capabilities but will really be the result of numerous collaborations assembled only when they're needed."[56] On a global level, the virtual corporation could combine the twin competencies of cost effectiveness and responsiveness; thus, it could pursue the "think globally, act locally" philosophy with ease. This reflects the trend toward "mass customization." The same forces that are driving the formation of the digital *keiretsu*—high-speed communication networks, for example—are embodied in the virtual corporation. As noted by William Davidow and Michael Malone in their book *The Virtual Corporation*, "The success of a virtual corporation will depend on its ability to gather and integrate a massive flow of information throughout its organizational components and intelligently act upon that information."[57]

Why has the virtual corporation suddenly burst onto the scene? Previously, firms lacked the technology to facilitate this type of data management. Today's distributed databases, networks, and open systems make possible the kinds of data flow required for the virtual corporation. In particular, these data flows permit superior supply chain management. Ford provides an interesting example of how technology is improving information flows among the far-flung operations of a single company. Ford's $6 billion "world car"—known as the Mercury Mystique and Ford Contour in the United States, the Mondeo in Europe—was developed using an international communications network linking computer workstations of designers and engineers on three continents.[58]

# MARKET EXPANSION STRATEGIES

Companies must decide whether to expand by seeking new markets in existing countries or, alternatively, seeking new country markets for already identified and served market segments.[59] These two dimensions in combination produce four **market expansion strategy** options, as shown in Table 9-9. Strategy 1, **country and market concentration**, involves targeting a limited number of customer segments in a few countries. This is typically a starting point for most companies. It matches

**Table 9-9**

*Market Expansion Strategies*

| | | Market | |
| --- | --- | --- | --- |
| | | Concentration | Diversification |
| Country | Concentration | 1. Narrow Focus | 2. Country Focus |
| | Diversification | 3. Country Diversification | 4. Global Diversification |

---

[56] John Byrne, "The Virtual Corporation," *Business Week* (February 8, 1993), p. 103.

[57] William H. Davidow and Michael S. Malone, *The Virtual Corporation: Structuring and Revitalizing the Corporation for the 21st Century* (New York: HarperBusiness, 1993), p. 59.

[58] Julie Edelson Halpert, "One Car, Worldwide, with Strings Pulled from Michigan," *The New York Times* (August 29, 1993), sec. 3, p. 7.

[59] This section draws on I. Ayal and J. Zif, "Market Expansion Strategies in Multinational Marketing," *Journal of Marketing* 43 (Spring 1979), pp. 84–94; and "Competitive Market Choice Strategies in Multinational Marketing," *Columbia Journal of World Business* (Fall 1978), pp. 72–81.

company resources and market investment needs. Unless a company is large and endowed with ample resources, this strategy may be the only realistic way to begin.

In Strategy 2, **country concentration and market diversification,** a company serves many markets in a few countries. This strategy was implemented by many European companies that remained in Europe and sought growth by expanding into new markets. It is also the approach of the American companies that decide to diversify in the U.S. market as opposed to going international with existing products or creating new global products. According to the U.S. Department of Commerce, more than 80 percent of U.S. companies that export limit their sales to five or fewer markets. This means that the majority of U.S. companies are pursuing Strategies 1 or 2.

Strategy 3, **country diversification and market concentration,** is the classic global strategy whereby a company seeks out the world market for a product. The appeal of this strategy is that, by serving the world customer, a company can achieve a greater accumulated volume and lower costs than any competitor and therefore have an unassailable competitive advantage. This is the strategy of the well-managed business that serves a distinct need and customer category.

Strategy 4, **country and market diversification,** is the corporate strategy of a global, multibusiness company such as Matsushita. *Overall*, Matsushita is multi-country in scope and its various business units and groups serve multiple segments. Thus, at the level of corporate strategy, Matsushita may be said to be pursuing Strategy 4. At the operating business level, however, managers of individual units must focus on the needs of the world customer in their particular global market. In Table 9-9, this is Strategy 3, country diversification and market segment concentration. An increasing number of companies all over the world are beginning to see the importance of market share not only in the home or domestic market but also in the world market. Success in overseas markets can boost a company's total volume and lower its cost position.

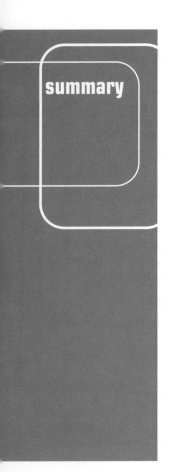

## summary

Companies that wish to move beyond exporting and importing can avail themselves of a wide range of alternative market entry strategies. Each alternative has distinct advantages and disadvantages associated with it; the alternatives can be ranked on a continuum representing increasing levels of investment, commitment, and risk. **Licensing** can generate revenue flow with little new investment; it can be a good choice for a company that possesses advanced technology, a strong brand image, or valuable intellectual property. **Contract manufacturing** and **franchising** are two specialized forms of licensing that are widely used in global marketing.

A higher level of involvement outside the home country may involve **foreign direct investment.** This can take many forms. **Joint ventures** offer two or more companies the opportunity to share risk and combine value chain strengths. Companies considering joint ventures must plan carefully and communicate with partners to avoid "divorce." Foreign direct investment can also be used to establish company operations outside the home country through **greenfield investment,** acquisition of a minority or majority **equity stake** in a foreign business, or taking **ownership** of an existing business entity through merger or outright acquisition.

Cooperative alliances known as **global strategic partnerships (GSPs)** represent an important market entry strategy in the twenty-first century. GSPs are ambitious, reciprocal, cross-border alliances that may involve business partners in a number of different country markets. GSPs are particularly well suited to emerging markets in Central and Eastern Europe, Asia, and Latin America. Western businesspeople should also be aware of two special forms of cooperation found in Asia, namely Japan's *keiretsu* and South Korea's *chaebol.*

To assist managers in thinking through the various alternatives, market expansion strategies can be represented in matrix form: **country and market concentration, country concentration and market diversification, country diversification and market concentration,** and **country and market diversification.** The preferred expansion strategy will be a reflection of a company's stage of development (i.e., whether it is international, multinational, global, or transnational). The Stage 5 transnational combines the strengths of these three stages into an integrated network to leverage worldwide learning.

1. What are the advantages and disadvantages of using licensing as a market entry tool? Give examples of companies from different countries that use licensing as a global marketing strategy.

2. The president of XYZ Manufacturing Company of Buffalo, New York, comes to you with a license offer from a company in Osaka. In return for sharing the Buffalo company's patents and know-how, the Japanese company will pay a license fee of 5 percent of the ex-factory price of all products sold based on the U.S. company's license. The president wants your advice. What would you tell him?

3. What is foreign direct investment (FDI)? What forms can FDI take?

4. Do you agree with Ford's decision to acquire Jaguar? What was more valuable to Ford—the physical assets or the name?

5. What is meant by the phrase *global strategic partnership*? In what ways does this form of market entry strategy differ from more traditional forms such as joint ventures?

6. What are *keiretsu*? How does this form of industrial structure affect companies that compete with Japan or that are trying to enter the Japanese market?

7. Which strategic options for market entry or expansion would a small company be likely to pursue? A large company?

# Case 9-1

## DHL Shakes Up the Global Package Express Business

Battle lines are being drawn in the global package delivery business. On one side are FedEx and United Parcel Service. The two are archrivals in the $47 billion U.S. package-delivery market. FedEx Corporation is headquartered in Memphis; its FedEx Express unit is the market leader in the overnight express segment. UPS ("What Can Brown Do For You?") is in second place. By contrast, in the ground package delivery market segment, UPS currently has a 60 percent share. UPS recently acquired the Mail Boxes Plus chain and converted its retail units into UPS Stores; for its part, FedEx acquired Kinko's, a leading provider of document services.

Globally, however, there is a different leader: DHL Worldwide Express. Brussels-based DHL commands a 40 percent share of the express business, more than twice as much as FedEx. DHL offers express service to more than 120,000 destinations worldwide and operates in more than 220 countries. DHL's corporate parent is Deutsche Post, 70 percent of whose shares are owned by the German government. With 2002 revenues of $44 billion, the German company is Europe's largest postal service provider. Sometimes known as the "yellow giant," it underwent a dramatic restructuring to make it more competitive in Europe's single market. Now Deutsche Post CEO Klaus Zumwinkel has set his sights on becoming the number-three competitor in the United States express market. To achieve this goal, he spent $1.1 billion in 2003 to acquire Airborne Inc.

The deal was complicated by the fact that Airborne's assets include a fleet of airplanes. Because U.S. law forbids U.S.-based airlines to be in foreign hands, DHL divested itself of Airborne's airline assets. A new entity, ABX Air, is a U.S.-owned business. DHL retained ownership of Airborne's ground assets. FedEx and UPS responded to the move by filing a complaint with the U.S. Department of Transportation (DOT). The complaint alleged that DHL Airways Inc., the carrier that DHL Worldwide Express used to fly packages into and out of the United States, is under the control of Deutsche Post. Until 2003, DHL did, in fact, own a minority stake in DHL Airways. In 2003, however, DHL Airways was acquired by Astar Air Cargo, a privately held company with American ownership. As John Daasburg, Astar's chief executive, noted recently, "There's more red, white, and blue in our blood than you'll see at a 4th of July parade." However, about 90 percent of Astar's business is generated by DHL.

At the heart of the matter is concern on the part of the American companies that Deutsche Post's monopoly position in the German mail market gives it unfair financial resources that will allow it to undercut delivery prices. For example, DHL recently won Nike's European $8 million delivery contract away from UPS by undercutting the UPS bid by 10 percent. Although Deutsche Post's U.S. business lost €150 million in 2002, the goal is to return to profitability by 2005. An unfavorable ruling

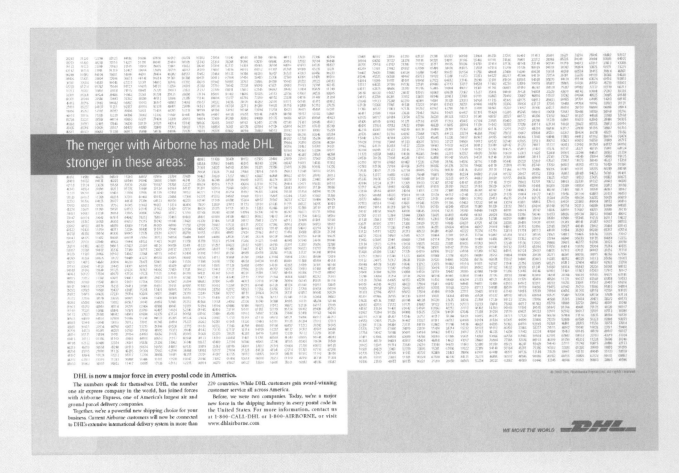

The merger with Airborne has made DHL stronger in these areas:

**DHL is now a major force in every postal code in America.**

The numbers speak for themselves. DHL, the number one air express company in the world, has joined forces with Airborne Express, one of America's largest air and ground parcel delivery companies.

Together, we're a powerful new shipping choice for your business. Current Airborne customers will now be connected to DHL's extensive international delivery system in more than 220 countries. While DHL customers gain award-winning customer service all across America.

Before, we were two companies. Today, we're a major new force in the shipping industry in every postal code in the United States. For more information, contact us at 1-800-CALL-DHL or 1-800-AIRBORNE, or visit www.dhlairborne.com

WE MOVE THE WORLD _DHL_

from the DOT would force Deutsche Post to find a new airline partner in the United States.

> *"Our objective is to build a yellow machine for Europe, as UPS has done with a brown machine for the U.S."*
>
> Klaus Zumwinkel, Chairman, Deutsche Post

The dispute comes at a low point in relations between the United States and Europe. In particular, many Americans faulted the German government for not supporting President Bush's military actions in Iraq. Ironically, DHL delivers mail to U.S. troops serving in Iraq. Now, DHL is fighting back on *its* home turf. Zumwinkel has asked the European Commission to investigate whether Star Air, an air cargo subsidiary of Denmark's Maersk A/S that serves UPS exclusively in Europe, is in compliance with EU law. In a recent interview, Zumwinkel said, "The way in which [FedEx and UPS] are trying to hinder a European company is clearly not in line with the rules that govern international trade. We've only just arrived in the U.S. and have been confronted with political issues to an unbelievable degree."

**Vital Stats**

UPS: 13 million packages and documents per business day; 88,000 motor vehicles, 575 airplanes, 1.8 million business customers

Fed Ex: 3 million packages (FedEx Express)

## Discussion Questions

1. Are you surprised by the aggressiveness of the FedEx and UPS response to DHL's acquisition of Airborne?

2. In 2004, the DOT ruled in favor of Astra. What must Fed Ex and UPS do to compete effectively with DHL?

*Sources:* Betty Liu, "Mail Services Aim to Stamp on German Competition," *Financial Times* (October 8, 2003), p. 14; A12; Matthew Karnitschnig, "Deutsche Post Girds for Battle," *The Wall Street Journal* (October 6, 2003), p. A12; Rick Brooks, "Package Delivery Battle Hinges on DHL Ruling," *The Wall Street Journal* (May 13, 2003), p. B1; Douglas Blackmon, "Post Mortem: National Mail Services Foil UPS's Big Strategy for Dominating Europe," *The Wall Street Journal* (November 4, 1999), pp. A1, A6.

# Case 9-2

## Harry Potter

J. K. Rowling conceived the idea for a Harry Potter (HP) novel while riding on a London train in 1990. The first HP book was released in mid-1997 by Bloomsbury Publishing, after being refused by three major publishers. Since then, the Potter phenomenon has reached the four corners of the globe. The first three books in the series have sold more than 66 million copies and have been translated into more than 200 languages. The success of the HP phenomenon can be attributed in part to the fact that the story itself—the trials and tribulations of an orphan with fantastic powers—has great appeal to both young people and adults. From a marketing point of view, the phenomenon demonstrates masterful management of a standardized core product (the story) and associated trademarked merchandise that has been adapted to local cultures. Today, thanks to her vivid imagination, personal determination, and some savvy global marketing, J.K. Rowling is the wealthiest woman in England.

### Harry Potter: The Phenomenon . . .

At the Harry Potter phenomenon's peak, the average Australian would be exposed to the Harry Potter brand 19 times a day through multiple media and environments. As a global brand consultant noted, "The really scary part is that I saw exactly the same situation 2 weeks ago in Japan as I did this week on Australia's Gold Coast." Except for the fact that it has been translated into dozens of languages, Harry Potter is identical all around the world, irrespective of whether it is read in book form on the London tube or a tuk tuk in Bangkok or is seen as a movie in Montreal or Jakarta. HP transcends both cultural and geographic boundaries.

U.S. media giant AOL Time Warner secured the rights to release the first four movies starting with *Harry Potter and the Philosopher's Stone* in December 2001. AOL Time Warner also held the right to allocate merchandise licenses for the brand. More than 87 global and local licenses were distributed. Global licensees such as Mattel, Lego, and Coca-Cola adopted a standardized orientation, distributing identical products, promotions, and pricing throughout global markets. Hallmark Cards had exclusive rights to sell HP-themed birthday supplies such as invitations and party favors. From Indonesia to Iceland, a child could purchase the same Mattel figurine, drink a Harry Potter–badged Coke, and pay identical amounts for a Harry Potter–themed Lego set.

Second-tier licenses were awarded somewhat haphazardly on a country-by-country basis. Products were adapted to suit the needs and wants of local consumers. For example, Johnson & Johnson produced "lightning bolt purple" toothpaste in Australia, while International Greetings produced note pads, calendars, and other stationery items in the United Kingdom. This activity led to an uncoordinated approach in controlling the Harry Potter brand internationally. Coca-Cola adopted a standardized approach to marketing Harry Potter and leveraged the brand effectively on an international scale.

## The Harry Potter Brand and Coca-Cola's Involvement

Coca-Cola secured the $150 million worldwide sponsorship rights to the first Harry Potter movie, placing the familiar Harry Potter logo on 850 million beverage bottles. Writing in *The Guardian*, Jerome Monahan noted, "Harry Potter has acquired the kind of popularity and recognition that makes him a 'fit' for a global product such as Coca-Cola. Harry Potter novels contain ideals such as friendship, optimism, and honesty, which Coca-Cola believe closely match their core brand values."

*The Deal* Prior to AOL Time Warner spending $120 million to produce the first Harry Potter movie, Coca-Cola approached the media giant with a $150 million licensing deal. Thus, before a single a ticket had been sold, AOL Time Warner had returned a $30 million profit, turning this children's fantasy into a mega deal. AOL Time Warner's terms stipulated no product placements in the movie and that no character faces were to appear on Coca-Cola packaging. In addition, Coca-Cola agreed to implement a literacy campaign that included donating 65 million books to schools around the world. Thanks to Coca-Cola's extensive distribution system, Harry Potter gained exposure even in remote areas of the world.

*What Has Harry Potter Offered Coca-Cola?* The Coca-Cola brand gained long-term leverage from the Harry Potter alliance. The Harry Potter logo became a standard fixture on Coca-Cola packaging worldwide during the promotion. This translated into greater awareness for both the Harry Potter and Coca-Cola brands. However, this awareness was not immediately converted into beverage sales. In fact, Coca Cola's volume share of the U.K. cola category slipped 5.4 percent in the 5 weeks following the launch of the Harry Potter movie. Bill Pecoriello, an analyst with Morgan Stanley, believes that the main objective of the sponsorship was to enhance Coca-Cola's brand image rather than to increase sales of the company's beverage products. It did, however, stimulate sales of Harry Potter books, movie tickets, and merchandise.

Coca-Cola's strategy has also been shrewd in other ways. Despite its overall popularity, Coke's target market is a global segment of older teenagers to late 20-year-olds. The benefit of aligning with the Harry Potter brand indirectly allowed Coca-Cola to broaden its age appeal to focus on younger children worldwide, without alienating parents and its original target market. Coca-Cola does not directly advertise to primary school children, but by association with Harry Potter, the brand could comfortably and persuasively move into new international targeting territory.

*Cobranding* The strategic partnership between the Harry Potter brand and Coca-Cola also represents global cobranding in a daring form, blurring the lines between entertainment and advertising. This made it a clever promotional tool. As Martin Lindstrom, author of *BRANDchild: Insights Into the Minds of Today's Global Kids*, said, "The two brands embrace a collaborative venture designed to advance the interests of both parties in a considered and strategic fashion." The viability of the partnership was measured against three principles and the outcomes were as follows:

- *Equal value for both parties* The Harry Potter brand gained worldwide exposure, and Coca-Cola leveraged Harry Potter for goodwill and his appeal to a young target market.

- *Brand value match* Harry Potter represents the ideals of friendship, honesty, and optimism which Coca-Cola executives viewed as being complementary to their company's core brand values.

- *Easy to understand* The alliance between the soft drink giant and the small publisher was a natural one; both companies target similar markets with global themes such as friendship.

*Ramifications from the Harry Potter Sponsorships* A formal backlash against the alliance manifested itself in SaveHarry.com, a Web site aimed at ending Coca-Cola's use of Harry Potter to market "junk" food to kids. The campaign was orchestrated by the global non-profit Center for Science in the Public Interest along with 40 cosponsoring organizations from Japan to Italy. Diane Levin, author of *Remote Control Childhood—Combating the Hazards of Media Culture*, opened: "It is wrong to use the power of children's love of Harry Potter to sell Coke. Children trust Harry and don't have the full cognitive ability to separate that trust from the exploitative power of the Coke message."

Other issues arose as well. Because some licenses were distributed on an ad hoc, country-by-country basis, inconsistent images of the Harry Potter brand appeared. Some observers noted that Harry Potter runs the risk of being overcommercialized if there is a lack of control of how his image is used. In France, for example, the local licensee produced a version of the boy wizard that bears little resemblance to Rowling's creation. This is likely to confuse children's perception of Harry Potter and, potentially, damage the brand.

On the positive side, the awareness of the Harry Potter brand created from the Coca-Cola alliance fueled sales of both the book and movie tickets in dozens of countries. In addition, Coca-Cola's literacy campaign contributed to the rising trend in children's reading, ignited by the Harry Potter series. Before Harry Potter, children's reading was not a popular pastime. Coca-Cola also gave the Harry Potter brand greater credibility in children's eyes, because they associate the already popular drink with the popular fictional hero.

## Conclusion

The Harry Potter–brand success is the result of a carefully orchestrated marketing mix of global standardization as well as local adaptation. The movie and book series are the core products of the brand and are uniform worldwide. The global licensing agreements with Lego, Mattel, and especially Coca-Cola demonstrate the effectiveness of a coordinated global approach to merchandising. The Harry Potter brand has been somewhat tarnished by the local licensees adapting their products to meet local needs to the detriment of Harry Potter's image and ideals. For a classic story such as Harry Potter, a global standardized marketing approach was optimal in achieving unprecedented success.

## Discussion Questions

1. Do you think that Harry Potter would have achieved the same success had Bloomsbury not aligned itself with global heavyweights such as Coca-Cola?

2. Is Harry Potter perceived differently around the world? Why or why not?

3. What measures could be taken to ensure that licensees do not tarnish the Harry Potter brand?

4. What, if any, are the risks to licensees such as Coca-Cola and Lego of aligning themselves with Harry Potter?

This case was prepared by Alexandra Kennedy-Scott, David Henderson, and Michel Phan, ESSEC Business School. Used by permission.

*Sources:* Leon Gettler, "The Buzzier the Better in World of Neo-Marketing," *The Age* (February 11, 2001), p. 2; Jerome Monahan, "Coca-Cola Is It. And So Is Harry Potter," *Guardian Education* (March 13, 2001), p. 55; Martin Lindstrom, "Brand + Brand = Success?" Part One **www.clickz.com** (May 5, 2002); Matthew Benns, "Harry Potter and the Spell of Big Money," *Sun Herald* (October 14, 2001), p. 34.

# 10 Product and Brand Decisions

"Thin is in." That is the verdict from consumers who have made wide screen, flat-panel TV sets one of the hottest new consumer electronics products in years. The new sets represent a dramatic departure from the cathode-ray tube (CRT) technology that has been an integral part of TV design for more than 50 years. Thanks to innovative liquid-crystal display (LCD) and plasma-gas technologies that were first used to manufacture screens for personal computers, today's TV sets are sleek, sexy, and cool. With their sharper, brighter pictures, they also enhance the enjoyment of viewing widescreen DVD movies at home. The consumer electronics industry desperately needs a new hit product. Global sales of CRT screens had been flat for years; annual revenues totaled $26 billion with no significant growth forecast. Meanwhile, in 2002, revenues for flat-panel displays surpassed those for CRTs for the first time; industry forecasts call for sales of flat-panel models to surpass the $60 billion mark by 2006. What is surprising is who the key players are. Sharp currently has more than 50 percent share of the global market for LCD monitors; its displays can be found in airplane cockpits, pinball machines, and PCs. Korea's Samsung is number two in the industry with a 19 percent market share. By contrast, Sony, long a world leader in TV manufacturing and a strong global brand name, has only 8 percent market share and is sourcing its LCDs from Hitachi and LG.Philips. Although Sony is legendary for its spirit of innovation, it was a late entry into the growing market for flat-panel displays. Sony focused on its Wega brand TVs that offered flat screens in a conventional CRT format; company engineers insisted that Sony's Trinitron CRT technology was superior to flat-panel technology which, in any event, the company had no experience producing.

Products are arguably the most crucial element of a company's marketing program. Product decisions are integral to the company's value proposition; in addition, every aspect of

The growing popularity of flat-panel LCD and plasma screen TVs has propelled LG Philips, Sharp, and Samsung Electronics to the front ranks of the world's consumer electronics companies. In 2003, Samsung had the largest share of the U.S. market for sets costing more than $3,000. Demand is growing most rapidly in Japan, where flat-panel TVs already account for 10 percent of the market.

the enterprise, including pricing, communication, and distribution policies, must fit the product. A firm's customers and competitors are determined by the products it offers. In many purchase situations, customers seek out particular brands, not just products. Sony's late entry into the flat-panel TV market highlights the challenges facing global companies today: Management must develop product and brand policies and strategies that are sensitive to market needs, competition, and company ambitions and resources on a global scale. Effective global marketing entails finding a balance between the payoff from extensively adapting products and brands to local market preferences and the benefits that come from concentrating company resources on relatively standardized global products and brands.

This chapter examines the major dimensions of global product and brand decisions. First is a review of basic product and brand concepts, followed by a discussion of local, international, and global products and brands. Product design criteria are identified and attitudes toward foreign products are explored. The next section outlines strategic alternatives available to global marketers. Finally, new product issues in global marketing are discussed.

## BASIC PRODUCT AND BRAND CONCEPTS

A **product** is a good, service, or idea with tangible and/or intangible attributes that collectively create value for a buyer or user. A product's *tangible* attributes can be assessed in physical terms such as weight, dimensions, or materials used. Consider, for example, a flat-panel TV with an LCD screen that measures 42 inches across. The unit weighs 100 pounds, is 4 inches thick, and has a tuner capable of receiving high-definition TV signals over the air. These tangible, physical features translate into benefits that enhance the enjoyment of watching prime time TV and movies on DVD. Accessories such as mounts and floor stands enhance the value offering by enabling great flexibility in placing the set in a living room or home theater. *Intangible* product attributes, including status associated with product ownership, a manufacturer's service commitment, and a brand's overall reputation or mystique, are also important. When shopping for a new TV set, for example, many people want "the best": They want a TV loaded with features (tangible product elements), as well as one that is "cool" and makes a status statement (intangible product element).

## Product Types

A frequently used framework for classifying products distinguishes between consumer and industrial goods. For example, Kodak offers products and services to both amateur and professional photographers worldwide. Consumer and industrial goods, in turn, can be further classified on the basis of criteria such as buyer orientation. Buyer orientation is a composite measure of the amount of effort a customer expends, the level of risk associated with a purchase, and buyer involvement in the purchase. The buyer orientation framework includes such categories as convenience, preference, shopping, and specialty goods. Although film is often a low-involvement purchase, many film buyers in the United States show a strong preference for Kodak film, and significant numbers of Japanese photographers prefer Fuji. Products can also be categorized in terms of their life span (durable, nondurable, and disposable). Kodak and other companies market both single-use (disposable) cameras as well as more expensive units that are meant to last for many years. As these examples from the photo industry suggest, traditional product classification frameworks are fully applicable to global marketing.

## Brands

A **brand** is a complex bundle of images and experiences in the customer's mind. A brand represents a promise by a particular company about a particular product; it is a sort of quality certification. Brands also enable customers to better organize their marketplace experience by helping them seek out and zero in on particular products. An important brand function is to differentiate a particular company's offering from all others. Customers integrate all their experiences of observing, using, or consuming a product with everything they hear and read about it. Information about products and brands comes from a variety of sources and cues, including advertising, publicity, sales personnel, and packaging. Perceptions of service after the sale, price, and distribution are also taken into account. The sum of impressions is a **brand image,** a single—but often complex—mental image about both the product itself and the company that markets it (see Figure 10-1). Another important brand concept is **brand equity,** which represents the added value that accrues to a product as a result of a company's prior investments in the marketing of the brand. Brand equity can also be thought of as an asset representing the value created by the relationship between the brand and customers over time. The stronger the relationship, the greater the equity. For example, the value of global megabrands such as Coca-Cola and Marlboro has been estimated to run in the tens of *billions* of dollars.[1]

Warren Buffett, the legendary American investor who heads Berkshire Hathaway, asserts that the global power of brands such as Coca-Cola and Gillette permits the companies that own them to set up a protective moat around their economic castles. Buffett explains, "The average company, by contrast, does battle daily without any such means of protection."[2] That protection often yields added profit, because the owners of powerful brand names can typically command higher prices for their products than can owners of lesser brands. In other words, the strongest global brands have tremendous brand equity.

As noted, the essence of a brand exists in the mind; as such, brands are intangible. However, companies develop logos, distinctive packaging, and other communication devices to provide visual representations of their brands. A logo can take a variety of forms, starting with the brand name itself. For example, the Coca-Cola

---

1  For a complete discussion of brand equity, see Kevin Lane Keller, *Strategic Brand Management* (Upper Saddle River, NJ: Prentice Hall, 1998), Chapter 2.
2  John Willman, "Labels that Say It All," *Financial Times—Weekend Money* (October 25–26, 1997), p. 1.

**Figure 10-1**

Components of a Brand Image

The diagram shows concentric circles with the following labels:

Center: Experience with product

Middle ring: Family, friends; Service by company employees; Packaging; Pricing; Company name; Brand name/logo

Outer ring: Advertising; Publicity, news stories; Distribution; Promotions, sponsored events

brand is expressed in part by a *word mark* consisting of the words "Coke" and "Coca-Cola" written in a distinctive white script. The "wave" that appears on red Coke cans and bottle labels is an example of a *non-word mark logo*, sometimes known as a *brand symbol*. Non-word marks such as the Nike swoosh, the three-pronged Mercedes star, and McDonald's golden arches have the great advantage of transcending language and are therefore especially valuable to global marketers. To protect the substantial investment of time and money required to build and sustain brands, companies register brand names, logos, and other brand elements as

## *global* MARKETING Q&A

**Wall Street Journal:** "BMW is one of the top brands in any industry. For you, as CEO, are there special responsibilities you have in maintaining or building your brand image?"

**Helmut Panke, Chief Executive Officer, BMW:** "As provocative as it sounds, the biggest task is to be able to say, 'No.' Because in the end, authentic brand management boils down to understanding that a brand is a promise that has to be fulfilled everywhere, at any time. So when something doesn't fit, you must make sure that that is not done. The most important role of senior management, not just the CEO, is to understand that the brand is not just a label that you can put on and take off. BMW . . . settles for fewer compromises, which goes back to what the brand stands for."

Source: Neal E. Boudette, "BMW's CEO Just Says 'No' to Protect Brand," The Wall Street Journal (November 26, 2003), p. B1.

### Wide Screen Flat-Panel TVs Rule

Sony is a good example of a company whose preference for its own technology has proven to be counterproductive. Innovation guru Henry Chesbrough notes that today, the technologies needed for products are so complex and rivals so numerous that no company—even one as big and capable as Sony—can develop all it needs internally. A case in point is the cost of building an LCD production facility. The price tag is about $2.7 billion, too high a cost for Sony to bear alone. Sony's strong track record as an innovator and inventor of whole classes of technologies blinded it to the merits of using technologies from other companies. It was hard hit by shrinking profit margins in its electronics business; in 2003, Sony it announced it would close 12 of 17 factories that make picture-tube TVs. It also announced a joint venture with Samsung to manufacture LCD sets. Meanwhile, new competitors have entered the TV market. Gateway, seeking fast-growing new segments as its PC business has slowed, introduced an LCD TV set with a retail price of less than $3,000; likewise, Dell announced it would begin selling TVs. Despite these new entrants into the industry, Sony's goal is to have 30 percent share of the global flat-panel market.

The new TVs do have some drawbacks, including high prices. Because the screen panel itself represents about 85 percent of the cost of an entire set, companies are innovating to bring the cost down. For example, Corning is a key supplier of glass products to the industry; the company recently found a way to ship 500 glass panel sheets in the space that would previously only accommodate 20 sheets. The result was a dramatic drop in shipping costs to Asian manufacturers. Likewise, Sharp and other manufacturers have found ways to reduce the amount of time required to insert the liquid-crystal substance between the glass panels. In 2001, 5 days were required to fabricate a finished screen; today, a 30-inch screen can be produced in just 2 hours.

There are other drawbacks as well. For one thing, plasma sets are more susceptible to "burn in," which occurs when an on-screen image leaves a permanent "ghost." Moreover, manufacturing limitations mean that LCD sets are only available in smaller sizes, up to 30 inches wide. By contrast, plasma sets can have screens as wide as 60 inches. However, plasma screens lose their brightness over time. They are also more difficult to manufacture because "dead" pixels leave tiny blank spots on the screen. As many as one in five plasma-screen sets have to be discarded during the manufacturing process because of dead pixels or other defects.

*Sources: Eric A. Taub, "Flat-Panel Sets to Enhance the Visibility of Samsung," The New York Times (January 8, 2004), pp. C1, C4; Andrew Ward, Kathrin Hille, Michiyo Nakamoto, Chris Nuttal, "Flat Out for Flat Screens: The Battle to Dominate the $29 bn Market Is Heating Up but the Risk of Glut Is Growing," Financial Times (December 24, 2003), p. 9; Evan Ramstad. "Rise of Flat-Screen TVs Reshapes Industry," The Wall Street Journal (November 20, 2003), p. B8; Phred Dvorak, "Facing a Slump, Sony to Revamp Product Lines," The New York Times (September 12, 2003), pp. B1, B2; Michiyo Nakamoto, "Sony Discusses Screen Venture with Samsung," Financial Times (September 23, 2003), p. 19; Elliot Spagat, "Is It Finally Time to Get a Flat-Panel TV?" The Wall Street Journal (September 12, 2002), p. D1; Peter Landers, "Sharp Covets the Sony Model: A Sexy, High-End Image," The Wall Street Journal (March 11, 2002), p. A13.*

> *"We have to shift to high value-added products, and to do that we need to improve our brand."*
>
> Noboru Fujimoto, President
> Sharp Electronics Corporation[3]

trademarks or service marks. As discussed in Chapter 5, safeguarding trademarks and other forms of intellectual property is a key issue in global marketing.

## Local Products and Brands

A **local product** or **local brand** is one that has achieved success in a single national market. Sometimes a global company creates local products and brands in an effort to cater to the needs and preferences of particular country markets. For example, Coca-Cola has developed several branded drink products for sale only in Japan, including a noncarbonated, ginseng-flavored beverage; a blended tea known as Sokenbicha; and Lactia-brand fermented milk drink. In Poland, B.A.T Industries recognized that consumption of local cigarette brands was much higher than that of premium-priced global brands such as Marlboro. In the mid-1990s, B.A.T introduced a new brand, Jan Sobieski, named for a Polish king. Thanks to high-quality packaging and a price that was 30 percent less than global brands, Jan Sobieski quickly captured 8 percent of total cigarette sales in Poland. Similarly, the rosters of the giant local record companies frequently include artists whose popularity is limited to a single country. For example, BMG International releases recordings by local stars such as B'z (Japan), Bronco (Mexico), and Joaquin Sabina (Spain). Artists such as these may sell one million CDs or cassettes in their home markets while remaining virtually unknown elsewhere.

> *"There is a strong local heritage in the brewing industry. People identify with their local brewery, which makes beer different from detergents or electronic products."*
>
> Karel Vuursteen, Chairman,
> Heineken[4]

---

[3]   Peter Landers, "Sharp Covets the Sony Model: A Sexy, High-End Image," *The Wall Street Journal* (March 11, 2002), p. A13

[4]   John Willman, "Time for Another Round," *Financial Times* (June 21, 1999), p. 15.

Local products and brands also represent the lifeblood of domestic companies. Entrenched local products and brands can represent significant competitive hurdles to global companies entering new country markets. In China, for example, a sports goods company started by Olympic gold medalist Li Ning sells more sneakers than global powerhouse Nike. In developing countries, global brands are sometimes perceived as overpowering local ones. Growing national pride can result in a social backlash that favors local products and brands. In China, a local TV set manufacturer, Changhong Electric Appliances, has built its share of the Chinese market from 6 percent to more than 22 percent by cutting prices and using patriotic advertising themes such as "Let Changhong hold the great flag of revitalizing our national industries." White-goods maker Haier Group has also successfully fought off foreign competition and now accounts for 40 percent of China's refrigerator sales. In addition, Haier enjoys a 30 percent share of both the washing machine and air conditioner markets. The aspirations of the company's president, Zhang Ruimin, can be glimpsed from slogans stenciled on office walls: "Haier—Tomorrow's Global Brand Name," and "Never Say 'No' to the Market."[5] In 2002, Haier Group announced a strategic alliance with Taiwan's Sampo Group. The deal, which is valued at $300 million, calls for each company to manufacture and sell the other's refrigerators and telecommunications products both globally and locally.

## International Products and Brands

**International products** and **international brands** are offered in several markets in a particular region. For example, there are a number of "Euro products" and "Euro brands" that are offered in Europe but not the rest of the world. Similarly, the two-seat Smart car developed by DaimlerChrysler is currently offered for sale in Europe only (see Case 10-2). The experience of General Motors with its Corsa model in the early 1990s provides a case study in how an international product or brand can be taken global. The Opel Corsa was a new model originally introduced in Europe. GM then decided to build different versions of the Corsa in China, Mexico, and Brazil. As David Herman, chairman of Adam Opel AG, noted, "The original concept was not that we planned to sell this car from the tip of Tierra del Fuego to the outer regions of Siberia. But we see its possibilities are limitless." GM calls the Corsa its "accidental world car."[6] One might describe GM's actions as "think international, act global."

## Global Products and Brands

The globalization of industry is putting pressure on companies to develop global products and to leverage brand equity on a worldwide basis. A **global product** meets the wants and needs of a global market. A true global product is offered in all world regions, including the Triad and in countries at every stage of development. A **global brand** has the same name and a similar image and positioning throughout the world. Some companies are well established as global brands. For example, when Nestlé asserts that it "Makes the very best," the quality promise is understood and accepted globally. The same is true for Gillette ("The best a man can get"), BMW ("The ultimate driving machine"), GE ("Imagination at work"),

[5] John Ridding, "China's Own Brands Get Their Acts Together," *Financial Times* (December 30, 1996), p. 6; Kathy Chen, "Global Cooling: Would America Buy a Refrigerator Labeled 'Made in Quingdao'?" *The Wall Street Journal* (September 17, 1997), pp. A1, A14.

[6] Diana Kurylko, "The Accidental World Car," *Automotive News* (June 27, 1994), p. 4.

Harley-Davidson ("An American legend"), and many other global companies. Former Gillette CEO Alfred Zeien explained his company's approach as follows:

> A multinational has operations in different countries. A global company views the world as a single country. We know Argentina and France are different, but we treat them the same. We sell them the same products, we use the same production methods, we have the same corporate policies. We even use the same advertising—in a different language, of course.[7]

As this quote implies, companies such as Gillette enjoy several benefits and advantages that derive from creating global products and utilizing global branding. These include economies of scale associated with creating a single ad campaign for the world and the advantages of executing a single brand strategy. All global companies are trying to increase the visibility of their brands, especially in the key U.S. market. Examples include Philips with its "Sense and simplicity" global image advertising and Siemens' recent "Be inspired" campaign.

Note that a global brand is not the same thing as a global product. For example, personal stereos are a category of global product; Sony is a global brand. Many companies, including Sony, make personal stereos. However, Sony created the category more than 20 years ago when it introduced the Walkman in Japan. The history of the Walkman illustrates the fact that global brands must be created by marketers. Initially, Sony's personal stereo was to be marketed under three brand names. In their book *Breakthroughs!*, Ranganath Nayak and John Ketteringham describe how the global brand as we know it today came into being when famed Sony Chairman Akio Morita realized that global consumers were one step ahead of his marketing staffers:

> At an international sales meeting in Tokyo, Morita introduced the Walkman to Sony representatives from America, Europe, and Australia. Within two months, the Walkman was introduced in the United States under the name "Soundabout"; two months later, it was on sale in the United Kingdom as "Stowaway." Sony in Japan had consented to the name changes because their English-speaking marketing groups had told them the name "Walkman" sounded funny in English. Nevertheless, with tourists importing the Walkman from Japan and spreading the original name faster than any advertising could have done, Walkman became the name most people used when they asked for the product in a store. Thus, *Sony managers found themselves losing sales because they had three different names for the same item*. Morita settled the issue at Sony's United States sales convention in May 1980 by declaring that, funny or not, Walkman was the name everybody had to use.[8]

The Sony Walkman is an excellent example of **combination** or **tiered branding**, whereby a corporate name (Sony) is combined with a product brand name (Walkman). By using multitiered branding, marketers can leverage a company's reputation while developing a distinctive identity for a line of products. A tiered-brand approach can be a powerful tool for introducing new products. Although Sony markets a number of local products, the company also has a stellar track record as a global corporate brand, a creator of global products, and a marketer of global brands. For example, using the Walkman brand name as a point of departure, Sony created the Discman portable CD player and the Watchman portable TV. Sony's recent global product-brand offerings include the Minidisc digital music recording-playback system, a full line of DVD players, and a new Super Audio Compact Disc (SACD) music system.

**Cobranding** is a variation on tiered branding in which two or more *different* company or product brands are featured prominently on product packaging or in advertising. Properly implemented, cobranding (or *dual branding*, as it is sometimes

---

7 Victoria Griffith, "As Close as a Group Can Get to Global," *Financial Times* (April 7, 1998), p. 21.
8 P. Ranganath Nayak and John M. Ketteringham, *Breakthroughs! How Leadership and Drive Create Commercial Innovations that Sweep the World* (San Diego, CA: Pfeiffer & Company, 1994), pp. 128–129.

called) can engender customer loyalty and allow companies to achieve synergy. However, cobranding can also confuse consumers and dilute brand equity. The approach works most effectively when the products involved complement each other. Credit card companies were the pioneers, and today it is possible to use cards to earn frequent flyer miles and discounts on automobiles. Another well-known example of cobranding is the Intel Inside campaign promoting both the Intel Corporation and its Pentium-brand processors in conjunction with advertising for various brands of personal computers. BellSouth International has successfully utilized a wireless cobranding strategy to penetrate the Latin American telecommunications market today, BellSouth is the largest provider of cellular services in the region.

Companies can also leverage strong brands by creating **brand extensions**. This strategy entails using an established brand name as an umbrella when entering new businesses or developing new product lines that represent new categories to the company. British entrepreneur Richard Branson is an acknowledged master of this approach: The Virgin brand has been attached to a wide range of businesses and products (**www.virgin.com**). Virgin is a global brand, and the company's businesses include an airline, a railroad franchise, retail stores, movie theaters, financial services, and soft drinks. Some of these businesses are global, and some are local. For example, Virgin Megastores are found in many parts of the world, while the operating scope of Virgin Rail Group is limited to the United Kingdom. The brand has been built on Branson's shrewd ability to exploit weaknesses in competitors' customer service skills, as well as a flair for self-promotion. Branson's business philosophy is that brands are built around reputation, quality, innovation, and price rather than image.[9] Although Branson is intent on establishing Virgin as *the* British brand of the new millennium, some industry observers wonder if the brand has been spread too thin (see Table 10-1).

## Global Brand Development

Table 10-2 shows global brands ranked in terms of their economic value at the beginning of the twenty-first century as determined by analysts at the Interbrand consultancy and Citigroup. To be included in the rankings, the brand had to generate at least 20 percent of sales outside the home country (brands owned by privately held companies such as Mars are not included). Not surprisingly, Coca-Cola tops the list. However, one of the telling findings of the rankings is that strong brand management is now being practiced by companies in a wide range of industries, not just by consumer packaged-goods marketers.[10]

**Table 10-1**

*The Virgin Group*

- Virgin Entertainment
  Virgin Megastores and MGM Cinemas
- Virgin Trading
  Virgin Cola and Virgin Vodka
- Virgin Radio
- Virgin Media Group
  Virgin Publishing, Virgin Television,
  Virgin Net
- Virgin Hotels
- Voyager Investments
  Virgin Bride

- Virgin Travel Group
  Virgin Atlantic Airways, Virgin Holidays
- Virgin Direct Personal Financial Services
- Virgin Rail Group
- V2 Records

- Victory Corporation
  Cosmetics and Clothing
- Virgin Express

---

9   Alison Smith, "A Genius for Publicity," *Financial Times* (August 4, 1997), p. 9.
10  Gerry Khermouch, "The Best Global Brands," *Business Week* (August 6, 2001), pp. 50+.

*Richard Branson has built a business empire by extending the Virgin brand name to a variety of products, including Virgin Cola and Virgin Vodka. In 2003, Virgin Cola was relaunched in the United States via an alliance with 7-Eleven stores.*

Developing a global brand is not always an appropriate goal. As David Aacker and Erich Joachimsthaler noted in the *Harvard Business Review*, managers who seek to build global brands must first consider whether such a move fits well with their company or their markets. First, managers must realistically assess whether anticipated scale economies will actually materialize. Second,

**Table 10-2**

*The World's Most Valuable Brands*

| Rank | Value ($ billions) |
|------|--------------------|
| 1. Coca-Cola | 69.9 |
| 2. Microsoft | 65.1 |
| 3. IBM | 52.8 |
| 4. GE | 42.4 |
| 5. Nokia | 35.0 |
| 6. Intel | 34.7 |
| 7. Disney | 32.6 |
| 8. Ford | 30.1 |
| 9. McDonald's | 25.3 |
| 10. AT&T | 22.8 |
| 11. Marlboro | 22.0 |
| 12. Mercedes | 21.7 |
| 13. Citibank | 19.0 |
| 14. Toyota | 18.6 |
| 15. Hewlett-Packard | 17.9 |
| 16. Cisco Systems | 17.2 |
| 17. American Express | 16.9 |
| 18. Gillette | 15.3 |
| 19. Merrill Lynch | 15.0 |
| 20. Sony | 15.0 |
| 21. Honda | 14.6 |
| 22. BMW | 13.9 |
| 23. Nescafé | 13.2 |
| 24. Compaq | 12.3 |
| 25. Oracle | 12.2 |

*Source: Adapted from "The 100 Top Brands," Business Week (August 8, 2001), pp. 60–61.*

they must recognize the difficulty of building a successful global brand team. Finally, managers must be alert to instances in which a single brand cannot be imposed on all markets successfully. Aacker and Joachimsthaler recommend that companies place a priority on creating strong brands in *all* markets through **global brand leadership**:

> Global brand leadership means using organizational structures, processes, and cultures to allocate brand-building resources globally, to create global synergies, and to develop a global brand strategy that coordinates and leverages country brand strategies.[11]

The following eight guidelines can assist marketing managers in their efforts to establish global brand leadership:

1. Create a compelling value proposition for customers in every market entered, beginning with the home country market. A global brand begins with this foundation of value.
2. Before taking a brand across borders, think about all elements of brand identity and select names, marks, and symbols that have the potential for globalization. Give special attention to the Triad and BEMs.

---

[11] David Aaker and Erich Joachimsthaler, "The Lure of Global Branding," *Harvard Business Review* 77, no. 6 (November–December 1999), pp. 137–144.

3. Companies with an established national brand should thoroughly research the alternatives of extending it versus adopting a new brand identity globally. For example, AT&T changed its name from American Telephone & Telegraph, and Bavarian Motor Works (Bayerische Motoren Weke AG) adopted the acronym BMW as its global brand.
4. Develop a company-wide communication system to share and leverage knowledge and information about marketing programs and customers in different countries.
5. Develop a consistent planning process across markets and products. Make a process template available to all managers in all markets.
6. Assign specific responsibility for managing branding issues to ensure that local brand managers accept global best practices. This can take a variety of forms, ranging from a business management team or a brand champion (led by senior executives) to a global brand manager or brand management team (led by middle managers).
7. Execute brand-building strategies that leverage global strengths and respond to relevant local differences.
8. When in doubt, harmonize, unravel confusion, and eliminate complexity. For example, a consumer packaged-goods marketer with 25 bar soap brands should ask whether 5 would work just as well in the markets served.[12]

Mars Inc. confronted the global brand issue with its chocolate-covered caramel bar that sold under a variety of national brand names such as Snickers in the United States and Marathon in the United Kingdom. Management decided to transform the candy bar—already a global product—into a global brand. This decision entailed some risk, such as the possibility that consumers in the United Kingdom would associate the name Snickers with knickers, the British slang for a woman's under-garment. Mars also changed the name of its successful European chocolate biscuit from Raider to Twix, the same name used in the United States. In both instances, a single brand name gives Mars the opportunity to leverage all of its product com-munications across national boundaries. Managers were forced to think globally about the positioning of Snickers and Twix, something that they were not obliged to do when the candy products were marketed under different national brand names. The marketing team rose to the challenge; as Lord Saatchi described it:

> Mars decided there was a rich commercial prize at stake in ownership of a single human need: hunger satisfaction. From Hong Kong to Lima, people would know that Snickers was "a meal in a bar." Owning that emotion would not give them 100 percent of the global confectionery market but it would be enough. Its appeal would be wide enough to make Snickers the number one confectionery brand in the world, which it is today.[13]

Coke is arguably the quintessential global product and global brand. Coke relies on similar positioning and marketing in all countries; it projects a global image of fun, good times, and enjoyment. The product itself may vary to suit local tastes; for example, Coke increased the sweetness of its beverages in the Middle East where customers prefer a sweeter drink. Also, prices may vary to suit local competitive conditions, and the channels of distribution may differ. Since the mid-1990s, Coke's advertising theme has been "Always Coca-Cola." Each new "always" campaign includes more than a dozen TV commercials with different story lines designed to appeal to audiences in different parts of the world. However, the basic, underlying strategic principles that guide the management of the brand are the same worldwide. Only an ideologue would insist that a "global product" cannot be adapted to meet

---

12  Warren J. Keegan, "Global Brands: Issues and Strategies," Center for Global Business Strategy, Pace University, Working Paper Series, 2002.
13  Lord Saatchi, "Battle for Survival Favours the Simplest," *Financial Times* (January 5, 1998), p. 19.

local preferences; certainly, no company building a global brand needs to limit itself to absolute uniformity of marketing mix elements. The issue is not exact uniformity but rather: Are we offering *essentially* the same product? As discussed in the next few chapters, other elements of the marketing mix—for example, price, communications appeal and media strategy, and distribution channels—may also vary.

At Avon Products, global brands generate $725 million in annual sales and account for approximately 25 percent of personal care product revenues. Avon's global fragrances include Far Away and Rare Gold. Even as it has created new global perfume brands, Avon has consolidated some of its national brands in an effort to improve quality and cut costs. Avon has found that uniform ingredients and packaging for global brands result in gross profit margins that are 4 percent higher than those of its regional and national brands.

## Local Versus Global Products and Brands: A Needs-Based Approach

Coca-Cola, McDonald's, Singapore Airlines, Mercedes-Benz, and Sony are a few of the companies that have transformed local products and brands into global ones. The essence of marketing is finding needs and filling them. Maslow's hierarchy of needs, a staple of sociology and psychology courses, provides a useful framework for understanding how and why local products and brands can be extended beyond home country borders. Maslow hypothesized that people's desires can be arranged into a hierarchy of five needs.[14] As an individual fulfills needs at each level, he or she progresses to higher levels (see Figure 10-2). At the most basic level of human existence, physiological and safety needs must be met. People need food, clothing, and shelter, and a product that meets these basic needs has potential for globalization. However, the basic human need to consume food and liquids is not the same thing as wanting or preferring a Big Mac or a Coke. Before the Coca-Cola Company and McDonald's conquered the world, they built their brands and business systems at home. Because their products fulfilled basic human needs

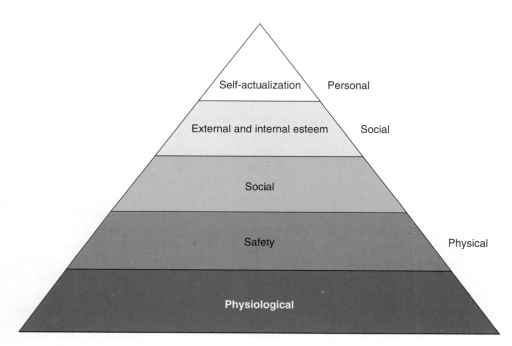

### Figure 10-2

*Maslow's Hierarchy of Needs*

Source: A. H. Maslow, "A Theory of Human Motivation," in Readings in Managerial Psychology, Harold J. Levitt and Louis R. Pondy, eds. (Chicago: University of Chicago Press, 1964), pp. 6–24.

---

[14] A. H. Maslow, "A Theory of Human Motivation," in *Readings in Managerial Psychology*, Harold J. Levitt and Louis R. Pondy, eds. (Chicago: University of Chicago Press, 1964), pp. 6–24.

and because both companies are masterful marketers, they were able to cross geographic boundaries and build global brand franchises. At the same time, Coca-Cola and McDonald's have learned from experience that some food and drink preferences remain deeply embedded in culture. Responding to those differences has meant creating local products and brands for particular country markets. Sony has prospered for a similar reason. Audio and video entertainment products fulfill important social functions. Throughout its history, Sony's corporate vision has called for developing new products such as the transistor radio and the Walkman personal stereo that fulfill the need for entertainment.

Mid-level needs in the hierarchy include self-respect, self-esteem, and the esteem of others. These social needs, which can create a powerful internal motivation driving demand for status-oriented products, cut across the various stages of country development. Gillette's Alfred Zeien understood this. Marketers in Gillette's Parker Pen subsidiary are confident that consumers in Malaysia and Singapore shopping for an upscale gift will buy the same Parker pen as Americans shopping at Neiman Marcus. "We are not going to come out with a special product for Malaysia," Zeien has said.[15] In Asia today, young women are taking up smoking as a status symbol—and showing a preference for Western brands such as Marlboro. However, as noted earlier, smokers' needs and wants may be tempered by economic circumstances. Recognizing this, companies such as B.A.T create local brands that allow individuals to indulge their desire or need to smoke at a price they can afford to pay.

Luxury goods marketers are especially skilled at catering to esteem needs on a global basis. Rolex, Louis Vuitton, and Dom Perignon are just a few of the global brands that consumers buy in an effort to satisfy esteem needs. Some consumers flaunt their wealth by buying expensive products and brands that others will notice. Such behavior is referred to as *conspicuous consumption* or *luxury badging*. Any company with a premium product or brand that has proven itself in a local market by fulfilling esteem needs should consider devising a strategy for taking the product global.

Products can fulfill different needs in different countries. Consider the refrigerator as used in industrialized, high-income countries. The *primary function* of the refrigerator in these countries is related to basic needs as fulfilled in that society. These include storing frozen foods for extended periods; keeping milk, meat, and other perishable foods fresh between car trips to the supermarket; and making ice cubes. In lower-income countries, by contrast, frozen foods are not widely available. Homemakers shop for food daily rather than weekly. Because of lower incomes, people are reluctant to pay for unnecessary features such as icemakers. These are luxuries that require high-income levels to support. The functions of the refrigerator in a lower-income country are merely to store small quantities of perishable food for 1 day and to store leftovers for slightly longer periods. Because the needs fulfilled by the refrigerator are limited in these countries as compared with advanced countries, a much smaller refrigerator is quite adequate. In some developing countries, refrigerators have an important *secondary purpose* related to higher-order needs: They fulfill a need for prestige. In these countries, there is demand for the largest model available, which is prominently displayed in the living room rather than hidden in the kitchen.

Hellmut Schütte has proposed a modified hierarchy to explain the needs and wants of Asian consumers (see Figure 10-3).[16] Although the two lower-level needs are the same as in the traditional hierarchy, the three highest levels emphasize the intricacy and importance of social needs. *Affiliation needs* in Asia are satisfied when an individual has been accepted by a group. Conformity with group norms becomes a key force driving consumer behavior. For example, when Tamagotchis

---

15  Louis Uchitelle, "Gillette's World View: One Blade Fits All," *The New York Times* (January 3, 1994), p. C3.
16  Hellmut Schütte, "Asian Culture and the Global Consumer," *Financial Times—Mastering Marketing* (September 21, 1998), p. 2.

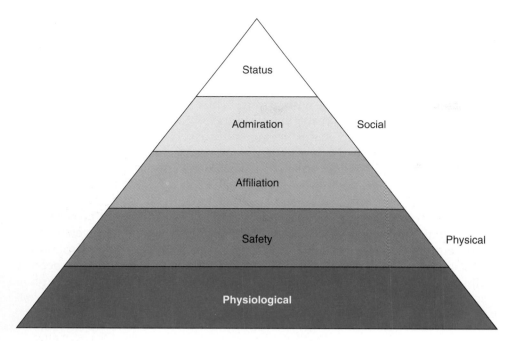

**Figure 10-3**

*Maslow's Hierarchy: The Asian Equivalent*

Source: Hellmutt Schutte, "Maslow's Hierarchy: The Asian Equivalent," Consumer Behavior in Asia (New York: New York University Press, 1998), p. 23.

and other brands of electronic pets were the "in" toy in Japan, every teenager who wanted to fit in bought one (or more). Knowing this, managers at Japanese companies develop local products specifically designed to appeal to teens. The next level is *admiration*, a higher-level need that can be satisfied through acts that command respect within a group. At the top of the Asian hierarchy is *status*, the esteem of society as a whole. In part, attainment of high status is character driven. However, the quest for status also leads to luxury badging. Support for Schütte's contention that status is the highest-ranking need in the Asian hierarchy can be seen in the geographic breakdown of the $35 billion global luxury goods market. Fully 20 percent of industry sales are generated in Japan alone, with another 22 percent of sales occurring in the rest of the Asia-Pacific region. Nearly half of all sales revenues of Italy's Gucci Group are generated in Asia.

> *"For Asians, face is very important, so you have to show you are up to date with the latest available product."*
>
> Alan Chang, View Sonic (Taiwan), explaining the popularity of flat-panel TVs in Japan[17]

## "COUNTRY OF ORIGIN" AS BRAND ELEMENT

One of the facts of life in global marketing is that perceptions about and attitudes toward particular countries often extend to products and brands known to originate in those countries. Such perceptions contribute to the **country-of-origin effect;** they become part of a brand's image and contribute to brand equity. This is particularly true for automobiles, electronics, fashion, beer, recorded music, and certain other product categories. Perceptions and attitudes about a product's origins can be positive or negative. On the positive side, as one marketing expert has pointed out, "'German' is synonymous with quality engineering, 'Italian' is synonymous with style, and 'French' is synonymous with chic."[18] Within a given country, consumers are likely to differ in terms of both the importance they ascribe to a product's country of origin and their perceptions of different countries. Moreover, as industries globalize, the origin issue is becoming more complex. Country-of-design, country-of-manufacture, and country sources for parts can all become relevant considerations.

---

[17] Andrew Ward, Kathrin Hille, Michiyo Nakamoto, Chris Nuttal, "Flat Out for Flat Screens: The Battle to Dominate the $29 bn Market Is Heating Up but the Risk of Glut Is Growing," *Financial Times* (December 24, 2003), p. 9.

[18] Dana Milbank, "Made in America Becomes a Boast in Europe," *The Wall Street Journal* (January 19, 1994), p. B1.

The manufacturing reputation of a particular country can change over time. Studies conducted during the 1970s and 1980s indicated that the "made in the USA" image lost ground to the "made in Japan" image. Today, however, U.S. brands are finding renewed acceptance globally. Examples include Jeep Cherokee sports utility vehicles, Lands' End clothing, and Budweiser beer, all of which are being successfully marketed with strong "USA" themes. Korea's image has improved greatly in recent years, thanks to the reputations of global companies such as Hyundai, Daewoo, and Samsung. Industry observers expect other Asian corporate megabrands to emerge in the coming years.

Finland is home to Nokia, which rose in stature from a local brand to a global brand in little more than a decade. However, as brand strategy expert Simon Anholt points out, other Finnish companies need to move quickly to capitalize on Nokia's success if Finland is to become a valuable nation-brand. For example, Raisio Oy has developed Benecol brand margarine that has been proven to lower cholesterol levels. If large numbers of health-conscious consumers around the world embrace so-called nutraceutical products, Raisio and Benecol may become well-known brands and further raise Finland's profile on the global scene. Anholt also notes that some countries are "launch brands" in the sense that they lack centuries of tradition and foreign interaction upon which to build their reputations:

> For a country like Slovenia to enhance its image abroad is a very different matter than for Scotland or China. Slovenia needs to be launched: Consumers around the world first must be taught where it is, what it makes, what it has to offer, and what it stands for. This in itself represents a powerful opportunity: The chance to build a modern country brand, untainted by centuries of possibly negative associations.[19]

Country stereotyping can present a disadvantage to a competitor in a given market. One study conducted in the early 1990s investigated the relationship between country of origin and American consumer perceptions of risk when buying microwave ovens and jeans. Overall, the study found a significant consumer bias in favor of U.S.-made microwaves and jeans. However, the study also showed no difference in perceived risk between microwave ovens in terms of "made in the USA" and "made in Taiwan." By contrast, respondents indicated a higher perceived risk for jeans manufactured in Taiwan compared with those from the United States. The same study revealed a negative country-of-origin bias for Mexican-made products. Finally, the survey indicated a significantly higher perceived risk for a Mexican microwave oven than for one made in Taiwan; there was no significant difference between Mexico and Taiwan in terms of perceived risk for jeans.[20] This study was published before NAFTA; since the mid-1990s, the "made in Mexico" image has gained enormous ground as local companies and global manufacturers have established world-class manufacturing plants in Mexico to supply world demand. For example, General Motors, Volkswagen, DaimlerChrysler, Nissan, Ford, and other global automakers have established Mexican operations that produce nearly two million vehicles per year, three-fourths of which are exported.[21]

If a country's manufacturers produce high-quality products that are nonetheless *perceived* as being of lower quality than similar goods from other countries, there are two alternatives. One is to disguise the foreign origin of the product. Package, label, and product design can minimize evidence of foreign derivation. A brand policy of using local names will contribute to a domestic identity. The other alternative is to continue the foreign identification of the product and

[19] Simon Anholt, "The Nation as Brand," *Across the Board* 37, no. 10 (November–December 2000), pp. 22–27.

[20] Jerome Witt and C. P. Rao, "The Impact of Global Sourcing on Consumers: Country-of-Origin Effects on Perceived Risk," *Journal of Global Marketing* 6, no. 3 (1992), pp. 105–128.

[21] Elliot Blair Smith, "Early PT Cruiser Took a Bruisin'," *USA Today* (August 8, 2001), pp. 1B, 2B. See also Joel Millman, "Trade Wins: The World's New Tiger on the Export Scene Isn't Asian; It's Mexico," *The Wall Street Journal* (May 9, 2000), pp. A1, A10.

attempt to change buyer attitudes toward the product. Over time, as consumers experience higher quality, the perception will change and adjust. It is a fact of life that perceptions of quality often lag behind reality.

In some product categories, foreign products have a substantial advantage over their domestic counterparts simply because of their "foreign-ness." Global marketers have an opportunity to capitalize on the situation by charging premium prices. The import segment of the beer industry is a case in point. In one study of American attitudes about beer, subjects who were asked to indicate taste preference for beer in a blind test indicated a preference for domestic beers over imports. The same subjects were then asked to indicate preference ratings for beers in an open test with labels attached. In this test, the subjects preferred imported beer. Increasing numbers of Americans are developing a taste for imported beers; 2000 import sales added up to about 20 million barrels, an increase of 12.3 percent over 1999. In 1997, thanks to a brilliant marketing campaign, Grupo Modelo's Corona Extra surpassed Heineken as the best-selling imported beer in America. With distribution in 150 countries, Corona is a textbook example of a local brand that has been built into a global powerhouse. Meanwhile, America's best-known beer brands are finding acceptance abroad as well. In the United Kingdom, for example, many pubs stock Budweiser and Michelob. Craft brew brands such as Pete's Wicked are also widely available.

> *"Consider labels such as 'Made in Brazil' and 'Made in Thailand.' Someday they may be symbols of high quality and value, but today many consumers expect products from those countries to be inferior."*
> Christopher A. Bartlett and Sumantra Ghoshal[22]

> The European Commission has proposed a mandatory "Made in the EU" label for goods manufactured in Europe. Walpole is an association that represents dozens of brands that are made in the United Kingdom. Walpole pledges to lobby against the label initiative on the grounds that the labels will dilute the value associated with the United Kingdom as a country of manufacture.

---

[22] Christopher A. Bartlett and Sumantra Ghoshal, "Going Global: Lessons from Late Movers," *Harvard Business Review* 78, no. 2 (March–April 2000), p. 133.

# PACKAGING

In many instances, packaging is an integral element of product-related decisions. Packaging is an important consideration for products that are shipped long distances to markets in all parts of the world. Moreover, the phrase "consumer packaged goods" applies to a wide variety of products whose packaging is designed to protect or contain the product during shipping, at retail locations, and at the point of use or consumption. "Eco-packaging" is a key issue today, and package designers must address environmental issues such as recycling and biodegradability. In Germany, for example, product packaging must conform to Green Dot regulations. Packaging also serves important communication functions: Packages (and labels attached to them) offer communication cues that provide consumers with a basis for making a purchase decision. Today, many industry experts agree that packaging must engage the senses, make emotional connections, and enhance a consumer's brand experience. According to Bernd Schmitt, director of Columbia University's Center on Global Brand Leadership, "Packages are creating an experience for the customer that goes beyond the functional benefits of displaying and protecting the object."[23] Absolut vodka, Altoids breath mints, and Godiva chocolates are a few examples of brands whose value proposition includes "experiential packaging."

Brewers, soft drink marketers, distillers, and other beverage firms typically devote considerable thought to ensuring that packages speak to consumers or provide some kind of benefit beyond simply holding liquid. For example, a critical element in the success of Corona Extra beer in export markets was management's decision to retain the traditional package design that consisted of a tall transparent bottle with "Made in Mexico" etched directly on the glass. At the time, the conventional wisdom in the brewing industry was that export beer bottles should be short, green or brown in color, with glued-on paper labels. The fact that consumers could see the beer inside the Corona Extra bottle made it seem more pure and natural. Today, Corona is the top-selling imported beer brand in the United States, Australia, Belgium, the Czech Republic, and several other countries.[24] Coca-Cola's distinctive (and trademarked) contour bottle comes in both glass and plastic versions and helps consumers seek out the "real thing." The Coke example also illustrates the point that packaging strategies can vary by country and region. In North America, where large refrigerators are found in many households, Coca-Cola's latest packaging innovation is the Fridge Pack, a long, slender carton that holds the equivalent of 12 cans of soda. The Fridge Pack fits on a refrigerator's lower shelf and includes a tap for easy dispensing. In Latin America, by contrast, Coca-Cola executives intend to boost profitability by offering Coke in several different sized bottles. Until recently, for example, 75 percent of Coke's volume in Argentina was accounted for by 2 liter bottles priced at 45 cents each. Coke has introduced cold, individual-serving bottles priced at 33 cents that are stocked in stores near the front; unchilled, 1.25 liter returnable glass bottles priced at 28 cents are available on shelves further back in the store.[25]

## Labeling

As noted on the first page of this textbook, one hallmark of the modern global marketplace is the abundance of multi-language labeling that appears on many products. In today's self-service retail environments, product labels may be

---

[23] Queena Sook Kim, "The Potion's Power Is in Its Packaging," *The Wall Street Journal* (December 21, 2000), p. B12.

[24] Sara Silver, "Modelo Puts Corona in the Big Beer League," *Financial Times* (October 30, 2002), p. 26.

[25] Betsy McKay, "Coke's Heyer Finds Test in Latin America," *The Wall Street Journal* (October 15, 2002), p. B4.

designed to attract attention, to support a product's positioning, and to help persuade consumers to buy. Labels can also provide consumers with various types of information. Obviously, care must be taken that all ingredient information and use and care instructions are properly translated. The content of product labels may also be dictated by country- or region-specific regulations. Regulations regarding mandatory label content vary in different parts of the world; for example, as noted in Chapter 5, the European Union now requires mandatory labeling for some foods containing genetically modified ingredients. Regulators in Australia, New Zealand, Japan, Russia, and several other countries have also proposed similar legislation. In the United States, the Nutrition Education and Labeling Act that went into effect in the early 1990s was intended to make food labels more informative and easier to understand. Today, virtually all food products sold in the United States must present information regarding nutrition (e.g., calories and fat content) and serving size in a standard format. The use of certain terms such as "light" and "natural" is also restricted. Other examples of labeling that impact global marketers include:

- Mandatory health warnings on tobacco products are required in most countries.
- The American Automobile Labeling Act clarifies the country of origin, the final assembly point, and percentages of the major sources of foreign content of every car, truck, and minivan sold in the United States (effective October 1, 1994).
- Since mid-2004, the European Union has required labels on all food products that include ingredients derived from genetically modified crops.

## Aesthetics

In Chapter 4, the subject of aesthetics was introduced in a discussion of varying perceptions of color in different parts of the world. Global marketers must understand the importance of *visual aesthetics* embodied in the color or shape of a product, label, or package. Likewise, *aesthetic styles*, such as the degree of complexity found on a label, are perceived differently in different parts of the world. (E.g., it has been said that German wines would be more appealing in export markets if the labels were simplified.) Aesthetic elements that are deemed appropriate, attractive, and appealing in one's home country may be perceived differently elsewhere. In some cases, a standardized color can be used in all countries; examples include the distinctive yellow color on Caterpillar's earth-moving equipment and its licensed outdoor gear and the red Marlboro chevron. In other instances, color choices should be changed in response to local perceptions. It was noted in Chapter 4 that white is associated with death and bad luck in some Asian countries; recall that when GM executives were negotiating with China for the opportunity to build cars there, they gave Chinese officials gifts from upscale Tiffany & Company in the jeweler's signature blue box. The Americans astutely replaced Tiffany's white ribbons with red ones, because red is considered a lucky color in China and white has negative connotations.

Packaging aesthetics are particularly important to the Japanese. This point was driven home to the chief executive of a small U.S. company that manufactures an electronic device for controlling corrosion. After spending much time in Japan, the executive managed to secure several orders for the device. Following an initial burst of success, Japanese orders dropped off; for one thing, the executive was told, the packaging was too plain. "We couldn't understand why we needed a five-color label and a custom-made box for this device, which goes under the hood of a car or in the boiler room of a utility company," the executive said. While waiting for the bullet train in Japan one day, the executive's local distributor purchased a cheap watch at the station and had it elegantly wrapped. The distributor asked the

American executive to guess the value of the watch based on the packaging. Despite all that he had heard and read about the Japanese obsession with quality, it was the first time the American understood that, in Japan, "a book is judged by its cover." As a result, the company revamped its packaging, seeing to such details as ensuring that strips of tape used to seal the boxes were cut to precisely the same length.[26]

## PRODUCT WARRANTIES

A warranty can be an important element of a product's value proposition. An **express warranty** is a written guarantee that assures the buyer is getting what he or she has paid for or that provides recourse in case a product's performance falls short of expectations. In global marketing, warranties can be used as a competitive tool to position a company in a positive way. For example, in the late 1990s, Hyundai Motor America chief executive Finbarr O'Neill realized that many American car buyers perceived Korean cars as "cheap" and were skeptical about the Hyundai nameplate's reliability. In fact, the company had made significant improvements in the quality and reliability of its vehicles, but consumer perceptions of the brand had not kept pace with the changes. O'Neill instituted a 10-year, 100,000-mile warranty program that represents the most comprehensive coverage in the auto industry. Concurrently, Hyundai launched several new vehicles and increased expenditures for advertising. The results are impressive: Hyundai's U.S. sales jumped from about 90,000 vehicles in 1998 to nearly 400,000 vehicles in 2003.

## EXTEND, ADAPT, CREATE: STRATEGIC ALTERNATIVES IN GLOBAL MARKETING

To capitalize on opportunities outside the home country, company managers must devise and implement appropriate marketing programs. Depending on organizational objectives and market needs, a particular program may consist of extension strategies, adaptation strategies, or a combination of the two. A company that has developed a successful local product or brand can implement an **extension strategy** that calls for offering a product virtually unchanged (i.e., "extending" it) in markets outside the home country. A second option is an **adaptation strategy;** this involves changing elements of design, function, or packaging in response to needs or conditions in particular country markets. These product strategies can be used in conjunction with extension or adaptation communication strategies. This is the type of strategic decision facing executives at a company such as Starbucks who build a brand and a product/service offering in the home country market before expanding into global markets. A third strategic option, **product invention,** entails developing new products "from the ground up" with the world market in mind.

The decision to extend, adapt, or create is contingent on a number of factors relating to company-specific objectives as well as the sociocultural, economic, and political environments described in earlier chapters. In some instances, the key to meeting market share or unit sales objectives is making product design changes in response to local market conditions. However, the benefits of achieving such objectives must be weighed against the cost of changing a product's design and testing it in the market. Also, despite the evidence cited in earlier chapters that tastes and preferences are converging around the globe, significant differences do still exist in terms of what customers want and need. Marketers who ignore such differences and pursue extension strategies for the sake of economy or expediency do so at their own peril.

---

[26] Nilly Landau, "Face to Face Marketing Is Best," *International Business* (June 1994), p. 64.

Laws and regulations in different countries frequently lead to obligatory product design adaptations. This may be seen most clearly in Europe, where one impetus for the creation of the single market was the desire to dismantle regulatory and legal barriers that prevented pan-European sales of standardized products. These were particularly prevalent in the areas of technical standards and health and safety standards. In the food industry, for example, there were 200 legal and regulatory barriers to cross-border trade within the EU in 10 food categories. Among these were prohibitions or taxes on products with certain ingredients and different packaging and labeling laws. As these barriers are dismantled, there will be less need to adapt product designs and many companies will be able to create standardized "Euro-products."

Despite the trend toward convergence, many product standards that remain on the books have not been harmonized. This situation can create problems for companies not based in the EU. Dormont Manufacturing, appropriately based in Export, Pennsylvania, makes hoses that hook up to deep-fat fryers and similar appliances used in the food industry. Dormont's gas hose is made of stainless-steel helical tubing with no covering. British industry requirements call for galvanized metal annular tubing and a rubber covering; Italian regulations specify stainless steel annual tubing with no covering. The cost of complying with these regulations effectively shuts Dormont out of the European market.[27] Moreover, the European Commission continues to set product standards that force many non-EU companies to adapt product or service offerings that satisfy domestic market regulations. For example, consumer safety regulations mean that McDonald's cannot give away soft-plastic toys with its Happy Meals in Europe. Microsoft has been forced to modify contracts with European software makers and Internet-service providers to ensure that consumers in the EU have access to a wide range of technologies. The commission has also set stringent guidelines on product content as it affects recyclability. As Maja Wessels, a Brussels-based lobbyist for United Technologies (UT), noted recently, "Twenty years ago, if you designed something to U.S. standards you could pretty much sell it all over the world. Now the shoe's on the other foot." Engineers at UT's Carrier division are redesigning the company's air conditioners to comply with pending European recycling rules, which are tougher than U.S. standards.[28]

As noted in Chapter 1, the extension/adaptation/creation decision is one of the most fundamental issues addressed by a company's global marketing strategy. Although it pertains to all elements of the marketing mix, extension/adaptation is of particular importance in product and communications decisions. As a framework for guiding product and communications decisions, the extend/adapt options can be represented in matrix form. Figure 10-4 shows four strategic alternatives available to Starbucks or any other company seeking to expand from its domestic base into new geographic markets. Extension strategies are employed by companies in the international, global, and transnational stages of development. The critical difference is one of execution and mind-set. In an international company, for example, the extension strategy reflects an ethnocentric orientation and the *assumption* that all markets are alike. A global company such as Gillette does not fall victim to such assumptions; the company's geocentric orientation allows it to thoroughly understand its markets and consciously take advantage of similarities in world markets. Likewise, a multinational company utilizes the adaptation strategy because of its polycentric orientation and the assumption that all markets are different. By contrast, the geocentric orientation of managers and executives in a global company has sensitized them to actual, rather than assumed, differences between markets.

---

[27] Timothy Aeppel, "Europe's 'Unity' Undoes a U.S. Exporter," *The Wall Street Journal* (April 1, 1996), p. B1.

[28] Brandon Mitchener, "Standard Bearers: Increasingly, Rules of Global Economy Are Set in Brussels," *The Wall Street Journal* (April 23, 2002), p. A1.

**Figure 10-4**

Global Product Planning:
Strategic Alternatives

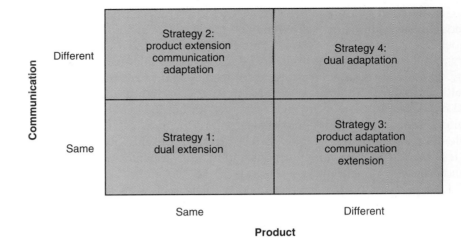

Note that the alternatives are not mutually exclusive: A company can simultaneously utilize different product/communication strategies in different parts of the world. For example, Nike has built a global brand by marketing technologically advanced, premium-priced athletic shoes in conjunction with advertising that emphasizes U.S.-style in-your-face brashness and "Just Do It" attitude. In the huge and strategically important China market, however, this approach had several limitations. For one thing, Nike's "bad boy" image is at odds with ingrained Chinese values such as respect for authority and filial piety. As a general rule, advertisements in China do not show disruption of harmony; this is due in part to a government that discourages dissent. Price was another issue: A regular pair of Nike shoes cost the equivalent of $60–$78 while average annual family income ranges from about $200 in rural areas to $500 in urban areas. In the mid-1990s, Nike responded by creating a shoe that could be assembled in China specifically for the Chinese market using less expensive material and sold for under $40. After years of running ads designed for Western markets by longtime agency Wieden & Kennedy, Nike hired Chinese-speaking art directors and copywriters working in WPP Group's J. Walter Thompson ad agency in Shanghai to create new advertising featuring local athletes that would appeal to Chinese nationalistic sentiments.[29]

## Strategy 1: Product-Communication Extension

Many companies employ **product-communication extension** (dual extension) as a strategy for pursuing opportunities outside the home market. Under the right conditions, this is the easiest product marketing strategy; it can be the most profitable one as well. Companies pursuing this strategy sell the same product with virtually no adaptation, using the same advertising and promotional appeals used domestically, in two or more country markets or segments.

As a general guideline, it should be noted that extension/standardization strategies can be utilized more frequently with industrial (business-to-business) products than with consumer products. Industrial products tend not to be as rooted in culture as consumer goods. Manufacturers of industrial products should be especially alert to extension possibilities. For example, Henkel KgaA's Loctite Corp. subsidiary manufactures industrial adhesives and sealants that are sold in more than 80 countries. Loctite's double-digit sales and earnings growth over the past several years can be partially attributed to top management's recognition that the products it had developed for the U.S. market could be sold without adaptation virtually anywhere.

---

[29]   Sally Goll Beatty, "Bad-Boy Nike Is Playing the Diplomat in China," *The Wall Street Journal* (November 10, 1997), p. B1.

Some marketers have learned the hard way that the dual extension approach does not work in every market. When Campbell Soup tried to sell its tomato soup in the United Kingdom, it discovered, after substantial losses, that the English prefer a more bitter taste than Americans. Campbell learned its lesson and subsequently succeeded in Japan by creating corn pottage and other flavors specifically for the Japanese market. In 2000, H.J. Heinz Company launched a new green ketchup in an easy-to-grasp squeeze bottle. The target market was American children who account for about 50 percent of ketchup consumption in the United States. The question now facing Heinz's marketing staff is whether EZ Squirt can be extended to other markets. In Canada, for example, research suggests that kids will embrace both the new bottle and the green ketchup inside. However, because parents will be making the actual purchase, it is important to win them over as well. As Susan Yorke, a manager at H.J. Heinz Co. of Canada, notes, "Coloured ketchup is definitely polarizing because you have your loyal users who have grown up with ketchup and can't imagine doing anything to it—certainly not a different color." Will an extension strategy work with EZ Squirt? Yorke is optimistic. "We have a skilled marketing team. . . . If we do launch these products, like every other launch, it's because we think it's going to be successful," she said.[30] Meanwhile, back in the United States, Heinz launched *purple* EZ Squirt in 2001.

The product-communication extension strategy has an enormous appeal to global companies because of the cost savings associated with this approach. The most obvious sources of savings are design and manufacturing economies of scale, inventory savings, and elimination of duplicate product R&D costs. Also important are the substantial economies associated with standardization of marketing communications. For a company with worldwide operations, the cost of preparing separate print and TV ads for each market can be enormous. Although these cost savings are important, they should not distract executives from the more important objective of maximum profit performance, which may require the use of an adaptation or invention strategy. As we have seen, product extension, in spite of its immediate cost savings, may in fact result in market failure.

## Strategy 2: Product Extension–Communication Adaptation

When taking a product beyond the home-country market, management sometimes discovers that consumer perceptions about "quality" and "value" are different from those in the home country. It may also turn out that a product fills a different need, appeals to a different segment, or serves a different function. Whatever the reason, market success may be achieved by extending the product while adapting the marketing communications program. The appeal of the **product extension–communication adaptation strategy** is its relatively low cost of implementation. Because the physical product is unchanged, expenditures for R&D, manufacturing setup, and inventory are avoided. The biggest costs associated with this approach are in researching the market and revising advertising, sales promotion, point-of-sale material, and other communication elements as appropriate.

For example, before executives at Ben & Jerry's Homemade launched their ice cream in the United Kingdom, the company conducted extensive research to determine whether the package design effectively communicated the brand's "super premium" position. The research indicated that British consumers perceived the colors differently than U.S. consumers. The package design was changed, and Ben & Jerry's was launched successfully in the U.K. market. Marketers of premium

---

[30] Heidi Staseson, "Not So Easy Being Green at Heinz," *Marketing Magazine* 105, no. 30 (July 31, 2000), p. 6.

American bourbon brands such as Wild Turkey have found that images of Delta blues music, New Orleans, and Route 66 appeal to upscale drinkers outside the United States. However, images that stress bourbon's rustic, backwoods origins do not appeal to Americans. Likewise, Jägermeister schnapps is marketed differently in key country markets. Chief executive Hasso Kaempfe believes that a diversity of images has been a key element in the success of Jägermeister outside of Germany, where the brown herb-based concoction originated. In the United States, Jägermeister was "discovered" in the mid-1990s by bar patrons, particularly college students. Eschewing traditional media advertising, Kaempfe's marketing team has capitalized on the brand's cult status by hiring "Jägerettes" girls to pass out free samples; the company's popular T-shirts and orange banners are also distributed at rock concerts. By contrast, in Italy, the brand's second-largest export market, Jägermeister is considered an up-market digestive to be consumed after dinner. In Germany, Austria, and Switzerland, where beer culture predominates, Jägermeister and other brands of schnapps have more traditional associations as a remedy for coughs, stomachaches, or hangovers.[31]

> "Europeans hate Americans when they think of them as being the policemen of the world, but they love Americans when they think about blue jeans and bourbon and ranches."
>
> Gary Regan, author of *The Book of Bourbon*[32]

Jägermeister is an example of **product transformation:** The same physical product ends up serving a different function or use than that for which it was originally designed or created. In some cases a particular country or regional environment will allow local managers a greater degree of creativity and risk taking when approaching the communication task. As a result, managers "push the envelope" in an effort to stand out amid the message clutter. For example, Europeans exhibit a higher tolerance for sexual innuendo in advertising than do Americans. A 1997 billboard campaign in Europe for VF Corporation's Lee brand boot-cut jeans showed a naked man lying on his stomach with a woman's stiletto-heeled foot poised over his buttocks. Although the visual left little to the imagination, the copy drove home the point by commanding, "Put the boot in." A London newspaper described the campaign as "one of the most provocative of the year"; it is safe to say that such billboards will never appear in the United States. Recently, European ad bureaus have responded to government complaints by clamping down on "porno-chic" ads. In particular, French authorities have objected to the portrayal of women in ads from Emanuel Ungaro, Christian Dior, and Benetton Group. Groups such as France's Truth in Advertising Bureau and Italy's Advertising Self-Regulation Bureau ask member agencies to voluntarily withdraw offending ads; most agencies comply.[33]

## Strategy 3: Product Adaptation–Communication Extension

A third approach to global product planning is to extend, without change, the basic home-market communications strategy while adapting the product to local use or preference conditions. Exxon adheres to this third strategy option, which is known as **product adaptation–communication extension.** Exxon adapts its gasoline formulations to meet the weather conditions prevailing in different markets without changing the basic communications appeal, "Put a Tiger in Your Tank." There are many other examples of products that have been adapted to perform the same function around the globe under different market conditions. Hon Industries of Muscatine, Iowa, markets value-priced office furniture throughout the United States and Canada. Its Hon International subsidiary is responsible for marketing in the rest of the world. When executives began to explore the possibility of exporting to Japan, they realized that they would have to scale down the size of their designs

---

[31] Bettina Wassener, "Schnapps Goes to College," *Financial Times* (September 4, 2003), p. 9.
[32] Kimberly Palmer, "Rustic Bourbon: A Hit Overseas, Ho-Hum in the U.S." *The Wall Street Journal* (September 2, 2003), p. B1.
[33] Allesandra Galloni, "Clampdown on 'Porno-chic' Ads Is Pushed by French Authorities," *The Wall Street Journal* (October 25, 2001), p. B4.

to accommodate the smaller Japanese physique. Similarly, soap and detergent manufacturers have adjusted their product formulations to meet local water and washing equipment conditions with no change in their basic communications approach. Household appliances have been scaled to sizes appropriate to different use environments, and clothing has been adapted to meet fashion criteria.

## Strategy 4: Product-Communication Adaptation

Sometimes, when comparing a new geographic market to the home market, marketers discover that environmental conditions or consumer preferences differ; the same may be true of the function a product serves or consumer receptivity to advertising appeals. In essence, this is a combination of the market conditions associated with Strategies 2 and 3. In such a situation, a company will utilize the **product-communication adaptation** (dual adaptation) strategy. Historically, this approach has been associated with the decentralized structure of the multinational corporation. Unilever's experience with fabric softener in Europe exemplifies the classic multinational road to adaptation. For years, the product was sold in 10 countries under seven different brand names, with different bottles and marketing strategies. Unilever's decentralized structure meant that product and marketing decisions were left to country managers. They chose names that had local-language appeal and selected package designs to fit local tastes. Today, rival Procter & Gamble is introducing competitive products with a pan-European strategy of standardized products with single names, suggesting that the European market is more similar than Unilever assumed. In response, Unilever's European brand managers are attempting to move gradually toward standardization.[34]

American computer manufacturers have discovered that Germans view computers as commodities. Germans will not pay extra for a well-known brand, and, because of their price sensitivity, it is difficult to convince them of the need for feature upgrades. As a result, despite the fact that its chairman was German, Compaq did not do well in Germany against local brands and no-name computers. Compaq has revised its product offering in Germany and its entire marketing mix to compete more effectively in the German computer market.

It is important to understand that these strategic options are not mutually exclusive. Sometimes, a company will draw upon all four of these strategies simultaneously when marketing a given product in different parts of the world. For example, H. J. Heinz utilizes a mix of strategies in its ketchup marketing. While a dual-extension strategy works in England, spicier, hotter formulations are also popular in central Europe and Sweden. Recent ads in France featured a cowboy lassoing a bottle of ketchup and thus reminded consumers of the product's American heritage. Swedish ads conveyed a more cosmopolitan message; by promoting Heinz as "the taste of the big world" and featuring well-known landmarks such as the Eiffel Tower, the ads disguised the product's origins.[35]

## Strategy 5: Product Invention

Extension and adaptation strategies are effective approaches to many but not all global market opportunities. For example, they do not respond to markets where there is a need but not the purchasing power to buy either the existing or adapted product. This latter situation applies to the emerging markets of the world, which are home to roughly three-quarters of the world's population. When potential customers have limited purchasing power, a company may need to develop an

[34] E. S. Browning, "In Pursuit of the Elusive Euroconsumer," *The Wall Street Journal* (April 23, 1992), p. B2.
[35] Gabriella Stern, "Heinz Aims to Export Taste for Ketchup," *The Wall Street Journal* (November 20, 1992), pp. B1, B9.

entirely new product designed to address the market opportunity at a price point that is within the reach of the potential customer. The converse is also true: Companies in low-income countries that have achieved local success may have to go beyond mere adaptation by "raising the bar" and bringing product designs up to world-class standards if they are to succeed in high-income countries. **Invention** is a demanding but potentially rewarding product strategy for reaching mass markets in less developed countries as well as important market segments in industrialized countries.

Two entrepreneurs working independently recognized that millions of people around the globe need low-cost eyeglasses. Robert J. Morrison, an American optometrist, created Instant Eyeglasses. These glasses utilize conventional lenses, can be assembled in minutes, and sell for about $20 per pair. Joshua Silva, a physics professor at Oxford University, took a more high-tech approach: glasses with transparent membrane lenses filled with clear silicone fluid. Using two manual adjusters, users can increase or decrease the power of the lenses by regulating the amount of fluid in them. Professor Silva hopes to sell the glasses in developing countries for about $10 per pair.[36] Another example of the invention strategy is the South African company that licensed the British patent for a hand-cranked, battery-powered radio. The radio was designed by an English inventor responding to the need for radios in low-income countries. Consumers in these countries do not have electricity in their homes, and they cannot afford the cost of replacement batteries. His invention is an obvious solution: a hand-cranked radio. It is ideal for the needs of low-income people in emerging markets. Users simply crank the radio, and it will play on the charge generated by a short cranking session for almost an hour.

Sometimes manufacturers in developing countries that intend to go global also utilize the product invention strategy. For example, Thermax, an Indian company, had achieved great success in its domestic market with small industrial boilers. Engineers developed a new design for the Indian market that significantly reduced the size of the individual boiler unit. However, the new design was not likely to succeed outside India. In India, where labor costs are low, relatively elaborate installation requirements are not an issue. The situation is different in higher-wage countries where industrial customers demand sophisticated integrated systems that can be installed quickly. The managing director at Thermax instructed his engineers to design for the world market. The gamble paid off: Today, Thermax is one of the world's largest producers of small boilers.[37]

Colgate pursued the product invention strategy in developing Total, a toothpaste brand whose formulation, imagery, and ultimate consumer appeal were designed from the ground up to readily cross national boundaries. The product was tested in six countries, each of which had a different cultural profile: the Philippines, Australia, Colombia, Greece, Portugal, and the United Kingdom. Total is now available in 100 countries and generates $150 million in annual revenues. According to John Steel, senior vice president for global business development at Colgate, Total's success results from the application of a fundamental marketing principle: Consumers are the ones who make or break brands. "There ain't no consumers at 300 Park Avenue," he says, referring to company headquarters. Steel explains, "You get a lot more benefit and you can do a lot more with a global brand than you can a local brand. You can bring the best advertising talent from the world on to a problem. You can bring the best research brains, the best

---

36 Amy Borrus, "Eyeglasses for the Masses," *Business Week* (November 20, 1995), pp. 104–105; Nicholar Thompson, "Self-Adjusted Glasses Could be Boon to Africa," *The New York Times* (December 10, 2002), p. D6.
37 Christopher A. Bartlett and Sumantra Ghoshal, "Going Global: Lessons from Late Movers," *Harvard Business Review* 78, no. 2 (March–April 2000), p. 137.

leverage of your organization onto something that is truly global. Then all your R&D pays off, the huge packaging costs pay off, the advertising pays off, and you can leverage the organization all at once."[38]

The winners in global competition are the companies that can develop products offering the most benefits, which in turn create the greatest value for buyers anywhere in the world. In some instances, value is not defined in terms of performance, but rather in terms of customer perception. The latter is as important for an expensive perfume or champagne as it is for an inexpensive soft drink. Product quality is essential—indeed, it is frequently a given—but it is also necessary to support the product quality with imaginative, value-creating advertising and marketing communications. Most industry experts believe that a global appeal and a global advertising campaign are more effective in creating the perception of value than a series of separate national campaigns.

*"Designing a Harley-Davidson motorcycle for international markets requires constant collaboration among design teams around the world. We use videoconferencing, phone calls, e-mail, and on-site meetings to enhance communications. We advise our engineers to stay close to the customers in the markets in which the customers are located so we can quickly react to changing customer desires and international regulations."*

Bruce Roberts, Harley-Davidson mechanical design engineer[39]

## How to Choose a Strategy

Most companies seek product-communications strategies that optimize company profits over the long term. Which strategy for global markets best achieves this goal? There is no general answer to this question. For starters, the considerations noted before must be addressed. In addition, it is worth noting that managers run the risk of committing two types of errors regarding product and communication decisions. One error is to fall victim to the **"not invented here" (NIH) syndrome,** *ignoring* decisions made by subsidiary or affiliate managers. Managers who behave in this way are essentially abandoning any effort to leverage product-communication policies outside the home-country market. The other error has been to *impose* policies upon all affiliate companies on the assumption that what is right for customers in the home market must also be right for customers everywhere.

German carmaker Volkswagen AG learned the consequences of this latter error; VW saw its position in the U.S. import market erode from leader to also-ran over the course of two decades. By the early 1970s, Volkswagen was manufacturing cars in Pennsylvania for the American market; a product extension strategy enabled the company to sell more cars in the United States than all other foreign automakers combined. By the early 1990s, however, VW commanded a scant 0.5 percent share of the U.S. auto market. By clinging to the assumption that vehicles designed for European tastes would continue to be embraced by American car buyers seduced by more stylish Japanese imports, Volkswagen fell victim to its own ethnocentricity. (Negative publicity about engines leaking oil and exploding didn't help either.) Volkswagen was offering a German-designed car built to American quality standards while competing with Japanese cars that incorporated much higher standards of quality. After becoming CEO in 1993, Ferdinand Piëch engineered a brilliant turnaround; the enthusiastic response of American car buyers to the new Beetle and updated Passat and Jetta models have boosted U.S. market share to 2.5 percent. Buoyed by a 14 percent increase in U.S. sales, VW's $1.8 billion profit in 2000 was double the previous year's figure.[40]

Companies differ in terms of both their willingness and capability to identify and produce profitable product adaptations. Unfortunately, in companies where an ethnocentric mind-set predominates, executives and managers are oblivious to

[38] Pam Weisz, "Border Crossings: Brands Unify Image to Counter Cult of Culture," *Brandweek* (October 31, 1994), p. 24.
[39] Bruce Wiebusch, "Deere, Hogs, and International Design," *Design News* (November 18, 2002).
[40] Christine Tierney, "Volkswagen," *Business Week* (July 23, 2001), pp. 60–65+.

the issues presented here. One new-product expert described three stages that a company must go through:

1. *Cave dweller.* The primary motivation behind launching new products internationally is to dispose of excess production or to better utilize plant capacity.
2. *Naive nationalist.* The company recognizes growth opportunities outside the domestic market. It realizes that cultures and markets differ from country to country and, as a result, sees product adaptation as the only possible alternative.
3. *Globally sensitive.* The company views regions or the entire world as the competitive marketplace. New product opportunities are evaluated across countries, with some standardization planned as well as some differentiation to accommodate cultural variances. New-product planning processes and control systems are reasonably standardized.[41]

To sum up, the choice of product-communication strategy in global marketing is a function of three key factors: (1) the product itself, defined in terms of the function or need it serves; (2) the market, defined in terms of the conditions under which the product is used, the preferences of potential customers, and the ability to buy the products in question; and (3) adaptation and manufacture costs to the company considering these product-communication approaches. Only after analysis of the product-market fit and of company capabilities and costs can executives choose the most profitable strategy.

## NEW PRODUCTS IN GLOBAL MARKETING

The matrix shown in Figure 10-4 provides a framework for assessing whether extension or adaptation strategies can be effective. However, the four strategic options described in the matrix do not necessarily represent the best possible responses to global market opportunities. To win in global competition, marketers, designers, and engineers must think outside the box and create innovative new products that offer superior value worldwide. In today's dynamic, competitive market environment, many companies realize that continuous development and introduction of new products are keys to survival and growth. That is the point of Strategy 5, product invention. Similarly, marketers should look for opportunities to create global advertising campaigns to support the new product or brand.

Gary Reiner, formerly a new-product specialist with the Boston Consulting Group and currently chief information officer at GE, has identified global companies that excel at new product development. His list includes Honda, Compaq, Motorola, Canon, Boeing, Merck, Microsoft, Intel, and Toyota. One common characteristic: They are global companies that pursue opportunities in global markets where competition is fierce, thus ensuring that new products will be world class. Other characteristics noted by Reiner are:

1. They focus on one or only a few businesses
2. Senior management is actively involved in defining and improving the product development process
3. They have the ability to recruit and retain the best and the brightest people in their fields
4. They understand that speed in bringing new products to market reinforces product quality[42]

---

[41] Thomas D. Kuczmarski, *Managing New Products: The Power of Innovation* (Upper Saddle River, NJ: Prentice Hall, 1992), p. 254.
[42] Gary Reiner, "Lessons from the World's Best Product Developers," *The Wall Street Journal* (April 4, 1990), p. A12.

# Identifying New-Product Ideas

What is a new product? A product's newness can be assessed in the context of its relation to those who buy or use it. Newness may also be organizational, as when a company acquires an already existing product with which it has no previous experience. Finally, an existing product that is not new to a company may be new to a particular market. The starting point for an effective worldwide new-product program is an information system that seeks new-product ideas from all potentially useful sources and channels these ideas to relevant screening and decision centers within the organization. Ideas can come from many sources, including customers, suppliers, competitors, company salespeople, distributors and agents, subsidiary executives, headquarters executives, documentary sources (e.g., information service reports and publications), and, finally, actual firsthand observation of the market environment.

The product may be an entirely new invention or innovation that requires a relatively large amount of learning on the part of users. When such products are successful, they create new markets and new consumption patterns that literally represent a break with the past; they are sometimes called **discontinuous innovations.**[43] For example, the VCR's revolutionary impact can be explained by the concept of time shifting: The device's initial appeal was that it freed TV viewers from the tyranny of network programming schedules. For the first time, it was possible to record television programming for viewing at a later time. The VCR's market growth and acceptance was also driven by the video rental industry, which sprang up to serve the needs of VCR owners. Likewise, the personal computer revolution that began two decades ago has resulted in the democratization of technology. When they were first introduced, PCs were a discontinuous innovation that dramatically transformed the way users live and work.

An intermediate category of newness is less disruptive and requires less learning on the part of consumers; such products are called **dynamically continuous innovations.** Products that embody this level of innovation share certain features with earlier generations while incorporating new features that offer added value such as a substantial improvement in performance or greater convenience. Such products cause relatively smaller disruptions of previously existing consumption patterns. The Sensor, SensorExcel, and MACH3 shaving systems represent Gillette's ongoing efforts to bring new technology to bear on wet shaving, an activity that is performed today pretty much as it has been for decades. The consumer electronics industry has been the source of many dynamically continuous innovations. Personal stereos such as Sony's Walkman provide music on the go, something that people had grown accustomed to since the transistor radio was introduced in the 1950s; the innovation was a miniaturized cassette playback system. The advent of the compact disc in the early 1980s provided an improved music listening experience but didn't require significant behavioral changes. Similarly, much to the delight of couch potatoes everywhere, widescreen TV sets with flat-panel LCD and plasma displays offer viewers significantly improved performance without enabling or requiring new behaviors.

Most new products fall into a third category, **continuous innovation.** Such products are typically "new and improved" versions of existing ones and require less R&D expenditure to develop than dynamically continuous innovations. Continuous innovations cause minimal disruption of existing consumption patterns and require the least amount of learning on the part of buyers. As noted previously, newness can be evaluated relative to a buyer or user. When a current PC user seeking an upgrade buys a new model with a faster processor or more memory, the PC can be viewed as a continuous innovation. However, to a first-time user, the same computer represents a discontinuous innovation. Consumer packaged goods

---

[43] The terminology and framework described here are adapted from Thomas Robertson, "The Process of Innovation and the Diffusion of Innovation," *Journal of Marketing* 31, no. 1 (January 1967), pp. 14–19.

## Figure 10-5

New-Product Continuum

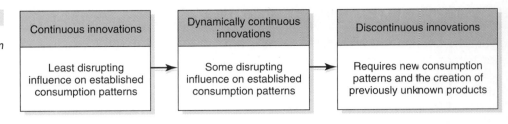

companies and food marketers rely heavily on continuous innovation when rolling out new products. These often take the form of **line extensions** such as new sizes, flavors, and low-fat versions. The three degrees of product newness can be represented in terms of a continuum as shown in Figure 10-5.

## New-Product Development

A major driver for the development of global products is the cost of product R&D. As competition intensifies, companies discover they can reduce the cost of R&D for a product by developing a global product design. Often the goal is to create a single **platform,** or core product design element or component, that can be quickly and cheaply adapted to various country markets. As Christopher Sinclair noted during his tenure as president and CEO of PepsiCo Foods and Beverages International, "What you really want to do is look at the four or five platforms that can allow you to cut across countries, become a scale operator, and do the things that global marketers do."[44]

Even products like automobiles, which must meet national safety and pollution standards, are now designed with global markets in mind. With a global product platform, companies can offer an adaptation of a global design as needed instead of unique designs for individual countries or geographic regions. The new Ford Focus, launched in Europe at the end of 1998 and in the United States in 1999, represented the company's first major new vehicle since the much-vaunted Ford 2000 reorganization. Focus is being marketed in Europe and the United States with a minimum of adaptation. The chief program engineer on the Focus project was from Great Britain, the chief technical officer was German, an Irishwoman managed the project, and an Anglo-Australian was chief designer. Under Ford 2000, about $1,000 per vehicle was cut out of the development cost.[45] The Focus platform will be used on the next generation Mazda 323, Volvo's S40 and V40 models, and a seven-passenger minivan as part of Ford's C1 Technologies program. Unfortunately, Ford has yet to reap the potential quality and cost-saving benefits associated with its platform strategy: Despite positive reviews in the automotive press, the Focus has been plagued with quality defects since it was brought across the Atlantic to the United States.

A standardized platform was also a paramount consideration when GM set about the task of redesigning its minivan. GM's globally minded board directed the design team to create a vehicle that would be popular in both the United States and Europe. Because roads in Europe are typically narrower and fuel is more expensive, the European engineers lobbied for a vehicle that was smaller than the typical minivan. In the end, interior designers were able to provide ample interior space in a slightly smaller body. By using lightweight metals such as magnesium for some components, vehicle weight was minimized, with a corresponding improvement in fuel economy. In the United States, the minivans are marketed as

---

[44] "Fritos 'Round the World," *Brandweek* (March 27, 1995), pp. 32, 35.
[45] Robert L. Simison, "Ford Hopes Its New Focus Will Be a Global Bestseller," *The Wall Street Journal* (October 8, 1998), p. B10.

the Chevrolet Venture, Pontiac Transport, and Oldsmobile Silhouette. The Opel Sentra version will be exported to Germany; the right-hand-drive Vauxhall Sintra is destined for the British market.[46]

Other design-related costs, whether incurred by the manufacturer or the end user, must also be considered. *Durability* and *quality* are important product characteristics that must be appropriate for the proposed market. In the United States and Europe, car buyers do not wish to incur high service bills. Ironically, the new Ford Focus was designed to be less expensive to maintain and repair. For example, engine removal takes only about 1.5 hours, about half the time required to remove the engine in the discontinued Escort. In addition, body panels are bolted together rather than welded, and the rear signal lights are mounted higher so they are less likely to be broken in minor parking lot mishaps.

## The International New-Product Department

As noted previously, a high volume of information flow is required to scan adequately for new-product opportunities, and considerable effort is subsequently required to screen these opportunities to identify candidates for product development. The best organizational design for addressing these requirements is a new-product department. Managers in such a department engage in several activities. First, they ensure that all relevant information sources are continuously tapped for new-product ideas. Second, they screen these ideas to identify candidates for investigation. Third, they investigate and analyze selected new-product ideas. Finally, they ensure that the organization commits resources to the most likely new-product candidates and is continuously involved in an orderly program of new-product introduction and development on a worldwide basis.

With the enormous number of possible new products, most companies establish screening grids in order to focus on those ideas that are most appropriate for investigation. The following questions are relevant to this task:

1. How big is the market for this product at various prices?
2. What are the likely competitive moves in response to our activity with this product?
3. Can we market the product through our existing structure? If not, what changes will be required, and what costs will be incurred to make the changes?
4. Given estimates of potential demand for this product at specified prices with estimated levels of competition, can we source the product at a cost that will yield an adequate profit?
5. Does this product fit our strategic development plan? (a) Is the product consistent with our overall goals and objectives? (b) Is the product consistent with our available resources? (c) Is the product consistent with our management structure? (d) Does the product have adequate global potential?

For example, the corporate development team at Virgin evaluates more than a dozen proposals each day from outside the company, as well as proposals from Virgin staff members. The team is headed by Brad Rosser, who is director of corporate management. When assessing new-product ideas, Rosser and his team look for synergy with existing Virgin products, pricing, marketing opportunities, risk versus return on investment, and whether the idea "uses or abuses" the Virgin brand. Recent ventures that have been given the green light are Virgin Jeans, a denim clothing store chain; Virgin Bride, a wedding consulting service; and Virgin Net, an Internet service provider.[47]

---

[46] Rebecca Blumenstein, "While Going Global, GM Slips at Home," *The Wall Street Journal* (January 8, 1997), pp. B1, B4.
[47] Elena Bowes, "Virgin Flies in Face of Conventions," *Ad Age International* (January 1997), p. i4.

## Testing New Products

The major lesson of new-product introduction outside the home market has been that whenever a product interacts with human, mechanical, or chemical elements, there is the potential for a surprising and unexpected incompatibility. Because virtually *every* product matches this description, it is important to test a product under actual market conditions before proceeding with full-scale introduction. A test does not necessarily involve a full-scale test-marketing effort. It may be simply observing the actual use of the product in the target market.

Failure to assess actual use conditions can lead to big surprises, as Unilever learned when it rolled out a new detergent brand in Europe without sufficient testing. Unilever spent $150 million to develop the new detergent, which was formulated with a stain-fighting manganese complex molecule intended to clean fabrics faster at lower temperatures than competing products such as Procter & Gamble's Ariel. Backed by a $300 million marketing budget, the detergent was launched in April 1994 as Persil Power, Omo Power, and other brand names. After a restructuring, Unilever had cut the time required to roll out new products in Europe from 3 years to 16 months. In this particular instance, the increased efficiency combined with corporate enthusiasm for the new formula resulted in a marketing debacle. Consumers discovered that some clothing items were damaged after being washed with Power. P&G was quick to capitalize on the situation; P&G ran newspaper ads denouncing Power and commissioned lab tests to verify that the damage did, in fact, occur. Unilever chairman Sir Michael Perry called the Power fiasco, "the greatest marketing setback we've seen." Unilever reformulated Power, but it was too late to save the brand. The company lost the opportunity to gain share against P&G in Europe.[48]

## summary

The product is the most important element of a company's marketing program. Global marketers face the challenge of formulating coherent product and brand strategies on a worldwide basis. A **product** can be viewed as a collection of tangible and intangible attributes that collectively provide benefits to a buyer or user. A **brand** is a complex bundle of images and experiences in the mind of the customer. In most countries, **local brands** compete with **international brands** and **global brands**. A **global product** meets the wants and needs of a global market. A **global brand** has the same name and a similar image and positioning in most parts of the world. Many global companies leverage favorable **brand images** and high **brand equity** by employing **combination (tiered) branding, cobranding,** and **brand extension** strategies. Companies can create strong brands in all markets through **global brand leadership**. **Maslow's hierarchy is** a needs-based framework that offers a way of understanding opportunities to develop local and global products in different parts of the world. Some products and brands benefit from the **country-of-origin effect.** Product decisions must also address packaging issues such as **labeling** and **aesthetics.** Also, **product warranty** policies must be appropriate for each country market.

Product and communications strategies can be viewed within a framework that allows for combination of three strategies: **extension strategy, adaptation strategy,** and **creation strategy.** Five strategic alternatives are open to companies pursuing geographic expansion: **product-communication extension; product extension–communication adaptation; product adaptation–communication extension; product-communication adaptation;** and **product invention.** The strategic alternative(s) that a particular company chooses will depend on the product and the need it serves, customer preferences and purchasing power, and the costs of adaptation versus standardization. **Product transformation** occurs when a product introduced into new country markets

---

48 Laurel Wentz, "Unilever's Power Failure a Wasteful Use of Haste," *Advertising Age* (May 6, 1995), p. 42.

serves a different function or is used differently than originally intended. When choosing a strategy, management should consciously strive to avoid the **"not invented here" syndrome.**

Global competition has put pressure on companies to excel at developing standardized product **platforms** that can serve as a foundation for cost-efficient adaptation. New products can be classified as **discontinuous, dynamically continuous,** or **continuous innovations.** A successful product launch requires an understanding of how markets develop: sequentially over time or simultaneously. Today, many new products are launched in multiple national markets as product development cycles shorten and product development costs soar.

discussion questions

1. What is the difference between a product and a brand?

2. How do local, international, and global products differ? Cite examples.

3. What are some of the elements that make up a brand? Are these elements tangible or intangible?

4. What criteria should global marketers consider when making product design decisions?

5. How can buyer attitudes about a product's country of origin affect marketing strategy?

6. Identify several global brands. What are some of the reasons for the global success of the brands you chose?

7. Briefly describe various combinations of product-communication strategies available to global marketers. When is it appropriate to use each?

# Case 10-1

## Boeing Versus Airbus: A Battle for the Skies

Executives at the Boeing Company, the world's largest manufacturer of commercial aircraft, have plenty of experience making "bet the company" type of product decisions. In the 1950s, when the company was best known for military aircraft such as the B-52 bomber, Boeing single-handedly created the commercial market for jet aircraft with the introduction of the 707. In the mid-1960s, Boeing gambled that the world's airlines would be enthusiastic about a new wide-body aircraft. The gamble paid off handsomely: Since its first passenger flight in 1970, the Boeing 747 jumbo jet has generated more than $130 billion in sales. In 2001, Boeing made headlines again when it announced plans for a revolutionary new delta-wing aircraft called the Sonic Cruiser. The new jet would carry between 100 and 300 passengers and fly just below the speed of sound (Mach 1) with a range of up to 10,000 miles. On the same day it announced the Sonic Cruiser, Boeing cancelled development of the 747X, a larger, updated version of the venerable jumbo jet.

The Sonic Cruiser project grew out of Boeing's belief that air travelers are keenly interested in saving time, especially on long routes; the Sonic Cruiser would cut travel time by 1 hour for each 3,000 miles flown. Boeing also predicted that airline deregulation in Europe and Asia will result in increased industry competition, a situation that will result in more direct flights between cities that bypass the congestion of major regional hubs. In addition, the Sonic Cruiser would be build with lightweight composite materials that would result in operating savings of up to 20 percent. The stakes were high for Boeing: The world's airlines are expected to spend $1.5 trillion on new aircraft during the next two decades, but it would cost a minimum of $10 billion to develop the new plane. Meanwhile, the company was booking fewer orders for older Boeing models such as the single-aisle 757 and the 767.

Boeing's announcement about the Sonic Cruiser came as a shock to the entire global aerospace industry, including archrival Airbus. Airbus, which until 2000 was a consortium of five European companies, had spent 10 years planning

a double-decker, super jumbo craft, the A380. The new jet, which will go into service in 2006, will cost as much as $12 billion to develop. Airbus executives believe *their* new aircraft is the one that will revolutionize air travel in the twenty-first century. After assessing strategic opportunities, Airbus executives arrived at a different conclusion than their counterparts at Boeing. Although agreeing that the business will become more fragmented as deregulation spreads around the world, they predict large increases in passenger traffic but a limited amount of new airport construction. The conclusion: The airlines will need a new super jumbo to carry more passengers while reducing the number of flights between key hubs.

Airbus executives also dismissed Boeing's announcement as a public relations tactic to divert the public's attention from its decision not to compete head-to-head with the A380. Moreover, some industry observers questioned whether Boeing could build a faster airplane for which the total cost of operation would be feasible. One issue was whether current aerospace technology, including supercomputers for design and new composite materials containing graphite, could be employed effectively. Roy V. Harris, a former assistant director of research at NASA, asked, "Can they do it? I can't say that for sure right now. I think it will be a challenge." Airbus conceded that it, too, had considered building a faster aircraft but, as one executive said, "We have seen no great change in the laws of economics and physics that have given us any hope." John Leahy, the top sales executive for Airbus, is skeptical as well. "If there is such a thing as a free lunch, I am sure we are all interested," he said. One competitor predicted that Boeing would ultimately cancel the Sonic Cruiser program and offer airlines a scaled down version of its 777 instead.

By 2002, Boeing was indeed backpedaling on the Sonic Cruiser plan. The airline industry was retrenching in the wake of the 9/11 terror attacks; United Airlines, a key Boeing customer, was in bankruptcy. Moreover, airline passengers appeared to be more concerned with ticket prices than with travel time. Accordingly, Boeing began assessing customer reaction to an alternative design for a more conventional aircraft. As one airline executive said in mid-2002, "The folks over at Boeing are sort of pulling their hair out right now trying to figure out which is the right avenue to take." In the past, Boeing had canceled new-product development programs such as a proposed fuel-efficient model 7J7. Alan Mulally, Boeing's top executive at its commercial airplane division, defended that record, saying that Boeing is a nimble, customer-driven company. "What a neat thing it is to look at your customers and the market and make your investments accordingly. The fact that Boeing is listening and flexible is a great thing," he said.

By the fall of 2003, the suspense was over: As some industry observers had predicted, Boeing announced it was scrapping plans for the Sonic Cruiser. Instead the company will develop a new 200-seat model, the 7E7 Dreamliner, that will offer passengers improved comfort in the air. The new aircraft will have arched ceilings and "mood-enhancing lighting," larger windows than those on the 777; and seats in economy class will be arranged 3-2-3 across rather than 2-4-2. This configuration will make it less likely that passengers will be stuck in a "bad" seat. Boeing's new baby would also represent a powerful value proposition for the airlines: The "E" stands for "efficiency," and Boeing predicted that the new aircraft will cost 20 percent less to operate than existing aircraft.

Boeing's strategy for the 7E7 includes dispersing design work to Russia, China, and Japan. Thanks to the Internet, engineers in these nations can collaborate in real time. Moreover, by tapping talent resources in key countries, Boeing hopes to increase the likelihood of booking orders from airlines and governments in those nations. The use of composite materials will not only lower the 7E7's operating costs, but it will also enable Boeing to reconfigure its supply chain. For example, the wings and most of the fuselage will be manufactured in Japan and transported to Seattle in specially modified 747-400 freightliners. Previously, parts from Japan had been transported by water, rail, and, finally, truck, a journey that could take 1 month. Boeing expects that, by cutting transport time to 1 day, it can save 40 percent in shipping and inventory expenses. Companies that wish to bid on parts of the 7E7 will not have to deal with Boeing headquarters. Instead, they have to deal with Boeing's new 7E7 Council, a group made up of top executives from several outside suppliers.

Boeing's strategy for the 7E7 has created some controversy. In the 2 years leading up to the 7E7 announcement, Boeing had already cut 35,000 jobs in the United States. The company had previously outsourced some aircraft production to other countries; for example, Japanese companies supply about one-fifth of the 777. One reason for outsourcing was that airlines would be more likely to buy an aircraft that had some local content. However, that strategy had not always paid off. For example, Boeing has a design center in Russia that employs more than seven hundred engineers. In 2002, however, Russia's largest airline, AeroFlot, ordered twice as many aircraft from Airbus than it did from Boeing. Similarly, Boeing helped establish a small plant in South Africa to perform work that had previously been done in Seattle. In 2002, South African Airways ordered 41 jets from Airbus.

In the eyes of some critics, there is more at stake than just orders for new airplanes: The 7E7 project marks the first time that Being is sharing its proprietary technology for wing design and manufacture. Jennifer MacKay is president of the Society of Professional Engineering Employees in Aerospace, a union that represents Boeing engineers and other technical workers. She is deeply concerned about the long-term consequences of sharing technology with other countries. "In the end, if we teach everybody how to make the major parts, why is Boeing even needed?" she asks. Mike Blair, senior vice president of the 7E7, has an answer. "Figuring out what the wings look like, figuring out how to put them on the airplane, understanding whether that's something our customers will buy, understanding how to integrate that stuff, that's the magic Boeing brings to this process," he said.

**Table 1**  *7E7 Suppliers*

| Supplier | Percent of Project |
|---|---|
| Boeing | 35 |
| Mitsubishi Heavy Industries/Fuji Heavy Industries/Kawasaki Heavy Industries | 35 |
| Vought Aircraft Industries (Dallas, Texas)/Alenia Aeronautica (Rome) | 26 |
| Others | 4 |

## Discussion Questions

1. Assess Boeing's plans to subcontract out significant portions of the 7E7's manufacture.
2. How can Boeing successfully compete in the airline industry with Airbus and others?
3. Contrast the difference in strategy for Boeing and Airbus.

*Sources:* J. Lynn Lunsford, "Boeing's New Baby," *The Wall Street Journal* (November 18, 2003), pp. B1, B8; Caroline Daniel, "Airbus Takes on Boeing with More than Banter," *Financial Times* (November 14, 2003), p. 23; Byron Acohido, "Boeing Rips a Page out of Airbus' Book," *USA Today* (October 22, 2003), p. 3B; Lunsford, "Boeing Explores Plan 'B'," *The Wall Street Journal* (June 11, 2002), p. D5; Lunsford, "Lean Times: With Airbus on Its Tail, Boeing Is Rethinking How It Builds Planes," *The Wall Street Journal* (September 5, 2001), pp. A1, A16; Lunsford, "Navigating Change: Boeing, Losing Ground to Airbus, Faces Key Choice," *The Wall Street Journal* Alan Levin, "Boeing's Sonic Cruiser: Gambling on Speed," *USA Today* (June 18, 2001), pp. 1A, 2A; Laurence Zuckerman, "Boeing Plays an Aerial Wild Card," *The New York Times* (June 17, 2001), sec. 3, pp. 1, 11; Daniel Michaels, "New Approach: Airbus Revamp Brings Sense to Consortium, Fuels Boeing Rivalry," *The Wall Street Journal* (April 3, 2001), pp. A1, A8; Jeff Cole, "Wing Commander: At Boeing, an Old Hand Provides New Tricks in Battle with Airbus," *The Wall Street Journal* (January 10, 2001), pp. A1, A12.

# Case 10-2

### The Smart Car

In 1991, Nicolas Hayek, chairman of Swatch, announced an agreement with Volkswagen to develop a battery-powered "Swatch car." At the time, Hayek said his goal was to build "an ecologically inoffensive, high-quality city car for two people" that would sell for about $6,400. The Swatchmobile concept was based on Hayek's conviction that consumers become emotionally attached to cars just as they do to watches. Like the Swatch, the Swatchmobile (officially named "Smart") was designed to be affordable, durable, and stylish. Early on, Hayek noted that safety would be another key selling point, declaring, "This car will have the crash security of a Mercedes." Composite exterior panels mounted on a cage-like body frame would allow owners to change colors by switching panels. Further, Hayek envisioned a car that emitted almost no pollutants, thanks to its electric engine. The car would also be capable of gasoline-powered operation, using a highly efficient, miniaturized engine capable of achieving speeds of 80 miles per hour. Hayek predicted that worldwide sales would reach one million units, with the United States accounting for about half the market.

Some observers attributed the hoopla surrounding the Swatchmobile concept to Hayek's charismatic personality. His automotive vision was dismissed as being overly optimistic; less ambitious attempts at extending the Swatch brand name to new categories, including a brightly colored unisex clothing line, had flopped. Other products such as Swatch telephones, pagers, and sunglasses also met with lukewarm consumer acceptance. The Swatchmobile represented Hayek's attempt to pioneer a completely new market segment. Industry observers warned, moreover, that the Swatch name could be hurt if the Smart car were plagued by recall or safety problems.

In 1993, the alliance with Volkswagen was dissolved; Hayek claimed it was because of disagreement on the concept of the car (Volkswagen officials said low profit projections were the problem). In the spring of 1994, Hayek announced that he had lined up a new joint venture partner. The Mercedes-Benz unit of Daimler-Benz AG would invest 750 million Deutsche marks in a new factory in Hambach-Saargemuend, France. In November 1998, after several months of production delays and repeated cost overruns, Hayek sold Swatch's remaining 19 percent stake in the venture, officially known as Micro Compact Car GmBH (MCC), to Mercedes. A spokesman indicated that Mercedes' refusal to pursue the hybrid gasoline/battery engine was the reason Swatch withdrew from the project.

The decision by Mercedes executives to take full control of the venture was consistent with its strategy for leveraging its engineering skills and broadening the company's appeal beyond the luxury segment of the automobile market. As Mercedes chairman Helmut Werner said, "With the new car, Mercedes wants to combine ecology, emotion, and intellect." Approximately 80 percent of the Smart's parts are components and modules engineered by and sourced from outside suppliers and subcontractors known as "system partners." The decision to locate the assembly plant in France disappointed German labor unions, but Mercedes executives expected to save 500 marks per car. The reason: French workers are on the job 275 days per year, while German workers average only 242 days; also, overall labor costs are 40 percent lower in France than in Germany.

MCC claims that at Smart Ville, as the factory is known, only 7.5 hours are required to complete a vehicle. This is 25 percent less time than required by the world's best automakers. The first 3 hours of the process are performed by systems partners. A Canadian company, Magna International, starts by welding the structural components, which are then painted by Eisenmann, a German company. Both operations are performed outside the central assembly hall; the body is then passed by conveyer into the main hall. There VDO, another German company, installs the instrument panel. At this point, modules and parts manufactured by Krupp-Hoesch, Bosch, Dynamit Nobel, and Ymos are delivered for assembly by MCC employees. To encourage integration of MCC employees and system partners and to underscore the need for quality, both groups share a common dining room overlooking the main assembly hall.

The Smart City Coupé officially went on sale in Europe in October 1998. Sales got off to a slow start amid concerns about the vehicle's stability. That problem was solved with a sophisticated electronic package that monitors wheel slippage. Late-night TV comedians gave the odd-looking car no respect and referred to it as "a motorized ski boot" and "a backpack on wheels." During the first quarter of 1999, the 150 Smart dealers in 19 countries in continental Europe sold a total of 8,400 cars, an average of 56 cars each. The sales picture was brightest in the United Kingdom, where a London dealer sold 160 vehicles between the Smart launch in October 1998 and May 1999. The brisk sales pace in Britain was especially noteworthy because MCC was only building left-hand drive models (the United Kingdom is the only country in Europe in which right-hand drive cars are the norm). Industry observers noted that Brits' affection for the Austin Mini, a tiny vehicle that first appeared in the 1960s, appeared to have been extended to the Smart. MCC reduced its annual sales target from 130,000 to 100,000. Robert Easton, joint chairman of DaimlerChrysler, went on record as being skeptical of the vehicle's future. In an interview with *Automotive News*, he said, "It's possible we'll conclude that it's a good idea but one whose time simply hasn't come."

In 2000, the Smart exceeded its revised sales target, and interest in the vehicle was growing. Wolf-Garten GmbH & Company, a German gardening equipment company, announced plans to convert the Smart to a lawn mower suitable for use on golf courses. A convertible and diesel-engine edition have been added to the product line. In 2001, executives at DaimlerChrysler announced plans to research the U.S. market to determine prospects for the Smart. The announcement came as Americans face steep increases in gasoline prices.

*Visit the Web site*
**www.smart.com**

## Discussion Questions

1. Assess the U.S. market potential for the Smart. Do you think the car will be a success? Why or why not?

2. Identify other target markets where you would introduce this car. What sequence of countries would you recommend for the introduction?

*Sources:* Dan McCosh, "Get Smart: Buyers Try to Jump the Queue," *The New York Times* (March 19, 2004), p. D1; Nicholas Foulkes "Smart Set Gets Even Smarter," *Financial Times* (February 14–15, 2004), p. W10; Will Pinkston and Scott Miller, "DaimlerChrysler Steers Toward 'Smart' Debut in U.S.," *The Wall Street Journal* (August 20, 2001), pp. B1, B4; Miller, "Daimler May Roll Out Its Tiny Car Here," *The Wall Street Journal* (June 9, 2001), p. B1; Miller, "DaimlerChrysler's Smart Car May Have a New Use," *The Wall Street Journal* (February 15, 2001), pp. B1, B4; Haig Simonian, "Carmakers' Smart Move," *Financial Times* (July 1, 1997), p. 12; William Taylor, "Message and Muscle: An Interview with Swatch Titan Nicolas Hayek," *Harvard Business Review* (March–April 1993), pp. 99–110; Kevin Helliker, "Swiss Movement: Can Wristwatch Whiz Switch Swatch Cachet to an Automobile?" *The Wall Street Journal* (March 4, 1994), pp. A1, A3; Ferdinand Protzman, "Off the Wrist, Onto the Road: A Swatch on Wheels," *The New York Times* (March 4, 1994), p. C1.

# 11 Pricing Decisions

In many countries, the government imposes price controls on prescription drugs. The United States is a notable exception, and drug makers set prices for that country that are the highest in the world. There is a reason for the high prices: The companies need to recover the high research and development costs associated with bringing a new drug to market. Elsewhere, governments set price ceilings that do not take R&D into account. For example, prices for Allegra, Lipitor, Viagra, Zocor, and other popular prescription drugs are as much as 85 percent lower in Canada than in the United States. High prices are one reason why, overall, the United States drug market rings up $200 billion in sales each year. High prices have also resulted in a thriving cross-border trade with Canada worth about $800 million per year. Many persons living near the Canadian border cross over by car or bus to shop. Americans who live farther from the border have several options: They can order drugs from Canadian pharmacies over the Internet or visit storefront operations such as RxDepot that fax prescriptions to Canada. Whichever option they choose, Americans who buy drugs in other countries are breaking the law.

In any country, two basic factors determine the boundaries within which market prices should be set. The first is product cost, which establishes a *price floor*, or minimum price. Although pricing a product below the cost boundary is certainly possible, few firms can afford to do this for long. Second, prices for comparable substitute products create a *price ceiling*, or upper boundary. In many instances, international competition puts pressure on the pricing policies and related cost structures of domestic companies. Generally speaking, international trade results in lower prices for goods. Lower prices, in turn, help keep a country's rate of inflation in check. Between the lower and upper boundary for every product there is an *optimum price*,

Americans are flocking north to Canada to save money on prescription medications. For example, bus tours from Detroit to a casino in Windsor, Ontario stop at Canadian pharmacies so that passengers can shop. On the West Coast, Rx Express buses and trains pick up passengers in several states en route to Vancouver. Americans purchase up to a 3-month's supply. However, the reimportation of prescription medicines into the United States is illegal.

which is a function of the demand for the product as determined by the willingness and ability of customers to buy. However, as the cross-border trade in prescription drugs illustrates, sometimes government controls or other factors affect the prices for products and services.

## BASIC PRICING CONCEPTS

In a true global market, the **law of one price** would prevail: All customers in the market could get the best product available for the best price. As Lowell Bryan and his collaborators note in *Race for the World*, a global market exists for certain products such as integrated circuits, crude oil, and commercial aircraft: A Boeing 777 costs the same worldwide. By contrast, beer, compact discs, and many other products that are available around the world are actually being offered in markets that are national rather than global in nature. That is, these are markets where national competition reflects differences in factors such as costs, regulation, and the intensity of the rivalry among industry members.[1] The beer market is extremely fragmented; as shown in Table 11-1, even though Budweiser is the leading global brand, it commands less than 4 percent of the total market. The nature of the beer market explains why; for example, a six-pack of Heineken varies in price by as much as 50 percent (adjusted for purchasing power parity, transportation, and other transaction costs) depending on where it is sold. In Japan, for example, the price is a function of the competition between Heineken, other imports, and five national producers—Kirin, Asahi, Sapporo, Suntory, and Orion—that collectively command 60 percent of the market.

Because of these differences in national markets, the global manager must develop pricing systems and pricing policies that address price floors, price ceilings, and optimum prices in each of the national markets in which his or her company operates. A firm's pricing system and policies must also be consistent with other uniquely global opportunities and constraints. For example, companies that are active in the 12 nations of the euro zone have had to adjust to the new cross-border transparency of prices. Similarly, the Internet has made price information for many products available around the globe. Companies must carefully

---

[1] Lowell Bryan, *Race for the World: Strategies to Build a Great Global Firm* (Boston: Harvard Business School Press, 1999), pp. 40–41.

**Table 11-1**

*Top 10 Global Beer Brands*

| Brand | Brewer | Market Share % |
|-------|--------|----------------|
| 1. Budweiser | Anheuser-Busch | 3.6 |
| 2. Bud Light | Anheuser-Busch | 2.6 |
| 3. Asahi Super Dry | Asahi Breweries | 1.8 |
| 4. Skol | Ambev | 1.8 |
| 5. Corona Extra | Grupo Modelo | 1.7 |
| 6. Heineken | Heineken | 1.6 |
| 7. Brahman Chopp | Ambev | 1.5 |
| 8. Miller Lite | Miller Brewing | 1.4 |
| 9. Coors Light | Coors Brewing | 1.4 |
| 10. Polar | Cerveceria Polar | 1.1 |

*Source:* "The Big Pitcher: Brewers Are Trying to Become Global Marketers," *The Economist* (January 20, 2001), p. 64. © 2001 The Economist Newspaper Ltd. All rights reserved. Reprinted with permission. Further reproduction prohibited. www.economist.com.

consider how customers in one country or region will react if they discover they are paying significantly higher prices for the same product as customers in other parts of the world.

There is another important internal organizational consideration besides cost. Within the typical corporation, there are many interest groups and, frequently, conflicting price objectives. Divisional vice presidents, regional executives, and country managers are each concerned about profitability at their respective organizational levels. Similarly, the director of global marketing seeks competitive prices in world markets. The controller and financial vice president are concerned about profits. The manufacturing vice president seeks long production runs for maximum manufacturing efficiency. The tax manager is concerned about compliance with government transfer pricing legislation. Finally, company counsel is concerned about the antitrust implications of global pricing practices. Ultimately, price generally reflects the goals set by members or the sales staff, product managers, corporate division chiefs, and/or the company's chief executive.

# GLOBAL PRICING OBJECTIVES AND STRATEGIES

Whether dealing with a single home country market or multiple country markets, marketing managers must develop pricing objectives as well as strategies for achieving those objectives. The overall goal may be to contribute to an internal performance measure such as unit sales, market share, or return on investment. However, a number of pricing issues are unique to global marketing. The pricing strategy for a particular product may vary from country to country; a product may be positioned as a low-priced, mass-market product in some countries and a premium-priced, niche product in others. Pricing objectives may also vary depending on a product's life-cycle stage and the country-specific competitive situation. In making global pricing decisions, it is also necessary to factor in external considerations such as the added cost associated with shipping goods long distances across national boundaries. The issue of global pricing can also be fully integrated in the product-design process, an approach widely used by Japanese companies.

## Market Skimming and Financial Objectives

Price can be used as a strategic variable to achieve specific financial goals, including return on investment, profit, and rapid recovery of product development costs. When financial criteria such as profit and maintenance of margins are the objectives, the product must be part of a superior value proposition for buyers; price is integral to the total positioning strategy. The **market skimming** pricing strategy is often part of a deliberate attempt to reach a market segment that is willing to pay a premium price for a particular brand or for a specialized or unique product. Companies that seek competitive advantage by pursuing differentiation strategies or positioning their products in the premium segment frequently use market skimming. LVMH and other luxury goods marketers that target the global elite market segment use skimming strategies. For years, Mercedes-Benz utilized a skimming strategy; however, this created an opportunity for Toyota to introduce its luxury Lexus line and undercut Mercedes.

The skimming pricing strategy is also appropriate in the introductory phase of the product life cycle when both production capacity and competition are limited. By setting a deliberately high price, demand is limited to innovators and early adopters who are willing and able to pay the price. When the product enters the growth stage of the life cycle and competition increases, manufacturers start to cut prices. This strategy has been used consistently in the consumer electronics industry; for example, when Sony introduced the first consumer VCRs in the 1970s, the retail price exceeded $1,000. The same was true when compact disc players were launched in the early 1980s. Within a few years, prices for these products dropped well below $500. This pattern was evident in the fall of 1998, when HDTV sets went on sale in the United States with prices starting at about $7,000. This price both maximizes revenue on limited volume and matches demand to available supply. Already, prices for HDTV sets are dropping significantly as more prime-time programming is broadcast in the new format and consumers become more familiar with HDTV and its advantages.

## Penetration Pricing and Nonfinancial Objectives

Some companies are pursuing nonfinancial objectives with their pricing strategy. Price can be used as a competitive weapon to gain or maintain market position. Market share or other sales-based objectives are frequently set by companies that enjoy cost-leadership positions in their industry. A **penetration pricing policy strategy** calls for setting price levels that are low enough to quickly build market share. Many companies that use this type of pricing are located in the Pacific Rim. Scale-efficient plants and low-cost labor allow these companies to blitz the market.

When Sony was developing the Walkman in 1979, initial plans called for a retail price of ¥50,000 ($249) to achieve breakeven. However, it was felt that a price of ¥35,000 ($170) was necessary to attract the all-important youth market segment. After the engineering team conceded that they could trim costs to achieve breakeven volume at a price of ¥40,000, Chairman Akio Morita pushed them further and insisted on a retail price of ¥33,000 ($165) to commemorate Sony's 33rd anniversary. At that price, even if the initial production run of 60,000 units sold out, the company would lose $35 per unit. The marketing department was convinced the product would fail: Who would want a tape recorder that couldn't record? Even Yasuo Kuroki, the project manager, hedged his bets: He ordered enough parts for 60,000 units but had only 30,000 actually produced. Although sales were slow immediately following the Walkman's launch in July 1979, they exploded in late summer. The rest, as the saying goes, is history.[2] Sony has used penetration strategies with numerous other product introductions. When the portable CD player was in development in the mid-1980s, the cost per unit at initial sales volumes was estimated to exceed $600. Because this was a no-go price in

[2]   P. Ranganath Nayak and John M. Ketteringham, *Breakthroughs! How Leadership and Drive Create Commercial Innovations That Sweep the World* (San Diego, CA: Pfeiffer, 1994), pp. 124–127.

the United States and other target markets, Chairman Morita instructed management to price the unit in the $300 range to achieve penetration. Because Sony was a global marketer, the sales volume it expected to achieve in these markets led to scale economies and lower costs.

It is not unusual for a company to change its objectives as a product proceeds through its life cycle and as competitive conditions change. For example, in 2000, Sony rolled out its next-generation game console, the PlayStation 2 (PS2), for $299; competing systems from Microsoft (Xbox) and Nintendo (GameCube) were launched 1 year later. By March 2001, Sony had shipped 10 million units to Asia, Europe, and the United States. As of mid-2002, Sony had sold more than 10 million units in the United States alone; according to industry estimates, one out of three American households owns a PlayStation. In an effort to further increase its customer base, Sony lowered PS2's price to $199 in May 2002. The price of the original PlayStation, which at this point was $99, was dropped to $49. In 2003, Nintendo responded by cutting GameCube's price from $149 to $99, a move that put Nintendo in second place behind PlayStation in terms of sales.[3]

It should be noted that a first-time exporter is unlikely to use penetration pricing. The reason is simple: Penetration pricing often means that the product may be sold at a loss for a certain length of time. Unlike Sony, many companies that are new to exporting cannot absorb such losses, nor are they likely to have the marketing system in place (including transportation, distribution, and sales organizations) that allows global companies like Sony to make effective use of a penetration strategy. Many companies, especially those in the food industry, launch new products that are not innovative enough to qualify for patent protection. When this occurs, penetration pricing is recommended as a means of achieving market saturation before competitors copy the product.

## Companion Products: "Razors and Blades" Pricing

One crucial element is missing from the discussion of video game console pricing in the previous section: the video games themselves. The biggest profits in the video industry come from sales of game software; thus, even though prices are dropping for PlayStation 2, Xbox, and GameCube, sales of hit titles are generating substantial revenues and profits. This illustrates the notion of *companion products*: AOL software is worthless without a personal computer, a modem, and a telephone line; a video game player is worthless without games, a DVD player is worthless without movies, a razor handle is worthless without blades, a cellular phone is worthless without a calling plan, and so on. As the saying goes, "If you make money on the blades, you can give away the razors." Thus, cellular phone companies heavily discount (or even give away) handsets to subscribers who sign long-term service contracts. Likewise, Gillette can sell a single Mach3 razor for less than $5; over a period of years, the company will make significant profits from selling packages of replacement blades. Moreover, a given household might own one or two consoles but dozens of games. Since launching the first PlayStation in 1995, Sony has sold more than 110 million game consoles worldwide. During the same time period, however, sales of PlayStation games have exceeded 880 million units. In the second quarter of 2000, as Sony rolled out PS2, it lost $23 million. Two years later, as sales shifted from consoles to games, Sony posted on operating profit of $34 million on sales of $2 billion in the same period.

---

[3] Lauren J. Flynn, "Deep Price Cuts Help Nintendo Climb to No. 2 in Game Sales," *The New York Times* (January 26, 2004), p. C3.

# Target Costing

The actual cost of producing the product will create a cost floor. Japanese companies have traditionally approached cost issues in a way that results in substantial savings. Western companies are beginning to adopt some of these money-saving ideas. The Japanese begin with market mapping and product definition and positioning. Up to this point, the processes are parallel in the United States and Japan. At the next step, the processes diverge. In Japan, the planned selling price minus the desired profit is calculated, resulting in a target cost figure. Only at this point are design, engineering, and supplier pricing issues dealt with; extensive consultation between all value chain members is used to meet the target. Once the necessary negotiations and trade-offs have been settled, manufacturing begins, followed by continuous cost reduction. In the U.S. process, cost is typically determined after design, engineering, and marketing decisions have been made in sequential fashion; if the cost is too high, the process cycles back to square one—the design stage.[4]

## Calculating Prices: Cost-Based Pricing and Price Escalation

The following is a list of eight basic considerations for persons whose responsibility includes setting prices outside the home country.[5]

1. Does the price reflect the product's quality?
2. Is the price competitive given local market conditions?
3. Should the firm pursue market penetration, market skimming, or some other pricing objective?
4. What type of discount (trade, cash, quantity) and allowance (advertising, trade-off) should the firm offer its international customers?
5. Should prices differ with market segment?
6. What pricing options are available if the firm's costs increase or decrease? Is demand in the international market elastic or inelastic?
7. Are the firm's prices likely to be viewed by the host-country government as reasonable or exploitative?
8. Do the foreign country's dumping laws pose a problem?

Companies frequently use a method known as cost-plus pricing when selling goods outside their home-country markets. **Cost-based pricing** is based on an analysis of internal (e.g., materials, labor, testing) and external costs. As a starting point, firms that comply with Western cost accounting principles typically use the *full absorption cost method*; this defines per-unit product cost as the sum of all past or current direct and indirect manufacturing and overhead costs. However, when goods cross national borders, additional costs and expenses such as transportation, duties, and insurance are incurred. If the manufacturer is responsible for them, they too must be included. By adding the desired profit margin to the cost-plus figure, managers can arrive at a final selling price. It is important to note that, in China and some other developing countries, many manufacturing enterprises are state run and state subsidized. This makes it difficult to calculate accurate cost figures and opens a country's exporters to charges that they are selling products for less than the "true" cost of producing them.

Companies using *rigid cost-plus pricing* set prices without regard to the eight considerations listed previously. They make no adjustments to reflect market

---

4   Robin Cooper and W. Bruce Chew, "Control Tomorrow's Costs Through Today's Designs," *Harvard Business Review* 74, no. 1 (January–February 1996), p. 95.
5   Adapted from "Price, Quotations, and Terms of Sale Are Key to Successful Exporting," *Business America* (October 4, 1993), p. 12.

# the rest of the story

## Stopping the Cross-Border Prescription Drug Trade

By complying with price controls, pharmaceutical companies are in effect subsidizing consumers who live outside the United States. Writing in *The New York Times*, columnist William Safire proposes two options. The first is a tough-minded approach that entails refusing to accept the price controls. Although such a move would effectively shut the companies out of Canada and other key markets, it would force Canadians to buy *their* drugs over the Internet at prices that reflect the industry's full costs. A more tenderhearted approach would be to estimate product demand in Canada and supply low-price drugs only in quantities sufficient to meet Canada's needs. That would put pressure on the price controls, and possibly force the government to impose rationing or to lift the price controls to eliminate the bargains.

In the United States, local and state leaders are rallying to the cause of consumers. Governors in several states are considering setting up drug importation programs for state employees and retirees. In Washington, a bipartisan coalition of lawmakers is working on legislation to legalize the importation of drugs from Canada and other countries. The measure was passed by the House in July 2003 and now goes to the Senate. Congress approved a limited Medicare prescription drug benefit in the fall of 2003; previously, many Americans over the age of 65 lacked an insurance plan for drugs. The pharmaceutical industry has a powerful presence in Washington; it employs more than 600 lobbyists—a ratio of approximately six lobbyists for each senator. According to Public Citizen, an advocacy group, the industry spent $91.4 million on lobbying activities in 2002. The industry donates money to both political parties, but most of the money goes to the GOP.

Why is it illegal for Americans to buy drugs abroad? Mark McClellan, commissioner of the United States Food and Drug Administration, says, "FDA's job is to assure drug safety in the United States, and unapproved, imported drugs are illegal because FDA does not have the resources under current law to assure their safety." Some U.S. pharmacy owners want the government to do more to prevent the cross-border trade; Craig Fuller, CEO of the National Association of Chain Drug Stores, says, "We have laws on the books, and those laws ought to be enforced." In fact, the government is beginning to crack down on illegal drug reimportation. For example, the Department of Justice filed suit in federal court against RxDepot; the judge ordered the company to cease operations. Some drug makers have begun cutting back on shipments to Canadian companies that are active participants in the illegal market. One pharmacist in Windsor, Ontario, summed up the situation this way: "The bottom line to this whole things is you have ordinary God-fearing people who live in the U.S. who cannot afford their medicine."

*Sources:* William Safire, "The Doughnut's Hole," The New York Times (October 27, 2003), p. A23; William M. Welch, "Once Just a Trickle, Canada's Rx Drugs Pouring into USA," USA Today (October 7, 2003), pp. 1A, 2A; Julie Appleby, "Firm Fights for Canadian Drugs," USA Today (October 7, 2003), p. 3B; Mark Meinzl and Tamsin Carlisle, "Canadian Pharmacies vs. Big Drug Makers," The Wall Street Journal (August 12, 2003), p. D4; Joel Baglole, "Getting the Gray Out," The Wall Street Journal (February 11, 2003), p. R6.

conditions outside the home country. The obvious advantage of rigid cost-based pricing is its simplicity: Assuming that both internal and external cost figures are readily available, it is relatively easy to arrive at a quote. The disadvantage is that this approach ignores demand and competitive conditions in target markets; the risk is that prices will either be set too high or too low. If the rigid cost-based approach results in market success, it is only by chance. A major U.S. appliance manufacturer introduced its line of household appliances in Germany and, using U.S. sourcing, set price by simply marking up every item in its line by 28.5 percent. The result of this pricing method was a line that contained a mixture of underpriced and overpriced products. The overpriced products did not sell because better values were offered by local companies. The underpriced products sold well, but they would have yielded greater profit at higher prices. What was needed was product line pricing, which took lower-than-normal margins in some products and higher margins in others to maximize the profitability of the full line. Rigid cost-plus pricing is attractive to inexperienced exporters, who are frequently less concerned with financial goals than with issues such as assessing market potential. Such exporters are typically responding to global market opportunities in a reactive manner, not proactively seeking them.

An alternative method, *flexible cost-plus pricing*, is used to ensure that prices are competitive in the context of the particular market environment. This approach is frequently used by experienced exporters and global marketers. They realize that the rigid cost-plus approach can result in severe **price escalation,** with the unintended result that exports are priced at levels above what customers can pay. Managers who utilize flexible cost-plus pricing are acknowledging the importance of the eight criteria listed earlier. Flexible cost plus sometimes incorporates the *estimated future cost method* to establish the future cost for all component elements.

For example, the automobile industry uses palladium in catalytic converters. Because the market price of heavy metals is volatile and varies with supply and demand, component manufacturers might use the estimated future cost method to ensure that the selling price they set enables them to cover their costs.

## Terms of the Sale

Every commercial transaction is based on a contract of sale, and the trade terms in that contract specify the exact point at which the ownership of merchandise is transferred from the seller to the buyer and which party in the transaction pays which costs. The following activities must be performed when goods cross international boundaries:

1. Obtaining an export license if required (in the United States, nonstrategic goods are exported under a general license that requires no specific permit)
2. Obtaining a currency permit if required
3. Packing the goods for export
4. Transporting the goods to the place of departure (this would normally involve transport by truck or rail to a seaport or airport)
5. Preparing a land bill of lading
6. Completing necessary customs export papers
7. Preparing customs or consular invoices as required by the country of destination
8. Arranging for ocean freight and preparation
9. Obtaining marine insurance and certificate of the policy

Who is responsible for carrying out these steps? It depends on the terms of the sale. The internationally accepted terms of trade are known as **Incoterms.** Two Incoterms apply to all modes of transportation. If a contract specifies **ex-works,** the seller places goods at the disposal of the buyer at the time specified in the contract. The buyer takes delivery at the premises of the seller and bears all risks and expenses from that point on. If, instead, the contract specifies **delivered duty paid,** the seller has agreed to deliver the goods to the buyer at the place he or she names in the country of import, with all costs, including duties, paid. Under this contract, the seller is also responsible for obtaining the import license if one is required.

Several Incoterms apply to sea and inland waterway transportation only. Some contracts call for the seller to place goods alongside, or available to, the vessel or other mode of transportation and pay all charges up to that point. This is known as **F.A.S. (free alongside ship) named port of destination.** The seller's legal responsibility ends once a clean wharfage receipt has been obtained. With **F.O.B. (free on board),** the responsibility and liability of the seller do not end until the goods have actually been placed aboard a ship. Terms should preferably be "F.O.B. ship (name port)." The term F.O.B. is frequently misused in international sales. F.O.B. means "goods must be loaded on board, *and* buyer pays freight." Because freight charges generally include loading the goods, in essence, a double payment is made; the buyer pays twice! Similar to F.O.B is **C.I.F. (cost, insurance, freight) named port of destination**. Under this contract, like the F.O.B. contract, the risk of loss or damage to goods is transferred to the buyer once the goods have passed the ship's rail. However, the seller has to pay the expense of transportation for the goods up to the port of destination, including the expense of insurance. If the terms of the sale are **C.F.R. (cost and freight),** the seller is not responsible for risk or loss at any point outside the factory.

Table 11-2 is a typical example of the kind of **price escalation** that can occur when some of these costs are added to the per-unit cost of the product itself. In this example, a Kansas City–based distributor of agricultural equipment is shipping a container load of farm implements to Yokohama, Japan, through the port of Seattle.

**Table 11-2**

| Item | | | Percentage of Ex-Works Price |
|------|------|------|------|
| Ex-works Kansas City | | $30,000 | 100 |
| Container freight charges from K.C. to Seattle | $1,475.00 | | |
| Terminal handling fee | 350.00 | | |
| Ocean freight for 20 ft. container | 2,280.00 | | |
| Currency Adjustment Factor (CAF) (51% of ocean freight) | 1,162.80 | | |
| Insurance (110% of C.I.F. value) | 35.27 | | |
| Forwarding fee | 150.00 | | |
| Total shipping charges | 5,453.07 | | 18 |
| Total C.I.F. Yokohama value | | 35,453.07 | |
| V.A.T. (3% of C.I.F. value) | | 1,063.69 | 3 |
| | | 36,516.76 | |
| Distributor markup (10%) | | 3,651.67 | 12 |
| | | 40,168.43 | |
| Dealer markup (25%) | | 10,042.10 | 33 |
| Total retail price | | $50,210.53 | 166 |

*This was loaded at the manufacturer's door, shipped by stack train to Seattle, and then transferred via ocean freight to Yokohama. Total transit time from factory door to foreign port is about 28 days.

A shipment of product that costs ex-works $30,000 in Kansas City ends up with a total retail price in excess of $50,000 in Yokohama. A line-by-line analysis of this shipment shows how price escalation occurs. First, there is the total shipping charge of $5,453.07, which is 18 percent of the ex-works Kansas City price. The principal component of this shipping charge is a combination of land and ocean freight totaling $5,267.80. A currency adjustment factor (CAF) is assessed to protect the seller from possible losses from disadvantageous shifts in the dollar-yen exchange rate. This figure will vary depending on the perceived volatility of exchange rates.

All import charges are assessed against the landed price of the shipment (C.I.F. value). Note that there is no line item for duty in this example; no duties are charged on agricultural equipment sent to Japan.[6] Duties may be charged in other countries. A nominal distributor markup of 10 percent ($3,652) actually represents 12 percent of the C.I.F. Yokohama price because it is a markup not only on the ex-works price but on freight and V.A.T. as well. (It is assumed here that the distributor's markup includes the cost of transportation from the port to Yokohama.) Finally, a dealer markup of 25 percent adds up to $10,042 (33 percent) of the C.I.F. Yokohama price. Like distributor markups, dealer markup is based on the total landed cost.

The net effect of this add-on accumulating process is a total retail price in Yokohama of $50,210, or 166 percent of the ex-works Kansas City price. This is price escalation. The example provided here is by no means an extreme case. Indeed, longer distribution channels or channels that require a higher operating margin, as are typically found in export marketing, can contribute to price escalation. Because of the layered distribution system in Japan, the markups in Tokyo could easily result in a price that is 200 percent of the C.I.F. value. An example of price escalation for a single product is shown in Table 11-3. A 2004 right-hand drive Jeep Grand Cherokee equipped with a V8 engine ends up costing ¥5 million—roughly $50,000—by the time it reaches a dealer in Japan. The final price represents a 166 percent increase over the U.S. sticker price of $30,000.

---

6  Since the Uruguay Round of GATT negotiations, Japan has lowered or eliminated duties on thousands of categories of imports. Japan's simple average duty rate as of 2003 was 2.5 percent; approximately 60 percent of tariff lines (including most industrial products) were rated 5 percent or lower.

| Item | Amount of Price Escalation | Total |
|---|---|---|
| Ex-works price | 0 | $30,000 |
| Exchange rate adj. | $2,100 | $32,100 |
| Shipping | $ 300 | $32,400 |
| Customs fees | $1,000 | $33,400 |
| Distributor margin | $3,700 | $37,100 |
| Inspection, accessories | $1,700 | $38,800 |
| Added options, prep | $3,000 | $41,800 |
| Final sticker price | $8,200 | $50,000 |

**Table 11-3**

*An American-Built Jeep Grand Cherokee Goes to Japan (estimates)*

These examples of cost-plus pricing show an approach that a beginning exporter might use to determine the C.I.F. price. This approach could also be used for differentiated products such as the Jeep Cherokee for which buyers are willing to pay a premium. However, as noted earlier, experienced global marketers are likely to take a more flexible approach and view price as a strategic variable that can help achieve marketing and business objectives.

# ENVIRONMENTAL INFLUENCES ON PRICING DECISIONS

Global marketers must deal with a number of environmental considerations when making pricing decisions. Among them are currency fluctuations, inflation, government controls and subsidies, and competitive behavior. Some of these factors work in conjunction with others; for example, inflation may be accompanied by government controls. Each is discussed in detail in the following paragraphs.

## Currency Fluctuations

In global marketing, the task of setting prices is complicated by fluctuating exchange rates. Currency fluctuations can create significant problems and opportunities for the classic international company that exports from the home country. Management faces different decision situations, depending on whether currencies in key markets have strengthened or weakened relative to the home-country currency. A weakening of the home country currency swings exchange rates in a favorable direction: Overseas earnings can result in windfall revenues when translated into the home-country currency. It is a different situation when a company's home currency strengthens; this is an unfavorable turn of events for the typical exporter because overseas revenues are reduced when translated into the home country currency. Today's business environment is characterized by "roller coaster," or "yo-yo"-style, swings in currency values; they may move in a favorable direction for several quarters and then abruptly reverse.

For the transnational corporation, however, it is not simply a matter of home-country currency value relative to the value of currencies in key markets. Honda Motor is a case in point; the company is heavily dependent on the North American market, which accounts for more than half its operating income. Although some Japanese automakers serve foreign markets primarily by exporting from Japan, about three-fourths of the cars Honda sells in America are produced in the United States. In late 2000, the dollar had fallen to ¥108 to $1 compared with ¥113 to $1 the previous year; the unfavorable shift had a direct negative impact on corporate profits. The situation was even more complicated in Europe; Honda serves the entire European market from a single plant in the United Kingdom. The pound's recent

| Table 11-4 | When Domestic Currency Is Weak | When Domestic Currency Is Strong |
|---|---|---|
| *Global Pricing Strategies* | 1. Stress price benefits. | 1. Engage in nonprice competition by improving quality, delivery and after-sale service. |
| | 2. Expand product line and add more costly features. | 2. Improve productivity and engage in cost reduction. |
| | 3. Shift sourcing to domestic market. | 3. Shift sourcing outside home country. |
| | 4. Exploit market opportunities in all markets. | 4. Give priority to exports to countries with stronger currencies. |
| | 5. Use full-costing approach, but employ marginal-cost pricing to penetrate new or competitive markets. | 5. Trim profit margins and use marginal-cost pricing. |
| | 6. Speed repatriation of foreign-earned income and collections. | 6. Keep the foreign-earned income in host country; slow down collections. |
| | 7. Minimize expenditures in local or host-country currency. | 7. Maximize expenditures in local or host-country currency. |
| | 8. Buy advertising, insurance, transportation, and other services in domestic market | 8. Buy needed services abroad and pay for them in local currencies. |
| | 9. Bill foreign customers in their own currency. | 9. Bill foreign customers in the domestic currency. |

Source: Reprinted from the *Columbia Journal of World Business*, Vol. 31, S. Tamer Cavusgil, *Pricing for Global Markets*, p. 4, Copyright © 2004, with permission from Elsevier.

strength relative to the euro has resulted in a significant decline in Honda's European sales. At the same time, the euro has weakened relative to the British pound as well. So, not only have currency fluctuations negatively affected sales on the continent, but the revenue that Honda realizes from those sales is reduced as well![7]

Needless to say, currency fluctuations can have an impact on prices as well as other elements of the marketing mix. Table 11-4 provides several guidelines. In some instances, slight upward price adjustments due to the strengthening of a country's currency have little effect on export performance, especially if demand is relatively inelastic. The first two strategies in the right-hand column of Table 11-4 call for focusing attention on competitive issues besides price including productivity and cost reduction efforts. Companies in the strong-currency country can also choose to absorb the cost of maintaining international market prices at previous levels—at least for a while. Companies using the rigid cost-plus pricing method described earlier may be forced to change to the flexible approach. The use of the flexible cost-plus method to reduce prices in response to unfavorable currency swings is an example of a **market holding** strategy and is adopted by companies that do not want to lose market share. If, by contrast, large price increases are deemed unavoidable, managers may find their products can no longer compete.

In the 3 years immediately after the euro zone was established, the euro declined in value more than 25 percent relative to the dollar. This situation forces American companies, in particular small exporters, to choose from among the options associated with strong currencies listed in Table 11-4. The strategy chosen varies according to a company's particular circumstances. For example, Vermeer Manufacturing of Pella, Iowa, with annual sales of $650 million, prices its products in euros for the European market. As 2000 came to an end, Vermeer had been forced to raise its European prices four times since the euro's introduction. Its subsidiary in the Netherlands pays employees in euros and also buys materials locally, illustrating strategies number 7 and 8. By contrast, Stern Pinball of Melrose Park, Illinois, prices its machines in dollars in export markets. Company president Gary Stern is utilizing the first strategy in Table 11-4: To offset price increases in Europe,

---

[7] Todd Zaun, "Honda Takes Currency Hit in Europe," *The Wall Street Journal* (March 28, 2001), p. A16.

the company is developing new features such as pinball machines that "speak" several European languages. It has also produced new products such as a soccer game themed to European interests as well as an Austin Powers game targeted at the United Kingdom. As Stern commented, "If I were bright enough to know which way the euro was going, I sure wouldn't be making pinball machines. I'd be trading currency."[8]

Consider an example based on the currency crisis in Asia in 1997 and 1998. The Thai baht, Indonesian rupiah, South Korean won, and other Asian currencies fell dramatically. The economic turmoil in the affected countries depressed domestic demand for many manufactured goods; at the same time, the prices for Asian goods in export markets fell dramatically. The left-hand column of Table 11-4 shows strategies to use when the domestic currency is weak. One approach is **marginal-cost pricing** to penetrate new markets. Marginal-cost pricing entails setting the selling price equal to the variable (incremental) costs of producing one additional unit of output. This approach makes sense for a manufacturer with excess capacity in a weak-currency country if the manufacturer has already achieved sales levels sufficient to cover fixed costs. With fixed costs covered, the manufacturer can price the product aggressively for export in a bid to penetrate new markets. A word of caution is in order, however: Companies that utilize marginal-cost pricing may be vulnerable to charges of dumping. According to Table 11-4, what else should Samsung, Hyundai, Daewoo, and other manufacturers do?

If a country's currency weakens relative to a trading partner's currency, a producer in a weak-currency country can choose to cut export prices to increase market share or maintain its prices and reap healthier profit margins. For example, as shown in Table 11-5, over a recent 16-month period the yen weakened approximately 29 percent relative to the dollar. The figures in the table should be interpreted in the following way: If the amount of yen (or other currency) per dollar increases in a given time period, it means the yen's value is decreasing. (Conversely, if the amount of yen per dollar had *decreased*, it would have indicated that the yen had strengthened relative to the dollar.) The currency shift indicated in Table 11-5 is a boon for Japanese companies such as Canon Inc. and Olympus Optical because each dollar in sales was worth ¥130 in April 2002. Indeed, according to Teruhisa Tokunaka, chief financial officer of Sony, a 1-yen shift in the yen-dollar exchange rate can raise or lower the company's annual operating profit by 8 billion yen.[9]

By early 2003, as the Bush administration prepared for war, the dollar was down 11 percent from its 2002 peak against a weighted portfolio of foreign currencies. This was good news for companies such as Caterpillar, but bad news for American consumers.

As noted earlier, price discrepancies across the euro zone should gradually disappear because manufacturers will no longer be able to cite currency fluctuations as a justification for the discrepancies. **Price transparency** means that buyers will be able to comparison shop easily because goods will be priced in euros as opposed to marks, francs, or lira. The European Commission publishes an annual

| | U.S. | Japan | **Table 11-5** |
| --- | --- | --- | --- |
| January 2000 | $1.00 | ¥101 | *Value of U.S. Dollar Versus* |
| April 2002 | $1.00 | ¥130 | *Japanese Yen* |

---

8 Christopher Cooper, "Euro's Drop Is Hardest for the Smallest," *The Wall Street Journal* (October 2, 2000), p. A21.
9 Robert A. Guth, Michael M. Phillips, and Charles Hutzler, "On the Decline: As the Yen Keeps Dropping, A New View of Japan Emerges," *The Wall Street Journal* (April 24, 2002), pp. A1, A8.

**Table 11-6**

*Automobile Price Differences in the EU*

| Small Segment | | Medium Segment | | Large Segment | |
|---|---|---|---|---|---|
| Opel Corsa | 24.0% | VW Golf | 43.5% | BMW 318I | 12.0% |
| Ford Fiesta | 44.7% | Opel Astra | 26.0% | Audi A4 | 13.0% |
| Renault Clio | 33.8% | Ford Escort/Orion | 33.8% | Ford Mondeo | 58.5% |
| Peugeot 106 | 21.1% | Renault Mégane | 27.9% | Opel Vectra | 18.2% |
| VW Polo | 36.7% | Peugeot 306 | 46.2% | VW Passat | 36.4% |

*Source:* European Commission, **europa.eu.int,** accessed May 2004.

*"The car industry is going to be hurt. There will be greater price transparency. Prices are higher in northern Europe and once consumers there get wind of this there will be a move down in prices towards the southern countries."*

Marcie Krempel, AT Kearney[10]

report comparing automobile price differences in the EU. For example, as shown in Tables 11-6, prices for a medium-sized Volkswagen Golf are as much as 43 percent higher depending on the country of purchase. In the large-size category, prices for a Ford Mondeo can vary by more than 50 percent. Not surprisingly, these differences encourage cross-border shopping, a phenomenon that is expected to decline in the next few years.

Some automobile price differences in Europe are due to different standards for safety equipment and different tax levels. For example, Denmark and Sweden have a value-added tax (VAT) of 25 percent, the highest rate in the European Union. Moreover, Denmark taxes luxury goods heavily. Taxes are also high in Finland, Belgium, Ireland, Austria, and Italy. Volkswagen has already begun to harmonize its wholesale prices for vehicles distributed in Europe.

## Inflationary Environment

Inflation, or a persistent upward change in price levels, is a problem in many country markets. Inflation can be caused by an increase in the money supply; as noted in the previous section, inflation is often reflected in the prices of imported goods in a country whose currency has been devalued. In 1998, for example, the Russian government defaulted on its foreign debt and devalued the ruble; prices for some goods in Russian stores rose as much as 300 percent. Likewise, in the Dominican Republic, the peso lost one-third of its value in 2002; suddenly, shoppers were faced with price increases of 40 to 50 percent. The situations in Russia and the Dominican Republic are extreme; overall, in 2000, the average rate of inflation in the world's advanced economies stood at a low 2.3 percent. In developing countries, inflation averaged about 6 percent. By comparison, inflation in 2000 was much higher in the transitional economies in Central and Eastern Europe with Russia experiencing inflation of 20 percent.

An essential requirement for pricing in an inflationary environment is the maintenance of operating profit margins. When present, inflation requires price adjustments, for a simple reason: Rising costs must be covered by increased selling prices. Regardless of cost accounting practices, if a company maintains its margins, it has effectively protected itself from the effects of inflation. This, in turn, requires manufacturers and retailers of all types to become more technologically adept. In Brazil, where the inflation rate was as high as 2,000 percent during the late 1980s, retailers sometimes changed prices several times each day. Shelf pricing, rather than individual unit pricing, became the norm throughout the retailing sector nearly 15 years before Wal-Mart arrived in the region. Because their warehouses contained goods that had been bought at different prices, local retailers were forced to invest in sophisticated computer and communications systems to help them keep pace with the volatile financial environment. They utilized sophisticated inventory management software to help them maintain financial control. As Wal-Mart came to Brazil in the mid-1990s, it discovered that local

---

[10] Graham Bowley, "On the Road to Price Convergence," *Financial Times* (November 12, 1998), p. 29.

# GLOBAL *marketing in action*

## Pricing Reeboks in India

When Reebok, the world's number two athletic shoe company, decided to enter India in 1995, it faced several basic marketing challenges. For one thing, Reebok was creating a market from scratch. Upscale sports shoes were virtually unknown, and the most expensive sneakers available at the time cost 1,000 rupees (about $23). Reebok officials also had to select a market entry mode. The decision was made to subcontract with four local suppliers, one of which, the Phoenix Group, became a joint venture partner. To reinforce Reebok's high-tech brand image, company officials decided to establish their own retail infrastructure. There were two other crucial pieces of the puzzle: product and price. Should Reebok create a line of mass-market shoes specifically for India and priced at Rs 1,000? The alternative was to offer the same designs sold in other parts of the world and price them at Rs 2,500 ($58), a figure that represents the equivalent of a month's salary for a junior civil servant.

In the end, Reebok decided to offer Indian consumers about 60 models chosen from the company's global offerings. The decision was based in part on a desire to sustain Reebok's brand image of high quality. Management realized that the decision could very well limit the size of the market; despite estimates that as many as 300 million Indians could be classified as "middle class," the number of people who could afford premium-priced products was estimated to be about 30 million.

Reebok's least expensive shoes were priced at about Rs 2,000 per pair; for the same amount of money, a farmer could buy a dairy cow or a homeowner could buy a new refrigerator. Nevertheless, consumer response was very favorable, especially among middle-class youths. As Muktesh Pant, a former regional manager who became the first CEO of Reebok India, noted, "For Rs 2,000 to Rs 3,000, people feel they can really make a statement. It's cheaper than buying a new watch, for instance, if you want to make a splash at a party. And though our higher-priced shoes put us in competition with things like refrigerators and cows, the upside is that we're now being treated as a prestigious brand."

Sneakers represented just one aspect of the larger marketing of professional sports and sports culture to Indian youth. India's middle class households were spending more time in the living room watching cricket matches on TV, a trend that created an opportunity for sports sponsorships and sports-related ads. Indeed, in the late 1990s, Reebok spent more than $1.5 million on event marketing and sponsoring teams such as the East Bengal Football Club.

Reebok quickly discovered that demand was strong outside of key metropolitan markets such as Delhi, Mumbai, and Chennai. The cost of living is lower in small towns, so consumers have more disposable income to spend. Reebok appointed distributors in each of India's 26 states to distribute lower price shoe models in a network of about 1,500 multi-brand footwear and apparel shops. One problem, however, is that knockoff versions of Reebok, Adidas, and Nike shoes were widely available. Reebok conducted several raids on outlets that were selling the counterfeit goods.

Reebok's agreement with the Phoenix Group called for the latter to create of chain of 50-plus stores. However, after the first 10 stores were opened, management at Phoenix decided to concentrate on marketing the company's own brands. Accordingly, Reebok began to identify individual partners to run stores in major cities; there are currently about 90 branded franchise stores in 50 cities. By establishing exclusive stores, promoting Reebok as a lifestyle brand, and offering a unique "sports fashion" shopping experience, Reebok was able to offer a taste of Western-style capitalist consumption for those so inclined. Between 1996 and 1999, Reebok's retail sales in India more than tripled, increasing from Rs 250 million to Rs 900 million.

Today, Reebok India exports hundreds of thousands of pairs of Indian-made shoes to Europe and the United States. CEO Pant was recently promoted to vice president of global brand marketing at Reebok International headquarters in Stoughton, Massachusetts. Reflecting on Reebok's Indian launch, he observed, "At first we were embarrassed about our pricing. But it has ended up serving us well."

*Sources: Bernard D'Mello, "Reebok and the Global Footwear Sweatshop," Monthly Review 54, no. 9 (February 2003), pp. 26–41; Mark Nicholson, "Where a Pair of Trainers Costs as Much as a Cow," Financial Times (August 18, 1998), p. 10.*

---

competitors had the technological infrastructure that allowed them to match its aggressive pricing policies.[11]

Low inflation presents pricing challenges of a different type. With inflation in the United States in the low single digits in the late 1990s and strong demand forcing factories to run at or near capacity, companies should have been able to raise prices. However, the domestic economic situation was not the only consideration. In the mid-1990s, excess manufacturing capacity in many industries, high rates of unemployment in many European countries, and the lingering recession in Asia made it difficult for companies to increase prices. As John Ballard, CEO of a California-based engineering firm, noted in 1994, "We thought about price increases. But our research of competitors and what the market would bear told us it was not worth pursuing." By the end of the decade, globalization, the Internet,

---

[11]  Pete Hisey, "Wal-Mart's Global Vision," *Retail Merchandiser* 41, no. 4 (April 2001), pp. 21–49.

a flood of low-cost exports from China, and a new cost-consciousness among buyers were also significant constraining factors.[12]

## Government Controls, Subsidies, and Regulations

Governmental policies and regulations that affect pricing decisions include dumping legislation, resale price maintenance legislation, price ceilings, and general reviews of price levels. Government action that limits management's ability to adjust prices can put pressure on margins. Under certain conditions, government action poses a threat to the profitability of a subsidiary operation. In a country that is undergoing severe financial difficulties and is in the midst of a financial crisis (e.g., a foreign exchange shortage caused in part by runaway inflation), government officials are under pressure to take some type of action. This was true in Brazil for many years. In some cases, governments take expedient steps such as selective or broad price controls.

When selective controls are imposed, foreign companies are more vulnerable to control than local ones, particularly if the outsiders lack the political influence over government decision that local managers have. For example, Procter & Gamble encountered strict price controls in Venezuela in the late 1980s. Despite increases in the cost of raw materials, P&G was only granted about 50 percent of the price increases it requested; even then, months passed before permission to raise prices was forthcoming. As a result, by 1988, detergent prices in Venezuela were less than what they were in the United States.[13]

Government control can also take other forms. As discussed in Chapter 8, companies are sometimes required to deposit funds in a noninterest-bearing escrow account for a specified period of time if they wish to import products. For example, Cintec International, an engineering firm that specializes in restoring historic structures, spent 8 years seeking the necessary approval from Egyptian authorities to import special tools to repair a mosque. In addition, the country's port authorities required a deposit of nearly $25,000 before allowing Cintec to import diamond-tipped drills and other special tools. Why would Cintec's management accept such conditions? Cairo is the largest city in the Muslim world, and there are hundreds of centuries-old historic structures in need of refurbishment. By responding to the Egyptian government's demands with patience and persistence, Cintec is positioning itself as a leading contender for more contract work.[14]

Cash deposit requirements such as the one described here clearly create an incentive for a company to minimize the stated value of the imported goods; lower prices mean smaller deposits. Other government requirements that affect the pricing decision are profit transfer rules that restrict the conditions under which profits can be transferred out of a country. Under such rules, a high transfer price paid for imported goods by an affiliated company can be interpreted as a device for transferring profits out of a country.

Also discussed in Chapter 8 were government subsidies. As noted earlier, the topic of agricultural subsidies is a sensitive one in the current round of global trade talks. Brazil and a bloc of more than 20 other nations are pressing Washington to end agricultural subsidies. For example, Washington spends between $2.5 and

---

12 Lucinda Harper and Fred R. Bleakley, "Like Old Times: An Era of Low Inflation Changes the Calculus for Buyers and Sellers," *The Wall Street Journal* (January 14, 1994), p. A1. See also Jacob M. Schlesinger and Yochi J. Dreazen, "Counting the Cost: Firms Start to Raise Prices, Stirring Fear in Inflation Fighters," *The Wall Street Journal* (May 16, 2000), pp. A1, A8.

13 Alecia Swasy, "Foreign Formula: Procter & Gamble Fixes Aim on Tough Market: The Latin Americans," *The Wall Street Journal* (June 15, 1990), p. A7.

14 Scott Miller, "In Trade Talks, the Gloves Are Off," *The Wall Street Journal* (July 15, 2003), p. A12. See also James Drummond, "The Great Conservation Debate," *Financial Times Special Report—Egypt* (October 22, 2003), p. 6.

$3 billion per year on cotton subsidies (the European Union spends about $700 million), a fact that was a focal point at the failed WTO ministerial meeting in Cancún, Mexico, in September 2003. Benin, Chad, Burkina Faso, and others complain that the subsidies keep U.S. cotton prices so low that it costs the African nations $250 million each year in lost exports.[15]

Government regulations can affect prices in other ways. In Germany, for example, price competition was historically severely restricted in a number of industries. This was particularly true in the service sector. The German government's recent moves toward deregulation have improved the climate for market entry by foreign firms in a range of industries, including insurance, telecommunications, and air travel. Deregulation is also giving German companies their first experience with price competition in the domestic market. In some instances, deregulation represents a *quid pro quo* that will allow German companies wider access to other country markets. For example, the United States and Germany recently completed an open-skies agreement that will allow Lufthansa to fly more routes within the United States. At the same time, the German air market has been opened to competition. As a result, air travel costs between German cities have fallen significantly. Change is slowly coming to the retail sector as well. The Internet and globalization have forced German policy makers to repeal two archaic laws. The first, the *Rabattgesetz* or Discount Law, limited discounts on products to 3 percent of the list price. The second, the *Zugabeverordnung* or Free Gift Act, banned companies from giving away free merchandise such as shopping bags.[16]

## Competitive Behavior

Pricing decisions are bounded not only by cost and the nature of demand but also by competitive action. If competitors do not adjust their prices in response to rising costs, management—even if acutely aware of the effect of rising costs on operating margins—will be severely constrained in its ability to adjust prices accordingly. Conversely, if competitors are manufacturing or sourcing in a lower-cost country, it may be necessary to cut prices to stay competitive.

In the United States, Levi Strauss & Company is under price pressure from several directions. First, Levi faces stiff competition from the Wrangler and Lee brands marketed by VF Corporation. A pair of Wrangler jeans retails for about $20 at Penney's and other department stores, compared with about $30 for a pair of Levi 501s. Second, Levi's two primary retail customers, J.C. Penney and Sears, are aggressively marketing their own private label brands. Finally, designer jeans from Calvin Klein, Polo, and Diesel are enjoying renewed popularity. An exclusive new fashion brand, Seven, retails for more than $100 per pair. Outside the United States, thanks to the heritage of the Levi brand and less competition, Levi jeans command premium prices—$80 or more for one pair of 501s. To support the prestige image, Levi's are sold in boutiques. Not surprisingly, Levi's non-U.S. sales represent about one-third of revenues but more than 50 percent of profits. In an attempt to apply its global experience and enhance the brand in the United States, Levi has opened a number of Original Levi's Stores in select American cities. Despite such efforts, Levi rang up only $4.1 billion in sales in 2003 compared with $7.1 billion in 1996. In 2002, officials announced plans to close six plants and move most of the company's North American production offshore in an effort to cut costs.[17]

---

[15] Neil King, Jr. and Scott Miller, "Trade Talks Fail amid Big Divide over Farm Issues," *The Wall Street Journal* (September 15, 2003), pp. A1, A18.

[16] Greg Steinmetz, "Mark Down: German Consumers Are Seeing Prices Cut in Deregulation Push," *The Wall Street Journal* (August 15, 1997), pp. A1, A4; David Wessel, "German Shoppers Get Coupons," *The Wall Street Journal* (April 5, 2001), p. A1.

[17] Leslie Kaufman, "Levi Strauss to Close 6 U.S. Plants and Lay Off 3,300," *The New York Times* (April 9, 2002), p. C2.

# Using Sourcing as a Strategic Pricing Tool

The global marketer has several options for addressing the problem of price escalation or the environmental factors described in the last section. The choices are dictated in part by product and market competition. Marketers of domestically manufactured finished products may be forced to switch to offshore sourcing of certain components to keep costs and prices competitive. In particular, China is quickly gaining a reputation as "the world's workshop." U.S. bicycle companies such as Huffy are relying more heavily on production sources in China and Taiwan.

Another option is a thorough audit of the distribution structure in the target markets. A rationalization of the distribution structure can substantially reduce the total markups required to achieve distribution in international markets. Rationalization may include selecting new intermediaries, assigning new responsibilities to old intermediaries, or establishing direct marketing operations. For example, Toys 'R' Us successfully targets the Japanese toy market by bypassing layers of distribution and adopting a warehouse style of selling similar to its U.S. approach. Toys 'R' Us was viewed as a test case of the ability of Western retailers—discounters in particular—to change the rules of distribution.

## GLOBAL PRICING: THREE POLICY ALTERNATIVES

What pricing policy should a global company pursue? Viewed broadly, there are three alternative positions a company can take on worldwide pricing.

## Extension or Ethnocentric

The first can be called an extension or ethnocentric pricing policy. An **extension** or **ethnocentric pricing policy** calls for the per-unit price of an item to be the same no matter where in the world the buyer is located. In such instances, the importer must absorb freight and import duties. The extension approach has the advantage of extreme simplicity because no information on competitive or market conditions is required for implementation. The disadvantage of the ethnocentric approach is that it does not respond to the competitive and market conditions of each national market and, therefore, does not maximize the company's profits in each national market or globally. When toymaker Mattel adapted U.S. products for overseas markets, for example, little consideration was given to price levels that resulted when U.S. prices were converted to local currency prices. As a result, Holiday Barbie and some other toys were overpriced in global markets.[18]

Similarly, Mercedes executives recently moved beyond an ethnocentric approach to pricing. As Dieter Zietsche, president and CEO of DaimlerChrysler Corporation, noted recently, "We used to say that *we* know what the customer wants, and he will have to pay for it . . . we didn't realize the world had changed."[19] Mercedes got its wake-up call when Lexus began offering "Mercedes quality" for $20,000 less. After assuming the top position in 1993, Mercedes CEO Helmut Werner boosted employee productivity, increased the number of low-cost outside suppliers, and invested in production facilities in the United States and

---

[18] Lisa Bannon, "Mattel Plans to Double Sales Abroad," *The Wall Street Journal* (February 11, 1998), pp. A3, A11.
[19] Alex Taylor III, "Speed! Power! Status!" *Fortune* (June 10, 1996), pp. 46–58.

Spain in an effort to move toward more customer- and competition-oriented pricing. The company also rolled out new, lower-priced versions of its E Class and S Class sedans. *Advertising Age* immediately hailed management's new attitude for transforming Mercedes from "a staid and smug purveyor into an aggressive, market-driven company that will go bumper-to-bumper with its luxury car rivals—even on price."[20]

## Adaptation or Polycentric

The second policy, **adaptation** or **polycentric pricing,** permits subsidiary or affiliate managers or independent distributors to establish whatever price they feel is most desirable in their circumstances. There is no requirement that prices be coordinated from one country to the next. One recent study of European industrial exporters found that companies utilizing independent distributors were the most likely to utilize polycentric pricing. Such an approach is sensitive to local market conditions; however, valuable knowledge and experience within the corporate system concerning effective pricing strategies are not brought to bear on each local pricing decision. Because the distributors or local managers are free to set prices as they see fit, they may ignore the opportunity to draw upon company experience. Arbitrage is also a potential problem with the polycentric approach; when disparities in prices between different country markets exceed the transportation and duty costs separating the markets, enterprising individuals can purchase goods in the lower-price country market and then transport them for sale in markets where higher prices prevail.

This is precisely what has happened in both the pharmaceutical and textbook publishing industries. Discounted drugs intended for AIDS patients in Africa have been smuggled into the European Union and sold at a huge profit (see Case 11-1). Similarly, Pearson (which publishes this text), McGraw-Hill, Thomson, and other publishers typically set lower prices in Europe and Asia than in the United States. The reason is that the publishers use polycentric pricing: They establish prices on a country-by-country basis using per capita income and economic conditions as a guide. (The wholesale price of the Chinese language version of this textbook is about $0.25!)

## Geocentric

The third approach, **geocentric pricing,** is more dynamic and proactive than the other two. A company using geocentric pricing neither fixes a single price worldwide, nor allows subsidiaries or local distributors to make independent pricing decisions. Instead, the geocentric approach represents an intermediate course of action. Geocentric pricing is based on the realization that unique local market factors should be recognized in arriving at pricing decisions. These factors include local costs, income levels, competition, and the local marketing strategy. Price must also be integrated with other elements of the marketing program. For example, when a "pull" strategy calls for using mass media advertising and intensive distribution, the price selected must be appropriate given the costs of advertising and the choice of distribution channels. The geocentric approach recognizes that price coordination from headquarters is necessary in dealing with international accounts and product arbitrage.

*"In the past, Mercedes vehicles would be priced for the European market, and that price was translated into U.S. dollars. Surprise, surprise: You're 20% more expensive than the Lexus LS400, and you don't sell too many cars."*

Joe Eberhardt, Chrysler Group Executive Vice President for Global Sales, Marketing and Service

*"The practice of selling U.S. products abroad at prices keyed to the local market is longstanding. It's not unusual, it doesn't violate public policy, and it's certainly not illegal."*

Allen Adler, American Association of Publishers[21]

---

[20] Raymond Serafin, "Mercedes-Benz of the '90s Includes Price in Its Pitch," *Advertising Age* (November 1, 1993), p. 1.
[21] Tamar Lewin, "Students Find $100 Textbooks Cost $50, Purchased Overseas," *The New York Times* (October 21, 2003), p. A16.

The geocentric approach also consciously and systematically seeks to ensure that accumulated national pricing experience is leveraged and applied wherever relevant.

Local costs plus a return on invested capital and personnel fix the price floor for the long term. In the short term, however, headquarters might decide to set a market penetration objective and price at less than the cost-plus return figure by using export sourcing to establish a market. This was the case described earlier with the Sony Walkman launch. Another short-term objective might be to arrive at an estimate of the market potential at a price that would be profitable given local sourcing and a certain scale of output. Instead of immediately investing in local manufacture, a decision might be made to supply the target market initially from existing higher-cost external supply sources. If the price and product are accepted by the market, the company can then build a local manufacturing facility to further develop the identified market opportunity in a profitable way. If the market opportunity does not materialize, the company can experiment with the product at other prices because it is not committed to a fixed sales volume by existing local manufacturing facilities.

For consumer products, local income levels are critical in the pricing decision. If the product is normally priced well above full manufacturing costs, the global marketer should consider accepting reduced margins and price below prevailing levels in low-income markets. *The important point here is that in global marketing there is no such thing as a "normal" margin.* Of the three methods described, the geocentric approach is best suited to global competitive strategy. A global competitor will take into account global markets and global competitors in establishing prices. Prices will support global strategy objectives rather than the objective of maximizing performance in a single country. Table 11-7 lists some comments by European exporters that provide insights into the real-world process of setting prices.

**Table 11-7**

*How Managers Calculate Export Prices for Industrial Products*

| Statement by Management | Implication/Interpretation |
| --- | --- |
| "We have the competitors' price list on our desk. I may speak frankly—who does not? We know exactly what our competitors charge for certain products, and we calculate accordingly." | When calculating prices for foreign markets, managers benchmark competitors' prices. |
| "An interesting way of evaluating whether a product will fit requirements of the market has emerged. You give some machines to an auction house and set a very low price limit. Your products are then auctioned off. That way, you get a feel for the right price level as well as the potential demand for the product. It is a very easy and cost-effective method." | As a practical matter, some companies use innovative, trial and error approaches to determine price elasticity. |
| "At trade shows, we go directly to our customers and try to find out what prices we can charge. We scan our price limits sensitively. This is how we get to a price list in the end." | Some companies take a methodical approach to determining price elasticity. |
| "We differentiate simply because there are some countries where we can get a better price. Then there are countries where we can't." | Rationale for differentiating prices using either polycentric or geocentric approach. |
| "I decided not to listen to people who advise me to differentiate prices. Wherever we are active, we want to have the image and the reputation of calculating our prices correctly and honestly." | Rationale for using standardized pricing. |

Source: Adapted from Barbara Stöttinger, "Strategic Export Pricing: A Long and Winding Road," *Journal of International Marketing* 9, no. 1 (2001), pp. 40–63.

# GRAY MARKET GOODS

**Gray market goods** are trademarked products that are exported from one country to another where they are sold by unauthorized persons or organizations. Consider the following illustration:

> Suppose that a golf equipment manufacturer sells a golf club to its domestic distributors for $200; it sells the same club to its Thailand distributor for $100. The lower price may be due to differences in overseas demand or ability to pay. Or, the price difference may reflect the need to compensate the foreign distributor for advertising and marketing the club. The golf club, however, never makes it to Thailand. Instead, the Thailand distributor resells the club to a gray marketer in the United States for $150. The gray marketer can then undercut the prices charged by domestic distributors who paid $200 for the club. The manufacturer is forced to lower the domestic price or risk losing sales to gray marketers, driving down the manufacturer's profit margins. Additionally, gray marketers make liberal use of manufacturer's trademarks and often fail to provide warranties and other services that consumers expect from the manufacturer and its authorized distributors.[22]

This practice, known as **parallel importing,** typically flourishes when a product is in short supply, when producers employ skimming strategies in certain markets, or when the goods are subject to substantial markups. This has happened with French champagne sold in the United States; it is also true of the European market for pharmaceuticals, where prices vary widely from country to country. In the United Kingdom and the Netherlands, for example, parallel imports account for as much as 10 percent of the sales of some pharmaceutical brands.

Sometimes, gray marketers bring a product produced in one country—French champagne, for example—into a second country market in competition with authorized importers. The gray marketers sell at prices that undercut those set by the legitimate importers. In another type of gray marketing, a company manufactures a product in the home country market as well as in foreign markets. In this case, products manufactured abroad by the company's foreign affiliate for sales abroad are sometimes sold by a foreign distributor to gray marketers. The latter then bring the products into the producing company's home-country market, where they compete with domestically produced goods. For example, in the mid-1980s, Caterpillar's U.S. dealers found themselves competing with gray market construction equipment manufactured in Europe. The strong dollar had provided gray marketers with an opportunity to bring Caterpillar equipment into the United States at lower prices than domestically produced equipment. Even though the gray market goods carry the same trademarks as the domestically produced ones, they may differ in quality, ingredients, or some other way. Manufacturers may not honor warranties on some types of gray market imports such as cameras and consumer electronics equipment.[23]

As these examples show, the marketing opportunity that presents itself requires gray market goods to be priced lower than goods sold by authorized distributors or domestically produced goods. Clearly, buyers gain from lower prices and increased choice. In the United Kingdom alone, for example, total annual retail sales of gray market goods are estimated to be as high as $1.6 billion. A recent case in Europe resulted in a ruling that strengthened the rights of brand owners. Silhouette, an Austrian manufacturer of upscale sunglasses, sued the Hartlauer discount chain after the latter obtained thousands of pairs of sunglasses

---

[22] Adapted from Perry J. Viscounty, Jeff C. Risher, and Collin G. Smyser, "Cyber Gray Market Is Manufacturers' Headache," *The National Law Journal* (August 20, 2001), p. C3.

[23] James E. Inman, "Gray Marketing of Imported Trademarked Goods: Tariffs and Trademark Issues," *American Business Law Journal* (May 1993), pp. 59–116; Paul Lansing and Joseph Gabriella, "Clarifying Gray Market Gray Areas," *American Business Law Journal* (September 1993), pp. 313–337.

that Silhouette had intended for sale in Eastern Europe. The European Court of Justice found in favor of Silhouette. In clarifying a 1989 directive, the court ruled that stores cannot import branded goods from outside the EU and then sell them at discounted prices without permission of the brand owner. The *Financial Times* denounced the ruling as "bad for consumers, bad for competition, and bad for European economies."[24]

In the United States, gray market goods are subject to a 75-year-old law, the Tariff Act of 1930. Section 526 of the act expressly forbids importation of goods of foreign manufacture without the permission of the trademark owner. There are, however, several exceptions spelled out in the act; the U.S. Customs Service, which implements the regulation, and the court system have considerable leeway in decisions regarding gray market goods. For example, in 1988, the U.S. Supreme Court ruled that trademarked goods of foreign manufacture such as champagne could legally be imported and sold by gray marketers. In many instances, however, the court's interpretation of the law differs from that of the U.S. Customs Service.

Because of problems associated with regulating gray markets, one legal expert has argued that, in the name of free markets and free trade, the U.S. Congress should repeal Section 526. In its place, a new law should require gray market goods to bear labels clearly explaining any differences between them and goods that come through authorized channels. Other experts believe that, instead of changing the laws, companies should develop proactive strategic responses to gray markets. One such strategy would be improved market segmentation and product differentiation to make gray market products less attractive; another would be to aggressively identify and terminate distributors that are involved in selling to gray marketers. Even as the debate over legal recourse continues, the Internet is emerging as a powerful new tool that allows would-be gray marketers to both access pricing information and reach customers.[26]

*To combat the gray market for Swiss watches, TAG Heuer runs print ads during the holiday shopping season urging consumers to buy its famous sports watch only from authorized dealers.*

[24] Peggy Hollinger and Neil Buckley, "Grey Market Ruling Delights Brand Owners," *Financial Times* (July 17, 1998), p. 8

[25] Ray Marcelo, "Officials See Red Over Handset Sales," *Financial Times* (October 3, 2003), p. 16.

[26] Perry J. Viscounty, Jeff C. Risher, and Collin G. Smyser, "Cyber Gray Market Is Manufacturers' Headache," *The National Law Journal* (August 20, 2001), p. C3.

# DUMPING

Dumping is an important global pricing strategy issue. GATT's 1979 antidumping code defined **dumping** as the sale of an imported product at a price lower than that normally charged in a domestic market or country of origin. In addition, many countries have their own policies and procedures for protecting national companies from dumping. For example, China has retaliated against years of Western antidumping rules by introducing rules of its own. China's State Council passed the Antidumping and Antisubsidy Regulations in March 1997. The regulations are designed to counter the effects of dumping or export subsidization that result in injury to an established Chinese industry or that substantially impede the establishment of a comparable Chinese industry. The Ministry of Foreign Trade and Economic Cooperation and the State Economic and Trade Commission have responsibility for antidumping matters.[27]

The U.S. Congress has defined *dumping* as an unfair trade practice that results in "injury, destruction, or prevention of the establishment of American industry." Under this definition, dumping occurs when imports sold in the U.S. market are priced either at levels that represent less than the cost of production plus an 8 percent profit margin or at levels below those prevailing in the producing country. The U.S. Commerce Department is responsible for determining whether products are being sold in the United States at below-market prices; the International Trade Commission (ITC) then determines whether the dumping has resulted in injury to U.S. firms.

In Europe, antidumping policy is administered by the European Commission; a simple majority vote by the Council of Ministers is required before duties can be imposed on dumped goods. Six-month provisional duties can be imposed; more stringent measures include definitive, 5-year duties. Low-cost imports from Asia have been the subject of dumping disputes in Europe. Another issue concerns $650 million in annual imports of unbleached cotton from China, Egypt, India, Indonesia, Pakistan, and Turkey. A dispute pitted an alliance of textile importers and wholesalers against Eurocoton, which represents textile weavers in France, Italy, and other EU countries. Eurocoton supports the duties as a means of protecting jobs from low-priced imports; the job issue is particularly sensitive in France. British textile importer Broome & Wellington maintains, however, that imposing duties would drive up prices and cost even more jobs in the textile finishing and garment industries.[28] As of January 2005, the global system of textile quotas will be abolished; the result should be lower prices worldwide.

Dumping was a major issue in the Uruguay round of GATT negotiations. Many countries took issue with the U.S. system of antidumping laws, in part because historically the commerce department almost always ruled in favor of the U.S. company that filed the complaint. For their part, U.S. negotiators were concerned that U.S. exporters were often targeted in antidumping investigations in countries with few formal rules for due process. The U.S. side sought to improve the ability of U.S. companies to defend their interests and understand the bases for rulings.

The result of the GATT negotiations was an agreement on interpretation of GATT Article VI. From the U.S. point of view, one of the most significant changes between the agreement and GATT's 1979 antidumping code is the addition of a "standard of review" that will make it harder for GATT panels to dispute U.S. antidumping determinations. There are also a number of procedural and methodological changes. In some instances, these have the effect of bringing GATT regulations more in line with U.S. law. For example, in calculating "fair

---

27  Lester Ross and Susan Ning, "Modern Protectionism: China's Own Antidumping Regulations," *China Business Review* (May/June 2000), pp. 30–33.
28  Neil Buckley, "Commission Faces Fight on Cotton 'Dumping'," *Financial Times* (December 2, 1997), p. 5; Emma Tucker, "French Fury at Threat to Cotton Duties," *Financial Times* (May 19, 1997), p. 3.

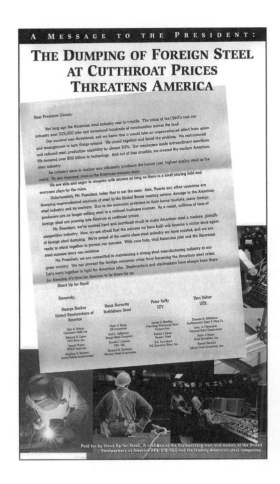

Representatives of the U.S. steel industry sponsored this 1998 ad to urge President Clinton to get tough on low-price steel that was sold in the United States by producers in Western Europe, Asia, and Russia. In 2001, the International Trade Commission launched an investigation to determine whether steel imports were hurting American steel producers. Based on the ITC's recommendation, in March 2002 President George W. Bush imposed sweeping tariffs of up to 30 percent on a wide range of steel imports for a 3-year period. The European Union responded by drawing up a list of U.S. product imports that would be taxed in retaliation for the president's action. In 2003, President Bush dropped the tariffs.

price" for a given product, any sales of the product at below-cost prices in the exporting country are not included in the calculations; inclusion of such sales would have the effect of exerting downward pressure on the fair price. The agreement also brought GATT standards in line with U.S. standards by prohibiting governments from penalizing differences between home market and export market prices of less than 2 percent.

As previously noted, the last few years have seen an increase of antidumping investigation and penalties. These have originated primarily in the United States but also in the EU, Canada, and Australia. Many of the dumping cases in the United States involve manufactured goods from Asia. Most of the U.S. cases involve a single or narrowly defined group of products and are initiated by U.S. companies that claim to be materially damaged by the low-priced imports. In some cases, like tungsten from China and nitrocellulose from Yugoslavia, the company bringing action is the sole U.S. producer. In 1996, the U.S. Department of Commerce issued a preliminary ruling that importers of large German and Japanese printing presses into the United States had engaged in dumping. Rockwell Graphic Systems filed an antidumping petition after *The Washington Post* bought presses from Mitsubishi Heavy Industries. Investigators from both the commerce department and the International Trade Commission reported that they had found evidence of injury to the U.S. producer, and antidumping duties ranging from 17.17 percent to 58.14 percent were put into effect.

In 1998, in the wake of the global financial crisis, 12 U.S. steel producers filed dumping complaints against producers of hot-rolled steel in Japan, Russia, and Brazil. Paul Wilhelm, president of U.S. Steel Group, declared, "We are in a crisis. I know what it costs to make a ton of steel, and these imports are clearly being dumped and subsidized." Although the U.S. steel producers believed they had a strong case, the steel industry has a reputation for using trade laws as a competitive tool. Steel makers routinely file complaints of unfair trade with the ITC; over the past two decades, the industry has been the instigator of 45 percent of all dumping complaints filed.[29]

For positive proof that dumping has occurred in the United States, both price discrimination and injury must be demonstrated. **Price discrimination** is the practice of setting different prices when selling the same quantity of "like-quality" goods to different buyers. The existence of either one without the other is an insufficient condition to constitute dumping. Companies concerned with running afoul of antidumping legislation have developed a number of approaches for avoiding the dumping laws. One approach is to differentiate the product sold from that in the home market so it does not represent "like quality." An example of this is an auto accessory that one company packaged with a wrench and an instruction book, thereby changing the "accessory" to a "tool." The duty rate in the export market happened to be lower on tools, and the company also acquired immunity from antidumping laws because the package was not comparable to competing goods in the target market. Another approach is to make nonprice competitive adjustments in arrangements with affiliates and distributors. For example, credit can be extended and essentially have the same effect as a price reduction.

## PRICE FIXING

In most instances, it is illegal for representatives of two or more companies to secretly set similar prices for their products. This practice, known as **price fixing,** is generally held to be an anticompetitive act. Companies that collude in this manner are generally trying to ensure higher prices for their products than would generally be available if markets were functioning freely. In *horizontal price fixing*, competitors within an industry that make and market the same product conspire to keep prices high. For example, in the 1990s, ArcherDanielsMidland (ADM) and several other companies were found guilty of colluding to prop up world prices for an enzyme used in animal feed. The term "horizontal" applies in this instance because ADM and its co-conspirators are all at the same supply-chain "level" (i.e., they are manufacturers). *Vertical price fixing* occurs when a manufacturer conspires with wholesalers or retailers (i.e., channel members at different "levels" from the manufacturer) to ensure certain retail prices are maintained. For example, the European Commission recently fined Nintendo nearly $150 million after it was determined that the video game company had colluded with European distributors to fix prices. During the 1990s, prices of Nintendo video game consoles varied widely across Europe. They were much more expensive in Spain than in Britain and other countries; however, distributors in countries with lower retail prices agreed not to sell to retailers in countries with high prices.[30] Another recent case of price fixing pits DeBeers SA, the South African diamond company, against the United States. The price fixing case involves industrial diamonds rather than gemstones; however, DeBeers is a well-known name in the United States thanks to a long-running advertising campaign keyed to the tagline "A Diamond Is Forever." Because the company itself has no American retail presence, DeBeers diamonds are marketed in the United States by intermediaries. DeBeers executives have indicated a willingness to plead guilty and pay a fine in exchange for

---

[29] Chris Adams, "Paper Victories: U.S. Steelmakers Win Even When They Lose an Unfair-Trade Case," *The Wall Street Journal* (March 27, 1998), pp. A1, A8; Nancy Dunne and Edward Alden, "Canadian, US Steel Makers Launch Anti-Dumping Cases," *Financial Times* (October 1, 1998), p. 7.
[30] Paul Meller, "Europe Fines Nintendo $147 Million for Price Fixing," *The Wall Street Journal* (February 24, 2004), p. W1.

access to the United States. As a spokesperson said, "The U.S. is the biggest market for diamond jewelry—accounting for 50 percent of global retail jewelry sales—and we would really, really like to resolve these issues."[31]

## TRANSFER PRICING

**Transfer pricing** refers to the pricing of goods, services, and intangible property bought and sold by operating units or divisions of the same company. In other words, transfer pricing concerns *intracorporate exchanges*, transactions between buyers and sellers that have the same corporate parent. For example, Toyota subsidiaries both sell to, and buy from, each other. Transfer pricing is an important topic in global marketing because goods crossing national borders represent a sale; therefore, their pricing is a matter of interest both to the tax authorities, who want to collect a fair share of income taxes, and to the customs service, which wants to collect an appropriate duty on the goods. Joseph Quinlan, chief marketing strategist at Bank of America, estimates that U.S. companies have 23,000 overseas affiliates; about 25 percent of U.S. exports represent shipments by American companies to affiliates and subsidiaries outside the United States. Similarly, intracorporate shipments by companies based outside America to U.S. units represent one-fourth of U.S. merchandise shipments. Transfer pricing is an issue for each such shipment.

In determining transfer prices to subsidiaries, global companies must address a number of issues, including taxes, duties and tariffs, country profit transfer rules, conflicting objectives of joint venture partners, and government regulations. Not surprisingly, tax authorities such as the Internal Revenue Service in the United States, Inland Revenue in the United Kingdom, and Japan's National Tax Administration Agency take a keen interest in transfer pricing policies. One unidentified company recently paid a fine of $1.6 billion to Inland Revenue to settle a transfer-pricing suit. Transfer pricing is proving to be a key corporate issue in Europe as the euro makes it easier for tax authorities to audit transfer-pricing policies.[32]

There are three major alternative approaches to transfer pricing. The approach used will vary with the nature of the firm, products, markets, and historical circumstances of each case. A **market-based transfer price** is derived from the price required to be competitive in the international market. In other words, it represents an approximation of an arm's-length transaction. The constraint on this price is cost. Today's global companies have many outsourcing options available to them. This puts additional pressure on intracorporate supply groups to control and cut costs in an effort to compete with outside vendors. In some instances, no market exists for a particular product; how, then, can one arrive at a market-based price? **Cost-based transfer pricing** can take the same forms as the cost-based pricing methods discussed earlier in the chapter, including full cost and estimated future cost. The way costs are defined may have an impact on tariffs and duties of sales to affiliates and subsidiaries by global companies. A third alternative is to allow the organization's affiliates to determine **negotiated transfer prices** among themselves. This method may be employed when market prices are subject to frequent changes. Table 11-8 summarizes the results of recent studies comparing transfer pricing methods by country. As shown in the table, market-based and cost-based transfer pricing are the two preferred methods in the United States, Canada, Japan, and the United Kingdom.

31 John R. Wilke, "DeBeers Is in Talks to Settle Price-Fixing Charge," *The Wall Street Journal* (February 24, 2004), pp. A1, A14.
32 Jim Kelly, "Time to Tackle the Most Taxing Issue," *Financial Times* (September 24, 1998), p. 25.

| Methods | United States (%) | Canada (%) | Japan (%) | United Kingdom (%) |
|---|---|---|---|---|
| 1. Market-based | 35 | 37 | 37 | 31 |
| 2. Cost-based | 43 | 33 | 41 | 38 |
| 3. Negotiated | 14 | 26 | 22 | 20 |
| 4. Other | 8 | 4 | 0 | 11 |
| | 100 | 100 | 100 | 100 |

Source: Adapted from Charles T. Horngren, Srikant M. Datar, and George Foster, Cost Accounting: A Managerial Emphasis (Upper Saddle River, NJ: Prentice Hall, 2003), p. 767.

**Table 11-8**

*Transfer Pricing Methods Used in Selected Countries*

## Tax Regulations and Transfer Prices

Because the global corporation conducts business in a world characterized by different corporate tax rates, there is an incentive to maximize system income in countries with the lowest tax rates and to minimize income in high-tax countries. Governments, naturally, are well aware of this situation. In recent years, many governments have tried to maximize national tax revenues by examining company returns and mandating reallocation of income and expenses.

## Sales of Tangible and Intangible Property

Section 482 of the U.S. Treasury regulations deals with controlled intracompany transfers of raw materials and finished and intermediate goods, as well as intangibles such as charges for the use of manufacturing technology. The general rule that applies to sales of tangible property is known as the "arm's-length" formula, defined as the price that would have been charged in independent transactions between unrelated parties under similar circumstances. The complete text of Section 482 appears in the appendix to this chapter.

## Competitive Pricing

Because Section 482 places so much emphasis on arm's-length price, a manager at a U.S. company who examines the regulations might wonder whether the spirit of these regulations permits pricing decisions to be made with regard to market and competitive factors. Clearly, if only the arm's-length standard is applied, a company may not be able to respond to the competitive factors that exist in every market, domestic and global. Fortunately, the regulations provide an opening for the company that seeks to be price competitive or to aggressively price U.S.-sourced products in its international operations. Many interpret the regulations to mean that it is proper for a company to reduce prices and increase marketing expenditures through a controlled affiliate to gain market share, even when it would not do so in an arm's-length transaction with an independent distributor. This is because market position represents, in effect, an investment and an asset. A company would invest in such an asset only if it controlled the reseller; that is, if the reseller is a subsidiary. The regulations may also be interpreted as permitting a company to lower its transfer price for the purpose of entering a new market or meeting competition in an existing market either by instituting price reductions or by increasing marketing efforts in the target markets. Companies must have and use this latitude in making price decisions if they are to achieve significant success in international markets with U.S.-sourced goods.

## Importance of Section 482 Regulations

Whatever the pricing rationale, executives and managers involved in international pricing policy decisions must familiarize themselves with the Section

482 regulations. The pricing rationale must conform with the intention of these regulations. In an effort to develop more workable transfer pricing rules, the IRS issued temporary regulations on January 13, 1993, calling for "contemporaneous documentation" that supports transfer price decisions. Such documentation will require participation of management and marketing personnel in transfer pricing decisions, as opposed to the tax department. Companies should be prepared to demonstrate that their pricing methods are the result of informed choice, not oversight.

Treasury regulations and IRS enforcement policies often seem perplexingly inscrutable. However, ample evidence exists that the government simply seeks to prevent tax avoidance and to ensure fair distribution of income from the operations of companies doing business internationally. Still, the government does not always succeed in its efforts to enforce Section 482 by reallocating income. In one long-running legal battle, the U.S. government is attempting to recover $2.7 billion plus interest from GlaxoSmithKline. The Internal Revenue Service charges that Glaxo did not pay enough tax on profits from Zantac, its hugely successful ulcer medication. Between 1989 and 1999, U.S. revenues from Zantac totaled $16 billion. Specifically, the IRS is charging that Glaxo's American unit overpaid royalties to the British parent company, thus reducing taxable U.S. income. The case may not come to trial until 2006.[33]

Even companies that make a conscientious effort to comply with the regulations and that document this effort may find themselves in tax court. Should a tax auditor raise questions, executives should be able to make a strong case for their decisions. Fortunately, consulting services are available to help managers deal with the arcane world of transfer pricing. It is not unusual for large global companies to invest hundred of thousands of dollars and hire international accounting firms to review of transfer pricing policies. For companies with tighter budgets, Worldwide Transfer Pricing Institute in Schaumburg, Illinois, offers a package of software, documentation, and training.

## COUNTERTRADE

In recent years, many exporters have been forced to finance international transactions by taking full or partial payment in some form other than money.[34] A number of alternative finance methods, known as *countertrade*, are widely used. In a **countertrade** transaction, a sale results in product flowing in one direction to a buyer; a separate stream of products and services, often flowing in the opposite direction, is also created. Countertrade generally involves a seller from the West and a buyer in a developing country; for example, the countries in the former Soviet bloc have historically relied heavily on countertrade. This approach, which reached a peak in popularity in the mid-1980s, is now used in some 100 countries. Within the former Soviet Union, countertrade has flourished in the 1990s, following the collapse of the central planning system.

As one expert notes, countertrade flourishes when hard currency is scarce. Exchange controls may prevent a company from expatriating earnings; the company may be forced to spend money in-country for products that are then exported and sold in third-country markets. Historically, the single most important driving force behind the proliferation of countertrade was the decreasing ability of developing countries to finance imports through bank loans. This

---

[33] Susannah Rodgers, "GlaxoSmithKline Gets Big Tax Bill," *The Wall Street Journal* (January 8, 2004), p. A8.
[34] Many of the examples in the following section are adapted from Matt Schaffer, *Winning the Countertrade War: New Export Strategies for America* (New York: John Wiley & Sons, 1989).

trend resulted in debt-ridden governments pushing for self-financed deals.[35] According to Pompiliu Verzariu of the U.S. Commerce Department:

> In the 1990s, countertrade pressures abated in many parts of the world, notably Latin America, as a result of debt reduction induced by the Brady plan initiative, lower international interest rates, policies that liberalized trade regimes, and the emergence of economic blocs such as NAFTA and Mercosur, which integrate regional trade based on free-market principles.[36]

Today, several conditions affect the probability that importing nations will demand countertrade. First is the priority attached to the Western import. The higher the priority, the less likely it is that countertrade will be required. The second condition is the value of the transaction; the higher the value, the greater the likelihood that countertrade will be involved. Third, the availability of products from other suppliers can also be a factor. If a company is the sole supplier of a differentiated product, it can demand monetary payment. However, if competitors are willing to deal on a countertrade basis, a company may have little choice but to agree or risk losing the sale altogether. Overall, the advantages to nonmarket and developing economies are access to Western marketing expertise and technology in the short term, and creation of hard currency export markets in the long term. The U.S. government officially opposes government-mandated countertrade, which represents the type of bilateral trade agreement that violates the free trading system established by GATT.

Two categories of countertrade are discussed here. Barter falls into one category; the mixed forms of countertrade, including counterpurchase, offset, compensation trading, and cooperation agreements belong in a separate category. They incorporate a real distinction from barter because money or credit is involved in the transaction.

## Barter

The term **barter** describes the least complex and oldest form of bilateral, nonmonetized countertrade. Simple barter is a direct exchange of goods or services between two parties. Although no money is involved, both partners construct an approximate shadow price for products flowing in each direction. One contract formalizes simple barter transactions, which are generally for less than 1 year to avoid problems in price fluctuations. However, for some transactions, the exchange may span months or years, with contract provisions allowing adjustments in the exchange ratio to handle fluctuations in world prices.

Companies sometimes seek outside help from barter specialists. For example, New York–based Atwood Richards engages in barter in all parts of the world. Generally, however, distribution is direct between trading partners, with no intermediary included. For example, during the Soviet era, General Electric sold a turbine generator to Romania. For payment, GE Trading Company accepted $150 million in chemicals, metals, nails, and other products that it then sold on the world market. One of the highest-profile companies involved in barter deals is PepsiCo, which has done business in the Soviet and post-Soviet market for more than 20 years. In the Soviet era, PepsiCo bartered soft-drink syrup concentrate for Stolichnaya vodka, which was, in turn, exported to the United States by the PepsiCo Wines & Spirits subsidiary and marketed by M. Henri Wines. In the post-Soviet market economy in the Commonwealth of Independent States, barter is not

[35] Pompiliu Verzariu, "Trends and Developments in International Countertrade," *Business America* (November 2, 1992), p. 2.
[36] Janet Aschkenasy, "Give and Take," *International Business* (September 1996), p. 11.

necessarily required. Today, Stolichnaya is imported into the United States and marketed by Carillon Importers, a unit of Diageo PLC.

## Counterpurchase

This form of countertrade, also termed *parallel trading* or *parallel barter*, is distinguished from other forms in that each delivery in an exchange is paid for in cash. For example, Rockwell International sold a printing press to Zimbabwe for $8 million. The deal went through, however, only after Rockwell agreed to purchase $8 million in ferrochrome and nickel from Zimbabwe, which it subsequently sold on the world market.

The Rockwell-Zimbabwe deal illustrates several aspects of **counterpurchase.** Generally, products offered by the foreign principal are not related to the Western firm's exports and thus cannot be used directly by the firm. In most counterpurchase transactions, two separate contracts are signed. In one the supplier agrees to sell products for a cash settlement (the original sales contract); in the other, the supplier agrees to purchase and market unrelated products from the buyer (a separate, parallel contract). The dollar value of the counterpurchase generally represents a set percentage—and sometimes the full value—of the products sold to the foreign principal. When the Western supplier sells these goods, the trading cycle is complete.

## Offset

**Offset** is a reciprocal arrangement whereby the government in the importing country seeks to recover large sums of hard currency spent on expensive purchases such as military aircraft or telecommunications systems. In effect, the government is saying, "If you want us to spend government money on your exports, you must import products from our country." Offset arrangements may also involve cooperation in manufacturing, some form of technology transfer, placing subcontracts locally, or arranging local assembly or manufacturing equal to a certain percentage of the contract value.[37] In one recent deal involving offsets, Lockheed Martin Corp. sold F-16 fighters to the United Arab Emirates for $6.4 billion. In return, Lockheed agreed to invest $160 million in the petroleum-related UAE Offsets Group.[38]

Offset may be distinguished from counterpurchase because the latter is characterized by smaller deals over shorter periods of time.[39] Another major distinction between offset and other forms of countertrade is that the agreement is not contractual but reflects a memorandum of understanding that sets out the dollar value of products to be offset and the time period for completing the transaction. In addition, there is no penalty on the supplier for nonperformance. Typically, requests range from 20 to 50 percent of the value of the supplier's product. Some highly competitive sales have required offsets exceeding 100 percent of the valuation of the original sale.

Offsets have become a controversial facet of today's trade environment. To win sales in important markets such as China, global companies are facing demands for offsets even when transactions do not involve military procurement.

---

[37] The commitment to local assembly or manufacturing under the supplier's specifications is commonly termed a *coproduction agreement*, which is tied to the offset but does not, in itself, represent a type of countertrade.

[38] Daniel Pearl, "Arms Dealers Get Creative with 'Offsets,'" *The Wall Street Journal* (April 20, 2000), p. A18.

[39] Patricia Daily and S. M. Ghazanfar, "Countertrade: Help or Hindrance to Less-Developed Countries?" *Journal of Social, Political, and Economic Studies* 18, no. 1 (Spring 1993), p. 65.

For example, the Chinese government requires Boeing to spend 20 to 30 percent of the price of each aircraft on purchases of Chinese goods. As Boeing executive Dean Thornton explained:

> "Offset" is a bad word, and it's against GATT and a whole bunch of other stuff, but it's a fact of life. It used to be twenty years ago in places like Canada or the UK, it was totally explicit, down to the decimal point. "You will buy 20 percent offset of your value." Or 21 percent or whatever. It still is that way in military stuff. [With sales of commercial aircraft], it's not legal so it becomes less explicit.[40]

## Compensation Trading

This form of countertrade, also called *buyback*, involves two separate and parallel contracts. In one contract, the supplier agrees to build a plant or provide plant equipment, patents or licenses, or technical, managerial, or distribution expertise for a hard currency down payment at the time of delivery. In the other contract, the supplier company agrees to take payment in the form of the plant's output equal to its investment (minus interest) for a period of as many as 20 years.

Essentially, the success of compensation trading rests on the willingness of each firm to be both a buyer and a seller. The People's Republic of China has used compensation trading extensively. Egypt also used this approach to develop an aluminum plant. A Swiss company, Aluswiss, built the plant and also exports alumina (an oxide of aluminum found in bauxite and clay) to Egypt. Aluswiss takes back a percentage of the finished aluminum produced at the plant as partial payment for building the plant. As this example shows, compensation differs from counterpurchase in that the technology or capital supplied is related to the output produced.[41] In counterpurchase, as noted before, the goods taken by the supplier typically cannot be used directly in its business activities.

## Switch Trading

Also called *triangular trade* and *swap*, **switch trading** is a mechanism that can be applied to barter or countertrade. In this arrangement, a professional switch trader, switch trading house, or bank steps into a simple barter or other countertrade arrangement when one of the parties is not willing to accept all the goods received in a transaction. The switching mechanism provides a "secondary market" for countertraded or bartered goods and reduces the inflexibility inherent in barter and countertrade. Fees charged by switch traders range from 5 percent of market value for commodities to 30 percent for high-technology items. Switch traders develop their own networks of firms and personal contacts and are generally headquartered in Vienna, Amsterdam, Hamburg, or London. If a party anticipates that the products received in a barter or countertrade deal will be sold eventually at a discount by the switch trader, the common practice is to price the original products higher, build in "special charges" for port storage or consulting, or require shipment by the national carrier.

---

[40] William Greider, *One World, Ready or Not: The Manic Logic of Global Capitalism* (Upper Saddle River, NJ: Simon & Schuster, 1997), p. 130.

[41] Patricia Daily and S. M. Ghazanfar, "Countertrade: Help or Hindrance to Less-Developed Countries?" *Journal of Social, Political, and Economic Studies* 18, no. 1 (Spring 1993), p. 66.

Pricing decisions are a critical element of the marketing mix that must reflect costs, competitive factors, and customer perceptions regarding value of the product. In a true global market, the **law of one price** would prevail. Pricing strategies include **market skimming, market penetration,** and **market holding.** Novice exporters frequently use **cost-plus pricing**. International terms of a sale such as **ex-works, F.A.S., F.O.B.,** and **C.I.F.** are known as **Incoterms,** and specify which party to a transaction is responsible for covering various costs. These and other costs lead to **price escalation,** the accumulation of costs that occurs when products are shipped from one country to another. Expectations regarding currency fluctuations, inflation, government controls, and the competitive situation must also be factored into pricing decisions. Global companies can maintain competitive prices in world markets by shifting production sources as business conditions change. Overall, a company's pricing

policies can be categorized as **ethnocentric, polycentric,** or **geocentric.**

Several additional pricing issues are related to global marketing. The issue of **gray market goods** arises because price variations between different countries lead to **parallel imports. Dumping** is another contentious issue that can result in strained relations between trading partners. In the United States, proof of **price discrimination** and injury are required in dumping cases. **Transfer pricing** is an issue because of the sheer monetary volume of intra-corporate sales and because governments are anxious to generate as much tax revenue as possible. Three options are available: **cost-based transfer pricing, market-based transfer pricing,** and **negotiated transfer pricing.** Various forms of **countertrade** play an important role in today's global environment. **Barter, counterpurchase, offset, compensation trading,** and **switch trading** are the main countertrade options.

1. What are the basic factors that affect price in any market? What considerations enter into the pricing decision?

2. Define the various types of pricing strategies and objectives available to global marketers.

3. Identify some of the environmental constraints on global pricing decisions.

4. Why do price differences in world markets often lead to gray marketing?

5. What is dumping? Why was dumping such an important issue during the Uruguay Round of GATT negotiations?

6. What is a transfer price? Why is it an important issue for companies with foreign affiliates? Why

did transfer pricing in Europe take on increased importance in 1999?

7. What is the difference between ethnocentric, polycentric, and geocentric pricing strategies? Which one would you recommend to a company that has global market aspirations?

8. If you were responsible for marketing CAT scanners worldwide (average price, $1,200,000), and your country of manufacture was experiencing a strong and appreciating currency against almost all other currencies, what options would be available to you to maintain your competitive advantage in world markets?

9. Compare and contrast the different forms of countertrade.

# Case 11-1

## Pricing AIDS Drugs in Emerging Markets

For years, the war against AIDS has been heavily dependent on drugs developed and produced by global pharmaceutical companies such as Merck & Co., Bristol-Myers Squibb Company, and GlaxoSmithKline PLC. The most effective treatment against the deadly virus is a "cocktail" consisting of several different drugs, and the per-person cost of a 1-year supply can run as high as $10,000 (see Table 1). Such prices are far beyond the means of AIDS victims in low-income nations; in Africa alone, an estimated 25 million people are infected with HIV, the virus that causes AIDS. At the end of the 1990s, AIDS patients in countries such as Uganda were paying approximately $6 per day for a drug cocktail such as Glaxo's Combivir.

In May 2000, following discussions with representatives of the United Nations AIDS Program (UNAIDS), Merck and four other major pharmaceutical companies announced an agreement to cut drug prices in developing countries by as much as 85 to 90 percent compared with prices in the United States. For example, Merck set a discounted price of $1,044 for its Crixivan protease inhibitor. Although many in the world community welcomed the announcement, it was clear that even these prices were still beyond the reach of many AIDS victims. Employers, governments, the World Bank, and other donor organizations would be required to provide subsidies if the drugs were to be truly affordable.

The announcement also highlighted the fact that pricing is only one element in the fight against the spread of AIDS. To be effective, AIDS drugs have to be taken in strict daily regimens. A patient's condition can worsen if the regimen is not followed faithfully; in addition, there are concerns in the medical community about the development of new drug-resistant strains of the disease. Thus, related issues include the need for improving the public health infrastructure in countries such as Uganda with an emphasis on drug distribution, counseling, AIDS education, HIV testing, and prevention.

The proposed price cuts also entailed potential risks to Glaxo and other industry leaders. The companies treat the costs associated with drug manufacturing as trade secrets. According to some estimates, profit margins are as high as 90 percent once research and development costs have been recovered. By cutting prices in developing countries, the companies were opening themselves to pressure to cut prices in developed countries as well. Also, there was a risk that the cheaper drugs would fall into the hands of black marketers who would then re-export them to developed countries and undercut established prices. Merck representatives planned to negotiate with government officials from each nation and seek assurance that the drugs would stay off the black market before actually implementing the price cuts.

There was one other critical factor in the decision to cut prices: the threat from manufacturers of low-priced generic AIDS drugs. Several manufacturers in India, Brazil, and Thailand had already created "generic" versions of Zerit, 3TC, Crixivan, and other name-brand drugs. Production of these "copycat" versions was possible because India currently does not recognize international patent laws. In February 2001, less than 1 year after the initiative with UNAIDS was announced, Yusuf K. Hamied, the president of India's Cipla Ltd., stunned the world community by announcing that he was prepared to offer a year's supply of three AIDS drugs to governments in sub-Saharan Africa for $600 per patient. That price was about 40 percent below the prices offered by GlaxoSmithKline and others. He also asserted that he would make the three-drug cocktail available to a private organization, Doctors Without Borders, for $350 per year. Another Indian manufacturer, Hetero Drugs Ltd., quickly followed suit and set a price of $347 per year.

The announcements were hailed by AIDS activists, even though there were two complications. First, the Indian companies would somehow have to circumvent laws in various African nations that protect the patent holders of drugs that had been copied. In South Africa, for example, the government filed a lawsuit against the Western pharmaceutical companies in an effort to secure distribution. Second, Cipla and other generic producers had to obtain approval from local regulatory agencies before their drugs could be made available. Meanwhile, activists continued to pressure the big drug companies for additional reductions beyond those originally announced as well as price cuts on drugs not covered in the UNAIDS agreement. For example, the University of Minnesota holds the patent on Ziagen, which is produced by GlaxoSmithKline but had not been among the discounted drugs. Student activists at the university have been urging administrators to consider asking Glaxo to add Ziagen to the list of AIDS drugs that will be discounted.

**Table 1**  Per Patient Per Year Price of AIDS Drugs

| Drug (Company) | U.S. Price | CIPLA | HETERO | Proposed Price in Africa |
|---|---|---|---|---|
| Zerit (Bristol-Myers) | $3,589 | $70 | $47 | $252 |
| 3TC (Glaxo) | 3,271 | 190 | 98 | 232 |
| Crixivan (Merck) | 6,016 | NA | 2,300 | 600 |
| Combivir (Glaxo) | 7,093 | 635 | 293 | 730 |
| Stocrin (Merck) | 4,730 | NA | 1,179 | 500 |
| Viramune (Boehringer) | 3,508 | 340 | 202 | 483 |

Several of the drug companies that had announced price cuts in 2000 responded quickly to the announcements from India. Less than a month after Cipla's announcement, a Merck spokesperson indicated that the company would slash prices in Africa by an additional 40 to 55 percent. The new price for Crixivan was set at $600; another Merck drug, Stocrin, was priced at $500 per year per patient. Thus, a Crixivan/Stocrin cocktail would cost about $1,100, compared with about $11,000 in the United States; at the discounted prices, Merck indicated it was generating zero profit. Merck also indicated that it would make the discounted drugs available to other low-income nations besides those in Africa. Bristol-Myers Squibb and GlaxoSmithKline also announced plans for a new round of price cuts.

Despite the moves, the global pharmaceutical giants appeared to be losing a public relations war in which AIDS activists portrayed them as both secretive and as withholding needed drugs from millions who need them. At the 1998 world AIDS conference in Geneva, UN officials announced a pilot program to reduce AIDS drug prices in low-income countries. However, Merck elected not to participate in the program; executives argued that issues pertaining to infrastructure and health-service networks had to be addressed first. AIDS activists responded by dismantling Merck's booth at the conference. Merck and other Western companies remained concerned that, if a broader base of public opinion turned against them, the ongoing controversy might ultimately undermine their international patents.

## Discussion Questions

1. Given the discount prices that Merck and the other global drug companies are making available in Africa and other developing countries, are they charging too much for AIDS drugs in the United States? Should they be required to disclose their cost structures?

2. Do you think intellectual property laws in countries such as South Africa should be changed to allow generic producers such as Cipla access to the market?

3. What should Merck, Glaxo, and other pharmaceutical manufacturers do to improve their image with the general public?

*Sources:* Michael Waldholz, "Into Africa: Makers of AIDS Drugs Agree to Slash Prices for Developing World," *The Wall Street Journal* (May 11, 2000), pp. A1, A12; Daniel Pearl and Alix Freedman, "The Catalyst: Behind Cipla's Offer of Cheap AIDS Drugs: Potent Mix of Motives," *The Wall Street Journal* (March 12, 2001), pp. A1, A8; Mark Schoofs and Michael Waldholz, "New Regimen: AIDS-Drug Price War Breaks Out in Africa, Goaded by Generics," *The Wall Street Journal* (March 7, 2001), pp. A1, A14; Rachel Zimmerman and Michael Waldholz, "Abbott to Cut African AIDS-Drug Prices," *The Wall Street Journal* (March 27, 2001), pp. A3, A8.

# Case 11-2

## LVMH and Luxury Goods Marketing

Do you know anyone who spends $1,700 on a suit plus $600 for a matching handbag? When it comes to champagne and perfume, do your friends spend $100 or more for a single bottle? Welcome to the rarefied world of luxury goods marketing. In this world, affluent consumers eagerly seek out luxury brands such as Armani, Christian Dior, Gucci, Louis Vuitton, Prada, and Versace. They are willing and able to pay high prices for top-quality merchandise from fashion houses whose names are synonymous with status, good taste, and prestige. In France, *haute couture* traditionally meant that one outfit was meticulously crafted for members of the aristocracy, "old money" socialites, or celebrities. Today, however, the concept and meaning of *haute couture* are being transformed.

Although the *couture* image of the supermodel strutting down the catwalk is still a mainstay of the fashion world, some of the world's best-known fashion houses are redefining the notion of luxury by catering to the needs of a more diverse, *nouveau riche* clientele. Whereas in years past, fashion houses produced only clothing, today numerous licensing deals are generating more cash than the clothing itself is. Countless items bearing the names of venerable *couture* houses are now available worldwide. Thanks to the stock market boom of the 1990s and rising prosperity levels in developing nations, a new class of affluent consumers has begun to develop a taste for luxury branded products, rang-ing from Gucci sunglasses to Dior pantyhose. In fact, apparel goods constitute less than 20 percent of total sales volume by Hermés. As Lord Thurso, chief executive of a luxury health spa in Great Britain, noted, "The trick is not to sell real luxury to very rich people. It's to sell a *perception* of luxury to aspiring people."

One fashion house that is changing with the times is LVMH Moët Hennessy Louis Vuitton SA, the largest marketer of luxury products and brands in the world. Chairman Bernard Arnault presides over a diverse empire of products and brands, sales of which totaled $15 billion (€11.6 billion) in 2003 (see Figure 1). Arnault, whom some refer to as "the pope of high fashion," recently summed up the luxury business as follows: "We are here to sell dreams. When you see a couture show on TV around the world, you dream. When you enter a Dior boutique and buy your lipstick, you buy something affordable, but it has the dream in it." Sales of luggage and leather fashion goods, including the 100-year old Louis Vuitton brand, account for 30 percent of revenues. The company's specialty group includes Duty Free Shoppers (DFS) and Sephora. DFS operates stores in international airports around the world; Sephora, which LVMH acquired in 1997, is Europe's second-largest chain of perfume and cosmetics stores. Driven by such well-known brands as Christian Dior, Givenchy, and Kenzo, perfumes and body products generate nearly 20 percent of LVMH's revenues. LVMH's wine and spirits unit includes such prestigious Champagne brands as Dom Perignon, Moët & Chandon, and Veuve Clicquot.

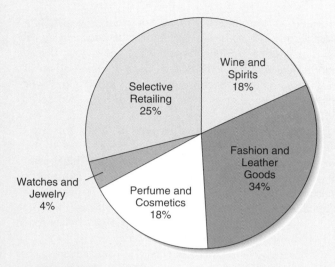

**Figure 1**

*LVMH Operating Units by 2003 Net Sales*

Despite the high expenses associated with operating elegant stores and purchasing advertising space in upscale magazines, the premium retail prices that luxury goods command translate into handsome profits. The Louis Vuitton brand alone accounts for about 60 percent of LVMH's operating profit. Not surprisingly, unscrupulous operators have taken note of the high margins associated with Vuitton handbags, gun cases, and luggage displaying the distinctive beige-on-brown latticework LV monogram. Louis Vuitton SA spends $10 million annually battling counterfeiters in Turkey, Thailand, China, Morocco, South Korea, and Italy. Some of the money is spent on lobbyists who

represent the company's interests in meetings with foreign government officials. Yves Carcelle, chairman of Louis Vuitton SA, recently explained, "Almost every month, we get a government somewhere in the world to destroy canvas, or finished products."

Another problem is a flourishing gray market. Givenchy and Christian Dior's Dune fragrance are just two of the luxury perfume brands that are sometimes diverted from authorized channels for sale at mass-market retail outlets. LVMH and other luxury goods marketers found a new way to combat gray market imports into the United States. In March 1995, the U.S. Supreme Court let stand an appeals court ruling prohibiting a discount drugstore chain from selling Givenchy perfume without permission. Parfums Givenchy USA had claimed that its distinctive packaging should be protected under U.S. copyright law. The ruling means that Costco, Wal-Mart, and other discounters will no longer be able to sell some imported fragrances without authorization.

Asia—particularly Japan—represents important markets for companies such as LVMH. The financial turmoil that began in July 1997 and the subsequent currency devaluations and weakening of the yen have translated into lower demand for luxury goods. Because price perceptions are a critical component of luxury goods' appeal, LMVH executives are making a number of adjustments in response to changing business conditions. For example, Patrick Choel, president of the perfume and cosmetics division, has raised wholesale prices in individual Asian markets. The goal is to discourage discount retailers from stocking up with designer products and then selling them to down-market consumers. Also, expenditures on perfume and cosmetics advertising have been reduced to maintain profitability in the face of a possible sales decline. Vuitton chairman Yves

Carcelle is also making adjustments. He has canceled plans for a new store in Indonesia; group managers have raised prices to counteract the effect of currency devaluations. Because the DFS chain depends on Japanese tourists in Asia and Hawaii for 75 percent of sales, Louis Vuitton managers also work with tour operators to predict the flow of Japanese tourists. When tourism is at a peak, price increases from 10 to 22 percent help maximize profits on merchandise sales.

Arnault was confident that the Asian crisis would not severely affect his company's performance in the long term. As Arnault explained in the spring of 1998, "One has to distinguish between Japan, where most of our business is, and the rest of Asia. Japan is in a growth slump, but it isn't going to have the same difficulties as Korea or Indonesia. And our business in Japan is doing very well." Because the Louis Vuitton unit controls its own distribution, management was even able to take advantage of the crisis by renegotiating store leases in key Asian cities. In some instances, the company has secured longer lease terms plus reductions in rates by as much as one-third. Arnault's optimism was well founded; with interests rate at record lows and a gloomy outlook for the stock market, Japanese consumers had few other spending options. In 2001, executives actually raised prices at Louis Vuitton's 45 Japanese stores.

*"One friend of mine has 10 Louis Vuitton bags. In Japan, it's a status symbol. It's very important to have European luxury goods."*

A 39-year-old flight attendant based in Tokyo

The United States is also a key market for LVMH. One particular marketing program focused on increasing awareness of Hennessy cognac. Thanks to a revival of "cocktail culture" in the United States, sales of hard spirits are up. To promote awareness and consumption among a younger demographic, in the mid-1990s Hennessy marketing managers recruited twentysomethings to go to upscale bars in major metropolitan markets and order drinks such as the "Hennessy martini" and "Hennessy sidecar" made with cognac. Although the notion of mixing cognac is considered heresy by traditionalists, it was essential to broadening the brand's appeal. If a bartender didn't know how to create a particular drink, the Hennessy agent helpfully explained the recipe while attracting the attention of other patrons. Hennessy also picked up the tab when their "secret agents" would buy rounds of cognac-based drinks for everyone at the bar. The promotion was designed to increase awareness among young adults and to communicate that cognac can be enjoyed by people other than "old fogies." The effort paid off in some unexpected ways: Cognac has been embraced by urban hip-hop culture, and cognac exports to the United States tripled over the past decade. LVMH's Hennessey is the brand of choice for many rap stars; the brand name has even popped up in more than 100 songs.

Such marketing tactics are a world away from the old days, when the companies that today make up LVMH were family-run enterprises focused more on prestige than on profit. They sold mainly to a small, very rich clientele. Even as he broadens the company's consumer base, Arnault has taken a number of steps to raise the level of professionalism of LVMH's management team. In 1997, Arnault implemented a corporate restructuring that groups the company's subsidiaries into divisions. Previously, the heads of individual subsidiaries reported directly to Arnault; now, division heads meet with him to discuss strategy. Notes Arnault, "It's much more efficient, because it allows us to put into practice all the synergies between the different brands in a coordinated way."

Changing times can also be seen in Arnault's choice of American designer Marc Jacobs to create the first-ever Louis Vuitton ready-to-wear line. The line is priced quite high, and to preserve its exclusivity, it is currently available only through Louis Vuitton boutiques. There will be no markdowns on unsold merchandise. Any stocks that remain at the end of the season will be destroyed. Jacobs' first collection included a plain white cotton poplin raincoat that prompted one observer to ask, "Is this luxury?" Ironically, the signature LV is hard to spot on many pieces in the collection, such as a white-on-white patent leather bag.

In the late 1990s, Arnault sensed that cosmetics-buying habits were changing in key markets. He opened Sephora stores in New York, Chicago, and San Francisco in conjunction with a new Web site, Sephora.com. Today, there are more than 70 Sephora stores in the United States; plans call for expanding into Japan and Latin America as well. Customers who visit Sephora USA stores are encouraged to wander freely and sample products on an open floor without waiting for sales clerks to assist them. However, high start-up and promotion costs have reduced the financial contribution that Sephora makes to LVMH, and some analysts have asked when Sephora will be profitable.

Profitability is also an issue with another of Arnault's acquisitions, Donna Karan International Inc. In 2001, Arnault paid more than $600 million for the company and its trademarks. Arnault had tried without success to acquire Giorgio Armani; Donna Karan is LVMH's first American designer label. As Arnault noted, "What appealed to us is the fact that it is one of the best-known brand names in the world." After the deal was completed, however, company executives were surprised to learn that some items from the DKNY line could be found in discount stores such as TJ Maxx. Arnault appointed Giuseppe Brusone, a former managing director of Armani, as Donna Karan's chief executive and instructed him to reshape the company. Brusone intends to improve quality, close company-owned outlet stores, and reduce shipments to department stores to keep the clothes from being marked down. He also intends to shift manufacturing out of New York; the move will both cut costs and lend the line the added prestige associated with garments that are "made in Italy."

All of these actions are designed to keep LVMH—and Arnault himself—at the forefront of the luxury goods business and one step ahead of an ever-changing business environment. Arnault is widely admired for his business instincts and acumen. However, some in the industry view his bold moves as emblematic of all that is wrong with luxury at the dawn of the new millennium. An executive at a competitor noted disapprovingly, "They run this thing like Procter & Gamble."

***Visit the Web Site***
**www.lvmh.com**
**www.sephora.com**

## Discussion Questions

1. Bernard Arnault has built LVMH into a luxury goods empire by making numerous acquisitions. What strategy is evident here?

2. How do LVMH executives adjust prices in response to changing economic conditions?

3. Do you think the high retail prices charged for luxury goods are worth paying?

4. How will luxury goods marketers be affected by the slowdown in tourism that followed the terror attacks of September 11, 2001?

*Sources:* Lisa Bannon and Alessandra Galloni, "Brand Manager Deluxe," *The Wall Street Journal* (October 10, 2003), p. B1; John Carreyrou and Christopher Lawton, "Napoleon's Nightcap Gets a Good Rap from Hip-Hop Set," *The Wall Street Journal* (July 14, 2003), pp. A1, A7; Teri Agins and Deborah Ball, "Changing Outfits: Did LVMH Commit a Fashion Faux Pas Buying Donna Karan?" *The Wall Street Journal* (March 21, 2002), pp. A1, A8; Ball, "Despite Downturn, Japanese Are Still Having Fits for Luxury Goods," *The Wall Street Journal* (April 24, 2001), pp. B1, B4; Bonnie Tsui, "Eye of the Beholder: Sephora's Finances," *Advertising Age* (March 19, 2001), p. 20; Lucia van der Post, "Life's Brittle Luxuries," *Financial Times* (July 18–19, 1998), p. I; Gail Edmondson, "LVMH: Life Isn't All Champagne and Caviar," *Business Week* (November 10, 1997), pp. 108+; Jennifer Steinhauer, "The King of Posh," *The New York Times* (August 17, 1997), sec. 3, pp. 1, 10–11; David Owen, "A Captain Used to Storms," *Financial Times* (June 21–22, 1997); Holly Brubach, "And Luxury for All," *The New York Times Magazine* (July 12, 1998), pp. 24–29+; Amy Barrett, "LVMH's Chairman Remains Calm Despite Turbulence," *The Wall Street Journal* (March 16, 1998), p. B4; Barrett, "Gucci's Big Makeover Is Turning Heads," *The Wall Street Journal* (August 26, 1997), p. 12; Stewart Toy, "100 Years of Louis Vuitton," *Cigar Aficionado* (Autumn 1996), pp. 378–379+.

# Appendix 11.1

# Section 482 of the Internal Revenue Code

In any case of two or more organizations, trades, or businesses (whether or not incorporated, whether or not organized in the United States, and whether or not affiliated) owned or controlled directly or indirectly by the same interests, the Secretary may distribute, apportion, or allocate gross income, deductions, credits, or allowances between or among such organizations, trades, or businesses, if he determines that such distribution, apportionment, or allocation is necessary in order to prevent evasion of taxes or clearly to reflect the income of any of such organizations, trades, or businesses. In the case of any transfer (or license) of intangible property (within the meaning of section 936(h)(3)(B)), the income with respect to such transfer or license shall be commensurate with the income attributable to the intangible.

Source: *Internal Revenue Code* (New York: The Research Institute of America, 1987), p. 695.

# 12 Global Marketing Channels and Physical Distribution

**H**ypermarkets are giant stores as big as four or more football fields. Part supermarket, part department store, they feature a wide array of product categories—groceries, toys, furniture, fast food, and financial services—all under one roof. Hypermarkets have flourished in Europe for more than three decades. France's Carrefour SA opened the first hypermarket in 1962; with help from the French government, zoning laws ensured that competing stores would be kept from the vicinity. By 1973, the hypermarket concept had been introduced in Spain; today, Carrefour operates 9,000 stores in 27 countries. It is the world's second largest retailer. Most of the European stores were well established before competing retailing concepts such as shopping malls and discount stores made the Atlantic crossing from America. Now the hypermarket concept is being transplanted around the globe. Carrefour has established a strong presence in Asia; in December 2000, it became the first foreign retailer to open a hypermarket in Japan.

Hypermarkets comprise just one of the many elements that make up distribution channels around the globe. The American Marketing Association defines **channel of distribution** as "an organized network of agencies and institutions which, in combination, perform all the activities required to link producers with users to accomplish the marketing task."[1] **Physical distribution** is the movement of goods through channels; as suggested by the definition, *channels* are made up of a coordinated group of individuals or firms that perform functions that add utility to a product or service. Hypermarket operators such as Carrefour serve an important distribution function; when Western retailers set up shop in developing countries such as Poland and Indonesia, they provide customers with access to more products and lower

---

[1] Peter D. Bennett, *Dictionary of Marketing Terms* (Chicago: American Marketing Association, 1988), p. 29.

Customers enter a Carrefour hypermarket in Toulouse, a city in southwestern France. In August 1999, Carrefour and food retailer Promodès announced a merger that created Europe's largest retail chain. The action represents a European counteroffensive against U.S. based Wal-Mart stores, which ranks as the world's #1 retailer.

prices than ever before. As Tadeusz Donocki, undersecretary of state at Poland's economics ministry, noted recently, "It's a way of bringing dreams closer to people, dreams which before they saw only in films."[2] In developed countries, the arrival of innovators such as Wal-Mart often serves as the catalyst for wrenching changes in long-established distribution traditions (see Case 12-1).

The appearance of hypermarkets around the world adds greater diversity to distribution channels, which already represent the most highly differentiated aspects of national marketing systems. On the opposite end of the spectrum from hypermarkets, for example, are small stores in Latin America called *pulperías*. The diversity of channels and the wide range of possible distribution strategies and market entry options can present challenges to managers responsible for designing global marketing programs. Smaller companies are often blocked by their inability to establish effective channel arrangements. In larger companies that operate via country subsidiaries, channel strategy is the element of the marketing mix that headquarters understands the least. It is important for managers responsible for world marketing programs to understand the nature of international distribution channels. Channels and physical distribution are crucial aspects of the total marketing program; without them, a great product at the right price and effective communications mean very little.

## CHANNEL OBJECTIVES

Marketing channels exist to create utility for customers. The major categories of channel utility are **place utility** (the availability of a product or service in a location that is convenient to a potential customer), **time utility** (the availability of a product or service when desired by a customer), **form utility** (the availability of the product processed, prepared, in proper condition and/or ready to use), and **information utility** (the availability of answers to questions and general communication about useful product features and benefits). Because these utilities can be a basic source of competitive advantage and comprise an important element of the firm's overall value proposition, choosing a channel strategy is one of the key policy decisions management must make. For example, the Coca-Cola Company's

---

[2]    Stefan Wagstyl, "Eastern Europe Takes a Shine to Hypermarket Shopping," *Financial Times* (January 20, 1999), p. 2.

leadership position in world markets is based in part on its ability to put Coke "within an arm's reach of desire"; in other words, to create place utility.

The starting point in selecting the most effective channel arrangement is a clear focus of the company's marketing effort on a target market and an assessment of the way(s) in which distribution can contribute to the firm's overall value proposition. Who are the target customers, and where are they located? What are their information requirements? What are their preferences for service? How sensitive are they to price? Customer preference must be carefully determined because there is as much danger to the success of a marketing program from creating too much utility as there is from creating too little. Moreover, each market must be analyzed to determine the cost of providing channel services. What is appropriate in one country may not be effective in another. Even marketers concerned with a single-country program can study channel arrangements in different parts of the world for valuable information and insight into possible new channel strategies and tactics. For example, retailers from Europe and Asia studied self-service discount retailing in the United States and then introduced the self-service concept in their own countries. Similarly, governments and business executives from many parts of the world have examined Japanese trading companies to learn from their success. Wal-Mart's formula has been closely studied and copied by competitors in the markets it has entered.

## DISTRIBUTION CHANNELS: TERMINOLOGY AND STRUCTURE

As defined previously, distribution channels are systems that link manufacturers to customers. Although channels for consumer products and industrial products are similar, there are also some distinct differences. In **business-to-consumer marketing** (b-to-c or B2C), consumer channels are designed to put products in the hands of people for their own use; as participants in a process known as **business-to-business marketing (b-to-b or B2B)**, industrial channels deliver products to manufacturers or other types of organizations that use them as inputs in the production process or in day-to-day operations. Distributors play important roles in both consumer and industrial channels; a **distributor** is a wholesale intermediary that typically carries product lines or brands on a selective basis. An **agent** is an intermediary who negotiates transactions between two or more parties but does not take title to the goods being purchased or sold.

### Consumer Products and Services

Figure 12-1 summarizes six channel structure alternatives for consumer products. The characteristics of both buyers and products have an important influence on channel design. The first alternative is to market directly to buyers via the Internet, mail order, various types of door-to-door selling, or manufacturer-owned retail outlets. The other options utilize retailers and various combinations of sales forces, agents/brokers, and wholesalers. The number of individual buyers and their geographic distribution, income, shopping habits, and reaction to different selling methods frequently vary from country to country and may require different channel approaches. Product characteristics such as degree of standardization, perishability, bulk, service requirements, and unit price have an impact as well. Generally speaking, channels tend to be longer (require more intermediaries) as the number of customers to be served increases and the price per unit decreases. Bulky products usually require channel arrangements that minimize the shipping distances and the number of times products change hands before they reach the ultimate customer.

## Figure 12-1

Marketing Channel Alternatives: Consumer Products

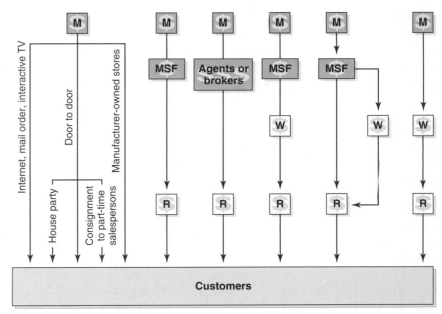

M = Manufacturer    MSF = Manufacturer's sales force
W = Wholesaler      R = Retailer

The Internet and related forms of new media are dramatically altering the distribution landscape. eBay pioneered a form of online commerce known as peer-to-peer (p-to-p) marketing; the Internet's potential was quickly recognized by traditional merchants. Now, eBay is assisting large companies such as Disney and IBM set up online "storefronts" to sell items for fixed prices in addition to conducting business-to-consumer (b-to-c) auctions. "As we evolved from auction-style bidding to adding Buy It Now last year, the logical next step for us was to give sellers a place to showcase their listings," said Bill Cobb, eBay's senior vice president for global marketing.[3] Some observers predict that interactive television (ITV) will also become a viable direct distribution channel in the coming years as more households are wired with the necessary two-way technology. Time-pressed consumers in many countries are increasingly attracted to the time and place utility created by the Internet and similar communication technologies.

Low-cost, mass-market nondurable products and certain services can be sold door-to-door via a direct sales force. Door-to-door selling is a form of distribution that is mature in the United States; however, it is growing in popularity elsewhere. For example, by the mid-1990s, AIG had 5,000 agents selling insurance policies door-to-door in China. This innovative channel strategy was so successful that domestic Chinese companies such as People's Insurance and Ping An Insurance copied it. Noted one local insurance executive, "We have to adjust ourselves to the rising competition."[4] However, in April 1998, the state council imposed a blanket ban on all types of direct selling. Although the ban was aimed most directly at illegal pyramid schemes, Mary Kay, Tupperware, Avon, and Amway have been forced to adapt their business models. In the United States, for example, Mary Kay sales representatives are independent entrepreneurs who buy products from the company and then resell them. By contrast, to comply with the new government

3  Nick Wingfield, "Ebay Allows Sellers to Set Up Storefronts Online in Bid to Expand Beyond Auctions," *The Wall Street Journal* (June 12, 2001), p. B8.
4  Craig Smith, "AIG Reshapes China's Insurance Industry," *The Wall Street Journal* (February 9, 1996), p. A8.

Russia represents the most successful new market entry in Avon's history. Between 1997 and 2002, Avon Russia's sales increased from $56 million to $142 million. The company forecasts that, by 2007, sales will triple again to $500 million. The 44,000 Russian sales representatives promote Avon cosmetics in factories, beauty parlors, and, occasionally, in the homes of friends. Avon has aggressively recruited highly qualified women from the ranks of doctors and engineers, offering them the opportunity to achieve financial independence despite Russia's uncertain economic environment.

regulations, members of Mary Kay's Chinese sales force act as agents selling on behalf of the company.[5]

In Japan, the biggest barrier facing U.S. auto manufacturers isn't high tariffs; rather, it's the fact that half the cars that are sold each year are sold door-to-door. Toyota and its Japanese competitors maintain showrooms, but they also employ more than 100,000 car salespeople. Unlike their American counterparts, many Japanese car buyers never visit dealerships. In fact, the close, long-term relationships between auto salespersons and the Japanese people can be thought of as a consumer version of the *keiretsu* system discussed in Chapter 9. Japanese car buyers expect numerous face-to-face meetings with a sales representative, during which trust is established. The relationship continues after the deal is closed; sales reps send cards and continually seek to ensure the buyer's satisfaction. American rivals such as Ford, meanwhile, try to generate showroom traffic. Nobumasa Ogura manages a Ford dealership in Tokyo. "We need to come up with some ideas to sell more cars without door-to-door sales, but the reality is that we haven't come up with any," he said.[6]

Another direct selling alternative is the *manufacturer-owned store* or *independent franchise store*. One of the first successful U.S.-based international companies, Singer, established a worldwide chain of company-owned and -operated outlets to sell and service sewing machines. More recently, the Walt Disney Company has revamped its chain of retail outlets that offer apparel, videos, toys, and other merchandise featuring the company's trademarked characters. The company will spend $300 million to establish 600 new stores around the world. The stores are designed to boost annual merchandise sales beyond the current level of $13 billion.[7] As noted in Chapter 9, Japanese consumer electronics companies integrate stores into their distribution groups. Nike, Levi Strauss, well-known fashion design houses, and other companies with strong brands sometimes establish one or a few flagship retail stores as product showcases or as a means of obtaining marketing intelligence. Such channels supplement, rather than replace, distribution through independent retail stores.

[5] Ricky Y. K. Chan, "At the Crossroads of Distribution Reform: China's Recent Ban on Direct Selling," *Business Horizons* 42, no. 5 (September–October 1999), pp. 41–46. See also Virginia A. Hulme, "Mary Kay in China: More than Makeup," *China Business Review* 28, no. 1 (January–February 2001), pp. 42–46.

[6] Valerie Reitman, "Toyota Calling: In Japan's Car Market, Big Three Face Rivals Who Go Door-to-Door," *The Wall Street Journal* (September 28, 1994), pp. A1, A6.

[7] Bruce Orwall, "Disney's Magic Transformation," *The Wall Street Journal* (October 4, 2000), pp. B1, B4.

# GLOBAL *marketing in action*

## Selling Cosmetics Door-to-Door

Amway and Avon are two companies that have succeeded in extending their direct sales systems outside the United States. Amway currently has operations in 42 countries; in 1997, foreign markets accounted for about three-fourths of the company's $6.8 billion in revenues. Amway's foreign prices tend to be relatively high because all products are exported from the company's Michigan headquarters. In the Philippines, for example, most Amway products are subject to a 30 percent import charge; a 150-milliliter tube of Glister toothpaste sells for $6.54 versus $1.50 for a comparable tube of Colgate.

Avon has successfully used door-to-door sales in dozens of countries identified by company executives as having weak retail infrastructures. Also, it recognized that low discretionary income levels translate into modest expenditures on cosmetics and toiletries. Thus, the role of the sales force is to communicate the benefits of cosmetics and build demand. In such countries as Hungary, the Czech Republic, and Russia, in-home direct selling is the perfect channel strategy. In fact, Avon became the first company permitted to sell door-to-door in China. Since 1990, Avon has operated a joint venture with Guangzhou Cosmetics Factory in the province of Old Canton. However, after the Chinese government banned direct selling in 1998, Avon shifted its strategy and opened beauty boutiques. Today, the company has more than 5,500 across China. Chief executive Andrea Jung expects to resume directly selling by 2005, when China lifts the ban to comply with World Trade Organization rules.

Avon has recruited several thousand distributors in India, but its efforts to date have been surpassed by Sweden's Oriflame International. Oriflame's cosmetics are available throughout India, thanks to the company's success at recruiting nearly 100,000 sales representatives. The scale and scope of Oriflame's effort make it the most ambitious direct sales effort ever launched in India. Traditionally, India has had a bias against direct selling because it was associated with salespeople hawking goods of dubious quality. However, Avon and Oriflame have succeeded in part by targeting Indian women who are active socially and in part because India has a tradition of "kitty" parties where women sell each other saris and jewelry.

*Sources: Lauren Foster, "Mistress of the Turnaround Answers Avon's Calling," Financial Times (November 6, 2003), p. 8; Emily Nelson and Ann Zimmerman, "Avon Goes Store to Store," The Wall Street Journal (September 18, 2000), pp. B1, B4; Erin White, "Ding-Dong, Avon Calling (on the Web, Not Your Door)," The Wall Street Journal (December 28, 1999), p. A1; Sumit Sharma, "Sell It Yourself: Direct Sales Help Makeup Brand Storm Across India," The Asian Wall Street Journal (April 28, 1997), p. 10; Yumiko Ono, "On a Mission: Amway Grows Abroad, Sending 'Ambassadors' to Spread the Word," The Wall Street Journal (May 14, 1997), pp. A1, A6.*

Other channel structure alternatives for consumer products include various combinations of a manufacturer's sales force and wholesalers calling on independent retail outlets, which in turn sell to customers (retailing is discussed in detail later in the chapter). For mass-market consumer products such as ice-cream novelties, cigarettes, and light bulbs that are bought by millions of consumers, a channel that links the manufacturer to distributors and retailers is generally required to achieve market coverage. A channel structure that appears to have more intermediaries than necessary may actually reflect rational adjustment to costs and preferences in a market; it may also present an opportunity to the innovative marketer to pursue competitive advantage by introducing more effective channel arrangements. A cornerstone of Wal-Mart's phenomenal growth in the United States is its ability to achieve significant economies by buying huge volumes of goods directly from manufacturers. However, individual country customs vary. For example, Toys 'R' Us faced considerable opposition from Japanese toy manufacturers that refused to engage in direct selling after the U.S. company opened its first stores in Japan.

Perishable products impose special form utility demands on channel members who must ensure that the merchandise is in satisfactory condition at the time of customer purchase. In developed countries, distribution of perishable food products is handled by a company's own sales force or by independent channel members; in either case, stock is checked by the distributor organization to ensure that it is fresh. In less-developed countries, public marketplaces are important channels; they provide a convenient way for producers of vegetables, bread, and other food products to sell their goods directly. Sometimes, a relatively simple channel innovation in a developing country can significantly increase a company's overall value proposition. In the early 1990s, for example, the Moscow Bread Company (MBC) needed to improve its distribution system in the Russian capital. For Russians, bread is truly the staff of life, with consumers queuing up daily to buy fresh loaves at numerous shops and kiosks. Unfortunately, MBC's staff was burdened by excessive paperwork that resulted in the delivery of stale bread. Andersen Consulting found that as much as one-third of the bread the company produced was wasted. In developed countries, about 95 percent of food is sold packaged; the figure is much lower in the former Soviet Union. Whether a consumer bought bread at an open air market or in an enclosed store, it was displayed unwrapped. Therefore, it was imperative for the bread to get from MBC's ovens to the stores in the shortest possible time. Barring an improvement in delivery time, the bread's shelf life had to be extended. The consulting team devised a simple solution—plastic bags to keep the bread fresh. Russian consumers responded favorably to the change; not only did the bags guarantee freshness and extend the shelf life of the bread by 600 percent, but also the bags themselves created utility. In a country where such extras are virtually unknown, the bags constituted a reusable "gift."[8]

**Piggyback marketing** is another channel innovation that has grown in popularity. In this arrangement, one manufacturer obtains product distribution by utilizing another company's distribution channels. Both parties can benefit: The active distribution partner makes fuller use of its distribution system capacity and thereby increases the total revenue generated by the channel members. The manufacturer using the piggyback arrangement does so at a cost that is much lower than that required for any direct arrangement. Successful piggyback marketing requires that the combined product lines be complementary. They must appeal to the same customer, and they must not compete with each other. If these requirements are met, the piggyback arrangement can be an effective way of fully utilizing a global channel system to the advantage of both parties.

A case in point is Avon Products, which has a network of direct sales representatives in more than 100 countries. Dozens of companies have taken advantage of the opportunity to piggyback with Avon. Several of Mattel's toy lines are being marketed in China by 85,000 Avon reps; Mattel reaps tens of millions of dollars in revenues from sales of Barbie dolls and cosmetics, Hot Wheel toys, and Sesame Street characters. As Andrea Jung, Avon's CEO and former global marketing chief, explained, "We knew we had a great thing in our hands. Our powerful distribution channel combined with their powerful brand is a huge opportunity." In Australia, New Zealand, Brazil, Canada, and France, Avon reps offer *Reader's Digest* subscriptions along with Avon's health and beauty products. The agreement is reciprocal; Avon's direct response offers "ride along" in *Reader's Digest* product shipments and targeted mailings. In emerging markets, Avon offers a second catalog featuring products from Timex, Duracell, Time-Life, and others. The products are sold on consignment; piggyback products already account for 15 percent of sales in some emerging markets.[9]

## Industrial Products

Figure 12-2 summarizes marketing channel alternatives for the industrial- or business-products company. As is true with consumer channels, product and customer characteristics have an impact on channel structure. Three basic elements are involved: the manufacturer's sales force, distributors or agents, and wholesalers. A manufacturer can reach customers with its own sales force, a sales force that calls on wholesalers who sell to customers, or a combination of these two arrangements. A manufacturer can sell directly to wholesalers without using a sales force, and wholesalers, in turn, can supply customers. Finally, a distributor or agent can call on wholesalers or customers for the manufacturer. For vendors serving a relatively small customer base, a shorter channel

[8] "Case Study: Moscow Bread Company," Andersen Consulting, 1993.
[9] Tara Parker-Pope and Lisa Bannon, "Avon's New Calling: Sell Barbie in China," *The Wall Street Journal* (May 1, 1997), pp. B1, B5; Clarence Murphy, "Scents and Sensibility," *The Economist* (July 13, 1996), p. 57.

# the rest of the story

## Hypermarkets

In the United States, retailing channels are quite diverse. In addition to long-entrenched shopping malls and discount stores, wholesale clubs such as Pace and Sam's offer rock-bottom prices, and Toys 'R' Us, Circuit City, and other "category killers" offer tremendous depth in particular product categories. In February 1988, Carrefour ("Crossroads" in French) opened its first U.S. hypermarket, a gigantic store in Philadelphia with 330,000 square feet of floor space. Carrefour soon built a second American unit, but then shut down both stores in October 1993. The problem? Many shoppers simply found the stores too big and too overwhelming. Also, although the product assortment was very broad, there was little depth in some product categories. For many products, only one brand or one flavor was available.

The stores' outsized physical scale also changed the economics of profitable operation. For example, consultants for Kmart noted that its hypermarket near Atlanta could only succeed if it attracted four times as many shoppers as a regular discount department store and if the average transaction equaled $43, double the average for discount stores. Meanwhile, costs associated with running the huge stores translated into gross margins of around 8 percent, half the margin of the typical discount store. Finally, Americans just didn't take to mixing food and nonfood purchases in one location. As retail consultant Kurt Barnard noted, "One-stop shopping did not take hold easily. Working parents don't have time for their kids, let alone a shopping expedition that takes hours."

*"In the future, we will have local companies or global companies but not much in between. Globalization will lead those who are not in the first team, or who are national retailers, to make alliances."*

Daniel Bernard, Chairman Carrefour

Despite problems in the United States, hypermarkets are thriving elsewhere. There are several reasons for this. First, in countries where shoppers must visit many smaller stores or markets to complete their shopping, the megastore concept is viewed as a welcome innovation, even though many customers feel loyalty to traditional family-owned stores. Also, hypermarket operators offer free parking in spacious lots, a lure to shoppers in countries where parking spaces are in short supply. A third reason is demographic: As more women enter the workforce, they have less time to shop. While U.S. shoppers can choose from many discount stores and supermarkets, consumers in other countries find that hypermarkets are the only convenient alternative to shopping store-to-store.

Venezuela's first hypermarket, Tiendas Exito, opened in May 2001. A French/Venezuelan/Colombian partnership opened the store despite Venezuela's relatively small population of 24 million people and an economy mired in recession. The partners reasoned that the soaring cost of living would motivate consumers to go bargain hunting.

Carrefour is still fine-tuning its global strategy. In November 1999, it acquired French rival Promodès; valued at $13.6 billion, the deal was the world's largest retail acquisition. In their quest to build a global brand, Carrefour executives changed the names of hundreds of Promodès' Pryca and Continent stores in Spain and France to Carrefour. Confused by the changes, shoppers are going elsewhere. Meanwhile a competitor, the Netherlands-based supermarket operator Royal Ahold NV, is retaining local store names as it expands around the globe. As the company's chief executive said, "Everything the customer sees, we localize. Everything they don't see, we globalize."

*Sources: Sarah Ellison, "Carrefour and Ahold Find Shoppers Like to Think Local," The Wall Street Journal (August 31, 2001), p. A5; Marc Lifsher, "Will Venezuelans Shun Mom and Pop for the Hypermarket?" The Wall Street Journal (June 28, 2001), p. A13; Peggy Hollinger, "Carrefour's Revolutionary," Financial Times (December 4, 1998), p. 14; Laurie Underwood, "Consumers at a Crossroad," Free China Review (February 2, 1995), pp. 66–67; Laurie M. Grossman, "Hypermarkets: A Sure-Fire Hit Bombs," The Wall Street Journal (June 25, 1992), p. B1.*

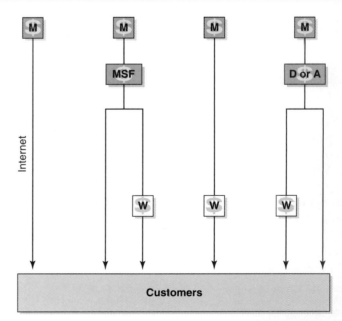

**Figure 12-2**

*Marketing Channel Alternatives: Industrial Products*

**M** = Manufacturer    **MSF** = Manufacturer's sales force
**W** = Wholesaler    **D or A** = Distributor or agent

design with relatively few (or no) intermediaries may be possible. For example, if there are only 10 customers for an industrial product in each national market, these 10 customers must be directly contacted by either the manufacturer or an agent.

Channel innovation can be an essential element of a successful marketing strategy. Dell's rise to a leading position in the global PC industry was based on Michael Dell's decision to bypass conventional channels by selling direct and by building computers to customers' specifications. Dell began life as a b-to-b marketer; its business model proved so successful that the company then began marketing direct to the home PC market. Consider Boeing aircraft, for example; given the price, physical size, and complexity of a jet airliner, it is easy to understand why Boeing utilizes its own sales force. Other products sold in this way include mainframe computers and large photocopy systems; these are expensive, complicated products that require both explanation and applications analysis focused on the customer's needs. A company-trained salesperson, sales engineer, or sales team is well suited for the task of creating information utility for computer buyers.

Before deciding which structure to use and which wholesalers and agents to select, managers must study each country individually. In general, the larger the market, the more feasible it is for a manufacturer to use its own sales force. Kyocera Corporation of Kyoto, Japan, has successfully used its own sales force to achieve leadership in the billion-dollar global market for ceramic microchip covers. Company founder Kazuo Inamori went to great lengths to make sure the spiritual drive of Kyocera's unique corporate culture extended to all parts of the company, including the sales force. Kyocera successfully entered the U.S. market by custom-tailoring ceramic chip housings to each customer's needs. Kyocera also became legendary for its service among California's Silicon Valley chipmakers. Breaking with the norm in the electronics industry of using independent distributors, Kyocera relied on a salaried sales force. Early on, Kyocera earned a reputation for answering customer questions overnight, while domestic suppliers often took weeks to respond. Employees worked around the clock to satisfy customer requests for samples. Another hallmark: No company is too small for Kyocera to serve. Jerry Crowley of Gazelle Microcircuits in Santa Clara reported, for example, that Kyocera salespeople began calling on him when he had only 11 employees. Gazelle has been buying custom chip packages from Kyocera ever since. Today, Kyocera has sales forces in the United States, Europe, and Japan that place unwavering emphasis on quality and customer service.

## ESTABLISHING CHANNELS AND WORKING WITH CHANNEL INTERMEDIARIES

A global company expanding across national boundaries must utilize existing distribution channels or build its own. Channel obstacles are often encountered when a company enters a competitive market where brands and supply relationships are already established. If management chooses *direct involvement*, the company establishes its own sales force or operates its own retail stores. As described earlier, Kyocera used this approach; Kodak adopted the direct approach in Japan, where Kodak Japan is a company-owned distributor. The other option is *indirect involvement*, which entails utilizing independent agents, distributors, and/or wholesalers. Channel strategy in a global marketing program must fit the company's competitive position and overall marketing objectives in each national market. Direct involvement in distribution in a new market can entail considerable expense. Sales representatives and sales management must be hired and trained. The sales organization will inevitably be a heavy loser in its early stage of operation in a new market because it will not have sufficient volume to cover its overhead costs. Therefore, any company contemplating establishing its own sales force should be prepared to underwrite losses for this sales force for a reasonable period of time. As noted previously, whichever strategy a company uses, the process of shaping international channels to fit overall company objectives is constrained by customer and product characteristics.

Channel decisions are important because of the number and nature of relationships that must be managed. Channel decisions typically involve long-term legal commitments and obligations to various intermediaries. Such commitments are often extremely expensive to terminate or change, so it is imperative for companies to document the nature of the relationship with the foreign partner. As the saying goes, "The shortest pencil is better than the longest memory." At a minimum, the written agreement should include a definition of what constitutes "good cause" for termination. Also, as noted in Chapter 5, it is often preferable to settle business disputes through arbitration rather than in a local court. Thus, the distributor or agent agreement should also provide for arbitration in a neutral forum in a third country. In many instances, local laws protect agents and distributors; even in the absence of a formal written agreement, in a civil code country the law will be applied. In addition to written obligations, commitments must be backed by good faith and feelings of mutual obligation. In short, the selection of distributors and agents in a target market is critically important. A good agent or distributor can make the difference between zero performance and performance that is much better than expected.

Companies entering emerging markets for the first time must exercise particular care in choosing a channel intermediary. Typically, a local distributor is required because the market entrant lacks knowledge of local business practices and needs a partner with links to potential customers. In addition, newcomers to a particular market generally want to limit their risk and financial exposure. Although initial results may be satisfactory, with time the local distributor may come to be perceived as performing poorly. This is when managers from the global company often intervene and attempt to take control from the local distributor. Former Harvard Business School professor David Arnold offers seven specific guidelines to help prevent such problems from arising.[10]

1. *Select distributors. Don't let them select you.* A company may link up with a distributor by default after being approached by representatives at a trade fair. In fact, such eager candidates may already be serving a company's competitors. Their objective may be to maintain control over the product category in a given market. A proactive market entrant can identify potential distributors by requesting a list from the U.S. Department of Commerce or its equivalent in other countries. The local chamber of commerce or trade association in a country can provide similar information.

2. *Look for distributors capable of developing markets, rather than those with a few good customer contacts.* A distributor with good contacts may appear to be the "obvious" choice in terms of generating quick sales and revenues. However, a better choice is often a partner willing both to make the investment necessary to achieve success and draw upon the marketing experience of the global company. Such a partner may, in fact, have no prior experience with a particular product category. In this case, the distributor may devote more effort and assign the new partner a higher priority simply because taking on the product line does not represent the status quo.

3. *Treat local distributors as long-term partners, not temporary market-entry vehicles.* A contractual agreement that provides strong financial incentives for customer acquisition, new product sales, or other forms of business development is a signal to the distributor that the market entrant is taking a long-term perspective. Such development can be done with the input of managers from the global company.

4. *Support market entry by committing money, managers, and proven marketing ideas.* In addition to providing sales personnel and technical support, management should consider demonstrating its commitment early on by investing in a minority equity stake in an independent distributor. The risks associated with such investment should be no greater than risks associated with independent distribution systems in the manufacturer's home country. The earlier such a commitment is made, the better the relationship that is likely to develop.

5. *From the start, maintain control over marketing strategy.* To exploit the full potential of global marketing channels, the manufacturer should provide solid leadership for marketing in terms of which products the distributor should sell and how to position them. Again, it is necessary to have employees on site or to have country or regional managers monitor the distributor's performance. As one manager noted, "We used to give far too much autonomy to distributors, thinking that they knew their markets. But our value proposition is a tough one to execute, and time and again we saw distributors cut prices to compensate for failing to target the right customers or to sufficiently train salespeople." This is not to say that the intermediary

---

[10] The following discussion is adapted from David Arnold, "Seven Rules of International Distribution," *Harvard Business Review* 78, no. 6 (November–December 2000), pp. 131–137.

should not be allowed to adapt the distribution strategy to suit local conditions. The point is for the manufacturer to take the lead.

6. *Make sure distributors provide you with detailed market and financial performance data.* Distributor organizations are often a company's best source—maybe the only source—of market information. The contract between a manufacturer and distributor should include specific language to the effect that local market information and financial data will be transferred back to the manufacturer. One sign that a successful manufacturer/distributor relationship can be established is the latter's willingness to provide such information.

7. *Build links among national distributors at the earliest opportunity.* A manufacturer should attempt to establish links between its networks of national distributors. This can be accomplished by setting up a regional corporate office or by establishing a distributor council. At any point in time, a company may have some excellent agents and distributors, others that are satisfactory, and a third group that is unsatisfactory. By creating opportunities for distributors to communicate, ideas for new product designs based on individual-market results can be leveraged, and overall distributor performance can be improved.

When devising a channel strategy, it is necessary to be realistic about the motives of the typical channel intermediary. On the one hand, it is the intermediary's responsibility to implement an important element of a company's marketing strategy. Left to their own devices, however, middle vendors may seek to maximize their own profit rather than the manufacturer's. These agents sometimes engage in **cherry picking,** the practice of accepting orders only from manufacturers with established demand for products and brands. Cherry picking can also take the form of selecting only a few choice items from a vendor's product lines. This is a rational course of action for the vendor, but it can present a serious obstacle to a manufacturer who is attempting to break into a market with a new product. The cherry picker is not interested in developing a market for a new product, which is a problem for the expanding international company. As noted previously, a manufacturer should provide leadership and invest resources to build the relationship with a desired distributor. A manufacturer with a new product or a product with a limited market share may find it more desirable to set up some arrangement for bypassing the cherry-picking channel member. In some cases, a manufacturer must incur the costs of direct involvement by setting up its own distribution organization to obtain a share of the market. When company sales finally reach critical mass, management may decide to shift from direct involvement to a more cost-effective independent intermediary. The move does not mean that intermediaries are "better" than direct distribution. Such a move is simply a response by a manufacturer to cost considerations and the newly acquired attractiveness of the company's product to independent distributors.

An alternative method of dealing with the cherry-picking problem does not require setting up an expensive direct sales force. Rather, a company may decide to rely on a distributor's own sales force by subsidizing the cost of the sales representatives the distributor has assigned to the company's products. This approach has the advantage of holding down costs by tying in with the distributor's existing sales management team and physical distribution system. With this approach, it is possible to place managed direct selling support and distribution support behind a product at the expense of only one salesperson per selling area. The distributor's incentive for cooperating in this kind of arrangement is that he or she obtains a "free" sales representative for a new product with the potential to be a profitable addition to his or her line. This cooperative arrangement is ideally suited to getting a new export-sourced product into distribution in a market. A company may also decide to provide special incentives to independent channel agents; however, this approach can be expensive. The company might offer outright payments, either direct cash bonuses or contest awards, tied to sales performance. In competitive markets with sufficiently high prices, incentives could take the form of gross margin guarantees.

### Channels in Less-Developed Countries

One of the conspicuous features of retail channels in less-developed countries is the remarkable number of people engaged in selling very small quantities of merchandise. In Ethiopia and other East African countries, for example, an open window in the side of a building is likely to be a *souk*, a small walk-up store whose proprietor sells everything from toilet paper and playing cards to rice and eggs. To maximize sales, *souks* are strategically interspersed throughout neighborhood areas. The proprietors know what customers want and need. For example, early in the day they may sell incense and a paper cone with enough coffee for the morning coffee ceremony. In the evening, cigarettes and gum may be in demand, especially if the *souk* is located near a neighborhood nightclub. If a *souk* is closed, it is often possible to rouse the proprietor by knocking on the window, because the store also serves as the proprietor's domicile. Some *souk* owners even provide curb service and bring items to a customer waiting in a car.

By comparison, government department stores in East Africa are less likely to display such a service orientation. Government stores may be stocked with mass quantities of items that are slow to sell. For example, the shelves may hold row after row of tinned tomatoes, even though fresh tomatoes are readily available year round in the market. Customers must go through several steps before actually taking possession of their purchases—determining what goods are available, making a purchase decision, moving to another area to pay, and finally, taking possession of the goods. This usually involves a substantial number of papers, seals, and stamps, as well as interaction with two or three clerks.

Clerk jobs are highly prized in countries where jobs are scarce; compared to the *souk* proprietor, who is willing to work from dawn to dusk, the government employee works from 9:00 A.M. to 5:00 P.M. with 2 hours off for lunch.

In Costa Rica, the privately owned *pulpería* is similar to the Western-style general store that was popular in the first part of the twentieth century. Customers enter the store, tell clerks what items are desired, and the clerks fetch the items, which may range from chicken feed to thumb tacks. A typical *pulpería* stocks staples such as sugar and flour in 50-kilo bags that the proprietor resells in smaller portions. Most *pulperías* have a refrigeration unit so they can sell ice cream novelties; in areas where there is no electricity, the *pulpería* owner will use a generator to provide power for the refrigerator. *Pulperías* are serviced by a fleet of private wholesalers; on any given day, the soft drink truck, the candy truck, or the staples truck may make deliveries. The *pulpería* serves as a central gathering place for the neighborhood and generally has a public telephone from which patrons can make calls for a fee. This attracts many people to the store in communities where there are few, if any, telephones.

Both the *souk* and the *pulpería* typically offer an informal system of credit. People who patronize these shops usually live in the neighborhood and are known to the proprietor. Often, the proprietor will extend credit if he or she knows that a customer has suffered a setback such as loss of a job or a death in the family. Informally, the proprietors of private retail shops fulfill the role of a lender, especially for people who do not have access to credit through regular financial institutions.

*Source: Private communication from Brian Larson of CARE Niger.*

# GLOBAL RETAILING

**Global retailing** is any retailing activity that crosses national boundaries. Since the mid-1970s, there has been growing interest among successful retailers in expanding globally. However, this not a new phenomenon. For centuries, entrepreneurial merchants have ventured abroad both to obtain merchandise and ideas and to establish retail operations. During the nineteenth and early twentieth centuries, British, French, Dutch, Belgian, and German trading companies established retailing organizations in Africa and Asia. International trading and retail store operation were two of the economic pillars of the colonial system of that era. In the twentieth century, Dutch retailer C&A expanded across Europe, and Woolworth crossed the Atlantic from the United States to the United Kingdom. Today's global retailing scene is characterized by great variety (the top 25 companies are listed in Table 12-1). Before proceeding to a detailed discussion of global retailing issues, we will briefly survey some of the different forms retailing can take. Retail stores can be divided into categories according to the amount of square feet of floor space, the level of service offered, width and depth of product offerings, or other criteria.

**Department stores** literally have several departments under one roof, each representing a distinct merchandise line and staffed with a limited number of salespeople. Departments in a typical store might include men's, women's, children's, beauty aids, housewares, and toys. Examples from around the world include Marks & Spencer, Macy's, Bay, Auchan, and Mitsukoshi.

**Specialty retailers** offer less variety than department stores. They are more narrowly focused and feature a relatively narrow merchandise mix aimed at a particular target market. Specialty stores offer a great deal of merchandise depth

**Table 12-1**

*Top 25 Global Retailers (2002 Sales; $ millions)*

| Rank | Company | Country | Formats | Sales ($) |
|------|---------|---------|---------|-----------|
| 1 | Wal-Mart Stores | USA | Discount store, Wholesale club | $244,524 |
| 2 | Carrefour (incl. Promodes) | France | Hypermarket | 64,942 |
| 3 | Royal Ahold | Netherlands | Supermarket/Hypermarket | 59,229 |
| 4 | Home Depot | USA | Home improvement | 58,247 |
| 5 | Kroger | USA | Supermarket | 51,760 |
| 6 | Metro AG | Germany | Diversified | 48,687 |
| 7 | Target | USA | Discount/Department store | 43,917 |
| 8 | Tesco | UK | Supermarket/Hypermarket | 41,489 |
| 9 | Sears Roebuck | USA | Department store/General merch. | 41,366 |
| 10 | Costco | USA | Food/General merch. | 37,993 |
| 11 | ITM Entreprises (incl. Spar) | France | Diversified | 36,284 |
| 12 | Albertson's | USA | Supermarket | 35,626 |
| 13 | Rewe | Germany | Diversified | 36,339 |
| 14 | Edeka Gruppe (incl. AVA) | Germany | Diversified | 34,063 |
| 15 | Safeway | USA | Supermarket | 32,399 |
| 16 | J.C. Penney | USA | Department store/Drug store | 32,347 |
| 17 | Kmart | USA | Discount store/Specialty | 30,762 |
| 18 | Aldi Gruppe | Germany | Food/Discount | 30,000 |
| 19 | Walgreen | USA | Drugstore | 28,681 |
| 20 | Ito-Yokada (incl. 7-Eleven) | Japan | Diversified | 28,330 |
| 21 | Tengelmann Gruppe | Germany | Diversified | 26,911 |
| 22 | Sainsbury (incl. Shaw's) | UK | Supermarket, Hypermarket, DIY | 26,818 |
| 23 | Lowe's | USA | Home improvement | 26,491 |
| 24 | Auchan | France | Hypermarket/Diversified | 26,079 |
| 25 | Pinault-Printemp-Redoute | France | Department store/Luxury goods | 25,890 |

*Source:* "100 Largest Global Retailers," **www.chainstoreage.com**, accessed January 2004.

(e.g., many styles, colors, and sizes), high levels of service from knowledgeable staff persons, and a marketing premise that is both clear and appealing to consumers. Laura Ashley, Body Shop, Victoria's Secret, Gap, Starbucks, and the Disney Store are examples.

**Supermarkets** are departmentalized retail establishments that offer a variety of food (e.g., produce, baked goods, meats) and nonfood items (e.g., paper products, health and beauty aids), mostly on a self-service basis. Tesco, Sainsbury, Safeway, A&P, and Sparr are some examples; on average, supermarkets have between 50,000 and 60,000 square feet of floor space. A comparison of food distribution in countries at different stages of development illustrates how channels reflect and respond to underlying market conditions in a country. In the United States, several factors combine to make the supermarket or the self-service one-stop food store the basic food-retailing unit: high incomes, large-capacity refrigerator-freezer units, high levels of automobile ownership, and high reliance on frozen and convenience foods. Many shoppers want to purchase a week's worth of groceries in one trip to the store. They have the money, ample storage space in the refrigerator, and the hauling capacity to move this large quantity of food from the store to the home. The supermarket, because it is efficient, can fill the food shoppers' needs at lower prices than butcher shops and other traditional full-service food stores. Additionally, supermarkets can offer more variety and a greater selection of merchandise than can smaller food stores, a fact that appeals to affluent consumers.[11]

In other parts of the world the supermarket revolution came many years later. France, Belgium, Spain, Brazil, and Colombia are some of the countries in which supermarket retailing quickly took hold as large, modern, highly efficient stores were built. In Italy, by contrast, legislation limiting the opening of large supermarkets has

---

[11] For an excellent account of the history of supermarket retailing in the United States, see David B. Sicilia, "Supermarket Sweep," *Audacity* (Spring 1997), pp. 10–19.

been a restraining force; as a result, large format stores grew in popularity more gradually. Asia is the next frontier for the grocery business; as Laurent Zeller, managing director of a French market research firm, commented, "When I got to Asia in 1996, retailers here were still very traditional compared to, say, South America, where hypermarkets had been growing for 10 years." Although Wal-Mart is generating headlines as it moves around the globe, American retailers lag behind the Europeans in moving outside their home countries. One reason is the sheer size of the domestic U.S. market.[12]

**Convenience stores** offer some of the same products as supermarkets, but the merchandise mix is limited to high-turnover convenience products. In terms of square footage, these are the smallest stores of the various retail categories discussed here. Prices for some products may be 15 to 20 percent higher than supermarket prices. As the name implies, these stores are located in high-traffic locations and offer expanded hours to accommodate commuters, students, and other highly mobile consumers. Some convenience store chains are regional (e.g., Casey's, Kum & Go, Tom Thumb, Love's); others, such as 7-Eleven, have operations in several countries.

**Discount stores** can be divided into several categories. The most general characteristic that they have in common is the emphasis on low prices. *Full-line discounters* typically offer a wide range of merchandise, including non-food items and nonperishable food, in a limited-service format. In Canada, for example, Hudson Bay's Zellers is the largest discount-store chain. French discounter Tati is going global; in addition to opening a store on New York's Fifth Avenue, Tati currently has stores in Lebanon, Turkey, Germany, Belgium, Switzerland, and the Côte d'Ivoire.

Wal-Mart is the reigning king of the full-line discounters, with many stores covering 120,000 square feet (or more) of floor space; food accounts for about a third of floor space and sales. Wal-Mart stores typically offer middle-class customers a folksy atmosphere and value-priced brands. Levi's recent launched a new jeans line for sale at Wal-Mart; historically, Wal-Mart carried the Rustler and Wrangler jeans brands. Levi's did not produce a line that could be sold for less than $30. However, because so many shoppers frequent the discount giant, Levi's was missing an important selling opportunity. In 2003, Levi created a new brand, Signature, for Wal-Mart.

Wal-Mart is also a leader in the **warehouse club** segment of discount retailing; consumers "join" the club to take advantage of low prices on products displayed in their shipping boxes in a "no frills" atmosphere. Wal-Mart has taken its Sam's Club stores into Mexico and Brazil.

**Hypermarkets,** which were discussed in the chapter introduction, are a hybrid retailing format combining the discounter, supermarket, and warehouse club approaches under a single roof. Size-wise, hypermarkets are huge, covering 200,000 to 300,000 square feet.

**Supercenters** offer a wide range of aggressively priced grocery items plus general merchandise in a space that occupies about half the size of a hypermarket. Supercenters are an important aspect of Wal-Mart's growth strategy, both at home and abroad. Wal-Mart opened its first supercenter in 1988; today, it operates more than 450 supercenters, including 75 stores in Mexico and units in Argentina and Brazil. Some prices at Wal-Mart's supercenters in Brazil are as much as 15 percent lower than competitors', and some observers wonder if the company has taken the discount approach too far. Company officials insist that profit margins are in the 20 to 22 percent range.[13]

[12] Michael Flagg, "In Asia, Going to the Grocery Increasingly Means Heading for a European Retail Chain," *The Wall Street Journal* (April 24, 2001), p. A21.

[13] Matt Moffett and Jonathan Friedland, "Wal-Mart Won't Discount Its Prospects in Brazil, Though Its Losses Pile Up," *The Wall Street Journal* (June 4, 1996), p. A15; Wendy Zellner, "Wal-Mart Spoken Here," *Business Week* (June 23, 1997), pp. 138–139+.

**Category killers** is the label many in the retailing industry use when talking about stores such as Toys 'R' Us, Home Depot, and IKEA. The name refers to the fact that such stores specialize in a particular product category such as toys or furniture and offer a vast selection at low prices. In short, these stores represent retailing's "900-pound gorillas" that essentially demolish smaller, more traditional competitors and prompt department stores to scale down merchandise sections that are in direct competition.

**Outlet stores** are retail operations that allow companies with well-known consumer brands to dispose of excess inventory, out-of-date merchandise, or factory seconds. To attract large numbers of shoppers, outlet stores are often grouped together in **outlet malls.** The United States is home to 320 outlet malls such as the giant Woodbury Common mall in Central Valley, New York. Now, the concept is catching on in Europe and Asia as well. The acceptance reflects changing attitudes among consumers and retailers; in both Asia and Europe, brand-conscious consumers are eager to save money.

Currently, a number of environmental factors have combined to push retailers out of their home markets in search of opportunities around the globe. Saturation of the home country market, recession or other economic factors, strict regulation on store development, and high operating costs are some of the factors that prompt management to look abroad for growth opportunities. Wal-Mart is a case in point; its international expansion in the mid-1990s coincided with disappointing financial results in its home market (see Case 12-1).

Even as the domestic retailing environment grows more challenging for many companies, an ongoing environmental scanning effort is likely to turn up markets in other parts of the world that are underdeveloped or where competition is weak. In addition, high rates of economic growth, a growing middle class, a high proportion of young people in the population, and less stringent regulation combine to make some country markets very attractive.[14] Laura Ashley, Body Shop, Disney Stores, and other specialty retailers are being lured to Japan by developers who need established names to fill space in large, suburban, American-style shopping malls.[15] Such malls are being developed as some local and national restrictions on retail development are being eased and as consumers tire of the aggravations associated with shopping in congested urban areas.

However, the large number of unsuccessful cross-border retailing initiatives suggests that anyone contemplating a move into global retailing should do so with a great deal of caution. Among those that have scaled back expansion plans in the face of disappointment are France's Galeries Lafayette and Shanghai-based Yaohan Group. Galeries Lafayette opened a New York store on fashionable Fifth Avenue; however, the merchandise mix suffered in comparison with offerings at posh competitors such as Henri Bendel and Bonwit Teller. Yaohan has more than 400 stores in 13 countries, including the United States and China. However, Chinese expansion plans are on hold because consumers have reacted indifferently to the 10-story megastore in Shanghai. As one Chinese consumer remarked, "It's just so-so. I'm not really impressed."[16] Speaking of global opportunities for U.S.-based retailers, one industry analyst noted, "It's awfully hard to operate across the water. It's one thing to open up in Mexico and Canada, but the distribution hassles are just too big when it comes to exporting an entire store concept overseas."[17]

---

[14] Ross Davies and Megan Finney, "Retailers Rush to Capture New Markets," *Financial Times—Mastering Global Business, Part 7* (1998), pp. 2–4.

[15] Norihiko Shirouzu, "Japanese Mall Mogul Dreams of American Stores," *The Wall Street Journal* (July 30, 1997), pp. B1, B10; Shirouzu, "Jusco Bets that U.S.-Style Retail Malls Will Revolutionize Shopping in Japan," *The Wall Street Journal* (April 21, 1997), p. A8.

[16] Norihiko Shirouzu and Fara Waner, "Asian Retailing Titan Hits a Great Wall," *The Wall Street Journal* (January 17, 1997), p. A10.

[17] Neil King, Jr., "Kmart's Czech Invasion Lurches Along," *The Wall Street Journal* (June 8, 1993), p. A11.

The critical question for the would-be global retailer is, "What advantages do we have relative to local competition?" The answer will often be, "Nothing," when competition, local laws governing retailing practice, distribution patterns, or other factors are taken into account. However, a company may possess competencies that can be the basis for competitive advantage in a particular retail market. A retailer has several things to offer consumers. Some are readily perceived by customers, such as selection, price, and the overall manner in which the goods are offered in the store setting. The last includes such things as store location, parking facilities, in-store atmosphere, and customer service. Competencies can also be found in less visible value chain activities such as distribution, logistics, and information technology.

For example, contrary to Japan's service-oriented reputation, Japanese retailers traditionally offered few extra services to their clientele. There were no special orders, no returns, and stock was chosen not according to consumer demand but, rather, according to purchasing preferences of the stores. Typically, a store would buy limited quantities from each of its favorite manufacturers and then, when the goods sold out, consumers had no recourse. Instead of trying to capitalize on the huge market, many retailers simply turned a deaf ear to customer needs. From the retailers' point of view, this came out fine in the end, however; most of their stock eventually sold because buyers were forced to purchase what was left over. They had no other choice. As Gap, Eddie Bauer, and other American retailers have entered Japan with liberal return policies, a willingness to take special orders, and a policy of replenishing stock, many Japanese consumers have switched loyalties. Also, thanks to economies of scale and modern distribution methods unknown to some Japanese department store operators, the American companies offer a greater variety of goods at lower prices. Although upscale foreign competition has hurt Japanese department store operators, Japan's depressed economy is another factor. Traditional retailers are also being squeezed from below as recession-pressed consumers flock to discounters such as the Y100 Shop chain.

J.C. Penney is expanding retailing operations internationally for a number of the reasons cited here. After touring several countries, Penney executives realized that retailers outside the United States often lack marketing sophistication when grouping and displaying products and locating aisles to optimize customer traffic. For example, a team visiting retailers in Istanbul in the early 1990s noted that one store featured lingerie next to plumbing equipment. As CEO William R. Howell noted at the time, Penney's advantage in such instances was its ability to develop an environment that invites the customer to shop. Although it struggled in Indonesia, the Philippines, and Chile, Penney has met with great success in Brazil. In 1999, the American retailer purchased a controlling stake in Renner, a regional chain with 21 stores. Crucially, Penney maintained the local name and local management team. Meanwhile, Renner, benefiting from Penney's expertise in logistics, distribution, and branding, has become Brazil's fastest-growing chain, with a total of 49 stores.[18]

A matrix-based scheme for classifying global retailers is shown in Figure 12-3.[19] One axis represents private or own-label focus versus a manufacturer brands focus. The other axis differentiates between retailers specializing in relatively few product categories and retailers that offer a wide product assortment. IKEA, in quadrant A, is a good example of a global retailer with a niche focus (assemble-yourself furniture for the home) as well as an own-label focus (IKEA sells its own brand). IKEA and other retailers in quadrant A typically use extensive advertising and product innovation to build a strong brand image.

In quadrant B, the private-label focus is retained, but many more product categories are offered. This is the strategy of Marks & Spencer (M&S), the British-based department store company whose St. Michael private label is found on a broad range

18  Miriam Jordan, "Penney Blends Two Business Cultures," *The Wall Street Journal* (April 5, 2001), p. A15.
19  The discussion in this section is adapted from Jacques Horovitz and Nirmalya Kumar, "Strategies for Retail Globalization," *Financial Times—Mastering Global Business, Part 7* (1998), pp. 4–8.

## Figure 12-3

### Global Retailing Categories

Source: Adapted from Jacques Horovitz and Nirmalya Kumar, "Strategies for Retail Globalization," Financial Times—Mastering Global Business, Part 7 (1998), p. 4.

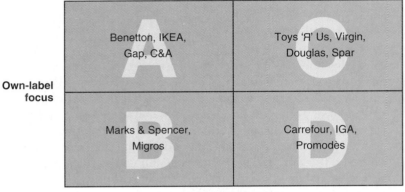

**Fewer categories**

| | |
|---|---|
| **A** Benetton, IKEA, Gap, C&A | **C** Toys 'Я' Us, Virgin, Douglas, Spar |
| **B** Marks & Spencer, Migros | **D** Carrefour, IGA, Promodès |

**Own-label focus** ... **Manufacturer brands focus**

**Many categories**

of clothing, food, home furnishings, jewelry, and other items. Private label retailers that attempt to expand internationally face a double-edged challenge: They must attract customers to both the store and the branded merchandise. M&S has succeeded by virtue of an entrepreneurial management style that has evolved over the last 100-plus years. M&S opened its first store outside the United Kingdom in 1974; it currently operates in 32 countries. In 1997, then-chairman Sir Richard Greenbury announced an ambitious plan to put M&S "well on its way to establishing a global business." It was his belief that consumer tastes are globalizing, at least with respect to fashion apparel. Food is a different story; because tastes are more localized, M&S executives anticipate that the proportion of revenues from food sales will be lower than they are in Great Britain.[20] The difficulty of today's retailing environment is underscored by Marks & Spencer's recent financial woes. The company's profits and share price plunged in the late 1990s amid a sales slump and infighting between top executives; Sir Richard left the company in 1998. A turnaround is underway, with a new human resources strategy as an important element.

Retailers in the upper right quadrant offer many well-known brands in a relatively tightly defined merchandise range. Here, for example, we find Toys 'R' Us, which specializes in toys and includes branded products from Mattel, Nintendo, and other marketers. Additional examples include such category killers as Blockbuster Video and Virgin Megastores. As noted earlier, this type of store tends to quickly dominate smaller established retailers by out-merchandizing local competition and offering customers superior value by virtue of extensive inventories and low prices. Typically, the low prices are the result of buyer power and sourcing advantages that local retailers lack. The retailing environment in which Richard Branson built the Virgin Megastore chain illustrates once again the type of success that can be achieved through an entrepreneurial management style:

It required little retailing expertise to see that the sleepy business practices of traditional record shops provided a tremendous opportunity. To rival the tiny neighborhood record shops, with their eclectic collections of records, a new kind of record store was coming into being. It was big; it was well-lit, and records were arranged clearly in alphabetical order by artist; it covered most tastes in pop music comprehensively; and it turned over its stock much faster than the smaller record retailer. . . . It was the musical equivalent of a supermarket.[21]

---

20  Rufus Olins, "M&S Sets Out Its Stall for World Domination," *The Sunday Times* (November 9, 1997), p. 6. See also Andrew Davidson, "The Andrew Davidson Interview: Sir Richard Greenbury," *Management Today* (November 2001), pp. 62–67; and Judi Bevan, *The Rise and Fall of Marks & Spencer* (London: Profile Books, 2001).

21  Tim Jackson, *Virgin King: Inside Richard Branson's Business Empire* (London: HarperCollins, 1995), p. 277.

Richard Branson, founder and chairman of the Virgin Group, at the opening of a megastore in New York's Time Square. The $15 million facility occupies 75,000 square feet of space on three levels and features more than one thousand music listening stations. The charismatic Branson is so closely associated with his company that, in the minds of many observers, the man is the brand.

Starting with one megastore location on London's Oxford Street in 1975, Branson's Virgin Retail empire now extends throughout Europe, North America, Japan, Hong Kong, and Taiwan.

Carrefour, Promodès, Wal-Mart, and other retailers fitting in the fourth quadrant offer the same type of merchandise available from established local retailers. What the newcomers bring to a market, however, is competence in distribution or some other value chain element. To date, Wal-Mart's international division has established more than 1,000 stores outside the United States; it is already the biggest retailer in Mexico and Canada. Other store locations include Argentina, Brazil, China, and Germany. International revenues for the fiscal year ended January 31, 2003, totaled $47.5 billion, compared with only $7.5 billion in 1997.

**Figure 12-4**

*Global Retailing Market Entry
Strategy Framework*

*Source: Adapted from Jacques Horovitz and
Nirmalya Kumar, "Strategies for Retail
Globalization," Financial Times—Mastering
Global Business, Part 7 (1998), p. 5.*

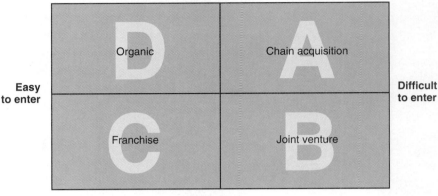

Four market entry expansion strategies are available to retailers that wish to cross borders. As shown in Figure 12-4, these strategies can be captured conceptually by a matrix that differentiates between (1) markets that are easy to enter versus those that are difficult to enter and (2) culturally close markets versus culturally distant ones. The upper half of the matrix encompasses quadrants A and D and represents markets in which shopping patterns and retail structures are similar to those in the home country. In the lower half of the matrix, quadrants C and B represent markets that are significantly different from the home country market in terms of one or more cultural characteristics. The right side of the matrix, in quadrants A and B, represents markets that are difficult to enter because of the presence of strong competitors, location restrictions, excessively high rent or real estate costs, or other factors. In quadrants C and D, any barriers that exist are relatively easy to overcome. The four entry strategies indicated by the matrix are organic, franchise, chain acquisition, and joint venture.

**Organic growth** occurs when a company uses its own resources to open a store on a greenfield site or to acquire one or more existing retail facilities from others. In 1997, for example, Marks & Spencer announced plans to expand from one store to four in Germany via the purchase of three stores operated by Cramer and Meerman. When Richard Branson set up the first Virgin Megastore in Paris, he did so by investing millions of pounds in a spectacular retail space on the Champs-Elysées. From the perspective of M&S and Virgin, the retail environments of Germany and France are both culturally close and easy to enter. Of course, the success of this strategy hinges on the availability of company resources to sustain the high cost of the initial investment.

**Franchising,** shown in quadrant C of Figure 12-4, is the appropriate entry strategy when barriers to entry are low yet the market is culturally distant in terms of consumer behavior or retailing structures. As defined in Chapter 9, franchising is a contractual relationship between two companies. The parent company-franchisor authorizes a franchisee to operate a business developed by the franchisor in return for a fee and adherence to franchise-wide policies and practices. The key to a successful franchise operation is the ability to transfer company know-how to new markets. Benetton, IKEA, and other focused, private-label retailers often use franchising as a market-entry strategy in combination with wholly owned stores that represent organic growth. IKEA has more than 100 company-owned stores across Europe and the United States; its stores in the Middle East and Hong Kong are franchise operations.

In global retailing, **acquisition** is a market-entry strategy that entails purchasing a company with multiple existing outlets in a foreign country. This strategy can provide the buyer with quick growth as well as access to existing brand suppliers, distributors, and customers. Marks & Spencer, for example, had no plans for organic growth in the United States; rather, it acquired the upscale private-label American retailer Brooks Brothers in 1988 for $750 million. Executives at Brooks Brothers spent most of the 1990s trying to expand the brand's customer base, and recent results have been promising. With hindsight, however, it is clear that M&S paid too much for the acquisition. As noted previously, M&S is currently in the midst of its own financial retrenchment; at the end of 2001, it was announced that Brooks Brothers would be sold to Retail Brand Alliance, a private holding company.

Joint ventures, the final entry strategy, have been examined in detail in an earlier chapter. With regard to global retailing, a joint-venture strategy is advisable when culturally distant, difficult-to-enter markets are targeted. Many Western retailers are using joint ventures to enter China, Japan, and other Asian countries. The ownership split can be adjusted in proportion to perceived entry difficulty and previous experience. Virgin Group's retail expansion in Asia provides a case study in the appropriateness of the joint-venture approach. In Japan, commercial landlords typically require millions in up-front payments before they will lease retail space. Accordingly, in 1992, Virgin established a joint venture called Virgin Megastores Japan with Marui, a local retailer with a good track record of catering to the preferences of young people. The first megastore was set up in the basement of an existing Marui department store in Japan's Shinjuku district. That and subsequent stores have been wildly successful; Virgin has duplicated the joint-venture approach elsewhere in Asia, including Hong Kong, Taiwan, and South Korea. In each location, Virgin establishes a joint venture with a leading industrial group.[22]

Of course, achieving retailing success outside the home country market is not simply a matter of consulting a matrix and choosing the recommended entry strategy. Management must also be alert to the possibility that the merchandise mix, sourcing strategy, distribution, or other format elements will have to be adapted. Management at Crate & Barrel, for example, is hesitant to open stores in Japan. Part of the reason is research indicating that at least half the company's product line would have to be modified to accommodate local preferences. Another issue is the company's ability to transfer its expertise to new country markets.

## INNOVATION IN GLOBAL RETAILING

As noted at the beginning of this chapter, distribution channels around the world are highly differentiated. On the surface, it appears this differentiation can be explained only in terms of culture and the income level that exists in the market. However, the incidence and rate of retail innovation can be explained in terms of the following four observations:

1. Innovation takes place only in the most highly developed systems. In general, channel agents in less-developed systems will adapt developments already tried and tested in more highly developed systems.
2. The ability of a system to successfully adapt innovations is directly related to its level of economic development. Certain minimum levels of economic development are necessary to support anything beyond the most simple retailing methods.
3. Even when the economic environment is conducive to change, the process of adaptation may be either hindered or helped by local demographic factors, geographic factors, social mores, government action, and competitive pressures.
4. The process of adaptation can be greatly accelerated by the actions of aggressive individual firms.

---

[22] Tim Jackson, *Virgin King: Inside Richard Branson's Business Empire* (London: HarperCollins, 1995), pp. 289–291.

## British Retailers

British retailers have had a difficult time in the United States because they often fail to appreciate that the United States is an extremely different retailing environment. What works in the United Kingdom, in spite of the common language and the apparent similarity in consumer tastes, will not automatically work in the United States. In the United Kingdom, retailers typically locate their stores on "high streets," which are roughly equivalent to downtown in the United States. However, America is the land of the mall; there are no "high streets" in most American cities. Site selection is critically important for retailing success, and the British have often done a poor job in this key area.

Other problems include breaking through to get the consumer's attention. Because U.S. consumers are brand loyal, overcoming their resistance to change requires huge marketing budgets, and the British sometimes skimp in this area. Product line policy and pricing are also areas of difference where many British retailers have tripped up. British retailers don't offer the variety that U.S. consumers expect, and they don't rely nearly as much on price discounting. In the United States, fresh product assortments and aggressive pricing drive retailing. Anita Roddick got her Body Shop off to a good start in the United States and then watched as Limited jumped into the category with Bath & Body Works, a division it launched in 1992. Bath & Body Works captured Body Shop's market by constantly changing products, entering as many malls as possible, and by keeping prices lower. Meanwhile, Body Shop did not even have a formal marketing department. Today, Bath & Body Works dominates the category that Body Shop created.

Until recently, the companies that avoided this trap were the exceptions to the rule. For example, Richard Branson, the entrepreneurial leader of Virgin, has built the Virgin brand in the United States the American way—by adding more and more products and by being noisy and loud about the brand. There is some evidence, however, that increasing numbers of British retailers are changing with the times. Harrods, Harvey Nichols, and other top retailers are improving the décor in key stores and offering shoppers an entertainment experience. For example, visitors to Fifth Floor Harvey Nichols will find a posh restaurant, a wine shop, and a gourmet food hall. Some of the biggest innovations have been at Selfridges, whose flagship store just off Oxford Street in London is home to Europe's largest cosmetics department. Window displays have featured buzz-building "performances" such as humans in animal costumes modeling lingerie. As Peter Williams, CEO of Selfridges, said recently, "Our competitors are not just other department stores. Our competitors are restaurants, theaters, a weekend away, or other entertainment venues."

Sources: Cecile Rohwedder, "Selling Selfridges," The Wall Street Journal (May 5, 2003), p. B1; Ernest Beck, "Marks & Spencer to Focus on Key Brands," The Wall Street Journal (July 15, 1999), p. B1; Jennifer Steinhauer, "The British Are Coming, and Going," The New York Times (September 22, 1998), pp. C1, C4.

Self-service is a major twentieth century channel innovation. It provides an excellent illustration of the four points just outlined. Self-service retailing, which allows customers to handle and select merchandise themselves in a store with minimal assistance from sales personnel, originated in the United States. The spread of self-service to other countries supports the tendency of an economic system to support innovations only after a certain level of economic development has been achieved. Self-service was first introduced internationally into the most highly developed countries. It has spread to the countries at middle and lower stages of development but serves very small segments of the total market in these countries.

If a country market has reached a stage of economic development that will support a channel innovation, it is clear that the action of well-managed firms can contribute considerably to the diffusion of the channel innovation. The rapid growth of Benetton and McDonald's is a testament to the skill and competence of these firms as well as to the appeal of their product. In some instances, retail innovations are improved, refined, and expanded outside the home country. For example, 7-Eleven stores in Japan are half the size of U.S. stores and carry one-third the inventory, yet they ring up twice as much in sales. They boast a fourth-generation electronic point-of-sale (EPOS) information system that is more sophisticated than the system used in the United States. Another Japanese 7-Eleven innovation is *Shop America*, an in-store catalog that allows Japanese shoppers to order imported luxury products from companies like Tiffany's and Cartier. The Japanese successes came even as Southland Corporation, the U.S.-based parent company, slipped into financial difficulty. Commenting on the comparison between the Japanese and American sides of the business, retailing analyst Takayuki Suzuki noted, "Their [U.S. management's] merchandising has been really backwards, and the gap between us is rather large.

The biggest reason is that they kept their old style and did not improve their methods and adapt to consumers' changing tastes. They became really rigid."[23] Eventually 7-Eleven Japan acquired the U.S.-based parent company; with 7,300 stores, it is now Japan's largest retailer.

## PHYSICAL DISTRIBUTION, SUPPLY CHAINS, AND LOGISTICS MANAGEMENT

In Chapter 1, marketing was described as one of the activities in a firm's **value chain.** The distribution "P" of the marketing mix plays a central role in a given firm's value chain; after all, Coca-Cola, IKEA, Nokia, Toyota, and other global companies create value by making sure their products are available where and when customers want to buy them. As defined at the beginning of this chapter, physical distribution consists of activities involved in moving finished goods from manufacturers to customers. However, the value chain concept is much broader, for two basic reasons. First, the value chain is a useful tool for assessing an organization's competence as it performs value-creating activities with a broader **supply chain** that includes *all* the firms that perform support activities by generating raw materials, converting them into components or finished products, and making them available to customers. Second, the particular industry in which a firm competes (for example, automobiles, pharmaceuticals, or consumer electronics) is characterized by a value chain. The specific activities an individual firm performs help define its position in the value chain. If a company is somewhat removed from the final customer, it is said to be *upstream* in the value chain. A company that is relatively close to customers—a retailer, for example—is said to be *downstream* in the value chain. **Logistics,** in turn, is the management process that integrates the activities of all companies—both upstream and downstream—to ensure an efficient flow of goods through the supply chain.

---

[23] James Sterngold, "New Japanese Lesson: Running a 7-11," *The New York Times* (May 9, 1991), p. C7. See also Bethan Hutton, "Japan's 7-Eleven Sets Store by Computer Links," *Financial Times* (March 17, 1998), p. 26.

An industry's value chain can change over time. In pharmaceuticals, for example, research, testing, and delivery are the three steps that historically defined the industry from its beginnings in the early nineteenth century. Then, starting in the mid-1960s, after Crick and Watson published their groundbreaking work on DNA, two new upstream steps in the industry's value chain emerged: basic research into genes associated with specific diseases and identification of the proteins produced by those genes. More recently, with the mapping of the human genome largely complete, value in the pharmaceuticals industry is migrating downstream to identifying, testing, and producing molecules that operate on the proteins produced by genes.[24]

The value chain, logistics, and related concepts are extremely important as supply chains stretch around the globe. As Beth Dorrell, the export administrator who was profiled in Chapter 8, noted, "A commodity raw material from Africa can be refined in Asia, then shipped to South America to be incorporated into a component of a final product that is produced in the Middle East and then sold around the world." Figure 12-5 illustrates some of these concepts and activities at IKEA, the global furniture marketer. IKEA purchases wood and other raw material inputs from a network of suppliers located in dozens of countries; these suppliers are upstream in the value chain, and the process by which wood is transported to the factories is known as *inbound logistics*. IKEA's factories add value to the inputs by transforming them into furniture kits that are then shipped on to IKEA's stores. The stores are downstream in IKEA's value chain; the activities associated with shipping furniture kits from factory to store are known as *outbound logistics*.[25]

Physical distribution and logistics are the means by which products are made available to customers when and where they want them. The most important distribution activities are order processing, warehousing, inventory management, and transportation.

## Order Processing

Activities relating to order processing provide information inputs that are critical in fulfilling a customer's order. Order processing includes order entry in which the order is actually entered into a company's information system; order handling, which involves locating, assembling, and moving products into distribution; and order delivery, the process by which products are made available to the customer.

## Warehousing

Warehouses are used to store goods until they are sold; another type of facility, the **distribution center,** is designed to efficiently receive goods from suppliers and then fill orders for individual stores or customers. Distribution centers represent such an automated, high-tech business today that many companies outsource this function. FedEx, DHL, and other shipping specialists leverage their hub systems by serving as distribution centers for a variety of companies.

## Inventory Management

Proper inventory management ensures that a company neither runs out of manufacturing components or finished goods nor incurs the expense and risk of carrying excessive stocks of these items. Another issue is balancing order-processing

---

[24] David Champion, "Mastering the Value Chain: An Interview with Mark Levin of Millennium Pharmaceuticals," *Harvard Business Review* 79, no. 6 (June 2001), pp. 108–115.

[25] A detailed analysis of IKEA's approach to value creation is found in Richard Normann and Rafael Ramirez, "From Value Chain to Value Constellation: Designing Interactive Strategy," *Harvard Business Review* 71, no. 4 (July–August 1993), pp. 65–77.

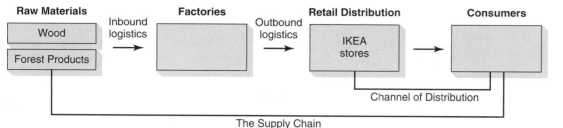

Figure 12-5

Supply Chain, Value
Chain, and Logistics
for IKEA

costs against inventory-carrying costs. The more often a product is ordered, the higher the order-processing costs associated with unloading, stocking, and related activities. The less frequently a product is ordered, the higher the inventory-carrying costs, because more product must be kept in inventory to cover the longer period between orders. An important new tool for inventory management is radio frequency identification (RFID). RFID utilizes small tags that are attached to pallets, containers, or individual inventory items (see Case 12-2).

## Transportation

Finally, transportation decisions concern the method or mode a company should utilize when moving products through domestic and global channels. The most important modes for the products discussed in this book are rail, truck, air, and water. Each of these modes has its advantages and disadvantages, as summarized in Table 12-2. However, a particular mode may be unavailable in some countries because of an underdeveloped infrastructure or geographic barriers. Pipelines are highly specialized and used by companies transporting energy-related resources such as oil and natural gas.

*Rail* provides an extremely cost-effective means for moving large quantities of merchandise long distances. In the United States, carriers such as Burlington Northern Santa Fe (BNSF) account for about 42 percent of all cargo moved when measured by ton miles; however, according to figures compiled by Eno Transportation Foundation, rail accounts for only about 10 percent of total U.S. freight transportation revenues. Rail's capability is second only to water in terms of the variety of products that can be transported. However, trains are less reliable than trucks. Poor track maintenance leads to derailments, and bottlenecks on heavily traveled lines can create delays.

*Trucks* are an excellent mode for both long-haul, transcontinental transport and local delivery of goods. In nations with well-developed highway systems, truck freight provides the highest level of accessibility of any mode. Thanks to modern information technology, truck shipments are also easily traced. According to the American Trucking Association, in the United States alone, the trucking industry handles nearly 70 percent of all freight tonnage; in 2003, the industry generated revenues of $610 billion. Thanks to government deregulation and a business trend toward focusing on core competencies, companies such as General Motors,

| Mode | Reliability | Cost | Speed | Accessibility | Capability | Ease of tracing |
|------|-------------|------|-------|---------------|------------|-----------------|
| Rail | average | average | average | average | high | low |
| Water | low | low | slow | low | high | low |
| Truck | high | varies | fast | high | high | high |
| Air | high | high | fast | low | moderate | high |
| Pipeline | high | low | slow | low | low | moderate |
| Internet | high | low | moderate to fast | moderate; increasing | low | high |

Table 12-2

Comparison of Major
International Transportation
Modes

Hewlett Packard, and PPG Industries are turning to transportation companies for assistance. Ryder System, BAX Global, CNF, and others are analyzing, designing, and managing logistics and supply chains for these and many other companies.[26]

There are two main types of water transportation. *Inland water transportation* is an extremely low-cost mode generally used to move agricultural commodities, petroleum, fertilizers, and other goods that, by their nature, lend themselves to bulk shipping via barge. However, inland water transportation can be slow and subject to weather-related delays. Virtually any product can be shipped via *ocean transportation*. The world's deep-water ports can receive a variety of types of ocean-going vessels, such as container vessels, bulk and break-bulk vessels, and ro-ro (roll-on, roll-off) vessels. Although sailing times are not competitive with air transportation, it is generally more cost effective to ship large quantities of merchandise via ocean than by air. Denmark's Maersk Sealand is the world's largest shipping container line (see Table 12-3). Why is water rated "low" in reliability? In any given year, approximately 200 freighters sink due to bad weather or other factors. Compounding the tragic loss of human lives is that fact that the cargo ends up on the ocean floor. Cargo can sometimes be lost without a ship sinking. For example, in 1997, a huge wave rocked the freighter Tokio Express in the waters off Lands' End, England. Several dozen shipping containers were tossed overboard, including one containing nearly 5 million Lego pieces. The container was bound for Connecticut, where the pieces were to be assembled in kits. One year later, Lego pieces began washing ashore in Florida!

*Air* is the fastest transport mode and the carrier of choice for perishable exports such as flowers or fresh fish, but it is also the most expensive. The size and the weight of an item may determine that it is more cost effective to ship via air than ocean. If a shipment's delivery is time sensitive, such as emergency parts replacement, air is also the logical mode.

Thanks to the digital revolution, the *Internet* is becoming an important transportation mode that is associated with several advantages and one major disadvantage. First, the bad news: the Internet's capability is low. As Nicolas Negroponte of MIT's Media Lab has famously observed, as long as something consists of atoms, it cannot be shipped via the Internet. However, anything that can be digitized—including text, voice, music, pictures, and video—can be sent via the Internet. Advantages include low cost and high reliability. Accessibility is increasing as global PC demand increases; by the end of 2003, an estimated 585 million households had Internet access. Accessibility is also growing thanks to telecommunications innovations that allow cell phones and other wireless digital devices to access the Internet. Speed depends on several factors, including bandwidth. As broadband technology becomes more widespread and compression technology improves, the

| Table 12-3 Leading Shipping Lines | Carrier | Number of Vessels | Capacity 20 ft. units (thousands) |
|---|---|---|---|
| | Maersk Sealand (Denmark) | 324 | 816 |
| | Evergreen Marine (Taiwan) | 209 | 493 |
| | P&O Nedlloyd (UK) | 155 | 414 |
| | Hanjin Shipping (South Korea) | 76 | 414 |
| | American President Lines (USA) | 78 | 260 |
| | Cosco (China) | 136 | 257 |
| | CP Ships (UK) | 85 | 193 |
| | CMA-CGM (France) | 74 | 191 |
| | NYK Line (Japan) | 61 | 189 |

*Source:* Containerization International

26 Jon Bigness, "Driving Force: In Today's Economy, There is Big Money to be Made in Logistics," *The Wall Street Journal* (September 6, 1995), pp. A1, A9.

A crane operator sits more than 100 feet above the pier as he works the controls of a monster crane and moves a 40-foot container from ship to shore at the Port of Tacoma.

speed at which large digital files such as full-length motion pictures can be downloaded will increase dramatically.

*Channel strategy* involves an analysis of each shipping mode to determine which mode, or combination of modes, will be both effective and efficient in a given situation. An aspect of transportation technology that has revolutionized global trade is containerization, a concept that was first utilized in the United States starting in the mid-1950s.

**Containerization** refers to the practice of loading ocean-going freight into steel boxes measuring 20 feet, 40 feet, or longer. Containerization offers many advantages, including flexibility in the product that can be shipped via container, as well as flexibility in shipping modes. **Intermodal transportation** of goods is a combination of land and water shipping from producer to customer.[27] In the United States alone, railroads handle more than $150 billion in seaport goods, a statistic that is a testament to intermodal transportation's growing importance. Unfortunately, lack of investment in America's rail infrastructure has resulted in delays at seaports. As Bernard LaLonde, a professor of transportation and logistics, noted "It's the Achilles' heel of global distribution. The ships keep getting bigger and faster. Trade keeps growing. But we don't have the rail links we need."[28]

Use of a particular mode of transportation may be dictated by a particular market situation, by the company's overall strategy, or by conditions at the port of importation. For example, every November, winemakers from France's Beaujolais region participate in a promotion celebrating the release of the current vintage. Although wine destined for Europe markets may travel by rail or truck, U.S.-bound wine is shipped via air freight. Normally, owing to weight and bulk considerations, French wine makes the transatlantic journey by water. Similarly, Acer Group ships motherboards and other high-tech components from Taiwan via air freight to ensure that the latest technology is incorporated into its computers. Bangladesh's primary port, Chittagong, is subject to frequent delays and strikes, which forces Gap and other clothing companies to ship via air. Every Christmas, supplies of the season's hottest-selling toys and electronics

---

[27] For an excellent case study of the evolution of intermodal technology in the United States, see Jon R. Katzenback and Douglas K. Smith, *The Wisdom of Teams: Creating the High-Performance Organization* (New York: HarperBusiness, 1994), Chapter 2.

[28] Daniel Machalaba, "Cargo Hold: As U.S. Seaports Get Busier, Weak Point Is a Surprise: Railroads," *The Wall Street Journal* (September 19, 1996), p. A1.

# behind the scenes

## Adding Utility to a Case of Wine Through Distribution Channels

Each year, wine and spirits worth more than $1 billion are exported from France, Germany, Italy, and other European countries to all parts of the world. Have you ever wondered how a case of wine finds its way from, say, France to your local liquor store? In fact, after leaving the winery, the wine may pass through the hands of brokers, freight forwarders, shipping agents, export agents, shippers, importers, wholesalers, and distributors before it finishes its journey at your local retailer.

In France, the structure of the wine industry is quite complex. An intermediary called a **négociant** plays an important role that varies according to region. *Négociants* sometimes act as brokers and have standing contracts to buy specified quantities of finished wine on behalf of various U.S. **importers.** The *négociant* also functions somewhat like a banker, paying the producer as much as 25 percent in advance of delivery. *Négociants* may also buy grapes from growers to make their own wine, blending and bottling them under their own labels. Wine may be bottled and packed in cases by the producer or by the *négociant*.

Wine destined for France or other European markets travels by truck. If the wine is to be exported to the United States or Japan, a **freight forwarder** or **shipping agent** sends a truck to the winery to pick up the wine. For the largest producers, the simplest type of consolidation takes place at the winery itself; a truck carrying a 20- or 40-foot shipping container is backed up to the door of the winery and loaded there for the ocean voyage. For smaller producers, the wines are picked up and then delivered to a warehouse. There, the shipping agent consolidates various deliveries before filling a container for the shipping line of the importer's choosing.

Shipping dates and rates will vary depending on the availability of containers. In general, a 20-foot container can hold 800 cases of wine; a single 40-foot container can take up to 1,300 cases. The weight of the wine is a consideration when determining how many cases to ship in a given container. Not only do wine bottles vary in size (750 ml bottles are the most common, with 12 bottles in a case), but there is likely to be a difference in weight between two cases of different types of wine. For example, heavier bottles are required for champagne and other sparkling wines because the contents are under pressure; bottles of fine Bordeaux are packaged in wooden crates that weigh more than ordinary cardboard cartons.

Shipping wine is a challenging venture because of the perishable nature of the product. Proper storage and transportation are vital; light, heat, and temperature fluctuations are wine's worst enemy. Ideally, wine should be kept at a constant temperature near 55 degrees. To prevent improper shipping from ruining a shipment, temperature-controlled containers (known as "reefers") are often used, even though they add about $3 per case to the cost of the shipment. To further protect the wine, some importers avoid shipping during the hot summer months. Because ownership of the wine is transferred to the importer at the moment the wine leaves the French storage warehouse, it is important to insure the shipment. Wine shipments can even be insured against possible losses due to war and terrorism. The best importers arrange for proper warehouse storage even before taking title to the wines.

The transatlantic trip for U.S.-bound wine takes a week or more. The port of entry depends on the location of the importer or **wholesaler/distributor.** The port of New York is used when wines are destined for the East Coast. Wine bound for the nation's midsection often enters through Baltimore or Norfolk, Virginia. Ships going to a western destination may chart a course through the Gulf of Mexico on their way to Houston; wines bound for the port of San Francisco pass through the Panama Canal. Once the wine enters the United States, it must clear U.S. customs. Customs agents and the importer or wholesaler make sure the shipment meets all government regulations and that paperwork is properly prepared. The Bureau of Alcohol, Tobacco, and Firearms is the U.S. government agency with jurisdiction over wines and spirits.

After it has cleared customs, the wine is shipped to the wholesaler's warehouse. Again, the importance of temperature-controlled shipping comes into play. If the wholesaler is too busy to pick up the container immediately, it may sit on the dock for a week or more in warm weather; without refrigeration, the wine—and the importer's investment—might be lost. If the distributor is located in Chicago, the wine often enters the country in Baltimore and completes the next leg of the trip via rail. Sometimes, trucks will bring a shipment of wine to the Midwest from the East Coast and return full of meat to make the trip cost effective. After the wine has been unloaded at the warehouse, the distributor's sales staff arranges for the cases of wine to be delivered by truck or van to individual retailers.

There is as much variety among retail channels for wine as there is among wine producers. Outlets vary from mom-and-pop grocery stores to wine sections in large supermarkets to huge wine and liquor discounters, with considerable variety in between. In some stores, wine is stored and displayed haphazardly, often in sunny windows or near heating vents. Other stores go to great lengths to make sure that the wine isn't ruined after its long journey in protective containers. One large retailer, Big Y in Northampton, Massachusetts, even goes so far as to keep the entire store at 55 degrees year around.

Still other factors have a major influence on sales. One is the marketing and merchandising skill of the retailer: Point-of-sale help from an informed retailer is important in selling fine wines. Also, the industry press can have a huge impact on sales. A good rating in publications such as *Wine Spectator* or *The Wine Advocate* can make the difference between obscurity and a sellout for a particular wine. Often, savvy wine retailers will display a press clipping with a positive rating on the bin of a certain wine so customers can educate themselves as they shop.

products are shipped via air from factories in Asia to ensure just-in-time delivery by Santa Claus. Sony's PlayStation 2 is a case in point; in October 2000, the company shipped the first 500,000 PS2 units by air to stores around the world. Likewise, in 2002, in the face of high demand for the new flat-screen iMac, Apple Computer shipped about half its Asian production by air. An estimated $1 billion is added to U.S. shipping costs each year because companies are forced to compensate for railway delays by keeping more components or parts in inventory or by shipping via air.

# Logistics Management: A Brief Case Study

The term logistics management describes the integration of activities necessary to ensure the efficient flow of raw materials, in-process inventory, and finished goods from producers to customers. J.C. Penney provides a case study in the changing face of logistics, physical distribution, and retail supply chains in the twenty-first century. Several years ago, Penney's management team made a key decision to outsource most elements of its private-label shirt supply chain to TAL Apparel Ltd. of Hong Kong. Penney's North American stores carry virtually no extra inventory of house-brand shirts; when an individual shirt is sold, EPOS scanner data is transmitted directly to Hong Kong. TAL's proprietary computer model then determines whether to replenish the store with the same size, color, and style. Replacement shirts are sent directly to stores without passing through Penney's warehouse system; sometimes the shirts are sent via air, sometimes by ship. This approach represents a dramatic departure from past practices; Penney typically carried 6 months' worth of inventory in its warehouses and 3 months' inventory in stores. By working more closely with TAL, Penney can lower its inventory costs, reduce the quantity of goods that have to be marked down, and respond more quickly to changing consumer tastes and fashion styles. As Wai-Chan Chan of McKinsey & Company Hong Kong notes, "You are giving away a pretty important function when you outsource your inventory management. That's something that not a lot of retailers want to part with."[29]

**summary**

A **channel of distribution** is the network of agencies and institutions that links producers with users. **Physical distribution** is the movement of goods through channels. **Business-to-consumer marketing** uses consumer channels; **business-to-business marketing** employs industrial channels to deliver products to manufacturers or other types of organizations. Channel decisions are difficult to manage globally because of the variation in channel structures from country to country. Marketing channels can create **place utility, time utility, form utility,** and **information utility** for buyers. The characteristics of customers, products, middle vendors, and environment all affect channel design and strategy.

Consumer channels may be relatively direct, utilizing direct mail or door-to-door selling, as well as manufacturer-owned stores. A combination of manufacturers' sales force, agents-brokers, and wholesalers may also be used. **Piggyback marketing** is a distribution innovation in which one manufacturer gains distribution in a particular country market by "riding along" with the products of another manufacturer. Channels for industrial products are less varied, with manufacturer's sales force, wholesalers, and dealers or agents utilized.

**Global retailing** is a growing trend as successful retailers expand around the world in support of growth objectives. **Retail distribution** takes many different forms, including **department stores, specialty retailers, supermarkets, convenience stores, discount stores, warehouse clubs, hypermarkets, supercenters, category killers,** and **outlet malls.** Selection, price, store location, and customer service are a few of the competencies that can be used strategically to enter a new market. It is possible to classify retailers in a matrix that distinguishes companies offering few product categories with an own-label focus; many categories-own-label focus; few categories-manufacturer-brand-focus; and many categories-manufacturer-brand focus. Global retail expansion can be achieved via **organic growth, franchising, acquisition,** and **joint venture.**

Transportation and physical distribution issues are critically important in global marketing because of the geographical distances involved in sourcing products and serving customers in different parts of the world. A company's **supply chain** includes all the firms that perform support activities such as generating raw materials or fabricating components. **Logistics** integrates the activities of all companies in a firm's value chain to ensure an efficient flow of goods through the supply chain. Important activities include **order processing, warehousing,** and **inventory management.** To cut costs and improve efficiency, many companies are reconfiguring their supply

[29] Gabriel Kahn, "Made to Measure: Invisible Supplier Has Penney's Shirts All Buttoned Up," *The Wall Street Journal* (September 11, 2003), pp. A1, A9.

chains by outsourcing some or all of these activities. Six transportation modes—**air, truck, water, rail, pipeline,** and **Internet**—are widely used in global distribution. Distributing products around the globe is made easier by **containerization** and **intermodal transportation**.

**discussion questions**

1. In what ways can channel intermediaries create utility for buyers?

2. What factors influence the channel structures and strategies available to global marketers?

3. What is *cherry picking*? What approaches can be used to deal with this problem?

4. Compare and contrast the typical channel structures for consumer products and industrial products.

5. Identify the different forms of retailing and cite an example of each form. Identify retailers from as many different countries as you can.

6. Identify the four retail market expansion strategies discussed in the text. What factors determine the appropriate mode?

7. Briefly discuss the global issues associated with physical distribution and transportation logistics. Cite one example of a company that is making efficiency improvements in its channel or physical distribution arrangements.

8. What special distribution challenges exist in Japan? What is the best way for a non-Japanese company to deal with these challenges?

**build your global marketing skills**

Each December, *Chain Store Age* magazine publishes its survey of the world's largest retailers. The top-ranked companies for 2003 were shown in Table 12-1. Browse through the list and choose any company that interests you. Compare its 2003 ranking with the most recent ranking (which you can find either by referring to the print version of *Chain Store Age* or by visiting www.chainstoreage.com). How have the industry rankings changed? Consult additional sources (e.g., magazine articles, annual reports, the company's Web site) to enhance your understanding of the factors and forces that contributed to the company's move up or down in the rankings. What do the current rankings tell you about changes in global retailing?

# Case 12-1

## Wal-Mart's Global Expansion

Wal-Mart, the discount retail giant whose very name strikes fear in the hearts of many small-town retailers in the United States, has gone global. The company utilizes a variety of different retail formats, including discount stores; supercenters that feature a full line of groceries and general merchandise; and Sam's Club, a warehouse operation offering goods in unbroken bulk packages. As Wal-Mart extends its reach around the globe, observers are using words such as "assault" and "invasion" to describe what it's like for a nation that the company has in its sights. As the chief executive of one supplier noted, "Wal-Mart is going to change the retailing landscape internationally exactly the same way it's done domestically." Some industry observers expect that, within a few years, four or five giant firms will dominate the world's retail scene. Retail consultant Daniel O'Connor summed up the situation this way: "We're really moving to boundaryless retailing." Needless to say, Wal-Mart executives intend to put their company in first place.

### North America

Wal-Mart's first foray outside the United States was in Mexico in 1991. Although Wal-Mart executives had no previous foreign experience, they recognized that there were substantial income and cultural differences in Mexico. Accordingly, the American retail giant established a 50–50 joint venture with Cifra SA, Mexico's largest retailer. Despite having a partner, the company made a number of blunders. Among them were poorly translated signs and a merchandise assortment that included inappropriate items such as ice skates, leaf blowers, and riding lawn mowers. To make matters worse, Wal-Mart's vaunted information system would automatically re-stock merchandise that local managers had tried to close out. The Mexican stores sold American-style packaged meat and vegetables, which many shoppers preferred to purchase from small neighborhood stores. Also, most Mexican suppliers shipped directly to stores rather than to retailer warehouses and distribution centers. Thus, Wal-Mart lacked the control that translates into low prices in the United States. As Sam Dunn, director of administration for Wal-Mart de Mexico, commented, "The key to this market is distribution. The retailer who solves that will dominate."

One sign of Wal-Mart's long-term commitment to Mexico was its decision in mid-1997 to convert its joint venture shares into Cifra common stock and purchase enough additional shares to have a controlling stake in the company; the new enterprise is called Wal-Mart de Mexico S.A. de C.V. (Walmex). Meanwhile, Wal-Mart turned its sights further south. In 1995, the company teamed up with Lojas Americanas SA and opened five stores in Brazil; operating without a partner in Argentina, Wal-Mart opened four stores. By 2000, the company was operating 12 supercenters and eight Sam's Clubs in Brazil and 11 supercenters in Argentina. The stores offer a staggering variety, with a typical mix of approximately 50,000 different products.

In 1994, Wal-Mart entered Canada by acquiring the 122-store Woolco chain. The market appeared attractive because a high percentage of the Canadian population lives within 100 miles of the U.S. border. In addition to a high

**Table 1** Wal-Mart International Division, Revenues

|  | 2001 | 2002 | 2003 | 2004 |
|---|---|---|---|---|
| Revenue (millions) | $32,100 | $35,485 | $40,794 | $47,572 |
| Operating Margin | 3.0% | 3.6% | 4.9% | 5.0% |

Source: Wal-Mart Annual Report, 2003 and 2004.

**Table 2** Wal-Mart Retail Operations by Country, 2003

|  | Discount Stores | Supercenters | Sam's Clubs | Neighborhood Markets |
|---|---|---|---|---|
| Argentina | 0 | 11 | 0 | 0 |
| Brazil | 0 | 12 | 8 | 2* |
| Canada | 213 | 0 | 0 | 0 |
| China | 0 | 20 | 4 | 2 |
| Germany | 0 | 94 | 0 | 0 |
| Korea | 0 | 15 | 0 | 0 |
| Mexico | 472** | 75 | 50 | 0 |
| Puerto Rico† | 9 | 1 | 9 | 33 |
| United Kingdom†† | 248 | 10 | 0 | 0 |
| **Total** | **942** | **238** | **71** | **37** |

*Brazil includes Todo Dias
**Mexico includes 118 Bodegas, 50 Suburbias, 44 Superamas, 260 Vips
†Puerto Rico includes 33 Amigos
††United Kingdom includes 248 Asda Stores
Source: Wal-Mart 2003 Annual Report, p. 7.

familiarity with Wal-Mart, Canadians also speak English and have a monetary system that is similar to the American one. The small size of existing Woolco stores resulted in disappointing sales; Wal-Mart responded by moving to new locations and expanding units. Much early sales growth came at the expense of existing department stores. Future growth may be hampered by the relatively small Canadian population and a trend toward cross border shopping to escape high value-added taxes. Also, management at Zeller's, Wal-Mart's main competitor in Canada, has responded by renovating stores and expanding beyond its traditional discount formula.

### South America

The retailing environment in South America is competitive, in part because Carrefour arrived first. The French company inked distribution deals with manufacturers of leading local brands; this is a key advantage, because well-known consumer packaged-goods brands such as Tide detergent are not widely accepted in South America. Moreover, Carrefour played hardball, undercutting Wal-Mart's prices on key items such as cooking oil, rice, and shampoo. Some observers noted that Carrefour's French heritage undoubtedly gave it the upper hand in presenting fresh fish, meat, and produce. Local retailers were strong as well; faced with rampant inflation in the late 1980s, they had invested in sophisticated cash registers and an inventory control system to help them make frequent, even daily, price adjustments.

*"You have to be culturally sensitive in the selection of merchandise in order to succeed in emerging markets, or in any foreign market. Carrefour is very good at making adjustments in local markets, and is very good at developing local management. I think that's the major lesson that the world's largest retailer can learn from the second largest retailer."*

Ira Kalish, director, Global Retail Intelligence, PricewaterhouseCoopers Los Angeles

Despite these competitive challenges, Wal-Mart quickly adapted to the unfamiliar environment. It hired local managers, who in turn helped develop the right product assortment and merchandising approaches. For example, the Wal-Mart Supercenters in Argentina initially kept fresh seafood in glass display cases. However, South Americans typically want to examine prospective food purchases up close and even touch them; Wal-Mart made the appropriate changes. Wal-Mart quickly discovered that, in South America, the entire family shops together; it turned out that Wal-Mart's aisles were not wide enough to accommodate such groups. Shoppers also were information deprived; Wal-Mart responded with clinics and in-store demonstrations such as weekly makeovers in the cosmetics departments. Wal-Mart also had to adjust the approach of its Sam's Club warehouse stores. Small business operators were expected to account for a significant amount of purchases at Sam's Club. However, even these buyers were unable to afford the bulk packs that are mainstays of Wal-Mart's wholesale club format. Sam's managers were forced to break down bulk quantities into smaller packs and even sell individual items.

### Europe

Market entry in Europe came in 1997 with the purchase of 21 hypermarkets from Wertkauf GmbH. The following year Wal-Mart acquired 74 additional hypermarkets from Spar Handels AG. The early going was difficult; the two acquired companies were merged under a centralized headquarters, a major remodeling program affecting most of the stores was launched, and distribution was centralized. In addition, the company's aggressive pricing resulted in a price war among Germany's retailers who had already been through traumatic changes related to the reunification with East Germany in 1990. Wal-Mart's losses in Germany for 1999 were estimated to run as high as $200 million. However, with the transition largely in place, in 2000, company officials announced plans to open 50 more stores in Germany and to double its share of the hypermarket sector to 20 percent within a few years.

In 1999, Wal-Mart shocked the European retailing world by offering more than $10 billion for Britain's third-largest supermarket chain, Asda Group PLC. It was the largest cash offer every made for a UK business. Industry observers noted that Asda had spent years studying such fundamental elements of the Wal-Mart approach as everyday low pricing and an "anti-management" management culture that, for example, calls for having a greeter at the front of the store and stresses the importance of calling store personnel "colleagues." As Asda chairman Archie Norman said, "The culture and attitude of Wal-Mart is one that we aspired to."

*"In order to be big globally we have to be big in Europe."*

Jay Fitzsimmons, Wal-Mart Senior Vice President

### Asia

Wal-Mart is also targeting Asia. With China now a member of World Trade Organization, Wal-Mart executives intend to capitalize on the coming economic expansion. Wal-Mart's earliest foray into China, a joint venture launched in 1996 with Thailand's Charoen Pokphand Group, was terminated after 18 months due to management differences. Although Beijing restricts the operations of foreign retailers, Wal-Mart executives have made a point of building relationships with government officials. In addition, Wal-Mart exports approximately $10 billion worth of goods from China each year. Joe Hatfield, Wal-Mart's chief in Asia, spent a great deal of time checking in local shops to better understand the type of merchandise the typical Chinese consumer wants to buy. Through trial-and-error, Wal-Mart has learned what type of merchandise sells and what doesn't. By the end of 2003, Wal-Mart had 26 stores in China. However, it still lags behind France's Carrefour SA, which operates 45 hypermarkets and 90 Dia discount stores. In April 2004, Carrefour opened China's first supermarket.

Wherever Wal-Mart goes, competitors are forced to adjust to the new retail climate. In China, Dutch retailer Royal Ahold NV and Hong Kong supermarket chain Park' N Shop have scaled back. In the face of Wal-Mart's voracious appetite for acquisitions, Metro AG, Germany's number one retailer, bought the Allfauf and Kriegbaum hypermarket chains. New slogans that closely resemble Wal-Mart's such as "ehrliche Niedrigpreise" ("honestly low prices") greet shoppers at Metro's Real hypermarkets, and the stores open earlier in the day. Still, the size and scale of Wal-Mart's operation give it tremendous buying power. For example, Wal-Mart buys 20 percent of all the Pampers brand disposable diapers produced by Procter & Gamble. In Mexico, Francisco Martínez, CFO of rival Comercial Mexicana SA, noted, "I buy 20,000 plastic toys, and Wal-Mart buys 20 million. Who do you think gets them cheaper?"

## Discussion Questions

1. Which of the market entry strategy options identified in Figure 12-4 has Wal-Mart utilized in its global expansion?

2. What are the keys to Wal-Mart's success in the United States? Will those factors help the company as it expands around the globe?

3. How do the ways in which Wal-Mart creates utility for buyers vary in different parts of the world?

4. If you were a small, independent retailer threatened by Wal-Mart, what would you do?

*Sources:* David Luhnow, "Crossover Success: How Nafta Helped Wal-Mart Reshape the Mexican Market," *The Wall Street Journal* (August 31, 2001), pp. A1, A2; William Boston, "Wal-Mart Girds for Major German Expansion," *The Wall Street Journal* (July 20, 2000), pp. A21, A22; Peter Wonacott, "Wal-Mart Finds Market Footing in China," *The Wall Street Journal* (July 17, 2000), p. A31; John Schmid, "In Germany, Wal-Mart Touches Off a Price War," *International Herald Tribune* (November 11, 1998), pp. 1, 10; Jonathan Friedland and Louise Lee, "Foreign Aisles: The Wal-Mart Way Sometimes Gets Lost in Translation Overseas," *The Wall Street Journal* (October 8, 1997), pp. A1, A12; Wendy Zellner, "Wal-Mart Spoken Here," *Business Week* (June 23, 1997), pp. 138–139+; Bob Ortega, "Tough Sale: Wal-Mart Is Slowed by Problems of Price and Culture in Mexico," *The Wall Street Journal* (July 28, 1994), pp. A1, A5.

# Case 12-2

## The Future of Radio Frequency Identification

Since the mid-1970s, shoppers in many parts of the world have been accustomed to laser scanners at checkout counters that scan bar codes on purchased items. Now, manufacturers and retailers are rolling out a new technology that could one day enable them to take a closer look at all the items in a person's grocery bag. Radio Frequency Identification (RFID) is a new technology employing tiny tags equipped with microchips and antennas. Developed at the Massachusetts Institute of Technology's Auto-ID Center, RFID has been used for such applications as security and access control and toll collection on roads and bridges. In October 2003, responsibility for commercializing RFID was turned over to EPCglobal, a joint venture created by the U.S.-based Uniform Code Council and Europe's EAN. Now, global companies are assessing the technology as a means of improving supply chain management. RFID tags can facilitate a company's efforts to track the location of components and parts as they move along an assembly line, or shipping containers as they move from global factories to retailers in various parts of the world. The tags currently cost about $0.25 each, and thus are too expensive to put on individual items. Even so, privacy advocates are already speaking out against the technology.

Katherine Albrecht is director of Citizens Against Supermarket Privacy Invasion and Numbering (CASPIAN), a consumer advocacy group that has previously targeted such common marketing techniques as shopper loyalty cards. Why all the fuss about an issue that is basically a matter of supply chain management? Albrecht, a doctoral student at Harvard University, is concerned that, if tags are embedded in clothing, companies—or government agencies—will be able to track the movements of the people wearing the clothes. She cautions, "Very few people grasp the enormity of this."

Albrecht established a Web site—**www.spychips.org**—to help spread the word worldwide. Concerned about these activities, the Grocery Manufacturers Association began delving into Albrecht's personal background in an attempt to discredit or embarrass her. The ploy backfired when an internal GMA e-mail was inadvertently sent to Albrecht; the GMA subsequently issued an apology.

Benetton has already responded to the negative publicity surrounding the tags by reassuring consumers that it does not attach tags to any individual clothing items in its stores. In spring 2003, Wal-Mart canceled an experimental program that would have placed radio tags on razors and blades. During a trial program at the Tesco supermarket chain in Great Britain, consumers who bought tagged Gillette razors were photographed. In this test, the goal was to prevent shoplifting; each photo was deleted when the shopper paid for the razor at checkout. Europe's Metro Group supermarket chain went ahead with a 2-month experiment that entailed setting up so-called smart shelves in German stores to track the presence of tagged items. After obtaining a Metro loyalty card, Albrecht discovered a hidden RFID chip in it. Metro could use the cards in conjunction with tagged grocery items to track all customer purchases. After Albrecht went public with the news, Metro recalled the cards and promised that it would no longer distribute tagged cards.

Despite the controversy, Wal-Mart is moving ahead with plans to integrate RFID into its supply chain. The company has told its top suppliers that, effective January 2005, they must attach RFIDs to each pallet and case of product. In typical Wal-Mart fashion, the retailer has stipulated that suppliers must absorb the cost of implementing the RFID program. Despite the cost involved and the controversy surrounding the privacy issue, RFID promises to benefit consumers and channel intermediaries alike. Even though Wal-Mart boasts the industry's most sophisticated inventory management system, one study found that, at any given moment, 7 percent of items that shoppers expect to find at Wal-Mart are temporarily out of stock. Because retailers will be able to pinpoint the exact location of a shipment, loss due to theft or simple error will be reduced. Stores can reduce the amount of excess inventory they carry, and consumers will be less likely to be disappointed by a stock-out situation.

## Discussion Questions

1. Why do you think Katherine Albrecht is suspicious of the retail industry's motives for employing RFID?

2. What should the retail industry do in response to the mounting controversy over RFID?

3. Should retailers be forced to disclose when they are using RFID chips on products?

*Sources:* Jack Neff, "Privacy Activist Albrecht Tackles Marketers Head On," *Advertising Age* (April 19, 2004), p. 54; Barnaby J. Feder, "Wal-Mart Hits More Snags in Its Push to Use Radio Tags to Track Goods," *The New York Times* (March 29, 2004), p. C4; John Gapper, "Privacy Gets a Price-Tag When Bugs Go Shopping," *Financial Times* (March 2, 2004), p. 13; Kevin J. Delaney, "Inventory Tool to Launch in Germany," *The Wall Street Journal* (January 12, 2004), p. B5; Jack Neff, "P&G Products to Wear Wire," *Advertising Age* (December 15, 2003), pp. 1, 32; Feder, "Wal-Mart Plan Could Cost Suppliers Millions," *The New York Times* (November 10, 2003), p. C2; Feder, "How to Find that Needle Hopelessly Lost in the Haystack," *The New York Times* (September 29, 2003), pp. C1, C4.

# 13 Global Marketing Communications Decisions I
## ADVERTISING AND PUBLIC RELATIONS

Scotch whiskey is a textbook example of a global product. Wealthy consumers with discerning palates do not hesitate to pay premium prices for top brands of blended scotch such as Chivas Regal and Johnnie Walker. Those seeking an even more expensive, exclusive tasting experience can choose single malt scotches such as Glenfiddich and Lagavulin that are produced by a single distillery. Until recently, Canada's Seagram owned the Chivas brand. Chivas had long enjoyed a reputation as *the* deluxe scotch whiskey, and the brand's promotional strategy frequently called for global advertising campaigns. For example, in the early 1990s a print campaign was keyed to the slogan "There will always be a Chivas Regal." The campaign featured a series of universal images and was translated into 15 languages. Managers in each of 34 countries were authorized to choose individual ads from the campaign that they deemed appropriate for their markets. Seagrams also launched a global billboard campaign to enhance the universal appeal for Chivas. The theory: The rich all over will sip the brand, no matter where they made their fortune. As the twentieth century came to a close, however, Seagram's management team was focusing its attention on the company's film business and on spirits brands such as Captain Morgan rum and Absolut vodka that appeal to younger drinkers. In the key U.S. market, Johnnie Walker Black overtook Chivas as the top-selling brand. In 2000, Seagram shed its wine and spirits unit, and Chivas Regal was sold to France's Pernod Ricard SA. Between 2000 and 2002, Chivas experienced a 10 percent overall decline in sales volume, while Johnnie Walker posted gains of 12 percent.

Advertising and other forms of communication are critical tools in the marketing of distilled spirits. Marketing communications—the promotion *P* of the marketing mix—refers to all forms of communication used by organizations to inform, remind, explain, persuade, and influence

the attitudes and buying behavior of customers and others. The primary purpose of marketing communications is to tell customers about the benefits and values that a company, product, or service offers. The elements of the promotion mix are advertising, public relations, personal selling, and sales promotion. All of these elements can be utilized in global marketing, either alone or in varying combinations. The challenge facing the new owners of Chivas Regal is finding a promotional strategy that will reverse the brand's sales slump.

The environment in which marketing communications programs and strategies are implemented also varies from country to country. The challenge of effectively communicating across borders is one reason that global companies and their advertising agencies are embracing a concept known as **integrated marketing communications (IMC).** Adherents of an IMC approach explicitly recognize that the various elements of a company's communication strategy must be carefully coordinated.[1] This chapter examines advertising and public relations from the perspective of the global marketer. The next chapter is devoted to the remaining elements of the promotion mix: sales promotion and personal selling.

---

[1]  Thomas R. Duncan and Stephen E. Everett, "Client Perception of Integrated Marketing Communications," *Journal of Advertising Research* (May–June 1993), pp. 119–122; see also Stephen J. Gould, Dawn B. Lerman, and Andreas F. Grein, "Agency Perceptions and Practices on Global IMC," *Journal of Advertising Research* 39, no. 1 (January–February 1999), pp. 7–20.

# GLOBAL ADVERTISING

**Advertising** may be defined as any sponsored, paid message that is communicated in a nonpersonal way. Some advertising messages are designed to communicate with persons in a single country or market area. Regional or pan-regional advertising is created for audiences across several country markets such as Europe or Latin America. **Global advertising** may be defined as messages whose art, copy, headlines, photographs, tag lines, and other elements have been developed expressly for their worldwide suitability. IBM ("Solutions for a small planet"), De Beers ("A diamond is forever"), BP ("Beyond Petroleum"), and Vodafone ("Your voice") are companies that have used global campaigns successfully. In Chapter 10, we noted that a global company may simultaneously offer local, international, and global products and brands to buyers in different parts of the world. The same is true with advertising: A global company may utilize single-country advertising in addition to campaigns that are regional and global in scope.

In Japan, for example, PepsiCo has achieved great success with a local campaign featuring Pepsiman, a superhero action figure. Prior to 1996, the ads shown in Japan were the same global spots used throughout the rest of the world. However, in Japan's $24 billion soft drink market, Pepsi trailed far behind Coca-Cola; Pepsi had a mere 3 percent market share compared with Coke's 30 percent share. The Pepsiman character was designed by local Japanese talent, but Industrial Light & Magic, the special-effects house owned by *Star Wars* creator George Lucas, was hired to give the TV spots a U.S.-style high-tech edge. By breaking with its usual strategy of running global ads and increasing the ad budget by 50 percent over 1995, Pepsi's 1996 sales in Japan rose by 14 percent. Pepsiman even has his own PlayStation video game; it is, essentially, a long-form interactive ad for Pepsi Cola.[2]

A global company that has the ability to successfully transform a domestic campaign into a worldwide one, or to create a new global campaign from the ground up, possesses a critical advantage. The first company to find a global market for any product is frequently at an advantage relative to competitors that make the same discovery later. The search for a global advertising campaign should bring together everyone involved with the product to share information and leverage their experiences. Global campaigns with unified themes can help to build long-term product and brand identities and offer significant savings by reducing the cost associated with producing ads. Regional market areas such as Europe are experiencing an influx of standardized global brands as companies align themselves, buy up other companies, and get their production plans and pricing policies organized for a united region. From a marketing point of view, there is a great deal of activity going on that will make brands truly pan-European in a short period of time. This phenomenon is accelerating the growth of global advertising.

The potential for effective global advertising also increases as companies recognize and embrace new concepts such as "product cultures." An example is the globalization of beer culture, which can be seen in the popularity of German-style beer halls in Japan and Irish-style pubs in the United States. Similarly, the globalization of coffee culture has created market opportunities for companies such as Starbucks. Companies also realize that some market segments can be defined on the basis of global demography—youth culture, for example—rather than ethnic or national culture. Athletic shoes and other clothing items, for instance, can be targeted to a worldwide segment of 18- to 25-year-old males. William Roedy, president of MTV Networks International, sees clear implications of such product

*"Today, pan-European campaigns account for up to 40 percent of what we do. Five years ago it might have been half that amount."*

Fernan Montera, chairman of European operations, Young & Rubicam[3]

---

[2]   John Herskovitz, "Pepsiman Comes Calling Again," *Advertising Age International* (January 11, 1999), p. 9.

[3]   Alison Smith, "Border Crossings," *Financial Times* (May 7, 1998), p. 22.

cultures for advertising. MTV is just one of the media vehicles that enable people virtually anywhere to see how the rest of the world lives and to learn about products that are popular in other cultures. Many human wants and desires are similar if presented within recognizable experience situations. People everywhere want value, quality, and the latest technology made available and affordable; everyone everywhere wants to be loved and respected, and we all get hungry.[4]

According to figures compiled by ZenithOptimedia, worldwide advertising expenditures in 2003 totaled $155 billion. Because advertising is often designed to add psychological value to a product or brand, it plays a more important communications role in marketing consumer products than in marketing industrial products. Frequently purchased, low-cost products generally require heavy advertising support to remind consumers about the product. Not surprisingly, consumer products companies top the list of big global advertising spenders. Procter & Gamble, Unilever, L'Oreal, and Nestlé are companies whose "globalness" can be inferred from the significant proportion of advertising expenditures outside the home-country markets. *Advertising Age*'s ranking of global marketers in terms of advertising expenditures is shown in Table 13-1. The top 100 advertisers spent a total of $74.2 billion in 2002; in addition, the top 100 spent $37.3 billion on U.S. advertising. A close examination of Table 13-1 provides clues to the extent of a company's globalization efforts. For example, packaged-goods giants P&G and Unilever spend significant amounts in all major world regions. By contrast, the table shows that the geographic scope of France's PSA Peugeot Citroën is largely limited to Europe.

**Table 13-1**

*Top 25 Global Marketers, 2002 ($ millions)*

| Company | Worldwide Ad Spending | U.S. Ad Spending | Asia Ad Spending* | Europe Ad Spending | Latin America Ad Spending |
|---|---|---|---|---|---|
| 1. Procter & Gamble | 4,479 | 2,032 | 539 | 1,647 | 120 |
| 2. Unilever | 3,315 | 689 | 705 | 1,713 | 145 |
| 3. General Motors Corp. | 3,218 | 2,447 | 63 | 522 | 197 |
| 4. Toyota Motor Corp. | 2,405 | 885 | 1,063 | 347 | 28 |
| 5. Ford Motor Co. | 2,387 | 1,407 | 89 | 746 | 92 |
| 6. Time Warner | 2,349 | 1,812 | 40 | 413 | 53 |
| 7. DaimlerChrysler | 1,800 | 1,341 | 21 | 356 | 31 |
| 8. L'Oreal | 1,683 | 545 | 65 | 1,001 | 38 |
| 9. Nestlé | 1,547 | 494 | 138 | 819 | 67 |
| 10. Sony Corp. | 1,513 | 875 | 135 | 417 | 38 |
| 11. Johnson & Johnson | 1,453 | 1,079 | 83 | 232 | 30 |
| 12. Walt Disney Co. | 1,428 | 1,154 | 32 | 191 | 14 |
| 13. Altria Group | 1,425 | 892 | 29 | 436 | 37 |
| 14. Honda Motor Corp. | 1,383 | 710 | 522 | 1C8 | 16 |
| 15. Volkswagen | 1,349 | 440 | 39 | 756 | 83 |
| 16. Nissan Motor Co. | 1,280 | 703 | 386 | 125 | 21 |
| 17. Coca-Cola Co. | 1,199 | 302 | 269 | 467 | 102 |
| 18. McDonald's Corp. | 1,183 | 574 | 181 | 353 | 34 |
| 19. Vivendi Universal | 1,176 | 485 | 20 | 645 | 7 |
| 20. GlaxoSmithKline | 1,157 | 777 | 60 | 269 | 31 |
| 21. PepsiCo | 1,096 | 757 | 92 | 138 | 66 |
| 22. Pfizer | 1,075 | 821 | 34 | 145 | 54 |
| 23. PSA Peugeot Citroën | 904 | 0 | 1 | 859 | 33 |
| 24. Mars Inc. | 870 | 325 | 54 | 470 | 19 |
| 25. Viacom | 827 | 756 | 5 | 20 | 3 |

*Asia includes Australia and New Zealand.
*Source:* Reprinted with permission from the November 2003 issue of *Advertising Age Global.* Copyright, Crain Communications Inc. 2003.

---

4   Dean M. Peebles, "Executive Insights: Don't Write Off Global Advertising," *International Marketing Review* 6, no. 1 (1989), pp. 73–78.

## A Global Ad Campaign for Chivas Regal

Prior to the acquisition, Pernod Ricard was best known for Ricard, an anise-flavored beverage known as a pastis. The company also owned single-market European brands such as Sambuca Ramazzotti (Italy) and Ouzo Mini (Greece). Pernod Ricard had gained some experience building global platforms for once-local brands such as Jameson whisky and Havana Club rum. Even so, some industry observers wondered whether a company that had focused on so-called "second tier" local brands had the skills to reinvigorate its new, truly global brands. As one analyst put it, "Pernod Ricard was a very big French company that has joined the big time. Now they're taking on the big global brands, which requires different skills. The question is, do they have the skills that it takes?"

Patrick Ricard is chairman, chief executive, and the son of the company's founder. He believes the management team at Pernod Ricard does indeed have the skills required to succeed in the global marketplace against giants such as Diageo. For one thing, the company's decentralized strategy is well matched to an industry sector characterized by local tastes.

In his quest to revitalize the Chivas brand, Ricard passed over British advertising agencies in favor of TBWA Paris. Martin Riley, international marketing director of Ricard's Chivas Brothers unit, explained the decision by noting that upscale British drinkers prefer single malt scotches to blended brands such as Chivas. *Impact*, an industry trade magazine, observed that "When you know," the enigmatic slogan developed for Seagram's final Chivas advertising campaign, was "utterly ineffective." As Riley noted, "When you get to a lot of countries that are not primarily English-speaking, like those in Asia or South America, they would like you to fill in the dots." The new slogan, "This is the Chivas Life," was designed to appeal to the aspirations of Chivas drinkers anywhere in the world.

Chivas was also a sponsor of the Playboy Club Tour, a 50-city marketing extravaganza commemorating *Playboy* magazine's fiftieth anniversary. Market research revealed that Hispanics account for 40 percent of Chivas' U.S. sales volume; in 2003 and 2004, Chivas sponsored a tour by La Ley, a Grammy-winning Chilean rock group popular with Hispanic audiences. "La Vida Chivas," the Spanish translation of the new ad slogan, was featured prominently during the tour, as was the sobriety message La Ley M = + D ("Moderation = More Entertainment"). A Web site (**www.chivaslaley.com**) provided tour date information; the site also offered fans the opportunity to sign up to be members of the "Chivas Circle" and to order personalized Chivas labels.

Sources: R. W. Apple Jr., "A Rugged Drink for a Rugged Land," *The New York Times* (July 16, 2003), pp. D1, D7; Adam Jones, "Pernod Mulls Next Wave of Consolidation," *Financial Times* (March 9, 2004), p. 14; Deborah Ball, "Scotch on the Rocks? 'Single Malt' Diversifies," *The Wall Street Journal* (December 30, 2003), pp. B1, B4; Adam Jones, "Global Media Campaign Aims to Stress the Importance of Being Chivas," *Financial Times Scotch Whiskey Special Report* (November 28, 2003), p. 10; Ball, "Pernod Acquisition has Mixed Well," *The Wall Street Journal* (November 11, 2002), p. B3.

Global advertising also offers companies economies of scale in advertising as well as improved access to distribution channels. Where shelf space is at a premium, as with food products, a company has to convince retailers to carry its products rather than those of competitors. A global brand supported by global advertising may be very attractive because, from the retailer's standpoint, a global brand is less likely to languish on the shelves. Landor Associates, a company specializing in brand identity and design, recently determined that Coke has the number one brand-awareness and esteem position in the United States, number two in Japan, and number six in Europe. However, standardization is not always required or even advised. Nestlé's Nescafé coffee is marketed as a global brand, even though advertising messages and product formulation vary to suit cultural differences.

## Global Advertising Content: The "Standardization" Versus "Adaptation" Debate

Communication experts generally agree that the overall requirements of effective communication and persuasion are fixed and do not vary from country to country. The same thing is true of the components of the communication process: The marketer is the source of the message; the message must be encoded, conveyed via the appropriate channel(s), and decoded by a member of the target audience. Communication takes place only when the intended meaning is transferred from the source to the receiver. Four major difficulties can compromise an organization's attempt to communicate with customers in any location:

1.  The message may not get through to the intended recipient. This problem may be the result of an advertiser's lack of knowledge about appropriate media for reaching certain types of audiences. For example, the effectiveness of television as a medium for reaching mass audiences will vary proportionately with the extent to which television viewing occurs within a country.

2.  The message may reach the target audience but may not be understood or may even be misunderstood. This can be the result of an improper encoding or an inadequate understanding of the target audience's level of sophistication.

3.  The message may reach the target audience and may be understood but still may not induce the recipient to take the action desired by the sender. This could result from a lack of cultural knowledge about a target audience.

4.  The effectiveness of the message can be impaired by *noise*. *Noise* in this case is an external influence such as competitive advertising, other sales personnel, and confusion at the receiving end. These factors can detract from the ultimate effectiveness of the communication.

The key question for global marketers is whether the *specific* advertising message and media strategy must be changed from region to region or country to country because of environmental requirements. Proponents of the "one world, one voice" approach to global advertising believe that the era of the global village is fast approaching and that tastes and preferences are converging worldwide. According to the standardization argument, because people everywhere want the same products for the same reasons, companies can achieve great economies of scale by unifying advertising around the globe. Advertisers who follow the localized approach are skeptical of the global village argument. Rather, they assert that consumers still differ from country to country and must be reached by advertising tailored to their respective countries. Proponents of localization point out that most blunders occur because advertisers have failed to understand—and adapt to—foreign cultures. Nick Brien, managing director of Leo Burnett, explains the situation this way:

> As the potency of traditional media declines on a daily basis, brand building locally becomes more costly and international brand building becomes more cost effective. The challenge for advertisers and agencies is finding ads that work in different countries and cultures. At the same time as this global tendency, there is a growing local tendency. It's becoming increasingly important to understand the requirements of both.[5]

During the 1950s, the widespread opinion among advertising professionals was that effective international advertising required assigning responsibility for campaign preparation to a local agency. In the early 1960s, this idea of local delegation was repeatedly challenged. For example, Eric Elinder, head of a Swedish advertising agency, wrote: "Why should three artists in three different countries sit drawing the same electric iron and three copywriters write about what, after all, is largely the same copy for the same iron?"[6] Elinder argued that consumer differences between countries were diminishing and that he would more effectively serve a client's interest by putting top specialists to work devising a strong international campaign. The campaign would then be presented with insignificant modifications that mainly entailed translating the copy into language well suited for a particular country.

As the decade of the 1980s began, Pierre Liotard-Vogt, then-CEO of Nestlé, expressed similar views in an interview with *Advertising Age*.

*Advertising Age:* Are food tastes and preferences different in each of the countries in which you do business?

---

5   Meg Carter, "Think Globally, Act Locally," *Financial Times* (June 30, 1997), p. 12.
6   Eric Elinder, "International Advertisers Must Devise Universal Ads, Dump Separate National Ones, Swedish Ad Man Avers," *Advertising Age* (November 27, 1961), p. 91.

*Liotard-Vogt:* The two countries where we are selling perhaps the most instant coffee are England and Japan. Before the war they didn't drink coffee in those countries, and I heard people say that it wasn't any use to try to sell instant coffee to the English because they drink only tea and still less to the Japanese because they drink green tea and they're not interested in anything else.

When I was very young, I lived in England and at that time, if you spoke to an Englishman about eating spaghetti or pizza or anything like that, he would just look at you and think that the stuff was perhaps food for Italians. Now on the corner of every road in London you find pizzerias and spaghetti houses.

So I do not believe [preconceptions] about "national tastes." They are "habits," and they're not the same. If you bring the public a different food, even if it is unknown initially, when they get used to it, they will enjoy it too.

To a certain extent we know that in the north they like a coffee milder and a bit acid and less roasted; in the south, they like it very dark. So I can't say that taste differences don't exist. But to believe that those tastes are set and can't be changed is a mistake.[7]

The "standardized versus localized" debate picked up tremendous momentum after the 1983 publication, noted in earlier chapters, of Professor Ted Levitt's *Harvard Business Review* article, "The Globalization of Markets." Recently, global companies have embraced a technique known as **pattern advertising.** This is analogous to the concept of global product platforms discussed in Chapter 10. Representing a middle ground between 100 percent standardization and 100 percent adaptation, a pattern strategy calls for developing a basic panregional or global communication concept for which copy, artwork, or other elements can be adapted as required by individual country markets. For example, ads in a 1997 European print campaign for Boeing shared basic design elements, but the copy and the visual elements were localized on a country-by-country basis.

Much of the research on this issue has focused on the match between advertising messages and local culture. For example, Ali Kanso surveyed two different groups of advertising managers; those adopting localized approaches to advertising and those adopting standardized approaches. One finding was that managers who are attuned to cultural issues tended to prefer the localized approach, whereas managers less sensitive to cultural issues preferred a standardized approach.[8] Bruce Steinberg, ad sales director for MTV Europe, discovered that the people responsible for executing global campaigns locally can exhibit strong resistance to a global campaign. Steinberg reported that he sometimes had to visit as many as 20 marketing directors from the same company to get approval for a pan-European MTV ad.[9]

As Kanso correctly notes, the debate over advertising approaches will probably continue for years to come. Localized and standardized advertising both have their place and both will continue to be used. Kanso's conclusion: What is needed for successful international advertising is a global commitment to local vision. In the final analysis, the decision of whether to use a global or localized campaign depends on recognition by managers of the trade-offs involved. On the one hand, a global campaign will result in the substantial benefits of cost savings, increased control, and the potential creative leverage of a global appeal. On the other hand, localized campaigns focus on the most important attributes of a product or brand in each nation or culture. The question of *when* to use each approach depends on the product involved and a company's objectives in a particular market.

McDonald's advertising has enjoyed a surge of popularity in Japan during the past several years. One explanation is that McDonald's is utilizing its global approach that invites consumers to associate the restaurant with family members

---

7  "A Conversation with Nestlé's Pierre Liotard-Vogt," *Advertising Age* (June 30, 1980), p. 31.
8  Ali Kanso, "International Advertising Strategies: Global Commitment to Local Vision," *Journal of Advertising Research* 32, no. 1 (January–February 1992), pp. 10–14.
9  Ken Wells, "Selling to the World: Global Ad Campaigns, After Many Missteps, Finally Pay Dividends," *The Wall Street Journal* (August 27, 1992), p. A1.

WAAR VIND JE DE SPECIALIST OP HET TERREIN VAN DE LUCHTWEERSTAND?

In Nederland. Een land, zo vlak dat de wind er volledig vrij spel heeft. En wij zouden natuurlijk geen Nederlanders zijn als wij met deze aërodynamica niet iets slims zouden doen. Denk bijvoorbeeld maar aan windenergie. "Ook bij het maken van delen van vliegtuigvleugels, draait het allemaal om luchtweerstand," vertelt Willemien Diks, al geruime tijd werkzaam bij Fokker Aerostructures in Papendrecht.

Zij is programmamanager en verantwoordelijk voor de productie van vleugeldelen voor de Boeing 737, 747, 757, 767 en de 777. "Dat Boeing de specialist zocht en vond in Nederland, is een logisch verhaal." En dat past precies in de werkwijze, die Boeing al meer dan 30 jaar voorstaat. Samenwerken met experts en hun bedrijven in heel Europa. Tenslotte komt er heel wat teamwork kijken bij het bouwen van een vliegtuig.

www.boeing.com

BOEING

WE CAN TRACE OUR LINEAGE TO ROW 4. SEAT 28. WHITE HART LANE.

When Megan Jones isn't in her seat at Tottenham Hotspur, she's wiring seats for Boeing. Megan is an electrician for Britax Rumbold in Camberley who make first class passenger seats for Boeing planes. Of the 500 apprentices on her course, Megan was the only woman to qualify. She also finished the 3 year course six months early. Boeing has been working with European experts like Megan and their companies for over 30 years. For one simple reason: we want to work with people who are best at what they do. Of course, building an airplane is a massive enterprise. It takes teamwork on a grand scale. Many individuals, many companies, many countries. But working together, we can do almost anything.

www.boeing.com

BOEING

*Ogilvy & Mather Worldwide created this corporate image campaign for Boeing in 1997. The ads, which appeared in European print media such as the London Times, Le Figaro, and Der Spiegel, communicate the point that Boeing relies extensively on European expertise in avionics. A textbook example of pattern advertising, the ads feature similar layouts (i.e., the dominant visual element is a photo in the upper half of the page; caption copy is reversed and superimposed on a black background in the lower half; a photo of an airplane is inset) whereas the copy and photos are localized for individual country markets.*

interacting in various situations. Starting in 1996, McDonald's campaign in Japan depicted various aspects of fatherhood. For example, one spot showed a father and son bicycling home with burgers and fries; another showed a father driving a van full of boisterous kids to McDonald's for milkshakes. The ads came at a time when many Japanese "salarymen" were reassessing the balance between work and family life. Although part of McDonald's global campaign, the spots have local elements as well: Japanese actors are used, and local musicians composed music reminiscent of Japanese prime time TV shows.[10]

Localized ads are less likely to be required for industrial products or for technology-oriented products sold to either consumers or business customers. For example, South Dakota–based Gateway commissioned Yankelovich Partners to conduct a survey of technology buying behavior in the United States, Great Britain, France, Australia, and Japan. As Luanne Flikkema, director of global research at Gateway, reported:

> We found that cultural differences had essentially no effect on the attitudes, motivators, and needs involved in purchasing technology. A first-time PC buyer in Japan was more similar to a first-time buyer in France than to a repeat buyer in Japan. An "Enthusiast" buyer was an Enthusiast buyer around the world. Were there any subtle regional differences? Of course. Did they make any appreciable difference in the purchase process? No.[11]

---

10 Yumko Ono, "Japan Warms to McDonald's Doting Dad Ads," *The Wall Street Journal* (May 8, 1997), pp. B1, B12.
11 Luanne Flikkema, "Global Marketing's Myth: Differences Don't Matter," *Marketing News* (July 20, 1998), p. 4.

## Thinking Globally, Acting Locally at Nissan

Generally speaking, Japanese companies prefer a localized approach to advertising. For example, Nissan officials perceive a great deal of variation in consumer tastes and values across the company's markets. As a Nissan spokesman said, "The marketing and advertising decisions are made by the individual markets." This attitude explains why it is unlikely that the recent campaign for Nissan created by TBWA Chiat/Day for the United States will be used in other markets. Keyed to the slogan "Life is a journey. Enjoy the ride," the campaign was designed to increase brand awareness among American car buyers. Bob Thomas, president and CEO of Nissan Motor Corporation USA, budgeted a record $200 million for the campaign; Thomas instructed the agency "to create advertising that everybody would be talking about." Recalling the origins of the campaign, Lee Clow, creative director at TBWA Chiat/Day, told *The New York Times*, "People don't really like car advertising. It's all the same; it's all sheet metal, features, and usually some kind of deal at the end. We're changing the rules of how car advertising can be done."

Each ad in the TV campaign features a cameo by a Japanese-American actor modeled on Yutaka Katayama, Nissan's U.S. executive in the company's early export days. In "Toys," one of the campaign's most memorable spots, stop-motion animation is set against Van Halen's version of "You Really Got Me." In the 60-second spot, a GI Joe-like doll drives a 300ZX to pick up a Barbie lookalike, much to the dismay of a third, preppy figure. Production costs for the "Toys" spot alone totaled $1 million, twice as much as Nissan usually spends on a commercial. Both ads received popular and critical acclaim; unfortunately, however, Nissan's U.S. sales actually fell. As marketing consultant Jack Trout said, "They're not doing very well, but they're being talked about. There's something wrong: They've spent too much time and effort and money trying to entertain people, and they're not really showing their cars effectively."

Responding to complaints from dealers that the ads were not building showroom traffic, hard sell regional ads without Mr. K were created. Tom Patten, president of TBWA Chiat/Day, explained, "We wanted to spend more time on the critical element of motivating people to get out of their chairs on a Saturday afternoon and go to a dealer. In doing that, we don't see a need to utilize Mr. K. He's not relevant at this level." By 1998, however, the brand image ads were gone. A campaign prominently featured later new models such as a four-door Frontier pickup truck. In one ad, a fisherman hooks a submarine, which he then lands with the help of his truck. Nissan dealers in the United States applaud the new approach. As one said, "Enough with the esoteric marketing concepts."

*Sources: Robert L. Simison, "Nissan's Crisis Was Made in the U.S.A.," The Wall Street Journal (November 25, 1998), pp. B1, B4; Yumiko Ono, "McCann Finds Global a Tough Sell in Japan," The Wall Street Journal (June 19, 1997), p. B12; Sally Goll Beatty, "Mixed Message: Nissan's Ad Campaign Was a Hit Everywhere but in the Showrooms," The Wall Street Journal (April 8, 1997), pp. A1, A14.*

By contrast, marketing and advertising managers at Pioneer Hi-Bred International frequently use both global and localized advertising executions. It is management's belief that some messages lend themselves to straight translation, while others need to be created in a way that is suited to the people, marketplace, and style of the particular country or region. Of the ads shown on page 444, the left is for the United States, and the ad on the right was created for Québec.

## ADVERTISING AGENCIES: ORGANIZATIONS AND BRANDS

Advertising is a fast-paced business, and the ad agency world is fluid and dynamic. New agencies are formed, existing agencies are dismantled, and cross-border investment, spin-offs, joint ventures, and mergers and acquisitions are a fact of life. There is also a great deal of mobility in the industry as executives and top talent move from one agency to another. The 20 largest global **advertising organizations** ranked by 2002 gross income are shown in Table 13-2. The key to understanding the table is the word *organization*; each firm identified in Table 13-2 is an umbrella corporation or holding company that includes one or more "core" advertising agencies, as well as units specializing in direct marketing, marketing services, public relations, or research.

> "Eighteen-year-olds in Paris have more in common with 18-year-olds in New York than with their own parents. They buy the same products, go to the same movies, listen to the same music, sip the same colas. Global advertising merely works on that premise."
>
> William Roedy,
> President, MTV International[12]

---

[12] Ken Wells, "Selling to the World: Global Ad Campaigns, After Many Missteps, Finally Pay Dividends," *The Wall Street Journal* (August 27, 1992), p. A1.

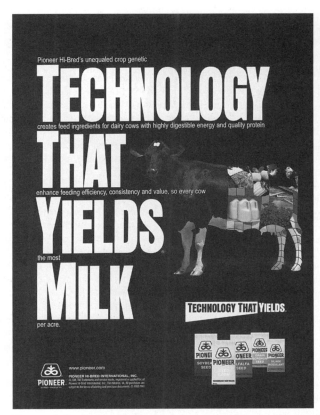

These ads for Pioneer Hi-Bred International exhibit localization that goes beyond translation of copy. The layouts, visual elements, and copy are different; elements common to the two ads are the trapezoid-shaped logo and the slogan "Technology That Yields."

| Table 13-2 | | |
|---|---|---|

Top 20 Global Advertising Organizations

| Organization and Headquarters Location | Worldwide Revenue 2002 ($ millions) |
|---|---|
| 1. Omnicom Group (New York) | 7,536.3 |
| 2. Interpublic Group of Cos. (New York) | 6,203.6 |
| 3. WPP Group (London) | 5,781.5 |
| 4. Publicis Group (Paris) | 2,711.9 |
| 5. Dentsu (Tokyo) | 2,060.9 |
| 6. Havas (Suresnes, France) | 1,841.6 |
| 7. Grey Global Group (New York) | 1,199.7 |
| 8. Hakuhodo (Tokyo) | 860.8 |
| 9. Cordiant Communications Group (London) | 788.5 |
| 10. Asatsu-DK (Tokyo) | 339.5 |
| 11. TMP Worldwide (New York) | 335.3 |
| 12. Carlson Marketing Group (Minneapolis) | 328.5 |
| 13. Incepta Group (London) | 240.9 |
| 14. Protocol Marketing Group (Deerfield, IL) | 225.0 |
| 15. Digitas (Boston) | 203.9 |
| 16. Daiko Advertising (Osaka) | 192.2 |
| 17. Tokyu Agency (Tokyo) | 180.4 |
| 18. Maxxcom (Toronto) | 169.5 |
| 19. Cheil Communications (South Korea) | 165.0 |
| 20. George P. Johnson Co (Auburn Hills, MI) | 149.3 |

Source: Reprinted with permission from the April 23, 2003 issue of Advertising Age. Copyright, Gain Communications Inc. 2003.

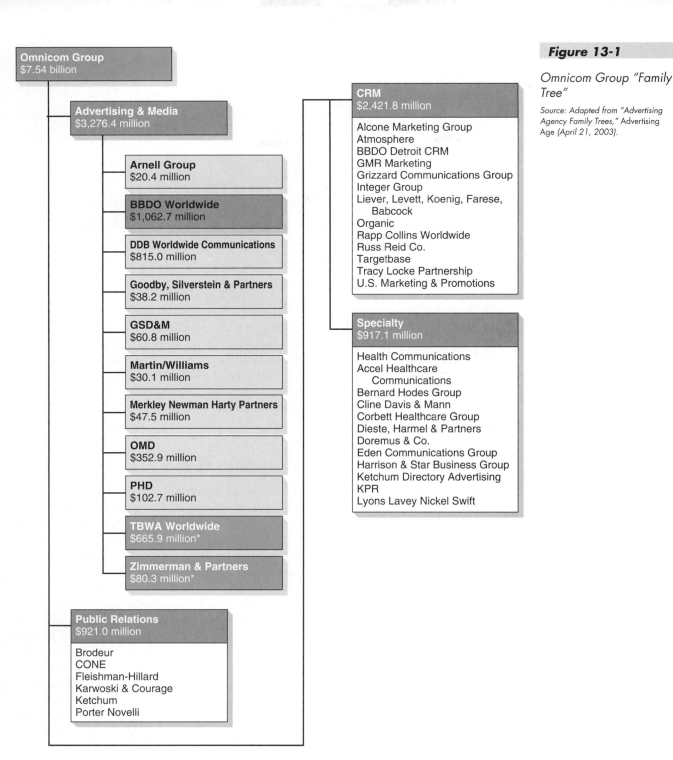

**Figure 13-1**

*Omnicom Group "Family Tree"*

Source: Adapted from "Advertising Agency Family Trees," Advertising Age (April 21, 2003).

**Omnicom Group**
$7.54 billion

**Advertising & Media**
$3,276.4 million

**Arnell Group**
$20.4 million

**BBDO Worldwide**
$1,062.7 million

**DDB Worldwide Communications**
$815.0 million

**Goodby, Silverstein & Partners**
$38.2 million

**GSD&M**
$60.8 million

**Martin/Williams**
$30.1 million

**Merkley Newman Harty Partners**
$47.5 million

**OMD**
$352.9 million

**PHD**
$102.7 million

**TBWA Worldwide**
$665.9 million*

**Zimmerman & Partners**
$80.3 million*

**Public Relations**
$921.0 million

Brodeur
CONE
Fleishman-Hillard
Karwoski & Courage
Ketchum
Porter Novelli

**CRM**
$2,421.8 million

Alcone Marketing Group
Atmosphere
BBDO Detroit CRM
GMR Marketing
Grizzard Communications Group
Integer Group
Liever, Levett, Koenig, Farese,
    Babcock
Organic
Rapp Collins Worldwide
Russ Reid Co.
Targetbase
Tracy Locke Partnership
U.S. Marketing & Promotions

**Specialty**
$917.1 million

Health Communications
Accel Healthcare
    Communications
Bernard Hodes Group
Cline Davis & Mann
Corbett Healthcare Group
Dieste, Harmel & Partners
Doremus & Co.
Eden Communications Group
Harrison & Star Business Group
Ketchum Directory Advertising
KPR
Lyons Lavey Nickel Swift

As shown in Figure 13-1, the family tree of Omnicom Group is quite complex. The group is comprised of several large agencies, including BBDO Worldwide, DDB Worldwide Communications, and TBWA Worldwide. Each of those agency "brands," in turn, includes a variety of firms. Omnicom generates about 45 percent of revenues from advertising and media; public relations accounts for 12.2 percent, customer relationship management (CRM) for 32.1 percent. Specialty services such as health care advertising account for the remaining 12.2 percent of revenues.

**Table 13-3**

*Top 10 Global Advertising
Agency Brands*

| Agency and Headquarters Location | Worldwide Revenue 2002 ($ millions) |
|---|---|
| 1. Dentsu (Tokyo) | 1,442.6 |
| 2. McCann-Erickson Worldwide (New York) | 1,238.5 |
| 3. BBDO Worldwide (New York) | 1,062.7 |
| 4. J. Walter Thompson Co. (New York) | 996.9 |
| 5. Publicis Worldwide (New York) | 909.9 |
| 6. Hakuhodo (Tokyo) | 860.8 |
| 7. DDB Needham Worldwide (New York) | 815.0 |
| 8. Leo Burnett Worldwide (Chicago) | 801.9 |
| 9. TBWA Worldwide (New York) | 665.9 |
| 10. Ogilvy & Mather Worldwide (New York) | 589.4 |

*Source:* Reprinted with permission from the April 21, 2003 issue of *Advertising Age.* Copyright, Crain Communications Inc. 2003.

Individual agencies (agency "brands") are ranked in Table 13-3 by 2002 worldwide income. Most of the agency brands identified in Table 13-3 are **full-service agencies:** In addition to creating advertising, they provide other services such as market research, media buying, and direct marketing. The agencies listed in Table 13-3 are not equally global; Dentsu, for example, derives approximately 85 percent of its revenue from the home market. The need for a broader scope was one reason that Dentsu executives acquired a stake in Leo Burnett at the end of 1998.

## Selecting an Advertising Agency

Companies can create ads in-house, use an outside agency, or combine both strategies. For example, Chanel, Benetton, and Diesel rely on in-house marketing and advertising staffs for creative work; Coca-Cola has its own agency, Edge Creative, but also uses the services of outside agencies such as Leo Burnett. When one or more outside agencies are used, they can serve product accounts on a multicountry or even global basis. It is possible to select a local agency in each national market or an agency with both domestic and overseas offices. Like Coca-Cola, Levi Strauss and Polaroid also use local agencies. Today, however, there is a growing tendency for Western clients to designate global agencies for product accounts to support the integration of the marketing and advertising functions; Japan-based companies are less inclined to use this approach. For example, in 1995, Colgate-Palmolive consolidated its $500 million in global billings with Young & Rubicam. That same year, IBM consolidated its ad account with Ogilvy & Mather for the launch of the "Solutions for a small planet" global campaign. Similarly, Bayer AG consolidated most of its $300 million consumer products advertising with BBDO Worldwide; Bayer had previously relied on 50 agencies around the globe. Agencies are aware of this trend and are themselves pursuing international acquisitions and joint ventures to extend their geographic reach and their ability to serve clients on a global account basis. In an effort to remain competitive, many small independent agencies in Europe, Asia, and the United States belong to the Transworld Advertising Agency Network. TAAN allows member agencies to tap into worldwide resources that would not otherwise be available to them.

In selecting an advertising agency, the following issues should be considered:

*Company organization.* Companies that are decentralized may want to leave the choice to the local subsidiary.
*National responsiveness.* Is the global agency familiar with local culture and buying habits in a particular country or should a local selection be made?
*Area coverage.* Does the candidate agency cover all relevant markets?

## global MARKETING Q&A

**Wall Street Journal:** "As a global marketer, do you believe in using a single global ad agency to serve all your marketing and media needs?"

**Peter Weedfald, Samsung Electronics, senior vice president of strategic marketing, North America:** "The responsibility of messaging for advertising, marketing and communications ought to come from inside the company. If you can find yourself a champion agency that can actually execute, that's magnificent. The problem for the agencies is that sometimes they come in and talk about advertising and maybe the client doesn't get it, or vice versa. We work with Interpublic Group's Foote Cone & Belding which we are very proud of, and our internal agency."

Ellen Byron, "Samsung Official Prepares for Consumer-Electronics Fight," The Wall Street Journal (December 24, 2003), p. B3.

*Buyer perception.* What kind of brand awareness does the company want to project? If the product needs a strong local identification, it would be best to select a national agency.

Despite an unmistakable trend toward using global agencies to support global marketing efforts, companies with geocentric orientations will adapt to the global market requirements and select the best agency or agencies accordingly. For example, Colgate recently acquired the Kolynos line of oral care products in Latin America; McCann-Erickson Worldwide is responsible for that account, even though Young & Rubicam has the bulk of Colgate's business elsewhere. Western agencies still find markets such as South Korea and Japan very complex; similarly, Japanese and Korean agencies find it just as difficult to establish local agency presence in Western markets.

As noted later in the chapter, advertising professionals face escalating pressure to achieve new heights of creativity. Some critics of advertising complain that agencies sometimes try to create advertising that will win awards and generate acclaim and prestige rather than advertising that serves clients' needs. The search for fresh answers to promotion challenges has prompted some client companies to look to new sources for creative ideas. For example, McDonald's historically relied on American agencies for basic creative direction. However, global marketing chief Larry Light recently staged a competition that included agencies from all over the world. A Germany agency devised the "I'm lovin' it" tagline.[13] Leo Burnett China's ideas included a hand signal for McDonald's global campaign. As Light noted, "China just blew our minds. We didn't expect that kind of expression and joy. Our expectation was for more conservatism, much less individuality, and more caution."[14]

## CREATING GLOBAL ADVERTISING

As suggested earlier in the discussion of the adaptation versus standardization debate, the *message* is at the heart of advertising. The particular message and the way it is presented will depend on the advertiser's objective. Is the ad designed to inform, entertain, remind, or persuade? Moreover, in a world characterized by information overload, ads must break through the clutter, grab the audience's

---

[13] Erin White and Shirley Leung, "How Tiny German Shop Landed McDonald's," *The Wall Street Journal* (August 6, 2003), pp B1, B3.

[14] Geoffrey A. Fowler, "Commercial Break: The Art of Selling," *Far Eastern Economic Review* (October 30, 2003), pp. 30–33.

## Regulation of Tobacco Advertising

### China

In 1994, the Chinese government banned tobacco advertising from television and radio; the ban also extended to newspaper, magazine, and cinema ads. With a population of 1.2 billion people, including one-third of the world's smokers, China is considered to be a massive potential market for cigarette manufacturers at a time when Western markets are shrinking. The ban was part of China's first law of advertisements. The World Health Organization has asked Chinese leaders to launch antismoking campaigns and impose tougher controls on cigarette smuggling and higher taxes on domestic cigarette producers.

### Central Europe

Tobacco companies face the prospect of tougher marketing regulations as countries in Central Europe work to meet requirements for entry into the EU. In the Czech Republic, the Association of Advertising Agencies (ARA) is battling a proposal to ban all cigarette advertising as of April 2001. Jiri Mikes, vice president of ARA, said his organization was not completely opposed to changes in the law, but questioned the government's implementation date since the EU's deadline for meeting tobacco advertising restrictions was not until 2006. In Lithuania, authorities began to enforce the country's 3-year-old tobacco advertising ban on May 1, 2000; some newspapers printed blank pages in protest. Jurga Karmanoviene, media director for Saatchi & Saatchi Lithuania, interprets the enforcement as evidence that the government is sending a signal that it is beginning to meet EU requirements. Similar developments are occurring in Poland, Hungary, Bulgaria, and Romania.

### Australia

In June 1994, the Philip Morris Company initiated legal action to overturn the Australian government's ban on cigarette advertising, contending that it infringed on the company's freedom of speech. Under legislation passed in 1992, tobacco advertising and sponsorship in Australia was phased out and banned entirely by 1996, except for international events such as Formula One racing. Philip Morris attempted to have the Commonwealth Tobacco Advertising Prohibition Act declared invalid on the grounds that the act went beyond preventing cigarette advertising and imposed a wide array of restrictions that infringe on basic rights. According to a company executive, "The Philip Morris Australian subsidiary says the anti-tobacco laws breach the Australian Constitution's implied guarantee of freedom of communication, breaches the states and is beyond the powers of the federal Government."

### European Union

A union-wide tobacco ad ban proposal was introduced in mid-1991 with the aim of fulfilling single-market rules of the Maastricht Treaty. The directive would have prohibited tobacco advertising on billboards as of July 2001; newspaper and magazine advertising was slated to end by 2002, with sports sponsorship banned by 2003 (such "world level" sports as Formula One racing would be excluded until 2006). Not surprisingly, the proposed ban was opposed by tobacco companies and advertising associations. The European Commission justified the directive on the grounds that various countries had or were considering restrictions on tobacco advertising and that there was a need for common rules on cross-border trade. Prior to the directive's implementation date, however, the German government took the issue to the European Court of Justice. The Germans argued that the directive was illegal because tobacco advertising is a health issue; thus, the directive could only be adopted if the member states agreed unanimously. The EU's advocate general concurred with the German government. On October 5, 2000, the court ruled that that the directive prohibiting tobacco ads should be annulled. A revised directive concerning cross-border tobacco advertising was adopted in December 2002; it is scheduled to take effect in July 2005. However, the German government is challenging the new directive on the grounds that it would restrict single-country print advertisements for local cigarette brands.

For RJ Reynolds International, Philip Morris International, B.A.T, and other tobacco marketers, the receding threat of a pan-European ban on tobacco ads comes as welcome news. The industry spends between $600 million and $1 billion on advertising in the EU annually. An EU ban would have hurt them most in the countries where they compete with entrenched state tobacco monopolies, namely, France, Italy, and Spain.

*Sources: Geoffrey A. Fowler, "Treaty May Stub Out Cigarette Ads in China," The Wall Street Journal (December 2, 2003), pp. B1, B6; Joyce-Ann Gatsoulis, "EU Aspirants Shake Up Tobacco Marketing Scene," Advertising Age International (July 2000), p. 15; Tony Koenderman and Paul Meller, "EU Topples Tobacco Ad Rules," Advertising Age (October 9, 2000), pp. 4, 97; Juliana Koranteng, "EU Ad Ban on Tobacco Under Fire as Illegal," Advertising Age (July 10, 2000), pp. 4, 49; "Australia's Ad Ban is Fought," The New York Times (June 7, 1994), p. 19; Marcus Brauchli, "China Passes Law in Move to Prohibit Ads for Tobacco," The Wall Street Journal, (October 31, 1994), p. B10; Lili Cui, "Mass Media Boycott Tobacco Ads," Beijing Review (June 6, 1994) p. 8; "Tobacco Adverts: Fuming," The Economist (February 5, 1994), pp. 60–61.*

attention, and linger in their minds. This requires developing an original and effective **creative strategy,** which is simply a statement or concept of what a particular message or campaign will say. Advertising agencies can be thought of as "idea factories"; in industry parlance, the Holy Grail in creative strategy development is something known as the **big idea.** Legendary ad man John O'Toole defined the *big idea* as "that flash of insight that synthesizes the purpose of the strategy, joins the product benefit with consumer desire in a fresh, involving way, brings the subject to life, and makes the reader or audience stop, look, and listen."[15] In his book about Subaru of America, Randall Rothenberg describes the big idea in the following way:

> The Big Idea is easier to illustrate than define, and easier to illustrate by what it is not than by what it is. It is not a "position" (although the place a product occupies in the consumer's mind may be a part of it). It is not an "execution" (although the writing or graphic style of an ad certainly contributes to it). It is not a slogan (although a tag line may encapsulate it).
>
> The Big Idea is the bridge between an advertising strategy, temporal and worldly, and an image, powerful and lasting. The theory of the Big Idea assumes that average consumers are at best bored and more likely irrational when it comes to deciding what to buy.[16]

Some of the world's most memorable advertising campaigns have achieved success because they originate from an idea that is so "big" that the campaign offers opportunities for a variety of new executions. Such a campaign is said to have *legs* because it can be used for long periods of time. The print campaign for Absolut vodka is a perfect example: Over the course two decades, Absolut's agency has created hundreds of two-word puns on the brand name linked with various pictoral renderings of the distinctive bottle shape. Other campaigns based on big ideas include MSN ("Life's better with the butterfly") and MasterCard ("There are some things in life money can't buy"). In 2003, McDonald's executives launched a search for an idea "big" enough to be used in multiple country markets even as the company faces disapproval in some countries from consumers who link it to unpopular U.S. government policies (See Case 1-1).

The **advertising appeal** is the communications approach that relates to the motives of the target audience. For example, ads based on a **rational appeal** depend on logic and speak to the audience's intellect. Rational appeals are based on consumers' needs for information. Ads using an **emotional appeal** may tug at the heartstrings or tickle the funny bone of the intended audience and evoke a feeling response that will direct purchase behavior. The message elements in a particular ad will depend in part on which appeal is being employed. The **selling proposition** is the promise or claim that captures the reason for buying the product or the benefit that ownership confers. Because products are frequently at different stages in their life cycle in various national markets, and because of cultural, social, and economic differences that exist in those markets, the most effective appeal or selling proposition for a product may vary from market to market.

Effective global advertising may also require developing different presentations of the product's appeal or selling proposition. The way an appeal or proposition is presented is called the **creative execution.** In other words, there can be differences between *what* one says and *how* one says it. Many execution alternatives are available including straight sell, scientific evidence, demonstration, comparison, testimonial, slice of life, animation, fantasy, and dramatization. The responsibility for deciding on the appeal, the selling proposition, and the appropriate execution lies with **creatives,** a term that applies to art directors and copywriters.

To illustrate the relationship between creative strategy, appeal, and execution, consider the creative challenge presented to Ogilvy & Mather in China. The client, Coca-Cola's Fanta, wanted a national TV ad that would communicate to consumers that "Fanta is an antidote to everyday pressures on Chinese youth." This was the overall creative strategy; in other words, what the message should say. What type of appeal would be appropriate? Not surprisingly, soft drinks lend themselves especially well to emotional appeals; that was the appeal Ogilvy & Mather preferred. The next step was to choose a specific execution. Soft drink marketers often utilize slice-of-life and fantasy executions, usually injected with an element of fun or

---

[15] John O'Toole, *The Trouble with Advertising* (New York: Random House, 1985), p. 131.
[16] Randall Rothenberg, *Where the Suckers Moon* (New York: Vintage Books, 1995), pp. 112–113.

humor. As Jeff Delkin, Ogilvy's regional business director in Shanghai, notes, for a U.S. ad, the creative strategy could be executed with a teen's fantasy or images of revenge on a mean teacher. However, in China, it is not acceptable to challenge or undermine the position of authority figures such as teachers and parents. The completed ad shows that drinking Fanta can create a fun experience in a classroom. When a student opens a can of Fanta, oranges begin to rain down. The teacher catches the oranges and juggles them—much to the delight of the students.[17]

## Art Directors and Art Direction

The visual presentation of an advertisement—the "body language"—is a matter of **art direction.** An **art director** is an advertising professional who has the general responsibility for the overall look of an ad. In addition, the art director chooses graphics, pictures, type styles, and other visual elements that appear in an ad. Some forms of visual presentation are universally understood. Revlon, for example, has used a French producer to develop television commercials in English and Spanish for use in international markets. These commercials are filmed in Parisian settings but communicate the universal appeals and specific benefits of Revlon products. By producing its ads in France, Revlon obtains effective television commercials at a much lower cost than it would have paid for commercials produced in the United States. PepsiCo has used four basic commercials to communicate its advertising themes. The basic setting of young people having fun at a party or on a beach has been adapted to reflect the general physical environment and racial characteristics of North America, South America, Europe, Africa, and Asia. The music in these commercials has also been adapted to suit regional tastes, ranging from rock 'n' roll in North America to bossa nova in Latin America to high life in Africa.

The global advertiser must make sure that visual executions are not inappropriately extended into markets. Benetton recently encountered a problem with its United Colors of Benetton campaign. The campaign appeared in scores of countries, primarily in print and on billboards. The art direction focused on striking, provocative interracial juxtapositions—a white hand and a black hand handcuffed together, for example. Another version of the campaign, depicting a black woman nursing a white baby, won advertising awards in France and Italy. However, because the image evoked the history of slavery in the United States, that particular creative execution was not used in the U.S. market (see Case 13-1).

## Copy

The words that are the spoken or written communication elements in advertisements are known as **copy. Copywriters** are language specialists who develop the headlines, subheads, and body copy used in print advertising and the scripts containing the words that are delivered by spokespeople, actors, or hired voice talents in broadcast ads. As a general rule, copy should be relatively short and avoid slang or idioms. Languages vary in terms of the number of words required to convey a given message; thus the increased use of pictures and illustrations. Some global ads feature visual appeals that convey a specific message with minimal use of copy. Low literacy rates in many countries seriously compromise the use of print as a communications device and require greater creativity in the use of audio-oriented media.

It is important to recognize overlap in the use of languages in many areas of the world (e.g., the European Union, Latin America, and North America).

*"There is a tradition in France of advertising as an extension of the arts, and the arts have always been seen as a sacrosanct area of free expression. You get the feeling that copywriters and photographers have the same extent of protected expression that Michelangelo or Andy Warhol might have claimed."*

Seth Goldschlager,
Publicis Groupe, Paris[18]

---

[17]  Geoffrey A. Fowler, "Commercial Break: The Art of Selling," *Eastern Economic Review* (October 30, 2003), p. 32.

[18]  Elaine Sciolino, "Advertising: A Campaign to Shock the Bourgeoisie in France," *The Wall Street Journal* (January 21, 2003), p. C14.

# OPEN *to* discussion

## Are Advertising Agencies Ready for the Twenty-First Century?

In a recent speech, Martin Sorrell, CEO of the WPP Group, warned of changes in the business environment that have enormous implications for the advertising industry. Quoting business gurus such as Harvard professor John Kao and management author-philosopher Charles Handy, Sorrell suggested that the information age is already giving way to the creative age, an era that will require not just creativity, but *actionable* creativity. The problem, in Sorrell's view, is twofold: client companies aren't yet asking for "actionable creativity," and few advertising agencies are prepared to offer it. Sorrell noted:

> We must first recognize ourselves, and then convey to others, that creativity is not simply about communications . . . I believe that, over the last 30 years and in most parts of the world, agencies have become more, rather than less, specialized in the forms of creativity they offer. By "more specialized," I mean more narrowly focused and therefore more limited.
>
> There was once a time when client companies would welcome an agency's thoughts on just about all aspects of their business: diversification, brand strategy, investment, internal training, presentation—as well as advertising and promotion. For a wide variety of reasons, all that has changed: certainly in the US and the UK. Increasingly, clients expect only creativity in their communications from their agencies—and, increasingly, that's all that agencies are organized to provide.

Sorrell continued by cautioning that in today's world, it is not enough for creativity to be the exclusive domain of agency creatives:

> In a business world that is going to put a higher and higher value on integrated creativity, we are in danger of losing what should be our overwhelming advantage—by allowing something called "creativity" to be confined to the creative compound. What we sell are pearls. Whether we are designers or planners or writers or art directors or corporate strategists, our raw material is knowledge. We turn that knowledge into ideas, insights, and objects that have a material, quantifiable value to our clients. They are all pearls: of wisdom, of beauty, of desire, of wonder.

Sorrell concluded his remarks by noting that advertising agencies will have to develop new organizational forms, structures, and processes to remain competitive in the twenty-first century. In particular, he suggests that agency personnel have much to learn from their "creative cousins"—those who work in the theater, the arts, and electronic publishing and design.

Capitalizing on this, global advertisers can realize economies of scale by producing advertising copy with the same language and message for these markets. Of course, the success of this approach will depend in part on avoiding unintended ambiguity in the ad copy. Then again, in some situations, ad copy must be translated into the local language. Translating copy has been the subject of great debate in advertising circles. Advertising slogans often present the most difficult translation problems. The challenge of encoding and decoding slogans and tag lines in different national and cultural contexts can lead to unintentional errors. For example, the Asian version of Pepsi's "Come alive" copy line was rendered as a call to bring ancestors back from the grave.

Advertising executives may elect to prepare new copy for a foreign market in the language of the target country or to translate the original copy into the target language. A third option is to leave some (or all) copy elements in the original (home-country) language. In choosing from these alternatives, the advertiser must consider whether a translated message can be received and comprehended by the intended foreign audience. Anyone with knowledge of two or more languages realizes that the ability to think in another language facilitates accurate communication. To be confident that a message will be understood correctly after it is received, one must understand the connotations of words, phrases, and sentence structures, as well as their translated meaning.

The same principle applies to advertising—perhaps to an even greater degree. A copywriter who can think in the target language and understands the consumers in the target country will be able to create the most effective appeals, organize the ideas, and craft the specific language, especially if colloquialisms, idioms, or humor are involved. For example, in southern China, McDonald's is careful not to advertise prices with multiple occurrences of the number 4. The reason is simple: In Cantonese, the pronunciation of the word *four* is similar to that of the word *death.*[19] In its efforts to develop a global brand image, Citicorp discovered that translations of its slogan "Citi never sleeps" conveyed the meaning that Citibank had a sleeping disorder such as insomnia. Company executives decided to retain the slogan but use English throughout the world.[20]

## Cultural Considerations

Knowledge of cultural diversity, especially the symbolism associated with cultural traits, is essential for creating advertising. Local country managers can share important information, such as when to use caution in advertising creativity. Use of colors and man-woman relationships can often be stumbling blocks. For example, in Japan, intimate scenes between men and women are considered to be in bad taste; they are outlawed in Saudi Arabia. Veteran adman John O'Toole offers the following insights to global advertisers:

> Transplanted American creative people always want to photograph European men kissing women's hands. But they seldom know that the nose must never touch the hand or that this rite is reserved solely for married women. And how do you know that the woman in the photograph is married? By the ring on her left hand, of course. Well, in Spain, Denmark, Holland, and Germany, Catholic women wear the wedding ring on the right hand.
>
> When photographing a couple entering a restaurant or theater, you show the woman preceding the man, correct? No. Not in Germany and France. And this would be laughable in Japan. Having someone in a commercial hold up his hand with the back of it to you, the viewer, and the fingers moving toward him should communicate "come here." In Italy it means "good-bye."[21]

Ads that strike viewers in some countries as humorous or irritating may not necessarily be perceived that way by viewers in other countries. American ads make frequent use of spokespeople and direct product comparisons; they use logical arguments to try to appeal to the reason of audiences. Japanese advertising is more image oriented and appeals to audience sentiment. In Japan, what is most important frequently is not what is stated explicitly but, rather, what is implied. Nike's U.S. advertising is legendary for its irreverent, "in your face" style and relies heavily on celebrity sports endorsers such as Michael Jordan. In other parts of the world, where soccer is the top sport, some Nike ads are considered to be in poor taste and its pitchmen have less relevance. Nike has responded by adjusting its approach; notes Geoffrey Frost, director of global advertising, "We have to root ourselves in the passions of other countries. It's part of our growing up."[22] Some American companies have canceled television ads created for the Latin American market portraying racial stereotypes that were offensive to persons of color. Nabisco, Goodyear, and other companies are also being more careful about the shows during which they buy airtime; some very popular Latin American programs feature content that exploits class, race, and ethnic differences.[23]

There are also widely varying standards for use of sexually explicit or provocative imagery. Partial nudity and same-sex couples are frequently seen in ads in Latin America and Europe. In the U.S. market, advertisers are constrained by network television decency standards and the threat of boycotts by conservative consumer

---

19 Jeanne Whalen, "McDonald's Cooks Worldwide Growth," *Advertising Age International* (July–August 1995), p. I4.
20 Stephen E. Frank, "Citicorp's Big Account Is at Stake as It Seeks a Global Brand Name," *The Wall Street Journal* (January 9, 1997), p. B6.
21 John O'Toole, *The Trouble with Advertising* (New York: Random House, 1985), pp. 209–210.
22 Roger Thurow, "Shtick Ball: In Global Drive, Nike Finds Its Brash Ways Don't Always Pay Off," *The Wall Street Journal* (May 5, 1997), p. A10.
23 Leon E. Wynter, "Global Marketers Learn to Say 'No' to Bad Ads," *The Wall Street Journal* (April 1, 1998), p. B1.

**Wall Street Journal:** "For more than a decade, international marketers have focused on creating global marketing strategies. Why do you maintain the pendulum is swinging back to a more local approach?"

**Sir Martin Sorrell, CEO, WPP Group:** "What's happened is that companies are trying to run things in black and white ways, where one size fits all. And there's a very simple message: One size doesn't fit all. Consumers are more interesting for their differences rather than their similarities."

**Wall Street Journal:** "If one size doesn't fit all, should companies be marketing to certain consumer groups, such as Muslims, with specific messages?"

**Sir Martin:** "Yes, just as they'd market to Hispanics, Afro-Americans, or Asians. Muslims are 26 percent of the world's population today; by 2014, they will be 30 percent. That same year, two-thirds of the world's population will be Asian. Muslims are coming into sharp relief because of Iraq and Afghanistan. But the central theme is that nobody in the West has really spent enough time thinking about what differentiates the Muslim mind. We assume that if it works in New York it will work in Baghdad, but there are significant differences. There has to be more sensitivity to this issue."

Source: Erin White and Jeffrey A. Trachtenberg, "One Size Doesn't Fit All," The Wall Street Journal (October 1, 2003), p. B1.

activists. Some industry observers note a paradoxical situation in which the programs shown on U.S. TV are frequently racy, but the ads that air during those shows are not. As Marcio Moreira, worldwide chief creative officer at the McCann-Erickson agency, noted "Americans want titillation in entertainment but when it comes to advertising they stop being viewers and become consumers and critics."[24] However, it is certainly not the case that anything goes outside the United States. Women in Monterrey, Mexico, recently complained about billboards for the Playtex unit of Sara Lee Corporation that featured supermodel Eva Herzegova wearing a Wonderbra. The campaign was created by a local agency, Perez Munoz Publicidad. Playtex responded by covering up the model on the billboards in some Mexican cities. French Connection UK made waves in the United States recently with print ads that prominently featured the British company's initials (i.e., FCUK). Public outcry prompted the company to tone down the ads by spelling out the name.

Food is the product category most likely to exhibit cultural sensitivity. Thus, marketers of food and food products must be alert to the need to localize their advertising. A good example of this is the effort by H. J. Heinz Company to develop the overseas market for ketchup. Heinz's strategy called for adapting both the product and advertising to target country tastes.[25] In Greece, for example, ads show ketchup pouring over pasta, eggs, and cuts of meat. In Japan, they instruct Japanese homemakers on using ketchup as an ingredient in Western-style food such as omelettes, sausages, and pasta. Barry Tilley, London-based general manager of Heinz's Western Hemisphere trading division, says Heinz uses focus groups to determine what foreign consumers want in the way of taste and image. Americans like a sweet ketchup, but Europeans prefer a spicier, more piquant variety. Significantly, Heinz's foreign marketing efforts are most successful when the company quickly adapts to local cultural preferences. In Sweden, the made-in-America theme is so muted in Heinz's ads that "Swedes don't realize Heinz is

---

24  Melanie Wells and Dottie Enrico, "U.S. Admakers Cover It Up; Others Don't Give a Fig Leaf," *USA Today* (June 27, 1997), pp. B1, B2.
25  Gary Levin, "Ads Going Global," *Advertising Age* (July 22, 1991), pp. 4, 42.

American. They think it is German because of the name," says Tilley. In contrast to this, American themes still work well in Germany. Kraft and Heinz are trying to outdo each other with ads featuring strong American images. In one of Heinz's TV ads, American football players in a restaurant become very angry when the 12 steaks they ordered arrive without ketchup. The ad ends happily, of course, with plenty of Heinz ketchup to go around.[26]

Much academic research has been devoted to the impact of culture on advertising. For example, Tamotsu Kishii identified seven characteristics that distinguish Japanese from American creative strategy:

1. Indirect rather than direct forms of expression are preferred in the messages. This avoidance of directness in expression is pervasive in all types of communication among the Japanese, including their advertising. Many television ads do not mention what is desirable about the brand in use and let the audience judge for themselves.
2. There is often little relationship between ad content and the advertised product.
3. Only brief dialogue or narration is used in television commercials, with minimal explanatory content. In the Japanese culture, the more one talks, the less others will perceive him or her trustworthy or self-confident. A 30-second advertisement for young menswear shows five models in varying and seasonal attire, ending with a brief statement from the narrator: "Our life is a fashion show!"
4. Humor is used to create a bond of mutual feelings. Rather than slapstick, humorous dramatizations involve family members, neighbors, and office colleagues.
5. Famous celebrities appear as close acquaintances or everyday people.
6. Priority is placed on company trust rather than product quality. Japanese tend to believe that if the firm is large and has a good image, the quality of its products should also be outstanding.
7. The product name is impressed on the viewer with short, 15-second commercials.[27]

Green, Cunningham, and Cunningham conducted a cross-cultural study to determine the extent to which consumers of different nationalities use the same criteria to evaluate soft drinks and toothpaste. Their subjects were college students from the United States, France, India, and Brazil. Compared to France and India, the U.S. respondents placed more emphasis on the subjective, as opposed to functional, product attributes. The Brazilian respondents appeared even more concerned with the subjective attributes than the Americans were. The authors concluded that advertising messages should not use the same appeal for these countries if the advertiser is concerned with communicating the most important attributes of its product in each market.[28]

In Chapter 4 we cited a study by Martin Ross that used Hofstede's social values framework to predict the effectiveness of advertising that presented functional, social, and sensory brand images in different countries. In another study, Zandpour and Harich combined Hofstede's social values framework with a culture's perceptions of

[26] Gabriella Stern, "Heinz Aims to Export Taste for Ketchup," *The Wall Street Journal* (November 20, 1992), p. B1.
[27] C. Anthony Di Benedetto, Mariko Tamate, and Rajan Chandran, "Developing Creative Advertising Strategy for the Japanese Marketplace," *Journal of Advertising Research* (January–February 1992), pp. 39–48. A number of recent studies have been devoted to comparing ad content in different parts of the world, including Mary C. Gilly, "Sex Roles in Advertising: A Comparison of Television Advertisements in Australia, Mexico, and the United States," *Journal of Marketing* (April 1988), pp. 75–85; Marc G. Weinberger and Harlan E. Spotts, "A Situation View of Information Content in TV Advertising in the U.S. and U.K.," *Journal of Advertising* 53 (January 1989), pp. 89–94.
[28] Robert T. Green, William H. Cunningham, and Isabella C. M. Cunningham, "The Effectiveness of Standardized Global Advertising," *Journal of Advertising* (Summer 1975), pp. 25–30.

Figure 13-2

"Think" and "Feel" Country Clusters

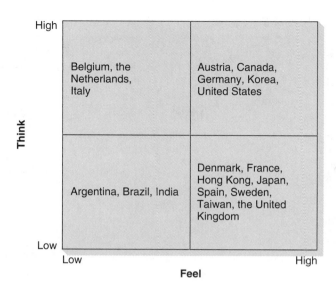

time (monochronic cultures focus on one thing at a time, while inhabitants of a polychronic culture do not display a preference for sequential schedules or presentation of information). Several relevant market factors were also studied, including advertising expenditures per capita, the presence or absence of U.S. advertising agencies or their affiliates, the availability of qualified advertising professionals, and the degree of government control over advertising. The researchers used these factors to group countries into "think" and "feel" clusters and predict whether rational or emotional appeals used in television advertising for food and beverage, personal care, and several other product categories would be most prevalent in a given country market.

The researchers divided rational appeals into *argument* (the ad relates facts or reasons why the purchase should be made) and *lecture* (ads are devoid of fictional characters or plot elements; rather, they include narration that directly addresses the audience and provides an explicit conclusion). Emotional appeals were classified as *dramatic* (narration, character, and plot are key message elements) and *psychological* (explicit statements of how the product will benefit the consumer; desire is created by appealing to a consumer's self-interest). The findings are summarized in Figure 13-2 and Table 13-4. Figure 13-2 places the countries studied in a matrix classifying them

| Type of Appeal | Cultural/Market Factors | Countries Where Appeal Is Appropriate |
|---|---|---|
| Rational/argument | Monochronic cultures with low power distance; high uncertainty avoidance; good supply of marketing professionals | Austria, Belgium, Germany, Italy, United States |
| Rational/lecture | Collectivist cultures with high power distance and high uncertainty avoidance | Belgium, Italy, Mexico |
| Emotional/psychological | Collectivist cultures with high power distance; high advertising expenditures; strict government control | Hong Kong, Taiwan, France, United States, South Korea, Spain |
| Emotional/dramatic | High power distance; high advertising expenditures; limited supply of advertising professionals | Hong Kong, France, Japan |

*Source:* Adapted from Fred Zandpour and Katrin R. Harich, "Think and Feel Country Clusters: A New Approach to International Advertising Standardization," *International Journal of Advertising* 15, no. 4 (1996), pp. 325–344.

in terms of the dimensions "think" and "feel." For example, the researchers rank Austria, Canada, Germany, South Korea, and the United States high on both dimensions; consumers in these countries are presumed to be receptive to television advertising employing either rational or emotional appeals.[29] Table 13-4 is intended to be a guide to creating standardized appeals in terms of the clusters; for example, a standardized ad employing a rational/argument appeal could be translated as appropriate and used to good effect in Austria, Belgium, Italy, and the United States. Many German companies, for example, prefer ads that contain plenty of copy that presents a rational argument for a product's superiority. This is typical of ads for beer, automobiles, and food products. However, many creative campaigns are based on the understanding that sometimes the best approach is to disregard guidelines and break some so-called rules. Recent German ads for the Mini Cooper are definitely offbeat when compared to mainstream auto ads.[30]

## GLOBAL MEDIA DECISIONS

The next issue facing advertisers is which medium or media to use when communicating with target audiences. In some instances, the agency that creates advertising also makes recommendations about media placement; however, many advertisers use the services of specialized media planning and buying organizations. The available alternatives can be broadly categorized as print media, electronic media, and other. Print media range in form from local daily and weekly newspapers to magazines and business publications with national, regional, or international audiences. Electronic media include broadcast television, cable television, radio, and the Internet. Additionally, advertisers may utilize various forms of outdoor, transit, and direct mail advertising. Globally, media decisions must take into account country specific regulations. For example, France bans retailers from advertising on television.

---

[29] Fred Zandpour and Katrin R. Harich, "Think and Feel Country Clusters: A New Approach to International Advertising Standardization," *International Journal of Advertising* 15, no. 4 (1996), pp. 325–344.

[30] Erin White, "German Ads Get More Daring, but Some Firms Aren't Pleased," *The Wall Street Journal* (November 22, 2002), p. B6.

Media availability can vary from country to country. Some companies use virtually the entire spectrum of available media; Coca-Cola is a good example. Other companies prefer to utilize one or two media categories. Benetton, for example, relied exclusively on print and outdoor media for many years. The same was true of the Swatch Group's advertising for Swatch watches. However, faced with increasing competition with Timex in the U.S. fashion watch market, Swatch rolled out a new line of metal watches in 1995. Simultaneously, Swatch began using television advertising for the first time in conjunction with its sponsorship of the 1996 Olympics. As Denise Benou, vice president of marketing at Swatch, noted, "People know our brand, but they don't have as clear an awareness of what Swatch is today. We needed to show that we don't have limited appeal."[31]

## Media Vehicles and Expenditures

As shown in Table 13-5, more money is spent on advertising in the United States than anywhere else in the world. In fact, expenditures in the United States are more than four times greater than in the second-ranked country, which is Japan. As one might expect, the largest per capita advertising expenditures occur in highly developed countries. The lowest per capita expenditures are in the less-developed countries. Television is the number one medium in seven of the nine nations included in Table 13-5; newspapers are the leading medium in Germany and Japan, with television ranked second. In Germany, outlays for newspaper advertising surpass those for television by a ratio of two to one. By contrast, in Brazil, expenditures on television advertising are nearly three times higher than those for newspapers. The availability of media to advertisers and the conditions affecting media buys vary greatly around the world. In Mexico, an advertiser that can pay for a full-page ad may get the front page, while in India, paper shortages may require booking an ad six months in advance. In some countries, especially those where the electronic media are government owned, television and radio stations can broadcast only a restricted number of advertising messages. In Saudi Arabia, no commercial television advertising was allowed prior to May 1986; currently, ad content and visual presentation are restricted.

The United States and Japan lead the world in television advertising with combined expenditures in 2000 of $67 billion. In real terms, television spending in the European Union increased by 78 percent between 1990 and 2000, compared with 26 percent for newspapers and 11 percent for magazines during the same period.

| Country | Total Ad Spending 2000 ($ billions) |
|---|---|
| United States | 134.3 |
| Japan | 33.2 |
| Germany | 21.6 |
| United Kingdom | 15.8 |
| France | 11.1 |
| Italy | 8.3 |
| Brazil | 6.9 |
| Spain | 5.4 |
| Canada | 5.3 |

**Table 13-5**

*Top Countries for Ad Expenditures*

Sources: Adapted from "Top Countries for Ad Expenditures." Zenith Media, *The Economist*.

---

[31] Fara Warner, "Timex, Swatch Get Set for Battle with Expensive Ad Campaigns," *The Wall Street Journal* (May 31, 1995), p. B8.

**Table 13-6**

*Media Allocation in Asia*

| Medium | 2004 (%) | 2003 (%) |
|---|---|---|
| Radio | 3 | 4 |
| CRM/digital/interactive | 8 | 6 |
| Out-of-home | 9 | 6 |
| Magazine | 15 | 14 |
| Total print | 28 | 30 |
| Total TV | 36 | 40 |

Source: Wall Street Journal. Online by JP Morgan. Copyright 2004 by Dow Jones & Co. Inc. Reproduced with permission of Dow Jones & Co, Inc. in the format Textbook via Copyright Clearance Center.

This trend is likely to continue as digital broadcasting gains acceptance in Europe. Television is also important in the Latin American market. Of the 10 countries where more than 50 percent of measured media expenditures are allocated to television, most are located in Central or South America or the Caribbean. In Brazil, for example, television accounts for 60 percent of advertising spending. As ownership of television sets increases in other areas of the world such as Southeast Asia, television advertising will become more important as a communication vehicle.

Worldwide, radio continues to be a less important advertising medium than print and television. In Asia, for example, radio's proportion of total measured media advertising expenditures trails considerably behind print, television, and direct advertising (see Table 13-6). However, in countries where advertising budgets are limited, radio's enormous reach can provide a cost-effective means of communicating with a large consumer market. Also, radio can be effective in countries where literacy rates are low. Table 13-6 also shows a trend that is gaining traction throughout the world: Spending on customer relationship management and interactive advertising is gaining ground at the expense of TV and print.

As countries add mass transportation systems and build and improve their highway infrastructures, advertisers are utilizing more indoor and outdoor posters and billboards to reach the buying public. Worldwide spending on outdoor advertising amounted to about 6 percent of total ad spending; in Europe, 6.4 percent of advertising spending is allocated to outdoor, compared with 4 percent in the United States (see Table 13-7). Key players in the outdoor advertising include Texas-based Clear Channel Communications, with more than 775,000 outdoor and transit displays worldwide, New York media conglomerate Viacom, and France's JCDecaux. Japan's population relies heavily on public transportation; the average Tokyo resident spends 70 minutes commuting to work. Consequently, spending on outdoor and transit advertising in Japan is much higher than in most other countries; an estimated $4.4 billion annual expenditures on outdoor media amounts to as much as 12 percent of total ad spending.[32]

**Table 13-7**

*Expenditures for Outdoor Advertising as Percentage of Total Ad Spending*

| Country | Percentage |
|---|---|
| France | 11.7 |
| United Kingdom | 5.8 |
| Spain | 5.4 |
| Italy | 4.3 |
| Canada | 4.2 |
| United States | 4.0 |
| Germany | 4.0 |
| Worldwide | 5.9 |

Source: Adapted from "Expenditures for Outdoor Advertising" Zenith Optimedia Group.

[32] Geoffrey A. Fowler and Sebastian Moffett, "Adidas's Billboard Ads Give a Kick to Japanese Pedestrians," *The Wall Street Journal* (August 29, 2003), pp. B1, B4.

# Media Decisions

Although markets are becoming increasingly similar in industrial countries, the availability of television, newspapers, and other forms of electronic and print media varies around the world. This fact of life has a direct impact on media decisions. For example, circulation figures of newspapers on a per capita basis cover a wide range. In Japan, readership is high; according to a recent study by RoperASW, 77 percent of adults in Japan read the newspaper regularly. There is one newspaper in circulation for every two people. By contrast, in the United States, 42 percent of adults read newspapers regularly. Approximately 65 million newspapers are in daily circulation in the United States, a per capita ratio of one to four. The ratio is one paper to approximately 20 people in Latin America, and one to 200 persons in Nigeria and Sweden.

Even when media availability is high, its use as an advertising vehicle may be limited. For example, in Europe, television advertising either does not exist or is extremely limited in Denmark, Sweden, and Norway. The time allowed for advertising each day varies from 12 minutes in Finland to 80 in Italy, with 12 minutes per hour per channel allowed in France and 20 in Switzerland, Germany, and Austria. Regulations concerning content of commercials vary, and there are waiting periods of up to 2 years in several countries before an advertiser can obtain broadcast time. In Germany, advertising time slots are reserved and paid for 1 year in advance.

In Saudi Arabia, where all advertising is subject to censorship, regulations prohibit a long list of subject matter, including the following:

> Advertisements of horoscope or fortune-telling books, publications, or magazines are prohibited.
>
> Advertisements that frighten or disturb children are to be avoided.
>
> Use of preludes to advertisements that appear to indicate a news item or official statement are to be avoided
>
> Use of comparative advertising claims is prohibited.
>
> Noncensored films cannot be advertised.
>
> Women may only appear in those commercials that relate to family affairs, and their appearance must be in a decent manner that ensures their feminine dignity.
>
> Female children under 6 years of age may appear in commercials, provided that their roles are limited to a childhood-like activity.
>
> Women should wear a long, suitable dress, which fully covers the body except face and palms. Sweat suits or similar garments are not allowed.[33]

# PUBLIC RELATIONS AND PUBLICITY

**Public relations** (PR) is the department or function responsible for evaluating public opinion about, and attitudes toward, the organization and its products and brands. Public relations personnel also are responsible for fostering goodwill, understanding, and acceptance among a company's various constituents and publics. Like advertising, public relations is one of four variables in the promotion mix. One of the tasks of the PR practitioner is to generate favorable **publicity.** By definition, publicity is communication about a company or product for which the company does not pay. (In the PR world, publicity is sometimes referred to as

---

[33] National Trade Data Bank: The Export Connection, USDOC, *International Trade Administration, Market Research Reports* (October 2, 1992). See also Mushtag Luqmani, Ugur Yavas, and Zahir Quraeshi, "Advertising in Saudi Arabia: Content and Regulation," *International Marketing Review* 6, no. 1 (1989), pp. 59–72.

"earned media," and advertising and promotions are known as "unearned media"). PR personnel also play a key role in responding to unflattering media reports or controversies that arise because of company activities in different parts of the globe. In such instances, PR's job is to make sure that the company responds promptly and gets its side of the story told. The basic tools of public relations include news releases, newsletters, media kits, press conferences, tours of plants and other company facilities, articles in trade or professional journals, company publications and brochures, TV and radio talk show appearances by company personnel, special events, and home pages on the Internet. In addition to the examples discussed in the following pages, Table 13-8 summarizes several recent instances of negative global publicity involving well-known firms.

As noted earlier, a company exerts complete control over the content of its advertising and pays for message placement in the media. However, the media typically receive many more press releases and other public relations materials than they can use. Generally speaking, a company has little control over when, or if, a news story runs, nor can the company directly control the spin, slant, or tone of the story. To compensate for this lack of control, many companies utilize **corporate advertising** which, despite the name, is generally considered part of the PR function. As with "regular" advertising, corporate advertising is created and paid for by a company or organization identified in the ad. However, unlike regular advertising, the objective of corporate advertising is not to generate demand by informing, persuading, entertaining, or reminding customers. In the context of integrated marketing communications, corporate advertising is often used to call attention to the company's other communications efforts.

**Image advertising** is designed to enhance the public's perception of a company, create goodwill, or announce a major change, such as a merger or acquisition. Following the merger of Daimler and Chrysler in the fall of 1998, a series of full-page print ads announced the formation of the new company. In 2004, Interbrew and Ambev placed full-page ads in the business press to announce their new alliance. Global companies frequently utilize image advertising an effort to present themselves as good corporate citizens in foreign countries. The Boeing ads

| Table 13-8 | Company or Brand (home country) | Nature of Publicity |
|---|---|---|
| *Negative Publicity Affecting Global Marketers* | Coca-Cola (USA) and PepsiCo (USA) | In India, allegations that soft drink products from both companies were contaminated with pesticide residue led to sharp sales drops in late summer 2003. |
| | Halliburton (USA) | Allegations that the company overcharged the United States government for supplies and services rendered in Iraq. |
| | Ford Motor Company (USA) and Bridgestone/Firestone (Japan/USA) | A rash of tire failures on Ford vehicles prompted a recall in 2000 of several tire models. Ultimately, Ford severed its decades-old relationship with Firestone. |
| | Nike (USA) | Since the mid-1990s, Nike has been responding to the criticism that its subcontractors operate factories in which sweatshop conditions prevail. Filmmaker Michael Moore featured an interview with Nike CEO Phil Knight in the anti-globalization documentary *The Big One*. |
| | McDonald's (USA) | Concerns about mad cow disease in Europe, a bitter legal battle in Great Britain, and extensive media reporting that linked fast food to obesity have all presented public relations challenges to the fast-food giant. |

that appear earlier in this chapter were part of a European print campaign launched in 1997 to enhance Boeing's image by raising awareness of the number of jobs the company created locally.

Other examples of image advertising by global companies include Nokia's purchase of full-page newspaper ads to congratulate the University of Florida Gators for winning the 1997 Sugar Bowl (which Nokia sponsored). The ads also mentioned the Nokia Sweepstakes, which featured a million-dollar prize if a contestant could throw a football through an inflated cellular phone at a distance of about 10 yards. Similarly, Japan's Fuji Photo Film asked its advertising agency, Angotti, Thomas, and Hedge, to develop an image campaign for the United States. At the time, Fuji was embroiled in a trade dispute with Kodak. Fuji had also invested more than $1 billion in U.S. production facilities and had won a long-term photofinishing contract with Wal-Mart. The campaign was designed to appeal both to Wal-Mart and to the giant retailer's customers. As a Wal-Mart spokesman told *The Wall Street Journal*, "We've long said we buy American when we can. The more people understand how American Fuji is, the better."[34]

In **advocacy advertising,** a company presents its point of view on a particular issue. A recent example of advocacy advertising is the full-page newspaper ad sponsored by Virgin Airlines, in which company founder Richard Branson attacked a proposed alliance between British Airways and American Airlines. Similarly, in 1995, Japanese car marketers hired Hill & Knowlton to create a public relations campaign designed to convince then President Bill Clinton that his plan to impose 100 percent tariffs on 13 luxury cars was ill-advised and could even cost him California's 54 electoral votes in the 1996 election. Nissan and other companies also sent position papers and information packets to dealers and the media. Interviews with representatives from auto dealers were carried by both print and electronic media.

Senior executives at some companies relish the opportunity to generate publicity. For example, Benetton's striking print and outdoor ad campaigns keyed to the "United Colors of Benetton" generated both controversy and wide media attention. Richard Branson, the flamboyant founder of the Virgin Group, is a one-man publicity machine. His personal exploits as a hot-air balloon pilot have earned him and his company a great deal of free ink. The company does employ traditional media advertising; however, as Will Whitehorn, Virgin's corporate affairs director, recently noted, "PR is the heart of the company. If we do things badly, it will reflect badly on the image of the brand more than most other companies." At Virgin, Whitehorn notes, "advertising is a subset of PR, not the other way around."[35]

Sometimes publicity is generated when a company simply goes about the business of global marketing activities. As noted in Case 8-1, Nike and other marketers have received a great deal of negative publicity regarding alleged sweatshop conditions in factories run by subcontractors. To date, Nike's public relations team has not done an effective job of counteracting the criticism by effectively communicating the positive economic impact Nike has had on the nations where its sneakers are manufactured.

Any company that is increasing its activities outside the home country can utilize PR personnel as boundary spanners between the company and employees, unions, stockholders, customers, the media, financial analysts, governments, and suppliers. Many companies have their own in-house PR staff. Companies may also choose to engage the services of an outside PR firm. During the past few years, some of the large advertising holding companies discussed previously have acquired PR agencies. For example, Omnicom Group bought Fleishman-Hillard, WPP Group acquired Canada's Hill & Knowlton, and Interpublic Group bought Golin/Harris

---

[34] Wendy Bounds, "Fuji Considers National Campaign to Develop All-American Image," *The Wall Street Journal* (October 1, 1996), p. B8.

[35] Elena Bowes, "Virgin Flies in Face of Conventions," *Ad Age International* (January 1997), p. i4.

# GLOBAL *marketing in action*

International. Other PR firms, including the London-based Shandwick PLC and Edelman Public Relations Worldwide, are independent. Several independent PR firms in the United Kingdom, Germany, Italy, Spain, Austria, and the Netherlands have joined together in a network known as Globalink. The purpose of the network is to provide members with various forms of assistance such as press contacts, event planning, literature design, and suggestions for tailoring global compaigns to local needs in a particular country or region.[36]

## The Growing Role of Public Relations in Global Marketing Communications

Public relations professionals with international responsibility must go beyond media relations and serve as more than a company mouthpiece; they are called upon to simultaneously build consensus and understanding, create trust and harmony, articulate and influence public opinion, anticipate conflicts, and resolve disputes.[37] As companies become more involved in global marketing and the globalization of industries continues, company management must recognize the value of international public relations. One recent study found that, internationally, PR expenditures are growing at an average of 20 percent annually. Fueled by soaring foreign investment, industry privatization, and a boom in initial public offerings (IPOs), PR expenditures in India are reported to be growing by 200 percent annually.

The number of international PR associations is growing as well. The new Austrian Public Relations Association is a case in point; many European PR trade

---

[36] Joe Mullich, "European Firms Seek Alliances for Global PR," *Business Marketing* 79 (August 1994), pp. 4, 31.

[37] Karl Nessman, "Public Relations in Europe: A Comparison with the United States," *Public Relations Journal* 21, no. 2 (Summer 1995), p. 154.

associations are part of the Confédération Européenne des Relations Publiques and the International Public Relations Association. Another factor fueling the growth of international PR is increased governmental relations between countries. Governments, organizations, and societies are dealing with broad-based issues of mutual concern such as the environment and world peace. Finally, the technology-driven communication revolution that has ushered in the information age makes public relations a profession with truly global reach. Faxes, satellites, high-speed modems, and the Internet allow PR professionals to be in contact with media virtually anywhere in the world.

In spite of these technological advances, PR professionals must still build good personal working relationships with journalists and other media representatives, as well as with leaders of other primary constituencies. Therefore, strong interpersonal skills are needed. One of the most basic concepts of the practice of public relations is to know the audience. For the global PR practitioner, this means knowing the audiences in both the home country and the host country or countries. Specific skills needed include the ability to communicate in the language of the host country and familiarity with local customs. Obviously, a PR professional who is unable to speak the language of the host country will be unable to communicate directly with a huge portion of an essential audience. Likewise, the PR professional working outside the home country must be sensitive to nonverbal communication issues in order to maintain good working relationships with host-country nationals. Commenting on the complexity of the international PR professional's job, one expert notes that, in general, audiences are "increasingly more unfamiliar and more hostile, as well more organized and powerful . . . more demanding, more skeptical and more diverse." International PR practioners can play an important role as "bridges over the shrinking chasm of the global village."[38]

## How Public Relations Practices Differ around the World

Public relations practices in specific countries can be affected by cultural traditions, social and political contexts, and economic environments. As noted earlier in the chapter, the mass media and the written word are important vehicles for information dissemination in many industrialized countries. In developing countries, however, the best way to communicate might be through the gongman, the town crier, the market square, or the chief's courts. In Ghana, dance, songs, and storytelling are important communication channels. In India, where half of the population cannot read, writing press releases will not be the most effective way to communicate.[39] In Turkey, the practice of PR is thriving in spite of that country's reputation for harsh treatment of political prisoners. Although the Turkish government still asserts absolute control as it has for generations, corporate PR and journalism are allowed to flourish so that Turkish organizations can compete globally.

Even in industrialized countries, there are some important differences between PR practices. In the United States, much of the news in a small, local newspaper is placed by means of the hometown news release. In Canada, on the other hand, large metropolitan population centers have combined with Canadian economic and climatic conditions to thwart the emergence of a local press. The dearth of small newspapers means that the practice of sending out hometown news releases is almost nonexistent.[40] In the United States, PR is increasingly

[38] Larissa A. Grunig, "Strategic Public Relations Constituencies on a Global Scale," *Public Relations Review* 18, no. 2 (Summer 1992), pp. 127–136.

[39] Carl Botan, "International Public Relations: Critique and Reformulation," *Public Relations Review* 18, no. 2 (Summer 1992), pp. 150–151.

[40] Melvin L. Sharpe, "The Impact of Social and Cultural Conditioning on Global Public Relations," *Public Relations Review* 18, no. 2 (Summer 1992), pp. 103–107.

viewed as a separate management function. In Europe that perspective has not been widely accepted; PR professionals are viewed as part of the marketing function rather than as distinct and separate specialists in a company. In Europe, fewer colleges and universities offer courses and degree programs in public relations than in the United States. Also, European coursework in PR is more theoretical; in the United States, PR programs are often part of mass communication or journalism schools and there is more emphasis on practical job skills.

A company that is ethnocentric in its approach to PR will extend home-country PR activities into host countries. The rationale behind this approach is that people everywhere are motivated and persuaded in much the same manner. Obviously, this approach does not take cultural considerations into account. A company adopting a polycentric approach to PR gives the host-country practitioner more leeway to incorporate local customs and practices into the PR effort. Although such an approach has the advantage of local responsiveness, the lack of global communication and coordination can lead to a PR disaster.[41]

The ultimate test of an organization's understanding of the power and importance of public relations occurs during a time of environmental turbulence, especially a potential or actual crisis. When disaster strikes, a company or industry often finds itself thrust into the spotlight. A company's swift and effective handling of communications during such times can have significant implications. The best response is to be forthright and direct, reassure the public, and provide the media with accurate information.

China's ongoing trade-related friction with the United States highlights the need for a better public relations effort on the part of the Chinese Foreign Ministry. Some sources of this friction have been discussed in earlier chapters, such as estimates that Chinese counterfeiting of copyrighted material alone costs U.S. companies $800 million annually or that 98 percent of the computer software used in China is pirated. Such revelations reflect poorly on China. Hong Kong businessman Barry C. Cheung notes, "China lacks skills in public relations generally and crisis management specifically, and that hurts them."[42] Part of the problem stems from the unwillingness of China's Communist leaders to publicly explain their views on these issues, to admit failure, and to accept advice from the West.

## summary

Marketing communications—the promotion *P* of the marketing mix—includes advertising, public relations, sales promotion, and personal selling. When a company embraces **integrated marketing communications,** it recognizes that the various elements of a company's communication strategy must be carefully coordinated. **Global advertising** consists of the same advertising appeals, messages, artwork, and copy in campaigns around the world. The effort required to create a global campaign forces a company to determine whether or not a global market exists for its product. The trade-off between standardized and adapted advertising is often accomplished by means of **pattern advertising,** which can be used to create localized global

advertising. Many advertising agencies are part of larger **advertising organizations.** Advertisers may place a single global agency in charge of worldwide advertising; it is also possible to use one or more agencies on a regional or local basis.

The starting point in ad development is the **creative strategy,** a statement of what the message will say. The people who create ads often seek a **big idea** that can serve as the basis for memorable, effective messages. The **advertising appeal** is the communication approach—rational or emotional—that best relates to buyer motives. The **selling proposition** is the promise that captures the reason for buying the product. The **creative execution** is the way an appeal or proposition is presented.

---

[41] Carl Botan, "International Public Relations: Critique and Reformulation," *Public Relations Review* 18, no. 2 (Summer 1992), p. 155.

[42] Marcus W. Brauchli, "A Change of Face: China Has Surly Image, but Part of the Reason Is Bad Public Relations," *The Wall Street Journal* (June 16, 1996), p. A1.

**Art direction** and **copy** must be created with cultural considerations in mind. Perceptions of humor, male-female relationships, and sexual imagery vary in different parts of the world. Media availability varies considerably from country to country. When selecting media, marketers are sometimes as constrained by laws and regulations as by literacy rates.

A company utilizes **public relations** (PR) to foster goodwill and understanding among constituents both inside and outside the company. In particular, the PR department attempts to generate favorable **publicity** about the company and its products and brands. The PR department must also manage corporate communications when responding to negative publicity. The most important PR tools are press releases, media kits, interviews, and tours. Many global companies make use of various types of **corporate advertising,** including **image advertising** and **advocacy advertising.** Public relations is also responsible for providing accurate, timely information, especially in the event of a crisis.

**discussion questions**

1. In what ways can global brands and global advertising campaigns benefit a company?

2. How does the "standardized versus localized" debate apply to advertising?

3. What is the difference between an advertising appeal and creative execution?

4. When creating advertising for world markets, what are some of the issues that art directors and copywriters should take into account?

5. How do the media options available to advertisers vary in different parts of the world? What can advertisers do to cope with media limitations in certain countries?

6. How does public relations differ from advertising? Why is PR especially important for global companies?

7. What are some of the ways public relations practices vary in different parts of the world?

**build your global marketing skills**

Each spring, *Advertising Age* magazine publishes its survey of the top 50 global advertising organizations. The top-ranked companies for 2002 were shown in Tables 13-2 and 13-3. Browse through either table and choose any agency organization or brand that interests you. Compare its 2002 ranking with the most recent ranking (which you can find either by referring to the print version of *Advertising Age* or by visiting www.adageglobal.com). How have the industry rankings changed? Consult additional sources (e.g., magazine articles, the company's Web site) to enhance your understanding of the factors and forces that contributed to the company's move up or down in the rankings. Has the agency been acquired by a large organization? Has it gained or lost an important account?

# Case 13-1

## Benetton Group S.p.A.: Raising Consciousness and Controversy with Global Advertising

Benetton Group S.p.A., the Italy-based global clothing retailer, exhibits something of a dual personality. Academics have hailed the company's information technology expertise (see Chapter 6); Benetton has also been cited as a textbook example of a flagship global firm that excels at building relationships (see Chapter 15). Moreover, the company continues to innovate in the area of upstream value chain activities: An article in *Sloan Management Review* explains how Benetton is rethinking its global supplier and distributor network.[43] By contrast, the company has garnered a great deal of publicity—much of it negative—for an advertising strategy that, over the course of nearly two decades, has emphasized social issues rather than the company's products.

Worldwide sales of Benetton's brightly colored knitware and contemporary clothing doubled between 1988 and 1993 to 2.75 trillion lire ($1.63 billion). In 1993 alone, sales were up about 10 percent, and net income increased by 13 percent. The strong showing in 1993 was due in part to the devaluation of the Italian lira, which enabled Benetton to cut prices for its clothing around the world. By contrast, 1994 results were discouraging. Sales were flat at $1.69 billion, operating profits fell 5 percent, to $245 million, and margins narrowed to 13.9 percent, down from 14.7 percent during 1991 to 1993. The sales slump was surprising in view of the fact that Benetton had opened stores in China, Eastern Europe, and India and extended the brand into new categories, such as footwear and cosmetics.

Some industry observers believed that Benetton's financial difficulties were due in part to a backlash to the company's controversial global advertising campaigns keyed to the theme "The United Colors of Benetton." Various executions of the ads, in magazines, on posters and billboards, and *Colors*, a bi-monthly publication produced inhouse, featured provocative, even shocking photos designed to focus public attention on social and political issues such as the environment, terrorism, racial issues, and sexually transmitted diseases. The creative concept of the ads reflected the views of Oliviero Toscani, who was creative director and chief photographer for Benetton from 1982 through 2000. "I have found out that advertising is the richest and most powerful medium existing today. Therefore, I feel responsible to do more than say, 'Our sweater is pretty,'" he told *The New York Times*. Noted Victorio Rava, worldwide advertising manager, "We believe our advertising needs to shock, otherwise people will not remember it."

One of the first ads to stir controversy depicted a white hand and a black hand joined by handcuffs; another showed an angelic white child embracing a black child whose hair was unmistakably styled to resemble the horns of a devil. An ad with a picture of a black woman nursing a white baby appeared in 77 countries; while banned in the United States and the United Kingdom, the ad won awards in France and Italy. In fall 1991, several U.S. magazine publishers refused to carry some of the ads; one depicted a nun kissing a priest. A picture of a newborn baby covered with a bloody placenta was also rejected. As Benetton's Rava noted in the early 1990s, "We didn't envision a political idea when we started this 'Colors' strategy five years ago, but now, with racist problems becoming more important in every country it has become political on its own."

With its next series of ads, Benetton used images associated with sexuality. As Peter Fressola, director of communications, explained the message strategy, "We're saying there are two important issues to be addressed, and they are over-population and sexually transmitted diseases such as AIDS. I think it is time to take the gloves off and put on the rubbers and address these issues." In an interview with *Advertising Age*, Toscani explained, "Everybody uses emotion to sell a product. The difference here is we are not selling a product. We want to show, in this case, human realities that we are aware of." The ads broke new ground for the images they presented: A man dying of AIDS surrounded by his family; a montage of multicolored condoms; a group of people with the initials *HIV* stamped on their arms; test tubes filled with blood labeled with the names of world leaders.

In France, the HIV ad caused a great deal of controversy. One man who was dying of AIDS ran an ad with a picture of his own face above a headline that read, "during the agony, the sales continue." In the United States, where the number of Benetton stores had been slowly dwindling, the ads were poorly received by many customers and Benetton retailers. The manager of a Benetton store in Biloxi, Mississippi, received telephone calls from people who said they refused to shop at stores selling products from a "sick" company. In Florida, one franchisee closed a dozen Benetton locations, noting, "It is not our function as retailers to raise the consciousness of people. I've had long, hard fights with Italy over the advertising." In an effort to help mollify its American licensees, Benetton began providing them with local ads featuring clothing instead of social issues. At the national level, however, Benetton continued the controversial ads. When asked about the possible negative impact of customer boycotts, Luciano Benetton, the president Benetton Group S.p.A., said, "It's silly to change direction because someone in the market thinks it's not right. We are sincere, and we are consistent in pursuing it this way."

Simon Anholt, an industry consultant and author of a book about international advertising, has asserted that the campaign's critics were missing the point. For one thing, notes Anholt, the goal of much youth-oriented advertising is to make a brand famous rather than to sell a product; Benetton's advertising has certainly accomplished this goal. A second point is that there is not meant to be a rational link between the message and the product per se; the target audience for the Benetton brand neither looks for nor desires such a link. Instead, Anholt believes, young people often wish to identify with a mind-set or a philosophy; the marketer's task in such instances is to link the

---

43  Arnald Camuffo, Pietro Romano, and Andrea Vinelli, "Back to the Future: Benetton Transforms Its Global Network," *Sloan Management Review* 43, no. 1 (Fall 2001), pp. 46–52.

philosophy to the company's brand. Finally, Anholt suggests that the Benetton campaign may well have been designed to shock the *parents* of Benetton's target consumers; according to this view, young people are often attracted to the "hot" brands or "cool" styles that an older demographic may find offensive.

In the spring of 1994, Toscani pushed the envelope even further. A new $15 million ad campaign that ran in 25 countries featured a picture of the bloody uniform of a Croatian soldier who had died in the Yugoslavian civil war. Although Benetton executives had come to expect criticism, they were unprepared for the latest reaction. The company was accused of exploiting the war for the sake of profit. In France, many of the offending posters were pulled down or covered with graffiti reading "boycott Benetton" and "this is blood for money." The French minister for humanitarian affairs even made a public announcement discouraging people from buying Benetton sweaters; he called for his fellow citizens to "pull [the sweaters] off people who are going to wear them." In some parts of Germany and Switzerland, the company's products were banned. Some media reports in Europe questioned the authenticity of the uniform and alleged it did not belong to the fallen soldier named in the ad. The Vatican newspaper charged Benetton with "advertising terrorism."

Luciano Benetton acknowledged that, "This is not what a corporate communications campaign should do. It should create interest." Still, he vowed the company would continue "to search for new facts and new emotions" to include in its ads. Indeed, when the Sarajevo daily newspaper *Oslo bodhenie* (Liberation) requested posters of the ad to put up around the city, Benetton supplied 10,000 copies.

Benetton occasionally put controversy aside and ran more mainstream ads. In 1995, the Chiat/Day agency created a television campaign that featured models posing and dancing against a white background while a voiceover presented the models' thoughts. In mid-1997, a new print campaign featured individual closeup portraits of young people from around the world juxtaposed with photos of Benetton apparel on the facing page. Benetton also teamed up with the United Nations for a campaign keyed to the International Year of Volunteers 2001. In 1998, aiming to boost sales and reach a broader market in the United States, Benetton reached an accord with retailer Sears, Roebuck and Co. A new, lower-priced clothing line, Benetton USA, was created especially for Sears.

By 1999, however, Toscani was championing a new cause: prisoners on death row in the United States. Helen Garrett, advertising director of Amnesty International, responded positively to the campaign. "I am in favor of efforts to raise public awareness and put a face on this difficult human rights issue. . . . I tip my hat to Benetton for this effort," she said. By contrast, a number of critics took the company to task. Bob Garfield, the highly regarded ad reviewer for *Advertising Age* magazine, awarded the campaign zero stars on a one- to four-star rating system. Garfield had dismissed some of Benetton's previous ads as "banal expressions of moral outrage over war, racism, and disease." Although Garfield acknowledged that the issue of capital punishment was worth exploring, he asserted that "No brand has the right to increase its sales on the backs, on the misery, on the fates of condemned men and women. . . ."

*"Spare us all the consciousness raising, please. There is nothing a sportswear company can add to the discussion."*
Bob Garfield
*Advertising Age* ad critic

In 2000, the state of Missouri filed a lawsuit against Benetton alleging that the company had misrepresented itself when requesting the interviews with death-row inmates. A week after the suit was filed, Sears cancelled its agreement with Benetton. (The lawsuit was settled after Benetton officials agreed to apologize to several Missouri families whose relatives were murder victims.) In May 2000, 3 months after the launch of the "We, On Death Row" campaign, Oliviero Toscani resigned from Benetton. In an interview with *Ad Age Global* in 2001, Toscani defended his body of work. "Most good ads are forgotten after six months, but who still remembers the Benetton ad with the priest kissing the nun? Ten years later and people remember! That's immortality!" he said. He also noted that Benetton's sales in 2000 were 20 times greater than they had been at the beginning of his career with the company.

Still, in 2000, U.S. sales accounted for just 11 percent of Benetton's $1.8 billion in revenues, and the number of stores in the United States had dwindled to 150. In 2001, Benetton launched a new $10 million campaign in the United States that sidestepped social issues. The new ads, which some observers viewed as similar to ads for Gap, featured lively multiethnic models dancing in the company's knitwear. Benetton also announced plans to open new megastores in key U.S. cities such as New York and Atlanta. In 2004, Kurt Anderson, founder of *Spy* magazine, was hired as the new editorial director of *Colors*. Acknowledging that, in past years, the magazine had been focused on misery and pain, Anderson promised that the revamped *Colors* would resemble a blend of venerable *Life* magazine and *National Geographic*. Also, in an unusual step for a family business in Italy, Luciano Benetton stepped down as chief executive and hired an outsider. Commenting on his decision, Luciano noted, "We were four brothers and sisters sharing a commitment. This is what united us and made us successful—family." He continued, "We wanted to guarantee a solid future for our company and make sure it remained competitive. You can only do this with professional management."

## Discussion Questions

1. Do you believe Benetton is sincere in its efforts to promote social causes through its advertising?

2. Compare and contrast the controversy surrounding the "We, On Death Row" advertising campaign with the controversies generated by Benetton's earlier campaigns of the 1990s. Do you think Americans responded differently than, say, Europeans? Why?

3. There is a saying in the marketing world that "there is no such thing as bad publicity." Does that apply in the Benetton case?

4. Assess Benetton's efforts to boost sales in the United States. What recommendations would you make to management?

*Sources:* Ellen Hale, "Business All in the *Famiglia*," USA *Today* (February 4, 2004), pp. 1A, 1B; Cathy Horyn, "Toning Down the Colors of Benetton," *The New York Times* (April 27, 2004), pp. B1, B6; Clark and Cecile Rohwedder, "Benetton Unveils Makeover Strategy," *The Wall Street Journal* (December 10, 2003), p. B4; Simon Anholt, *Another One Bites the Grass: Making Sense of International Advertising* (New York: John Wiley & Sons, 2000), pp. 138–139; Leigh Gallagher, "About Face," *Forbes* (March 19, 2001), pp. 178–180; Jerry Della Famina, "Benetton Ad Models are Dressed to Kill Sales," *The Wall Street Journal* (March 20, 2000), p. A35; Bob Garfield, "The Colors of Exploitation: Benetton on Death Row," *Advertising Age* (January 10, 2000), p. 45; Eleftheria Parpis, "Consumer Republic," *Adweek* (January 10, 2000), p. 20; John Rossant, "The Faded Colors of Benetton," *Business Week* (April 10, 1995), pp. 87, 90; Peter Gumbel, "Benetton is Stung by Backlash Over Ad," *The Wall Street Journal* (March 4, 1994), p. A8; Gary Levin, "Benetton Ad Lays Bare the Bloody Toll of War," *Advertising Age* (February 21, 1994); Dennis Rodkin, "How Colorful Can Ads Get?" *Mother Jones* (January 1990), p. 52; Stuart Elliott, "Benetton Stirs More Controversy," *The New York Times* (July 23, 1991), p. 19; Gary Levin, "Benetton Brouhaha," *Advertising Age* (February 17, 1992), p. 62; Teri Agins, "Shrinkage of Stores and Customers in U.S., Causes Italy's Benetton to Alter Its Tactics," *The Wall Street Journal* (June 24, 1992), pp. B1, B10.

# Case 13-2

## Adidas-Salomon AG

In February 1993, a group of investors headed by Robert Louis-Dreyfus, former CEO of Saatchi & Saatchi Advertising, bought a controlling interest in Adidas AG. Optimistic about Adidas's future, Dreyfus's group raised its stake to full ownership in 1995. Two years later, Dreyfus acquired Salomon, a French company. The move created Adidas-Salomon AG, the second largest sports equipment company in the world after Nike. Today, the company markets sports shoes, athletic clothing, and equipment in nearly 200 countries.

Adidas has an illustrious history dating back many decades; in fact, when Jesse Owens won four gold medals at the 1936 Olympic games, he was wearing track shoes made by Adi Dassler. A few years later, Dassler founded Adidas (Dassler's brother Rudolph started rival shoemaker Puma). Public triumphs such as Owens' Olympic wins helped make Adidas the world leader in the sports shoe market; the company's Trefoil logo is iconic for the brand. By successfully leveraging its heritage, the company generated revenues of $7.8 billion in 2003.

This financial performance represents a sweet victory for the new owners. Years of financial controversy and changing ownership had diverted management's attention from the market and gradually eroded the company's fortunes. In Germany, Adidas's share of sports shoe sales declined from 60 percent to 40 percent from the early 1980s to the early 1990s, including a 10-point slide in a 2-year period. Sneaker sales doubled in Europe between 1985 and 1995, and Nike and Reebok's share of the market jumped to 50 percent from 5 percent despite extremely high import duties. The Americans' success was due in part to big spending on advertising. Nike and Reebok each spent about $100 million annually to promote their shoes in Europe; Adidas's ad spending in Europe was considerably less. The popularity of American sneakers got an extra boost thanks to the high visibility of the American Dream

**ADIDAS'** global print campaign by independent **180 AMSTERDAM** tells the authentic stories of runners who let nothing stand in the way of their passion. One subject, Fauja Singh, is not only a 92-year-old marathoner. Mr. Singh's real achievement is that he has shaved an hour off his time over the past three years. Other runners withstand extreme weather, fatigue and danger to complete their course. Copywriters: Peter McHugh, Clare Buchanan. Art director: Heath Lowe.

Team at the 1992 Olympics; NBA stars endorse both Reebok and Nike.

The American athletic shoe companies are skilled global marketers. In 2003, Nike rang up $10.6 billion in worldwide sales, while Reebok's sales totaled $3.1 billion in 2002. Reebok is the market leader in France, Spain, and England, and Nike is number one in many other European countries. Although advertising taglines such as "Just Do It" and "Planet Reebok" are presented in English, other parts of the message are adapted to reflect cultural differences. In France, for example, violence in ads is unacceptable, so Reebok replaced boxing scenes with images of women running on a beach. Also, European participation in sports is lower than in America; accordingly, Europeans are less likely to visit sporting goods stores. In France, Reebok shoes are now sold in nearly 1,000 traditional shoe stores.

Even in the face of such tough and growing competition, Adidas still enjoys high brand loyalty among older Europeans. The company recruits young people and pays them to wear Adidas shoes in public; they are also paid to work at sporting goods stores and promote Adidas products in other ways. Adidas also updated its image among younger European consumers by creating a new sport called Streetball. Ads airing on MTV Europe feature players outfitted in the company's new Streetball apparel line. Unlike its American rivals, Adidas does not utilize a global ad campaign. For example, a 1995 campaign that ran outside the United States featured Emil Zatopke, a Czechoslovakian Olympic runner.

As the twenty-first century began, company executives realized the need for a new global strategy. The first step was unveiling a new brand position: "Forever Sport—from Competition to Lifestyle." As global marketing chief Erich Stamminger noted in 2001, "We want to mean more to more people. We want to expand our customer base and gain deeper market penetration in our existing markets." To achieve these goals, the company's three divisions were restructured along product lines: performance products, leisure products, and multifunctional products. In January 2002, the company dropped the advertising agency with which it had been affiliated for many years, London-based Leagas Delany. Adidas' new agency, Los Angeles–based TBWA, will work in conjunction with 180, a Dutch agency. Explaining the rationale for the change, Stamminger noted, "By appointing one global agency network, we are continuing our strategy of strengthening the Adidas brand worldwide."

TBWA got right to work. Its Japanese unit developed a billboard featuring two people playing vertical soccer. The company received a boost at the 2003 World Athletic Championships in Paris, where a Caribbean sprinter named Kim Collins won the 100 meter final in a pair of retro-styled Adidas track and field shoes. Adidas executives were looking forward to the 2004 Olympic Games in Athens, where the field included 18 teams sponsored by Adidas. As Mike Riehl, head of global sports marketing, noted, "Athletics [track and field] goes back all the way for us—it is a fixed part of our philosophy to make products for all Olympic disciplines." Riehl asserted that the renewed focus on athletics was "all about brand positioning and our claim to be the Olympic brand."

*"Adidas has been in sports for four times as long as its competition, but the U.S. still doesn't appreciate the brand for what it is."*

Lee Clow, creative director, 180/TBWA

Retro-style shoes are enjoying increased popularity in Europe, where track and field events are popular. However, the picture is not so clear in the United States, which is the world's largest market for athletic shoes. In spring 2003, Nike outmaneuvered its rivals by signing basketball phenomenon LeBron James to a sponsorship deal. Reebok was enjoying surging demand for new shoes endorsed by rappers Jay-Z and 50 Cent. Meanwhile, the integrity of athletics was coming under increased scrutiny after revelations that a new "designer steroid," tetrahydrogestrinon (THG), was being widely used. In fact, Dwain Chambers, a British sprinter who endorsed Adidas, had tested positive for THG. As 2003 came to a close, it was clear that the Adidas strategy was not paying off. Orders in the key U.S. market were down; it remained to be seen whether U.S. interest in the Olympics would translate into greater sales. Nike was the clear industry leader, with nearly 40 percent share of the athletic shoe market. The company's T-Mac shoe, endorsed by Tracy McGrady of the Orlando Magic, was the top selling basketball shoe in the United States in 2001 and 2002. However, sales of a new T-Mac model launched in fall 2003 were below expectations.

To turn the situation around, Stamminger was dispatched to Portland, Oregon and put in charge of the North American region. In spring 2004, Adidas launched a $50 million global print and TV campaign keyed to the tagline "Nothing is impossible." Some of the ads feature boxing legend Muhammad Ali and tell a "past and present" story linking sports figures from earlier eras with modern-day stars. In May, Stamminger announced the fruits of a secret, 3-year development effort: The Adidas 1, a shoe with an onboard microchip that adjusts the cushioning level to an athlete's weight and performance needs. In a press release, Stamminger noted, "This is the world's first intelligent shoe. It senses, understands, and adapts."

## Discussion Questions:

1. Do you think that ads proclaiming Adidas' heritage will be effective in helping build the brand in the United States?

2. Assess the new "Nothing is impossible" advertising tagline. Do you think this phrase will become part of popular culture the way Nike's "Just do it" tagline has?

3. With an initial price tag of $250, the high-tech Adidas 1 is not targeted at a broad market. What role can the Adidas 1 play in the company's public relations plan?

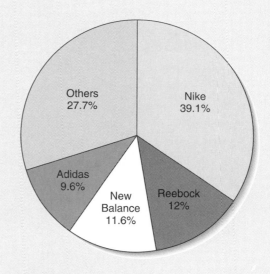

**Figure 1**

*Sources:* Stephanie Kang, "Adidas Gets Artsy with its U.S. Ads," *The Wall Street Journal* (February 5, 2004), p. B3; Doug Cameron, "Adidas Puts Focus on US," *Financial Times* (December 11, 2003), p. 16; Uta Harnischfeger and Matthew Garrahan, "Adidas — Off the Pace and More Hurdles Ahead," *Financial Times* (November 10, 2003), p. 6; Geoffrey A. fowler and Sebastian Moffett, "Adidas's Billboard Ads Give a Kick to Japanese Pedestrians," *The Wall Street Journal* (August 29, 2003), pp. B1, B4; J. Lacap, "Adidas Embraces New Global Strategy," *Sporting Goods Business* (November 2001), p. 8; Claire Cozens, "Adidas Drops Leagas Delaney," *MediaGuardian.co.uk* (January 9, 2002); Dagmar Mussey, "Adidas Strides on its Own Path," *Advertising Age* (February 13, 1995), p. 6; Kevin Goldman, "Adidas Tries to Fill its Rivals' Big Shoes," *The Wall Street Journal* (March 17, 1994), p. B5; Joseph Pereira, "Off and Running: Pushing U.S. Style, Nike and Reebok Sell Sneakers to Europe," *The Wall Street Journal* (July 22 1993), pp. A1, A8; Stephen Barr, "Adidas on the Rebound," *CFO* (September 1991), pp. 48–56; Igor Reichlin, "Where Nike and Reebok Have Plenty of Running Room," *Business Week* (March) 11, 1991, pp. 56–60.

# 14 Global Marketing Communications Decisions II

SALES PROMOTION, PERSONAL SELLING, SPECIAL FORMS
OF MARKETING COMMUNICATION

In 2001, Microsoft Corporation made its first foray in the video game industry by launching Xbox. Armed with a $500 million global promotional campaign, Xbox chief Robbie Bach intended to serve notice that Microsoft had created a gaming system that could compete with Sony's popular PlayStation 2 and Nintendo's GameCube. To succeed, Xbox would have to be embraced by gamers in the United States, Europe, and Japan. Bach used a variety of promotional tactics, timed in three phases: prelaunch, launch (November and December 2001), and sustain. To build awareness and give avid gamers a chance to try the system, the prelaunch phase included a partnership with SoBe, a unit of PepsiCo whose fruit juices and sports drinks are popular with young people. Three hundred SoBe "Love Buses" were outfitted with Xbox consoles and sent to tour rock concerts and festivals. Microsoft also teamed up with the Taco Bell restaurant chain for a massive promotion; one Xbox system was given away at each of Taco Bell's 6,500 locations. PepsiCo's Frito-Lay snack unit was tapped for an instant-win sweepstakes on 55 million packages of Doritos Extreme. The grand-prize winners received a complete RCA home theater system and an Xbox. In addition, Microsoft teamed up with Linkin Park, a popular American band that spotlighted Xbox during its "Projekt: Revolution" tour. Band members autographed Xbox consoles that were then given away during local radio promotions at each tour stop. Fans could also get a chance to win an Xbox on the Internet by logging onto the ProjektRevolution.com and Xbox.com Web sites.

Sales promotion has been a crucial marketing tool for Microsoft in the worldwide launch of Xbox. When developing integrated marketing communications solutions and strategies, global companies and advertising agencies are giving sales promotion an

To give its target market plenty of opportunities to interact with the brand, the Xbox promotion strategy calls for partnering with sports and music events. For example, in 2003, Xbox was presenting sponsor for the Lollapalooza tour. The sponsorship package included multiple "Presented by Xbox" references; in addition, the Xbox logo appeared on concert tickets. Attendees had the opportunity to visit the Xbox Game Riot tent to take part in competitions.

increasingly prominent role; in the first decade of the twenty-first century, worldwide expenditures on sales promotion are growing at double-digit rates. Direct marketing, event sponsorship, and specialized forms of marketing communication such as infomercials and the Internet are also growing in importance. Of course, personal selling remains an important promotional tool as well. Taken together, the marketing mix elements discussed in this chapter and Chapter 13 can be used to create highly effective integrated campaigns that support global brands.

## SALES PROMOTION

**Sales promotion** refers to any paid consumer or trade communication program of limited duration that adds tangible value to a product or brand. In a *price promotion*, tangible value may take the form of a price reduction, coupon, or mail-in refund. *Nonprice promotions* may take the form of free samples, premiums, "buy one, get one free" offers, sweepstakes, and contests. **Consumer sales promotions** may be designed to make consumers aware of a new product, to stimulate nonusers to sample an existing product, or to increase overall consumer demand. **Trade sales promotions** are designed to increase product availability in distribution channels. At many companies, expenditures for sales promotion activities have surpassed expenditures for media advertising. At any level of expenditure, however, sales promotion is only one of several marketing communication tools. Sales promotion plans and programs should be integrated and coordinated with those for advertising, public relations, and personal selling.

Worldwide, the increasing popularity of sales promotion as a marketing communication tool can be explained in terms of several strengths and advantages. Besides providing a tangible incentive to buyers, sales promotions also reduce the perceived risk buyers may associate with purchasing the product. From the point of view of the sponsoring company, sales promotion provides accountability; the manager in charge of the promotion can immediately track the results of the

| Company/Country Market for Promotion | Promotion |
|---|---|
| Seagram Spirits and Wine Group/global | Online charity auction in fall 2001 to celebrate two hundredth anniversary of Chivas Regal scotch. |
| Mars/global | Global Color Vote promotion invited consumers in 200 countries to vote whether a new M&M candy should be purple, aqua, or pink. Purple won. |
| Wm. Wrigley Co./USA | U.S. launch of European Orbit brand gum with Orbit Institute advertising tied to Orbit Institute Sampling Initiative that included "field research teams" dressed like the characters in the ads who distributed 7 million gum samples. |
| Guinness/Malaysia, Singapore, Hong Kong | Promotion to select new bottle shape from four different design options for Guinness, e.g., "bullhorn" shape, and guitar shape. Contest was advertised in magazines, billboards, and table tent cards. |

**Table 14-1**

*Sales Promotions by Global Marketers*

promotion. Overall, promotional spending is increasing at many companies as they shift advertising allocations away from traditional print and broadcast advertising. Several company-specific examples of sales promotion programs are shown in Table 14-1.

In addition, sweepstakes, rebates, and other forms of promotion require consumers to fill out a form and return it to the company, which can then build up information in its database for use when communicating with customers in the future. For example, Clicquot, a unit of LVMH Moët Hennessy Louis Vuitton, markets Hine cognac and other fine wines and spirits. In an effort to build the company's in-house mailing list, managers offered cognac drinkers a prize for filling out a Hine Cognac crossword puzzle. Clicquot rented a list with the addresses of persons who had attended cigar "smoker" events in major cities.

A global company can sometimes leverage experience gained in one country market and use it in another market. For example, PepsiCo experienced great success in Latin America with its Numeromania contest. When soft drink sales stalled in Poland during the summer of 1996, Pepsi rolled out Numeromania there; lured by the promise of big cash prizes, many economically squeezed Poles rushed out to buy Pepsi so they could enter the contest.[1] International managers can learn about American-style promotion strategies and tactics by attending seminars such as those offered by the Promotional Marketing Association of America (PMAA). Sometimes adaptation to country-specific conditions is required; for example, TV ads in France cannot have movie tie-ins. Ads must be designed to focus on the promotion rather than the movie. Such regulations would have an impact on Disney, for example.

As with other aspects of marketing communication, a key issue is whether promotion efforts should be directed by headquarters or left to local country managers. The authors of one study noted that Nestlé and other large companies that once had a polycentric approach to consumer and trade sales promotion have redesigned their efforts. Kashani and Quelch identify four factors that contribute

---

[1] Roderick Oram, "Brand Experiences," *Financial Times* (October 30, 1996), FT Survey, p. III.

to more headquarters involvement in the sales promotion effort: cost, complexity, global branding, and transnational trade:[2]

1. As sales promotions command ever-larger budget allocations, headquarters naturally takes a greater interest
2. The formulation, implementation, and follow-up of a promotion program may require skills that local managers lack
3. The increasing importance of global brands justifies headquarters involvement to maintain consistency from country to country and ensure that successful local promotion programs are leveraged in other markets
4. As mergers and acquisitions lead to increased concentration in the retail industry and as the industry globalizes, retailers will seek coordinated promotional programs from their suppliers

The level of headquarters involvement notwithstanding, in most cases, local managers in the market know the specific local situation. They should be consulted before a promotion is launched. A number of factors must be taken into account when determining the extent to which the promotion must be localized:

- In countries with low levels of economic development, low incomes limit the range of promotional tools available. In such countries, free samples and demonstrations are more likely to be used than coupons or on-pack premiums.
- Market maturity can also be different from country to country; consumer sampling and coupons are appropriate in growing markets, but mature markets might require trade allowances or loyalty programs.
- Local perceptions of a particular promotional tool or program can vary. Japanese consumers, for example, are reluctant to use coupons at the checkout counter. A particular premium can be seen as a waste of money.
- Local regulations may rule out use of a particular promotion in certain countries. Table 14-2 lists regulations governing coupon distribution in several countries.
- Trade structure in the retailing industry can affect the use of sales promotions. For example, in the United States and parts of Europe, the retail industry is highly concentrated, that is, dominated by a few key players such as Wal-Mart. This situation requires significant promotional activity at both the trade and consumer level. By contrast, in countries where retailing is more fragmented—Japan is a case in point—there is less pressure to engage in promotional activities.

## Sampling

Sampling is a sales promotion technique that provides consumers with the opportunity to try a product or service at no cost. As Marc Pritchard, vice president of global cosmetics and personal care at Procter & Gamble, noted recently, "The most fundamental thing that consumers want to do is try before they buy."[3] A typical sample is an individual portion of a consumer packaged product such as breakfast cereal, shampoo, cosmetics, or detergent distributed through the mail, door to door, or at a retail location. The average cost-per-sample for such promotional programs can range from 10 cents to 50 cents; 2 million to 3 million samples are distributed in a typical sampling program. Cost is one of the major disadvantages associated with sampling; another problem is that it is sometimes difficult for marketing managers

---

[2] Kamran Kashani and John A. Quelch, "Can Sales Promotion Go Global?" *Business Horizons* 33, no. 3 (May–June 1990), pp. 37–43.
[3] Sarah Ellison, "Taking the 'Free' out of Free Samples," *The Wall Street Journal* (September 25, 2002), p. D1.

| Country | Coupons by Mail | Home Delivery Coupons | On-Pack Coupons | In-Pack Coupons |
|---|---|---|---|---|
| England | Legal | Legal | Legal | Legal |
| France | Legal for discount on same product. No cross coupons. | Legal for discount on same product. No cross coupons. | Legal for discount on same product. No cross coupons. | Legal for discount on same product. No cross coupons. |
| Germany | Legal for samples only. Price-off coupons not allowed. | Legal for samples only. Price-off coupons not allowed. | Price reduction cannot be made by retailer. Consumers mail on-pack code directly to manufacturer. | Prohibited in most cases. |
| Sweden | Legal to persons age 16 and over; illegal to send to persons younger than 16. Restrictions when sending to parents of new baby. | Legal to persons age 16 and over; illegal to send to persons younger than 16. Restrictions when sending to parents of new baby. | Legal | Legal |
| USA | Legal. Restrictions on alcohol, tobacco, and drugs. | Legal. Restrictions on alcohol, tobacco, and drugs. | Legal; all terms must be disclosed. Minimum 6-month redemption period required. | Legal; all terms must be disclosed. Minimum 6-month redemption period required. |

**Table 14-2**

*Coupon Promotion Regulation in Select Countries*

*Source:* Adapted from *Promo* magazine.

# the rest of the story

## Xbox

Xbox's design reflects its corporate heritage. The console itself contains an 8-gigabyte hard drive, which allows users to save games without using memory cards. The system boasts a 733-megahertz Intel processor and an ethernet port. It also was designed to play music CDs and DVDs. Microsoft's promotional strategy for Xbox paid off. One year after the launch, the new system quickly reached the number 2 position in the market in the key U.S. market with sales of 4.1 million units. Nintendo fell to number 3, but Sony remained the clear leader with more than 17 million units sold. Worldwide, Sony commands about 70 percent of the gaming market.

There were some problems, however. For example, in Japan, some game developers refused to create software for the American system. By the end of 2002, approximately 300 games were available for PS2 compared with about 30 for Xbox. In 2003, Microsoft hired Yoshihiro Maruyama to head its games unit in Japan. Microsoft is counting on Maruyama to help boost Xbox's share of console sales in Japan from its current low-single digit level and to win over skeptical Japanese game developers. Previously, Maruyama had been chief operating officer of the U.S. unit of Square Enix, a game developer.

Microsoft has extensive experience with the Internet and networking capabilities, and chairman Bill Gates believes that gamers will increasingly want to plan online. More and more households are equipped with the broadband Web services necessary for high-speed connectivity, and Microsoft executives believe that broadband will be quite common by 2005. Gates and his team are betting that online gaming represents the future of the video game industry; Xbox Live, launched in 2002, now has about 1 million subscribers. In 2004, Microsoft announced that it had reached an agreement with Electronic Arts, a leading supplier of game software, to develop versions of popular sports games for Xbox Live.

Meanwhile, Xbox marketers were making strategic use of key marketing and promotion mix elements to support Xbox. The Xbox logo can be seen in major and minor league ballparks. In fall 2003, Xbox was featured on the CBS TV series *Two and a Half Men*. In March 2004, Microsoft cut the retail price of the Xbox console from $179 to $149.

*Sources: Robert A Guth, "Microsoft Is Taking Games Up a Notch," The Wall Street Journal (May 11, 2004), p. B10; Phred Dvorak, "Microsoft Hires Chief for Xbox Games Unit in Japan," The Wall Street Journal (September 26, 2003), p. B4; Kenneth Hein, "We Know What Guys Want," Brandweek (November 14, 2002), p. M48; Khan T. L. Tran, "Trailing Sony, Microsoft Xbox Bets on the Web," The Wall Street Journal (November 8, 2002), p. B1; "Console Wars," Economist (June 22, 2002), p. 57; Rebecca Buckman, "What Mircrosoft Really Sees in Xbox," The Wall Street Journal (November 9, 2001), p. B1; Robert Guth, "Microsoft Weighs Options as Sales of Xbox Sag in Japan," The Wall Street Journal (September 23, 2002), p. B1; Guth, "Fighting Chance: In Battle for the Future, Microsoft Must Woo Japan's Game Makers," The Wall Street Journal (March 26, 2002), p. A1.*

to assess the contribution a sampling program makes to return on investment. Today, many companies utilize *event marketing* and *sponsorships* to distribute samples at concerts, sports events, or special events such as food and beverage festivals attended by large numbers of people. In the information age, sampling may also consist of a week's free viewing of a cable TV channel or a no-cost trial subscription to an online computer service; Internet users can also request free samples through a company's Web site.

Compared with other forms of marketing communication, sampling is more likely to result in actual trial of the product. To ensure trial, consumer products companies are increasingly using a technique known as "point-of-use" sampling. For example, Starbucks dispatches "chill patrols" in the summertime to pass out samples of frozen Frappucino to overheated commuters during rush hour in busy metropolitan areas. In an example of "point-of-dirt" sampling, Unilever recently hired a promotional marketing firm to pass out Lever2000 hand wipes in food courts and petting zoos. As Michael Murphy, director of home and personal-care promotions at Unilever, noted, "We're getting smarter. You must be much more precise in what, where, and how you deliver samples."[4]  Sampling can be especially important if consumers are not persuaded by claims made in advertising or other channels. In China, for example, shoppers are reluctant to buy full-sized packages of imported consumer products that they haven't tried—especially because the price may be several times higher than the price of local brands. Procter & Gamble's dominance in China's shampoo market can be attributed to the company's skillful use of market segmentation coupled with an aggressive sampling program. P&G offers four shampoo brands in China: Rejoice ("soft and beautiful hair"), Pantene ("nutrition"), Head & Shoulders (dandruff relief), and Vidal Sassoon (fashion).[5] P&G distributed millions of free samples of its shampoo products; after the no-risk trial, many consumers became adopters.

## Couponing

A **coupon** is a printed certificate that entitles the bearer to a price reduction or some other special consideration for purchasing a particular product or service. In the United States and Great Britain, marketers rely heavily on newspapers to deliver coupons; nearly 90 percent of all coupons are distributed in a printed ride-along vehicle known as a *free-standing insert* (FSI). Sunday papers carry the vast majority of FSIs. *On-pack coupons* are attached to, or part of, the product package; they can frequently be redeemed immediately at check out. *In-pack coupons* are placed inside the package. Coupons can also be handed out in stores, offered on a self-service basis from on-shelf dispensers, delivered to homes by mail, or distributed electronically at the checkout counter. Also, the number of coupons distributed via the Internet is growing. *Cross coupons* are distributed with one product but redeemable for a different product. For example, a toothpaste coupon might be distributed with a toothbrush. The United States is by far the world leader in terms of the number of coupons issued. NCH Marketing Services tracks coupon trends; according to a recent study, in 2002, 248 billion coupons were distributed in the United States of which consumers redeemed about 1.5 percent with an average value of 89 cents.

Coupons are a favorite promotion tool of consumer packaged goods companies such as Procter & Gamble and Unilever. The goal is to reward loyal users and stimulate product trial by nonusers. In the European Union, couponing is widely used in the United Kingdom and Belgium. Couponing is not as widely used in Asia where saving face is important. Although Asian consumers have a

---

4  Geoffrey Fowler, "When Free Samples Become Saviors," *The Wall Street Journal* (August 14, 2001), p. B1.
5  "Winning the China FMCG Market," ATKearney, 2003.

reputation for thriftiness, some are reluctant to use coupons because doing so might bring shame upon them or their families. According to Joseph Potacki, who teaches a "Basics of Promotion" seminar for the PMAA, couponing is the aspect of the promotion mix for which the practices in the United States differ the most from those in other countries. In the United States, couponing accounts for 70 percent of consumer promotion spending. Elsewhere, the percentage is much lower. According to Potacki, "It is far less—or nonexistent—in most other countries simply because the cultures don't accept couponing." Potacki notes that one reason couponing is gaining importance in countries such as the United Kingdom is because retailers are learning more about its advantages.[6] Table 14-2 gives an overview of regulations concerning coupon promotions in selected countries.

## Sales Promotions: Issues and Problems

As noted earlier, many companies are being more strategic in targeting their sampling programs. In the case of coupons, retailers must bundle the redeemed coupons together and ship them to a processing point. Many times, coupons are not validated at the point of purchase; fraudulent redemption costs marketers hundreds of millions of dollars each year. Human nature being what it is, fraud can take other forms as well. For example, during the 2004 Super Bowl broadcast, PepsiCo launched a joint promotion with Apple Computer's iTunes Music Store. Apple planned to give away 100 million songs for free (regular price: $0.99); consumers could obtain a code from the caps of Pepsi bottles and enter the code online to quality for the download. The promotion was designed so that anyone purchasing a bottle of Pepsi had a 1-in-3 chance of being a winner. However, many people discovered that, by tilting the bottles to one side, they could tell whether the bottle was a winner. Moreover, they could read the code without having to pay for the Pepsi!

Companies must take extreme care when formulating and executing sales promotions. In some emerging markets, sales promotion efforts can raise eyebrows if companies appear to be exploiting regulatory loopholes and lack of consumer resistance to intrusion. Sales promotion in Europe is highly regulated. Sales promotions are popular in Scandinavia because of restrictions on broadcast advertising, but promotions in the Nordic countries are themselves subject to regulations. If such regulations are relaxed as the single market develops in Europe and regulations are harmonized, companies may be able to roll out pan-European promotions.

A recent study examined coupon usage and attitudes toward both coupons and sweepstakes in Taiwan, Thailand, and Malaysia. The study has particular relevance to global companies that are targeting these and other developing nations in Asia where consumers have relatively little experience with coupons. The study utilized Hofstede's social values framework as a guide. All three countries in the study are collectivist, and the researchers found that an individual's positive attitude toward coupons and coupon usage was influenced by positive attitudes of family members and society as a whole. However, the three nations show some differences in value orientation. For example, Malaysia has a higher power distance and lower uncertainty avoidance than the others. For Malaysians, the fear of public embarrassment was a constraint on coupon usage. In all three countries, media consumption habits were also a factor; persons who were not regular readers of magazines or newspapers were less likely to be aware that coupons were available. Consumers in Taiwan and Thailand look more favorably upon coupons than sweepstakes. The impact of

---

[6] Leslie Ryan, "Sales Promotion: Made in America," *Brandweek* (July 31, 1995), p. 28.

religion surprised the researchers. In Malaysia, where the population is primarily Muslim, the researchers assumed that consumers would avoid sweepstakes promotions. Sweepstakes can be compared to gambling, which is frowned on by Islam. However, Malaysians showed a preference for sweepstakes over coupons. In Taiwan, where Buddhism, Confucianism, and Taoism are all practiced, religion appeared to have little impact on attitudes toward promotions. One implication for marketing in developing countries is that, despite cultural differences, increased availability of promotions will result in higher levels of consumer utilization.[7]

## LESSONS
# from the global marketplace

### AOL

America Online, or AOL as it is known, is the world's largest Internet service provider. One measure of the company's strength can be seen in its recent $156 billion merger with media giant TimeWarner. In the United States, nearly 20 million subscribers pay monthly fees of approximately $25 for unlimited use of the service. The company is known for its easy-to-use technology; AOL's signature greeting, "You've got mail," has become a cultural icon in the United States. The TimeWarner acquisition greatly increased the amount of media content available to subscribers. AOL was one of the stars of the tech boom in the 1990s; its subscription base grew rapidly as the company utilized an aggressive direct mail campaign to distribute its software via free computer disc and CD-ROM. Typically, AOL also offers new subscribers a free trial period (as much as 1000 hours). The company quickly surpassed established online companies such as Prodigy; AOL eventually acquired the well-known CompuServe. To maintain its fast-paced growth, AOL executives are looking to new markets in Europe, Latin America, and Asia. Currently, AOL and CompuServe have about 4.5 million subscribers. However, leadership status has eluded AOL outside its home country: The company ranks tenth in Japan and fourth in Brazil. A key question for AOL is whether the marketing strategy that built the business at home will work abroad.

By the middle of 2001, America Online Latin America reached the 1-million subscriber milestone. Market entry in Brazil had come at the end of 1998 via a joint venture with Cisnero Group, a Latin American media firm with offices in Florida. Brazil was identified as the best opportunity because it is home to half the Internet users in Latin America. However, AOL made several missteps. Following its practice in other countries, AOL distributed free CD-ROMs loaded with software in shopping malls and video stores. However, due to a manufacturing error, several hundred of the disks contained music rather than computer software. There was also a problem with the disks that weren't faulty; as the software loaded, it updated a user's Web browser and changed the appearance of home pages. The problems were reported in local newspapers and represented a minor public relations crisis for AOL.

Some observers also took exception to AOL's advertising claims that it was the "biggest" ISP. In fact, that distinction belonged to Universo Online SA (UOL), a local company that claimed to have 500,000 subscribers at the time of the AOL launch. AOL executives maintained that the claim was accurate because it referred to the company's global position. Another problem was the fact that a local Brazilian company had registered the domain name aol.com.br. The two sides are trying to resolve the issue in court. Another issue was a significant currency devaluation in Brazil. Despite these problems, AOL Latin America proceeded with launches in Mexico, Argentina, and Puerto Rico.

As the new millennium got underway, AOL Latin America President Charles Herington was upbeat about prospects in the region. Although industry observers questioned when the company would break even, Herington maintained that the company's strategy was on track. One indicator was the fact that subscriber revenue was growing at a faster rate than subscriber growth. In short, that meant that once the promotional trial period ended, users were converting to paying subscribers. "We've been successful at growing our membership faster than anybody else, but at the same time we have grown our revenue even more aggressively. Sometimes this message gets lost," Herington said. Because many subscribers lacked credit cards, they agreed to make monthly payments in cash at local banks. Many subscribers simply didn't pay, and their service was terminated. AOL shifted to requesting that subscribers pay cash in advance for a year's service. Another problem was the fact that local telephone companies charged high per-minute fees that drove up the cost of staying online. The venture posted a $233 million operating loss in 2001 on sales of only $66 million. By the end of 2003, the number of subscribers had dropped below 500,000.

*Sources: Julia Angwin, "America Online Seeks to Cut Losses Overseas," The Wall Street Journal (October 7, 2002), pp. A19, A21; Pamela Druckerman and Nick Wingfield, "Lost in Translation: AOL's Big Assault on Latin America Hits Snags in Brazil," The Wall Street Journal (July 11, 2000), pp. A1, A16; Matt Pottinger, "AOL to Unveil China Venture of $200 Million," The Wall Street Journal (June 4, 2001), p. A19; Druckerman, "Brazil is Test Case for Free Web Access," The Wall Street Journal (February 7, 2000), p. A28.*

---

[7] Lenard C. Huff and Dana L. Alden, "An Investigation of Consumer Response to Sales Promotions in Developing Markets: A Three Country Analysis," *Journal of Advertising Research* 38, no. 3 (May–June 1998), pp. 47–57.

# PERSONAL SELLING

**Personal selling** is person-to-person communication between a company representative and a prospective buyer. The seller's communication effort is focused on informing and persuading the prospect, with the short-term goal of making a sale and with a longer-term goal of building a relationship with that buyer. The salesperson's job is to correctly understand the buyer's needs, match those needs to the company's product(s), and then persuade the customer to buy. Because selling provides a two-way communication channel, it is especially important in marketing industrial products that may be expensive and technologically complex. Sales personnel can often provide headquarters with important customer feedback that can be utilized in design and engineering decisions.

Effective personal selling in a salesperson's home country requires building a relationship with the customer; global marketing presents additional challenges because the buyer and seller may come from different national or cultural backgrounds. Despite such challenges, it is difficult to overstate the importance of a face-to-face, personal selling effort for industrial products in global markets. In 1993, a Malaysian developer, YTL Corp., sought bids on a $700 million contract for power-generation turbines. Siemens of Germany and General Electric were among the bidders. Datuk Francis Yeoh, managing director of YTL, requested meetings with top executives from both companies. "I wanted to look them in the eye to see if we can do business," Yeoh said. Siemens complied with the request, GE did not send an executive, and Siemens was awarded the contract.[8]

Personal selling is also a popular marketing communication tool in countries with various restrictions on advertising. As noted in Chapter 13, it is difficult to obtain permission to present product comparisons in any type of advertising in Japan. In such an environment, selling is the best way to provide hard-hitting, side-by-side comparisons of competing products. Personal selling is also used frequently in countries where low wage rates allow large local sales forces to be hired. For example, Home Box Office built its core of subscribers in Hungary by selling door-to-door. In fact, the cost effectiveness of personal selling in certain parts of the world has been a key driver behind the decision at many U.S.-based firms to begin marketing products and services overseas. A company is more likely to test a new territory or product if the entry price is relatively low. For example, some high-tech firms have utilized lower-cost sales personnel in Latin America to introduce new product features to their customers. Only if the response is favorable do the firms commit major resources to a U.S. rollout.

The challenge to companies that wish to pursue low-cost personal selling overseas, however, is to establish and maintain acceptable quality among members of the sales team. The old saying, "You get what you pay for" has come to haunt more than one company that has undertaken global expansion. When MCI Communications first entered Latin America several decades ago, it was attracted in part by the prospect of achieving inexpensive market penetration for its large multinational client companies. Management's initial enthusiasm quickly gave way to an alarming realization that the quality of support in this part of the world was not on a level with what MCI's major accounts were used to in the United States. As a result, there was a period when both MCI and its competition chose the costlier sales approach of using U.S.-based personnel to provide remote, but higher quality, support to the Latin American sites of their respective global customer bases. However, MCI's upper management ultimately decided to invest more to create in-country sales and service teams whose output more closely mirrored that of their U.S. counterparts.

---

8   Marcus W. Brauchili, "Looking East: Asia, on the Ascent, Is Learning to Say No to 'Arrogant' West," *The Wall Street Journal* (April 13, 1994), pp. A1, A8.

The risks inherent in establishing a personal selling structure overseas remain today. The crucial issue is not whether in-country sales and marketing people can provide more benefit than a remote force. Today, it's a given that, in the vast majority of scenarios, they can. The issue is whether the country team should consist of in-country nationals or **expatriates** (also known as expats); that is, employees who are sent from their home countries to work abroad. It should be noted that many of the environmental issues and challenges identified in earlier chapters often surface as a company completes the initial stages of implementing a personal selling strategy. These include:

- *Political risks.* Unstable or corrupt governments can completely change the rules for the sales team. Establishing new operations in a foreign country is especially tricky if a coup is imminent or if a dictator demands certain "considerations" (which has been the case in many developing countries). For example, Colombia offers great market potential and its government projects an image of openness. However, many companies have found the unspoken rules of the Cabal to be inordinately burdensome. In a country ruled by a dictatorship, the target audience and accompanying message of the sales effort tend to be far narrower and restricted because government planners mandate how business will be conducted. Firms selling in Hong Kong were concerned that China would impose its will and dramatically alter the selling environment after the transfer of power in 1997. In response to such concerns, British Telecom brought many members of its Hong Kong sales staff back to London prior to the changeover. However, to the great relief of Hong Kong's business community, Chinese officials ultimately recognized that a policy of minimal intervention would be the wisest approach.

- *Regulatory hurdles.* Governments sometimes set up quota systems or impose tariffs that affect entering foreign sales forces. In part, governments consider such actions to be an easy source of revenue, but, even more important, policy makers want to ensure that sales teams from local firms retain a competitive edge in terms of what they can offer and at what price. Regulations can also take the form of rules that disallow certain types of sales activities. In 1998, for example, the Chinese government banned door-to-door selling, effectively blocking Avon's business model. Avon responded by establishing a network of store representatives; today, China is Avon's fastest growing global market. Avon CEO Andrea Jung expects annual sales in China to reach $400 million by 2007.

- *Currency fluctuations.* There have been many instances where a company's sales effort has been derailed not by ineffectiveness or lack of market opportunity, but by fluctuating currency values. In the mid-1980s, for example, Caterpillar's global market share declined when the dollar's strength allowed Komatsu to woo U.S. customers away. Then, while Caterpillar's management team was preoccupied with domestic issues, competitors chipped away at the firm's position in global markets.

- *Market unknowns.* When a company enters a new region of the world, its selling strategy may unravel because of a lack of knowledge of market conditions, the accepted way of doing business, or the positioning of its in-country competitors. When a game plan is finally crafted to counter the obstacles, it is sometimes too late for the company to succeed. However, if management devotes an inordinate amount of time conducting market research prior to entry, it may discover that its window of opportunity has been lost to a fastmoving competitor that did not fall victim to the "analysis paralysis" syndrome. Thus, it is difficult to make generalizations about the optimal time to enter a new country.

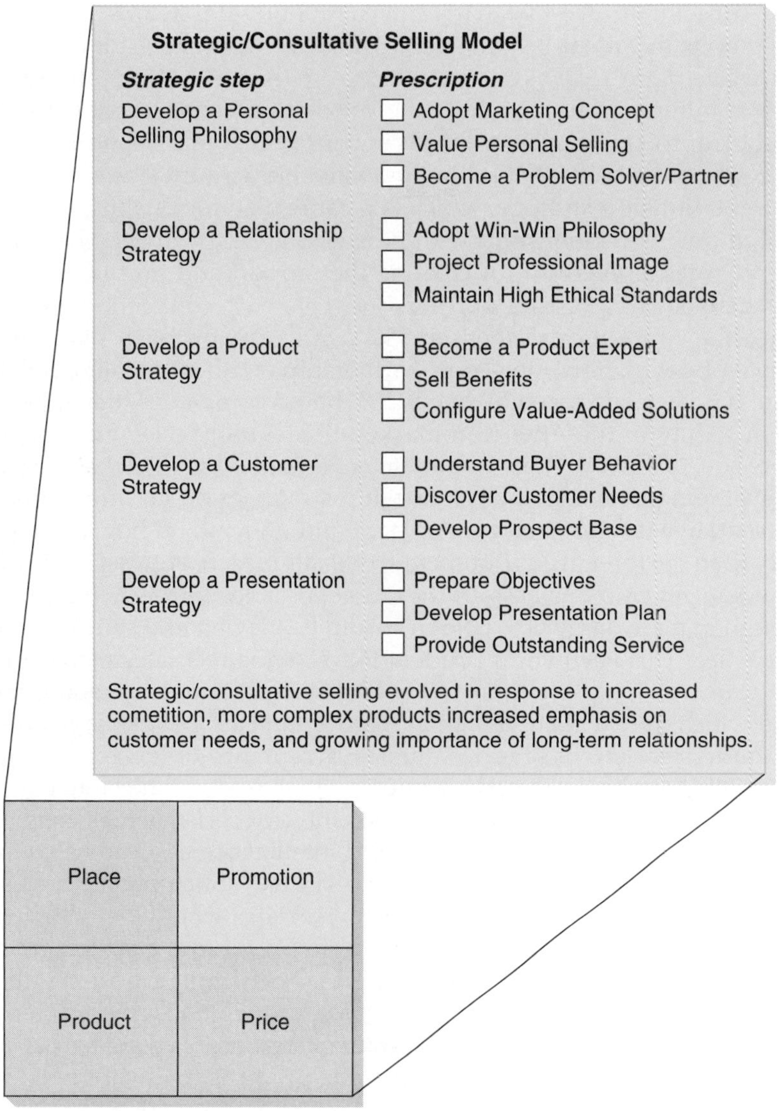

**Figure 14-1**

The Strategic/Consultative Selling Model

Source: Gerald L. Manning and Barry L. Reece,
Selling Today: Creating Customer Value, 9th ed.
(Upper Saddle River, NJ: Prentice Hall, 2004),
p. 15.

**Strategic/Consultative Selling Model**

| Strategic step | Prescription |
|---|---|
| Develop a Personal Selling Philosophy | ☐ Adopt Marketing Concept |
| | ☐ Value Personal Selling |
| | ☐ Become a Problem Solver/Partner |
| Develop a Relationship Strategy | ☐ Adopt Win-Win Philosophy |
| | ☐ Project Professional Image |
| | ☐ Maintain High Ethical Standards |
| Develop a Product Strategy | ☐ Become a Product Expert |
| | ☐ Sell Benefits |
| | ☐ Configure Value-Added Solutions |
| Develop a Customer Strategy | ☐ Understand Buyer Behavior |
| | ☐ Discover Customer Needs |
| | ☐ Develop Prospect Base |
| Develop a Presentation Strategy | ☐ Prepare Objectives |
| | ☐ Develop Presentation Plan |
| | ☐ Provide Outstanding Service |

Strategic/consultative selling evolved in response to increased cometition, more complex products increased emphasis on customer needs, and growing importance of long-term relationships.

| Place | Promotion |
|---|---|
| Product | Price |

If all of these challenges can be overcome, or at least minimized, the personal selling endeavor can be implemented with the aid of a tool known as the Strategic/Consultative Selling Model.

## The Strategic/Consultative Selling Model

Figure 14-1 shows the **Strategic/Consultative Selling Model,** which has gained wide acceptance in the United States. The model consists of five interdependent steps, each with three prescriptions that can serve as a checklist for sales personnel.[9] Many U.S. companies have begun developing global markets and have established face-to-face sales teams either directly, using their own personnel, or indirectly, through contracted sales agents. As a result, the Strategic/Consultative Selling Model is increasingly utilized on a worldwide basis. The key to ensuring that the model produces the desired outcome—building quality partnerships with customers—is to have it implemented and followed on a consistent basis. This is

---

[9] This discussion of the Strategic/Consultative Selling Model is adapted from Gerald L. Manning and Barry L. Reece, *Selling Today: Creating Customer Value*, 9th ed. (Upper Saddle River, NJ: Prentice Hall, 2004), Chapter 1. The authors are also indebted to Larry Sirhall, a marketing consultant based in Bend, Oregon.

far more difficult to achieve with international sales teams than it is with U.S.-based units that are much more accessible to corporate headquarters.

First, a sales representative must develop a **personal selling philosophy.** This requires a commitment to the marketing concept and a willingness to adopt the role of problem solver or partner in helping customers. A sales professional must also be secure in the belief that selling is a valuable activity. The second step is to develop a **relationship strategy,** which is a game plan for establishing and maintaining high-quality relationships with prospects and customers. The relationship strategy provides a blueprint for creating the rapport and mutual trust that will serve as the basis of a lasting partnership. This step connects sales personnel directly to the concept of *relationship marketing*, an approach that stresses the importance of developing long-term partnerships with customers. Relationship marketing has been embraced by many U.S.-based companies that apply the concept when selling in the American market; it is equally relevant—and perhaps even more so—to any company hoping to achieve success in global marketing.

In developing personal and relationship strategies on an international level, the representative is wise to take a step back and understand how these strategies will likely fit in the foreign environment. For example, an aggressive "I'll do whatever it takes to get your business" is the worst possible approach in some cultures, even though in many large U.S. cities it would be viewed as a standard, even preferred, practice. This is why it is prudent for a company's sales management and sales rep teams to invest the time and energy necessary to learn about the global market in which they will be selling. In many countries, people have only a rudimentary understanding of sales techniques; acceptance of those techniques may be low as well. A sophisticated sales campaign that excels in the United States may never hit the mark in other countries. In-country experts such as consultants or agents can be excellent sources of real world intelligence that can help a sales rep create an effective international relationship strategy. Such people are especially helpful if the sales force will include many expatriates who will not have resident nationals as colleagues whom they can turn to for advice. Sales representatives must understand that patience and a willingness to assimilate host-country norms and customs are important attributes in developing relationships built on respect.

The third step, developing a **product strategy,** results in a plan that can assist the sales representative in selecting and positioning products that will satisfy customer needs. A sales professional must be an expert who possesses not only a deep understanding of the features and attributes of each product he or she represents but also an understanding of competitive offerings. That understanding is then used to position the product and communicate benefits that are relevant to the customer's wants and needs. As with the selling philosophy and relationship strategy, this step must include comprehension of the target market's characteristics and the fact that prevailing needs and wants may mandate products that are different than those offered in the home country. Until recently, most American companies engaged in international selling have offered products rather than services. For example, John Deere did a marvelous job of increasing its global market share by supplying high quality but relatively mundane farming equipment to countries where agriculture remains a mainstay of local economies. Today, however, with exploding worldwide demand for technology-related services, the picture is changing. For example, in 2003, services accounted for 48 percent of IBM's revenues and 41 percent of profits.

Next comes a **customer strategy,** a plan that ensures that the sales professional will be maximally responsive to customer needs. Doing so requires a general understanding of consumer behavior; in addition, the salesperson must collect and analyze as much information as possible about the needs of each customer or prospect. The customer strategy step also includes building a prospect base, consisting of current customers as well as potential customers (or leads). A qualified lead is someone whose probability of wanting to buy the product is high. Many sales organizations diminish their own productivity by chasing after

**Figure 14-2**

*Building a High-Quality Sales Partnership*

Source: Gerald L. Manning and Barry L. Reece, Selling Today: Creating Customer Value, 9th ed. (Upper Saddle River, NJ: Prentice Hall, 2004), p. 18.

too many nonqualified leads. This issue can be extremely challenging for an international sales unit because customer cues or "buying signs" may not coincide with those that have been proven in the sales rep's home country.

The final step, the actual face-to-face selling situation, requires a **presentation strategy.** This consists of setting objectives for each sales call and establishing a presentation plan to meet those objectives. The presentation strategy must be based on the sales representative's commitment to provide outstanding service to customers. As shown in Figure 14-2, when these four strategies are integrated with an appropriate personal selling philosophy, the result is a high-quality partnership.

The **presentation plan** that is at the heart of the presentation strategy is typically divided into six stages: approach, presentation, demonstration, negotiation, closing, and servicing the sale (see Figure 14-3). The relative importance of each

| The Six-Step Presentation Plan | |
|---|---|
| **Step One:**<br>Approach | ☐ Review Strategic/Consultative Selling Model<br>☐ Initiate customer contact |
| **Step Two:**<br>Presentation | ☐ Determine prospect needs<br>☐ Select product or service<br>☐ Initiate sales presentation |
| **Step Three:**<br>Demonstration | ☐ Decide what to demonstrate<br>☐ Select selling tools<br>☐ Initiate demonstration |
| **Step Four:**<br>Negotiation | ☐ Anticipate buyer concerns<br>☐ Plan negotiating methods<br>☐ Initiate win-win negotiations |
| **Step Five:**<br>Close | ☐ Plan appropriate closing methods<br>☐ Recognize closing clues<br>☐ Initiate closing methods |
| **Step Six:**<br>Servicing the Sale | ☐ Suggestion selling<br>☐ Follow through<br>☐ follow-up calls |

Service, retail, wholesale, and manufacturer selling

**Figure 14-3**

*The Six-Step Presentation Plan*

Source: Gerald L. Manning and Barry L. Reece, Selling Today: Creating Customer Value, 9th ed. (Upper Saddle River, NJ: Prentice Hall, 2004), p. 209.

stage can vary by country or region. As mentioned several times already, the global salesperson *must* understand cultural norms and proper protocol, from proper exchange of business cards to the volume of one's voice during a discussion to the level of eye contact made with the decision maker. In some countries, the approach is drawn out, as the buyer gets to know or takes the measure of the salesperson on a personal level with no mention of the pending deal. In such instances, the presentation comes only after rapport has been firmly established. In some regions of Latin America and Asia, rapport development may take weeks, even months. The customer may place more importance on what occurs *following* work than on what is accomplished during the formal work hours of 8 A.M. to 5 P.M.

In the six-step presentation plan, the first step, *approach*, is the sales representative's initial contact with the customer or prospect. The most crucial element of the step is to completely understand the decision-making process and the roles of each participant, such as decision maker, influencer, ally, or blocker. In some societies, it is difficult to identify the highest-ranking individual based on observable behavior during group meetings. This crucial bit of strategic information often is uncovered only after the rep has spent considerable time developing rapport and getting to know the overall customer organization from various perspectives and in various contexts.

In the *presentation* step, the prospect's needs are assessed and matched to the company's products. To communicate effectively with a foreign audience, the style and message of the presentation must be carefully thought out. In the United States, the presentation is typically designed to sell and persuade, whereas the intent of the international version should be to educate and inform. High-pressure tactics rarely succeed in global selling, despite the fact that they are natural components of many American sales pitches. The message is equally critical because what may be regarded as fully acceptable in U.S. discussions may either offend or confuse the overseas sales audience. A humorous example of this occurred during a session between representatives from Adolph Coors Company and a foreign prospect. The first slide in the presentation contained a translation of Coors's slogan "Turn It Loose," but within seconds of this slide being shown, the audience began to chuckle. As translated, the slogan described diarrhea—obviously something that the presenter had no desire to convey to this group!

Next comes the *sales demonstration*, during which the salesperson has the opportunity to tailor the communication effort to the customer and alternately tell and show how the product can meet the customer's needs. This step represents one of selling's important advantages as a promotional tool. The prospect's senses become involved, and he or she can actually see the product in action, touch it, taste it, or hear it, as the case may be.

During the presentation, the prospect may express concerns or objections about the product itself, the price, or some other aspect of the sale. Dealing with objections in an international setting is a learned art. In some cases, this is simply part of the sales ritual and the customer expects the representative to be prepared for a lively debate on the pros and cons of the product in question. In some instances, it is taboo to initiate an open discussion where any form of disagreement is apparent; such conversations are to be handled in a one-to-one situation or in a small group with a few key individuals present. A common theme in sales training is the concept of **active listening;** naturally, in global sales, verbal and nonverbal communication barriers of the type discussed in Chapter 4 present special challenges. When objections are successfully overcome, serious negotiations can begin.

*Negotiation* is required to ensure that both the customer and the salesperson come away from the presentation as winners. Experienced American sales reps know that persistence during the negotiation stage is one tactic often needed to win an order in the United States. However, American-style persistence inferring tenacity or arm-twisting can be considered rude and offensive by some foreign customers. This can end the negotiations quickly—or, in the worst case, such behavior can be taken as a display of self-perceived American superiority, which then must be countered aggressively or brought to an immediate end. Inappropriate application of American-style negotiation tactics has plagued some U.S. sales reps attempting to assertively close deals with Canadian companies. Conversely, in other countries, persistence often means endurance, a willingness to patiently invest months or years before the effort results in an actual sale. For example, a company wishing to enter the Japanese market must be prepared for negotiations to take from 3 to 10 years.

Having completed the negotiation step, the sales representative is able to move on to the *close* and thus ask for the order. Attitudes toward the degree of bluntness that is acceptable in making this request vary among countries. In Latin America, a bold closing statement is respected, whereas in Asia, it is something that must be done with more deference toward the decision maker. As with objection handling and negotiation, the close is a selling skill that comes with both knowledge and experience in global business and sales.

The final step is *servicing the sale*. A successful sale does not end when the order is written; to ensure customer satisfaction with the purchase, an implementation process (which may include delivery and installation) must be outlined and a customer service program established. Implementation can be complicated because of logistical and transportation issues as well as potential problems with the in-country resources to handle all the necessary steps. Transportation alternatives were discussed in Chapter 12. Decisions regarding resources for implementation and after-sale service are similar to decisions about the personal selling structure described in the following paragraphs. There are cost benefits to using in-country nationals for implementation, but quality control is more difficult to guarantee. Establishing expatriates for the primary function of implementation is costly and normally cannot be justified until international operations are more mature and profitable. However, sending an implementation team to the host country creates a variety of expense and regulatory concerns. Even when implementation has been adequately addressed, the requirement for sold customer service raises all of the same questions again: in-country nationals, expatriates, or third-country nationals?

## Sales Force Nationality

As noted previously, a basic issue for companies that sell globally is the composition of the sales force in terms of nationality. It is possible to utilize expatriate salespersons, hire host country nationals, or utilize third-country sales personnel. The staffing decision is contingent on several factors, including management's orientation, the technological sophistication of the product, and the stage of economic development exhibited by the target country. These are summarized in Table 14-3.

**Table 14-3**

Contingency Factors in Selecting Sales Force Nationality

| Technology Level | Management Orientation | | | | | |
| | Ethnocentric | | Polycentric | | Regiocentric | |
| | Developed | Less Developed | Developed | Less Developed | Developed | Less Developed |
| High | Expatriates | Expatriates | Expatriates | Host-country nationals | Expatriates | Third-country nationals |
| Low | Expatriates | Expatriates | Host-country nationals | Host-country nationals (agents) | Third-country nationals | Third-country nationals (agents) |

*Source:* Earl D. Honeycutt Jr. and John B. Ford, "Guidelines for Managing an International Sales Force," *Industrial Marketing Management* 24, p. 139. © Copyright 1999–2003, with permission from Elsevier.

Not surprisingly, a company with an ethnocentric orientation is likely to prefer expatriates and adopt a standardized approach without regard to technology or the level of economic development in the target country. Polycentric companies selling in developed countries should opt for expatriates to sell technologically sophisticated products; a host-country sales force can be used when technological sophistication is lower. In less-developed countries, host-country nationals should be used for products in which technology is a factor; host-country agents should be used for low-tech products. The widest diversity of sales force nationality is found in a company in which a regiocentric orientation prevails. Except in the case of high-tech products in developed countries, third-country nationals are likely to be used in all situations.

In addition to the factors just cited, management must also weigh the advantages and disadvantages of each nationality type (see Table 14-4). First, because they come from the home country, expatriates often possess a high level of product knowledge and are likely to be thoroughly versed in their company's commitment to after-sales service. They come with corporate philosophies and culture well engrained. Also, they are better able to institute the acceptable practices and follow the policies of the home office and, generally, there is less potential for control or loyalty issues to arise. Finally, a foreign assignment can also provide employees with valuable experience that can enhance promotion prospects. There are also several disadvantages to utilizing expatriates. If the headquarters mind-set is *too* firmly ingrained, the expat may have a difficult time understanding the foreign environment and assimilating into it. This can eventually lead to significant losses; the sales effort may be poorly received in the market or homesickness can lead to a costly reversal of the relocation process. Indeed, maintaining expat sales personnel is extremely expensive; the average annual cost to U.S. companies of posting employees and their families overseas exceeds $250,000. In addition to paying expat salaries, companies must pay moving expenses, cost-of-living adjustments, and host-country taxes. Despite the high investment, many expats fail to complete their assignments because of inadequate training and orientation prior to the cross-border transfer. In addition, studies have shown that one-quarter of U.S. expats leave their companies within a year of returning home.

An alternative is to build a sales force with host-country personnel. Locals offer several advantages, including intimate knowledge of the market and business environment, language skills, and superior knowledge of local culture. The last

**Table 14-4**

*Advantages and Disadvantages of Different Sales Types*

| Category | Advantages | Disadvantages |
|---|---|---|
| Expatriates | Superior product knowledge<br>Demonstrated commitment to high customer service standards<br>Train for promotion<br>Greater HQ control | Highest cost<br>High turnover<br>Cost for language and cross-cultural training |
| Host country | Economical<br>Superior market knowledge<br>Language skills<br>Superior cultural knowledge<br>Implement actions sooner | Needs product training<br>May be held in low esteem<br>Language skills may not be important<br>Difficult to ensure loyalty |
| Third country | Cultural sensitivity<br>Language skills<br>Economical<br>Allows regional sales coverage | Faces identity problems<br>Blocked promotions<br>Income gaps<br>Needs product or company training<br>Loyalty not assured |

*Source:* Adapted from Earl D. Honeycutt Jr. and John B. Ford, "Guidelines for Managing an International Sales Force," *Industrial Marketing Management* 24, p. 138. © Copyright 1999–2003, with permission from Elsevier.

consideration can be especially important in Asia and Latin America. In addition, because in-country personnel are already in place in the target country, there is no need for expensive relocations. However, host-country nationals may possess work habits or selling styles that do not mesh with those of the parent company. Furthermore, the firms' corporate sales executives tend to have less control over an operation that is dominated by host-country nationals. Headquarters executives may also experience difficulty cultivating loyalty, and host-country nationals are likely to need hefty doses of training and education regarding both the company and its products.

A third option is to hire persons who are not natives of either the headquarters country or the host country; such persons are known as *third-country nationals.* For example, a U.S.-based company might hire someone from Thailand to represent it in China. This option has many advantages in common with the host-country national approach. In addition, if conflict, diplomatic tension, or some other form of disagreement has driven a wedge between the home country and the target sales country, a sales representative from a third country may be perceived as sufficiently neutral or "at arm's length" to enable the company to continue its sales effort. However, there are several disadvantages of the third-country option. For one thing, sales prospects may wonder why they have been approached by someone who is neither a local national nor a native of the headquarters country. Third-country nationals may lack motivation if they are compensated less generously than expats or host-country sales personnel; also, they may find themselves passed over for promotions as coveted assignments go to others.

After much trial and error in creating sales forces, most companies today attempt to establish a hybrid sales force comprised of a balanced mix of expatriates and in-country nationals. The operative word for this approach is *balanced,* because there always remains the potential for conflict between the two groups. It is also the most expensive proposition in terms of up-front costs because, both relocation of expats and extensive training of in-country nationals are required. However, the short-term costs are usually deemed necessary in order to do business and conduct personal selling overseas.

After considering the options shown in Table 14-4, management may question the appropriateness of trying to create personal selling units made up of their own people. A fourth option is to utilize the services of **sales agents.** Agents work under contract rather than as full-time employees. In the United States, companies have used sales agents for many years, often with mixed results. From a global perspective, it often makes a great deal of sense to set up one or more agent entities to at least gain entry to a selected country or region. In some cases, because of the remoteness of the area or the lack of revenue opportunity (beyond servicing satellite operations of customers headquartered elsewhere), agents are retained on a fairly permanent level. To this day, the majority of U.S., Asian, and European companies with an Africa-based sales presence maintain agent groups to represent their interests.

Agents are much less expensive than full-time employees and possess the same advantage of understanding the market as a team of in-country nationals. Subsequently, if a certain degree of success is achieved, the role of agents can be diminished in favor of employee-based teams. Conversely, if the market does not prove to be financially viable, it is much less costly to pull out from an agent-oriented territory. However, the challenge of control that was discussed earlier is even greater due to the fact that agents frequently have other sources of income available to them. Thus, a company may find itself in a relatively weak bargaining position when coming to terms with agents. Additionally, because there are other job opportunities for agents (especially with the growing trend of firms in the same industry concurrently targeting the same overseas markets), the question of loyalty is significant. A company that employs foreign sales agents has to determine just what to provide in terms of product and strategic training because of the very real possibility that a competitor will lure those agents away with more attractive compensation packages.

Agents have even used their remote locations as a shield to avoid detection as they accept assignments from competing firms, offering customers the best deal among the several options they represent. Situations such as this mean that companies must create some type of monitoring system within agent territories, either through an in-country manager or regular visits from the home office sales department.

Other international personal selling approaches that fall somewhere between sales agents and full-time employee teams include:

- *Exclusive license arrangements* in which a firm will pay commissions to an in-country company's sales force to conduct personal selling on its behalf. For example, when Canada's regulatory agency prevented U.S. telephone companies from entering the market on their own, AT&T, MCI, Sprint, and other firms crafted a series of exclusive license arrangements with Canadian telephone companies.
- *Contract manufacturing or production* with a degree of personal selling made available through warehouses or showrooms that are open to potential customers. Sears has employed this technique in various overseas markets, with the emphasis placed on the manufacturing and production but with the understanding that opportunities for some sales results do exist.
- *Management-only agreements* through which a corporation will manage a foreign sales force in a mode that is similar to franchising. Hilton Hotels has these types of agreements all over the world; not only for hotel operations but also for personal selling efforts aimed at securing conventions, business meetings, and large group events.
- *Joint ventures* with an in-country (or regional) partner. Because many countries place restrictions on foreign ownership within their borders, partnerships can serve as the best way for a company to obtain both a personal sales capability as well as an existing base of customers.

## SPECIAL FORMS OF MARKETING COMMUNICATIONS: DIRECT MARKETING, EVENT SPONSORSHIP, AND PRODUCT PLACEMENT

The Direct Marketing Association defines **direct marketing** as any communication with a consumer or business recipient that is designed to generate a response in the form of an order, a request for further information, and/or a visit to a store or other place of business. Companies use direct mail, telemarketing, television, print, and other media to generate responses and build databases filled with purchase histories and other information about customers. By contrast, mass marketing communications are typically aimed at broad segments of consumers with certain demographic, psychographic, or behavioral characteristics in common. Other differences between direct marketing and "regular" marketing are shown in Table 14-5. Although direct marketing dates back decades, more sophisticated techniques and tools are being used today. For example, Don Peppers and Martha Rogers advocate an approach known as **one-to-one marketing.** Building on the notion of customer relationship management (CRM), one-to-one marketing calls for treating different customers differently based on their previous purchase history or past interactions with the company. Peppers and Rogers describe the four steps in one-to-one marketing as follows:[10]

1. *Identify* customers and accumulate detailed information about them
2. *Differentiate* customers and rank them in terms of their value to the company

---

[10] Don Peppers, Martha Rogers, and Bob Dorf, "Is Your Company Ready for One-to-One Marketing?" *Harvard Business Review* 77, no. 1 (January–February 1999).

| Direct Marketing | Mass Marketing | Table 14-5 |
|---|---|---|
| Marketer adds value (creates place utility) by arranging for delivery of product to customer's door. | Product benefits do not typically include delivery to customer's door. | *Comparison of Direct Marketing and Mass Marketing* |
| Marketer controls the product all the way through to delivery. | Marketer typically loses control as product is turned over to distribution channel intermediaries. | |
| Direct response advertising is used to generate an immediate inquiry or order. | Advertising is used for cumulative effect over time to build image, awareness, loyalty, and benefit recall. Purchase action is deferred. | |
| Repetition is used within the ad or offer. | Repetition is used over a period of time. | |
| Customer perceives higher risk because product is bought unseen. Recourse may be viewed as distant or inconvenient. | Customer perceives less risk due to direct contact with product. Recourse is viewed as less distant. | |

Source: Adapted from Direct Marketing Association.

3. *Interact* with customers and develop more cost efficient and effective forms of interaction
4. *Customize* the product or service offered to the customer, e.g., by personalizing direct mail offers

Worldwide, the popularity of direct marketing has been steadily increasing in recent years. One reason is the availability of credit cards—widespread in some countries, growing in others—as a convenient payment mechanism for direct response purchases. (In fact, Visa, American Express, and MasterCard generate enormous revenues by sending direct mail offers to their cardholders.) Another reason is societal: Whether in Japan, Germany, or the United States, dual-income families have money to spend but less time to shop outside the home. Technological advances have made it easier for companies to reach customers directly. Cable and satellite television allow advertisers to reach specific audiences on a global basis. As noted in Chapter 7, MTV reaches nearly 400 million households worldwide and attracts a young viewership. A company wishing to reach businesspeople can buy time on CNN, Fox News Network, or CNBC.

Direct marketing's popularity in Europe increased sharply during the 1990s. The European Commission expects investment in direct marketing to surpass expenditures for traditional advertising in the near future. One reason is that direct marketing programs can be readily made to conform to the "think global, act local" philosophy. Notes Tony Coad, managing director of a London-based direct marketing and database company, "Given the linguistic, cultural, and regional diversity of Europe, the celebrated idea of a Euro-consumer is Euro-baloney. Direct marketing's strength lies in addressing these differences and adapting to each consumer."[11] Obstacles still remain, however, including the European Commission's concerns about data protection and privacy, high postal rates in some countries, and the relatively limited development of the mailing list industry. Rainer Hengst of Deutsche Post offers the following guidelines for U.S.-based direct marketers that wish to go global:[12]

● The world is full of people who are not Americans. Be sure not to treat them like they are.

---

[11] Bruce Crumley, "European Market Continues to Soar," *Advertising Age* (February 21, 1994), p. 22.
[12] Rainer Hengst, "Plotting Your Global Strategy," *Direct Marketing* 63, no. 4 (August 2000), pp. 52–57.

- Like politics, all marketing is local. Just because your direct mail campaign worked in Texas, do not assume it will work in Toronto.
- Although there may be a European Union, there is no such thing as a "European."
- Pick your target, focus on one country, and do your homework.
- You'll have a hard time finding customers in Paris, France, if your return address is Paris, Texas. Customers need to be able to return products locally or at least believe there are services available in their country.

## Direct Mail

Direct mail uses the postal service as a vehicle for delivering an offer to prospects targeted by the marketer. Direct mail is the primary marketing tool for retail specialists such as L.L. Bean and Lands' End; it is also popular with banks, insurance companies, and other financial services providers. As customers respond to direct mail offers, the marketer adds information to its database. That information, in turn, allows the marketer to refine subsequent offers and generate more precisely targeted lists. In the United States, there is a well-developed mailing list industry. A company can rent a list to target virtually any type of buyer; naturally, the more selective and specialized the list, the more expensive it is. The availability of good lists and the sheer size of the market are important factors in explaining why Americans receive more direct mail than anyone else (see Table 14-6). However, on a per capita basis, German consumers are world-leader mail-order shoppers, buying more than $500 each in merchandise annually. Americans rank second, with annual per capita spending of $379 (see Table 14-7).

Compared with the United States, list availability in Europe and Japan is much more limited. The lists that are available may be lower in quality and contain more errors and duplications than lists from the United States. Despite such problems, direct mail is growing in popularity in some parts of the world. In Europe, for example, regulators are concerned about the extent that children are exposed to, or even targeted by, traditional cigarette advertising. Faced with the threat of increased restrictions on it advertising practices, the tobacco industry is making a strategy shift toward direct mail. As David Robottom, development director at the Direct Marketing Association, noted, "Many of the promotions on cigarette packets are about collected data. [The tobacco companies] are working very hard at building up loyalty." Table 14-8 lists direct mail volume for selected European countries. The data shown in the table confirm the widespread use of direct mail in Germany; with the exception of Denmark and the Netherlands, the countries listed in Table 14-7 are experiencing healthy growth in direct mail volume.

Following the economic crisis in Asia, a number of companies in that region have turned to direct mail in an effort to use their advertising budgets more effectively. Historically, the Asian direct marketing sector has lagged behind its

***Table 14-6***

*Annual Number of Direct Mail Pieces Received Per Capita*

| Country | Number of Direct Mail Pieces |
|---|---|
| United States | 350+ |
| Switzerland | 107 |
| Germany | 68 |
| France | 65 |
| Norway | 53 |
| Denmark | 50 |
| Finland | 46 |
| Great Britain | 40 |
| Ireland | 20 |

*Source:* Deutsche Post.

| Country | Per Capita Sales |
|---|---|
| Germany | $528 |
| United States | 379 |
| Switzerland | 333 |
| United Kingdom | 280 |
| France | 231 |
| Denmark | 227 |
| Norway | 219 |
| Finland | 212 |

**Table 14-7**

*Annual Mail Order Sales*

Source: Deutsche Post.

counterparts in the United States and Europe. Grey Global Group established a Kuala Lumpur office of Grey Direct Interactive in 1997; OgilvyOne Worldwide is the Malaysian subsidiary of Ogilvy & Mather Group specializing in direct marketing. Companies in the banking and telecommunications sectors have been at the forefront of direct marketing initiatives in Asia, using their extensive databases to target individual consumers by mail or Internet. In 2000, Nestlé launched a successful direct mail campaign in Malaysia that offered cat owners free samples of Friskies brand cat food, coupons for discounts on purchases of Friskies, and the opportunity to join the Friskies Cat Club. Nestlé expanded its existing database of 450,000 names by placing newspaper ads offering coupons to readers who wrote to the company, distributing questionnaires in conjunction with in-store sampling, and by hosting contests on its Web site. The 20 percent response rate to the Friskies mailing was well above the single-digit rates typical of direct mail campaigns in the United States. As Leong Ming Chee, marketing and communications director for Nestlé Products, noted, "You can spend 100,000 ringgit ($26,320) on TV ads for a product like this and have no idea how many viewers have cats and so how much of it goes to waste. This way, you can target those exact consumers directly."[13]

A recent campaign by Mercedes-Benz shows the role that direct mail can play in a coordinated communications program. Prior to the launch of the new American-built All Activity Vehicle (AAV), the company targeted 135,000 prospective buyers with a mailing designed to build traffic at dealerships. An initial mailing consisted of a detailed questionnaire covering topics that ranged from the appropriate number of cupholders to safety. After the questionnaires were analyzed, respondents received a second mailing customized according to their earlier responses. For example, prospects interested in safety received information about airbags. Because production of the vehicle had not yet begun, Mercedes

| Country | 1999 | 2000 | 2001 | % change 2000 vs 2001 |
|---|---|---|---|---|
| Denmark | 235 | 237 | 222 | −6.3 |
| France | 4,252 | 4,501 | 4,591 | +2.0 |
| Germany | 6,398 | 6,442 | 6,508 | +1.0 |
| Netherlands | 1,449 | 1,532 | 1,494 | −2.5 |
| Norway | 377 | 374 | 400 | +7.0 |
| Poland | 295 | 291 | 307 | +5.7 |
| Switzerland | 1,300 | 1,535 | 1,703 | +10.9 |
| United Kingdom | 4,345 | 4,664 | 4,939 | +5.9 |

**Table 14-8**

*Addressed European Direct Mail Volume* (millions of items)

Source: Direct Mail Information Service (DMIS).

---

[13] Cris Prystay, "In Malaysia, Advertisers Adopt Direct Mail to Keep Sales Purring," *Asian Wall Street Journal* (March 26–April 1, 2001), p. 12.

managers were able to make some minor changes in accordance with respondent preferences, such as placing the spare tire inside the vehicle and offering a roof rack as standard equipment. As the launch date approached, potential customers were able to reserve an AAV by mail and specify the color and options that they wanted.

## Catalogs

Worldwide, mail order represents a $200 billion market. A **catalog** is a magazine-style publication that features photographs, illustrations, and extensive information about a company's products. (The term "magalog" is sometimes used to describe this communication medium.) Catalogs have a long and illustrious history as a direct marketing tool in both Europe and the United States.[14] The European catalog market flourished after World War II as consumers sought convenience, bargain prices, and access to a wider range of goods. U.S.-based catalog marketers include Lands' End, L.L. Bean, The Sharper Image, and Victoria's Secret; in Europe, Great Universal Stores, Littlewoods, Freemans, and Otto GmbH & Co KG (which includes Spiegel and Eddie Bauer) are well-known catalog companies. Catalogs are widely recognized as an important part of an integrated marketing communications program, and many companies use catalogs in tandem with traditional retail distribution. The U.S. mail order market generates $90 billion in annual revenues; U.S. companies are the world's leading catalog marketers, accounting for 50 percent of global catalog sales. European companies rank second, with a 40 percent share.

Historically, catalogers in the United States benefited from the ability to ship goods from one coast to the other, crossing multiple state boundaries with relatively few regulatory hurdles. By contrast, prior to the advent of the single market, catalog sales in Europe were hindered by the fact that mail order products passing through customs at national borders were subject to value-added taxes (VAT). Because VAT drove up prices of goods that crossed borders, a particular catalog tended to be targeted at intracountry buyers. In other words, Germans bought from German catalogs, French consumers bought from French catalogs, and so on. Market-entry strategies were also affected by the customs regulations; catalogers grew by acquiring existing companies in various countries. For example, Otto GmbH & Co KG distributes more than 600 different catalogs in 21 countries.

Today, the single market means that mail order goods can move freely throughout the EU without incurring VAT charges. Also, since January 1993, VAT exemptions have been extended to goods bound to the European Free Trade Area countries (Norway, Iceland, Switzerland, and Liechtenstein). Some predict robust growth in Europe's mail order business, thanks to the increased size of the potential catalog market and the VAT-free environment. The single market is also attracting American catalog retailers, who will be faced with higher costs for paper, printing, and shipping as well as the familiar issue of whether to adapt their offerings to local tastes. Stephen Miles, director of international development, Lands' End, said, "The most difficult thing is to know in which areas to be local. We're proud that we're an American sportswear company, but that doesn't mean your average German consumer wants to pick up the phone and speak English to someone."[15]

In Japan, the domestic catalog industry is well developed. Leading catalog companies include Cecile, with $1 billion in annual sales of women's apparel and lingerie; Kukutake Publishing, which sells educational materials; and

---

[14] One of the authors of this book lives in a home that was ordered in kit form from the 1910 Sears catalog.
[15] Joshua Levine, "Give Me One of Those," *Forbes* (June 3, 1996), p. 134.

Shaddy, a general merchandise company. As noted in Chapter 12, Japan's fragmented distribution system represents a formidable obstacle to market entry by outsiders. An increasing number of companies use direct marketing to circumvent the distribution bottleneck. Annual revenues for all forms of consumer and business direct response advertising in Japan passed the $1 trillion mark in the mid-1990s; they declined to $525 billion in 2000 as Japan's economic difficulties continued. Direct mail (including catalogs) accounted for about $175 billion in 2000 direct response sales. Success can be achieved using different strategies. For example, Patagonia dramatically increased sales after publishing a Japanese-language catalog, whereas L.L. Bean offers a Japanese-language insert in its traditional catalog.

Even as they continue to develop the Japanese market, Western catalogers are now turning their attention to other Asian countries. In Hong Kong and Singapore, efficient postal services, highly educated populations, wide use of credit cards, and high per capita income are attracting the attention of catalog marketers. Notes Michael Grasee, the former director of international business development at Lands' End, "We see our customer in Asia as pretty much the same customer we have everywhere. It's the time-starved, traveling, hardworking executive."[16] Catalogers are also targeting Asia's developing countries. Otto GmbH & Co KG with 2003 revenues of $15 billion and about 9 percent of global mail order sales, is planning to enter China, Korea, and Taiwan. Because these countries have few local mail order companies for acquisition, executives at Otto have mapped out an entry strategy based on acquiring a majority stake in joint ventures with local retailers.[17]

## Infomercials and Teleshopping

An **infomercial** is a form of paid television programming in which a particular product is demonstrated, explained, and offered for sale to viewers who call a toll-free number shown on the TV screen. Thomas Burke, president of Saatchi & Saatchi's infomercial division, calls infomercials "the most powerful form of advertising ever created." With **teleshopping** home shopping channels such as QVC, the Home Shopping Network (HSN), and ValueVision taking the infomercial concept one step further; the programming is *exclusively* dedicated to product demonstration and selling. Worldwide, home shopping is a multibillion dollar industry. The leading home shopping channels are also leveraging the Internet; in 2001, HSN generated $2 billion in sales through television and the company's **www.hsn.com** Web site. Industry observers expect the popularity of home shopping will increase over the next few years as interactive television (ITV or t-commerce) technology finds its way into more households. ITV has a greater presence in Europe than in the United States; in the United Kingdom alone, more than half of all pay-TV subscribers take advantage of ITV services.[18]

The cost of producing a single infomercial can reach $3 million; advertisers then pay as much as $500,000 for time slots on U.S. cable and satellite systems and local TV channels. Because infomercials are typically 30 minutes in length and often feature studio audiences and celebrity announcers, many viewers believe they are watching regular talk show-type programming. Although originally associated with personal care, fitness, and household products such as those from legendary direct-response pitchman Ron Popeil, infomercials have

---

[16] James Cox, "Catalogers Expand in Asia," *USA Today* (October 18, 1996), p. 4B.

[17] Dagmar Mussey, "Otto Expands Family-Owned Catalog Empire," *Advertising Age International* (September 1996), p. i4.

[18] "Europe Wants Its ITV," *Chain Store Age* 77, no. 7 (July 2001), pp. 76–78.

gone up-market in recent years. For example, Philips Electronics produced a groundbreaking infomercial during the launch of its CD-i multiplayer in the early 1990s. Unfortunately, Philips's execution of the infomercial was flawed—callers were given the name of a local dealer but not given a chance to order CD-i directly—and CD-i ultimately failed. By contrast, Lexus generated more than 40,000 telephone inquiries after launching its used-car program with an infomercial; 2 percent of those who responded ultimately purchased a Lexus automobile. Mainstream advertisers have also discovered the power of teleshopping; for example, Saks Fifth Avenue rang up $1 million in sales after its private-label apparel was featured on QVC.

As these figures indicate, infomercials and home shopping television are important marketing communications channels for global marketers. Both formats have proven viable outside the United States. E4L (formerly National Media Corp.) produces infomercials that are shown in more than 200 million homes worldwide. As Mark Hershorn, the company's former president and CEO, told *Advertising Age International*:

> We're realizing very significant opportunities in the global marketplace. Our goal isn't to be an infomercial company, but a global marketer that goes direct to the consumer through the TV. Infomercials represent a powerful marketing vehicle that is not limited by geographic borders. U.S. manufacturers are in a fierce competition to create brands and infomercials that can create shelf space for products in consumers' homes on a global basis. Down the road, we'll be able to put a product simultaneously into the homes of 300 to 500 million people around the globe. Now *that's* powerful.[19]

E4L relies heavily on alliances with TV stations in individual country markets. For many of the products the company offers, "not available in stores" is a powerful selling point. However, advertisers whose products are also available through traditional channels can use infomercials and home shopping television to identify prospective buyers, to support advertising campaigns in other media, and to help educate consumers by offering them a complete product demonstration.

In Asia, infomercials generate several hundred million dollars in annual sales. Costs for a late-night time slot range from $100,000 in Japan to $20,000 in Singapore. Infomercials are also playing a part in the development of China's market sector. The government has given its blessing by allowing China Central Television, the state-run channel, to air infomercials and give Chinese consumers access to Western goods. Despite low per capita incomes, Chinese consumers are thought to achieve a savings rate as high as 40 percent because housing and health care are provided by the state. China Shop-A-Vision is in the vanguard, signing up 20,000 "TV shopping members" in its first year of airing infomercials. As these and other pioneers in Chinese direct-response television have learned, however, many obstacles remain, including the limited number of private telephones, low penetration of credit cards, high product prices due to import tariffs, and problems with delivery logistics in crowded cities such as Shanghai.[20]

Although home shopping giants QVC and Home Shopping Network are staying out of China for now, QVC's agreement with Rupert Murdoch's British Sky Broadcasting (BSkyB) satellite company enables it to reach England, Ireland, and parts of the European continent. Similarly, Mexico's Grupo Televisa beams QVC into Mexico and South America. A number of local and regional teleshopping

---

[19] Kim Cleland, "Infomercial Audience Crosses over Cultures," *Advertising Age International* (January 15, 1996), p. i8.
[20] Jon Hilsenrath, "In China, a Taste of Buy-Me TV," *The New York Times* (November 17, 1996), Sec. 3, pp. 1, 11.

channels have sprung up in Europe. Germany's HOT (Home Order Television) is a joint venture with Quelle Schickedanz, a mail order company. Sweden's TV-Shop is available in 15 European countries. Europeans are likely to be more discriminating than the average American teleshopping customer. As QVC executive Francis Edwards explained, "European customers respond in different ways, though the basic premise and concept is the same. The type of jewelry is different. German consumers wouldn't buy 14-karat gold. They go for a higher karat. We can sell wine in Germany, but not in the U.S."[21]

## Sponsorship

**Sponsorship** is an increasingly popular form of marketing communications whereby a company pays a fee to have its name associated with a particular event, team or athletic association, or sports facility. Sponsorship combines elements of public relations and sales promotion. From a public relations perspective, sponsorship generally ensures that a corporate or brand name will be mentioned numerous times by on-air or public-address commentators. Large-scale events also draw considerable media attention that typically includes multiple mentions of the sponsoring company or brand in news reports or talk shows. Because event sponsorship typically provides numerous contact points with large numbers of people, it is a perfect vehicle for sampling and other sales promotion opportunities. An Olympic Games or World Cup soccer sponsorship can help a company reach a global audience; sponsors are also drawn to events that reach national or regional audiences, such as professional team sports, car racing, hot air balloon competitions, rodeos, and music concerts.

Sony recently became an official U.S. sponsor of the National Basketball Association with the signing of a $10 million per year deal. One part of the deal calls for recordings by musicians on the Sony Music label—Aerosmith, Pearl Jam, and Mariah Carey, for example—to get priority consideration for air time during games.

*For more than twenty years, the Coca-Cola Company has been the official soft-drink sponsor of World Cup soccer. For one year of sponsorship, Coca-Cola and other sponsors pay the International Federation of Football Associations (FIFA) approximately $35 million; each sponsor typically spends an equivalent amount on promotion. Televised World Cup matches reach an estimated 44 billion viewers in more than 200 countries.*

---

[21] Michelle Pentz, "Teleshopping Gets a Tryout in Europe but Faces Cultural and Legal Barriers," *The Wall Street Journal* (September 9, 1996), p. A8.

Hoping to achieve higher levels of brand awareness in the United States, Nokia sponsors the Sugar Bowl; Ericsson paid to have its name emblazoned on the new stadium where the Carolina Panthers football team plays. In 1997, Fila and Adidas engaged in a bidding war for sponsorship rights to the New York Yankees baseball team. Adidas eventually won a 10-year deal with a total value of $100 million; although that deal sets a record for sponsorship of an American sport, it is dwarfed by Nike's $200 million deal to sponsor the Brazilian national soccer team.

Sponsorship can be an effective component of an integrated marketing communications program. It can be used in countries where regulations limit the extent to which a company can use advertising or other forms of marketing communication. In China, for example, where tobacco advertising is prohibited, B.A.T and Philip Morris spend tens of millions of dollars sponsoring events such as a Hong Kong-Beijing car rally and China's national soccer tournament. Sponsorship is also popular in the United Kingdom, where Benson & Hedges paid £4 million for a 5-year contract to sponsor cricket matches, and Rothman's spends £15 million annually to sponsor a Formula One racing team. However, to comply with the EU directive on tobacco advertising, tobacco sponsorship of all sports—including Formula One racing—will be phased out by 2006.

## Product Placement in Motion Pictures, Television Shows, and Other Performances

Companies can achieve a unique kind of exposure by using **product placement:** arranging for their products and brand names to appear in popular television programs, movies, and other types of performances. Movies are a popular entertainment medium; worldwide audience figures for a blockbuster hit can equal tens of millions of people. In many instances, the placements generate media interest and result in additional publicity. Placements can be accomplished in several different ways. Sometimes companies pay a fee for the placement; alternatively, a show's producers will write the product into the script in exchange for marketing and promotion support of the new production. A brand's owners can also strike a barter agreement whereby the company, Sony, for example, supplies the filmmakers with products that serve as props in exchange for licensing rights to the James Bond name in retail promotions. Product placement agencies such as Switzerland's Propaganda and Hollywood-based Hero Product Placement function like talent agencies for products. As such, the agencies fulfill several important functions such as obtaining legal clearances from a brand's owners, promoting their clients' products to producers, and arranging for products to be delivered to a soundstage.

In the case of television placement, the blurring of advertising and programming content comes as companies increasingly question the effectiveness of traditional advertising. In fact, there is research evidence suggesting that a prominent product placement in a television program leads to better recall than a traditional ad. Many viewers use VCRs or PVRs such as TiVo to "zap" commercials; consumers are, in effect, ignoring commercials. This trend forces advertisers to find new ways to expose viewers to their messages. In addition to the effectiveness issue, prop masters and set dressers facing budget pressures are compelled to obtain props for free whenever possible. Moreover, as the cost of marketing major feature films has increased (it is not unusual for a studio to spend $20 to $30 million on marketing alone), studios are increasingly looking for partnerships to share the cost and attract the broadest possible viewing audience. The James Bond films are a case in point: the first 19 films featuring the suave British agent have grossed more than $3 billion in worldwide ticket sales. However, the most recent film in the series, *Die Another Day*, cost nearly $100 million to produce.

Not surprisingly, some companies are eager to be associated with a high-profile project like a Bond film. In 1996, when BMW introduced a sporty new

Agent 007 is always equipped with sophisticated, high-tech gadgets, so a promotional tie in with Sony Ericsson's T68i smart phone was a perfect match. Die Another Day, the twentieth James Bond movie, showcased some key features of the T68i such as high-quality color imaging capability and polyphonic ring signals.

Z3 convertible, it wanted to make a major global splash. BMW garnered extensive publicity by placing the Z3 in *Goldeneye*, the eighteenth James Bond film. In the film, gadget chief Q gives 007 a Z3 in place of his Aston-Martin; the Z car also figured prominently in movie previews and print ads. BMW dealers were provided with "BMW 007 kits" that allowed prospective buyers to learn more about both the movie and the car before either was available. As *Advertising Age* observed, "BMW has shaken, not just stirred, the auto industry with unprecedented media exposure and awareness for the Z3 and BMW in the U.S."[22]

*Tomorrow Never Dies*, the follow-up to *Goldeneye*, featured global brand promotional tie-ins worth an estimated $100 million. Ericsson, Heineken, Omega, Brioni, and Visa International all placed products in the film. Bond star Pierce Brosnan also appeared as Agent 007 in specially filmed television commercials. When *Die Another Day*, the twentieth installment in the series, was released at the end of 2002, BMW took a back seat to Ford. The U.S. automaker persuaded the producers to bring back the Aston-Martin (the nameplate is now owned by Ford); Jaguars and the new Thunderbird are also prominent in the film.

Product placement raises an interesting issue for global marketers, especially consumer packaged-goods companies. This tactic virtually dictates a product

---

[22] Jon Rappoport, "BMW Z3," *Advertising Age* (June 24, 1996), p. S37; see also Tim Burt, "His Name's Bond, and He's Been Licensed to Sell," *Financial Times* (October 5–6, 2002), p. 22.

standardization approach, because once footage of a scene is shot and incorporated into a movie or television program, the image of the product is "frozen" and will be seen without adaptation everywhere in the world.[23]

For better or for worse, product placements have even reached the world of live theater and opera: In fall 2002, a new Broadway production of Puccini's *La Bohème* was set in Paris circa 1957. The stage set included billboards for luxury pen maker Montblanc and Piper-Heidsieck champagne; during a crowd scene at Café Momus, Piper-Heidsieck was served. Not surprisingly, some industry observers warn of a backlash. Ethical concerns are sometimes raised when controversial products such as cigarettes are featured prominently or glamorized. When advertising appears in conventional forms such as broadcast commercials, most consumers are aware of the fact that they are being exposed to an ad. This is not necessarily the case with product placement; in effect, viewers are being marketed to subliminally without their consent. What constitutes proper use of product placement? As Joe Uva, an executive of Omnicom's media planning group, noted, "It shouldn't be forced; it shouldn't be intrusive. If people say 'It's a sell out, it's product placement,' it didn't work." Eugene Secunda, a media studies professor at New York University, is skeptical. "I think it's a very dangerous plan. The more you get the audience to distrust the content of your programming, to look at it with suspicion in terms of your real agenda, the less likely they are to be responsive to the message because they're going to be looking at everything cynically and with resistance."[24]

*Samsung Electronics' DIGITall tie-in with The Matrix: Reloaded motion picture was awarded the grand prize 2004 Super Reggie Award by the Promotional Marketing Association. Samsung was also the 2004 Gold Award winner for best international consumer promotion. In a product-placement coup, a special Matrix-themed Samsung cell phone was used by lead characters in the movie. Created by FCB Worldwide, the integrated global promotional campaign included print and broadcast advertisements, consumer and trade promotions, event marketing, and a special Web site.*

23  Stephen J. Gould, Pola B. Gupta, and Sonja Grabner-Krauter, "Product Placements in Movies: A Cross-Cultural Analysis of Austrian, French and American Consumers' Attitudes Toward this Emerging, International Promotional Medium," *Journal of Advertising* 29, no. 4 (Winter 2000) pp. 41–58.
24  Richard Tompkins, "How Hollywood Brings Brands into Your Home," *Financial Times* (November 5, 2002), p. 15.

**Sales promotion** is any paid, short-term communication program that adds tangible value to a product or brand. **Consumer sales promotions** are targeted at ultimate consumers; **trade sales promotions** are used in business-to-business marketing. **Sampling** gives prospective customers a chance to try a product or service at no cost. A **coupon** is a certificate that entitles the bearer to a price reduction or other value-enticing consideration when purchasing a product or service.

**Personal selling** is face-to-face communication between a prospective buyer and a company representative. The **strategic/consultative selling model** that is widely used in the United States is also being utilized worldwide. The model's five strategic steps call for developing a **personal selling philosophy**, a **relationship strategy**, a **product strategy**, a **customer strategy**, and a **presentation strategy.** The six steps in the presentation plan are: **approach, presentation, demonstration, negotiation, closing,** and **servicing the sale.** Successful

global selling may require adaptation of one or more steps in the presentation plan. An additional consideration in global selling is the composition of the sales force, which may include **expatriates,** or sales agents.

Several others forms of communication can be used in global marketing. These include **direct marketing,** a measurable system that uses one or more media to start or complete a sale. One-to-one marketing is an updated approach to direct marketing that calls for treating each customer in a distinct way based on his or her previous purchase history or past interactions with the company. **Direct mail, catalogs, infomercials,** and **teleshopping** are some of the direct marketing tools that have been successfully used on a global basis. Global marketers frequently try to place their products in blockbuster movies that will reach global audiences. **Sponsorships** and **product placement** are also becoming vital communication tools that can be used on a global basis.

summary

1. Briefly review how the main tools of sales promotion (e.g., sampling and couponing) can be used in global markets. What issues and problems can arise in different country markets?

2. What potential environmental challenges must taken into account by a company that uses personal selling as a promotional tool outside the home country?

3. Identify the six steps in the Strategic/Consultative Selling Model and the outlined six-step presentation plan. Do these steps have global applicability, or are they only used for selling in the home-country market? What special challenges face a sales representative outside his or her home country?

4. How does management's orientation (i.e., ethnocentric, polycentric, or regiocentric) correlate with decisions about sales force nationality? What other factors affect sales force composition?

5. What role does direct marketing have in a global company's promotion mix? Name three companies that have successfully used direct mail or other forms of direct-response advertising.

6. Why are infomercials, sponsorship, and product placement growing in importance for global marketers?

discussion questions

Located in the United Kingdom, the Direct Mail Information Service compiles statistics on direct mail in Europe. To review current statistics, log on to: **www.dmis. co.uk**

LucJam, a brand strategy firm based in San Francisco, has a Web site that tracks product placement in movies, TVs shows, and other media. Find it at: **www.americabrand stand.com.**

visit the web site

# Case 14-1

## Marketing an Industrial Product in Latin America

The government of a Latin American republic had decided to modernize one of its communication networks at a cost of several million dollars. Because of its reputation for quality, the government approached American company "Y." Company management, having been sounded out informally, considered the size of the order and decided to bypass its regular Latin American representative and send its sales manager instead. The following describes what took place.

The sales manager arrived and checked into the leading hotel. He immediately had some difficulty pinning down just who his business contact was. After several days without results, he called at the American Embassy where he found the commercial attaché had the necessary up-to-the-minute information. The commercial attaché listened to his story. The attaché realized the sales manager had already made a number of mistakes but, figuring that the locals were used to American blundering, he reasoned that all was not lost. The attaché informed the sales manager that the Minister of Communications was the key man and that whoever got the nod from him would get the contract. He also briefed the sales manager on methods of conducting business in Latin America and offered some pointers about dealing with the minister.

The attaché's advice ran somewhat as follows:

1. "You don't do business here the way you do in the States; it is necessary to spend much more time. You have to get to know your man and vice versa."

2. "You must meet with him several times before you talk business. I will tell you at what point you can bring up the subject. Take your cues from me." (At this point, our American sales manager made a few observations to himself about "cookie pushers" and wondered how many payrolls had been met by the commercial attaché.)

3. "Take that price list and put it in your pocket. Don't get it out until I tell you to. Down here price is only one of the many things taken into account before closing a deal. In the United States, your past experience will prompt you to act according to a certain set of principles, but many of these principles will not work here. Every time you feel the urge to act or to say something, look at me. Suppress the urge and take your cues from me. This is very important."

4. "Down here people like to do business with men who are somebody. 'Being somebody' means having written a book, lectured at a university, or developed your intellect in some way. The man you are going to see is a poet. He has published several volumes of poetry. Like many Latin Americans, he prizes poetry highly. You will find that he will spend a good deal of business time quoting his poetry to you, and he will take great pleasure in this."

5. "You will also note that the people here are very proud of their past and of their Spanish blood, but they are also exceedingly proud of their liberation from Spain and their independence. The fact that they are a democracy, that

they are free, and also that they are no longer a colony is very, very important to them. They are warm and friendly and enthusiastic if they like you. If they don't, they are cold and withdrawn."

6. "And another thing, time down here means something different. It works in a different way. You know how it is back in the States when a certain type blurts out whatever is on his mind without waiting to see if the situation is right. He is considered an impatient bore and somewhat egocentric. Well, down here you have to wait much, much longer, and I really mean much, *much* longer, before you can begin to talk about the reason for your visit."

7. "There is another point I want to caution you about. At home, the man who sells takes the initiative. Here, *they* tell you when they are ready to do business. But most of all, don't discuss price until you are asked and don't rush things."

## The Pitch

The next day the commercial attaché introduced the sales manager to the Minister of Communications. First, there was a long wait in the outer office while people went in and out. The sales manager looked at his watch, fidgeted, and finally asked whether the minister was really expecting him. The reply he received was scarcely reassuring, "Oh yes, he is expecting you but several things have come up that require his attention. Besides, one gets used to waiting down here." The sales manager irritably replied, "But doesn't he know I flew all the way down here from the United States to see him, and I have spent over a week already of my valuable time trying to find him?" "Yes, I know," was the answer, "but things just move much more slowly here."

At the end of about 30 minutes, the minister emerged from the office, greeted the commercial attaché with a double abrazo, throwing his arms around him and patting him on the back as though they were long-lost brothers. Now, turning and smiling, the minister extended his hand to the sales manager, who, by this time, was feeling rather miffed because he had been kept in the outer office so long.

After what seemed to be an all-too-short chat, the minister rose, suggesting a well-known cafe where they might meet for dinner the next evening. The sales manager expected, of course, that, considering the nature of their business and the size of the order, he might be taken to the minister's home, not realizing that the Latin home is reserved for family and very close friends.

Until now, nothing at all had been said about the reason for the sales manager's visit, a fact which bothered him somewhat. The whole setup seemed wrong; additionally he did not like the idea of wasting another day in town. He told the home office before he left that he would be gone for a week or 10 days at most and made a mental note that he would clean this order up in 3 days and enjoy a few days in Acapulco or Mexico City. Now the week had already gone and he would be lucky if he made it home in 10 days.

Voicing his misgivings to the commercial attaché, he wanted to know if the minister really meant business, and if he did, why could they not get together and talk about it? The commercial attaché by now was beginning to show the strain of constantly having to reassure the sales manager. Nevertheless, he tried again: "What you don't realize is that part of the time we were waiting, the minister was rearranging a very tight schedule so that he could spend tomorrow night with you. You see, down here they don't delegate responsibility the way we do in the States. They exercise much tighter control than we do. As a consequence, this man spends up to 15 hours a day at his desk. It may not look like it to you, but I assure you he really means business. He wants to give your company the order; if you play your cards right, you will get it."

The next evening was more of the same. Much conversation about food and music, about many people of whom the sales manager had never heard. They went to a night club, where the sales manager brightened up and began to think that perhaps he and the minister might have something in common after all. It bothered him, however, that the principal reason for his visit was not even alluded to tangentially. However, every time he started to talk about electronics, the commercial attaché would nudge him and proceed to change the subject.

The next meeting was to be held over morning coffee at a café. By now the sales manager was having difficulty hiding his impatience. To make matters worse, the minister had a mannerism that he did not like. When they talked, he was likely to put his hand on him; he would take hold of his arm and get so close that he nearly spit in his face. Consequently,

the sales manager kept trying to dodge and put more distance between himself and the minister.

Following coffee, they walked in a nearby park. The minister expounded on the shrubs, the birds, and the beauties of nature, and at one spot he stopped to point at a statue and said: "There is a statue of the world's greatest hero, the liberator of mankind!" At this point, the worst happened. The sales manager asked who the statue was of and, when told the name of a famous Latin American patriot, said, "I never heard of him," and walked on. After this meeting, the American sales manager was never able to see the minister again. The order went to a Swedish concern.

## Discussion Questions

1. What impression do you think the sales manager made on the minister?
2. How would you critique the quality of the communication between all parties in this case?
3. Is a high-context culture or a low-context culture at work in this case? Explain your answer.

*Sources:* Edward T. Hall, "The Silent Language in Overseas Business," *Harvard Business Review* (May–June 1960), pp. 93–96; Philip R. Harris and Robert T. Moran, "Doing Business with Latin Americans—Mexico, Central & South America," Chapter 14 *Managing Cultural Differences: High Performance Strategies for a New World of Business,* 3rd ed. (Houston, TX: Gulf Publishing Company, 1991); Paul Leppert, *Doing Business with Mexico* (Fremont, CA: Jain Publishing Company, 1995); Lawrence Tuller, *Doing Business in Latin America and the Caribbean* (Chicago: Amacom, 1993).

# 15 Strategic Elements of Competitive Advantage

2003 was a difficult year for IKEA, the $8 billion global furniture powerhouse based in Sweden. The euro's strength dampened financial results, as did an economic downturn in Central Europe. The company faces increasing competition from hypermarkets, "do-it-yourself" retailers such as Wal-Mart, and supermarkets that are expanding into home furnishings. Looking to the future, CEO Anders Dahlvig stresses three areas for improvement: product assortment, customer service, and product availability. With more than 160 stores in 22 countries, the company's success to date reflects founder Ingvar Kamprad's "social ambition" of selling a wide range of stylish, functional home furnishings at prices so low that the majority of people can afford to buy them. The store exteriors are painted bright blue and yellow, Sweden's national colors. Shoppers view furniture on the main floor in scores of realistic settings arranged throughout the cavernous showrooms. In a departure from standard industry practice, IKEA's furniture bears names such as "Ivar" and "Sten" instead of model numbers. At IKEA, shopping is a self-service activity; after browsing and writing down the names of desired items, shoppers can pick up their furniture on the lower level. There they find "flat packs" containing the furniture in kit form; one of the cornerstones of IKEA's strategy is having customers take their purchases home in their own vehicles and assemble the furniture themselves. The lower level of a typical IKEA store also contains a restaurant, a grocery store called the Swede Shop, a supervised play area for children, and a baby care room.

The essence of marketing strategy is successfully relating the strengths of an organization to its environment. As the horizons of marketers have expanded from domestic to regional and global, so too have the horizons of competitors. The reality in almost every industry today, including home furnishings, is global competition. This fact of life puts an organization under

increasing pressure to master techniques for conducting industry analysis and competitor analysis, and understanding competitive advantage at both the industry and national levels. These topics are covered in detail in this chapter.

## INDUSTRY ANALYSIS: FORCES INFLUENCING COMPETITION

A useful way of gaining insight into competitors is through industry analysis. As a working definition, an *industry* can be defined as a group of firms that produce products that are close substitutes for each other. In any industry, competition works to drive down the rate of return on invested capital toward the rate that would be earned in the economist's "perfectly competitive" industry. Rates of return that are greater than this so-called competitive rate will stimulate an inflow of capital either from new entrants or from existing competitors making additional investment. Rates of return below this competitive rate will result in withdrawal from the industry and a decline in the levels of activity and competition.

According to Michael E. Porter of Harvard University, a leading theorist of competitive strategy, there are five forces influencing competition in an industry: the threat of new entrants, the threat of substitute products or services, the bargaining power of buyers, the bargaining power of suppliers, and the competitive rivalry among current members of the industry. In industries such as soft drinks, pharmaceuticals, and cosmetics, the favorable nature of the five forces has resulted in attractive returns for competitors. However, pressure from any of the forces can limit profitability, as evidenced by the recent fortunes of some competitors in the personal computer and semiconductor industries. A discussion of each of the five forces follows.

## Threat of New Entrants

New entrants to an industry bring new capacity, a desire to gain market share and position, and, quite often, new approaches to serving customer needs. The decision to become a new entrant in an industry is often accompanied by a major commitment of resources. New players mean prices will be pushed downward and margins squeezed, resulting in reduced industry profitability in the long run. Porter describes eight major sources of barriers to entry, the presence or absence of which determines the extent of threat of new industry entrants.[1]

The first barrier, **economies of scale,** refers to the decline in per-unit product costs as the absolute volume of production per period increases. Although the concept of scale economies is frequently associated with manufacturing, it is also applicable to R&D, general administration, marketing, and other business functions. Honda's efficiency at engine R&D, for example, results from the wide range of products it produces that feature gasoline-powered engines. When existing firms in an industry achieve significant economies of scale, it becomes difficult for potential new entrants to be competitive.

**Product differentiation,** the second major entry barrier, is the extent of a product's perceived uniqueness; in other words, whether or not it is a commodity. Differentiation can be achieved as a result of unique product attributes or effective marketing communications, or both. Product differentiation and brand loyalty "raise the bar" for would-be industry entrants who would be required to make substantial investments in R&D or advertising. For example, Intel achieved differentiation and erected a barrier in the microprocessor industry with its "Intel Inside" advertising campaign and logo that appear on many brands of personal computers.

A third entry barrier relates to **capital requirements.** Capital is required not only for manufacturing facilities (fixed capital) but also for financing R&D, advertising, field sales and service, customer credit, and inventories (working capital). The enormous capital requirements in such industries as pharmaceuticals, mainframe computers, chemicals, and mineral extraction present formidable entry barriers.

A fourth barrier to entry are the one-time **switching costs** caused by the need to change suppliers and products. These might include retraining, ancillary equipment costs, the cost of evaluating a new source, and so on. The perceived cost to customers of switching to a new competitor's product may present an insurmountable obstacle preventing industry newcomers from achieving success. For example, Microsoft's huge installed base of PC operating systems and applications presents a formidable entry barrier.

A fifth barrier to entry is access to **distribution channels.** If channels are full, or unavailable, the cost of entry is substantially increased because a new entrant must invest time and money to gain access to existing channels or to establish new channels. Some Western companies have encountered this barrier in Japan.

**Government policy** is frequently a major entry barrier. In some cases, the government will restrict competitive entry. This is true in a number of industries, especially those outside the United States that have been designated as "national" industries by their respective governments. Japan's postwar industrialization strategy was based on a policy of reserving and protecting national industries in their development and growth phases. The result was a market that proved difficult for non-Japanese competitors to enter, an issue that was targeted by the Clinton administration. American business executives in a wide range of industries urged adoption of a government policy that would reduce some of these barriers and open the Japanese market to more U.S. companies.

Established firms may also enjoy **cost advantages independent of scale economies** that present barriers to entry. Access to raw materials, a large pool of low-cost labor, favorable locations, and government subsidies are several examples.

Finally, expected **competitor response** can be a major entry barrier. If new entrants expect existing competitors to respond strongly to entry, their expectations about the rewards of entry will certainly be affected. A potential competitor's belief that entry into an industry or market will be an unpleasant experience

---

[1]   Michael E. Porter, *Competitive Strategy* (New York: Free Press, 1980), pp. 7–33.

may serve as a strong deterrent. Bruce Henderson, former president of the Boston Consulting Group, used the term "brinkmanship" to describe a recommended approach for deterring competitive entry. Brinkmanship occurs when industry leaders convince potential competitors that any market entry effort will be countered with vigorous and unpleasant responses. This is an approach Microsoft has used many times to maintain its dominance in software operating systems and applications.

In the quarter century since Porter first described the five forces model, the digital revolution appears to have altered the entry barriers in many industries. First and foremost, technology has lowered the cost for new entrants. For example, Barnes & Noble watched an entrepreneurial upstart, Amazon.com, storm the barriers protecting traditional "brick-and-mortar" booksellers. Amazon.com founder Jeff Bezos identified and exploited a glaring inefficiency in book distribution: Bookstores ship unsold copies of books back to publishers to be shredded and turned into pulp. Amazon's centralized operations and increasingly personalized online service enable customers to select from millions of different titles at discount prices and have them delivered to their homes within days. For a growing number of book-buying consumers, Amazon.com eclipses the value proposition of local bookstores that offer "only" a few thousand titles and gourmet coffee bars. Since Bezos founded Amazon.com in 1995, sales have grown to $5.2 billion and the company has expanded into new product lines such as CDs and videos. To date, the company has served tens of millions of customers in 160 countries. Barnes & Noble has responded by entering the online book market itself even as it continues to be profitable in its traditional bricks-and-mortar business. In the meantime, Bezos has repositioned Amazon.com as an Internet superstore selling electronics and general merchandize. In 2003, the company earned a first-ever full-year profit of $35 million.

## Threat of Substitute Products

A second force influencing competition in an industry is the threat of substitute products. The availability of substitute products places limits on the prices market leaders can charge in an industry; high prices may induce buyers to switch to the substitute. Once again, the digital revolution is dramatically altering industry structures. In addition to lowering entry barriers, the digital era means that certain types of products can be converted to bits and distributed in pure digital form. For example, the development of the MP3 file format for music was accompanied by the increased popularity of peer-to-peer (p-to-p) file swapping among music fans. Napster and other online music services offer a substitute to consumers who are tired of paying $15 or more for a CD. Although a U.S. court severely curtailed Napster's activities, other services—including several outside the United States— have sprung up in its place. Bertelsmann, Sony, and the top players in the music industry were taken by surprise, and even now are struggling to develop a coherent response to the threat to their core businesses (see Case 17-1).

## Bargaining Power of Buyers

In Porter's model, "buyers" refers to manufacturers (e.g., GM) and retailers (e.g., Wal-Mart), rather than consumers. The ultimate aim of such buyers is to pay the lowest possible price to obtain the products or services that they require. Usually, therefore, if they can, buyers drive down profitability in the supplier industry. To accomplish this, the buyers have to gain leverage over their vendors. One way they can do this is to purchase in such large quantities that supplier firms are highly dependent on the buyers' business. Second, when the suppliers' products are viewed as commodities—that is, as standard or

*Wal-Mart has become one of the biggest sellers of recorded music in the United States. Much of the discounter's growth in this area has come at the expense of specialty music stores whose share of the market fell from 70 percent in 1990 to 44.5 percent in 1999. One way that Wal-Mart exercises its buying power is by refusing to stock recordings bearing "Parental Advisory" stickers; many artists release edited versions so that Wal-Mart will carry them.*

undifferentiated—buyers are likely to bargain hard for low prices, because many firms can meet their needs. Buyers will also bargain hard when the supplier industry's products or services represent a significant portion of the buying firm's costs. A fourth source of buyer power is the willingness and ability to achieve backward integration.

For example, because it purchases massive quantities of goods for resale, Wal-Mart is in a position to dictate terms to any vendor wishing to distribute its products at the retail giant's stores. This includes the recorded music industry; Wal-Mart accounts for approximately 10 percent of the market for CD sales. Wal-Mart refuses to stock CDs stickered with parental advisories for explicit lyrics or violent imagery. Artists who want their recordings available at Wal-Mart have the option of altering lyrics and song titles or deleting offending tracks. Likewise, artists are sometimes asked to change album cover art if Wal-Mart deems it offensive. Nina Crowley, executive director of the Massachusetts Music Industry Coalition, objects to such changes. "What really upsets us is that they're using their financial power to change art," she said. A Wal-Mart spokesperson noted, "We do not quibble or argue with anyone's right to sing what they want, to print what they want, and say what they want. But we reserve the right to sell what we want."[2]

## Bargaining Power of Suppliers

Supplier power in an industry is the converse of buyer power. If suppliers have enough leverage over industry firms, they can raise prices high enough to significantly influence the profitability of their organizational customers. Suppliers' ability to gain leverage over industry firms is determined by several factors. Suppliers will have the advantage if they are large and relatively few in number. Second, when the suppliers' products or services are important inputs to user firms, are highly differentiated, or carry switching costs, the suppliers will have considerable leverage over buyers. Suppliers will also enjoy bargaining power if their business is not threatened by alternative products. A fourth source of supplier power is the willingness and ability of suppliers to develop their own products and

---

[2]   "Wal-Mart Rules Prompt Changes in Music," *Associated Press*, November 19, 1996.

brand names if they are unable to get satisfactory terms from industry buyers. In the tech world, Microsoft and Intel are two excellent examples of companies with substantial supplier power. Because about 90 percent of the world's nearly 600 million PCs use Microsoft's operating systems and Intel's microprocessors, the two companies enjoy a great deal of leverage relative to Dell, Compaq, and other computer manufacturers. In fact, it was precisely because Microsoft became so powerful that the U.S. government and the European Union launched separate antitrust investigations.

## Rivalry Among Competitors

Rivalry among firms refers to all the actions taken by firms in the industry to improve their positions and gain advantage over each other. Rivalry manifests itself in price competition, advertising battles, product positioning, and attempts at differentiation. To the extent that rivalry among firms forces companies to rationalize costs, it is a positive force. To the extent that it drives down prices, and therefore profitability, and creates instability in the industry, it is a negative factor. Several factors can create intense rivalry. Once an industry becomes mature, firms focus on market share and how it can be gained at the expense of others. Second, industries characterized by high fixed costs are always under pressure to keep production at full capacity to cover the fixed costs. Once the industry accumulates excess capacity, the drive to fill capacity will push prices—and profitability— down. A third factor affecting rivalry is lack of differentiation or an absence of switching costs, which encourages buyers to treat the products or services as commodities and shop for the best prices. Again, there is downward pressure on prices and profitability. Fourth, firms with high strategic stakes in achieving success in an industry generally are destabilizing because they may be willing to accept below-average profit margins to establish themselves, hold position, or expand.

The personal computer industry is a case in point. For years, demand for PCs grew at an annual rate of 15 percent. Since the tech bubble burst in early 2000, however, firms have been dealing with a worldwide slowdown in demand; recent growth has been in the single digits. Dell has responded by aggressively cutting prices in a bid to boost share. With profit margins collapsing, competitors are struggling to adjust. The price war has claimed one victim already; in mid-2001, key rival Compaq agreed to be acquired by Hewlett-Packard. Dell is legendary for its lean operating philosophy; just 11.5 cents of every sales dollar go to overhead, compared with 16 cents at Gateway, 21 cents at Compaq, and 22.5 cents at Hewlett-Packard. The company can assemble a complete PC in 3 minutes. With a build-to-order strategy at the heart of its business model, Dell's sales staff maintains close ties with customers. This approach gives Dell a great deal of flexibility when making pricing decisions.[3]

*"Our goal is to shrink the profit pool and take the biggest slice."*

Kevin Rollins,
President and COO, Dell Inc.[4]

## COMPETITIVE ADVANTAGE

**Competitive advantage** exists when there is a match between a firm's distinctive competencies and the factors critical for success within its industry. Any superior match between company competencies and customers' needs permits the firm to outperform competitors. There are two basic ways to achieve competitive advantage. First, a firm can pursue a low-cost strategy that enables it to offer products

---

[3] Gary McWilliams, "Lean Machine: How Dell Fine-Tunes Its PC Pricing to Gain Edge in a Slow Market," *The Wall Street Journal* (June 8, 2001), p. A1.

[4] Richard Waters, "Dell Aims to Stretch Its Way of Business," *Financial Times* (November 13, 2003), p. 8.

at lower prices than competitors. Competitive advantage may also be gained by a strategy of differentiating products so that customers perceive unique benefits, often accompanied by a premium price. Note that both strategies have the same effect: They both contribute to the firm's overall value proposition. Michael E. Porter explored these issues in two landmark books, *Competitive Strategy* (1985) and *Competitive Advantage* (1990); the latter is widely considered to be one of the most influential management books in recent years.

The quality of a firm's strategy is ultimately decided by customer perception. Operating results such as sales and profits are measures that depend on the level of psychological value created for customers: The greater the perceived consumer value, the better the strategy. A firm may market a better mousetrap, but the ultimate success of the product depends on customers deciding for themselves whether or not to buy it. Value is like beauty; it's in the eye of the beholder. In sum, competitive advantage is achieved by creating more value than is done by the competition, and value is defined by customer perception.

Two different models of competitive advantage have received considerable attention. The first offers "generic strategies," four routes or paths that organizations choose to offer superior value and achieve competitive advantage. According to the second model, generic strategies alone don't account for the astonishing success of many Japanese companies in the 1980s and 1990s. The more recent model, based on the concept of "strategic intent," proposes four different sources of competitive advantage. Both models are discussed in the following paragraphs.

> "The only way to gain lasting competitive advantage is to leverage your capabilities around the world so that the company as a whole is greater than the sum of its parts. Being an international company — selling globally, having global brands or operations in different countries — isn't enough."
>
> David Whitwam, CEO, Whirlpool[5]

## Generic Strategies for Creating Competitive Advantage

In addition to the "five forces" model of industry competition, Michael Porter has developed a framework of so-called generic business strategies based on the two types or sources of competitive advantage mentioned previously: *low-cost* and *differentiation*. The relationship of these two sources with the scope of the target market served (narrow or broad) or product mix width (narrow or wide) yields four **generic strategies:** *cost leadership*, *product differentiation*, *cost focus*, and *focused differentiation*.

Generic strategies aiming at the achievement of competitive advantage or superior marketing strategy demand that the firm make choices. The choices concern the *type* of competitive advantage it seeks to attain (based on cost or differentiation) and the *market scope* or *product mix width* within which competitive advantage will be attained.[6] The nature of the choice between types of advantage and market scope is a gamble, and it is the nature of every gamble that it entails *risk*: By choosing a given generic strategy, a firm always risks making the wrong choice.

### Broad Market Strategies: Cost Leadership and Differentiation

**Cost leadership advantage** is based on a firm's position as the industry's low-cost producer, in broadly defined markets or across a wide mix of products. This strategy has gained widespread appeal in recent years as a result of the popularization of the experience curve concept. In general, a firm that bases its competitive strategy on overall cost leadership must construct the most efficient facilities (in terms of scale or technology) and obtain the largest share of market so that its cost per

---

5    Regina Fazio Maruca, "The Right Way to Go Global: An Interview with Whirlpool CEO David Whitwam," *Harvard Business Review* 72, no. 2 (March–April 1994), p. 135.
6    Michael E. Porter, *Competitive Advantage: Creating and Sustaining Superior Performance* (New York: Free Press, 1985), p. 12.

unit is the lowest in the industry. These advantages, in turn, give the producer a substantial lead in terms of experience with building the product. Experience then leads to more refinements of the entire process of production, delivery, and service, which leads to further cost reductions.

Whatever its source, cost leadership advantage can be the basis for offering lower prices (and more value) to customers in the late, more-competitive stages of the product life cycle. In Japan, companies in a range of industries—35mm cameras, consumer electronics and entertainment equipment, motorcycles, and automobiles—have achieved cost leadership on a worldwide basis.

Cost leadership, however, is a sustainable source of competitive advantage only if barriers exist that prevent competitors from achieving the same low costs. In an era of increasing technological improvements in manufacturing, manufacturers constantly leapfrog over one another in pursuit of lower costs. At one time, for example, IBM enjoyed the low-cost advantage in the production of computer printers. Then the Japanese took the same technology and, after reducing production costs and improving product reliability, gained the low-cost advantage. IBM fought back with a highly automated printer plant in North Carolina, where the number of component parts was slashed by more than 50 percent and robots were used to snap many components into place. Despite these changes, IBM ultimately chose to exit the business; the plant was sold.

When a firm's product has an actual or perceived uniqueness in a broad market, it is said to have a **differentiation advantage.** This can be an extremely effective strategy for defending market position and obtaining above-average financial returns; unique products often command premium price. Examples of successful differentiation include Maytag in large home appliances, Caterpillar in construction equipment, and almost any successful branded consumer product. Maytag has been called "the Rolls-Royce of washers and dryers;" half the washers sold in the United States are priced at $399 or less, and Maytag does offer a model at that price point. However, the Maytag line also includes the Neptune, a high-tech, water-saving machine; the two Neptune models are priced at $999 and $1,399. IBM traditionally has differentiated itself with a strong sales service organization and the security of the IBM standard in a world of rapid obsolescence. Among athletic shoe manufacturers, Nike stands out as the technological leader thanks to unique product features found in a wide array of shoes.

## Narrow Target Strategies: Cost Focus and Focused Differentiation

The preceding discussion of cost leadership and differentiation considered only the impact on broad markets. By contrast, strategies to achieve a narrow focus advantage target a narrowly defined market/customer. This advantage is based on an ability to create more customer value for a narrowly targeted segment and results from a better understanding of customer needs and wants. A narrow-focus strategy can be combined with either cost- or differentiation-advantage strategies. In other words, while a *cost focus* means offering a narrow target market low prices, a firm pursuing *focused differentiation* will offer a narrow target market the perception of product uniqueness at a premium price.

German's *Mittelstand* companies have been extremely successful pursuing **focused differentiation** strategies backed by a strong export effort. The world of "high-end" audio equipment offers another example of focused differentiation. A few hundred small companies design speakers, amplifiers, and related hi-fi gear that costs thousands of dollars per component. While audio components represent a $21 billion market worldwide, annual sales in the high-end segment are only about $1.1 billion. American companies such as Audio Research, Conrad-Johnson, Krell, Mark Levinson, Martin-Logan, and Thiel dominate the segment, which also includes hundreds of smaller enterprises with annual sales of less than $10 million. The state-of-the-art equipment these companies offer is distinguished by superior

*In keeping with the design aesthetics of high-end audio gear, Aragon's 7-channel surround sound preamp and matching amplifier are the epitome of classic, minimalist design. The amplifier alone (bottom unit) retails for about $3,000.*

craftsmanship and performance and is highly sought after by audiophiles in Asia (especially Japan and Hong Kong) and Europe. Industry growth is occurring as companies learn more about overseas customers and build relationships with distributors in other countries.[7]

The final strategy is **cost focus,** when a firm's lower cost position enables it to offer a narrow target market and lower prices than the competition. In the shipbuilding industry, for example, Polish and Chinese shipyards offer simple, standard vessel types at low prices that reflect low production costs.[8] IKEA, the Swedish furniture company described in the chapter introduction, has grown into a successful global company by combining both the focused differentiation and cost focus strategies. As George Bradley, president of Levitz Furniture in

## *global* MARKETING Q&A

**Wall Street Journal:** "Sixty percent of the operating profit of LVMH comes from Vuitton. Doesn't that worry you?"

**Bernard Arnault, Chairman and Chief Executive Officer, LVMH Moët Hennessy Louis Vuitton:** "Not at all, because I think Vuitton is the brand that has the most growth potential and no direct, comparable competitor. There is a real economic reason people buy Vuitton. There's some fashion, but it's not really fashion. The real motivation is that it's the best value in leather goods. The price is high, but it's not crazy. Vuitton is like Microsoft. You cannot imitate the business model. It's impossible."

**Wall Street Journal:** "How concerned are you about Louis Vuitton counterfeits?"

**Bernard Arnault:** "Very concerned. On the other hand, this summer when I was on the beaches in Italy and France, all the counterfeit bags were Vuitton and Dior, so maybe it's a sign that the product is doing well—the price of success. We try to seize the counterfeits, but it's a constant struggle."

*Source: Lisa Bannon and Allesandra Galloni, "Brand Manager Deluxe," The Wall Street Journal (October 10, 2003), pp. B1, B4.*

---

[7]   Personal communication from Kerry Moyer, Senior Director, Industry Programs, Consumer Electronics Association, Arlington, Virginia, 2003.
[8]   Michael E. Porter, *The Competitive Advantage of Nations* (New York: Free Press, 1990), p. 39.

Boca Raton, Florida, noted, "[IKEA] has really made a splash. They're going to capture their niche in every city they go into." Of course, such a strategy can be risky. As Bradley explains, "Their market is finite because it is so narrow. If you don't want contemporary, knock-down furniture, it's not for you. So it takes a certain customer to buy it. And remember, fashions change."[9]

The issue of sustainability is central to this strategy concept. As noted, cost leadership is a sustainable source of competitive advantage only if barriers exist that prevent competitors from achieving the same low costs. Sustained differentiation depends on continued perceived value and the absence of imitation by competitors.[10] Several factors determine whether or not focus can be sustained as a source of competitive advantage. First, a cost focus is sustainable if a firm's competitors are defining their target markets more broadly. A focuser doesn't try to be all things to all people: Competitors may diminish their advantage by trying to satisfy the needs of a broader market segment—a strategy which, by definition, means a blunter focus. Second, a firm's differentiation focus advantage is only sustainable if competitors cannot define the segment even more narrowly. Also, focus can be sustained if competitors cannot overcome barriers that prevent imitation of the focus strategy, and if consumers in the target segment do not migrate to other segments that the focuser doesn't serve.

# the rest of the story

## IKEA

IKEA's unconventional approach to the furniture business has enabled it to rack up impressive growth in a $30 billion industry in which overall sales have been flat. Sourcing furniture from a network of more than 1,600 suppliers in 55 countries helps the company maintain its low-cost, high-quality position. During the 1990s, IKEA expanded into Central and Eastern Europe. Because consumers in those regions have relatively low purchasing power, the stores offer a smaller selection of goods; some furniture was designed specifically for the cramped living styles typical in former Soviet bloc countries. Throughout Europe, IKEA benefits from the perception that Sweden is the source of high-quality products and efficient service. Currently, Germany and the United Kingdom are IKEA's top two markets. The United Kingdom represents the fastest-growing market in Europe; although Britons initially viewed the company's less-is-more approach as cold and "too Scandinavian," they were eventually won over. IKEA currently has 10 stores in the United Kingdom and plans to open 20 more in the next decade. As Allan Young, creative director of London's St. Luke's advertising agency, noted, "IKEA is anticonventional. It does what it shouldn't do. That's the overall theme for all IKEA ads: liberation from tradition."

In 2005, IKEA will open two stores near Tokyo; more stores are on the way as the company expands in Asia. IKEA's first attempt to develop the Japanese market in the mid-1970s resulted in failure. Why? As Tommy Kullberg, chief executive of IKEA Japan explains, "In 1974, the Japanese market from a retail point of view was closed. Also, from the Japanese point of view, I do not think they were ready for IKEA, with our way of doing things, with flat packages and asking the consumers to put things together and so on." However, demographic and economic trends are much different today. After years of recession, consumers are seeking alternatives to paying high prices for quality goods. Also, IKEA's core customer segment—post-baby boomers in their 30s—will grow by nearly 10 percent between 2000 and 2010. In Japan, IKEA will offer home delivery and an assembly service option.

*"To succeed in Japan, I think we have to tell the whole story of why we can sell our products at affordable prices."*

Tommy Kullberg

Industry observers predict that North America will eventually rise to the number one position in terms of IKEA's worldwide sales. The company opened its first U.S. store in Philadelphia in 1985; as of 2003, IKEA operated 16 stores in the United States and 11 in Canada. As Goran Carstedt, president of IKEA North America, explains, "Our customers understand our philosophy, which calls for each of us to do a little in order to save a lot. They value our low prices. And almost all of them say they will come back again." As one industry observer noted, "IKEA is on the way to becoming the Wal-Mart Stores of the home-furnishing industry. If you're in this business, you'd better take a look."

*Sources: Mariko Sanchanta, "IKEA's Second Try at Japan's Flat-Pack Fans," Financial Times (March 4, 2004), p. 11; Christopher Brown-Humes, "An Empire Built on a Flat Pack," Financial Times (November 24, 2003), p. 8; Brown-Humes, "IKEA Aims to Fill Up Homes One Catalogue at a Time," Financial Times (August 14, 2003), p. 14; Alan M. Rugman and Joseph R. D'Cruz, Multinationals as Flagship Firms (Oxford, England: Oxford University Press, 2000), Chapter 3; Ernest Beck, "IKEA Sees Quirkiness as Selling Point in UK," The Wall Street Journal (January 4, 2001), pp. A1, A5; Loretta Roach, "IKEA: Furnishing the World," Discount Merchandiser (October 1994), pp. 46, 48; "Furnishing the World," The Economist (November 19, 1994), pp. 79–80.*

---

9   Jeffrey A. Trachtenberg, "Home Economics: IKEA Furniture Chain Pleases with Its Prices, Not with Its Service," *The Wall Street Journal* (September 17, 1991), pp. A1, A5.
10  Michael E. Porter, *Competitive Advantage: Creating and Sustaining Superior Performance* (New York: Free Press, 1985), p. 158.

# The Flagship Firm: The Business Network with Five Partners[11]

According to Professors Alan Rugman and Joseph D'Cruz, Porter's model is too simplistic given the complexity of today's global environment. Rugman and D'Cruz have developed an alternative framework based on business networks that they call the flagship model (see Figure 15-1). Japanese vertical *keiretsu* and Korean *chaebol* have succeeded, Rugman and D'Cruz argue, by adopting strategies that are mutually reinforcing within a business system and by fostering a collective long-term outlook among partners in the system. Moreover, the authors note, "long-term competitiveness in global industries is less a matter of rivalry between firms and more a question of competition between business systems." A major difference between their model and Porter's is that Porter's is based on the notion of corporate individualism and individual business transactions. For example, as discussed previously, Microsoft's tremendous supplier power allows it to dictate to, and even prosper at the expense of, the computer manufacturers it supplies with operating systems and applications. The flagship model is evident in the strategies of Ford, Volkswagen, and other global automakers; Sweden's IKEA and Italy's Benetton are additional examples.

As shown in Figure 15-1, the flagship firm is at the center of a collection of five partners; together, they form a business system that consists of two types of relationships. The flagship firm provides the leadership, vision, and resources to "lead the network in a successful global strategy." *Key suppliers* are those that perform some value-creating activities, such as manufacturing of critical components, better than the flagship. The double-headed arrows that penetrate the flagship and key suppliers in Figure 15-1 indicate that this is a network

## Figure 15-1

### The Flagship Model

Source: Alan M. Rugman and Joseph R. D'Cruz, Multinationals as Flagship Firms (Oxford, England: Oxford University Press, 2000), p. 9. By permission of Oxford University Press.

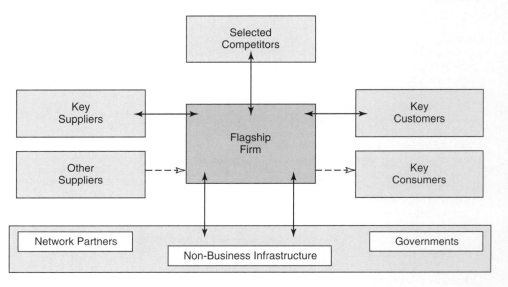

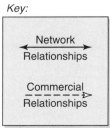

---

[11] The following discussion is adapted from Alan M. Rugman and Joseph R. D'Cruz, *Multinationals as Flagship Firms* (Oxford, England: Oxford University Press, 2000).

relationship, with a sharing of strategies, resources, and responsibility for the success of the network. Other suppliers are kept at "arm's length"; these traditional commercial relationships are depicted diagrammatically by arrows that stop at the border of the flagship. Likewise, the flagship has network relationships with *key customers* and more traditional, arm's length commercial relationships with *key consumers*. In the case of Volkswagen, for example, dealers are its key customers while individual car buyers are key consumers; similarly, Benetton's key customers are its retail outlets while the individual clothes shopper is the key consumer. *Key competitors* are companies with which the flagship develops alliances such as those described at the end of Chapter 9. The fifth partner is the *nonbusiness infrastructure* (NBI), comprised of universities, governments, trade unions, and other entities that can supply the network with intangible inputs such as intellectual property and technology. In the flagship model, flagship firms often play a role in the development of a country's industrial policy.

Benetton's success in the global fashion industry illustrates the flagship model (for a discussion of Benetton's advertising, see Case 13-1). Benetton is the world's largest purchaser of wool, and its centralized buying enables the company to reap scale economies. The core activities of cutting and dyeing are retained in-house, and Benetton has made substantial investments in computer-assisted design and manufacturing. However, Benetton is linked to approximately 400 subcontractors that produce finished garments in exclusive supply relationships with the company. In turn, the subcontractors are linked to the 5,000 Benetton retail shops by a network of 80 agents who find investors, train managers, and assist with merchandising. As Rugman and D'Cruz note, "Benetton is organized to reward cooperation and relationship building and the company's structure has been created to capitalize on the benefits of long-term relationships."

## Creating Competitive Advantage via Strategic Intent

An alternative framework for understanding competitive advantage focuses on competitiveness as a function of the pace at which a company implants new advantages deep within its organization. This framework identifies **strategic intent,** growing out of ambition and obsession with winning, as the means for achieving competitive advantage. Writing in the *Harvard Business Review*, Gary Hamel and C. K. Prahalad note:

> Few competitive advantages are long lasting. Keeping score of existing advantages is not the same as building new advantages. The essence of strategy lies in creating tomorrow's competitive advantages faster than competitors mimic the ones you possess today. An organization's capacity to improve existing skills and learn new ones is the most defensible competitive advantage of all.[12]

This approach is founded on the principles of W. E. Deming, who stressed that a company must commit itself to continuing improvement in order to be a winner in a competitive struggle. For years, Deming's message fell on deaf ears in the United States, while the Japanese heeded his message and benefited tremendously. Japan's most prestigious business award is named after him. Finally, however, U.S. manufacturers are starting to respond.

---

[12] Gary Hamel and C. K. Prahalad, "Strategic Intent," *Harvard Business Review* 67, no. 3 (May–June 1989), pp. 63–76. See also Hamel and Prahalad, "The Core Competence of the Corporation," *Harvard Business Review* 68, no. 3 (May–June 1990), pp. 79–93.

The significance of Hamel and Prahalad's framework becomes evident when comparing Caterpillar and Komatsu. As noted earlier, Caterpillar is a classic example of differentiation: The company became the largest manufacturer of earthmoving equipment in the world because it was fanatical about quality and service. Caterpillar's success as a global marketer has enabled it to achieve a 35 percent share of the worldwide market for earthmoving equipment, more than half of which represents sales to developing countries. The differentiation advantage was achieved with product durability, global spare parts service (including guaranteed parts delivery anywhere in the world within 48 hours), and a strong network of loyal dealers.

Caterpillar faced a very challenging set of environmental forces during the last several decades. Many of Caterpillar's plants were closed by a lengthy strike in the early 1980s; a worldwide recession at the same time caused a downturn in the construction industry. This hurt companies that were Caterpillar customers. In addition, the strong dollar gave a cost advantage to foreign rivals.

Compounding Caterpillar's problems was a new competitive threat from Japan. Komatsu was the world's number-two construction equipment company and had been competing with Caterpillar in the Japanese market for years. Komatsu's products were generally acknowledged to offer a lower level of quality. The rivalry took on a new dimension after Komatsu adopted the slogan "*Maru-c,*" meaning "encircle Caterpillar." Emphasizing quality and taking advantage of low labor costs and the strong dollar, Komatsu surpassed Caterpillar as number one in earthmoving equipment in Japan and made serious inroads in the United States and other markets. However, the company continued to develop new sources of competitive advantage even after it achieved world-class quality. For example, new-product development cycles were shortened and manufacturing was rationalized. Caterpillar struggled to sustain its competitive advantage because many customers found that Komatsu's combination of quality, durability, and lower price created compelling value. Yet even as recession and a strong yen put new pressure on Komatsu, the company sought new opportunities by diversifying into machine tools and robots.[13]

The Komatsu/Caterpillar saga is just one example of how global competitive battles are shaped by more than the pursuit of generic strategies. Many firms have gained competitive advantage by *disadvantaging* rivals through "competitive innovation." Hamel and Prahalad define *competitive innovation* as "the art of containing competitive risks within manageable proportions" and identify four successful approaches utilized by Japanese competitors. These are: *building layers of advantage, searching for loose bricks, changing the rules of engagement*, and *collaborating*.

**Layers of Advantage** A company faces less risk in competitive encounters if it has a wide portfolio of advantages. Successful companies steadily build such portfolios by establishing layers of advantage on top of one another. Komatsu is an excellent example of this approach. Another is the TV industry in Japan. By 1970, Japan was not only the world's largest producer of black-and-white TV sets but was also well on its way to becoming the leader in producing color sets. The main competitive advantage for such companies as Matsushita at that time was low labor costs.

Because they realized that their cost advantage could be temporary, the Japanese also added an additional layer of *quality and reliability* advantages by building plants large enough to serve world markets. Much of this output did not carry the manufacturer's brand name. For example, Matsushita Electric sold products to other companies such as RCA that marketed them under their own brand

---

13 Robert L. Rose and Masayoshi Kanabayashi, "Komatsu Throttles Back on Construction Equipment," *The Wall Street Journal* (May 13, 1992), p. B4.

names. Matsushita was pursuing a simple idea: A product sold was a product sold, no matter whose label it carried.[14]

In order to build the next layer of advantage, the Japanese spent the 1970s investing heavily in marketing channels and Japanese brand names to gain recognition. This strategy added yet another layer of competitive advantage: the *global brand franchise*; that is, a global customer base. By the late 1970s, channels and brand awareness were established well enough to support the introduction of new products that could benefit from global marketing; VCRs and photocopy machines, for example. Finally, many companies have invested in *regional manufacturing* so their products can be differentiated and better adapted to customer needs in individual markets.

The process of building layers illustrates how a company can move along the value chain to strengthen competitive advantage. The Japanese began with manufacturing (an upstream value activity) and moved on to marketing (a downstream value activity) and then back upstream to basic R&D. All of these sources of competitive advantage represent mutually reinforcing layers that are accumulated over time.

**Loose Bricks** A second approach takes advantage of the "loose bricks" left in the defensive walls of competitors whose attention is narrowly focused on a market segment or a geographic area to the exclusion of others. For example, Caterpillar's attention was focused elsewhere when Komatsu made its first entry into the Eastern Europe market. Similarly, Taiwan's Acer Inc. prospered by following founder Stan Shih's strategy of approaching the world computer market from the periphery. Shih's inspiration was the Asian board game *Go*, in which the winning player successfully surrounds opponents. Shih gained experience and built market share in countries overlooked by competitors such as IBM and Compaq. By the time Acer was ready to target the United States in earnest, it was already the number one PC brand in key countries in Latin America, Southeast Asia, and the Middle East.[15] Intel's loose brick was its narrow focus on complex microprocessors for personal computers. Even as it built its core business to a commanding 90 percent share of the market, markets for non-PC consumer electronics products were exploding. The new products, which include television desk-top boxes, digital cameras, and so-called smart cards, require chips that are far cheaper than those produced by Intel. Competitors such as NEC Corp and LSI Logic recognized the opportunity and beat Intel into an important new market.[16]

**Changing the Rules** A third approach involves changing the so-called "rules of engagement" and refusing to play by the rules set by industry leaders. For example, in the copier market, IBM and Kodak imitated the marketing strategies used by market leader Xerox. Meanwhile Canon, a Japanese challenger, wrote a new rulebook.

While Xerox built a wide range of copiers, Canon built standardized machines and components, reducing manufacturing costs. While Xerox employed a huge direct sales force, Canon chose to distribute through office-product dealers. Canon also designed serviceability, as well as reliability, into its products so that it could rely on dealers for service rather than incurring the expense required to create a national service network. Canon further decided to sell rather than lease its machines, freeing the company from the burden of

[14] James Lardner, *Fast Forward: Hollywood, The Japanese, and the VCR Wars* (New York: New American Library, 1987) p. 135.
[15] Dan Shapiro, "Ronald McDonald, Meet Stan Shih," *Sales & Marketing Management* (November 1995), p. 86.
[16] Dean Takahashi, "Hand-Held Combat: How the Competition Got Ahead of Intel in Making Cheap Chips," *The Wall Street Journal* (February 12, 1998), pp. A1, A10.

financing the lease base. In another major departure, Canon targeted its copiers at secretaries and department managers rather than at the heads of corporate duplicating operations.[17]

Canon introduced the first full-color copiers and the first copiers with "connectivity," the ability to print images from such sources as video camcorders and computers. The Canon example shows how an innovative marketing strategy—with fresh approaches to the product, pricing, distribution, and selling—can lead to overall competitive advantage in the marketplace. Canon is not invulnerable, however; in 1991 Tektronix, a U.S. company, leapfrogged past Canon in the color copier market by introducing a plain-paper color copier that offered sharper copies at a much lower price.[18]

**Collaborating** A final source of competitive advantage is using know-how developed by other companies. Such *collaboration* may take the form of licensing agreements, joint ventures, or partnerships. History has shown that the Japanese have excelled at using the collaborating strategy to achieve industry leadership. As noted in Chapter 9, one of the legendary licensing agreements of modern business history is Sony's licensing of transistor technology from AT&T's Western Electric subsidiary in the 1950s for $25,000. This agreement gave Sony access to the transistor and allowed the company to become a world leader. Building on its initial successes in the manufacturing and marketing of portable radios, Sony has grown into a superb global marketer whose name is synonymous with a wide assortment of high-quality consumer electronics products.

More recent examples of Japanese collaboration are found in the aircraft industry. Today, Mitsubishi Heavy Industries Ltd. and other Japanese companies manufacture airplanes under license to U.S. firms and also work as subcontractors for aircraft parts and systems. Many observers fear that the future of the American aircraft industry may be jeopardized as the Japanese gain technological expertise. Various examples of "collaborative advantage" are discussed in the next section.[19]

## GLOBAL COMPETITION AND NATIONAL COMPETITIVE ADVANTAGE[20]

An inevitable consequence of the expansion of global marketing activity is the growth of competition on a global basis. In industry after industry, global competition is a critical factor affecting success. As Yoshino and Rangan have explained, **global competition** occurs when a firm takes a global view of competition and sets about maximizing profits worldwide, rather than on a country-by-country basis. If, when expanding abroad, a company encounters the same rival in market

---

[17] Gary Hamel and C. K. Prahalad, "Strategic Intent," *Harvard Business Review* 67, no. 3 (May–June 1989), p. 69.

[18] G. Pascal Zachary, "Color Printer Gives Tektronix Jump on Canon," *The Wall Street Journal* (June 14, 1991), p. B1.

[19] Hamel and Prahalad have continued to refine and develop the concept of strategic intent since it was first introduced in their groundbreaking 1989 article. During the 1990s, the authors outlined five broad categories of resource leverage that managers can use to achieve their aspirations: Concentrating resources on strategic goals via convergence and focus; accumulating resources more efficiently via extracting and borrowing; complementing one resource with another by blending and balancing; conserving resources by recycling, co-opting, and shielding; and rapid recovery of resources in the marketplace. Gary Hamel and C. K. Prahalad, "Strategy as Stretch and Leverage," *Harvard Business Review* 71, no. 2 (March–April 1993), pp. 75–84.

[20] This section draws heavily on Chapter 3, "Determinants of National Competitive Advantage," and Chapter 4, "The Dynamics of National Advantage," in Porter 1990. For an extended country analysis based on Porter's framework, see Michael Enright, Antonio Francés, and Edith Scott Assavedra, *Venezuela: The Challenge of Competitiveness* (New York: St. Martin's Press, 1996).

---

after market, then it is engaged in global competition.[21] In some industries, global companies have virtually excluded all other companies from their markets. An example is the detergent industry, in which three companies—Colgate, Unilever, and Procter & Gamble—dominate an increasing number of detergent markets in Latin America and the Pacific Rim. Many companies can make a quality detergent, but brand-name muscle and the skills required for quality packaging overwhelm local competition in market after market.[22]

The automobile industry has also become fiercely competitive on a global basis. Part of the reason for the initial success of foreign automakers in the United States was the reluctance—or inability—of U.S. manufacturers to design and manufacture high-quality, inexpensive small cars. The resistance of U.S. manufacturers was based on the economics of car production: the bigger the car, the higher the list price. Under this formula, small cars meant smaller unit profits. Therefore, U.S. manufacturers resisted the increasing preference in the U.S. market for smaller cars, a classic case of ethnocentrism and management myopia. European and Japanese manufacturers' product lines have always included cars smaller than those made in the United States. In Europe and Japan, market conditions were much different than in the Unites States: less space, high taxes on engine displacement and on fuel, and greater market interest in functional design and engineering innovations. First Volkswagen, then Japanese automakers such as Nissan and Toyota, discovered a growing demand for their cars in the U.S. market. It is noteworthy that many significant innovations and technical advances—including radial tires, anti-lock brakes, and fuel injection—also came from Europe and Japan. Airbags are a notable exception.

The effect of global competition has been highly beneficial to consumers around the world. In the two examples cited, detergents and automobiles, consumers have benefited. In Central America, detergent prices have fallen as a result of global competition. In the United States, foreign companies have provided consumers with the automobile products, performance, and price characteristics they wanted. If smaller, lower-priced imported cars had not been available, it is unlikely that Detroit manufacturers would have provided a comparable product as quickly. What is true for automobiles in the United States is true for every product class around the world. Global competition expands the range of products and increases the likelihood that consumers will get what they want.

The downside of global competition is its impact on the producers of goods and services. Global competition creates value for consumers, but it also has the potential to destroy jobs and profits. When a company offers consumers in other countries a better product at a lower price, this company takes customers away from domestic suppliers. Unless the domestic supplier can create new values and find new customers, the jobs and livelihoods of the domestic supplier's employees are threatened.

This section addresses the following issue: Why is a particular nation a good home base for specific industries? Why, for example, is the United States the home base for the leading competitors in PCs, software, credit cards, and movies? Why is Germany the home of so many world leaders in printing presses, chemicals, and luxury cars? Why are so many leading pharmaceutical, chocolate/confectionery, and trading companies located in Switzerland? Why are the world leaders in consumer electronics home based in Japan?

Harvard professor Michael E. Porter addressed these issues in his landmark 1990 book *The Competitive Advantage of Nations*. Many observers hailed the book as a groundbreaking guide for shaping national policies on competitiveness. According to Porter, the presence or absence of particular attributes in individual countries influences industry development, not just the ability of individual firms to create

---

[21] Michael Y. Yoshino and U. Srinivasa Rangan, *Strategic Alliances: An Entrepreneurial Approach to Globalization* (Boston: Harvard Business School Press, 1995), p. 56.

[22] See Joseph Kahn, "Cleaning Up: P&G Viewed China as a National Market and Is Conquering It," *The Wall Street Journal* (September 12, 1995), pp. A1, A6.

**Figure 15-2**

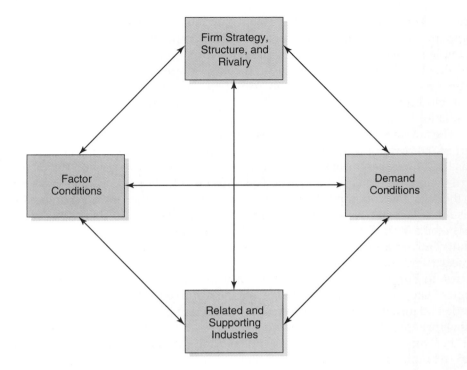

core competences and competitive advantage.[23] Porter describes these attributes—factor conditions, demand conditions, related and supporting industries, and firm strategy, structure, and rivalry—in terms of a national "diamond." (see Figure 15-2). The diamond shapes the environment in which firms compete. Activity in any one of the four points of the diamond impacts on all the others and vice versa.

## Factor Conditions

The phrase *factor conditions* refers to a country's endowment with resources. Factor resources may have been created or inherited. *Basic factors* may be inherited or created without much difficulty; because they can be replicated in other nations, they are not sustainable sources of national advantage. Specialized factors, by contrast, are more advanced and provide a more sustainable source for advantage. Porter describes five categories of factor conditions: human, physical, knowledge, capital, and infrastructure.

**Human Resources** The quantity of workers available, the skills possessed by these workers, the wage levels, and the overall work ethic of the workforce together constitute a nation's human resource factor. Countries with a plentiful supply of low-wage workers have an obvious advantage in the production of labor-intensive products. On the other hand, such countries may be at a *disadvantage* when it comes to the production of sophisticated products requiring highly skilled workers capable of working without extensive supervision.

**Physical Resources** The availability, quantity, quality, and cost of land, water, minerals, and other natural resources determine a country's physical resources. A country's size and location are also included in this category, because proximity to markets and sources of supply, as well as transportation costs, are strategic considerations. These factors are obviously important advantages or disadvantages to industries dependent on natural resources.

---

[23]   Michael E. Porter, *The Competitive Advantage of Nations* (New York: Free Press, 1990).

**Knowledge Resources** The availability within a nation of a significant population having scientific, technical, and market-related knowledge means that the nation is endowed with knowledge resources. The presence of this factor is usually a function of the number of research facilities and universities—both government and private—operating in the country. This factor is important to success in sophisticated products and services, and to doing business in sophisticated markets. This factor relates directly to Germany's leadership in chemicals; for some 150 years, Germany has been home to top university chemistry programs, advanced scientific journals, and apprenticeship programs.

**Capital Resources** Countries vary in the availability, amount, cost, and types of capital available to the country's industries. The nation's savings rate, interest rates, tax laws, and government deficit all affect the availability of this factor. The advantage enjoyed by industries in countries with low capital costs versus those located in nations with relatively high capital costs is sometimes decisive. Firms paying high capital costs are frequently unable to stay in a market where the competition comes from a nation with low capital costs. The firms with the low cost of capital can keep their prices low and force the firms paying high costs to either accept low returns on investment or leave the industry.

**Infrastructure Resources** Infrastructure includes a nation's banking system, health care system, transportation system, communications system, as well as the availability and cost of using these systems. More sophisticated industries are more dependent on advanced infrastructures for success.

Competitive advantage accrues to a nation's industry if the mix of factors available to the industry is such that it facilitates pursuit of a generic strategy; that is, low-cost production or the production of a highly differentiated product or service. Competitive advantage may also be created indirectly by nations that have selective factor *disadvantages*. For example, the absence of suitable labor may force firms to develop forms of mechanization that give the nation's firms an advantage. High transportation costs may motivate firms to develop new materials that are less expensive to transport.

## Demand Conditions

The nature of home demand conditions for the firm's or industry's products and services is important because it determines the rate and nature of improvement and innovation by the firms in the nation. These are the factors that either train firms for world-class competition or that fail to adequately prepare them to compete in the global marketplace. Three characteristics of home demand are particularly important to creation of competitive advantage: the composition of home demand, the size and pattern of growth of home demand, rapid home market growth, and the means by which a nation's home demand pulls the nation's products and services into foreign markets.

**Composition of Home Demand** This demand element determines how firms perceive, interpret, and respond to buyer needs. Competitive advantage can be achieved when the home demand sets the quality standard and gives local firms a better picture of buyer needs, at an earlier time, than is available to foreign rivals. This advantage is enhanced when home buyers pressure the nation's firms to innovate quickly and frequently. The basis for advantage is the fact that the nation's firms can stay ahead of the market when firms are more sensitive to and more responsive to home demand and when that demand, in turn, reflects or anticipates world demand.

**Size and Pattern of Growth of Home Demand** These are important only if the composition of the home demand is sophisticated and anticipates foreign demand. Large home markets offer opportunities to achieve economies of scale and learning while dealing with familiar, comfortable markets. There is less apprehension about investing in large-scale production facilities and expensive R&D programs when the home market is sufficient to absorb the increased capacity. If the home demand accurately reflects or anticipates foreign demand, and if the firms do not become content with serving the home market, the existence of large-scale facilities and programs will be an advantage in global competition.

**Rapid Home Market Growth** This is yet another incentive to invest in and adopt new technologies faster and to build large, efficient facilities. The best example of this is in Japan, where rapid home market growth provided the incentive for Japanese firms to invest heavily in modern automated facilities. *Early home demand*, especially if it anticipates international demand, gives local firms the advantage of getting established in an industry sooner than foreign rivals. Equally important is *early market saturation*, which puts pressure on a company to expand into international markets and innovate. Market saturation is especially important if it coincides with rapid growth in foreign markets.

**Means by Which a Nation's Products and Services Are Pushed or Pulled into Foreign Countries** The issue here is whether a nation's people and businesses go abroad and then demand the nation's products and services in those second countries. For example, when the U.S. auto companies set up operations in foreign countries, the auto parts industry followed. The same is true for the Japanese auto industry. Similarly, when overseas demand for the services of U.S. engineering firms skyrocketed after World War II, those firms in turn established demand for U.S. heavy construction equipment. This provided an impetus for Caterpillar to establish foreign operations.

A related issue is that of a nation's people going abroad for training, pleasure, business, or research. After returning home, they are likely to demand the products and services with which they became familiar while abroad. Similar effects can result from professional, scientific, and political relationships between nations. Those involved in the relationships begin to demand the products and services of the recognized leaders.

It is the interplay of demand conditions that produces competitive advantage. Of special importance are those conditions that lead to initial and continuing incentives to invest and innovate, and to continuing competition in increasingly sophisticated markets.

## Related and Supporting Industries

A nation has an advantage when it is home to internationally competitive industries in fields that are related to, or in direct support of, other industries. Internationally competitive supplier industries provide inputs to downstream industries. The latter, in turn, are likely to be internationally competitive in terms of price and quality and thus gain competitive advantage from this situation. Downstream industries will have easier access to these inputs and the technology that produced them, and to the managerial and organizational structures that have made them competitive. Access is a function of proximity both in terms of physical distance and cultural similarity. It is not the inputs in themselves that give advantage. It is the *contact* and *coordination* with the suppliers, the opportunity to structure the value chain so that linkages with suppliers are optimized. These opportunities may not be available to foreign firms.

Similar advantages are present when there are internationally competitive, related industries in a nation. Opportunities are available for coordinating and sharing value chain activities. Consider, for example, the opportunities for sharing between computer hardware manufacturers and software developers. Related industries also create "pull through" opportunities as described previously. For example, non-U.S. sales of PCs from Compaq, Dell, IBM, and others have bolstered demand for software from Microsoft and other U.S. companies. Porter notes that the development of the Swiss pharmaceuticals industry can be attributed in part to Switzerland's large synthetic dye industry; the discovery of the therapeutic effects of dyes in turn led to the development of pharmaceutical companies.[24]

## Firm Strategy, Structure, and Rivalry

Domestic rivalry in a single national market is a powerful influence on competitive advantage. The personal computer industry in the United States is a good example of how a strong domestic rivalry keeps an industry dynamic and creates continual pressure to improve and innovate. The rivalry between Dell, Gateway, Compaq, Apple, and others forces all the players to develop new products, improve existing ones, lower costs and prices, develop new technologies, and continually improve quality and service to keep customers happy. Rivalry with foreign firms may lack this intensity. Domestic rivals have to fight each other not just for market share, but also for employee talent, R&D breakthroughs, and prestige in the home market. Eventually, strong domestic rivalry will push firms to seek international markets to support expansions in scale and R&D investments, as Japan amply demonstrates. The absence of significant domestic rivalry can lead to complacency in the home firms and eventually cause them to become noncompetitive in the world markets.

It is not the number of domestic rivals that is important; rather, it is the intensity of the competition and the quality of the competitors that make the difference. It is also important that there be a fairly high rate of new business formations to create new competitors and safeguard against the older companies becoming comfortable with their market positions and products and services. As noted earlier in the discussion of the five forces model, new industry entrants bring new perspectives and new methods. They frequently define and serve new market segments that established companies have failed to recognize.

Differences in management styles, organizational skills, and strategic perspectives also create advantages and disadvantages for firms competing in different types of industries, as do differences in the intensity of domestic rivalry. In Germany, for example, company structure and management style tend to be hierarchical. Managers tend to come from technical backgrounds and to be most successful when dealing with industries that demand highly disciplined structures, like chemicals and precision machinery. Italian firms, on the other hand, tend to look like, and be run like, small family businesses that stress customized over standardized products, niche markets, and substantial flexibility in meeting market demands.

Capital markets and attitudes toward investments are important components of the national environments. For example, U.S. laws prohibit banks from taking an equity stake in companies to which they extend loans. This drives a short-term focus on quarterly and annual gains and losses. This focus is carried into equity markets where low profits produce low share prices and the threat of a takeover. As a result, U.S. firms tend to do well in new-growth industries and other rapidly expanding markets. They do not do well in more mature industries where return on investment is lower and patient searching for innovations is required. Many other countries have an opposite orientation. Banks are allowed to take equity stakes in the customer companies to which they loan, which therefore take a long-term view and are less concerned about short-term results.

There are two final external variables to consider in the evaluation of national competitive advantage—chance and government.

---

[24] Michael E. Porter, *The Competitive Advantage of Nations* (New York: Free Press, 1990), p. 324.

# Chance

Chance events play a role in shaping the competitive environment. Chance events are occurrences that are beyond the control of firms, industries, and usually governments. Included in this category are such things as wars and their aftermaths; major technological breakthroughs; sudden dramatic shifts in factor or input cost, such as an oil crisis; dramatic swings in exchange rates; and so on.

Chance events are important because they create major discontinuities in technologies that allow nations and firms that were not competitive to leapfrog over old competitors and become competitive, even leaders, in the changed industry. For example, the development of microelectronics allowed many Japanese firms to overtake U.S. and German firms in industries that had been based on electromechanical technologies—areas traditionally dominated by the Americans and Germans.

From a systemic perspective, the role of chance events lies in the fact that they alter conditions in the diamond. The nation with the most favorable "diamond," however, will be the one most likely to take advantage of these events and convert them into competitive advantage. For example, Canadian researchers were the first to isolate insulin, but they could not convert this breakthrough into an internationally competitive product. Firms in the United States and Denmark were able to do that because of their respective national "diamonds."

# Government

Although it is often argued that government is a major determinant of national competitive advantage, the fact is that government is not a determinant, but rather an influence on determinants. Government influences determinants by virtue of its role as a buyer of products and services, and by its role as a maker of policies on labor, education, capital formation, natural resources, and product standards. It also influences determinants by its role as a regulator of commerce, for example, by telling banks and telephone companies what they can and cannot do.

By reinforcing determinants in industries where a nation has competitive advantage, government improves the competitive position of the nation's firms. Governments devise legal systems that influence competitive advantage by means of tariffs and nontariff barriers and laws requiring local content and labor. In the United States, for example, the dollar's decline over the past decade has been due in part to a deliberate policy to enhance U.S. export flows and stem imports. In other words, government can improve or lessen competitive advantage, but it cannot create it.

# CURRENT ISSUES IN COMPETITIVE ADVANTAGE

Porter's work on national competitive advantage has stimulated a great deal of further research. The Geneva-based World Economic Forum issues an annual report ranking countries in terms of their competitiveness. A recent study by Morgan Stanley used the Porter framework to identify 238 companies with a sustainable competitive advantage worldwide. "National advantage" was then assessed by analyzing how many of these companies were headquartered in a particular country. The United States ranked first, with 125 companies identified as world leaders (see Table 15-1). Among the world's automakers, Morgan Stanley's analysts considered only BMW, Toyota, and Honda to have worldwide competitive advantage.[25]

---

[25] Tony Jackson, "Global Competitiveness Observed from an Unfamiliar Angle," *Financial Times* (November 21, 1996), p. 18.

| Country | Number of Companies | Table 15-1 |
|---|---|---|
| 1. United States | 125 | |
| 2. United Kingdom | 21 | *Location of Companies With* |
| 3. Japan | 19 | *Global Competitive Advantage* |
| 4. France | 12 | |
| 5. Germany | 10 | |
| 6. Netherlands | 7 | |
| 7. Canada | 6 | |
| 8. Switzerland | 6 | |
| 9. Sweden | 3 | |
| 10. Finland | 3 | |

In his book, Dartmouth College professor Richard D'Aveni suggests that the Porter strategy frameworks fail to adequately address the dynamics of competition in the 1990s and the new millennium.[26] D'Aveni takes a different approach. He notes that, in today's business environment, market stability is undermined by short product life cycles, short product design cycles, new technologies, and globalization. The result is an escalation and acceleration of competitive forces. In light of these changes, D'Aveni believes the goal of strategy has shifted from sustaining to disrupting advantages. The limitation of the Porter models, D'Aveni argues, is that they are static; that is, they provide a snapshot of competition at a given point in time. Acknowledging that Hamel and Prahalad broke new ground in recognizing that few advantages are sustainable, D'Aveni aims to build upon their work in order to shape "a truly dynamic approach to the creation and destruction of traditional advantages." D'Aveni uses the term **hypercompetition** to describe a dynamic competitive world in which no action or advantage can be sustained for long. In such a world, D'Aveni argues, "everything changes" because of the dynamic maneuvering and strategic interactions by hypercompetitive firms such as Microsoft and Gillette.

According to D'Aveni's model, competition unfolds in a series of dynamic strategic interactions in four arenas: cost/quality timing and know-how, entry barriers, and deep pockets. Each of these arenas is "continuously destroyed and recreated by the dynamic maneuvering of hypercompetitive firms." According to D'Aveni, the only source of a truly sustainable competitive advantage is a company's ability to manage its dynamic strategic interactions with competitors by means of frequent movements and countermovements that maintain a relative position of strength in each of the four arenas.

Competition in the first arena, cost/quality, occurs via seven dynamic strategic interactions: price wars, quality and price positioning, "the middle path," "cover all niches," outflanking and niching, the move toward an ultimate value marketplace, and escaping from the ultimate value marketplace by restarting the cycle. D'Aveni cites the global watch industry as an example of hypercompetitive behavior in the cost/quality arena. In the 1970s, the center of the industry shifted from Switzerland to Japan as the Japanese created high-quality quartz watches that could be sold cheaply. In the early 1980s, the merger of two Swiss companies into Suisse Microelectronique et d'Horlogerie SA (SMH) was followed by a highly automated manufacturing innovation that allowed a quartz movement to be integrated into a stylish plastic case. As a result of this innovation and a strong marketing effort in support of the Swatch brand, the center of the watch industry shifted back to Switzerland. The watch industry continues to be highly segmented, with prestige brands competing on

---

[26] Richard D'Aveni, *Hypercompetition: Managing the Dynamics of Strategic Maneuvering* (New York: Free Press, 1994).

reputation and exclusivity; as with many other luxury goods, higher prices are associated with higher perceived quality. In the low-cost segment, brands compete on price and value.

The second arena for hypercompetition is based on organizational advantages derived from timing and know-how. As described by D'Aveni, a firm that has the skills to be a "first mover" and arrive first in a market has achieved a *timing advantage*. A *know-how advantage* is the technological knowledge—or other knowledge of a new method of doing business—that allows the firm to create an entirely new product or market. [27] D'Aveni identifies six dynamic strategic interactions that drive competition in this arena: capturing first-mover advantages; imitation and improvement by followers; creating impediments to imitation; overcoming the impediments; transformation or leapfrogging; and downstream vertical integration. As the consumer electronics industry has globalized, Sony and its competitors have exhibited hypercompetitive behavior in this second arena. Sony has an enviable history of first-mover achievements based on its know-how in audio technology: first pocket-sized transistor radio, first consumer VCR, first portable personal stereo, and first compact disc player. Although each of these innovations literally created an entirely new market, Sony has fallen victim to the risks associated with being a first mover. The second dynamic strategic interaction—imitation and improvement by followers—can be seen in the successful efforts of JVC and Matsushita to enter the home VCR market a few months after Sony's Betamax launch. VHS technology offered longer recording times and now, two decades later, is the dominant consumer format worldwide. In the 1990s, Sony found technological leaps harder to achieve, as evidenced by the slow market acceptance of its MiniDisc digital recording/playback units. Sony has also shown a willingness to be a follower; the company only entered the video game industry in 1994, but its 64-bit PlayStation outsold a competitive product from Sega. After Sony launched the PlayStation 2 in 2000, Sega halted production of its Dreamcast game player; the company is now concentrating on developing game software.

After years of moves and countermoves between Sony and its imitators, Sony progressed to downstream vertical integration with the 1988 purchase of CBS Records for $2 billion and then, later, the purchase of Columbia Pictures. The acquisitions, which represent the sixth dynamic strategic interaction, were intended to complement Sony's core "hardware" businesses (e.g., TVs, VCRs, and hi-fi equipment) with "software" (e.g., videocassettes and CDs). However, Matsushita quickly imitated Sony by paying $6 billion for MCA Inc. Neither Sony nor Matsushita has proved successful at managing the acquisitions. Sony took a $2.7 billion pre-tax write-off in 1995 for losses relating to its motion picture group; Matsushita sold 80 percent of its MCA stake to Seagram. Meanwhile, Sony has faced a more fundamental challenge: personal computers are dramatically changing the consumer electronics industry. Digital storage devices may soon render Sony's core competencies in analog audio technology obsolete. Sony executives must develop new know-how resources if the company is to continue to lead in the information age.

Industries in which barriers to entry have been built up comprise the third arena in which hypercompetitive behavior is exhibited. As described earlier in the chapter, these barriers include economies of scale, product differentiation, capital investments, switching costs, access to distribution channels, cost advantages other than scale, and government policies. D'Aveni describes how aggressive competitors erode these traditional entry barriers via eight strategic interactions. For example, a cornerstone of Dell's global success in the PC industry is a direct-sales

---

[27] Richard D'Aveni, *Hypercompetition: Managing the Dynamics of Strategic Maneuvering* (New York: Free Press, 1994), p. 71.

approach that bypasses dealers and other distribution channels. Similarly, in the long distance telephone industry, ring-back services based in the United States and elsewhere enable persons making long-distance calls from Europe to sidestep exorbitant rates charged by government-owned PTTs.

The first dynamic strategic interaction comes as a company builds a geographic "stronghold" by creating and reinforcing barriers. After securing a market—especially the home-country market—competitors begin to seek markets outside the stronghold. Thus, the second dynamic strategic interaction takes place when companies target the product market strongholds of competitors in other countries. Honda's geographic expansion outside Japan with motorcycles and automobiles—a series of forays utilizing guerrilla tactics—is a case in point. The third dynamic strategic interaction comes when incumbents make short-term counterresponses to the guerrilla attacks. Strong incumbents may try to turn back the invader with price wars, factory investment, or product introductions, or they may adopt a wait-and-see attitude before responding. In the case of both Harley-Davidson and the Detroit-based U.S. auto industry, management originally underestimated and rationalized away the full potential of the threat from Honda and other Japanese companies. Realizing that their company was a weak incumbent, Harley-Davidson management had little choice but to appeal for government protection. The resulting "breathing room" allowed Harley to put its house in order. Similarly, the U.S. government heeded Detroit's pleas for relief and imposed tariffs and quotas on Japanese auto imports. This gave the Big Three time to develop higher quality, fuel-efficient models to offer U.S. consumers.

The fourth dynamic strategic interaction occurs when the incumbent realizes it must respond fully to the invader by making strategic responses to create new hurdles. U.S. automakers, for example, waged a public relations campaign urging U.S. citizens to "Buy American." The fifth dynamic strategic interaction takes place when competitors react to these new hurdles. In an effort to circumvent import quotas as well as co-opt the "Buy American" campaign, the Japanese automakers built plants in the United States. The sixth dynamic strategic interaction consists of long-run counterresponses to the attack via defensive moves or offensive moves. GM's 1990 introduction of Saturn is a good illustration of a well-formulated and executed defensive move. As the first decade of the twenty-first century continues, GM is launching another defensive move; in an effort to defend its Cadillac nameplate from Lexus, Acura, and Infiniti, GM is developing a global strategy for Cadillac. Competition in the third arena continues to escalate; in the seventh dynamic strategic interaction, competition between the incumbent and entrant is exported to the entrant's home turf. President Clinton's threat of trade sanctions against Japanese automakers in 1995 was intended to send a message that Japan needed to open its auto market. In 1997, GM intensified its assault on Japan with the introduction there of Saturn. The eighth and final dynamic strategic interaction in this arena consists of an unstable standoff between the competitors. Over time the stronghold erodes as entry barriers are overcome, leading competitors to the fourth arena.

As the preceding discussion shows, the irony and paradox of the hypercompetition framework is that, in order to achieve a sustainable advantage, companies must seek a series of *unsustainable* advantages! D'Aveni is in agreement with Peter Drucker, who has long counseled that the role of marketing is innovation and the creation of new markets. Innovation begins with abandonment of the old and obsolete. In Drucker's words, "Innovative organizations spend neither time nor resources on defending yesterday. Systematic abandonment of yesterday alone can transfer the resources . . . for work on the new."

D'Aveni urges managers to reconsider and reevaluate the use of what he believes are old strategic tools and maxims. He warns of the dangers of commitment to a given strategy or course of action. The flexible, unpredictable player may have an advantage over the inflexible, committed opponent. D'Aveni notes that, in hypercompetition, pursuit of generic strategies results in short-term advantage at best. The winning companies are the ones that successfully move up the ladder of escalating competition, not the ones that lock into a fixed position. D'Aveni is also critical of the five forces model. The best entry barrier, he argues, is maintaining the initiative, not mounting a defensive attempt to exclude new entrants.

Other researchers have challenged Porter's thesis that a firm's home-base country is the main source of core competencies and innovation. For example, Indiana University Professor Alan Rugman argues that the success of companies based in small economies such as Canada and New Zealand stems from the "diamonds" found in a particular set or combination of home and related countries. For example, a company based in a European Union nation may rely on the national "diamond" of one of the 24 other EU members. Similarly, one impact of NAFTA on Canadian firms is to make the U.S. "diamond" relevant to competency creation. Rugman argues that, in such cases, the distinction between the home nation and the host nation becomes blurred. He proposes that Canadian managers must look to a "double diamond" and assess the attributes of both Canada and the United States when formulating corporate strategy.[28] In other words, he argues that, for smaller countries, the nation is not the relevant unit of analysis in formulating strategy. Rather, corporate strategists must look beyond the nation to the region or to sets of closely linked countries. Other critics have argued that Porter generalized inappropriately from the American experience, while confusing industry-level competition with trade at the national level. In the *Journal of Management Studies*, Howard Davies and Paul Ellis assert that nations can, in fact, achieve sustained prosperity without becoming innovation driven; the authors also note the absence of strong diamonds in the home bases of many internationally successful industries.[29]

As for Michael Porter himself, his views on corporate strategy and competitive advantage evolved throughout the 1990s. In an interview, he emphasized the difference between operational efficiency and strategy. The former, in Porter's view, concerns improvement via time-based competition or total quality management; the latter entails "making choices." Porter explains, "'Choice' arises from doing things differently from the rival. And strategy is about trade-offs, where you decide to do this and not that. Strategy is the deliberate choice not to respond to some customers, or choosing which customer needs you are going to respond to." Porter is not convinced of the validity of competitive advantage models based on core competency or hypercompetitive industries. As for core competencies, Porter notes:

> Any individual thing that a company does can usually be imitated. The whole notion that you should rest your success on a few core competencies is an idea that invites destructive competition. Successful companies don't compete that way. They fit together the things they do in a way that is very hard to replicate. [Competitors] have to match everything, or they've basically matched nothing.

On the subject of hypercompetition, Porter says:

> I don't think we're moving towards a hypercompetitive world in which there are no tradeoffs. We're probably moving in the other direction. There are more customer segments than ever before, more technological options, more distribution channels. That ought to create lots of opportunities for unique positions.[30]

---

28  Alan M. Rugman and Lain Verbeke, "Foreign Subsidiaries and Multinational Strategic Management: An Extension and Correction of Porter's Single Diamond Framework," *Management International Review* 3, no. 2 (1993), pp. 71–84.

29  Howard Davies and Paul Ellis, "Porter's Competitive Advantage of Nations: Time for the Final Judgment?" *Journal of Management Studies* 37 no. 8 (December 2000) pp. 1189–1213.

30  Tony Jackson, "Why Being Different Pays," *Financial Times* (June 23, 1997), p. 14.

In this chapter we focus on factors that help industries and countries achieve **competitive advantage.** According to Porter's **five forces model,** industry competition is a function of the threat of new entrants, the threat of substitutes, the bargaining power of suppliers and buyers, and rivalry among existing competitors. Porter's **generic strategies** model can be used by managers to conceptualize possible sources of competitive advantage. A company can pursue broad market strategies of **cost leadership** and **differentiation** or the more targeted approaches of **cost focus** and **focused differentiation.** Rugman and D'Cruz have developed a framework known as the **flagship model** to explain how networked business systems have achieved success in global industries. Hamel and Prahalad have proposed an alternative framework for pursuing competitive advantage, growing out of a firm's **strategic intent** and use of competitive innovation. A firm can build **layers of advantage,** search for **loose bricks** in a competitor's defensive walls, **change the rules of engagement,** or **collaborate with competitors** and utilize their technology and know-how.

Today, many companies are discovering that industry competition is changing from a purely domestic to a global phenomenon. Thus, competitive analysis must also be carried out on a global scale. Global marketers must also have an understanding of national sources of competitive advantage. Porter has described four determinants of **national advantage. Factor conditions** include human, physical, knowledge, capital, and infrastructure resources. **Demand conditions** include the composition, size, and growth pattern of home demand. The rate of home market growth and the means by which a nation's products are pulled into foreign markets also affect demand conditions. The final two determinants are the presence of **related and supporting industries** and the **nature of firm strategy,** structure, and **rivalry.** Porter notes that chance and government also influence a nation's competitive advantage. Porter's work has been the catalyst for promising new research into strategy issues, including D'Aveni's work on **hypercompetition** and Rugman's recent **double-diamond framework** for national competitive advantage.

1. How can a company measure its competitive advantage? How does a firm know if it is gaining or losing competitive advantage? Cite a global company and its source of competitive advantage.

2. Outline Porter's five forces model of industry competition. How are the various barriers to entry relevant to global marketing?

3. How does the five partners, or flagship model, developed by Rugman and D'Aveni differ from Porter's five forces model?

4. Give an example of a company that illustrates each of the four generic strategies that can lead to competitive advantage: overall cost leadership, cost focus, differentiation, and differention focus.

5. Briefly describe Hamel and Prahalad's framework for competitive advantage.

6. How can a nation achieve competitive advantage?

7. According to current research on competitive advantage, what are some of the shortcomings of Porter's models?

8. What is the connection, if any, between *national* competitive advantage and *company* competitive advantage? Explain and discuss.

# Case 15-1

## Kodak in the Twenty-First Century: The Search for New Sources of Competitive Advantage

Eastman Kodak Company is at a crossroads. After inventing the famous Brownie camera in 1900, Kodak reigned as the undisputed leader in the silver-halide chemical processes that formed the basis of the photography industry throughout the twentieth century. Today, the company's color film business is a classic cash cow, accounting for as much as 70 percent of Kodak's revenues. However, the company's long-entrenched conservative corporate culture, bureaucratic organizational structure, and go-slow approach to innovation resulted in sluggish, ill-fated responses to changes in the photography market. Although management understood that the digital revolution was changing the way consumers take, store, and access photos, the speed of the changeover from film-based photography to digital came as a shock. In the late 1990s, Kodak invested $1 billion in an alternative film-based format known as Advanced Photo System. It flopped. Meanwhile, the company maintained a premium pricing strategy, allowing competitors such as Fuji to undercut it and gain market share.

Now, management is attempting to remake company's business model in fundamental ways. CEO Daniel Carp has replaced most of Kodak's executive team with newcomers who have worked at technology-oriented companies such as Hewlett-Packard, Lexmark International, and General Electric. To shore up its core film business, Kodak will make private-label film for sale outside the United States. Kodak has also vowed to fight more aggressively for market share with its branded film by cutting prices. Perhaps the most dramatic move is the decision to stop selling film-based cameras for the consumer market in the United States, Canada, and Europe. The only exception is disposable single-use cameras, which remain popular with consumers. The company will continue to develop and market film cameras in China, India, Eastern Europe, and Latin America, where management believes the traditional photography format still has potential for growth.

In an even riskier move, management intends to branch out into new, nonphotographic product lines such as ink-jet printers. One foray into digital printers took the form of Phogenix, a joint venture with Hewlett-Packard. The goal was to use Kodak's thermal dye transfer process in conjunction with H-P's printers; however, the technology was obsolete by the time the product was launched. Likewise, a joint project with Lexmark to develop a desktop photo ink-jet printer resulted in failure, in part because its direct-to-camera interface was not compatible with consumer usage patterns. Kodak currently sells ink-jet paper; expanding into the hardware side of the business will bring the company into head-to-head competition with H-P, Canon, and Seiko Epson. Those companies offer many models of printers for

$100 or less. To fund its investment in the printer market, Kodak is counting on continued revenue flow from its film business. Kodak is also targeting the market for expensive commercial digital printing systems, a move that will position it against Xerox and H-P. Kodak has a joint venture with Heidelberger Druckmaschinen AG, a German company that is the world's number one manufacturer of printing equipment. The venture produces printers under the brand name NexPress. Kodak intends to increase its level of involvement in the venture and roll out a new line of less-expensive equipment.

> *"The trick is to get the cost structure of the traditional consumer business down. We are a business in transition."*
>
> Daniel Carp, CEO, Eastman Kodak

Managing the transition away from film will also require Kodak to redefine its relationship with key business partners. For example, Kodak was for many years the exclusive supplier of traditional photo processing services for the Walgreen drugstore chain; the relationship, which includes 1-hour services, generates about one-half billion dollars in annual revenue for Kodak. Archrival Fuji has a close partnership with Wal-Mart. Now, Fuji is making inroads at Walgreen as well. The minilabs supplied by Kodak were subject to frequent breakdowns; despite the fact the Walgreen was bound by long-term leases; the retailer began installing Fuji minilabs at a cost of $115,000 per unit. Presently, about one-third of Walgreen's 4,290 stores now use Fuji's 1-hour minilab equipment. Fuji also supplies in-store kiosks that enables customers to print photos from their digital cameras. Walgreen's photo-processing Web site also uses Fuji to process prints.

Kodak is enjoying some successes in its transformation to the digital world. Indeed, sales of digital products grew from zero to $1 billion over a 5-year period. Its Easy Share camera is the number two best selling digital camera in the United States; Sony is the market leader.

### Discussion Questions

1. Assess Kodak's situation in terms of Porter's five forces model and generic strategies. Which forces are driving competition in the photo industry? What has happened to Kodak's traditional sources of competitive advantage?

2. Do you think the digital photography revolution will spread to China and India more quickly than Kodak's management expects?

*Sources:* James Bandler, "Losing Focus: As Kodak Eyes, Digital Future, A Big Partner Starts to Fade," *The Wall Street Journal* (January 23, 2004), pp. A1, A8; Bandler, "Ending Era, Kodak Will Stop Selling Most Film Cameras," *The Wall Street Journal* (January 14, 2004), p. B1, B4; Bandler, "Kodak Shifts Focus from Film, Betting Future on Digital Lines," *The Wall Street Journal* (September 29, 2003), pp. A1, A12.

# Case 15-2

## Lego

The Lego Company is a $1.6 billion global business built out of the humblest of materials: interlocking plastic toy bricks. From its base in Denmark, the family-owned Lego empire extends around the world and today includes theme parks, clothing, and toys that can be controlled by computer. Each year, the company produces about 14 billion plastic blocks as well as tiny human figures to populate towns and operate gizmos that spring from the imaginations of young people. Lego products, which are especially popular with boys, are available in more than 130 countries; in the key North American market, the company's overall share of the construction-toy market has been as high as 80 percent. Kjeld Kirk Kristiansen, Lego's chief executive and the grandson of the founder, says that Lego products stand for "exuberance, spontaneity, self-expression, concern for others, and innovation." (The company's name comes from the Danish phrase "leg godt," which means "play well.") Kristiansen also attributes his company's success to the esteem the brand enjoys among parents. "Parents consider Lego not as just a toy company but as providing products that help learning and developing new skills" he says.

For the past several years, however, some of those parents have been switching loyalties. Mega Bloks Inc., a rival company in Montreal, Canada, has been aggressively gaining market share with its own colorful plastic blocks. Some are compatible with Lego products, and all generally cost less than comparable Lego products. Lego executives believe that Lego's proprietary mix of resin results in a higher quality toy. By contrast, Mega Bloks holds costs down by using commodity-grade resin. While Lego dominates the 7- to 12-year-old segment, Mega Bloks is the number one player in the preschool market. Because the bricks in Mega Bloks' original line are larger and softer than Lego, some parents believe they are easier for very young children to use. Lego responded by introducing a Duplo line of oversized blocks made of the same material as the company's core brick line. In recent years, Mega Bloks has introduced a midsized line as well as a line called Micro for the elementary school set. Micro bricks can be used interchangeably with Legos. Lego filed a lawsuit alleging that the Micro line copied the "look" of the knobs on Lego bricks and thus violated Canadian trademark law. Canada's Federal Court of Appeal dismissed the claim in 2003, concluding that the bricks' design is functional and thus entitled to trademark protection. In 2004, Canada's Supreme Court announced that it would hear Lego's appeal.

*"For many people, the biggest part of the brand equity is the brick — which is why we must ensure a significant proportion of the business stays in the brick arena."*

Francesco Ciccolella, Senior Vice President for Corporate Development, Lego Company

In short, Mega Bloks has prospered at Lego's expense. Mega Bloks' sales doubled between 2000 and 2003; by contrast, the Danish company reported its first loss ever—$44 million—in 1988. Meanwhile, Hasbro and other competitors are also targeting the $600 million market for construction toys. In the 1990s, Lego's strategy called for new sources of growth beyond the core block category. The company developed its own line of original robot action figures. Known as Bionicles, the figures can be integrated with the traditional construction materials. Currently, the Bionicle line is Lego's best seller; in 2003, a direct-to-DVD animated feature, *Bionicle—Mask of Light*, was released by Miramax. Another new product, Mybots, was a $70 toy set that included blocks with computer chips embedded to provide lights and sound. A $200 Mindstorms Robotics Invention System allowed users to build computer-controlled creatures. To further leverage the Lego brand, the company also formed alliances with Walt Disney Company and Lucasfilms, creator of the popular *Star Wars* series. For several years, sales of licensed merchandise relating to the popular Harry Potter and Star Wars movie franchises sold extremely well.

More recently, however, while the Harry Potter movie series continued to enjoy great success, interest in the Potter themed play sets was waning. After a disappointing Christmas 2003 season, Lego was left with millions of dollars worth of unsold goods. The difficult retail situation was compounded by the dollar's weakness relative to the Danish krone; Lego posted a record loss of $166 million for 2003. The company unveiled a number of new initiatives aimed at restoring profitability. Its new Quattro line of large, soft bricks is targeted directly at the preschool market. Clikits is a line of pastel-colored bricks targeted at young girls who want to create jewelry.

## Discussion Questions

1. What is the most important decision currently facing Kjeld Kirk Kristiansen?

2. In 2004, Lego continued its entertainment promotional and product tie-ins with new Harry Potter and Spiderman movies. Do you think this is the right strategy?

3. Using Porter's generic strategies framework, compare and contrast Lego and Mega Bloks in terms of their respective pursuit of competitive advantage.

*Sources:* Joseph Pereira and Christopher J. Chipello, "Battle of the Block Makers," *The Wall Street Journal* (February 4, 2004), pp. B1, B4; Clare MacCarthy, "Deputy Chief Sacked as Lego Tries to Rebuild," *Financial Times* (January 9, 2004), p. 19; Majken Schultz and Mary Jo Hatch, "The Cycles of Corporate Branding: The Case of the Lego Company," *California Management Review* 46, no. 1 (Fall 2003), pp. 6–26; Meg Carter, "Building Blocks of Success," *Financial Times* (October 30, 2003), p. 8; Peter Marsh, "Lego Builds Its Future," *Financial Times* (March 16–17, 1996), p. 9.

# 16

# Leading, Organizing, and Controlling the Global Marketing Effort

Germany's Bertelsmann AG has experienced its share of turmoil in the past few years. From humble beginnings in 1835 as a hymnal publisher, Bertelsmann has grown into a $21 billion media powerhouse. Its businesses include the Gruner + Jahr magazine division, Random House book publishing, the Direct Group book club, BMG Music, and RTL, its highly profitable television unit. When Thomas Middelhoff was named chief executive in 1997 at the age of 44, he was described variously as a "media industry Wunderkind" and a "visionary" whose futuristic strategy entailed moving Bertelsmann away from its traditional base of academic and educational publishing. An early decision to buy a stake in AOL Europe paid off handsomely when the unit was resold for $7 billion. However, Middelhoff's relentless focus on acquisitions also resulted in some bad bets, including money-losing Internet start-ups and an ill-fated decision to loan $80 million to the Napster file-sharing service. In July 2002, in the face of differences between the executive board and Bertelsmann's supervisory board, Middelhoff left the company. New chief executive Gunter Thielen is expected to close or sell some of the "visionary" businesses acquired by his predecessor.

This chapter focuses on the integration of each element of the marketing mix into a total plan that addresses opportunities and threats in the global marketing environment. Thomas Middelhoff's abrupt departure from Bertelsmann illustrates some of the challenges facing business leaders in the twenty-first century. Leaders must be capable of articulating a coherent global vision and strategy that integrates local responsiveness, global efficiency, and leverage. The leader is also the architect of an organization design that is appropriate for the company's strategy. The leader must also ensure that appropriate control mechanisms are in place so that, in a world in which industries and markets are rapidly globalizing, organizational goals can be achieved.

Since assuming the chief executive position at Bertelsmann, Gunter Thielen has moved quickly to refocus the company on core businesses such as publishing and printing. Recent book releases include former president Bill Clinton's best-selling memoir. To underscore Bertelsmann's European roots, Thielen sold the company's U.S. headquarters in New York City. In addition, Thielen also helped negotiate the merger of Bertelsmann's BMG division with the Sony Music Group. This makes Sony BMG the world's second largest music company, behind Universal Vivendi's Universal Music Group.

## LEADERSHIP

Global marketing demands exceptional leadership. As noted throughout this book, the hallmark of a global company is the capacity to formulate and implement global strategies that leverage worldwide learning, respond fully to local needs and wants, and draw on the talent and energy of every member of the organization. This heroic task requires global vision and sensitivity to local needs. Overall, the leader's challenge is to direct the efforts and creativity of everyone in the company toward a global effort that best utilizes organizational resources to exploit global opportunities. As Hewlett-Packard CEO Carly Fiorina said in her 2000 commencement address at the Massachusetts Institute of Technology:

> Leadership is not about hierarchy or title or status: It is about having influence and mastering change. Leadership is not about bragging rights or battles or even the accumulation of wealth; it's about connecting and engaging at multiple levels. It's about challenging minds and capturing hearts. Leadership in this new era is about empowering others to decide for themselves. Leadership is about empowering others to reach their full potential. Leaders can no longer view strategy and execution as abstract concepts, but must realize that both elements are ultimately about people.[1]

An important leadership task is articulating beliefs, values, policies, and the intended geographic scope of a company's activities. Using the mission statement or similar document as a reference and guide, members of each operating unit must address their immediate responsibilities and at the same time cooperate with functional, product, and country experts in different locations. However, it is one thing to spell out the vision and another thing entirely to secure commitment to it throughout the organization. As noted in Chapter 1, global marketing entails engaging in significant business activities outside the home country. This means exposure to different languages and cultures. In addition, global marketing involves skillful application of specific concepts, considerations, and strategies. Such endeavors may

---

[1] Carleton "Carly" S. Fiorina, Commencement Address, Massachusetts Institute of Technology, Cambridge, MA, June 2, 2000. See also "It's Death if You Stop Trying New Things," *Financial Times* (November 20, 2003), p. 8.

*Hewlett-Packard CEO Carly Fiorina has shown decisive leadership in one of the world's most challenging industries. In 2002, Fiorina prevailed in her quest to acquire rival computer maker Compaq. Now, she is facing off against Dell in a price war. Betting that H-P can generate profits with its popular printers and consumer electronics products such as digital music players and flat-panel TVs, Fiorina has slashed prices on the company's PCs.*

represent substantial change, especially in U.S. companies with a long tradition of domestic focus. When the "go global" initiative is greeted with skepticism, the CEO must be a change agent who prepares and motivates employees.

Whirlpool CEO David Whitwam recently described his own efforts in this regard in the early 1990s:

> When we announced the Philips acquisition, I traveled to every location in the company, talked with our people, explained why it was so important. Most opposed the move. They thought, "We're spending a billion dollars on a company that has been losing money for 10 years? We're going to take resources we could use right here and ship them across the Atlantic because we think this is becoming a 'global' industry? What the hell does that mean?"[2]

Jack Welch encountered similar resistance at GE. "The lower you are in the organization, the less clear it is that globalization is a great idea," he said. As Paolo Fresco, a former GE vice chairman, explained:

> To certain people, globalization is a threat without rewards. You look at the engineer for X-ray in Milwaukee and there is no upside on this one for him. He runs the risk of losing his job, he runs the risk of losing authority—he might find his boss is a guy who does not even know how to speak his language.[3]

In addition to "selling" their visions, top management at both Whirlpool and GE face the formidable task of building a cadre of globally oriented managers. Similar challenges are facing corporate leaders in other parts of the world. For example, Uichiro Niwa, president of Itochu Corp., took steps to ensure that more of the trading company's $115 billion in annual transactions would be conducted online.[4] He is also radically changing the way he communicates with employees. He is relying more on e-mail, a practice that until recently was virtually unknown in Japan. He also

2   William C. Taylor and Alan M. Webber, *Going Global: Four Entrepreneurs Map the New World Marketplace* (New York: Penguin Books USA, 1996), p. 12.
3   Noel M. Tichy and Stratford Sherman, *Control Your Destiny or Someone Else Will* (New York: HarperBusiness, 1994), p. 227.
4   Robert Guth, "Facing a Web Revolution, a Mighty Japanese Trader Reinvents Itself," *The Wall Street Journal* (March 27, 2000), p. B1.

convenes face-to-face meetings and conferences with employees to solicit suggestions and to hear complaints. This too represents a dramatic change in the way Japanese companies are being led; traditionally, low-level employees were expected to accept the edicts of top management without questioning them.

## Top Management Nationality

Many globally minded companies realize that the best person for a top management job or board position is not necessarily someone born in the home country. Speaking of U.S. companies, Christopher Bartlett of the Harvard Business School has noted:

> Companies are realizing that they have a portfolio of human resources worldwide, that their brightest technical person might come from Germany, or their best financial manager from England. They are starting to tap their worldwide human resources. And as they do, it will not be surprising to see non-Americans rise to the top.[5]

The ability to speak foreign languages is one difference between managers born and raised in the United States and those born and raised elsewhere. For example, according to one report, 20,000 Japanese businesspeople who are fluent in English are working in the United States, but only 200 American businesspersons doing business in Japan can speak Japanese.[6] Roberto Goizueta, the Cuban-born CEO of Coca-Cola who died in 1997, spoke English, Spanish, and Portuguese; Ford's former chief executive, Alexander Trotman, was born in England and speaks English, French, and German. Sigismundus W. W. Lubensen, the former president and CEO of Quaker Chemical Corporation, is a good example of today's cosmopolitan executive. Born in the Netherlands and educated in Rotterdam as well as New York, Lubensen, who speaks Dutch, English, French, and German, says, "I was lucky to be born in a place where if you drove for an hour in any direction, you were in a different country, speaking a different language. It made me very comfortable traveling in different cultures."[7] Additional examples of corporate leaders who are not native to the headquarters country are shown in Table 16-1.

Generally speaking, Japanese companies have been reluctant to place non-Japanese nationals in top positions. For years, only Sony, Mazda, and Mitsubishi

*global* MARKETING Q&A

**Wall Street Journal:** "A lot of your management team is Nokia born and bred. What do you do to encourage global, international thinking?"

**Jorma Ollila, Chief Executive Officer, Nokia:** "The fact is that we are $35.75 billion in revenue, and global, truly global, so that we are present in all major markets. And 1 percent of our sales is in our home market, where 65 percent of R&D happens and the senior management team sits. It really is an issue.

"You have to have had good international exposure, hopefully working abroad so you have really hit some hard international challenges. Then we rotate a lot, so there are a lot of Finnish expats outside. And one-third of our expats are non-Finns—Americans in Thailand and Canadians in China. It is a modus operandi. But it is a tough issue."

Source: David Pringle and Raju Narisetti, "Guiding Nokia in Technology's Rough Seas," The Wall Street Journal (November 24, 2003), pp. B1, B2.

---

[5] Kerry Peckter, "The Foreigners Are Coming," *International Business* (September 1993), p. 53.
[6] Charlene Marmer Solomon, "Success Abroad Depends on More than Job Skills," *Personnel Journal* (April 1994), p. 52.
[7] Peckter, p. 58.

**Table 16-1**

*Who's in Charge? Executives of 2004*

| Company (Headquarters Country) | Executive (Nationality) | Position |
|---|---|---|
| Nissan Motor (Japan) | Carlos Ghosn (Brazil) | President and CEO |
| Pearson PLC (Great Britain) | Marjorie Scardino (USA) | CEO |
| Cadbury Schweppes PLC (Great Britain) | Todd Stitzer (USA) | CEO |
| Ford Motor Company (USA) | Nick Scheele (Great Britain) | President and COO |
| Goodyear Tire and Rubber (USA) | Samir Gibara (Egypt) | Chairman, president, and CEO |
| Schering-Plough (USA) | Fred Hassan (Pakistan) | Chairman, president, and CEO |
| Hoechst AG (Germany) | Ernest Drew (USA) and Claudio Sonder (Brazil) | Named to management board |
| Samsung Electronics (S. Korea) | David Steel (Great Britain) | Vice president of business development |
| Mitsubishi Motors (Japan) | Rolf Eckrodt (Germany) | CEO |
| Hyundai Motors America (USA) | Finbarr O'Neill (Ireland) | CEO |
| L'Oreal SA (France) | Lindsay Owen-Jones (Great Britain) | CEO |
| Reuters Group PLC (Great Britain) | Tom Glocer (USA) | CEO |
| Wolters Kluwer NV (Netherlands) | Nancy McKinstry (USA) | Chairman and CEO |
| Sual (Russia) | Chris Norval (South Africa) | CEO |

*"In the end it does not matter whether the CEO is Japanese or not. Mitsubishi is a Japanese company."*

Rolf Eckrodt, CEO
Mitsubishi Motors[9]

had foreigners on their boards. In March 1999, however, after Renault SA bought a 36.8 percent stake in Nissan Motor, the French company installed a Brazilian, Carlos Ghosn, as president. An outsider, Ghosn was required to move aggressively to cut costs and make drastic changes in Nissan's structure. He also introduced two new words into Nissan's lexicon: speed and commitment. Ghosn's turnaround effort was so successful that his life story and exploits have been celebrated in Big Comic Story, a comic that is popular with Japan's salarymen.[8]

## Leadership and Core Competence

Core competence, a concept developed by global strategy experts C. K. Prahalad and Gary Hamel, was introduced in Chapter 15. In the 1980s, many business executives were assessed on their ability to reorganize their corporations. In the 1990s, Prahalad and Hamel believe executives were judged on their ability to identify, nurture, and exploit the core competencies that make growth possible. Core competence must provide potential access to a wide variety of markets, make a significant contribution to the perceived customer benefits of the end product, and be difficult for competitors to imitate. Few companies are likely to build world leadership in more than five or six fundamental competencies. In the long run, an organization will derive its global competitiveness from its ability to bring high-quality, low-cost products to market faster than its competitors. To do this, an organization must be viewed as a portfolio of competencies rather than a portfolio of businesses. In some instances, a company has the technical resources to build competencies, but key executives lack the vision to do so. As Jorma Ollila, chairman and chief executive of Finland's Nokia, noted recently, "Design is a fundamental building block of the [Nokia] brand. It is central to our product creation and is a core competence integrated into the entire

---

8    Norihiko Shirouzu, "U-Turn: A Revival at Nissan Shows There's Hope for Ailing Japan Inc.," *The Wall Street Journal* (November 16, 2000), pp. A1, A10. See also Todd Zaun, "Look! Up in the Sky! It's Nissan's Chief Executive!" *The Wall Street Journal* (December 27, 2001), p. B1.
9    Todd Zaun, "Now at the Helm, Eckrodt Must Produce Results at Mitsubishi," *The Wall Street Journal* (March 29, 2002), p. A11.

**Table 16-2**

*Responsibility for Global Marketing*

| Company (Headquarters Country) | Executive | Position |
| --- | --- | --- |
| DaimlerChrysler (USA/Germany) | George Murphy | Senior Vice President for Global Marketing |
| McDonald's (USA) | Larry Light | Global Chief Marketing Officer |
| Reebok International (USA) | Muktesh Pant | Vice President of Global Brand Marketing |
| Adidas-Solomon (Germany) | Erich Stamminger | Senior Vice President of Global Marketing |
| Kraft Foods (USA) | Betsy D. Holden | President, Global Marketing and Category Development |
| Calvin Klein (USA) | Kim Vernon | Senior Vice President, Global Advertising, Marketing, and Communications |
| Procter & Gamble (USA) | Jim Stengel | Global Chief Marketing Officer |

company."[10] Ollila's comment underscores the fact that today's executives must rethink the concept of the corporation if they wish to operationalize the concept of core competencies. In addition, the task of management must be viewed as building both competencies and the administrative means for assembling resources spread across multiple businesses.[11] Table 16-2 lists some of the individuals responsible for global marketing at select companies.

# ORGANIZATION

The goal in organizing for global marketing is to find a structure that enables the company to respond to relevant market environment differences while ensuring the diffusion of corporate knowledge and experience from national markets throughout the entire corporate system. The pull between the value of centralized knowledge and coordination and the need for individualized response to the local situation creates a constant tension in the global marketing organization. A key issue in global organization is how to achieve balance between autonomy and integration. Subsidiaries need autonomy to adapt to their local environment, but the business as a whole needs integration to implement global strategy.[12]

When management at a domestic company decides to pursue international expansion, the issue of how to organize arises immediately. Who should be responsible for this expansion? Should product divisions operate directly or should an international division be established? Should individual country subsidiaries report directly to the company president or should a special corporate officer be appointed to take full-time responsibility for international activities? After the decision of how to organize initial international operations has been reached, a growing company is faced with a number of reappraisal points during the development of its international business activities. Should a company abandon its international division, and, if so, what alternative structure should be adopted? Should an area or regional headquarters be formed? What should be the relationship of staff executives at corporate, regional, and subsidiary offices? Specifically, how should the marketing function be organized? To what extent

---

[10] Neil McCartney, "Squaring Up to Usability at Nokia," *Financial Times—IT Review Telecom World* (October 13, 2003), p. 4.

[11] C. K. Prahalad and Gary Hamel, "The Core Competence of the Corporation," *Harvard Business Review* 68, no. 3 (May–June 1990), pp. 79–86.

[12] George S. Yip, *Total Global Strategy* (Upper Saddle River, NJ: Prentice Hall, 1992), p. 179.

# *global* MARKETING Q&A

**USA Today:** "What keeps you up at night?"

**Jim Press, U.S. COO, Toyota:** "How I could have done what we just finished better?"

**Carlos Ghosn, CEO, Nissan:** "The temptation of complacency. There still are people in the company who are used to mediocre performance . . . That would be the beginning of the end."

**USA Today:** "What's the biggest hole in your lineup?"

**Jim Press:** "We need more derivatives of the products we have—different engine offerings of the vehicles we have and performance versions."

**Carlos Ghosn:** "An entry-level car below the Sentra, a top-of-the-line luxury car, and a luxury truck."

**USA Today:** "What competitor gets most of your attention?"

**Jim Press:** "Always Honda, but GM is steaming back in a hurry."

**Carlos Ghosn:** "Honda for return on invested capital. VW for brand management. Renault for purchasing costs."

Source: James R. Healey, David Kiley, Earle Eldridge, "Auto Execs Shed Game Faces to Answer 3 Tough Questions," USA Today (January 19, 2004), p. 4B.

should regional and corporate marketing executives become involved in subsidiary marketing management?

Even companies with years of experience competing around the globe find it necessary to adjust their organizational designs in response to environmental change. It is perhaps not surprising that, during his tenure at Quaker Chemical, Sigismundus Lubensen favored a global approach to organizational design over a domestic/international approach. He advised Peter A. Benoliel, his predecessor CEO, to have units in Holland, France, Italy, Spain, and England report to a regional vice president in Europe. "I saw that it would not be a big deal to put all of the European units under one common denominator," Lubensen recalled.[13]

As markets globalize and as Japan opens its own market to more competition from overseas, more Japanese companies are likely to break from traditional organization patterns. Many of the Japanese companies discussed in this text qualify as global or transnational companies because they serve world markets, source globally, or do both. Typically, however, knowledge is created at headquarters in Japan and then transferred to other country units. For example, Canon enjoys a high reputation for world-class, innovative imaging products such as bubble-jet printers and laser printers. In recent years, Canon has shifted more control to subsidiaries, hired more non-Japanese staff and management personnel, and assimilated more innovations that were not developed in Japan. In 1996, R&D responsibility for software was shifted from Tokyo to the United States, responsibility for telecommunication products to France, and computer language translation to Great Britain. As Canon President Fujio Mitarai explained in an interview, "The Tokyo headquarters cannot know everything. Its job should be to provide low-cost capital, to move top management between regions, and come up with investment initiatives. Beyond that, the local subsidiaries must assume total responsibility for management. We are not there yet, but we are

---

[13] Kerry Peckter, "The Forigens Are Coming," *International Business* (September 1993), p. 58.

moving step by step in that direction." Toru Takahashi, director of R&D, shares this view. "We used to think that we should keep research and development in Japan, but that has changed," he said. Despite these changes, Canon's board of directors includes only Japanese nationals.[14]

No single correct organizational structure exists for global marketing. Even within a particular industry, worldwide companies have developed different strategic and organizational responses to changes in their environments.[15] Still, it is possible to make some generalizations. Leading-edge global competitors share one key organizational design characteristic: Their corporate structure is flat and simple, rather than tall and complex. The message is clear: The world is complicated enough, so there is no need to add to the confusion with a complex internal structuring. Simple structures increase the speed and clarity of communication and allow the concentration of organizational energy and valuable resources on learning, rather than on controlling, monitoring, and reporting.[16] According to David Whitwam, CEO of Whirlpool, "You must create an organization whose people are adept at exchanging ideas, processes, and systems across borders, people who are absolutely free of the 'not-invented-here' syndrome, people who are constantly working together to identify the best global opportunities and the biggest global problems facing the organization."[17]

A geographically dispersed company cannot limit its knowledge to product, function, and the home territory. Company personnel must acquire knowledge of the complex set of social, political, economic, and institutional arrangements that exist within each international market. Many companies start with ad hoc arrangements such as having all foreign subsidiaries report to a designated vice president or to the president. Eventually, such companies establish an international division to manage their geographically dispersed new businesses. It is clear, however, that the international division in the multiproduct company is an unstable organizational arrangement. As a company grows, this initial organizational structure frequently gives way to various alternative structures.

In the fast-changing competitive global environment of the twenty-first century, corporations will have to find new, more creative ways to organize. New forms of flexibility, efficiency, and responsiveness are required to meet the demands of globalizing markets. The need to be cost effective, to be customer driven, to deliver the best quality, and to deliver that quality quickly are some of today's global realities. Recently, several authors have described new organization designs that represent responses to today's the competitive environment. These designs acknowledge the need to find more responsive and flexible structures, to flatten the organization, and to employ teams. There is the recognition of the need to develop networks, to develop stronger relationships among participants, and to exploit technology. These designs also reflect an evolution in approaches to organizational effectiveness. At the turn of the twentieth century, Frederick Taylor claimed that all managers had to see the world the same way. Then came the contingency theorists who said that effective organizations design themselves to match their conditions. These two basic theories are reflected in today's popular management writings. As Henry Mintzberg has observed, "To Michael Porter, effectiveness resides in strategy, while to Tom Peters it is the operations that count—executing any strategy with excellence."[18]

---

[14] William Dawkins, "Time to Pull Back the Screen," *Financial Times* (November 18, 1996), p. 12. See also Sumatra Ghoshal and Christopher A. Bartlett, *The Individualized Corporation* (New York: Harper Perennial, 1999), pp. 179–181.

[15] Christopher Bartlett and Sumantra Ghoshal, *Managing Across Borders: The Transnational Solution* (Boston: Harvard Business School Press, 1989), p. 3.

[16] Vladimir Pucik, "Globalization and Human Resource Management," in V. Pucik, N. Tichy, and C. Barnett (eds.), *Globalizing Management: Creating and Leading the Competitive Organization* (New York: J. Wiley & Sons, 1992), p. 70.

[17] Regina Fazio Maruca, "The Right Way to Go Global: An Interview with Whirlpool CEO David Whitwam," *Harvard Business Review* 72, no. 2 (March–April 1994), p. 137.

[18] Henry Mintzberg, "The Effective Organization: Forces and Forms," *Sloan Management Review* 32, no. 2 (Winter 1991), pp. 54–55.

Kenichi Ohmae has written extensively on the implications of globalization on organization design. He recommends a type of "global superstructure" at the highest level that provides a view of the world as a single unit. The staff of this unit are responsible for ensuring that work is performed in the best location and coordinating efficient movement of information and products across borders. Below this level, Ohmae envisions organizational units assigned to regions "governed by economies of service and economies of scale in information." In Ohmae's view of the world, there are 30 regions with populations ranging from 5 million to 20 million people. For example, China would be viewed as several distinct regions; the same is true of the United States. The first task of the CEO in such an organization is to become oriented to the single unit that is the borderless business sphere, much as an astronaut might view the earth from space. Then, zooming in, the CEO attempts to identify differences. As Ohmae explains,

> A CEO has to look at the entire global economy and then put the company's resources where they will capture the biggest market share of the most attractive regions. Perhaps as you draw closer from outer space you see a region around the Pacific Northwest, near Puget Sound, that is vibrant and prosperous. Then you recognize the region stretching from New York to Boston that is still doing awful. You might see a booming concentration of computer companies and software publishers around Denver, and similar concentrations around Dallas-Fort Worth. Along the coast of California and in parts of New England you will see regions that are strong centers for health care and biotechnology. As a CEO, that's where you put your resources and shift your emphasis.[19]

## the rest of the story

### Turmoil at the Top of Bertelsmann

Thomas Middelhoff's agenda included taking Bertelsmann public in 2005; even as he was championing that proposal, it was becoming apparent that revenue increases were the result of acquisitions rather than improved operations. Middelhoff's actions and relative lack of interest in operations began to grate on Reinhard Mohn, the company patriarch and great-grandson of the founder. Mohn came to view Middelhoff as a dealmaker rather than a manager; also, as one observer noted, Middlehoff "wanted to pursue an aggressive expansion strategy to ensure the group's status as a global player, but for the family he was going too fast."

After taking over the top spot, Gunter Thielen moved quickly to shore up the company and improve profitability. His growth target calls for achieving operating profit margins of 10 percent by 2005. Meanwhile, however, internal political struggles and external disputes have provided further distractions. For example, at the end of 2003, Thielen placed a huge strategic bet by merging Bertelsmann's BMG music unit with Sony's recorded music business. However, the move was opposed by Gerd Schulte-Hillen, chairman of Bertelsmann's supervisory board with more than 30 years of experience; the disagreement resulted in Schulte-Hillen's resignation.

Bertelsmann was embarrassed by a lawsuit brought in California court by two former executives involved in AOL Europe who alleged that the company had violated its contractual obligations to them. The court found in favor of the plaintiffs and awarded the men €200 million in damages. Another widely publicized court battle pitted Gruner + Johr against Rosie O'Donnell, whose magazine was shut down a short time after it was launched. Yet another suit brought by a record industry group charged Bertelsmann with contributing to copyright violations by investing money in Napster.

Thielen has the support of Liz Mohn, who is married to Reinhard Mohn. In 2002, Ms. Mohn became chairperson of the trust that controls the Mohn family's stake in Bertelsmann. Thielen's current contract runs through 2005, but some industry observers believe he will stay longer. As Jürgen Strube, former CEO of BASF AG and current member of its supervisory board, noted recently, "Mr. Thielen is very energetic. There's no reason he shouldn't be able to continue in this position for years to come."

*Sources: Matthew Karrnitschnig, "Bertelsmann Reviews Strategy," The Wall Street Journal (December 17, 2003), p. B7; Martin Peers, Matthew Rose, and Matthew Karnitschnig, "Digital Divide: At Bertelsmann, Another Blow to Futuristic Media Visions," The Wall Street Journal (July 29, 2002), pp. A1, A10; Matthew Karnitschnig and Neal E. Boudette, "History Lesson: Battle for the Soul of Bertelsmann Led to CEO Ouster," The Wall Street Journal (July 30, 2002), pp. A1, A6; Matthew Rose and Martin Peers, "Revising Bertelsmann," The Wall Street Journal (July 30, 2002), pp. B1, B4.*

---

[19] William C. Taylor and Alan M. Webber, *Going Global: Four Entrepreneurs Map the New World Marketplace* (New York: Penguin, 1996), pp. 48–58.

We believe that successful companies, the real global winners, must have both good strategies and good execution.

## Patterns of International Organizational Development

Organizations vary in terms of the size and potential of targeted global markets and local management competence in different country markets. Conflicting pressures may arise from the need for product and technical knowledge; functional expertise in marketing, finance, and operations; and area and country knowledge. Because the constellation of pressures that shape organizations is never exactly the same, no two organizations pass through organizational stages in exactly the same way, nor do they arrive at precisely the same organizational pattern. Nevertheless, some general patterns hold.

A company engaging in limited export activities often has a small in-house export department as a separate functional area. Most domestically oriented companies undertake initial foreign expansion by means of foreign sales offices or subsidiaries that report directly to the company president or other designated company officer. This person carries out his or her responsibilities without assistance from a headquarters staff group. This is a typical initial arrangement for companies getting started in international marketing operations.

**International Division Structure** As a company's international business grows, the complexity of coordinating and directing this activity extends beyond the scope of a single person. Pressure is created to assemble a staff that will take responsibility for coordination and direction of the growing international activities of the organization. Eventually, this pressure leads to the creation of the international division, as illustrated in Figure 16-1. The executive in charge of the international division typically has a direct reporting relationship to corporate staff and thus

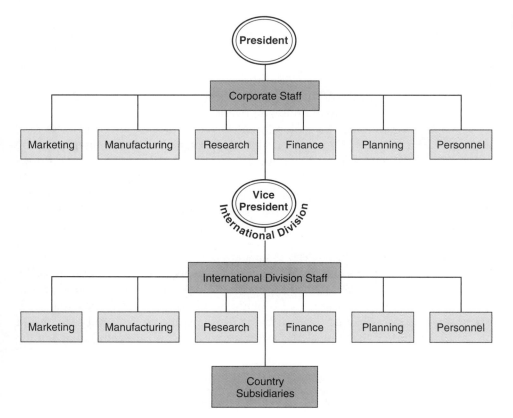

**Figure 16-1**

*Functional Corporate Structure, Domestic Corporate Staff Orientation, International Division*

ranks at the same level as the executives in charge of finance, marketing, operations, and other functional areas. Wal-Mart, Levi Strauss, and Anheuser-Busch are examples of companies whose structures include international divisions.

Four factors contribute to the establishment of an international division. First, top management's commitment to global operations has increased enough to justify an organizational unit headed by a senior manager. Second, the complexity of international operations requires a single organizational unit whose management has sufficient authority to make its own determination on important issues such as which market entry strategy to employ. Third, an international division is frequently formed when the firm has recognized the need for internal specialists to deal with the special demands of global operations. A fourth contributing factor is management's recognition of the importance of proactively scanning the global horizon for opportunities and competitive threats rather than simply responding to situations as they arise.

**Regional Management Centers** When business is conducted in a single region that is characterized by similarities in economic, social, geographical, and political conditions, there is both justification and need for a management center. Thus, another stage of organizational evolution is the emergence of an area or regional headquarters as a management layer between the country organization and the international division headquarters. The increasing importance of the European Union as a regional market has prompted a number of companies to change their organizational structures by setting up regional headquarters there. In the mid-1990s, Quaker Oats established its European headquarters in Brussels; Electrolux, the Swedish home appliance company, has also regionalized its European operations.[20] A regional center typically coordinates decisions on pricing, sourcing, and other matters. Executives at the regional center also participate in the planning and control of each country's operations with an eye toward applying company knowledge on a regional basis and optimally utilizing corporate resources on a regional basis. This organizational design is illustrated in Figure 16-2.

Regional management can offer a company several advantages. First, many regional managers agree that an on-the-scene regional management unit makes sense where there is a real need for coordinated, pan-regional decision making. Coordinated regional planning and control are becoming necessary as the national subsidiary continues to lose its relevance as an independent operating unit. Regional management can probably achieve the best balance of geographical, product, and functional considerations required to implement corporate objectives effectively. By shifting operations and decision making to the region, the company is better able to maintain an insider advantage.[21]

A major disadvantage of a regional center is its cost. The cost of a two-person office could exceed $600,000 per year. The scale of regional management must be in line with scale of operations in a region. A regional headquarters is inappropriate if the size of the operations it manages is inadequate to cover the costs of the additional layer of management. The basic issue with regard to the regional headquarters is "Does it contribute enough to organizational effectiveness to justify its cost and the complexity of another layer of management?"

**Geographical and Product Division Structures** As a company becomes more global, management frequently faces the dilemma of whether to organize by geography or by product lines. The geographical structure involves the assignment of operational responsibility for geographic areas of the world to line managers. The corporate headquarters retains responsibility for worldwide planning and control, and each area of the world—including the "home" or base market—is organizationally equal. For the

---

[20] "... And Other Ways to Peel the Onion," *The Economist* (January 7, 1995), pp. 52–53.
[21] Allen J. Morrison, David A. Ricks, and Kendall Roth, "Globalization Versus Regionalization: Which Way for the Multinational?" *Organizational Dynamics* (Winter 1991), pp. 17–29.

company with French origins, France is simply another geographic market under this organizational arrangement. This structure is most common in companies with closely related product lines that are sold in similar end-use markets around the world. For example, the major international oil companies utilize the geographical structure, which is illustrated in Figure 16-3. McDonald's organizational design integrates the international division and geographical structures. McDonald's U.S. is organized into five geographical operating divisions and McDonald's International has four.

When an organization assigns regional or worldwide product responsibility to its product divisions, manufacturing standardization can result in significant economies. For example, Whirlpool recently reorganized its European operations, switching from a geographic or country orientation to one based on product lines. One potential disadvantage of the product approach is that local input from individual country managers may be ignored with the result that products will not be sufficiently tailored to local markets. The essence of the Ford 2000 reorganization initiated in 1995 was to integrate North American and European operations. Over a 3-year period, the company saved $5 billion in development costs. However, by 2000, Ford's European market share had slipped nearly 5 percent. In a shift back toward the geographic model, then-CEO Jacques Nasser returned to regional executives some of the authority they had lost.[22]

---

[22] Joann S. Lublin, "Division Problem: Place vs. Product: It's Tough to Choose a Management Model," *The Wall Street Journal* (June 27, 2001), pp. A1, A4.

**Figure 16-3**

*Geographic Corporate Structure, World Corporate Staff Orientation, Area Divisions Worldwide*

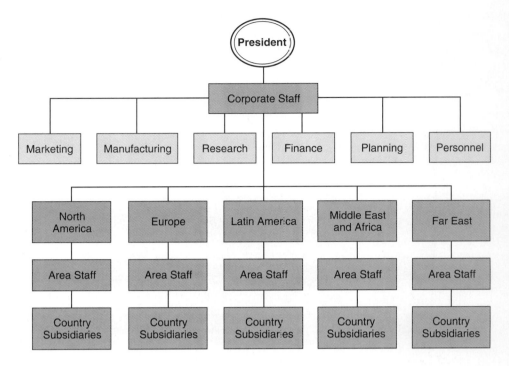

The challenges associated with devising the structure that is best suited to improving global sales can be seen in Procter & Gamble's ambitious Organization 2005 plan. Initiated by CEO Durk Jager in 1999, this reorganization entailed replacing separate country organizations with five global business units for key product categories such as paper products and feminine hygiene. A number of executives were reassigned; in Europe alone, 1,000 staff members were transferred to Geneva. Many managers, upset about the transfers and news that P&G intended to cut 15,000 jobs worldwide, quit the company; the resulting upheaval cost CEO Jager his job. To appease middle managers, new CEO A. G. Lafley restored some of the previous geographic focus.[23]

**The Matrix Design** In the fully developed large-scale global company, product or business, function, area, and customer know-how are simultaneously focused on the organization's worldwide marketing objectives. This type of total competence is a **matrix organization.** Management's task in the matrix organization is to achieve an organizational balance that brings together different perspectives and skills to accomplish the organization's objectives. In 1998, both Gillette and Ericsson announced plans to reorganize into matrix organizations. Ericsson's matrix is focused on three customer segments: network operators, private consumers, and commercial enterprises.[24] Gillette's new structure separates product-line management from geographical sales and marketing responsibility.[25] Likewise, Boeing has reorganized its commercial transport design and manufacturing engineers into a matrix organization built around five platform or aircraft model-specific groups. Previously, Boeing was organized along functional lines; the new design is expected to lower costs and quicken updates and problem solving. It will also unite essential design, engineering, and manufacturing processes between Boeing's commercial transport factories and component plants, enhancing product consistency.[26] Why are

23 Emily Nelson, "Rallying the Troops at P&G: New CEO Lafley Aims to End Upheaval by Revamping Program of Globalization," *The Wall Street Journal* (August 31, 2000), pp. B1, B4.
24 "Ericsson to Simplify Business Structure," *Financial Times* (September 29, 1998), p. 21.
25 Mark Maremont, "Gillette to Shut 14 of Its Plants, Lay Off 4,700," *The Wall Street Journal* (September 29, 1998), pp. A3, A15.
26 Paul Proctor, "Boeing Shifts to 'Platform Teams,'" *Aviation Week & Space Technology* (May 17, 1999), pp. 63–64.

executives at these and other companies implementing matrix designs? The matrix form of organization is well-suited to global companies because it can be used to establish a multiple-command structure that gives equal emphasis to functional and geographical departments.

Professor John Hunt of the London Business School suggests four considerations regarding the matrix organizational design. First, the matrix is appropriate when the market is demanding and dynamic. Second, employees must accept higher levels of ambiguity and understand that policy manuals cannot cover every eventuality. Third, in country markets where the command-and-control model persists, it is best to overlay matrices on only small portions of the workforce. Finally, management must be able to clearly state what each axis of the matrix can and cannot do. However, this must be accomplished without creating a bureaucracy.[27]

Having established that the matrix is appropriate, management can expect the matrix to integrate four basic competencies on a worldwide basis:

1. *Geographic knowledge.* An understanding of the basic economic, social, cultural, political, and governmental market and competitive dimensions of a country is essential. The country subsidiary is the major structural device employed today to enable the corporation to acquire geographical knowledge.
2. *Product knowledge and know-how.* Product managers with a worldwide responsibility can achieve this level of competence on a global basis. Another way of achieving global product competence is simply to duplicate product management organizations in domestic and international divisions, achieving high competence in both organizational units.
3. *Functional competence in such fields as finance, production, and, especially, marketing.* Corporate functional staff with worldwide responsibility contributes toward the development of functional competence on a global basis. In a handful of companies, the appointment of country subsidiary functional managers is reviewed by the corporate functional manager who is responsible for the development of his or her functional activity in the organization on a global basis.
4. *A knowledge of the customer or industry and its needs.* Certain large and extremely sophisticated global companies have staff with a responsibility for serving industries on a global basis to assist the line managers in the country organizations in their efforts to penetrate specific customer markets.

Under this arrangement, instead of designating national organizations or product divisions as profit centers, both are responsible for profitability, the national organization for country profits and the product divisions for national and worldwide product profitability. Figure 16-4 illustrates the matrix organization. This organization chart starts with a bottom section that represents a single-country responsibility level, moves to representing the area or international level, and finally moves to representing global responsibility from the product divisions to the corporate staff, to the chief executive at the top of the structure.

At Whirlpool, North American operations are organized in matrix form. CEO David Whitwam expects to extend this structure into Europe and other regional markets. Whirlpool managers from traditional functions such as operations, marketing, and finance also work in teams devoted to specific products, such as dishwashers or ovens. To encourage interdependence and integration, the cross-functional teams are headed by "brand czars" such as the brand chief for Whirlpool or Kenmore. As Whitwam explains, "The Whirlpool-brand czar still worries about the Whirlpool

---

[27] John W. Hunt, "Is Matrix Management a Recipe for Chaos?" *Financial Times* (January 12, 1998), p. 10.

**Figure 16-4**

*The Matrix Structure*

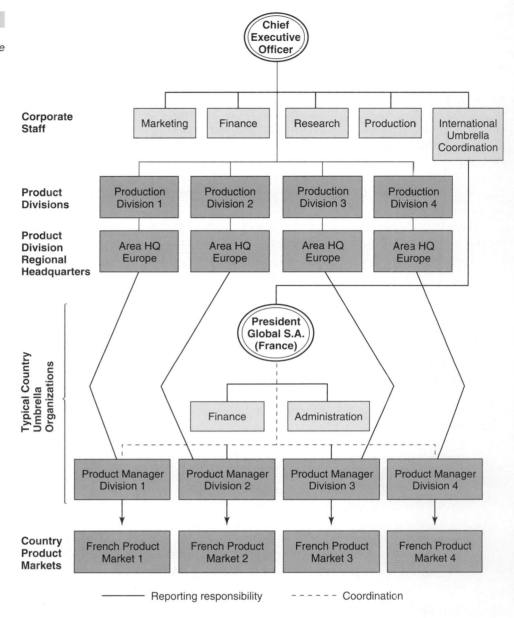

| —————— Reporting responsibility | ------ Coordination |

name. But he also worries about all the refrigerator brands that we make because he heads that product team. It takes a different mind-set."[28]

Some companies are moving away from the matrix in response to changing competitive conditions. For nearly a decade, ABB was a matrix organized along regional lines. Local business units—factories that make motors or power generators, for example—reported both to a country manager and to a business area manager who set strategy for the whole world. This structure allowed ABB to execute global strategies while still thriving in local markets. However, in 1998, new chairman Göran Lindahl dissolved the matrix. As the chairman explained in a press release, "This is an aggressive move aimed at greater speed and efficiency by further focusing and flattening the organization. This step is possible now thanks to our strong, decentralized presence in all local and global markets around the world." In January 2001, Lindahl stepped down and his successor, Jorgen Centerman, revamped the organizational structure yet again. The new design was

28 William C. Taylor and Alan M. Webber, *Going Global: Four Entrepreneurs Map the New World Marketplace* (New York: Penguin USA, 1996), p. 25 .

intended to improve the focus on industries and large corporate customers; Centerman wants to ensure that all of ABB's products were designed to the same systems standards.[29] However, in 2002, with the chief executive under pressure to sell assets, ABB's board replaced Centerman with Jürgen Dorman.

The key to successful matrix management is ensuring that managers are able to resolve conflicts and achieve integration of organization programs and plans. The mere adoption of a matrix design or structure does not create a matrix organization. The matrix organization requires a fundamental change in management behavior, organizational culture, and technical systems. In a matrix, influence is based on technical competence and interpersonal sensitivity, not on formal authority. In a matrix culture, managers recognize the absolute need to resolve issues and choices at the lowest possible level and do not rely on higher authority.

In the twenty-first century, an important task of top management is to eliminate a one-dimensional approach to decisions and encourage the development of multiple management perspectives and an organization that will sense and respond to a complex and fast-changing world. By thinking in terms of changing behavior rather than changing structural design, company management can free itself from the limitations of the structural chart and focus instead on achieving the best possible results with available resources.

## LEAN PRODUCTION: ORGANIZING THE JAPANESE WAY

In the automobile industry, a comparison of early craft production processes, mass production, and modern "lean" production provides an interesting case study of the effectiveness of new organizational structures in the twentieth century.[30] Dramatic productivity differences existed between craft and mass producers in the first part of the twentieth century. The mass producers—most notably Ford Motor Company—gained their substantial advantage by changing their value chains so that each worker was able to do far more work each day than the craft producers. The innovation that made this possible was the moving assembly line, which required the originators to conceptualize the production process in a totally new way. The assembly line also required a new approach to organizing people, production machinery, and supplies. By rearranging their value chain activities, the mass producers were able to achieve reductions in effort ranging from 62 percent to 88 percent over the craft producers. These productivity improvements provided an obvious competitive advantage.

The advantage of the mass producers lasted until the Japanese auto companies further revised the value chain and created **lean production,** thereby gaining for themselves the kinds of dramatic competitive advantages that mass producers had previously gained over craft producers. For example, the Toyota Production System (TPS), as the Japanese company's manufacturing methods are known, achieves efficiencies of about 50 percent over typical mass production systems. Even with the reduced assembly time, the lean producer's vehicles have significantly fewer defects than the mass-produced vehicles. The lean producer is also using about 40 percent less factory space and maintaining only a fraction of the inventory stored

29 David Woodruff, "New ABB Chairman Unveils Overhaul, Reacting to Rival GE," *The Wall Street Journal* (January 12, 2001), p. A16. A detailed discussion of ABB's matrix structure is found in Ghoshal and Bartlett (1999), pp. 183–190.
30 This section is adapted from the following sources: James P. Womack, Daniel T. Jones, and Daniel Roos, *The Machine that Changed the World: The Story of Lean Production* (New York: HarperCollins, 1990); Ranganath Nayak and John M. Ketteringham, *Breakthroughs!* (San Diego, CA: Pfeiffer, 1994), Chapter 9; and Michael Williams, "Back to the Past: Some Plants Tear Out Long Assembly Lines, Switch to Craft Work," *The Wall Street Journal* (October 24, 1994), pp. A1, A4.

| **Table 16-3** | **Traditional Assumptions** | **Ohno and Shingo's Insights** |
|---|---|---|
| *Five Assumptions About Mass Production Versus Toyota Production System* | 1. Maximize machine utilization | Labor is more costly than machines |
| | 2. Fixed set up times | Setup time can be reduced |
| | 3. Build to inventory to reduce unit cost | Minimize inventory to cut cost, waste |
| | 4. Inspect at end of process | Inspect to prevent defective production |
| | 5. Maximize backwards integration | Outsource from supplier specialists |

*Source:* Adapted from Adrian Slywotzky, *Value Migration* (Cambridge, MA: Harvard Business School Press, 1996), pp. 31–33.

by the mass producer. Again, the competitive advantages are obvious. Whether the strategy is based on differentiation or low cost, the lean producer has the advantage.

To achieve these gains at Toyota, production gurus Taiichi Ohno and Shigeo Shingo challenged several assumptions traditionally associated with automobile manufacturing. They made changes to operations within the auto company itself such as reducing setup times for machinery. The changes also applied to operations within supplier firms and the interfaces between Toyota and its suppliers and to the interfaces with distributors and dealers. Ohno and Shingo's innovations have been widely embraced in the industry; as a result, individual producers' value chains have been modified, and interfaces between producers and suppliers have been optimized to create more effective and efficient value systems (see Table 16-3).

**Assembler Value Chains** Employee ability is emphasized in a lean production environment. Before being hired, people seeking jobs with Toyota participate in the Day of Work, a 12-hour assessment test to determine who has the right mix of physical dexterity, team attitudes, and problem-solving ability. Once hired, workers receive considerable training to enable them to perform any job in their section of the assembly line or area of the plant, and they are assigned to teams in which all members must be able to perform the functions of all other team members. Workers are also empowered to make suggestions and to take actions aimed at improving quality and productivity. Quality control is achieved through *kaizen*, a devotion to continuous improvement that ensures that every flaw is isolated, examined in detail to determine the ultimate cause, and then corrected. Mechanization, and particularly flexible mechanization, is increased within the lean production firm. Toyota's Sienna minivan, for example, is produced on the same assembly line in Georgetown, Kentucky, as the company's Camry models. The Sienna and Camry share the same basic chassis and 50 percent of their parts. There are 300 different stations on the assembly line, and Sienna models require different parts at only 26 stations. Toyota expects to build one Sienna for every three Camrys that come off the assembly line.[31]

In contrast to the lean producers, U.S. mass producers typically maintain operations with greater direct labor content, less mechanization, and much less flexible mechanization. They also divide their employees into a large number of discrete specialties with no overlap. Employee initiative and teamwork are not encouraged. Quality control is expressed as an acceptable number of defects per vehicle.

Even when the comparisons are based on industry averages, the Japanese lean producers continue to enjoy substantial productivity and quality advantages. Again, these advantages put the lean producers in a better position to exploit low cost or differentiation strategies. They are getting better productivity out of their workers and machines, and they are making better use of their factory floor space. The relatively small size of the repair area reflects the higher quality of their products. A high number of "suggestions per employee" provides some insight into why lean producers outperform mass producers. First, they invest a great deal more in the training of their workers. They also rotate all workers through all

---

[31] Micheline Maynard, "Camry Assembly Line Delivers New Minivan," *USA Today* (August 11, 1997), p. 3B.

jobs for which their teams are responsible. Finally, all workers are encouraged to make suggestions, and management acts on those suggestions. These changes to the value chain translate into major improvements in the value of their products.

It should come as no surprise that many of the world's automakers are studying lean production methods and introducing them in both existing and new plants throughout the world. In 1999, for example, GM announced plans to spend nearly $500 million to overhaul its Adam Opel plant in Germany. Pressure for change came from several sources, including increasing intense rivalry in Europe's car market, worldwide overcapacity, and a realization that price transparency in the euro zone will exert downward pressure on prices. GM hopes to transform the plant into a state-of-the-art lean production facility with a 40 percent workforce reduction by 2005. As GM Europe President Michael J. Burns said, "Pricing is more difficult today. . . . You have to work on product costs, structural costs . . . everything."[32]

**Downstream Value Chains** The differences between lean producers and U.S. mass producers in the way they deal with their respective dealers, distributors, and customers are as dramatic as the differences in the way they deal with their suppliers. U.S. mass producers follow the basic industry model and maintain an "arm's-length" relationship with dealers that is often characterized by a lack of cooperation and even open hostility. There is often no sharing of information because there is no incentive to do so. The manufacturer is often trying to force on the dealer models the dealer knows will not sell. The dealer, in turn, is often trying to pressure the customer into buying models he or she does not want. All parties are trying to keep information about what they really want from the others. This does little to ensure that the industry is responsive to market needs.

The problem starts with the market research, which is often in error. It is compounded by lack of feedback from dealers regarding real customer desires. It continues to worsen when the product planning divisions make changes to the models without consulting the marketing divisions or the dealers. This process invariably results in production of models that are unpopular and almost impossible to sell. The manufacturer uses incentives and other schemes to persuade the dealers to accept the unpopular models, such as making a dealer accept one unpopular model for every five hot-selling models it orders. The dealer then has the problem of persuading customers to buy the unpopular models.

Within the mass assembler's value chain, the linkage between the marketing elements and the product planners is broken. The external linkage between the sales divisions and the dealers is also broken. The production process portion of the value chain is also broken in that it relies on the production of thousands of unsold models that then sit on dealer lots, at enormous cost, while the dealer works to find customers. Within the dealerships, there are even more problems. The relationship between the salesperson and the customer is based on sparring and trying to outsmart each other on price. When the salesperson gets the upper hand, the customer gets stung. It is very much like the relationship between the dealer and the manufacturer. Each is withholding information from the other in the hope of outsmarting the other. Too often, salespeople do not investigate customers' real needs and try to find the best product to satisfy those needs. Rather, they provide only as much information as is needed to close the deal. Once the deal is closed, the salesperson has virtually no further contact with the customer. No attempt is made to optimize the linkage between dealers and manufacturers or the linkage between dealers and customers.

The contrast with the lean producer is again striking. In Japan, the dealer's employees are true product specialists. They know their products and deal with all aspects of the product, including financing, service, maintenance, insurance,

---

[32] Joseph B. White, "GM Plans to Invest $445 Million, Cut Staff," *The Wall Street Journal* (May 27, 1999), p. A23.

registration and inspection, and delivery. A customer deals with one person in the dealership, and that person takes care of everything from the initial contact through eventual trade-in and replacement and all the problems in between. Dealer representatives are included on the manufacturer's product development teams and provide continuous input regarding customer desires. The linkages between dealers, marketing divisions, and product development teams are totally optimized.

The stress caused by large inventories of finished cars is also absent. A car is not built until there is a customer order for it. Each dealer has only a stock of models for the customer to view. Once the customer has decided on the car he or she wants, the order is sent to the factory and in a matter of a couple of weeks the car is delivered, by the salesperson, to the customer's house.

Once a Japanese dealership gets a customer, it is absolutely determined to hang on to that customer for life. It is also determined to acquire all of the customer's family members as customers. A joke among the Japanese says that the only way to escape from the salesperson who sold a person a car is to leave the country. Japanese dealers maintain extensive databases on actual and potential customers. These databases deal with demographic data and preference data. Customers are encouraged to help keep the information in the database current and they cooperate in this. This elaborate store of data becomes an integral part of the market research effort and helps ensure that products match customer desires. The fact that there are no inventories of unpopular models because every car is custom ordered for each customer and the fact that the dealer has elaborate data on the needs and desires of its customers change the whole nature of the interaction between the customer and the dealer. The customer literally builds the car she or he wants and can afford. There is no need to try to outsmart each other.

The differences between U.S. mass producers and the Japanese lean producers reflect their fundamental differences in business objectives. The U.S. producers focus on short-term income and return on investment. Today's sale is a discrete event that is not connected to upstream activities in the value chain and has no value in tomorrow's activities. Efforts are made to reduce the cost of the sales activities. The Japanese see the process in terms of the long-term perspective. There are two major goals of the sales process. The first is to maximize the income stream from each customer over time. The second is to use the linkage with the production processes to reduce production and inventory costs and to maximize quality and therefore differentiation.

## GLOBAL MARKETING MANAGEMENT CONTROL

Global marketing presents formidable problems to managers responsible for marketing control. Each national market is different from every other market. Distance and differences in language, custom, and practice create communications problems. As noted earlier in the chapter, in larger companies, the size of operations and number of country subsidiaries often result in the creation of an intermediate headquarters. This adds an organizational level to the control system. This section reviews global marketing control practices, compares these practices with domestic marketing control, and identifies the major factors that influence the design of a global control system.

In the managerial literature, **control** is defined as the process by which managers ensure that resources are used effectively and efficiently in the accomplishment of organizational objectives. Control activities are directed toward marketing programs and other programs and projects initiated by the planning process. Data measures and evaluations generated by the control process are also a major input to the planning process. Thus, planning and control are intertwined and interdependent. The planning process can be divided into two related phases. *Strategic* planning is the selection of product and market opportunities and the commitment of human and financial resources to achieve these objectives. *Operational* planning is the process in which strategic product or market objectives and resource commitments to these objectives are translated into specific projects and programs. The relationship of strategic planning, operational planning, and control is illustrated in Figure 16-5.

For companies with global operations, marketing control presents additional challenges. The rate of environmental change in a global company is a dimension of each of the national markets in which it operates. In Chapters 2 through 6 of this book, we examined these environments; each is changing at a different rate and each exhibits unique characteristics. The multiplicity of national environments challenges the global marketing control system with much greater environmental diversity and, therefore, greater complexity in its control. Finally, global marketing can create special communications problems associated with the great distance between markets and headquarters and the differences among managers in languages, customs, and practices.

When company management decides that it wants to develop a global strategy, control of subsidiary operations must be shifted from the subsidiary to the headquarters. The subsidiary will continue to provide vital input into the strategic planning process; even so, such a shift in the organization's balance of power may

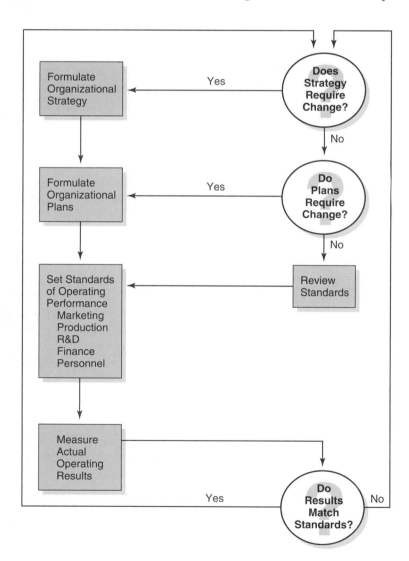

**Figure 16-5**

*Strategic and Operational Planning and Control*

result in strong resistance to change. In many companies, a tradition of subsidiary autonomy and self-sufficiency limits the influence of headquarters. To overcome such limits, headquarters must facilitate the shift in the perception of self-interest from subsidiary autonomy to global business performance. The conflicts that inevitably arise should be anticipated to the extent possible and the appropriate interventions made. In addition, headquarters can use both formal and informal approaches to maintain control.

## Formal Control Methods

Planning and budgeting are two basic tools of formal marketing control. Planning is determining desired sales and profit objectives and projected marketing program expenditures in unit and money terms. The formal document in which these objectives and expenditures are expressed is a budget. How is the budget established? In practice, many companies rely on two standards: last year's actual performance and some kind of industry average or historical norm. For global companies, a better approach is for headquarters to develop an estimate of the kind of growth that would be desirable and attainable in each national market. This estimate can be based on company studies of national and industry growth patterns.

Control consists of measuring actual sales and expenditures. In the case of no variance (or a favorable variance) between actual and budget, no action is usually taken. An unfavorable variance—lower unit sales than planned, for example—acts as a red flag that attracts the attention of line and staff executives at regional and international headquarters. They will investigate and attempt to determine the cause of the unfavorable variance and what might be done to improve performance.

Larger companies may have sufficient business volume to justify staff product specialists at corporate headquarters who follow the performance of products worldwide. Global marketing product managers have staff responsibility for their product(s) from introduction to termination. Because markets are at different stages of development, a company's products may be at different stages of the product life cycle in different geographical areas. A major responsibility of staff specialists is to ensure that lessons learned in world markets are applied to the management of products worldwide. The task of the global marketing product manager is to try to avoid making the same mistake twice and to capitalize on what the company has learned in world markets; in short, to ensure that all learning is applied wherever relevant. This includes transfers from markets that are at similar stages of development, as well as transfers across stages of development.

Smaller companies focus on key products in key markets. Key products are those that are important to the company's sales, profit objectives, and competitive position. They are frequently new products that require close attention in their introductory stage in a market. If any budget variances develop with a key product, headquarters intervenes directly to learn about the nature of the problem and to assist local management in dealing with the problem.

Another principal measure of marketing performance is share of market, which compares company performance with that of other competitors in the market. Companies that do not obtain this measure, even if it is an estimate, are flying blind. In larger markets, data are reported for subsidiaries and, where significant sales are involved, on a product-by-product basis. Share-of-market data in larger markets are often obtained from independent market audit groups. In smaller markets, share-of-market data are often not available because the market is not large enough to justify the development of an independent commercial marketing audit service. In smaller markets, it is possible for a country manager or agent to hide a deteriorating market position or share of market behind absolute gains in sales and earnings.

## Influences on Marketing Budgets

In preparing a budget or plan, the following factors are important.

**Market Potential** How large is the potential market for the product being planned? In every domestic market, management must address this question in formulating a product plan. A company that introduces a product in more than one national market must answer this question for each market.

**Competition** A marketing plan or budget must be prepared in light of the competitive level in the market. The more entrenched the competition, the more difficult it is to achieve market share and the more likely it is that a competitive reaction will meet any move that promises significant success in the target market. Competitive moves are particularly important as a variable in international market planning because many companies are moving from strong competitive positions in their base markets to foreign markets where they have a minor position and must compete against entrenched companies. Domestic market standards and expectations of marketing performance are based on experience in markets where the company has a major position. These standards and expectations are simply not relevant to a market where the company is in a minor position and trying to break into the market.

**Impact of Substitute Products** One of the sources of competition for a product in a market is availability of substitute products. As a product is moved into markets at different stages of development, improbable substitute products often emerge. For example, in Colombia a major source of competition for manufactured boxes and other packaging products is woven bags and wood boxes made in the handicraft sector of the economy. Marketing officials of global companies in the packaging industry report that the garage-based small business producing a handmade product is extremely difficult competition because of costs of materials and labor in Colombia.

**Process** The manner in which performance targets are communicated to subsidiary management is as important as the way in which they are derived. One of the most sophisticated methods used today is the *indicative planning method*. Headquarters estimates of regional potential are disaggregated and communicated to subsidiary management as *guidance*. The subsidiaries are in no way bound by guidance. They are expected to produce their own plan by taking into account the headquarters guidance that is based on global data and their own data from the market, including a detailed review of customers, competitors, and other relevant market developments. This method produces excellent results because it combines a global perspective and estimate with specific country marketing plans that are by the country management teams themselves.

Headquarters, in providing guidance, does not need to understand a market in depth. For example, the headquarters of a manufacturer of electrical products does not need to know how to sell electric motors to a French consumer. What headquarters can do is gather data on the expected expansion in generating capacity in France and use experience tables drawn from world studies that indicate what each megawatt of additional generating capacity will mean in terms of the growth in demand in France for electrical motors. The estimate of total market potential, together with information on the competitiveness of the French subsidiary, can be the basis for guidance in terms of expected sales and earnings in France. The guidance may not be accepted by the French subsidiary. If the indicative planning method is used properly, the subsidiary educates the headquarters if its guidance is unrealistic. When headquarters does its job well, it will select an attainable but ambitious target. If subsidiary personnel doubt they can achieve the headquarters goal, discussion and headquarters involvement in the planning process will lead to either a plan that will achieve the guidance objective or a revision of the guidance by headquarters.

# Informal Control Methods

In addition to budgeting, informal control methods, especially the transfer of people from one market to another, play an important role. When people are transferred, they take with them their experience in previous markets, which normally includes some standards for marketing performance. Investigation of a new market that has lower standards than a previous market leads to revised standards or to discovery of a reason for the difference. Another valuable informal control device is face-to-face contact between subsidiary staff and headquarters staff, as well as contact among subsidiary staff. These contacts provide the opportunity for an exchange of information and judgments that can be valuable input into the planning and control process. Annual meetings that bring together staff from throughout a region of the world often result in informal inputs to the process of setting standards.

# THE GLOBAL MARKETING AUDIT

A **global marketing audit** can be defined as a comprehensive, systematic examination of the marketing environment and company objectives, strategies, programs, policies, and activities. The audit can be company-wide in scope or it can encompass a particular line of business or organizational subunit. The objective of periodic audits is to identify existing and potential problems and opportunities in a company's marketing performance and to recommend a plan of action for improving that performance. In other words, the global marketing audit is a tool for evaluating and improving a company's (or business unit's) global marketing operations.

A full marketing audit has two basic characteristics. First, it is formal and systematic. Random questions may result in useful insights, but this is not a marketing audit. The effectiveness of an audit normally increases to the extent that it involves a sequence of orderly diagnostic steps. Second, a marketing audit should be conducted periodically. Most companies in trouble are well on their way to disaster before the trouble is fully apparent. An audit can reveal such troubles while there is still time to deal with them. The audit may be broad or it may be a narrowly focused assessment. A full marketing audit is comprehensive. It reviews the company's marketing environment, competition, objectives, strategies, organization, systems, procedures, and practices in every area of the marketing mix, including product, pricing, distribution, communications, customer service, and research strategy and policy.

There are two types of audit: independent and internal. An independent marketing audit is conducted by someone who is free from the influence of the organization being audited. The independent audit may or may not be objective: It is quite possible for company management to influence the consultant or professional firm. The company that wants a truly independent audit should understand the importance of objectivity. A potential limitation of an independent marketing audit is the auditor's lack of understanding of the industry. In many industries, there is no substitute for experience: An industry outsider may simply not see the subtle clues that an industry veteran would easily recognize. Then again, the independent auditor may see obvious indicators that the veteran may be unable to see.

An internal audit or self-audit may be quite valuable because it is conducted by marketers who understand the industry. However, it may lack the objectivity of an independent audit. Because the two types of audits have complementary strengths and limitations, both should be conducted periodically for the same scope and time period so that the results may be compared. The comparison may lead to insights on how to strengthen the performance of the marketing team.

# Setting Objectives and Scope of the Audit

The first step of an audit is a meeting between company executives and the auditor to agree on objectives, coverage, depth, data sources, report format, and time period for the audit.

**Gathering Data** One of the major tasks in conducting an audit is data collection. A detailed plan of interviews, secondary research, review of internal documents, and the like is required. This effort usually involves an auditing team. A basic rule in data collection is not to rely solely on the opinion of people being audited for data. In auditing a sales organization, it is absolutely essential to talk to field sales personnel as well as to sales management, and, of course, no audit is complete without direct contact with customers and suppliers.

Creative auditing techniques should be encouraged and explored by the auditing team. For example, if an auditor wants to determine whether top executives are really in touch with the organization and all of its activities, the auditor should speak with mailroom personnel and find out if chief executives have ever visited the facility. If they have never been there, it speaks volumes about the management style and the degree of hands-on management in the organization. Similarly, if an organization has developed an elaborate marketing incentive program that is purported to generate results with customers, an audit should involve customer contact to find out if, indeed, the program is actually having any impact.

**Preparing and Presenting the Report** The next step after data collection and analysis is the preparation and presentation of the audit report. This presentation should restate the objectives and scope of the audit, present the main findings, and list major recommendations, conclusions, and topics for further study and investigation.

**Components of the Marketing Audit** There are six major components of a full global marketing audit:

1. The marketing environment audit
2. The marketing strategy audit
3. The marketing organization audit
4. The marketing systems audit
5. The marketing productivity audit
6. The marketing function audit

The marketing audit presents a number of potential problems and pitfalls. Setting objectives can be a pitfall if, indeed, the objectives fail to anticipate major problems or contingencies. The auditor must have the authority to revise objectives and priorities during the course of the audit itself. Similarly, new data sources may appear during the audit, and the auditor should be open to such sources. The approach of the auditor should be simultaneously systematic, following a predetermined outline, and perceptive and open to new directions and sources that appear in the course of the audit investigation.

**Report Presentation** One of the biggest problems in marketing auditing is that the executive who commissions the audit may have unrealistically high expectations about what the audit will do for the company. An audit is valuable even if it does not identify major new directions or offer cure-alls. All concerned must recognize that improvements at the margin make the difference between success and mediocrity. Experienced marketers don't look for dramatic revolutionary findings or cure-alls; rather, they know that incremental improvements can lead to success in global marketing. Global marketers, even more than their domestic counterparts, need marketing audits to assess far-flung efforts in

# global MARKETING Q&A

**Wall Street Journal:** "The SonyBMG merger reduced the number of major record labels to four from five. How many majors does the industry need?"

**Gunter Thielen, Chief Executive Officer, Bertelsmann AG:** "I think the four majors that now exist can survive quite well. The independents as well, as long as they find good niches. Maybe there will be three at some point. In the music industry, size is really an asset because you can run your national affiliates more efficiently. At SonyBMG, we're combining operations in every country and are going to save a lot of money."

**Wall Street Journal:** "If you look beyond music at the rest of the media industry, what do you think the dominant trend in the media world in the coming years will be?"

**Gunter Thielen:** "The entire business is becoming more international. Up until now, the big U.S. majors—the world's three biggest media companies—have concentrated their business in the U.S. I think the process of globalization will mean that these companies will become much more active abroad."

**Wall Street Journal:** "What about Bertelsmann?"

**Gunter Thielen:** "For us, this is nothing new. We've been operating outside of Germany for 40 years because Germany is much smaller than the U.S. We reached the limits of our home market decades ago. That led us first into other European markets and then to the U.S. Now, we're in the midst of expanding into the third major global region—Asia. I think the big American companies are also doing this. In any case, I always run into people from Viacom, TimeWarner and so forth on my trips to Asia. They're exploring just like we are."

**Wall Street Journal:** "Thomas Middelhoff, your predecessor, once described himself as 'an American with a German passport.' What are you?"

**Gunter Thielen:** "I feel more European. Not as much German as European."

*Source: Matthew Karnitschnig, "Bertelsmann's Latest Tune," The Wall Street Journal, September 27, 2004, pp. B1, B3.*

highly diverse environments. The global marketing audit should be at the top of the list of programs for strategic excellence and implementation excellence for the winning global company.

## summary

To respond to the opportunities and threats in the global marketing environment, organizational **leaders** must develop a global vision and strategy. Leaders must also be able to communicate that vision throughout the organization and build global competencies. Global companies are increasingly realizing that the "right" person for top jobs is not necessarily a home-country national.

In **organizing** for the global marketing effort, the goal is to create a structure that enables the company to respond to significant differences in international market environments and to extend valuable corporate knowledge. Alternatives include an **international division structure, regional management centers,** **geographical structure, regional** or **worldwide product division structure,** and the **matrix** design. Whichever form of organization is chosen, balance between autonomy and integration must be established. Many companies are adopting the organizational principle of **lean production** that was pioneered by Japanese automakers.

The differences between global marketing **control** practices and purely domestic control must be recognized. Appropriate adjustments should be made to the way in which global planning and control practices are formulated and implemented. The **global marketing audit** can be an effective tool for improving global marketing performance.

1. Are top executives of global companies likely to be home-country nationals?

2. In a company involved in global marketing, which activities should be centralized at headquarters and which should be delegated to national or regional subsidiaries?

3. Identify some of the factors that lead to the establishment of an international division as an organization increases its global business activities.

4. "A matrix structure integrates four competencies on a worldwide scale." Explain.

5. In the automobile industry, how does "lean production" differ from the traditional assembly line approach?

6. In preparing a marketing budget or plan, what factors should managers should take into account?

# Case 16-1

## A Marketer Takes the Wheel at Volkswagen AG

Bernd Pischetsrieder has a lot on his mind these days. Since becoming chairman of Volkswagen AG in April 2002, he has presided over the launch of several key new vehicles. The $35,000 Volkswagen Touareg is the company's first SUV. Named after a nomadic African tribe that makes an annual journey across the Sahara, the Touareg appeared on the market just as SUV sales were starting to decline in the United States. *Car and Driver* magazine named the Touareg the "best luxury SUV" of 2003. Another new vehicle is the Phaeton, the first super luxury model to bear the VW nameplate. Developed at a cost of $700 million, Phaeton boasts the world's finest automotive air conditioning system and carries a price tag of $85,000. Together, the Touareg and Phaeton illustrate Volkswagen's strategy of moving upmarket. Finally, in mid-2003, the fifth generation of the venerable compact Golf was unveiled. Since being launched in 1974, 22 million Golfs have been sold worldwide, and Pischetsrieder set a 2004 sales target of 600,000 units (see Table 1).

**Table 1** *Worldwide Sales of Golf*

| Year Launched | Total Sales ($ millions) |
| --- | --- |
| Golf I (1974) | 6.8 |
| Golf II (1983) | 6.3 |
| Golf III (1990) | 4.8 |
| Golf IV (1997) | 4.4 |
| Golf V (2003) | na |

Away from the fanfare associated with product launches, Pischetsrieder has been quietly going about the task of transforming Volkswagen's organization. Pischetsrieder's predecessor was Ferdinand Piech, the former head of VW's Audi AG subsidiary and grandson of legendary auto designer Ferdinand Porsche. Piech, an autocratic leader with an engineering background who was "steely eyed and intense," had assumed the top post in 1993 when Volkswagen was reeling from the effects of a devastating economic recession. At the time, the company had stakes in Spain's SEAT and Skoda, a Czech company. He immediately declared a state of crisis in the company and began taking drastic actions; cost cutting topped the list. Piech trimmed VW's worldwide employment, starting with 20,000 jobs in 1993. Piech also pledged to slash the number of auto platforms underlying VW's nameplates from 16 to 4 by 1998. During his tenure, a new car, the Passat, was launched, as were redesigned Jetta and Beetle models. He acquired three luxury automakers: Lamborghini, Bugatti, and Bentley. Piech also elevated the status of engineering in the company and spending on R&D soared. Piech quickly gained a reputation for making key decisions himself.

Comparing and contrasting his business style with that of his predecessor, Pischetsrieder recently noted that Piech "tends to view the business from an engineering stand-point, whereas I look at things with more of a marketing orientation." One approach Piech favored was pitting engineering teams one against the other; the result, in some instances, was a duplication of effort. Also, as the number of underlying vehicle platforms shrank, some models closely resembled others, even though the vehicles had different nameplates. Pischetsrieder has indicated that he will cut back the amount of money spent on R&D. Also, he will tie executive compensation to financial performance. By introducing a measure of return on investment known as economic value added (EVA), Pischetsrieder is sending a message that managers must reduce capital spending. Bonuses will also be based on group performance rather than on the performance of the seven different automotive brands in the company's portfolio. The chairman has also bundled the company's seven car brands into two groups. One consists of VW, Skoda, Bentley, and Bugatti. The second group is comprised of Audi, SEAT, and Lamborghini.

## Company Background

Volkswagen enjoys the distinction of being the number one carmaker in Europe and the fourth largest in the world. Worldwide, the company sells more than five million vehicles each year. The compact Golf is the best-selling car in Europe, where VW commands a 17 percent market share. Initial European demand for the new midsize Passat was so strong that there was an 8-month waiting list. The company can boast that its giant Wolfsburg plant is home to the most automated production line in the world, capable of completing 80 percent of a car's assembly by machine. VW ranks as the second-largest company in Germany; only DaimlerChrysler is bigger. Outside Europe, Volkswagen has also achieved considerable success. In Mexico, for example, the company's share of the passenger car market is 40 percent. Volkswagen is also the number one Western auto manufacturer in China, where it commands 55 percent of the market.

A deeper understanding of Volkswagen's place in the auto industry requires an overview of former chairman Carl Hahn's attempts to implement his vision of VW as Europe's first global automaker. Indeed, management guru Peter Drucker credits Volkswagen for developing the first truly global strategy more than 30 years ago. By 1970, the Beetle was a mature product in Europe; sales were still moderately strong in the United States, and booming in Brazil. Drucker describes what happened next:

> The chief executive officer of Volkswagen proposed switching the German plants entirely to the new model, the successor to the Beetle, which the German plants would also supply to the United States market. But the continuing demand for Beetles in the United States would be satisfied out of Brazil, which would then give Volkswagen do Brasil the needed capability to enlarge its plants and to maintain for another ten years the Beetle's leadership in the growing Brazilian market. To assure the American customers of the "German quality" that was one of the Beetle's main attractions, the critical parts such as engines and transmissions for all cars sold in North America would, however, still be made in

What color do you dream in?

©1998 Volkswagon. 1-800 DRIVE VW or WWW.VW.COM

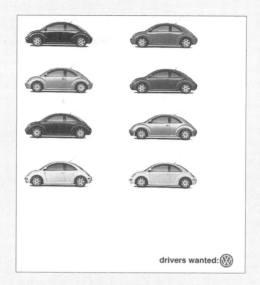

drivers wanted: Ⓥ

Germany. The finished car for the North American market would be assembled in the United States.[33]

Unfortunately, this visionary strategy failed. One problem was resistance on the part of German unions. A second problem was confusion among American dealers about a car that was equally "made in Germany," "made in Brazil," and "made in the USA." Two decades later, as described in an interview with *Harvard Business Review*, Hahn's strategic plan for the 1990s and beyond called for a decentralized structure of four autonomous divisions. In pursuit of this vision, Hahn invested tens of billions of dollars in Czechoslovakia's Skoda autoworks and SEAT in Spain. The Volkswagen, Audi, Skoda, and SEAT units each would have its own chief executive. As a whole, the company would be capable of turning out more than four million cars annually in low-cost plants located close to buyers. The company's R&D center, however, would continue to be in Germany. Highly automated plants in Germany would provide components such as transmissions, engines, and axles to assembly operations in other parts of the world.

In Spain, VW hoped to take advantage of labor rates 50 percent lower than in the former West Germany and roughly on par with those paid by Japanese companies with factories in Britain. Because labor makes up a larger share of production costs for subcompacts than for larger models, and because annual demand in Spain amounts to 500,000 cars, Spain was an attractive location for small-car production. Besides serving the domestic market, VW intended to use Spain as a production source that would allow it to cut prices and boost margins in Europe. Between 1986 and 1990, VW paid the Spanish government a total of $600 million in exchange for 100 percent ownership of SEAT. The company increased Spanish production from 350,000 to 500,000 vehicles; the popular Golf model represents about one-quarter of the output. VW invested $1.9 billion in a new plant in Martorell capable of producing 300,000 cars each year.

---

[33] Peter F. Drucker, *Innovation and Entrepreneurship: Practice and Principles* (New York: Harper & Row, 1985), p. 87.

Similar reasoning was behind VW's 1991 purchase of a 31 percent stake in Skoda from the Czechoslovak government. Located northeast of Prague in the city of Mlada Boleslav, the Skoda works enjoyed distinction as the most efficient plant in the former Soviet bloc. However, product quality was low and the plant was a major source of pollution. With an eye to doubling production to 450,000 cars, VW pledged to invest $5 billion by the end of the 1990s. VW's presence also persuaded TRW, Rockwell International, and other parts suppliers interested in serving Skoda in Central and Eastern Europe, to establish operations in the Czech Republic which split from Slovakia in 1992. However, to maintain their low-cost position and ensure quality control, VW and Skoda executives went a step beyond the Japanese-style "lean production" system that emphasizes just-in-time delivery from nearby suppliers. Several different suppliers manufacture components such as seats, instrument panels, and rear axles *inside* the plant itself. As Skoda CFO Volkhard Kohler explained in 1994, "We have to organize better than in the Western world and use supplier integration. Wages will increase, so we have to find other ways of being cost-effective. Supplier integration is part of the new thinking and what we do here can be a model for the West." Professor Daniel Jones of the Cardiff University Business School supports the effort. "It's physically integrated, but in terms of management and performance each runs his own show. It makes a lot of sense because you have the direct integration of people making the parts and the people putting them in the car," he said in an interview.

Hahn also earmarked $3 billion for a project in which he took a keen personal interest: investment in the former East Germany, where he was born. On October 3, 1990, German reunification added 16 million people to Volkswagen's home-country market virtually overnight. Under communism, the citizens of East Germany had a choice of basically one car: the notoriously low-quality Trabant. Hahn's strategy for a reunited Germany included building a new $1.9 billion factory that would employ 6,500 workers and produce a quarter of a million Golf and Polo models each year. The investment was justified in part by forecasts that East Germans would buy 750,000 cars each year; VW aimed to capture a third of the market, equal to its share in West Germany.

As noted earlier, Ferdinand Piech succeeded Hahn as chairman in 1993. With great fanfare, VW announced in March 1993 that it had succeeded in luring a new production chief away from General Motors. José Ignacio Lopéz de Arriortúa was expected to play a major role in cost cutting at VW, but he arrived amid accusations of industrial espionage. The controversy did not stop López from doing what he had been hired to do. He broke long-term contracts with many of VW's suppliers and put new contracts up for bid; as a result, a higher percentage of components are now sourced outside Germany. At VW's new General Pachecho plant in Buenos Aires, López subcontracted various aspects of production to a dozen outside companies. VW workers build a few crucial parts such as the chassis and power train; suppliers are responsible for various other tasks such as assembling instrument panels. In the end, the espionage controversy cost López his job and Piech settled the civil case by agreeing to pay GM $100 million and buy $1 billion in GM parts.

Even though his tenure at VW was brief and stormy, the positive aspects of the López legacy endured. Maryann Kellar, author of a book about VW, calls the Czech and Argentine experiment "something that has been talked about for years as the next great productivity and cost enhancement move by the industry." In 1996, Skoda rolled out the Octavia, the first new car developed by the Czech plant during the Volkswagen era and the first to use a VW chassis platform. Piech also won concessions from IG Metall, the German autoworkers union. The union agreed to 2.5 percent annual pay raises and a pledge of job security. In addition, the work day for many assembly line workers has been reduced to 5 hours and 46 minutes; in essence, a 4-day week. CFO Bruno Adelt estimated that all the agreed-upon changes would boost productivity 4 to 5 percent.

Even as VW expanded production in emerging markets and introduced production efficiencies, it was devising a comeback strategy for the United States. Mexican production of a new version of the legendary Beetle began in 1997 with a U.S. launch in 1998. As board member Jens Neumann said, "The Beetle is the core of the VW soul. If we put it back in people's minds, they'll think of our products more." Like its predecessor, the new Beetle has curved body panels and running boards. However, it is a front-wheel-drive model with more headroom and legroom. Despite being priced at about $15,000, 10 percent higher than the company's entry-level Golf, the new Beetle was initially a huge success. Sales were strong through 2000; then, as the buzz surrounding the vehicle died down, sales began to slip. In 2003, hoping to recapture some "cool" and re-energize the Beetle brand, a convertible model was introduced.

## Pischetsrieder Looks to the Future

One could easily imagine some of the questions going through chairman Pischetsrieder's mind as he sat in his office in Wolfsburg. How would VW's engineers respond to their loss of influence within the company? After nearly a decade of Piech's autocratic style, would company personnel respond positively to Pischetsrieder's attempts to delegate authority and decision making responsibility? According to recent J.D. Powers and Associates Initial Quality Index, Volkswagen ranks last among the world's top seven automakers in terms of buyer-reported problems during the first 90 days of ownership. What should be done to address the company's quality problems? At the end of 2002, sales of the Phaeton amounted to slightly more than 3,000 vehicles. Could VW successfully shed its image as the "people's car" and move upmarket, thus fulfilling a goal established by Ferdinand Piech? And, would the company's newfound attention to customer desires pay off in the form of increased brand loyalty and market share? Would he be able to move quickly to fill gaps in the company's product lineup? Should he authorize the development of a new version of the Microbus, the beloved icon that is virtually synonymous with American counterculture in the 1960s?

## Discussion Questions

1. What key decisions are currently facing Bernd Pischetsrieder?

2. Some critics say it is a strategic mistake to reposition Volkswagen as a more upscale brand. Do you agree with the criticism?

3. In Europe, a well-equipped 4-door Golf carries a sticker price equivalent to about $24,000. This price represents a premium of about 8 percent compared with competing models such as the Opel Astra. Although the new Golf's styling remains relatively unchanged from previous models, performance enhancements such as a multilink axle for a smoother ride have resulted in higher production costs. Hans Dieter Potsch, Volkswagen's chief financial officer, says, "The market is willing to pay more for the additional quality." Discuss.

Sources: James Mackintosh, "Volkswagen Misfires: The Carmaker Counts the Cost of Its High Spending and Its Faltering Search for Luxury," *Financial Times* (March 9, 2004), p. 9; Mackintosh, "VW's Iconic Golf Seems to be Running Out of Gas," *Financial Times* (February 12, 2004), p. 14; Mackintosh, "VW Chief Signals Passing of the Age of the Engineers," *Financial Times* (September 8, 2003), p. 8; Mackintosh, "Touareg to Drive VW's Move Upmarket," *Financial Times* (July 22, 2003), p. 20; Neal Boudette, "Drivers Wanted: Volkswagen Stalls on Several Fronts After Luxury Drive, " *The Wall Street Journal* (May 8, 2003), pp. A1, A17; Gabriella Stern, "VW's U.S. Comeback Rides on Restyled Beetle," *The Wall Street Journal* (May 6, 1997), pp. B1, B2; Haig Simonian, "Alliances Forged in the Factories," *Financial Times* (November 4, 1996), p. 10; David Woodruff, "VW is Back—But for How Long?" *Business Week* (March 4, 1996), pp. 66–67; Jonathan Friedland, "VW Puts Suppliers on Production Line," *The Wall Street Journal* (February 15, 1996), p. A11; James Bennet, "Eurocars: On the Road Again," *The New York Times* (August 20, 1995), sec. 3, p. 1; Jane Perlez, "Skoda Gives Its Suppliers a Place in the Auto Plant," *The New York Times* (November 19, 1994), pp. 41, 52; Richard W. Stevenson, "In a Czech Plant, VW Shows How to Succeed in the East," *The New York Times* (November 19, 1994), pp. D1, D6; Steven Greenhouse, "Carl Hahn's East European Homecoming," *The New York Times* (September 23, 1990), sec. 3, pp. 1, 6; Bernard Avishai, "A European Platform for Global Competition: An Interview with VW's Carl Hahn," *Harvard Business Review* 69, no. 4 (July-August 1991), pp. 103–113; Ferdinand Protzman, "New Leadership for Volkswagen," *The New York Times* (March 30, 1992), pp. C1, C2. Timothy Aeppel, "VW Chief Declares a Crisis and Prescribes Bold Action," *The Wall Street Journal* (April 1, 1993), p. B3; Peter Drucker, *Innovation and Entrepreneurship: Practice and Principles* (New York: Harper & Row, 1985).

# Case 16-2

## Kazuo Inamori: Spiritual Leadership at Kyocera Corp.

With headquarters in Kyoto, Japan, Kyocera Corp. is a $10.2 billion company that built its global reputation by developing and manufacturing products and product components containing high-tech synthetic ceramics. Although Kyocera (the name is short for Kyoto Ceramics) is unknown to most people, the company has for many years been *the* world leader in the production and sales of ceramic housings for computer microchips. The housings serve as a ceramic "cocoon" to protect the fragile chips during transit. Like many other Japanese companies, Kyocera's original competitive advantage stemmed from its ability to make high-quality products faster and cheaper than competitors.

In other ways, however, Kyocera breaks the mold usually associated with Japan Inc. The company is one of only a handful of companies in Japan with foreign directors on its board. Its San Diego-based subsidiary is mostly run by Americans. Rather than recruit graduates of prestigious schools, Kyocera prefers to hire its employees from second-tier technical schools. Company founder Kazuo Inamori and chairman emeritus believes his employees work harder because they are grateful to be given a chance to work for a top company. And while most Japanese companies strive for consensus and adherence to company norms, Inamori encourages creativity and independence within Kyocera.

In Kyocera's early days, Inamori often spent a great deal of time on the plant floor, personally overseeing the kilns and the mixing of raw materials. It was precisely this approach that helped it win its first crucial contract with Texas Instruments. Making chip packages is both an art and a science; they must be baked for 18 hours at temperatures as high as 1,600 degrees Celsius. Recalls Inamori, "We got the contract because we were so good at mixing and baking, because the top people in the company were in front of the kilns all the time, and they could control the variances and keep the quality consistent, which is very hard in ceramics." Inamori earned the nickname "Mr. A.M." because he stayed at work until 3 or 4 in the morning.

Despite this close attention to production details, as Inamori explains in his recently published autobiography, the secret to Kyocera's growth is not its grasp of technology. Rather, it is the "spiritual energy of the workers." In an interview with *Business Japan*, Inamori said, "I feel that the strength of an enterprise is determined by the number of workers who really understand the spiritual qualities which enable a business to succeed. That is why I always endeavor to get my thoughts across to them. My time is often taken up in that connection rather than in dealing with technological problems concerning ceramic manufacture."

Inamori exhorted his employees to ever-higher levels of performance with Inamorisms, such as "When a company is no longer on the offensive, that company is already beginning to go downhill." Part of Inamori's directness and driven nature may be explained by the fact that, as a young man, his goal was to become a kamikaze pilot (the term used to describe Japanese volunteers who flew suicide attacks) during World War II. However, because the war ended before he could fulfill his dream, he dedicated his life to staging offensive maneuvers in marketing, rather than in the military. Inamori believes that when a company is first founded, the employees have a burning drive for work and military-style discipline. When such organizations grow in size, however, top management's attention shifts away from the maintenance of worker energy. According to Inamori, the spiritual drive that was present when Kyocera was founded has not waned. This fact distinguishes Kyocera from most other organizations—Japanese, American, or otherwise.

Inamori implements that spiritual drive by striving for efficiency. He insists that all employees work at holding down costs and engage in high-quality work. For example, instead of following the electronics industry norm of using distributors for its products, Kyocera relies on a salaried sales force. The result: Kyocera spends 12 to 13 percent of revenues on general, administrative, and sales expenses compared to the 20 percent that is normal for other companies. There has never been a layoff at Kyocera's U.S. plant in San Diego; in return, the company enjoys high employee loyalty. These are just a few of the reasons why Kyocera is such a tough competitor.

Kyocera's early opportunities were tied to the fledgling semiconductor industry in the United States; ceramic components play a significant role in high-technology products because they are heat resistant and do not conduct electricity. The road to Kyocera's domination of the chip package market began in the mid-1960s, when it bid successfully against a West German firm for a Texas Instruments contract to build ceramic insulating rods for silicon transistors. Soon thereafter, Fairchild Semiconductor (the forerunner to Intel) drafted technically demanding designs for housings to protect the chips it manufactured. However, Fairchild was unable to find any U.S. company willing to build the housings for a reasonable price, even though Coors Electronic Packaging was the world leader in ceramic semiconductor package manufacturing at the time. Fairchild turned to Kyocera, which was anxious to expand into electronic applications for its ceramic business. Asa Jonishi, Kyocera's first U.S. salesman, worked hard for the account; not only was Kyocera willing to take on the Fairchild project for a low price but also it delivered its first order against a seemingly impossible deadline of 3 months.

Kyocera's success in the U.S. market can also be attributed to its willingness to custom tailor chip housings to each customer's needs. Among California's Silicon Valley chipmakers, Kyocera has become legendary for its service. Kyocera backs up its $100 million-per-year R&D expenditures with sales forces in both the United States—50 direct salespeople at 12 direct sales offices—and Japan that pay heed to Inamori's unwavering emphasis on quality and customer service. Early on, Kyocera earned a reputation for answering customer questions overnight, whereas U.S. suppliers often took weeks to respond. Employees would work around the clock to satisfy customer requests for samples.

Today, Kyocera is targeting new applications for ceramics, including replacements for human body parts, automobile engines, and knives. (The History Channel has even profiled Kyocera's innovative ceramic cutlery and production processes in a program titled "Axes, Swords, and Knives.") Soaring demand for portable communications devices has translated into strong sales of the miniature electronic parts that are Kyocera's specialty. Despite its past successes, however, Kyocera faces new challenges in the future. Plastic packaging has replaced ceramics for some types of integrated circuits; by the late 1990s, for example, Intel was substituting cheaper resins in its microprocessor packaging. Kyocera's engineers responded by developing heat-resistant plastic packages and plastic/ceramic hybrids. Kyocera has diversified; acquisitions include Elco Corporation, a U.S. manufacturer of electrical connectors, Japanese camera maker Yashica Corporation, and Mita Industrial, a photocopier producer. Kyocera's environmentally friendly laser printers are particularly popular in Germany. Kyocera has also gotten out of unattractive business segments such as PCs and fax machines. Kyocera lost a bet big on the now-bankrupt Iridium satellite-telephone venture; Kyocera was a handset supplier and also handled sales in Japan and other Asian countries. However, Kyocera started marketing regular cellular phones in 2001;

company executives hope to challenge Nokia and other leading suppliers.

## Discussion Questions

1. What factors have helped Kyocera succeed in serving organizational markets?
2. How is Kyocera different from the "typical" Japanese company?
3. How important was Inamori's spiritual drive to Kyocera's success? What will happen to the company's culture now that Inamori has retired?

*Sources:* Benjamin Fulford, "Kyocera's Pay Dirt," *Forbes* (September 20, 1999), pp. 113–114; Kazuo Inamori, *A Passion for Success: Practical, Inspiration, and Spiritual Insight from Japan's Leading Entrepreneur* (New York: McGraw-Hill, 1995); George Taninecz, "Kazuo Inamori: 'Respect the Divine and Love People,'" *Industry Week* (June 5, 1995), pp. 47–51; "Kyocera's Secrets: Flexibility, Spirituality and Teamwork," *Business Japan* (January 1987), pp. 31–32; Gene Bylinsky, "The Hottest High-Tech Company in Japan," *Fortune* (January 1990), pp. 83–84 + ; "Cult of Personality," *Business Month* (August 1990), pp. 42–44; David Halberstam, "Coming In from the Cold War," *The Washington Monthly* (January–February 1991), pp. 32–34; Jacob M. Schlesinger, "Kyocera Plays an Ambivalent Role in U.S. Weaponry," *The Wall Street Journal* (February 1991), p. A15; Jonathan Friedland, "Samurai Sorcerer," *Far Eastern Economic Review* (June 3, 1993), pp. 60–65.

# 17 The Digital Revolution and Global Electronic Marketplace

**B**arry Diller has always been a man with big plans. He began his career in the mailroom at the fabled William Morris talent agency. His next stop was ABC Television, where his programming innovations included the "Movie of the Week" and the mini-series. Television proved to be a stepping-stone to Hollywood; in 1974, at the age of 34, Diller became chairman of Paramount Pictures. In 1984, having presided over such blockbuster hits as *Raiders of the Lost Ark*, he moved on to 20th Century Fox. Cable television was next; Diller took the top spot at QVC, the home shopping channel. After resigning from QVC in the mid-1990s, Diller began building a media company that he named USA Networks. He bought the Home Shopping Network (HSN) and a family of TV stations. During the next few years, however, the burgeoning dotcom scene caught his eye. He was intrigued by the possibilities for e-commerce, especially online retailing. In 2001, only 1 year after the dotcom bubble had burst, he bought a 64 percent stake in Expedia, the online travel service. To raise additional money to invest, he sold USA Networks to Vivendi Universal, the French media company, for $11 billion. Diller's vision is to make his new company, IAC/InterActiveCorp, the world's largest e-commerce enterprise. Indeed, today IAC is the world's largest provider of online travel services through its Hotels.com and Expedia.com Web sites. InterActive also owns Ticketmaster, the world's leading ticketing service, and online personals listing services Match.com and uDate.com.

As Barry Diller's experience with IAC/InterActiveCorp illustrates, the digital revolution is bringing about the creation of new companies, industries, and markets. The same process is also contributing to the *destruction* of companies, industries, and markets. In short, the revolution is dramatically transforming the world in which we live. In this final chapter, we will begin by briefly reviewing the key innovations that served as precursors to the digital revolution. In the next two sections, convergence, the disruptive nature of Internet technology, and its effect on global

companies are discussed. Then key e-commerce issues that face global marketers are examined; Figure 17-2 (page 568) presents a categorization of Web sites in matrix form. Next comes an overview of Web site design issues as they pertain to global marketing. The final section of the chapter examines some of the new products and services made possible by the digital revolution.

## THE DIGITAL REVOLUTION: A BRIEF HISTORY

The **digital revolution** is a paradigm shift resulting from technological advances that allow for the digitization—that is, conversion to binary code—of analogue sources of information, sounds, and images. The origins of the digital revolution can be traced back to the mid-twentieth century. Over a 5-year period between 1937 and 1942, John Vincent Atanasoff and Clifford Berry developed the world's first electronic digital computer at Iowa State University. The Atanasoff-Berry Computer (ABC) incorporated several major innovations in computing including the use of binary arithmetic, regenerative memory, parallel processing, and separation of the memory and computing functions. In 1947, William Shockley and two colleagues at AT&T's Bell Laboratories invented a "solid state amplifier," or transistor, as it became known. This was a critical innovation because the vacuum tubes that were used in computers and electronics products at that time were large, consumed a large amount of power, and generated a great deal of heat. Shockley and collaborators John Bardeen and William Brattain were awarded the Nobel Prize in physics in 1956 for their invention. In the mid-1950s, Sony licensed the transistor from Bell Labs; Sony engineers boosted the yield of the transistor and created the market for transistor radios. The sound was "lo-fi" but the devices were portable and stylish, which is what consumers—especially teenagers—wanted. Also during the 1950s, Robert Noyce and Jack Kilby independently invented the silicon chip (also known as the **integrated circuit** or IC).[1] The IC gave the transistor its modern form and allowed its power to be harnessed in a reliable, low-cost way.

---

[1]   Noyce founded Fairchild Semiconductor and later, Intel. His Intel co-founder was Gordon Moore, who is famous for formulating "Moore's Law," according to which computer power doubles every 18 months. Kilby was the founder of Texas Instruments.

The IC permitted the development of the personal computer, whose appearance marked the next phase of the digital revolution. Many of the events during this era have become the stuff of legend. For example, pioneering companies such as Atari and Osborne appeared and then disappeared. Steve Jobs and Steve Wozniak started Apple Computer in a garage in the late 1970s. The company's Apple II is widely regarded as the first "true" personal computer; the Apple II's popularity received a big boost in 1979 when a spreadsheet program known as VisiCalc was introduced. A computer **spreadsheet** is an electronic ledger that automatically calculates the effect of a change to one figure on other figures across rows and down columns; previously, these changes had to be done manually. While such powerful, time-saving functionality is taken for granted today, VisiCalc was a true milestone in the digital revolution. IBM brought its first PC to market in 1981; Bill Gates initially declined an offer to write an operating system for IBM's new machine. Gates later changed his mind and developed the Microsoft Disk Operating System (MS-DOS). In 1984, Apple introduced the revolutionary Macintosh, with its user-friendly graphical interface and point-and-click mouse. A few years, later, Microsoft replaced MS-DOS with Windows. Meanwhile, component manufacturers were innovating as well; Intel began marketing the 286 microprocessor in 1982. This was followed in quick succession by the 386 and 486 versions; in 1993, Intel unveiled the Pentium.

The rise of the Internet and the World Wide Web marks the next phase of the digital revolution. The Internet's origins can be traced back to an initiative by the Defense Advanced Research Projects Agency (DARPA) that created a computer network that could maintain lines of communication in the event of a war. In 1969, the ARPAnet was unveiled; this was a network linking computer research centers at colleges and universities. E-mail within a computer network was made possible by the creation of a file-transfer program in 1972. There was a problem, however; it was not possible to send e-mail that was created on one network to a computer on a different network. This problem was solved the following year when Vint Serf and Bob Kahn created a cross-network protocol; thus, in 1973, a "network of networks"—in other words, the Internet—was born.

The ability to exchange e-mail messages on the Internet had a revolutionary impact on society, as technology guru Stewart Brand noted in the mid-1980s:

> Marshall McLuhan used to remark, "Gutenburg made everybody a reader. Xerox made everybody a publisher." Personal computers are making everybody an author.

E-mail, word processing programs that make revising as easy as thinking, and laser printers collapse the whole writing-publishing-distributing process into one event controlled entirely by the individual. If, as alleged, the only real freedom of the press is to own one, the fullest realization of the First Amendment is being accomplished by technology, not politics.[2]

Of course, the Internet revolution did not end with the advent of e-mail. More innovations were yet to come. In 1990, a software consultant named Tim Berners-Lee invented the **uniform resource locator** (URL), an Internet site's address on the World Wide Web; **hypertext markup language** (HTML), a format language that controls the appearance of Web pages; and **hypertext transfer protocol** (http), which enables hypertext files to be transferred across the Internet.[3] These innovations allowed Web sites to be linked and visually rich content to be posted and accessed. In short, Berners-Lee is the father of the World Wide Web. In 1993, Marc Andreesen created the first commercial browser; called Mosaic, it put images and words together on the same screen. Andreesen went on to create Netscape. Within 5 years of the Web's debut, the number of users increased from 600,000 to 40 million. In the following decade, search engines such as Yahoo! and Google were created and encryption and security features were built into the Web. Search engines have also been dramatically improved; for example, an earlier technology known as "link analysis" has been superceded by Google's novel "page ranking." As the twenty-first century gets underway, Internet usage is exploding around the world; in 2003, an estimated 580 million PCs were able to access the Internet.

Not surprisingly, the Internet's powerful capabilities have resulted in a backlash from various sources. For example, the Chinese government, alarmed by the free flow of information across the Internet, closely monitors the content on Web sites that its citizens access. In addition, policymakers in some countries, including Brazil, South Africa, Syria, and Egypt, are concerned that the nonprofit Internet Corporation for Assigned Names and Numbers (Icann) is based in the United States and managed by the U.S. government. These countries are seeking to have the United Nations assume a role in Internet governance.[4] As companies become more adept at using the Internet to gather, store, and access information about customers, privacy issues are becoming a focal point of concern among policy makers and the general public. In the European Union, for example, a privacy protection directive was established in 1995; in 2002, the EU adopted a privacy and electronic communications directive.

## CONVERGENCE

The digital revolution is causing dramatic changes in industry structure. **Convergence** is a term that refers to the coming together of previously separate industries and product categories (see Figure 17-1). New technologies affect the business sector(s) in which a company competes. What business is Sony in? Originally, it was a consumer electronics company best known for innovative products such as transistor radios, Trinitron televisions, VCRs and other stereo components, and the Walkman line of personal music players. Then, Sony entered new businesses by acquiring a record company and a motion picture studio. These acquisitions themselves did not represent convergence, because they occurred in the early days of the digital revolution. Motion pictures, recorded music, and consumer electronics were still separate industries. Today, however, Sony is in the "bits" business: Its core businesses incorporate digital technology and involve digitizing and distributing sound, images, and data. Now, Sony's competitors include Dell (computers and consumer electronics), Kodak (digital cameras), and Nokia (cell phones).

---

[2] Stewart Brand, *The Media Lab: Inventing the Future at MIT* (New York: Penguin Books, 1988), p. 253.
[3] Hypertext is any text that contains links to other documents.
[4] "A Free Internet," *Financial Times* (November 14, 2003), p. 15.

*Figure 17-1*

*Industry Convergence*

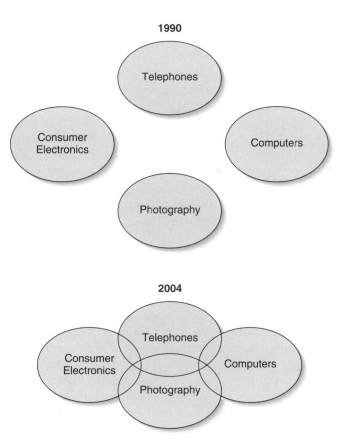

What kind of challenges does convergence present? Consider the plight of Kodak, the undisputed leader in photography-related products for more than a century. The company has been struggling to remake its business model as its sales of digital-related products grew from zero to $1 billion in 5 years (see Case 15-1). Because of convergence, Kodak's competitors include companies such as Gateway. In 2003, both companies introduced five-megapixel digital cameras at a break-through price of $399. In a recent column, Walter Mossberg, technology reporter for *The Wall Street Journal*, compared Gateway's DC-T50 to the Kodak EasyShare DX4530. Mossberg wrote, "Surprisingly, we preferred the Gateway, from a company new to cameras, over the Kodak. In every important respect—picture quality, design, and convenience—the Gateway surpassed the Kodak."[5] This type of product review suggests that Kodak executives and managers have much work to do if Kodak is going to successfully adapt to the changing competitive landscape.

## VALUE NETWORKS AND DISRUPTIVE TECHNOLOGIES[6]

As noted at the beginning of the chapter, the digital revolution provides both opportunities and threats. IBM, Kodak, Xerox, and Motorola are examples of global companies that have struggled to remake their businesses in the face of technological innovation. IBM missed out on the minicomputer market, in part because management believed minicomputers promised lower margins and represented a smaller

---

[5]    Walter Mossberg, "High-End Digital Cameras Fall Below $400," *The Wall Street Journal* (September 3, 2003), p. D1.

[6]    Much of the material in this section is adapted from Clayton Christensen, *The Innovator's Dilemma* (New York: HarperBusiness, 2003). See also Simon London, "Digital Discomfort: Companies Struggle to Deal With the 'Inevitable Surprise' of the Transition from Atoms to Bits," *Financial Times* (December 17, 2003), p. 17.

market than the established mainframe market. DEC, Data General, and Prime created the minicomputer market, but these companies, in turn, missed the PC revolution. This time, however, IBM's executive team demonstrated that it had learned its lesson: It set up an independent organizational unit to create the company's first PC. However, IBM subsequently was slow to recognize growing market demand for laptops; new entrants included Toshiba, Sharp, and Zenith. In an era when environmental scanning, strategic planning, and other conceptual tools of the type discussed in Chapter 15 are widely known and used, how is it that managers at many companies have failed to respond to change in a timely manner? According to Harvard professor Clayton Christensen, the problem is that executives become so committed to a current, profitable technology that they fail to provide adequate levels of investment in new, apparently riskier technologies. Ironically, companies fall into this trap by adhering to prevailing marketing orthodoxy, namely, listening to and responding to the needs of established customers. Christensen calls this situation the **innovator's dilemma**.

In every industry, companies are embedded in a **value network**. Each value network has a cost structure associated with it that dictates the margins needed to achieve profitability. The boundaries of the network are defined, in part, by the unique rank ordering of the importance of various product performance attributes. Parallel value networks, each built around a different definition of what makes a product valuable, may exist within the same broadly-defined industry. Each network has its own "metrics of value." For example, for laptop computers, the metrics are small size, low weight and power consumption, and rugged design. During the 1980s, customers who bought portable computers were willing to pay a premium for smaller size; buyers of mainframe computers did not value this attribute. Conversely, mainframe buyers valued (i.e., were willing to pay more for) memory capacity as measured by megabytes; portable computer buyers placed less value on this attribute. In short, the value networks for mainframe computers and portable computers are different.

As firms gain experience within a given network, they are likely to develop capabilities, organizational structures, and cultures tailored to the distinctive requirements of their respective value networks. The industry's dominant firms— typically with reputations as "well managed" firms—lead in developing and/or adopting **sustaining technologies**, that is, incremental or radical innovations that improve product performance. According the Christensen, most new technologies developed by established companies are sustaining in nature; indeed, the vast majority of innovations are of this type.

However, new entrants to an industry lead in developing **disruptive technologies** that redefine performance. The benefits associated with disruptive technologies go beyond enhancing product performance; disruptive technologies enable something to be done that was previously deemed impossible. Disruptive technologies typically enable new markets to emerge. As Christensen explains, "An innovation that is disrupting to one firm can be sustaining to another firm. The Internet was sustaining technology to Dell Computer, which already sold PCs direct by telephone. But it was disruptive technology to Compaq, whose major distribution channel was retailers."[7]

To help managers recognize the innovator's dilemma and develop appropriate responses to environmental change, Christensen has developed five principles of disruptive innovations:

1. Companies depend on customers and investors for resources. As management guru Rosabeth Moss Kanter points out, the best innovations are user-driven; paradoxically, however, if management listens to established customers, opportunities for disruptive innovation may be missed.[8]

---

[7] Simon London, "Why Disruption Can Be Good For Business," *Financial Times* (October 3, 2003), p. 8.
[8] Rosabeth Moss Kanter, John Kao, and Fred Wiersema, *Innovation: Breakthrough Thinking at 3M, Dupont, GE, Pfizer, and Rubbermaid* (New York: HarperBusiness, 1997), p. 24.

2. Small markets don't solve the growth needs of large companies. Small organizations can most easily respond to the opportunities for growth in a small market. This fact may require large organizations to create independent units to pursue new technologies, as IBM did in developing its PC.
3. Markets that don't exist can't be analyzed. Christensen recommends that companies embrace **agnostic marketing.** This is the explicit assumption that *no one*—not company personnel, not the company's customers—can know whether, how, or in what quantities a disruptive product can or will be used before they have experienced using it.
4. An organization's capabilities define its disabilities.
5. Technology supply may not equal market demand. Some products offer a greater degree of sophistication than the market requires. For example, developers of accounting software for small businesses overshot the functionality required by the market, thus creating an opportunity for a disruptive software technology that provided adequate, not superior, functionality and was simple and more convenient to use. This was the opportunity seized by Scott Cook, developer of Quicken and Quickbooks.

# GLOBAL E-COMMERCE

The term **e-commerce** refers to the general exchange of goods and services using the Internet as a communication channel. In 2003, global e-commerce revenues stood at $1.6 trillion and growing. Consider the following:

- According to a report released by the University of California-Berkeley, in 2002, five exabytes of information—an amount equal to every word spoken by humans—were generated worldwide[9]
- China has more than 68 million Internet users; in Shanghai, Beijing, and Guangzhou, one-third of all residents use the Internet[10]
- Japan has about 60 million Internet users, and Japan accounted for $1.6 billion in online revenue in 2004

E-commerce activities can be divided into three broad categories: business-to-consumer (B2C or b-to-c), business-to-business (B2B or b-to-b), and consumer-to-consumer (or peer-to-peer or P2P). Many people associate e-commerce with well-known commerce service providers (CSPs) such as Amazon.com and Yahoo!. NUA Surveys projected worldwide e-commerce revenues of $2.7 trillion in 2004, with the United States accounting for more than half of the total. eMarketer, Forrester Research, Gartner Group, and Ovum are firms that track e-commerce trends; Ovum estimates that online consumer spending will rise to $361 billion by 2007. However, in the United States alone, B2B transactions in 2003 totaled $700 billion. In short, B2B commerce constitutes the biggest share of the Internet economy and will likely continue to do so for the foreseeable future. About three-fourths of 2001 revenue was generated in North America; that figure is expected to drop to 50 percent as online sales in Europe and elsewhere increase over the next few years (see Table 17-1).

Web sites can be classified by purpose: *promotion sites* promote goods or services, *content sites* provide news and entertainment and support a company's public relations efforts, and *transaction sites* are cyberspace retail operations that allow customers to purchase goods and services. Web sites can be categorized in terms of content and audience focus (see Figure 17-2). When studying the categories, keep in mind that, overall, the Internet can be used as an advertising channel, as a public

---

[9] Kevin Maney, "Computing Power Tries to Keep Up With Information Flood," *USA Today* (November 19, 2003), p. B3.
[10] Charles Hutzler, "Internet Use in China Gains Breadth," *The Wall Street Journal* (November 18, 2003), p. B4.

**Table 17-1**

*Projections from 2001 for Worldwide B2C Revenues, by Region, 2000–2004 (billions)*

| Region | 2000 | 2001 | 2002 | 2003 | 2004 |
|--------|------|------|------|------|------|
| North America | $47.5 | $ 74.4 | $110.6 | $135.2 | $197.9 |
| Europe | $ 8.1 | $ 16.5 | $ 37.1 | $ 81.8 | $183.5 |
| Asia | $ 3.2 | $ 8.3 | $ 15.6 | $ 26.4 | $ 38.0 |
| Latin America | $ 0.7 | $ 1.8 | $ 3.3 | $ 5.5 | $ 8.1 |
| Africa/Middle East | $ 0.2 | $ 0.3 | $ 0.6 | $ 1.1 | $ 1.6 |
| World | $59.7 | $101.3 | $167.2 | $250.0 | $429.1 |

*Source: eGlobal Report, e-Marketer, 2001.*

relations tool, as a means for running a contest or sales promotion, and as support for the personal selling effort. In Quadrant 1, the focus is on providing information and service to domestic or local-country customers. Quadrant 2 companies such as iTunes Music Store maintain transaction-oriented e-commerce sites with a domestic focus (see Case 17-1). Companies in both Quadrants 1 and 2 do attract international traffic, but the focus is still local. For example, international students at your college may have learned about your school via the Internet, even though home-country prospective students constitute the primary target audience for the Web site. Companies that initially fall into quadrants 1 and 2 can transition into quadrants 3 and 4; for example, in 2004, Apple's iTunes Music Store was rolled out in Germany, France, and the United Kingdom.

Problems can arise when a transaction site that is not designed to serve foreign customers nevertheless attracts them. Customer service can be a problem when customers are located in different time zones. For example, BlueTie is a small company based in Rochester, New York, that markets e-mail and office-software applications by subscription. The company's servers continually update customer calendars and e-mail. When non-U.S. orders began to come in, BlueTie managers found it challenging to deliver correct times and dates. Fixing the problem required spending tens of thousands of dollars and tied up precious employee time. Payment can be another problem; in some countries, credit card use is low. Customers who do not have credit cards must arrange payment by bank check. Another issue is credit card fraud; Indonesia, Russia, Croatia, and Bosnia are among the countries where fraud is rampant. Extra identity measures may have to be taken, such as requiring buyers to fax the actual credit card they are using as well as photo IDs.[11]

**Figure 17-2**

*Categories of Web Sites*

*Source: Adapted from "The Internet and International Marketing," by John A. Quelch and Lisa R. Klein, MIT Sloan Management Review 37, no. 3 (Spring 1996), p. 65.*

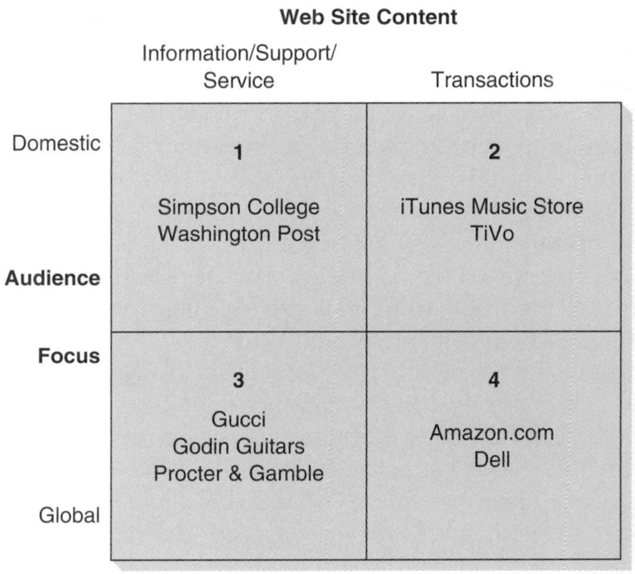

**Web Site Content**

| | Information/Support/Service | Transactions |
|--|--|--|
| Domestic | **1**<br>Simpson College<br>Washington Post | **2**<br>iTunes Music Store<br>TiVo |
| Global | **3**<br>Gucci<br>Godin Guitars<br>Procter & Gamble | **4**<br>Amazon.com<br>Dell |

Audience Focus

---

[11] Peter Loftus, "Internet Turns Firms into Overseas Businesses," *The Wall Street Journal* (December 16, 2003), p. B4. See also Matt Richtel, "Credit Card Theft Is Thriving Online as Global Market," *The New York Times* (May 13, 2002), p. A1.

When IBM CEO Sam Palmisano introduced his company's new On Demand advertising campaign in fall 2002, it signaled a shift in the company's e-commerce strategy. The change was intended to convey the fact that IBM was moving away from "what we are selling" (i.e., e-business solutions), to "what our customers want to become" (i.e., on-demand organizations). Headlines in the print campaign identify some key clients and industries that IBM serves. Highlights include "Napster Is On," "Acura Is On," and "China in On."

Procter & Gamble Far East Inc., the consumer products company's operation in Japan, is using the Web to build its portfolio of brands in the region. The company has launched **shufufufu.com**, Japan's first virtual community for women. The Web address combines *shufu* ("housewife") and *fu-fu-fu* (the sound of a woman's laughter); the P&G logo has been de-emphasized. The site was created by the digital division of Beacon Communications K.K. As Fergus Kibble, digital director at Beacon, noted, "Our research showed that Japanese housewives often feel very isolated."[12] The site's success can be attributed in part to the popularity of Harumi Kurihara, the "Japanese Martha Stewart" who writes a weekly essay on the site and provides tips on cooking, homemaking, and personal care.

In Quadrant 3, the audience focus is global. Companies such as FedEx and Gucci are already global in scope, and the Internet constitutes a powerful, cost-effective communication tool. Unilever PLC has begun digitizing its vast library of television commercials. Computer users can download the full-frame, full-motion videos for products such as Salon Selectives shampoo and watch them at any time. Although some industry observers are skeptical, Unilever's interactive marketing staff believes that the Web may represent an important new, low-cost channel for showing ads.[13] McDonald's is also putting digitized versions of its ads on the Web,

12. Tom Boatman, "Interactive Marketing Strategies in Japan," *Japan Inc.* (June 2001).
13. Vanessa O'Connell, "Unilever to Run Some TV Spots, Digitized, Online," *The Wall Street Journal* (March 2, 2001), pp. B1, B5.

but for a different purpose. The fast-food giant has established an online digital commercial archive, **www.mcdcommercials.com,** that allows McDonald's ad agencies anywhere in the world to review a library of 15,000 TV commercials. The agency can then request pre-existing footage to incorporate into new ads.[14]

Procter & Gamble also has ambitious plans for exploiting the Internet as a global promotional and informational tool. P&G has registered a number of Internet domains based on brand names, including **www.covergirl.com, www.oldspice.com,** and **www.sunnyd.com.** P&G has also registered nearly 100 other generic domains that relate to its various product lines, including cakemix.com, laundry.com, and nails.com. Although it is possible that these domains will not ultimately be developed into Web sites, P&G's actions sent a signal to others in the industry that it is striving for a first mover advantage on the Net. George Rosenbaum, CEO of the Chicago-based Leo Shapiro & Associates market research firm, commented, "P&G's commitment means that all major competitors will also have to play seriously. This is going to raise the tempo of advertising on the Internet."[15]

In Quadrant 4, companies seek e-commerce transactions with customers on a worldwide basis. Amazon.com is perhaps the most successful example of the global audience-transaction business model. Online book shoppers can chose from more than 2.5 million titles; many titles carry discounted prices. After assessing a number of potential products in terms of their suitability for online sales, company founder Jeffrey Bezos settled on books for two reasons. First, there are too many titles for any one "brick-and-mortar" store to carry. The second reason is related to industry structure: The publishing industry is highly fragmented, with 4,200 publishers in the United States alone. That means that no single publisher has a high degree of supplier power. Bezos' instincts proved sound: Sales exploded after Amazon.com's Web site became operational in mid-1995. Within a year, orders were coming in from 66 countries.

Obviously, some products are inherently not suitable candidates for sale via the Internet: McDonald's doesn't sell hamburgers from its Web site, and Procter & Gamble does not sell shampoo. In some instances, global marketers make the strategic decision to establish a presence on the Web without offering transaction opportunities even though the product could be sold that way. Rather, such companies limit their Web activities to promotion and information in support of offline retail distribution channels. There are several reasons for this. First, many companies lack the infrastructure necessary to process orders from individual customers. Second, it can cost anywhere from $20 million to $30 million to establish a fully functioning e-commerce site. There may be other, product-specific reasons. The Web site for Godin Guitars, for example, provides a great deal of product information and a directory of the company's worldwide dealer network. Company founder Robert Godin believes that the best way for a person to select a guitar is to play one, and that requires a visit to a music store. Likewise, visitors to Web sites for some luxury goods purveyors, including Burberry, Prada, and Gucci, are not given the opportunity to buy. Top design houses strive to create an overall retail shopping experience that enhances the brand; this objective is basically at odds with e-commerce. As a spokesperson for Prada noted recently, "Miuccia Prada is trying to combine fashion with architecture and design. It's a 360-degree experience."[16] One notable exception is LVMH, whose **www.eluxury.com** Web site offers a limited selection of ready-to-wear items by Marc Jacobs and other designers. However, the site has yet to show a profit.

[14] Kata MacArthur, "Fast Food Meets the Internet," *Advertising Age* (June 19, 2000), p. 28.
[15] Raju Narisetti, "P&G Steps Up Ad Cyber-Surfing: Tide Could Have a Major Effect," *The Wall Street Journal* (April 18, 1997), p. B10.
[16] Sally Beatty, "Fashion Tip: Get Online," *The Wall Street Journal* (October 31, 2003), pp. B1, B3.

As the Internet has developed into a crucial global communication tool, decision makers in virtually all organizations are realizing that they must include this new medium in their communications planning. Many companies purchase banner ads on popular Web browsers such as AOL or Yahoo!; typically, the ads are linked to the company's home page or product- or brand-related sites. Although creative possibilities are limited with banner ads, and **click-through rates**—the percentage of users who click on an advertisement that has been presented—are typically low, the number of companies that use the Web as a medium for global advertising is expected to increase dramatically over the next few years.

The increased importance of the Internet in global marketing can also be seen in the number and variety of alliances that advertisers are establishing with Web sites. For example, Unilever PLC sponsors the Microsoft Network (MSN) and MSN WomenCentral in the United States, France, Germany, and the United Kingdom. This type of sponsorship generally means banner ads and links to other brand-related sites are featured prominently.[17] The trend toward consolidation among media companies enables advertisers to efficiently achieve greater reach across media platforms. For example, Toyota Motors advertised its 2002 Camry on AOL Time Warner's various media properties. One of Toyota's objectives was to reposition Camry from a brand associated with older women to a brand that appeals to younger men. In fall 2001, Toyota sponsored a special issue of *Time* titled "Music Goes Global." Part of AOL's "Music Goes Global" Web site was dedicated to the Camry. Also, Toyota sponsored some music programming on CNN and TNT, which are also part of the AOL Time Warner family.[18] An important trend is **paid search advertising,** whereby companies pay to have their ads appear when users type certain search terms. Yahoo! recently paid $1.6 billion to acquire Overture, a company specializing in paid search advertising. As a Yahoo! spokesperson noted, "Paid search is just starting to take off globally. So this acquisition wasn't just part of our strategy for search, it was important for our international strategy as well."[19]

*Technology Forecast*

*Online music spending is forecast to increase from $800 million (7 percent of total music sales) in 2003 to $3.3 billion (26 percent of music sales) in 2008.*

Jupiter Research[20]

# WEB SITE DESIGN[21]

To fully exploit the Internet's potential, company executives must be willing to integrate interactive media into their marketing mixes. Web sites can be developed in-house, or an outside firm can be contracted to do the job. During the past few years, a new breed of interactive advertising agency has emerged to help companies globalize their Internet offerings (see Table 17-2). Whichever approach a company adopts, several issues must be addressed when setting up for global e-commerce. A critical first step is registering a country-specific domain name. Thus, Amazon.com has a family of different domain names, including one for each country in which it operates (see Table 17-3 on page 573). Although it is certainly possible for a person living in France to browse Amazon.com's U.S. site, he or she would likely prefer a direct link to a French-language site. From both a marketing and consumer perspective, this makes sense: The Web site of choice will be one that quotes prices in euros rather than dollars, offers a product selection tailored to French tastes, and ships from local distribution points. Moreover, research suggests that visitors spend more time at

---

[17] Sarah Ellison, "Unilever, Microsoft in European Net Deal," *The Wall Street Journal* (February 2, 2000), p. B8.

[18] Julia Angwin, "AOL Lands Toyota for Multimedia Pact," *The Wall Street Journal* (August 28, 2001), p. B7.

[19] Bob Tedeschi, "E-Commerce Report," *The New York Times* (January 12, 2004), p. C6.

[20] Nick Wingfield and Ethan Smith, "Microsoft Plans to Sell Music Over the Web," *The Wall Street Journal* (November 17, 2003), p. B5.

[21] Much of the discussion in this section is adapted from Alexis D. Gutzman, *The E-Commerce Arsenal* (New York: Amacom, 2001).

### Ebay's Japanese Failure

Ebay, the company whose name is synonymous with online auctions in the United States, is one of the legendary success stories of the digital revolution. Today, the company is a cultural phenomenon, boasting 95 million registered users who can bid on 45,000 different categories of goods. In 2003, eBay took in $2.1 billion in revenues; net income was a healthy $442 million. Between 2002 and 2003, revenue and net income both increased nearly 80 percent. To sustain this type of growth, eBay's executive team has set its sights on international expansion. Today, the company has successfully established a presence in several countries, including Australia, Brazil, Spain, and Switzerland.

However, one of eBay's first forays outside the United States ended in defeat. Yahoo opened its Internet portal in Japan in April 1996, 4 years ahead of eBay's entry. Yahoo Japan was a joint venture between Yahoo! Inc. and Japan's Softbank Corp. Yahoo Japan was modeled on its U.S. parent; a variety of free services was available, including news, chat rooms, and e-mail. As more users logged on, increasing numbers of advertisers paid to post banner ads on the site. In due course, Yahoo founder Jerry Yang and Softbank chairman Masayoshi Son encouraged Yahoo Japan chief Masahiro Inoue to start offering online auctions. Yang had been blindsided by eBay's U.S. success and did not want to repeat the mistake a second time. Inoue resisted, noting that the Japanese have little experience with auctions of any kind. He was also skeptical that status-conscious Japanese consumers would buy products from complete strangers. However, Yang continued to press his case, stressing that eBay was gearing up for a Japanese launch. Moreover, with advertising providing 80 percent of Yahoo's revenues in the United States, Yang was anxious to diversify the venture's revenue stream.

In the end, Inoue relented; his team of engineers had Yahoo Japan's auction site operational in September 1999. Ebay launched its Japanese service in February 2000. Taking its cue from eBay's early development in the United States, management stressed used collectibles. This turned out to be a mistake; Japanese users showed more interest in bidding on new goods. Ebay also erred by charging a commission on each transaction; initially, Yahoo Japan users did not pay commissions or monthly fees. By the end of 2001, between 20,000 and 25,000 items were listed on eBay's Japanese site; by contrast, Yahoo Japan had more than 3 million items. As eBay CEO Meg Whitman noted, "We're definitely in catch-up mode." In March 2001, after barely more than a year, eBay closed down the service.

Despite the setback in Japan, eBay continues to expand in Asia. In 2003, the company paid $180 million to acquire Eachnet, a popular Chinese consumer auction site. Once again, eBay faces competition from Yahoo, which has invested in a Chinese language search development company and formed a joint venture auction site with Sina.com. Other competitors include Taobao.com, a local auction site launched by Chinese Internet entrepreneur Jack Ma. Ma believes that global Internet companies are prone to making three types of mistakes in approaching China: They underestimate the differences between China and the U.S. market; they incur higher costs than local companies; and they go global too quickly. Ma summarizes the situation by observing, "[Ebay and Yahoo] are the sharks in the ocean, and we are the crocodiles in the Yangtze River. When they fight in the Yangtze River, they will be in trouble. The smell of the water is different."

*Sources: Mure Dickie, "China's Crocodiles Ready for a Fight," Financial Times (July 14, 2004), p. 18; Nick Wingfield, "Ebay, Conceding Missteps, Will Close Its Site in Japan," The Wall Street Journal (February 27, 2002), p. B4; Ken Belson, Rob Hof, and Ben Elgin, "How Yahoo! Japan Beat eBay at Its Own Game," Business Week (June 4, 2001), p. 58; Robert A. Guth, "Yahoo Japan Learns from Parent's Achievements and Errors," The Wall Street Journal (December 11, 2000), p. A28.*

sites that are in their own language; they also tend to view more pages and make more purchases. Many people will seek information about sites on local versions of well-known search engines. For example, in France, Yahoo's local site is **fr.Yahoo.com**. In addition, local country search engines and directories will recognize sites that are intended for a particular country audience. In France,

*Table 17-2*

*Top 5 Interactive Agencies by U.S. Interactive Marketing Revenue*

| Agency (HQ Location) | Clients | 2003 Revenues ($ millions) |
|---|---|---|
| Digitas (Boston) | Saab, FedEx, Morgan Stanley, AT&T Wireless | $84 |
| SBI.Razorfish (New York) | Adidas, Dell, BP, Ford Motor | $72 |
| Modem Media (New York) | Delta Air Lines, Michelin, General Motors, Sony, Unilever | $49 |
| aQuantive (Avenue A; Seattle) | Apple, AstraZeneca, Nike, Victoria's Secret | $44 |
| AKQA (Seattle) | Accenture, BMW Group, Microsoft, Sainsbury's, Xbox | $36 |

*Source:* Adapted from "Top 50 Marketing Services Agencies by Discipline," *Advertising Age* (May 17, 2004), p. S-6.

| Domain Name | Country | **Table 17-3** |
|---|---|---|
| amazon.co.uk | United Kingdom | *Amazon.com Domain Names* |
| amazon.de | Germany | |
| amazon.fr | France | |
| amazon.co.jp | Japan | |
| amazon.at | Austria | |

voila.fr is such a site. A complete listing of search engines by country can be found at **www.searchenginecolossus.com**.

A note of caution is in order: It is not enough to simply translate a Web site from the home country language into other languages. Thus, another basic step is localizing a Web site in the native language and business nomenclature of the target country. From a technical point of view, Web sites designed to support English, French, German, and other languages that use the Latin alphabet only store a maximum of 256 characters in ASCII (American Standard Code for Information Interchange) format. Even so, there are language-specific needs; for example, a German language Web site requires more than double the capacity of an English language site because German copy takes more space.[22] However, languages such as Japanese and Chinese require a database that supports double-ASCII. For this reason, it is wise to start with a double-ASCII platform when designing a Web site's architecture. The site's architecture should also be flexible enough to allow different date, currency, and money

# the rest of the story

## Barry Diller and IAC/InterActive

The travel industry experienced a steep downturn in the aftermath of the terror attacks of September 11, 2001. In an effort to put "heads in beds," InterContinental, Marriott, and other major hotel chains sold excess room inventory at a discount to Hotels.com and other online services. When a traveler books a room through, say, Hotels.com, the price he or she pays is 20 to 30 percent more than Hotels.com's cost; thus, each transaction nets a tidy gross margin for Hotels.com. According to estimates compiled by Smith Travel Research, in the United States alone, online services redirected $1 billion in revenues away from the hotel operators. Six percent of all U.S. hotel reservations were made online in 2003; travel consultant PhoCus Wright expects that, by 2005, that figure will increase to 20 percent.

Not surprisingly, hotel operators are taking notice and developing their own online services. InterContinental has been especially aggressive, launching brand-neutral sites such as Accomodations.info and DealsonHotels.com that direct users to various hotel properties run by InterContinental. The company has also launched Web sites in French, German, Spanish, and Chinese. As Eric Pearson, vice president of e-commerce at InterContinental, noted, "There's a huge demand from consumers traveling abroad. That shows proof positive that if you're a global company, you need to provide services around the world."

For the moment, hotel bookings remain an extremely lucrative source of revenue and profit for IAC/InterActiveCorp. By contrast, financial results from the Match.com and uDate personals services have been less stable. For example, in the fourth quarter of 2003, profits from personals were only $1.5 billion, a decline of 84 percent. Match.com logs 60,000 new subscribers each day; however, that figure is offset by a significant number of cancellations. As Diller explained, "We went from a few thousand subscribers to 880,000. We changed the model, thinking we could change the pricing and get people to stay subscribed for longer, which turned out to be just dumb." Still, Diller sees great potential for cross selling between the personals and his company's other services.

Diller is also keenly aware of global market opportunities. Currently, about 17 percent of IAC/InterActiveCorp's revenues are generated outside the United States; Diller wants to double that figure. Some industry observers predict Diller's next move will be to acquire a British travel site such as Lastminute.com or eBookers.com. As Diller explains, "The aim is to be the largest e-commerce player with a multi-brand strategy. In some cases, we're going to set up new ventures; in some cases it's more efficient to acquire, where a brand is already established."

*Sources: Tim Burt and Peter Thal Larsen, "The Negotiator-in-Chief," Financial Times (April 27, 2004), p. 11; Betty Liu and Amy Lee, "Hoteliers Try to Evict an Unwelcome Visitor," Financial Times (April 19, 2004), p. 6; Timothy J. Mullaney and Ronald Grover, "The Web Mogul," Business Week (October 13, 2003), pp. 62–66 +; Burt and Larsen, "Inside Barry Diller's Hive of Interactivity," Financial Times (September 19, 2003), p. 10.*

---

[22] Patricia Riedman, "Think Globally, Act Globally," *Advertising Age* (June 19, 2000), p. S-48.

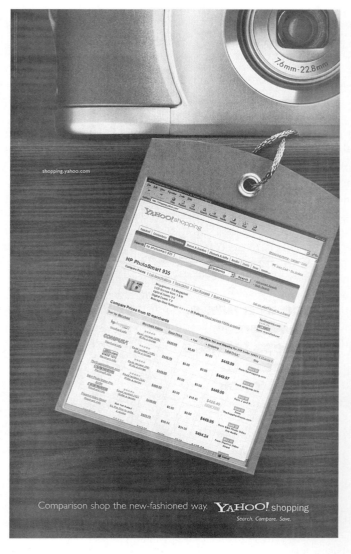

*Yahoo! is the Internet's most visited site. The company boasts more than 140 million registered users; one of Yahoo's strengths is the number of services it offers besides search. For example, Yahoo! users can access GeoCities, My.Yahoo, Games On Demand; send instant messages; and, as shown here, compare prices with Yahoo! Shopping. The company currently has 25 global sites in 13 different languages; Yahoo! Shopping's country-specific sites include Denmark, Germany, and India.*

Comparison shop the new-fashioned way. YAHOO! shopping
Search. Compare. Save.

*"Shopping on the Internet is no different than traditional sales channels. It's all about trusting the brand and having a strong relationship with one's customers."[23]*

Ron Fry, Internet Business Manager, Lands' End

formatting. For example, to someone living in the United Kingdom, "7/10/05" means October 7, 2005. To an American, it means July 10, 2005.

Ideally, each country-specific site should reflect local culture, customs, and aesthetic preferences. Logos and other elements of brand identity should be included on the site, with adjustments for color preferences and meaning differences when necessary. For example, the shopping cart icon is familiar to online shoppers in the United States and many European countries. However, online companies must determine whether that icon is appropriate in all country markets. Local translators should be used to ensure that copy reflects current language usage. It is also important not to "reinvent the wheel" by translating the same terms over and over again. Local translators should have access to an in-house dictionary that contains preferred translations of company-specific terms. The system should be capable of identifying content that has already been translated and then reusing that content. Product descriptions may also vary from country to country; as noted in Chapter 4, American-themed merchandise is very popular in Japan. Table 17-4 compares a sample product descriptions in English and Japanese.[24]

Another critical global e-commerce issue is privacy. The European Union's regulations are among the world's strictest; companies are limited in terms of how much personal information—a customer's age, marital status, and buying patterns, for example—can be gathered and how long the information can be retained. Customers

---

[23] Christopher Price, "Fashion Suits the Internet Shopper," *Financial Times* (June 24, 1998), p. 23.
[24] Alexis D. Gutzman, *The E-Commerce Arsenal* (New York: Amacom, 2001), p. 165.

| United States | Japan | Table 17-4 |
|---|---|---|
| "New York Yankees hat with white stitching on black canvas." | "Authentic baseball hat for the New York Yankees baseball team. Just like they wear in New York City! White stitching on black canvas reflects the team's colors." | Product Descriptions: An English Versus Japanese Comparison |
| "These warm-weather cargos are made from our popular tropic-weight cotton. The 6 oz. cloth is dyed with rich pigment color that weathers gradually. Garment-washed to feel comfortably broken-in right away. Our Natural Fit offers extra room at the seat and thighs. Quarter front pockets, two flapped back pockets and roomy cargo pockets on legs. Double-needle stitching at stress seams. Fit belts up to 13/4". Imported. Machine wash and dry." | "Cargo Pants have high breathability for hot weather. This garment is made from tropic-weight cotton and dyed with rich pigment color and weathers gradually. Enjoy the way this cargo's fabric feels comfortably broken in. This fits you naturally for your movement. Front pockets for both sides, two flapped back pockets and roomy cargo pockets on legs. Double-needle stitching at stress seams. Fit belts up to 4cm. Cotton 100%. Washable by machine." | |

have the right to view the information contained in company databases and correct errors. Moreover, the EU's standards have been adopted in other parts of the world, including Canada, Australia, and Asia. Spain's regulations are particularly stringent; taking advantage of a common language, Chile and Argentina have copied the drafts of Spain's laws. By contrast, Washington's reluctance to protect privacy is due in part to First Amendment issues as well as to national security concerns stemming from the terror attacks of 2001. To help ensure compliance with privacy laws, American companies have created a new executive-level job position: chief privacy officer.[25]

What makes a "good" Web site? Each year, *Financial Times* publishes Web-ranking surveys. The ranking is primarily a measure of Web sites' usefulness to investors and members of the financial community in terms of providing information; however, as pointed out in the *Times*, sites that do a good job with investor relations are likely to be good at everything. The metrics of evaluation include the following:[26]

- *Technology and functionality.* This category includes layout, ease of navigation, and print-out opportunities. Does the site offer interactive functions such as order forms and e-mail subscriptions?
- *Content.* This category includes e-mail address information for key people or corporate functions; corporate information such as mission, vision, and company history; and financial information such as quarterly reports in PDF or HTML format. Does the company monitor and respond to incoming e-mails?

The study of European Web sites was produced by a Swedish firm, Halvorsson and Halvorsson. Stora Enso, a paper company based in Finland, had the top-ranked European site Table 17-5. One reason for its ranking is the attention to detail evident at the site: Visitors can use various interactive online tools such as pop-up windows with interactive calculators for converting currencies and metric/imperial measures for determining cost savings associated with changing the weight of a paper product.[27] BlueRiverStone, an Internet research firm located in South Africa, produced a study of U.S. corporate Web sites. UPS.com, United Parcel Service's top-ranked U.S. site, received high marks for both functionality and content. The site provides share quotes from the New York Stock Exchange; summaries of current activity in the Dow Jones Industrial Average, the S&P 500, and NASDAQ; a stock chart; an archive of historical stock prices; financial data downloadable as Excel files; and an annual report with a drop-down table of contents.

[25] David Scheer, "For Your Eyes Only: Europe's New High-Tech Role: Playing Privacy Cop to the World," *The Wall Street Journal* (October 10, 2003), p. A1.
[26] Niklas Franck and Andreas Leifsson, "Better Sites Are Boost for Investors," *Financial Times–IT Review* (November 26, 2003), p. 3.
[27] David Bowen, "Winners Exploit What the Web Is Good At," *Financial Times–IT Review* (November 26, 2003), p. 3.

| Europe | | United States |
| --- | --- | --- |
| Company | Country | Company |
| 1. Stora Enso | Finland | 1. UPS |
| 2. SCA | Sweden | 2. Anthem |
| 3. British American Tobacco | United Kingdom | 3. 3M |
| 4. UBS | Switzerland | 4. Intel |
| 5. ThyssenKrupp | Germany | 5. Chevron Texaco |
| 6. Nordea | Sweden | 6. ExxonMobil |
| 7. Siemens | Germany | 7. Duke Energy |
| 8. Bayer | Germany | 8. EDS |
| 9. Henkel | Germany | 9. Cendant |
| 10. Novartis | Switzerland | 10. Home Depot |
| 11. Volvo | Sweden | 11. McDonald's |
| 12. Credit Suisse | Switzerland | 12. Tenet Healthcare |
| 13. SABMiller | United Kingdom | 13. Sprint |
| 14. DaimlerChrysler | Germany | 14. Federated Department Stores |
| 15. TPG | Netherlands | 15. Gap |
| 16. Novo Nordisk | Denmark | 16. Citigroup |
| 17. BT | United Kingdom | 17. Delta Air Lines |
| 18. BP | United Kingdom | 18. Georgia-Pacific |
| 19. Cadbury Schweppes | United Kingdom | 19. IBM |
| 20. Deutsche Telekom | Germany | 20. Allstate |
| 21. Nokia | Finland | 21. Motorola |
| 22. BASF | Germany | 22. Qwest Communications |
| 23. Ericsson | Sweden | 23. Wachovia |
| 24. Prudential | United Kingdom | 24. American Electric |
| 25. Shell | Netherlands/UK | 25. Lucent Technologies |

Source: Financial Times.

## NEW PRODUCTS AND SERVICES

As a result of the digital revolution, a new generation of products, services, and technologies is being developed by a variety of companies in all parts of the world. These include broadband networks, mobile commerce, wireless connectivity, and "smart" cell phones.

### Broadband

A **broadband** communication system is one that has sufficient capacity to carry multiple voice, data, or video channels simultaneously. *Bandwidth* determines the range of frequencies that can pass over a given transmission channel. For example,

*global* MARKETING Q&A

**Wall Street Journal:** "What's next after cell phones that take photos, play games, and pay at soda machines? Will cell phones with personal-organizer functions become a mass-market product?"

**Jorma Ollila, Chief Executive Officer, Nokia:** "The important thing will be the camera industry converging into mobile phones. Expressing emotions with pictures, where everyone has a suitable device, just makes so much sense. In terms of PDAs, there will be an enterprise [business] segment that will want the PDA functionality integrated with good phone capability."

Source: David Pringle and Raju Narisetti, "Guiding Nokia in Technology's Rough Seas," The Wall Street Journal (November 2, 2003), p. B2.

# challenges of the global marketplace

## Open Source Software

Global software sales have been very, very good to Microsoft. The company's Windows operating system is found in more than 90 percent of the world's personal computers, and popular software programs such as Office Suite are used virtually everywhere. Because of its dominant position in the industry, Microsoft has a global pricing policy that calls for charging approximately the same amount in every world market. Today, however, Microsoft's pricing structure faces a threat from open source software that is distributed for free.

The term *open source software* is used to describe a software program for which the source code—the original program instructions—is made available so that users can make modifications. In the mid-1970s, a programmer named Richard Stallman wrote a macro editor for Unix that he called Emacs. Other programmers wanted to use Emacs, so Stallman published the GNU ("GNU's not Unix") Public License (GPL) in association with the concept of "copyleft" (a play on the notion of copyright). In essence, Stallman granted permission for others to run, copy, modify, and distribute his operating system software, with one caveat: No one could place restrictions on their modifications. In 1991, a 21-year-old Helsinki University student named Linus Torvalds developed a Unix-compatible operating system that he called Linux (a combination of Linus and Minix, a Unix clone widely used by college students). Today, numerous free versions of Linux are available, including Mandrakelinux. Worldwide, fully 25 percent of servers run Linux software; increasingly, Linux is being used in PCs as well.

What does the Linux phenomenon mean for Microsoft? In short, it means that the software giant's virtual monopoly on PC operating systems may be at risk. In developing countries such as Malaysia and Thailand, government initiatives are aimed at putting as many PCs as possible into the hands of ordinary citizens and small business owners. Not surprisingly, government agencies are looking for the best price, making free Linux software a very attractive choice. For example, working with the Association of Thai Computer Manufacturers, the Thai government made Linux-equipped "People's PCs" available for about 10,900 baht ($260). Microsoft responded by creating a Thai-language version of Windows XP and bundling it with Microsoft Office for a price of about $36. By mid-2003, roughly one quarter of the 134,000 PCs ordered by Thais were equipped with Windows. Similarly, in Malaysia, PCs running Linux are available at prices as low as about $263. Microsoft has responded by making a Malaysian version of Windows XP available on a PC for about $302.

Developing countries are not the only ones hoping to find cheaper alternatives to Microsoft. France, for example, needs to reduce its deficit to be in compliance with euro-zone regulations. To do so, the French government is considering open source options such as OpenOffice, a version of Sun Microsystem's StarOffice; Mozilla, a Web browser; and other open source programs. In Asia, representatives from Japan and South Korea are holding meetings in an effort to set joint policies regarding information technology.

*Sources: Rebecca Buckman, "Microsoft's Malaysia Policy," The Wall Street Journal (May 20, 2004), p. B1; Buckman, "Face-Off Over People's PC," The Wall Street Journal (August 14, 2003), p. B1;* **www.gnu.org** *(accessed June 2004).*

---

traditional telephone networks offered quite limited bandwidth compared with state-of-the art digital telephone networks. As a result, a traditional telephone call sounds "lo-fi." Bandwidth is measured in bits-per-second; a full page of English text is about 16,000 bits. For example, a 56Kbs modem connected to a conventional telephone line can move 16,000 bits in less than one second; by comparison, a broadband Internet connection that utilizes coaxial cable can move up to 10 gigabits per second. Consumer broadband service is typically available from cable TV companies or telephone companies via digital subscriber lines (DSL). In addition to faster download times and greater capacity, broadband offers other advantages. For example, it is always on (in other words, there is no need to access the Internet via phone dial-up service). Roughly one-third of American households currently have high-speed Internet access. Even so, according to figures compiled by the Organization for Economic Cooperation and Development, at the end of 2003 the United States ranked tenth in the world in terms of broadband penetration.[28]

What opportunities does broadband offer to companies outside the telecommunications industry? Broadband Internet enables users to access streaming audio, streaming video, and streaming media. **Streaming audio** enables users to listen to Internet radio stations. **Streaming video** is a sequence of moving images that are sent in compressed form over the Internet and displayed by the viewer as they arrive. **Streaming media** combines streaming video with sound. With streaming video or streaming media, a Web user does not have to wait to download

---

[28] Demetri Sevastopulo, "Rocky Road to the US's Broadband Future," *Financial Times* (December 9, 2003), p. 10.

a large file before seeing the video or hearing the sound. Instead, the media is sent in a continuous stream and is played as it arrives. Apple, Microsoft, RealNetworks, and MacroMedia are some of the companies that sell the software necessary to view streaming media. Streaming media represents a huge market opportunity for the video game industry, which includes electronics companies (e.g., Microsoft and Sony); game publishers (e.g., Electronic Arts); and Internet portals (e.g., Yahoo!). Yahoo! currently ranks as the top Web destination for online gaming, with more than 5.5 billion minutes of gaming hosted on its servers each month. Most of these are simple, Java-based games such as chess that are available without charge. However, in 2002, Yahoo! launched Games On Demand (GOD), a service that allows users to download and play PC games such as Zoo Tycoon. Another trend is online gaming: Gamers in different locations, even different countries, compete against each other using PCs, Xbox, or PlayStation 2 consoles. These are sometimes known as massively multiplayer online games (MMOG); popular titles include EverQuest, Second Life, and Final Fantasy IX. As of mid-2003, Microsoft's Xbox Live service had attracted 500,000 subscribers worldwide.[29] Next generation game consoles, which will reach the market in 2005, are expected to fuel consumer interest in online gaming. Broadband also permits publishers to offer full-featured games for sale online via downloads.

***Technology Forecast***

*By 2008, 18 percent of U.S. households will be playing online PC games.*

Forrester Group[30]

However, the promise of broadband goes far beyond gaming. Many industry observers and policymakers believe that broadband will be a critical economic tool in the coming decades. Broadband will provide opportunities for online education, medical diagnosis and treatment, and, of course, e-commerce. It is a key productivity tool that allows employees to save time by tapping online resources and by sharing electronic documents on desktop PCs in real time. South Korea currently leads the world in broadband penetration, with 21.3 subscribers per 100 residents; overall, 70 percent of Korean households are broadband subscribers. By comparison, the United States has 6.5 subscribers per 100 residents, a figure that represents roughly one quarter of U.S. households. South Korea's government budgeted $50 billion in an effort to link 80 major cities and towns via broadband; moreover, South Korea's network is extremely fast, offering standard speeds of 8 megabits per second (Mbps); by comparison, much of Europe's broadband currently operates at less than 1 Mbps. As Stephen Ward, a consultant with Deloitte, explains, "Koreans tend to be early adopters of technology and, more significantly, are fast followers. They are always conscious of the need not to get left behind by the Japanese and the young have a great desire to conform with the gadget-carrying norm of their peers."[31]

Singapore offers businesses grants of up to $200,000 to pay for broadband equipment and consulting services. The European Union also wants to increase broadband access throughout its member nations. Several factors help explain broadband's relatively slow start in the United States. For one thing, one quarter of the U.S. population lives in rural areas; this means that broadband is more expensive to roll out than in densely populated nations such as South Korea. Also, U.S. telecom companies where reluctant to invest in broadband lines because of concern that the U.S. Federal Communications Commission would force them to lease the lines to rival service providers. Concerned about the lack of broadband capacity, Michigan and other states are launching their own initiatives.[32]

---

29  Chris Nuttal, "Everything to Play For," *Financial Times IT Review—Mobile and Online Games* (December 10, 2003), p. 4.

30  Ben King, "Heavenly Time Playing GOD," *Financial Times IT Review—Mobile and Online Games* (December 10, 2003), p. 4.

31  Andrew Ward, "Where High-Speed Access is Going Mainstream," *Financial Times IT Review—Next-Generation Broadband* (June 9, 2004), p. 4.

32  Jim Hopkins, "Other Nations Zip by USA in High-Speed Net Race," *USA Today* (January 19, 2004), pp. 1B, 2B.

# MOBILE COMMERCE AND WIRELESS CONNECTIVITY

**Mobile commerce (m-commerce)** is the term for conducting commercial transactions using wireless handheld devices such as personal digital assistants (PDAs) and cell phones. Many companies are developing ways to provide Internet access without the need for a wire, DSL, or cable connection. For example, **wi-fi** (wireless fidelity) permits laptop and PDA users to establish high-speed wireless connections to the Internet and corporate intranets via "hot spots" located in airports, cafes, or other public places. Laptops are more popular in the United States than in Europe; this helps explain the fact that, by the end of 2003, there were about 12,000 hot spots in the United States. That number is expected to grow significantly in the coming years. The popularity of hotspots can also be explained in part by the need for so-called knowledge workers or "laptop warriors" to maintain high levels of productivity during trips. At the moment, South Korea is home to the world's largest wi-fi network of more than 17,000 hot spots from local telecom company KT.

A similar technology known as **Bluetooth** is gaining popularity in Europe; because it consumes less power than wi-fi, Bluetooth is well suited to use with cell phones.[33] However, Bluetooth works over shorter distances than wi-fi. Each week, approximately 1 million Bluetooth-enabled devices are shipped to stores. In addition to cell phone handsets, Bluetooth has been incorporated into automobiles and home appliances such as refrigerators and microwave ovens. Currently, British Telecommunications (BT) has about 4,000 Bluetooth hot spots in place. In addition, BT is testing a service called Blue Phone that will allow Bluetooth users to connect to BT's phone line network from a mobile unit.[34]

Wi-fi connections require a subscription to a service provider; one problem is getting a connection in a hot spot supported by a different provider than the one to which a user subscribes.[35] In the United States, Starbucks is partnering with T-Mobile USA (the American arm of Deutsche Telekom's T-Mobile International) to offer wi-fi service; the strategy is to encourage patrons to stay in Starbucks coffee shops longer and, presumably, spend more money on coffee and other items. In the United States, T-Mobile also has deals with Border's bookstores, Kinko's business centers, Texaco service stations, and major airports. Current wi-fi technology can only handle data, not voice. However, many industry observers expect that in the near future, hot spots will enable cell phone users to switch to the Internet for telephone calls.

Wireless technology is being used in other ways. In the automotive world, there is a trend toward **telematics,** which is a car's ability to exchange information about the vehicle's location or mechanical performance. Cars are also being equipped with online access so passengers can send and receive e-mails. BMW Online illustrates some of telematics' potential. The system, which is available in Germany and the United Kingdom in 7 Series BMWs, provides access to a wide range of information and services, including the availability of parking spaces. The service also assists users who wish to book hotel rooms or make restaurant reservations. Mercedes-Benz is rolling out a similar service.[36]

---

[33] "Bluetooth" is the English translation of Harald Blatand, a Danish Viking and king who lived in the 10th century.

[34] Jonathan Moules, "Bluetooth and the Quest for a Wireless World," *Financial Times* (December 3, 2003), p. 9.

[35] Dennis K. Berman and Jesse Drucker, "Wi-Fi Industry Bets 'Roaming' Will Lure Users," *The Wall Street Journal* (November 6, 2003), p. B1.

[36] Chris Reiter, "Web-Rigged Cars Get Second Look," *The Wall Street Journal* (December 11, 2003), p. D2.

# Smart Cell Phones

Cell phones have been one of the biggest new product success stories of the digital revolution. Worldwide, 400 million cellular handsets are sold each year. The popularity of cell phones has been a boon to manufacturers such as Nokia, Motorola, Samsung, and Ericsson as well as service providers such as Deutsche Telekom, U.S. Cellular, Verizon, and others. New features such as color displays and cameras give consumers a reason to upgrade their equipment on a regular basis; a new generation of "smart phones" gives phones some of the capabilities of computers. Though smart phones only represent about 5 percent of the market at present, they have the potential to boost the fortunes of the manufacturers as well as to create new sources of revenue for the service providers. The marketing possibilities of cell phone-based e-commerce are suggested by the following:[37]

- In Europe, France's Orange SA, Spain's Telefonica Moviles SA, Germany's T-Mobile International AG, and Britain's Vodafone Group have formed a consortium called Simpay to offer m-commerce services to 250 million cellular subscribers throughout the European Union.
- In Australia, a thirsty traveler can pay for a Coke at Central Station in Sydney by calling "Dial-a-Coke," making a beverage selection, and then collecting their selection from a vending machine. Charges for the purchase appear on the customer's cell phone bills.
- In Norway, mobile operator Telenor ASA has teamed with a finance group to offer mobile purchases of flowers, compact discs, bus tickets, and food.

While these and other new mobile services are in development, individuals are already using their cell phones for tasks other than calling. For example, text messaging has exploded in popularity; worldwide, about 10 billion peer-to-peer messages are sent each month. Now, advertisers are taking advantage of this capability by using **short message service (SMS),** a globally accepted wireless standard for sending alphanumeric messages of up to 160 characters. Of course, SMS can be used to send **spam,** which is unsolicited "junk" e-mail sent to large numbers of people to promote products or services. (The term "spam" is borrowed from a famous Monty Python comedy routine in which the brand name of Hormel Foods Corporation's canned meat product is used so often that it crowds everything else out.) A new global industry trade group, the Mobile Marketing Association, has been formed to address this and other issues (**www.mmaglobal.com**). Coca-Cola, 20th Century Fox, and other companies are using SMS for m-commerce purposes. Industry experts expect marketers to integrate SMS with communication via other digital channels such as interactive digital TV, the Internet, and e-mail.

*"Wireless phone booths are the Starbucks of telephony in South America."*

Ralph de la Vega, BellSouth Latin America[38]

## Ring Tones and Ring Tunes

Because of rampant illegal sharing of music files, record companies are searching for new sources of revenue (see Case 17-1). One opportunity is to license the rights to popular songs for use as cell phone ring tones. Cell phone users bought nearly 5 million ring tones in 2003; sales are strongest in Europe and Japan. Currently, however, the primary beneficiaries of this growing market are music publishers and songwriters. The reason is simple: Many ring tones are re-recordings and thus represent instrumental "soundalike" or "cover" versions rather than the original versions by the original recording artists; therefore, a song's publisher and writer receive royalties of approximately 15 percent each time a tone is downloaded. The situation is changing, however, as the record companies prepare to make original recordings available. Ring tunes, also

---

[37] Gren Manuel, "Dialing for Dollars," *The Wall Street Journal—E-Commerce* (October 20, 2003), p. R3.
[38] Almar Latour, "Latin Lessons: BellSouth Finds Pocket of Growth in an Odd Place," *The Wall Street Journal* (November 20, 2003), p. A8.

known as music tones, song tunes, TruTones, and master tones, are digitized clips of original songs by the original recording artists. Licensing fees for ring tunes will be higher, because they include master recording royalties of 30 to 50 percent. As John Rose, executive vice president of EMI Group, notes, "This is quite an attractive market to us. We think it'll be a significant multi-billion-dollar market over the next couple of years as the new handsets roll out."[39] This attitude has some industry players concerned. For example, Simon Buckingham is chief executive of PhoneFurniture, which does business as **www.ringtones.com**. He says, "Record companies are in danger of killing the golden goose before it has laid its eggs by charging excessive royalty rates, and are doing so more out of ignorance of the mobile market and value chain than greed."[40] Meanwhile, a Web-based company called Xingtones has begun offering software that allows users to create their own ring tunes from compact discs and digital music files.

*Technology Forecast*

*By 2008, annual cell phone music purchases in the United States could reach $1 billion.*

The Yankee Group[41]

## Mobile Gaming

As noted above, broadband's role in the console video-game market is growing in importance. At the same time, many consumers are playing simple, inexpensive games on their cell phones. In the United States, Verizon Wireless sells games for about $4; in Europe, mm02 plc sells games for an equivalent amount. Because cell phones have small screens and limited storage space and computing power, mobile gaming appeals more to occasional users such as commuters rather than hard-core gamers. Industry growth may also be slow due to the large number of different technical standards incorporated into different brands of telephones. Currently, the economics of mobile gaming do not favor game developers; cell phone service providers keep 10 percent to 70 percent of the selling price of each game downloaded. Moreover, for games based on popular motion pictures, game developers are required to pay licensing fees to the film studios.[42] For this reason, some big industry players, including Electronic Arts, are not investing heavily in mobile games. Some simple multi-player games written in the Java programming language are currently available for downloading on cell phones. However, mobile games are quickly becoming more sophisticated as phone makers add more features. For example, some phones are equipped with a **global positioning system** (GPS) that allows users to determine their exact geographic position. GPS capability will lead to location-based games in which players compete by trying to physically approach their opponents.

*Technology Forecast*

*By 2008, the global market for cell phone games could reach $7 billion.*

Strategy Analytics[43]

# Internet Phone Service

For the telecommunications industry, Internet telephone service is the "next big thing." Thanks to a technology known as **voice over Internet protocol (VoIP)**, the human voice can be digitized and broken into data packets that can be transmitted over the Internet and converted back into normal speech. If a call is placed to a conventional phone, it must be switched from the Internet to a traditional phone network; local telephone companies generally own the lines into residences and businesses. However, if the call is made between two subscribers to the same VoIP provider, it bypasses the traditional network altogether. The implications are clear: VoIP has the potential to render the current telecommunications

---

39 Bob Tedeschi, "E-Commerce Report," *The Wall Street Journal* (February 23, 2004), p. C5.
40 Yinka Adegoke, "Record Labels Bank on a Ring Tone Boom," *Financial Times* (December 16, 2003), p. 8.
41 Bob Tedeschi, "E-Commerce Report," *The Wall Street Journal* (February 23, 2004), p. C5.
42 David Pringle, "Making Games for Cellphones Is No Easy Play," *The Wall Street Journal* (October 17, 2003), p. B1.
43 David Pringle, "Making Games for Cellphones Is No Easy Play," *The Wall Street Journal* (October 17, 2003), p. B1.

infrastructure—consisting primarily of twisted copper and fiber optic cable—obsolete. Currently, VoIP accounts for only 3 percent of global calling; however, the promise of a global growth market has resulted in soaring stock values for start-up companies in the United States such as SpectraLink Corporation and Verso Technologies Inc. In Europe, Niklas Zennstrom, co-founder of the KaZaA music file sharing service, has started Skyper Ltd (**www.skype.co.uk**). The company offers peer-to-peer software for Internet calls.[44]

Not to be outmaneuvered, AT&T, SBC Communications, and other established phone companies are setting up their own Internet phone services. Meanwhile, a controversy is brewing, because traditional phone companies are subject to heavy regulation. By contrast, in most countries, the Internet is still unregulated; this is to encourage innovation and promote acceptance by businesses and the general public. For example, the European Commission is relying on regulators in member nations to establish rules for Internet calls. Likewise, in the United States, the Federal Communications Commission classifies VoIP as an information service. At the state level, some regulators are taking a similar "hands off" approach. In Minnesota, a district court judge ruled that Vonnage, based in Edison, New Jersey is, indeed, an information service provider. As a result, Vonnage and other Internet phone service companies do not have to pay the taxes and fees that conventional telecom companies pay. This, in turn, allows them to set lower prices for their services.[45]

## CONCLUSION

This is an exciting time to prepare for a career in global marketing. Until recently, one sure way to put your career at risk in many companies (especially U.S. companies) was to go overseas. There was nothing wrong with being overseas per se, but management did not always recognize the value of global experience and turned to executives who were close at hand for promotions.

Today, global experience counts. We are in a global market with global competition, and those with global experience have a definite advantage. Top U.S. executives with international experience include Samir F. Gibara, president and CEO of Goodyear Tire & Rubber; Michael Hawley, president and COO of Gillette; Lucio A. Noto, chairman and CEO of Mobil; and Raymond G. Viault, vice chairman of General Mills.[46]

How do you establish a career in global marketing? There are two broad paths:

1. Get directly into a job outside your home country or into a multicountry headquarters job in a global company
2. Get company experience in an industry that prepares you for promotion to a job with multicountry responsibility or to an assignment outside your home country

For many, the second choice is better than the first. There is no substitute for solid industry experience and your best opportunity to get it may be in your home country. You speak the language, understand the culture, and are trained in business and marketing. You are ready to learn. An option is to get this basic experience in another country. The advantage of this move is that you will learn a new culture and language and broaden your international experience while you learn about a company and industry. Good luck!

[44] Jonathan Moules, "Online Upstarts Target the Titans," *Financial Times* (November 20, 2003), p. 9.
[45] Peter Grant and Almar Latour, "Circuit Breaker: Battered Telecoms Face New Challenge: Internet Calling," *The Wall Street Journal* (October 9, 2003), pp. A1, A9. See also Anne Marie Squeo, "Internet Phone Service Threatens Industry's Giants," *The Wall Street Journal* (November 28, 2003), pp. B1, B2.
[46] Joann S. Lublin, "An Overseas Stint Can Be a Ticket to the Top," *The Wall Street Journal* (January 29, 1996), p. B1.

The **digital revolution** has created a global electronic marketplace. The revolution has gained momentum over the course of 70-plus years, during which time technological breakthroughs included the digital mainframe computer, the transistor, the integrated circuit, the personal computer, operating systems, DARPAnet, the Internet, and the World Wide Web. The digital revolution has resulted in a process known as **convergence,** meaning that previously separate industries and markets are coming together. The revolution has also unleashed a wave of **disruptive technologies** that are creating new markets and reshaping industries and **value networks. E-commerce,** or marketing exchanges conducted over the Internet, is growing in importance for both consumer and industrial goods marketers. Generally, commercial Web sites can have a domestic or global focus; in addition, sites can be information or transaction oriented. Global marketers must take care when designing Web sites. Country-specific domain names must be registered and local-language sites developed. In addition to addressing issues of technology and functionality, content must reflect local culture, customs, and aesthetic preferences. New products and services spawned by the digital revolution include: **broadband; wi-fi, Bluetooth,** and other forms of **wireless connectivity; telematics;** and **smart cell phones** that can be used for **mobile gaming** and **Internet phone service.**

1. Briefly review the key innovations that culminated in the digital revolution. What is the basic technological process that made the revolution possible?

2. What is convergence? How is convergence affecting Sony? Kodak? Nokia?

3. What is the innovator's dilemma? What is the difference between sustaining technology and disruptive technology? Briefly review Christensen's five principles of disruptive innovation.

4. What key issues must be addressed by global companies that engage in e-commerce?

5. Briefly outline Web design issues as they pertain to global marketing.

6. Review the key products and services that have emerged during the digital revolution. What are some products and services that are not mentioned in the chapter?

# Case 17-1

## Napster and the Global Music Industry

Although the online revolution has affected many industries, perhaps none has been more directly impacted than the recorded music business. In a 4-year period between 1999 and 2003, shipments of recorded music declined 26 percent and industry revenues fell by 14 percent. In Germany, one of Europe's top music markets, sales fell by one-third between 1998 and 2003. Some industry observers place the blame for the decline squarely on Internet piracy in the form of rampant swapping of music files. Other possible causes cited are the relative lack of exciting new artists and the global economic downturn. Whichever explanation is the right one, on a weekly, even daily basis, media reports paint a picture of an industry in turmoil and locked in a desperate struggle to adapt to a changed business environment. Key events included the following:

- The Record Industry Association of America (RIAA) filed a lawsuit against 261 individuals who were accused of breaking federal law by sharing music files

- Collectively, the major record companies fired about 8,000 employees in an effort to bring costs under control

- Several retail music chains, including Wherehouse and Tower Records, filed for bankruptcy

- Universal, one the world's top four music companies, cut wholesale CD prices in the United States by 25 percent

- Apple Computer and several other companies launched online music services that allow consumers to legally buy music online for as little as $0.99 per song

Few doubt that online distribution will play an increasingly important role in the music industry. Indeed, one study suggested that revenues from online music could exceed $3 billion by 2008. Less clear was which companies would succeed in the years to come.

### The Digital Revolution and the Music Industry: A Brief Overview

Prior to 1999, annual worldwide sales of recorded music totaled about $40 billion. Five global players dominate the industry: Sony BMG (Japan/Germany), Warner Music Group (United States), Universal Music (France), and EMI (Great Britain). With the exception of EMI and Warner Music, the music companies are divisions of larger diversified global companies. The music industry's troubles can be traced back to a number of technological developments. Ironically, for many years, the digital revolution was a boon to the industry. From the time of its introduction in 1983, consumers responded enthusiastically to the compact disc format. Attracted by the format's pristine sound and convenience, consumers bought new releases on CD and replaced many older recordings they owned with digitally-mastered CD versions. Within a few years, vinyl LPs and singles (and the turntables necessary to play them) had become specialty products purchased primarily by collectors, audiophiles, and hip-hop DJs. Buoyed by relatively high prices, the recorded music industry enjoyed several boom years.

Even as the CD format matured, CD-ROM drives had become standard equipment on most PCs by the mid-1990s. In 1999, a technology known as MP3 was introduced that enabled music files from CDs to be compressed so they were much smaller and easier to copy. A new generation of software enabled users to "rip" songs by copying them from CDs, converting them into MP3 files, and storing them on a PC's hard drive. Moreover, the advent of recordable CDs enabled individuals to "burn" CDs with their favorite songs. Portable devices that could store and play MP3 files became increasingly popular as their functionality improved and prices came down. Finally, and perhaps most important, the Internet became an integral part of the daily lives of millions of consumers.

These trends converged into a "perfect storm" in 1999 when a college dropout named Shawn Fanning developed Napster, a Web site that enabled individuals to swap songs for free. Other sites, including MP3.com and Gnutella.com, offered similar services. Tens of millions of music fans—college students, in particular—flocked to Napster; in February 2001 alone, an estimated 2.75 billion songs were downloaded from the site. It was not unusual for individuals to have hundreds of downloaded songs residing in the hard drives of their PCs. The songs could also be transferred to portable MP3 players to provide music on the go. In short, Napster appeared to offer an attractive alternative to paying $15 for a CD that contained one or two hit songs out of a total of 10 to 15 tracks.

The popularity of Napster and similar services caught the music industry by surprise; company executives, trade groups such as the RIAA, and many recording artists denounced Napster for infringing on the copyrights of songwriters and recording artists. More broadly, Napster and other sites threatened the foundations of a business model that hadn't changed significantly for decades. Record companies discovered new artists, signed them to contracts, provided career guidance, paid the expenses associated with recording albums and creating videos, and then distributed the finished recordings through retail stores, mail-order clubs, and other outlets. Unknown to the general public was the fact that record companies lose money on most releases. The companies rely on multi-million-selling albums by superstars such as Norah Jones, Linkin Park, and Britney Spears to subsidize recordings by other artists whose sales figures are too low to enable expenses to be recouped. However, this fact was lost on the average consumer; many had seen music celebrities' palatial homes featured on shows such as MTV's *Cribs* and concluded, as one college student put it, "Rock stars have tons of money already; they don't need my $15!"

Songwriters Have Rights, Too

Record company executives finally realized that their industry was undergoing gut-wrenching change. Many challenges had to be confronted and resolved; a critical one was devising a mechanism that would enable artists to be paid for downloaded songs. This issue was of particular concern to the National Music Publishers' Association, a trade group that controls the publishing rights to most songs in the United States. The association collects $0.075 for every individual song on a compact disc; a portion of that amount is then distributed to the song's publisher and the songwriter. The association is pushing the record labels for a better deal for songs distributed online; their argument is based in part on the fact that the labels will have lower expenses. A Copyright Arbitration Royalty Panel was established to conduct hearings on the issue.

The music business environment in Europe is more complex than in the United States; although the EU has passed a uniform copyright protection law, the law must be ratified by each member state. Meanwhile, individual countries have their own copyright laws and their own collecting societies for channeling royalty payments to artists. This situation requires online music services to obtain a separate license for each country in which they do business. Another problem is the fact that, with the exception of the United Kingdom, the collecting societies charge €0.20 (about $0.24) for each download; in the United States and the United Kingdom, by contrast, the licensing fee is $0.08. As Hans-Herwig Geyer, spokesman for the German Copyright Society (GEMA), said, "It's not our problem that online business models all call for music to be cheap."

In fact, the artists' community was divided on the issue of free Napster-style file swapping. Some artists noted that they were disenchanted by restrictive radio playlists that tend to ignore artists on independent labels. They also expressed disdain for record company executives (or "suits" as they are sometimes called) who didn't appreciate the music. Such artists viewed the Internet as a way of building an audience without the support or backing of a major label. Other artists shared a less charitable view, believing that unauthorized file swapping was theft.

"See You in Court," Part One

The major labels responded to Napster on several different fronts. Acting on behalf of the industry, in December 1999, the RIAA filed suit in U.S. court in an effort to shut Napster down.

An initial court ruling found that Napster violated copyright laws, and on Wednesday, July 26, 2000, district judge Marilyn Hall Patel ordered Napster shut down. Napster immediately filed an appeal; on February 12, 2001, the Ninth Circuit Court of Appeals upheld the lower court's ruling. In March, to comply with a preliminary injunction, the company installed a filter that blocked approximately 1 million copyrighted titles from being downloaded. Hank Barry, Napster's chief executive, offered to pay the record labels $1 billion over a 5-year period. Barry proposed a basic subscription service costing between $2.95 per month and $4.95 per month that would entitle a user to a fixed number of downloads. The record companies rejected that proposal. In January 2000, the RIAA filed suit against MP3.com for copyright infringement following the launch of a My.MP3.com, a service that enabled users to store copies of their CDs on MP3.com's servers. The artists themselves even took legal steps; in 2000, the heavy metal band Metallica filed its own suit against Napster, calling it a "corrupt organization" and alleging that it was engaged in copyright infringement and racketeering. As Metallica drummer Lars Ulrich said, "We take our craft—whether it be the music, the lyrics, or the photos and artwork—very seriously, as do most artists. It is therefore sickening to know that our art is being traded like a commodity rather than the art that it is."

Legal Online Music Services, Version 1.0

While the legal challenges to online music piracy moved through the court system, executives from the major labels were under increased pressure from the U.S. Congress to make online music available legally and to do so quickly. In a series of hearings, congressional leaders made it clear that if the record companies couldn't create acceptable licensing arrangements for Internet music distribution, Congress would make such licensing compulsory. A number of issues confronted the companies. Different technologies, including Windows Media Player, Macintosh iTunes, and Realplayer, were available for ripping and digitizing music, and several of the formats were incompatible with the others. Another fundamental question facing the majors was: How much are people willing to pay for access to online music?

While these issues were being debated, the record companies began creating alliances that would enable them to establish online music subscription services. Three of the five major record companies, Warner Music, BMG, and EMI, formed MusicNet in conjunction with Seattle-based RealNetworks. RealNetworks had become a key player in online entertainment with its RealPlayer software that allows PC users to listen to Internet radio stations by using streaming audio technology. Universal Music and Sony teamed up to form PressPlay, a rival subscription service available through Yahoo! for $9.95 per month.

These first-generation sites had various shortcomings. For example, songs by artists who recorded on labels distributed by Warner, BMG, or EMI weren't available on PressPlay; conversely, artists who recorded for Universal Music or Sony couldn't sell their songs on MusicNet. Only PressPlay allowed songs to be burned onto CDs or transferred to portable music players. (PressPlay was later sold to Roxio in 2003 and relaunched as Napster). Also, to the dismay of some consumers, the pay-for-play services incorporated a technology that obliterated downloaded music files if a user canceled his or her sub-

scription. Industry analysts also noted that consumers would not be satisfied if a subscription service gave them access to catalog offerings of only a few record labels. Another issue was ease of use: Some existing sites that offered songs encrypted with copy-prevention codes were prone to crashing.

By the summer of 2000, MP3.com had reached settlements with four of the five major record companies. In May 2001, Vivendi acquired MP3.com for $372 million after the online service paid millions in damages to Universal Music to settle the copyright suit. Meanwhile, Bertelsmann, the corporate parent of BMG, angered its competitors by striking an agreement with Napster to provide a "secure membership-based service." Thomas Middelhoff, Bertelsmann's chief executive at the time, noted, "Now the show begins. We have to evolve Napster and make it the best service available to people who love music." Within a few months, however, Middelhoff had resigned from Bertlesmann.

As these example show, the fledging online music industry was suffering growing pains. But there was more turmoil to come. For example, Viacom's MTV was jockeying for position as well. Its MTV.com Web site attracted about six million visitors each month. The cable giant took an equity stake in RioPort, a technology company that had signed licensing deals with the major labels. RioPort's business model was different in that the company proposed a "pay-per-download" approach instead of subscriptions. Music files could be downloaded into portable players, and the system was capable of handling most available digital formats. However, in 2003, Ecast, RioPort's corporate parent, shut the site down to concentrate on other business opportunities.

"See You in Court," Part Two

In 2003, the record industry struck back against file swappers. Acting on behalf of the music companies, the RIAA sued Verizon Communications to obtain the name of a suspected file swapper. The RIAA also subpoenaed colleges in an effort to obtain the names of students who actively swapped songs that were stored on the colleges' servers. Most significantly, in September 2003, the RIAA filed lawsuits in federal court against 261 individuals who allegedly had large libraries of copyrighted music on their computers that they made available to others on file-sharing networks such as KaZaA and Grokster. The individuals included a 12-year-old New York girl whose parents agreed to pay a $2,000 fine to settle the suit. The industry also offered amnesty to file swappers who had not been sued; individuals would agree to delete illegal copies of songs from their hard drives. The industry's court actions provoked protests from public advocacy groups such as the Electronic Frontier Foundation, Internet service providers, and even some recording artists.

*"Nobody likes playing the heavy and resorting to litigation, but when you're being victimized by illegal activity there is a time you have to stand up and take action."*

Cary Sherman, President, Recording Industry Association of America

Legal Online Music Services, Version 2.0

Even as the industry was seeking recourse against file sharing in court, a number of new, legal, online services were being launched. The most successful was iTunes Music Store; launched by Apple Computer, it built upon the company's popular software for storing and cataloging music files on Macintosh computers. Apple had also begun marketing a wildly successful digital music player, the iPod. A 2003 *Time* magazine cover story hailed iTunes as the "Innovation of the Year." Apple sold 10 million songs during iTunes' first 6 months of operation. In July 2004, sales passed the 100-million-song mark; Steve Jobs and iPod were featured in another cover story, this time in *Newsweek* magazine. Meanwhile, Napster was relaunched as a legitimate service; the familiar "kittyhead" logo appeared in numerous print ads. Napster 2.0 became the first computer-only service to sell 5 million downloads in the United States; Napster also offered a subscription service for a monthly fee. Comparing his company's online strategy with Apple's, Napster CEO Chris Gorog noted:

> The à la carte model is a great catalyst for the online industry because it's simple to understand. But it's also limiting. Right now, for example, in the U.S., with iTunes if you spend $9.95 you can listen to 10 songs. With Napster, if you spend $9.95 a month you can listen to half a million. We think that's the model of the future, and we also think for us it's the model with greater financial reward, because of the margins.

Other companies were joining the fray as well. For example, MusicMatch Downloads was a Windows-based service that, like iTunes, offered liberal usage rules. However, MusicMatch uses the Windows Media format, which is not compatible with Apple's iPod. Dell Computer launched MusicMatch under its own brand, and RealNetworks launched a service called Rhapsody. Meanwhile, solo recording artist and former Genesis front man Peter Gabriel was the driving force behind OD2, Europe's first legal site for downloading songs. In 2001, after several years of careful planning and negotiating with record labels, OD2 was launched in seven European countries in conjunction with Microsoft's MSN Music Club. OD2 has also partnered with MTV Europe, Virgin, HMV, and the Coca-Cola Company; the latter uses OD2 as a source for its MyCokeMusic store in the United Kingdom. Wal-Mart, which already accounts for 20 percent of recorded music sales in the United States, announced it was launching an online service. Industry observers expected that Wal-Mart would use its retail strength to undercut the prevailing 99-cents-per-download pricing structure. Table 1 shows a listing of leading legal online services as of mid-2004.

***Visit the Web site***

*The Electronic Frontier Foundation is a nonprofit organization co-founded by Lotus Corporation founder Mitch Kapor and John Perry Barlow, lyricist for the Grateful Dead.*

**www.eff.org**

## Discussion Questions

1. How did the record companies find themselves in this situation? Are any of their wounds self-inflicted? What mistakes did they make?

2. Do you agree with the RIAA's decision to sue individuals who share music files on the Internet? Will the lawsuits deter others from sharing files or will they alienate consumers?

3. Compare Napster's subscription-based business model with iTunes' "a la carte" approach. Which of these business models will be most successful?

4. Put yourself in the shoes of a well-meaning, law-abiding individual who is speaking to a group of high school seniors about ethics. In your presentation, you explain that the unauthorized swapping of music files online is against the law. During a question-and-answer session, an audience member says, "Maybe the law is wrong and should be changed." How do you respond?

*Sources:* Paul Sexton, "Napster Returns for Another Bite of the Apple," *Financial Times* (March 3, 2004), p. 7; Brandon Mitchener, "European Download Blues," *The Wall Street Journal* (November 10, 2003), pp. B1, B6; Richard Milne, "The Genesis of a New Musical Partnership," *Financial Times* (September 1, 2003), p. 6; Nick Wingfield and Ethan Smith, "The High Costs of Sharing," *The Wall Street Journal* (September 8, 2003), pp. B1, B8; "E-Music Sites Settle on Prices. It's a Start," *The New York Times* (March 3, 2003), pp. C1, C5; Martin Peers and William Boston, "Sour Note: Plugging into the Web Is a Jarring Experience for the Music Industry," *The Wall Street Journal* (April 12, 2001), pp. A1, A10; Devin Leonard, "The Music Men Are Out of Tune," *Fortune* (June 11, 2001), pp. 144–146 + ; Don Clark, "Napster Offers Annual Fees to CD Labels," *The Wall Street Journal* (February 21, 2001), p. B6; Anna Wilde Mathews, "The Flip Side: Royalty Fight Threatens Record Industry's Plans to Deliver Songs Online," *The Wall Street Journal* (May 1, 2001), pp. A1, A8; Lee Gomes, "Napster Ruling May Be Just the Overture," *The Wall Street Journal* (July 28, 2000), pp. B1, B4; Ted Bridis, "Online Music: Is It Time to Rewind or Fast Forward?" *The Wall Street Journal* (April 4, 2001), p. B3; Gomes, "Bertelsmann, Napster Agree on Service," *The Wall Street Journal* (November 1, 2000), pp. A3, A8.

***Table 1*** *Online Music Services*

| Music Service/Corporate Parent (Headquarters) | Overview |
| --- | --- |
| iTunes Music Store/ Apple Computer (USA) | Downloaded songs can easily be transferred to Apple iPod music player. Compatible with Windows. |
| Napster 2.0/Roxio (USA) | The notorious file swapping site reborn as a legitimate subscription-based service. |
| OD2/On Demand Distribution PLC (United Kingdom) | Cofounded by rock star Peter Gabriel. Sold to LoudEye for $40 million in 2004. |
| MusicMatch/ MusicMatch Inc. (USA) | Creator of popular MusicMatch Jukebox software. |
| Rhapsody/ RealNetworks (USA) | RealNetworks pioneered RealPlayer software that enables hundreds of millions of users to listen to streaming audio and view streaming video online. |

# GLOSSARY

The chapter number follows the definition.

**acquisition** A market-entry strategy that entails investing in assets outside the home country. (9)

**ad valorem duty** A duty that is expressed as a percentage of the value of goods. (8)

**adaptation approach** Management's use of highly localized marketing programs in different country markets. (1)

**adopter categories** In the adoption process developed by Everett Rogers, a typology of buyers at different stages of the "adoption" or product life cycle. The categories are innovators, early majority, late majority, and laggards. (4)

**adoption process** A model developed by Everett Rogers that describes the "adoption" or purchase decision process. The stages consist of awareness, interest, evaluation, trial, and adoption. (4)

**advertising** Any sponsored, paid message that is communicated through a nonpersonal channel. Advertising is one of four variables in the promotion mix. (13)

**advertising appeal** The communications approach that relates to the motives of the target audience. (13)

**advertising organization** A corporation or holding company that includes one or more "core" advertising agencies, as well as units specializing in direct marketing, marketing services, public relations, or research. (13)

**advocacy advertising** A form of corporate advertising in which a company presents its point of view on a particular issue. (13)

**aesthetics** A shared sense within a culture of what is beautiful as opposed to ugly and what represents good taste as opposed to tastelessness. (4)

**agent** An intermediary who negotiates transactions between two or more parties but does not take title to the goods being purchased or sold. (12)

**Andean Community** A customs union comprised of Bolivia, Colombia, Ecuador, Peru, and Venezuela. (3)

**antidumping duties** Duties imposed on products whose prices government officials deem too low. (8)

**arbitration** A negotiation process between two or more parties to settle a dispute outside of the court system. (5)

**arbitrary monetary policy** Policy that, in effect, raises the price of foreign goods by the cost of money for the term of the required deposit. (8)

**art direction** The visual presentation of an advertisement. (13)

**art director** An ad agency "creative" with general responsibility for the overall look of an advertisement. The art director chooses graphics, pictures, type styles, and other visual elements. (13)

**Association of Southeast Asian Nations (ASEAN)** A trade bloc comprised of Brunei, Cambodia, Indonesia, Malaysia, Laos, Myanmar, the Philippines, Singapore, Thailand, and Vietnam. (3)

**attitude** In culture, a learned tendency to respond in a consistent way to a given object or entity. (4)

**balance of payments** The record of all economic transactions between the residents of a country and the rest of the world. (2)

**barter** The least complex and oldest form of bilateral, non-monetized countertrade consisting of a direct exchange of goods or services between two parties. (11)

**behavioral market segmentation** The process of performing market segmentation utilizing user status, usage rate, or some other measure of product consumption. (7)

**belief** In culture, an organized pattern or knowledge that an individual holds to be true about the world. (4)

**benefit segmentation** The process of segmenting markets on the basis of the benefits sought by buyers. (7)

**big emerging markets (BEMs)** Countries that have experienced rapid economic growth and represent significant marketing opportunities. (2)

**big idea** A concept that can serve as the basis for a memorable, effective advertising message. (13)

**bill of exchange** A written order from one party directing a second party to pay to the order of a third party. (8)

**Bluetooth** Technology that permits access to the Internet from a cell phone when the user is within range of a hot spot. (17)

**brand** A representation of a promise by a particular company about a particular product; a complex bundle of images and experiences in the customer's mind. (10)

**brand equity** The reflection of the brand's value to a company as an intangible asset. (10)

**brand extensions** A strategy that uses an established brand name as an umbrella when entering new businesses or developing new product lines that represent new categories to the company. (10)

**brand image** A single, but often complex, mental image about both the physical product and the company that markets it. (10)

**bribery** The corrupt business practice of demanding or offering some type of consideration—typically cash payment—when negotiating a cross-border deal. (5)

**broadband** A digital communication system with sufficient capacity to carry multiple voice, data, or video channels simultaneously. (17)

**business-to-business marketing** Marketing products and services to other companies and organizations. Contrasts with business-to-consumer (B2C) marketing. (12)

**call centers** Sophisticated telephone operations that provide customer support and other services to in-bound callers from around the world. May also provide outsourcing services such as telemarketing. (8)

**call option** The right to buy a specified amount of foreign currency at a fixed price, up to the option's expiration date. (2)

**capital account** In a country's balance of payments, the record of all long-term direct investment, portfolio investment, and other short- and long-term capital flows. (2)

**capital requirements** Costs that can be seen as fixed capital, as in manufacturing facilities, or working capital, as in financing R&D, advertising, field sales and service, customer credit, and inventories. (15)

**CARICOM (Caribbean Community and Common Market)** Formed in 1973, it is a free trade area whose members include Antigua and Barbuda, Bahamas, Barbados, Belize, Dominica, Grenada, Guyana, Haiti, Jamaica, Montserrat, St. Kitts and Nevis, St. Lucia, St. Vincent and the Grenadines, and Trinidad and Tobago. (3)

**cartel** A group of separate companies or countries that collectively set prices, control output, or take other actions to maximize profits. (5)

**category killer** A store that specializes in a particular product category and offers a vast selection at low prices. (12)

**Central American Integration System** A customs union comprised of El Salvador, Honduras, Guatemala, Nicaragua, Costa Rica, and Panama. (3)

**centrally planned capitalism** An economic system characterized by command resource allocation and private resource ownership. (2)

**centrally planned socialism** An economic system characterized by command resource allocation and state resource ownership. (2)

**C.F.R. (cost and freight)** A contract in which the seller is not responsible for risk or loss at any point outside the factory. (11)

*chaebol* In South Korea, a type of corporate alliance group composed of dozens of companies and centered around a central bank or holding company and dominated by a founding family. (9)

**channel of distribution** An organized network of agencies and institutions that, in combination, perform all the activities required to link producers with users to accomplish the marketing task. (12)

**characteristics of innovations** In Roger's diffusion of innovation framework, five factors that affect the rate at which a new product is accepted by buyers: relative advantage, compatibility, complexity, divisibility, and communicability. (4)

**cherry picking** In distribution, a situation in which a channel intermediary such as a distributor only accepts new lines from manufacturers whose products and brands already enjoy strong demand. (12)

**C.I.F. (cost, insurance, freight) named port of destination** The Incoterm for a contract requiring the seller to retain responsibility and liability for goods until they have physically passed over the rail of a ship. (11)

**click-through rate** The percentage of visitors to an Internet site who click on an advertisement link presented on the computer screen. (17)

**cluster analysis** In market research, a quantitative data analysis technique that groups variables into clusters that maximize within-group similarities and between-group differences. Can be used in psychographic segmentation. (6)

**cobranding** A variation on tiered branding in which two or more different company or product brands are featured prominently on product packaging or in advertising. (10)

**collaborating with competitors** Seeking competitive advantage by utilizing know-how developed by other companies. (15)

**collaborative agreements** Linkages between companies from different countries for the purpose of pursuing common goals. (9)

**collectivism** In Hofstede's social values typology, the extent to which group cohesiveness and harmony are emphasized in a culture. A shared concern for the well-being of all members of society is also evident. (4)

**combination branding** A strategy in which a corporate name is combined with a product brand name; also called tiered or umbrella branding. (10)

**common agricultural policy (CAP)** Legislation adopted by European countries after World War II to aid and protect the interests of farmers. (8)

**common external tariff (CET)** A tariff agreed upon by members of a preferential trading bloc. Implementation of a CET marks the transition from a free trade area to a customs union. (3)

**common-law country** A country in which the legal system relies on past judicial decisions (cases) to resolve disputes. (5)

**common market** A preferential trade agreement that builds on the foundation of economic integration provided by a free trade area and a customs union. (3)

**Common Market of the South (Mercosur)** A customs union comprised of Argentina, Brazil, Paraguay, Uruguay, and Chile. (3)

**comparability** The degree to which research results from different countries can be used to make valid comparisons. (6)

**compensation trading (buyback)** A countertrade deal typically involving sale of plant equipment or technology licensing in which the seller or licensor agrees to take payment in the form of the products produced using the equipment or technology for a specified number of years. (11)

**competitive advantage** The result of a match between a firm's distinctive competencies and the factors critical for creating superior customer value in an industry. (1)

**competitor response** The reaction of existing competitors to a new entrant's arrival in an industry or market. (15)

**concentrated global marketing** The target market strategy that calls for creating a marketing mix to reach a niche segment of global consumers. (7)

**confiscation** Governmental seizure of a company's assets without compensation. (5)

**conjoint analysis** In market research, a quantitative data analysis technique that can be used to gain insights into the combination of product features that will be attractive to potential buyers. (6)

**consumer panel** Primary data collection using a sample of consumers or households whose behavior is tracked over time; frequently used for television audience measurement. (6)

**consumer sales promotions** Promotion designed to make consumers aware of a new product, to stimulate nonusers to sample an existing product, or to increase overall consumer demand. (14)

**containerization** In physical distribution, the practice of loading long-haul truck or ocean-going freight into steel boxes measuring 20 feet, 40 feet, or longer. (12)

**continuous innovation** A product that is "new and improved" but requires little R&D expenditure to develop and causes minimal disruption of existing consumption patterns and requires the least amount of learning on the part of buyers. (10)

**contract manufacturing** A licensing arrangement in which a global company provides technical specifications to a subcontractor or local manufacturer. (9)

**control** The process by which managers ensure that resources are used effectively and efficiently in the accomplishment of organizational objectives. (16)

**convenience stores** A form of retail distribution that offers some of the same products as supermarkets, but the merchandise mix is limited to high turnover convenience products. (12)

**convergence** The aspect of the digital revolution that pertains to the merging, overlapping, or coming together of previously distinct industries or product categories. (17)

**cooperative exporter** An export organization of a manufacturing company retained by other independent manufacturers to sell their products in some or all foreign markets. (8)

**copy** The words that are the spoken or written communication elements in advertisements. (13)

**copyright** The establishment of ownership of a written, recorded, performed, or filmed creative work. (5)

**copywriter** An advertising agency "creative" who is responsible for developing the headlines, subheads, and body copy used in print advertising and the scripts for broadcast ads. (13)

**corporate advertising** Advertising that is not designed to directly stimulate demand for a specific product. Image advertising and advocacy advertising are two types of corporate advertising. (13)

**cost focus** In Porter's generic strategies framework, one of four options for building competitive advantage. When a firm that serves a small (niche) market has a lower cost structure than its competitors, it can offer customers the lowest prices in the industry. (15)

**cost-based pricing** Pricing based on an analysis of internal costs (e.g., material, labor, etc.) and external costs. (11)

**cost-based transfer pricing** A transfer pricing policy that uses costs as a basis for setting prices in intracorporate transfers. (11)

**cost leadership advantage**  A broad market strategy based on a firm's position as the industry's low-cost producer. (15)

**cost-plus pricing**  The price that results from adding the additional costs and expenses not directly related to the manufacturing cost to the full-cost price. (11)

**counterfeiting**  The unauthorized copying and production of a product. (5)

**counterpurchase**  A monetized countertrade deal in which the seller agrees to purchase products of equivalent value that it must then sell in order to realize revenue from the original deal. (11)

**countertrade**  An export transaction in which a sale results in product flowing in one direction to a buyer, and a separate stream of products and services, often flowing in the opposite direction. (11)

**countervailing duties (CVDs)**  Additional duties levied to offset subsidies granted in the exporting country. (8)

**country-of-origin effect**  Perceptions of, or attitudes toward, products or brands on the basis of the country of origin or manufacture. (10)

**coupon**  A sales promotion tool consisting of a printed certificate that entitles the bearer to a price reduction or some other value-enhancing consideration when purchasing a particular product or service. (14)

**creative**  In an advertising agency, a person who is responsible for developing the appropriate advertising appeal, selling proposition, and creative execution of an advertisement. (13)

**creative execution**  In advertising, the way an appeal or selling proposition is presented. Creative execution is the "how," creative strategy is the "what." (13)

**creative strategy**  A statement or concept of what a particular advertising message or campaign will say. (13)

**culture**  A society's ways of living are transmitted from one generation to another. Culture's manifestations include attitudes, beliefs, values, aesthetics, dietary customs, and language. (4)

**current account**  A record of all recurring trade in merchandise and services, private gifts, and public aid transactions between countries. (2)

**customer relationship management**  The process of storing and analyzing data collected from customer "touchpoints" for the purpose of identifying a firm's best customers and serving their needs as efficiently, effectively, and profitably as possible. (6)

**customer strategy**  A sales representative's plan for collecting and analyzing information about the needs of each customer or prospect. (14)

**customs procedures**  Procedures that are considered restrictive if they are administered in a way that makes compliance difficult and expensive. (8)

**customs union**  A preferential trade bloc whose members agree to seek a greater degree of economic integration than is provided by a free trade agreement. In addition to reducing tariffs and quotas, a customs union is characterized by a common external tariff (CET). (3)

**data warehouse**  A database, part of a company's MIS, that is used to support management decision making. (6)

**delivered duty paid**  A type of contract in which the seller has agreed to deliver the goods to the buyer at the place he or she names in the country of import, with all costs, including duties, paid. (11)

**demand conditions**  Conditions that determine the rate and nature of improvement and innovations by the firms in the nation. (10)

**demographic segmentation**  The process of segmenting markets on the basis of measurable characteristics such as country income, population, age, or some other measure. (7)

**department store**  A category of retail operations characterized by multiple sections or areas under one roof, each representing a distinct merchandise line and staffed with a limited number of salespeople. (12)

**devaluation**  The decline in value of a currency relative to other currencies. (2)

**developed countries**  Countries that can be assigned to the high-income category. (2)

**developing countries**  Countries that can be assigned to the upper ranks of the low-income category, the lower-middle income category, or the upper-middle-income category. (2)

**differentiated global marketing**  A strategy that calls for targeting two or more distinct market segments with multiple marketing mix offerings. (7)

**differentiation**  In Porter's generic strategies framework, one of four options for building competitive advantage. Differentiation advantage is present when a firm serves a broad market and its products are perceived as unique; this allows the firm to charge premium prices compared with the competition. (15)

**diffusion of innovations**  A framework developed by Everett Rogers to explain the way that new products are adopted by a culture over time. Framework includes the 5-stage innovation adoption process, characteristics of innovations, and innovation adopter categories. (4)

**digital revolution**  The paradigm shift resulting from technological advances allowing for the digitization—i.e., conversion to binary code—of analogue sources of information, sounds, and images. (17)

**direct mail**  A direct marketing technique that uses the postal service as a vehicle for delivering an offer to prospects targeted by the marketer. (14)

**direct marketing**  Any communication with a consumer or business recipient that is designed to generate a response in the form of an order, a request for further information, and/or a visit to a store or other place of business. (14)

**direct perception**  In environmental scanning, the reliance on immediate sensory input (e.g., seeing, hearing, tasting) to supplement documentary information sources. (6)

**discontinuous innovation**  A new product that, upon its success, creates new markets and new consumption patterns. (10)

**discount stores**  A category of retail operations that emphasizes low merchandise prices. (12)

**discriminatory exchange rate policies**  Policies that distort trade in much the same way as selective import duties and export subsidies. (8)

**discriminatory procurement policies**  Policies that can take the form of government rules and administrative regulations, as well as formal or informal company policies that discriminate against foreign suppliers. (8)

**disruptive technology**  A technology that redefines product or industry performance and enables new markets to emerge. (17)

**distribution**  One of the four Ps of the marketing mix; the physical flow of goods through channels. (12)

**distribution center**  A facility designed to efficiently receive goods from suppliers and then fill orders for individual stores or customers. (12)

**distribution channels**  A barrier to entry into an industry created by the need to create and establish new channels. (12)

**distributor**  A wholesale channel intermediary that typically carries product lines or brands on a selective basis. (13)

**domestic company**  A company that limits the geographic scope of its resource commitment and marketing activities to opportunities in the home country. (1)

**domestic market**  A company's "home turf," generally the country or countries in which the organization's headquarters is located. (1)

**double diamond model**  A framework for understanding national competitive advantage in terms of a "double diamond" instead of the single diamond found in Michael Porter's national advantage model. (15)

**dumping**  The sale of a product in an export market at a price lower than that normally charged in the domestic market or country of origin. (8)

**duties**  Rate schedule; can sometimes be thought of as a tax that punishes individuals for making choices of which their government disapprove. (8)

**dynamically continuous innovation**  An intermediate category of newness that is less disruptive and requires less learning on the part of consumers. (10)

**Economic Community of West African States (ECOWAS)**  An association of 16 nations that includes Benin, Burkina Faso, Cape Verde, The Gambia, Ghana, Guinea, Guinea-Bissau, Ivory Coast, Liberia, Mali, Mauritania, Niger, Nigeria, Senegal, Sierra Leone, and Togo. (3)

**economic exposure**  The degree to which exchange rates affect a company's market value as measured by its stock price. (2)

**economic freedom index**  A league table of country rankings based on key economic variables such as trade policy, taxation policy, government consumption, monetary policy, capital flows and foreign investment, etc. (2)

**economic union**  A highly evolved form of cross-border economic integration involving reduced tariffs and quotas; a common external tariff; reduced restrictions on the movement of labor and capital; and the creation of unified economic policies and institutions such as a central bank. (3)

**economies of scale**  The decline in per-unit product costs as the absolute volume of production per period increases. (15)

**efficient consumer response (ECR)**  An MIS tool that enables retailers to work more closely with vendors to facilitate stock replenishment. (6)

**80/20 rule**  In behavioral market segmentation, the rule of thumb that 20 percent of a company's products or customers account for 80 percent of revenues or profits. (7)

**electronic data interchange (EDI)**  An MIS tool that allows a company's business units to submit orders, issue invoices, and transact business electronically with other company units as well as outside companies. (6)

**electronic point of sale (EPOS)**  Purchase data gathered by checkout scanners that help retailers identify product sales patterns and the extent to which consumer preferences vary with geography. (6)

**emic analysis**   Global market research that analyzes a country in terms of its local system of meanings and values. (6)

**emotional appeal**   In advertising, an appeal intended to evoke a feeling response (as opposed to an intellectual response) that will direct purchase behavior. (13)

**environmental scanning**   Gathering information about global markets. Two modes can be used: surveillance and search. (6)

**environmental sensitivity**   A measure of the extent to which products must be adapted to the culture-specific needs of different country markets. Generally, consumer products show a higher degree of environmental sensitivity than industrial products. (4)

**EPRG framework**   A developmental framework for analyzing organizations in terms of four successive management orientations: ethnocentric, polycentric, regiocentric, and geocentric. (1)

**equity stake**   Market entry strategy involving foreign direct investment for the purpose of establishing partial ownership of a business. (9)

**ethnocentric orientation**   The first level in the EPRG framework: the conscious or unconscious belief that one's home country is superior. (1)

**ethnocentric pricing**   The practice of extending a product's home-country price to all country markets. Also known as extension pricing policy. (11)

**etic analysis**   Global market research that analyzes a country from an outside perspective. (6)

**euro**   The single European currency. (3)

**euro zone**   Austria, Belgium, Finland, Ireland, the Netherlands, France, Germany, Greece, Italy, Luxembourg, Portugal, and Spain. (3)

**expanded Triad**   The dominant economic centers of the world: the Pacific region, North America, and Europe. (2)

**expatriate**   An employee who is sent from his or her home country to work abroad. (14)

**export broker**   A broker who receives a fee for bringing together the seller and the overseas buyer. (8)

**export commission representative**   Representative assigned to all or some foreign markets by the manufacturer. (8)

**export distributor**   An individual or organization that has the exclusive right to sell a manufacturer's products in all or some markets outside the country of origin. (8)

**export management company (EMC)**   Term used to designate an independent export firm that acts as the export department for more than one manufacturer. (8)

**export marketing**   Exporting using the product offered in the home market as a starting point and modifying it as needed to meet the preferences of international target markets. (8)

**export merchants**   Merchants who seek out needs in foreign markets and make purchases in world markets to fill these needs. (8)

**export selling**   Exporting without tailoring the product, the price, or the promotional material to suit individual country requirements. (8)

**exporting**   Selling or marketing goods or services to buyers located outside the home country. (8)

**express warranty**   A written guarantee that assures a buyer that he or she is getting what was paid for or provides recourse in the event that a product's performance falls short of expectations. (10)

**expropriation**   Governmental seizure of a company's assets in exchange for compensation that is generally lower than market value. (5)

**extension approach**   Management's use of domestic country marketing programs and strategies when entering new country markets. (1)

**ex-works**   A type of contract in which the seller places goods at the disposal of the buyer at the time specified in the contract. (11)

**factor analysis**   In market research, a computerized quantitative data analysis technique that is used to perform data reduction. Responses from questionnaires that contain multiple items about a product's benefits serve as input; the computer generates factor loadings that can be used to create a perceptual map. (6)

**factor conditions**   A country's endowment with resources. (15)

**femininity**   In Hofstede's social values framework, the extent to which the social roles of men and women overlap in a culture. (4)

**first-mover advantage**   Orthodox marketing wisdom suggesting that the first company to enter a country market has the best chance of becoming the market leader. (7)

**flagship model**   A model of competitive advantage developed by Alan Rugman that describes how networked business systems can create competitive advantage in global industries. (15)

**focus**   The concentration of resources on a core business or competence. (1)

**focus group**   Primary data collection method involving a trained moderator who facilitates discussion among the members of a group at a specially equipped research facility. (6)

**focused differentiation**   In Porter's generic strategies framework, one of four options for building competitive advantage. When a firm serves a small (niche) market and its products are perceived as unique, the firm can charge premium prices. (15)

**foreign consumer culture positioning**   A positioning strategy that seeks to differentiate a product, brand, or company by associating it with its country or culture of origin. (7)

**Foreign Corrupt Practices Act (FCPA)**   A law that makes it illegal for U.S. corporations to bribe an official of a foreign government or political party to obtain or retain business. (5)

**foreign direct investment**   The market entry strategy in which companies invest in or acquire plants, equipment, or other assets outside the home country. (9)

**foreign purchasing agents**   Purchasing agents who operate on behalf of, and are remunerated by, an overseas customer. (8)

**forward market**   A mechanism for buying and selling currencies at a preset price for future delivery. (2)

**franchising**   A contract between a parent company–franchisor and franchisee that allows the franchisee to operate a business developed by the franchisor in return for a fee and adherence to franchise-wide policies and practices. (9)

**F.A.S. (free alongside ship) named port of destination**   The Incoterm for a contract that calls for the seller to place goods alongside, or available to, the vessel or other mode of transportation and pay all charges up to that point. (11)

**F.O.B. (free on board)**   The Incoterm for a contract in which the responsibility and liability of the seller do not end until the goods have actually been placed aboard a ship. (11)

**free trade agreement (FTA)**   An agreement that leads to the creation of a free trade area (also abbreviated FTA). A free trade agreement represents a relatively low level of economic integration. (3)

**free trade area (FTA)**   A preferential trading bloc whose members have signed a free trade agreement (also abbreviated FTA) that entails reducing or eliminating tariffs and quotas. (3)

**free trade zone**   A geographical entity that may include a manufacturing facility and a warehouse. (8)

**freight forwarders**   Specialists in traffic operations, customs clearance, and shipping tariffs and schedules. (8)

**full-service advertising agency**   An advertising agency that provides services such as market research, media buying, and direct marketing in addition to creative campaign development. (13)

**General Agreement on Tariffs and Trade (GATT)**   The organization established at the end of World War II to promote free trade; also, the treaty signed by member nations. (3)

**generic strategies**   Michael Porter's model describing four different options for achieving competitive advantage: cost leadership, differentiation, cost focus, focused differentiation. (15)

**geocentric orientation**   The fourth level in the EPRG framework: the understanding that the company should seek market opportunities throughout the world. Management also recognizes that country markets may be characterized by both similarities and differences. (1)

**geocentric pricing**   The practice of using both extension and adaptation pricing policies in different country markets. (11)

**geographical structure**   A pattern of organization in which the operational responsibility for a geographical area of the world is assigned to line managers; the corporate headquarters retains responsibility for worldwide planning and control. (16)

**global advertising**   An advertising message whose art, copy, headlines, photographs, tag lines, and other elements have been developed expressly for their worldwide suitability. (13)

**global brand**   A brand that has the same name and a similar image and positioning throughout the world. (10)

**global brand leadership**   The act of allocating brand-building resources globally with the goal of creating global synergies and developing a global brand strategy that coordinates and leverages country brand strategies. (10)

**global company**   A company exhibiting a geocentric orientation that pursues marketing opportunities in all parts of the world using one of two strategies: either serving world markets by exporting goods manufactured in the home country market or by sourcing products from a variety of different countries with the primary goal of serving the home country market. Global operations are integrated and coordinated. (1)

**global competition**   A success strategy in which a firm takes a global view of competition and sets about maximizing profits worldwide, rather than on a country-by-country basis. (15)

**global consumer culture positioning**   A positioning strategy that seeks to differentiate a product, brand, or company as a symbol of, or associated with, global culture or a global market segment. (7)

**global elite**   A global market segment comprised of well-traveled, affluent consumers who spend heavily on prestige or luxury products and brands that convey an image of exclusivity. (7)

**global industry** An industry in which competitive advantage can be achieved by integrating and leveraging operations on a worldwide scale. (1)

**global market research** The project-specific gathering and analysis of data on a global basis or in one or more markets outside the home country. (6)

**global market segmentation** The process of identifying specific segments of potential customers with homogeneous attributes who are likely to exhibit similar buying behavior irrespective of their country of residence. (7)

**global marketing** The commitment of organizational resources to pursuing global market opportunities and responding to environmental threats in the global marketplace. (1)

**global marketing audit** A comprehensive, systematic examination of the marketing environment and company objectives, strategies, programs, policies, and activities. (16)

**global marketing strategy (GMS)** A firm's blueprint for pursuing global market opportunities that addresses four issues: whether a standardization approach or localization approach will be used; whether key marketing activities will be concentrated in relatively few countries or widely dispersed around the globe; guidelines for coordinating marketing activities around the globe; and the scope of global market participation. (1)

**global positioning system (GPS)** A digital communication system that uses satellite feeds to determine the geographic position of a mobile device. (17)

**global product** A product that satisfies the wants and needs of buyers in all parts of the world. (10)

**global retailing** Engaging in or owning retail operations in multiple national markets. (12)

**global strategic partnerships (GSP)** A sophisticated market entry strategy via an alliance with one or more business partners for the purpose of serving the global market. (9)

**global teens** A global market segment comprised of persons aged 12–19 whose purchase behavior is shaped by shared interest in fashion, music, and youth lifestyle issues. (7)

**government policy** A barrier to entry into an industry created by the policies instituted by the government. (15)

**gray market goods** Products that are exported from one country to another without authorization from the trademark owner. (11)

**greenfield investment** A market entry strategy that entails foreign direct investment in a factory, retail outlet, or some other form of new operations in a target country. (9)

**Group of Seven (G7)** Seven nations—the United States, Japan, Germany, France, Great Britain, Canada, and Italy—whose representatives meet regularly to deal with global economic issues. (2)

**Gulf Cooperation Council (GCC)** An association of oil-producing states that includes Bahrain, Kuwait, Oman, Qatar, Saudi Arabia, and the United Arab Emirates. (3)

**Harmonized Tariff System (HTS)** A system in which importers and exporters have to determine the correct classification number for a given product or service that will cross borders. (8)

**hedging** An investment made to protect a company from possible financial losses due fluctuating currency exchange rates. (2)

**high-context culture** A culture in which a great deal of information and meaning resides in the context of communication, including the background, associations, and basic values of the communicators. (4)

**high-income country** A country in which per capita GNP is $9,266 or greater. (2)

**hot spot** Any location that offers Wi-Fi access, e.g. hotels, airports, coffee shops, restaurants, etc. (17)

**hypercompetition** A strategy framework developed by Richard D'Aveni that views competition and the quest for competitive advantage in terms of the dynamic maneuvering and strategic interactions of firms in an industry. (15)

**hypermarket** A category of retail operations characterized by very large scale facilities that combine elements of discount store, supermarket, and warehouse club approaches. (12)

**image advertising** A type of corporate advertising that is used to inform the public about a major event such as a name change, merger, etc. (13)

**importing** Purchasing goods or services from companies located outside the home country. (8)

**incipient market** A market in which demand will materialize if particular economic, political, or sociocultural trends continue. (6)

**Incoterms** Internationally accepted terms of trade that impact prices. (11)

**individualism** In Hofstede's social values typology, the extent to which each member of society is primarily concerned with his or her interests and those of the immediate family. (4)

**infomercial** A form of paid television programming in which a particular product is demonstrated, explained, and offered for sale to viewers who call a toll-free number shown on the screen. (14)

**information overload** Overload that occurs when executives and other company personnel cannot effectively assimilate all the information available to them. (6)

**information technology (IT)** An organization's processes for creating, storing, exchanging, using, and managing information. (6)

**innovation adopter categories** In Rogers' diffusion of innovation framework, a way of classifying buyers in terms of their receptivity to new products: innovators, early adopters, early majority, late majority, laggards. (4)

**innovation adoption process** In Rogers' diffusion of innovation framework, a five-stage hierarchy that a person goes through when deciding to buy a new product: awareness, interest, evaluation, trial, and adoption. (4)

**integrated circuit (IC)** The silicon chip that gave modern form to the transistor and represented a milestone in the digital revolution. (17)

**integrated marketing communications (IMC)** An approach to the promotion element of the marketing mix that values coordination and integration of a company's marketing communication strategy. (13)

**intellectual property protection** The aspect of a country's legal environment pertaining to patent, trademark, and copyright protection. (5)

**intermodal transportation** The aspect of physical distribution that involves transferring shipping containers between land and water transportation modes. (12)

**international brand** A brand that is available throughout a particular world region. (10)

**international company** A company that pursues market opportunities outside the home country via an extension strategy. (1)

**international division structure** A pattern of organization design in which the executive in charge of the international division has a direct reporting relationship to corporate staff. (16)

**Internet** A network of computer networks across which e-mail and other digital files can be sent. (17)

**intranet** An electronic system that allows authorized company personnel or outsiders to share information electronically in a secure fashion while reducing the amount of paper generated. (6)

**invention** A demanding but potentially rewarding product strategy for reaching mass markets in less developed countries. (10)

**inventory management** The aspect of physical distribution that seeks to ensure that sufficient quantities of goods are available to meet demand or fulfill orders without incurring the extra costs associated with high inventory levels. (12)

**Islamic law** A legal system used in the Middle East that is based on a comprehensive code known as the sharia. (5)

**joint venture** A market entry strategy in which two companies share ownership of a newly-created business entity. (9)

**jurisdiction** The aspect of a country's legal environment that deals with a court's authority to rule on particular types of controversies arising outside of a nation's borders or exercise power over individuals or entities from different countries. (5)

*keiretsu* In Japan, an enterprise alliance consisting of businesses that are joined together in mutually reinforcing ways. (9)

**latent market** An undiscovered market segment in which demand for a product would materialize if an appropriate product were offered. (6)

**law of one price** A market in which all customers have access to the best product at the best price. (11)

**layers of advantage** A strategy for creating competitive advantage by building a wide portfolio of advantages. (15)

**leader** Someone whose job is to direct the efforts and creativity of everyone in the company toward a global effort that best utilizes organizational resources to exploit global opportunities. (16)

**lean production** An extremely effective, efficient, and streamlined manufacturing system such as the Toyota Production System. (16)

**least-developed countries (LDCs)** Terminology adopted by the United Nations to refer to the fifty countries that rank lowest in per capita GNP. (2)

**legal environment** A nation's system of laws, courts, attorneys, legal customs, and practices. (5)

**letter of credit (L/C)** A payment method in export/import in which a bank substitutes its creditworthiness for that of the buyer. (8)

**leverage** Some type of advantage—for example, experience transfers, leverage, or scale economies—that a company enjoys by accumulating experience in multiple country markets. (1)

**licensing** A contractual market entry strategy whereby one company makes an asset available to another company in exchange for royalties or some other form of compensation. (9)

**line extension** A variation of an existing product such as a new flavor or new design. (10)

**local brand** A brand that is available in a single country market. (10)

**local consumer culture positioning** A positioning strategy that seeks to differentiate a product, brand, or company in terms of its association with local culture, local production, or local consumption. (7)

**localization (adaptation) approach** The pursuit of global market opportunities using an adaptation strategy of significant marketing mix variation in different countries. (1)

**logistics management** The management process that integrates the activities of various suppliers and distribution intermediaries to ensure an efficient flow of goods through a firm's supply chain. (12)

**long-term orientation (LTO)** The fifth dimension in Hofstede's social values framework, LTO is a reflection of a society's concern with immediate gratification versus persistence and thrift over the long term. (4)

**loose bricks** A strategy for creating competitive advantage by taking advantage of a competitor whose attention is narrowly focused on a market segment or geographic area to the exclusion of others. (15)

**low-context culture** A culture in which messages and knowledge are more explicit and words carry most of the information in communication. (4)

**low-income country** A country with per capita GNP of less than $755. (2)

**lower-middle-income country** A country with GNP per capita between $756 and $2,995. (2)

**Maastricht Treaty** The 1991 treaty that set the stage for the transition from the European monetary system to an economic and monetary union. (3)

**management information system (MIS)** A system that provides managers and other decision makers with a continuous flow of information about company operations. (6)

**manufacturers' export representatives** Combination export management firms. (8)

**maquiladora** A program that allows manufacturing, assembly, or processing plants to import materials, components, and equipment duty-free; in return they use Mexican labor. (2)

**marginal-cost pricing** A pricing strategy that sets the selling price equal to the variable costs of producing one additional unit of output. (11)

**market** People or organizations with needs and wants and both the ability and willingness to buy. (2)

**market-based transfer price** A transfer pricing policy that sets prices for intracorporate transactions at levels that are competitive in the global market. (11)

**market capitalism** An economic system characterized by market allocation of resources and private resource ownership. (2)

**market entry strategy** The manner in which company management decides to pursue market opportunities outside the home country. (9)

**market expansion strategy** The particular combination of product-market and geographic alternatives that management chooses when expanding company operations outside the home country. (9)

**market holding** A pricing strategy that allows management to maintain market share; prices are adjusted up or down as competitive or economic conditions change. (11)

**market penetration** A pricing strategy that calls for setting price levels that are low enough to quickly build market share. (11)

**market skimming** A pricing strategy designed to reach customers willing to pay a premium price for a particular brand or for a specialized product. (11)

**market socialism** An economic system characterized by limited market resource allocation within an overall environment of state ownership. (2)

**marketing mix** Product, price, place, and promotion—the four Ps. (1)

**marketing model drivers** Key elements or factors that must be taken into account when evaluating countries as potential target markets. (7)

**marketing research** The project-specific, systematic gathering of data in the search scanning mode. (6)

**masculinity** In Hofstede's social values framework, the extent to which a culture's male population is expected to be assertive, competitive, and concerned with material success. (4)

**Maslow's hierarchy** A classic framework for understanding how human motivation is linked to needs. (10)

**matrix organization** A pattern of organization design in which management's task is to achieve an organizational balance that brings together different perspectives and skills to accomplish the organization's objectives. (16)

**merchandise trade surplus** A figure in a country's balance of payments showing that the value of the country's exports of manufactured goods exceeds the value of its imports of manufactured goods. (2)

**mixed allocation system** A system containing elements of both market and command allocation systems. (2)

**mobile commerce (m-commerce)** Conducting commercial transactions using wireless handheld devices such as personal digital assistants (PDAs) and cell phones. (17)

**most favored nation (MFN)** A privileged trading status in which a GATT signatory nation agrees to apply its favorable tariff or lowest tariff rate to all nations that are also signatories to GATT. (8)

**multidimensional scaling (MDS)** In market research, a quantitative data analysis technique that can be used to create perceptual maps. MDS helps marketers gain insights into consumer perceptions when a large number of products or brands are available. (6)

**multinational company** A company that pursues market opportunities outside the home country market via an adaptation strategy, i.e., different product, price, place, and/or promotion strategy than used in the domestic market. In a typical multinational, country managers are granted considerable autonomy; there is little integration or coordination of marketing activities across different country markets. (1)

**multisegment targeting** A marketing strategy that entails targeting two or more distinct market segments with multiple marketing mix offerings. (7)

**national advantage** Strategy guru Michael E. Porter's competitive advantage framework for analysis at the nation-state level. The degree to which a nation develops competitive advantage depends on four elements: factor conditions, demand conditions, the presence of related and supporting industries, and the nature of firm strategy. (15)

**nationalization** Broad transfer of industry management and ownership in a particular country from the private sector to the government. (5)

**negotiated transfer price** A transfer pricing policy that establishes prices for intracorporate transactions on the basis of the organization's affiliations. (11)

**newly industrializing economies (NIEs)** A term used to refer to upper-middle-income countries with high rates of economic growth. (2)

**niche** A single segment of the global market. (7)

**nontariff barriers (NTBs)** Any restriction besides taxation that restricts or prevents the flow of goods across borders, ranging from "buy local" campaigns to bureaucratic obstacles that make it difficult for companies to gain access to some individual country and regional markets. (1)

**normal trade relations (NTR)** A trading stratus under WTO rules that entitles a country to low tariff rates. (8)

**North American Free Trade Agreement (NAFTA)** A free trade area encompassing Canada, the United States, and Mexico. (3)

**observation** A method of primary data collection using trained observers who watch and record the behavior of actual or prospective customers. (6)

**offset** A countertrade deal in which a government recoups hard-currency expenditures by requiring some form of cooperation by the seller, such as importing products or transferring technology. (11)

**one-to-one marketing** An updated framework for direct marketing that calls for treating each customer in a distinct way based on his or her previous purchase history or past interactions with the company. (14)

**order processing** The aspect of physical distribution that includes order entry, order handling, and order delivery. (12)

**organic growth** In global retailing, a market expansion strategy whereby a company uses its own resources to open a store on a greenfield site or to acquire one or more existing retail facilities or sites from another company. (12)

**Organization for Economic Cooperation and Development (OECD)** A group of 30 nations that work together to aid in the development of economic systems based on market capitalism and pluralistic democracy. (2)

**organizing** The goal of creating a structure that enables the company to respond to significant differences in international market environments and to extend valuable corporate knowledge. (16)

**outlet mall** A grouping of outlet stores. (12)

**outlet store** A category of retail operations that allows marketers of well-known consumer brands to dispose of excess inventory, out-of-date merchandise, or factory seconds. (12)

**outsourcing** Shifting jobs or work assignments to another company to cut costs. When the work moves abroad to a low-wage country such as India or China, the term "offshoring" is sometimes used. (8)

**ownership** A market entry strategy that involves foreign direct investment for the purpose of acquiring or merging with another company. (9)

**paid search advertising** An Internet communication tactic in which companies pay to have their ads appear when users type certain search terms. (17)

**parallel importing** The act of importing goods from one country to another without authorization from the trademark owner. Parallel import schemes exploit price differentials between country markets. (11)

**patent** A formal legal document that gives an inventor the exclusive right to make, use, and sell an invention for a specified period of time. (5)

**pattern advertising** A communication strategy that calls for developing a basic panregional or global concept for which copy, artwork, or other elements can be adapted as required for individual country markets. (13)

**penetration pricing policy** A pricing strategy of setting price levels that are low enough to quickly build market share. (11)

**personal interview** Primary data collection via interactive communication (e.g., face-to-face, telephone, etc.) that allows interviewers to ask "Why"-type questions. (6)

**personal selling** One of four variables in the promotion mix; face-to-face communication between a prospective buyer and a company sales representative. (14)

**personal selling philosophy** A sales representative's commitment to the marketing concept coupled with a willingness to adopt the role of problem solver or partner in helping customers. The first step in the Strategic/Consultative Selling Model. (14)

**physical distribution** All activities involved in moving finished goods from manufacturers to customers. Includes order processing, warehousing, inventory management, and transportation. (12)

**piggyback marketing** A distribution strategy in which one manufacturer obtains product distribution by utilizing another company's channels. (12)

**platform** A core product design element or component that can be quickly and cheaply adapted to various country markets. (10)

**political environment** The set of governmental institutions, political parties, and organizations that are the expression of the people in the nations of the world. (5)

**political risk** The risk of a change in political environment or government policy that would adversely affect a company's ability to operate effectively and profitably. (5)

**polycentric orientation** The second level in the EPRG framework: the view that each country in which a company does business is unique. In global marketing, this orientation results in high levels of marketing mix adaptation, often implemented by autonomous local managers in each country market. (1)

**polycentric pricing** The practice of setting different price levels for a given product in different country markets. Also known as adaptation pricing policy. (11)

**positioning** The act of differentiating a product or brand in the minds of customers or prospects relative to competing products or brands. (7)

**positioning by benefit** A positioning strategy that seeks to differentiate a company, product, or brand in terms of one or more specific benefits (e.g., reliability) offered to buyers. (7)

**positioning by competition** A positioning strategy that seeks to differentiate a company, product, or brand by comparing it. (7)

**positioning by quality/price** A positioning strategy that seeks to differentiate a product, brand, or company in terms expensiveness/exclusivity, acceptable quality/good value, etc. (7)

**positioning by use or user** A positioning strategy that seeks to differentiate a product by associating it with users whose expertise or accomplishments are admired by potential buyers. (7)

**power distance** In Hofstede's social values typology, the cultural dimension that reflects the extent to which it is acceptable for power to be distributed unequally in a society. (4)

**preferential tariff** A reduced tariff rate applied to imports from certain countries. (8)

**preferential trading agreement** A trade agreement between a relatively small number of signatory nations, often on a regional or subregional basis. Such trade agreements can be characterized by different levels of economic integration. (3)

**presentation plan** In personal selling, the heart of the presentation strategy. The plan has six stages: approach, presentation, demonstration, negotiation, closing, and servicing the sale. (14)

**presentation strategy** Setting objectives for each sales call and establishing a presentation plan to meet those objectives. (14)

**price discrimination** The practice of setting different prices when selling the same quantity of like-quality goods to different buyers. (11)

**price escalation** The increase in an imported product's price due to expenses associated with transportation, currency fluctuations, etc. (11)

**price fixing** Secret agreements between representatives of two or more companies to set prices. (11)

**price transparency** Euro-denominated prices for goods and services that enable consumers and organizational buyers to comparison shop across Europe. (11)

**primary data** In market research, data gathered through research pertaining to the particular problem, decision, or issue under study. (6)

**private international law** The body of law that applies to disputes arising from commercial transactions between companies of different nations. (5)

**product** One of the four Ps of the marketing mix: a good, service, or idea with tangible and/or intangible attributes that collectively create value for a buyer or user. (10)

**product adaptation–communication extension strategy** A strategy of extending, without change, the basic home-market communications strategy while adapting the product to local use or preference conditions. (10)

**product-communication adaptation** A dual-adaptation strategy that uses a combination of marketing conditions. (10)

**product-communication extension** A strategy for pursuing opportunities outside the home market. (10)

**product differentiation** A product's perceived uniqueness that can serve as a barrier to entry in an industry. (10)

**product extension–communications adaptation strategy** The strategy of marketing an identical product by adapting the marketing communications program. (10)

**product invention** In global marketing, developing new products with the world market in mind. (10)

**product market** A market defined in terms of a particular product category. E.g., in the automotive industry, "the SUV market," "the sports car market," etc. (7)

**product placement** A marketing communication tool that involves a company paying a fee to have one or more products and brand names appear in popular television programs, movies, and other types of performances. (14)

**product saturation level** The percentage of customers or households that own a product in a particular country market; a measure of market opportunity. (2)

**product strategy** In personal selling, a sales representative's plan for selecting and positioning products that will satisfy customer needs. The third step in the Strategic/Consultative Selling Model. (14)

**product transformation** When a product that has been introduced into multiple country markets via a product extension/communication adaptation strategy serves a different function or use than originally intended. (10)

**pro forma invoice** A document that sets an export/import transaction into motion. The pro forma specifies the amount and the means by which an exporter wants to be paid; also specifies the items to be purchased. (8)

**psychographic segmentation** The process of assigning people to market segments on the basis of their attitudes, interests, opinions, and lifestyles. (7)

**public international law** The body of international law that pertains to non-commercial disputes between nations. (5)

**public relations (PR)** One of four variables in the promotion mix. Within an organization, the department or function responsible for evaluating public opinion about, and attitudes toward, the organization and its products and brands. PR personnel also are responsible for fostering goodwill, understanding, and acceptance among a company's various constituents and the public. (13)

**publicity** Communication about a company or product for which the company does not pay. (13)

**purchasing power parity (PPP)** A concept that permits adjustment of national income measurements in various countries to reflect what a unit of each country's currency can actually buy. (2)

**put option** The right to sell a specified number of foreign currency units at a fixed price, up to the option's expiration date. (2)

**quota** Government-imposed limit or restriction on the number of units or the total value of a particular product or product category that can be imported. (8)

**rational appeal** In advertising, an appeal to the target audience's logic and intellect. (13)

**reactivity** The tendency of research subjects to behave differently because they are being studied. (6)

**regiocentric orientation** The third level in the EPRG framework: the view that specific regions of the world are characterized by similarities as well as differences. In global marketing, a regiocentric orientation is evident when a company develops an integrated strategy for a particular geographic area. (1)

**regional management center** A pattern of organization in which there is an area or regional headquarters as a management layer between the country organization and the international division headquarters. (16)

**regional or worldwide product division structure** A pattern of organization in which the international responsibility is shifted from a corporate international division to the product division international departments, which in turn shift to total divisional organization. (16)

**regulatory environment** Governmental and non-governmental agencies and organizations that enforce laws or establish guidelines for conducting business. (5)

**relationship strategy** In personal selling, a sales representative's game plan for establishing and maintaining high-quality relationships with prospects and customers. The second step in the Strategic/Consultative Selling Model. (14)

**restrictive administrative and technical regulations** Regulations that can create barriers to trade; it may take the form of antidumping, size, or safety and health regulations. (8)

**ring tone**   A digital sound file that is an instrumental version of a song or composition. (17)

**ring tune**   A digital sound file of a song or composition featuring the original recording artist. (17)

**rules of engagement**   A strategy for creating competitive advantage that involves breaking these rules and refusing to play by the rules set by industry leaders. (15)

**rules of origin**   A system of certification that verifies the country of origin of a shipment of goods. (3)

**sales agent**   An agent who works under contract rather than as a full-time employee. (14)

**sales force automation (SFA)**   An information technology tool that automates lead assignment, contact follow up, and other routine tasks associated with personal selling. (6)

**sales promotion**   One of the four elements of the promotion mix. A paid, short-term communication program that adds tangible value to a product or brand. (14)

**sampling**   A sales promotion technique that provides potential customers with the opportunity to try a product or service at no cost. (14)

**search**   The environmental scanning mode characterized by formal information gathering activity. (6)

**secondary data**   Existing data in personal files, published sources, and databases. (6)

**self-reference criterion (SRC)**   The unconscious human tendency to interpret the world in terms of one's own cultural experience and values. (4)

**selling proposition**   In advertising, the promise or claim that captures the reason for buying the product or the benefit that product ownership confers. (14)

**short message service (SMS)**   A globally accepted wireless standard for sending alphanumeric messages of up to 160 characters. (17)

**single-column tariff**   A schedule of duties in which the rate applies to imports from all countries on the same basis; the simplest type of tariff. (8)

**social values typology**   A study by Dutch organizational anthropologist Geert Hofstede that classifies national cultures according to five dimensions: individualism versus collectivism; masculinity versus femininity; power distance; uncertainty avoidance; and long-term orientation versus short-term orientation. (4)

**sourcing decision**   A strategic decision that determines whether a company makes a product itself or buys products from other manufacturers as well as where it makes or buys. (8)

**Southern African Development Community (SADC)**   An association whose member states are Angola, Botswana, Democratic Republic of Congo, Lesotho, Malawi, Mauritius, Mozambique, Namibia, Seychelles, South Africa, Swaziland, Tanzania, Zambia, and Zimbabwe. (3)

**sovereignty**   A country's supreme and independent political authority. (5)

**spam**   Unsolicited "junk" e-mail received via the Internet; often sent to a large number of people to promote products or services. (17)

**specialty retailer**   A category of retail operations characterized by a more narrow focus than a department store and offering a relatively narrow merchandise mix aimed at a particular target market. (12)

**specific duty**   A duty expressed as a specific amount of currency per unit of weight, volume, length, or other unit of measurement. (8)

**sponsorship**   A form of marketing communication that involves payment of a fee by a company to have its name associated with a particular event, team or athletic association, or sports facility. (14)

**spreadsheet**   A software application in the form of an electronic ledger that automatically recalculates changes made to figures entered in rows and columns. (17)

**standardized (extension) approach**   The pursuit of global market opportunity using an extension strategy of minimal marketing mix variation in different countries. (1)

**standardized global marketing**   A target market strategy that calls for creating the same marketing mix for a broad mass market of potential buyers. (7)

**strategic alliance**   A partnership among two or more firms created to minimize risk while maximizing leverage in the marketplace. (9)

**Strategic/Consultative Selling Model**   A five-step framework for approaching the personal selling task: personal selling philosophy; relationship strategy; product strategy; customer strategy; and presentation strategy. (14)

**strategic intent**   A competitive advantage framework developed by strategy experts Gary Hamel and C. K. Prahalad. (15)

**streaming media**   The transmission of combined audio and video content via a broadband network. (17)

**streaming video**   A sequence of moving images sent in compressed form via the Internet and displayed on a computer screen. (17)

**subculture** Within a culture, a small group of people with their own shared subset of attitudes, beliefs, and values. (4)

**supercenter** A category of retail operations that combines elements of discount stores and supermarkets in a space that occupies about half the size of a hypermarket. (12)

**supermarket** A category of retail operations characterized by a departmentalized, single-story retail establishment that offers a variety of food and non-food items on a self- service basis. (12)

**supply chain** A group of firms that perform support activities by generating raw materials, converting them into components of finished goods, and making them available to buyers. (12)

**surveillance** The environmental scanning mode in which a marketer engages in informal information gathering via viewing or monitoring. (6)

**survey research** Primary data collection via questionnaire-based studies designed to generate qualitative responses, quantitative responses, or both. (6)

**switch trading** A transaction in which a professional switch trader, switch trading house, or bank steps into a simple barter arrangement or other countertrade arrangement in which one of the parties is not willing to accept all the goods received in the transaction. (11)

**switching costs** A barrier to entry into an industry created by the need to change suppliers and products. (15)

**targeting** The process of evaluating market segments and focusing marketing efforts on a country, region, or group of people. (7)

**tariffs** The rules, rate schedules (duties), and regulations of individual countries affecting goods that are imported. (8)

**telematics** A car's ability to exchange information about the vehicle's location or mechanical performance via a wireless Internet connection. (17)

**temporary surcharge** Surcharges introduced from time to time to provide additional protection for local industry and, in particular, in response to balance-of-payments deficits. (8)

**tiered branding** A strategy in which a corporate name is combined with a product brand name; also called combination or umbrella branding. (10)

**trade deficit** A negative number in the balance of payments showing that the value of a country's imports exceeds the value of its exports. (2)

**trade mission** A state- or federally sponsored show outside the home country organized around a product, a group of products, an industry, or an activity at which company personnel can learn about new markets as well as competitors. (8)

**trade sales promotion** Promotion designed to increase product availability in distribution channels. (14)

**trade show** A gathering of company representatives organized around a product, a group of products, or an industry, at which company personnel can meet with prospective customers and gather competitor intelligence. (8)

**trade surplus** A positive number in the balance of payments showing that the value of a country's exports exceeds the value of its imports. (2)

**trademark** A distinctive mark, motto, device, or emblem that a manufacturer affixes to a particular product or package to distinguish it from goods produced by other manufacturers. (5)

**transaction exposure** In global finance, the type of risk that is created when a company's sales or purchases of products or services are denominated in a foreign currency. (11)

**transfer pricing** The pricing of goods, services, and intangible property bought and sold by operating units or divisions of a company doing business with an affiliate in another jurisdiction. (11)

**transistor** A "solid state amplifier" that replaced vacuum tubes in electronics products; it was a milestone in the digital revolution. (17)

**transnational company** A company exhibiting a geocentric orientation that pursues marketing opportunities in all parts of the world. However, a transnational company differs from a global company by fully integrating and coordinating two strategies: both sourcing products from a variety of different countries and serving multiple country markets across most world regions. (1)

**transportation** The aspect of physical distribution that involves moving or transferring goods from one location to another. (12)

**transportation mode** In physical distribution, the particular means by which goods are shipped. The six main transportation modes are rail, water, truck, air, pipeline, and Internet. (12)

**Triad** The three regions of Japan, Western Europe, and the United States, which represented the dominant economic centers of the world. (2)

**two-column tariff** General duties plus special duties indicating reduced rates determined by tariff negotiations with other countries. (8)

**uncertainty avoidance** In Hofstede's social values framework, the extent to which members of a culture are uncomfortable with unclear, ambiguous, or unstructured situations. (4)

**upper-middle-income country** A country with GNP per capita between $2,996 and $9,266. (2)

**usage rate** In behavioral market segmentation, an assessment of the extent to which a person uses a product or service. (7)

**user status** In behavioral market segmentation, an assessment of whether a person is a present user, potential user, non user, former user, etc. (7)

**value** A customer's perception of a firm's product or service offering in terms of the ratio of benefits (product, place, promotion) relative to price. This ratio can be represented by the value equation: $V = B/P$. (1)

**value chain** The various activities that a company performs—e.g., research and development, manufacturing, marketing, physical distribution, and logistics—in order to create value for customers. (1)

**value equation** $V = B/P$, where V stands for "perceived value," B stands for "product, price, and place," and P stands for "price." (1)

**value network** The cost structure in a particular industry that dictates the margins needed to achieve profitability. A broadly-defined industry—e.g., computers—may have parallel value networks, each with its own metrics of value. (17)

**values** In culture, enduring beliefs or feelings that a specific mode of conduct is personally or socially preferable to another mode of conduct. (4)

**variable import levies** A system of levies applied to certain categories of imported agricultural products. (8)

**warehouse club** A form of retailing that offers low merchandise prices in a no-frills format. Consumers typically pay a nominal fee to join the club and gain entrance to the store. (12)

**warehousing** The aspect of physical distribution that involves the storage of goods. (12)

**wireless connectivity** Technology that allows a computer, cell phone, PDA, or other digital device to access the Internet without using a cable connection. (17)

**wireless fidelity (wi-fi)** Technology based on a low-power radio signal that permits access to the Internet from a laptop computer or PDA when the user is within range of a base station transmitter ("hot spot"). (17)

**World Trade Organization (WTO)** The successor to the General Agreement on Tariffs and Trade. (3)

# CREDITS

**CHAPTER 1**
Page 2: © 2004 R. Griggs Ltd. All rights reserved. Page 6: Used by permission of Southern Company. All rights reserved. Page 11: Courtesy of the Coca-Cola Company. Page 12: Courtesy of HSBC Bank USA. Page 24: Used by permission of Pfizer. All rights reserved. Page 31: Courtesy of AP Wide World Photos. Page 35: Courtesy of Getty Images, Inc-Liaison/Dan Hartung.

**CHAPTER 2**
Page 46: Courtesy of Network Photographers, Ltd. Page 50: Courtesy of AP Wide World Photos. Page 52: Courtesy of Corbis/Bettmann/Reuters. Page 55: Courtesy of Shawn G. Henry Photographer, Inc./Shawn G. Henry. Page 58: Courtesy of Library of Congress/Miguel Luis Fairbanks. Page 59: Courtesy of Bilderberg Archiv der Fotografen/Peter Ginter. Page 63: Courtesy of Peter Menzel Photography/Peter Menzel. Page 65: Courtesy of AP Wide World Photos. Page 79: Courtesy of AP Wide World Photos.

**CHAPTER 3**
Page 82: Courtesy of AP Wide World Photos. Page 93: Courtesy of Corbis/Bettmann/O'Rear.

**CHAPTER 4**
Page 118: Courtesy of Corbis/Bettmann/Michael Appleton. Page 118: Courtesy of Getty Images, Inc-Liaison/Pascal Le Segretain. Page 122: Courtesy of Rachel Donnan. Page 122: Courtesy of Getty Images, Inc-Liaison/Hugo Philpott. Page 127: Courtesy of AP Wide World Photos/Nathan Martin. Page 130: Courtesy of The Image Works/© Fujifotos. Page 147: Courtesy of Cafedirect. Page 147: Courtesy of The Image Works.

**CHAPTER 5**
Page 152: Courtesy of AP World Wide Photos. Page 158: Courtesy of IBERIA. Page 161: Courtesy of Corbis/Sygma/U.N. Page 163: Courtesy of The Image Works/Lee Snider. Page 166: Courtesy of Kimberly-Clark Corporation. Page 167: Reprinted by permission from the World Intellectual Property Organization, which owns the copyright. Page 184: Courtesy of AP Wide World Photos. Page 185: Courtesy of Landov LLC/Alejandro Ernesto.

**CHAPTER 6**
Page 193: Courtesy of Siebel Systems, Inc. Page 218: Courtesy of Corbis/Sygma/Copes Van Hasselt Johan. Page 224: Courtesy of Whirlpool Corporation.

**CHAPTER 7**
Page 252: Courtesy of U.S.A. Corporate Headquarters. Page 226: Courtesy of AP Wide World Photos. Page 239: Courtesy of Getty Images, Inc-Liaison/Oleg Nikishin. Page 256: © Apple Computer, Inc. Used with permission. All rights reserved. Apple® and the Apple logo are registered trademarks of Apple Computer, Inc. Page 259: Courtesy of AP Wide World Photos. Page 260: Courtesy of American Honda Motor Co. Inc.

## CHAPTER 8

Page 263: Courtesy of Corbis/Bettmann/Dean Conger. Page 277: Courtesy of Getty Images, Inc-Liaison/Barry Johnson. Page 283: Courtesy of Corbis/Bettmann/CRASTO/Reuters. Page 288: Used by permission of Bill Butcher. All rights reserved. Page 290: DOONESBURY © 1997 G. B. Trudeau. Reprinted by permission of UNIVERSAL PRESS SYNDICATE. All rights reserved.

## CHAPTER 9

Page 294: Courtesy of SABMiller. Page 296: Courtesy of The Image Works. Page 307: Courtesy of Ford Motor Company. Page 324: © 2004 DHL Express (USA), Inc. All rights reserved. Page 325: Courtesy of AP Wide World Photos.

## CHAPTER 10

Page 329: Courtesy of Landov LLC/Seokyong Lee/Bloomberg News. Page 343: Used by permission of The Walpole Committee Limited. All rights reserved. Page 360: Courtesy of AP Wide World Photos. Page 362: Courtesy of DaimlerChrysler Corporation.

## CHAPTER 11

Page 365: Courtesy of The Image Works/Jim West.

## CHAPTER 12

Page 402: Courtesy of AP Wide World Photos. Page 405: Courtesy of The Image Works/R. Lord. Page 409: © Copyright 2004. Dell Inc. Used by permission. All rights reserved. Page 418: Courtesy of Magnum Photos, Inc./I. Uimonen. Page 419: Courtesy of AP Wide World Photos/Richard Drew. Page 423: Courtesy of Corbis/SABA Press Photos, Inc. Page 427: Courtesy of AP Wide World Photos/Geff Hinds/The News Tribune. Page 433: Courtesy of Intermec Technologies Corporation.

## CHAPTER 13

Page 436: Used by permission of Chivas Brothers Import Co. Page 456: Used by permission of MINI Division. All rights reserved. Page 467: Courtesy of Landov LLC/Bloomberg News. Page 468: Courtesy of Adidas America.

## CHAPTER 14

Page 472: Courtesy of Getty Images, Inc – Liaison/Amanda Edwards. Page 495: Courtesy of AP Wide World Photos. Page 497: © Copyright Sony Ericsson. All rights reserved. Page 498: Courtesy of Samsung.

## CHAPTER 15

Page 503: Courtesy of The Image Works/Mark Antman. Page 506: Courtesy of PhotoEdit/David Young-Wolff. Page 510: Courtesy of Klipsch Audio Technologies. Page 529: Courtesy of AP Wide World Photos.

## CHAPTER 16

Page 531: Courtesy of Bertelsmann AG. Page 532: Courtesy of Landov LLC/Greg Stidham/HP/Via Bloomberg News.

## CHAPTER 17

Page 562: Courtesy of IAC InterActive Corporation. Page 563: Courtesy of Iowa State University Library. Page 569: © IBM. Used by permission. All rights reserved. Page 574: Reproduced with permission of Yahoo! Inc. © 2004 by Yahoo! Inc. YAHOO! and the YAHOO! logo are trademarks of Yahoo! Inc. Page 584: Courtesy of UMG. Page 584: Courtesy of Recording Industry Association of America (RIAA). Page 584: Copyright 2004. Electronic Frontier Foundation. Creative Commons license: Attribution Non Commercial 2.0. Some rights reserved. http://creativecommons.org/licenses/by-nc/2.0/

# AUTHOR/NAME INDEX

## A

Aaker, David A., 251n47, 337, 337n
Abramovich, Roman, 48
Adami, Norman, 300
Adams, Chris, 387n29
Adegoke, Yinka, 581n40
Adelman, David, 308
Adelt, Bruno, 558
Adler, Allen, 381
Aeppel, Timothy, 347n27
Ahluwalia, M. S. "Titoo," 124–125, 189
Ajami, Riad, 214n36
Albrecht, Katherine, 433–434
Albright, Katherine, 174n33
Alden, Dana L., 119n4, 254n48, 478n
Alden, Edward, 387n29
Alford, William P., 165n
Allen, John M., Jr., 179n40
Amerman, John, 148
Amorim, Celso, 85
Andreas, Wayne, 186
Andreesen, Marc, 564
Andrews, Edmund L., 267n3
Angell, Philip S., 159
Angwin, Julia, 571n18
Anholt, Simon, 342, 342n19, 466–467
Anthony, Myrvin L., 94n6
Arnault, Bernard, 396, 398, 510
Arnold, David, 205–206, 205n, 218, 218n41, 242n37, 245, 294n, 411, 411n,
Arnold, Wayne, 158n
Arriortúa, José Ignacio López de, 164, 198
Aschkenasy, Janet, 391n36
Ashcroft, Elizabeth, 5n7
Atanasoff, John Vincent, 562
Ayal, I., 321n59
Ayers, Richard H., 305

## B

Bach, Robbie, 471
Bahree, Bhushan, 83n
Bailey, James, 18
Ballard, John, 377
Bannon, Lisa, 38n18, 407n9
Barad, Jill, 149
Bardeen, John, 562
Barnard, Kurt, 408
Barnett, C., 537n16
Barnevik, Percy, 7
Barocha, Cyrus, 229
Barone, Michael, 242n36
Barrett, Amy, 132n33, 218n39
Barry, Hank, 586
Bartlett, Christopher A., 246n, 343, 343n, 352n37, 533, 537n14, 537n15, 545n29
Batra, Rajeev, 119n4, 254n48
Bean, Bruce, 159
Beatty, Sally, 348n, 237n28, 570n16
Beck, Ernest, 128n24, 240n31
Bell, Charlie, 35
Bell, Daniel, 61–62
Benetton, Luciano, 199, 467
Benezra, Karen, 213n33
Benner, Mike, 185

Bennett, Peter D., 3n, 401n, 200n12
Benoliel, Peter A., 536
Benou, Denise, 457
Berman, Dennis K., 579n35
Bernard, Daniel, 408
Berners-Lee, Tim, 564
Bernstein, Richard, 121n10
Berry, Clifford, 562
Bevan, Judi, 418n
Bezos, Jeff, 505, 570
Bhagwati, Jagdish, 93
Bickers, Charles, 256
Bigness, Jon, 426n
Bilkey, Warren J., 264n
Bingaman, Anne, 172
Blair, Tony, 62
Blanford, Larry, 22
Blatand, Harald, 579n33
Bleakley, Fred R., 75n, 378n12
Block, Paul, 248
Blumenstein, Rebecca, 21n30, 123n14, 357n46
Boatman, Tom, 569n12
Bond, Michael Harris, 119n2, 133n
Bono, 65
Borga, Maria, 298n11
Borrus, Amy, 175n35, 352n36
Botan, Carl, 463n39, 464n41
Boudette, Neal E., 244n40
Boulton, Leyla, 156n
Bounds, Wendy, 461n34
Bourgeois, Jacques C., 144n
Bové, Jose, 33
Bowen, David, 575n27
Bowes, Elena, 357n47, 461n35
Bowley, Graham, 194n7, 376n
Bowman, Hank, 223
Bradley, George, 510
Brand, Stewart, 563, 563n
Branson, Richard, 335, 336, 419, 420, 422, 461
Brattain, William, 562
Brauchli, Marcus W., 48n, 286n, 464n42, 479n
Brien, Nick, 440
Briscoe, Andrew, 291
Britt, Bill, 121n7
Brittan, Leon, 187
Bronfman, Edgar, Jr., 7
Brown, Chris, 236
Brown, Frank, 227
Brown, John, 176
Brown, Ron, 211
Browning, E. S., 351n34
Brusone, Giuseppe, 398
Buckingham, Simon, 581
Buckley, Neil, 227n8, 384n24, 385n28
Buckman, Rebecca, 47n5
Buffett, Warren, 330
Burke, Thomas, 493
Burns, Michael J., 547
Burns, Tom, 118n
Burrows, Steve, 185
Burt, Tim, 497n22
Burton, Thomas M., 129n31
Busch, Adolphus, 184
Busch, August, III, 184

Bush, George W., 77, 81, 83, 85, 104, 117, 125, 158, 188, 267, 291, 325, 386
Buss, Christian W., 144n
Byran, Lowell, 46n, 365, 365n
Byrne, John, 321n56

## C

Calian, Sara, 305n22
Camuffo, Arnald, 466n
Cantalupo, Jim, 34
Carcelle, Yves, 398
Cardoso, Henrique, 85
Carey, John, 168n19
Carey, Mariah, 495
Carey, Susan, 122n
Carp, Daniel, 528
Carrión, Julio, 114
Carter, Jimmy, 174
Carter, Meg, 121n8, 440n5
Castro, Fidel, 185–188
Cavanagh, John, 289
Cavusgil, S. Tamer, 9n12
Centerman, Jörgen, 7, 544–545
Champion, David, 424n24
Chandran, Rajan, 129n30, 454n27
Chan, Ricky Y. K., 405n5
Chang, Alan, 341
Chebat, Jean-Charles, 121n6
Chen, Kathy, 333n5
Chesbrough, Henry, 332
Cheung, Barry C., 464
Chew, W. Bruce, 369n4
Chipperfield, Lynn, 268
Chirac, Jacques, 58, 117, 291
Choel, Patrick, 398
Christensen, Clayton, 565n6, 566
Chwang, Ronald, 80
Ciccolella, Francesco, 529
Cipollaro, Michael, 308
Clark, C. David, 145
Clark, Don, 171n27
Clark-Meads, Jeff, 101n13
Clarke, Nigel, 237
Cleland, Kim, 494n19
Clinton, Bill, 77, 85, 109, 185–188, 288, 290, 386, 461
Clow, Lee, 468–470
Coad, Tony, 489
Cobb, Bill, 404
Cohon, George, 33
Coker, Robert, 291
Cole, Jeff, 286n
Coleman, Brian, 73n26
Coleman, Calmetta, 13n
Collins, Kim, 468–470
Colosio, Donaldo, 66
Cooper, Christopher, 375n8
Cooper, Helene, 58n, 83n
Cooper, Robin, 369n4
Corniou, Jean-Pierre, 190, 190n
Cox, James, 493n16
Craig, C. Samuel, 7, 7n
Crossen, Cynthia, 210n24
Crowley, Jerry, 410
Crumley, Bruce, 489n11

Cunningham, Isabella C. M., 454, 454n28
Cunningham, William H., 454, 454n28
Cutler, Bob D., 137, 137n42
Cutts, Robert L., 316n43
Czinkota, Michael R., 200, 200n13, 203n, 204, 204n, 265n

**D**

da Costa, Synesio Batista, 149
Daft, Douglas, 5
Dahlvig, Anders, 502
Daily, Patricia, 392n39, 393n41
D'Aveni, Richard, 296, 296n5, 523–525, 523n, 524, 524n
Davidow, William, 321, 321n57
Davidson, Andrew, 418n
Davies, Howard, 526, 526n29
Davies, Ross, 416n14
Davis, Bob, 180n42
Dawkins, William, 537n14
D'Cruz, Joseph, 512, 512n
Dean, James, 270n
Deane, Daniela, 227n9
de Gortari, Carlos Salinas, 153
de Leon, Rudy, 267
Delkin, Jeff, 450
Dell, Michael, 409
della Cava, Marco R., 145n52
Deming, W. E., 513
Deogun, Nikhil, 9n15
DePalma, Anthony, 302n16
Dholakia, Nikhilesh, 214n37
Di Benedetto, C. Anthony, 129n30, 454n27
Dickie, Jim, 192
Dickson, Richard, 150
Dierks, Michael, 173n31
Diller, Barry, 62, 561–562, 573
DiMasi, Joseph A., 23n
DiMassimo, Mark, 35
Dinh, Do Duc, 78
Dion, Celine, 134
Domzal, Teresa J., 254n49
Doney, Patricia M., 49n
Donnan, Shawn, 121n9
Donocki, Tadeusz, 402
Dorman, Jürgen, 7, 545
Dorrell, Beth, 272, 424
Douglas, Susan P., 7, 7n
Dovgan, Vladimir, 239
Doyle, Patrick, 227
Doz, Yves L., 311n34, 312n35
Draper, Matthew, 213
Dreazen, Yochi J., 378n12
Drew, Ernest, 534
Drossos, Basil, 21
Drucker, Jesse, 579n35
Drucker, Peter, 207, 208n21, 525, 556, 557n
Drummond, James, 378n14
Duncan, Thomas R., 436n
Dunne, Nancy, 157n, 387n29

**E**

Easton, Robert, 362
Eaton, Robert, 315
Eberhardt, Joe, 381
Eckert, Robert, 148, 150
Eckrodt, Rolf, 534
Edmonston, Jack, 213n35
Edwards, Francis, 495
Eggleton, Art, 187
Einstein, Albert, 121
Eisner, Michael, 139

Eizenstat, Stuart, 187
Elinder, Eric, 440, 440n6
Elkin, Tobi, 237n29
Elliot, Stuart, 237n26
Ellis, Paul, 526, 526n29
Ellison, Sarah, 241n33, 251n46, 474n3, 571n17
Emanuel, Carlos, 113
Enrico, Dottie, 453n24
Enright, Michael, 516n20
Erdem, S. Altan, 137n42
Erena, Sertab, 1
Everett, Stephen E., 436n

**F**

Fand, Jimmy, 282
Fatt, Arther C., 227n5
Feils, Dorothee J., 179n41
Ferreira, Joe, Jr., 75
Finney, Megan, 416n14
Fiorina, Carleton "Carly" S., 60, 531–532, 531n
Fireman, Paul, 211
Fisher, George, 217
Flagg, Michael, 415n12
Flask, A. Paul, 129
Fleming, Charles, 177n38
Flikkema, Luanne, 442, 442n11
Flynn, Lauren J., 368n
Fogel, Marya, 167n17
Ford, Richard, 235
Forelle, Charles, 226n1
Fortes, Isabela, 61
Fowler, Geoffrey A., 447n14, 450n17, 458n, 476n4
Fox, Vicente, 85
Fram, Eugene H., 214n36
Francés, Antonio, 516n20
Franck, Niklas, 575n26
Frank, Robert, 129n31, 227n9
Frank, Stephen E., 452n20
Fraone, Gina, 193n
Freidheim, Cyrus, 320
Fresco, Paolo, 532
Fressola, Peter, 466
Freston, Tom, 126
Friedland, Jonathan, 415n13
Friedman, Thomas L., 5, 5n4, 22, 26n34, 51, 71n
Friedrich, Jacqueline, 126n23
Frith, Katherine Toland, 137n41
Fritsch, Peter, 56n
Frost, Geoffrey, 452
Fry, Ron, 574
Fujimoto, Noboru, 332
Fuller, Chief Justice, 153
Fuller, Craig, 370

**G**

Gabriel, Peter, 587
Gabriella, Joseph, 383n23
Gallacher, Suzanne, 234–235
Galloni, Allesandra, 350n33
Gandhi, 189
Gandhi, Rajiv, 56
Garfield, Bob, 300, 467
Garten, Jeffrey E., 54n
Gates, Bill, 475, 563
George, Mike, 226
Gerlach, Michael L., 316n44
Gerstner, Lou, 7
Geyer, Hans-Herwig, 584
Ghazanfar, S. M., 392n39, 393n41

Ghoshal, Sumantra, 246n, 343, 343n, 352n37, 537n14, 537n15, 545n29
Ghosn, Carlos, 534, 536
Ghymn, Kyung-I, 123n13
Gibara, Samir, 534, 582
Gibson, Richard, 305n22
Gidwitz, Ronald, 305
Gifford, Kathie Lee, 288–289
Gilad, Benjamin, 220n
Gillis, Malcolm, 230n13
Gilly, Mary C., 454n27
Gilson, Ronald L., 316n45
Glocer, Tom, 534
Godin, Robert, 570
Goizueta, Roberto, 533
Golden, Peggy A., 49n
Goldschlager, Seth, 450
Gorbachev, Mikhail, 51
Gorog, Chris, 587
Gould, Stephen J., 436n, 497n23
Govindarajan, Vijay, 5n6
Grabner-Krauter, Sonja, 497n23
Grabowski, Henry G., 23n
Grant, Peter, 582n45
Grasee, Michael, 493
Greenberg, Jack M., 34
Greenberger, Robert S., 231n15
Greenbury, Richard, 418, 418n
Green, Peter S., 27n
Green, Robert T., 454, 454n28
Greider, William, 16, 47n2, 50, 50n, 52, 52n11, 393n40
Grein, Andreas, 436n
Gresser, Charis, 296n6
Griffith, Victoria, 334n7
Grunig, Larissa A., 463n38
Gupta, Anil, 5n6
Gupta, Pola B., 497n23
Gupwell, Yvonne, 78
Guth, Robert A., 6n9, 15n20, 375n9, 532n4
Gutierrez, Lucio, 112, 114
Gutzman, Alexis, D., 571n21, 575n24
Guyon, James A., 302n17

**H**

Hagenbaugh, Barbara, 285n
Hahn, Carl, 556, 557, 558
Halder, Dipankar, 20
Hall, Edward T., 132–133, 132n35
Hallett, Andrew Hughes, 94n6
Hallinan, Joseph T., 295n3
Halper, Donald G., 59n
Halpert, Julie Edelson, 321n58
Halstead, L. Lindsay, 307
Hamel, Gary, 310, 311n34, 312n35, 513–514, 513n, 516n17, 516n19, 534, 535n11
Hamied, Yusuf K., 395
Hamilton, David P., 303n18
Handler, Ruth, 148
Handy, Charles, 451
Hansell, Saul, 18n25
Hansen, Ronald W., 23n
Harding, James, 209n
Harich, Katrin R., 456n29
Harper, Lucinda, 378n12
Harris, Roy V., 360
Hassan, Fred, 534
Hassan, Salah S., 227n3
Hatfield, Joe, 198
Hauser, John R., 214n37
Hawkins, Lee, Jr., 243n
Hawkins, Tony, 108n
Hawley, Michael, 582
Hayek, Nicolas, 283

Healy, James R., 211n26
Heenan, David A., 311n32, 311n33, 313n
Hein, Kenneth, 199n11
Helms, Jesse, 186
Henderson, Angelo B., 315n
Henderson, Bruce, 505
Hengst, Rainer, 489, 489n12
Herington, Charles, 478
Herman, David, 333
Hershman, Michael, 63n21
Hershorn, Mark, 494
Herskovitz, John, 437n2
Herzegova, Eva, 453
Hewett, Kelly, 123n12
Higgins, Andrew, 159n
Hill, Jeffrey, 239
Hille, Kathrin, 341n17
Hilsenrath, Jon E., 47n5, 494n20
Hisey, Pete, 377n
Hoff, Edward J., 10n17
Hofstede, Geert, 119, 119n2, 133–138, 133n
Holden, Betsy D., 535
Hollinger, Peggy, 384n24
Holman, Michael, 107n, 108n
Holness, Stewart, 194
Holusha, John, 314n39
Hood, Marlowe, 126n22
Hopkins, Jim, 578n32
Hopp, Dietmar, 194
Horovitz, Jacques, 417n19
Houlder, Vanessa, 194n6, 197n
Howard, Donald G., 278n
Howell, Llewellyn D., 155
Howell, William R., 417
Hudgins, Edward L., 93, 267n5
Huff, Lenard C., 478n
Hughes, Louis R., 21
Hulme, Virginia, 405n5
Hunt, John, 543, 543n
Hussein, Saddam, 104
Hutton, Bethan, 137n43, 191n4, 432n
Hutzler, Charles, 375n9, 567n10
Hwang, Suein L., 242n36

I

Ibrahim, Abala, 149
Ibuka, Masaru, 136, 296
Illingworth, J. Davis, 207
Inamori, Kazuo, 409, 559–560
Inman, James E., 383n23
Iskander, H. F., 26

J

Jackson, Janet, 225
Jackson, Jesse, Jr., 109
Jackson, John, 187
Jackson, Michael, 184
Jackson, Paul, 259
Jackson, Tim, 419n, 421n
Jackson, Tony, 522n, 526n30
Jacobs, Laurence E., 123n13
Jacobs, Marc, 398, 570
Jager, Durk, 542
Jager, Melvin, 172
Jagger, Mick, 236
Jain, Dipak, 142, 142n
James, Canute, 94n7
Jansky, Petr, 185
Javalgi, Rajshekhar G., 137n42
Jayson, Darryl, 196
Jehl, Douglas, 149
Joachimsthaler, Erich, 337, 337n
Jobs, Steve, 297, 563
Johnson, David, 145

Johnson, Denise M., 49n
Jones, Daniel T., 545n30, 557
Jones, Harry, 162n10
Jones, Kevin K., 312n36
Jones, Norah, 585
Jonishi, Asa, 559
Jonquières, Guy de, 175n37
Joosten, Stan, 211
Jordan, Michael, 289
Jordan, Miriam, 61n, 239n, 417n18
Jung, Andrea, 407, 480

K

Kaempfe, Hasso, 350
Kahn, Bob, 563
Kahn, Gabriel, 207n19, 429n
Kahn, Joseph, 228n11, 269n7, 286n, 517n22
Kalish, Ira, 432
Kamm, Thomas, 98n11
Kamprad, Ingvar, 502
Kanabayashi, Masayoshi, 514n
Kanso, Ali, 441, 441n8
Kanter, James, 171n27
Kanter, Rosabeth Moss, 566, 566n8
Kao, John, 566n8
Kardisch, Josh, 164n13
Karmanoviene, Jurga, 448
Karp, Jonathan, 9n15, 98n10
Kashani, Kamran, 473–474, 474n2
Kasparov, Garry, 462
Katayama, Yutaka, 443
Katsanis, Lea Prevel, 227n3
Katsh, Salem M., 173n31
Katzenback, Jon R., 427n27
Kaufman, Leslie, 379n17
Kavner, Robert, 313
Kazmin, Amy, 97n
Keegan, Warren J., 338n12
Kellar, Maryann, 558
Keller, Kevin Lane, 330n1
Kelly, Jim, 388n32
Kelso, Charles D., 162n9
Kelso, Randall, 162n9
Kennedy, John F., 186
Keown, Charles, 123n13
Kerber, Ross, 304n
Kernaghan, Charles, 288
Kerwin, Kathleen, 207n20
Ketteringham, John, 334, 334n8,
    367n, 545n30
Khalaf, Roula, 106n
Khermouch, Gerry, 335n10
Khodorkovsky, Mikhail, 48
Kibble, Fergus, 569
Kilby, Jack, 562, 562n
Kim Dae Jung, 320
Kimmelman, Louis B., 177n39
King, Ben, 578n30
King, Neil, Jr., 175n36, 269n6, 379n15, 416n17
Kipkorir, Benjamin, 109
Kirk, Don, 27n
Kirkpatrick, David, 60n
Klaus-Dieter, Borchardt, 181n44, 181n45
Knight, Phil, 460
Kohler, Volkhard, 557
Kohnstamm, Abby, 7
Kotabe, Masaaki, 265n
Koykka, John, 185
Kranhold, Kathryn, 98n10, 212n30
Krempel, Marcie, 376
Krieger, Andrew, 70
Kristiansen, Kjeld Kirk, 529
Krugman, Paul, 49, 289
Kuczmarski, Thomas D., 354n41
Kullberg, Tommy, 511

Kumar, Nirmalya, 417n19
Kumar, V., 219n
Kuner, John, 259
Kurihara, Harumi, 569
Kuroki, Yasuo, 367
Kurylko, Diana, 333n6

L

Lafley, A. G., 542
LaLonde, Bernard, 427
Landau, Nilly, 346n
Landers, Peter, 332n3
Lansing, Paul, 383n23
Lardner, James, 136n38, 515n14
Lardy, Nicholas R., 51n
Latour, Almar, 580n38, 582n45
Lawton, Christopher, 246n
Lazareff, Alexandre, 126
Leavitt, Harold J., 339n
Lebedev, Platon, 48
Lee, James, 138–139, 138n45
Lee, Louise, 124n18
Leech, Paul, 298
Lei, David, 314n40
Leifsson, Andreas, 575n26
Lenicov, Jorge Remes, 92
Lenin, Vladimir, 50, 52
Leno, Jay, 125
Leong Ming Chee, 491
Lerman, Dawn B., 436n
Le Sante, William, 298
Leung, Shirley, 447n13
Levin, Diane, 326
Levin, Doron, P., 284n
Levin, Gary, 255n, 453n25
Levine, Ellen, 128
Levine, Joshua, 492n15
Levitt, Theodore, 9, 227, 441
Lewin, Tamar, 381n21
Lidstone, Digby, 121n7
Lifsher, Marc, 92n
Light, Larry, 34, 447, 535
Limbaugh, Rush, 125
Lindahl, Göran, 7, 544
Lindstrom, Martin, 326
Ling, Dennis, 75
Li Ning, 333
Linton, Ralph, 119n3
Liotard-Vogt, Pierre, 440
Lipin, Steven, 124n19
Lipman, Joanne, 9n13
Lister, John, 462
Loeb, Ronald, 150
Loftus, Peter, 568n
Londa, Bruce, 179n40
London, Simon, 566n7
Long Yongtu, 51
López de Arriortúa, José Ignacio, 558
Louis-Dreyfus, Robert, 468
Lubensen, Sigismundus W. W., 533, 536
Lublin, Joann S., 541n, 582n
Luqmani, Mushtaq, 164n12, 459n

M

Ma, Jack, 572
MacArthur, Kata, 570n14
Machalaba, Daniel, 427n28
Machan, Dyan, 239n
Mackintosh, James, 305n21
Macquin, Anne, 137n40
Madden, Thomas J., 123n12
Madonna, 134
Main, Jeremy, 310n28, 310n30
Major, John, 236

Malnight, T. W., 18n23
Malone, Michael, 321, 321n57
Maney, Kevin, 567n9
Manning, Gerald, 481n
Manuel, Gren, 580n37
Marcelo, Ray, 384n25
Maremont, Mark, 232n, 542n25
Margolis, Jonathan, 256
Marineau, Phil, 237
Marsh, Peter, 306n24
Martinez, Francisco, 433
Martinez-Mont, Lucy, 95n
Maruca, Regina Fazio, 508n5, 537n17
Maruyama, Yoshihiro, 475
Marx, Karl, 50, 51
Maslow, A. H., 339–341, 339n
Mason, John, 175n37
Mataloni, Raymond J., Jr., 298n11
Mathews, Anna Wilde, 172n29
Mathlouthi, Tawfik, 121
Maucher, Helmut, 5
Maynard, Micheline, 546n
McCartney, Neil, 535n10
McClellan, Mark, 370
McKay, Betsy, 6n8, 237n27, 240n31, 344n25
McKay, Graham, 293, 300
McKinstry, Nancy, 534
McLuhan, Marshall, 134, 563
McMenamin, Brigid, 172n30
McWilliams, Gary, 507n3
Meller, Paul, 387n30
Merchant, Khozem, 244n39
Merritt, Bruce G., 179n40
Micklethwait, John, 5, 5n5, 227, 227n7, 235n22, 267n4
Middelhoff, Thomas, 530, 538, 586
Mikes, Jiri, 448
Milbank, Dana, 341n18
Miles, Stephen, 492
Miller, Scott, 6n10, 102n, 378n14, 379n15
Miller, Stephen, 246
Millman, Joel, 89n, 241n34, 342n21
Mintzberg, Henry, 537, 537n18
Mitarai, Fujio, 536
Mitchener, Brandon, 121n10, 170n24, 171n27, 180n43, 347n28
Miyashita, Kenichi, 317n46
Moffett, Matt, 58n, 415n13
Moffett, Sebastian, 283n, 458n
Mohindroo, Pankaj, 384
Mohn, Liz, 538
Mohn, Reinhard, 538
Monahan, Jerome, 326
Mondavi, Michael, 18
Mondavi, Robert, 18n24
Montague, Claudi, 215n
Montera, Fernan, 437
Monti, Mario, 170
Moon, H. Chang, 59n
Moore, Gordon, 562n
Moore, Michael, 125, 460
Moore, Stephen D., 295n4
Moreira, Marcio, 453
Morita, Akio, 334, 367–368
Morrison, Allen J., 20n28, 540n21
Morrison, Dale, 218
Morrison, Robert J., 352
Morton, Ian, 236n24
Mossberg, Walter, 565, 565n5
Mote, Nick, 212
Moules, Jonathan, 579n34, 582n44
Moyer, Kerry, 510n7
Muhuad, Jamil, 112, 114
Mullich, Joe, 462n36
Münchau, Wolfgang, 63n20

Munk, Nina, 13n
Murdock, George P., 119, 119n3, 144
Murphy, Clarence, 407n9
Murphy, George, 535
Murphy, Michael, 476
Murray, Sarah, 298n10
Mussey, Dagmar, 493n17
Muthaura, Francis, 107

## N

Nairn, Geoffrey, 191n2
Nakamoto, Michiyo, 341n17
Nanoo, Suresh, 124
Narisetti, Raju, 570n15
Nasser, Jacques, 19, 46, 541
Naughton, Keith, 301n14
Nayak, Ranganath, 334, 334n8, 367n, 545n30
Nayak, Sapna, 32, 228
Negroponte, Nicolas, 426
Nelson, Emily, 211n28, 239n, 241n33, 542n23
Nelson, Mark M., 163n
Nessman, Karl, 462n37
Neumann, Gerhard, 313
Neumann, Jens, 558
Ning, Susan, 385n27
Niwa, Uichiro, 532–533
Nixon, Richard, 173–174
Noboa, Gustavo, 112
Normann, Richard, 424n25
Norval, Chris, 534
Noto, Lucio A., 582
Noyce, Robert, 562, 562n
Nuttal, Chris, 341n17, 578n29

## O

O'Connell, Vanessa, 569n13
O'Donnell, Rosie, 538
Ogura, Nobumasa, 405
Ohmae, Kenichi, 9n14, 10, 63, 310n29, 538
Ohno, Taiichi, 546
Okui, Toshifumi, 249
Olins, Rufus, 418n
Ollila, Jorma, 259, 533, 534, 576
O'Neill, Finbarr, 346, 534
Ono, Yumiko, 124n17, 128n25, 169n23, 296n7, 301n13, 442n10
Ore, Norbert, 285
Ortego, Joseph, 164n13
Orwall, Bruce, 405n7
Osborne, Magz, 227n6
O'Toole, John, 448, 449n15, 452, 452n21
Ouaki, Fabien, 130
Owen-Jones, Lindsay, 534
Owens, Jesse, 468

## P

Palmer, Kimberly, 350n32
Palmer, Stephen, 295
Panke, Helmut, 6, 244, 331
Pant, Muktesh, 377, 535
Parker-Pope, Tara, 66n, 250n44, 407n9
Parkes, Christopher, 210n25
Parveen, Zahida, 121
Patel, Marilyn Hall, 586
Patten, Tom, 443
Pawle, John, 206n
Pearl, Daniel, 98n10, 392n38
Pearson, Eric, 573
Peckter, Kerry, 533n5, 533n7, 536n
Pecoriello, Bill, 326
Peebles, Dean M., 438n
Pennar, Karen, 154n

Pentz, Michelle, 495n
Peppers, Don, 488, 488n
Pereira, Joseph, 212n29
Perlez, Jane, 270n
Perlmutter, Howard, 15n21, 311n32, 311n33, 313n
Perot, Ross, 66
Perry, Michael, 358
Peters, Tom, 537
Petsch, Greg, 284
Phillips, Michael M., 375n9
Phuc, Vu Tien, 78
Piëch, Ferdinand, 284, 353, 556, 558
Piirto, Rebecca, 236n25
Pines, Daniel, 174n34
Pischetsrieder, Bernd, 556–558
Pitofsky, Robert, 169
Platinin, Sergei, 237
Pondy, Louis R., 339n
Pope, Kyle, 98n11
Popeil, Ron, 493
Porter, Eduardo, 241n35
Porter, Michael, 5, 221, 503–526
Posner, Michael, 288
Potacki, Joseph, 477
Prahalad, C. K., 311n34, 312n35, 513–514, 513n, 516n17, 516n19, 534, 535n11
Press, Jim, 536
Prestowitz, Clyde, 319, 319n51, 319n52
Price, Christopher, 574n
Pringle, David, 581n42, 43
Pritchard, Marc, 474
Proctor, Paul, 542n26
Prystay, Cris, 212n31, 234n18, 491n
Pucik, Vladimir, 537n16
Putin, Vladimir, 45, 48, 156, 159
Pynder, Richard, 168n20

## Q

Queena Sook Kim, 345n23
Quelch, John A., 10n17, 473–474, 474n2
Quickel, Stephen W., 145n50
Quinlan, Joseph, 388
Quinlan, Michael R., 34
Quintanilla, Carl, 128n26
Quraeshi, Zahir, 164n12, 459n

## R

Raghavan, Anita, 170n24
Rai, Saritha, 228n10
Ramachandran, K., 234
Ramirez, Rafael, 424n25
Rangan, U. Srinivasa, 21n29, 309n25, 309n26, 310n31, 314, 314n41, 516, 517n21
Rao, C. P., 342n20
Rao, P. V. Narasimha, 56
Rapoport, Carla, 318n, 319n53
Rappoport, Jon, 497n22
Ratliff, William, 78
Ravaud, René, 313
Rawsthorn, Alice, 101n13, 128n27, 171n28, 234n19
Reagan, Ronald, 165, 174
Reece, Barry L., 481n
Reed, John, 19
Regan, Gary, 350
Regev, Motti, 124, 124n16
Reiling, Peter A., 148
Reiner, Gary, 354, 354n42
Reiter, Chris, 579n36
Reitman, Valerie, 405n6
Revzin, Philip, 182n46

Reynolds, Kim, 115
Ricard, Patrick, 439
Rice, Paul, 147–148
Richtel, Matt, 568n
Ricks, David A., 20n28, 540n21
Ridding, John, 333n5
Ridgley, Marie, 125
Riedman, Patricia, 573n
Ries, Al, 250, 250n45, 251
Risher, Jeff C., 383n22
Ritzer, George, 130, 130n
Roberts, Bruce, 353
Robertson, Thomas, 355n
Robottom, David, 490
Roddick, Anita, 253
Rodgers, Susannah, 390n33
Roedy, William, 229, 437, 443
Roe, Mark J., 316n45
Rogers, Everett, 139–143, 139n, 264n
Rogers, Martha, 488, 488n
Rohter, Larry, 28n
Rohwedder, Cecilie, 218n40, 295n3
Rokeach, Milton, 120n
Rollins, Kevin, 507
Romano, Pietro, 466n
Ronkainen, Ilkka, 200, 200n, 203n,
    204, 204n
Roos, Daniel, 545n30
Root, Franklin, 160n7, 167n18, 295n2,
    297n, 299n
Rose, John, 581
Rose, Robert L., 514n
Rosenbaum, George, 570
Rosser, Brad, 357
Ross, Lester, 385n27
Ross, Martin, 137, 138, 138n44, 454
Rosso, Renzo, 128, 234
Roth, Kendall, 20n28, 540n21
Roth, Martin S., 123n12
Rothenberg, Randall, 449, 449n16
Rothman, Randall, 4n3
Rouziès, Dominique, 137n40
Rowe, Brian, 313
Rowling, J. K., 325–327
Ruggiero, Renato, 83
Rugman, Alan, 512, 512n, 526, 526n28
Russel, George, 101n12
Russell, David, 317n46
Ryan, Leslie, 477n
Ryans, John K., Jr., 227n4

S

Saatchi, Lord, 338, 338n13
Sabac, Florin M., 179n41
Safire, William, 370
Salgado, Ricardo, 89
Samli, A. Coskun, 227
Saporito, Bill, 145n51
Scardino, Marjorie, 534
Schaffer, Matt, 390n34
Schaninger, Charles M., 144n
Scheele, Nick, 534
Scheer, David, 575n25
Schifrin, Matthew, 310n27
Schill, Walter E., 312n36
Schlesinger, Jacob M., 378n12
Schmitt, Bernd, 344
Schrage, Elliot, 289
Schulte-Hillen, Gerd, 538
Schütte, Hellmut, 143n, 340, 340n16
Schwab, Charles M., 173
Schwartz, John, 210n25
Schweitzer, Louis, 27
Sciolino, Elaine, 450n18

Scott, Edith, 516n20
Sculley, John, 297
Secunda, Eugene, 497
Selya, Bruce, 169
Sengupta, Subir, 137n41
Serafin, Raymond, 381n20
Serf, Vint, 563
Sevastopulo, Demetri, 577n
Severino, Rodolfo, 97
Shaiken, Harley, 66
Shane, Scott A., 136n39
Shansby, J. Gary, 251n47
Shapiro, Alan C., 47n3
Shapiro, Dan, 515n15
Shari, Michael, 208n22
Sharpe, Melvin L., 463n40
Sherman, Cary, 587
Sherman, Stratford, 532n3
Shih, Stan, 35–37, 79–80, 515
Shingo, Shigeo, 546
Shirouzu, Norihiko, 17n, 231n14,
    317n49, 416n15,
    416n16, 534n8
Shockley, William, 562
Shriver, Jerry, 132n34
Shuh, Arnold, 104n
Sicilia, David B., 414n
Siddiqi, Moin A., 105n
Silva, Joshua, 352
Silver, Sara, 344n24
Simison, Robert L., 356n45
Simon, Hermann, 250n43
Sinclair, Christopher, 356
Singh, Manmohan, 56, 98
Sinha, Yashwant, 57
Sirhall, Larry, 481n
Sloan, Pat, 248n
Slocum, John W., Jr., 314n40
Slomanson, William R., 160n8
Slywotzky, Adrian J., 35, 230, 230n12
Smith, Alison, 335n9, 437n3
Smith, Craig S., 123n14, 158n, 286n, 404n4
Smith, Douglas K., 427n27
Smith, Elliot Blair, 342n21
Smith, Ethan, 571n20
Smith, Jerald R., 49n
Smith, Roland, 310
Smyser, Collin G., 383n22
Solomon, Charlene Marmer, 533n6
Son, Masayoshi, 572
Sonder, Claudio, 534
Song, Meeyoung, 128n28
Sorrell, Martin, 451, 453
Soss, Neal, 154
Spears, Britney, 585
Spielvogel, Carl, 9
Spodek-Dickey, Cindy, 199
Spotts, Harlan E., 454n27
Squeo, Anne Marie, 582n45
Stallman, Richard, 577
Stamminger, Erich, 535
Stanislaw, Joseph, 25, 25n, 51, 52n10
Stanley, Richard, 153
Staseson, Heidi, 349n
Steel, David, 534
Steel, John, 352
Steenkamp, Jan-Benedict, 119n4, 254n48
Steinberg, Bruce, 441
Steinmetz, Greg, 128n26, 379n16
Stengel, Jim, 535
Stepanowsky, Paula, 234n20
Stern, Gabriella, 351n35, 454n26
Sterngold, James, 423n
Stille, Alexander, 132n34
Stitzer, Todd, 534

St. Laurent, Yves, 166
Stobel, Klaus, 249
Stokes, Martin, 123n15
Strube, Jürgen, 538
Sugiyama, Sam, 149–150
Suharto, President, 33, 57, 153, 156
Sutai, Yuan, 303
Suzuki, Takayuki, 422
Swasy, Alecia, 378n13

T

Tagliabue, John, 27n, 234n21
Tahmincioglu, Eve, 298n9
Takada, Hirokazu, 142, 142n
Takahashi, Dean, 515n16
Takahashi, Toru, 537
Tamate, Miriko, 129n30, 454n27
Tan, Tony, 127
Tarantino, Quentin, 2
Taylor, Alex, III, 235n23, 380n19
Taylor, Frederick, 537
Taylor, William C., 10n16, 26n33, 532n2,
    538n, 544n
Tedeschi, Bob, 571n19, 581n39, 581n41
Thielen, Gunter, 530, 538, 554
Thomas, Bob, 443
Thornton, Dean, 393
Thurow, Roger, 452n22
Thurso, Lord, 396
Tichy, Noel M., 532n3, 537n16
Tierney, Christine, 353n40
Tilley, Barry, 453–454
Tingzon, Manolo, 127
Tokunaka, Teruhisa, 375
Tomkins, Richard, 497n24
Torvalds, Linus, 577
Toscani, Oliviero, 466, 467
Trachtenberg, Jeffrey A., 511n9
Tran, Khanh T. L., 212n32
Tran, Phil, 78
Trani, John, 306
Trichet, Jean-Claude, 116
Trotman, Alexander, 19, 533
Trout, Jack, 250, 250n45, 251
Trudeau, Garry, 290
Tucker, Emma, 170n25, 171n28, 385n28
Tuckman, Johanna, 90n

U

Uchitelle, Louis, 306n23, 340n15
Unger, Lynette, 254n49
Urban, Glen L., 214n37
Uva, Joe, 497

V

Vagts, Detlev, 171n26
Valdez, Humberto Garza, 241
Valle, Emerson do, 224
Varoli, John, 240n32
Vega, Ralph de la, 580
Verbeke, Lain, 526n28
Verity, John W., 194n6
Vermeulen, Karla, 166n16
Vernon, Kim, 535
Verzariu, Pompiliu, 391, 391n35
Viault, Raymond, 582
Villalonga, Juan, 118
Vinelli, Andrea, 466n
Viscounty, Perry J., 383n22
Voigt, Kevin, 128n29
Von Braun, Wernher, 121
Vuursteen, Karel, 332

## W

Wagoner, Rick, 305
Wagstyl, Stefan, 402
Wai-Chan Chan, 429
Walsh, Nick Paton, 240n32
Walton, Sam, 229
Waner, Fara, 416n16
Wang, J. T., 80
Ward, Andrew, 341n17, 578n31
Ward, Stephen, 578
Warner, Fara, 124n19,
        125n, 457n
Waslekar, Sundeep, 233n
Wassener, Bettina, 350n31
Waters, Richard, 226n2, 507n4
Watson, Alexander, 186
Watson, Brian, 77
Webber, Alan M., 10n16, 26n33, 532n2,
        538n, 544n
Weedfald, Peter, 447
Weinberger, Marc G., 454n27
Weiss, Nelio, 169
Weisz, Pam, 353n38
Welch, Jack, 14, 19, 532
Wells, Ken, 441n9, 443n
Wells, Melanie, 453n24
Wentz, Laurel, 358n
Werner, Helmut, 362, 380
Wessel, David, 62n18, 379n16
Wessels, Maja, 347
Westhead, Keith, 259
Whalen, Jeanne, 452n19
Whelen, Tensie, 148
While, Gregory, 211n27
White, Erin, 447n13, 456n30

White, Gregory L., 302n15
White, Joseph B., 121n6, 243n, 547n
Whitehorn, Will, 461
Whitwam, David, 8, 25–26, 223, 224, 508,
        532, 537, 543–544
Wiebusch, Bruce, 353n39
Wiersema, Fred, 566n8
Wijm, Annemieke, 148
Wilhelm, Paul, 386–387
Wilke, Jerry G., 249
Wilke, John R., 169n21,
        22, 388n31
Williams, Frances, 11n, 166n15
Williams, Michael, 545n30
Williams, Peter, 422
Williams, Venus, 212
Williamson, Marlene, 36
Willman, John, 73n25, 126n21,
        330n2, 332n4
Wingfield, Nick, 404n3, 571n20
Winterhalter, Jürgen, 250
Witt, Jerome, 342n20
Womack, James P., 545n30
Wonacott, Peter, 199n10, 243n
Wong, Karen, 212
Won, Grace, 174n33
Woo-Choong, Kim, 303
Woodruff, David, 545n29
Woodside, Arch G., 121n6
Wooldridge, Adrian, 5, 5n5, 227, 227n7,
        235n22, 267n4
Worthly, Reginald, 123n13
Wozniak, Steve, 563
Wynter, Leon E., 452n23
Wysocki, Bernard, 314n38

## Y

Yajima, Hiroshi, 230–231
Yang, Michael, 303–304
Yasin, Yevgeny, 48
Yavas, Ugur, 164n12, 459n
Yeats, Alexander, 93
Yeltsin, Boris, 45, 156
Yeoh, Datuk Francis, 479
Yergin, Daniel, 25, 25n, 51, 52n10
Yip, George S., 535n12
Yorke, Susan, 349
Yoshino, Michael Y., 21n29, 309n25,
        309n26, 310n31, 314, 314n41,
        516, 517n21
Young, Andrew, 290
Yudashkin, Valentin, 237

## Z

Zachary, G. Pascal, 213n34, 516n18
Zandpour, Fred, 456n29
Zaun, Todd, 374n, 534n9
Zeien, Alfred, 334, 340
Zeller, Laurent, 415
Zellner, Wendy, 415n13
Zennstrom, Niklas, 582
Zhang Ruimin, 333
Zhu Rongji, 56
Zietsche, Dieter, 380
Zif, J., 321n59
Zimmerman, Ann, 191n3
Zoellick, Robert, 81, 159
Zou, Shaoming, 9n12
Zuccaro, Bruno, 199
Zumwinkel, Klaus, 324, 325

# SUBJECT/ORGANIZATION INDEX

## A

ABB Inc., 7, 27, 544
ABC Television, 561
Absolut vodka, 344, 435, 449
Abstract culture, 119
ACC. *See* Arab Cooperation Council
Accommodations.info, 573
Acer Group, 427
Acer, Inc., 35–37, 64, 244, 515
Acquisition, 420–421
Acquisitions and mergers, 298–299, 303, 306
    driving force behind, 305
    Jaguar PLC, by Ford, 307
Actionable creativity, 451
Active listening, 484
Adam Opel AG, 333
Adaptation, 244, 248
    global product platform and, 356–357
Adaptation approach, to marketing, 18
Adaptation pricing, 381
Adaptation strategy. *See* Product and brand
        decisions
Adaptation versus standardization, 8–9
Adidas AG, 191, 254, 377, 496
Adidas-Salomon AG, 290, 468–479, 535
Administrative Council of Economic
        Defense (Brazil), 169
Admiration needs, 341
Adolph Coors, 484
Adopter categories (diffusion theory),
        141–142, 143
Adoption process (diffusion theory), 140
ADR. *See* Alternative dispute resolution
        (ADR)
Ad valorem duty, 274
Advanced countries, 61–63
Advanced Micro Devices (AMD), 320
Advertising. *See also* Public relations and
        publicity
    across national boundaries, 22
    actionable creativity, 451
    advocacy, 461
    agencies, 443–447
    appeal, 449
    art directors and direction, 450
    big idea, 448–449
    color perceptions and, 452
    content, 439–443
    copy and copywriters, 450–452
    corporate, 154, 460
    creating, 447–456
    creative execution, 449
    creative strategy, 448
    cross-national collective/individual
        differences, 137
    cultural considerations, 441, 452–456
    defined, 437
    difficulties, 439–449
    economies of scale and, 439
    emotional appeal, 449
    expenditures for, top countries (table), 457
    focus groups for, 211–212
    food and, 453–454
    Hofstede's social values framework and,
        454–455
    humorous, 452

image, 460–461
Internet, 569–571
"in your face," 452
Japanese versus American, 454
localized, 441–443
man-woman relationships, 452
McDonald's, 31, 34
media decisions, 456–459
memorable campaigns, 449
music in, 124
one world, one voice, 440
paid search (Web), 571
pattern, 441
rational appeal, 449
selling proposition, 449
sexual innuendo in, 350
sexually explicit or provocative imagery,
        452–453
standardization versus adaptation
        debate, 439–443
of tampons, 238–239
television, 210
tobacco, 448
top 20 organizations (table), 444
top marketers (table), 438
uncertainty avoidance and, 136
word-of-mouth buzz, 137
worldwide expenditures, 438
Advertising agencies, 443–447
Advertising appeal, 449
Advertising organizations, 443
Advisory, Conciliation and Arbitration
        Service (ACAS), 179
Advocacy advertising, 461
AeroFlot, 361
Aerosmith, 495
Aesthetics, 121–124
    of products, 345–346
Aesthetic styles, 122, 345
Affiliation needs, 340–341
Affluent Materialists (European
        consumer), 236
Affluent (Sony's U.S. consumer
        segment), 237
Afghanistan, 104
Africa, 62, 103, 147, 286, 567. *See also*
        Regional markets
    market attractiveness, 60
    McDonald's sales in, 31
African Americans, 148, 229, 241
African Growth and Opportunities
        Act, 109
AFTA. *See* ASEAN Free Trade Area (AFTA)
AGB, 210
Age. *See also* Generation Y; Global teens
    of car buyers, and brands bought
        (table), 260
    demographic of, 228
    of European Union population, 228
    under-16 age segment (Asia), 124
Age segmentation, 234
Agent, 276, 403
Agility, as marketing company principle, 42
Agnostic marketing, 567
Agreement on Customs Valuations, 274
Agreement on Textiles and Clothing, 109

Agreement on Trade-Related Aspects of
        Intellectual Property Rights
        (TRIPs), 173
Agriculture, subsidies for, 291, 378–379. *See
        also* Farmers
AIDS
    drugs for, smuggling and, 381
    pricing drugs in emerging markets,
        395–396
AIG, 154, 404
Air Canada, 310
Air New Zealand, 310
Air transportation, 426
Airborne, 324, 424
Airbus, 313, 360–361
Airline industry, 17, 171
Airlines Group, 310
Albania, 53, 156
Albertson's, 414
Aldi Gruppe, 414
Algeria, 53, 105
Allegra, 364
Alliance, 303
Allianz, 15
Alternative dispute resolution (ADR), 177
Altoids breath mints, 344
Altria Group, 10, 17
Aluswiss, 393
Amazon.com, 191, 505, 567, 570, 571, 573
Amazonia handbags, 60–61
America Online (AOL), 170, 478. *See
        also* AOL
America Online Latin America, 478
American Arbitration Association (AAA),
        178, 179
American Automobile Labeling Act, 345
American Brands, 186
American Express, 57, 69, 209, 234, 336, 489
American Furniture Manufacturers
        Committee for Legal Trade, 268
American International Group, 14, 15
American Marketing Association, 200, 401
American Standard, 78
American Sugarbeet Growers
        Association, 291
American Trucking Association, 425
Ammirati Puris Lintas, 208
Amstel, 293
AMU. *See* Arab Maghreb Union
Amway, 404, 406
Analogy, market estimation by, 217–218
Analysis of variance (ANOVA), 215
Analysis paralysis, 480
Anatomy of marketing, 43
Andean Community, 85, 90–92, 95
Andean Pact, 90
Andersen Consulting, 197, 407
Angola, 53, 108, 109, 174
Angotti, Thomas, and Hedge, 461
Anheuser-Busch, 184–185, 300, 301, 540
ANOVA. *See* Analysis of variance (ANOVA)
Anti-American sentiment, 121
Anticipation, as marketing company
        principle, 39
Antidumping and Antisubsidy Regulations
        (China), 385

Antidumping duties and regulations, 268, 271, 275
Antigua, 94
Antitrust laws, 153, 169–172
    investigations (table), 170
    keiretsu system and, 317
AOL, 571. *See also* America Online
    Europe, 530
    software, 368
    Time Warner, 27, 325, 326, 571
A&P, 414
A.P. Moller/Maersk, 171
Apple Computer, 48, 521
    beginning of, 563
    iPod, 256, 297, 587
    iTunes, 587
    iTunes Music Store, 297, 568, 586
    lost opportunity, 297
    new era for, 297
    online music services, 583
    positioning of products, 256
    sales promotion, 477
    shipping method, 428
    Singapore and, 97
    streaming media software, 578
Approach step, in personal selling presentation plan, 484
Arab Cooperation Council (ACC), 105
Arab Maghreb Union (AMU), 105
Arbitrary monetary policy, 271
Arbitration, 177–178, 179
Archer Daniels Midland, 186, 387
Argentina, 53, 113, 123, 139, 149, 415, 419
    big emerging market (BEM), 54
    Coca-Cola in, 344
    GNP, 92
    population, 92
    privacy issues, 575
    as upper-middle-income country, 58
Armani, 17, 396–399
Armenia, 53, 299
Arm's-length formula, 389
Arrival draft, 281
Art directors and direction (advertising), 450
Artificial intelligence, 197
Asatsu-DK, 444
ASCII (American Standard Code for Information), 573
ASEAN. *See* Association of Southeast Asian Nations (ASEAN)
ASEAN Free Trade Area (AFTA), 97
Asia, 315, 386, 421, 487, 511, 567. *See also individual countries*
    coupon use in, 476–477
    direct marketing in, 490–491
    infomercials in, 494
    media allocation in (advertising; table), 458
    MTV in, 229
    nonverbal communication in, 129
    privacy issues, 575
    under-16 age segment, 124
    Wal-Mart in, 432–433
Asia-Pacific, 66
    ASEAN, 96–97
    Disney sales, 295
    economic growth of, 265
    marketing issues in, 97–98
    McDonald's sales in, 31–33
Asiana, 310
Asian Americans, 148, 229, 241
Asian consumers, hierarchy of needs of, 340–341
Asian economic miracle, 64

"Asian flu," 54, 78, 375
Asian tigers, 54
AsiaSatI, 234
Assembly lines, 283
Assets, seizure of, 160–161
Association of Southeast Asian Nations (ASEAN), 77, 96
Associative counterfeit, 165
Asunción Treaty, 92
Atanasoff-Berry Computer (ABC), 562
Atari, 563
AT&T, 77, 192, 220, 296–297, 313–314, 320, 336, 338, 562, 582
Attitudes, 119, 120
Attributes, of products, 251, 329
Atwood Richards, 391
Auchan, 413, 414
Auctions, online, 404. *See also* eBay
Audio Research, 509
Audits. *See* Global marketing audit
Australia
    antidumping regulations, 386
    Avon Products in, 407
    Colgate Total toothpaste testing in, 352
    Corona beer in, 344
    corruption ranking, 174
    "Dial-a-Coke," 580
    e-Bay in, 572
    European Union sugar exporting policy and, 291
    free trade agreements, 84
    Gateway survey in, 442
    GMOs and, 151
    Harley-Davidson in, 249
    index of economic freedom, 53
    mandatory labeling in, 345
    McDonald's in, 233
    Patent Cooperation Treaty and, 167
    privacy issues, 575
    technology transfer laws, 172
    tobacco advertising regulations, 448
Austria
    beer culture of, 350
    cultural perceptions in, 455–456
    EU member, 101
    euro zone charter member, 100
    Euroland member, 115
    Globalink in, 463
    GNP, 99
    Hofstede's cultural typology rankings (table), 135
    index of economic freedom, 53
    low-power distance and, 133
    masculinity behavior, 134
    population, 99
    salesperson characteristics needed, 136
    tariff elimination, 268
    taxes in, 376
    television advertising in, 459
Austrian, 310
Austrian Public Relations Association, 462
Authoritarian state capitalism, in Singapore, 52
Automobile industry. *See also individual makers*
    currency fluctuations and, 373
    foreign consumer culture positioning (FCCP) in, 257
    foreign, United States market and, 243
    Generation Y and, 260–261
    global competition in, 517
    as global industry, 13
    global product platform and, 356–357
    Hispanic market and, 241

    incipient market in China, 208–209
    Jaguar PLC acquisition, by Ford, 307
    joint ventures, 301–302, 310–311
    lean production in, 545–548
    market entry options (table), 304
    marketing mix offerings, 250
    price differences in European Union (table), 376
    in Russia, 302
    sport utility vehicles (SUVs), 243
    threats to U.S. industry, 24
    Volkswagen in the United States, 353
AutoPacific Toyota, 243
Aventis, 23
Avon Products, 56, 189, 404
    Asian currency crisis as opportunity, 74–75
    in China, 406
    as global brand, sales and, 339
    global door-to-door selling, 406
    market entry, 306
    Mexican sales, 66, 72–73
    piggyback marketing, 407
    in Russia, 405
    store representatives, in, 480
AvtoVAZ, 302
Azerbaijan, 53, 174, 299

**B**

BAA McArthurGlen, 128
Back translation, 209
Backer Spielvogel Bates Worldwide, 9, 77
Bahamas, 53, 94
Bahrain, 53, 104, 105
Baja Fresh, 31
Balance of payments, 66–68
*Balance of Payments Statistics Yearbook* (IMF), 67
Banana exports, 113
Bandai, 149
Bandwidth, 576
Bangkok Declaration, 96
Bangladesh, 53, 174, 266, 427
    per capita GNP, 55
    population, 233
    textile manufacturing in, 55–56
Bang & Olufsen, 256
Bank for International Settlements, 70
Bank of America, 14
Bank of Mexico, 66
Bankers Trust, 70
Barbados, 53, 94
Barbie doll, 148–150, 201
Barbuda, 94
Bargaining power of buyers, 505–506
Bargaining power of suppliers, 506–507
Barter, 391–392
Baskin Robbins, 34
Bath & Body Works, 253, 422
B.A.T. Industries, 17, 332, 340, 448
Bauma, 264
Bavarian Motor Works, 338. *See also* BMW
BAX Global, 426
Bay, 413
Bayer AG, 166–167, 172, 303, 446
Bayerische Moteren Werke AG, 338. *See also* BMW
BBDO Worldwide, 446
Beer brands, 366
Behavior segmentation, 237–240
Beijing Conciliation Center, 179
Being strategy, of a company, 43
Belarus, 34, 53, 56, 57, 299

Belgium
  church-state separation vote, in
      European constitution, 121
  Corona beer in, 344
  coupon use in, 476
  cultural perceptions in, 455–456
  euro zone member, 100
  Euroland member, 115
  European Union member, 99
  Frito-Lay in, 139
  GNP, 99
  Hofstede's cultural typology rankings
      (table), 135
  index of economic freedom ranking, 53
  per capita income, 231
  population, 99
  St. Laurent Champagne perfume in, 166
  Stella Artois beer advertising, 251
  supermarket retailing in, 414
  Tati stores in, 415
  taxes in, 376
Belief, 120
Belize, 53, 94
Bell Laboratories, 136, 562
BellSouth, 335
Belvedere vodka, 252
BEMs. See Big emerging markets (BEMs)
Benecol, 342
Benefit segmentation, 240–241
Benefits, of a product, 4, 251
Benetton
  advertising controversies, 350, 450,
      466–468
  country identification, 1
  distribution system, 10
  English, in all advertising tag lines, 256
  flagship model, 513
  franchising as market-entry strategy, 420
  global teen segment, 234
  growth of, 422
  in-house advertising and marketing, 446
  management information system (MIS)
      of, 191, 199
  media types used, 457, 461
  positioning of, 254
  radio frequency identification use
      refused, 433
Benevolent openness, 16
Benin, 53, 106, 107, 379
Ben & Jerry's Homemade ice cream, 349
Berkshire Hathaway, 14, 330
Berne Convention (1992), 167, 168
Bertelsmann, 134, 505, 530, 538, 586
Bestfoods, 144
Beverage Partners Worldwide, 310
Bharatiya Janata Party (BJP), 98
Big emerging markets (BEMs), 54,
      301–302, 337
Big idea, 448–449
Big Mac Index, 71–72
"Big One, The," 460
Big six (Japan), 316–317
Bilateral arrangements, 81
Bill Blass, 295
Bill of exchange, 280–281
Bill of lading, 279
Biotechnology industry, 151–152
Bipolar fashion, 255
Black Africa, 106
Blancpain, 283
Blockbuster Video, 212, 418
"Blocking statute," 187
Blue (color), 122–123
Blue Moon, 122
BlueRiverStone, 575

BlueTie, 568
Bluetooth, 122, 579
BMG, 17, 584, 586
BMG International, 332, 538
BMG Music, 530
bmi, 310
BMW, 243, 244, 251, 302, 315, 331, 333, 336,
      338, 497
BMW Online, 579
Body language, 127
Body Shop International PLC, 249, 253, 298,
      414, 416, 422
Boeing, 191, 197, 267, 310, 313, 314, 320, 409,
      441, 442, 542
  Airbus versus, 360–361
  in China, 393
Bolivia, 53, 84, 90, 91, 92, 93
Bombardier, 17
Bon Vivants (Porsche demographic), 235
Bonwit Teller, 416
Book of Bourbon, The (Regan), 350
Booz, Allen, & Hamilton, 320
Borden Inc., 296, 297, 306
Border's bookstores, 579
Bosch, 362
Bosch-Siemens, 8, 17
Bosnia, 53, 568
Botswana, 53, 84, 108, 109
Bottom-up segmentation analysis, 245
Boundaries, of market prices, 364
Boundaryless marketing, 3, 4
Bowling for Columbine, 125
BP, 14, 15, 48, 437
BRANDchild: Insights into the Minds of Today's
      Global Kids (Lindstrom), 326
Branded products, 182
Brand equity, 330
Brand extensions, 335
Brand identification, 1
Brand image, 137, 330, 331
Brand symbol, 331
Brand value, 326
Branding
  cobranding, 334–335
  combination or tiered, 334
  dual, 334–335
Brands. See also Product and brand decisions
  defined, 330
  global, 10
  launch brands, 342
  marketing company principle, 39–40
  value indicator of a company, 44
  world's most valuable (table), 336
Brazil
  agricultural subsidies, 378
  AIDS, generic drugs for, 395
  Avon Products in, 407
  Barbie dolls and, 149
  big emerging market (BEM), 54
  Coca-Cola in, 10
  coffee sales, 148
  currency, sliding, 113
  Daimler Chrysler and farmers'
      cooperative, 60
  e-Bay in, 572
  global operations, increase in, 16
  gross national product (GNP), 92, 232
  hyperinflation, 58
  index of economic freedom ranking, 53
  Internet Corporation for Assigned Names
      and Numbers (Icann) and, 546
  JC Penney in, 417
  Kolynos acquisition by Colgate-
      Palmolive, 169
  majority equity position in companies, 160

  music of, 123
  natural resources, 58
  nonsignatory to United Nations
      Convention on the Recognition
      and Enforcement of Foreign
      Arbitral Awards, 177
  OECD applicant, 63
  Patent Cooperation Treaty (PCT)
      and, 167
  per capita income, 59
  population, 92, 233
  size variants, 58
  soft drink preferences, 1
  subjective attributes of products and, 454
  sugar exports, 291
  supermarket retailing, 414
  television advertising in, 457, 458
  time orientation, 135–136
  trade-related issues, 95
  upper-middle-income country, 57, 58
  Volkswagen in, 556
  Wal-Mart in, 376–377, 415, 419
Brazilian Association of Toy
      Manufacturers, 149
Breakthroughs! (Nayak and
      Ketteringham), 334
Breguet, 283
Bribery, 173–176
"Brick-and-mortar" booksellers, 505, 570
Bridgestone/Firestone, negative publicity, 460
Brinkmanship, 505
Bristol-Myers Squibb, 23, 295, 395–396
British Airways, 320
British Petroleum, 77
British Telecommunications (BT), 64,
      480, 579
BRL Hardy, 246
Broadband communication
      system, 576–578
Bronco, 332
Brooks Brothers, 421
Broome & Wellington, 385
Brown (color), 123
"Brown shoes," 290
Brunei, 96
Buddhism, 120, 478
Budgets, 550. See also Marketing budgets
Budweiser beer, 184–185, 257, 343, 365
Buggles, 225
Buka puasa, 121
Bulgaria, 53, 99
Bundle of benefits, 4
Burberry, 570
Burger King, 31, 33, 34
Burkina Faso, 53, 107, 379
Burlington Northern Santa Fe (BNSF), 425
Burma, 53, 96–97
Burundi, 53, 56
Bush administration, 375
Business arbitration, 179
Business Environment Risk Intelligence
      (BERI), 155
Business-to-business (b-to-b/B2B)
  e-commerce category, 567
  marketing, 403
Business-to-consumer (b-to-c/B2B)
  e-commerce category, 567
  marketing, 403, 404
  revenues, 567
Buy American Act (1933), 270
Buyer for export, 275
Buyer of last resort, 16
Buyers, bargaining power of, 505–506
BuyUSA, 270
B'z, 332

# C

Cable & Wireless PLC, 175
CACM. *See* Central American Common
   Market
Cadbury, 245, 247
Cadbury Schweppes PLC, 534
Cadillac, 211, 243, 525
CAFTA. *See* Central American Free Trade
   Agreement
Calculating prices, 369–371
California, avocado-growers'
   problem, 88–89
Call centers, 282–283, 286
Call option, 74
Calvin Klein, 235, 250, 379, 535
Calvo Doctrine, 179–180
Carlson Marketing Group, 444
Cambodia, 53, 96
Cameroon, 53, 174
Campbell Soup Company, 144–145, 218,
   240, 349
Canada. *See also* North American Free Trade
   Agreement
   advertising expenditures, 457, 458
   antidumping and, 275, 386
   apparel and textile exports to the United
      States, 266
   automobile exports to Mexico, 66
   Avon Products in, 407
   common law in, 163
   Cuba and, 186, 187
   expanded Triad membership, 64
   Export Development Corporation, 157
   export organizations, 204
   export/import ranking, 68
   free trade agreements, 84
   Gap stores in, 13
   global competitive advantage and, 523
   gross national product (GNP), 88, 232
   high-income country, 62
   index of economic freedom ranking, 53
   international lawsuits, 179
   ketchup preferences, 349
   McDonald's in, 31, 233
   MMT gasoline additive and, 160
   newspaper business, 463
   OECD membership, 63
   per capita income, 231
   population, 88
   privacy issues, 575
   regional market, 87–89
   Swatchmobile and, 362
   "think" and "feel" country designation,
      455, 456
   transfer pricing, 388–389
   Virtual Trade Commissioner, 204
   Wal-Mart in, 419, 431–432
   Zeller's discount store, 415
Canadean Limited, 200
Canon, 244, 254, 283, 286, 318, 375, 515–516,
   536–537
Canon Kabushiki Kaisah, 168
CAP. *See* Common Agricultural Policy
Cape Verde, 53, 107
Capital account, 67
Capital costs, 284
Capital investments, 48
Capital movements, 47
Capital requirements, 504
Capital resources, 519
Captain Morgan rum, 435
Caribbean, 89, 103, 458
Caribbean Basin Initiative (CBI) of 1984,
   95, 269
Caribbean Basin Trade Partnership Act, 95

Caribbean Community and Common
   Market (CARICOM), 94, 95
CARICOM. *See* Caribbean Community and
   Common Market
Carillon Importers, 392
Carlson Companies, 186
Carrefour, 192, 229–230, 401, 402, 408, 414, 419
Cartels, 171
Case-based reasoning (CBR), 197
Case Europe, 101
Cases
   Acer, Inc., 35–37, 79–80
   Adidas-Salomon AG, 468–470
   America's Cuban Conundrum, 185–188
   Barbie: The American Girl Goes Global,
      148–150
   Benetton Group S.p.A.: Raising
      Consciousness and Controversy
      with Global Advertising, 466–468
   Boeing Versus Airbus: A Battle for the
      Skies, 360–361
   Bud Versus Bud, 184–185
   Carmakers Target Gen Y, 260–261
   Concerns About Factory Safety and
      Worker Exploitation in
      Developing Countries, 288–290
   DHL Shakes Up the Global Package
      Express Business, 324–325
   Ecuador Adopts the Dollar, 112–114
   Euro Yo-yo, 114–116
   Fair Trade Coffee: Ethics, Religion, and
      Sustainable Production, 147–148
   Harry Potter, 325–327
   Kazuo Inamori: Spiritual Leadership at
      Kyocera Corp., 559–560
   Kodak in the Twenty-First Century: The
      Search for New Sources of
      Competitive Advantage, 528
   Lego, 529
   LVMH and Luxury Goods Marketing,
      396–399
   A Marketer Takes the Wheel at
      Volkswagen AG, 556–557
   Marketing an Industrial Product in
      Latin America, 500–501
   McDonald's Expands Globally While
      Adjusting Its Local Recipe, 31–35
   Napster and the Global Music Industry,
      584–587
   Nokia Segments the Global Cell Phone
      Market, 259–260
   Pricing AIDS Drugs in Emerging
      Markets, 395–396
   Research Helps Whirlpool Act Local in
      the Global Market, 223–224
   The Smart Car, 361–363
   U.S. Sugar Subsidies: Too Sweet a
      Deal?, 291
   Vietnam's Market Potential, 77–79
   Wal-Mart's Global Expansion, 431–433
Casey's, 415
Cash in advance, 281
Castro government, 160
Catalogs, 492–493
Category killers, 408, 416, 418
Caterpillar, 1, 24, 84, 244, 375
   competitive threats, 514, 515
   currency fluctuation influences, 480
   differentiation advantage, 509, 514
   gray market competition, 383
   information technology investment, 191
   market size, 17
   merchandise sales, 295
   network of dealers, 10
   patent infringement possibilities, 168

strategic approach to world market, 306
Vietnam and, 77
yellow color, 122, 345
Catholic Relief Services (CRS), 147
Cave dweller stage, in new-product
   strategy, 354
CBS Records, 524
CE Alphas (Sony's U.S. consumer
   segment), 237
CEFTA. *See* Central European Free Trade
   Association
Cell phones, 17, 254, 256, 259–260, 579–582.
   *See also* Mobile phones
Cell production, 283
Celtic Tiger (Ireland), 64
Central African Republic, 53
Central America, 58, 89, 148, 458, 517. *See
   also individual countries*
Central American Common Market
   (CACM), 89
Central American Free Trade Agreement
   (CAFTA), 84, 291
Central American Integration System
   (SICA), 85, 89–90, 95
Central Europe. *See also individual countries;*
   Regional markets
   Barbie dolls in, 148
   Dawoo Group investment in, 300
   economic downturn, 502
   European Council aspirations, 181
   foreign direct investment in, 299
   IKEA in, 511
   inflation, 376
   legal system development, 163
   McDonald's in, 33–34
   political environment, 156
   Revlon in, 248
   risks and opportunities in, 286
   strategic alliance opportunities, 315
   tobacco advertising regulations, 488
   trade secret laws, 173
   Unilever in, 66
Central European Free Trade Association
   (CEFTA), 103–104
Centrally planned capitalism, 50–52
Centrally planned socialism, 49–50
Cereal Partners Worldwide, 139, 310
Cervejaria Brahma SA, 169
CET. *See* Common external tariffs (CETs)
C.F.R. (cost and freight), 371
CFTA. *See* U.S.–Canada Free Trade
   Agreement
Chad, 53, 379
Chaebol system, 319–320, 512
Chance, in competitive environment, 522
Chanel, 249, 446
Changhong Electric Appliances, 333
Channel decisions, 410
Channel distributors, 410–413
Channels of distribution. *See also* Physical
   distribution
   as barrier to entry, 504
   channel objectives, 402–403
   consumer products and services, 403–407
   defined, 401
   establishing channels/channel
      intermediaries, 410–412
   global retailing, 413–423
   guidelines for choosing a local
      distributor, 411–412
   industrial products, 407–410
   in less-developed countries (LDCs), 413
   marketing channel alternatives, 403–410
Channel strategy, 427
Channel V, 134

Chase Manhattan Bank, 255
Cheil Communications, 444
Chemical Tariff Harmonization Agreement
        (CTHA), 86
Cherry picking (channel distribution), 412
Chevrolet, 46, 260, 302, 357
Chevron, 26
Chevron Texaco, 15
Chicago Mercantile Exchange, 70
Child labor issues, 289
Chile, 53, 81, 149, 161, 417
    associate member of Mercosur, 92–93
    free trade agreements of (table), 84
    GNP, 92
    population, 92
    privacy issues, 575
    as upper-middle-income country, 57
China
    Acer, Inc. in, 80
    advertising language in, 451–452
    appliance brands, competition among, 1
    ASEAN trade and, 97
    average individual annual income, 228
    Avon Products in, 406, 407, 480
    beer market, 300
    big emerging market (BEM), 54, 56
    Boeing in, 286, 361
    civil-law jurisdiction, 163
    Closer Economic Partnership
            Agreement, 84
    Coca-Cola advertising in, 449–450
    color perceptions in, 123, 345
    compensation trading in, 393
    cost calculating problems in, 369
    devaluation of the yuan, 70
    dispersal of productive wealth in, 16
    door-to-door selling in, 404
    dumping rules, 385, 386
    duties and taxes, 157–158
    eBay in, 572
    economic growth of, 25, 265
    economic reforms, 50
    export/import ranking, 68
    exports, 265–266
    foreign investment in, 266
    furniture exports, 262–264, 268
    gross national product (GNP), 232
    growth of, 97
    Hong Kong business and, 480
    human rights issues, 56
    incipient market for automobiles, 208–209
    index of economic freedom ranking, 53
    infomercials in, 494
    intellectual property and, 56, 165, 168, 464
    Internet control, 564
    Internet users in, 567
    joint ventures in, 301–302, 303,
            310–311, 421
    Jollibee restaurants in, 127
    local products and brands, 333
    market access, 286
    market segmentation and, 244
    market selection framework (table), 245
    market socialism, 51
    Mattel in, 407
    McDonald's in, 10–11, 32
    Nike in, 348
    nonconvertible currency, 156
    NTR status, 273
    OECD applicant, 63
    offsets and, 392–393
    offshore sourcing in, 380
    open market, 50
    outsourcing, 282
    per capita income, 231

    personal selling ban, 480
    piggyback marketing in, 407
    pirated software in, 69
    population, 232, 233
    private sector, 51
    product saturation levels, 65–66
    public relations needs, 464
    sales force nationality in, 487
    sampling in, 476
    segment size and growth potential, 243
    shark fin and sea cucumber demand, 114
    signatory to the United Nations
            Convention on the Recognition
            and Enforcement of Foreign
            Arbitral Awards, 177
    smuggling and, 158
    sweatshops, 289, 290
    tariffs of, 265
    tobacco advertising regulations, 448
    trade secret laws, 173
    Tsingtao Brewery, 184
    TV-advertising market, 206–207
    U.S. imports from, 67
    U.S. trade partner, 87
    Visa's strategy in, 243
    Wal-Mart and, 2, 198–199, 419, 432–433
    "world's workplace," 284
    Yaohan stores in, 416
China Great Wall Computer Group, 301
China triangle, 266
Chinese Value Survey (CVS), 135
Chipotle Mexican Grill, 34
Chivas Regal scotch, 435, 439
Chocolate Manufacturers Association, 114
Chowkin restaurants, 127
Christian Dior, 350, 396–399
Christianity, 120
Chrysler Corporation, 4, 13, 120, 208, 315
Cia. Cervejaria Brahma SA, 169
C.I.F. (cost, insurance, freight) named port
        of destination, 371
Cigarettes. See Tobacco industry
Cintec International, 378
Circuit City, 25, 408
Cisco Systems, 14, 336
Citibank, 57, 336
Citicorp, 18, 70, 220, 452
Citigroup, 14, 15
Citizens Against Supermarket Privacy
        Invasion and Numbering
        (CASPIAN), 433–434
Citroen, 46
Civil law, common law versus, 162–163
Civil-law country, 162–163
Claritas/NPDC, 215
Cleaning data, 214
Clear Channel Communications, 458
Click-through rates, 571
Clicquot, 473
Clinton administration, 66, 85, 157, 269–270
Close, in presentation, 485
Closer Economic Partnership Agreement, 84
Club Med, 272
"Club Med" nations, 98
Cluster analysis, 215
CMEA. See Council for Mutual Economic
        Assistance
CNF, 426
Cobranding, 326, 334–335
Coca-Cola
    advertising, 212, 449–450
    anti-American sentiment, effect on,
            121, 125
    brand building in Southeast and West
            Asia, 54

    broadcast advertising decisions, 210
    Cuba and, 186
    "Dial-a-Coke," 580
    dietary and health needs in low-income
            countries, 60
    economic value ranking (table), 336
    efficient consumer response (ECR), 192
    European Union food safety laws and, 102
    focus groups for, 212–213
    foreign direct investment, in Russia, 298
    global establishment of, during World
            War II, 246
    global marketing, importance of, 13
    global music industry and, 587
    global strategic partnerships, 310
    global teenage market, 234
    GMOs in, 151
    Harry Potter and, 325–327
    India and, 51, 98, 189, 190
    in-house advertising and marketing
            staff, 446
    Japan and, 9–10, 332
    licensing, 295
    logo, 12, 330–331
    market value, 14
    MTV Europe and, 229
    negative publicity, 460
    Nestlé and, 5
    packaging, 344
    physiological needs met by, 339–340
    place utility and, 402–403
    power of, as protection, 330
    quintessential global product and brand,
            338–339
    strongest brand in world, 9
    Turkey and, 57
    value chain and, 423
    Vietnam and, 77
Code law, 162–163
Coffee market, 147–148
Cold War, 48, 51
Colgate, 6, 128, 352, 517
Colgate-Palmolive, 169, 446
Collaboration, 308, 326, 516
Collaborative agreements, 309
Collectivist cultures, 133–138, 477
Collusion, 169
Colombia, 53, 81, 84, 90, 91, 113, 148, 352,
        414, 480
Color perceptions, among cultures, 122–123,
        139, 345–346, 452
Combination branding, 334
Comfortable Belongers (European
        consumers), 236
Command allocation approach, 51
Commerce service providers (CSPs), 567
Commercial Fan Moteur (CFM)
        International, 313
Commission of East African
        Cooperation, 107
Common Agricultural Policy (CAP),
        267, 291
Common external tariffs (CETs), 84, 89–90, 92
Common law, civil law versus, 162–163
Common-law countries, 162–163
Common market, 85, 86
Common Market, 291
Common Market of the South. See Mercosur
Commonwealth of Independent States, 34
Communicability, 141
Communication. See also Advertising;
        Public relations and publicity
    face-to-face, 198–199
    global marketing and, 23
    language and, among cultures, 126–129

Communications decisions. *See*
 Advertising; Direct marketing;
 Personal selling; Product place-
 ment; Public relations and public-
 ity; Sales promotion; Sponsorship
Communism, demise of, 48
Community, as marketing company
 principle, 38
Community Party of Vietnam (CPV), 78
Community Patent Convention, 165
Companion products, 368
Company, as marketing company
 principle, 38
Compaq, 284, 336, 507, 521, 566
Comparability, 219
Comparative analysis, 216–217
Compatability, 141, 244
Compensation trading, 393
Competence, 543
Competition
 bargaining power of buyers, 505–506
 bargaining power of suppliers, 506–507
 as budget influence, 551
 joint venture partners as, 303
 as marketing company principle, 38–39
 market segmentation and, 243–244
 as positioning strategy, 253
 rivalry among competitors, 507
 threat of new entrants, 503–505
 threat of substitute products, 505
Competitive advantage, 4–5, 7, 245
 current issues in, 522–526
 defined, 507
 flagship model, 512–513
 generic strategies for creating cost focus,
 510–511
 cost leadership advantage, 508–509
 differentiation advantage, 509
 focused differentiation, 509–510
 Kodak and, 528
 national, global competition and, 516–518
 demand conditions, 519–520
 firm strategy, structure, and rivalry,
 521–522
 related and supporting industries,
 520–521
 strategic intent, creating with, 513
 changing the rules, 515–516
 collaborating, 516
 layers of advantage, 514–515
 loose bricks, 515
*Competitive Advantage of Nations, The*
 (Porter), 517–518
*Competitive Advantage* (Porter), 508
Competitive behavior, 379
Competitive innovation, 514
Competitive pricing, 389
*Competitive Strategy* (Porter), 508
Competitor response, 504–505
Complexity, 141
Compressor Control Corporation, 281
Concentrated global marketing, 249–250
Concentration of marketing activities, 8–9
Confédération Européenne des Relations
 Publiques, 463
Confiscation, 160–161
Conflict, in joint ventures, 302–303
Conflict resolution, 176–180
Confucianism, 478
Congo. *See* Democratic Republic of Congo
Conjoint analysis, 217
Conrad-Johnson, 509
Consignment, sales on, 282
Consolidated Cigar Corporation, 186
Conspicuous consumption, 340

Consten, 171
Consumer behavior, in India, 189–190
Consumer electronics industry, continuous
 innovations in, 355
Consumer loyalty, 192
Consumer packaged goods, 344
Consumer panel, 210
Consumer products and services. *See*
 Channels of distribution
Consumer sales promotions, 472
Consumer-to-consumer, e-commerce
 category, 567
Consumers, needs and wants, 227
Consumption, 119–120
"Contagion," 54
Containerization, 427
Content sites (Web), 567
Contests, 472
Continuous innovation, 355–356
Contract manufacturing, 294, 297, 488
Control, 548. *See also* Management control
Controls, government, 378
Convenience sample, 214
Convenience stores, 415
Conventional wisdom, 227
Convergence, 564–565
Cooperative exporter, 276
Cooperative strategies
 digital future, 320–321
 in Japan (keiretsu), 316–319
 in South Korea (chaebol), 319–320
Coordination of marketing activities, 9
Coors Electronic Packaging, 559
Copy and copywriters (advertising),
 255, 450–452
Copyleft, 577
Copyright, 165–168
 cell phone ring tunes and, 581
 packaging and, 397
Copyright Arbitration Royalty Panel, 585
Cordiant Communications Group, 444
Core competence, 534–535
Corning Glass, 302
Corona Extra beer, 1, 241–242, 256, 343, 344
Corporacion Andina de Fomento, 114
Corporate advertising, 460
Corporate culture, 157
Corporate taxation, 158–159
Correlation analysis, 215
Corruption, 173–176
Cosi, 31
Cosmair, 250
Cosmetics industry
 door-to-door selling, 406
 marketing mix offerings, 250
Cossacks (Russian consumer type), 236
Cost, insurance, and freight (CIF), 274
Cost advantages independent of scale
 economies, 504
Cost-based pricing, 369
Cost-based transfer pricing, 388–389
Cost focus, 510–511
Cost leadership advantage, 508–509
Cost-plus pricing, 369–371
Costa Rica, 53, 58, 81, 89, 90, 413
Costco, 397, 414
Cote d'Ivoire, 415
Cotonou Agreement, 103
Cotton subsidies, 379
Council for Mutual Economic Assistance
 (CMEA), 103
Counterfeiting, 165
Counterpurchase, 392
Countertrade
 barter, 391–392

compensation trading, 393
counterpurchase, 392
 defined, 390
 offset, 392–393
 switch trading, 393
Counterveiling duties (CVDs), 275
Country and market concentration, 321–322
Country and segment diversification, 322
Country concentration and segment
 diversification, 322
Country diversification and market
 concentration, 322
Country infrastructure, 285
Country-of-origin effect, 341–343
Country stereotyping, 342
Couponing, 475, 476–477
CPC International, 144
Craft brew, 343
Crate & Barrel, 421
Cray computer, 319
Creation tactic, 44
Creative execution, 449
Creative strategy, 448
Credit card fraud, 568
Credit Suisse, 192
Creeping expropriation, 160
Crises, public relations and, 464
CRM. *See* Customer relationship
 management (CRM)
Croatia, 34, 53, 568
Cross-border prescription drug trade, 370
Cross coupons, 476
CSX Corporation, 285
CTHA. *See* Chemical Tariff Harmonization
 Agreement
Cuba, 53, 103, 123, 160, 177, 273
 command allocation approach, 51
 economic freedom ranking, 52
 U.S. relations with, 185–188
Cuban-American National
 Foundation, 186
Cuban Liberty and Democratic Solidarity
 Act, 185
Cultural gap, 117
Cultural imperialism, 86
Cultural megashock, 200
Cultural myopia, 138
Cultural norms, 119
Cultural typology. *See* Hofstede's cultural
 typology
Cultural universals, 119, 144
Culture. *See also* Social and cultural
 environments
 advertising considerations, 452–456
 Barbie dolls and, 149
 corporate, 157
 defined, 119
 of global strategic partnerships
 (GSPs), 311
 influence on consumption and goods
 ownership, 144
 "McDonaldization" of, 130
 in personal selling, 484
 political, 152
Culture gap, 117
Culture shock, 118–119
Cummins Engine, 306
Currency crisis
 in Asia, 375
 in Mexico, 66
Currency depreciation, 156
Currency fluctuations, 73, 373–376, 480
Currency values, 71
Current account, 67
Customer needs, 285

Customer relationship management (CRM), 17, 192–194, 488
Customer strategy, 482–483
Customer value, 4
Customs Cooperation Council, 268
Customs duties, 274–275
Customs procedures, 270–271
Customs union, 84, 86
CVDs. *See* Counterveiling duties (CVDs)
CVS. *See* Chinese Value Survey (CVS)
Cyprus, 53, 104, 115
Czech Republic, 53, 99, 103, 113, 115, 163, 184, 300, 304, 344, 406, 448, 557
Czechoslovakia, 99

## D

Daewoo Corporation, 62, 77, 299, 300, 303, 320, 342, 375
Daiko Advertising, 444
Daimler-Benz, 13, 120
DaimlerChrysler, 10, 15, 27, 60, 61, 73, 74, 79, 266, 304, 333, 342, 362, 535
DaimlerChrysler Aerospace Airbus (Dasa), 73
D'arcy Massius Benton & Bowles (DMBB), 236
*Das Kapital* (Marx), 51
Data analysis
    cluster analysis, 215
    comparative analysis, 217–218
    conjoint analysis, 217
    data cleaning, 214
    dependence techniques, 216–217
    factor analysis, 215
    forecasting by analogy, 218
    interdependence techniques, 215
    multidimensional scaling (MDS), 215–216
    tabulation, 214–215
    time-series displacement, 218
Data availability, 203–205
Data collection, 193–194, 206–209
Data gathering, 205–206
Data General, 565
Data warehouses, 194
Datamonitor, 200
Date draft, 281
Davidoff of Geneva, 226
DDB Needham Worldwide, 446
DDB Worldwide, 34–35
DealsonHotels.com, 573
De Beers diamond cooperative, 59, 387–388, 437
DEC, 565
Defense Advanced Research Projects Agency (DARPA), 563
Def Jam, 226
Delivered duty paid, 371
Dell Computer, 17, 79, 191, 226, 244, 285, 409, 507, 521, 564, 566, 587
Demand, price elasticity of, 73
Demand conditions, 519–520
Democratic Republic of Congo, 53, 108, 109
Democratization of information, 22
Demographic data, 203
Demographic segmentation. *See* Segmentation
Denmark, 53, 98, 136, 171, 174, 187, 325, 376, 426, 459
    direct mail and, 490–491
    GNP, 99
    Hofstede's cultural typology rankings (table), 135
    per capita income, 231
    population, 99
Dentsu, 201, 444, 446

Department stores, 413
Dependence techniques (data analysis), 216–217
Deregulation, 89, 379
Desk research, 203
Deutsche Bank, 259
Deutsche Post, 324
Deutsche Telecom, 579, 580
Devaluation, 70
Developed countries, 57, 61–63, 406
Developing countries, 57–59
    cost calculating problems in, 369
    factory safety and worker exploitation in, 288–290
    international partnerships in, 315–316
    marketing opportunities in, 59–61
    product invention strategy in, 352
    public relations in, 463
Developing economy, 153
Developing nations, 179
DG Environment, 159
DG Sanco, 159
DHL Airways, 324
DHL Worldwide Express, 324–325
Diageo PLC, 191, 239–240, 392
*Die Another Day*, 497
Diesel jeans, 128, 379, 446
Dietary preferences, among cultures, 124–126
Differentiated global marketing, 250
Differentiation
    as marketing company principle, 41
    as marketing tactic, 44
    of products, in vodka industry, 252, 253
Differentiation advantage, 509
*Diffusion of Innovations* (Rogers), 143
Diffusion theory, 139
    adopter categories, 141–142, 143
    adoption process, 140
    innovations, 140–141
    in Pacific Rim countries, 142–143
Digital future, 320–321
Digital keiretsu, 320
Digital revolution, 505, 561–564, 584–587
Digital subscriber line (DSL), 577
Digitas, 444
Direct investment, 294
Direct involvement (channel distribution), 410
Direct labor costs, 284
Direct mail, 490–492
Direct marketing, 488
Direct Marketing Association, 488
Direct market representation, 278–279
Direct selling, 404–407
Direct sensory perception, 198–199
Disadvantaging rivals, 514
Disaffected Survivors (European consumer), 236
Discontinuous innovations, 355–356
Discount stores, 415
Discovery, 177
Discretionary protectionism, 88–89
Discriminatory exchange rate policies, 271
Discriminatory procurement policies, 270
Discriminatory tariffs, 160
Disney, 34, 404
    economic value ranking (table), 336
    licensing by, 295
Disney Stores, 414, 416
Disproportionality, law of, 238
Dispute settlement, 176–180
Dispute Settlement Body (DSB; of WTO), 82
Distilled spirits, 435

Distribution center, 424
Distribution channels, 504
Distribution strategies, of the European union (table), 102
Distributor, 403
Divisibility, 141
Djibouti, 53
DKB, 316
Doctors Without Borders, 395
Documentary collections (sight or time drafts), 280–281
Documentary credit, 279–280, 281
Documents against payment (DP), 272, 281
Dodwell Marketing Consultants, 319
Doha Development Round, 83, 268
Dollar
    most heavily traded currency, 70
    yen versus, value of (table), 375
Dollarization, 112
Dom Perignon, 340
Domestic companies, 16
Domestic rivalry, 521
Dominica, 94
Dominican Republic, 53, 123, 266, 269, 376
Domino effect, 54
Domino's Pizza, 32
Donna Karan, 398–399
Door-to-door selling, 404–405, 406
Dormont Manufacturing, 347
Downstream industries, 520
Downstream value chains, 423, 547–548
Draft, 280–281
Drawee, 280
Drawer, 280
Dr. Martens, 1, 2
Dr. Pepper, 125
Drugs, illegal, from Ecuador, 113–114
Dual adaptation, 351
Dual branding, 334–335
Dual extension, 348–349
Dual-income families, 489
Dumping, 17, 275, 304, 385–387
Dunkin' Donuts, 66
DuPont, 98, 151
Durability, 357
Duracell battery, 252–253
Duties, 372n. *See also* Customs duties; Taxes
    in China, 157–158
    defined, 267
    zero, 83–84
Dynamically continuous innovations, 355–356
Dynamit Nobel, 362

## E

E4L, 494
Early adopters, 142
"Early harvest" agreements, 85
Early home demand, 520
Early majority, 142
Early market saturation, 520
Earned media, 460
Earnings stripping, 160
East Africa, 413
Eastern Europe. *See also individual countries*; Regional markets
    arbitration with Western Europe, 179
    Daewoo Group investment in, 300
    European Council aspirations, 181
    foreign direct investment in, 299
    IKEA in, 511
    inflation, 376
    Komatsu in, 515
    legal system development, 163

McDonald's in, 33–34
political environment, 156
Revlon in, 248
risks and opportunities in, 286
strategic alliance opportunities, 315
Unilever in, 66
Eastman Kodak, 165, 267, 528
Eating habits, 139
eBay, 48, 404, 572
Economic Community of West African
    States (ECOWAS), 106, 107, 108
Economic cooperation, 81
Economic exposure, 72–73
Economic freedom. *See* Index of economic
    freedom
Economic growth, 24–25
Economic integration, regional forms
    (table), 86
Economic systems
    centrally planned capitalism, 50–52
    centrally planned socialism, 49–50
    index of economic freedom (table), 53
    market capitalism, 49
    market socialism, 50–52
Economic union, 85–86
Economies (developing, industrialized,
    newly industrializing,
    nonmarket, 153)
Economies of scale, 439, 504
Economist Intelligence Unit (EIU), 155
*Economist* (journal), 204
Eco-packaging, 344
ECOWAS. *See* Economic Community of
    West African States
ECR. *See* Efficient consumer response
ECU. *See* European Currency Unit
Ecuador, 53, 90
    banana exports, 113
    GNP, 91
    growth of, due to oil, 113
    population, 91
    U.S. dollar adopted by, 112–114
Eddie Bauer, 417, 492
Edeka Gruppe, 414
Edelman Public Relations Worldwide, 462
EDI. *See* Electronic data interchange
EEA. *See* European Economic Area
"Effects doctrine" of international law, 186
Efficient consumer response (ECR), 192
EFTA. *See* European Free Trade Area
Egypt, 53, 104, 105, 106, 149, 385, 393, 564
80/20 rule, 238
Eisenmann, 362
Elaz-GM, 302
Electrolux, 1, 6, 8, 17, 58, 223
Electronic Arts, 78, 578, 581
Electronic commerce (e-commerce), 62,
    568–570
    2003 revenues, 567
    broadband, 576–578
    categories of activities, 567
    mobile commerce (m-commerce), 579–582
    privacy issues, 575
    Web site design, 571–576
    wireless connectivity, 579–582
Electronic data interchange (EDI), 191
Electronic Frontier Foundation, 587
Electronic point of sale (EPOS), 192, 422
Electronic smart cards, 192
Eli Lilly, 17–18
Elitists (Porsche demographic), 235
El Salvador, 53, 58, 84, 89, 90
E-mail, early years, 563
Emanuel Ungaro, 350
eMarketer, 567

Embargo, U.S.–Vietnam, 77. *See also* Trade
    embargo
Embraer, 17
"Emerging Mena" countries, 106
EMI, 17, 134, 584, 586
Emic analysis, 219
Emotional appeal, 449
Emotional/dramatic advertising, 455
Emotional/psychological advertising, 455
Emotional response, 255
Employment, productivity and, 47
EMS. *See* European Monetary System
EMU. *See* European Monetary Union
Enabling conditions, 245–247
*Endaka* (strong yen), 286
Endesa, 177
English language
    American style, 129, 131
    as marketing tool in Japan, 130, 256
    world-wide, 128
Enterprise for the Americas Initiative, 95
Entrepreneurial globalization, 308–309
Environmentalism, 60–61, 114, 361–363
Environmental scanning modes, 195–197
Environmental sensitivity, 143–145
EPOS. *See* Electronic point of sale (EPOS)
EPRG framework, 16, 18
Equatorial Guinea, 53
Equity stakes, investment via, 303–306
Ericsson, 231, 542, 580
Estee Lauder, 250
Esteem, 340
Estimated future cost method, 370–371
Estonia, 53, 99, 115
Estrela, 149
Ethics, 147–148, 497
Ethiopia, 53, 413
Ethnic segmentation, 241–242
Ethnocentric orientation, to marketing,
    16–18, 20, 485, 486
Ethnocentric pricing policy, 380–381
Ethyl Corporation, 160
Etic analysis, 219
Euro, 100, 114–116, 374
"Euroconsumer: Marketing Myth or
    Cultural Certainty?," 236
Eurocoton, 385
Europe, 234, 351, 459, 567, 580, 582
    antidumping policy, 385
    catalog difficulties in, 492
    direct marketing in, 489
    Harley-Davidson in, 249
    laptop computers in, 579
    McDonald's in, 31, 33
    pet food market, 241
    regional market and sales, 17
    segmenting the single market, 238
    Wal-Mart in, 432
European Agreements, 99
European Commission, 101, 169, 170, 180,
    186–187, 343, 347, 385, 387
European Community (EC), 98, 180
European Court of Justice, 180, 181–182, 384
European Currency Unit (ECU), 100
European Economic Area (EEA), 84, 100–101
European Free Trade Area (EFTA),
    100–101, 492
European Monetary System (EMS), 100
European Monetary Union (EMU), 114
European Parliament, 180
European Patent Convention, 168
European Patent Office, 165–166, 168
European Union (EU), 21, 46, 83, 84, 153,
    180, 230, 268, 381, 386. *See also*
    *individual countries*

age of population, 228
agricultural support from, 291
antitrust suit against Microsoft, 171
ASEAN trade and, 97
automobile price differences in
    (table), 376
banana imports in, 113
broadband goals, 578
copyright law and, 585
coupon use in, 476
customs union with Turkey, 84
enlargement of, 116
export/import ranking, 68
farm subsidies and, 267
GDP, 115
genetically modified organisms (GMOs)
    and, 151, 159
mandatory labeling for, 345
income and population (table), 99
map of (figure), 100
marketing issues in, 101–102
members, newest (table), 99
objective of, 99
origins of, 98
pacts, 100–101
population and GNP, 99
privacy issues, 564, 575
regional economic organizations, 180–182
sacrifices for improved market
    success, 154
sugar subsidies, 86
technology transfer laws, 172
tobacco advertising regulations, 448
Euro products and brands, 333, 347
Euro zone, 68, 100, 115
Event marketing, 476
Exchange rate exposure, 73–75
Exclusive license arrangements, 488
Exclusive supply arrangements, 317–318
Ex-Im Bank, 157
Existing markets, 206
Expanded Triad, 64
Expatriates, 480, 486
Expedia.com, 62, 561
Experience transfers, 25–26
Experiential packaging, 344
Export broker, 276
Export commission house, 275
Export commission representative, 276
Export confirming house, 275
Export Development Corporation, 157
Export distributor, 276
Export-Import Bank, 16, 109, 282
Exporting/importing, 262–292, 294
    China's furniture industry, 261–264, 268
    cotton imports, 385
    customs duties, 274–275
    export participants, 275–276
    financing and methods of payment
        cash in advance, 281
        documentary collections (sight or
            time drafts), 280–281
        documentary credit, 279–280
        sales on a consignment basis, 282
        sales on open account, 282
    manufacturer's country, 277–278
    market country, 278–279
    national policies governing, 265
        discouraging imports and blocking
            market access, 267–271
        support of exports, 266–267
    organizational activities, 264–265
    potential problems (table), 265
    price calculations for, 382
    reasons for not exporting, 270

Exporting/importing *(Continued)*
  sourcing, 282
    country infrastructure, 285
    customer needs, 285
    factor costs and conditions, 284
    foreign exchange rates, 286
    logistics, 285
    management vision, 283
    political factors, 286
  stages, 264–265
  Taiwan, 79–80
  tariff systems, 271–275
  top countries (table), 68
  U.S.–Vietnam, 79
Export management company (EMC), 276
Export marketing, 262–263
Export merchants, 276
Export selling, 262
Export vendor, 276
Express warranty, 346
Expropriation, 160–161
Expropriation and compensation rule, in
    NAFTA, 160
Extension approach, to marketing, 16
Extension pricing policy, 380–381
Extension strategy. *See* Product and brand
    decisions
Ex-works, 371
Exxon, 350
Exxon Mobil, 14, 15

## F

Face-to-face communication, 198–199, 533
Face-to-face selling. *See* Strategic/
    Consultative Selling Model
Factor analysis, 215
Factor costs, 284
Factor loadings, 215
Factor scores, 215
Factory safety, 288–290
Fahrvergnügen, 257
Fairchild Semiconductor, 559, 562n
Fair Labor Standards Act, 288
"Fair price," 385–386
Fair trade, 147–148
Fair Trade Commission (Japan), 169
Fairtrade Foundation, 147
Fairtrade Labeling Organization
    International (FLO), 147
Families (Sony's U.S. consumer segment), 237
Famso, 241
Fantasists (Porsche demographic), 235
FAO Schwartz, 137
Farmers, 81. *See also* Agriculture
  genetically modified organisms and,
    151–152
  subsidies for, 267
  sugar subsidies, 291
F.A.S. (free alongside ship) named port of
    destination, 371
Fast food, world-wide, 125
FCCP. *See* Foreign consumer culture
    positioning
FCPA. *See* Foreign Corrupt Practices Act
FDI. *See* Foreign direct investment
Feasibility, in market segmentation, 244
Federal Express, 191, 324, 424, 569
Femininity, 134–138
Ferrari, 208
Fiat, 6, 58, 302
Fiji, 53, 291
File swapping. *See* MP3 file swapping;
    Napster
*Financial Times*, 204

Financing, of exports. *See*
    Exporting/importing
Finland, 10, 53, 100, 101, 115, 128, 174, 235,
    268, 291, 306, 376, 523
  country-of-origin effect, 342
  dietary preferences, 124
  direct mail and, 490–491
  GNP, 99
  Hofstede's cultural typology rankings
    (table), 135
  population, 99
Firm strategy, structure, and rivalry, 521–522
First-mover advantage, 60, 246, 524
First-mover disadvantages, 246
Fisher-Price, 289
Fitzsimmons, Jay, 432
Flagship model, 512–513
Fleishman-Hillard, 461
Flexible cost-plus pricing, 370
Float, 54, 70–71
Fly American Act, 270
F.O.B. (free on board), 371
Focus, 5, 7
Focused differentiation, 509–510
Focus groups, 211–212
FoE. *See* Friends of the Earth
Food
  advertising of, 453–454
  benefit segmentation example, 240
  dietary preferences among cultures,
    124–126, 189, 196
  globalization of, 139
  legal and regulatory barriers, 347
  McDonald's global expansion, 31–35
  need for, 339
Food and Agriculture Organization, 291
Food safety, in the European Union, 102
Ford Motor Company
  age of buyers, 260
  assembly line innovation, 545
  Brazil and, 58
  China, pursuit of opportunities in, 56
  competition success, 4, 24
  economic value ranking (table), 336
  equity stake, 304
  Ford 2000 restructuring plan, 46, 541
  global product platform and, 356–357
  Hispanic market, 241
  India and, 98
  information technology and, 191
  Jaguar PLC acquisition, 307
  joint venture expectations, 302
  Mexican operations, 342
  negative publicity, 460
  price differences in the European
    Union, 376
  reorganization into global company, 19
  revenues, 15
  Russia and, 103
  Thailand and, 298
  Vietnam and, 79
Forecasting, by analogy, 217–218
Foreign Commercial Service, 204
Foreign consumer culture positioning
    (FCCP), 251, 252, 256–257
Foreign Corrupt Practices Act
    (FCPA), 173–175
Foreign direct investment (FDI), 77–78,
    298–299
Foreign exchange market, 69–71
Foreign exchange rates, 286
Foreign language study, 129
Foreign purchasing agents, 275
Foreign sales corporation (FSC), 266–267
Forrester Research, 567

Fortress Europe, 271
Forward market, 70, 74
Foster's Brewing Group, 256–257
France
  advertising in, 350
    adaptations for ketchup, 351
    expenditures, 457, 458
  automakers in, 27
  Avon Products in, 407
  Barbie dolls and, 148
  Benetton advertising controversy, 466
  budget deficit, 115
  Carrefour hypermarkets, 229–230,
    401–402
  church-state separation vote, on
    European constitution, 121
  country-of-origin effect, 341
  culture clash with America, 125
  dietary preferences, 124
  direct mail and, 490–491
  equity stakes, 304
  euro zone member, 100
  Euroland member, 115
  European Community member, 98
  exports, to America, 125
  Frito-Lay in, 139
  functional product attributes valued
    in, 454
  Galeries Lafayette, 416
  Gap stores in, 13
  Gateway survey in, 442
  global competitive advantage and, 523
  Grey Goose vodka, 252
  gross national product (GNP), 99, 232
  high-income country, 62
  historic relationship with America, 117
  Hofstede's cultural typology rankings
    (table), 135
  index of economic freedoms
    ranking, 53
  investment insurance, 157
  language use regulations, 153
  McDonald's in, 33, 233
  Microsoft and, 577
  motion picture box office receipts, 1
  music industry, 584
  music regulations, 153
  parallel imports problem, 171
  Patent Cooperation Treaty (PCT), 167
  piggyback marketing in, 407
  population, 99
  power distance culture (high), 133, 136
  recorded music sales, 23
  Pernod Ricard SA, purchase of Chivas
    Regal, 435
  smart cell phones in, 580
  state tobacco monopoly, 448
  supermarket retailing in, 414
  Tati stores, 415
  television advertising, 456, 459
  "think" and "feel" country
    designation, 455
  U.S. trade partner, 87
  wine industry, structure of, 428
Franchising, 297–298
  global retailing market entry and, 420
  independent franchise store, 405
"Frankenfoods," 159
Fraud
  credit card, 568
  in sales promotions, 477
Free economy, 53
Free markets, 89
Free-standing insert (FSI), 476
Free trade agreement (FTA), 83–84

Free trade area (FTA), 83–84, 86, 93
Free Trade Area of the Americas (FTAA), 81, 94
  creation of, 85
  Ecuador and, 114
  importance of, 95
  opposition to, 85
Free trade zone (FTZ), 282
Freemans, 492
Freescale Semiconductor, 320
Freight forwarders, 276, 428
Friends of the Earth (FoE), 159
Friskies Cat Club, 491
Frito-Lay, 139, 213, 471
FTA. See Free trade area
FTZ. See Free trade zone
Fuji bicycles, 254
Fuji Photo Film, 165, 244, 304, 330, 461
Fujitsu, 98
Full absorbtion cost method, 369
Full-line discounters, 415
Full-service agencies (advertising), 446
Functional brand image, 137–138
Functional competence, 543
Fur Council of Canada, 61
Fuyo, 316

# G

G3 (Group of Three), 84
Gabon, 53
Galeries Lafayette, 416
Gallaher Group, 17
Gaman (persistence), 136
Gambia, 53, 107
GameCube, 368, 471
Gamers, 578
Games on Demand (GOD), 578
Gaming, 581
Gap, 12, 13, 20, 235, 414, 417, 427
Gartner Group, 567
Gartner Group Asia, 206
Gateway, 64, 442, 507, 521, 564–565
GATT. See General Agreement on Tariffs and Trade
GCC. See Gulf Cooperation Council
GCCP. See Global consumer culture positioning
GDP. See Gross domestic product
Gender segmentation, 234–235
General Agreement on Tariffs and Trade (GATT), 21, 28, 81, 268, 274, 372n
  customs valuation code, 273–274
  dumping issue and, 385–386
  intent of, 82
  patents and, 168
  rounds, history of, 86
General Dynamics, 186
General Electric (GE), 14, 15, 73, 87, 168, 191, 313, 333, 336, 391, 479, 532
General Mills, 310, 582
General Motors (GM)
  China and, 56, 123, 233, 243, 266, 301–302
  competition success, 4
  equity stake, 304
  foreign sales corporation (FSC) upheaval and, 266–267
  Hispanic market, 241
  India and, 98
  joint venture with Daewoo Group, 303
  lean production, 547
  Mexican currency crisis and, 66
  Mexican operations, 342
  revenues, 15
  standardized platform of minivan, 356

strategic interaction (defensive moves), 525
trade dispute with Volkswagen, jurisdiction of, 164–165
transportation companies and, 425–426
Vietnam and, 79
General Packet Radio Service (GPRS), 259
Generation Y
  carmakers and, 260–261
  European demographic, 238
Generic strategies. See Competitive advantage
Genetically modified organisms (GMOs), 151–152, 159, 345
Gen Y (Sony's U.S. consumer segment), 237
Geocentric orientation, to marketing, 18, 19–21
Geocentric pricing, 381–382
Geodemographic data, 215
Geographic knowledge, 543
Geographic stronghold, 525
Geographical division structures, 540–542
George P. Johnson Co., 444
Georgia, 53, 174, 299
Gerber, 27, 299, 305, 308
German Copyright Society (GEMA), 585
Germany. See also Daimler-Chrysler; Mercedes-Benz; Volkswagen AG
  antitrust and, 182
  Barbie dolls and, 148
  beer culture of, 350
  catalog sales in, 218
  Caterpillar purchases, 306
  Coca-Cola in, 10
  computer preferences in, 351
  country-of-origin effect, 341
  coupons in (table), 475
  deregulation, 379
  direct labor costs, 284
  direct marketing in, 489
  dumping by, 386
  economic success of, 47–48
  equity stakes and, 304
  euro zone member, 100
  Euroland member, 115
  European Community member, 98
  exporting of, 270
  Fairtrade Labeling Organization, 147
  Gap stores in, 13
  global competitive advantage and, 523
  Globalink member, 462
  gross national product (GNP), 99, 232
  high-income country, 62
  Hofstede's cultural typology rankings (table), 135
  illegal payment by firms, 175
  index of economic freedom ranking, 53
  investment insurance, 157
  Jewish objections to DaimlerChrysler advertising, 120–121
  low-context culture, 132
  mail-order shopping in, 490–491
  McDonald's in, 233
  Mittelstand, Internet use, and, 194
  music industry, 584
  newspaper advertising outlays, 457
  niche market of Winterhalter, 249–250
  outdoor advertising outlays, 458
  packaging regulations in, 344
  Patent Cooperation Treaty (PCT), 167
  personal selling for industrial products, 479
  Poland as trading partner, 57
  population, 99
  power distance score (low), 133

price competition, 379
privatization by, 184
product-communication strategy error, 353
Rabattgesetz (Discount Law), 379
regulatory environment, 180
smart cars and, 362
smart cell phones, 580
St. Laurent Champagne perfume in, 166
subsidiaries in Ireland, 64
target of Lexus, 248
Tati stores in, 415
telematics in, 579
teleshopping, 495
television advertising, 457, 459
think and feel country designation, 455–456
tobacco advertising regulations, 448
trademark loophole, 166–167
U.S. trade partner, 87
United Kingdom rivalry with, 98
Wal-Mart in, 419
Zugabeverordung (Free Gift Act), 379
Gestures, 127
GfK, 201, 210
Ghana, 53, 463, 107
Gillette, 28, 10, 77, 189, 252–253, 330, 333, 334, 336, 347, 355, 368, 542, 582
Giorgio Armani, 17, 396–399
Glass Egg Digital Media, 78
Glaverbel, 296
GlaxoSmithKline, 14, 23, 390, 395–396
GlaxoWellcome, 20
Glenfiddich scotch, 435
Global advertising, 437. See also Advertising; Public relations and publicity
Global brand development, 335–339
Global brand franchise, 513
Global brand leadership, 337
Global capital movements, 47
Global company, 20
Global competition. See Competitive advantage
Global consumer culture positioning (GCCP), 120, 254–256
Global e-commerce. See Electronic commerce
Global elite, 234
Global growth, managing, 7
Global industry, 5
Global localization, 9–10
Global marketing. See also Marketing; Market research
  challenges of, 577
  defined, 3
  driving forces
    leverage, 25–27
    market needs, wants, and the information revolution, 22–23
    product development costs, 23
    quality, 23–24
    regional economic agreements, 21–22
    restraining forces, 27–28
    transportation and communication improvements, 23
    world economic trends, 24–25
  importance of, 13–15
  information technology for, 190–195
  management orientations, 15
    ethnocentric, 16–18
    geocentric, 19–21
    polycentric, 18–19
    regiocentric, 19–21

Global marketing *(Continued)*
  strategic alternatives (extend, adapt, create), 346–354
  strategies (table), 8
  what it is and is not, 8–13
Global marketing audit, 552–554
Global marketing strategy (GMS), 8–9, 10, 12
Global market integration, 154
Global market participation, 8
Global market research, 200
  leading companies (table), 201
  spending totals, 200
Global market segmentation. *See* Segmentation
Global positioning system (GPS), 581
Global pricing strategies (table), 374
Global product planning, strategic alternatives (figure), 348
Global products, 333–335
  benefits to company, 334
  development of, 335–339
  distinguished from global brand, 334
  local brands versus, 339–341
Global retailing, 413–423
Global strategic partnerships (GSPs), 306
  alliances with Asian competitors, 312–313
  AT&T and Olivetti, 313–314
  attractiveness of, 310
  attributes of, 311
  Boeing and Japan, 314–315
  CFM International, GE, and Snecma, 313
  defined, 309
  examples of (table), 310
  market entry modes distinguished from, 310–311
  reasons for entering, 310
  success factors of, 311–315
  upward trend, 309–310
Global strategy, 26–27
Global teens, 234, 242–243, 254
Globalink, 462
Globalization of food, 139
Globally sensitive stage, in new product strategy, 354
Globaphobia, 28
Globerations (European demographic), 238
GMOs. *See* Genetically modified organisms (GMOs)
GNP. *See* Gross national product (GNP)
Godin Guitars, 570
Godiva chocolates, 344
Golden Grays (European demographic), 238
*Goldeneye*, 497
Goldstar, 62
Golin/Harris International, 461
*Good Housekeeping* magazine, 128
Goodyear, 452
Goodyear Tire and Rubber, 534, 582
Google, 48, 564
Governance, of global strategic partnerships (GSPs), 311
Government controls, 378
Government policy, as entry barrier, 504
Government regulations, 379
Government subsidies, 378–379
Governmental assistance to exporters, 267
Gray market goods, 383–384, 397
Grease payments, 174
Great Britain, 98, 157, 158, 166, 351, 442, 492, 580, 584. *See also* United Kingdom
  Coca-Cola in, 10
  coupons in (table), 475
  direct mail and, 490
  as high-income country, 62

McDonald's in, 33
  retailing style, 422
Great Universal Stores, 492
Greece, 53, 98, 99, 100, 103, 115, 134, 135, 352, 453
Green consumers, 61
Greenfield investment, 303, 304
Greenfield operations, 303
Green Giant Foods, 125
Greenpeace, 159
Grenada, 94
Grenadines, 94
Grey China Advertising, 206
Grey ChinaBase Annual Customer Study, 206
Grey Direct Interactive, 491
Grey Global Group, 444, 491
Grey Goose Vodka, 234, 252
Grokster, 586
Gross domestic product (GDP), 47, 47n.4. *See also* GDP
Gross national product (GNP). *See also* GNP; *individual countries*
  defined, 47n.4
  of high-income countries, 61
  of lower-middle-income countries, 57
  of low-income countries, 55
  top 10 nations (table), 232
  in the Triad, 230
  of upper-middle-income countries, 57
Group of Seven (G-7), 62
Group of Three (G3), 84
Grundig, 171
Grupo Comercial Chedraui SA, 241
Grupo Domos, 187
Grupo Gigant SA, 241
Grupo Modelo, 256, 343
Grupo Sol Melia, 186
Grupo Televisa, 494
Guam, 127
Guatemala, 53, 58, 84, 89, 90, 95, 269, 291
Gucci, 396–399, 569, 570
Gucci Group, 341
Guidance, 551
Guiding principles of the marketing company, 38–44. *See also* Marketing
  agility, 42
  anticipation, 39
  brand, 39–40
  community, 38
  company, 38
  competition, 38–39
  differentiation, 41
  integration, 39
  marketing mix, 41
  positioning, 41
  process, 40
  retention, 39
  segmentation, 40
  selling, 41–42
  service, 40
  targeting, 40–41
  totality, 42
  utility, 42
Guinea-Bissau, 53, 107
Guinness, 64, 293
Gulf Cooperation Council (GCC), 104–106
Guyana, 53, 94

**H**

Häagen-Dazs, 257
Hadith, 164
Haier Group, 1, 333
Haiti, 53, 94, 174
Hakuhodo, 444, 446

Halliburton, 460
Hallmark Cards, 325
Halvorsson and Halvorsson, 575
*Haram* (forbidden), 164
Harley-Davidson, 11, 13, 20, 244, 249, 257, 334, 525
Harmonized Tariff System (HTS), 268, 273
Harry Potter, 325–327
Hartlauer, 383–384
Hasbro, 289
Haute couture, 396–399
Havas, 444
Hawley, Michael, 582
HDTV sets, 367
Hearst Corporation, 128
Heart share of target market, 44
Hedging, of exchange rate exposure, 74
Heineken beer, 125, 242, 254, 293, 300, 365
Helene Curtis, 27, 305
Helms-Burton Act, 185, 186–188
Henkel, 103, 192, 348
Hennessey, 396–398
Henri Bendel, 416
Heritage Foundation, 52
Hermes, 60, 61
Hewlett-Packard, 17, 60, 97, 168, 192, 266, 320, 336, 426, 507, 531–532
Hidden trade barriers, 269
High-context culture, 132–133
High-income countries, 61–63
High-tech products, 254
High-touch products, 254–255
Hill & Knowlton, 461
Hinduism, 120, 124
Hispanics, 229
  automobile preferences, 241
  Barbie dolls and, 148
  beer preferences, 241
  income, 241
  U.S. demographics, 241
Hitachi, 35, 79, 168, 317, 318, 319, 328
HIV. *See* AIDS
H.J. Heinz, 151, 308, 349, 351, 453–454
HMV, 587
Hoechst AG, 534
Hofstede's cultural typology, 133–138
Hofstede's social values framework
  advertising and, 454–455
  sales promotion study and, 477
Holland, 98
Home Box Office, 479
Home demand, 519–520
Home Depot, 414, 416
Home Shopping Network (HSN), 493, 494, 561
Honda, 11, 56, 77, 235–236, 241, 244, 260, 336, 504, 525
Honda Motor, 373
Honduras, 53, 58, 84, 89, 90, 266
Hong Kong
  advertising appeals, 455
  apparel and textile exports to the United States, 266
  arbitration center, 179
  Asian flu and, 54
  catalog marketers in, 493
  China and, 139, 480
  China triangle market, 266
  cigarette smuggling and, 158
  Closer Economic Partnership Agreement, 84
  common-law jurisdiction, 163
  container port, 97
  economic system, 51
  export/import ranking, 68

Hofstede's cultural dimension rankings (Triad), 135
index of economic freedom ranking, 53
JC Penney outsourced supply chain to, 429
joint venture with Virgin Group, 421
Jollibee restaurants in, 127
managed dirty float with SDRs, 71
movie promotions to, 124
MTV Asia, 229
per capita income, 231
tariff reductions, 268
tiger status, 64
uncertainty avoidance and, 136
Hon Industries, 350
Horizontal keiretsu, 317
Horizontal price fixing, 387
Host country sales types, 486
Hotels.com, 62, 561, 573
House of Lauder, 249
HSBC Holdings, 11, 14
HTS. *See* Harmonized Tariff System
Hudson Bay, 415
Huffy bicycles, 380
Hugo Boss, 295
Human resources, 518
Humor, in advertising, 452
Hungarian Research Institute for Physics, 316
Hungary, 51, 53, 99, 103, 115, 156, 163, 248, 300, 406
    alliance opportunities in, 316
    door-to-door selling in, 479
    as upper-middle-income country, 57, 58
Hunger, 144
Hush Puppies, 290
Hypercompetition, 523–524, 526
Hyperinflation, in Ecuador, 112
Hypermarkets, 401, 408, 415, 432, 502
Hypertext, 564n.3
Hypertext markup language (HTML), 564
Hypertext transfer protocol (HTTP), 564
Hyundai Corporation, 62, 98, 260–261, 320, 342, 375
Hyundai Motor America, 346
Hyundai Motors, 534

**I**

IAC/InterActiveCorp, 561, 573
Iams, 17
IBM, 6–7, 14, 15, 17, 69, 79, 87, 97, 98, 168, 220, 320, 336, 404, 437, 462, 509, 515, 565, 566
IBM Germany, 194
I Can't Believe It's Not Butter, 125
ICC. *See* International Chamber of Commerce
Iceland, 84, 101, 174, 231, 492
ICJ. *See* International Court of Justice
Ideas, 119
IKEA, 48, 231, 416, 417, 420, 423, 424, 502–503, 510, 511
iMac, 297
Image advertising, 460–461
Imitation, 165
IMP Group, 179
Import charges, 275
Importers, 428
Importing. *See* Exporting/importing
Imports
    American, from France, 125
    parallel, 171
IMS Health, 200, 201
Inbound logistics, 424
Incepta Group, 444
Incipient markets, 208–209

Income
    per capita, of selected nations (table), 231
    as segmentation variable, 230–234
Incoterms, 371
Independent franchise store, 405
Independent marketing audit, 552
Index of economic freedom, 52, 53, 104
India, 53, 59–60, 62, 63, 65, 135–136, 160, 163, 266, 289, 315, 385, 395, 454, 463
    Barbie dolls and, 149
    big emerging market (BEM), 54, 56
    Coca-Cola in, 51
    consumer behavior in, 189–190
    dietary preferences, 124–125
    economic history, 56–57
    economic reforms, 50
    enabling conditions in, 245
    food preferences, 189, 196
    foreign direct investment in (table), 299
    marketing opportunities in, 98
    McDonald's in, 32
    MTV in, 229
    music in, 134
    outsourcing, 282
    population, 232, 233, 243
    pricing Reeboks in, 377
    product invention strategy in, 352
    regional market and sales, 17
    segment size and growth potential, 243
Indicative planning method, 551
Indirect involvement (channel distribution), 410
Individualist cultures, 133–138, 135
Indochina, 163
Indonesia, 51, 53, 63, 70, 74, 127, 153, 160, 163, 229, 266, 289–290, 375, 385, 417
    big emerging market (BEM), 54
    credit card fraud in, 568
    foreign investment in, 57
    GNP, 96
    incipient market for cigarettes, 208
    McDonald's in, 32–33
    per capita GNP, 57
    political risk in, 156–157
    population, 96, 233
Industrialized countries, 61–63
    national income, 231
    public relations in, 463–464
Industrialized economy, 153
Industrializing countries, 57–59
Industrial products, channels of distribution for, 407–410
Industry analysis, 503–507
Industry, defined, 503
Infineon Technologies, 320
Inflationary environment, 376–378
Infomercials, 493–495
Information. *See* Market information, sources of
Information Age, 60, 476
Information collection, integrated approach to, 220–221
Information overload, 196–197
Information revolution, 22–23
Information subject agenda. *See* Subject agenda
Information technology (IT)
    customer relationship management (CRM), 192–194
    data warehouses, 194
    defined, 190
    efficient consumer response (ECR), 192
    electronic data interchange (EDI), 191
    electronic point of sale (EPOS), 192

electronic smart cards, 192
global marketing and, 23
management information systems (MISs), 190–191
privacy issues, 193–194
sales force automation (SFA), 192
Information utility, 402
Infrastructure resources, 519
ING Group, 15
Inland water transportation, 426
Innovations
    in channels of distribution, 409–410
    characteristics of, 140–141
    continuous and discontinuous, 355–356
    demographic changes and, 229–230
    diffusion theory and, 139–143
    in global retailing, 421–423
    Internet, 563–564
    in postindustrial countries, 62
Innovators, 142
Innovator's dilemma, 566
In-pack coupons, 476
Instant Eyeglasses, 352
Institute on the World Economy, 78
Intangible attributes, 329
Integrated circuit (IC), 562–563
Integrated marketing communications (IMC), 436
Integration, as marketing company principle, 39
Integration of competitive moves, 9
Intel, 14, 64, 143, 320, 335, 336, 515, 563
Intellectual property, 69, 165–168, 332
Intelligent agent software, 197
Interaction effect, 142
InterActiveCorp (IAC), 62
Interactive television (ITV), 404, 493
InterAmerican Development Bank, 114
InterContinental hotels, 573
Interdependence techniques (data analysis), 215
Interfaith Coffee Program of Equal Exchange, 147
Intermodal transportation, 427
Internal audits, 552–553
Internal Revenue Service (IRS), 388
International Arbitration Tribunal, 177
International Chamber of Commerce (ICC), 179
International commercial arbitration, 178
International companies, 16
International Convention for the Protection of Industrial Property, 167
International Council for Commercial Arbitration (ICCA), 179
International Court of Arbitration, 179
International Court of Justice (ICJ), 161, 162
International finance, 69
    economic exposure, 72–73
    exchange rate exposure, 73–75
    foreign exchange market dynamics, 71
    managed dirty float with SDRs, 70–71
    purchasing power parity (PPP), 71–72
International law, 161
    antitrust, 169–172
    bribery and corruption, 173–176
    common law versus civil law, 162–163
    conflict resolution, dispute settlement, and litigation, 176–180
    "effects doctrine," 186
    intellectual property, 165–168
    Islamic law, 164
    jurisdiction, 164–165
    licensing and trade secrets, 172–173
International Law Commission, 162

International Monetary Fund (IMF), 54, 67, 68, 112, 114, 204
International Monetary Market (IMM), 70
International new-product department, 357
International partnerships, in developing countries, 315–316
International products and brands, 333
International Public Relations Association, 463
International trade, 1–3
International Trade Commission, 275, 385, 386
International Union for the Protection of Literary and Artistic Property, 167
Internet. *See also* Electronic commerce (e-commerce)
    backlash toward, 564
    control of, in China, 564
    corporate information processing and, 194
    country-specific sites, 574
    direct marketing on, 491
    in distribution, 404
    driving force for global marketing, 22–23
    early years, 563–564
    effect of, on world economy, 48
    English as primary language, 256
    importance of, 571
    market information through, 190
    prescriptions drugs through, 370
    price information on, 365–366
    as transportation mode, 426–427
    use among American men aged 18–34, 210
    user numbers, in China and Japan, 567
    Web site classification, 568–571
Internet Corporation for Assigned Names and Numbers (Icann), 564
Internet phone service, 581–582
Interpublic Group of Cos., 444, 461
Intracorporate exchanges, 388
Intranet, 191
Invention, 352. *See also* Product invention
Inventory management, 424–425
Investigation (information collection), 195
Investment. *See* Market entry strategies
iPod, 256, 297, 587
Iran, 53, 104, 149, 273
Iran and Libya Sanctions Act, 187
Iraq, 53, 104, 105, 158
Ireland, 47n. 4, 20, 53, 98, 100, 115, 121, 376
    as Celtic tiger, 64
    direct mail and, 490
    GNP, 99
    Hofstede's cultural typology rankings (table), 135
    per capita income, 231
    population, 99
Iridium, 208
Irrevocable letter of credit, 279–280
Islam, 120–121, 149
Islamic law, 164
Islands of integrity, 175
Israel, 53, 84, 101, 104
Isuzu Motors, 301
Italy. *See also* Benetton
    advertising appeals, 445–456
    advertising expenditures, 457–458
    apparel and textile exports to the United States, 266
    AT&T and Olivetti partnership failure, 313–314
    Barbie dolls and, 148
    "Club Med" nation stigma, 98
    country-of-origin effect, 341
    Cuba and, 186
    euro zone member, 100
    Euroland member, 115

European constitution, references to God, 121
Globalink member, 462
gross national product (GNP), 99, 232
Gucci Group sales in Asia, 341
high-income country, 62
Hofstede's cultural dimensions rankings (table), 135
index of economic freedom ranking, 53
joint venture with Cummins Engine, 306
population, 99
product regulations, 347
state tobacco monopoly, 448
taxes in, 376
U.S. trade partner, 87
wine and spirits industry, 428
ITM Enterprises, 414
Itochi, 15
Itochu Corp., 532
Ito-Yokada, 414
ITT, 186
iTunes, 586
iTunes Music Store, 297, 568, 586
Ivory Coast, 53

**J**

Jackson-Vanik amendment, 77
Jägermeister schnapps, 350
Jamaica, 53, 94, 123
James Bond films, product placement in, 496–498
James River, 302
Jamiroquai, 134
Jamont, 302, 306
Jan Sobieski cigarettes, 332
Japan
    advertising in, localized approach, 443
    affluent market, 230
    age of population, 228
    American style in, 13
    ASEAN and, 96
    attitudes, beliefs, and values in, 120
    auto dealers as specialists for life, 547–548
    automakers, 4
    automobile industry investment in the United States, 286
    Avon factors in, 74
    Barbie dolls and, 149–150, 201
    Boeing design work in, 361
    catalog industry, 492–493
    channel innovation in, 409–410
    civil-law jurisdiction, 163
    Coca-Cola in, 9–10, 332
    collaboration in, 516
    collectivist culture of, 137
    color perceptions in, 123
    competitive global advantage and, 523
    creative strategy of, 454
    cultural perceptions, 135–136, 455–456
    Cummins Engine joint venture, 306
    dietary preferences, 124
    diffusion of innovations in, 142–143
    direct marketing in, 489
    distribution system, 493
    door-to-door car sales, 405
    dumping by, 386–387
    duties, reduction or elimination of, 372n
    e-Bay's failure in, 572
    economic success of, 47–48
    *endaka*, 286
    English as a marketing tool in, 130, 256
    export strategies, 266
    export/import ranking, 68

fax machine industry, 207–208
food preferences in, 139
Foreign Corrupt Practices Act (FCPA), 175
foreign direct investment in India, 299
foreign exchange market and, 71
*gaman*, 136
global strategic partnership with Boeing, 314
GMO regulations, 151
*Good Housekeeping* magazine in, 128
gross national product (GNP), 232
hamburger restaurants per capita, 31
high-context culture, 132
high-income country, 62
Hofstede's cultural typology rankings (table), 135
ice cream industry in, 296
IKEA in, 511
index of economic freedom, 53
Indonesia auto industry controversy, 153
infomercials in, 494
intellectual property and, 168
Internet users in, 567
investment in the United States, 298
investment insurance by, 157
joint ventures in, 301, 421
keiretsu system, 316–319, 512
knowledge creation, 536–537
Kyocera Corporation, 559–560
lean production, 545–548
lifestyle features, 63
lifestyle in, 63
low-cost advantage, 509
mandatory labeling, 345
market complexities, 97–98
marketing agency complexities, 447
masculinity behavior, 134
McDonald's in, 31–32, 442
monocultural society, 120
MTV in, 229
music industry and, 584
nationality of top management, 533–534
newspaper readership, 459
Nippon Telegraph and Telephone (NTT), 14–15
nonverbal communication in, 129
online business in, 532–533
package aesthetics and, 345–346
Patent Cooperation Treaty (PCT), 167
PepsiCo advertising in, 437
per capita income, 231
personal selling in, 479
population, 233
postindustrial country, 61
Ralston Purina joint venture, ending of, 303
recorded music sales, 23
regional market and sales, 17
regulatory environment, 180
retailing style, 417
Shop America stores, 422–423
soup market, 240
tariff elimination, 268
tariffs and trade agreements, 269
technology transfer laws, 172
television advertising in, 457
television industry in, 514–515
Toyota Lexus sales in, 248
trade dispute with the United States (mid-1990s), 98
trade secret laws, 173
trade with United States, 67–68, 87
transfer pricing, 388–389
Treaty of Rome, 170–171
Triad membership, 64

uncertainty avoidance and, 136
unfair trade practices, 271
video games in, 475
Vietnam and, 77
virtual community for women, 569
"Japanese English," 130
Japan Tobacco, 17
Jay-Z, 226
J.C. Penney, 414, 417, 429
J.D. Powers and Associates Initial Quality
  Index, 558
Jeep, 250, 342
JetBlue Airways, 122
Jiangling Motors, 301
Joaquin Sabina, 332
Jobbers, 276
John Deere, 482
Johnnie Walker scotch, 435
Johnson & Johnson, 14, 159, 160, 232, 325
Joint ventures, 170, 294, 306
  advantages, 299–300
  in big emerging markets (BEMs), 301–302
  defined, 299
  disadvantages, 302–303
  global retailing market entry and, 421
  Japan and, difficulties, 301
  in personal selling, 488
  in Russia, 315
  traditional, 310
Jollibee restaurants, 1, 127, 246
Jordan, 53, 84, 104, 105, 106
J.P. Morgan, 70
Judaism, 120
Jurisdiction, 164–165, 177–178
Just-in-time system, 317
JVC, 524
J. Walter Thompson, 77, 348, 446

## K

Kader Industrial Toy Company, 289
Kaizen, 546
KamAZ, 306
Kantar Group, 201
Kao, 232
KaZaA, 582, 586
Kazakhstan, 53, 299
Keiretsu system, 98, 316–319, 320, 321, 405, 512
Kellogg, 139, 189, 196
Kentucky Fried Chicken, (KFC) 32, 66,
  182, 121
Kenya, 53, 107, 109
Ketel One vodka, 252
Key suppliers/customers/competitors,
  512–513
Kia, 160
*Kiki*, 1
Kirin Brewery, 184, 301
Kleenex, 166
KLM, 171
Kmart, 408, 414
Knorr dehydrated soups, 144
Know-how, 543
Know-how advantage, 524
Knowledge
  ascendancy of, over capital, 62
  competencies from, 543
  creation of, in home territory, 536–537
Knowledge resources, 518–519
Kodak, 57, 217, 244, 330, 515, 528, 564–565
Kolynos, 169
Komatsu, 17, 244, 480, 514
Koran, 164
Korea, 51, 128, 163, 229, 342, 456. *See also*
  North Korea; South Korea

Kraft, 102, 147, 148, 454, 535
Krell, 509
Kroger, 414
Krupp-Hoesch, 362
*Kuchikomi* (word of mouth), 137
Kukutake Publishing, 492
Kum & Go, 415
*Kuptsy* (Russian consumer type), 236–237
Kuwait, 53, 104, 105
Kyocera Corporation, 409, 559–560
Kyrgyzstan, 53, 299

## L

Labeling, 344–345
Labor, 284
  low-cost sources of, 77, 78, 289
Laboratoire UPSA, 167
Lagavulin scotch, 435
Laggards, 142
Land, 284
Landor Associates, 439
Lands' End, 342, 490, 492
Language and communication, 126–129
  in advertising, 450–452
  English in international business, 256
  Web site translations and, 573–574
Lanham Act, 165
Laos, 52, 53, 96
Laptop warriors, 579
Late majority, 142
Late movers, 246
Latent market, 207
Latin America, 81, 95, 134, 147, 266, 286,
  447, 473, 479, 487, 515, 567. *See
  also* Regional markets; *individual
  countries*
  advertising in, 458
  Barbie dolls and, 149
  Calvo Doctrine, 179–180
  Coca-Cola in, 344
  GDP, 113
  "lost decade," 160–161
  market attractiveness, 60
  marketing in, 500–501
  McDonald's sales in, 31
Latvia, 53, 99, 115, 156
Launch brands, 342
Laura Ashley, 414, 416
Law of disproportionality, 238
Law of one price, 365
Lawyers, 176–180
Lawyers Committee for Human
  Rights, 288
Layers of advantage, 514–515
LCCP. *See* Local consumer culture
  positioning (LCCP)
LCDs. *See* Less-developed countries (LCDs)
Leadership
  core competence and, 534–535
  examples of, 531–533
  top management nationality, 533–534
Lean production
  assembler value chains, 546–547
  defined, 545
  downstream value chains, 547–548
Learning, 312
Lebanon, 53, 104, 106, 415
Lee jeans, 379
Legal environment. *See* International law
Lego Group, 64, 325, 326, 529
Leo Burnett, 440, 446
Leo Sharpio & Associates, 570
Lesotho, 53, 84, 108, 109
Less-developed countries (LDCs), 57

channels of distribution in, 413
distribution of perishable foods, 406
marketing opportunities in, 59–61
sales forces in, 486
Letter of credit (L/C), 272, 279–280
Leverage
  defined, 25
  experience transfers, 25–26
  global strategy, 26–27
  resource utilization, 26
  scale economies, 26
Levi Strauss, 229, 234–235, 237, 256, 379,
  405, 415, 446, 540
Lexus, 210–211, 247–248
LG Electronics, 62, 298, 320, 337
LG.Philips, 17, 328
Liberia, 107
Libya, 53, 105, 273
Licensed asset, 295
Licensee, 295
Licensing, 172–173, 294
  advantages, 295–296
  cell phone ring tunes and, 581
  contract manufacturing, 297
  defined, 295
  disadvantages and opportunity costs,
    296–297
  franchising, 297–298
  of Harry Potter, 325–327
  Mattel and Barbie, 149
  patent-licensing arrangements,
    178–179
  second-tier, 325
Licensing Executives Society, 172
Licensor, 295
Licensor-competitor, 297
Liechtenstein, 84, 101, 492
Line extensions, 356
Link analysis, 564
Linkin Park, 471, 585
Linux, 577
Lipitor, 364
Listening, 484
Lithuania, 52, 53, 99, 115
Litigation, 176–180
Littlewoods, 492
Living wage, 288
Liz Claiborne, 288
L.L. Bean, 490, 492
Local consumer culture positioning
  (LCCP), 257
Localized approach
  to advertising, 439–443
  to marketing, 18
  to sales promotion, 474
Local products and brands, 332–333,
  339–341
Lockheed Martin Corp., 392
Logistics, 285, 423–424, 429
Logo, 330–331
Lomé Convention, 103
London International Financial Futures
  Exchange (LIFFE), 70
Lone Star Cement, 186
Long-term orientation (LTO), 135–138
Long-term values, 135
Loose bricks, 515
*Lord of the Rings*, 252–253
L'Oreal, 438, 534
LOT Polish Airlines, 310
Louis Vuitton, 340, 396–399
Love's, 415
Low-context culture, 132–133
Lower-middle-income countries, 57
Lowe's, 414

Low-income countries
    market development stages in, 55–57
    standard of living in, 231
Low-wage labor force, 77, 78
Loyalty programs, 192
LSI Logic, 515
LTI International Hotels, 186
Lucky Ali, 134
Lufthansa, 310
Luxembourg, 53, 98, 100, 115, 139, 181
    GNP, 99
    per capita income, 231
    population, 99
    standard of living, 230
Luxury badging, 340
Luxury goods, 340, 367, 376
    gray market and, 397
    marketing of, 396–399
    market size and key players, 17
LVMH Moët Hennessy Louis Vuitton SA,
    17, 367, 396–399, 473 570

# M

Maastricht Treaty (1991), 100, 115
Macedonia, 53
MacroMedia, 578
Macy's, 413
Madagascar, 53
Mad cow disease, 33, 159, 460
"Made in the EU," 343
Madrid agreement of 1891, 166
Maersk A/S, 325
Maersk Sealand, 426
Magalog, 492
Magna International, 362
MaK, 306
Malawi, 53, 108, 109
Malaysia, 53, 54, 69, 70, 160, 163, 229,
    289–290, 304, 340, 577
    direct marketing in, 491
    GNP, 96
    population, 96
    sales promotion and, 477–478
    as upper-middle-income country, 57
Mali, 53, 107
Malta, 53, 115
Managed dirty float with SDRs, 70–71
Managed trade, 269
Management
    of global strategic partnerships
        (GSPs), 311
    nationality of, 533–534
Management control, 548–550
Management information systems (MISs),
    190–191
Management myopia, 27
Management-only agreements, 488
Management orientations. See also Global
        marketing
    ethnocentric, 485, 486
    polycentric, 485, 486
    regiocentric, 485
Manufacturer-owned store, 405
Manufacturer's country, organizing for
        exporting in, 277–278
Manufacturer's export representatives, 276
Manufacturing keiretsu, 317
Mapping strategy of a company, 43
Maquiladora, 59
Marginal-cost pricing, 375
Markel Corp., 115
Market access, as political factor in
        exporting/importing, 286
Market access, blocking of, 267–271

Market-based transfer price, 388–389
Market capitalism, 49
Market country, organizing for exporting
        in, 278–279
Market development, stages of, 53
    big emerging markets (BEMs), 54–55
    GNP and population (table), 55
    high-income countries, 61–63
    lower-middle-income countries, 57
    low-income countries, 55–57
    marketing implications of, 65–66
    marketing opportunities in LDCs and
        developing countries, 59–61
    the Triad, 63–64
    upper-middle-income countries, 57–59
Market entry strategies
    acquisition and (table), 305
    cooperative strategies
        digital future, 320–321
        in Japan (keiretsu), 316–319
        in South Korea (chaebol), 319–320
        evolution and interaction of
            (figure), 315
        expansion strategies, 420–421
        global retailing framework (figure), 420
        global strategic partnerships, 306,
            308–315
        international partnerships in developing
            countries, 315–316
    investment
        foreign direct investment, 298–299
        joint ventures, 299–303
        ownership or equity stakes, 303–306
    licensing, 295–298
    market expansion strategies, 321–322
    risk levels for (figure), 294
Market expansion strategies, 321–322
Market holding strategy, 374
Market information, sources of, 197–199
Market-oriented democracy, 153
Market potential, as budget influence, 551
Market potential, assessing. See Target
        markets, choosing
Market research, 199
    data collection process, 202
    defined, 200
    headquarters control of, 219–220
    integrated approach to information
        collection, 220–221
    objectives, 200
    search for new products, 224
    step 1: identify the information
        requirement, 200–201
    step 2: problem definition, 201, 203
    step 3: choose unit of analysis, 203
    step 4: examine data availability,
        203–205
    step 5: assess value of research, 205
    step 6: research design
        data collection issues, 206–209
        data gathering guidelines, 205–206
        research methodologies, 209–213
        scale development, 213–214
        tasks, 206
    step 7: analyzing data, 214–218
    step 8: presenting the findings, 218–219
    top firms, 201
Market scope, 508
Market segmentation, 225. See also
        Segmentation
Market selection framework (table), 245
Market share, 550
Market skimming, 366–367
Market socialism, 50–52
Market unknowns, 480

Marketing. See also Global marketing;
        Guiding principles of the market-
        ing company anatomy of, 43
    conventional and unconventional
        wisdom, 227–228
    culture and, 129–130, 132
    overview, 3–8
    role of, 60
    in social and cultural environments,
        143–145
Marketing activities
    concentration of, 8–9
    coordination of, 9
Marketing budgets, influences on,
        551–552
Marketing communications, 435–436. See
        also Advertising; Public relations
        and publicity
Marketing mix, 4
    as marketing company principle, 41
    as marketing tactic, 44
Marketing model drivers, 245–247
Marketing strategies, 43
    single-country and global (table), 8
Marketing tactic, 43–44
Marketing value, 44
MarketResearch.com, 204, 205
Markets
    existing, 206
    incipient, 208–209
    latent, 207
    potential, 207
Mark Levinson, 509
Marks & Spencer, 159, 209, 413, 417–418,
        420–421
Marlboro cigarettes, 10, 256, 336, 340, 345
Marriott hotels, 573
Mars Inc., 338
Martin-Logan, 509
Marubeni, 15
Marvel Enterprises, 269
Marxism, 50
Mary Kay Cosmetics, 206, 404
Masculinity, 133–138, 135
Maslow's Hierarchy of Needs, 144,
        339–341
Mass customization, 321
Mass-market consumer products, 406
Mass marketing, 489
Mass production, 545–546
Massachusetts Institute of Technology
        (MIT), 64
Massively multiplayer online games
        (MMOG), 578
MasterCard, 124, 489
Master tones, 581
Match.com, 561, 573
Material culture, 119
Matrix organization, 542–545
Matsushita Electric Industrial Company, 24,
        26, 128, 168, 322, 514–515, 524
Mattel, 148–150, 201, 325, 326, 380, 407
Mauritania, 53, 105, 107
Mauritius, 53, 108, 109, 291, 299
Max Factor, 253
Maxxcom, 444
May Department Stores, 288
Maytag, 509
Mazda, 304, 319, 356, 533–534
MCC, 362
McCann-Erickson Worldwide, 446, 447
"McDonaldization of culture," 130
McDonald's, 182, 535
    adaptation of menu to local tastes,
        31–35, 144, 237

advertising in Japan, 442
big idea and, 449
Central Europe, approach in, 103
China, pursuit of opportunities in, 56
country identification, 1
economic value ranking (table), 336
European Commission consumer safety standards and, 347
franchising, 298
global expansion, 31–35, 233
global marketing strategy, 10, 12
Jollibee restaurants and, 127
lawsuit in Britain, 33
McDonald's International, 31–35
Mexican currency crisis and, 66
negative publicity, 460
non-word mark logo, 331
organizational design, 541
physiological needs met by, 339–340
promotions for, 34
representation at European Commission, 180
skill and competence of, 422
strategy alternatives, 238
U.S. refocus, 34–35
Web ads, 569–570
MCI Communications, 479
McKinsey & Company, 206, 312–313
Mecca-Cola, 121
Media, in global advertising, 456–459
Media Lab Europe, 64
Media Player, 586
Medium Is the Message, The (McLuhan), 134
Meiji Milk, 296
"Mena" region, 106
Mercado Comun del Sur. See Mercosur
Mercedes-Benz, 234, 243, 256, 331, 336, 339, 362, 367, 380, 491, 579
Merchandise, world trade in, 68–69
Merck & Co., 14, 23, 395–396
Mercosur (Mercado Comun del Sur; Common Market of the South), 58, 92–93, 95
Mergers and acquisitions, 170, 298–299, 303
Merrill Lynch, 220, 336
Message, in advertising, 447
Metrics of value, 566
Metro AG, 123, 192, 414
Mexico
    advertising appeals in, 455
    apparel and textile exports to the United States, 266
    arbitration centers in, 179
    avocado-growers' problem, 88–89
    Avon Products in, 66, 72–73
    big emerging market (BEM), 54
    Bronco (recording artist), 332
    Coca-Cola in, 10
    coffee sales, 148
    country-of-origin effect, 342, 343
    Cuba, entry into, 186–187
    currency crisis in, 66
    direct labor costs, 284
    expanded Triad member, 64
    export/import ranking, 68
    free trade agreements, 84, 95
    gross national product (GNP), 87, 88, 232
    Group of Three (G3) member, 84
    Harley-Davidson in, 249
    index of economic freedom ranking, 53
    joint venture with Corning Glass, 302
    labor, low-cost, 289
    long-term orientation (LTO), 135, 136
    market selection framework (table), 245
    opportunities for entry, 315

population, 88
power distance score (high), 136
privatization in, 153
regional market, 87–89
QVC (homeshopping), 494
Sam's Club in, 415
trade secret laws, 173
trade surplus with the United States, 69
upper-middle-income country, 58–59
Volkswagen Beetle production in, 558
Wal-Mart in, 415, 419, 431
MGM/UA, 171
M. Henry Wines, 391
Michelob, 343
Micron Technology, 168
Microsoft, 14, 17, 69, 168, 171, 191, 199, 297, 336, 347, 368, 471–472, 475, 507, 563, 577, 578, 587
Microsoft Network (MSN), 571
MicroStrategy, 194
Midas Muffler, 182
Middle East, 127, 515, 567. See also Regional markets
    Barbie dolls and, 149
    bribery in, 173
    color perceptions in, 123
    index of economic freedom and, 104
    Islamic law, 164
    marketing issues in, 106
    McDonald's sales in, 31
    nonverbal communication in, 129
    oil prices and business, 104
    pan-Arabism and, 104
Miller Brewing, 169, 293
Mini Cooper, 456
Ministry for International Trade and Industry (MITI; Japan), 204, 266
MIS. See Management information systems (MISs)
Mission, of global strategic partnerships (GSPs), 311
Mitsubishi, 15, 168, 260, 533–534
Mitsubishi Group, 316, 317, 318
Mitsubishi Heavy Industries, 386, 516
Mitsubishi Motors, 230, 534
Mitsui Group, 15, 316
Mitsukoshi, 413
Mittelstand companies, 194
mm02 plc, 581
MMT gasoline additive, 160
Mobil, 154, 582
Mobile commerce (m-commerce), 579–582
Mobile gaming, 581
Mobile Marketing Association, 580
Mobile phones, 128, 254. See also Cell phones
Moet Chandon, 272
Moldova, 53, 299
Mongolia, 53
Monitoring (information collection), 195
Monsanto, 151, 159, 303
Montenegro, 53
Montserrat, 94
Moody's Investors Service, 48
Moore's Law, 562n
Morocco, 53, 84, 105, 106
Morphology, 126, 127
Morris, 46
Mosaic, 564
Moscow Bread Company (MBC), 406–407
Most-favored nation (MFN), 272
Mostly free economy, 53, 104
Mostly unfree economy, 53, 104
Mother hen, 276
Motorcycle industry, 244
Motorola, 17, 56, 64, 208, 226, 259, 565, 580

Movie industry, 1, 124. See also Product placement
Movie tie-ins, 473
Movies, 124
Mozambique, 53, 108, 109
MP3 file swapping, 101, 505, 584
MP3 players, 254
MSN Music Club, 587
MSN WomenCentral, 571
MTV, 225, 229, 242–243, 437–438, 489
MTV Asia, 229
MTV Europe, 226, 587
MTV Video Music Awards (1998), 134
Muhammad, 164
Multidimensional scaling (MDS), 215–216, 217
Multifiber Arrangement (MFA), 56
Multilateral Agreement on Investment, 188
Multinational company, 18
Multinational corporations (MNCs), 179
Multisegment targeting, 250
Multitiered branding, 334
Munich Convention, 168
Music
    cultures and, 123–124
    in India, 134
    MTV and, 225
Music industry, 1
    cell phone ring tunes and, 580–581
    file swapping, 505
    local recording stars, 332
    market size and key players, 17
    Napster and, 584–587
    transshipment and (Europe), 101
    Wal-Mart's influence on, 506
Music tones, 581
MusicMatch Downloads, 587
MusicNet, 586
Muslims, 121. See also Islam; Islamic law
Myanmar, 96, 97, 174
MyCokeMusic store, 587
Myopia
    cultural, 138
    management, 27

## N

Nabisco, 452
NAFTA. See North American Free Trade Agreement
Naive nationalist stage, in new-product strategy, 354
Namesake companies, 295
Namibia, 53, 84, 108, 109
Napoleonic Code, 163
Napster, 505, 530, 538, 584
National Association of Manufacturers, 85
National Basketball Association, 295, 495
National Bipartisan Commission on Cuba, 188
National competitive advantage. See Competitive advantage
National controls, 28
National Music Publishers' Association, 585
National pride, 333
National Trade Data Base (NTDB), 203
Nationalist backlash, 126
Nationality, of top management, 533–534
Nationalization, 160–161
Nation-states, 153–154
NCH Marketing Services, 476
NEC Corp, 168, 515
Need-base approach to brands, 339–341

Needs, 22, 144–145, 227, 339
Négociant, 428
Negotiated transfer prices, 388–389
Negotiation, 484–485
Neiman Marcus, 237
Nepal, 53
Nescafé, 255, 336, 439
Nestlé
    advertising expenditures, 438
    approach to consumer and trade sales, 473
    brand loyalty, building, 308
    Cereal Partners Worldwide, 310
    Coca-Cola alliance, 5–6
    coffee trader, 147
    currency exposure issue, 73
    direct mail campaign, 491
    global brand, 333
    GMOs and, 151
    high-touch, emotional appeal, 255
    India and, 196, 245, 247
    logo, non-country specific, 256
    Nescafé, 255, 336, 439
    pet food market, 17, 241
    Russia and, 237
    transnational company, 20
Netherlands
    corruption ranking, 174
    direct mail in, 490
    euro zone member, 100
    Euroland member, 115
    Frito-Lay in, 139
    global competitive advantage and, 523
    Globalink member, 462
    GNP, 99
    Hofstede's cultural typology rankings
        (table), 135
    index of economic freedom ranking, 53
    Ketel One vodka, 252
    masculinity score (low), 134
    parallel imports in, 383
    Patent Cooperation Treaty (PCT), 167
    population, 99
    power distance score (low), 133
    Royal Ahold NV, 408, 414
    Royal Philips Electronics, positioning
        of, 22
    U.S. investments in, 298
Netscape, 564
Neumann Gruppe, 147
Nevis, 94
New entrants, 503–505
New products
    characteristics needed to excel, 354
    continuum (figure), 356
    development of, 354, 356–357
    ideas for, 355–356
    international department, 357
    stages, 354
    testing, 358
New York Convention, 177
New Zealand, 53, 151, 174, 268, 345, 407
Newly industrializing economy, 153
Newly industrializing economy (NIE), 58
Newness, 355
News Corporation, 20
Newspaper advertising, 456–459
N-Gage, 226, 259
Nicaragua, 53, 58, 84, 89, 90
Niche marketing, 120, 249–250
Nickelodeon, 225
Nielsen Media Research, 200, 210
Niger, 53, 107
Nigeria, 53, 107, 160, 174, 133
Nike, 57, 59, 180, 191, 229, 234, 256, 288, 331,
    333, 377, 405, 452, 468, 509

in China, 348
    negative publicity, 460, 461
    sweatshop controversy, 289–290
Nikon, 78
Nintendo, 368, 387, 471, 475
Nippon Paper Industries, 169
Nippon Telegraph and Telephone (NTT),
    14–15
Nissan, 4, 17, 24, 27, 46, 124, 243, 319, 342,
    443, 534, 536
Noise, 440
Nokia, 1, 10, 17, 128, 226, 235, 256, 259–260,
    308, 336, 342, 423, 461, 496,
    534–535, 564, 580
Nominal scale, 213
Nonbusiness infrastructure (NBI), 513
Nonmanufacturing jobs, 284
Nonmarket economy, 153
Nonmaterial culture, 119
Nonprice promotion, 472
Nonprobability samples, 213
Nontariff barriers, 28, 160
Nontariff trade barrier (NTB), 269
Nonverbal communication, 127, 129
Non-word mark logo, 331
Normal trade relations (NTR), 77, 272–273
North Africa, 106
North America, 230, 567. See also Canada;
        Mexico; United States
    economic integration of, 87
    as a regional market, 87–89
North American Free Trade Agreement, 21,
        28, 58–59, 66, 69, 84, 87–89, 93,
        187, 342
    countries (figure), 88
    expropriation and compensation rule, 160
    GNP of, 88
    income and population (table), 88
    regiocentric orientation, 19
    trade secret laws, 173
North American Free Trade area, 46
North Korea, 52, 53, 167, 273. See also Korea;
        South Korea
North Yemen, 105
Northern Telecom, 20
Northwestern airlines, 171
Norway, 53, 84, 101, 174, 268, 459, 492, 580
    direct mail and, 490–491
    per capita income, 231
Not invented here (NIH) syndrome, 353
Nouveau riche clientele, 396–399
Novartis, 14, 23, 151
NTB. See Nontariff trade barrier (NTB)
NTT DoCoMo, 14
Nutrition Education and Labeling Act, 345

## O

Obesity, 291
Observation, 210–211
Ocean transportation, 426
OD2, 587
OECD. See Organization for Economic
        Cooperation and Development
        (OECD)
Offset, 392–393
"Offshoring, 282"
Ogilvy & Mather, 77, 446
Ogilvy & Mather Worldwide, 442
OgilvyOne Worldwide, 491
Oil
    Africa and, 106
    as business driver in Middle East, 104
    as growth driver for Ecuador, 113
Oligarchs, 48

Olivetti, 313–314
Olympus Optical, 375
Oman, 53, 104, 105
Omega, 283
Omnibus Trade and Competitiveness
        Act, 174
Omnicom Group, 444, 445, 461
One-to-one marketing, 488–489
One World, Ready or Not (Grieder), 16
Online storefronts, 404
On-pack coupons, 476
Onyx Software, 193
OPEC, 171
Opel, 547
Open-account sales, 282
Open economies, 89
Open-ended questions, 209, 212
Open source software, 577
Operational planning, 549
OPIC. See Overseas Private Investment
        Corporation (OPIC)
Opportunity costs, with licensing,
        296–297
Option, foreign currency, 74
Opt out option, 194
Oracle, 17, 336
Orange SA, 580
Ordering relationships, 135
Order processing, 424
Organic growth, 420
Organization, 535–538. See also Lean
        production
    of global strategic partnerships
        (GSPs), 311
    international, patterns of development
        division structure, 539–540
        geographical and product division
        structures, 540–542
        matrix organization, 542–545
        regional management centers, 540
Organizational culture, 27
Organization for Economic Cooperation
        and Development (OECD), 62–63,
        86, 169, 577
    farm subsidies and, 267
    standard against bribery, 175
Organized intelligence, 220
ORG-MARG, 189, 200
Oriflame International, 406
Original equipment manufacturer (OEM),
        35, 79
Osborne, 563
Otis Elevator, 77, 186
Otto GmbH & Co. KG, 492, 493
Outbound logistics, 424
Outlet malls, 416
Outlet stores, 416
Outsourcing. See Exporting/importing
Overland Ltd., 295
Overseas Private Investment Corporation
        (OPIC), 77, 157, 161
Ovum, 567
Ovum Limited, 200
Ownership, investment via, 303–306
Ownership levels, for basic products, 62
Oxfam, 147, 148

## P

Pacific Rim countries, diffusion of
        innovations in, 142–143
Packaging
    aesthetics, 345–346
    copyright law and, 397
    cultural differences in, 139

Kyocera Corporation and, 559–560
labeling, 344–345
Paid search advertising, 571
Pakistan, 53, 163, 233, 266, 385
Panama, 53, 89, 90, 112, 175
Pan-Arabism, 104
Panera Bread, 31
Paraguay, 53, 92, 149, 174
Parallel barter, 392
Parallel imports, 171, 383
Parallel trading, 392
Parallel translations, 209
Paramount, 171
Paramount Pictures, 561
Pareto's Law, 238
Paris Convention, 167
Paris Union, 167
Parker Pen, 28, 340
Partnerships. 483. *See also* Global strategic
partnerships (GSPs);
International partnerships, in
developing countries
Patent, 58, 165–168, 178–179
Patent Cooperation Treaty (PCT), 167
Pattern advertising, 441
Payee, 280
Payment methods, for exports. *See*
Exporting/importing
Peace of Westphalia, 161
Pearl Jam, 495
Pearson PLC, 534
Peer-to-peer (P2P)
e-commerce category, 567
file swapping, 505
marketing, 404
Penetration pricing policy strategy, 367–368
Peoplemeter, 210
People's Republic of China, 266. *See also*
China
PepsiCo, 182, 213, 471, 473
advertising by, 450
advertising in Japan, 437
in India, 190
integrated marketing communications
and, 462
negative publicity, 460
Soviet Union (former) and, 391
Per capita income. *See* Income; *individual
countries*
Perceptual blockage, 138
Perestroika, 51
Perishable products, 406
Permanent Court of International Justice, 162
Pernod Ricard SA, 435
Perrier, 234
Persian Gulf War, 104
Persistence, 135
Personal computers, 507, 563
laptops, 579
market size and key players, 17
revolution of, 48
Personal digital assistants(PDAs), 579
Personal interaction, 198–199
Personal interviews, 210
Personal selling
defined, 479
issues and challenges, 480
other approaches, 488
sales force nationality, 485–488
Strategic/Consultative Selling Model,
481–485
Personal selling philosophy, 482
Personal sources, of information, 197–198
Peru, 53, 90, 91
Pete's Wicked beer, 343

Peugeot, 27, 46, 77, 208
Pfizer, 14, 23
Pharmaceutical industry, 23, 381
Pharmaceutical Research and
Manufacturers Association, 23
Phasing, 129
Philadelphia Stock Exchange (PSE), 70
Philip Morris, 10, 158, 169, 293, 448
Philippines, 1, 53, 74, 83, 96, 160, 229, 246,
266, 352, 406, 417
Philips Electronics, 97, 103, 254, 320,
334, 494
Phillips-Van Heusen (PVH), 288
PhoCus Wright, 573
Phoenix Group, 377
PhoneFurniture, 581
Phonology, 126, 127, 128
Physical component, of culture, 119
Physical culture, 119
Physical distribution, 423. *See also* Channels
of distribution
defined, 401
inventory management, 424–425
logistics management, 429
order processing, 424
transportation, 425–428
warehousing, 424
Physical resources, 518
Physiological needs, 144–145, 339
Piggyback exporter, 276
Piggyback marketing, 407
Pilkington, 295–296
Pioneer Hi-Bred International, 151, 443, 444
Pipelines, 425
Piracy, 69, 165
Pizza Hut, 32, 34, 182
Place utility, 402–403
Planning
budgeting and, 550
strategic and operational, 549
Platform, 356
PlayStation 2, 368, 471, 524, 578
Playtex, 453
Pluralization of consumption, 227
Plymouth, 46
Point-of-use sampling, 476
Poland, 53, 54, 57, 99, 103, 113, 115, 121, 163,
300, 332, 402
Polaroid, 446
Political culture, 152
Political environment, 152
nation-states and sovereignty, 153–154
political risk, 154–157
seizure of assets, 160–161
taxes, 157–160
Political risk
categories of (table), 155
causes of, 155–156
defined, 154–155
in exporting and importing, 286
expressions and symptoms of, 156–157
income versus (figure), 157
in Indonesia, 156–157
in personal selling, 480
in Russia, 158–159
Polo, 379
Polycentric orientation, to marketing,
18–19, 485, 486
Polycentric pricing, 381
PolyGram, 7, 134
Pontiac, 260, 357
Population, as segmentation variable, 230–234
Porno-chic, 350
Porsche AG, 235
Port of Singapore, 97

Portugal, 53, 98, 99, 100, 103, 115, 134, 135,
139, 352
Positioning
attribute or benefit, 251
competition, 253
defined, 225, 250
foreign consumer culture positioning
(FCCP), 256–257
global consumer culture positioning
(GCCP), 254–256
local consumer culture positioning
(LCCP), 257
as marketing company principle, 41
as marketing strategy, 43
quality and price, 251–252
use or user, 252–253
Postindustrial countries, 61–63
Potential markets, 207
Power distance, 133–138, 135, 477
PPG, 296, 426
Prada, 396, 570
Preferential tariff, 273
Preferential trade agreements
common market, 85
customs union, 84
defined, 83
economic union, 85–86
free trade area (FTA), 83–84
Premiums, 472
Prescription drugs, 364, 370
Presentation plan, 483–485
Presentation strategy, 483
PressPlay, 586
Price, as positioning strategy, 251–252
Price ceilings, 364
Price discrimination, 317–318, 387
Price elasticity of demand, 73
Price escalation, 370–372
Price-fixing, 169, 317–318, 387–388
Price promotion, 472
Price transparency, 375–376
Pricing decisions, 364
adaptation (polycentric) pricing, 381
basic concepts, 365–366
calculating, for exports, 382
companion products, 368
competitive behavior, 379
cost-plus pricing, 369–370
countertrade, 390
barter, 391–392
compensation trading, 393
counterpurchase, 392
offset, 392–393
switch trading, 393
currency fluctuations, 373–376
dumping, 384–387
environmental influences on, 373–380
extension (ethnocentric) pricing policy,
380–381
geocentric pricing, 381–382
government controls, subsidies, and
regulations, 378–379
gray market goods, 383–384
inflationary environment, 376–378
market skimming and financial
objectives, 366–367
objectives and strategies, 366–373
penetration pricing and nonfinancial
objectives, 367–368
policy alternatives, 380–382
price escalation, 370–371
price fixing, 387–388
sourcing, as a strategic pricing tool, 380
target costing, 369
terms of the sale, 371–373

Pricing decisions    (*Continued*)
  transfer pricing, 388–390
    competitive pricing, 389
    sales of tangible and intangible
        property, 389
    Section 482 regulations, 389–390
    tax regulations and, 389
Pricing strategies, of the European union
        (table), 102
Primary data, 205
Primary function, 340
Prime, 565
Principles. *See* Guiding principles of the
        marketing company
Print media, 456
Privacy
    data collection and, 193–194
    e-commerce issues, 575
    Internet concerns, 564
Private international law, 162
Private label retailers, 418
Private sector, in China, 51
Privatization
    in Mexico, 153
    Russian oligarchs and, 48
Probability samples, 213–214
Problem definition. *See* Market research
Process, as marketing value, 44
Process, as marketing company principle, 40
ProChile, 93
Procter & Gamble, 102, 169, 267, 358, 474, 517
    advertising decisions, 210
    advertising expenditures, 438
    China market, 56, 232–233, 476
    coffee trading of, 147
    data collection by, 211
    Internet use by, 570
    joint ventures in China, 301
    market value, 14
    pet food market, 17, 241
    positioning by, 250–251
    reorganization plan, 542
    Turkey and, 57
    Venezuela and, 378
Procter & Gamble Far East Inc., 569
Product adaptation, 248
Product adaptation-communication
        extension, 350–351
Product and brand decisions, 328
    basic concepts, 329
        brands, 330–332
        global brand development, 335–339
        global products and brands, 333–335
        international products and brands, 333
        local products and brands, 332–333
        local versus global: needs-based
            approach, 339–341
        product types, 330
    country-of-origin effect, 341–343
    extend, adapt, create strategies, 346–347
        how to choose strategy, 353–354
        product adaptation-communication
            extension, 350–351
        product-communication
            adaptation, 351
        product-communication extension,
            348–349
        product extension-communication
            adaptation, 349–350
        product invention, 351–353
    new products in global marketing, 354
        development of, 356–357
        ideas for, 355–356
        international department, 357
        testing, 358

packaging
    aesthetics, 345–346
    labeling, 344–345
    product warranties, 346
Product attribute, 251
Product-communication adaptation, 351
Product-communication extension, 348–349
Product cultures, 437
Product, defined, 329
Product design adaptations, 347
Product development costs, 23
Product differentiation, 252, 253, 504
Product division structures, 540–542
Product extension-communication
        adaptation strategy, 349–350
Product invention, 351–353. *See also* Product
        and brand decisions
Product knowledge, 543
Product-market, 245
Product-market decisions, 247–248
Product-market profile, 246–247
Product mix width, 508
Product placement, 496–498
Product platform, 356–357
Product saturation levels, 65
Product strategies
    of the European union (table), 102
    in personal selling, 482
Product transformation, 350
Product types, 330
Product warranties, 346
Products. *See* Channels of distribution
Productivity, employment and, 47
Pro forma invoice, 279
Projective technique, 212
Promodès, 419
Promotion sites (Web), 567
Promotion strategies, of the European
        union (table), 102
Promotional Marketing Association of
        America (PMAA), 473
Pronuptia, 182
Property, tangible and intangible, sales of, 389
Protectionist sentiment, 286
Protocol Marketing Group, 444
Proton, 304
Proud Patrons (Porsche demographic), 235
PRS Group, 155
Psychographic segmentation, 235–237
Public international law, 162
Public relations and publicity, 460–461. *See
        also* Advertising
    defined, 459
    differences worldwide, 463–464
    in global marketing communications,
        462–463
    negative, 460
Publicis Group, 444
Publicis Worldwide, 446
Pull strategy, 381
"Pull through" opportunities, 520
Purchasing power parity (PPP), 71–72
Purple (color), 123
Put option, 74

**Q**

Qatar, 53, 104, 105
Qibla Cola, 121
Quaker Oats, 151
Quality
    global marketing and, 23–24
    as positioning strategy, 251–252
    as product characteristic, 357
Questionnaires, 209

Quick service restaurant (QSR), 31
Quota sample, 214
Quotas, 214, 305
    avocado-growers' problem, 89
    defined, 269
    Ecuador and, 113
QVC, 493, 494

**R**

Rabattgesetz (Discount Law; Germany), 379
*Race for the World* (Bryan), 365
Radio advertising, 458
Radio frequency identification tags (RFID),
        192, 425, 433–434
Radisson Hotel, 186
Rado, 283
"Raiders of the Lost Ark," 561
Rail transportation, 425
Rain forest, 114
Rainforest Alliance, 147, 148
Raisio Oy, 342
Ralston Purina, 17, 303
Ramadan, 121
Random House, 530
Rational appeal, 449
Rational/argument advertising, 455
Rational/lecture advertising, 455
Ray Ban, 78
Raytheon, 58
"Razors and blades" pricing, 368
RCA, 514–515
Reactivity, 211
*Reader's Digest*, 407
Reading activity, by management staff, 197
Real, 92
Real operating exposure, 73
RealNetworks, 578, 586, 587
Realplayer, 586
Real-time enterprises (RTEs), 191
Rebates, 473
Reckitt Benckiser, 125
Record Industry Association of America
        (RIAA), 584–587
Red (color), 123, 345
Reebok, 191, 211–212, 288, 289–290, 377,
        468, 535
"Reefers" (shipping containers), 428
Regiocentric orientation, to marketing, 18,
        19–21, 485
Regional economic organizations, 180–182
Regional management centers, 540
Regional manufacturing, 515
Regional markets. *See also* General
        Agreement on Tariffs and Trade
        (GATT); Preferential trade agree-
        ments; World Trade Organization
        (WTO)
    Africa
        Commission of East African
            Cooperation, 107
        Economic Community of West
            African States (ECOWAS),
            106–107, 108
        Southern African Development
            Community (SADC), 108, 109
    ASEAN (Association of Southeast Asian
        Nations), 96–98
    Europe
        Central European Free Trade
            Association (CEFTA), 103–104
        Cotonou Agreement, 103
        European Economic Area (EEA),
            100–101
        European Free Trade Area (EFTA),
            100–101

European Union (EU), 98–100
Lomé Convention, 103
marketing issues in the European
Union, 101–102
Gulf Cooperation Council (GCC), 104–106
Latin America
Andean Community, 90–92
CARICOM (Caribbean Community
and Common Market), 94–95
current trade relations, 95
Mercosur (Mercado Comun del Sur;
Common Market of the South),
92–93
SICA (Sistema de la Integración
Centroamericana; Central
American Integration System),
89–90
Middle East, 104–106
North America, 87–89
Regression analysis, 215
Regulatory environment, 180–182
personal selling and, 480
Relationship marketing, 482
Relationship strategy, 482
Relative advantage, 140
Religion, 147–148
Barbie dolls and, 149
as source of society's attitudes, beliefs,
and values, 120–121
Remedies, for trade secret infringements, 173
*Remote Control Childhood—Combating
the Hazards of Media Culture*
(Levin), 326
Renault, 27, 46, 302, 304, 534
Repressed economy, 53, 56, 104
Republic of South Africa, 106
Research, in information collection, 195
Research design. *See* Market research
Research methodologies. *See* Market research
Resource utilization, 26
Resources, kinds of, 518–519
Restraining forces, of global marketing
management myopia and organizational
culture, 27
national controls, 28
opposition to globalization, 28
Restrictive administrative and technical
regulations, 271
Retail Brand Alliance, 421
Retailing, global, 413–423
Retention, as marketing company
principle, 39
Reuters Group, 534
Revlon, 164, 248, 250, 450
Rewe, 414
RFID. *See* Radio frequency identification tags
R. Griggs Group, 2
Rigid cost-based pricing, 369–370
Ring tones and ring tunes, 580–581
Risk, 508
Rivalry among competitors, 507
Riverdance, 64
RJ Reynolds, 448
Robert Mondavi Corporation, 18
Rockwell Graphic Systems, 386
Rockwell International, 392
Rolex, 340
Roman Catholicism, 120
Romania, 34, 53, 99, 300, 391
Rounds, 86
Rover, 243, 250
Royal Ahold, 408, 414
Royal Dutch/Shell Group, 14, 15
Royal Philips Electronics, 20, 22
Royalties, 581

RTEs. *See* Real-time enterprises
RTL, 530
Rule of engagement, changing, 515–516
Rules of origin, 84
Russia, 51, 53, 63, 163, 166, 252, 299, 300,
345, 361, 386
alliance opportunities in, 315
automakers in, 302
Avon Products in, 405, 406
budget deficit and taxes, 159
Coca-Cola in, 298
credit card fraud in, 568
dietary preferences, 124
economic collapse of, 45–46
economic rebound, 48
growth opportunities, 46
inflation in, 376
joint venture in, 302
market selection framework (table), 245
McDonald's in, 33–34
population, 233
psychographic profile of market, 236–237
reforms in, 156
restriction of foreign ownership in joint
ventures, 303
taxation in, 158–159
vodka consumption, 239–240
*Russian and Commonwealth Business Law
Report, The*, 163
Russian Souls (consumer type), 236
Rwanda, 53, 56
Rx Depot, 370
Ryder System, 426

# S
Saab, 231
SABMiller, 293, 300
SACU. *See* Southern African Customs Union
SADC. *See* Southern African Development
Community
Safe Harbor agreement, 193–194
Safety needs, 339
Safeway, 414
SAFTDA. *See* Southern Africa Free Trade
and Development Agreement
Sainsbury, 159, 213, 414
Saint-Gobain, 296
Sale, terms of, 371–373
Sales agents, 487–488
Sales demonstration, 484
Sales force automation (SFA), 192–193
Sales force nationality, 485–488
Sales of tangible and intangible property, 389
Sales on a consignment basis, 282
Sales on open account, 282
Sales promotion
cost, complexity, global branding, and
transnational trade, 474
couponing, 476–477
defined, 472
examples of (table), 473
issues and problems, 477–478
localized, 474
regulation of, 477
sampling, 474–476
Salient attributes, 216
Sampling, 472, 474, 476
Sampo Group, 333
Sam's Club, 415, 432
Samsung, 17, 62, 168, 303, 320, 328, 342, 375,
534, 580
Sanctions. *See* Embargo; Trade embargo
Sandoz, 299, 308
Sanofi-Aventis, 295

Sanwa, 316
SAP, 17
SARS outbreak, 68, 268
SAS, 310
Sassaby Inc., 250
Saudi Arabia, 53, 104, 457
advertising censorship, 459
GNP, 105
as high-context culture, 132
population, 105
SBC Communications, 582
SBU. *See* Strategic Business Unit
Scalar bias, 213
Scalar equivalence, 213
Scale development, 213–214
Scale economies, 26, 439
Scandinavia, 133, 134, 477
Scanning modes, 195–197
Schering-Plough, 534
Schick-Wilkinson Sword. 226
Science Foundation Ireland (SFI), 64
S.C. Johnson & Sons, 172
Seagram Company, 7, 239, 435, 473
Sea-Land Service, 171
Search engines, 564
Search mode (information collection),
195–197
Sears, 25, 220, 288, 414
Seattle Coffee Company, 145
Secondary data, 203
Secondary purpose, 340
Section 482, U.S. Treasury regulations,
389–390, 400
Securities and Exchange Commission, 174
Segmentation
assessing attractiveness of segments. *See*
Target markets, choosing
behavior, 237–240
benefit, 240–241
contrasting views of (table), 228
demographic
age, 234
changes in, and market innovation,
229–230
defined, 228
gender, 234–235
income and population, 230–234
worldwide facts and trends,
228–229
ethnic, 241–242
examples, by global companies, 226
global market segmentation,
defined, 226–227
as marketing company principle, 40
as marketing strategy, 43
psychographic, 235–237
screening criteria for market segments
(figure), 246
Segment simultaneity, 227
Seizure of assets, 160–161
Self-audit, 552–553
Self-esteem, 340
Self-reference criterion (SRC), 138–139, 209
in market research, 201, 203
Self-respect, 340
Self-service retailing, 422, 502
Selling
as marketing company principle, 41–42
as marketing tactic, 44
Selling proposition, 449
Semantics, 126, 127, 128
Sematech, 320
Semiotics, 127
Semi-slave labor, 289
Senegal, 53, 107

Sense of shame, 135
Sensory appeal, 137–138
Sequencing, 129
Serbia, 53
7-Eleven, 191, 414, 415, 422–423
Service
    as marketing company principle, 40
    as market value, 44
Service sector, 62
Services. *See also* Channels of distribution
    fastest-growing sector of world trade, 69
    world trade in, 68–69
Servicing the sale, 485
Sexual innuendo, 350
Sexually explicit or provocative imagery, in
    advertising, 452–453
Seychelles, 108, 109
SFA. *See* Sales force automation
Shaddy, 493
Shame, sense of, 135
Shandwick PLC, 462
Shanghai Automotive Industry, 301
*Sharia* (Muslim code of conduct), 164
Sharp, 17, 328, 332, 566
Sharper Image, 492
Sherman Act of 1890, 169
Sherritt International Corp., 187
Shipping Act of 1916, 171–172
Shipping agent, 428
Shipping lines (table), 426
Short message service (SMS), 580
Short-term orientation, 135
SICA. *See* Central American Integration
    System
Siebel Systems, 17, 193
Siemens, 15, 35, 56, 57, 308, 320, 479
Sierra Leone, 53, 107
Sight draft, 281
Silhouette, 383–384
Silicon chip, 562
Silk Road, 2
Silk Route, 134
Simpay, 580
Singapore, 33, 53, 54, 64, 84, 87, 124, 135,
    163, 174, 229, 268, 289, 340, 493
    broadband in, 578
    Coca-Cola in, 212
    economic freedom ranking, 52
    export/import ranking, 68
    GNP, 96
    per capita income, 231
    population, 96
    U.S.–ASEAN trading activities and, 97
Singapore Airlines, 310, 339
Single-column tariff, 271
Single European Act, 98, 180
Single Market era, 181–182
Sistema de la Intergracion
    Centroamericana. *See* Central
    American Integration System
Skimming pricing strategy, 367
Skoda, 304, 557
Skyy vodka, 122–123
Slovak Republic, 53
Slovakia, 34, 99, 103, 115, 284
Slovenia, 53, 99, 115
Slow Food movement, 132
Small and medium-sized enterprises
    (SMEs), 270
Smart Car, 361–363
Smart cards, 192
Smart cell phones, 580–581
SMEs. *See* Small and medium-sized
    enterprises
Smirnoff vodka, 239–240

Smuggling
    in China, 158
    Vietnam/Thailand, 78
Snecma, 313, 320
Social and cultural environments, 117–150
    aesthetics, 121–124
    attitudes, beliefs, and values, 120
    dietary preferences, 124–126
    diffusion theory, 139–143
    high- and low-context cultures, 132–133
    Hofstede's cultural typology, 133–138
    language and communication, 126–129
    marketing implications of, 143–145
    marketing's impact on culture, 129–132
    religion, 120–121
    self-reference criterion and perception,
    138–139
Social brand image, 137–138
Social institutions, 119
Socialism, 48
Softbank Corp., 572
Software
    global patent protection for, 168
    intelligent agent, 197
    sales force automation (SFA), 192–193
Software piracy, 69
Software Publishers Association, 69
SoHo (Sony's U.S. consumer segment), 237
Song tunes, 581
Sony Corp., 128, 132, 199, 339–340, 538
    convergence in, 564
    distribution networks, 134
    economic value ranking, 336
    first-mover achievements, 524
    global teen segment, 234, 254
    market size, 17
    music industry, 584, 586
    PlayStation2, 368, 471, 524, 578
    reorganization of marketing function, 237
    sponsorship by, 495
    substitute products threat, 505
    television market, 328–329, 332
    top management nationality, 533–534
    transistor development, 136,
    296–297, 562
    U.S. patents of, 168
    uniform pricing policies, 101
    Vietnam and, 77
Sony Electronics, 237
Sony Music, 584
Sony Walkman, 334, 367–368, 382
Sourcing, 380. *See also* Exporting/importing
South Africa, 53, 84, 108, 387, 395, 564, 575
    big emerging market (BEM), 54
    GNP, 109
    population, 109
    product invention strategy in, 352
    as upper-middle-income country, 59
South Africa Breweries PLC, 293, 300
South African Development Coordination
    Council, 108
South America, 66, 89, 432, 458, 494. *See also*
    *individual countries*
Southeast Asia, 57, 156, 269, 515
    market attractiveness, 60
    MTV in, 229
    political risk in, 156–157
Southern Africa Free Trade and
    Development Agreement
    (SAFTDA), 84
Southern African Customs Union
    (SACU), 108
Southern African Development Community
    (SADC), 108, 109
Southern Company, 6

South Korea, 53, 54, 64, 69, 77, 87, 95, 134,
    153, 160, 167, 266, 268, 289, 298,
    303, 375, 421, 447, 455. *See also*
    Korea; North Korea
    big emerging market (BEM), 54
    broadband penetration in, 578
    chaebol in, 319–320, 513
    color perceptions in, 123
    diffusion of innovations in, 142–143
    export/import ranking, 68
    as high-income country, 62
    per capita income, 62
    trade secret laws, 173
Southland Corporation, 422–423
Sovereignty, 153–154
Soviet Union (former), 56, 167, 248, 299
    countertrade in, 390
    economic reforms, 50
    foreign direct investment in (table), 299
    McDonald's in, 33
    PepsiCo in, 391
    perestroika, 51
    pirated software in, 69
"Spaghetti bowl" of trade agreements, 93
Spain, 53, 98, 100, 103, 115, 121, 134, 139,
    158, 186, 187, 332, 381, 414, 448,
    455, 457, 458, 462, 557, 572, 580
    Coca-Cola in, 10
    GNP, 99
    Hofstede's cultural typology rankings
    (table), 135
    population, 99
    privacy issues, 575
Spam, 580
SpanAir, 310
Spar Handels AG, 432
Sparr, 414
Specialty retailers, 413–414
Specific duty, 274
SpectraLink Corporation, 582
Spiegel, 492
Spoken (verbal) language, 126–129
SpongeBob SquarePants, 34
Sponsorships, 476, 495–496
Sport utility vehicles (SUVs), in China, 243
Spot market, 70
Sprint, 170
SRC. *See* Self-reference criterion
SRI International, 235, 236
Sri Lanka, 53
Standardization versus adaptation, 8–9
Standard of living
    in low-income countries, 231
    United States, 230
Standard Oil, 186
Standardized approach
    to advertising, 439–443
    to marketing, 16
Standardized global marketing, 248
Stanley Works, 305–306
Star Air, 325
Star Alliance, 310
Starbucks, 31, 145, 147, 347, 414, 476, 579
State Committee for Cooperation and
    Investment (SCCI; Vietnam), 78
State trade controls, 269
*Statistical Abstract of the United States*, 203
*Statistical Yearbook of the United Nations*, 204
STAT-USA/Internet, 203
Status needs, 341
Status-oriented products, 340
Steel industry, 81
    dumping complaints against Japan,
    386–387
    tariff on imports, 386

Stella Artois beer, 251
Stereotyping, country-of-origin effect and, 341–343
Stern Pinball, 374
St. Kitts, 94
St. Lucia, 94
Stockholm Chamber of Commerce, 179
Stolichnaya Gold vodka, 250, 252, 392
Stora Enso, 575
Strategic alliances, 309, 315
    relationship enterprises and, 320–321
Strategic Business Unit (SBU), 43
Strategic/Consultative Selling Model, 481–485
Strategic intent. See Competitive advantage
Strategic international alliances, 309
Strategic planning, 549
Strategy, of global strategic partnerships (GSPs), 311
Strategy Analytics, 581
Strategy options. See Target markets, choosing
Streaming audio, 577
Streaming media, 577–578
Streaming video, 577
St. Vincent, 94
STV (strategy, tactic, and value) model, 43–44
Sual, 534
Subaru, 4
Subcultures, 120
    language and, 128
Subject agenda, 195–197
Subjective culture, 119
Sub-Saharan Africa, 106
Subsidies, 378–379
    exports and, 267
    sugar, 86, 291
Substitute products, 505
    as budget influence, 551
Subway, 31
Successful Idealists (European consumer), 236
Sudan, 53
Südzucker AG, 103
Sugar Act of 1934, 291
Sugar Association, 291
Sugar subsidies, 86
Suisse Microelectronique et d'Horlogerie SA (SMH), 523
Sumimoto, 15, 316
Summit of the Americas, 81, 85
Sun Microsystems, 577
Suntory, 301
Supercenters, 415
Supermarkets, 414–415
Supreme Court. See U.S. Supreme Court
Suppliers, bargaining power of, 506–507
Supply chain, 423
Suriname, 53, 94
Surveillance mode (information collection), 195–197
Survey research, 209
Sustainable production, 147–148
Sustaining technologies, 566
SUVs. See Sport utility vehicles (SUVs)
Suzuki, 98
Swap, 393
Swarski Crystal, 272
Swatch AG, 64
Swatch car, 361–363
Swatch Group, 1, 234, 283, 457, 523
Swaziland, 53, 84, 108, 109
Sweatshops, 288–290

Swede Shop, 502
Sweden, 53, 101, 115, 174, 268, 291, 351, 376, 406, 459, 502, 523
    coupons in (table), 475
    GNP, 99
    Hofstede's cultural typology rankings (table), 135
    per capita GNP, 231
    per capita income, 231
    population, 99
    as postindustrial country, 61
Swedish Arbitration Institute, 179
Sweepstakes, 472, 473, 478
Swiss Bank Corporation (SBC), 197
Switch trading, 393
Switching costs, 504
Switzerland, 53, 101, 128, 167, 174, 268, 350, 393, 415, 459, 492, 523, 572
    direct mail and, 490–491
    as low-context culture, 132
    per capita income, 231
Symbols, 119
Synergy, 300
Syntax, 126, 127
Syria, 53, 104, 564

## T

Tabulation, 214–215
Taco Bell, 471
TAG Heuer, 384
Taiwan
    Acer, Inc., 35–37, 79–80, 427, 525
    apparel and textile exports to the United States, 266
    civil-law jurisdiction, 163
    country-of-origin effect, 342
    coupon/sweepstake use in, 477–478
    diffusion of innovations in, 142–143
    economic system, 51
    export/import ranking, 68
    Guatemala and, 95
    Hofstede's cultural dimension rankings (table), 135
    index of economic freedom ranking, 53
    joint venture with Virgin Group, 421
    masculinity score (low), 134
    movie promotion in, 124
    MTV Asia, 229
    strategic alliance with China's Haier Group, 333
    "think" and "feel" country designation, 455
    tiger status, 64
    U.S. machine tool agreements, 269
    U.S. trade partner, 87
    wage development in, 289
Tajikistan, 53, 56, 174, 299
TAL Apparel, Ltd., 429
Tamagotchi craze, 137, 340–341
Tampons, marketing of, 238–239
Tangible attributes, 329
Tanzania, 53, 107, 108, 109, 231
Taoism, 478
Target, 414
Target costing, 369
Target markets, choosing
    current size and growth potential, 242–243
    feasibility and compatibility, 244
    framework for selecting, 245–247
    Harley-Davidson and, 249
    potential competition, 243–244
    product-market decisions, 247–248
    strategy options

concentrated global marketing, 249–250
differentiated global marketing, 250
standardized global marketing, 248
Targeting
    defined, 225
    as marketing company principle, 40–41
    as marketing strategy, 43
Tariff Act of 1930 (U.S.), 384
Tariffs, 28, 169, 244, 305. See also Harmonized Tariff System (HTS); Nontariff trade barrier (NTB)
    1945–1994, 86
    common external, 89–90
    defined, 267
    discriminatory, 160
    Ecuador and, 113
    preferential, 273
    single-column, 271
    South American banana growers and the EU, 102
    on steel imports, 386
    two-column, 271–272
    United States classifications, 269
    Uruguay round and, 268
Tartarstan, 306
Tatarstan republic, 302
Tati, 415
Taxes, 157–160, 376
    transfer pricing and, 389
Tax incentives, export/import, 266–267
T-commerce, 493
Technology
    forecasts, 571, 578, 581
    linguistics and, 128
    in newly industrializing countries, 58
    software, patent protection for, 168
Technology transfer laws, 172
Technoserve, 148
Tektronix, 516
Telefonica Moviles SA, 580
Telematics, 579
Telenor ASA, 580
Telephones. See Cell phones; Mobile phones
Teleshopping, 493–495, 514
Television advertising, 456–459, 489
Television sets, 328–329, 332
    interactive television (ITV), 404
Temporary surcharges, 275
Tengelmann Gruppe, 414
Tenneco Automotive, 319
Terms of the sale, 371–373
Terrorism, 285
Tesco, 414
Testing, of new products, 358
Texaco, 186
Texas Instruments, 191, 297, 320, 559, 562n
Textbook industry, pricing in, 381
Textile industry
    Bangladesh, 55–56
    in Kenya and Mauritius, 109
Text messaging, 128
Thai, 310
Thailand, 33, 51, 53, 54, 69, 70, 75, 77, 83, 96, 163, 213, 229, 266, 289, 291, 298, 375, 395, 477, 577
Thermax, 352
"Think" and "feel" country clusters, 455–456
Think globally, act locally, 321, 443
Third-country nationals, sales types, 486, 487
Thirst, 145
Thomson Financial, 310
Thomson Financial Securities Data, 303
Threat of new entrants, 503–505

Threat of substitute products, 505
3G addresses, 238
360-degree view of the customer, 192
3M International, 103
Three Tigers, 134–135
Thrift, 135
Tiendas Exito, 408
Tiered branding, 334
Tiffany & Company, 123, 345
Tiger, 64
Tile Connection, 282
Timberland, 290
Time draft, 281
Time orientation, 135–136
Time-series displacement, 218
Time utility, 402
Time Warner, 170, 478
Timing advantage, 524
TiVo, 192, 496
T-Mobile International AG, 580
T-Mobile USA, 579
TMP Worldwide, 444
TNS, 201, 210
TNT, 320
Tobacco industry
    direct mail advertising by, 490
    in India, 196
    mandatory warning labels, 345
    market size and key players, 17
    regulation of advertising in, 448
Tobacco Merchants Association (TMA), 196
Tobago, 53, 94
Togo, 53, 107
Tokyo round, 86
Tokyu Agency, 444
*Tomorrow Never Dies*, 497
Tom Thumb, 415
Top-down segmentation analysis, 245
Top Guns (Porsche demographic), 235
Toshiba, 6, 77, 317, 566
Total, 14, 15
Total Request Live (TRL), 225
Total Research Corporation, 213
Total toothpaste, 352
Totality, as marketing company principle, 42
Touching, 127
Touchpoint, 192
Tourism
    American/French, reduction in, 125
    in Ecuador, 114
Tower Records, 584
Toy Biz, 269
Toyota, 4, 11, 13, 14, 15, 46, 54, 180, 207,
        210–211, 241, 247–248, 260, 302,
        303, 317, 336, 388, 423, 536, 571
Toys "R" Us, 179, 289, 380, 406, 408, 416, 418
TPA. *See* Trade promotion authority
Trade Act (1988), 271
Trade and Tariff Act of 1984, 275
Trade barriers, 28, 169, 270, 306
    nontariff, 269
    restrictive, regional, 271
Trade deficit, 67
Trade embargo, U.S.–Cuba, 186. *See also*
        Embargo
Trade Marks Act (United Kingdom, 1994), 181
Trade mission, 264
Trade negotiation, between 1947 and 1994, 86
Trade promotion authority (TPA), 85
Trade sales promotions, 472
Trade secrets, 164–165, 172–173
Trade show, 264
Trade surplus, 67
Trademark, 165–168, 332
Trademark Act of 1946, 165

Trademark Law Revision Act (1988), 165
Transaction exposure, 73
Transaction sites (Web), 567
Transaction value, 274
TransFair USA, 147
Transfer pricing, 378
    competitive pricing, 389
    defined, 388
    market-based, cost-based, and
        negotiated, 388–389
    sales of tangible and intangible
        property, 389
    Section 482 regulations, 389–390, 400
    tax regulations and, 389
Transgenic crops, 151
Transnational commerce culture, 254
Transnational company, 20
Transparency International Corruption
        Perceptions Index, 173, 174
Transportation
    global marketing and, 23
    technology in, 23
Transportation bill of lading, 279
Transportation (physical distribution),
        425–428
Transshipment, 101
Transworld Advertising Agency Network
        (TAAN), 446
Travel industry, 573
Treaty of Lagos (1975), 106
Treaty of Rome (1958), 98, 180, 181
    interstate trade clause, 170–171
Triad nations, 63–64, 86, 136, 156, 286,
        333, 337
    GNP in, 230
    Hofstede's cultural typology rankings
        (table), 135
*Triad Power* (Ohmae), 63
Triangular trade, 393
Trinidad, 53, 94
Trinitron televisions, 564
TRIPS. *See* Agreement on Trade-Related
        Aspects of Intellectual Property
        Rights (TRIPs)
Truck transportation, 425–426
True market, 70
Trust, 136
TruTones, 581
Tsingtao Brewery, 184
TSMC, 320
Tunisia, 53, 105, 106
Tupperware, 404
Turkey, 1, 53, 57, 101, 121, 385, 415, 463
    big emerging market (BEM), 54, 57
    customs union with the European
        Union, 84
    European Union (EU) and, 57
    lower-middle-income country, 57
Turkmenistan, 53, 56, 299
TWBA Worldwide, 446
20th Century Fox, 561, 580
Two-column tariff, 271–272
Tyumen Oil, 48

## U

U2, 64, 65
uDate.com, 561
Uganda, 53, 107, 395
Ukraine, 34, 53, 269–270, 299
Uncertainty avoidance, 134–138, 477
Unconventional wisdom, 227–228
Undifferentiated target marketing, 248
Unearned media, 460
Uniform Commercial Code (U.S.), 162–163

Uniform Customs and Practice for
        Documentary Credits, 279
Uniform resource locator (URL), 564
Uniform Trade Secrets Act (UTSA), 173
Unilever, 20, 66, 78, 98, 144, 189, 210, 232,
        250, 305, 358, 438, 476, 517, 571
United Airlines, 310
United Arab Emirates, 53, 104, 105, 392
United Auto Workers, 289
United International Pictures (UIP), 171
United Kingdom. *See also* Great Britain
    advertising expenditures, 457, 458
    Advisory, Conciliation and Arbitration
        Service, in industrial disputes, 179
    Ben & Jerry's Homemade ice cream
        in, 349
    Cable & Wireless PLC in Panama, 175
    Colgate Total toothpaste testing in, 352
    coupon use in, 476
    economic system, 51
    European Court of Justice
        involvement, 181
    Fairtrade Foundation, 147
    foreign direct investment in India, 299
    Frito-Lay in, 139
    Gap stores in, 13
    global brand issues, 338
    global competitive advantage and, 523
    Globalink membership, 462
    gray market goods, dollar amount, 383
    gross national product (GNP), 99, 232
    Hofstede's cultural typology rankings
        (table), 135
    IKEA in, 511
    index of economic freedom, 53
    McDonald's in, 233
    MyCokeMusicStore in, 579
    parallel imports in, 383
    population, 99
    recorded music sales, 23
    right-hand drive cars, 362
    second-tier licensing of Harry Potter
        products in, 325
    subsidiaries in Ireland, 64
    telematics in, 579
    Trade Marks Act protections, 181
    transfer pricing, 388–389
    U.S. investment in, 298
    U.S. trade partner, 87
United Nations International Court of
        Justice (ICJ), 161, 162
United Nations AIDS Program, 395
United Nations Conference on International
        Trade Law (UNCITRAL), 179–180
United Nations Convention on the
        Recognition and Enforcement of
        Foreign Arbitral Awards, 177
United Nations Security Council, 162
United Overseas Limited (UOL), 164
United Parcel Service (UPS), 298, 324, 575
United States
    advertising expenditures, 458
    Agreement on Customs Valuations, 274
    American Arbitration Association
        (AAA), 179
    antitrust laws, 169–172
    ASEAN trade and, 97
    balance of payments, 1990–2003 (table), 67
    brand images, 137
    CARICOM and, 95
    cartels and, 171
    catalog marketers in, 492
    color perceptions in, 123
    common law foundation, 163
    copyright law and, 585

Corona beer in, 344
country-of-origin effect, 342
coupon use in, 475, 476
creative strategy of, 454
culture clash with France, 125
customs valuation code, 273–274
demographics of, 229
diffusion of innovations in, 142
direct investment abroad, dollars, 305
direct labor costs, 284
direct mail and, 490–491
direct marketing guidelines, 489–490
dumping from Asia, 386
economic system, 51
export/import ranking, 68
exports, percent of, 270
foreign automakers and, 243
foreign direct investment in India, 299
free trade agreement with Chile, 82, 84
Fuji Foto Film Company, dumping
    charge, 304
Gateway survey in, 442
genetically modified organisms
    (GMOs), 151–152
global competitive advantage and, 523
gray market law, 384
gross national product (GNP), 88, 232
hamburger restaurants per capita, 31
high-income country, 62
historic relationship with France, 117
Hofstede's cultural typology rankings
    (table), 135
import totals, 265
index of economic freedom ranking, 53
individualistic culture, 133
Indonesia' automobile industry problem
    and, 153
inflation in, 377
infomercials and home shopping
    television, 494
intellectual property, 165–168
international dispute arbiter, 179
investment insurance by, 157
Jollibee restaurants in, 127
laptop computers in, 579
lawyers and lawsuits, 176–177
Lexus market, 248
low-context culture, 132
main ethnic groups, 229, 241
manufacturing's share of GDP, 47
market size, 13
market uniqueness, 87
McDonald's refocus on, 34–35
Mexican currency crisis and exports
    to, 66
music industry in, 584
music of, 123
OECD membership, 63
Patent Cooperation Treaty (PCT) and,
    167–168
per capita income, 230, 231
population, 88, 233
postindustrial country, 61
public relations in, 463–464
recorded music sales, 23
regional market, 17, 87–89
regulatory environment, 180
Russia, legal influence on, 163
St. Laurent Champagne perfume in, 166
start-up companies in, 582
subjective attributes of products in, 454
Tariff Act of 1930, 384
tariff classifications, 269
tax minimization, 160
television advertising in, 457

"think" and "feel" country designation,
    455, 456
trade balance on services and
    merchandise trade (figure), 69
trade deficits, 67
trade partners (figure), 87
trade secrets, 173
trade with Japan, 67–68
transfer pricing, 388–389
Triad membership, 64
uncertainty avoidance and, 136
Volkswagen in, 556
United Technologies, 77, 186, 347
Univac, 6–7
Universal, 171
Universal Music, 17, 584, 586
University of Minnesota, 395
Unspoken (nonverbal)
    communication, 127
Unsustainable advantages, 525
Upper-middle-income countries, 57–59
Upstream/value chain, 423
Uruguay, 53, 92, 113, 149
Uruguay round, 86, 268, 274, 275, 372n,
    385–386
U.S. Act of State Doctrine, 161
US Airways, 310
U.S.–Canada Free Trade Agreement
    (CFTA), 87
U.S. Cellular, 580
U.S. Central Intelligence Agency, 204
U.S. Commerce Department, 275
U.S. Commercial Service, 270
U.S. Court of International Trade, 269
U.S.–Cuba trade embargo, 186
U.S. Customs Service, 285, 384
U.S. Department of Commerce, 263, 270,
    322, 386
U.S. Department of Justice, 174, 370
U.S. Department of Transportation,
    286, 324
U.S. Export-Import Bank. See Export-Import
    Bank
U.S. Federal Communications Commission,
    578, 582
U.S. Federal Trade Commission, 169, 317–318
U.S. Food and Drug Administration, geneti-
    cally modified organisms
    (GMOs) and, 159
U.S.–Japan Semiconductor Agreement, 269
U.S. Justice Department, 318
U.S. Labor Department, 288
U.S. Patent and Trademark Office, 168
U.S. Steel Group, 386–387
U.S. Sugar Corporation, 291
U.S. Supreme Court
    European Court of Justice and, 181–182
    packaging and copyright law, 397
    on sovereign states, 153
    trademarked goods and the gray
        market, 384
U.S. Treasury Department, 274, 286
    Section 482 regulations, 389–390, 400
U.S. Uniform Commercial Code, 162–163
U.S.–Vietnam free trade area, 77, 79
USA Networks, 561
Usage rates, 237–238
Use or user, as positioning strategy,
    252–253
User status, 238
Utilities, 217
Utility
    distribution channels and, 428
    as marketing company principle, 42
Uzbekistan, 53, 56, 299, 300

## V

Value, 7
Value added, 220
Value-added tax (VAT), 157–158, 376, 492
Value chain, 3, 4, 423–424, 546–548
Value enabler of a company, 44
Value enhancer of a company, 44
Value equation, 3–4
Value indicator of a company, 44
Value networks, 565–567, 566
Values, 119
    defined, 120
    long term, 135
ValueVision, 493
Van Halen, 124, 134
Variable import levies, 275
Varig, 310
VAT. See Value-added tax
Venezuela, 51, 53, 84, 90, 91, 378, 408
Verizon Communications, 15, 580, 586
Verizon Wireless, 581
Vermeer Manufacturing, 374
Versace, 396
Verso Technologies Inc., 582
Vertical keiretsu, 317, 512
Vertical price fixing, 387
VH1, 225
Viagra, 364
Victoria's Secret, 414, 492
Video games, 471–472
Vietnam, 53, 84, 299
    coffee production in, 147
    food preferences in, 139
    foreign direct investment in, 77–78
    GNP, 96
    market potential, 77–79
    per capita income, 78
    population, 96
Viewing (information collection), 195–197
Virgin brand, 335, 336, 357, 587
Virgin Group, 421, 461
Virgin Stores, 418, 419, 420, 422
Virtual Corporation, The (Davidow and
    Malone), 321
Virtual Trade Commissioner (Canada), 204
Visa, 243, 251, 489
Visa International, 124
Visual aesthetics, 122, 345
Vitango, 60
Vitro, 302
Vivendi Universal, 7, 27, 561, 586
VNU, 200, 201, 210
Vodafone Group, 14, 437, 580
Vodka consumption, 239–240
Vodka industry, 250
    positioning in, 252
    product differentiation, 253
Voice over Internet protocol (VoIP), 581–582
Volcafe, 147
Volkswagen AG, 15, 56, 164, 208, 243, 257,
    260, 271, 304, 342, 376
    history of, 556–558
    home market versus world market
        lesson, 353
Volvo, 6, 17, 46, 251
Vonnage, 582
V&S Vin & Spirit AB, 239

## W

Walgreen, 414
Wal-Mart, 14, 15, 123, 229, 237, 267, 288, 397,
    402, 414, 419, 461, 540, 587
    in Asia, 432–433
    bargaining power of buyer, 506

Wal-Mart (*Continued*)
   in Brazil, 376–377
   in Canada, 431–432
   in China, 198–199
   Cuban products in, 187
   EDI system, 191
   in Europe, 432
   global expansion, 431–433
   international revenues (table), 431
   Levi's and, 415
   in Mexico, 431
   purchases from China, 2
   radio frequency identification (RFID)
      and, 433–434
   in South America, 432
   supercenters, 415
   volume buying, 406
   warehouse clubs, 415
Walpole, 343
Walt Disney Company, 69, 138–139, 201, 405
Wants, 22, 144–145, 227, 339
Warehouse club, 415
Warehousing, 424
Warner, 101, 134
Warner Music Group, 17, 584, 586
Waterford, 1, 20, 64
Waterford Wedgwood PLC, 255
Web site design, 571–576
Weighted currencies, 100
Wendy's, 31
Wertkauf GmbH, 432
Western Europe, 33, 64, 148, 179, 386. *See
   also* Regional markets
West Germany, 98
Wherehouse, 584
Whirlpool, 1, 8, 17, 25, 58, 128, 212, 532, 537,
   541, 543–544
White (color), 123, 345
WHO. *See* World Health Organization
   (WHO)
Wholesaler/distributor, 428

Wieden & Kennedy, 348
Wi-fi connections, 579
Wild Turkey, 350
William Morris talent agency, 561
Wine industry, shipping in, 428
Winterhalter, 249
WIPO. *See* World Intellectual Property
   Organization (WIPO)
Wireless connectivity, 579–582
Wolf-Garten GmbH & Company, 362
Wolters Kluwer, 534
Word mark, 331
Word-of-mouth, 137
Worker exploitation, 288–290
World Arbitration Institute, 179
World Bank, 53, 114, 204, 395
World Bank Investment Dispute Settlement
   Center, 161
World Court, 162
World Customs Organization, 268
World economy, 24–25, 46–48
World e-Inclusion, 60
*World Factbook*, 204
World Health Organization (WHO), 291, 448
World Intellectual Property Organization
   (WIPO), 166
World Summit on Sustainable
   Development, 291
World Trade Organization (WTO), 21, 28,
   56, 77, 81, 85, 153, 156, 165, 180,
   187, 267, 406
   creation of, 82
   as dispute mediator, 82–83
   purpose of, 82
   recent cases (table), 83
WorldCom, 170
World Wide Web. *See* Internet
Worldwide Transfer Pricing Institute, 390
WPP Group, 201, 348, 444, 461
Wrangler jeans, 379
WTO. *See* World Trade Organization (WTO)

**X**
Xbox, 199, 368, 471, 475, 578
Xerox, 244, 565
Xingtones, 581

**Y**
Yahoo!, 564, 567, 571, 572, 578
Yankee Group, 581
Yankelovich Partners, 442
Yaohan Group, 416
Yellow (color), 123, 345
Yemen, 53, 104
Ymos, 362
Young professionals/D.I.N.K.S. (Sony's
   U.S. consumer segment), 237
Young & Rubicam, 446
YTL Corp., 479
Yugoslavia, 386
Yukos Oil, 48

**Z**
Zaibatsu, 317
Zaire, 108
Zambia, 53, 108, 109, 159
Zantac, 390
Zappa, Frank, 52
Zellers, 415
Zeneca PLC, 151, 159
Zenith, 566
Zenith brand, 337
Zenith Electronics, 298
ZenithOptimedia, 438
Zimbabwe, 53, 108, 109. 392
Zoomers (Sony's U.S. consumer
   segment), 237
Zoo Tycoon, 578
Zugabeverordung (Free Gift Act;
   Germany), 379